•BLOOMSBURY
DICTIONARY OF QUOTATIONS

• BLOOMSBURY DICTIONARY OF QUOTATIONS

BLOOMSBURY

First published 1987

This edition published 1991

Copyright © Bloomsbury Publishing Limited
Bloomsbury Publishing Limited, 2 Soho Square,
London W1V 5DE

Extracts from the Authorized King James Version of the
Bible, which is Crown Copyright, are reproduced by
permission of Eyre and Spottiswoode, Her Majesty's
Printers.

British Library Cataloguing in Publication Data

Bloomsbury dictionary of quotations.
   1.   Quotations, English
   080   PN6081

ISBN 0 7475 0897 6 Cased edition
ISBN 0 7475 0997 2 Paperback edition

Compiled and typeset by
Market House Books, Ltd., Aylesbury
Printed and bound in Great Britain by
Mackays of Chatham PLC, Chatham, Kent

• Contents

• Introduction

What is a quotation?

A quotation can be defined as:

'a phrase or passage from a book, poem or play etc, remembered and spoken, especially to illustrate succinctly or support a point or an argument'.

This is the definition we've used in our search for interesting, amusing or revealing phrases or passages that people have written or spoken during the last 3000 years.

Why do people consult dictionaries of quotations?

There seem to be several possible reasons:

• To check the details about a familiar quotation, or to find a half remembered one.
Who, for example, said, 'I am dying, with the help of too many physicians'?
Didn't Churchill once say something about his troubles never happening?
• To find unfamiliar quotations about a particular topic—love, death, marriage, etc.
• To find out something about an author through their sayings or writings.
• To browse through to find unexpected and interesting quotations.

We kept all these needs in mind when compiling the *Bloomsbury Dictionary of Quotations*. The extensive index enables you to find quotations easily; it is based on key words, listed alphabetically. For example, to find the quotations mentioned above you would look up the words 'physicians' and 'troubles'. So, if you can only remember a snippet of a quotation use the index. Each key word is followed by a short identifying phrase so that you can find the quotation, or types of quotation you want. Reference is to the author's name and to the quotation number.

It's easy to find out something by or about a particular author —they are all listed in alphabetical order and each has a biographical note telling you when they lived, with a brief comment on their lives and works.

Of course, you may simply enjoy browsing through the first part of the book. The juxtaposition of quotations by authors from different periods can make for fascinating and amusing reading.

From Confucius to Kinnock

In the *Bloomsbury Dictionary of Quotations* we have departed from established tradition in older works in that we have included both familiar quotations and perceptive or witty sayings that are less well known. We have, especially, sought quotations that reflect contemporary issues as well as those from literature and the Bible.

How the entries are set out

In an entry under a particular author the entries are arranged according to the references. First come the subject's own works, arranged in alphabetical order (but ignoring the 'A' and 'The'). Then follow works by other people in which the subject is quoted, again listed in alphabetical order. Next come speeches, letters etc, which are generally arranged in date order. These are followed by quotations referenced as Attrib. which are sayings or remarks that are widely and generally attributed to the person involved.

We have broken these rules when it seemed logical to do so—for example by putting 'last words' at the end of the entries.

In certain entries we have included quotations **about** the author —i.e. quotations by other writers about Shakespeare, Churchill, and other famous or quotable people. These are always placed at the start of the entry.

Who said what?

There are a few cases in which problems arise in attributing quotations. Some are widely ascribed to two or more people. For these we have included explanatory notes after the quotation. Another problem is that of co-authors such as Lennon and McCartney. In these cases the quotations are included under the first named, with a cross reference from the second. This does not, of course, imply that one is in any way more important.

Mae West exemplifies another difficulty. Many of her sayings are lines from films, and the author should, strictly, be the script writer. However, remarks such as 'Come up and see me (sometime)' are so closely associated with her that it would be perverse not to include them under her name.

Yet another problem involves such quotations as those of Goldwyn and Spooner, who almost certainly never made some of the remarks attributed to them. We decided to include these, if only because they are too good to leave out. Some indication of the difficulties in attributing quotations is given by the reaction of one person we telephoned about a quotation. 'Yes,' she said, 'it is often said to be by me, but I was only repeating something I heard years ago.' And the difficulty in selection is illustrated by her next remark. 'But I have said lots of other clever things that nobody has noticed.'

We hope that you will bear with us in our solutions to these problems and will find our selection both informative and enjoyable reading.

The Editors
1990

• Acknowledgments

Editors

John Daintith
Anne Stibbs
Edmund Wright
David Pickering

Contributors

Elizabeth Bonham
Sue Cope
Eve Daintith
Rosalind Fergusson
Joanna Gosling
Jock Graham
Lawrence Holden
Alan Isaacs
Amanda Isaacs
Valerie Illingworth
Stephen Jones
Elizabeth Martin
Sandra McQueen
Jennifer Monk
David Pickering
Ruth Salomon
Jessica Scholes
Gwynneth Shaw
Mary Shields
Kate Smith

•DICTIONARY OF QUOTATIONS

A

Abbott, Berenice (1898–) US photographer.

1 Photography can never grow up if it imitates some other medium. It has to walk alone; it has to be itself.

Infinity, 'It Has to Walk Alone'

Abel, Niels Henrik (1809–29) Norwegian mathematician. He was noted for his work on group theory and the theory of equations.

1 By studying the masters – not their pupils.

When asked how he had become a great mathematician so quickly
Men of Mathematics (E. T. Bell)

Accius, Lucius (170–c. 85 BC) Roman tragic playwright, who also wrote treatises on grammar, poetry, and agriculture. Of his plays, which were mostly on mythological subjects, about 700 lines survive.

1 Let them hate, so long as they fear.

Atreus, 'Seneca'

Acheson, Dean Gooderham (1893–1971) US lawyer and statesman. Noted for his strong stance against Soviet expansionism, he was prominent in the development of the Truman Doctrine, the Marshall Plan, and NATO.

Quotations about Acheson

1 Washington's number 1 number 2 man.

Anonymous

2 Not only did he not suffer fools gladly; he did not suffer them at all.

Lester Pearson (1897–1972) Canadian statesman. *Time*, 25 Oct 1971

Quotations by Acheson

3 It hasn't taken Winston long to get used to American ways. He hadn't been an American citizen for three minutes before attacking an ex-secretary of state!

At a ceremony in 1963 to make Churchill an honorary American citizen, Churchill obliquely attacked Acheson's reference to Britain losing an empire.
Randolph Churchill (K. Halle)

4 It is worse than immoral, it's a mistake.

Describing the Vietnam war. *See also* BOULAY DE LA MEURTHE. Quoted by Alistair Cooke in his radio programme *Letter from America*

5 I will undoubtedly have to seek what is happily known as gainful employment, which I am glad to say does not describe holding public office.

Remark made on leaving his post as secretary of state, 1952; he subsequently returned to private legal practice

6 Great Britain has lost an Empire and has not yet found a role.

Speech, Military Academy, West Point, 5 Dec 1962

7 A memorandum is written not to inform the reader but to protect the writer.

Attrib.

Acton, John Emerich Edward Dalberg Acton, 1st Baron (1834–1902) British historian; planning editor of the *Cambridge Modern History*. A friend and adviser to Gladstone, he served as a Whig MP (1859–65).

1 The danger is not that a particular class is unfit to govern. Every class is unfit to govern.

Letter to Mary Gladstone, 1881

2 Power tends to corrupt, and absolute power corrupts absolutely. Great men are almost always bad men . . . There is no worse heresy than that the office sanctifies the holder of it.

Often misquoted as 'Power corrupts   '
Letter to Bishop Mandell Creighton, 5 Apr 1887

Adamov, Arthur (1908–70) Russian-born French dramatist. An exponent of the theatre of the absurd, his plays include *La Parodie* (1947), featuring a handless clock, and *Le Ping Pong* (1955) in which human destiny is controlled by a pinball machine.

1 The reason why Absurdist plays take place in No Man's Land with only two characters is primarily financial.

Said at the Edinburgh International Drama Conference, 13 Sept 1963

Adams, Abigail (1744–1818) US feminist campaigner and a prolific letter writer. She was the wife of the second US president, John Adams, and mother of John Quincy Adams.

1 I am more and more convinced that man is a dangerous creature and that power, whether vested in many or a few, is ever grasping, and like the grave, cries 'Give, give.'

Letter to John Adams, 27 Nov 1775

2 . . . a habit the pleasure of which increases with practise, but becomes more urksome with neglect.

Referring to letter-writing
Letter to her daughter, 8 May 1808

Adams, F(ranklin) P(ierce) (1881–1960) US journalist and humorist. His columns in the New York *Herald-Tribune* (1931–37) and New York *Post* (1938–41) were widely read. His books include *Tobogganing on Parnassus* (1910).

1 The rich man has his motor car,
His country and his town estate.
He smokes a fifty-cent cigar
And jeers at Fate.

The Rich Man

2 Yet though my lamp burns low and dim,
Though I must slave for livelihood –
Think you that I would change with him?
You bet I would!

The Rich Man

Adams, John Quincy (1767–1848) Sixth president of the USA (1825–29). As secretary of state to President James Monroe (1817–25), he formulated the Monroe Doctrine opposing foreign intervention in American affairs.

Quotations about Adams

1 A man must be a born fool who voluntarily engages in controversy with Mr. Adams on a question of fact. I doubt whether he was ever mistaken in his life.

Henry Clay (1777–1852) US politician. Remark, 1823

2 He is no literary old gentleman, but a bruiser, and loves the melee.

Ralph Waldo Emerson (1803–82) US poet and essayist. *Journal*

Quotations by Adams

3 Think of your forefathers! Think of your posterity!

Speech, Plymouth, Massachusetts, 22 Dec 1802

4 I inhabit a weak, frail, decayed tenement; battered by the winds and broken in on by the storms, and, from all I can learn, the landlord does not intend to repair.

Said during his last illness
Attrib.

Adams, Richard (1920–) British novelist. A civil servant until the success of his children's book *Watership Down* (1972), he later wrote *Shardik* (1974), *The Plague Dogs* (1977), *The Girl in a Swing* (1980), and *Traveller* (1989).

1 I had vaguely supposed that marriage in a registry office while lacking both sanctity and style, was at least a swift, straightforward business. If not, then what was the use of it, even to the heathen? A few enquiries, however, showed it to be no such thing.

The Girl in a Swing, Ch. 13

2 Karin needed nothing from God. He just had the power to kill her that's all: to destroy her flesh and blood, the tools without which she could not work.

The Girl in a Swing, Ch. 28

3 Many human beings say that they enjoy the winter, but what they really enjoy is feeling proof against it.

Watership Down, Ch. 50

Adams, Samuel (1722–1803) US revolutionary leader. A leader of the agitation known as the Boston Tea Party, he became governor of Massachusetts (1794–97).

1 A nation of shop-keepers are very seldom so disinterested.

Referring to Britain, following the Declaration of Independence, 4 July 1776
Speech, Philadelphia, 1 Aug 1776

Adams, Sarah F(lower) (1805–48) British poet and hymn writer.

1 Nearer, my God, to thee,
Nearer to thee!

Nearer My God to Thee

Adcock, Sir Frank Ezra (1886–1968) British classicist; coeditor of the *Cambridge Ancient History* and professor of ancient history at Cambridge University.

1 That typically English characteristic for which there is no English name – *esprit de corps*.

Presidential address

Addams, Jane (1860–1935) US social worker and founder of Hull House, Chicago. She won the Nobel Peace Prize in 1931.

1 Old-fashioned ways which no longer apply to changed conditions are a snare in which the feet of women have always become readily entangled.

Newer Ideals of Peace, 'Utilization of Women in City Government'

2 In his own way each man must struggle, lest the moral law become a far-off abstraction utterly separated from his active life.

Twenty Years at Hull House

3 Civilization is a method of living, an attitude of equal respect for all men.

Speech, Honolulu, 1933

Addison, Joseph (1672–1719) British essayist. A Whig politician, he entered parliament in 1708. Addison contributed numerous essays to the *Tatler* and was cofounder (with Richard Steele) of *The Spectator* (1711).

Quotations about Addison

1 Whoever wishes to attain an English style, familiar but not coarse and elegant but not ostentatious, must give his days and nights to the volumes of Addison.

Samuel Johnson (1709–84) British lexicographer. *Lives of the Poets*

2 A parson in a tye-wig.

Bernard Mandeville (?1670–1733) Dutch-born British doctor, writer, and wit. Remark

Quotations by Addison

3 Pray consider what a figure a man would make in the republic of letters.

Ancient Medals

4 'Tis not in mortals to command success,
But we'll do more, Sempronius; we'll deserve it.

Cato, I:2

5 And if the following day, he chance to find
A new repast, or an untasted spring,
Blesses his stars, and thinks it luxury.

Cato, I:4

6 The woman that deliberates is lost.

Cato, IV:1

7 When vice prevails, and impious men bear sway,
The post of honour is a private station.

Cato, IV:1

8 What pity is it
That we can die but once to serve our country!

See also Nathan HALE
Cato, IV:4

9 A reader seldom peruses a book with pleasure until he knows whether the writer of it be a black man or a fair man, of a mild or choleric disposition, married or a bachelor.
The Spectator, 1

10 Thus I live in the world rather as a Spectator of mankind, than as one of the species, by which means I have made myself a speculative statesman, soldier, merchant, and artisan, without ever meddling with any practical part of life.
The Spectator, 1

11 Nothing is capable of being well set to music that is not nonsense.
The Spectator, 18

12 The infusion of a China plant sweetened with the pith of an Indian cane.
Referring to tea
The Spectator, 69

13 *Sir Roger* told them, with the air of a man who would not give his judgment rashly, that 'much might be said on both sides'.
Sir Roger de Coverley was a fictional archetype of the old-fashioned and eccentric country squire
The Spectator, 122

14 I have often thought, says Sir Roger, it happens very well that Christmas should fall out in the Middle of Winter.
The Spectator, 269

15 The Hand that made us is divine.
The Spectator, 465

16 A woman seldom asks advice until she has bought her wedding clothes.
The Spectator, 475

17 We are always doing something for posterity, but I would fain see posterity do something for us.
The Spectator, 583

18 I have but ninepence in ready money, but I can draw for a thousand pounds.
Comparing his ability to make conversation and to write
Life of Johnson (Boswell)

19 See in what peace a Christian can die.
Last words

Ade, George (1866–1944) US dramatist and humorist. Books include *Breaking into Society* (1903) and *The Old-Time Saloon* (1931); *The College Widow* (1904) and *Father and the Boys* (1907) were his best-known plays.

1 'Whom are you?' said he, for he had been to night school.
Bang! Bang!: The Steel Box

2 The music teacher came twice each week to bridge the awful gap between Dorothy and Chopin.
Attrib.

Adenauer, Konrad (1876–1967) German statesman; first chancellor of the Federal Republic (1949–63).

1 I haven't asked you to make me young again. All I want is to go on getting older.
Replying to his doctor
Attrib.

Adler, Alfred (1870–1937) Austrian psychiatrist. After breaking with Freud he based his work on the importance of the inferiority complex. His books include *The Neurotic Constitution* (1912) and *The Pattern of Life* (1930).

1 It is easier to fight for one's principles than to live up to them.
Alfred Adler (P. Bottome)

2 Against whom?
Said when he heard that an egocentric had fallen in love
Some of My Best Friends (J. Bishop), 'Exponent of the Soul'

Ady, Thomas (17th century) British poet, who wrote on the subject of witchcraft.

1 Matthew, Mark, Luke and John,
The bed be blest that I lie on.
A Candle in the Dark

Aesop (6th century BC) Reputed Greek writer of fables said by Herodotus to have been a slave from the island of Samos. Aesop's fables, popularized by the Roman poet Phaedrus (1st century AD), use animal characters to portray human frailties.

1 Beware that you do not lose the substance by grasping at the shadow.
Fables, 'The Dog and the Shadow'

2 I am sure the grapes are sour.
Fables, 'The Fox and the Grapes'

3 Thinking to get at once all the gold that the goose could give, he killed it, and opened it only to find – nothing.
Fables, 'The Goose with the Golden Eggs'

4 The gods help them that help themselves.
Fables, 'Hercules and the Waggoner'

5 It is not only fine feathers that make fine birds.
Fables, 'The Jay and the Peacock'

6 While I see many hoof-marks going in, I see none coming out.
Fables, 'The Lion, the Fox, and the Beasts'

7 I will have nothing to do with a man who can blow hot and cold with the same breath.
Fables, 'The Man and the Satyr'

8 Don't count your chickens before they are hatched.
Fables, 'The Milkmaid and her Pail'

9 The boy cried 'Wolf, wolf!' and the villagers came out to help him.
Fables, 'The Shepherd's Boy'

10 The lamb that belonged to the sheep whose skin the wolf was wearing began to follow the wolf in the sheep's clothing.
Fables, 'The Wolf in Sheep's Clothing'

Agar, Herbert Sebastian (1897–1980) US writer. His works include *The People's Choice* (1933), *The Pursuit of Happiness* (1938), and *A Time for Greatness* (1942).

1 The truth that makes men free is for the most part the truth which men prefer not to hear.
A Time for Greatness

Agassiz, Jean Louis Rodolphe (1807–73) Swiss naturalist.

1 I can't afford to waste my time making money.
When asked to give a lecture for a fee
Attrib.

Agate, James (Evershed) (1877–1947) British theatre critic. His articles and reviews were collected in his series *Ego* (1–9; 1935–47).

1 Long experience has taught me that in England nobody goes to the theatre unless he or she has bronchitis.
See also SCHNABEL
Ego, 6

2 The English instinctively admire any man who has no talent and is modest about it.
Attrib.

3 Theatre director: a person engaged by the management to conceal the fact that the players cannot act.
Attrib.

Agathon (c. 446–401 BC) Athenian poet and playwright.

1 Even God cannot change the past.
Nicomachean Ethics (Aristotle), VI

Agnew, Spiro T(heodore) (1918–) US politician. Republican vice-president (1969–73), he was forced to resign as a result of a federal tax case.

1 I agree with you that the name of Spiro Agnew is not a household name. I certainly hope that it will become one within the next couple of months.
TV interview, 8 Aug 1968

2 To some extent, if you've seen one city slum you've seen them all.
Election speech, Detroit, 18 Oct 1968

3 A spirit of national masochism prevails, encouraged by an effete corps of impudent snobs who characterize themselves as intellectuals.
Speech, New Orleans, 19 Oct 1969

4 An intellectual is a man who doesn't know how to park a bike.
Attrib.

Akins, Zoë (1886–1958) US dramatist. Among her most successful plays were the satirical comedy *The Greeks Had a Word for It* (1930) and *The Old Maid* (1935).

1 The Greeks Had a Word for It.
Play title

Albee, Edward (1928–) US dramatist. Originally an exponent of the theatre of the absurd, his first success was with *Who's Afraid of Virginia Woolf?* (1962). Later plays include *A Delicate Balance* (1967), *Seascape* (1975), and *Marriage Play* (1986).

1 Who's Afraid of Virginia Woolf?
Play title

2 I have a fine sense of the ridiculous, but no sense of humour.
Who's Afraid of Virginia Woolf?, I

3 You gotta have a swine to show you where the truffles are.
Who's Afraid of Virginia Woolf?, I

Albert, Prince (1819–61) The son of Ernest, Duke of Saxe-Coburg-Gotha, and consort of Queen Victoria, whom he married in 1840. He organized the Great Exhibition of 1851.

1 The works of art, by being publicly exhibited and offered for sale, are becoming articles of trade, following as such the unreasoning laws of markets and fashion; and public and even private patronage is swayed by their tyrannical influence.
Referring to the Great Exhibition
Speech, Royal Academy Dinner, 3 May 1851

Alcott, Louisa May (1832–88) US novelist. She wrote *Flower Fables* (1854) and, her most famous book, *Little Women* (1868–69).

1 Housekeeping ain't no joke.
Little Women, Pt. I

2 It takes people a long time to learn the difference between talent and genius, especially ambitious young men and women.
Little Women, Pt. II

3 . . . girls are so queer you never know what they mean. They say No when they mean Yes, and drive a man out of his wits for the fun of it . . .
Little Women, Pt. II

Alcuin (c. 735–804) English theologian and scholar. Adviser to Charlemagne, he made significant contributions to the development of education.

1 *Vox populi, vox dei.*
The voice of the people is the voice of God.
Letter to Charlemagne

Aldiss, Brian (1925–) British science-fiction writer. His novels include *Hothouse* (1962), *Frankenstein Unbound* (1973), the *Heliconia* trilogy (1982–85), and *Forgotten Life* (1988); he has also edited many anthologies.

1 Science fiction is no more written for scientists than ghost stories are written for ghosts.
Penguin Science Fiction, Introduction

Aldrich, Dean (1647–1710) English poet.

1 If all be true that I do think,
There are five reasons we should drink;
Good wine – a friend – or being dry –
Or lest we should be by and by –
Or any other reason why.
Reasons for Drinking

Alençon, Sophie-Charlotte, Duchesse d' (d. 1897) Bavarian-born duchess.

1 Because of my title, I was the first to enter here. I shall be the last to go out.

Refusing help during a fire, 4 May 1897, at a charity bazaar in Paris. She died along with 120 others.
Attrib.

Alexander, C. F. (1818–95) British hymn writer. Her popular hymns include *All Things Bright and Beautiful*, *Once in Royal David's City*, and *There is a Green Hill Far Away*.

1 All things bright and beautiful,
All creatures great and small,
All things wise and wonderful,
The Lord God made them all.
All Things Bright and Beautiful

2 Once in royal David's city
Stood a lowly cattle shed,
Where a Mother laid her Baby
In a manger for His bed:
Mary was that Mother mild,
Jesus Christ her little Child.
Once in Royal David's City

3 There is a green hill far away,
Without a city wall,
Where the dear Lord was crucified,
Who died to save us all.
There is a Green Hill Far Away

Alexander (III) the Great (356–323 BC) King of Macedon, who conquered most of the ancient world from Asia Minor to Egypt and India. He was both an outstanding general and an inspired administrator.

1 I am dying with the help of too many physicians.
Attrib.

Alfonso (X) the Wise (c. 1221–84) King of Castile and Léon. His court at Toledo was a centre for Christian, Muslim, and Jewish scholars.

1 Had I been present at the Creation, I would have given some useful hints for the better ordering of the universe.

Referring to the complicated Ptolemaic model of the universe.
Often quoted as, 'Had I been consulted I would have recommended something simpler'.
Attrib.

Ali, Muhammad (Cassius Clay; 1942–) US boxer noted for his extrovert personality. He was three times world heavyweight champion (1964–71, 1974–78, 1978–80).

1 I'm the greatest!
Remark, often said before, during, and after his fights

2 Float like a butterfly
Sting like a bee
Describing his boxing style
Remark

3 Only the nose knows
Where the nose goes
When the door close.
When asked whether a boxer should have sex before a big fight
Remark, reported by Al Silverman

4 You don't want no pie in the sky when you die. You want something here on the ground while you're still around.
Attrib.

Alison, Richard (fl. c. 1606) English poet.

1 There cherries grow, that none can buy
Till cherry ripe themselves do cry.
An Hour's Recreation in Music

2 There is a garden in her face,
Where roses and white lilies grow.
An Hour's Recreation in Music

Allainval, Abbé Lénor Jean d' (1700–53) French dramatist.

1 *L'embarras des richesses.*
A superfluity of good things.
Play title

Allen, Fred (1894–1956) US comedian.

1 A celebrity is a person who works hard all his life to become known, then wears dark glasses to avoid being recognized.
Treadmill to Oblivion

2 Where were you fellows when the paper was blank?
Said to writers who heavily edited one of his scripts
Attrib.

3 A gentleman is any man who wouldn't hit a woman with his hat on.
Attrib.

Allen, Woody (Allen Stewart Konigsberg; 1935–) US film actor and director. His films include *Play It Again, Sam* (1972), *Annie Hall* (1977), and *The Purple Rose of Cairo* (1985).

1 Is sex dirty? Only if it's done right
All You've Ever Wanted to Know About Sex

2 It was the most fun I ever had without laughing
Referring to sex
Annie Hall

3 Don't knock it, it's sex with someone you love.
Referring to masturbation
Annie Hall

4 I'm short enough and ugly enough to succeed on my own.
Play It Again Sam

5 I'm really a timid person – I was beaten up by Quakers.
Sleeper

6 My brain: it's my second favourite organ.
Sleeper

7 It's not that I'm afraid to die. I just don't want to be there when it happens.
Without Feathers, 'Death (A Play)'

8 The lion and the calf shall lie down together but the calf won't get much sleep.
Without Feathers, 'The Scrolls'

9 And my parents finally realize that I'm kidnapped and they snap into action immediately: they rent out my room.
Woody Allen and His Comedy (E. Lax)

10 I don't want to achieve immortality through my work . . . I want to achieve it through not dying.

Woody Allen and His Comedy (E. Lax)

11 I want to tell you a terrific story about oral contraception. I asked this girl to sleep with me and she said 'no'.

Woody Allen: Clown Prince of American Humor (Adler and Feinman), Ch. 2

Altman, Robert (1925–) US film director. His best-known film is *M*A*S*H* (1970). Subsequent films include *The Long Goodbye* (1973) and *Three Women* (1977).

1 What's a cult? It just means not enough people to make a minority.

The Observer, 1981

Ambrose, St (c. 339–97) Bishop of Milan (374–97). Born at Trier, he settled in Milan as a provincial governor. An eloquent preacher, he was responsible for the conversion of St Augustine.

1 When in Rome, live as the Romans do: when elsewhere, live as they live elsewhere.

Advice to St Augustine

Amery, Leopold Charles Maurice Stennett (1873–1955) British statesman. He played an important part in the downfall of Chamberlain's government (1940).

1 Speak for England.

Shouted to Arthur Greenwood, Labour Party spokesman, before he began to speak in a House of Commons debate immediately preceding the declaration of war, 2 Sept 1939

2 You have sat too long here for any good you have been doing. Depart, I say, and let us have done with you. In the name of God, *go!*

Said to Neville Chamberlain using Oliver CROMWELL's words
Speech, House of Commons, May 1940

Amis, Sir Kingsley (1922–) British novelist. He made his name with *Lucky Jim* (1954). Subsequent novels include *Jake's Thing* (1978), *The Old Devils* (1986), and *Difficulties With Girls* (1988). He has also published several volumes of verse.

1 Outside every fat man there is an even fatter man trying to close in.

See also CONNOLLY
One Fat Englishman, Ch. 3

2 It was no wonder that people were so horrible when they started life as children.

One Fat Englishman, Ch. 14

3 Lucky Jim.

Title of novel

Amis, Martin (1949–) British novelist, son of author Kingsley Amis. His works include *The Rachel Papers* (1974), *The Moronic Inferno* (1986), *Einstein's Monsters* (1987), and *London Fields* (1989).

1 Such precepts are arguable, I know, but I've always gone along with the view that, first, the surest guarantee of sexual success is sexual success (you can't have one without the other and you can't have the other without the one), and, second, that the trappings of sexual success are only fleetingly distinguishable from sexual success itself.

Success

Andersen, Hans Christian (1805–75) Danish writer, known for his fairy tales, including *The Snow Queen* and *The Ugly Duckling*.

1 'But the Emperor has nothing on at all!' cried a little child.

The Emperor's New Clothes

2 The Ugly Duckling.

Story title

3 Most of the people who will walk after me will be children, so make the beat keep time with short steps.

Planning the music for his funeral
Hans Christian Andersen (R. Godden)

Anderson, Elizabeth Garrett (1836–1917) British physician, who, despite being refused entry to medical school, studied privately and was granted a licence to practise in 1865.

1 Because I prefer to earn a thousand rather than twenty pounds a year.

Reply when asked why she did not train to be a nurse
Dr. Elizabeth Garrett Anderson (Louisa Garrett Anderson)

2 I was a young woman living at home with nothing to do in what authors call 'comfortable circumstances.' But I was wicked enough not to be comfortable. I was full of energy and vigour and of the discontent that goes with unemployed activies. Everything seemed wrong to me.

Draft for speech

Anne, the Princess Royal (1950–) The only daughter of Queen Elizabeth II, she married Mark Phillips (1948–) in 1973. She is an accomplished horsewoman, and has also made a worldwide reputation as an active and resourceful President of the Save the Children Fund.

1 When I appear in public people expect me to neigh, grind my teeth, paw the ground and swish my tail – none of which is easy.

The Observer, 'Sayings of the Week', 22 May 1977

2 It's a very boring time. I am not particularly maternal – it's an occupational hazard of being a wife.

TV interview, talking about pregnancy
Daily Express, 14 Apr 1981

3 Why don't you naff off!

To reporters
Daily Mirror, 17 Apr 1982

4 It could be said that the Aids pandemic is a classic own-goal scored by the human race against itself.

Remark, Jan 1988

Anonymous This includes a selection of sayings, rhymes, epitaphs, ballads, mottoes, etc., for which the author is unknown. They are arranged in alphabetical order of the first line. Further anonymous quotations are given under the entries for Nursery Rhymes and Proverbs.

1 Adieu, adieu, kind friends, adieu, adieu, adieu,
I can no longer stay with you, stay with you.
I'll hang my harp on a weeping willow-tree.
And may the world go well with thee.
There is a Tavern in the Town

2 *Ad majorem Dei gloriam.*
To the greater glory of God.
Motto of the Jesuits

3 All human beings are born free and equal in dignity and rights.
Universal Declaration of Human Rights (1948), Article 1

4 All present and correct.
Report by the orderly sergeant to the officer of the day
King's Regulations (Army).

5 All who come my grave to see
Avoid damp beds and think of me.
Epitaph of Lydia Eason, St Michael's, Stoke

6 Any officer who shall behave in a scandalous manner, unbecoming the character of an officer and a gentleman shall . . . be cashiered.
The words 'conduct unbecoming the character of an officer' are a direct quotation from the Naval Discipline Act (10 Aug 1860), Article 24
Articles of War (1872), *Disgraceful Conduct*, 79

7 Are we downhearted? No!
A favourite expression of the British soldiers during World War I
Attrib.

8 As I sat on a sunny bank,
On Christmas Day in the morning,
I spied three ships come sailing by.
As I sat on a Sunny Bank

9 *Ave Caesar, morituri te salutant.*
Hail Caesar; those who are about to die salute you.
Greeting to the Roman Emperor by gladiators

10 Begone, dull care! I prithee begone from me!
Begone, dull care, you and I shall never agree.
Begone Dull Care

11 Beneath this stone, in hope of Zion,
Doth lie the landlord of the 'Lion'.
His son keeps on the business still,
Resign'd unto the Heavenly will.
Epitaph, Upton-on-Severn churchyard

12 Come landlord, fill the flowing bowl,
Until it doth run over . . .
For tonight we'll merry, merry be,
Tomorrow we'll be sober.
Come, Landlord, Fill the Flowing Bowl

13 Come lasses and lads, get leave of your dads,
And away to the Maypole hie,
For every he has got him a she,
And the fiddler's standing by.
Come Lasses and Lads

14 Conduct . . . to the prejudice of good order and military discipline.
Army Act, 40

15 Dear Sir, Your astonishment's odd:
I am always about in the Quad.
And that's why the tree
Will continue to be,
Since observed by Yours faithfully, God.
The response to EWER's limerick

16 Early one morning, just as the sun was rising.
I heard a maid singing in the valley below:
'Oh, don't deceive me; Oh, never leave me!
How could you use a poor maiden so?'
Early One Morning

17 Everyman, I will go with thee, and be thy guide.
In thy most need to go by thy side.
Everyman, Pt. 1

18 Farewell and adieu to you,
Fair Spanish Ladies,
Farewell and adieu to you, Ladies of Spain.
Spanish Ladies

19 From ghoulies and ghosties and long-leggety beasties
And things that go bump in the night,
Good Lord, deliver us!
Cornish prayer

20 God be in my head,
And in my understanding;
God be in my eyes,
And in my looking;
God be in my mouth,
And in my speaking;
God be in my heart,
And in my thinking;
God be at my end,
And at my departing.
Sarum Missal

21 God rest you merry, gentlemen,
Let nothing you dismay.
God Rest you Merry

22 Greensleeves was all my joy,
Greensleeves was my delight,
Greensleeves was my heart of gold,
And who but Lady Greensleeves.
Greensleeves

23 Ha, ha, ha, you and me,
Little brown jug, don't I love thee!
The Little Brown Jug

24 Hail Mary, full of grace, the Lord is with thee:
Blessed art thou among women, and blessed is the fruit of thy womb, Jesus.
Ave Maria, 11th century

25 Here lie I and my four daughters,
Killed by drinking Cheltenham waters.
Had we but stick to Epsom salts,
We wouldn't have been in these here vaults.
Cheltenham Waters

26 Here lie I by the chancel door;
They put me here because I was poor.
The further in, the more you pay,
But here lie I as snug as they.

Epitaph, Devon churchyard

27 Here lies a man who was killed by lightning;
He died when his prospects seemed to be
brightening.
He might have cut a flash in this world of
trouble,
But the flash cut him, and he lies in the stubble.

Epitaph, Torrington, Devon

28 Here lies a valiant warrior
Who never drew a sword;
Here lies a noble courtier
Who never kept his word;
Here lies the Earl of Leicester
Who governed the estates
Whom the earth could never living love,
And the just heaven now hates.

Attrib. to Ben Jonson in *Collection of Epitaphs* (Tissington), 1857

29 Here lies father and mother and sister and I,
We all died within the space of one short year;
They all be buried at Wimble, except I,
And I be buried here.

Epitaph, Staffordshire churchyard

30 Here lies Fred,
Who was alive and is dead:
Had it been his father,
I had much rather;
Had it been his brother,
Still better than another;
Had it been his sister,
No one would have missed her;
Had it been the whole generation,
Still better for the nation:
But since 'tis only Fred,
Who was alive and is dead, –
There's no more to be said.

Referring to Frederick, Prince of Wales, eldest son of George II
and father of George III.
Memoirs of George II (Horace Walpole)

31 Here lies my wife,
Here lies she;
Hallelujah!
Hallelujee!

Epitaph, Leeds churchyard

32 Here lies the body of Mary Ann Lowder,
She burst while drinking a seidlitz powder.
Called from the world to her heavenly rest,
She should have waited till it effervesced.

Epitaph

33 Here lies the body of Richard Hind,
Who was neither ingenious, sober, nor kind.

Epitaph

34 Here lies Will Smith – and, what's something
rarish,
He was born, bred, and hanged, all in the same
parish.

Epitaph

35 Here's a health unto his Majesty . . .
Confusion to his enemies, . . .
And he that will not drink his health,
I wish him neither wit nor wealth,
Not yet a rope to hang himself.

Here's a Health unto his Majesty

36 Here's tae us wha's like us?
Gey few, and they're a' deid.

Scottish toast

37 Here we come gathering nuts in May
Nuts in May,
. . .
On a cold and frosty morning.

Children's song

38 He that fights and runs away
May live to fight another day.

Musarum Deliciae

39 *Honi soit qui mal y pense.*
Evil be to him who evil thinks.

Motto for the Order of the Garter

40 'How different, how very different from the
home life of our own dear Queen!'

Remark about the character of Cleopatra as performed by Sarah
Bernhardt

41 I always eat peas with honey
I've done it all my life,
They do taste kind of funny,
But it keeps them on the knife.

Peas

42 If all the world were paper,
And all the sea were ink,
And all the trees were bread and cheese,
What should we do for drink?

If All the World were Paper

43 I feel no pain, dear mother, now
But oh, I am so dry!
O take me to a brewery
And leave me there to die.

Shanty

44 I know two things about the horse,
And one of them is rather coarse.

The Horse

45 I'll sing you twelve O.
Green grow the rushes O.
What is your twelve O?
Twelve for the twelve apostles,
Eleven for the eleven who went to heaven,
Ten for the ten commandments,
Nine for the nine bright shiners,
Eight for the eight bold rangers,
Seven for the seven stars in the sky,
Six for the six proud walkers,
Five for the symbol at your door,
Four for the Gospel makers,
Three for the rivals,
Two, two, the lily-white boys,
Clothed all in green O,
One is one and all alone
And ever more shall be so.

The Dilly Song

46 I met wid Napper Tandy, and he took me by the hand,
And he said, 'How's poor ould Ireland, and how does she stand?'
She's the most disthressful country that iver yet was seen,
For they're hangin' men an' women there for the wearin' o' the Green.

The Wearin' o' the Green

47 In Dublin's fair city, where the girls are so pretty,
I first set my eyes on sweet Molly Malone,
As she wheeled her wheelbarrow, through streets broad and narrow,
Crying, Cockles and mussels! alive, alive, O!

She was a fishmonger, but sure 'twas no wonder,
For so were her father and mother before.

Cockles and Mussels

48 In good King Charles's golden days,
When loyalty no harm meant,
A zealous High Churchman was I,
And so I got preferment.

And this is law, that I'll maintain,
Unto my dying day, Sir,
That whatsoever King shall reign,
I'll be the Vicar of Bray, Sir.

The Vicar of Bray

49 In Scarlet town, where I was born,
There was a fair maid dwellin',
Made every youth cry *Well-a-way!*
Her name was Barbara Allen.

All in the merry month of May,
When green buds they were swellin',
Young Jemmy Grove on his death-bed lay,
For love of Barbara Allen.

So slowly, slowly rase she up,
And slowly she came nigh him,
And when she drew the curtain by –
'Young man, I think you're dyin'!'.

Barbara Allen's Cruelty

50 *Liberté! Égalité! Fraternité!*
Freedom! Equality! Brotherhood!

Motto for French Revolutionaries

51 Little Willy from his mirror
Licked the mercury right off,
Thinking in his childish error,
It would cure the whooping cough.
At the funeral his mother
Smartly said to Mrs Brown:
"Twas a chilly day for Willie
When the mercury went down'.

Willie's Epitaph

52 Lizzie Borden took an axe
And gave her mother forty whacks;
When she saw what she had done
She gave her father forty-one!

On 4 Aug 1892 in Fall River, Massachusetts, Lizzie Borden was acquitted of the murder of her stepmother and her father

53 Lo, Hudled up, together Lye
Gray Age, Grene youth, White Infancy.
If Death doth Nature's Laws dispence,
And reconciles All Difference
Tis Fit, One Flesh, One House Should have
One Tombe, One Epitaph, One Grave:
And they that Liv'd and Lov'd Either,
Should Dye and Lye and Sleep together.

Good Reader, whether go or stay
Thou must not hence be Long Away

Epitaph, of William Bartholomew (died 1662), his wife and some of their children, St John the Baptist, Burford

54 Love is blind; friendship closes its eyes.

Proverb

55 Mary Ann has gone to rest,
Safe at last on Abraham's breast,
Which may be nuts for Mary Ann,
But is certainly rough on Abraham.

Epitaph

56 Miss Buss and Miss Beale
Cupid's darts do not feel.
How different from us,
Miss Beale and Miss Buss.

Written about the headmistresses of North London Collegiate School and Cheltenham Ladies' College, respectively

57 My Bonnie lies over the ocean,
My Bonnie lies over the sea,
My Bonnie lies over the ocean,
Oh, bring back my Bonnie to me.

My Bonnie

58 My Love in her attire doth show her wit,
It doth so well become her:
For every season she hath dressings fit,
For winter, spring, and summer.
No beauty she doth miss,
When all her robes are on;
But beauty's self she is,
When all her robes are gone.
Madrigal

59 My name is George Nathaniel Curzon,
I am a most superior person.
My face is pink, my hair is sleek,
I dine at Blenheim once a week.
The Masque of Balliol

60 My sledge and anvil lie declined
My bellows too have lost their wind
My fire's extinct, my forge decayed,
And in the Dust my Vice is laid
My coals are spent, my iron's gone
My Nails are Drove, My Work is done.
An epitaph to William Strange, blacksmith, died 6 June 1746 and buried in Nettlebed churchyard

61 Nation shall speak peace unto nation.
Motto of the British Broadcasting Corporation

62 No one provokes me with impunity.
Motto of the Crown of Scotland

63 Now I am a bachelor, I live by myself and I work
at the weaving trade,
And the only only thing that I ever did wrong
Was to woo a fair young maid.

She sighed, she cried, she damned near died:
she said 'What shall I do?'
So I took her into bed and covered up her head
Just to save her from the foggy, foggy dew.
Weaver's Song

64 Now I lay me down to sleep,
I pray the Lord my soul to keep.
If I should die before I wake,
I pray the Lord my soul to take.
New England Primer, 1781

65 O Death, where is thy sting-a-ling-a-ling,
O Grave, thy victoree?
The bells of hell go ting-a-ling-a-ling
For you but not for me.
Song of World War I

66 O, Shenandoah, I long to hear you
Away, you rolling river.
Shenandoah

67 O ye'll tak' the high road, and I'll tak' the low
road,
And I'll be in Scotland afore ye,
But me and my true love will never meet again,
On the bonnie, bonnie banks o' Loch Lomon'.
The Bonnie Banks o' Loch Lomon'

68 *Per ardua ad astra.*
Through endeavour to the stars!
Motto of the Royal Air Force

69 Please to remember the Fifth of November,
Gunpowder Treason and Plot.
We know no reason why gunpowder treason
Should ever be forgot.
Traditional

70 Sacred to the memory of
Captain Anthony Wedgwood
Accidentally shot by his gamekeeper
Whilst out shooting
"Well done thou good and faithful servant"
Epitaph

71 She was poor but she was honest
Victim of a rich man's game.
First he loved her, then he left her,
And she lost her maiden name.

See her on the bridge at midnight,
Saying 'Farewell, blighted love.'
Then a scream, a splash and goodness,
What is she a-doin' of?

It's the same the whole world over,
It's the poor wot gets the blame,
It's the rich wot gets the pleasure.
Ain't it all a bleedin' shame?
She was Poor but she was Honest

72 Since wars begin in the minds of men, it is in the
minds of men that the defences of peace must
be constructed.
Constitution of UNESCO

73 Some talk of Alexander, and some of Hercules,
Of Hector and Lysander, and such great names
as these;
But of all the world's brave heroes there's none
that can compare
With a tow, row, row, row, row, row for the
British Grenadiers.
The British Grenadiers

74 Stranger! Approach this spot with gravity!
John Brown is filling his last cavity.
Epitaph of a dentist

75 Sumer is icumen in,
Lhude sing cuccu!
Groweth sed, and bloweth med,
And springth the wude nu.
Cuckoo Song, c. 1250

76 Swing low sweet chariot,
Comin' for to carry me home,
I looked over Jordan an' what did I see?
A band of Angels coming after me,
Comin' for to carry me home.
Swing Low, Sweet Chariot

77 That this house will in no circumstances fight for
its King and country.
Motion passed at the Oxford Union, 9 Feb 1933

78 The animals went in one by one,
There's one more river to cross.
One More River

79 The Campbells are comin', oho, oho.
The Campbells are Comin'

80 The fault is great in man or woman
Who steals a goose from off a common;
But what can plead that man's excuse
Who steals a common from a goose?
The Tickler Magazine, 1 Feb 1821

81 The holly and the ivy,
When they are both full grown,
Of all the trees that are in the wood,
The holly bears the crown.
The rising of the sun
And the running of the deer,
The playing of the merry organ,
Sweet singing in the choir.
The Holly and the Ivy

82 The King over the Water.
Jacobite toast

83 The king sits in Dunfermline town
Drinking the blude-red wine.

'I saw the new moon late yestreen
Wi' the auld moon in her arm;
And if we gang to sea master,
I fear we'll come to harm.'

O lang, lang may the ladies sit,
Wi' their fans into their hand,
Before they see Sir Patrick Spens
Come sailing to the strand!
Sir Patrick Spens

84 The rabbit has a charming face;
Its private life is a disgrace.
The Rabbit, 20th century

85 There are twelve months in all the year,
As I hear many men say,
But the merriest month in all the year
Is the merry month of May.
Robin Hood and the Widow's Three Sons

86 There is a lady sweet and kind,
Was never face so pleased my mind;
I did but see her passing by,
And yet I love her till I die.
Passing By

87 There is a tavern in the town,
And there my dear love sits him down,
And drinks his wine 'mid laughter free,
And never, never thinks of me.

Fare thee well, for I must leave thee,
Do not let this parting grieve thee,
And remember that the best of friends must
part.
There is a Tavern in the Town

88 There is so much good in the worst of us,
And so much bad in the best of us,
That it hardly becomes any of us
To talk about the rest of us.
Good and Bad

89 There's a wonderful family called Stein,
There's Gert and there's Epp and there's Ein;
Gert's poems are bunk,
Epp's statues are junk,
And no one can understand Ein.

90 There was a faith-healer of Deal,
Who said, 'Although pain isn't real,
If I sit on a pin
And it punctures my skin,
I dislike what I fancy I feel.'

91 There was an old man from Darjeeling,
Who boarded a bus bound for Ealing,
He saw on the door:
'Please don't spit on the floor',
So he stood up and spat on the ceiling.

92 There was an old man of Boulogne
Who sang a most topical song.
It wasn't the words
That frightened the birds,
But the horrible double-entendre.

93 There was a young lady of Riga,
Who went for a ride on a tiger;
They returned from the ride
With the lady inside,
And a smile on the face of the tiger.

94 There was a young man of Japan
Whose limericks never would scan;
When they said it was so,
He replied, 'Yes, I know,
But I always try to get as many words into the
last line as ever I possibly can.'

95 There was a young woman called Starkie,
Who had an affair with a darky.
The result of her sins
Was quadruplets, not twins –
One black, and one white, and two khaki.

96 There were three ravens sat on a tree,
They were as black as they might be.
The one of them said to his mate,
'Where shall we our breakfast take?'
The Three Ravens

97 There were twa sisters sat in a bour;
Binnorie, O Binnorie!
There came a knight to be their wooer,
By the bonnie milldams o' Binnorie.
Binnorie

98 The sons of the prophet were brave men and
bold,
And quite unaccustomed to fear,
But the bravest by far in the ranks of the Shah
Was Abdul the Bulbul Amir.
Abdul the Bulbul Amir

99 Thirty days hath September,
April, June, and November;
All the rest have thirty-one,
Excepting February alone,
And that has twenty-eight days clear

And twenty-nine in each leap year.
Stevins Manuscript, c. 1555

100 This animal is very bad; when attacked it defends itself.
La Ménagerie (P. K. Théodore), 1828

101 This is a rotten argument, but it should be good enough for their lordships on a hot summer afternoon.
A note on a ministerial brief read out by mistake in the House of Lords
The Way the Wind Blows (Lord Home), 1976

102 This the grave of Mike O'Day
Who died maintaining his right of way.
His right was clear, his will was strong.
But he's just as dead as if he'd been wrong.
Epitaph

103 'Tom Pearse, Tom Pearse, lend me your grey mare,
All along, down along, out along, lee
For I want for to go to Widdicombe Fair,
Wi' Bill Brewer, Jan Stewer, Peter Gurney,
Peter Davey, Dan'l Whiddon, Harry Hawk;
Old Uncle Tom Cobbleigh and all.
Old Uncle Tom Cobbleigh and all.'
Widdicombe Fair

104 Warm summer sun shine kindly here:
Warm summer wind blow softly here:
Green sod above lie light, lie light:
Good-night, Dear Heart: good-night, good-night.
Memorial to Clorinda Haywood, St Bartholomew's, Edgbaston

105 What shall we do with the drunken sailor
Early in the morning?
Hoo-ray and up she rises
Early in the morning.
What shall we do with the Drunken Sailor?

106 When I am dead, and laid in grave,
And all my bones are rotten,
By this may I remembered be
When I should be forgotten.
On a girl's sampler, 1736

107 When Israel was in Egypt land,
Let my people go,
Oppressed so hard they could not stand,
Let my people go.
*Go down, Moses,
Way-down in Egypt land,
Tell old Pharaoh
To let my people go.*
Negro spiritual

108 Whose Finger do you want on the Trigger When the World Situation Is So Delicate?
Headline from the *Daily Mirror* on the day before the General Election, Oct 1951
Publish and Be Damned (Hugh Cudlipp), 1953

109 Ye Highlands and ye Lawlands,
O where hae ye been?
They hae slain the Earl of Murray,
And hae laid him on the green.

He was a braw gallant,
And he rid at the ring;
And the bonny Earl of Murray,
O he might hae been a king!

O lang will his Lady
Look owre the Castle Downe,
Ere she see the Earl of Murray
Come sounding through the town!
The Bonny Earl of Murray

Anouilh, Jean (1910–87) French dramatist, whose plays have enjoyed considerable success on the English stage. His most famous works include *Antigone* (1944), *Ring Round the Moon* (1950), *The Lark* (1953), and *Becket* (1959).

1 Oh, love is real enough, you will find it some day, but it has one arch-enemy – and that is life.
Ardèle

2 Love is, above all, the gift of oneself.
Ardèle

3 All evil comes from the old. They grow fat on ideas and young men die of them.
Catch as Catch Can

4 Every man thinks God is on his side. The rich and powerful know that he is.
The Lark

5 The object of art is to give life a shape.
The Rehearsal

6 What fun it would be to be poor, as long as one was *excessively* poor! Anything in excess is most exhilarating.
Ring Round the Moon

7 When you are forty, half of you belongs to the past . . . And when you are seventy, nearly all of you.
Attrib.

Anthony, Susan B. (1820–1906) US editor and worker for women's suffrage.

1 Men their rights and nothing more; women their rights and nothing less.
The Revolution, Motto

2 . . . there never will be complete equality until women themselves help to make laws and elect lawmakers.
In *The Arena*, (May 1897) 'The Status of Women, Past, Present and Future'

3 And yet, in the schoolroom more than any other place, does the difference of sex, if there is any, need to be forgotten.
Elizabeth Cady Stanton (ed. Theodore Stanton and Harriot Stanton Blatch), Vol. II

4 . . . and I shall earnestly and persistently continue to urge all women to the practical recognition of the old Revolutionary maxim, 'Resistance to tyranny is obedience to God.'
Speech in court, 18 June 1873
Jailed for Freedom (Doris Stevens)

Antrim, Minna (b. 1861) US writer.

1 A homely face and no figure have aided many women heavenward.
Naked Truth and Veiled Allusions

2 A fool bolts pleasure, then complains of moral indigestion.
Naked Truth and Veiled Allusions

3 Experience is a good teacher, but she sends in terrific bills.
Naked Truth and Veiled Allusions

Apollinaire, Guillaume (Wilhelm de Kostrowitzky; 1880–1918) Italian-born French poet. Collections of verse include *Alcools* (1913) and *Calligrammes* (1918). He also wrote the surrealist play *Les Mamelles de Tirésias* (1917).

1 Memories are hunting horns whose sound dies on the wind.
Cors de Chasse

Appius Caecus (4th–3rd century BC) Roman statesman (censor c. 312 BC; consul 307 and 296 BC) whose reforms benefitted the plebeians. He is regarded as the founder of Latin prose and oratory.

1 Each man the architect of his own fate.
De Civitate (Sallust), Bk. I

Appleton, Sir Edward Victor (1892–1965) British physicist. He discovered the layer of ionized gas in the upper atmosphere that reflects radio waves back to earth. This is now known as the Appleton layer.

1 I do not mind what language an opera is sung in so long as it is a language I don't understand.
The Observer, 'Sayings of the Week,' 28 Aug 1955

Appleton, Thomas Gold (1812–84) US writer, poet, and patron of the arts.

1 Good Americans, when they die, go to Paris.
See WILDE
Autocrat of the Breakfast Table (O. W. Holmes), Ch. 6

2 A Boston man is the east wind made flesh.
Attrib.

Aquinas, St Thomas (1225–74) Italian Dominican theologian and philosopher. His two most influential works are the *Summa contra gentiles* (1259–64) and the unfinished *Summa theologica* (1266–73).

1 Human law is law only by virtue of its accordance with right reason, and by this means it is clear that it flows from Eternal law. In so far as it deviates from right reason it is called an Unjust law; and in such a case, it is no law at all, but rather an assertion of violence.
Summa theologica

The Arabian Nights (c. 1500) A collection of tales from the East linked together by the story that the sultan Shahriyar decreed that all his wives should be executed on the morning after their wedding. One wife, Scheherazade, delayed her execution by telling the sultan a series of stories, promising to tell the ending the next evening. After a thousand and one nights she was reprieved.

1 Who will change old lamps for new ones? . . . new lamps for old ones?
The History of Aladdin

2 Open Sesame!
The History of Ali Baba

Arabin, William (1773–1841) British judge.

1 If ever there was a case of clearer evidence than this of persons acting in concert together, this case is that case.
Arabinesque at Law (Sir R. Megarry)

2 They will steal the very teeth out of your mouth as you walk through the streets. I know it from experience.
Referring to the people of Uxbridge
Arabinesque at Law (Sir R. Megarry)

3 Prisoner, God has given you good abilities, instead of which you go about the country stealing ducks.
Arabinesque at Law (Sir R. Megarry)

Arbuthnot, Dr John (1667–1735) Scottish writer and physician. A member of the Scriblerus Club, he wrote *The History of John Bull* (1712), introducing this character.

1 He warns the heads of parties against believing their own lies.
The Art of Political Lying

Archilochus (c. 680–c. 640 BC) Greek poet. Only fragments of his poems survive. He became a mercenary and probably died in battle.

1 The fox knows many things – the hedgehog knows one *big* thing.
Attrib.

Archimedes (c. 287–212 BC) Greek mathematician, born in Sicily. He invented a number of mechanical devices, notably Archimedes' screw, and is believed to have discovered Archimedes' principle while taking a bath.

1 Give me a firm place to stand, and I will move the earth.
On the Lever

2 *Eureka!*
I have found it!
An exclamation of joy supposedly uttered as, stepping into a bath and noticing the water overflowing, he saw the answer to a problem and began the train of thought that led to his principle of buoyancy
Attrib.

Arendt, Hannah (1906–75) German-born US philosopher and historian.

1 The defiance of established authority, religious and secular, social and political, as a world-wide phenomenon may well one day be accounted the outstanding event of the last decade.
Crises of the Republic, 'Civil Disobedience'

2 It is quite gratifying to feel guilty if you haven't done anything wrong: how noble! Whereas it is rather hard and certainly depressing to admit guilt and to repent.
Eichmann in Jerusalem, Ch. 15

Ariosto, Ludovico (1474–1533) Italian poet. He spent most of his life serving the Este family of Ferrara and is remembered for his epic poem *Orlando furioso* (1516).

1 Nature made him, and then broke the mould.
Referring to Charlemagne's paladin, Roland
Orlando furioso

Aristotle (384–322 BC) Greek philosopher and scientist. A former pupil of Plato and tutor to Alexander the Great, he founded a school at the Lyceum in Athens.

1 What we have to learn to do, we learn by doing.
Nicomachean Ethics, Bk. II

2 The man who gets angry at the right things and with the right people, and in the right way and at the right time and for the right length of time, is commended.
Nicomachean Ethics, Bk. IV

3 Obstinate people can be divided into the opinionated, the ignorant, and the boorish.
Nicomachean Ethics, Bk. VII

4 Now a whole is that which has a beginning, a middle, and an end.
Referring specifically to the dramatic form of tragedy
Poetics, Ch. 7

5 For this reason poetry is something more philosophical and more worthy of serious attention than history.
Poetics, Ch. 9

6 Man is by nature a political animal.
Politics, Bk. I

7 Either a beast or a god.
Politics, Bk. I

8 Where some people are very wealthy and others have nothing, the result will be either extreme democracy or absolute oligarchy, or despotism will come from either of those excesses.
Politics, Bk. IV

9 Inferiors revolt in order that they may be equal and equals that they may be superior. Such is the state of mind which creates revolutions.
Politics, Bk. V

10 Plato is dear to me, but dearer still is truth.
Attrib.

Arminstead, Lewis Addison (1817–63) US general. A brigadier general in the Confederate army, he was killed at Gettysburg.

1 Give them the cold steel, boys!
Exhortation given to his troops during the US Civil War
Attrib.

Armstrong, Louis (1900–71) US jazz trumpeter.

1 A lotta cats copy the Mona Lisa, but people still line up to see the original.
When asked whether he objected to people copying his style
Attrib.

2 Musicians don't retire; they stop when there's no more music in them.
The Observer, 'Sayings of the Week', 21 Apr 1968

Armstrong, Neil Alden (1930–) US astronaut. In July 1969, as commander of the Apollo 11 lunar mission, he became the first person to step onto the moon.

1 That's one small step for man, one giant leap for mankind.
Said on stepping onto the moon. Armstrong later claimed that he had said, 'small step for a man . . . ', but that the 'a' had been lost in the radio transmission
Remark, 21 July 1969

2 Tranquillity Base here – the Eagle has landed.
The first words spoken on touchdown of the space module Apollo XI on the moon

Armstrong, Sir Robert (Temple) (1913–) British civil servant; secretary of the cabinet (1979–87).

1 It contains a misleading impression, not a lie. I was being economical with the truth.
Giving evidence on behalf of the British government in an Australian court case, Nov 1986. Armstrong was, in fact, quoting Edmund Burke (1729–97).

Arnold, George (1834–65) US poet and humorist. His collected poems were published posthumously in 1866 and 1867.

1 The living need charity more than the dead.
The Jolly Old Pedagogue

Arnold, Matthew (1822–88) British poet and critic, who served for 35 years as inspector of schools.

Quotations about Arnold

1 He is not as handsome as his photographs – or his poetry.
Henry James (1843–1916) US novelist. Letter to Charles Eliot Norton, 31 Mar 1873

2 Arnold is a dandy Isaiah, a poet without passion . . .
George Meredith (1829–1909) British novelist. *Fortnightly Review*, July 1909

Quotations by Arnold

3 Culture being a pursuit of our total perfection by means of getting to know, on all the matters which most concern us, the best which has been thought and said in the world.
Culture and Anarchy, Preface

4 Our society distributes itself into Barbarians, Philistines, and Populace; and America is just ourselves, with the Barbarians quite left out, and the Populace nearly.
Culture and Anarchy, Preface

5 The pursuit of perfection, then, is the pursuit of sweetness and light. . . . He who works for sweetness and light united, works to make reason and the will of God prevail.
Culture and Anarchy, Ch. 1

6 One has often wondered whether upon the whole earth there is anything so unintelligent, so unapt to perceive how the world is really going, as an ordinary young Englishman of our upper class.
Culture and Anarchy, Ch. 2

7 For this class we have a designation which now has become pretty well known, and which we may as well still keep for them, the designation of Philistines.
Referring to the middle class
Culture and Anarchy, Ch. 3

8 I often, therefore, when I want to distinguish clearly the aristocratic class from the Philistines proper, or middle class, name the former, in my own mind *the Barbarians*.
Culture and Anarchy, Ch. 3

9 But that vast portion, lastly, of the working-class which, raw and half-developed, has long lain half-hidden amidst its poverty and squalor, and is now issuing from its hiding-place to assert an Englishman's heaven-born privilege of doing as he likes, and is beginning to perplex us by marching where it likes, meeting where it likes, bawling what it likes, breaking what it likes – to this vast residuum we may with great propriety give the name of Populace.
Culture and Anarchy, Ch. 3

10 The sea is calm to-night,
The tide is full, the moon lies fair
Upon the Straits.
Dover Beach

11 And we are here as on a darkling plain
Swept with confused alarms of struggle and flight,
Where ignorant armies clash by night.
Dover Beach

12 Is it so small a thing
To have enjoy'd the sun,
To have lived light in the spring,
To have loved, to have thought, to have done?
Empedocles on Etna

13 Home of lost causes, and forsaken beliefs, and unpopular names, and impossible loyalties!
Referring to Oxford
Essays in Criticism, First Series, Preface

14 I am bound by my own definition of criticism: a disinterested endeavour to learn and propagate the best that is known and thought in the world.
Essays in Criticism, First Series, 'Functions of Criticism at the Present Time'

15 A criticism of life under the conditions fixed for such a criticism by the laws of poetic truth and poetic beauty.
Essays in Criticism, Second Series, 'The Study of Poetry'

16 Come, dear children, let us away;
Down and away below.
The Forsaken Merman

17 She left lonely for ever
The kings of the sea.
The Forsaken Merman

18 A wanderer is man from his birth.
He was born in a ship
On the breast of the river of Time.
The Future

19 Wandering between two worlds, one dead,
The other powerless to be born.
The Grande Chartreuse

20 Years hence, perhaps, may dawn an age,
More fortunate, alas! than we,
Which without hardness will be sage,
And gay without frivolity.
The Grande Chartreuse

21 The great apostle of the Philistines, Lord Macaulay.
Joubert

22 Culture, the acquainting ourselves with the best that has been known and said in the world, and thus with the history of the human spirit.
Literature and Dogma, Preface

23 Culture is the passion for sweetness and light, and (what is more) the passion for making them prevail.
Literature and Dogma, Preface

24 The eternal *not ourselves* that makes for righteousness.
Literature and Dogma, Ch. 8

25 It always seems to me that the right sphere for Shelley's genius was the sphere of music, not of poetry.
Maurice de Guérin, Footnote

26 When Byron's eyes were shut in death,
We bow'd our head and held our breath.
He taught us little: but our soul
Had *felt* him like the thunder's roll.
Memorial Verses

27 He spoke, and loos'd our heart in tears.
He laid us as we lay at birth
On the cool flowery lap of earth.
Referring to Wordsworth
Memorial Verses

28 Time may restore us in his course
Goethe's sage mind and Byron's force:
But where will Europe's latter hour
Again find Wordsworth's healing power?
Memorial Verses

29 We cannot kindle when we will
The fire which in the heart resides,
The spirit bloweth and is still,
In mystery our soul abides.
Morality

30 Now he is dead! Far hence he lies
In the lorn Syrian town;
And on his grave, with shining eyes,
The Syrian stars look down.
Obermann Once More

31 He will find one English book and one only,
where, as in the *Iliad* itself, perfect plainness of
speech is allied with perfect nobleness; and that
book is the Bible.
On Translating Homer

32 I think it will be found that the grand style arises
in poetry, when a noble nature, poetically gifted, treats with simplicity or with severity a
serious subject.
Closing words
On Translating Homer

33 Cruel, but composed and bland,
Dumb, inscrutable and grand,
So Tiberius might have sat,
Had Tiberius been a cat.
Poor Matthias

34 Go, for they call you, Shepherd, from the hill.
The Scholar Gipsy

35 All the live murmur of a summer's day.
The Scholar Gipsy

36 Tired of knocking at Preferment's door.
The Scholar Gipsy

37 Before this strange disease of modern life,
With its sick hurry, its divided aims.
The Scholar Gipsy

38 Still nursing the unconquerable hope,
Still clutching the inviolable shade.
The Scholar Gipsy

39 Resolve to be thyself: and know, that he
Who finds himself, loses his misery.
Self-Dependence

40 Others abide our question, Thou art free,
We ask and ask: Thou smilest and art still,
Out-topping knowledge.
Referring to Shakespeare
Shakespeare

41 Truth sits upon the lips of dying men.
Sohrab and Rustum

42 Who saw life steadily, and saw it whole:
The mellow glory of the Attic stage.
Sonnets to a Friend

43 And see all sights from pole to pole,
And glance, and nod, and bustle by;
And never once possess our soul
Before we die.
A Southern Night

44 The difference between genuine poetry and the
poetry of Dryden, Pope, and all their school, is
briefly this: their poetry is conceived and
composed in their wits, genuine poetry is conceived and composed in the soul.
Thomas Gray

45 That sweet City with her dreaming spires
She needs not June for beauty's heightening.
Referring to Oxford
Thyrsis

46 And sigh that one thing only has been lent
To youth and age in common – discontent.
Youth's Agitations

47 I am past thirty, and three parts iced over.
Letter to A. H. Clough, 12 Feb 1853

Arnold, Thomas (1795–1842) British educator; father of
Matthew Arnold. As headmaster of Rugby school (1828–42), his
reforms influenced many 19th-century public schools.

1 My object will be, if possible to form Christian
men, for Christian boys I can scarcely hope to
make.
Letter on appointment as Headmaster of Rugby, 1828

2 What we must look for here is, first, religious
and moral principles; secondly, gentlemanly conduct; thirdly, intellectual ability.
Address to the Scholars at Rugby

Asaf, George (George H. Powell; 1880–1951) US
songwriter.

1 What's the use of worrying?
It never was worth while,
So, pack up your troubles in your old kit-bag,
And smile, smile, smile.
Pack up Your Troubles in Your Old Kit-bag

Ashburton, Baron *See* Dunning, John.

Ashdown, Paddy (Jeremy John Dunham Ashdown; 1941–)
British politician. He became leader of the Social and Liberal
Democratic Party in 1988.

1 I have made it clear that the period of coalitions,
necessary though it was, is now over. We are
on our own.
The Observer, 'Sayings of the Eighties', 31 July 1988

2 We are not rootless vagabonds. We are on our
way to power.
Speech, SLD annual conference, Blackpool, Sept 1988

3 I do not believe that our place is at the comfortable mid-point between the extremes of left and
right.
Speech, SLD annual conference, Brighton, Sept 1989

Asimov, Isaac (1920–) Russian-born US science fiction
writer. His science fiction works include the *Foundation* series, *I,
Robot* (1950), and *The Edge of Tomorrow* (1986).

1 A candy store is a good thing in some ways. You work for yourself and the work is steady. The profits are small but they're there, and we went through the entire period of the Great Depression without missing a meal and without ever having to spend one moment's anxiety that my father might lose his job and that we might all be on the bread lines.
Before the Golden Age, Pt. I

2 . . . things called Stars appeared, which robbed men of their souls and left them unreasoning brutes, so that they destroyed the civilization they themselves had built up.
On the fictional world of Lagash, night comes once every 2049 years
Nightfall

Asquith, Herbert Henry, 1st Earl of Oxford and Asquith (1852–1928) British statesman; Liberal prime minister (1908–16). His government introduced old-age pensions, national insurance, and other social reforms.

1 One to mislead the public, another to mislead the Cabinet, and the third to mislead itself.
Explaining why the War Office kept three sets of figures
The Price of Glory (Alastair Horne), Ch. 2

2 It is fitting that we should have buried the Unknown Prime Minister by the side of the Unknown Soldier.
Said at Bonar Law's funeral, 5 Nov 1923
Attrib.

3 Wait and see.
In various speeches, 1910

Asquith, Margot (1865–1945) The second wife of Herbert Asquith, Earl of Oxford and Asquith. She wrote an outspoken *Autobiography* (1922).

1 To marry a man out of pity is folly; and, if you think you are going to influence the kind of fellow who has 'never had a chance, poor devil,' you are profoundly mistaken. One can only influence the strong characters in life, not the weak; and it is the height of vanity to suppose that you can make an honest man of anyone.
The Autobiography of Margot Asquith, Ch. 6

2 Rich men's houses are seldom beautiful, rarely comfortable, and never original. It is a constant source of surprise to people of moderate means to observe how little a big fortune contributes to Beauty.
The Autobiography of Margot Asquith, Ch. 17

3 If Kitchener was not a great man, he was, at least, a great poster.
Kitchener: Portrait of an Imperialist (Sir Philip Magnus), Ch. 14

Astley, Jacob, Baron (1579–1652) English Royalist general, who commanded the infantry at Edgehill during the Civil War.

1 O Lord! thou knowest how busy I must be this day: if I forget thee, do not thou forget me.
Prayer before taking part in the Battle of Edgehill
Memoires (Sir Philip Warwick)

Astor, John Jacob (1763–1848) US fur trader and property millionaire.

1 A man who has a million dollars is as well off as if he were rich.
Attrib.

Astor, Nancy Witcher, Viscountess (1879–1964) US-born British politician. A campaigner for women's rights, she became the first woman MP to sit in the House of Commons.

1 I married beneath me – all women do.
Dictionary of National Biography

2 Take a close-up of a woman past sixty! You might as well use a picture of a relief map of Ireland!
When asked for a close-up photograph
Attrib.

3 The penalty of success is to be bored by people who used to snub you.
Sunday Express, 12 Jan 1956

4 Jakie, is it my birthday or am I dying?
To her son on her death bed. He replied, 'A bit of both, Mum'.

Atkinson, E. L. (1882–1929) British naval physician, who accompanied Captain Scott on his last voyage to the Antarctic.

1 Hereabouts died a very gallant gentleman, Captain L. E. G. Oates of the Inniskilling Dragoons. In March 1912, returning from the Pole, he walked willingly to his death in a blizzard, to try and save his comrades, beset by hardships.
Epitaph on the memorial to OATES in the Antarctic

Attlee, Clement, Earl (1883–1967) British statesman and Labour prime minister (1945–51). As leader of the Labour Party, he was deputy prime minister in Churchill's wartime coalition government. His post-war government introduced the welfare state and granted independence to India.

1 Democracy means government by discussion but it is only effective if you can stop people talking.
Anatomy of Britain (Anthony Sampson)

2 Russian communism is the illegitimate child of Karl Marx and Catherine the Great.
Speech, 11 Apr 1956

3 The House of Lords is like a glass of champagne that has stood for five days.
Attrib.

Auber, David François Esprit (1782–1871) French composer.

1 This is the last time that I will take part as an amateur.
Said at a funeral
Das Buch des Lachens (W. Scholz)

2 Aging seems to be the only available way to live a long time.
Dictionnaire Encyclopédique (E. Guérard)

Aubrey, John (1626–97) English antiquary. His biographical anecdotes were posthumously collected as *Lives of Eminent Men* (1813) and *Brief Lives* (1898).

1 Sir Walter, being strangely surprised and put out of his countenance at so great a table, gives his son a damned blow over the face. His son, as rude as he was, would not strike his father, but strikes over the face the gentleman that sat next to him and said 'Box about: 'twill come to my father anon'.

Brief Lives, 'Sir Walter Raleigh'

2 How these curiosities would be quite forgot, did not such idle fellows as I am put them down.

Brief Lives, 'Venetia Digby'

3 He was so fair that they called him *the lady of* Christ's College.

Brief Lives, 'John Milton'

Auden, W(ystan) H(ugh) (1907–73) British poet; professor of poetry at Oxford University (1956–61). Auden made his name in the 1930s with such volumes as *Poems* (1930) and *Look, Stranger* (1936); later works included verse dramas and opera libretti.

Quotations about Auden

1 We have one poet of genius in Auden who is able to write prolifically, carelessly and exquisitely, nor does he seem to have to pay any price for his inspiration.

Cyril Connolly (1903–74) British journalist. *Enemies of Promise*

2 The high watermark, so to speak, of Socialist literature is W. H. Auden, a sort of gutless Kipling.

George Orwell (Eric Blair; 1903–50) British novelist. *The Road to Wigan Pier*

Quotations by Auden

3 Yet no one hears his own remarks as prose.

At a Party

4 Political history is far too criminal and pathological to be a fit subject of study for the young. Children should acquire their heroes and villains from fiction.

A Certain World

5 All sin tends to be addictive, and the terminal point of addiction is what is called damnation.

A Certain World

6 Happy the hare at morning, for she cannot read The Hunter's waking thoughts.

The Dog Beneath the Skin (with Christopher Isherwood)

7 When I find myself in the company of scientists, I feel like a shabby curate who has strayed by mistake into a drawing-room full of dukes.

The Dyer's Hand

8 The true men of action in our time, those who transform the world, are not the politicians and statesmen, but the scientists. Unfortunately, poetry cannot celebrate them, because their deeds are concerned with things, not persons and are, therefore, speechless.

The Dyer's Hand

9 Man is a history-making creature who can neither repeat his past nor leave it behind.

The Dyer's Hand, 'D. H. Lawrence'

10 Some books are undeservedly forgotten; none are undeservedly remembered.

The Dyer's Hand, 'Reading'

11 No poet or novelist wishes he were the only one who ever lived, but most of them wish they were the only one alive, and quite a number fondly believe their wish has been granted.

The Dyer's Hand, 'Writing'

12 Let us honour if we can
The vertical man
Though we value none
But the horizontal one.

Epigraph for Poems

13 To save your world you asked this man to die:
Would this man, could he see you now, ask why?

Epitaph for an Unknown Soldier

14 Alone, alone, about the dreadful wood
Of conscious evil runs a lost mankind,
Dreading to find its Father.

For the Time Being, 'Chorus'

15 To us he is no more a person
Now but a climate of opinion.

In Memory of Sigmund Freud

16 Now Ireland has her madness and her weather still,
For poetry makes nothing happen.

In Memory of W. B. Yeats, II

17 Earth, receive an honoured guest:
William Yeats is laid to rest.
Let the Irish vessel lie
Emptied of its poetry.

In Memory of W. B. Yeats, III

18 It is time for the destruction of error.
The chairs are being brought in from the garden,
The summer talk stopped on that savage coast
Before the storms.

It is time

19 Look, stranger, at this island now
The leaping light for your delight discovers.

Look, Stranger

20 Lay your sleeping head, my love,
Human on my faithless arm.

Lullaby

21 To the man-in-the-street, who, I'm sorry to say
Is a keen observer of life,
The word Intellectual suggests straight away
A man who's untrue to his wife.
Note on Intellectuals

22 God bless the USA, so large,
So friendly, and so rich.
On the Circuit

23 Only those in the last stage of disease could believe that children are true judges of character.
The Orators, 'Journal of an Airman'

24 My Dear One is mine as mirrors are lonely.
The Sea and the Mirror

25 Their fate must always be the same as yours,
To suffer the loss they were afraid of, yes,
Holders of one position, wrong for years.
Since you are going to begin today

26 When it comes, will it come without warning
Just as I'm picking my nose?
Will it knock on my door in the morning,
Or tread in the bus on my toes?
Will it come like a change in the weather?
Will its greeting be courteous or rough?
Will it alter my life altogether?
O tell me the truth about love.
Twelve Songs, XII

27 Our researchers into Public Opinion are content
That he held the proper opinions for the time of year;
When there was peace, he was for peace; when there was war, he went.
The Unknown Citizen

28 If there are any of you at the back who do not hear me, please don't raise your hands because I am also nearsighted.
Starting a lecture in a large hall
In *Book of the Month Club News*, Dec 1946

29 A professor is one who talks in someone else's sleep.
Attrib.

Augustine of Hippo, St (354–430) Bishop of Hippo in north Africa (396–430). Converted to Christianity in 386, he produced a number of influential theological works.

1 Thou hast created us for Thyself, and our heart is not quiet until it rests in Thee.
Confessions, Bk. I, Ch. 1

2 Give me chastity and continence, but not yet.
Confessions, Bk. VIII, Ch. 7

3 There is no salvation outside the church.
De Bapt., IV

4 *Roma locuta est; causa finita est.*
Rome has spoken; the case is concluded.
Sermons, Bk. I

5 We make ourselves a ladder out of our vices if we trample the vices themselves underfoot.
Sermons, Bk. III, 'De Ascensione'

Augustus (63 BC–14 AD) Roman emperor, known as Octavian until 27 BC. The adopted son of Julius Caesar, he formed a triumvirate with Mark Antony and Lepidus in 43 BC, becoming supreme head of the Roman Republic in 31 BC.

1 I found it brick and left it marble.
Referring to the improvements he had made to Rome
The Lives of the Caesars (Suetonius), 'Augustus'

Austen, Jane (1775–1817) British novelist. Her novels of middle-class life combine humour with perceptive characterization; her six major works were *Sense and Sensibility* (1811), *Pride and Prejudice* (1813), *Mansfield Park* (1814), *Emma* (1815–16), *Northanger Abbey* (1818), and *Persuasion* (1818).

Quotations about Austen

1 More can be learnt from Miss Austen about the nature of the novel than from almost any other writer.
Walter Allen (1911–) British author and literary journalist. *The English Novel*

2 That young lady has a talent for describing the involvements and feelings and characters of ordinary life which is to me the most wonderful thing I ever met with.
Walter Scott (1771–1832) Scottish novelist. *Journals*, 14 Mar 1826

3 Jane Austen's books, too, are absent from this library. Just that one omission alone would make a fairly good library out of a library that hadn't a book in it.
Mark Twain (Samuel Langhorne Clemens; 1835–1910) US writer. *Following the Equator*, Pt. II

Quotations by Austen

4 One half of the world cannot understand the pleasures of the other.
Emma, Ch. 9

5 Nobody is healthy in London, nobody can be.
Emma, Ch. 12

6 A man . . . must have a very good opinion of himself when he asks people to leave their own fireside, and encounter such a day as this, for the sake of coming to see him. He must think himself a most agreeable fellow.
Emma, Ch. 13

7 Human nature is so well disposed towards those who are in interesting situations, that a young person, who either marries or dies, is sure to be kindly spoken of.
Emma, Ch. 22

8 The sooner every party breaks up the better.
Emma, Ch. 25

9 Business, you know, may bring money, but friendship hardly ever does.
Emma, Ch. 34

10 One has no great hopes from Birmingham. I always say there is something direful in the sound.
Emma, Ch. 36

11 One of Edward's Mistresses was Jane Shore, who has had a play written about her, but it is a tragedy and therefore not worth reading.
The History of England

12 She was nothing more than a mere good-tempered, civil and obliging young woman; as such we could scarcely dislike her – she was only an Object of Contempt.
Love and Friendship

13 Let other pens dwell on guilt and misery.
Mansfield Park, Ch. 48

14 But are they all horrid, are you sure they are all horrid?
Northanger Abbey, Ch. 6

15 Oh! who can ever be tired of Bath?
Northanger Abbey, Ch. 10

16 A woman, especially if she have the misfortune of knowing anything, should conceal it as well as she can.
Northanger Abbey, Ch. 14

17 One does not love a place the less for having suffered in it unless it has all been suffering, nothing but suffering.
Persuasion, Ch. 20

18 It is a truth universally acknowledged, that a single man in possession of a good fortune must be in want of a wife.
The opening words of the book
Pride and Prejudice, Ch. 1

19 She was a woman of mean understanding, little information, and uncertain temper.
Pride and Prejudice, Ch. 1

20 A lady's imagination is very rapid; it jumps from admiration to love, from love to matrimony in a moment.
Pride and Prejudice, Ch. 6

21 Happiness in marriage is entirely a matter of chance.
Pride and Prejudice, Ch. 6

22 It is happy for you that you possess the talent of flattering with delicacy. May I ask whether these pleasing attentions proceed from the impulse of the moment, or are the result of previous study?
Pride and Prejudice, Ch. 14

23 You have delighted us long enough.
Pride and Prejudice, Ch. 18

24 Next to being married, a girl likes to be crossed in love a little now and then.
Pride and Prejudice, Ch. 24

25 One cannot be always laughing at a man without now and then stumbling on something witty.
Pride and Prejudice, Ch. 40

26 For what do we live, but to make sport for our neighbours, and laugh at them in our turn?
Pride and Prejudice, Ch. 57

27 I have been a selfish being all my life, in practice, though not in principle.
Pride and Prejudice, Ch. 58

28 What dreadful hot weather we have! It keeps me in a continual state of inelegance.
Letter, 18 Sept 1796

29 Mrs Hall of Sherbourne was brought to bed yesterday of a dead child, some weeks before she expected, owing to a fright. I suppose she happened unawares to look at her husband.
Letter, 27 Oct 1798

30 I do not want people to be very agreeable, as it saves me the trouble of liking them a great deal.
Letter, 24 Dec 1798

31 We met . . . Dr Hall in such very deep mourning that either his mother, his wife, or himself must be dead.
Letter to Cassandra Austen, 17 May 1799

32 The little bit (two inches wide) of ivory on which I work with so fine a brush as produces little effect after much labour.
Letter, 16 Dec 1816

Austin, Alfred (1835–1913) British poet. His appointment as poet laureate in 1896 provoked widespread derision.

1 Across the wires the electric message came: 'He is no better, he is much the same.'
Generally attrib. to Austin but there is no definite evidence that he wrote it
On the Illness of the Prince of Wales

2 I dare not alter these things; they come to me from above.
When accused of writing ungrammatical verse
A Number of People (E. Marsh)

Austin, Warren Robinson (1877–1962) US politician and diplomat.

1 It is better for aged diplomats to be bored than for young men to die.
When asked if he got tired during long debates at the UN
Attrib.

2 The Jews and Arabs should sit down and settle their differences like good Christians.
Attrib.

Avery, Oswald Theodore (1877–1955) Canadian bacteriologist.

1 Whenever you fall, pick up something.
Attrib.

Avicenna (980–1037) Persian philosopher and physician. He wrote an encyclopedia of philosophy, the *Ash-Shifa*, and the *Canon of Medicine*, used throughout the Middle East and Europe.

1 Writing about erotics is a perfectly respectable function of medicine, and about the way to make the woman enjoy sex; these are an important part of reproductive physiology.
Sex in Society (Alex Comfort)

Ayckbourn, Alan (1939–) British dramatist. His first success was *Relatively Speaking* (1967); subsequent plays include *Absurd Person Singular* (1973), *The Norman Conquests* (a trilogy; 1974), *A Chorus of Disapproval* (1985), and *Body Language* (1990).

1 Few women care to be laughed at and men not at all, except for large sums of money.
   The Norman Conquests, Preface

Ayer, Sir Alfred Jules (1910–89) British philosopher. His *Language, Truth and Logic* (1936) is an exposition of logical positivism. Later works include the autobiographical *Part of My Life* (1977) and *More of My Life* (1984).

1 No morality can be founded on authority, even if the authority were divine.
   Essay on Humanism

2 The principles of logic and metaphysics are true simply because we never allow them to be anything else.
   Language, Truth and Logic

B

Babbage, Charles (1792–1871) British mathematician and inventor of a computing machine, which was never built but is regarded as the forerunner of the computer.

1 Every moment dies a man,
   Every moment one and one sixteenth is born.
   A parody of TENNYSON's *Vision of Sin*
   Letter to Tennyson

Bacon, Francis (1909–) British painter, born in Dublin. His pictures are characterized by strong colours and distorted human figures.

1 How can I take an interest in my work when I don't like it?
   Francis Bacon (Sir John Rothenstein)

Bacon, Francis, 1st Baron Verulam, Viscount St Albans (1561–1626) English philosopher, lawyer, and politician. While lord chancellor (1618–21) he was charged with corruption and dismissed from public office. His writings include *Novum Organum* (1620), advocating the inductive method of logical reasoning.

1 For all knowledge and wonder (which is the seed of knowledge) is an impression of pleasure in itself.
   The Advancement of Learning, Bk. I, Ch. 1

2 If a man will begin with certainties, he shall end in doubts, but if he will be content to begin with doubts, he shall end in certainties.
   The Advancement of Learning, Bk. I, Ch. 5

3 They are ill discoverers that think there is no land, when they can see nothing but sea.
   The Advancement of Learning, Bk. II, Ch. 7

4 Just as it is always said of slander that something always sticks when people boldly slander, so it might be said of self-praise (if it is not entirely shameful and ridiculous) that if we praise ourselves fearlessly, something will always stick.
   The Advancement of Learning

5 One of the Seven was wont to say: 'That laws were like cobwebs; where the small flies were caught, and the great brake through.'
   Apothegms

6 I have often thought upon death, and I find it the least of all evils.
   An Essay on Death

7 I do not believe that any man fears to be dead, but only the stroke of death.
   An Essay on Death

8 Prosperity doth best discover vice; but adversity doth best discover virtue.
   Essays, 'Of Adversity'

9 God never wrought miracle to convince atheism, because his ordinary works convince it.
   Essays, 'Of Atheism'

10 For none deny there is a God, but those for whom it maketh that there were no God.
   Essays, 'Of Atheism'

11 Virtue is like a rich stone, best plain set.
   Essays, 'Of Beauty'

12 There is no excellent beauty that hath not some strangeness in the proportion.
   Essays, 'Of Beauty'

13 There is in human nature generally more of the fool than of the wise.
   Essays, 'Of Boldness'

14 Mahomet made the people believe that he would call a hill to him . . . when the hill stood still, he was never a whit abashed, but said, 'If the hill will not come to Mahomet, Mahomet will go to the hill.'
   Often misquoted as 'If the mountain will not come to Mohammed . . . '
   Essays, 'Of Boldness'

15 Houses are built to live in and not to look on; therefore let use be preferred before uniformity, except where both may be had.
   Essays, 'Of Building'

16 A wise man will make more opportunities than he finds.
   Essays, 'Of Ceremonies and Respects'

17 When he wrote a letter, he would put that which was most material in the postscript, as if it had been a by-matter.
   Essays, 'Of Cunning'

18 Men fear death, as children fear to go in the dark; and as that natural fear in children is increased with tales, so is the other.
   Essays, 'Of Death'

19 It is natural to die as to be born; and to a little infant, perhaps, the one is as painful as the other.
Essays, 'Of Death'

20 To choose time is to save time.
Essays, 'Of Dispatch'

21 It is a miserable state of mind to have few things to desire and many things to fear.
Essays, 'Of Empire'

22 Nothing destroyeth authority so much as the unequal and untimely interchange of power pressed too far, and relaxed too much.
Essays, 'Of Empire'

23 Riches are for spending.
Essays, 'Of Expense'

24 Whosoever is delighted in solitude is either a wild beast or a god.
Essays, 'Of Friendship'

25 Cure the disease and kill the patient.
Essays, 'Of Friendship'

26 God Almighty first planted a garden. And indeed it is the purest of human pleasures.
Essays, 'Of Gardens'

27 In charity there is no excess.
Essays, 'Of Goodness, and Goodness of Nature'

28 If a man be gracious and courteous to strangers, it shews he is a citizen of the world.
Essays, 'Of Goodness and Goodness of Nature'

29 As in nature things move violently to their place and calmly in their place, so virtue in ambition is violent, in authority settled and calm.
Essays, 'Of Great Place'

30 He that will not apply new remedies must expect new evils: for time is the greatest innovator.
Essays, 'Of Innovations'

31 The place of justice is a hallowed place.
Essays, 'Of Judicature'

32 Nuptial love maketh mankind; friendly love perfecteth it; but wanton love corrupteth and embaseth it.
Essays, 'Of Love'

33 He that hath wife and children hath given hostages to fortune; for they are impediments to great enterprises, either of virtue or mischief.
See also LUCAN
Essays, 'Of Marriage and Single Life'

34 Wives are young men's mistresses, companions for middle age, and old men's nurses.
Essays, 'Of Marriage and Single Life'

35 He was reputed one of the wise men, that made answer to the question, when a man should marry? A young man not yet, an elder man not at all.
Essays, 'Of Marriage and Single Life'

36 Nature is often hidden, sometimes overcome, seldom extinguished.
Essays, 'Of Nature in Men'

37 A man's nature runs either to herbs, or to weeds; therefore let him seasonably water the one, and destroy the other.
Essays, 'Of Nature in Men'

38 The joys of parents are secret, and so are their griefs and fears.
Essays, 'Of Parents and Children'

39 Children sweeten labours, but they make misfortunes more bitter.
Essays, 'Of Parents and Children'

40 Fame is like a river, that beareth up things light and swoln, and drowns things weighty and solid.
Essays, 'Of Praise'

41 Dreams and predictions ought to serve but for winter talk by the fireside.
Essays, 'Of Prophecies'

42 Age will not be defied.
Essays, 'Of Regiment of Health'

43 Revenge is a kind of wild justice; which the more man's nature runs to, the more ought law to weed it out.
Essays, 'Of Revenge'

44 A man that studieth revenge keeps his own wounds green.
Essays, 'Of Revenge'

45 Money is like muck, not good except it be spread.
Essays, 'Of Seditions and Troubles'

46 The remedy is worse than the disease.
Essays, 'Of Seditions and Troubles'

47 The French are wiser than they seem, and the Spaniards seem wiser than they are.
Essays, 'Of Seeming Wise'

48 Nakedness is uncomely as well in mind, as body.
Essays, 'Of Simulation and Dissimulation'

49 Studies serve for delight, for ornament, and for ability.
Essays, 'Of Studies'

50 Some books are to be tasted, others to be swallowed, and some few to be chewed and digested.
Essays, 'Of Studies'

51 Reading maketh a full man; conference a ready man; and writing an exact man.
Essays, 'Of Studies'

52 It were better to have no opinion of God at all, than such an opinion as is unworthy of him.
Essays, 'Of Superstition'

53 Suspicions amongst thoughts are like bats amongst birds, they ever fly by twilight.
Essays, 'Of Suspicion'

54 Travel, in the younger sort, is a part of education; in the elder, a part of experience.
Essays, 'Of Travel'

55 Let diaries, therefore, be brought in use.
Essays, 'Of Travel'

56 What is truth? said jesting Pilate, and would not stay for an answer.
Essays, 'Of Truth'

57 All colours will agree in the dark.
Essays, 'Of Unity in Religion'

58 It was prettily devised of Aesop, 'The fly sat upon the axletree of the chariot-wheel and said, what a dust do I raise.'
Essays, 'Of Vain-Glory'

59 Be so true to thyself, as thou be not false to others.
Essays, 'Of Wisdom for a Man's Self'

60 It is the wisdom of the crocodiles, that shed tears when they would devour.
Essays, 'Of Wisdom for a Man's Self'

61 A man that is young in years may be old in hours, if he have lost no time.
Essays, 'Of Youth and Age'

62 Nature, to be commanded, must be obeyed.
Novum Organum

63 Books must follow sciences, and not sciences books.
Proposition touching Amendment of Laws

64 *Nam et ipsa scientia potestas est.*
Knowledge itself is power.
Religious Meditations, 'Of Heresies'

65 Universities incline wits to sophistry and affectation.
Valerius Terminus of the Interpretation of Nature, Ch. 26

66 The house is well, but it is you, Your Majesty, who have made me too great for my house.
Reply when Elizabeth I remarked on the smallness of his house
After-dinner Stories and Anecdotes (L. Meissen)

67 I have taken all knowledge to be my province.
Letter to Lord Burleigh, 1592

68 For my name and memory, I leave it to men's charitable speeches, and to foreign nations, and the next ages.
Will, 19 Dec 1625

Baden-Powell, Robert Stephenson Smyth, 1st Baron (1857–1941) British general and founder of the Boy Scouts. He became famous for his defence of Mafeking during the Boer war (1899–90).

1 A Scout smiles and whistles under all circumstances.
Scouting for Boys

2 Be Prepared . . . the meaning of the motto is that a scout must prepare himself by previous thinking out and practising how to act on any accident or emergency so that he is never taken by surprise; he knows exactly what to do when anything unexpected happens.
Motto of the Scout movement
Scouting for Boys

Bader, Sir Douglas (1910–82) British fighter pilot. He lost both legs in a flying accident but still fought in World War II. He was knighted in 1976 for his work with the disabled.

1 . . . As he opened the gate, he noticed me about 800 feet above and in front of him. They both remained motionless, staring. I then realized that my appearance was a bit odd. My right leg was no longer with me . . . the leather belt which attached it to my body had broken under the strain, and the leg, the Spitfire, and I had all parted company.
Fight for the Sky

2 Don't listen to anyone who tells you that you can't do this or that. That's nonsense. Make up your mind, you'll never use crutches or a stick, then have a go at everything. Go to school, join in all the games you can. Go anywhere you want to. But never, never let them persuade you that things are too difficult or impossible.
Speaking to a fourteen-year-old boy who had had a leg amputated after a road accident
Flying Colours (Laddie Lucas)

Baedeker, Karl (1801–59) German publisher. His guidebooks became internationally famous.

1 Oxford is on the whole more attractive than Cambridge to the ordinary visitor; and the traveller is therefore recommended to visit Cambridge first, or to omit it altogether if he cannot visit both.
Baedeker's Great Britain, 'From London to Oxford'

Bagehot, Walter (1826–77) British economist and journalist; editor of *The Economist* (1860–77).

1 *The Times* has made many ministries.
The English Constitution, 'The Cabinet'

2 A severe though not unfriendly critic of our institutions said that 'the cure for admiring the House of Lords was to go and look at it.'
The English Constitution, 'The House of Lords'

3 The best reason why Monarchy is a strong government is that it is an intelligible government. The mass of mankind understand it, and they hardly anywhere in the world understand any other.
The English Constitution, 'The Monarchy'

4 It has been said that England invented the phrase, 'Her Majesty's Opposition'.
The English Constitution, 'The Monarchy'

5 Women – one half the human race at least – care fifty times more for a marriage than a ministry.

The English Constitution, 'The Monarchy'

6 But of all nations in the world the English are perhaps the least a nation of pure philosophers.

The English Constitution, 'The Monarchy'

7 The Sovereign has, under a constitutional monarchy such as ours, three rights – the right to be consulted, the right to encourage, the right to warn.

The English Constitution, 'The Monarchy'

8 Writers, like teeth, are divided into incisors and grinders.

Estimates of some Englishmen and Scotchmen, 'The First Edinburgh Reviewers'

9 No man has come so near our definition of a constitutional statesman – the powers of a first-rate man and the creed of a second-rate man.

Historical Essays, 'The Character of Sir Robert Peel'

10 He believes, with all his heart and soul and strength, that there *is* such a thing as truth; he has the soul of a martyr with the intellect of an advocate.

Historical Essays, 'Mr Gladstone'

11 Poverty is an anomaly to rich people. It is very difficult to make out why people who want dinner do not ring the bell.

Literary Studies, II

Bailly, Jean Sylvain (1736–93) French astronomer and mayor of Paris (1789–91). He was guillotined during the French Revolution.

1 It's time for me to enjoy another pinch of snuff. Tomorrow my hands will be bound, so as to make it impossible.

Said on the evening before his execution
Anekdotenschatz (H. Hoffmeister)

Bainbridge, Kenneth (1904–) US physicist. He directed the first atomic-bomb tests in 1945.

1 Now we are all sons of bitches.

After the first atomic test
The Decision to Drop the Bomb

Bairnsfather, (Charles) Bruce (1888–1959) British cartoonist, creator of the character Old Bill.

1 Well, if you knows of a better 'ole, go to it.

Fragments from France

Baker, Sir H. W. (1821–77) British hymn writer.

1 The King of love my Shepherd is,
Whose goodness faileth never;
I nothing lack if I am His,
And He is mine for ever.

The King of Love My Shepherd Is

Baldwin, James Arthur (1924–87) US writer. A Harlem-born black, he made his name with the novel *Go Tell It on the Mountain* (1953). Later books include *Just Above My Head* (1979) and *The Price of The Ticket* (1985).

1 If the concept of God has any validity or use, it can only be to make us larger, freer, and more loving. If God cannot do this, then it is time we got rid of Him.

The Fire Next Time

2 Money, it turned out, was exactly like sex, you thought of nothing else if you didn't have it and thought of other things if you did.

Nobody Knows My Name

3 The price one pays for pursuing any profession or calling is an intimate knowledge of its ugly side.

Nobody Knows My Name

4 Children have never been very good at listening to their elders, but they have never failed to imitate them.

Esquire, 1960

5 The future is . . . black.

The Observer, 'Sayings of the Week', 25 Aug 1963

6 It is a great shock at the age of five or six to find that in a world of Gary Coopers you are the Indian.

Speech, Cambridge Union, 17 Feb 1965

Baldwin, Stanley, 1st Earl Baldwin of Bewdley (1867–1947) British statesman; Conservative prime minister (1923–24, 1924–29, 1935–37). He was criticized for his failure to re-arm in the face of German militarism.

1 A lot of hard-faced men who look as if they had done very well out of the war.

Referring to the first House of Commons elected after World War I (1918)
Economic Consequences of the Peace (J. M. Keynes), Ch. 5

2 Then comes Winston with his hundred-horse-power mind and what can I do?

Stanley Baldwin (G. M. Young), Ch. 11

3 What the proprietorship of these papers is aiming at is power, and power without responsibility – the prerogative of the harlot through the ages.

Attacking the press barons Lords Rothermere and Beaverbrook. It was first used by KIPLING. *See also* DEVONSHIRE (10th Duke)
Speech, election rally, 18 Mar 1931

4 The only defence is in offence, which means that you have to kill more women and children more quickly than the enemy if you want to save yourselves.

Speech, Nov 1932

5 I met Curzon in Downing Street, from whom I got the sort of greeting a corpse would give to an undertaker.

After he became prime minister in 1933
Attrib.

6 When you think about the defence of England you no longer think of the chalk cliffs of Dover. You think of the Rhine. That is where our frontier lies to-day.

Speech, House of Commons, 30 July 1934

7 There is a wind of nationalism and freedom blowing round the world, and blowing as strongly in Asia as elsewhere.

Speech, London, 4 Dec 1934

8 I have seldom spoken with greater regret, for my lips are not yet unsealed. Were these troubles over I would make a case, and I guarantee that not a man would go into the Lobby against us.

Referring to the Abyssinian crisis; usually misquoted as 'My lips are sealed'
Speech, House of Commons, 10 Dec 1935

9 God grant him peace and happiness but never understanding of what he has lost.

Referring to Edward VIII's abdication

10 I would rather be an opportunist and float than go to the bottom with my principles round my neck.

Attrib.

11 The intelligent are to the intelligentsia what a man is to a gent.

Attrib.

12 There are three groups that no British Prime Minister should provoke: the Vatican, the Treasury and the miners.

A similar remark is often attributed to Harold MACMILLAN
Attrib.

13 A platitude is simply a truth repeated till people get tired of hearing it.

Attrib.

Balfour, Arthur James, 1st Earl of (1848–1930) British statesman; Conservative prime minister (1902–05). As foreign secretary (1916–19) he issued the Balfour Declaration supporting a Jewish national state in Palestine.

1 I rather think of having a career of my own.

When asked whether he was going to marry Margot Tennant
Autobiography (Margot Asquith), Ch. 9

2 'Christianity, of course but why journalism?'

In reply to Frank Harris's remark, '. . . all the faults of the age come from Christianity and journalism'
Autobiography (Margot Asquith), Ch. 10

3 I thought he was a young man of promise; but it appears he was a young man of promises.

Said of Winston Churchill on his entry into politics, 1899
Winston Churchill (Randolph Churchill), Vol. I

4 His Majesty's Government views with favour the establishment in Palestine of a national home for the Jewish people . . .

The so-called 'Balfour Declaration'
Letter to Lord Rothschild, 2 Nov 1917

5 It is unfortunate, considering that enthusiasm moves the world, that so few enthusiasts can be trusted to speak the truth.

Letter to Mrs Drew, 1918

6 Nothing matters very much, and very few things matter at all.

Attrib.

Ball, John (d. 1381) English priest and rebel; a leader of the Peasants' Revolt (1381). He was executed after the collapse of the rebellion.

1 When Adam delved and Eve span,
Who was then the gentleman?

Text of sermon

Balzac, Honoré de (1799–1850) French novelist. After several popular novels written under pseudonyms, his first success came with *Les Chouans* (1829). Later novels include *Le Père Goriot* (1834) and *La Cousine Bette* (1846). His entire output – over 40 novels – was organized under the title *La Comèdie humaine*.

1 Equality may perhaps be a right, but no power on earth can ever turn it into a fact.

La Duchesse de Langeais

2 There is no such thing as a great talent without great will-power.

La Muse du département

3 The majority of husbands remind me of an orangutang trying to play the violin.

La Physiologie du mariage

4 I am laughing to think what risks you take to try to find money in a desk by night where the legal owner can never find any by day.

Said on waking to find a burglar in the room
Attrib.

5 I should like one of these days to be so well known, so popular, so celebrated, so famous, that it would permit me . . . to break wind in society, and society would think it a most natural thing.

Attrib.

6 It is easier to be a lover than a husband, for the same reason that it is more difficult to show a ready wit all day long than to produce an occasional *bon mot*.

Attrib.

Banda, Dr Hastings (1906–) Malawi statesman. A physician, who trained and practised in the UK and the USA, he returned to his native Nyasaland in 1958. With independence he became president (1964).

1 I wish I could bring Stonehenge to Nyasaland to show there was a time when Britain had a savage culture.

The Observer, 'Sayings of the Week', 10 Mar 1963

Bangs, Edward (fl. 1775) US songwriter.

1 Yankee Doodle came to town
Riding on a pony;
Stuck a feather in his cap
And called it Macaroni.
Yankee Doodle; or Father's Return to Camp

Bankhead, Tallulah (1903–68) US actress, famous for her extravagant lifestyle.

Quotations about Bankhead

1 More of an act than an actress.
Anonymous

2 She was always a star, but only intermittently a good actress.
Brendan Gill *The Times*, 4 Aug 1973

3 She was an open, wayward, free, cosmopolitan, liberated, sensuous human being. In thus systematically invading her own privacy she was the first of the modern personalities.
Lee Israel *Miss Tallulah Bankhead*

Quotations by Bankhead

4 I have three phobias which, could I mute them, would make my life as slick as a sonnet, but as dull as ditch water: I hate to go to bed, I hate to get up, and I hate to be alone.
Tallulah, Ch. 1

5 It's one of the tragic ironies of the theatre that only one man in it can count on steady work – the night watchman.
Tallulah, Ch. 1

6 I've been called many things, but never an intellectual.
Tallulah, Ch. 15

7 Cocaine isn't habit-forming. I should know – I've been using it for years.
Pentimento (Lillian Hellman), 'Theatre'

8 There is less in this than meets the eye.
Referring to a revival of a play by Maeterlink
Shouts and Murmurs (A. Woollcott), 'Capsule Criticism'

9 Don't bother to thank me. I know what a perfectly ghastly season it's been for you Spanish dancers.
Said on dropping fifty dollars into a tambourine held out by a Salvation Army collector
With Malice Toward All (D. Hermann)

10 I'm as pure as the driven slush.
The Observer, 'Sayings of the Week', 24 Feb 1957

11 I'll come and make love to you at five o'clock. If I'm late start without me.
Somerset Maugham (E. Morgan)

12 I thought I told you to wait in the car.
When greeted by a former admirer after many years
Attrib.

13 Only good girls keep diaries. Bad girls don't have the time.
Attrib.

Baring, Maurice (1874–1945) British writer and journalist. He wrote several books on Russian literature, as well as plays, novels, and some verse.

1 If you would know what the Lord God thinks of money, you have only to look at those to whom He gives it.
Writers at Work, First Series (ed. Malcolm Gowley)

Baring-Gould, Sabine (1834–1924) British author, clergyman, and hymn writer. He wrote a 15-volume *Lives of the Saints* (1872–77), a number of novels, and many hymns.

1 Now the day is over,
Night is drawing nigh,
Shadows of the evening
Steal across the sky.
The Evening Hymn

2 Onward, Christian soldiers,
Marching as to war,
With the Cross of Jesus
Going on before.
Onward Christian Soldiers

3 Through the night of doubt and sorrow
Onward goes the pilgrim band,
Singing songs of expectation,
Marching to the Promised Land.
Through the Night of Doubt and Sorrow

Barker, Ronnie (1929–) British comedian, best known in his partnership with Ronnie Corbett ('The Two Ronnies').

1 The marvellous thing about a joke with a double meaning is that it can only mean one thing.
Sauce, 'Daddie's Sauce'

Barnard, Lady Ann (1750–1825) British poet. Her best-known ballad is *Auld Robin Gray* (1771).

1 My father argued sair – my mother didna speak,
But she looked in my face till my heart was like to break;
They gied him my hand but my heart was in the sea;
And so auld Robin Gray, he was gudeman to me.
Auld Robin Gray

Barnard, Christiaan Neethling (1922–) South African surgeon. He performed the world's first successful heart transplant operation in 1967.

1 The prime goal is to alleviate suffering, and not to prolong life. And if your treatment does not alleviate suffering, but only prolongs life, treatment should be stopped.
Attrib.

Barnum, Phineas Taylor (1810–91) US showman. After converting the American Museum into a showplace for freaks and curiosities, he created 'The Greatest Show on Earth' (1871) and finally joined his rival in founding the Barnum and Bailey Circus (1881).

1 There's a sucker born every minute.
Attrib.

2 How were the receipts today in Madison Square Garden?
Last words

Barrie, Sir J(ames) M(atthew) (1860–1937) British novelist and dramatist, born in Scotland; author of *Peter Pan* (1904). His other works include *The Admirable Crichton* (1902) and *Dear Brutus* (1917).

1 If it's heaven for climate, it's hell for company.
The Little Minister, Ch. 3

2 It's grand, and ye canna expect to be baith grand and comfortable.
The Little Minister, Ch. 10

3 When the first baby laughed for the first time, the laugh broke into a thousand pieces and they all went skipping about, and that was the beginning of fairies.
Peter Pan, I

4 Every time a child says 'I don't believe in fairies' there is a little fairy somewhere that falls down dead.
Peter Pan, I

5 To die will be an awfully big adventure.
Peter Pan, III

6 What is algebra exactly; is it those three-cornered things?
Quality Street, II

7 One's religion is whatever he is most interested in, and yours is Success.
The Twelve-Pound Look

8 It's a sort of bloom on a woman. If you have it, you don't need to have anything else; and if you don't have it, it doesn't much matter what else you have.
Referring to charm
What Every Woman Knows, I

9 A young Scotsman of your ability let loose upon the world with £300, what could he not do? It's almost appalling to think of; especially if he went among the English.
What Every Woman Knows, I

10 You've forgotten the grandest moral attribute of a Scotsman, Maggie, that he'll do nothing which might damage his career.
What Every Woman Knows, II

11 There are few more impressive sights in the world than a Scotsman on the make.
What Every Woman Knows, II

12 I have always found that the man whose second thoughts are good is worth watching.
What Every Woman Knows, III

13 Never ascribe to an opponent motives meaner than your own.
Speech, St Andrews, 3 May 1922

14 Some of my plays peter out, and some pan out.
Attrib.

Barth, Karl (1886–1968) Swiss Protestant theologian. His writings include *The Epistle to the Romans* (1919) and the monumental *Church Dogmatics* (1932–67).

1 Men have never been good, they are not good, they never will be good.
Time, 12 Apr 1954

Baruch, Bernard Mannes (1870–1965) US financier and presidential adviser; he was involved in the Paris Peace Conference (1919).

1 I will never be an old man. To me, old age is always fifteen years older than I am.
The Observer 'Sayings of the Week', 21 Aug 1955

2 Let us not be deceived – we are today in the midst of a cold war.
Speech, South Carolina Legislature, 16 Apr 1947

Bates, Katharine Lee (1859–1929) US writer and poet. Collections of verse include *Sunshine and Other Verses for Children* (1890) and *America the Beautiful and Other Poems* (1911).

1 O beautiful for spacious skies,
For amber waves of grain,
For purple mountain majesties
Above the fruited plain!
America! America!
God shed His grace on thee
And crown thy good with brotherhood
From sea to shining sea!
America the Beautiful

Baudelaire, Charles (1821–67) French poet. After a dissolute life spending his inherited money, he published *La Fanfarlo* (1847), a novel, and ten years later the collection of verse for which he is best known, *Les Fleurs du mal*.

1 No task is a long one but the task on which one dare not start. It becomes a nightmare.
My Heart Laid Bare

2 I have more memories than if I were a thousand years old.
Spleen

Bax, Sir Arnold (1883–1953) British composer. His seven symphonies and the tone poem *Tintagel* (1917) are his best-known works. He became Master of the King's Music in 1941.

1 One should try everything once, except incest and folk-dancing.
Farewell to My Youth

Bayly, Thomas Haynes (1797–1839) British writer of songs, ballads, plays, and novels.

1 Absence makes the heart grow fonder,
Isle of Beauty, Fare thee well!
Isle of Beauty

2 It was a dream of perfect bliss,
Too beautiful to last.
It was a Dream

3 She wore a wreath of roses,
The night that first we met.
She Wore a Wreath of Roses

Beachcomber *See* Morton, J. B.

Beatty, David, 1st Earl (1871–1936) British admiral.
Appointed commander of the grand fleet after the Battle of Jutland
in 1916, he served as first sea lord (1919–27).

1 There's something wrong with our bloody ships
today.
Remark during Battle of Jutland, 30 May 1916
Attrib.

Beaumarchais, Pierre-Augustin Caron de (1732–
99) French dramatist. His comedies *Le Barbier de Séville* (1775)
and *Le Mariage de Figaro* (1778) were made into operas by
Rossini and Mozart, respectively.

1 I make myself laugh at everything, so that I do
not weep.
Le Barbier de Séville, I:2

2 Drinking when we are not thirsty and making
love all year round, madam; that is all there is to
distinguish us from other animals.
Le Mariage de Figaro, II:21

Beaumont, Francis (1584–1616) English dramatist, who
wrote a number of plays in collaboration with John Fletcher. These
include *Philaster* (1609), and *A King and No King* (1611).

1 You are no better than you should be.
The Coxcomb, IV:3

2 But what is past my help is past my care.
With John Fletcher
The Double Marriage, I:1

3 It is always good
When a man has two irons in the fire.
The Faithful Friends, I:2

4 Let's meet, and either do, or die.
The Island Princess, II:2

5 I'll put a spoke among your wheels.
The Mad Lover, III:6

6 Those have most power to hurt us that we love.
The Maid's Tragedy, V:6

7 Nothing's so dainty sweet as lovely melancholy.
The Nice Valour, III:3

8 All your better deeds
Shall be in water writ, but this in marble.
The Nice Valour, V:3

9 Mortality, behold and fear!
What a change of flesh is here!
On the Tombs in Westminster Abbey

10 As men
Do walk a mile, women should talk an hour,
After supper. 'Tis their exercise.
Philaster, II:4

11 I'll have a fling.
Rule a Wife and have a Wife, III:5

12 Kiss till the cow comes home.
Scornful Lady, II:2

13 Whistle and she'll come to you.
Wit Without Money, IV:4

Beauvoir, Simone de (1908–86) French writer. A lifelong
companion of Jean-Paul Sartre, she wrote novels on existentialist
themes, notably *The Mandarins* (1954).

1 What is an adult? A child blown up by age.
La Femme rompue

2 A man would never get the notion of writing a
book on the peculiar situation of the human
male.
Le Deuxième Sexe (trans. *The Second Sex*)

3 One is not born a woman, one becomes one.
Le Deuxième Sexe (trans. *The Second Sex*)

4 If you live long enough, you'll see that every victory turns into a defeat.
Tous les hommes sont mortels

Beaverbrook, Max Aitken, Baron (1879–1964)
Canadian-born British newspaper proprietor and politician. He
owned the *Daily Express* and *Evening Standard.* In World War I
he was minister of information and in World War II he became
minister of aircraft production.

1 I am the cat that walks alone.
Beaverbrook (A. J. P. Taylor)

2 He did not care in which direction the car was
travelling, so long as he remained in the driver's seat.
Referring to Lloyd George
New Statesman, 14 June 1963

3 If you want to make mischief come and work on
my papers.
Inviting the journalist Anthony Howard to join his staff
Radio Times, 27 June 1981

4 Go out and speak for the inarticulate and the
submerged.
Somerset Maugham (E. Morgan)

5 Buy old masters. They fetch a better price than
old mistresses.
Attrib.

Beckett, Samuel (1906–89) Irish novelist, dramatist, and
poet. Having settled in Paris in 1937, he wrote in both English
and French. His best-known work is *Waiting for Godot* (1952).

1 CLOV. Do you believe in the life to come?
HAMM. Mine was always that.
Endgame

2 Nothing happens, nobody comes, nobody goes,
it's awful!
Waiting for Godot, I

3 VLADIMIR. That passed the time.
ESTRAGON. It would have passed in any case.
VLADIMIR. Yes, but not so rapidly.
Waiting for Godot, I

4 ESTRAGON. . . . Let's go.
VLADIMIR. We can't.
ESTRAGON. Why not?
VLADIMIR. We're waiting for Godot.
Waiting for Godot, I

5 We all are born mad. Some remain so.
Waiting for Godot, II

6 Habit is a great deadener.
Waiting for Godot, III

Beckford, William (1759–1844) British writer; author of the oriental novel *Vathek* (1782). He commissioned the gothic Fonthill Abbey, where he lived as a recluse until 1822.

1 I am not over-fond of resisting temptation.
Vathek

Becon, Thomas (1512–67) English Protestant churchman and chaplain to Thomas Cranmer.

1 For when the wine is in, the wit is out.
Catechism, 375

Becque, Henry (1837–99) French dramatist. He is best known for the plays *Les Corbeaux* (1882) and *La Parisienne* (1885).

1 What makes equality such a difficult business is that we only want it with our superiors.
Querelles littéraires

Bede, St (The Venerable Bede; c. 673–735 AD) English churchman and historian. The author of many grammatical and historical works, his *Ecclesiastical History of the English People* (c. 731) was his major book.

1 The present life of men on earth, O king, as compared with the whole length of time which is unknowable to us, seems to me to be like this: as if, when you are sitting at dinner with your chiefs and ministers in wintertime, . . . one of the sparrows from outside flew very quickly through the hall; as if it came in one door and soon went out through another. In that actual time it is indoors it is not touched by the winter's storm; but yet the tiny period of calm is over in a moment, and having come out of the winter it soon returns to the winter and slips out of your sight. Man's life appears to be more or less like this; and of what may follow it, or what preceded it, we are absolutely ignorant.
Ecclesiastical History of the English People, Bk. II, Ch. 13

Bee, Barnard Elliot (1824–61) US soldier. An officer in the Confederate army, he was killed at the Battle of Bull Run in 1861.

1 Let us determine to die here, and we will conquer.
There is Jackson standing like a stone wall. Rally behind the Virginians.
Said at the First Battle of Bull Run, 1861; hence Gen Thomas Jackson's nickname, 'Stonewall Jackson'
Reminiscences of Metropolis (Poore), II

Beecham, Sir Thomas (1879–1961) British conductor. Using his inherited wealth, he popularized the works of Richard Strauss and Delius in Britain as well as founding the London Philharmonic Orchestra (1932) and the Royal Philharmonic Orchestra (1947).

1 A musicologist is a man who can read music but can't hear it.
Beecham Remembered (H. Procter-Gregg)

2 There are two golden rules for an orchestra: start together and finish together. The public doesn't give a damn what goes on in between.
Beecham Stories (H. Atkins and A. Newman)

3 Ball . . . how very singular.
To a man called Ball
Sir Thomas Beecham (N. Cardus)

4 The English may not like music – but they absolutely love the noise it makes.
The Wit of Music (L. Ayre)

5 I have recently been all round the world and have formed a very poor opinion of it.
Speech at the Savoy
The News Review, 22 Aug 1946

6 Too much counterpoint; what is worse, Protestant counterpoint.
Said of J. S. Bach
The Guardian, 8 Mar 1971

7 The sound of the harpsichord resembles that of a bird-cage played with toasting-forks.
Attrib.

8 Brass bands are all very well in their place – outdoors and several miles away.
Attrib.

Beecher, Henry Ward (1813–87) US Congregational minister and author.

1 I have known many an instance of a man writing a letter and forgetting to sign his name, but this is the only instance I have ever known of a man signing his name and forgetting to write the letter.
Said on receiving a note containing the single word: 'Fool'
The Best Stories in the World (T. Masson)

Beeching, H. C. (1859–1919) British academic and clergyman.

1 First come I; my name is Jowett.
There's no knowledge but I know it.
I am Master of this college:
What I don't know isn't knowledge.
Referring to Benjamin Jowett, master of Balliol College, Oxford
The Masque of Balliol

Beerbohm, Sir Max (1872–1936) British writer and caricaturist. His only novel, *Zuleika Dobson* (1911), is set in Oxford.

Quotations about Beerbohm

1 The Incomparable Max.
George Bernard Shaw (1856–1950) Irish dramatist and critic.
Dramatic Opinions and Essays, Vol. II.

2 He has the most remarkable and seductive genius – and I should say about the smallest in the world.
Lytton Strachey (1880–1932) British writer. Letter to Clive Bell, 4 Dec 1917

Quotations by Beerbohm

3 There is always something rather absurd about the past.
1880

4 To give an accurate and exhaustive account of that period would need a far less brilliant pen than mine.
1880

5 Great men are but life-sized. Most of them, indeed, are rather short.
And Even Now

6 I believe the twenty-four hour day has come to stay.
A Christmas Garland, 'Perkins and Mankind'

7 Most women are not so young as they are painted.
A Defence of Cosmetics

8 Anything that is worth doing has been done frequently. Things hitherto undone should be given, I suspect, a wide berth.
Mainly on the Air

9 It is Oxford that has made me insufferable.
More, 'Going back to School'

10 The lower one's vitality, the more sensitive one is to great art.
Seven Men, 'Enoch Soames'

11 The dullard's envy of brilliant men is always assuaged by the suspicion that they will come to a bad end.
Zuleika Dobson

12 It needs no dictionary of quotations to remind me that the eyes are the windows of the soul.
Zuleika Dobson, Ch. 4

13 Women who love the same man have a kind of bitter freemasonry.
Zuleika Dobson, Ch. 4

14 You will find that the woman who is really kind to dogs is always one who has failed to inspire sympathy in men.
Zuleika Dobson, Ch. 6

15 Beauty and the lust for learning have yet to be allied.
Zuleika Dobson, Ch. 7

16 You will think me lamentably crude: my experience of life has been drawn from life itself.
Zuleika Dobson, Ch. 7

17 You cannot make a man by standing a sheep on its hind legs. But by standing a flock of sheep in that position you can make a crowd of men.
Zuleika Dobson, Ch. 9

18 She was one of the people who say, 'I don't know anything about music really, but I know what I like'.
Zuleika Dobson, Ch. 16

19 It's not in support of cricket but as an earnest protest against golf.
Said when giving a shilling towards W. G. Grace's testimonial
Carr's Dictionary of Extraordinary English Cricketers

20 Of course we all know that Morris was a wonderful all-round man, but the act of walking round him has always tired me.
Referring to William Morris
Conversations with Max (S. N. Behrman)

21 They were a tense and peculiar family, the Oedipuses, weren't they?
Max: A Biography (D. Cecil)

22 What were they going to do with the Grail when they found it, Mr Rossetti?
Caption to a cartoon

Beethoven, Ludwig van (1770–1827) German composer. About 600 of his works survive, including such masterpieces as the nine symphonies, the opera *Fidelio* (1805–14), chamber music (particularly the piano sonatas and string quartets), and the *Missa Solemnis* (1818–23).

1 Off with you! You're a happy fellow, for you'll give happiness and joy to many other people. There is nothing better or greater than that!
Said to Franz Liszt when Liszt, aged 11, had visited Beethoven and played for him
Beethoven: Letters, Journals and Conversations (M. Hamburger)

2 When I composed that, I was conscious of being inspired by God Almighty. Do you think I can consider your puny little fiddle when He speaks to me?
Said when a violinist complained that a passage was unplayable
Music All Around Me (A. Hopkins)

3 Do not let that trouble Your Excellency; perhaps the greetings are intended for me.
Said when walking with Goethe, when Goethe complained about greetings from passers-by.
Thayer's Life of Beethoven (E. Forbes)

Behan, Brendan (1923–64) Irish playwright. His best-known works are *The Quare Fellow* (1954), the autobiographical *Borstal Boy* (1958), and *The Hostage* (1958). Behan's alcoholism led to his premature death.

1 PAT. He was an Anglo-Irishman.
MEG. In the blessed name of God, what's that?
PAT. A Protestant with a horse.
The Hostage, I

2 When I came back to Dublin, I was courtmartialled in my absence and sentenced to death in my absence, so I said they could shoot me in my absence.
The Hostage, I

3 He was born an Englishman and remained one for years.
The Hostage, I

4 I wish I'd been a mixed infant.

The Hostage, II

5 I am a sociable worker.

The Hostage, II

6 I think weddings is sadder than funerals, because they remind you of your own wedding. You can't be reminded of your own funeral because it hasn't happened. But weddings always make me cry.

Richard's Cork Leg, I

7 Other people have a nationality. The Irish and the Jews have a psychosis.

Richard's Cork Leg, I

8 The English and Americans dislike only *some* Irish – the same Irish that the Irish themselves detest, Irish writers – the ones that *think*.

Richard's Cork Leg, I

9 Come in, you Anglo-Saxon swine
And drink of my Algerian wine.
'Twill turn your eyeballs black and blue,
And damn well good enough for you.

Painted as an advert on the window of a Paris café (the owner of which could not speak English)
My Life with Brendan (B. Behan)

10 I am married to Beatrice Salkeld, a painter. We have no children, except me.

Attrib.

11 Thank you, sister. May you be the mother of a bishop!

Said to a nun nursing him on his deathbed
Attrib.

Behn, Aphra (1640–89) English novelist and dramatist. Her writings include the novel *Oroonoko* (1688) and the play *The Rover* (1677–81).

1 Love ceases to be a pleasure, when it ceases to be a secret.

The Lover's Watch, 'Four o'clock'

2 Faith, Sir, we are here to-day, and gone tomorrow.

The Lucky Chance, IV

Bell, Alexander Graham (1847–1922) Scottish scientist, who settled in the USA in 1873 and became professor of vocal physiology at Boston University. He patented the telephone in 1876.

1 Mr Watson, come here; I want you.

The first telephone conversation, 10 Mar 1876, in Boston
Attrib.

Bell, (Arthur) Clive (Heward) (1881–1964) British art critic, who married Virginia Woolf's sister Vanessa Stephen in 1907. His books include *Art* (1914) and *Civilization* (1928).

1 It would follow that 'significant form' was form behind which we catch a sense of ultimate reality.

Art, Pt. I, Ch. 3

2 I will try to account for the degree of my aesthetic emotion. That, I conceive, is the function of the critic.

Art, Pt. II, Ch. 3

3 Only reason can convince us of those three fundamental truths without a recognition of which there can be no effective liberty: that what we believe is not necessarily true; that what we like is not necessarily good; and that all questions are open.

Civilization, Ch. 5

Belloc, (Joseph) Hilaire (Pierre) (1870–1953) French-born British poet, essayist, and historian; Liberal MP for Salford (1906–10). Publications include *Cautionary Tales* (1907) and biographies of major historical figures. He was an ardent Roman Catholic.

Quotations about Belloc

1 He cannot bear isolation or final ethical responsibility; he clings to the Roman Catholic Church; he clung to his French nationality because one nation was not enough for him.

George Bernard Shaw (1856–1950) Irish dramatist and critic.
Lives of the Wits (H. Pearson)

2 He is conscious of being decrepit and forgetful, but not of being a bore.

Evelyn Waugh (1903–66) British novelist. Diary, 1 May 1945

Quotations by Belloc

3 Child! do not throw this book about;
Refrain from the unholy pleasure
Of cutting all the pictures out!
Preserve it as your chiefest treasure.

The Bad Child's Book of Beasts, 'Dedication'

4 Alas! That such affected tricks
Should flourish in a child of six!

Cautionary Tales, 'Godolphin Horne'

5 The Chief Defect of Henry King
Was chewing little bits of String.

Cautionary Tales, 'Henry King'

6 'Oh, my Friends, be warned by me,
That Breakfast, Dinner, Lunch and Tea
Are all the Human Frame requires . . . '
With that the Wretched Child expires.

Cautionary Tales, 'Henry King'

7 A trick that everyone abhors
In little girls is slamming doors.

Cautionary Tales, 'Rebecca'

8 They died to save their country and they only saved the world.

The English Graves

9 The accursed power which stands on Privilege
(And goes with Women, and Champagne, and Bridge)
Broke – and Democracy resumed her reign:
(Which goes with Bridge, and Women and Champagne).

Epigrams, 'On a Great Election'

10 When I am dead, I hope it may be said:
'His sins were scarlet, but his books were read.'
Epigrams, 'On His Books'

11 I'm tired of Love: I'm still more tired of Rhyme.
But Money gives me pleasure all the Time.
Fatigue

12 Whatever happens, we have got
The Maxim Gun, and they have not.
Referring to African natives
The Modern Traveller

13 The Microbe is so very small
You cannot make him out at all.
More Beasts for Worse Children, 'The Microbe'

14 Like many of the upper class
He liked the sound of broken glass.
New Cautionary Tales, 'About John'

15 The fleas that tease in the high Pyrenees.
Tarantella

16 I always like to associate with a lot of priests because it makes me understand anti-clerical things so well.
Letter to E. S. P. Haynes, 9 Nov 1909

17 I am a Catholic. As far as possible I go to Mass every day. As far as possible I kneel down and tell these beads every day. If you reject me on account of my religion, I shall thank God that he has spared me the indignity of being your representative.
Said in his first election campaign
Speech, Salford, 1906

18 Candidates should not attempt more than six of these.
Suggested addition to the Ten Commandments
Attrib.

Benchley, Robert Charles (1889–1945) US humorist and drama critic. He published many volumes of collected essays, including *Love Conquers All* (1922) and *From Bed to Worse* (1934).

1 Even nowadays a man can't step up and kill a woman without feeling just a bit unchivalrous.
Chips off the Old Benchley, 'Down in Front'

2 A great many people have come up to me and asked how I manage to get so much work done and still keep looking so dissipated.
Chips off the Old Benchley, 'How to Get Things Done'

3 I have been told by hospital authorities that more copies of my works are left behind by departing patients than those of any other author.
Chips off the Old Benchley, 'Why Does Nobody Collect Me?'

4 One cubic foot less of space and it would have constituted adultery.
Describing an office shared with Dorothy Parker
Attrib.

5 I don't trust a bank that would lend money to such a poor risk.
To a bank that granted his request for a loan. *See also* Groucho
MARX
Attrib.

6 I do most of my work sitting down; that's where I shine.
Attrib.

7 So who's in a hurry?
When asked whether he knew that drinking was a slow death
Attrib.

8 Streets full of water. Please advise.
Telegram sent to his editor on arriving in Venice
Attrib.

Benjamin, Judah Philip (1811–84) US politician.

1 The gentleman will please remember that when his half-civilized ancestors were hunting the wild boar in Silesia, mine were princes of the earth.
Replying to a senator of Germanic origin who had made an antisemitic remark
Attrib.

Benn, Tony (Anthony Neil Wedgwood-Benn; 1925–) British left-wing Labour politician. He became 2nd Viscount Stansgate in 1960 but renounced his peerage in 1963 under the Peerage Act of that year.

1 If I rescued a child from drowning, the Press would no doubt headline the story 'Benn grabs child'.
The Observer, 'Sayings of the Week', 2 Mar 1975

2 The Marxist analysis has got nothing to do with what happened in Stalin's Russia; it's like blaming Jesus Christ for the Inquisition in Spain.
The Observer, 27 Apr 1980

Bennett, Alan (1934–) British playwright and actor in comic reviews, such as *Beyond the Fringe* (1960). His plays include *Forty Years On* (1968), *An Englishman Abroad* (1982), and *Single Spies* (1988).

1 Life is rather like a tin of sardines – we're all of us looking for the key.
Beyond the Fringe

2 I have never understood this liking for war. It panders to instincts already catered for within the scope of any respectable domestic establishment.
Forty Years On, I

3 It's the one species I wouldn't mind seeing vanish from the face of the earth. I wish they were like the White Rhino – six of them left in the Serengeti National Park, and all males.
Referring to dogs
Getting On, I

4 Your whole life is on the other side of the glass. And there is nobody watching.
The Old Country, I

5 We were put to Dickens as children but it never quite took. That unremitting humanity soon had me cheesed off.
The Old Country, II

Bennett, (Enoch) Arnold (1867–1931) British novelist. His novels, set in his native Staffordshire, include *Anna of the Five Towns* (1902) and *Clayhanger* (1910).

Quotations about Bennett

1 Bennett – a sort of pig in clover.

D. H. Lawrence (1885–1930) British novelist. Letter to Aldous Huxley, 27 Mar 1928

2 I remember that once, beating his knee with his clenched fist to force the words through his writhing lips, he said, 'I am a nice man.' He was.

W. Somerset Maugham (1874–1965) British novelist. *The Vagrant Mood*

Quotations by Bennett

3 'Ye can call it influenza if ye like,' said Mrs Machin. 'There was no influenza in my young days. We called a cold a cold.'

The Card, Ch. 8

4 The people who live in the past must yield to the people who live in the future. Otherwise the world would begin to turn the other way round.

Milestones

5 Pessimism, when you get used to it, is just as agreeable as optimism.

Things that have Interested Me, 'The Slump in Pessimism'

6 Well, my deliberate opinion is – it's a jolly strange world.

The Title, I

7 Being a husband is a whole-time job. That is why so many husbands fail. They cannot give their entire attention to it.

The Title, I

8 Journalists say a thing that they know isn't true, in the hope that if they keep on saying it long enough it will be true.

The Title, II

9 Good taste is better than bad taste, but bad taste is better than no taste.

The Observer, 'Sayings of the Week', 24 Aug 1930

Bennett, James Gordon (1841–1918) US newspaper owner and editor. He became editor of the *New York Herald*, which had been founded by his father in 1867. He inherited the ownership in 1872.

1 Deleted by French censor.

Used to fill empty spaces in his papers during World War I when news was lacking
Americans in Paris (B. Morton)

2 Price of Herald three cents daily. Five cents Sunday. Bennett.

Telegram to William Randolph Hearst, when he heard that Hearst was trying to buy his paper and had asked for a price
The Life and Death of the Press Barons (P. Brandon)

Benny, Jack (Benjamin Kubelsky; 1894–1974) US actor and comedian. His many films included *Charley's Aunt* (1941) and *To Be or Not To Be* (1942).

1 I don't deserve this, but I have arthritis, and I don't deserve that either.

Said when accepting an award
Attrib.

Benson, A(rthur) C(hristopher) (1862–1925) British writer, schoolmaster, and master of Magdalene College, Cambridge. He wrote the anthem *Land of Hope and Glory*, essays, biographical studies, and works of criticism.

1 Land of Hope and Glory, Mother of the Free, How shall we extol thee, who are born of thee? Wider still and wider shall thy bounds be set; God who made thee mighty, make thee mightier yet.

Land of Hope and Glory

Bentham, Jeremy (1748–1832) British philosopher. Works include *Principles of Morals and Legislation* (1789), presenting his theory of utilitarianism.

1 The greatest happiness of the greatest number is the foundation of morals and legislation.

The Commonplace Book

2 Lawyers are the only persons in whom ignorance of the law is not punished.

Attrib.

Bentley, Edmund Clerihew (1875–1956) British writer and journalist, inventor of the witty four-line verse form known as the 'clerihew'. His writings include the detective novel *Trent's Last Case* (1913).

1 When their lordships asked Bacon How many bribes he had taken He had at least the grace To get very red in the face.

Baseless Biography

2 The Art of Biography Is different from Geography. Geography is about Maps, But Biography is about Chaps.

Biography for Beginners

3 What I like about Clive Is that he is no longer alive. There is a great deal to be said For being dead.

Biography for Beginners

4 Sir Humphry Davy Abominated gravy. He lived in the odium Of having discovered Sodium.

Biography for Beginners

5 John Stuart Mill By a mighty effort of will Overcame his natural bonhomie And wrote 'Principles of Political Economy'.

Biography for Beginners

6 Sir Christopher Wren Said, 'I am going to dine with some men. If anybody calls Say I am designing St Paul's.'

Biography for Beginners

Bentley, Richard (1662–1742) English academic. He became master of Trinity College, Cambridge, in 1700. He is known for his critical books on classical authors.

1 He is believed to have liked port, but to have said of claret that 'it would be port if it could'.
Bentley (R. C. Jebb)

2 I hold it as certain, that no man was ever written out of reputation but by himself.
The Works of Alexander Pope (W. Warburton), Vol. IV

Beresford, Charles William de la Poer, Baron (1846–1919) British naval officer and author of *The Life of Nelson and his Times* (1898–1905).

1 Very sorry can't come. Lie follows by post.
Reply, by telegram, to a dinner invitation at short notice from Edward, Prince of Wales
The World of Fashion 1837–1922 (R. Nevill), Ch. 5

Bergman, Ingrid (1915–82) Swedish actress. She became an international film star, appearing in such films as *Casablanca* (1942) and *Gaslight* (1944).

1 I have no regrets. I wouldn't have lived my life the way I did if I was going to worry about what people were going to say.
Attrib.

2 It's not whether you really cry. It's whether the audience thinks you are crying.
Attrib.

Berkeley, George, Bishop (1685–1753) Irish churchman and philosopher. His philosophy of idealism is set out in his *Principles of Human Knowledge* (1710). Later works include *Siris* (1744).

1 It is impossible that a man who is false to his friends and neighbours should be true to the public.
Maxims Concerning Patriotism

2 We have first raised a dust and then complain we cannot see.
Principles of Human Knowledge, Introduction

Berlin, Irving (Israel Baline; 1888–1989) Russian-born US composer and lyricist. His works include 'Alexander's Rag Time Band' and 'White Christmas'; and the scores for musicals including *Annie Get Your Gun* (1946).

1 Got no check books, got no banks.
Still I'd like to express my thanks –
I got the sun in the mornin' and the moon at night.
Annie Get Your Gun, 'I Got the Sun in the Mornin''

2 There's No Business Like Show Business.
Song title

3 The world would not be in such a snarl, had Marx been Groucho instead of Karl.
Telegram to Groucho Marx on his seventy-first birthday

4 Listen kid, take my advice, never hate a song that has sold half a million copies.
Giving advice to Cole Porter
Attrib.

Berlioz, (Louis) Hector (1803–69) French composer. His first success was the *Symphonie Fantastique* (1830–31); later works include the symphony *Harold in Italy* (1834), the *Requiem* (1837), and the opera *Les Troyens* (1856–59). He also wrote a treatise on orchestration.

1 Time is a great teacher, but unfortunately it kills all its pupils.
Almanach des lettres françaises

Bernard, Tristan (1866–1947) French dramatist.

1 In the theatre the audience want to be surprised – but by things that they expect.
Contes, Repliques et Bon Mots

Bernard, W. B. (1807–75) British dramatist.

1 A Storm in a Teacup.
Play title

Bernhardt, Sarah (Sarah Henriette Rosine Bernard; 1844–1923) French actress and theatre manager, noted especially for her passionate performances in tragedy. Among her famous roles were Cordelia, Phèdre, and Hamlet.

1 For the theatre one needs long arms; it is better to have them too long than too short. An *artiste* with short arms can never, never make a fine gesture.
Memories of My Life, Ch. 6

2 I do love cricket – it's so very English.
On seeing a game of football
Nijinsky (R. Buckle)

Betjeman, Sir John (1906–84) British poet; poet laureate (1972–84). Publications include *Collected Poems* (1958), *High and Low* (1976), and a verse autobiography, *Summoned by Bells* (1960).

Quotations about Betjeman

1 By appointment: Teddy Bear to the Nation.
Alan Bell *The Times*, 20 Sept 1982

2 You've no idea how original it was to write like Tennyson in the 1930s, rather than Eliot or Auden.
Lord David Cecil (1902–86) British writer and critic. Remark

3 We invite people like that to tea, but we don't marry them.
Lady Chetwode. Lady Chetwode later became Betjeman's mother-in-law. Remark

Quotations by Betjeman

4 Spirits of well-shot woodcock, partridge, snipe
Flutter and bear him up the Norfolk sky.
Death of King George V

5 You ask me what it is I do. Well actually, you know,
I'm partly a liaison man and partly P.R.O.
Essentially I integrate the current export drive
And basically I'm viable from ten o'clock till five.
Executive

6 Phone for the fish knives Norman,
As Cook is a little unnerved;
You kiddies have crumpled the serviettes
And I must have things daintily served.
How to get on in Society

7 I know what I wanted to ask you;
Is trifle sufficient for sweet?
How to get on in Society

8 Rumbling under blackened girders, Midland,
bound for Cricklewood,
Puffed its sulphur to the sunset where the Land
of Laundries stood.
Rumble under, thunder over, train and tram alternate go.
Parliament Hill Fields

9 I have a vision of the future, chum.
The workers' flats in fields of soya beans
Tower up like silver pencils.
The Planster's Vision

10 Come, friendly bombs, and fall on Slough
It isn't fit for humans now.
There isn't grass to graze a cow
Swarm over, Death!
. . .
Come, friendly bombs, and fall on Slough
To get it ready for the plough.
The cabbages are coming now:
The earth exhales.
Slough

11 Miss J. Hunter Dunn, Miss J. Hunter Dunn,
Furnish'd and burnish'd by Aldershot sun.
A Subaltern's Love Song

Bevan, Aneurin (1897–1960) British Labour politician and editor of the left-wing *Tribune* (1940–45). As minister of health (1945–51) he introduced the National Health Service.

1 Its relationship to democratic institutions is that of the death watch beetle – it is not a Party, it is a conspiracy.
Referring to the Communist Party
Tribune

2 The language of priorities is the religion of Socialism.
Aneurin Bevan (Vincent Brome), Ch. 1

3 He is a man suffering from petrified adolescence.
Referring to Churchill
Aneurin Bevan (Vincent Brome), Ch. 11

4 I know that the right kind of political leader for the Labour Party is a desiccated calculating machine.
Usually regarded as a gibe at Hugh Gaitskell
Speech during Labour Party Conference, 29 Sept 1954

5 We know what happens to people who stay in the middle of the road. They get run over.
The Observer, 'Sayings of the Week', 9 Dec 1953

6 I read the newspaper avidly. It is my one form of continuous fiction.
The Observer, 'Sayings of the Week', 3 Apr 1960

7 This island is almost made of coal and surrounded by fish. Only an organizing genius could produce a shortage of coal and fish in Great Britain at the same time.
Speech, Blackpool, 18 May 1945

8 No amount of cajolery, and no attempts at ethical and social seduction, can eradicate from my heart a deep burning hatred for the Tory Party . . . So far as I am concerned they are lower than vermin.
Speech, Manchester, 4 July 1949

9 There is no reason to attack the monkey when the organ-grinder is present.
The 'monkey' was Selwyn Lloyd; the 'organ-grinder' was Harold Macmillan
Speech, House of Commons

10 We know what happens to people who stay in the middle of the road. They get run over.
The Observer, 9 Dec 1953

11 If you carry this resolution and follow out all its implications and do not run away from it, you will send a Foreign Secretary, whoever he may be, naked into the conference chamber.
Referring to unilateral disarmament
Speech, Labour Party Conference, 2 Oct 1957

12 Fascism is not itself a new order of society. It is the future refusing to be born.
Attrib.

13 I stuffed their mouths with gold!
Explaining how he persuaded doctors not to oppose the introduction of the National Health Service
Attrib.

Beveridge, William Henry, Baron (1879–1963) British economist. He is best known for the so-called Beveridge Report, *The Report on Social Insurance and Allied Services* (1942), upon which the welfare state was based.

1 The object of government in peace and in war is not the glory of rulers or of races, but the happiness of the common man.
Social Insurance

2 The trouble in modern democracy is that men do not approach to leadership until they have lost the desire to lead anyone.
The Observer, 'Sayings of the Week', 15 Apr 1934

3 Scratch a pessimist, and you find often a defender of privilege.
The Observer, 'Sayings of the Week', 17 Dec 1943

Bevin, Ernest (1881–1951) British trade-union leader and politician. Elected chairman of the TUC in 1937, he became minister of labour in Churchill's wartime coalition government. In the post-war Labour government he was foreign secretary.

1 Not while I'm alive, he ain't.
When told that Aneurin Bevan was 'his own worst enemy'. Also attributed to others
Aneurin Bevan (M. Foot)

2 If you open that Pandora's Box you never know what Trojan 'orses will jump out.

Referring to the Council of Europe
Ernest Bevin and the Foreign Office (Sir Roderick Barclay)

3 My policy is to be able to take a ticket at Victoria Station and go anywhere I damn well please.

The Spectator, 20 Apr 1951

Bible Quotations are taken from the Authorized Version of the Bible unless otherwise stated. The Books of the Bible are arranged in a single alphabetical order (not all books are represented). *See also* Book of Common Prayer, Psalms.

Acts

1 And when he had spoken these things, while they beheld, he was taken up; and a cloud received him out of their sight.

1:9

2 And when the day of Pentecost was fully come, they were all with one accord in one place.
And suddenly there came a sound from heaven as of a rushing mighty wind, and it filled all the house where they were sitting.
And there appeared unto them cloven tongues like as of fire, and it sat upon each of them.
And they were all filled with the Holy Ghost, and began to speak with other tongues, as the Spirit gave them utterance.

2:1–4

3 Others mocking said, These men are full of new wine.

2:13

4 Then Peter said, Silver and gold have I none; but such as I have give I thee: In the name of Jesus Christ of Nazareth rise up and walk.

3:6

5 When they heard these things, they were cut to the heart, and they gnashed on him with their teeth.

7:54

6 And as he journeyed, he came near Damascus: and suddenly there shined round about him a light from heaven:
And he fell to the earth, and heard a voice saying unto him, Saul, Saul, why persecutest thou me?
And he said, Who art thou, Lord? And the Lord said, I am Jesus whom thou persecutest: it is hard for thee to kick against the pricks.

9:3–5

7 And the Lord said unto him, Arise, and go into the street which is called Straight, and enquire in the house of Judas for one called Saul, of Tarsus: for, behold, he prayeth.

9:11

8 But the Lord said unto him, Go thy way: for he is a chosen vessel unto me, to bear my name before the Gentiles, and kings, and the children of Israel.

9:15

9 But Peter took him up, saying, Stand up; I myself also am a man.

10:26

10 Then Peter opened his mouth, and said, Of a truth I perceive that God is no respecter of persons.

10:34

11 And the people gave a shout, saying, It is the voice of a god, and not of a man.
And immediately the angel of the Lord smote him, because he gave not God the glory: and he was eaten of worms, and gave up the ghost.

12:22–23

12 God that made the world and all things therein, seeing that he is Lord of heaven and earth, dwelleth not in temples made with hands.

17:24

13 For in him we live, and move, and have our being; as certain also of your own poets have said, For we are also his offspring.

17:28

14 And now, behold, I go bound in the spirit unto Jerusalem, not knowing the things that shall befall me there.

20:22

15 And the chief captain answered, With a great sum obtained I this freedom. And Paul said, But I was free born.

22:28

16 Then said Paul unto him, God shall smite thee, thou whited wall: for sittest thou to judge me after the law, and commandest me to be smitten contrary to the law?

23:3

17 Then Festus, when he had conferred with the council, answered, Hast thou appealed unto Caesar? Unto Caesar shalt thou go.

25:12

Amos

18 Seek him that maketh the seven stars and Orion, and turneth the shadow of death into the morning, and maketh the day dark with night: that calleth for the waters of the sea, and poureth them out upon the face of the earth: The Lord is his name.

5:8

Colossians

19 Beware lest any man spoil you through philosophy and vain deceit, after the tradition of men, after the rudiments of the world, and not after Christ.

2:8

20 Where there is neither Greek nor Jew, circumcision nor uncircumcision, Barbarian, Scythian, bond nor free; but Christ is all, and in all.

3:11

21 Husbands, love your wives, and be not bitter against them.

3:19

22 Fathers, provoke not your children to anger, lest they be discouraged.

3:21

23 Let your speech be alway with grace, seasoned with salt, that ye may know how ye ought to answer every man.

4:6

I Corinthians

24 For after that in the wisdom of God the world by wisdom knew not God, it pleased God by the foolishness of preaching to save them that believe.
For the Jews require a sign, and the Greeks seek after wisdom:
But we preach Christ crucified, unto the Jews a stumblingblock, and unto the Greeks foolishness.

1:21–23

25 But as it is written, Eye hath not seen, nor ear heard, neither have entered into the heart of man, the things which God hath prepared for them that love him.

2:9

26 For the kingdom of God is not in word, but in power.

4:20

27 Meats for the belly, and the belly for meats: but God shall destroy both it and them. Now the body is not for fornication, but for the Lord; and the Lord for the body.

6:13

28 What? know ye not that your body is the temple of the Holy Ghost which is in you, which ye have of God, and ye are not your own?

6:19

29 Let the husband render unto the wife due benevolence: and likewise also the wife unto the husband.

7:3

30 But if they cannot contain, let them marry: for it is better to marry than to burn.

7:9

31 But he that is married careth for the things that are of the world, how he may please his wife.

7:33

32 Now as touching things offered unto idols, we know that we all have knowledge. Knowledge puffeth up, but charity edifieth.

8:1

33 Know ye not that they which run in a race run all, but one receiveth the prize? So run, that ye may obtain.
And every man that striveth for the mastery is temperate in all things. Now they do it to obtain a corruptible crown; but we an incorruptible.

9:24–25

34 All things are lawful for me, but all things are not expedient: all things are lawful for me, but all things edify not.

10:23

35 For the earth is the Lord's, and the fulness thereof.

10:26

36 Conscience, I say, not thine own, but of the other: for why is my liberty judged of another man's conscience?

10:29

37 But if a woman have long hair, it is a glory to her: for her hair is given her for a covering.

11:15

38 Though I speak with the tongues of men and of angels, and have not charity, I am become as sounding brass, or a tinkling cymbal.
And though I have the gift of prophecy, and understand all mysteries, and all knowledge; and though I have all faith, so that I could remove mountains, and have not charity, I am nothing.
And though I bestow all my goods to feed the poor, and though I give my body to be burned, and have not charity, it profiteth me nothing.
Charity suffereth long, and is kind; charity envieth not; charity vaunteth not itself, is not puffed up,
Doth not behave itself unseemly, seeketh not her own, is not easily provoked, thinketh no evil;
Rejoiceth not in iniquity, but rejoiceth in the truth;
Beareth all things, believeth all things, hopeth all things, endureth all things.
Charity never faileth: but whether there be prophecies, they shall fail; whether there be tongues, they shall cease; whether there be knowledge, it shall vanish away.
For we know in part, and we prophesy in part.
But when that which is perfect is come, then that which is in part shall be done away.
When I was a child, I spake as a child, I understood as a child, I thought as a child: but when I became a man, I put away childish things.
For now we see through a glass, darkly; but then face to face: now I know in part; but then shall I know even as also I am known.
And now abideth faith, hope, charity, these three; but the greatest of these is charity.

13:1–13

39 Let all things be done decently and in order.

14:40

40 If after the manner of men I have fought with beasts at Ephesus, what advantageth it me, if the dead rise not? let us eat and drink; for to-morrow we die.
Be not deceived: evil communications corrupt good manners.
15:32–33

41 There is one glory of the sun, and another glory of the moon, and another glory of the stars: for one star differeth from another star in glory.
So also is the resurrection of the dead. It is sown in corruption; it is raised in incorruption.
15:41–42

42 Behold, I shew you a mystery; We shall not all sleep, but we shall all be changed,
In a moment, in the twinkling of an eye, at the last trump: for the trumpet shall sound, and the dead shall be raised incorruptible, and we shall be changed.
For this corruptible must put on incorruption, and this mortal must put on immortality.
So when this corruptible shall have put on incor-ruption, and this mortal shall have put on im-mortality, then shall be brought to pass the saying that is written, Death is swallowed up in victory.
O death, where is thy sting? O grave, where is thy victory?
15:51–55

43 If any man love not the Lord Jesus Christ, let him be Anathema Maranatha.
The grace of our Lord Jesus Christ be with you.
16:22–23

II Corinthians

44 For we walk by faith, not by sight.
5:7

45 Every man according as he purposeth in his heart, so let him give; not grudgingly, or of ne-cessity: for God loveth a cheerful giver.
9:7

46 For ye suffer fools gladly, seeing ye yourselves are wise.
11:19

47 And lest I should be exalted above measure through the abundance of the revelations, there was given to me a thorn in the flesh, the mes-senger of Satan to buffet me, lest I should be exalted above measure.
12:7

Daniel

48 That at what time ye hear the sound of the cor-net, flute, harp, sackbut, psaltery, dulcimer, and all kinds of musick, ye fall down and worship the golden image that Nebuchadnezzar the king hath set up:

And whoso falleth not down and worshippeth shall the same hour be cast into the midst of a burning fiery furnace.
3:5–6

49 Then was Nebuchadnezzar full of fury, and the form of his visage was changed against Sha-drach, Meshach, and Abed-nego: therefore he spake, and commanded that they should heat the furnace one seven times more than it was wont to be heated.
3:19

50 The same hour was the thing fulfilled upon Neb-uchadnezzar: and he was driven from men, and did eat grass as oxen, and his body was wet with the dew of heaven, till his hairs were grown like eagles' feathers, and his nails like birds' claws.
4:33

51 In the same hour came forth fingers of a man's hand, and wrote over against the candlestick upon the plaster of the wall of the king's palace: and the king saw the part of the hand that wrote.
5:5

52 And this is the writing that was written, MENE, MENE, TEKEL, UPHARSIN.
This is the interpretation of the thing: MENE; God hath numbered thy kingdom, and finished it.
TEKEL; Thou art weighed in the balances, and art found wanting.
PERES; Thy kingdom is divided, and given to the Medes and Persians.
5:25–28

53 Then the king commanded, and they brought Daniel, and cast him into the den of lions. Now the king spake and said unto Daniel, Thy God whom thou servest continually, he will deliver thee.
6:16

Deuteronomy

54 For the Lord thy God bringeth thee into a good land, a land of brooks of water, of fountains and depths that spring out of valleys and hills;
A land of wheat, and barley, and vines, and fig trees, and pomegranates; a land of oil olive, and honey;
A land wherein thou shalt eat bread without scarceness, thou shalt not lack any thing in it; a land whose stones are iron, and out of whose hills thou mayest dig brass.
When thou hast eaten and art full, then thou shalt bless the Lord thy God for the good land which he hath given thee.
8:7–10

55 Take heed to yourselves, that your heart be not deceived, and ye turn aside, and serve other gods, and worship them.
11:16

56 Thou shalt not hearken unto the words of that prophet, or that dreamer of dreams.
13:3

57 I call heaven and earth to record this day against you, that I have set before you life and death, blessing and cursing: therefore choose life, that both thou and thy seed may live.
30:19

58 Be strong and of a good courage, fear not, nor be afraid of them: for the Lord thy God, he it is that doth go with thee; he will not fail thee, nor forsake thee.
31:6

59 He found him in a desert land, and in the waste howling wilderness; he led him about, he instructed him, he kept him as the apple of his eye.
32:10

60 And there arose not a prophet since in Israel like unto Moses, whom the Lord knew face to face.
34:10

Ecclesiastes

61 Vanity of vanities, saith the Preacher, vanity of vanities; all is vanity.
What profit hath a man of all his labour which he taketh under the sun?
One generation passeth away, and another generation cometh: but the earth abideth for ever.
1:2–4

62 All the rivers run into the sea; yet the sea is not full; unto the place from whence the rivers come, thither they return again.
All things are full of labour; man cannot utter it: the eye is not satisfied with seeing, nor the ear filled with hearing.
The thing that hath been, it is that which shall be; and that which is done is that which shall be done: and there is no new thing under the sun.
1:7–9

63 There is no remembrance of former things; neither shall there be any remembrance of things that are to come with those that shall come after.
1:11

64 And I gave my heart to seek and search out by wisdom concerning all things that are done under heaven: this sore travail hath God given to the sons of man to be exercised therewith.
I have seen all the works that are done under the sun; and, behold, all is vanity and vexation of spirit.
1:13–14

65 For in much wisdom is much grief: and he that increaseth knowledge increaseth sorrow.
1:18

66 The wise man's eyes are in his head; but the fool walketh in darkness: and I myself perceived also that one event happeneth to them all.
2:14

67 To every thing there is a season, and a time to every purpose under the heaven:
A time to be born, and a time to die; a time to plant, and a time to pluck up that which is planted;
A time to kill, and a time to heal; a time to break down, and a time to build up;
A time to weep, and a time to laugh; a time to mourn, and a time to dance;
A time to cast away stones, and a time to gather stones together; a time to embrace, and a time to refrain from embracing;
A time to get, and a time to lose; a time to keep, and a time to cast away;
A time to rend, and a time to sew; a time to keep silence, and a time to speak;
A time to love, and a time to hate; a time of war, and a time of peace.
3:1–8

68 Wherefore I praised the dead which are already dead more than the living which are yet alive.
Yea, better is he than both they, which hath not yet been, who hath not seen the evil work that is done under the sun.
4:2–3

69 Two are better than one; because they have a good reward for their labour.
For if they fall, the one will lift up his fellow: but woe to him that is alone when he falleth; for he hath not another to help him up.
4:9–10

70 And if one prevail against him, two shall withstand him; and a threefold cord is not quickly broken.
4:12

71 Better is a poor and a wise child than an old and foolish king, who will no more be admonished.
4:13

72 Then I commended mirth, because a man hath no better thing under the sun, than to eat, and to drink, and to be merry: for that shall abide with him of his labour the days of his life, which God giveth him under the sun.
8:15

73 Whatsoever thy hand findeth to do, do it with thy might; for there is no work, nor device, nor knowledge, nor wisdom, in the grave, whither thou goest.
9:10

74 I returned, and saw under the sun, that the race is not to the swift, nor the battle to the strong, neither yet bread to the wise, nor yet riches to men of understanding, nor yet favour to men of skill; but time and chance happeneth to them all.
9:11

75 The words of wise men are heard in quiet more than the cry of him that ruleth among fools.
9:17

76 A feast is made for laughter, and wine maketh merry: but money answereth all things.
10:19

77 Cast thy bread upon the waters: for thou shalt find it after many days.
11:1

78 And further, by these, my son, be admonished: of making many books there is no end; and much study is a weariness of the flesh.
12:12

79 Let us hear the conclusion of the whole matter: Fear God, and keep his commandments: for this is the whole duty of man.
12:13

Ecclesiasticus

80 My son, if thou come to serve the Lord, prepare thy soul for temptation.
2:1

81 Be not curious in unnecessary matters: for more things are shewed unto thee than men understand
3:23

82 Miss not the discourse of the elders: for they also learned of their fathers, and of them thou shalt learn understanding, and to give answer as need requireth.
8:9

83 Forsake not an old friend; for the new is not comparable to him: a new friend is as new wine; when it is old, thou shalt drink it with pleasure.
9:10

84 The physician cutteth off a long disease; and he that is today a king tomorrow shall die.
10:10

85 Desire not a multitude of unprofitable children, neither delight in ungodly sons.
16:1

86 Be not made a beggar by banqueting upon borrowing, when thou hast nothing in thy purse: for thou shalt lie in wait for thine own life, and be talked on.
18:33

87 If thou hast gathered nothing in thy youth, how canst thou find any thing in thine age?
25:3

88 Leave off first for manners' sake: and be not unsatiable, lest thou offend.
31:17

89 Let thy speech be short, comprehending much in few words; be as one that knoweth and yet holdeth his tongue.
32:8

90 The wisdom of a learned man cometh by opportunity of leisure: and he that hath little business shall become wise.
How can he get wisdom that holdeth the plough, and that glorieth in the goad, that driveth oxen, and is occupied in their labours, and whose talk is of bullocks?
38:24 – 25

91 Let us now praise famous men, and our fathers that begat us.
44:1

92 And some there be, which have no memorial; who are perished, as though they had never been; and are become as though they had never been born; and their children after them.
44:9

93 Their bodies are buried in peace; but their name liveth for evermore.
44:14

Ephesians

94 Wherefore putting away lying, speak every man truth with his neighbour: for we are members one of another.
Be ye angry, and sin not: let not the sun go down upon your wrath:
Neither give place to the devil.
Let him that stole steal no more: but rather let him labour, working with his hands the thing which is good, that he may have to give to him that needeth.
4:25 – 28

95 Children, obey your parents in the Lord: for this is right.
6:1

96 Finally, my brethren, be strong in the Lord, and in the power of his might.
Put on the whole armour of God, that ye may be able to stand against the wiles of the devil.
For we wrestle not against flesh and blood, but against principalities, against powers, against the rulers of the darkness of his world, against spiritual wickedness in high places.
6:10 – 12

II Esdras

97 Then had I pity upon your mournings, and gave you manna to eat; so ye did eat angels' bread.
1:19

98　Then were the entrances of this world made narrow, full of sorrow and travail: they are but few and evil, full of perils, and very painful. For the entrances of the elder world were wide and sure, and brought immortal fruit.

7:12–13

99　For the world hath lost his youth, and the times begin to wax old.

14:10

100　And come hither, and I shall light a candle of understanding in thine heart, which shall not be put out, till the things be performed which thou shalt begin to write.

14:25

Esther

101　And the king loved Esther above all the women, and she obtained grace and favour in his sight more than all the virgins; so that he set the royal crown upon her head, and made her queen instead of Vashti.

2:17

Exodus

102　Now there arose up a new king over Egypt, which knew not Joseph.

1:8

103　And when she could not longer hide him, she took for him an ark of bulrushes, and daubed it with slime and with pitch, and put the child therein; and she laid it in the flags by the river's brink.

2:3

104　He called his name Gershom: for he said, I have been a stranger in a strange land.

2:22

105　And the angel of the Lord appeared unto him in a flame of fire out of the midst of a bush: and he looked, and, behold, the bush burned with fire, and the bush was not consumed.

3:2

106　And I am come down to deliver them out of the hand of the Egyptians, and to bring them up out of that land unto a good land and a large, unto a land flowing with milk and honey; unto the place of the Canaanites, and the Hittites, and the Amorites, and the Perizzites, and the Hivites, and the Jebusites.

3:8

107　And God said unto Moses, I AM THAT I AM: and he said, Thus shalt thou say unto the children of Israel, I AM hath sent me unto you.

3:14

108　For they cast down every man his rod, and they became serpents: but Aaron's rod swallowed up their rods.

7:12

109　Your lamb shall be without blemish, a male of the first year: ye shall take it out from the sheep, or from the goats.

12:5

110　And thus shall ye eat it; with your loins girded, your shoes on your feet, and your staff in your hand; and ye shall eat it in haste: it is the Lord's passover.
For I will pass through the land of Egypt this night, and will smite all the firstborn in the land of Egypt, both man and beast; and against all the gods of Egypt I will execute judgment: I am the Lord.

12:11–12

111　And the Lord went before them by day in a pillar of a cloud, to lead them the way; and by night in a pillar of fire, to give them light; to go by day and night.

13:21

112　And the children of Israel went into the midst of the sea upon the dry ground: and the waters were a wall unto them on their right hand, and on their left.

14:22

113　The Lord is a man of war: the Lord is his name.

15:3

114　And mount Sinai was altogether on a smoke, because the Lord descended upon it in fire: and the smoke thereof ascended as the smoke of a furnace, and the whole mount quaked greatly.

19:18

115　I am the Lord thy God, which have brought thee out of the land of Egypt, out of the house of bondage.
Thou shalt have no other gods before me.
Thou shalt not make unto thee any graven image, or any likeness of any thing that is in heaven above, or that is in the earth beneath, or that is in the water under the earth:
Thou shalt not bow down thyself to them, nor serve them: for Lord thy God am a jealous God, visiting the iniquity of the fathers upon the children unto the third and fourth generation of them that hate me;
And shewing mercy unto thousands of them that love me, and keep my commandments.
Thou shalt not take the name of the Lord thy God in vain; for the Lord will not hold him guiltless that taketh his name in vain.
Remember the sabbath day, to keep it holy.
Six days shalt thou labour, and do all thy work:
But the seventh day is the sabbath of the Lord thy God: in it thou shalt not do any work, thou, nor thy son, nor thy daughter, thy manservant, nor thy maidservant, nor thy cattle, nor thy stranger that is within thy gates:

For in six days the Lord made heaven and earth, the sea, and all that in them is, and rested the seventh day: wherefore the Lord blessed the sabbath day, and hallowed it.

Honour thy father and thy mother: that thy days may be long upon the land which the Lord thy God giveth thee.

Thou shalt not kill.

Thou shalt not commit adultery.

Thou shalt not steal.

Thou shalt not bear false witness against thy neighbour.

Thou shalt not covet thy neighbour's house, thou shalt not covet thy neighbour's wife, nor his manservant, nor his maidservant, nor his ox, nor his ass, nor any thing that is thy neighbour's.

20:2–17

116 And if any mischief follow, then thou shalt give life for life,

Eye for eye, tooth for tooth, hand for hand, foot for foot,

Burning for burning, wound for wound, stripe for stripe.

21:23–25

117 Thou shalt not suffer a witch to live.

22:18

118 The first of the firstfruits of thy land thou shalt bring into the house of the Lord thy God. Thou shalt not seethe a kid in his mother's milk.

23:19

119 And the Lord said unto Moses, Come up to me into the mount, and be there: and I will give thee tables of stone, and a law, and commandments which I have written; that thou mayest teach them.

24:12

120 And he received them at their hand, and fashioned it with a graving tool, after he had made it a molten calf: and they said, These be thy gods, O Israel, which brought thee up out of the land of Egypt.

32:4

121 And he said, Thou canst not see my face: for there shall no man see me, and live.

33:20

122 And it shall come to pass, while my glory passeth by, that I will put thee in a clift of the rock, and will cover thee with my hand while I pass by.

33:22

Ezekiel

123 And thou, son of man, be not afraid of them, neither be afraid of their words, though briers and thorns be with thee, and thou dost dwell among scorpions: be not afraid of their words, nor be dismayed at their looks, though they be a rebellious house.

2:6

124 Son of man, thou dwellest in the midst of a rebellious house, which have eyes to see, and see not; they have ears to hear, and hear not: for they are a rebellious house.

12:2

125 Behold, every one that useth proverbs shall use this proverb against thee, saying, As is the mother, so is her daughter.

16:44–45

126 What mean ye, that ye use this proverb concerning the land of Israel, saying, The fathers have eaten sour grapes, and the children's teeth are set on edge?

18:2

127 Again, when the wicked man turneth away from his wickedness that he hath committed, and doeth that which is lawful and right, he shall save his soul alive.

18:27

128 And he said unto me, Son of man, can these bones live? And I answered, O Lord God, thou knowest.

Again he said unto me, Prophesy upon these bones, and say unto them, O ye dry bones, hear the word of the Lord.

37:3–4

129 So I prophesied as I was commanded: and as I prophesied, there was a noise, and behold a shaking, and the bones came together, bone to his bone.

37:7

Ezra

130 The people could not discern the noise of the shout of joy from the noise of the weeping of the people: for the people shouted with a loud shout, and the noise was heard afar off.

3:13

Galatians

131 O foolish Galatians, who hath bewitched you, that ye should not obey the truth, before whose eyes Jesus Christ hath been evidently set forth, crucified among you?

3:1

132 There is neither Jew nor Greek, there is neither bond nor free, there is neither male nor female: for ye are all one in Christ Jesus.

3:28

133 But Jerusalem which is above is free, which is the mother of us all.
4:26

134 For the flesh lusteth against the Spirit, and the Spirit against the flesh: and these are contrary the one to the other: so that ye cannot do the things that ye would.
5:17

135 But the fruit of the Spirit is love, joy, peace, longsuffering, gentleness, goodness, faith, Meekness, temperance: against such there is no law.
5:22–23

136 Be not deceived: God is not mocked: for whatsoever a man soweth, that shall he also reap.
6:7

Genesis

137 In the beginning God created the heaven and the earth.
And the earth was without form, and void; and darkness was upon the face of the deep. And the Spirit of God moved upon the face of the waters.
And God said, Let there be light: and there was light.
And God saw the light, that it was good: and God divided the light from the darkness.
And God called the light Day, and the darkness he called Night. And the evening and the morning were the first day.
1:1–5

138 Fiat lux.
Vulgate 1:3

139 And God called the dry land Earth; and the gathering together of the waters called he Seas: and God saw that it was good.
And God said, Let the earth bring forth grass, the herb yielding seed, and the fruit tree yielding fruit after his kind, whose seed is in itself, upon the earth: and it was so.
1:10–11

140 And God made two great lights: the greater light to rule the day, and the lesser light to rule the night: he made the stars also.
1:16

141 And God said, Let the earth bring forth the living creature after his kind, cattle, and creeping thing, and beast of the earth after his kind: and it was so.
1:24

142 And God said, Let us make man in our image, after our likeness: and let them have dominion over the fish of the sea, and over the fowl of the air, and over the cattle, and over all the earth, and over every creeping thing that creepeth upon the earth.

So God created man in his own image, in the image of God created he him; male and female created he them.
And God blessed them, and God said unto them, Be fruitful, and multiply, and replenish the earth, and subdue it: and have dominion over the fish of the sea, and over the fowl of the air, and over every living thing that moveth upon the earth.
1:26–28

143 And on the seventh day God ended his work which he had made; and he rested on the seventh day from all his work which he had made.
2:2

144 But there went up a mist from the earth, and watered the whole face of the ground.
And the Lord God formed man of the dust of the ground, and breathed into his nostrils the breath of life; and man became a living soul.
And the Lord God planted a garden eastward in Eden; and there he put the man whom he had formed.
And out of the ground made the Lord God to grow every tree that is pleasant to the sight, and good for food; the tree of life also in the midst of the garden, and the tree of knowledge of good and evil.
And a river went out of Eden to water the garden.
2:6–10

145 And the Lord God took the man, and put him into the garden of Eden to dress it and to keep it.
And the Lord God commanded the man, saying, Of every tree of the garden thou mayest freely eat:
But of the tree of the knowledge of good and evil, thou shalt not eat of it: for in the day that thou eatest thereof thou shalt surely die.
2:15–17

146 And the Lord God said, It is not good that the man should be alone; I will make him an help meet for him.
And out of the ground the Lord God formed every beast of the field, and every fowl of the air; and brought them unto Adam to see what he would call them: and whatsoever Adam called every living creature, that was the name thereof.
2:18–19

147 And the Lord God caused a deep sleep to fall upon Adam, and he slept: and he took one of his ribs, and closed up the flesh instead thereof;
And the rib, which the Lord God had taken from man, made he a woman, and brought her unto the man.
And Adam said, This is now bone of my bones, and flesh of my flesh: she shall be called Woman, because she was taken out of Man.

Therefore shall a man leave his father and his mother, and shall cleave unto his wife: and they shall be one flesh.

And they were both naked, the man and his wife, and were not ashamed.

2:21–25

148 Now the serpent was more subtil than any beast of the field which the Lord God had made.

3:1

149 God doth know that in the day ye eat thereof, then your eyes shall be opened, and ye shall be as gods, knowing good and evil.

And when the woman saw that the tree was good for food, and that it was pleasant to the eyes, and a tree to be desired to make one wise, she took of the fruit thereof, and did eat, and gave also unto her husband with her; and he did eat.

And the eyes of them both were opened, and they knew that they were naked; and they sewed fig leaves together; and made themselves aprons.

And they heard the voice of the Lord God walking in the garden in the cool of the day: and Adam and his wife hid themselves from the presence of the Lord God amongst the trees of the garden.

3:5–8

150 And he said, I heard thy voice in the garden, and I was afraid, because I was naked; and I hid myself.

And he said, Who told thee that thou wast naked?

3:10–11

151 And the man said, The woman whom thou gavest to be with me, she gave me of the tree, and I did eat.

And the Lord God said unto the woman, What is this that thou hast done? And the woman said, The serpent beguiled me, and I did eat.

And the Lord God said unto the serpent, Because thou hast done this, thou art cursed above all cattle, and above every beast of the field; upon thy belly shalt thou go, and dust shalt thou eat all the days of thy life.

3:12–14

152 In the sweat of thy face shalt thou eat bread, till thou return unto the ground; for out of it wast thou taken: for dust thou art and unto dust shalt thou return.

And Adam called his wife's name Eve; because she was the mother of all living.

3:19–20

153 Abel was a keeper of sheep, but Cain was a tiller of the ground.

4:2

154 And the Lord said unto Cain, Where is Abel thy brother? And he said, I know not: Am I my brother's keeper?

4:9

155 And the Lord said unto him, Therefore whosoever slayeth Cain, vengeance shall be taken on him sevenfold. And the Lord set a mark upon Cain, lest any finding him should kill him.

And Cain went out from the presence of the Lord, and dwelt in the land of Nod, on the east of Eden.

4:15–16

156 And all the days of Methuselah were nine hundred sixty and nine years: and he died.

5:27

157 And it repented the Lord that he had made man on the earth, and it grieved him at his heart.

6:6

158 And they went in unto Noah into the ark, two and two of all flesh, wherein is the breath of life.

And they that went in, went in male and female of all flesh, as God had commanded him: and the Lord shut him in.

And the flood was forty days upon the earth; and the waters increased, and bare up the ark, and it was lift up above the earth.

7:15–17

159 And the dove came in to him in the evening; and, lo, in her mouth was an olive leaf plucked off: so Noah knew that the waters were abated from off the earth.

8:11

160 Who so sheddeth man's blood, by man shall his blood be shed: for in the image of God made he man.

9:5

161 I do set my bow in the cloud, and it shall be for a token of a covenant between me and the earth.

9:13

162 He was a mighty hunter before the Lord: wherefore it is said, Even as Nimrod the mighty hunter before the Lord.

10:9

163 And the whole earth was of one language, and of one speech.

11:1

164 Therefore is the name of it called Babel; because the Lord did there confound the language of all the earth: and from thence did the Lord scatter them abroad upon the face of all the earth.

11:9

165 Now the Lord had said unto Abram, Get thee out of thy country, and from thy kindred, and from thy father's house, unto a land that I will shew thee:
And I will make of thee a great nation, and I will bless thee, and make thy name great; and thou shalt be a blessing:
And I will bless them that bless thee, and curse him that curseth thee: and in thee shall all families of the earth be blessed.
12:1–3

166 But the men of Sodom were wicked and sinners before the Lord exceedingly.
13:13

167 Then the Lord rained upon Sodom and upon Gomorrah brimstone and fire from the Lord out of heaven.
19:24

168 But his wife looked back from behind him, and she became a pillar of salt.
19:26

169 And Abraham said, My son, God will provide himself a lamb for a burnt offering: so they went both of them together.
22:8

170 And Abraham lifted up his eyes, and looked, and behold behind him a ram caught in a thicket by his horns: and Abraham went and took the ram, and offered him up for a burnt offering in the stead of his son.
22:13

171 And Jacob said to Rebekah his mother, Behold, Esau my brother a hairy man, and I am a smooth man.
27:11

172 And he dreamed, and behold a ladder set up on the earth, and the top of it reached to heaven: and behold the angels of God ascending and descending on it.
28:12

173 Leah was tender eyed; but Rachel was beautiful and well favoured.
29:17

174 Now Israel loved Joseph more than all his children, because he was the son of his old age: and he made him a coat of many colours.
37:3

175 And they said one to another, Behold, this dreamer cometh.
Come now therefore, and let us slay him, and cast him into some pit, and we will say, Some evil beast hath devoured him: and we shall see what will become of his dreams.
37:19–20

176 And all his sons and all his daughters rose up to comfort him; but he refused to be comforted; and he said, For I will go down into the grave unto my son mourning. Thus his father wept for him.
37:35

177 And Judah said unto Onan, Go in unto thy brother's wife, and marry her, and raise up seed to thy brother.
And Onan knew that the seed should not be his; and it came to pass, when he went in unto his brother's wife, that he spilled it on the ground, lest that he should give seed to his brother.
38:8–9

178 And the seven thin ears devoured the seven rank and full ears. And Pharaoh awoke, and, behold, it was a dream.
41:7

179 And the famine was sore in the land.
43:1

180 And take your father and your households, and come unto me: and I will give you the good of the land of Egypt, and ye shall eat the fat of the land.
45:18

181 Issachar is a strong ass couching down between two burdens:
And he saw that rest was good, and the land that it was pleasant; and bowed his shoulder to bear, and became a servant unto tribute.
49:14–15

182 Benjamin shall ravin as a wolf: in the morning he shall devour the prey, and at night he shall divide the spoil.
49:27

Habakkuk

183 But the Lord is in his holy temple: let all the earth keep silence before him.
2:20

Haggai

184 Now therefore thus saith the Lord of hosts; Consider your ways.
Ye have sown much, and bring in little; ye eat, but ye have not enough; ye drink, but ye are not filled with drink; ye clothe you, but there is none warm; and he that earneth wages earneth wages to put it into a bag with holes.
1:5–6

Hebrews

185 For the word of God is quick, and powerful, and sharper than any two-edged sword, piercing even to the dividing asunder of soul and spirit, and of the joints and marrow, and is a discerner of the thoughts and intents of the heart.
4:12

186 By faith the walls of Jericho fell down, after they were compassed about seven days.
11:30

187 Let brotherly love continue.
Be not forgetful to entertain strangers: for thereby some have entertained angels unawares.
13:1-2

188 And almost all things are by the law purged with blood; and without shedding of blood is no remission.
9:22

189 Now faith is the substance of things hoped for, the evidence of things not seen.
11:1

Hosea

190 For they have sown the wind, and they shall reap the whirlwind: it hath no stalk: the bud shall yield no meal: if so be it yield, the strangers shall swallow it up.
8:7

Isaiah

191 Come now, and let us reason together, saith the Lord: though your sins be as scarlet, they shall be as white as snow; though they be red like crimson, they shall be as wool.
1:18

192 How is the faithful city become an harlot! it was full of judgment; righteousness lodged in it; but now murderers.
1:21

193 And it shall come to pass in the last days, that the mountain of the Lord's house shall be established in the top of the mountains, and shall be exalted above the hills; and all nations shall flow unto it.
2:2

194 And he shall judge among the nations, and shall rebuke many people: and they shall beat their swords into plowshares, and their spears into pruning-hooks: nation shall not lift up sword against nation, neither shall they learn war any more.
2:4

195 Woe unto them that rise up early in the morning, that they may follow strong drink; that continue until night, till wine inflame them!
5:11

196 Woe unto them that call evil good, and good evil; that put darkness for light, and light for darkness; that put bitter for sweet, and sweet for bitter!
5:20

197 In the year that king Uzziah died I saw also the Lord sitting upon a throne, high and lifted up, and his train filled the temple.
Above it stood the seraphims: each one had six wings; with twain he covered his face, and with twain he covered his feet, and with twain he did fly.
And one cried unto another, and said, Holy, holy, holy, is the Lord of hosts: the whole earth is full of his glory.
6:1-3

198 Therefore the Lord himself shall give you a sign; Behold, a virgin shall conceive, and bear a son, and shall call his name Immanuel.
Butter and honey shall he eat, that he may know to refuse the evil, and choose the good.
7:14-15

199 And he shall be for a sanctuary; but for a stone of stumbling and for a rock of offence to both the houses of Israel, for a gin and for a snare to the inhabitants of Jerusalem.
8:14

200 The people that walked in darkness have seen a great light: they that dwell in the land of the shadow of death, upon them hath the light shined.
9:2

201 For unto us a child is born, unto us a son is given: and the government shall be upon his shoulder: and his name shall be called Wonderful, Counsellor, The mighty God, The everlasting Father, The Prince of Peace.
9:6

202 And there shall come forth a rod out of the stem of Jesse, and a Branch shall grow out of his roots:
And the spirit of the Lord shall rest upon him, the spirit of wisdom and understanding, the spirit of counsel and might, the spirit of knowledge and of the fear of the Lord.
11:1-2

203 The wolf also shall dwell with the lamb, and the leopard shall lie down with the kid; and the calf and the young lion and the fatling together: and a little child shall lead them.
And the cow and the bear shall feed; their young ones shall lie down together: and the lion shall eat straw like the ox.
And the sucking child shall play on the hole of the asp, and the weaned child shall put his hand on the cockatrice' den.

They shall not hurt nor destroy in all my holy mountain: for the earth shall be full of the knowledge of the Lord, as the waters cover the sea.
11:6–9

204 He calleth to me out of Seir, Watchman, what of the night? Watchman, what of the night? The watchman said, The morning cometh, and also the night: if ye will enquire, enquire ye: return, come.
21:11–12

205 And behold joy and gladness, slaying oxen, and killing sheep, eating flesh, and drinking wine: let us eat and drink; for tomorrow we shall die.
22:13

206 They shall not drink wine with a song; strong drink shall be bitter to them that drink it.
24:9

207 In that day the Lord with his sore and great and strong sword shall punish leviathan the piercing serpent, even leviathan that crooked serpent; and he shall slay the dragon that is in the sea.
27:1

208 For precept must be upon precept, precept upon precept; line upon line, line upon line; here a little, and there a little.
28:10

209 Then the eyes of the blind shall be opened, and the ears of the deaf shall be unstopped.
Then shall the lame man leap as an hart, and the tongue of the dumb sing: for in the wilderness shall waters break out, and streams in the desert.
And the parched ground shall become a pool, and the thirsty land springs of water: in the habitation of dragons, where each lay, shall be grass with reeds and rushes.
35:5–7

210 The voice of him that crieth in the wilderness, Prepare ye the way of the Lord, make straight in the desert a highway for our God. Every valley shall be exalted, and every mountain and hill shall be made low: and the crooked shall be made straight, and the rough places plain.
40:3–4

211 He shall feed his flock like a shepherd: he shall gather the lambs with his arm, and carry them in his bosom, and shall gently lead those that are with young.
40:11

212 The isles saw it, and feared; the ends of the earth were afraid, drew near, and came.
They helped every one his neighbour; and every one said to his brother, Be of good courage.
41:5–6

213 There is no peace, saith the Lord, unto the wicked.
48:22

214 All we like sheep have gone astray; we have turned every one to his own way; and the Lord hath laid on him the iniquity of us all. He was oppressed, and he was afflicted, yet he opened not his mouth: he is brought as a lamb to the slaughter, and as a sheep before her shearers is dumb, so he openeth not his mouth.
53:6–7

215 The righteous perisheth, and no man layeth it to heart: and merciful men are taken away, none considering that the righteous is taken away from the evil to come.
57:1

James

216 Blessed is the man that endureth temptation: for when he is tried, he shall receive the crown of life, which the Lord hath promised to them that love him.
1:12

217 Wherefore, my beloved brethren, let every man be swift to hear, slow to speak, slow to wrath:
For the wrath of man worketh not the righteousness of God.
1:19–20

218 Submit yourselves therefore to God. Resist the devil, and he will flee from you.
Draw nigh to God, and he will draw nigh to you. Cleanse your hands, ye sinners; and purify your hearts, ye double minded.
4:7–8

219 Grudge not one against another, brethren, lest ye be condemned: behold, the judge standeth before the door.
5:9

220 Let him know, that he which converteth the sinner from the error of his way shall save a soul from death, and shall hide a multitude of sins.
5:20

Jeremiah

221 Can the Ethiopian change his skin, or the leopard his spots? then may ye also do good, that are accustomed to do evil.
13:23

Job

222 And the Lord said unto Satan, Hast thou considered my servant Job, that there is none like him in the earth, a perfect and an upright man, one that feareth God, and escheweth evil?

Then Satan answered the Lord, and said, Doth Job fear God for nought?
1:8-9

223 Naked came I out of my mother's womb, and naked shall I return thither: the Lord gave, and the Lord hath taken away; blessed be the name of the Lord.
1:21

224 Then said his wife unto him, Dost thou still retain thine integrity? curse God, and die.
2:9

225 Let the day perish wherein I was born, and the night in which it was said, There is a man child conceived.
3:3

226 The eye of him that hath seen me shall see me no more: thine eyes are upon me, and I am not.
7:8

227 Wherefore then hast thou brought me forth out of the womb? Oh that I had given up the ghost, and no eye had seen me!
10:18

228 With the ancient is wisdom; and in length of days understanding.
12:12

229 They grope in the dark without light, and he maketh them to stagger like a drunken man.
12:25

230 Man that is born of a woman is of few days, and full of trouble.
14:1

231 Then Job answered and said, I have heard many such things: miserable comforters are ye all.
16:1-2

232 I have said to corruption, Thou art my father: to the worm, Thou art my mother, and my sister.
17:14

233 For I know that my redeemer liveth, and that he shall stand at the latter day upon the earth:
And though after my skin worms destroy this body, yet in my flesh shall I see God.
19:25-26

234 No mention shall be made of coral, or of pearls: for the price of wisdom is above rubies.
28:18

235 I was eyes to the blind, and feet was I to the lame.
29:15

236 Then the Lord answered Job out of the whirlwind, and said,
Who is this that darkeneth counsel by words without knowledge?

Gird up now thy loins like a man; for I will demand of thee, and answer thou me.
Where wast thou when I laid the foundations of the earth? declare, if thou hast understanding.
Who hath laid the measures thereof, if thou knowest? or who hath stretched the line upon it?
Whereupon are the foundations thereof fastened? or who laid the corner stone thereof;
When the morning stars sang together, and all the sons of God shouted for joy?
38:1-7

237 Canst thou draw out leviathan with an hook? or his tongue with a cord which thou lettest down?
41:1

John

238 In the beginning was the Word, and the Word was with God, and the Word was God.
The same was in the beginning with God.
All things were made by him; and without him was not any thing made that was made.
In him was life; and the life was the light of men.
And the light shineth in darkness; and the darkness comprehended it not.
1:1-5

239 He it is, who coming after me is preferred before me, whose shoe's latchet I am not worthy to unloose.
1:27

240 The next day John seeth Jesus coming unto him, and saith, Behold the Lamb of God, which taketh away the sin of the world.
1:29

241 Jesus saith unto her, Woman, what have I to do with thee? mine hour is not yet come.
2:4

242 When the ruler of the feast had tasted the water that was made wine, and knew not whence it was: (but the servants which drew the water knew;) the governor of the feast called the bridegroom,
And saith unto him, Every man at the beginning doth set forth good wine; and when men have well drunk, then that which is worse: but thou hast kept the good wine until now.
2:9-10

243 Jesus answered and said unto him, Verily, verily, I say unto thee, Except a man be born again, he cannot see the kingdom of God.
3:3

244 Jesus answered, Verily, verily, I say unto thee, Except a man be born of water and of the Spirit, he cannot enter into the kingdom of God.

That which is born of the flesh is flesh; and that which is born of the Spirit is spirit.
3:5 – 6

245 For God so loved the world, that he gave his only begotten Son, that whosoever believeth in him should not perish, but have everlasting life.
3:16

246 And this is the condemnation, that light is come into the world, and men loved darkness rather than light, because their deeds were evil.
3:19

247 Afterward Jesus findeth him in the temple, and said unto him, Behold, thou art made whole: sin no more, lest a worse thing come unto thee.
5:14

248 Verily, verily, I say unto you, He that heareth my word, and believeth on him that sent me, hath everlasting life, and shall not come into condemnation; but is passed from death unto life.
Verily, verily, I say unto you, The hour is coming, and now is, when the dead shall hear the voice of the Son of God: and they that hear shall live.
5:24 – 25

249 There is a lad here, which hath five barley loaves, and two small fishes: but what are they among so many?
And Jesus said, Make the men sit down. Now there was much grass in the place. So the men sat down, in number about five thousand.
6:9 – 10

250 And Jesus said unto them, I am the bread of life: he that cometh to me shall never hunger; and he that believeth on me shall never thirst.
6:35

251 So when they continued asking him, he lifted up himself, and said unto them, He that is without sin among you, let him first cast a stone at her.
8:7

252 She said, No man, Lord. And Jesus said unto her, Neither do I condemn thee: go, and sin no more.
8:11

253 Then spake Jesus again unto them, saying, I am the light of the world: he that followeth me shall not walk in darkness, but shall have the light of life.
8:12

254 And ye shall know the truth, and the truth shall make you free.
8:32

255 He answered and said, Whether he be a sinner or no, I know not: one thing I know, that, whereas I was blind, now I see.
9:25

256 Jesus said unto her, I am the resurrection, and the life: he that believeth in me, though he were dead, yet shall he live.
11:25

257 When Jesus therefore saw her weeping, and the Jews also weeping which came with her, he groaned in the spirit, and was troubled,
And said, Where have ye laid him? They said unto him, Lord, come and see.
Jesus wept.
11:33 – 35

258 In my Father's house are many mansions: if it were not so, I would have told you. I go to prepare a place for you.
14:2

259 Jesus saith unto him, I am the way, the truth, and the life: no man cometh unto the Father, but by me.
14:6

260 Greater love hath no man than this, that a man lay down his life for his friends.
15:13

261 But now I go my way to him that sent me; and none of you asketh me, Whither goest thou?
16:5

262 Quo vadis?
Vulgate 16:5

263 A woman when she is in travail hath sorrow, because her hour is come: but as soon as she is delivered of the child, she remembereth no more the anguish, for joy that a man is born into the world.
16:21

264 Now Caiaphas was he, which gave counsel to the Jews, that it was expedient that one man should die for the people.
18:14

265 Pilate saith unto him, What is truth? And when he had said this, he went out again unto the Jews, and saith unto them, I find in him no fault at all.
18:38

266 Then cried they all again, saying, Not this man, but Barabbas. Now Barabbas was a robber.
18:40

267 Then came Jesus forth, wearing the crown of thorns, and the purple robe. And Pilate saith unto them, Behold the man!
19:5

268 Ecce homo.
Vulgate 19:5

269 Pilate answered, What I have written I have written.

19:22

270 When Jesus therefore saw his mother, and the disciple standing by, whom he loved, he saith unto his mother, Woman, behold thy son! Then saith he to the disciple, Behold thy mother! And from that hour that disciple took her unto his own home.

19:26–27

271 When Jesus therefore had received the vinegar, he said, It is finished: and he bowed his head, and gave up the ghost.

19:30

272 Consummatum est.

Vulgate 19:30

273 Now in the place where he was crucified there was a garden; and in the garden a new sepulchre, wherein was never man yet laid.

19:41

274 The first day of the week cometh Mary Magdalene early, when it was yet dark, unto the sepulchre, and seeth the stone taken away from the sepulchre.
Then she runneth, and cometh to Simon Peter, and to the other disciple, whom Jesus loved, and saith unto them, They have taken the Lord out of the sepulchre, and we know not where they have laid him.

20:1–2

275 Jesus saith unto her, Woman, why weepest thou? whom seekest thou? She, supposing him to be the gardener, saith unto him, Sir, if thou have borne him hence, tell me where thou hast laid him, and I will take him away. Jesus saith unto her, Mary. She turned herself, and saith unto him, Rabboni; which is to say, Master.
Jesus saith unto her, Touch me not; for I am not yet ascended to my Father: but go to my brethren, and say unto them, I ascend unto my Father, and your Father; and to my God, and your God.

20:15–17

276 Noli me tangere.

Vulgate 20:17

277 The other disciples therefore said unto him, We have seen the Lord. But he said unto them, Except I shall see in his hands the print of the nails, and put my finger into the print of the nails, and thrust my hand into his side, I will not believe.

20:25

278 Then saith he to Thomas, Reach hither thy finger, and behold my hands; and reach hither thy hand, and thrust it into my side: and be not faithless, but believing.
And Thomas answered and said unto him, My Lord and my God.

Jesus saith unto him, Thomas, because thou hast seen me, thou hast believed: blessed are they that have not seen, and yet have believed.

20:27–29

279 So when they had dined, Jesus saith to Simon Peter, Simon, son of Jonas, lovest thou me more than these? He saith unto him, Yea, Lord; thou knowest that I love thee. He saith unto him, Feed my lambs.

21:15

280 He saith unto him the third time, Simon, son of Jonas, lovest thou me? Peter was grieved because he said unto him the third time, Lovest thou me? And he said unto him, Lord, thou knowest all things; thou knowest that I love thee. Jesus saith unto him, Feed my sheep.

21:17

I John

281 If we say that we have no sin, we deceive ourselves, and the truth is not in us.
If we confess our sins, he is faithful and just to forgive us our sins, and to cleanse us from all unrighteousness.

1:8–9

282 Beloved, let us love one another: for love is of God; and every one that loveth is born of God, and knoweth God.
He that loveth not knoweth not God; for God is love.

4:7–8

283 There is no fear in love; but perfect love casteth out fear: because fear hath torment. He that feareth is not made perfect in love.

4:18

284 If a man say, I love God, and hateth his brother, he is a liar: for he that loveth not his brother whom he hath seen, how can he love God whom he hath not seen?

4:20

Jonah

285 So the shipmaster came to him, and said unto him, What meanest thou, O sleeper? arise, call upon thy God, if so be that God will think upon us, that we perish not.
And they said every one to his fellow, Come, and let us cast lots, that we may know for whose cause this evil is upon us. So they cast lots, and the lot fell upon Jonah.

1:6–7

286 Now the Lord had prepared a great fish to swallow up Jonah. And Jonah was in the belly of the fish three days and three nights.

1:17

Joshua

287 And the priests that bare the ark of the covenant of the Lord stood firm on dry ground in the midst of Jordan, and all the Israelites passed over on dry ground, until all the people were passed clean over Jordan.

3:17

288 So the people shouted when the priests blew with the trumpets: and it came to pass, when the people heard the sound of the trumpet, and the people shouted with a great shout, that the wall fell down flat, so that the people went up into the city, every man straight before him, and they took the city.

6:20

289 And the princes said unto them, Let them live; but let them be hewers of wood and drawers of water unto all the congregation; as the princes had promised them.

9:21

Jude

290 Mercy unto you, and peace, and love, be multiplied.

1:2

Judges

291 And when he shewed them the entrance into the city, they smote the city with the edge of the sword; but they let go the man and all his family.

1:25

292 They fought from heaven; the stars in their courses fought against Sisera.

5:20

293 Blessed above women shall Jael the wife of Heber the Kenite be, blessed shall she be above women in the tent.
He asked water, and she gave him milk; she brought forth butter in a lordly dish.
She put her hand to the nail, and her right hand to the workmen's hammer; and with the hammer she smote Sisera, she smote off his head, when she had pierced and stricken through his temples.
At her feet he bowed, he fell, he lay down: at her feet he bowed, he fell: where he bowed, there he fell down dead.
The mother of Sisera looked out at a window, and cried through the lattice, Why is his chariot so long in coming? why tarry the wheels of his chariots?

5:24–28

294 And he said unto them, Out of the eater came forth meat, and out of the strong came forth sweetness. And they could not in three days expound the riddle.

14:14

295 And the men of the city said unto him on the seventh day before the sun went down, What is sweeter than honey? and what is stronger than a lion? And he said unto them, If ye had not plowed with my heifer, ye had not found out my riddle.

14:18

296 In those days there was no king in Israel, but every man did that which was right in his own eyes.

17:6

I Kings

297 So David slept with his fathers, and was buried in the city of David.

2:10

298 Then the king answered and said, Give her the living child, and in no wise slay it: she is the mother thereof.
And all Israel heard of the judgment which the king had judged; and they feared the king: for they saw that the wisdom of God was in him, to do judgment.

3:27–28

299 And when the queen of Sheba heard of the fame of Solomon concerning the name of the Lord, she came to prove him with hard questions.

10:1

300 And he said, Go forth, and stand upon the mount before the Lord. And, behold, the Lord passed by, and a great and strong wind rent the mountains, and brake in pieces the rocks before the Lord; but the Lord was not in the wind: and after the wind an earthquake; but the Lord was not in the earthquake:
And after the earthquake a fire; but the Lord was not in the fire: and after the fire a still small voice.

19:11–12

II Kings

301 And it came to pass, as they still went on, and talked, that, behold, there appeared a chariot of fire, and horses of fire, and parted them both asunder; and Elijah went up by a whirlwind into heaven.
And Elisha saw it, and he cried, My father, my father, the chariot of Israel, and the horsemen thereof. And he saw him no more: and he took hold of his own clothes, and rent them in two pieces.

2:11–12

302 And when Jehu was come to Jezreel, Jezebel heard of it; and she painted her face, and tired her head, and looked out at a window.

9:30

303 And they went to bury her: but they found no
more of her than the skull, and the feet, and
the palms of her hands.
9:35

304 In those days was Hezekiah sick unto death.
And the prophet Isaiah the son of Amoz came
to him, and said unto him, Thus saith the
Lord, Set thine house in order; for thou shalt
die, and not live.
Then he turned his face to the wall.
20:1–2

Lamentations

305 And I said, My strength and my hope is perished from the Lord:
Remembering mine affliction and my misery,
the wormwood and the gall.
3:18–19

306 It is good for a man that he bear the yoke in
his youth.
3:27

307 Waters flowed over mine head; then I said, I
am cut off.
3:54

Luke

308 And the angel came in unto her, and said, Hail,
thou that art highly favoured, the Lord is with
thee: blessed art thou among women.
And when she saw him, she was troubled at
his saying, and cast in her mind what manner
of salutation this should be.
1:28–29

309 And Mary said, My soul doth magnify the
Lord,
And my spirit hath rejoiced in God my Saviour.
For he hath regarded the low estate of his
handmaiden: for, behold, from henceforth all
generations shall call me blessed.
1:46–48

310 He hath shewed strength with his arm; he hath
scattered the proud in the imagination of their
hearts.
He hath put down the mighty from their seats,
and exalted them of low degree.
He hath filled the hungry with good things; and
the rich he hath sent empty away.
1:51–53

311 And the child grew, and waxed strong in spirit,
and was in the deserts till the day of his
shewing unto Israel.
1:80

312 And it came to pass in those days, that there
went out a decree from Caesar Augustus,
that all the world should be taxed.
2:1

313 And she brought forth her firstborn son, and
wrapped him in swaddling clothes, and laid him
in a manger; because there was no room for
them in the inn.
2:7

314 And there were in the same country shepherds
abiding in the field, keeping watch over their
flock by night.
And, lo, the angel of the Lord came upon
them, and the glory of the Lord shone round
about them: and they were sore afraid.
And the angel said unto them, Fear not: for,
behold, I bring you good tidings of great joy,
which shall be to all people.
2:8–10

315 Glory to God in the highest, and on earth
peace, good will toward men.
2:14

316 But Mary kept all these things, and pondered
them in her heart.
2:19

317 Lord, now lettest thou thy servant depart in
peace, according to thy word:
For mine eyes have seen thy salvation,
Which thou hast prepared before the face of all
people;
A light to lighten the Gentiles, and the glory of
thy people Israel.
2:29–32

318 And it came to pass, that after three days they
found him in the temple, sitting in the midst
of the doctors, both hearing them, and asking them questions.
And all that heard him were astonished at his
understanding and answers.
2:46–47

319 And the devil, taking him up into an high mountain, shewed unto him all the kingdoms of the
world in a moment of time.
4:5

320 And he said unto them, Ye will surely say unto
me this proverb, Physician, heal thyself:
whatsoever we have heard done in Caperna-
um, do also here in thy country.
4:23

321 No man also having drunk old wine straightway
desireth new: for he saith, The old is better.
5:39

322 And he said to the woman, Thy faith hath
saved thee; go in peace.
7:50

323 Go your ways: behold, I send you forth as
lambs among wolves.
Carry neither purse, nor scrip, nor shoes: and
salute no man by the way.
And into whatsoever house ye enter, first say,
Peace be to this house.
10:3–5

324 And Jesus answering said, A certain man went down from Jerusalem to Jericho, and fell among thieves, which stripped him of his raiment, and wounded him, and departed, leaving him half dead.

And by chance there came down a certain priest that way: and when he saw him, he passed by on the other side.

10:30–31

325 But a certain Samaritan, as he journeyed, came where he was: and when he saw him, he had compassion on him,

And went to him, and bound up his wounds, pouring in oil and wine, and set him on his own beast, and brought him to an inn, and took care of him.

And on the morrow when he departed, he took out two pence, and gave them to the host, and said unto him, Take care of him; and whatsoever thou spendest more, when I come again, I will repay thee.

10:33–35

326 And he said, He that shewed mercy on him. Then said Jesus unto him, Go, and do thou likewise.

10:37

327 Woe unto you, lawyers! for ye have taken away the key of knowledge: ye entered not in yourselves, and them that were entering in ye hindered.

11:52

328 Are not five sparrows sold for two farthings, and not one of them is forgotten before God?

12:6

329 And they all with one consent began to make excuse. The first said unto him, I have bought a piece of ground, and I must needs go and see it: I pray thee have me excused.

And another said, I have bought five yoke of oxen, and I go to prove them: I pray thee have me excused.

And another said, I have married a wife, and therefore I cannot come.

So that servant came, and shewed his lord these things. Then the master of the house being angry said to his servant, Go out quickly into the streets and lanes of the city, and bring in hither the poor, and the maimed, and the halt, and the blind.

14:18–21

330 What man of you, having an hundred sheep, if he lose one of them, doth not leave the ninety and nine in the wilderness, and go after that which is lost until he find it?

And when he hath found it, he layeth it on his shoulders, rejoicing.

And when he cometh home, he calleth together his friends and neighbours, saying unto them, Rejoice with me; for I have found my sheep which was lost.

I say unto you, that likewise joy shall be in heaven over one sinner that repenteth, more than over ninety and nine just persons, which need no repentance.

15:4–7

331 And he would fain have filled his belly with the husks that the swine did eat: and no man gave unto him.

And when he came to himself, he said, How many hired servants of my father's have bread enough and to spare, and I perish with hunger!

I will arise and go to my father, and will say unto him, Father, I have sinned against heaven, and before thee,

And am no more worthy to be called thy son: make me as one of thy hired servants.

And he arose, and came to his father. But when he was yet a great way off, his father saw him, and had compassion, and ran, and fell on his neck, and kissed him.

15:16–20

332 And bring hither the fatted calf, and kill it; and let us eat, and be merry:

For this my son was dead, and is alive again; he was lost, and is found. And they began to be merry.

15:23–24

333 There was a certain rich man, which was clothed in purple and fine linen, and fared sumptuously every day:

And there was a certain beggar named Lazarus, which was laid at his gate, full of sores,

And desiring to be fed with the crumbs which fell from the rich man's table: moreover the dogs came and licked his sores.

And it came to pass, that the beggar died, and was carried by the angels into Abraham's bosom: the rich man also died, and was buried;

16:19–22

334 And when he was demanded of the Pharisees, when the kingdom of God should come, he answered them and said, The kingdom of God cometh not with observation:

Neither shall they say, Lo here! or, lo there! for, behold, the kingdom of God is within you.

17:20–21

335 Remember Lot's wife.

17:32

336 And he saith unto him, Out of thine own mouth will I judge thee, thou wicked servant. Thou knewest that I was an austere man, taking up that I laid not down, and reaping that I did not sow.

19:22

337 And he answered and said unto them, I tell you that, if these should hold their peace, the stones would immediately cry out.
19:40

338 And when they were come to the place, which is called Calvary, there they crucified him, and the malefactors, one on the right hand, and the other on the left.
23:33

339 Then said Jesus, Father, forgive them; for they know not what they do. And they parted his raiment, and cast lots.
23:34

340 And when Jesus had cried with a loud voice, he said, Father, into thy hands I commend my spirit: and having said thus, he gave up the ghost.
23:46

I Maccabees

341 I perceive therefore that for this cause these troubles are come upon me, and, behold, I perish through great grief in a strange land.
6:13

Malachi

342 Have we not all one father? hath not one God created us? why do we deal treacherously every man against his brother, by profaning the covenant of our fathers?
2:10

343 But unto you that fear my name shall the Sun of righteousness arise with healing in his wings; and ye shall go forth, and grow up as calves of the stall.
4:2

Mark

344 And he said unto them, The sabbath was made for man, and not man for the sabbath: Therefore the Son of man is Lord also of the sabbath.
2:27–28

345 And he asked him, What is thy name? And he answered, saying. My name is Legion: for we are many.
5:9

346 And forthwith Jesus gave them leave. And the unclean spirits went out, and entered into the swine: and the herd ran violently down a steep place into the sea, (they were about two thousand;) and were choked in the sea.
5:13

347 For what shall it profit a man, if he shall gain the whole world, and lose his own soul? Or what shall a man give in exchange for his soul?
8:36–37

348 But when Jesus saw it, he was much displeased, and said unto them. Suffer the little children to come unto me, and forbid them not: for of such is the kingdom of God.
10:14

349 And there came a certain poor widow, and she threw in two mites, which make a farthing. And he called unto him his disciples, and saith unto them, Verily I say unto you, That this poor widow hath cast more in, than all they which have cast into the treasury: For all they did cast in of their abundance; but she of her want did cast in all that she had, even all her living.
12:42–44

350 And he said unto them, Go ye into all the world, and preach the gospel to every creature.
16:15

Matthew

351 Now when Jesus was born in Bethlehem of Judaea in the days of Herod the king, behold, there came wise men from the east to Jerusalem,
Saying, Where is he that is born King of the Jews? for we have seen his star in the east, and are come to worship him.
When Herod the king had heard these things, he was troubled, and all Jerusalem with him.
2:1–3

352 And when they were come into the house, they saw the young child with Mary his mother, and fell down, and worshipped him: and when they had opened their treasures, they presented unto him gifts; gold, and frankincense, and myrrh.
And being warned of God in a dream that they should not return to Herod, they departed into their own country another way.
2:11–12

353 For this is he that was spoken of by the prophet Esaias, saying, The voice of one crying in the wilderness, Prepare ye the way of the Lord, make his paths straight.
And the same John had his raiment of camel's hair, and a leathern girdle about his loins; and his meat was locusts and wild honey.
3:3–4

354 But when he saw many of the Pharisees and Sadducees come to his baptism, he said unto them, O generation of vipers, who hath warned you to flee from the wrath to come?
3:7

355 And Jesus answering said unto him, Suffer it to be so now: for thus it becometh us to fulfil all righteousness. Then he suffered him.

And Jesus, when he was baptized, went up straightway out of the water: and, lo, the heavens were opened unto him, and he saw the Spirit of God descending like a dove, and lighting upon him:

And lo a voice from heaven, saying, This is my beloved Son, in whom I am well pleased.

3:15–17

356 Then was Jesus led up of the Spirit into the wilderness to be tempted of the devil.

And when he had fasted forty days and forty nights, he was afterward an hungred.

And when the tempter came to him, he said, If thou be the Son of God, command that these stones be made bread.

But he answered and said, It is written, Man shall not live by bread alone, but by every word that proceedeth out of the mouth of God.

4:1–4

357 Jesus said unto him, It is written again, Thou shalt not tempt the Lord thy God.

Again, the devil taketh him up into an exceeding high mountain, and sheweth him all the kingdoms of the world, and the glory of them.

4:7–8

358 From that time Jesus began to preach, and to say, Repent: for the kingdom of heaven is at hand.

4:17

359 And he saith unto them, Follow me, and I will make you fishers of men.

4:19

360 Blessed are the poor in spirit: for theirs is the kingdom of heaven.

Blessed are they that mourn: for they shall be comforted.

Blessed are the meek: for they shall inherit the earth.

Blessed are they which do hunger and thirst after righteousness: for they shall be filled.

Blessed are the merciful: for they shall obtain mercy.

Blessed are the pure in heart: for they shall see God.

Blessed are the peacemakers: for they shall be called the children of God.

Blessed are they which are persecuted for righteousness' sake: for theirs is the kingdom of heaven.

5:3–10

361 Ye are the salt of the earth: but if the salt have lost his savour, wherewith shall it be salted? it is thenceforth good for nothing, but to be cast out, and to be trodden under foot of men.

Ye are the light of the world. A city that is set on an hill cannot be hid.

Neither do men light a candle, and put it under a bushel, but on a candlestick; and it giveth light unto all that are in the house.

Let your light so shine before men, that they may see your good works, and glorify your Father which is in heaven.

5:13–16

362 For verily I say unto you, Till heaven and earth pass, one jot or one tittle shall in no wise pass from the law, till all be fulfilled.

5:18

363 And if thy right eye offend thee, pluck it out, and cast it from thee: for it is profitable for thee that one of thy members should perish, and not that thy whole body should be cast into hell.

5:29

364 But I say unto you, That ye resist not evil: but whosoever shall smite thee on thy right cheek, turn to him the other also.

And if any man will sue thee at the law, and take away thy coat, let him have thy cloke also.

And whosoever shall compel thee to go a mile, go with him twain.

5:39–41

365 But I say unto you, Love your enemies, bless them that curse you, do good to them that hate you, and pray for them which despitefully use you, and persecute you;

That ye may be the children of your Father which is in heaven: for he maketh his sun to rise on the evil and on the good, and sendeth rain on the just and on the unjust.

For if ye love them which love you, what reward have ye? do not even the publicans the same?

5:44–46

366 Be ye therefore perfect, even as your Father which is in heaven is perfect.

5:48

367 But when ye pray, use not vain repetitions, as the heathen do: for they think that they shall be heard for their much speaking.

Be not ye therefore like unto them: for your Father knoweth what things ye have need of, before ye ask him.

After this manner therefore pray ye: Our Father which art in heaven, Hallowed be thy name.

Thy kingdom come. Thy will be done in earth, as it is in heaven.

Give us this day our daily bread.

And forgive us our debts, as we forgive our debtors.

And lead us not into temptation, but deliver us from evil: For thine is the kingdom, and the power, and the glory, for ever. Amen.

6:7–13

368 Lay not up for yourselves treasures upon earth, where moth and rust doth corrupt, and where thieves break through and steal:

But lay up for yourselves treasures in heaven, where neither moth nor rust doth corrupt, and where thieves do not break through nor steal:

For where your treasure is, there will your heart be also.

6:19-21

369 No man can serve two masters: for either he will hate the one, and love the other; or else he will hold to the one, and despise the other. Ye cannot serve God and mammon.

6:24

370 Behold the fowls of the air: for they sow not, neither do they reap, nor gather into barns; yet your heavenly Father feedeth them. Are ye not much better than they?

Which of you by taking thought can add one cubit unto his stature?

And why take ye thought for raiment? Consider the lilies of the field, how they grow; they toil not, neither do they spin:

And yet I say unto you, That even Solomon in all his glory was not arrayed like one of these. Wherefore, if God so clothe the grass of the field, which today is, and tomorrow is cast into the oven, shall he not much more clothe you, O ye of little faith?

6:26-30

371 Take therefore no thought for the morrow: for the morrow shall take thought for the things of itself. Sufficient unto the day is the evil thereof.

6:33

372 Judge not, that ye be not judged.

7:1

373 And why beholdest thou the mote that is in thy brother's eye, but considerest not the beam that is in thine own eye?

7:3

374 Give not that which is holy unto the dogs, neither cast ye your pearls before swine, lest they trample them under their feet, and turn again and rend you.

7:6

375 Ask, and it shall be given you; seek, and ye shall find; knock, and it shall be opened unto you:

For every one that asketh receiveth; and he that seeketh findeth; and to him that knocketh it shall be opened.

7:7-8

376 Or what man is there of you, whom if his son ask bread, will he give him a stone?

7:9

377 Enter ye in at the strait gate: for wide is the gate, and broad is the way, that leadeth to destruction, and many there be which go in thereat:

Because strait is the gate, and narrow is the way, which leadeth unto life, and few there be that find it.

7:13-14

378 Beware of false prophets, which come to you in sheep's clothing, but inwardly they are ravening wolves.

7:15

379 Ye shall know them by their fruits. Do men gather grapes of thorns, or figs of thistles? Even so every good tree bringeth forth good fruit; but a corrupt tree bringeth forth evil fruit.

A good tree cannot bring forth evil fruit, neither can a corrupt tree bring forth good fruit.

Every tree that bringeth not forth good fruit is hewn down, and cast into the fire.

Wherefore by their fruits ye shall know them.

7:16-20

380 Therefore whosoever heareth these sayings of mine, and doeth them, I will liken him unto a wise man, which built his house upon a rock:

And the rain descended, and the floods came, and the winds blew, and beat upon that house; and it fell not: for it was founded upon a rock.

And every one that heareth these sayings of mine, and doeth them not, shall be likened unto a foolish man, which built his house upon the sand:

And the rain descended, and the floods came, and the winds blew, and beat upon that house; and it fell: and great was the fall of it.

7:24-27

381 But the children of the kingdom shall be cast out into outer darkness: there shall be weeping and gnashing of teeth.

8:12

382 But Jesus said unto him, Follow me; and let the dead bury their dead.

8:22

383 And his disciples came to him, and awoke him, saying, Lord, save us: we perish.

And he saith unto them, Why are ye fearful, O ye of little faith? Then he arose, and rebuked the winds and the sea; and there was a great calm.

But the men marvelled, saying, What manner of man is this, that even the winds and the sea obey him!

8:25-27

384 Neither do men put new wine into old bottles: else the bottles break, and the wine runneth out, and the bottles perish: but they put new wine into new bottles, and both are preserved.

9:17

385 Heal the sick, cleanse the lepers, raise the dead, cast out devils: freely ye have received, freely give.
10:8

386 And ye shall be hated of all men for my name's sake: but he that endureth to the end shall be saved.
10:22

387 Think not that I am come to send peace on earth: I came not to send peace, but a sword.
10:34

388 He that hath ears to hear, let him hear.
11:15

389 O generation of vipers, how can ye, being evil, speak good things? for out of the abundance of the heart the mouth speaketh.
12:34

390 For whosoever shall do the will of my Father which is in heaven, the same is my brother, and sister, and mother.
12:50

391 And he spake many things unto them in parables, saying, Behold, a sower went forth to sow;
And when he sowed, some seeds fell by the way side, and the fowls came and devoured them up:
Some fell upon stony places, where they had not much earth: and forthwith they sprung up, because they had no deepness of earth:
And when the sun was up, they were scorched; and because they had no root, they withered away.
And some fell among thorns; and the thorns sprung up, and choked them:
But other fell into good ground, and brought forth fruit, some an hundredfold, some sixtyfold, some thirtyfold.
13:3–8

392 And they were offended in him. But Jesus said unto them, A prophet is not without honour, save in his own country, and in his own house.
13:57

393 But when Herod's birthday was kept, the daughter of Herodias danced before them, and pleased Herod.
Whereupon he promised with an oath to give her whatsoever she would ask.
And she, being before instructed of her mother, said, Give me John Baptist's head in a charger.
14:6–8

394 And in the fourth watch of the night Jesus went unto them, walking on the sea.
And when the disciples saw him walking on the sea, they were troubled, saying, It is a spirit; and they cried out for fear.

But straightway Jesus spake unto them, saying, Be of good cheer; it is I; be not afraid.
14:25–27

395 And immediately Jesus stretched forth his hand, and caught him, and said unto him, O thou of little faith, wherefore didst thou doubt?
14:31

396 And besought him that they might only touch the hem of his garment: and as many as touched were made perfectly whole.
14:36

397 And I say also unto thee, That thou art Peter, and upon this rock I will build my church; and the gates of hell shall not prevail against it.
And I will give unto thee the keys of the kingdom of heaven: and whatsoever thou shalt bind on earth shall be bound in heaven: and whatsoever thou shalt loose on earth shall be loosed in heaven.
16:18–19

398 Then said Jesus unto his disciples, If any man will come after me, let him deny himself, and take up his cross, and follow me.
16:24

399 And said, Verily I say unto you, Except ye be converted, and become as little children, ye shall not enter into the kingdom of heaven.
18:3

400 And whoso shall receive one such little child in my name receiveth me.
But whoso shall offend one of these little ones which believe in me, it were better for him that a millstone were hanged about his neck, and that he were drowned in the depth of the sea.
18:5–6

401 For where two or three are gathered together in my name, there am I in the midst of them.
18:20

402 Then came Peter to him, and said, Lord, how oft shall my brother sin against me, and I forgive him? till seven times?
Jesus saith unto him, I say not unto thee, Until seven times: but, Until seventy times seven.
18:21–22

403 Wherefore they are no more twain, but one flesh. What therefore God hath joined together, let not man put asunder.
19:6

404 Jesus said unto him, If thou wilt be perfect, go and sell that thou hast, and give to the poor, and thou shalt have treasure in heaven: and come and follow me.
But when the young man heard that saying, he went away sorrowful: for he had great possessions.
19:21–22

405 Then said Jesus unto his disciples, Verily I say unto you, That a rich man shall hardly enter into the kingdom of heaven.
And again I say unto you, It is easier for a camel to go through the eye of a needle, than for a rich man to enter into the kingdom of God.
19:23–24

406 But many that are first shall be last; and the last shall be first.
19:30

407 And a very great multitude spread their garments in the way; others cut down branches from the trees, and strawed them in the way.
And the multitudes that went before, and that followed, cried, saying, Hosanna to the Son of David: Blessed is he that cometh in the name of the Lord; Hosanna in the highest.
21:8–9

408 And said unto them, It is written, My house shall be called the house of prayer; but ye have made it a den of thieves.
21:13

409 For many are called, but few are chosen.
22:14

410 And he saith unto them, Whose is this image and superscription?
They say unto him, Caesar's. Then saith he unto them, Render therefore unto Caesar the things which are Caesar's; and unto God the things that are God's.
22:20–21

411 Jesus said unto him, Thou shalt love the Lord thy God with all thy heart, and with all thy soul, and with all thy mind.
This is the first and great commandment.
And the second is like unto it, Thou shalt love thy neighbour as thyself.
On these two commandments hang all the law and the prophets.
22:37–40

412 Woe unto you, scribes and Pharisees, hypocrites! for ye are like unto whited sepulchres, which indeed appear beautiful outward, but are within full of dead men's bones, and of all uncleanness.
23:27

413 And ye shall hear of wars and rumours of wars: see that ye be not troubled: for all these things must come to pass, but the end is not yet.
For nation shall rise against nation, and kingdom against kingdom: and there shall be famines, and pestilences, and earthquakes, in divers places.
All these are the beginning of sorrows.
24:6–8

414 Immediately after the tribulation of those days shall the sun be darkened, and the moon shall not give her light, and the stars shall fall from heaven, and the powers of the heavens shall be shaken:
And then shall appear the sign of the Son of man in heaven: and then shall all the tribes of the earth mourn, and they shall see the Son of man coming in the clouds of heaven with power and great glory.
And he shall send his angels with a great sound of a trumpet, and they shall gather together his elect from the four winds, from one end of heaven to the other.
24:29–31

415 Heaven and earth shall pass away, but my words shall not pass away.
24:35

416 And at midnight there was a cry made, Behold, the bridegroom cometh; go ye out to meet him.
Then all those virgins arose, and trimmed their lamps.
And the foolish said unto the wise, Give us of your oil; for our lamps are gone out.
25:6–8

417 And unto one he gave five talents, to another two, and to another one; to every man according to his several ability; and straightway took his journey.
25:15

418 His lord said unto him, Well done, thou good and faithful servant: thou hast been faithful over a few things, I will make thee ruler over many things: enter thou into the joy of thy lord.
25:21

419 For unto every one that hath shall be given, and he shall have abundance: but from him that hath not shall be taken away even that which he hath.
And cast ye the unprofitable servant into outer darkness: there shall be weeping and gnashing of teeth.
25:29–30

420 And before him shall be gathered all nations: and he shall separate them one from another, as a shepherd divideth his sheep from the goats:
And he shall set the sheep on his right hand, but the goats on the left.
25:32–33

421 For I was an hungred, and ye gave me meat: I was thirsty, and ye gave me drink: I was a stranger, and ye took me in:
Naked, and ye clothed me: I was sick, and ye visited me: I was in prison, and ye came unto me.
25:35–36

422 And the King shall answer and say unto them, Verily I say unto you, Inasmuch as ye have done it unto one of the least of these my brethren, ye have done it unto me.

25:40

423 And he answered and said, He that dippeth his hand with me in the dish, the same shall betray me.

The Son of man goeth as it is written of him: but woe unto that man by whom the Son of man is betrayed! it had been good for that man if he had not been born.

Then Judas, which betrayed him, answered and said, Master, is it I? He said unto him, Thou hast said.

26:33 35

424 And as they were eating, Jesus took bread, and blessed it, and brake it, and gave it to the disciples, and said, Take, eat; this is my body.

And he took the cup, and gave thanks, and gave it to them, saying, Drink ye all of it;

For this is my blood of the new testament, which is shed for many for the remission of sins.

26:26 – 28

425 Jesus said unto him, Verily I say unto thee, That this night, before the cock crow, thou shalt deny me thrice.

26:34

426 Watch and pray, that ye enter not into temptation: the spirit indeed is willing, but the flesh is weak.

26:41

427 And forthwith he came to Jesus, and said, Hail, master; and kissed him.

And Jesus said unto him, Friend, wherefore art thou come? Then came they, and laid hands on Jesus, and took him.

26:49 – 50

428 Then said Jesus unto him, Put up again thy sword into his place: for all they that take the sword shall perish with the sword.

26:52

429 Then Judas, which had betrayed him, when he saw that he was condemned, repented himself, and brought again the thirty pieces of silver to the chief priests and elders,

Saying, I have sinned in that I have betrayed the innocent blood. And they said, What is that to us? see thou to that.

27:3 – 4

430 When Pilate saw that he could prevail nothing, but that rather a tumult was made, he took water, and washed his hands before the multitude, saying, I am innocent of the blood of this just person: see ye to it.

Then answered all the people, and said, His blood be on us, and on our children.

27:24 – 25

431 And about the ninth hour Jesus cried with a loud voice, saying, Eli, Eli, lama sabachthani? that is to say, My God, my God, why hast thou forsaken me?

27:46

432 Jesus, when he had cried again with a loud voice, yielded up the ghost.

And, behold, the veil of the temple was rent in twain from the top to the bottom; and the earth did quake, and the rocks rent;

And the graves were opened; and many bodies of the saints which slept arose.

27:50 – 52

433 Teaching them to observe all things whatsoever I have commanded you: and, lo, I am with you alway, even unto the end of the world. Amen.

28:20

Micah

434 Trust ye not in a friend, put ye not confidence in a guide: keep the doors of thy mouth from her that lieth in thy bosom.

7:5

Nehemiah

435 And I said, Should such a man as I flee? and who is there, that, being as I am, would go into the temple to save his life? I will not go in.

6:11

Numbers

436 The Lord bless thee, and keep thee:

The Lord make his face shine upon thee, and be gracious unto thee:

The Lord lift up his countenance upon thee, and give thee peace.

6:24 – 26

437 And Moses lifted up his hand, and with his rod he smote the rock twice: and the water came out abundantly, and the congregation drank, and their beasts also.

20:11

438 And the Lord opened the mouth of the ass, and she said unto Balaam, What have I done unto thee, that thou hast smitten me these three times?

22:28

439 But if ye will not do so, behold, ye have sinned against the Lord: and be sure your sin will find you out.

32:23

I Peter

440 Being born again, not of corruptible seed, but of incorruptible, by the word of God, which liveth and abideth for ever.
For all flesh is as grass, and all the glory of man as the flower of grass. The grass withereth, and the flower thereof falleth away.
1:23–24

441 Honour all men. Love the brotherhood. Fear God. Honour the king.
2:17

442 Even as Sara obeyed Abraham, calling him lord: whose daughters ye are, as long as ye do well, and are not afraid with any amazement. Likewise, ye husbands, dwell with them according to knowledge, giving honour unto the wife, as unto the weaker vessel, and as being heirs together of the grace of life; that your prayers be not hindered.
3:6–7

Philippians

443 That at the name of Jesus every knee should bow, of things in heaven, and things in earth, and things under the earth.
2:10

444 Rejoice in the Lord alway: and again I say, Rejoice.
4:4

445 And the peace of God, which passeth all understanding, shall keep your hearts and minds through Christ Jesus.
4:7

446 Finally, brethren, whatsoever things are true, whatsoever things are honest, whatsoever things are just, whatsoever things are pure, whatsoever things are lovely, whatsoever things are of good report; if there be any virtue; and if there be any praise, think on these things.
4:8

Proverbs

447 For the lips of a strange woman drop as an honeycomb, and her mouth is smoother than oil:
But her end is bitter as wormwood, sharp as a two-edged sword.
5:3–4

448 Wisdom hath builded her house, she hath hewn out her seven pillars.
9:1

449 Stolen waters are sweet, and bread eaten in secret is pleasant.
9:17

450 He that spareth his rod hateth his son: but he that loveth him chasteneth him betimes.
13:24

451 Pride goeth before destruction, and an haughty spirit before a fall.
16:18

452 He that is slow to anger is better than the mighty; and he that ruleth his spirit than he that taketh a city.
16:32

453 Wine is a mocker, strong drink is raging: and whosoever is deceived thereby is not wise.
20:1

454 For thou shalt heap coals of fire upon his head, and the Lord shall reward thee.
25:22

455 As cold waters to a thirsty soul, so is good news from a far country.
25:25

456 Answer a fool according to his folly, lest he be wise in his own conceit.
26:5

457 Boast not thyself of tomorrow; for thou knowest not what a day may bring forth.
27:1

458 Who can find a virtuous woman? for her price is far above rubies
The heart of her husband doth safely trust in her, so that he shall have no need of spoil. She will do him good and not evil all the days of her life.
31:10–12

Revelations

459 Behold, he cometh with clouds; and every eye shall see him, and they also which pierced him: and all kindreds of the earth shall wail because of him. Even so, Amen.
I am Alpha and Omega, the beginning and the ending, saith the Lord, which is, and which was, and which is to come, the Almighty.
1:7–8

460 And I saw in the right hand of him that sat on the throne a book written within and on the backside, sealed with seven seals.
And I saw a strong angel proclaiming with a loud voice, Who is worthy to open the book, and to loose the seals thereof?
5:1–2

461 Saying with a loud voice, Worthy is the Lamb that was slain to receive power, and riches, and wisdom, and strength, and honour, and glory, and blessing.
5:12

462 And I looked, and behold a pale horse: and his name that sat on him was Death, and Hell followed with him. And power was given unto them over the fourth part of the earth, to kill with sword, and with hunger, and with death, and with the beasts of the earth.
6:8

463 And one of the elders answered, saying unto me, What are these which are arrayed in white robes? and whence came they?
And I said unto him, Sir, thou knowest. And he said to me, These are they which came out of great tribulation, and have washed their robes, and made them white in the blood of the Lamb.
7:13–14

464 And the name of the star is called Wormwood: and the third part of the waters became wormwood; and many men died of the waters, because they were made bitter.
8:11

465 And there was war in heaven: Michael and his angels fought against the dragon; and the dragon fought and his angels,
And prevailed not; neither was their place found any more in heaven.
And the great dragon was cast out, that old serpent, called the Devil, and Satan, which deceiveth the whole world: he was cast out into the earth, and his angels were cast out with him.
12:7–9

466 And that no man might buy or sell, save he that had the mark, or the name of the beast, or the number of his name.
Here is wisdom. Let him that hath understanding count the number of the beast: for it is the number of a man; and his number is Six hundred threescore and six.
13:17–18

467 Behold, I come as a thief. Blessed is he that watcheth, and keepeth his garments, lest he walk naked, and they see his shame.
And he gathered them together into a place called in the Hebrew tongue Armageddon.
16:15–16

468 And there came one of the seven angels which had the seven vials, and talked with me, saying unto me, Come hither; I will shew unto thee the judgment of the great whore that sitteth upon many waters.
17:1

469 And the woman was arrayed in purple and scarlet colour, and decked with gold and precious stones and pearls, having a golden cup in her hand full of abominations and filthiness of her fornication:
And upon her forehead was a name written, MYSTERY, BABYLON THE GREAT, THE MOTHER OF HARLOTS AND ABOMINATIONS OF THE EARTH.
And I saw the woman drunken with the blood of the saints, and with the blood of the martyrs of Jesus: and when I saw her, I wondered with great admiration.
17:4–6

470 And I saw heaven opened, and behold a white horse; and he that sat upon him was called Faithful and True, and in righteousness he doth judge and make war.
19:11

471 Blessed and holy is he that hath part in the first resurrection: on such the second death hath no power, but they shall be priests of God and of Christ, and shall reign with him a thousand years.
And when the thousand years are expired, Satan shall be loosed out of his prison,
And shall go out to deceive the nations which are in the four quarters of the earth, Gog and Magog, to gather them together to battle: the number of whom is as the sand of the sea.
20:6–8

472 And I saw a great white throne, and him that sat on it, from whose face the earth and the heaven fled away; and there was found no place for them.
And I saw the dead, small and great, stand before God; and the books were opened: and another book was opened, which is the book of life: and the dead were judged out of those things which were written in the books, according to their works.
And the sea gave up the dead which were in it; and death and hell delivered up the dead which were in them: and they were judged every man according to their works.
20:11–13

473 And I saw a new heaven and a new earth: for the first heaven and the first earth were passed away; and there was no more sea.
And I John saw the holy city, new Jerusalem, coming down from God out of heaven, prepared as a bride adorned for her husband.
21:1–2

474 And he shewed me a pure river of water of life, clear as crystal, proceeding out of the throne of God and of the Lamb.
In the midst of the street of it, and on either side of the river, was there the tree of life, which bare twelve manner of fruits, and yielded her fruit every month: and the leaves of the tree were for the healing of the nations.
22:1–2

Ruth

475 And Ruth said, Intreat me not to leave thee, or to return from following after thee: for whither thou goest, I will go; and where thou lodgest, I will lodge: thy people shall be my people, and thy God my God:
Where thou diest, will I die, and there will I be buried: the Lord do so to me, and more also, if ought but death part thee and me.
1:16–17

476 And he shall be unto thee a restorer of thy life and a nourisher of thine old age: for thy daughter in law, which loveth thee, which is better to thee than seven sons, hath born him.
4:15

I Samuel

477 Therefore Eli said unto Samuel, Go, lie down: and it shall be, if all thee, that thou shalt say, Speak, Lord; for thy servant heareth. So Samuel went and lay down in his place.
3:9

478 But now thy kingdom shall not continue: the Lord hath sought him a man after his own heart, and the Lord hath commanded him to be captain over his people, because thou hast not kept that which the Lord commanded thee.
13:14

479 And the people said unto Saul, Shall Jonathan die, who hath wrought this great salvation in Israel? God forbid: as the Lord liveth, there shall not one hair of his head fall to the ground; for he hath wrought with God this day. So the people rescued Jonathan, that he died not.
14:45

480 And he took his staff in his hand, and chose him five smooth stones out of the brook, and put them in a shepherd's bag which he had, even in a scrip; and his sling was in his hand: and he drew near to the Philistine.
17:40

481 And the women answered one another as they played, and said, Saul hath slain his thousands, and David his ten thousands.
18:7

II Samuel

482 Saul and Jonathan were lovely and pleasant in their lives, and in their death they were not divided: they were swifter than eagles, they were stronger than lions.
1:23–24

483 I am distressed for thee, my brother Jonathan: very pleasant hast thou been unto me: thy love to me was wonderful, passing the love of women.
How are the mighty fallen, and the weapons of war perished!
1:26–27

484 And a certain man saw it, and told Joab, and said, Behold, I saw Absalom hanged in an oak.
18:10

485 And the king was much moved, and went up to the chamber over the gate, and wept: and as he went, thus he said, O my son Absalom, my son, my son Absalom! would God I had died for thee, O Absalom, my son, my son!
18:33

Song of Solomon

486 I am the rose of Sharon, and the lily of the valleys.
As the lily among thorns, so is my love among the daughters.
2:1–2

487 He brought me to the banqueting house, and his banner over me was love.
Stay me with flagons, comfort me with apples: for I am sick of love.
His left hand is under my head, and his right hand doth embrace me.
2:4–6

488 The voice of my beloved! behold, he cometh leaping upon the mountains, skipping upon the hills.
2:8

489 My beloved spake, and said unto me, Rise up, my love, my fair one, and come away.
For, lo, the winter is past, the rain is over and gone;
The flowers appear on the earth; the time of the singing of birds is come, and the voice of the turtle is heard in our land.
2:10–12

490 Take us the foxes, the little foxes, that spoil the vines: for our vines have tender grapes.
2:15

491 My beloved is mine, and I am his: he feedeth among the lilies.
Until the day break, and the shadows flee away, turn, my beloved, and be thou like a roe or a young hart upon the mountains of Bether.
2:16–17

492 A fountain of gardens, a well of living waters, and streams from Lebanon.
4:15

493 I am come into my garden, my sister, my spouse: I have gathered my myrrh with my spice; I have eaten my honeycomb with my honey; I have drunk my wine with my milk: eat, O friends; drink, yea, drink abundantly, O beloved.
I sleep, but my heart waketh: it is the voice of my beloved that knocketh, saying, Open to me, my sister, my love, my dove, my undefiled: for my head is filled with dew, and my locks with the drops of the night.
5:1–2

494 My beloved put in his hand by the hole of the door, and my bowels were moved for him.
5:4

495 My beloved is gone down into his garden, to the beds of spices, to feed in the gardens, and to gather lilies.

I am my beloved's, and my beloved is mine: he feedeth among the lilies.

6:2–3

496 Who is she that looketh forth as the morning, fair as the moon, clear as the sun, and terrible as an army with banners?

6:10

497 Return, return, O Shulamite; return, return, that we may look upon thee. What will ye see in the Shulamite? As it were the company of two armies.

6:13

498 How fair and how pleasant art thou, O love, for delights!

7:6

499 I am my beloved's, and his desire is toward me.

7:10

500 Who is this that cometh up from the wilderness, leaning upon her beloved? I raised thee up under the apple tree: there thy mother brought thee forth: there she brought thee forth that bare thee.

8:5

501 Make haste, my beloved, and be thou like to a roe or to a young hart upon the mountains of spices.

8:14

I Thessalonians

502 Remembering without ceasing your work of faith, and labour of love, and patience of hope in our Lord Jesus Christ, in the sight of God and our Father.

1:3

503 For yourselves know perfectly that the day of the Lord so cometh as a thief in the night.

5:2

504 Prove all things; hold fast that which is good.

5:21

II Thessalonians

505 For even when we were with you, this we commanded you, that if any would not work, neither should he eat.

3:10

I Timothy

506 This is a faithful saying, and worthy of all acceptation, that Christ Jesus came into the world to save sinners; of whom I am chief.

1:15

507 This is a true saying, If a man desire the office of a bishop, he desireth a good work.
A bishop then must be blameless, the husband of one wife, vigilant, sober, of good behaviour, given to hospitality, apt to teach;

Not given to wine, no striker, not greedy of filthy lucre; but patient, not a brawler, not covetous.

3:1–3

508 For every creature of God is good, and nothing to be refused, if it be received with thanksgiving.

4:4

509 Drink no longer water, but use a little wine for thy stomach's sake and thine often infirmities.

5:23

510 For we brought nothing into this world, and it is certain we carry nothing out.

6:7

511 For the love of money is the root of all evil: which while some coveted after, they have erred from the faith, and pierced themselves through with many sorrows.

6:10

512 Fight the good fight of faith, lay hold on eternal life, whereunto thou art also called, and hast professed a good profession before many witnesses.

6:12

513 But evil men and seducers shall wax worse and worse, deceiving, and being deceived.

3:13

514 For I am now ready to be offered, and the time of my departure is at hand.
I have fought a good fight, I have finished my course, I have kept the faith:
Henceforth there is laid up for me a crown of righteousness, which the Lord, the righteous judge, shall give me at that day: and not to me only, but unto all them also that love his appearing.

4:6–8

Titus

515 One of themselves, even a prophet of their own, said, The Cretians are alway liars, evil beasts, slow bellies.

1:12

Tobit

516 Be not greedy to add money to money: but let it be as refuse in respect of our child.

5:18

517 Be of good comfort, my daughter; the Lord of heaven and earth give thee joy for this thy sorrow: be of good comfort, my daughter.

7:18

Wisdom

518 For the ear of jealousy heareth all things: and the noise of murmurings is not hid.

1:10

519 For the bewitching of naughtiness doth obscure things that are honest; and the wandering of concupiscence doth undermine the simple mind.
He, being made perfect in a short time, fulfilled a long time.
4:12–13

520 For all men have one entrance into life, and the like going out.
7:6

521 Wisdom reacheth from one end to another mightily: and sweetly doth she order all things.
8:1

522 For thou hast power of life and death: thou leadest to the gates of hell, and bringest up again.

Bickerstaffe, Isaac (c. 1735–c. 1812) Irish dramatist, especially of comedies and comic operas.

1 There was a jolly miller once,
Lived on the river Dee;
He worked and sang from morn till night;
No lark more blithe than he.
Love in a Village, I

2 And this the burthen of his song,
For ever us'd to be,
I care for nobody, not I,
If no one cares for me.
Love in a Village, I

Bidault, Georges (1899–1983) French statesman. A leader of the resistance during World War II, he was twice prime minister (1946, 1949–50).

1 The weak have one weapon: the errors of those who think they are strong.
The Observer, 1962

Bierce, Ambrose Gwinnett (1842–?1914) US writer and journalist. His short stories were published in such collections as *In the Midst of Life* (1892). He also compiled *The Devil's Dictionary* (1906).

Quotations about Bierce

1 There was nothing of the milk of human kindness in old Ambrose.
H. L. Mencken (1880–1956) US journalist. *Prejudices*, 'Ambrose Bierce'

2 I have heard one young woman declare, 'I can feel him ten feet away!'
George Sterling *American Mercury*, Sept 1925

Quotations by Bierce

3 *Bore*, n. A person who talks when you wish him to listen.
The Devil's Dictionary

4 *Brain*, n. An apparatus with which we think that we think.
The Devil's Dictionary

5 *Debauchee*, n. One who has so earnestly pursued pleasure that he has had the misfortune to overtake it.
The Devil's Dictionary

6 *Egotist*, n. A person of low taste, more interested in himself than in me.
The Devil's Dictionary

7 *Future*, n. That period of time in which our affairs prosper, our friends are true and our happiness is assured.
The Devil's Dictionary

8 *Marriage*, n. The state or condition of a community consisting of a master, a mistress and two slaves, making in all two.
The Devil's Dictionary

9 *Patience*, n. A minor form of despair, disguised as a virtue.
The Devil's Dictionary

10 *Peace*, n. In international affairs, a period of cheating between two periods of fighting.
The Devil's Dictionary

Binyon, (Robert) Laurence (1869–1943) British poet and dramatist. His poetic works include *The Sirens* (1924), *The Idols* (1928), and the wartime elegy 'For the Fallen' (1914).

1 Now is the time for the burning of the leaves.
The Burning of the Leaves

2 With proud thanksgiving, a mother for her children,
England mourns for her dead across the sea.
In response to the slaughter of World War I
Poems For the Fallen

3 They shall grow not old, as we that are left grow old:
Age shall not weary them, nor the years condemn.
At the going down of the sun and in the morning
We will remember them.
Poems For the Fallen

Birkenhead, F(rederick) E(lwin) Smith, Earl of (1872–1930) British lawyer and politician. As attorney general (1915–19), he prosecuted Roger Casement; he was lord chancellor from 1919 to 1922.

1 We have the highest authority for believing that the meek shall inherit the Earth; though I have never found any particular corroboration of this aphorism in the records of Somerset House.
Contemporary Personalities, 'Marquess Curzon'

2 JUDGE WILLIS. You are extremely offensive, young man.
F. E. SMITH. As a matter of fact, we both are, and the only difference between us is that I am trying to be, and you can't help it.
Frederick Elwin, Earl of Birkenhead (Lord Birkenhead), Vol. I, Ch. 9

3 JUDGE WILLIS. What do you suppose I am on the Bench for, Mr Smith?
SMITH. It is not for me to attempt to fathom the inscrutable workings of Providence.
Frederick Elwin, Earl of Birkenhead (Lord Birkenhead), Vol. I, Ch. 9

4 The world continues to offer glittering prizes to those who have stout hearts and sharp swords.
Speech, Glasgow University, 7 Nov 1923

Bismarck, Otto Eduard Leopold, Prince von
(1815–98) German statesman. As prime minister of Prussia (1862–90), he played a major role in the creation (1871) of the German Empire, which he then dominated as chancellor (1871–90).

1 The great questions of our day cannot be solved by speeches and majority votes . . . but by iron and blood.
Usually misquoted as 'blood and iron' – a form Bismarck himself used in 1886
Speech, Prussian Chamber, 30 Sept 1862

2 Politics is not an exact science.
Speech, Prussian Chamber, 18 Dec 1863

3 Politics is the art of the possible.
Said to Meyer von Waldeck, 11 Aug 1867

4 We will not go to Canossa.
A declaration of his anti-Roman Catholic policy; the Emperor Henry IV had submitted to Pope Gregory VII at Canossa, N. Italy, in 1077
Speech, Reichstag, 14 May 1872

5 The healthy bones of a single Pomeranian grenadier.
A price too high for Germany to pay regarding the Eastern Question
Speech, Reichstag, 5 Dec 1876

6 An honest broker.
His professed role in the diplomacy of 1878, including the Congress of Berlin
Speech, Reichstag, 19 Feb 1878

7 Politics is not a science . . . but an art.
Speech, Reichstag, 15 Mar 1884

8 If there is ever another war in Europe, it will come out of some damned silly thing in the Balkans.
Remark to Ballen, shortly before Bismarck's death

Blacker, Valentine (1778–1823) British soldier, who served in India.

1 Put your trust in God, my boys, and keep your powder dry.
Oliver Cromwell's Advice

Blackmore, R(ichard) D(oddridge) (1825–1900) British novelist. His best-known work is the historical romance *Lorna Doone* (1869).

1 I was launched into this vale of tears on the 7th of June 1825, at Longworth in Berkshire. Before I was four months old, my mother was taken to a better world, and so I started crookedly.
Lorna Doone, Introduction

2 Here was I, a yeoman's boy, a yeoman every inch of me, even where I was naked; and there was she, a lady born, and thoroughly aware of it, and dressed by people of rank and taste, who took pride in her beauty, and set it to advantage.
Lorna Doone, Ch. 8

3 However, for a moralist I never set up, and never shall, while common sense abides with me. Such a man must be truly wretched, in this pure dearth of morality; like a fisherman where no fish be; and most of us have enough to do, to attend to our own morals.
Lorna Doone, Ch. 69

Blackstone, Sir William (1723–80) British jurist, author of the classic *Commentaries on the Laws of England* (1765–69).

1 Man was formed for society.
Commentaries on the Laws of England, Introduction

2 The king never dies.
Commentaries on the Laws of England, Bk. I, Ch. 7

3 Time whereof the memory of man runneth not to the contrary.
Commentaries on the Laws of England, Bk. I, Ch. 18

4 That the king can do no wrong, is a necessary and fundamental principle of the English constitution.
Commentaries on the Laws of England, Bk. III, Ch. 17

5 It is better that ten guilty persons escape than one innocent suffer.
Commentaries on the Laws of England, Bk. IV, Ch. 27

Blackwell, Antoinette Brown (1825–1921) US feminist writer and minister.

1 Mr. Darwin . . . has failed to hold definitely before his mind the principle that the difference of sex, whatever it may consist in, must itself be subject to natural selection and to evolution.
The Sexes Throughout Nature

Blackwood, Helen Selina, Countess of Dufferin (1807–67) British poet. As Impulsia Gushington she wrote humorous ballads.

1 I'm sitting on the stile, Mary,
Where we sat, side by side.
Lament of the Irish Emigrant

2 They say there's bread and work for all,
And the sun shines always there:
But I'll not forget old Ireland,
Were it fifty times as fair.
Lament of the Irish Emigrant

Blair, Eric *See* Orwell, George.

Blair, Robert (1699–1746) Scottish poet and churchman. He is best remembered for the poem *The Grave* (1743), which was later illustrated by William Blake.

1 The schoolboy, with his satchel in his hand,
Whistling aloud to bear his courage up.
The Grave

2 Its visits,
Like those of angels, short, and far between.
The Grave

Blake, Charles Dupee (1846–1903) British writer of nursery rhymes.

1 Rock-a-bye baby on the tree top,
When the wind blows the cradle will rock,
When the bough bends the cradle will fall,
Down comes the baby, cradle and all.
Attrib.

Blake, William (1757–1827) British poet, painter, engraver, and visionary. Blake's mystical engravings and watercolours illustrate such works as *Songs of Innocence* (1789) and the poem *Jerusalem* (1804–20).

Quotations about Blake

1 William Blake's insanity was worth more than the sanity of any number of artistic mediocrities.
Gerald Abraham *Radio Times*, 10 Dec 1937

2 Where other poets use reality as a springboard into space, he uses it as a foothold when he returns from flight.
Arthur Symons (1865–1945) British poet. *William Blake*

Quotations by Blake

3 For everything that lives is holy, life delights in life.
America

4 The strongest poison ever known
Came from Caesar's laurel crown.
Auguries of Innocence

5 Every wolf's and lion's howl
Raises from Hell a human soul.
Auguries of Innocence

6 A truth that's told with bad intent
Beats all the lies you can invent.
Auguries of Innocence

7 Every tear from every eye
Becomes a babe in Eternity.
Auguries of Innocence

8 He who shall teach the child to doubt
The rotting grave shall ne'er get out.
Auguries of Innocence

9 To see a World in a grain of sand,
And a Heaven in a wild flower,
Hold Infinity in the palm of your hand,
And Eternity in an hour.
Auguries of Innocence

10 A robin redbreast in a cage
Puts all Heaven in a rage.
Auguries of Innocence

11 Does the Eagle know what is in the pit
Or wilt thou go ask the Mole?
Can Wisdom be put in a silver rod,
Or love in a golden bowl?
The Book of Thel, 'Thel's Motto'

12 'What,' it will be questioned, 'when the sun rises, do you not see a round disc of fire somewhat like a guinea?' 'O no, no, I see an innumerable company of the heavenly host crying, "Holy, Holy, Holy is the Lord God Almighty!"'
Descriptive Catalogue, 'The Vision of Judgment'

13 Humility is only doubt,
And does the sun and moon blot out.
The Everlasting Gospel

14 Great things are done when men and mountains meet;
This is not done by jostling in the street.
Gnomic Verses

15 He who bends to himself a Joy
Doth the wingèd life destroy;
But he who kisses the Joy as it flies
Lives in Eternity's sunrise.
Gnomic Verses

16 He who would do good to another must do it in Minute Particulars.
General Good is the plea of the scoundrel, hypocrite, and flatterer.
Jerusalem

17 I care not whether a man is Good or Evil; all that I care
Is whether he is a Wise Man or a Fool. Go! put off Holiness,
And put on Intellect.
Jerusalem

18 Without Contraries is no progression. Attraction and Repulsion, Reason and Energy, Love and Hate, are necessary to Human existence.
The Marriage of Heaven and Hell, 'The Argument'

19 If the doors of perception were cleansed everything would appear to man as it is, infinite.
The Marriage of Heaven and Hell, 'A Memorable Fancy'

20 Prisons are built with stones of Law, brothels with bricks of Religion.
The Marriage of Heaven and Hell, 'Proverbs of Hell'

21 Sooner murder an infant in its cradle than nurse unacted desires.
The Marriage of Heaven and Hell, 'Proverbs of Hell'

22 In seed time learn, in harvest teach, in winter enjoy.
The Marriage of Heaven and Hell, 'Proverbs of Hell'

23 The cut worm forgives the plough.
The Marriage of Heaven and Hell, 'Proverbs of Hell'

24 What is now proved was once only imagined.
The Marriage of Heaven and Hell, 'Proverbs of Hell'

25 The road of excess leads to the palace of Wisdom.
The Marriage of Heaven and Hell, 'Proverbs of Hell'

26 He who desires but acts not, breeds pestilence.
The Marriage of Heaven and Hell, 'Proverbs of Hell'

27 A fool sees not the same tree that a wise man sees.
The Marriage of Heaven and Hell, 'Proverbs of Hell'

28 Damn braces. Bless relaxes.
The Marriage of Heaven and Hell, 'Proverbs of Hell'

29 Exuberance is Beauty.
The Marriage of Heaven and Hell, 'Proverbs of Hell'

30 Those who restrain Desire, do so because theirs is weak enough to be restrained.
The Marriage of Heaven and Hell, 'Those who restrain Desire . . . '

31 Man has no Body distinct from his Soul; for that called Body is a portion of Soul discerned by the five Senses, the chief inlets of Soul in this age.
The Marriage of Heaven and Hell, 'The Voice of the Devil'

32 Energy is Eternal Delight.
The Marriage of Heaven and Hell, 'The Voice of the Devil'

33 And did those feet in ancient time
Walk upon England's mountains green?
And was the holy lamb of God
On England's pleasant pastures seen?
   . . .
I will not cease from mental fight,
Nor shall my sword sleep in my hand,
Till we have built Jerusalem
In England's green and pleasant land.
Better known as the hymn 'Jerusalem', with music by Sir Hubert Parry; not to be confused with Blake's longer poem *Jerusalem*. *Milton*, Preface

34 Mock on, mock on, Voltaire, Rousseau;
Mock on, mock on; 'tis all in vain!
You throw the sand against the wind,
And the wind blows it back again.
Mock on, mock on, Voltaire, Rousseau

35 When Sir Joshua Reynolds died
All Nature was degraded;
The King dropped a tear in the Queen's ear,
And all his pictures faded.
On Art and Artists

36 Love seeketh not itself to please,
Nor for itself hath any care,
But for another gives its ease,
And builds a Heaven in Hell's despair.
Songs of Experience, 'The Clod and the Pebble'

37 Love seeketh only Self to please,
To bind another to its delight,
Joys in another's loss of ease,
And builds a Hell in Heaven's despite.
Songs of Experience, 'The Clod and the Pebble'

38 My mother groan'd, my father wept,
Into the dangerous world I leapt;
Helpless, naked, piping loud,
Like a fiend hid in a cloud.
Songs of Experience, 'Infant Sorrow'

39 Tiger! Tiger! burning bright
In the forests of the night,
What immortal hand or eye
Could frame thy fearful symmetry?
Songs of Experience, 'The Tiger'

40 When the stars threw down their spears,
And watered heaven with their tears,
Did he smile his work to see?
Did he who made the Lamb make thee?
Songs of Experience, 'The Tiger'

41 Piping down the valleys wild,
Piping songs of pleasant glee,
On a cloud I saw a child.
Songs of Innocence, Introduction

42 'Pipe a song about a Lamb!'
So I piped with merry cheer.
Songs of Innocence, Introduction

43 To Mercy, Pity, Peace, and Love
All pray in their distress.
Songs of Innocence, 'The Divine Image'

44 For Mercy has a human heart,
Pity a human face,
And Love, the human form divine,
And Peace, the human dress.
Songs of Innocence, 'The Divine Image'

45 'Twas on a Holy Thursday, their innocent faces clean,
The children walking two and two, in red and blue and green.
Songs of Innocence, 'Holy Thursday'

46 Little Lamb, who made thee?
Dost thou know who made thee?
Songs of Innocence, 'The Lamb'

47 When the green woods laugh with the voice of joy.
Songs of Innocence, 'Laughing song'

48 My mother bore me in the southern wild.
And I am black, but O! my soul is white;
White as an angel is the English child,
But I am black, as if bereav'd of light.
Songs of Innocence, 'The Little Black Boy'

49 Man's Desires are limited by his Perceptions; none can desire what he has not perceived.
There is no Natural Religion

50 The Desire of Man being Infinite, the possession is Infinite, and himself Infinite.
There is no Natural Religion

51 I mock thee not, though I by thee am mockèd;
Thou call'st me madman, but I call thee blockhead.
To Flaxman

52 To generalize is to be an idiot.

Life of Blake (Gilchrist)

Blyton, Enid (1897–1968) British children's writer. Her most famous character is Noddy, introduced in 1949; her most successful adventure series include the *Famous Five* and the *Secret Seven*.

1 I shut my eyes for a few minutes, with my portable typewriter on my knee – I make my mind a blank and wait – and then, as clearly as I would see real children, my characters stand before me in my mind's eye. I see them in detail – hair, eyes, feet, clothes, expression – and I always know their Christian names but never their surname. (I get these out of a telephone directory afterwards!)

Letter to Professor Peter McKellar, 15 Feb 1953

2 One librarian thought my books were far too popular and the hordes of children swarming into the library for them on Saturday morning became a nuisance. 'If only you could see the children swamping the shelves,' he told me. 'It makes us far too busy.'

The Blyton Phenomenon, Ch. 5 (Sheila Ray)

3 As I found a lack of suitable poems of the types I wanted, I began to write them myself for the children under my supervision, taking, in many cases, the ideas, humorous or whimsical, of the children themselves, as the theme of the poems!

Enid Blyton, Ch. 3 (Barbara Stoney)

Boccaccio, Giovanni (1313–75) Italian writer and poet. He is chiefly known for the *Decameron*: a hundred stories told by young people escaping from the plague in Florence in 1348. Other works include *Filostrato*, which provided the plot for Chaucer's *Troilus and Criseyde*, and *Teseida* which formed the basis of the *Knights' Tale*.

1 It often happens, that he who endeavours to ridicule other people, especially in things of a serious nature, becomes himself a jest, and frequently to his great cost.

Decameron, The Second Day, I

2 There are some people so indiscreet in appearing to know what they had better be unacquainted with, that they think, by reproving other people's inadvertencies, to lessen their own shame: whereas they make that vastly greater.

Decameron, The Third Day, II

3 Although love dwells in gorgeous palaces, and sumptuous apartments, more willingly than in miserable and desolate cottages, it cannot be denied but that he sometimes causes his power to be felt in the gloomy recesses of forests, among the most bleak and rugged mountains, and in the dreary caves of a desert.

Decameron, The Third Day, X

4 Whoever rightly considers the order of things may plainly see the whole race of woman-kind is by nature, custom, and the laws, made subject to man, to be governed according to his discretion: therefore it is the duty of every one of us that desires to have ease, comfort, and repose, with those men to whom we belong, to be humble, patient, and obedient, as well as chaste . . .

Decameron, The Ninth Day, IX

Boethius, Anicius Manlius Severinus (c. 480–524) Roman statesman, philosopher, and scholar. His writings include translations of Aristotle, treatises on theology, music, and mathematics, and philosophical works, notably *The Consolation of Philosophy*.

1 In every adversity of fortune, to have been happy is the most unhappy kind of misfortune.

The Consolation of Philosophy

Bogarde, Dirk (Derek van den Bogaerde; 1921–) British film actor and writer who received international acclaim for such films as *The Damned* (1969), *Death in Venice* (1970), and *Providence* (1978). His books include the autobiographies *A Postillion Struck by Lightning* (1977), *Snakes and Ladders* (1978), *An Orderly Man* (1983), and *Backcloth* (1986) and the novels *A Gentle Occupation* (1980) and *West of Sunset* (1984).

1 I am an orderly man. I say this with no sense of false modesty, or of conceit . . . Being orderly, as a matter of fact, can be excessively tiresome and it often irritates me greatly, but I cannot pull away.

An Orderly Man, Ch. 1

2 I love the camera and it loves me. Well, not very much sometimes. But we're good friends.

Halliwell's Filmgoer's and Video Viewer's Companion

Bogart, Humphrey (1899–1957) US film star. His films incude *Casablanca* (1942), *The African Queen* (1951), and a host of others in which he played tough gangsters.

1 Here's looking at you, kid.

Casablanca

2 Play it, Sam. Play 'As Time Goes By'.

Often misquoted as 'Play it again, Sam'
Casablanca

3 Of all the gin joints in all the towns in all the world, she walks into mine!

Casablanca

Bogart, John B. (1845–1920) US journalist.

1 When a dog bites a man that is not news, but when a man bites a dog that is news.

Sometimes attributed to Charles Dana and Amos Cummings
Attrib.

Bohr, Niels Henrik David (1885–1962) Danish physicist. He made great contributions to the theory of atomic structure. His laboratory in Copenhagen was a haven for many Jewish scientists expelled by Hitler and he took to America the news that an atom bomb had become possible.

1 Of course I don't believe in it. But I understand that it brings you luck whether you believe in it or not.

When asked why he had a horseshoe on his wall
Attrib.

2 An expert is a man who has made all the mistakes, which can be made, in a very narrow field.

Attrib.

Boileau, Nicolas (1636–1711) French writer and poet. His *L'Art poétique* (1674) was widely read in Europe. *Le Lutrin* (1674) was a mock epic poem.

1 No one who cannot limit himself has ever been able to write.

L'Art poétique, I

2 Often the fear of one evil leads us into a worse.

L'Art poétique, I

3 A fool always finds a greater fool to admire him.

L'Art poétique, I

4 The dreadful burden of having nothing to do.

Épitres, XI

Boleyn, Anne (1507–36) Second wife (1533–36) of King Henry VIII of England. She was the mother of Elizabeth I, but failed to produce the male heir that Henry wanted. When he tired of her, she was accused of treason through adultery and executed.

1 The king has been very good to me. He promoted me from a simple maid to be a marchioness. Then he raised me to be a queen. Now he will raise me to be a martyr.

Notable Women in History (W. Abbot)

Bolt, Robert (1924–) British playwright. His plays include *A Man for All Seasons* (1960). He has also written several screenplays including *Lawrence of Arabia* (1962) and *The Mission* (1986).

1 Morality's not practical. Morality's a gesture. A complicated gesture learnt from books.

A Man for All Seasons

2 The nobility of England, my lord, would have snored through the Sermon on the Mount.

A Man for All Seasons

Bone, Sir David (1874–1959) British sea captain and writer, especially of seafaring novels.

1 It's 'Damn you, Jack – I'm all right!' with you chaps.

The Brassbounder, Ch. 3

Bone, James (1872–1962) British journalist.

1 He made righteousness readable.

Referring to C. P. Scott, former editor of *The Manchester Guardian*
Attrib.

Bonhoeffer, Dietrich (1906–45) German theologian. An anti-Nazi, he was imprisoned and hanged in Buchenwald. His posthumous *Letters and Papers from Prison* (1953) were widely read.

1 Man has learned to cope with all questions of importance without recourse to God as a working hypothesis.

See also LAPLACE
Letters and Papers from Prison, 8 June 1944

2 A God who let us prove his existence would be an idol.

No Rusty Swords

Bono, Edward de (1933–) British physician and writer. His books include *The Use of Lateral Thinking* (1967), *The Mechanism of Mind* (1969), and *Beyond Yes and No* (1972).

1 Unhappiness is best defined as the difference between our talents and our expectations.

The Observer, 'Sayings of the Week', 12 June 1977

Book of Common Prayer, The *See also* Bible, Psalms.

1 O all ye Works of the Lord, bless ye the Lord.

Benedicite

2 Man that is born of a woman hath but a short time to live, and is full of misery.

Burial of the Dead, First anthem

3 In the midst of life we are in death.

Burial of the Dead, First anthem

4 Almighty God, give us the grace that we may cast away the works of darkness, and put upon us the armour of light, now in the time of this mortal life.

Collect, 1st Sunday in Advent

5 Increase and multiply upon us they mercy; that, thou being our ruler and guide, we may so pass through things temporal, that we finally lose not the things eternal.

Collect, 4th Sunday after Trinity

6 Grant that those things which we ask faithfully we may obtain effectually.

Collect, 23rd Sunday after Trinity

7 Read, mark, learn and inwardly digest.

Collect, 2nd Sunday in Advent

8 All our doings without charity are nothing worth.

Collect, Quinquagesima Sunday

9 Lighten our darkness, we beseech thee, O Lord; and by thy great mercy defend us from all perils and dangers of this night.

Evening Prayer, Third Collect

10 Ye that do truly and earnestly repent you of your sins, and are in love and charity with your neighbours, and intend to lead a new life, following the commandments of God, and walking from henceforth in his holy ways; Draw near with faith, and take this holy Sacrament to your comfort; and make your humble confession to Almighty God, meekly kneeling upon your knees.

Holy Communion, The Invitation

11 The blessing of God Almighty, the Father, the Son, and the Holy Ghost, be amongst you and remain with you always.

Holy Communion, The Blessing

12 All the deceits of the world, the flesh, and the devil.

The Litany

13 We have erred, and strayed from thy ways like lost sheep.

Morning Prayer, General Confession

14 We have left undone those things which we ought to have done; and we have done those things we ought not to have done.

Morning Prayer, General Confession

15 As it was in the beginning, is now, and ever shall be: world without end.

Morning Prayer, Gloria

16 When two or three are gathered together in thy Name thou wilt grant their requests.

Morning Prayer, Prayer of St Chrysostom

17 Grant that this day we fall into no sin, neither run into any kind of danger.

Morning Prayer, Third Collect, for Grace

18 In the hour of death, and in the day of judgement.

The Litany

19 Being now come to the years of discretion.

Order of Confirmation

20 Defend, O Lord, this thy Child with thy heavenly grace, that he may continue thine for ever; and daily increase in thy holy Spirit more and more, until he come unto thy everlasting kingdom.

Order of Confirmation

21 O merciful God, grant that the old Adam in this Child may be so buried, that the new man may be raised up in him.

Publick Baptism of Infants, Invocation of blessing on the child.

22 Renounce the devil and all his works.

Publick Baptism of Infants

23 If any of you know cause, or just impediment, why these two persons should not be joined together in holy Matrimony, ye are to declare it.

Solemnization of Matrimony, The Banns

24 First, It was ordained for the procreation of children, to be brought up in the fear and nurture of the Lord, and to the praise of his holy Name.

Solemnization of Matrimony, Exhortation

25 Let him now speak, or else hereafter for ever hold his peace.

Solemnization of Matrimony, Exhortation

26 Wilt thou love her, comfort her, honour, and keep her in sickness and in health; and, forsaking all other, keep thee only unto her, so long as ye both shall live?

Solemnization of Matrimony, Betrothal

27 To have and to hold from this day forward, for better for worse, for richer for poorer, in sickness and in health, to love and to cherish, till death us do part.

Solemnization of Matrimony, Betrothal

28 With this Ring I thee wed, with my body I thee worship, and with all my wordly goods I thee endow.

Solemnization of Matrimony, Wedding

29 Those whom God hath joined together let no man put asunder.

Solemnization of Matrimony, Wedding

Boone, Daniel (1734–1820) US pioneeer, who led the settlement of Kentucky.

1 I can't say I was ever lost, but I was bewildered once for three days.

Reply when asked if he had ever been lost
Attrib.

Boorstin, Daniel J. (1914–) US writer. His books include *The Image* (1961).

1 The celebrity is a person who is known for his well-knownness.

The Image, 'From Hero to Celebrity: The Human Pseudo-event'

2 A best-seller was a book which somehow sold well simply because it was selling well.

The Image, 'From Shapes to Shadows: Dissolving Forms'

Booth, William (1829–1912) British preacher and founder of the Salvation Army.

1 A population sodden with drink, steeped in vice, eaten up by every social and physical malady, these are the denizens of Darkest England amidst whom my life has been spent.

In Darkest England, and the Way Out

2 This Submerged Tenth – is it, then, beyond the reach of the nine-tenths in the midst of whom they live.

In Darkest England, and the Way Out

Borges, Jorge Luis (1899–1986) Argentinian writer. *A Universal History of Infamy* (1935) was the first of his several volumes of short stories; he also wrote poetry, especially in the blindness of his later life.

1 I have known uncertainty: a state unknown to the Greeks.

Ficciones, 'The Babylonian Lottery'

2 The visible universe was an illusion or, more precisely, a sophism. Mirrors and fatherhood are abominable because they multiply it and extend it.

Ficciones, 'Tlön, Uqbar, Orbis Tertius'

3 The original is unfaithful to the translation.

Referring to Henley's translation of Beckford's *Vathek*
Sobre el 'Vathek' de William Beckford

4 The Falklands thing was a fight between two bald men over a comb.

Referring to the war with the UK over the Falklands (1982)
Time, 14 Feb 1983

Borrow, George Henry (1803–81) British writer. His extensive travels in Britain and Europe inspired such works as *Lavengro* (1851) and *The Romany Rye* (1857).

1 There are no countries in the world less known by the British than these selfsame British Islands.

Lavengro, Preface

2 If you must commit suicide . . . always contrive to do it as decorously as possible; the decencies, whether of life or of death, should never be lost sight of.

Lavengro, Ch. 23

3 Youth will be served, every dog has his day, and mine has been a fine one.

Lavengro, Ch. 92

Bosquet, Pierre (1810–61) French marshal, who served with distinction during the Crimean War, especially at the Battle of Alma.

1 *C'est magnifique, mais ce n'est pas la guerre.*
It is magnificent, but it is not war.

Referring to the Charge of the Light Brigade at the Battle of Balaclava, 25 Oct 1854
Attrib.

Bossidy, John Collins (1860–1928) US writer.

1 And this is good old Boston,
The home of the bean and the cod,
Where the Lowells talk only to Cabots,
And the Cabots talk only to God.

Toast at Holy Cross Alumni dinner, 1910

Boswell, James (1740–95) Scottish lawyer and writer. His biography of Dr Johnson, published in 1791, is still widely read.

1 JOHNSON. Well, we had a good talk.
BOSWELL. Yes, Sir; you tossed and gored several persons.

Life of Johnson, Vol. II

2 A man, indeed, is not genteel when he gets drunk; but most vices may be committed very genteelly: a man may debauch his friend's wife genteelly: he may cheat at cards genteelly.

Life of Johnson, Vol. II

Bottomley, Horatio William (1860–1933) British newspaper editor and proprietor. An MP, he was imprisoned for misappropriation of funds held in trust.

1 VISITOR. Ah, Bottomley, sewing?
BOTTOMLEY. No, reaping.

When found sewing mail bags
Horatio Bottomley (Julian Symons)

Boucicault, Dion (Dionysius Lardner Boursiquot; 1820–90) Irish-born US actor and dramatist. His plays include *The Octoroon* (1859) and *The Jilt* (1886).

1 Men talk of killing time, while time quietly kills them.

London Assurance, II:1

Boulay de la Meurthe, Antoine (1761–1840) French politician. A member of the Council of Five Hundred, he was banished by Louis XVIII.

1 It is worse than a crime, it is a blunder.

See also ACHESON. Referring to the summary execution of the Duc d'Enghien by Napoleon, 1804
Attrib.

Boulton, Sir H. E. (1859–1935) Scottish songwriter.

1 Speed, bonny boat, like a bird on the wing;
'Onward', the sailors cry;
Carry the lad that's born to be king
Over the sea to Skye.

Skye Boat Song

Bowen, Charles Synge Christopher, Baron (1835–94) British judge.

1 The rain it raineth on the just
And also on the unjust fella:
But chiefly on the just, because
The unjust steals the just's umbrella.

Sands of Time (Walter Sichel)

2 A blind man in a dark room – looking for a black hat – which isn't there.

Characterization of a metaphysician
Attrib.

Bowen, E. E. (1836–1901) British writer.

1 Forty years on, when afar and asunder
Parted are those who are singing to-day.

Forty Years On (the Harrow school song)

2 Follow up! Follow up! Follow up! Follow up! Follow up!
Till the field ring again and again,
With the tramp of the twenty-two men,
Follow up!

Forty Years On (the Harrow school song)

Bowen, Elizabeth (1899–1973) Irish novelist. Her books include *The Hotel* (1927), *The Death of the Heart* (1938), and *The Heat of the Day* (1949).

1 Experience isn't interesting till it begins to repeat itself – in fact, till it does that, it hardly *is* experience.

The Death of the Heart, Pt. I, Ch. 1

2 Art is the only thing that can go on mattering once it has stopped hurting.

The Heat of the Day, Ch. 16

3 Nobody speaks the truth when there's something they must have.

The House in Paris

4 Jealousy is no more than feeling alone among smiling enemies.

The House in Paris

5 No, it is not only our fate but our business to lose innocence, and once we have lost that, it is futile to attempt a picnic in Eden.

Orion III, 'Out of a Book'

Bowra, Sir Maurice (1898–1971) British scholar and classicist. His books include *The Heritage of Symbolism* (1943) and *The Creative Experiment* (1949).

1 I'm a man
More dined against than dining.

Summoned by Bells (J. Betjeman)

2 Any amusing deaths lately?

Attrib.

3 Splendid couple – slept with both of them.

Referring to a well-known literary couple
Attrib.

Brabazon of Tara, Derek Charles Moore-Brabazon, Baron (1910–74) British businessman and Conservative politician.

1 I take the view, and always have done, that if you cannot say what you have to say in twenty minutes, you should go away and write a book about it.

Attrib.

Bracken, Brendan, 1st Viscount (1901–58) British newspaper publisher and politician. He served as parliamentary private secretary to Winston Churchill (1940–41), minister of information (1941–45), and first lord of the Admiralty (1945).

1 It's a good deed to forget a poor joke.

The Observer, 'Sayings of the Week', 17 Oct 1943

Bradbury, Malcolm (1932–) British academic, novelist, and critic. Novels include *Eating People is Wrong* (1954), *Rates of Exchange* (1983), and *Cuts* (1988). His *The Social Context of Modern English Literature* (1972) is widely read.

1 Sympathy – for all these people, for being foreigners – lay over the gathering like a woolly blanket; and no one was enjoying it at all.

Eating People is Wrong, Ch. 2

2 I like the English. They have the most rigid code of immorality in the world.

Eating People is Wrong, Ch. 5

3 'We stay together, but we distrust one another.'
'Ah, yes . . . but isn't that a definition of marriage?'

The History Man, Ch. 3

4 I've noticed your hostility towards him . . . I ought to have guessed you were friends.

The History Man, Ch. 7

5 Reading someone else's newspaper is like sleeping with someone else's wife. Nothing seems to be precisely in the right place, and when you find what you are looking for, it is not clear then how to respond to it.

Stepping Westward, Bk. I, Ch. 1

6 The English are polite by telling lies. The Americans are polite by telling the truth.

Stepping Westward, Bk. II, Ch. 5

7 If God had meant us to have group sex, I guess he'd have given us all more organs.

Who Do You Think You Are?, 'A Very Hospitable Person'

Bradford, John (?1510–55) English Protestant martyr. Chaplain to King Edward VI and popular preacher, he was burned as a heretic after the accession of Queen Mary.

1 There, but for the grace of God, goes John Bradford.

Said on seeing some criminals being led to execution
Remark

Bradley, F(rancis) H(erbert) (1846–1924) British philosopher. *Appearance and Reality* (1893) outlined his idealist metaphysics.

1 The hunter for aphorisms on human nature has to fish in muddy water, and he is even condemned to find much of his own mind.

Aphorisms

2 This is the temple of Providence where disciples still hourly mark its ways and note the system of its mysteries. Here is the one God whose worshippers prove their faith by their works and in their destruction still trust in Him.

Referring to Monte Carlo
Aphorisms

3 It is good to know what a man is, and also what the world takes him for. But you do not understand him until you have learnt how he understands himself.

Aphorisms

4 The propriety of some persons seems to consist in having improper thoughts about their neighbours.

Aphorisms

5 Metaphysics is the finding of bad reasons for what we believe upon instinct; but to find these reasons is no less an instinct.

Appearance and Reality, Preface

6 His mind is open; yes, it is so open that nothing is retained; ideas simply pass through him.

Attrib.

Bradley, Omar Nelson (1893–1981) US general. He was responsible for successful campaigns in North Africa, Sicily, and France during World War II.

1 The way to win an atomic war is to make certain it never starts.

The Observer, 'Sayings of the Week', 20 Apr 1952

2 The wrong war, at the wrong place, at the wrong time, and with the wrong enemy.

Said in evidence to a Senate inquiry, May 1951, over a proposal by MacArthur that the Korean war should be extended into China

Bragg, Melvyn (1939–) British novelist, journalist, and broadcaster. Best known as a presenter of arts programmes on television, he has also written such novels as *A Hired Man* (1969), *Josh Lawton* (1972), and *The Maid of Buttermere* (1987).

1 Patriotism is seen not only as the last refuge of the scoundrel but as the first bolt-hole of the hypocrite.

Speak for England, Introduction

2 On the whole, despite pollution, resource recklessness and waste, I'm glad of the boom. I'm glad that people I know can move out of two-roomed damp gardenless slums into three-bedroomed council houses with bathrooms and lawns . . . I'm glad that the sons are six inches taller than their fathers and that *their* sons show signs even of overtopping them.

Speak for England, Ch. 5

Brahms, Johannes (1833–97) German composer, who worked in Vienna after 1863. A musical conservative, his works include four symphonies, two piano concertos, and *A German Requiem* (1868).

1 If there is anyone here whom I have not insulted, I beg his pardon.

Said on leaving a gathering of friends
Brahms (P. Latham)

2 A master is dead. Today we sing no more.

Stopping a choral rehearsal on hearing of the death of Wagner
Brahms (P. Latham)

Braine, John (1922–86) British novelist. His novel *Room at the Top* (1957) and its sequel *Life at the Top* (1962), depicting the rise of the working-class hero Joe Lampton, earned him a place as one of the 'Angry Young Men' of the 1950s.

1 Room at the Top.

From Daniel Webster's remark 'There is always room at the top'
Book title

2 Time, like a loan from the bank, is something you're only given when you possess so much that you don't need it.

Room at the Top, Ch. 15

3 Today I was driving a little more slowly because of the rain, but that was the only difference between yesterday and today.
My wife had been unfaithful to me but there was still the same number of traffic lights to obey . . . I should still have to take the turning to the left past the Christadelphian Chapel.

Life at the Top, Ch. 16

Bramah, Ernest (1868–1942) British writer. He is best known for the adventures of his blind detective Max Carrados.

1 One cannot live for ever by ignoring the price of coffins.

Kai Lung Unrolls His Mat

2 Although there exist many thousand subjects for elegant conversation, there are persons who cannot meet a cripple without talking about feet.

The Wallet of Kai Lung

Brancusi, Constantin (1876–1957) Romanian sculptor.

1 Nothing grows well in the shade of a big tree.

Refusing Rodin's invitation to work in his studio
Compton's Encyclopedia

Brando, Marlon (1924–) US film star. Originally a 'method' actor, he made many successful films, including *A Streetcar Named Desire* (1951), *On the Waterfront* (1954), and *The Godfather* (1972).

1 Acting is the expression of a neurotic impulse. It's a bum's life. Quitting acting, that's the sign of maturity.

Halliwell's Filmgoer's and Video Viewer's Companion

2 I'm not interested in making an assessment of myself and stripping myself for the general public to view.

Halliwell's Filmgoer's and Video Viewer's Companion

3 An actor's a guy who, if you ain't talking about him, ain't listening.

The Observer, 'Sayings of the Year', Jan 1956

Braun, Wernher von (1912–77) German rocket engineer who designed the V-2 rocket that was used to bomb London in World War II. After the war he was taken to the USA, where he worked on US space rockets.

1 Everything in space obeys the laws of physics. If you know these laws and obey them, space will treat you kindly. And don't tell me that man doesn't belong out there. Man belongs wherever he wants to go; and he'll do plenty well when he gets there.

Time, 17 Feb 1958

2 It was very successful, but it fell on the wrong planet.

Referring to the first V2 rocket to hit London during World War II
Attrib.

Brecht, Bertolt (1898–1956) German dramatist and poet. A Marxist, he lived in exile from 1933 to 1949. His best-known works are *The Threepenny Opera* (1928), in collaboration with Kurt Weil, *Mother Courage* (1941), and *The Caucasian Chalk Circle* (1949).

1 Those who have had no share in the good fortunes of the mighty often have a share in their misfortunes.

The Caucasian Chalk Circle

2 ANDREA. Unhappy the land that has no heroes.
GALILEO. No, unhappy the land that needs heroes.

Galileo, 13

3 What they could do with round here is a good war.

Mother Courage, I

4 When he told men to love their neighbour, their bellies were full. Nowadays things are different.
Mother Courage, II

5 I don't trust him. We're friends.
Mother Courage, III

6 The finest plans have always been spoiled by the littleness of those that should carry them out. Even emperors can't do it all by themselves.
Mother Courage, VI

7 A war of which we could say it left nothing to be desired will probably never exist.
Mother Courage, VI

8 What happens to the hole when the cheese is gone?
Mother Courage, VI

9 War is like love, it always finds a way.
Mother Courage, VI

10 Don't tell me peace has broken out.
Mother Courage, VIII

11 The wickedness of the world is so great you have to run your legs off to avoid having them stolen from under you.
The Threepenny Opera, I:3

Brenan, Gerald (Edward Fitzgerald Brenan; 1894–1987) British writer. His works include *The Face of Spain* (1950), *A Holiday by the Sea* (1961), and *Thoughts in a Dry Season* (1978).

1 When we attend the funerals of our friends we grieve for them, but when we go to those of other people it is chiefly our own deaths that we mourn for.
Thoughts in a Dry Season, 'Death'

2 Intellectuals are people who believe that ideas are of more importance than values. That is to say, their own ideas and other people's values.
Thoughts in a Dry Season, 'Life'

3 Old age takes away from us what we have inherited and gives us what we have earned.
Thoughts in a Dry Season, 'Life'

4 The cliché is dead poetry. English, being the language of an imaginative race, abounds in clichés, so that English literature is always in danger of being poisoned by its own secretions.
Thoughts in a Dry Season, 'Literature'

5 Miller is not really a writer but a non-stop talker to whom someone has given a typewriter.
Referring to Henry Miller
Thoughts in a Dry Season, 'Literature'

6 Poets and painters are outside the class system, or rather they constitute a special class of their own, like the circus people and the gipsies.
Thoughts in a Dry Season, 'Writing'

7 We confess our bad qualities to others out of fear of appearing naive or ridiculous by not being aware of them.
Thoughts in a Dry Season

Bridges, Robert Seymour (1844–1930) British poet and physician. He gave up medicine in 1882 and published several verse collections as well as an edition of the verse of his friend, Gerard Manley Hopkins. His own books include *Eros and Psyche* (1885), *The Spirit of Man* (1916), and *The Testament of Beauty* (1926). He was poet laureate from 1913.

1 For beauty being the best of all we know
Sums up the unsearchable and secret aims
Of nature.
The Growth of Love

2 Beauty sat with me all the summer day,
Awaiting the sure triumph of her eye;
Nor mark'd I till we parted, how, hard by,
Love in her train stood ready for his prey.
The Growth of Love

3 The day begins to droop, –
Its course is done:
But nothing tells the place
Of the setting sun.
Winter Nightfall

Brien, Alan (1925–) British critic and journalist. Books include *Domes of Fortune* (1979) and various collections of his articles.

1 I have done almost every human activity inside a taxi which does not require main drainage.
Punch, 5 July 1972

Bright, John (1811–89) British radical politician and orator. With Richard Cobden he campaigned successfully for the abolition of the Corn Laws.

1 The Angel of Death has been abroad throughout the land: you may almost hear the beating of his wings.
Referring to the Crimean War
Speech, House of Commons, 23 Feb 1855

2 England is the mother of parliaments.
Speech, Birmingham, 18 Jan 1865

3 Force is not a remedy.
Speech, Birmingham, 16 Nov 1880

4 And he adores his maker.
Comment when informed that Disraeli should be admired for being a self-made man
Attrib.

Brittain, Vera (Mary) (1893–1970) British writer and feminist. Her best-known book, *Testament of Youth* (1933), relates her experiences as an army nurse in World War I.

1 It is probably true to say that the largest scope for change still lies in men's attitude to women, and in women's attitude to themselves.
Lady into Woman, Ch. 15

2 The idea that it is necessary to go to a university in order to become a successful writer, or even a man or woman of letters (which is by no means the same thing), is one of those phantasies that surround authorship.
On Being an Author, Ch. 2

3 Politics are usually the executive expression of human immaturity.

The Rebel Passion

Bronowski, Jacob (1908–74) British scientist and writer, born in Poland. His television series *The Ascent of Man* (1973) was highly successful. His critical works on William Blake are also well-known.

1 Every animal leaves traces of what it was; man alone leaves traces of what he created.

The Ascent of Man, Ch. 1

2 That is the essence of science: ask an impertinent question, and you are on the way to the pertinent answer.

The Ascent of Man, Ch. 4

3 Physics becomes in those years the greatest collective work of science – no, more than that, the great collective work of art of the twentieth century.

Referring to the period around the turn of the century marked by the elucidation of atomic structure and the development of the quantum theory
The Ascent of Man, Ch. 10

4 The wish to hurt, the momentary intoxication with pain, is the loophole through which the pervert climbs into the minds of ordinary men.

The Face of Violence, Ch. 5

5 The world is made of people who never quite get into the first team and who just miss the prizes at the flower show.

The Face of Violence, Ch. 6

Brontë, Anne (1820–49) British novelist and poet. She was the younger sister of Charlotte and Emily; her first novel was published under the pseudonym Acton Bell. She wrote *Agnes Grey* (1847) and *The Tenant of Wildfell Hall* (1848).

1 Well, but you affirm that virtue is only elicited by temptation; – and you think that a woman cannot be too little exposed to temptation, or too little acquainted with vice, or anything connected therewith. It must be either that you think she is essentially so vicious, or so feeble-minded, that she cannot withstand temptation.

The Tenant of Wildfell Hall, Ch. 3

2 What is it that constitutes virtue, Mrs. Graham? Is it the circumstance of being able and willing to resist temptation; or that of having no temptations to resist.

The Tenant of Wildfell Hall, Ch. 3

3 Keep a guard over your eyes and ears as the inlets of your heart, and over your lips as the outlet, lest they betray you in a moment of unwariness.

The Tenant of Wildfell Hall, Ch. 16

Brontë, (Patrick) Branwell (1817–48) British artist, brother of Anne, Charlotte, and Emily. His alcoholism and addiction to opium caused much suffering to his family.

1 I shall never be able to realise the too sanguine hopes of my friends, for at twenty-eight I am a thoroughly *old man* – mentally and bodily. Far more so, indeed, than I am willing to express.

Letter to Joseph Leyland, 24 Jan 1847

Brontë, Charlotte (1816–55) British novelist. She was the elder sister of Emily and Anne; her first works were published under the pseudonym Currer Bell. Her novels include *Jane Eyre* (1847), *Shirley* (1849), and *Villette* (1853).

1 I grant an ugly *woman* is a blot on the fair face of creation; but as to the *gentlemen*, let them be solicitous to possess only strength and valour: let their motto be: – Hunt, shoot, and fight: the rest is not worth a fillip.

Jane Eyre, Ch. 17

2 The soul fortunately, has an interpreter – often an unconscious, but still a truthful interpreter – in the eye.

Jane Eyre, Ch. 28

3 Reader, I married him.

Jane Eyre, Ch. 38

4 An abundant shower of curates has fallen upon the north of England.

Shirley, Ch. 1

Brontë, Emily (Jane) (1818–48) British novelist and poet. She was the sister of Anne and Charlotte; her first works were published under the pseudonym Ellis Bell. Her romantic novel *Wuthering Heights* (1847) was published one year before her death from tuberculosis.

1 No coward soul is mine,
No trembler in the world's storm-troubled sphere:
I see Heaven's glories shine,
And faith shines equal, arming me from fear.

Last Lines

2 Vain are the thousand creeds
That move men's hearts: unutterably vain;
Worthless as wither'd weeds.

Last Lines

3 O! dreadful is the check – intense the agony –
When the ear begins to hear, and the eye begins to see;
When the pulse begins to throb – the brain to think again –
The soul to feel the flesh, and the flesh to feel the chain.

The Prisoner

4 Once drinking deep of that divinest anguish,
How could I seek the empty world again?

Remembrance

Brooke, Rupert (Chawner) (1887–1915) British poet, who became a national hero after the publication of his war poems *1914 and Other Poems* (1915). He died of blood poisoning in the Aegean before seeing action.

1 For England's the one land, I know,
   Where men with Splendid Hearts may go;
   And Cambridgeshire, of all England,
   The shire for Men who Understand.
   The Old Vicarage, Grantchester

2 Just now the lilac is in bloom
   All before my little room.
   The Old Vicarage, Grantchester

3 Unkempt about those hedges blows
   An unofficial English rose.
   The Old Vicarage, Grantchester

4 Stands the Church clock at ten to three?
   And is there honey still for tea?
   The Old Vicarage, Grantchester

5 War knows no power. Safe shall be my going,
   Secretly armed against all death's endeavour;
   Safe though all safety's lost; safe where men fall;
   And if these poor limbs die, safest of all.
   Safety

6 If I should die, think only this of me:
   That there's some corner of a foreign field
   That is forever England.
   The Soldier

Brookner, Anita (1938–) British novelist and art historian. Her novels include *Hotel du Lac* (1984), *Family and Friends* (1985), *Friends from England* (1987), and *Latecomers* (1988).

1 Young women have a duty to flirt, to engage in heartless and pointless stratagems, to laugh, pretend, tease, have moods, enslave and discard. The purpose of these manoeuvres is to occupy their time, the time that women of later generations are to give to their careers.
   Family and Friends, Ch. 1

2 In real life, of course, it is the hare who wins. Every time. Look around you. And in any case it is my contention that Aesop was writing for the tortoise market . . . Hares have no time to read. They are too busy winning the game.
   Hotel du Lac

3 It was clear that wealth had rendered her helpless.
   A Misalliance, Ch. 9

Brooks, Mel (Melvyn Kaminsky; 1926–) US film actor and director. His films include *The Producers* (1968), *Blazing Saddles* (1974), and *High Anxiety* (1977).

1 When I write, I keep Tolstoy around because I want great limits. I want big thinking.
   Halliwell's Filmgoer's and Video Viewer's Companion

2 That's it, baby, if you've got it, flaunt it.
   The Producers

3 Tragedy is if I cut my finger. Comedy is if I walk into an open sewer and die.
   New Yorker, 30 Oct 1978

Brooks, Phillips (1835–93) US Episcopal bishop and evangelist. His books include *New Starts in Life* (1896) and he wrote the hymn *O Little Town of Bethlehem*.

1 O little town of Bethlehem,
   How still we see thee lie;
   Above thy deep and dreamless sleep
   The silent stars go by.
   O Little Town of Bethlehem

Brougham, Henry Peter, Baron (1778–1868) Scottish lawyer and politician. He advocated the abolition of slavery and defended Queen Caroline at her trial (1820). He was also a founder of London University and the designer of the horse-drawn carriage that bears his name.

1 The great Unwashed.
   Attrib.

Brown, Thomas (1663–1704) English satirist and translator; author of numerous lampoons and epigrams.

1 I do not love thee, Doctor Fell,
   The reason why I cannot tell;
   But this alone I know full well,
   I do not love thee, Doctor Fell.
   Translation of Martial's *Epigrams*

Brown, Thomas Edward (1830–97) British poet. Born in the Isle of Man, he produced a number of works in the Manx dialect, notably *Foc's'le Yarns* (1881).

1 A rich man's joke is always funny.
   The Doctor

2 A garden is a lovesome thing, God wot!
   My Garden

Browne, Charles Farrar *See* Ward, Artemus.

Browne, Sir Thomas (1605–82) English physician and writer. The reflective *Religio Medici* (1642), not originally intended for publication, established his reputation as a writer. Later works included *Pseudodoxia Epidemia* (1646).

1 He who discommendeth others obliquely commendeth himself.
   Christian Morals, Pt. I

2 They do most by Books, who could do much without them, and he that chiefly owes himself unto himself, is the substantial Man.
   Christian Morals, Pt. II

3 All things are artificial, for nature is the art of God.
   Religio Medici, Pt. I

4 Thus the devil played at chess with me, and yielding a pawn, thought to gain a queen of me, taking advantage of my honest endeavours.
   Religio Medici, Pt. I

5 For my part, I have ever believed, and do now know, that there are witches.
   Religio Medici, Pt. I

6 It is the common wonder of all men, how among so many million of faces, there should be none alike.
   Religio Medici, Pt. II

7 No man can justly censure or condemn another, because indeed no man truly knows another.

Religio Medici, Pt. II

8 Charity begins at home, is the voice of the world.

Religio Medici, Pt. II

9 Lord, deliver me from myself.

Religio Medici, Pt. II

10 For the world, I count it not an inn, but an hospital, and a place, not to live, but to die in.

Religio Medici, Pt. II

11 There is surely a piece of divinity in us, something that was before the elements, and owes no homage unto the sun.

Religio Medici, Pt. II

12 Man is a noble animal, splendid in ashes, and pompous in the grave.

Urn Burial, Ch. 5

Browning, Elizabeth Barrett (1806–61) British poet. A semi-invalid, she married the poet Robert Browning in 1846 and lived with him in Italy. Her books include *Sonnets from the Portuguese* (1850), *Aurora Leigh* (1856), and *Poems Before Congress* (1860).

1 Since when was genius found respectable?

Aurora Leigh, Bk. VI

2 Do you hear the children weeping, O my brothers,
Ere the sorrow comes with years?

The Cry of the Children

3 God's gifts put man's best gifts to shame.

Sonnets from the Portuguese, XXVI

4 I love thee with a love I seemed to lose
With my lost saints – I love thee with the breath,
Smiles, tears, of all my life! – and, if God choose,
I shall but love thee better after death.

Sonnets from the Portuguese, XLIII

Browning, Robert (1812–89) British poet. *Men and Women* (1855), *Dramatis Personae* (1864), and *The Ring and the Book* (1868–69), were written after his marriage to the poet Elizabeth Barrett, with whom he eloped to Italy in 1846.

Quotations about Browning

1 Browning used words with the violence of a horse-breaker, giving out the scent of a he-goat. But he got them to do their work.

Ford Madox Ford (1873–1939) British novelist. *The March of Literature*

2 He might have passed for a politician, or a financier, or a diplomatist or, indeed, for anything but a poet.

George William Russell (1867–1965) Irish poet and dramatist. *Portraits of the Seventies*

Quotations by Browning

3 So free we seem, so fettered fast we are!

Andrea del Sarto

4 Ah, but a man's reach should exceed his grasp,
Or what's a heaven for?

Andrea del Sarto

5 Why need the other women know so much?

Any Wife to any Husband

6 My sun sets to rise again.

At the 'Mermaid'

7 Best be yourself, imperial, plain and true!

Bishop Blougram's Apology

8 We mortals cross the ocean of this world
Each in his average cabin of a life.

Bishop Blougram's Apology

9 Just when we are safest, there's a sunset-touch,
A fancy from a flower-bell, some one's death,
A chorus-ending from Euripides, –
And that's enough for fifty hopes and fears
As old and new at once as Nature's self,
To rap and knock and enter in our soul.

Bishop Blougram's Apology

10 The grand Perhaps!

Bishop Blougram's Apology

11 All we have gained then by our unbelief
Is a life of doubt diversified by faith,
For one of faith diversified by doubt:
We called the chess-board white, – we call it black.

Bishop Blougram's Apology

12 No, when the fight begins within himself,
A man's worth something.

Bishop Blougram's Apology

13 He said true things, but called them by wrong names.

Bishop Blougram's Apology

14 'Tis the Last Judgment's fire must cure this place,
Calcine its clods and set my prisoners free.

Childe Roland to the Dark Tower Came, XI

15 As for the grass, it grew as scant as hair
In leprosy.

Childe Roland to the Dark Tower Came, XIII

16 I never saw a brute I hated so;
He must be wicked to deserve such pain.

Childe Roland to the Dark Tower Came, XIV

17 Dauntless the slug-horn to my lips I set,
And blew. *Childe Roland to the Dark Tower came.*

Childe Roland to the Dark Tower Came, XXXIV

18 Though Rome's gross yoke
Drops off, no more to be endured,
Her teaching is not so obscured
By errors and perversities,
That no truth shines athwart the lies.
Christmas Eve, XI

19 Such ever was love's way; to rise, it stoops.
A Death in the Desert

20 For I say, this is death, and the sole death,
When a man's loss comes to him from his gain,
Darkness from light, from knowledge ignorance,
And lack of love from love made manifest.
A Death in the Desert

21 Man partly is and wholly hopes to be.
A Death in the Desert

22 How very hard it is
To be a Christian!
Easter-Day, I

23 At last awake
From life, that insane dream we take
For waking now.
Easter-Day, XIV

24 No, at noonday in the bustle of man's worktime
Greet the unseen with a cheer!
Epilogue to Asolando

25 Oh, to be in England
Now that April's there.
Home Thoughts from Abroad

26 And after April, when May follows,
And the whitethroat builds, and all the swallows!
Home Thoughts from Abroad

27 That's the wise thrush; he sings each song twice over,
Lest you should think he never could recapture
The first fine careless rapture!
Home Thoughts from Abroad

28 I sprang to the stirrup, and Joris, and he;
I galloped, Dirck galloped, we galloped all three.
How they brought the Good News from Ghent to Aix

29 Oh, good gigantic smile o' the brown old earth.
James Lee's Wife, VII

30 And, Robert Browning, you writer of plays,
Here's a subject made to your hand!
A Light Woman, XIV

31 Just for a handful of silver he left us,
Just for a riband to stick in his coat.
The Lost Leader

32 Blot out his name, then, record one lost soul more,
One task more declined, one more footpath untrod,
One more devils'-triumph and sorrow for angels,
One wrong more to man, one more insult to God!
The Lost Leader

33 Then let him receive the new knowledge and wait us,
Pardoned in heaven, the first by the throne!
The Lost Leader

34 Where the quiet-coloured end of evening smiles,
Miles and miles.
Love among the Ruins, I

35 She had
A heart – how shall I say? – too soon made glad,
Too easily impressed.
My Last Duchess

36 Never the time and the place
And the loved one all together!
Never the Time and the Place

37 What's come to perfection perishes.
Things learned on earth, we shall practise in heaven.
Works done least rapidly, Art most cherishes.
Old Pictures in Florence, XVII

38 There remaineth a rest for the people of God:
And I have had troubles enough, for one.
Old Pictures in Florence, XVII

39 Suddenly, as rare things will, it vanished.
One Word More, IV

40 God be thanked, the meanest of his creatures
Boasts two soul-sides, one to face the world with,
One to show a woman when he loves her!
One Word More, XVII

41 Hamelin Town's in Brunswick,
By famous Hanover city;
The river Weser, deep and wide,
Washes its wall on the southern side;
A pleasanter spot you never spied.
The Pied Piper of Hamelin

42 Rats!
They fought the dogs and killed the cats,
And bit the babies in the cradles.
The Pied Piper of Hamelin

43 And the muttering grew to a grumbling;
And the grumbling grew to a mighty rumbling;
And out of the houses the rats came tumbling.
The Pied Piper of Hamelin

44 'You threaten us, fellow? Do your worst,
Blow your pipe there till you burst!'
The Pied Piper of Hamelin

45 The year's at the spring,
And day's at the morn;
Morning's at seven;
The hill-side's dew-pearled;
The lark's on the wing;
The snail's on the thorn;
God's in His heaven –
All's right with the world.
Pippa Passes, Pt. I

46 A king lived long ago,
In the morning of the world,
When earth was nigher heaven than now.
Pippa Passes, Pt. I

47 Such grace had kings when the world begun!
Pippa Passes, Pt. I

48 All service ranks the same with God –
With God, whose puppets, best and worst,
Are we: there is no last or first.
Pippa Passes, Pt. I

49 Therefore I summon age
To grant youth's heritage.
Rabbi ben Ezra, XIII

50 How good is man's life, the mere living! how fit
to employ
All the heart and the soul and the senses for
ever in joy!
Saul, IX

51 Leave the flesh to the fate it was fit for! the spirit be thine!
Saul, XIII

52 Gr-r-r- there go, my heart's abhorrence!
Water your damned flower-pots, do!
Soliloquy of the Spanish Cloister

53 I the Trinity illustrate,
Drinking watered orange-pulp –
In three sips the Arian frustrate;
While he drains his at one gulp.
Soliloquy of the Spanish Cloister

54 There's a great text in Galatians,
Once you trip on it, entails
Twenty-nine distinct damnations,
One sure, if another fails.
Soliloquy of the Spanish Cloister

55 My scrofulous French novel
On grey paper with blunt type!
Soliloquy of the Spanish Cloister

56 She looked at him, as one who awakes:
The past was a sleep, and her life began.
The Statue and the Bust

57 What of soul was left, I wonder, when the kissing had to stop?
A Toccata of Galuppi's

58 What's become of Waring
Since he gave us all the slip?
Waring

Bruce, Lenny (1925–66) US comedian.

1 Every day people are straying away from the church and going back to God. Really.
The Essential Lenny Bruce (ed. J. Cohen), 'Religions Inc.'

2 It was just one of those parties which got out of hand.
Referring to the Crucifixion
The Guardian, 10 May 1979

Brummel, 'Beau' (George Bryan Brummell; 1778–1840)
British dandy and friend of George IV.

1 Who's your fat friend?
Referring to George, Prince of Wales
Reminiscences (Gronow)

Bruno, Giordano (1548–1600) Italian philosopher. A Dominican, his determination to discuss philosophical views, regardless of their religious orthodoxy, eventually caused his execution for heresy.

1 Perhaps your fear in passing judgement is greater than mine in receiving it.
Said to the cardinals who excommunicated him, 8 Feb 1600
Attrib.

Buchan, John, 1st Baron Tweedsmuir (1875–1940)
British novelist and diplomat. His adventure stories include *Prester John* (1910) and *The Thirty Nine Steps* (1915), filmed by Hitchcock in 1935. He became governor-general of Canada in 1935.

1 Presently a girl came on the stage and danced, a silly affair, all a clashing of tambourines and wriggling.
Greenmantle, Ch. 11

2 I'm afraid I was not free from bitterness myself on that subject. I said things about my own country that I sometimes wake in the night and sweat to think of.
Greenmantle, Ch. 13

3 In this plain story of mine there will be so many wild doings ere the end is reached, that I beg my reader's assent to a prosaic digression.
Prester John, Ch. 2

Buchanan, Robert Williams (1841–1901) British poet, novelist, and dramatist, famous for his criticism of the Pre-Raphaelites.

1 She just wore
Enough for modesty – no more.
White Rose and Red, I

2 The Fleshly School of Poetry.
Referring to Swinburne, William Morris, D. G. Rossetti, etc.
Title of article in the *Contemporary Review*, Oct 1871

Buck, Pearl S(ydenstricker) (1892–1973) US novelist. Winner of the Nobel Prize in 1938, her novels include *The Good Earth* (1931) and *The Three Daughters of Madame Liang* (1969).

1 Euthanasia is a long, smooth-sounding word, and it conceals its danger as long, smooth words do, but the danger is there, nevertheless.
The Child Who Never Grew, Ch. 2

2 Nothing and no one can destroy the Chinese people. They are relentless survivors. They are the oldest civilized people on earth. Their civilization passes through phases but its basic characteristics remain the same. They yield, they bend to the wind, but they never break.
China, Past and Present, Ch. 1

3 Ah well, perhaps one has to be very old before one learns how to be amused rather than shocked.
China, Past and Present, Ch. 6

4 No one really understood music unless he was a scientist, her father had declared, and not just a scientist, either, oh, no, only the real ones, the theoreticians, whose language was mathematics.
The Goddess Abides, Pt. I

5 It is better to be first with an ugly woman than the hundredth with a beauty.
The Good Earth, Ch. 1

6 I feel no need for any other faith than my faith in human beings.
I Believe

Buckingham, George Villiers, 2nd Duke of
(1628–87) English politician; a member of the Cabal. He also wrote poetry and satirical works, notably the comedy *The Rehearsal* (1671).

1 Ay, now the plot thickens very much upon us.
The Rehearsal, III:1

2 The world is made up for the most part of fools and knaves.
To Mr Clifford, on his Humane Reason

Buddha (Gautama Siddhartha; c. 563–c. 483 BC) Indian prince, who at the age of about 20 renounced his family and his rich indolent life to search for enlightenment, which he traditionally achieved beneath a banyan tree. The rest of his life was spent teaching his findings and formulating the principles of Buddhism.

1 All things, oh priests, are on fire . . . The eye is on fire; forms are on fire; eye-consciousness is on fire; impressions received by the eye are on fire.
The Fire Sermon

2 I have never yet met with anything that was dearer to anyone than his own self. Since to others, to each one for himself, the self is dear, therefore let him who desires his own advantage not harm another.
Buddhism (Edward Conze)

3 I do not fight with the world but the world fights with me.
Buddhism (Edward Conze)

4 This Aryan Eightfold Path, that is to say: Right view, right aim, right speech, right action, right living, right effort, right mindfulness, right contemplation.
Some Sayings of the Buddha (F. L. Woodward)

5 Ye must leave righteous ways behind, not to speak of unrighteous ways.
Some Sayings of the Buddha (F. L. Woodward)

Buffon, Georges-Louis Leclerc, Comte de (1707–88) French naturalist. In his monumental *Histoire naturelle* (1749–89), he formulated an early theory of evolution.

1 Style is the man himself.
Discours sur le style

Buller, Arthur Henry Reginald (1874–1944) British botanist and mycologist, who worked at the Royal Botanic Gardens, Kew.

1 There was a young lady named Bright,
Whose speed was far faster than light;
She set out one day
In a relative way,
And returned home the previous night.
Limerick

Bullock, Alan, Baron (1914–) British academic and historian. His books include *Hitler, A Study in Tyranny* (1952), *The Liberal Tradition* (1956), and *The Life and Times of Ernest Bevin* (1960–83).

1 The people Hitler never understood, and whose actions continued to exasperate him to the end of his life, were the British.
Hitler, A Study in Tyranny, Ch. 8

2 Hitler showed surprising loyalty to Mussolini, but it never extended to trusting him.
Hitler, A Study in Tyranny, Ch. 11

Bulmer-Thomas, Ivor (1905–) British writer and politician. His books include *The Socialist Tragedy* (1949) and *The Growth of the British Party System* (1965).

1 If ever he went to school without any boots it was because he was too big for them.
Referring to Harold Wilson
Remark, Conservative Party Conference, 1949

Bulwer-Lytton, Edward George Earle, 1st Baron Lytton (1803–73) British novelist and politician, who served in parliament first as a Liberal member, then as a Tory. He wrote many historical novels, including *The Last Days of Pompeii* (1834).

1 Beneath the rule of men entirely great,
The pen is mightier than the sword.
Richelieu, II:2

2 Nothing is so contagious as enthusiasm. It is the real allegory of the tale of Orpheus; it moves stones and charms brutes. It is the genius of sincerity and truth accomplishes no victories without it.
Dale Carnegie's Scrapbook (Dale Carnegie)

Buñuel, Luis (1900–83) Spanish film director, who made his name with the surrealist *Un Chien andalou* (1928) and *L'Âge d'or* (1930). Many of his later films were produced in Mexico, where he settled in 1947.

1 I am an atheist still, thank God.
Luis Buñuel: an Introduction (Ado Kyrou)

Bunyan, John (1628–88) English writer and preacher. During imprisonment for illegal preaching (1660–72) he wrote the autobiographical *Grace Abounding* (1666) and began work on his allegory *The Pilgrim's Progress* (1684).

1 As I walked through the wilderness of this world.
The Pilgrim's Progress, Pt. I

2 The name of the slough was Despond.
The Pilgrim's Progress, Pt. I

3 The gentleman's name that met him was Mr Worldly Wiseman.
The Pilgrim's Progress, Pt. I

4 A very stately palace before him, the name of which was Beautiful.
The Pilgrim's Progress, Pt. I

5 It beareth the name of Vanity Fair, because the town where 'tis kept is lighter than vanity.
The Pilgrim's Progress, Pt. I

6 So soon as the man overtook me, he was but a word and a blow.
The Pilgrim's Progress, Pt. I

7 A castle called Doubting Castle, the owner whereof was Giant Despair.
The Pilgrim's Progress, Pt. I

8 So I awoke, and behold it was a dream.
The Pilgrim's Progress, Pt. I

9 One Great-heart.
The Pilgrim's Progress, Pt. II

10 He that is down needs fear no fall;
He that is low, no pride.
The Pilgrim's Progress, 'Shepherd Boy's Song'

Burgess, Anthony (John Burgess Wilson; 1917–   ) British novelist and critic. His books include *A Clockwork Orange* (1962), *Earthly Powers* (1980), and *Any Old Iron* (1989).

1 Not a future. At least not in Europe. America's different, of course, but America's really only a kind of Russia. You've no idea how pleasant it is not to have any future. It's like having a totally efficient contraceptive.
Honey for the Bears, Pt. II, Ch. 6

2 Laugh and the world laughs with you; snore and you sleep alone.
Inside Mr. Enderby

3 Bath twice a day to be really clean, once a day to be passably clean, once a week to avoid being a public menace.
Mr Enderby, Pt. I, Ch. 2

4 Rome's just a city like anywhere else. A vastly overrated city, I'd say. It trades on belief just as Stratford trades on Shakespeare.
Mr Enderby, Pt. II, Ch. 2

5 The possession of a book becomes a substitute for reading it.
New York Times Book Review

6 Without class differences, England would cease to be the living theatre it is.
The Observer, 'Sayings of the Week', 26 May 1985

Burke, Edmund (1729–97) British politician and political philosopher. He entered parliament as a Whig in 1765. In *Reflections on the Revolution in France* (1790) he condemned the French Revolution.

Quotations about Burke

1 Burke was a damned wrong-headed fellow, through his whole life jealous and obstinate.
Charles James Fox (1749–1806) British Whig politician. Attrib.

2 If a man were to go by chance at the same time with Burke under a shed, to shun a shower, he would say – 'this is an extraordinary man.'
Samuel Johnson (1709–84) British lexicographer. *Life of Johnson* (J. Boswell), Vol. IV

Quotations by Burke

3 Example is the school of mankind, and they will learn at no other.
Letters on a Regicide Peace, letter 1

4 The only infallible criterion of wisdom to vulgar minds – success.
Letter to a Member of the National Assembly

5 There is, however, a limit at which forbearance ceases to be a virtue.
Observations on a Publication, 'The Present State of the Nation'

6 I am convinced that we have a degree of delight, and that no small one, in the real misfortunes and pains of others.
On the Sublime and Beautiful, Pt. I

7 Beauty in distress is much the most affecting beauty.
On the Sublime and Beautiful, Pt. III

8 Vice itself lost half its evil, by losing all its grossness.
Reflections on the Revolution in France

9 But the age of chivalry is gone. That of sophisters, economists, and calculators, has succeeded; and the glory of Europe is extinguished for ever.
Reflections on the Revolution in France

10 That chastity of honour, that felt a stain like a wound.
Reflections on the Revolution in France

11 Man is by his constitution a religious animal.
Reflections on the Revolution in France

12 Superstition is the religion of feeble minds.
Reflections on the Revolution in France

13 The concessions of the weak are the concessions of fear.
Speech on Conciliation with America (House of Commons, 22 Mar 1775)

14 All government, indeed every human benefit and enjoyment, every virtue, and every prudent act, is founded on compromise and barter.
Speech on Conciliation with America (House of Commons, 22 Mar 1775)

15 The use of force alone is but *temporary*. It may subdue for a moment; but it does not remove the necessity of subduing again: and a nation is not governed, which is perpetually to be conquered.
Speech on Conciliation with America (House of Commons, 22 Mar 1775)

16 I do not know the method of drawing up an in-
dictment against an whole people.
Speech on Conciliation with America (House of Commons, 22
Mar 1775)

17 Kings are naturally lovers of low company.
Speech on the Economical Reform (House of Commons, 11 Feb
1780)

18 The people are the masters.
Speech on the Economical Reform (House of Commons, 11 Feb
1780)

19 And having looked to government for bread, on
the very first scarcity they will turn and bite
the hand that fed them.
Thoughts and Details on Scarcity

20 When bad men combine, the good must associate; else they will fall one by one, an unpitied
sacrifice in a contemptible struggle.
Thoughts on the Cause of the Present Discontents

21 Liberty, too, must be limited in order to be
possessed.
Letter to the Sheriffs of Bristol, 1777

22 Among a people generally corrupt, liberty cannot
long exist.
Letter to the Sheriffs of Bristol, 1777

23 Nothing is so fatal to religion as indifference,
which is, at least, half infidelity.
Letter to William Smith, 29 Jan 1795

24 Somebody has said, that a king may make a nobleman, but he cannot make a gentleman.
Letter to William Smith, 29 Jan 1795

25 The greater the power, the more dangerous the
abuse.
Speech, House of Commons, 7 Feb 1771

26 Your representative owes you, not his industry
only, but his judgement; and he betrays instead
of serving you if he sacrifices it to your
opinion.
Speech to the electors of Bristol, 3 Nov 1774

27 He was not merely a chip off the old block, but
the old block itself.
Referring to William Pitt the Younger's first speech in the House
of Commons, 26 Feb 1781
Remark

28 A thing may look specious in theory, and yet be
ruinous in practice; a thing may look evil in theory, and yet be in practice excellent.
Impeachment of Warren Hastings, 19 Feb 1788

29 Dangers by being despised grow great.
Speech, House of Commons, 11 May 1792

Burke, Johnny (1908–64) US songwriter.

1 Don't you know each cloud contains
Pennies from Heaven?
Pennies from Heaven

Burnet, Gilbert (1643–1715) English bishop and historian,
born in Scotland. He was appointed Bishop of Salisbury in 1689.
His autobiographical *History of His Own Times* was published
posthumously.

1 He had said that he had known many kicked
downstairs, but he never knew any kicked upstairs before.
Recalling Halifax's observation
Original Memoirs

Burney, Fanny (Frances Burney D'Arblay; 1752–1840)
British novelist. Her novels include *Evelina* (1778), *Camilla*
(1796), and *The Wanderer* (1814). From 1802 to 1812 she lived in
Paris with her French husband, General D'Arblay.

1 Now I am ashamed of confessing that I have
nothing to confess.
Evelina, Letter 59

Burns, George (1896–) US comedian.

1 Too bad all the people who know how to run the
country are busy driving cabs and cutting hair.

Burns, John Elliot (1858–1943) British Labour politician
and trade union leader.

1 I have seen the Mississippi. That is muddy
water. I have seen the St Lawrence. That is
crystal water. But the Thames is liquid history.
Attrib.

Burns, Robert (1759–96) Scottish poet. A farmer's son,
Burns established his reputation with *Poems, Chiefly in the Scottish
Dialect* (1786). He subsequently wrote many songs, notably *Auld
Lang Syne*, and the narrative poem *Tam o' Shanter*, all of which
made him the national poet of Scotland.

Quotations about Burns

1 The largest soul of all the British lands came
among us in the shape of a hard-handed Scottish
peasant.
Thomas Carlyle (1795–1881) Scottish historian and poet. *On
Heroes, Hero-Worship and the Heroic in History*, Lecture V

2 If you can imagine a Scotch commercial traveller
in a Scotch commercial hotel leaning on the bar
and calling the barmaid 'Dearie' then you will
know the keynote of Burns' verse.
A. E. Housman (1859–1936) British scholar and poet. *Electric
Delights* (William Plumer)

Quotations by Burns

3 O Thou! Whatever title suit thee –
Auld Hornie, Satan, Nick, or Clootie.
Address to the Devil

4 Should auld acquaintance be forgot,
And never brought to min'?
Auld Lang Syne

5 We'll tak a cup o' kindness yet,
For auld lang syne.
Auld Lang Syne

6 Gin a body meet a body
Coming through the rye;
Gin a body kiss a body,
Need a body cry?
Coming through the Rye

7 I wasna fou, but just had plenty.
Death and Doctor Hornbrook

8 On ev'ry hand it will allow'd be,
He's just – nae better than he should be.
A Dedication to Gavin Hamilton

9 Here lie Willie Michie's banes;
O Satan, when ye tak him,
Gie him the schoolin' of your weans,
For clever deils he'll mak them!
Epitaph on a Schoolmaster

10 A man's a man for a' that.
For a' that and a' that

11 Green grow the rashes O,
Green grow the rashes O,
The sweetest hours that e'er I spend,
Are spent amang the lasses O!
Green Grow the Rashes

12 John Anderson my jo, John,
When we were first acquent,
Your locks were like the raven,
Your bonnie brow was brent.
John Anderson My Jo

13 Let them cant about decorum
Who have characters to lose.
The Jolly Beggars

14 Man's inhumanity to man
Makes countless thousands mourn!
Man was Made to Mourn

15 My heart's in the Highlands, my heart is not here;
My heart's in the Highlands a-chasing the deer;
Chasing the wild deer, and following the roe,
My heart's in the Highlands, wherever I go.
My Heart's in the Highlands

16 My love is like a red red rose
That's newly sprung in June:
My love is like the melodie
That's sweetly play'd in tune.
A Red, Red Rose

17 Scots, wha hae wi' Wallace bled,
Scots, wham Bruce has aften led,
Welcome to your gory bed,
Or to victorie.
Scots, Wha Hae

18 Liberty's in every blow!
Let us do or die!
Scots, Wha Hae

19 Some hae meat, and canna eat,
And some wad eat that want it,
But we hae meat and we can eat,
And sae the Lord be thankit.
The Selkirk Grace

20 Ah, gentle dames! It gars me greet
To think how mony counsels sweet,
How mony lengthen'd sage advices,
The husband frae the wife despises!
Tam o' Shanter

21 Wee, sleekit, cow'rin', tim'rous beastie,
O what a panic's in thy breastie!
To a Mouse

22 The best laid schemes o' mice an' men
Gang aft a-gley,
An' lea'e us nought but grief an' pain
For promis'd joy.
To a Mouse

23 But yet the light that led astray
Was light from Heaven.
The Vision

24 Ye banks and braes o' bonnie Doon,
How can ye bloom sae fresh and fair?
How can ye chant, ye little birds,
And I sae weary fu' o' care?
Ye Banks and Braes

Burroughs, Edgar Rice (1875–1950) US novelist. He became famous with *Tarzan of the Apes* (1914), which has been the basis of many films.

1 Me Tarzan.
The line 'Me Tarzan, you Jane' comes from the films and does not appear in the books
Tarzan of the Apes

Burton, Richard (Richard Jenkins; 1925–84) British actor, born in Wales. He began his career as an outstanding Shakespearean actor but from the 1950s acted almost exclusively in films, which included *Look Back in Anger* (1959), *Becket* (1964), *Who's Afraid of Virginia Woolf?* (1966), and *1984* (1984). He was married several times, twice to Elizabeth Taylor, with whom he often co-starred.

1 When I played drunks I had to remain sober because I didn't know how to play them when I was drunk.
Halliwell's Filmgoer's and Video Viewer's Companion

2 An actor is something less than a man while an actress is something more than a woman.
Halliwell's Filmgoer's and Video Viewer's Companion

Burton, Robert (1577–1640) English scholar and churchman. He is remembered for *Anatomy of Melancholy* (1621).

1 All my joys to this are folly,
Naught so sweet as Melancholy.
Anatomy of Melancholy, Abstract

2 If there is a hell upon earth, it is to be found in a melancholy man's heart.
Anatomy of Melancholy, Pt. I

3 From this it is clear how much more cruel the pen is than the sword.
Anatomy of Melancholy, Pt. I

4 England is a paradise for women, and hell for horses: Italy a paradise for horses, hell for women.
Anatomy of Melancholy, Pt. III

Bush, George (Herbert Walker) (1924–) US Republican president (1989–).

1 The United States is the best and fairest and most decent nation on the face of the earth.
Speech, May 1988

2 Learning is good in and of itself . . . the mothers of the Jewish ghettoes of the east would pour honey on a book so the children would know that learning is sweet. And the parents who settled hungry Kansas would take their children in from the fields when a teacher came.
Accepting his nomination as presidential candidate
Speech, Republican Party Convention, New Orleans, Aug 1988

3 The Congress will push me to raise taxes and I'll say no, and they'll push, and I'll say no, and they'll push again. And I'll say to them, read my lips, no new taxes.
Often misquoted as 'Watch my lips'
Speech, Republican Party Convention, New Orleans, Aug 1988

4 I will draw a line in the sand.
Speech (1990) referring to US forces defending Saudi Arabia following the Iraq invasion of Kuwait

Bussy-Rabutin (Roger de Rabutin, Comte de Bussy; 1618–93) French soldier and writer. His scandalous *Histoire amoureuse des Gaules* (1665) led to imprisonment and exile.

1 Absence is to love what wind is to fire; it extinguishes the small, it inflames the great.
Histoire amoureuse des Gaules

Butler, Joseph (1692–1752) British churchman. He became Bishop of Durham in 1750. *The Analogy of Religion* (1736) is his best-known work.

1 That which is the foundation of all our hopes and of all our fears; all our hopes and fears which are of any consideration: I mean a Future Life.
The Analogy of Religion, Introduction

Butler, R(ichard) A(usten), Baron (1902–82) British Conservative politician. A successful minister of education and chancellor of the exchequer, he twice failed to become prime minister. *The Art of the Possible* (1971) is his autobiography.

1 Politics is the art of the possible.
Often attrib. to Butler but used earlier by others, including Bismarck
The Art of the Possible, Epigraph

2 Mr Macmillan is the best prime minister we have.
Often quoted in the form above. In fact, Butler simply answered 'Yes' to the question 'Would you say that this is the best prime minister we have?'
Interview, London Airport

Butler, Samuel (1612–80) English satirist, secretary to George Villiers, 2nd Duke of Buckingham. The satirical poem *Hudibras* (1663–78), a mock romance, is his most famous work.

1 When civil fury first grew high,
And men fell out they knew not why.
Hudibras, Pt. I

2 For every why he had a wherefore.
Hudibras, Pt. I

3 To swallow gudgeons ere they're catched,
And count their chickens ere they're hatched.
Hudibras, Pt. II

4 Love is a boy, by poets styl'd,
Then spare the rod, and spoil the child.
Hudibras, Pt. II

5 Through perils both of wind and limb,
Through thick and thin she follow'd him.
Hudibras, Pt. II

6 Oaths are but words, and words but wind.
Hudibras, Pt. II

7 What makes all doctrines plain and clear?
About two hundred pounds a year.
Hudibras, Pt. III

8 He that complies against his will,
Is of his own opinion still.
Hudibras, Pt. III

9 The souls of women are so small,
That some believe they've none at all.
Miscellaneous Thoughts

Butler, Samuel (1835–1902) British writer. *Erewhon*, a satirical novel published anonymously in 1872, established his reputation; subsequent works include the autobiographical *The Way of All Flesh* (1903).

1 Some who had received a liberal education at the Colleges of Unreason, and taken the highest degrees in hypothetics, which are their principal study.
Erewhon, Ch. 9

2 Straighteners, managers and cashiers of the Musical Banks.
Erewhon, Ch. 9

3 While to deny the existence of an unseen kingdom is bad, to pretend that we know more about it than its bare existence is no better.
Erewhon, Ch. 15

4 The wish to spread those opinions that we hold conducive to our own welfare is so deeply rooted in the English character that few of us can escape its influence.
Erewhon, Ch. 20

5 An art can only be learned in the workshop of those who are winning their bread by it.
Erewhon, Ch. 20

6 It has been said that the love of money is the root of all evil. The want of money is so quite as truly.
Erewhon, Ch. 20

7 Spontaneity is only a term for man's ignorance of the gods.
Erewhon, Ch. 25

8 I keep my books at the British Museum and at Mudie's.
The Humour of Homer, 'Ramblings in Cheapside'

9 Life is one long process of getting tired.

Notebooks

10 Life is the art of drawing sufficient conclusions from insufficient premises.

Notebooks

11 All progress is based upon a universal innate desire on the part of every organism to live beyond its income.

Notebooks

12 When a man is in doubt about this or that in his writing, it will often guide him if he asks himself how it will tell a hundred years hence.

Notebooks

13 An apology for the Devil – it must be remembered that we have only heard one side of the case. God has written all the books.

Notebooks

14 God is Love – I dare say. But what a mischievous devil Love is!

Notebooks

15 The public buys its opinions as it buys its meat, or takes in its milk, on the principle that it is cheaper to do this than to keep a cow. So it is, but the milk is more likely to be watered.

Notebooks

16 The healthy stomach is nothing if not conservative. Few radicals have good digestions.

Notebooks

17 Though analogy is often misleading, it is the least misleading thing we have.

Notebooks

18 Some men love truth so much that they seem to be in continual fear lest she should catch a cold on overexposure.

Notebooks

19 Marriage is distinctly and repeatedly excluded from heaven. Is this because it is thought likely to mar the general felicity?

Notebooks

20 Man is the only animal that can remain on friendly terms with the victims he intends to eat until he eats them.

Notebooks

21 To be at all is to be religious more or less.

Notebooks

22 A client is fain to hire a lawyer to keep from the injury of other lawyers – as Christians that travel in Turkey are forced to hire Janissaries, to protect them from the insolencies of other Turks.

Prose Observations

23 Every man's work, whether it be literature or music or pictures or architecture or anything else, is always a portrait of himself.

The Way of All Flesh, Ch. 14

24 That vice pays homage to virtue is notorious; we call it hypocrisy.

The Way of All Flesh, Ch. 19

25 Pleasure after all is a safer guide than either right or duty.

The Way of All Flesh, Ch. 19

26 The advantage of doing one's praising for oneself is that one can lay it on so thick and exactly in the right places.

The Way of All Flesh, Ch. 34

27 'Tis better to have loved and lost than never to have lost at all.

The Way of All Flesh, Ch. 77

28 When you have told anyone you have left him a legacy the only decent thing to do is to die at once.

Samuel Butler: A Memoir (Festing Jones), Vol. 2

29 Brigands demand your money or your life; women require both.

Attrib.

Byrom, John (1692–1763) British poet and hymn writer. His collected poems were published in 1773 and a diary was published in the 19th century.

1 Christians awake, salute the happy morn,
Whereon the Saviour of the world was born.

Hymn for Christmas Day

Byron, George Gordon, 6th Baron (1788–1824) British poet. The melancholy *Childe Harold's Pilgrimage* (1812) brought him to the attention of literary society. After scandalizing London with his sexual exploits he lived abroad, largely in Italy; his later works include the poetic drama *Manfred* (1817) and the epic satire *Don Juan* (1819–24).

Quotations about Byron

1 When Byron's eyes were shut in death,
We bow'd our head and held our breath.
He taught us little: but our soul
Had *felt* him like the thunder's roll.

Matthew Arnold (1822–88) British poet and critic. *Memorial Verses*

2 If they had said the sun and the moon was gone out of the heavens it could not have struck me with the idea of a more awful and dreary blank in the creation than the words: Byron is dead.

Jane Welsh Carlyle (1801–66) The wife of Thomas Carlyle. Letter to Thomas Carlyle, 1824

3 Mad, bad, and dangerous to know.

Lady Caroline Lamb (1785–1828) The wife of William Lamb. Said of Byron in her *Journal*

Quotations by Byron

4 The 'good old times' – all times when old are good –
Are gone.

The Age of Bronze, I

5 The land self-interest groans from shore to
   shore,
   For fear that plenty should attain the poor.
   The Age of Bronze, XIV

6 In short, he was a perfect cavaliero,
   And to his very valet seem'd a hero.
   Beppo

7 I like the weather, when it is not rainy,
   That is, I like two months of every year.
   Beppo

8 Maidens, like moths, are ever caught by glare,
   And Mammon wins his way where Seraphs
   might despair.
   Childe Harold's Pilgrimage, I

9 Adieu, adieu! my native shore
   Fades o'er the waters blue.
   Childe Harold's Pilgrimage, I

10 My native Land – Good Night!
   Childe Harold's Pilgrimage, I

11 War, war is still the cry, 'War even to the knife!'
   Childe Harold's Pilgrimage, I

12 Hereditary bondsmen! know ye not
   Who would be free themselves must strike the
   blow?
   Childe Harold's Pilgrimage, I

13 There was a sound of revelry by night,
   And Belgium's capital had gather'd then
   Her Beauty and her Chivalry, and bright
   The lamps shone o'er fair women and brave
   men.
   Childe Harold's Pilgrimage, III

14 On with the dance! let joy be unconfined;
   No sleep till morn, when Youth and Pleasure
   meet
   To chase the glowing Hours with flying feet.
   Childe Harold's Pilgrimage, III

15 While stands the Coliseum, Rome shall stand;
   When falls the Coliseum, Rome shall fall;
   And when Rome falls – the World.
   Childe Harold's Pilgrimage, IV

16 There is a pleasure in the pathless woods,
   There is a rapture on the lonely shore,
   There is society, where none intrudes,
   By the deep Sea, and music in its roar:
   I love not Man the less, but Nature more.
   Childe Harold's Pilgrimage, IV

17 The spirit burning but unbent,
   May writhe, rebel – the weak alone repent!
   The Corsair, II

18 'Tis sweet to hear the watch-dog's honest bark
   Bay deep-mouthed welcome as we draw near
   home;
   'Tis sweet to know there is an eye will mark
   Our coming, and look brighter when we come.
   Don Juan, I

19 What men call gallantry, and gods adultery,
   Is much more common where the climate's
   sultry.
   Don Juan, I

20 Man's love is of man's life a thing apart,
   'Tis woman's whole existence.
   Don Juan, I

21 Man, being reasonable, must get drunk;
   The best of life is but intoxication.
   Don Juan, II

22 All tragedies are finish'd by a death,
   All comedies are ended by a marriage.
   Don Juan, III

23 Cost his enemies a long repentance,
   And made him a good friend, but bad
   acquaintance.
   Don Juan, III

24 Though sages may pour out their wisdom's
   treasure,
   There is no sterner moralist than Pleasure.
   Don Juan, III

25 Agree to a short armistice with truth.
   Don Juan, III

26 The isles of Greece, the isles of Greece!
   Where burning Sappho loved and sung,
   Where grew the arts of war and peace,
   Where Delos rose, and Phoebus sprung!
   Eternal summer gilds them yet,
   But all, except their sun, is set.
   Don Juan, III

27 The mountains look on Marathon –
   And Marathon looks on the sea:
   And musing there an hour alone,
   I dream'd that Greece might still be free.
   Don Juan, III

28 Nothing so difficult as a beginning
   In poesy, unless perhaps the end.
   Don Juan, IV

29 I thought it would appear
   That there had been a lady in the case.
   Don Juan, V

30 The women pardoned all except her face.
   Don Juan, V

31 There is a tide in the affairs of women,
   Which, taken at the flood, leads – God knows
   where.
   Don Juan, VI

32 A lady of a 'certain age', which means
   Certainly aged.
   Don Juan, VI

33 Now hatred is by far the longest pleasure;
   Men love in haste, but they detest at leisure.
   Don Juan, XIII

34 Society is now one polish'd horde,
Form'd of two mighty tribes, the *Bores* and
Bored.
Don Juan, XIII

35 'Tis strange – but true; for truth is always
strange;
Stranger than fiction: if it could be told,
How much would novels gain by the exchange!
Don Juan, XIV

36 I'll publish, right or wrong:
Fools are my theme, let satire be my song.
English Bards and Scotch Reviewers

37 'Tis pleasant, sure, to see one's name in print;
A book's a book, although there's nothing in't.
English Bards and Scotch Reviewers

38 A man must serve his time to every trade
Save censure – critics all are ready made.
English Bards and Scotch Reviewers

39 With death doomed to grapple,
Beneath this cold slab, he
Who lied in the chapel
Now lies in the Abbey.
Epitaph for William Pitt

40 She walks in beauty, like the night
Of cloudless climes and starry skies;
And all that's best of dark and bright
Meet in her aspect and her eyes.
She Walks in Beauty

41 So, we'll go no more a roving
So late into the night,
Though the heart be still as loving,
And the moon be still as bright.
So, we'll go no more a roving

42 Though the night was made for loving,
And the day returns too soon,
Yet we'll go no more a roving
By the light of the moon.
So, we'll go no more a roving

43 A better farmer ne'er brushed dew from lawn,
A worse king never left a realm undone!
Referring to George III
The Vision of Judgment, VIII

44 If I should meet thee
After long years,
How should I greet thee? –
With silence and tears.
When we two parted

45 I awoke one morning and found myself famous.
Remark made after the publication of *Childe Harold's Pilgrimage*
(1812)
Entry in Memoranda

Byron, Henry James (1834–84) British dramatist and
actor. He wrote numerous comedies and farces, notably *Cyril's
Success* (1868) and *Our Boys* (1875).

1 Life's too short for chess.
Our Boys, I

C

Cabell, James Branch (1879–1958) US novelist and
journalist. He was editor of the *American Spectator* (1932–35). His
novels include *The Rivet in Grandfather's Neck* (1915), *Jurgen*
(1919), *The Silver Stallion* (1926), and *The First Gentleman of
America* (1942).

1 I am willing to taste any drink once.
Jurgen, Ch. 1

2 The optimist proclaims we live in the best of all
possible worlds; and the pessimist fears this is
true.
The Silver Stallion

Caesar, (Gaius) Julius (100–44 BC) Roman general and
statesman. A member of the first Triumvirate (60 BC) with
Pompey and Crassus, his military campaigns in Gaul and Britain
won adulation. After the death of Crassus, conflict with Pompey
led to civil war, from which Caesar emerged as dictator of Rome.
He was assassinated by republican conspirators.

1 All Gaul is divided into three parts.
De Bello Gallico, Vol. I, Ch. 1

2 Caesar's wife must be above suspicion.
Said in justification of his divorce from Pompeia, after she was
unwittingly involved in a scandal
Lives, 'Julius Caesar' (Plutarch)

3 The die is cast.
Said on crossing the Rubicon (49 BC) at the start of his campaign
against Pompey
Remark

4 *Veni, vidi, vici.*
I came, I saw, I conquered.
The Twelve Caesars (Suetonius)

5 *Et tu, Brute?.*
You too, Brutus?
Last words

Cagney, James (1899–1986) US actor.

1 You dirty double-crossing rat!
Usually misquoted by impressionists as 'You dirty rat'
Blonde Crazy

Cage, John (1912–) US composer of avant garde music.
His book *Silence* (1961) gives an account of his indeterminist
philosophy; his works include *Sonatas and Interludes* (1946–48),
4 minutes 33 seconds (1954), *Apartment Building 1776* (1976), and
Europeras 3 and 4 (1990).

1 I have nothing to say, I am saying it, and that is
poetry.
In *The Sunday Times* (quoted by Cyril Connolly), 10 Sep 1972

Cahn, Sammy (Samuel Cohen; 1913–) US songwriter.
Many of his songs, including *Three Coins in the Fountain* and *Call
Me Irresponsible* were featured in Hollywood films.

1 Love and marriage, love and marriage,
Go together like a horse and carriage.
Our Town, 'Love and Marriage'

Calderón de la Barca, Pedro (1600–81) Spanish dramatist and poet. He became chaplain to Philip IV and wrote many plays, including *La Vida es Sueño* and *Astrólogo Fingido*.

1 For man's greatest crime is to have been born.
La Vida es Sueño, I

2 For I see now that I am asleep that I dream when I am awake.
La Vida es Sueño, II

Caligula (Gaius Caesar; 12–41 AD) Roman Emperor. His tyrannical and extravagant behaviour led to accusations of madness and eventually to his assassination.

1 Would that the Roman people had but one neck!
Life of Caligula (Suetonius), Ch. 30

Callaghan, Sir (Leonard) James, Baron (1912–) British Labour statesman. He became prime minister (1976–79) after Harold Wilson's resignation.

1 A lie can be half-way round the world before the truth has got its boots on.
Speech, 1 Nov 1976

2 Either back us or sack us.
Speech, Labour Party Conference, Brighton, 5 Oct 1977

Calverley, C(harles) S(tuart) (1831–84) British poet. He is remembered for his humorous collections *Verses and Translations* (1862) and *Fly Leaves* (1872).

1 The heart which grief hath cankered
Hath one unfailing remedy – the Tankard.
Beer

2 Jones – (who, I'm glad to say,
Asked leave of Mrs J. –)
Daily absorbs a clay
After his labours.
Ode to Tobacco

3 Yet it is better to drop thy friends, O my daughter, than to drop thy 'H's'.
Proverbial Philosophy, 'Of Friendship'

Camden, William (1551–1623) English antiquary and historian. His *Britannia*, a topographical and historical survey of the British Isles, was first published (in Latin) in 1586 and translated in 1610.

1 Betwixt the stirrup and the ground
Mercy I asked, mercy I found.
Epitaph for a Man killed by falling from his Horse

Campbell, Jane Montgomery (1817–78) British hymn writer.

1 We plough the fields, and scatter
The good seed on the land,
But it is fed and watered
By God's Almighty Hand.
He sends the snow in winter,
The warmth to swell the grain,
The breezes and the sunshine,
And soft refreshing rain.
Hymn

Campbell, Joseph (1879–1944) Irish poet. His works include *The Rushlight* (1906) and *The Mountainy Singer* (1909).

1 As a white candle
In a holy place,
So is the beauty
Of an aged face.
The Old Woman

Campbell, Mrs Patrick (Beatrice Stella Tanner; 1865–1940) British actress. She appeared in several plays by her friend G. B. Shaw.

1 It doesn't matter what you do in the bedroom as long as you don't do it in the street and frighten the horses.
The Duchess of Jermyn Street (Daphne Fielding), Ch. 2

2 Wedlock – the deep, deep peace of the double bed after the hurly-burly of the chaise-longue.
Jennie (Ralph G. Martin), Vol. II

3 Do you know why God withheld the sense of humour from women? That we may love you instead of laughing at you.
To a man
The Life of Mrs Pat (M. Peters)

Campbell, (Ignatius) Roy(ston Dunnachie) (1901–57) South African poet. His works include *The Flaming Terrapin* (1924); *The Georgiad* (1931), satirizing the Bloomsbury group; and the autobiographical *Broken Record* (1934) and *Light on a Dark Horse* (1951).

1 Now Spring, sweet laxative of Georgian strains,
Quickens the ink in literary veins,
The Stately Homes of England ope their doors
To piping Nancy-boys and Crashing Bores.
The Georgiad

2 Translations (like wives) are seldom faithful if they are in the least attractive.
Poetry Review

Campbell, Thomas (1777–1844) British poet, who made his name with *The Pleasures of Hope* (1799).

1 O leave this barren spot to me!
Spare, woodman, spare the beechen tree.
The Beech-Tree's Petition

2 On Linden, when the sun was low,
All bloodless lay the untrodden snow,
And dark as Winter was the flow
of Iser, rolling rapidly.
Hohenlinden

3 'Tis distance lends enchantment to the view,
And robes the mountain in its azure hue.
Pleasures of Hope, I

4 The proud, the cold untroubled heart of stone,
That never mused on sorrow but its own.
Pleasures of Hope, I

5 What millions died – that Caesar might be great!
Pleasures of Hope, II

6 Ye Mariners of England
That guard our native seas,
Whose flag has braved, a thousand years,
The battle and the breeze –
Your glorious standard launch again
To match another foe!
And sweep through the deep,
While the stormy winds do blow, –
While the battle rages loud and long,
And the stormy winds do blow.

Ye Mariners of England

7 Gentlemen, you must not mistake me. I admit
that he is the sworn foe of our nation, and, if you
will, of the whole human race. But, gentlemen,
we must be just to our enemy. We must not
forget that he once shot a bookseller.

Excusing himself in proposing a toast to Napoleon at a literary
dinner
The Life and Letters of Lord Macaulay (G. O. Trevelyan)

8 Now Barabbas was a publisher.

Attrib.

Campion, Thomas (1567–1620) English poet, composer,
and physician. In *Observations in the Art of English Poesie* (1602)
he attacked the use of rhyme.

1 Follow thy fair sun, unhappy shadow.

Follow Thy Fair Sun

2 There is a garden in her face,
Where roses and white lilies grow;
A heav'nly paradise is that place,
Wherein all pleasant fruits do flow.
There cherries grow, which none may buy
Till 'Cherry ripe' themselves do cry.

See also HERRICK
Fourth Book of Airs

3 The man of life upright,
Whose guiltless heart is free
From all dishonest deeds
Or thought of vanity.

The Man of Life Upright

4 Good thoughts his only friends,
His wealth a well-spent age,
The earth his sober inn
And quiet pilgrimage

The Man of Life Upright

5 The Summer hath his joys,
And Winter his delights.
Though Love and all his pleasures are but toys,
They shorten tedious nights.

Now Winter Nights Enlarge

Camus, Albert (1913–60) French existentialist novelist,
essayist, and dramatist, born in Algiers. His works include the
novels *The Outsider* (1942) and *The Plague* (1947); the play
Caligula (1944); and *The Myth of Sisyphus* (1942), an essay on the
absurd.

Quotations about Camus

1 His work presents the feeling of the *Absurd*, the
plight of man's need for clarity and rationality in
confrontation with the unreasonable silence of
the universe.

William Benét *The Reader's Encyclopedia*

2 His refusal to take solace in a concept of divine
or cosmic meaning for human life did not conflict with Camus' humanistic attitude that man
is capable of a certain degree of dignity in honestly facing his solitary condition.

William Benét *The Reader's Encyclopedia*

3 The Humphrey Bogart of Absurdism.

Herbert Lottmann *Albert Camus*

Quotations by Camus

4 Alas, after a certain age every man is responsible for his face.

The Fall

5 Style, like sheer silk, too often hides eczema.

The Fall

6 A single sentence will suffice for modern man:
he fornicated and read the papers.

The Fall

7 How many crimes committed merely because
their authors could not endure being wrong!

The Fall

8 No man is a hypocrite in his pleasures.

The Fall

9 Don't wait for the Last Judgement. It takes place
every day.

The Fall

10 Politics and the fate of mankind are shaped by
men without ideals and without greatness. Men
who have greatness within them don't go in for
politics.

Notebooks, 1935–42

11 An intellectual is someone whose mind watches
itself.

Notebooks, 1935–42

12 The future is the only kind of property that the
masters willingly concede to slaves.

The Rebel

13 One cannot be a part-time nihilist.

The Rebel

14 What is a rebel? A man who says no.

The Rebel

15 All modern revolutions have ended in a reinforcement of the power of the State.

The Rebel

16 He who despairs over an event is a coward, but
he who holds hopes for the human condition is
a fool.

The Rebel

Canetti, Elias (1905–) Bulgarian born novelist. His books, all written in German, include *Auto da Fé* (1946). He won the Nobel Prize for Literature in 1981.

1 Whenever you observe an animal closely, you feel as if a human being sitting inside were making fun of you.
The Human Province

2 It is important what a man still plans at the end. It shows the measure of injustice in his death.
The Human Province

3 The great writers of aphorisms read as if they had all known each other well.
The Human Province

Canning, George (1770–1827) British statesman. He was Tory foreign secretary (1807–09, 1822–27) and prime minister for the four months preceding his death.

1 But of all plagues, good Heaven, thy wrath can send,
Save me, oh, save me, from the candid friend.
New Morality

2 Pitt is to Addington
As London is to Paddington.
The Oracle

3 I called the New World into existence to redress the balance of the Old.
Speech, 12 Dec 1826

Capone, Al (1899–1947) Italian-born US gangster. His gang terrorized the underworld of Chicago until his imprisonment (1931) for tax evasion.

1 I've been accused of every death except the casualty list of the World War.
The Bootleggers (Kenneth Allsop), Ch. 11

2 This is virgin territory for whorehouses.
Talking about suburban Chicago
The Bootleggers (Kenneth Allsop), Ch. 16

3 They can't collect legal taxes from illegal money.
Objecting to the US Bureau of Internal Revenue claiming large sums in unpaid back tax
Capone (J. Kobler)

Capote, Truman (1924–84) US novelist. He made his name with *Other Voices, Other Rooms* (1948). Subsequent books include *Breakfast at Tiffany's* (1958) and *Music for Chameleons* (1980).

1 Venice is like eating an entire box of chocolate liqueurs at one go.
The Observer, 'Sayings of the Week', 26 Nov 1961

Caracciolo, Domenico, Marquis (1715–89) Governor of Sicily (1781, 1786).

1 In England there are sixty different religions, and only one sauce.
Attrib.

Carew, Thomas (c. 1595–1640) English poet. A diplomat for much of his life, he is remembered for his *Elegy on the Death of Dr Donne* and his love lyrics.

1 Here lies a King that ruled, as he thought fit,
The universal monarchy of wit.
Referring to John Donne
Elegy on the Death of Dr Donne

Carey, John (1934–) British critic and journalist.

1 Only change enraged him, because it touched the quick of his fear.
Original Copy, The English Scene

2 At Oxford you wear subfusc for exams, which means, for girls, black stockings, black skirts, white blouses and black ties. This severe costume, designed, I suppose, to quell all thought of sex, had, as I recall it, rather the opposite effect. Being surrounded by demure, black-stockinged creatures does not induce academic calm – or not when you're twenty-three.
Original Copy, Self

3 For words portray their users, and if literary criticism has any public function it ought to help us assess the mental health of the three main parties by comparing their different ways of destroying the English language.
Original Copy, The strange death of political language

Carey, Henry (c. 1690–1743) English poet, musician, and writer of burlesques and farces. *Sally in our Alley* is his best-known work; the words and music of *God Save the King* have also been attributed to him.

1 God save our Gracious King,
Long live our noble King,
God save the King.
Send him victorious,
Happy and glorious,
God Save the King

2 Of all the days that's in the week
I dearly love but one day –
And that's the day that comes betwixt
A Saturday and Monday.
Sally in our Alley

3 Of all the girls that are so smart
There's none like pretty Sally;
She is the darling of my heart
And she lives in our alley.
Sally in our Alley

Carlyle, Jane Welsh (1801–66) The wife of Thomas Carlyle. Clearly a writer of some talent, her output was restricted by her difficult life with her husband. Her letters and journal are often witty and stringent.

1 When one has been threatened with a great injustice, one accepts a smaller as a favour.
Journal, 21 Nov 1855

2 He has his talents, his vast and cultivated mind, his vivid imagination, his independence of soul and his high-souled principles of honour. But then – ah, these Buts! Saint Preux never kicked the fireirons, nor made puddings in his tea cup.
Referring to her husband, Thomas Carlyle
Letter to a friend, July 1821

3 If they had said the sun and the moon was gone out of the heavens it could not have struck me with the idea of a more awful and dreary blank in the creation than the words: Byron is dead.
Referring to the death of Byron
Letter to Thomas Carlyle, 1824

4 Medical men all over the world having merely entered into a tacit agreement to call all sorts of maladies people are liable to, in cold weather, by one name; so that one sort of treatment may serve for all, and their practice thereby be greatly simplified.
Letter to John Welsh, 4 Mar 1837

Carlyle, Thomas (1795–1881) Scottish historian and essayist. *Sartor Resartus*, a philosophical work, appeared in 1836; his subsequent writings include *The French Revolution* (1837) and *Heroes, Hero-Worship and the Heroic in History* (1841).

Quotations about Carlyle

1 It was very good of God to let Carlyle and Mrs Carlyle marry one another and so make only two people miserable instead of four.
Samuel Butler (1835–1902) British writer. Attrib.

2 Carlyle is a poet to whom nature has denied the faculty of verse.
Alfred, Lord Tennyson (1809–92) British poet. Letter to W. E. Gladstone

Quotations by Carlyle

3 A poet without love were a physical and metaphysical impossibility.
Critical and Miscellaneous Essays, 'Burns'

4 A witty statesman said, you might prove anything by figures.
Critical and Miscellaneous Essays, 'Chartism'

5 All reform except a moral one will prove unavailing.
Critical and Miscellaneous Essays, 'Corn Law Rhymes'

6 History is the essence of innumerable biographies.
Critical and Miscellaneous Essays, 'History'

7 A well-written Life is almost as rare as a well-spent one.
Critical and Miscellaneous Essays, 'Richter'

8 Literary men are . . . a perpetual priesthood.
Critical and Miscellaneous Essays, 'The State of German Literature'

9 The three great elements of modern civilization, Gunpowder, Printing, and the Protestant Religion.
Critical and Miscellaneous Essays, 'The State of German Literature'

10 Genius (which means transcendent capacity of taking trouble, first of all).
Frederick the Great, Vol. IV, Ch. 3

11 No great man lives in vain. The history of the world is but the biography of great men.
Heroes and Hero-Worship, 'The Hero as Divinity'

12 The true University of these days is a collection of books.
Heroes and Hero-Worship, 'The Hero as Man of Letters'

13 Burke said that there were Three Estates in Parliament; but, in the Reporters' Gallery yonder, there sat a *Fourth Estate*, more important far than they all.
Heroes and Hero-Worship, 'The Hero as Man of Letters'

14 France was a long despotism tempered by epigrams.
History of the French Revolution, Pt. I, Bk. I, Ch. 1

15 To a shower of gold most things are penetrable.
History of the French Revolution, Pt. I, Bk. III, Ch. 7

16 A whiff of grapeshot.
Describing how Napoleon, early in his career, quelled a minor riot in Paris
History of the French Revolution, Pt. I, Bk. V, Ch. 3

17 The difference between Orthodoxy or My-doxy and Heterodoxy or Thy-doxy.
History of the French Revolution, Pt. II, Bk. IV, Ch. 2

18 The seagreen Incorruptible.
Referring to Robespierre
History of the French Revolution, Pt. II, Bk. IV, Ch. 4

19 The Public is an old woman. Let her maunder and mumble.
Journal, 1835

20 Respectable Professors of the Dismal Science.
Referring to economics
Latter-Day Pamphlets, 1

21 Nature admits no lie.
Latter-Day Pamphlets, 5

22 Captains of industry.
Past and Present, Bk. IV, Ch. 4

23 No man who has once heartily and wholly laughed can be altogether irreclaimably bad.
Sartor Resartus, Bk. I, Ch. 4

24 Be not the slave of Words.
Sartor Resartus, Bk I, Ch. 8

25 Lives there the man that can figure a naked Duke of Windlestraw addressing a naked House of Lords?
Sartor Resartus, Bk. I, Ch. 9

26 Sarcasm I now see to be, in general, the language of the devil.
Sartor Resartus, Bk. II, Ch. 4

27 A good book is the purest essence of a human soul.
Speech made in support of the London Library
Carlyle and the London Library (F. Harrison)

28 If Jesus Christ were to come to-day, people would not even crucify him. They would ask him to dinner, and hear what he had to say, and make fun of it.
Carlyle at his Zenith (D. A. Wilson)

29 Macaulay is well for a while, but one wouldn't *live* under Niagara.
Notebook (R. M. Milnes)

30 The crash of the whole solar and stellar systems could only kill you once.
Letter to John Carlyle, 1831

31 Work is the grand cure of all the maladies and miseries that ever beset mankind.
Speech, Edinburgh, 2 Apr 1886

32 I never heard tell of any clever man that came of entirely stupid people.
Speech, Edinburgh, 2 Apr 1886

33 I don't pretend to understand the Universe – it's a great deal bigger than I am . . . People ought to be modester.
Attrib.

34 There they are cutting each other's throats, because one half of them prefer hiring their servants for life, and the other by the hour.
Referring to the American Civil War
Attrib.

35 MARGARET FULLER. I accept the universe. CARLYLE. Gad! she'd better!
Attrib.

36 Thirty millions, mostly fools.
When asked what the population of England was
Attrib.

Carnegie, Dale (1888–1955) US lecturer and writer. A teacher of public speaking, he also produced a number of books and broadcasts on this and related subjects.

1 How to Win Friends and Influence People.
Book title

2 There is only one way under high heaven to get the best of an argument – and that is to avoid it.
Dale Carnegie's Scrapbook

Carroll, Lewis (Charles Lutwidge Dodgson; 1832–98) British writer and mathematician; author of the children's classics *Alice's Adventures in Wonderland* (1865) and *Through the Looking-Glass* (1872).

Quotations about Carroll

1 Carroll's ego, a Humpty Dumpty (egg), was in perpetual peril of falling, never to be put together again. . . . His defensive hypersensitivity to a little girl's curiosity is a reflection of a boy too long exposed to feminine eyes. It is the anguished cry of a little boy forced to spend the first years of his life in the almost exclusive company of sisters (of which Carroll ultimately had seven).
Judith Bloomingdale *Aspects of Alice* (Robert Phillips)

2 . . . Carroll was not selfish, but a liberal-minded, liberal-handed egotist, but his egotism was all but second childhood.
Harry Furniss *Confessions of a Caricaturist*

3 Carroll's special genius, perhaps, lies in his ability to disguise charmingly the seriousness of his own concern, to make the most playful quality of his work at the same time its didactic crux.
Patricia Spacks *Logic and Language in Through the Looking-Glass*

Quotations by Carroll

4 'What is the use of a book,' thought Alice, 'without pictures or conversation?'
Alice's Adventures in Wonderland, Ch. 1

5 'Curiouser and curiouser!' cried Alice.
Alice's Adventures in Wonderland, Ch. 2

6 'You are old, Father William,' the young man said,
'And your hair has become very white;
And yet you incessantly stand on your head –
Do you think at your age, it is right?'
Alice's Adventures in Wonderland, Ch. 5

7 'If everybody minded their own business,' the Duchess said in a hoarse growl, 'the world would go round a deal faster than it does.'
Alice's Adventures in Wonderland, Ch. 6

8 This time it vanished quite slowly, beginning with the end of the tail, and ending with the grin, which remained some time after the rest of it had gone.
Describing the Cheshire Cat
Alice's Adventures in Wonderland, Ch. 6

9 'Then you should say what you mean,' the March Hare went on. 'I do,' Alice hastily replied; 'at least – at least I mean what I say – that's the same thing, you know.'
'Not the same thing a bit!' said the Hatter. 'Why, you might just as well say that 'I see what I eat' is the same thing as 'I eat what I see!''
Alice's Adventures in Wonderland, Ch. 7

10 Twinkle, twinkle, little bat!
How I wonder what you're at!
Up above the world you fly!
Like a teatray in the sky.
Alice's Adventures in Wonderland, Ch. 7

11 'Take some more tea,' the March Hare said to Alice, very earnestly.
'I've had nothing yet,' Alice replied in an offended tone, 'so I can't take more.'
'You mean you can't take *less*,' said the Hatter: 'it's very easy to take *more* than nothing.'
Alice's Adventures in Wonderland, Ch. 7

12 'Off with his head!'
Alice's Adventures in Wonderland, Ch. 8

13 Everything's got a moral, if only you can find it.
Alice's Adventures in Wonderland, Ch. 9

14 Take care of the sense, and the sounds will take care of themselves.

Alice's Adventures in Wonderland, Ch. 9

15 'Reeling and Writhing, of course, to begin with,' the Mock Turtle replied; 'and then the different branches of Arithmetic – Ambition, Distraction, Uglification, and Derision.'

Alice's Adventures in Wonderland, Ch. 9

16 'Will you walk a little faster?' said a whiting to a snail,
'There's a porpoise close behind us, and he's treading on my tail.'

Alice's Adventures in Wonderland, Ch. 10

17 Will you, won't you, will you, won't you, will you join the dance?

Alice's Adventures in Wonderland, Ch. 10

18 Soup of the evening, beautiful Soup!

Said by the Mock Turtle
Alice's Adventures in Wonderland Ch. 10

19 The Queen of Hearts, she made some tarts,
All on a summer day:
The Knave of Hearts, he stole those tarts,
And took them quite away!

Alice's Adventures in Wonderland, Ch. 11

20 'Where shall I begin, please your Majesty?' he asked.
'Begin at the beginning' the King said, gravely, 'and go on till you come to the end: then stop.'

Alice's Adventures in Wonderland, Ch. 11

21 'No, no!' said the Queen. 'Sentence first – verdict afterwards.'

Alice's Adventures in Wonderland, Ch. 12

22 For the Snark *was* a Boojum, you see.

The Hunting of the Snark

23 'Twas brillig, and the slithy toves
Did gyre and gimble in the wabe;
All mimsy were the borogoves,
And the mome raths outgrabe.

Through the Looking-Glass, Ch. 1

24 Now, *here,* you see, it takes all the running *you* can do, to keep in the same place. If you want to get somewhere else, you must run at least twice as fast as that!

Through the Looking-Glass, Ch. 2

25 Tweedledum and Tweedledee
Agreed to have a battle;
For Tweedledum said Tweedledee
Had spoiled his nice new rattle.

Through the Looking-Glass, Ch. 4

26 'Contrariwise,' continued Tweedledee, 'if it was so, it might be; and if it were so, it would be: but as it isn't, it ain't. That's logic.'

Through the Looking-Glass, Ch. 4

27 The Walrus and the Carpenter
Were walking close at hand;
They wept like anything to see
Such quantities of sand:
'If this were only cleared away,'
They said, 'it *would* be grand!'

Through the Looking-Glass, Ch. 4

28 'The time has come,' the Walrus said,
'To talk of many things:
Of shoes – and ships – and sealing-wax –
Of cabbages – and kings –
And why the sea is boiling hot –
And whether pigs have wings.'

Through the Looking-Glass, Ch. 4

29 But answer came there none –
And this was scarcely odd because
They'd eaten every one.

Through the Looking-Glass, Ch. 4

30 The rule is, jam tomorrow and jam yesterday – but never jam today.

Through the Looking-Glass, Ch. 5

31 'They gave it me,' Humpty Dumpty continued thoughtfully, . . . 'for an un-birthday present.'

Through the Looking-Glass, Ch. 6

32 'When *I* use a word,' Humpty Dumpty said in rather a scornful tone, 'it means just what I choose it to mean – neither more nor less.'

Through the Looking-Glass, Ch. 6

33 He's an Anglo-Saxon Messenger – and those are Anglo-Saxon attitudes.

Through the Looking-Glass, Ch. 7

34 It's as large as life, and twice as natural!

Through the Looking-Glass, Ch. 7

35 The Lion looked at Alice wearily. 'Are you animal – or vegetable – or mineral?' he said, yawning at every other word.

Through the Looking-Glass, Ch. 7

36 'Speak when you're spoken to!' the Red Queen sharply interrupted her.

Through the Looking-Glass, Ch. 9

37 'You look a little shy; let me introduce you to that leg of mutton,' said the Red Queen. 'Alice – Mutton; Mutton – Alice.'

Through the Looking-Glass, Ch. 9

Carson, Rachel Louise (1907–64) US biologist. *The Sea Around Us* (1951) and *Silent Spring* (1962) warned of the dangers of polluting the environment.

1 For all at last return to the sea – to Oceanus, the ocean river, like the ever-flowing stream of time, the beginning and the end.

The closing words of the book
The Sea Around Us

2 As cruel a weapon as the cave man's club, the chemical barrage has been hurled against the fabric of life.

The Silent Spring

3 Over increasingly large areas of the United States, spring now comes unheralded by the return of the birds, and the early mornings are strangely silent where once they were filled with the beauty of bird song.

The Silent Spring

Carter, Jimmy (1924–) US statesman; president (1977–81). A democrat, he was governor of Georgia (1970–74) before succeeding Gerald Ford as president.

1 I'm surprised that a government organization could do it that quickly.

Visiting Egypt, when told that it took twenty years to build the Great Pyramid
Presidential Anecdotes (P. Boller)

Carter, ('Miz') Lillian (1902–83) The mother of Jimmy Carter (US president, 1977–81).

1 I love all my children, but some of them I don't like.

In *Woman*, 9 Apr 1977

Cartland, Barbara (1902–) British romantic novelist.

1 Of course they have, or I wouldn't be sitting here talking to someone like you.

When asked in a radio interview whether she thought that British class barriers had broken down
Class (J. Cooper)

Cartwright, John (1740–1824) British writer and supporter of American colonists. He was also a parliamentary reformer and agitated for the abolition of slavery.

1 One man shall have one vote.

People's Barrier Against Undue Influence

Caruso, Enrico (1873–1921) Italian tenor noted for his singing in the operas of Verdi and Puccini.

1 You know whatta you do when you shit? Singing, it's the same thing, only up!

Whose Little Boy Are You? (H. Brown)

Cary, (Arthur) Joyce (Lunel) (1888–1957) British novelist. *Mister Johnson* (1939), set in West Africa, was followed by a trilogy about artists, which included his best-known book, *The Horse's Mouth* (1944).

1 Sara could commit adultery at one end and weep for her sins at the other, and enjoy both operations at once.

The Horse's Mouth, Ch. 8

2 Remember I'm an artist. And you know what that means in a court of law. Next worst to an actress.

The Horse's Mouth, Ch. 14

Cary, Phoebe (1824–71) US poet. Her verse collections include *Poems of Alice and Phoebe Cary* (1850), compiled in collaboration with her sister Alice (1820–71).

1 And though hard be the task, 'Keep a stiff upper lip.'

Keep a Stiff Upper Lip

Case, Phila Henrietta (fl. 1864) British poet.

1 Oh! why does the wind blow upon me so wild? – Is it because I'm nobody's child?

Nobody's Child

Casson, Sir Hugh (1910–) British architect. Director of architecture for the Festival of Britain (1951), he subsequently became president of the Royal Academy of Arts (1976–84); his books include *Victorian Architecture* (1948).

1 The British love permanence more than they love beauty.

The Observer, 'Sayings of the Week', 14 June 1964

Castling, Harry (19th cent.) British songwriter.

1 Let's all go down the Strand.

Song title

Castro, (Ruz) Fidel (1926–) Cuban president (1976–). He established a socialist government in 1959 after a long guerrilla war.

1 A revolution is not a bed of roses. A revolution is a struggle to the death between the future and the past.

Speech, Havana, Jan 1961 (2nd anniversary of the Cuban Revolution)

2 I was a man who was lucky enough to have discovered a political theory, a man who was caught up in the whirlpool of Cuba's political crisis long before becoming a fully fledged Communist . . . discovering Marxism . . . was like finding a map in the forest.

Speech, Chile, 18 Nov 1971

Caswall, Edward (1814–78) British hymn writer.

1 Days and moments quickly flying,
Blend the living with the dead;
Soon will you and I be lying
Each within our narrow bed.

Hymn

Cather, Willa (Siebert) (1873–1947) US writer and poet.

1 The history of every country begins in the heart of a man or woman.

O Pioneers!, Pt. II, Ch. 4

Catherwood, Mary (Hartwell) (1847–1901) US writer.

1 Two may talk together under the same roof for many years, yet never really meet; and two others at first speech are old friends.

Mackinac and Lake Stories, 'Marianson'

Cato the Elder (Marcius Porcius C; 234–149 BC) Roman statesman, orator, and writer. Elected censor in 184 BC, he wrote on a variety of subjects, notably agriculture and Roman history.

1 Carthage must be destroyed.

Life of Cato (Plutarch)

Catullus, Gaius Valerius (c. 84–c. 54 BC) Roman poet, remembered for his love poems addressed to Lesbia and his satirical attacks on Julius Caesar.

1 For the godly poet must be chaste himself, but there is no need for his verses to be so.
Carmina, XVI

2 *Odi et amo.*
I hate and love.
Carmina, LXXXV

3 *Atque in perpetuum, frater, ave atque vale.*
And for ever, brother, hail and farewell!
Carmina, CI

Causley, Charles (1917–) British poet and broadcaster. Publications include *Hands to Dance* (1951), *Johnny Alleluia* (1961), and *Collected Poems 1951–1975* (1975).

1 Ears like bombs and teeth like splinters:
A blitz of a boy is Timothy Winters.
Timothy Winters

Cavell, Edith (Louisa) (1865–1915) British nurse. During World War I she became involved in the escape of Allied soldiers from Belgium, which led to her execution by the Germans in 1915.

1 I realize that patriotism is not enough. I must have no hatred or bitterness towards anyone.
Last words

Cawein, Madison Julius (1865–1914) US poet. Verse collections include *Lyrics and Idyls* (1890), *Poems of Nature and Love* (1893), and *Kentucky Poems* (1902).

1 An old Spanish saying is that 'a kiss without a moustache is like an egg without salt.'
Nature-Notes

Cecil, Lord David (1902–86) British writer and critic. The author of biographies of Jane Austen, Thomas Hardy, and Max Beerbohm, he also wrote *A Portrait of Charles Lamb* (1983).

1 It does not matter that Dickens' world is not life-like; it is alive.
Early Victorian Novelists

Cervantes (Saavedra), Miguel de (1547–1616) Spanish novelist and dramatist; creator of *Don Quixote* (1605; 1615), a satirical romance of chivalry.

Quotations about Cervantes

1 Casting my mind's eye over the whole of fiction, the only absolutely original creation that I can think of is Don Quixote.
W. Somerset Maugham (1874–1965) British novelist. *10 Novels and their Authors*, Ch. 1

2 Cervantes laughed chivalry out of fashion.
Horace Walpole (1717–97) British writer. Letter to Sir Horace Mann, 19 July 1774

Quotations by Cervantes

3 A silly remark can be made in Latin as well as in Spanish.
The Dialogue of the Dogs

4 Take care, your worship, those things over there are not giants but windmills.
Don Quixote, Pt. I, Ch. 8

5 Didn't I tell you, Don Quixote, sir, to turn back, for they were not armies you were going to attack, but flocks of sheep?
Don Quixote, Pt. I, Ch. 18

6 The Knight of the Doleful Countenance.
Sancho Panza describing Don Quixote; sometimes translated as 'knight of the sad countenance'
Don Quixote, Pt. I, Ch. 19

7 Fear has many eyes and can see things underground.
Don Quixote, Pt. I, Ch. 20

8 A leap over the hedge is better than good men's prayers.
Don Quixote, Pt. I, Ch. 21

9 I have always heard, Sancho, that doing good to base fellows is like throwing water into the sea.
Don Quixote, Pt. I, Ch. 23

10 Let them eat the lie and swallow it with their bread. Whether the two were lovers or no, they'll have accounted to God for it by now. I have my own fish to fry.
Don Quixote, Pt. I, Ch. 25

11 A knight errant who turns mad for a reason deserves neither merit nor thanks. The thing is to do it without cause.
Don Quixote, Pt. I, Ch. 25

12 One shouldn't talk of halters in the hanged man's house.
Don Quixote, Pt. I, Ch. 25

13 She isn't a bad bit of goods, the Queen! I wish all the fleas in my bed were as good.
Don Quixote, Pt. I, Ch. 30

14 In me the need to talk is a primary impulse, and I can't help saying right off what comes to my tongue.
Don Quixote, Pt. I, Ch. 30

15 Every man is as Heaven made him, and sometimes a great deal worse.
Don Quixote, Pt. II, Ch. 4

16 The best sauce in the world is hunger.
Don Quixote, Pt. II, Ch. 5

17 Well, now, there's a remedy for everything except death.
Don Quixote, Pt. II, Ch. 10

18 Never meddle with play-actors, for they're a favoured race.
Don Quixote, Pt. II, Ch. 11

19 He's a muddle-headed fool, with frequent lucid intervals.
Sancho Panza describing Don Quixote
Don Quixote, Pt. II, Ch. 18

20 There are only two families in the world, my old grandmother used to say, The *Haves* and the *Have-Nots*.
Don Quixote, Pt. II, Ch. 20

21 A private sin is not so prejudicial in the world as a public indecency.
Don Quixote, Pt. II, Ch. 22

22 Tell me what company thou keepest, and I'll tell thee what thou art.
Don Quixote, Pt. II, Ch. 23

23 Good painters imitate nature, bad ones spew it up.
El Licenciado Vidriera

Chalmers, Patrick Reginald (1872–1942) British banker and novelist. His novels include *The Golden Bee* and *Prior's Mead*.

1 What's lost upon the roundabouts we pulls up on the swings!
Green Days and Blue Days: Roundabouts and Swings

Chamberlain, Joseph (1836–1914) British politician. Having entered parliament as a Liberal in 1876, he came into conflict with Gladstone over Irish Home Rule and transferred his support to the Conservatives.

1 Provided that the City of London remains as at present, the Clearing-house of the World.
Speech, Guildhall, London, 19 Jan 1904

2 The day of small nations has long passed away. The day of Empires has come.
Speech, Birmingham, 12 May 1904

Chamberlain, (Arthur) Neville (1869–1940) British statesman; son of Joseph Chamberlain. As Conservative prime minister (1937–40) his negotiations with Hitler preceding World War II led him finally to abandon his policy of appeasement and to declare war on Germany. He died shortly after resigning in favour of Churchill.

Quotations about Chamberlain

1 The people of Birmingham have a specially heavy burden for they have given the world the curse of the present British Prime Minister.
Sir Stafford Cripps (1889–1952) British politician. Speech, 18 Mar 1938

2 Well, he seemed such a nice old gentleman, I thought I would give him my autograph as a souvenir.
Adolf Hitler (1889–1945) German dictator. Attrib.

3 He was a meticulous housemaid, great at tidying up.
A. J. P. Taylor (1906–90) British historian. *English History 1914–1945*

Quotations by Chamberlain

4 In war, whichever side may call itself the victor, there are no winners, but all are losers.
Speech, Kettering, 3 July 1938

5 How horrible, fantastic, incredible, it is that we should be digging trenches and trying on gas-masks here because of a quarrel in a far-away country between people of whom we know nothing.
Referring to Germany's annexation of the Sudetenland
Radio broadcast, 27 Sept 1938

6 I believe it is peace for our time . . . peace with honour.
Broadcast after Munich Agreement, 1 Oct 1938

7 Hitler has missed the bus.
Speech, House of Commons, 4 Apr 1940

Chamfort, Nicolas (1741–94) French writer. He wrote many comedies, essays, and poems, but is best known for his *Maximes et pensées*.

1 Someone said of a very great egotist: 'He would burn your house down to cook himself a couple of eggs.'
Caractères et anecdotes

2 The most wasted of all days is that on which one has not laughed.
Maximes et pensées

3 Our gratitude to most benefactors is the same as our feeling for dentists who have pulled our teeth. We acknowledge the good they have done and the evil from which they have delivered us, but we remember the pain they occasioned and do not love them very much.
Maximes et pensées

Chandler, John (1806–76) British clergyman, writer, and translator of Latin hymns. His works include *The Hymns of the Primitive Church* (1837) and *Life of William of Wykeham* (1842).

1 Conquering kings their titles take.
Poem title

Chandler, Raymond (1888–1959) US novelist, famous for his detective stories and thrillers. His detective, Philip Marlowe, first appeared in *The Big Sleep* (1939).

1 It was a blonde. A blonde to make a bishop kick a hole in a stained-glass window.
Farewell, My Lovely, Ch. 13

2 She gave me a smile I could feel in my hip pocket.
Farewell, My Lovely, Ch. 18

3 Alcohol is like love: the first kiss is magic, the second is intimate, the third is routine. After that you just take the girl's clothes off.
The Long Good-bye

4 Down these mean streets a man must go who is not himself mean; who is neither tarnished nor afraid.
The Simple Art of Murder

5 If my books had been any worse I should not have been invited to Hollywood, and if they had been any better I should not have come.
The Life of Raymond Chandler (F. MacShane)

6 When I split an infinitive, god damn it, I split it so it stays split.
Letter to his English publisher

Chanel, Coco (1883–1971) French dress designer.

1 There goes a woman who knows all the things that can be taught and none of the things that cannot be taught.
Coco Chanel, Her Life, Her Secrets (Marcel Haedrich)

2 Youth is something very new: twenty years ago no one mentioned it.
Coco Chanel, Her Life, Her Secrets (Marcel Haedrich)

3 Wherever one wants to be kissed.
When asked where one should wear perfume
Coco Chanel, Her Life, Her Secrets (Marcel Haedrich)

4 Fashion is architecture: it is a matter of proportions.
Coco Chanel, Her Life, Her Secrets (Marcel Haedrich)

Chaplin, Charlie (Sir Charles Spencer C.; 1889–1977) British film actor. He developed the character of the pathetic tramp – with baggy trousers, bowler hat, and walking stick – in such films as *The Kid* (1921), *The Gold Rush* (1925), and *Modern Times* (1936)

Quotations about Chaplin

1 Chaplin is no business man. All he knows is that he can't take less.
Samuel Goldwyn (Samuel Goldfish; 1882–1974) Polish-born US film producer. *My Autobiography* (Chaplin)

2 The Zulus know Chaplin better than Arkansas knows Garbo.
Will Rogers (1879–1935) US actor and humorist. *Atlantic Monthly*, Aug 1939

3 . . . somehow importing to the peeling of a banana the elegant nonchalance of a duke drawing a monogrammed cigarette from a platinum case.
Alexander Woolcott (1887–1943) US journalist. *While Rome Burns*

Quotations by Chaplin

4 Wars, conflict, it's all business. One murder makes a villain. Millions a hero. Numbers sanctify.
Monsieur Verdoux

5 All I need to make a comedy is a park, a policeman and a pretty girl.
My Autobiography

6 The saddest thing I can imagine is to get used to luxury.
My Autobiography

7 I am for people. I can't help it.
The Observer, 'Sayings of the week', 28 Sept 1952

8 I remain just one thing, and one thing only – and that is a clown.
It places me on a far higher plane than any politician.
The Observer, 'Sayings of the Week', 17 June 1960

9 Life is a tragedy when seen in close-up, but a comedy in long-shot.
In *The Guardian*, Obituary, 28 Dec 1977

Charles, Elizabeth (Rundle) (1828–96) British writer.

1 To know how to say what others only know how to think is what makes men poets or sages; and to dare to say what others only dare to think makes men martyrs or reformers – or both.
Chronicle of the Schönberg-Cotta Family

Charles, Hughie *See* Parker, Ross.

Charles Francis Joseph (1887–1922) Emperor of Austria.

1 What should I do? I think the best thing is to order a new stamp to be made with my face on it.
On hearing of his accession to emperor
Anekdotenschatz (H. Hoffmeister)

Charles I (1600–49) King of England, Scotland, and Ireland (1625–49); son of James I. Charles' early reign was marked by conflict with parliament; from 1629 to 1640 he ruled without it. This caused widespread unrest and led finally to the Civil War (1642), culminating in the king's execution.

1 Never make a defence or apology before you be accused.
Letter to Lord Wentworth, 3 Sept 1636

2 I die a Christian, according to the Profession of the Church of England, as I found it left me by my Father.
Speech on the scaffold, 30 Jan 1649

Charles II (1630–85) King of England, Scotland, and Ireland (1660–85); son of Charles I. Exiled during Cromwell's Protectorate (1653–59), he returned to England at the Restoration of the monarchy in 1660. Charles' Roman Catholic sympathies led to conflict with parliament; anti-Catholic feeling intensified after the Popish Plot of 1678.

1 Brother, I am too old to go again to my travels.
Referring to his exile, 1651–60
History of Great Britain (Hume), Vol. II, Ch. 7

2 Not a religion for gentlemen.
Referring to Presbyterianism
History of My Own Time (Burnet), Vol. I, Bk. II, Ch. 2

3 This is very true: for my words are my own, and my actions are my ministers'.
Replying to Lord ROCHESTER's suggested epitaph
King Charles II (A. Bryant)

4 I am sure no man in England will take away my life to make you King.
To his brother James following revelation of the Popish Plot fabricated by Titus Oates
Attrib.

5 Better than a play.
Referring to House of Lords debate on the Divorce Bill
Attrib.

6 Let not poor Nelly starve.
Referring to Nell Gwynne
Said on his death bed

7 He had been, he said, a most unconscionable time dying; but he hoped that they would excuse it.
History of England (Macaulay), Vol. I, Ch. 4

Charles V (1500–58) Holy Roman Emperor (1519–56).
Warfare with France and the Turks dominated much of his reign,
which also saw the religious struggles of the Reformation: Charles
presided at the Diet of Worms (1521) where Luther was
condemned.

1 My cousin Francis and I are in perfect accord –
he wants Milan, and so do I.

Referring to his dispute with Francis I of France over Italian
territory
The Story of Civilization (W. Durant), Vol. 5

2 I make war on the living, not on the dead.

After the death of Martin Luther, when it was suggested that he
hang the corpse on a gallows
Attrib.

3 I speak Spanish to God, Italian to women,
French to men, and German to my horse.

Attrib.

Charles X (1757–1836) King of France (1824–30). After the
French Revolution, he lived abroad, returning in 1815 with the
restoration of the Bourbons. Following his overthrow, he went into
exile in England.

1 I would rather hew wood than be a king under
the conditions of the King of England.

Encyclopaedia Britannica

2 There is no middle course between the throne
and the scaffold.

Said to Talleyrand, who is said to have replied 'You are forgetting
the postchaise'
Attrib.

Charles, Prince of Wales (1948–) Eldest son of
Elizabeth II and heir to the throne of the United Kingdom. He is
noted for his controversial views on architecture and the
environment.

1 All the faces here this evening seem to be
bloody Poms.

Remark at Australia Day dinner, 1973

2 British management doesn't seem to understand
the importance of the human factor.

Speech, Parliamentary and Scientific Committee lunch, 21 Feb
1979

3 Like a carbuncle on the face of an old and valued
friend.

Referring to a proposed modern extension to the National
Gallery
Speech, 1986

4 You have to give this much to the Luftwaffe –
when it knocked down our buildings it did not
replace them with anything more offensive than
rubble. We did that.

The Observer, 'Sayings of the Week', 6 Dec 1987

5 Well, frankly, the problem as I see it at this moment in time is whether I should just lie down
under all this hassle and let them walk all over
me, or whether I should just say OK, I get the
message, and do myself in.

I mean, let's face it, I'm in a no-win situation,
and quite honestly, I'm so stuffed up to here
with the whole stupid mess that I can tell you
I've just got a good mind to take the easy way
out. That's the bottom line. The only problem is,
what happens if I find, when I've bumped myself off, there's some kind of . . . ah, you
know, all that mystical stuff about when you die,
you might find you're still – know what I
mean?

At the presentation of the Thomas Cranmer Schools Prize
(1989), suggesting a possible modern English version of Hamlet's
soliloquy. The original version is:

To be, or not to be: that is the question:
Whether 'tis nobler in the mind to suffer
The slings and arrows of outrageous fortune,
Or to take arms against a sea of troubles,
And by opposing end them? To die: to sleep;
No more; and, by a sleep to say we end
The heartache and the thousand natural shocks
That flesh is heir to, 'tis a consummation
Devoutly to be wish'd. To die, to sleep; To
sleep: perchance to dream: aye, there's the rub:
For in that sleep of death what dreams may
come
When we have shuffled off this mortal coil,
Must give us pause.

Chateaubriand, Vicomte François-René de
(1768–1848) French diplomat and writer. His publications include
Le Génie du Christianisme (1802) and *Mémoires d'Outre-tombe*
(1849).

1 An original writer is not one who imitates nobody, but one whom nobody can imitate.

Génie du Christianisme

2 One is not superior merely because one sees the
world in an odious light.

Attrib.

Chaucer, Geoffrey (c. 1342–1400) English poet. *The
Canterbury Tales* is a collection of stories told by pilgrims on their
way to Canterbury. His other works include the poem *The Book of
the Duchess* and *Troilus and Criseyde*.

Quotations about Chaucer

1 Chaucer, notwithstanding the praises bestowed
on him, I think obscene and contemptible; he
owes his celebrity merely to his antiquity.

Lord Byron (1788–1824) British poet. Attrib.

2 I read Chaucer still with as much pleasure as any
of our poets. He is a master of manners and of
description and the first tale-teller in the true
enlivened, natural way.

Alexander Pope (1688–1744) British poet. Attrib.

Quotations by Chaucer

3 Whan that Aprille with his shoures sote
The droghte of Marche hath perced to the rote.

The Canterbury Tales, Prologue

4 He was a verray parfit gentil knight.

Referring to the knight
The Canterbury Tales, Prologue

5 He was as fresh as is the month of May.
Referring to the squire
The Canterbury Tales, Prologue

6 Ful wel she song the service divyne,
Entuned in hir nose ful semely.
Referring to the prioress
The Canterbury Tales, Prologue

7 A Clerk ther was of Oxenford also,
That un-to logik hadde longe y-go.
The Canterbury Tales, Prologue

8 As lene was his hors as is a rake.
The Canterbury Tales, Prologue

9 Souninge in moral vertu was his speche,
And gladly wolde he lerne, and gladly teche.
Referring to the clerk
The Canterbury Tales, Prologue

10 No-wher so bisy a man as he ther nas,
And yet he semed bisier than he was.
Referring to the man of law
The Canterbury Tales, Prologue

11 For gold in phisik is a cordial,
Therfore he lovede gold in special.
Referring to the doctor
The Canterbury Tales, Prologue

12 She was a worthy womman al hir lyve,
Housbondes at chirche-dore she hadde fyve,
Withouten other companye in youthe.
Referring to the wife of Bath
The Canterbury Tales, Prologue

13 The smyler with the knyf under the cloke.
The Canterbury Tales, 'The Knight's Tale'

14 This world nis but a thurghfare ful of wo,
And we ben pilgrimes, passinge to and fro;
Deeth is an ende of every worldly sore.
The Canterbury Tales, 'The Knight's Tale'

15 Tragedie is to seyn a certeyn storie,
As olde bokes maken us memorie,
Of him that stood in greet prosperitee
And is y-fallen out of heigh degree
Into miserie, and endeth wrecchedly.
The Canterbury Tales, 'The Monk's Prologue'

16 Whan that the month in which the world bigan,
That highte March, whan God first maked man.
The Canterbury Tales, 'The Nun's Priest's Tale'

17 Mordre wol out, that see we day by day.
The Canterbury Tales, 'The Nun's Priest's Tale'

18 So was hir joly whistle wel y-wet.
The Canterbury Tales, 'The Reve's Tale'

19 That lyf so short, the craft so long to lerne,
Th' assay so hard, so sharp the conquerynge.
See also HIPPOCRATES
The Parliament of Fowls

20 For of fortunes sharp adversitee
The worst kinde of infortune is this,
A man to have ben in prosperitee,
And it remembren, what is passed is.
Troilus and Criseyde, 3

21 Go, litel book, go litel myn tragedie.
O moral Gower, this book I directe To thee.
Troilus and Criseyde, 5

Chekhov, Anton Pavlovich (1860–1904) Russian
dramatist and writer. Plays include *The Seagull* (1896), *Uncle
Vanya* (1897), *The Three Sisters* (1901), and *The Cherry Orchard*
(1904).

Quotations about Chekhov

1 Politically speaking, he might as well have been
living on the moon as in Imperial Russia.
Ronald Hingley (1920–) Scottish writer. *A New Life of Anton
Chekhov*

2 We are certainly entitled to deduce that he was
somewhat undersexed.
Ronald Hingley (1920–) Scottish writer. *A New Life of Anton
Chekhov*

3 When I had read this story to the end, I was
filled with awe. I could not remain in my room
and went out of doors. I felt as if I were
locked up in a ward too.
On reading *Ward Number Six* (1892)
Lenin (Vladimir Ilich Ulyanov; 1870–1924) Russian revolutionary
leader. *Anton Chekhov* (W. H. Bruford)

Quotations by Chekhov

4 LIBOV ANDREEVNA. Are you still a student?
TROFIMOV. I expect I shall be a student to the
end of my days.
The Cherry Orchard, I

5 When a lot of remedies are suggested for a disease, that means it can't be cured.
The Cherry Orchard, II

6 Before the cherry orchard was sold everybody
was worried and upset, but as soon as it was
all settled finally and once for all, everybody
calmed down, and felt quite cheerful.
The Cherry Orchard, IV

7 MEDVEDENKO. Why do you wear black all the
time?
MASHA. I'm in mourning for my life, I'm
unhappy.
The Seagull, I

8 NINA. Your play's hard to act, there are no living
people in it.
TREPLEV. Living people! We should show life
neither as it is nor as it ought to be, but as we
see it in our dreams.
The Seagull, I

9 The time's come: there's a terrific thunder-cloud
advancing upon us, a mighty storm is coming to
freshen us up. . . . It's going to blow away all
this idleness and indifference, and prejudice
against work. . . . I'm going to work, and in
twenty-five or thirty years' time every man and
woman will be working.
Three Sisters, I

10 Man has been endowed with reason, with the power to create, so that he can add to what he's been given. But up to now he hasn't been a creator, only a destroyer. Forests keep disappearing, rivers dry up, wild life's become extinct, the climate's ruined and the land grows poorer and uglier every day.
Uncle Vanya, I

11 A woman can become a man's friend only in the following stages – first an acquaintance, next a mistress, and only then a friend.
Uncle Vanya, II

12 SONYA. I'm not beautiful.
HELEN. You have lovely hair.
SONYA. No, when a woman isn't beautiful, people always say, 'You have lovely eyes, you have lovely hair.'
Uncle Vanya, III

13 When all is said and done, no literature can outdo the cynicism of real life; you won't intoxicate with one glass someone who has already drunk up a whole barrel.
Letter, 1887

Chesterfield, Philip Dormer Stanhope, 4th Earl of (1694–1773) English statesman and diplomat; author of the famous *Letters* (1774) to his illegitimate son. Appointed ambassador to The Hague in 1728, he subsequently served in Ireland and as secretary of state (1746–48).

Quotations about Chesterfield

1 This man I thought had been a Lord among wits; but, I find, he is only a wit among Lords.
Samuel Johnson (1709–84) British lexicographer. *Life of Johnson* (J. Boswell), Vol. I

2 They teach the morals of a whore, and the manners of a dancing master.
Samuel Johnson *Life of Johnson* (J. Boswell), Vol. I, Referring to Lord Chesterfield's letters

3 The only Englishman who ever maintained that the art of pleasing was the first duty in life.
Voltaire (François-Marie Arouet; 1694–1778) French writer. Letter to Frederick the Great, 16 Aug 1774

4 He was a man of much wit, middling sense, and some learning; but as absolutely void of virtue as any Jew, Turk or Heathen that ever lived.
John Wesley (1703–91) British religious leader. *Journal*, 11 Oct 1775

Quotations by Chesterfield

5 Be wiser than other people if you can, but do not tell them so.
Letter to his son, 19 Nov 1745

6 Whatever is worth doing at all is worth doing well.
Letter to his son, 10 Mar 1746

7 An injury is much sooner forgotten than an insult.
Letter to his son, 9 Oct 1746

8 Take the tone of the company you are in.
Letter to his son, 9 Oct 1747

9 Do as you would be done by is the surest method that I know of pleasing.
Letter to his son, 16 Oct 1747

10 I knew once a very covetous, sordid fellow, who used to say, 'Take care of the pence, for the pounds will take care of themselves.'
Possibly referring to William Lowndes
Letter to his son, 6 Nov 1747

11 I recommend you to take care of the minutes: for hours will take care of themselves.
Letter to his son, 6 Nov 1747

12 Advice is seldom welcome; and those who want it the most always like it the least.
Letter to his son, 29 Jan 1748

13 It must be owned, that the Graces do not seem to be natives of Great Britain; and I doubt, the best of us here have more of rough than polished diamond.
Letter to his son, 18 Nov 1748

14 Due attention to the inside of books, and due contempt for the outside, is the proper relation between a man of sense and his books.
Letter to his son, 10 Jan 1749

15 Idleness is only the refuge of weak minds.
Letter to his son, 20 July 1749

16 Women are much more like each other than men: they have, in truth, but two passions, vanity and love; these are their universal characteristics.
Letter to his son, 19 Dec 1749

17 Every woman is infallibly to be gained by every sort of flattery, and every man by one sort or other.
Letter to his son, 16 Mar 1752

18 A chapter of accidents.
Letter to his son, 16 Feb 1753

19 Religion is by no means a proper subject of conversation in a mixed company.
Letter to his godson

20 We, my lords, may thank heaven that we have something better than our brains to depend upon.
Speech, House of Lords
The Story of Civilization (W. Durant), Vol. 9

21 Make him a bishop, and you will silence him at once.
When asked what steps might be taken to control the evangelical preacher George Whitefield
Attrib.

22 When your ladyship's faith has removed them, I will go thither with all my heart.
Said to his sister, Lady Gertrude Hotham, when she suggested he go to a Methodist seminary in Wales to recuperate, recommending the views
Attrib.

23 Give Dayrolles a chair.

Said on his deathbed when visited by his godson, Solomon Dayrolles
Last words

Chesterton, G(ilbert) K(eith) (1874–1936) British essayist, novelist, and poet. His detective stories feature the priest Father Brown and his novels include *The Napoleon of Notting Hill* (1904). After conversion to Roman Catholicism (1933) much of his writing was religious.

Quotations about Chesterton

1 Chesterton is like a vile scum on a pond. . . . All his slop – it is really modern catholicism to a great extent, the *never* taking a hedge straight, the mumbo-jumbo of superstition dodging behind clumsy fun and paradox . . . I believe he creates a milieu in which art is impossible. He and his kind.

Ezra Pound (1885–1972) US poet. Letter to John Quinn, 21 Aug 1917

2 Chesterton's resolute conviviality is about as genial as an *auto da fé* of teetotallers.

George Bernard Shaw (1856–1950) Irish dramatist and critic. *Pen Portraits and Reviews*

3 Here lies Mr Chesterton,
Who to heaven might have gone,
But didn't when he heard the news
That the place was run by Jews.

Humbert Wolfe (1886–1940) British poet. *Lampoons*

Quotations by Chesterton

4 A great deal of contemporary criticism reads to me like a man saying: 'Of course I do not like green cheese: I am very fond of brown sherry.'

All I Survey

5 The modern world . . . has no notion except that of simplifying something by destroying nearly everything.

All I Survey

6 Talk about the pews and steeples
And the cash that goes therewith!
But the souls of Christian peoples . . .
Chuck it, Smith!

Antichrist, or the Reunion of Christendom

7 The strangest whim has seized me . . . After all I think I will not hang myself today.

A Ballade of Suicide

8 'My country, right or wrong' is a thing that no patriot would thing of saying, except in a desperate case. It is like saying 'My mother, drunk or sober.'

The Defendant

9 There is a road from the eye to the heart that does not go through the intellect.

The Defendant

10 The one stream of poetry which is continually flowing is slang.

The Defendant

11 All slang is metaphor, and all metaphor is poetry.

The Defendant

12 The devil's walking parody
On all four-footed things.

The Donkey

13 Fools! For I also had my hour;
One far fierce hour and sweet;
There was a shout about my ears,
And palms before my feet.

The Donkey

14 The rich are the scum of the earth in every country.

The Flying Inn

15 One sees great things from the valley; only small things from the peak.

The Hammer of God

16 The word 'orthodoxy' not only no longer means being right; it practically means being wrong.

Heretics, Ch. 1

17 There is no such thing on earth as an uninteresting subject; the only thing that can exist is an uninterested person.

Heretics, Ch. 1

18 As enunciated today, 'progress' is simply a comparative of which we have not settled the superlative.

Heretics, Ch. 2

19 We ought to see far enough into a hypocrite to see even his sincerity.

Heretics, Ch. 5

20 Happiness is a mystery like religion, and should never be rationalized.

Heretics, Ch. 7

21 Charity is the power of defending that which we know to be indefensible. Hope is the power of being cheerful in circumstances which we know to be desperate.

Heretics, Ch. 12

22 Carlyle said that men were mostly fools. Christianity, with a surer and more reverend realism, says that they are all fools.

Heretics, Ch. 12

23 A good novel tells us the truth about its hero; but a bad novel tells us the truth about its author.

Heretics, Ch. 15

24 The artistic temperament is a disease that afflicts amateurs.

Heretics, Ch. 17

25 To be clever enough to get all that money, one must be stupid enough to want it.

The Innocence of Father Brown

26 Evil comes at leisure like the disease; good comes in a hurry like the doctor.

The Man who was Orthodox

27 You can only find truth with logic if you have already found truth without it.
The Man who was Orthodox

28 The human race, to which so many of my readers belong.
The Napoleon of Notting Hill, Vol. I, Ch. 1

29 The madman is not the man who has lost his reason. The madman is the man who has lost everything except his reason.
Orthodoxy, Ch. 1

30 The cosmos is about the smallest hole that a man can hide his head in.
Orthodoxy, Ch. 1

31 Reason is itself a matter of faith. It is an act of faith to assert that our thoughts have any relation to reality at all.
Orthodoxy, Ch. 3

32 Mr Shaw is (I suspect) the only man on earth who has never written any poetry.
Referring to George Bernard Shaw
Orthodoxy, Ch. 3

33 All conservatism is based upon the idea that if you leave things alone you leave them as they are. But you do not. If you leave a thing alone you leave it to a torrent of change.
Orthodoxy, Ch. 7

34 Angels can fly because they take themselves lightly.
Orthodoxy, Ch. 7

35 Before the Roman came to Rye or out to Severn strode,
The rolling English drunkard made the rolling English road.
The Rolling English Road

36 Smile at us, pay us, pass us; but do not quite forget.
For we are the people of England, that never have spoken yet.
The Secret People

37 Is ditchwater dull? Naturalists with microscopes have told me that it teems with quiet fun.
The Spice of Life

38 He could not think up to the height of his own towering style.
Speaking of Tennyson
The Victorian Age in Literature, Ch. 3

39 Compromise used to mean that half a loaf was better than no bread. Among modern statesmen it really seems to mean that half a loaf is better than a whole loaf.
What's Wrong with the World

40 Mankind is not a tribe of animals to which we owe compassion. Mankind is a club to which we owe our subscription.
Daily News, 10 Apr 1906

41 Just the other day in the Underground I enjoyed the pleasure of offering my seat to three ladies.
Suggesting that fatness had its consolations
Das Buch des Lachens (W. Scholz)

42 There is nothing the matter with Americans except their ideals. The real American is all right; it is the ideal American who is all wrong.
New York Times, 1 Feb 1931

43 Democracy means government by the uneducated, while aristocracy means government by the badly educated.
New York Times, 1 Feb 1931

44 Education is simply the soul of a society as it passes from one generation to another.
The Observer, 'Sayings of the Week', 6 July 1924

45 I want to reassure you I am not this size, really – dear me no, I'm being amplified by the mike.
At a lecture in Pittsburgh
The Outline of Sanity: A Life of G. K. Chesterton (S. D. Dale)

46 Am in Birmingham. Where ought I to be?
Telegram to his wife during a lecture tour
Portrait of Barrie (C. Asquith)

47 The only way to be sure of catching a train is to miss the one before it.
Vacances à tous prix, 'Le Supplice de l'heure' (P. Daninos)

48 How beautiful it would be for someone who could not read.
Referring to the lights on Broadway
Attrib.

49 A puritan's a person who pours righteous indignation into the wrong things.
Attrib.

50 New roads: new ruts.
Attrib.

Chevalier, Albert (1861–1923) British music-hall artist. He introduced many popular songs, such as *The Future Mrs. 'Awkins* and *My Old Dutch*.

1 There ain't a lady livin' in the land
As I'd swop for my dear old Dutch!
My Old Dutch

2 Laugh! I though I should 'ave died,
Knocked 'em in the Old Kent Road.
Wot Cher or *Knocked 'em in the Old Kent Road*

Chevalier, Maurice (1888–1972) French singer, actor, and entertainer. His films include *Love Me Tonight* (1932) and *Gigi* (1958).

1 Many a man has fallen in love with a girl in a light so dim he would not have chosen a suit by it.
Attrib.

2 I prefer old age to the alternative.
Attrib.

Child, Lydia M. (1802–80) US abolitionist campaigner.

1 But men never violate the laws of God without suffering the consequences, sooner or later.
The Freedmen's Book, 'Toussaint L'Ouverture'

2 Not in vain is Ireland pouring itself all over the earth . . . The Irish, with their glowing hearts and reverent credulity, are needed in this cold age of intellect and skepticism.
Letters from New York, Vol. I, No. 33, 8 Dec 1842

3 England may as well dam up the waters from the Nile with bulrushes as to fetter the step of Freedom, more proud and firm in this youthful land.
The Rebels, Ch. 4

Chomsky, Noam (1928–) US academic linguist. His *Syntactic Structures* (1957) and *Aspects of the Theory of Syntax* (1965) set out his development of transformational grammar; later works include *Language and Responsibility* (1979) and *Towards a New Cold War* (1982).

1 Colourless green ideas sleep furiously.
Used by Chomsky to demonstrate that an utterance can be grammatical without having meaning
Syntactic Structures

Chopin, Kate (1851–1904) US writer.

1 The voice of the sea speaks to the soul. The touch of the sea is sensuous, enfolding the body in its soft, close embrace.
The Awakening, Ch. 6

2 The past was nothing to her; offered no lesson which she was willing to heed. The future was a mystery which she never attempted to penetrate. The present alone was significant.
The Awakening, Ch. 15

3 There are some people who leave impressions not so lasting as the imprint of an oar upon the water.
The Awakening, Ch. 34

Chou En Lai (1898–1976) Chinese statesman. He became political commissar to the Red Army in 1932. He was prime minister of the People's Republic of China (1949–76) and foreign minister (1949–58).

1 All diplomacy is a continuation of war by other means.
Compare CLAUSEWITZ

Christie, Dame Agatha (1891–1976) British detective-story writer. Her detective Hercule Poirot first appeared in *The Mysterious Affair at Styles* (1920). Among her 50 or so other stories are *Murder on the Orient Express* (1934) and *Death on the Nile* (1937). Her play *The Mousetrap* (1952) has had the longest run of any London play (over 35 years).

1 One doesn't recognize in one's life the really important moments – not until it's too late.
Endless Night, Bk. II, Ch. 14

2 Where large sums of money are concerned, it is advisable to trust nobody.
Endless Night, Bk. II, Ch. 15

3 Hercule Poirot tapped his forehead. 'These little grey cells, It is 'up to them' – as you say over here.'
The Mysterious Affair at Styles

4 If one sticks too rigidly to one's principles one would hardly see anybody.
Toward's Zero, I

5 Curious things, habits. People themselves never knew they had them.
Witness for the Prosecution

6 An archaeologist is the best husband any woman can have: the older she gets, the more interested he is in her.
Attrib.

Chuang Tse (*or* Zhuangzi; c. 369–286 BC) Chinese philosopher. The book to which he gave his name has influenced the development of Buddhism.

1 I do not know whether I was then a man dreaming I was a butterfly, or whether I am now a butterfly dreaming I am a man.
Chuang Tse (H. A. Giles), Ch. 2

Churchill, Charles (1731–64) British poet. His satirical verse includes *The Rosciad* (1761) and *The Prophecy of Famine* (1763), an attack on the government.

1 The danger chiefly lies in acting well,
No crime's so great as daring to excel.
Epistle to William Hogarth

2 Be England what she will,
With all her faults, she is my country still.
The Farewell

3 A joke's a very serious thing.
The Ghost, Bk. IV

4 Old-age, a second child, by Nature curs'd
With more and greater evils than the first,
Weak, sickly, full of pains; in ev'ry breath
Railing at life, and yet afraid of death.
Gotham, I

5 Keep up appearances; their lies the test
The world will give thee credit for the rest.
Night

Churchill, Jennie Jerome (1854–1921) US-born British hostess and writer, who married Lord Randolph Churchill in 1874. She was the mother of Sir Winston Churchill.

1 ALMA. I rather suspect her of being in love with him.
MARTIN. Her own husband? Monstrous! What a selfish woman!
His Borrowed Plumes

2 . . . we owe something to extravagance, for thrift and adventure seldom go hand in hand. . . .
Pearson's, 'Extravagance'

3 You seem to have no real purpose in life and won't realize at the age of twenty-two that for a man life means work, and hard work if you mean to succeed. . . .
Letter to Winston Churchill, 26 Feb 1897
Jennie (Ralph G. Martin), Vol. II

Churchill, Lord Randolph Henry Spencer (1849–95) British Conservative politician; father of Sir Winston Churchill. He was appointed secretary for India in 1885 and served for a few months as chancellor of the exchequer (1886).

1 The duty of an opposition is to oppose.
Lord Randolph Churchill (W. S. Churchill)

2 I never could make out what those damned dots meant.
Referring to decimal points
Lord Randolph Churchill (W. S. Churchill)

3 Ulster will fight; Ulster will be right.
Letter, 7 May 1886

4 An old man in a hurry.
Referring to Gladstone
Speech, June 1886

5 I expect you know my friend Evelyn Waugh, who, like you, your Holiness, is a Roman Catholic.
Remark made during an audience with the Pope

Churchill, Sir Winston Leonard Spencer (1874–1965) British statesman and writer, prime minister (1940–45, 1951–55). After service as a war correspondent in the Boer War, he became first Lord of the Admiralty in World War I and led a coalition government in World War II. He was celebrated for his skill as an orator and was the author of several historical books.

Quotations about Churchill

1 It hasn't taken Winston long to get used to American ways. He hadn't been an American citizen for three minutes before attacking an ex-secretary of state!
Dean Acheson (1893–1971) US lawyer and statesman. At a ceremony in 1963 to make Churchill an honorary American citizen, Churchill obliquely attacked Acheson's reference to Britain losing an empire. *Randolph Churchill* (K. Halle)

2 Then comes Winston with his hundred-horse-power mind and what can I do?
Stanley Baldwin (1867–1947) British statesman. *Stanley Baldwin* (G. M. Young), Ch. 11

3 I thought he was a young man of promise; but it appears he was a young man of promises.
Arthur Balfour (1848–1930) British statesman. Said of Winston Churchill on his entry into politics, 1899. *Winston Churchill* (Randolph Churchill), Vol. I

4 He is a man suffering from petrified adolescence.
Aneurin Bevan (1897–1960) British Labour politician. *Aneurin Bevan* (Vincent Brome), Ch. 11

5 The nation had the lion's heart. I had the luck to give the roar.
Winston Churchill (1874–1965) British statesman. Said on his 80th birthday

6 The first time you meet Winston you see all his faults and the rest of your life you spend in discovering his virtues.
Lady Constance Lytton (1869–1923) British suffragette. *Edward Marsh* (Christopher Hassall), Ch. 7

7 Winston had devoted the best years of his life to preparing his impromptu speeches.
F. E. Smith (1872–1930) British lawyer and politician. Attrib.

8 Simply a radio personality who outlived his prime.
Evelyn Waugh (1903–66) British novelist. *Evelyn Waugh* (Christopher Sykes)

Quotations by Churchill

9 Well, the principle seems the same. The water still keeps falling over.
When asked whether the Niagara Falls looked the same as when he first saw them
Closing the Ring, Ch. 5

10 I said that the world must be made safe for at least fifty years. If it was only for fifteen to twenty years then we should have betrayed our soldiers.
Closing the Ring, Ch. 20

11 We must have a better word than 'prefabricated'. Why not 'ready-made'?
Closing the Ring, Appendix C

12 The redress of the grievances of the vanquished should precede the disarmament of the victors.
The Gathering Storm, Ch. 3

13 I felt as if I were walking with destiny, and that all my past life had been but a preparation for this hour and this trial.
The Gathering Storm, Ch. 38

14 I have only one purpose, the destruction of Hitler, and my life is much simplified thereby. If Hitler invaded Hell I would make at least a favourable reference to the Devil in the House of Commons.
The Grand Alliance

15 When you have to kill a man it costs nothing to be polite.
Justifying the fact that the declaration of war against Japan was made in the usual diplomatic language
The Grand Alliance

16 Before Alamein we never had a victory. After Alamein we never had a defeat.
The Hinge of Fate, Ch. 33

17 By being so long in the lowest form I gained an immense advantage over the cleverest boys . . . I got into my bones the essential structure of the normal British sentence – which is a noble thing.
My Early Life, Ch. 2

18 Headmasters have powers at their disposal with which Prime Ministers have never yet been invested.
My Early Life, Ch. 2

19 So they told me how Mr Gladstone read Homer for fun, which I thought served him right.
My Early Life, Ch. 2

20 Which brings me to my conclusion upon Free Will and Predestination, namely – let the reader mark it – that they are identical.
My Early Life, Ch. 3

21 It is a good thing for an uneducated man to read books of quotations.
My Early Life, Ch. 9

22 Everyone threw the blame on me. I have noticed that they nearly always do. I suppose it is because they think I shall be able to bear it best.
My Early Life, Ch. 17

23 Those who can win a war well can rarely make a good peace and those who could make a good peace would never have won the war.
My Early Life, Ch. 26

24 I have never seen a human being who more perfectly represented the modern conception of a robot.
Referring to the Soviet statesman Molotov
The Second World War

25 I must point out that my rule of life prescribed as an absolutely sacred rite smoking cigars and also the drinking of alcohol before, after, and if need be during all meals and in the intervals between them.
Said during a lunch with the Arab leader Ibn Saud, when he heard that the king's religion forbade smoking and alcohol
The Second World War

26 In Franklin Roosevelt there died the greatest American friend we have ever known and the greatest champion of freedom who has ever brought help and comfort from the New World to the Old.
The Second World War

27 In war, resolution; in defeat, defiance; in victory, magnanimity; in peace, goodwill.
Epigram used by Sir Edward Marsh after World War II; used as 'a moral of the work' in Churchill's book
The Second World War

28 No one can guarantee success in war, but only deserve it.
Their Finest Hour

29 Wars are not won by evacuations.
Referring to Dunkirk
Their Finest Hour

30 When I look back on all these worries I remember the story of the old man who said on his deathbed that he had had a lot of trouble in his life, most of which had never happened.
Their Finest Hour

31 Peace with Germany and Japan on our terms will not bring much rest. . . . As I observed last time, when the war of the giants is over the wars of the pygmies will begin.
Triumph and Tragedy, Ch. 25

32 Dictators ride to and fro upon tigers which they dare not dismount. And the tigers are getting hungry.
While England Slept

33 In defeat unbeatable; in victory unbearable.
Referring to Viscount Montgomery
Ambrosia and Small Beer (E. Marsh), Ch. 5

34 You may take the most gallant sailor, the most intrepid airman, or the most audacious soldier, put them at a table together – what do you get? *The sum of their fears.*
Talking about the Chiefs of Staffs system, 16 Nov 1943
The Blast of War (H. Macmillan), Ch. 16

35 Don't talk to me about naval tradition. It's nothing but rum, sodomy, and the lash.
Former Naval Person (Sir Peter Gretton), Ch. 1

36 Jellicoe was the only man on either side who could lose the war in an afternoon.
The Observer, 'Sayings of the Week', 13 Feb 1927

37 Everybody has a right to pronounce foreign names as he chooses.
The Observer, 'Sayings of the Week', 5 Aug 1951

38 This is the sort of English up with which I will not put.
The story is that Churchill wrote the comment in the margin of a report in which a Civil Servant had used an awkward construction to avoid ending a sentence with a preposition. An alternative version substitutes 'bloody nonsense' for 'English'.
Plain Words (E. Gowers), Ch. 9

39 Men will forgive a man anything except bad prose.
Election speech, Manchester, 1906

40 It cannot in the opinion of His Majesty's Government be classified as slavery in the extreme acceptance of the word without some risk of terminological inexactitude.
Speech, House of Commons, 22 Feb 1906

41 *The Times* is speechless and takes three columns to express its speechlessness.
Referring to Irish Home Rule
Speech, Dundee, 14 May 1908

42 He is one of those orators of whom it was well said, 'Before they get up they do not know what they are going to say; when they are speaking, they do not know what they are saying; and when they sit down, they do not know what they have said'.
Referring to Lord Charles Beresford
Speech, House of Commons, 20 Dec 1912

43 The maxim of the British people is 'Business as usual'.
Speech, Guildhall, 9 Nov 1914

44 Labour is not fit to govern.
Election speech, 1920

45 I remember, when I was a child, being taken to the celebrated Barnum's circus, which contained an exhibition of freaks and monstrosities, but the exhibit . . . which I most desired to see was the one described as 'The Boneless Wonder'. My parents judged that that spectacle would be too revolting and demoralising for my youthful eyes, and I have waited 50 years to see the boneless wonder sitting on the Treasury Bench.
Referring to Ramsey MacDonald
Speech, House of Commons, 28 Jan 1931

46 India is a geographical term. It is no more a united nation than the Equator.
Speech, Royal Albert Hall, 18 Mar 1931

47 We have sustained a defeat without a war.
Speech, House of Commons, 5 Oct 1938

48 I cannot forecast to you the action of Russia. It is a riddle wrapped in a mystery inside an enigma.
Broadcast talk, 1 Oct 1939

49 I have nothing to offer but blood, toil, tears and sweat.
On becoming prime minister
Speech, House of Commons, 13 May 1940

50 Victory at all costs, victory in spite of all terror, victory however long and hard the road may be; for without victory there is no survival.
Speech, House of Commons, 13 May 1940

51 We shall not flag or fail. We shall fight in France, we shall fight on the seas and oceans, we shall fight with growing confidence and growing strength in the air, we shall defend our island, whatever the cost may be, we shall fight on the beaches, we shall fight on the landing grounds, we shall fight in the fields and in the streets, we shall fight in the hills; we shall never surrender.
Speech, House of Commons, 4 June 1940

52 This was their finest hour.
Referring to the Dunkirk evacuation
Speech, House of Commons, 18 June 1940

53 The battle of Britain is about to begin.
Speech, House of Commons, 1 July 1940

54 Never in the field of human conflict was so much owed by so many to so few.
Referring to the Battle of Britain pilots
Speech, House of Commons, 20 Aug 1940

55 We are waiting for the long-promised invasion. So are the fishes.
Radio broadcast to the French people, 21 Oct 1940

56 Give us the tools, and we will finish the job.
Referring to Lend-lease, which was being legislated in the USA
Radio Broadcast, 9 Feb 1941

57 You do your worst, and we will do our best.
Addressed to Hitler
Speech, 14 July 1941

58 Do not let us speak of darker days; let us rather speak of sterner days. These are not dark days: these are great days – the greatest days our country has ever lived.
Address, Harrow School, 29 Oct 1941

59 When I warned them that Britain would fight on alone whatever they did, their Generals told their Prime Minister and his divided Cabinet: 'In three weeks England will have her neck wrung like a chicken.'
Some chicken! Some neck!
Referring to the French Government
Speech, Canadian Parliament, 30 Dec 1941

60 This is not the end. It is not even the beginning of the end. But it is, perhaps, the end of the beginning.
Referring to the Battle of Egypt
Speech, Mansion House, 10 Nov 1942

61 I have not become the King's First Minister in order to preside over the liquidation of the British Empire.
Speech, Mansion House, 10 Nov 1942

62 The Almighty in His infinite wisdom did not see fit to create Frenchmen in the image of Englishmen.
Speech, House of Commons, 10 Dec 1942

63 There is no finer investment for any community than putting milk into babies.
Radio Broadcast, 21 Mar 1943

64 There are few virtues which the Poles do not possess and there are few errors they have ever avoided.
Speech, House of Commons, 1945

65 An iron curtain has descended across the Continent.
Address, Westminster College, Fulton, USA, 5 Mar 1946

66 We must build a kind of United States of Europe.
Speech, Zurich, 19 Sept 1946

67 Perhaps it is better to be irresponsible and right than to be responsible and wrong.
Party Political Broadcast, London, 26 Aug 1950

68 To jaw-jaw is better than to war-war.
Speech, Washington, 26 June 1954

69 They are the only people who like to be told how bad things are – who like to be told the worst.
Referring to the British
Speech, 1921

70 An appeaser is one who feeds a crocodile – hoping that it will eat him last.
Attrib.

Cibber, Colley (1671–1757) British actor and dramatist. His plays include the comedies *Love's Last Shift* (1696) and *The Careless Husband* (1704).

1 One had as good be out of the world, as out of the fashion.
Love's Last Shift, II

2 Stolen sweets are best.

The Rival Fools, I

Cicero, Marcus Tullius (106–43 BC) Roman orator and statesman. Elected consul in 63 BC, he was exiled (58–57 BC) and subsequently opposed Caesar in the civil war. After Caesar's assassination he delivered a famous series of speeches (the *Philippics*) against Mark Antony.

1 There is nothing so absurd but some philosopher has said it.

De Divinatione, II

2 The good of the people is the chief law.

De Legibus, III

3 *Summum bonum.*
The greatest good.

De Officiis, I

4 *O tempora! O mores!*
What times! What customs!

In Catilinam, I

5 *Cui bono?*
To whose profit?

Pro Milone, IV

Clarke, Arthur C. (1917–) British science-fiction writer. His novels include *Childhood's End* (1953), *2001: A space odyssey* (1968), and *Tales from Planet Earth* (1989).

1 When a distinguished but elderly scientist states that something is possible, he is almost certainly right. When he states that something is impossible, he is very probably wrong.

Profiles of the Future

Clarke, John (fl. 1639) English scholar; author of *Paroemiologia Anglo-Latina* (1639), a collection of English and Latin proverbs.

1 Home is home, though it be never so homely.

Paroemiologia Anglo-Latina

Clausewitz, Karl von (1780–1831) Prussian general. His military writings include *Vom Kriege*, which influenced strategy in World War I.

1 War is the continuation of politics by other means.

The usual misquotation of 'War is nothing but a continuation of politics with the admixture of other means'; *compare* CHOW EN LAI
Vom Kriege

Clay, Henry (1777–1852) US politician, nicknamed 'the great compromiser (or pacificator)'. He was secretary of state to the Republican president John Quincy Adams (1825–29).

1 I had rather be right than be President.

Speech, 1850

Clemenceau, Georges (1841–1929) French statesman. Prime minister (1906–09, 1917–20), he led France to victory at the end of World War I.

1 America is the only nation in history which miraculously has gone directly from barbarism to degeneration without the usual interval of civilization.

Attrib.

2 War is too important to be left to the generals.

Attrib.

Clemens, Samuel Langhorne *See* Twain, Mark

Clive of Plassey, Robert, Baron (1725–74) British soldier and governor of Bengal. He went to Madras with the East India Company in 1743 and distinguished himself in the Anglo-French conflict: his victory at the Battle of Plassey (1757) helped to establish British supremacy.

1 By God, Mr Chairman, at this moment I stand astonished at my own moderation!

Reply during Parliamentary Inquiry, 1773

Clough, Arthur Hugh (1819–61) British poet. His works include *The Bothie of Tober-na-Vuolich* (1848), 'Amours de Voyage' (1858), and 'The Latest Decalogue' (1862).

1 *Action will furnish belief,* – but will that belief be the true one?
This is the point, you know.

Amours de voyage, V

2 A world where nothing is had for nothing.

The Bothie of Tober-na-Vuolich, Bk. VIII, Ch. 5

3 How pleasant it is to have money.

Dipsychus, Bk. I

4 This world is very odd we see,
We do not comprehend it;
But in one fact we all agree,
God won't, and we can't mend it.

Dipsychus, Bk. II

5 Thou shalt have one God only; who
Would be at the expense of two?

The Latest Decalogue, 1

6 Thou shalt not kill; but needst not strive
Officiously to keep alive.

The Latest Decalogue, 11

7 'Tis better to have fought and lost,
Than never to have fought at all.

Peschiera

Cobbett, William (1763–1835) British journalist and writer, editor of the *Political Register* (1802–35). His controversial articles led to imprisonment and temporary exile; on returning to England he compiled his famous *Rural Rides* (1830).

1 To be poor and independent is very nearly an impossibility.

Advice to Young Men

2 From a very early age, I had imbibed the opinion, that it was every man's duty to do all that lay in his power to leave his country as good as he had found it.

Political Register, 22 Dec 1832

3 But what is to be the fate of the great wen of all?

Referring to London
Rural Rides

Cobden, Richard (1804–65) British politician. An outstanding orator, he was an advocate of free trade. With John Bright he formed the Anti-Corn Law League.

1 I believe it has been said that one copy of *The Times* contains more useful information than the whole of the historical works of Thucydides.

Speech, Manchester, 27 Dec 1850

Coborn, Charles (1852–1945) US songwriter.

1 Two lovely black eyes,
Oh, what a surprise!
Only for telling a man he was wrong.
Two lovely black eyes!

Two Lovely Black Eyes

Cocks, Sir (Thomas George) Barnett (1907–)
British political writer, clerk of the House of Commons (1962–73).

1 A committee is a cul-de-sac down which ideas are lured and then quietly strangled.

New Scientist, 1973

Cocteau, Jean (1889–1963) French poet and artist. He made his name with *Les Enfants terribles* (1929), which he later (1950) made into a film. His poetry included *L'Ange Heurtebise* (1925) and he also wrote *Orphée* (1926), a play.

1 A true poet does not bother to be poetical. Nor does a nursery gardener scent his roses.

Professional Secrets

2 Tact consists in knowing how far we may go too far.

In *Treasury of Humorous Quotations*

Cohen, Leonard (1934–) Canadian poet and singer. His albums include *The Songs of Leonard Cohen* (1967) and *I am the Man* (1988).

1 To the men and women who own men and women

those of us meant to be lovers
we will not pardon you
for wasting our bodies and time

The Energy of Slaves

2 They locked up a man
who wanted to rule the world
The fools
They locked up the wrong man

The Energy of Slaves

3 And Jesus was a sailor when he walked upon the water
And he spent a long time watching from his lonely wooden tower
And when he knew for certain only drowning men could see him
He said: 'All men will be sailors then, until the sea shall free them.'

Suzanne

Coke, Desmond (1879–1931) British writer. His works include *Sandford of Merton* (1903), *The Golden Key* (1909), and *The Worm* (1927).

1 All rowed fast but none so fast as stroke.

Popular misquotation, derived from the passage: 'His blade struck the water a full second before any other . . . until . . . as the boats began to near the winning post, his own was dipping into the water *twice* as often as any other.'
Sandford of Merton

Coke, Sir Edward (1552–1634) English lawyer and politician. A lifelong rival of Francis Bacon, he became attorney general in 1594 and served as chief justice of the King's Bench under James I (1613–16).

1 The house of every one is to him as his castle and fortress.

Semayne's Case

2 Magna Charta is such a fellow, that he will have no sovereign.

Speaking on the Lords Amendment to the Petition of Right, 17 May 1628
Hist. Coll. (Rushworth), I

Colby, Frank More (1865–1925) US editor. His works included *The New International Encyclopedia* (1900–03).

1 Men will confess to treason, murder, arson, false teeth, or a wig. How many of them will own up to a lack of humour?

Essays, I

2 I have found some of the best reasons I ever had for remaining at the bottom simply by looking at the men at the top.

Essays, II

Coleridge, (David) Hartley (1796–1849) British poet. The son of Samuel Taylor Coleridge, he wrote many sonnets and songs.

1 But what is Freedom? Rightly understood,
A universal licence to be good.

Liberty

Coleridge, Samuel Taylor (1772–1834) British poet, chiefly remembered for such works as 'Kubla Khan' (composed in 1797, under the influence of opium) and *The Rime of the Ancient Mariner* (1798). His *Lyrical Ballads* (1798), written with William Wordsworth, was extremely influential.

Quotations about Coleridge

1 A weak, diffusive, weltering, ineffectual man.

Thomas Carlyle (1795–1881) Scottish historian and essayist. Attrib.

2 His face when he repeats his verses hath its ancient glory, an Archangel a little damaged.

Charles Lamb (1775–1834) British essayist. Letter, 26 Apr 1816

Quotations by Coleridge

3 He who begins by loving Christianity better than Truth will proceed by loving his own sect or church better than Christianity, and end by loving himself better than all.

Aids to Reflection: Moral and Religious Aphorisms,

4 If a man could pass through Paradise in a dream, and have a flower presented to him as a pledge that his soul had really been there, and if he found that flower in his hand when he awoke – Aye, and what then?

Anima Poetae

5 The primary imagination I hold to be the living power and prime agent of all human perception, and as a repetition in the finite mind of the eternal act of creation in the infinite I AM.

Biographia Literaria, Ch. 13

6 The Fancy is indeed no other than a mode of memory emancipated from the order of time and space.

Biographia Literaria, Ch. 13

7 Nothing can permanently please, which does not contain in itself the reason why it is so, and not otherwise.

Biographia Literaria, Ch. 14

8 That willing suspension of disbelief for the moment, which constitutes poetic faith.

Biographia Literaria, Ch. 14

9 Our myriad-minded Shakespeare.

Biographia Literaria, Ch. 15

10 A sight to dream of, not to tell!

Christabel, I

11 I may not hope from outward forms to win
The passion and the life, whose fountains are within.

Dejection: An Ode

12 Swans sing before they die – 'twere no bad thing,
Did certain persons die before they sing.

Epigram on a Volunteer Singer

13 On awaking he . . . instantly and eagerly wrote down the lines that are here preserved. At this moment he was unfortunately called out by a person on business from Porlock.

Kubla Khan (preliminary note)

14 In Xanadu did Kubla Khan
A stately pleasure-dome decree:
Where Alph, the sacred river, ran
Through caverns measureless to man
Down to a sunless sea.

Kubla Khan

15 It was a miracle of rare device,
A sunny pleasure-dome with caves of ice!

Kubla Khan

16 A savage place! as holy and enchanted
As e'er beneath a waning moon was haunted
By woman wailing for her demon-lover!

Kubla Khan

17 And all should cry, Beware! Beware!
His flashing eyes, his floating hair!
Weave a circle round him thrice,
And close your eyes with holy dread,
For he on honey-dew hath fed,
And drunk the milk of Paradise.

Kubla Khan

18 Poetry is not the proper antithesis to prose, but to science. Poetry is opposed to science, and prose to metre.

Lectures and Notes of 1818, I

19 Reviewers are usually people who would have been poets, historians, biographers, . . . if they could; they have tried their talents at one or at the other, and have failed; therefore they turn critics.

Lectures on Shakespeare and Milton, I

20 The faults of great authors are generally excellences carried to an excess.

Miscellanies, 149

21 With Donne, whose muse on dromedary trots,
Wreathe iron pokers into true-love knots.

On Donne's Poetry

22 The most happy marriage I can picture or imagine to myself would be the union of a deaf man to a blind woman.

Recollections (Allsop)

23 If men could learn from history, what lessons it might teach us! But passion and party blind our eyes and the light which experience gives is a lantern on the stern, which shines only on the waves behind us!

Recollections (Allsop)

24 It is an ancient Mariner,
And he stoppeth one of three.
'By thy long grey beard and glittering eye,
Now wherefore stopp'st thou me?'

The Rime of the Ancient Mariner, I

25 The Sun came up upon the left,
Out of the sea came he!
And he shone bright, and on the right
Went down into the sea.

The Rime of the Ancient Mariner, I

26 The ice was here, the ice was there,
The ice was all around:
It cracked and growled, and roared and howled,
Like noises in a swound!

The Rime of the Ancient Mariner, I

27 With my cross-bow
I shot the albatross.

The Rime of the Ancient Mariner, I

28 As idle as a painted ship
Upon a painted ocean.

The Rime of the Ancient Mariner, I

29 The fair breeze blew, the white foam flew,
The furrow followed free;
We were the first that ever burst
Into that silent sea.
The Rime of the Ancient Mariner, II

30 Water, water, every where,
And all the boards did shrink;
Water, water, every where,
Nor any drop to drink.
The Rime of the Ancient Mariner, II

31 Alone, alone, all, all alone,
Alone on a wide wide sea!
And never a saint took pity on
My soul in agony.
The Rime of the Ancient Mariner, IV

32 The many men, so beautiful!
And they all dead did lie:
And a thousand thousand slimy things
Lived on; and so did I.
The Rime of the Ancient Mariner, IV

33 The moving Moon went up the sky,
And no where did abide:
Softly she was going up,
And a star or two beside.
The Rime of the Ancient Mariner, IV

34 Oh sleep! it is a gentle thing,
Beloved from pole to pole!
The Rime of the Ancient Mariner, V

35 Quoth he, 'The man hath penance done,
And penance more will do.'
The Rime of the Ancient Mariner, V

36 Like one, that on a lonesome road
Doth walk in fear and dread,
And having once turned round walks on,
And turns no more his head;
Because he knows, a frightful fiend
Doth close behind him tread.
The Rime of the Ancient Mariner, VI

37 No voice; but oh! the silence sank
Like music on my heart.
The Rime of the Ancient Mariner, VI

38 He prayeth well, who loveth well
Both man and bird and beast.
The Rime of the Ancient Mariner, VII

39 He prayeth best, who loveth best
All things both great and small;
For the dear God who loveth us,
He made and loveth all.
The Rime of the Ancient Mariner, VII

40 A sadder and a wiser man,
He rose the morrow morn.
The Rime of the Ancient Mariner, VII

41 I wish our clever young poets would remember
my homely definitions of prose and poetry; that
is, prose = words in their best order; – poetry = the best words in the best order.
Table Talk

42 No mind is thoroughly well organized that is deficient in a sense of humour.
Table Talk

43 What comes from the heart, goes to the heart.
Table Talk

44 The misfortune is, that he has begun to write
verses without very well understanding what
metre is.
Referring to Tennyson
Table Talk

45 To see him act, is like reading Shakespeare by
flashes of lightning.
Referring to Kean
Table Talk

46 Summer has set in with its usual severity.
Quoted in Lamb's letter to V. Novello, 9 May 1826

47 I believe the souls of five hundred Sir Isaac
Newtons would go to the making up of a Shake-
speare or a Milton.
Letter to Thomas Poole, 23 Mar 1801

Colette, Sidonie Gabrielle (1873–1954) French novelist.
Colette's early works, the 'Claudine' stories, were published under
her first husband's pen-name; her later independent novels include
La Vagabonde (1910), *Chéri* (1920), and *Gigi* (1944).

1 Total absence of humour renders life impossible.
Chance Acquaintances

2 When she raises her eyelids it's as if she were
taking off all her clothes.
Claudine and Annie

3 My virtue's still far too small, I don't trot it out
and about yet.
Claudine at School

4 Don't ever wear artistic jewellery; it wrecks a
woman's reputation.
Gigi

5 Don't eat too many almonds; they add weight to
the breasts.
Gigi

Collingbourne, William (d. 1484) English landowner.

1 The Cat, the Rat, and Lovell our dog
Rule all England under a hog.
The cat was Sir William Catesby; the rat Sir Richard Ratcliffe;
the dog Lord Lovell, who had a dog on his crest. The hog
refers to the emblem of Richard III, a wild boar.
Chronicles (R. Holinshed), III

Collings, Jesse (1831–1920) British politician. He was an
active agitator for land reform and later became undersecretary to
the Home Office.

1 Three acres and a cow.
Slogan used in his land-reform propaganda

Collingwood, Cuthbert, Baron (1750–1810) British
admiral. He blockaded Cádiz under Nelson, and took command at
Trafalgar after Nelson's death.

1 Now, gentlemen, let us do something today which the world may talk of hereafter.

Said before Trafalgar, 21 Oct 1805
Correspondence and Memoir of Lord Collingwood (G. L. Newnham; ed. Collingwood)

Collingwood, Robin George (1889–1943) British philosopher and archaeologist. His books include *The New Leviathan* (1946) and *The Idea of History* (1946).

1 So, perhaps, I may escape otherwise than by death the last humiliation of an aged scholar, when his juniors conspire to print a volume of essays and offer it to him as a sign that they now consider him senile.

Autobiography

Collins, Michael (1890–1922) Irish nationalist. Imprisoned for his part in the Easter Rising (1916), he later became finance minister in the Republican government. He played an important part in setting up the Irish Free State, but was shot by republicans who opposed the Anglo-Irish Treaty.

1 I am signing my death warrant.

Said on signing the agreement with Great Britain, 1921, that established the Irish Free State. He was assassinated in an ambush some months later.
Peace by Ordeal (Longford), Pt. 6, Ch. 1

Collins, Mortimer (1827–76) British writer. His novels include *Sweet Anne Page* (1868); he also wrote poems and a collection of essays, *The Secret of Long Life* (1871).

1 A man is as old as he's feeling,
A woman as old as she looks.

The Unknown Quantity

Collins, (William) Wilkie (1824–89) British novelist. He is best remembered for his mystery novel *The Woman in White* (1860) and the first whodunnit, *The Moonstone* (1868).

1 His eyes, of a steely light grey, had a very disconcerting trick, when they encountered your eyes, of looking as if they expected something more from you than you were aware of yourself.

Describing Sergeant Cuff
The Moonstone, Ch. 12

2 Cultivate a superiority to reason, and see how you pare the claws of all the sensible people when they try to scratch you for your own good!

The Moonstone, Ch. 21

3 There, in the middle of the broad, bright high-road . . . stood the figure of a solitary Woman, dressed from head to foot in white garments, her face bent in grave inquiry on mine, her hand pointing to the dark cloud over London, as I faced her.

The Woman in White

Colman, George, The Elder (1732–94) British dramatist. He became famous with his play *The Clandestine Marriage* (1766).

1 Love and a cottage! Eh, Fanny! Ah, give me indifference and a coach and six!

The Clandestine Marriage, I:2

Colman, George, The Younger (1762–1836) British dramatist and manager of the Haymarket Theatre (1789–1820). His plays include *The Battle of Hexham* (1789), *The Heir-at-Law* (1797), and *John Bull* (1803).

1 Mum's the word.

The Battle of Hexham, II:1

2 Lord help you! Tell 'em Queen Anne's dead.

Heir-at-Law, I:1

3 Not to be sneezed at.

Heir-at-Law, II:1

Colton, Charles Caleb (?1780–1832) British clergyman and writer. *Lacon* (1820), his most famous work, is a collection of aphorisms; he also wrote essays and poems.

1 Men will wrangle for religion; write for it; fight for it; anything but – live for it.

Lacon, Vol. I

2 When you have nothing to say, say nothing.

Lacon, Vol. I

3 Imitation is the sincerest form of flattery.

Lacon, Vol. I

4 Examinations are formidable even to the best prepared, for the greatest fool may ask more than the wisest man can answer.

Lacon, Vol. II

5 The debt which cancels all others.

Lacon, Vol. II

Columbus, Christopher (1451–1506) Italian navigator. In 1492 he discovered America under the patronage of the Spanish monarchs, Ferdinand and Isabella.

1 I believe that the earthly Paradise lies here, which no one can enter except by God's leave. I believe that this land which your Highnesses have commanded me to discover is very great, and that there are many other lands in the south of which there have never been reports.

From the narrative of his third voyage, on which he discovered South America

Compton-Burnett, Dame Ivy (1892–1969) British novelist. *Pastors and Masters* (1925) was her first successful novel. This was followed by some 16 others, including *Brothers and Sisters* (1929) and *Mother and Son* (1955).

1 Appearances are not held to be a clue to the truth. But we seem to have no other.

Manservant and Maidservant

2 There is more difference within the sexes than between them.

Mother and Son

3 'She still seems to me in her own way a person born to command,' said Luce . . .
'I wonder if anyone is born to obey,' said Isabel. 'That may be why people command rather badly, that they have no suitable material to work on.'

Parents and Children, Ch. 3

Confucius (K'ung Fu-tzu; 551–479 BC) Chinese philosopher, whose sayings are collected in the *Analects*.

1 When you meet someone better than yourself, turn your thoughts to becoming his equal. When you meet someone not as good as you are, look within and examine your own self.
Analects

2 Chi Wen Tzu always thought three times before taking action. Twice would have been quite enough.
Analects

3 Men's natures are alike; it is their habits that carry them far apart.
Analects

4 Study the past, if you would divine the future.
Analects

5 Learning without thought is labour lost; thought without learning is perilous.
Analects

6 Fine words and an insinuating appearance are seldom associated with true virtue.
Analects

7 Have no friends not equal to yourself.
Analects

8 When you have faults, do not fear to abandon them.
Analects

9 To be able to practise five things everywhere under heaven constitutes perfect virtue . . . gravity, generosity of soul, sincerity, earnestness, and kindness.
Analects

10 The superior man is satisfied and composed; the mean man is always full of distress.
Analects

11 The people may be made to follow a course of action, but they may not be made to understand it.
Analects

12 Recompense injury with justice, and recompense kindness with kindness.
Analects

13 The superior man is distressed by his want of ability.
Analects

14 What you do not want done to yourself, do not do to others.
Analects

Congreve, William (1670–1729) British Restoration dramatist, whose comedies include *Love for Love* (1695) and *The Way of the World* (1700). He also wrote a tragedy, *The Mourning Bride* (1697).

Quotations about Congreve

1 William Congreve is the only sophisticated playwright England has produced; and like Shaw, Sheridan, and Wilde, his nearest rivals, he was brought up in Ireland.
Kenneth Tynan (1927–80) British theatre critic. *Curtains*, 'The Way of the World'

2 He spoke of his works as trifles that were beneath him.
Voltaire (François-Marie Arouet; 1694–1778) French writer. *Letters concerning the English nation*

Quotations by Congreve

3 She lays it on with a trowel.
The Double Dealer, III:10

4 See how love and murder will out.
The Double Dealer, IV:6

5 I am always of the opinion with the learned, if they speak first.
Incognita

6 O fie miss, you must not kiss and tell.
Love for Love, II:10

7 I know that's a secret, for it's whispered every where.
Love for Love, III:3

8 Music has charms to soothe a savage breast.
The Mourning Bride, I

9 Heaven has no rage like love to hatred turned, Nor hell a fury like a woman scorned.
The Mourning Bride, III

10 SHARPER. Thus grief still treads upon the heels of pleasure:
Marry'd in haste, we may repent at leisure.
SETTER. Some by experience find those words mis-plac'd:
At leisure marry'd, they repent in haste.
The Old Bachelor, V:8

11 Courtship to marriage, as a very witty prologue to a very dull Play.
The Old Bachelor, V:10

12 Alack he's gone the way of all flesh.
Squire Bickerstaff Detected, attrib.

13 Say what you will, 'tis better to be left than never to have been loved.
The Way of the World, II:1

14 Lord, what is a lover that it can give? Why one makes lovers as fast as one pleases, and they live as long as one pleases, and they die as soon as one pleases: and then if one pleases one makes more.
The Way of the World, II:4

15 I nauseate walking; 'tis a country diversion, I loathe the country and everything that relates to it.
The Way of the World, IV:4

16 I hope you do not think me prone to any iteration of nuptials.
The Way of the World, IV:12

17 O, she is the antidote to desire.
The Way of the World, IV:14

Connell, James (1852–1929) British socialist; author of *The Red Flag* and other socialist songs and poems.

1 The people's flag is deepest red;
It shrouded oft our martyred dead,
And ere their limbs grew stiff and cold,
Their heart's blood dyed its every fold.
Then raise the scarlet standard high!
Within its shade we'll live or die.
Tho' cowards flinch and traitors sneer,
We'll keep the red flag flying here.
Traditionally sung at the close of annual conferences of the British Labour Party
The Red Flag, in *Songs that made History* (H. E. Piggot), Ch. 6

Connolly, Cyril (Vernon) (1903–74) British journalist and writer. A contributor to the *New Statesman*, the *Sunday Times*, and other papers, he published several collections of essays, such as *Enemies of Promise* (1938).

Quotations about Connolly

1 Writers like Connolly gave pleasure a bad name.
E. M. Forster (1879–1970) British novelist. Attrib.

2 The key to his behaviour was self-indulgence, which he made almost a rule of life.
Stephen Spender (1909–   ) British poet. *The Observer*, 10 July 1983

Quotations by Connolly

3 It is closing time in the gardens of the West.
The Condemned Playground

4 A great writer creates a world of his own and his readers are proud to live in it. A lesser writer may entice them in for a moment, but soon he will watch them filing out.
Enemies of Promise, Ch. 1

5 The ape-like virtues without which no one can enjoy a public school.
Enemies of Promise, Ch. 1

6 Literature is the art of writing something that will be read twice; journalism what will be grasped at once.
Enemies of Promise, Ch. 3

7 An author arrives at a good style when his language performs what is required of it without shyness.
Enemies of Promise, Ch. 3

8 As repressed sadists are supposed to become policemen or butchers so those with irrational fear of life become publishers.
Enemies of Promise, Ch. 3

9 Whom the gods wish to destroy they first call promising.
Enemies of Promise, Ch. 3

10 There is no more sombre enemy of good art than the pram in the hall.
Enemies of Promise, Ch. 3

11 All charming people have something to conceal, usually their total dependence on the appreciation of others.
Enemies of Promise, Ch. 16

12 I have always disliked myself at any given moment; the total of such moments is my life.
Enemies of Promise, Ch. 18

13 Boys do not grow up gradually. They move forward in spurts like the hands of clocks in railway stations.
Enemies of Promise, Ch. 18

14 The only way for writers to meet is to share a quick pee over a common lamp-post.
The Unquiet Grave

15 Life is a maze in which we take the wrong turning before we have learnt to walk.
The Unquiet Grave

16 In the sex-war thoughtlessness is the weapon of the male, vindictiveness of the female.
The Unquiet Grave

17 There is no fury like an ex-wife searching for a new lover.
The Unquiet Grave

18 Imprisoned in every fat man a thin one is wildly signalling to be let out.
Similar sentiments have been stated by others. *See* AMIS, ORWELL.
The Unquiet Grave

19 Better to write for yourself and have no public, than write for the public and have no self.
Turnstile One (ed. V. S. Pritchett)

20 The man who is master of his passions is Reason's slave.
Turnstile One (ed. V. S. Pritchett)

Conrad, Joseph (Teodor Josef Konrad Korzeniowski; 1857–1924) Polish-born British novelist. His 20 years at sea provided the background for most of his novels and stories, notably *The Nigger of the Narcissus* (1897) and *Lord Jim* (1900).

1 Exterminate all brutes.
Heart of Darkness

2 The horror! The horror!
Heart of Darkness

3 Mistah Kurtz – he dead.
Heart of Darkness

4 You shall judge of a man by his foes as well as by his friends.
Lord Jim, Ch. 34

5 A work that aspires, however humbly, to the condition of art should carry its justification in every line.
The Nigger of the Narcissus, Preface

6 The terrorist and the policeman both come from the same basket.

The Secret Agent, Ch. 4

7 The belief in a supernatural source of evil is not necessary; men alone are quite capable of every wickedness.

Under Western Eyes, Part 2

8 I remember my youth and the feeling that will never come back any more – the feeling that I could last for ever, outlast the sea, the earth, and all men; the deceitful feeling that lures us on to perils, to love, to vain effort – to death . . .

Youth

9 This could have occurred nowhere but in England, where men and sea interpenetrate, so to speak.

Youth

Conran, Shirley (1932–) British designer and journalist. Formerly married (1955–62) to Sir Terence Conran, her books include *Superwoman* (1975), *Action Woman* (1979), and the novels *Lace* (1982) and *Savages* (1987).

1 Our motto: Life is too short to stuff a mushroom.

Superwoman, Epigraph

2 I make no secret of the fact that I would rather lie on a sofa than sweep beneath it. But you have to be efficient if you're going to be lazy.

Superwoman, 'The Reason Why'

Constable, John (1776–1837) British landscape painter, who specialized in paintings of the Suffolk countryside.

1 There is nothing ugly; *I never saw an ugly thing in my life:* for let the form of an object be what it may, – light, shade, and perspective will always make it beautiful.

Letter to John Fisher, 23 Oct 1821

Cook, A(rthur) J(ames) (1885–1931) British trade-union leader. He was influential in bringing the miners out on strike in 1926, which led to the General Strike.

1 Not a penny off the pay; not a minute on the day.

Slogan used in the miners' strike, 1925

Cook, Peter (1937–) British writer and entertainer. He made his name in the revue *Beyond The Fringe* (1959) and has since appeared in many plays and revues, especially with Dudley Moore.

1 I am very interested in the Universe – I am specializing in the universe and all that surrounds it.

Beyond the Fringe

2 You know, I go to the theatre to be entertained . . . I don't want to see plays about rape, sodomy and drug addiction . . . I can get all that at home.

The Observer, caption to cartoon, 8 July 1962

Cook, Captain James (1728–79) British navigator and cartographer. He discovered and charted New Zealand and the east cost of Australia before being murdered on a visit to Hawaii.

1 At daylight in the morning we discovered a bay which appeared to be tolerably well sheltered from all winds, into which I resolved to go with the ship.

Recording his arrival at Botany Bay
Journal, 20 Apr 1770

Coolidge, (John) Calvin (1872–1933) 30th president of the USA (1923–29). A Republican, he served as governor of Massachusetts and as vice-president to Warren G. Harding before succeeding to the presidency.

Quotations about Coolidge

1 He looks as if he had been weaned on a pickle.

Alice Roosevelt Longworth (1884–1980) US hostess. *Crowded Hours*

2 How could they tell?

Dorothy Parker (1893–1967) US writer. On being told that Coolidge had died. *You Might As Well Live* (J. Keats)

Quotations by Coolidge

3 The business of America is business.

Speech, Washington, 17 Jan 1925

4 There is no right to strike against the public safety by anybody, anywhere, any time.

Referring to the Boston police strike
Remark, 14 Sept 1919

5 He said he was against it.

Reply when asked what a clergyman had said regarding sin in his sermon
Attrib.

Cooper, James Fenimore (1789–1851) US novelist. His works include *The Pioneers* (1823), *The Last of the Mohicans* (1826), and *The Pathfinder* (1840).

1 The Last of the Mohicans.

Title of Novel

Corbusier, Le *See* Le Corbusier.

Coren, Alan (1938–) British humorist and writer. He has been editor of *Punch* and columnist in a number of national papers. Books include *Golfing for Cats* (1975), *The Lady from Stalingrad Mansions* (1977), and *Bin Ends* (1987).

1 No visit to Dove Cottage, Grasmere, is complete without examining the outhouse where Hazlitt's father, a Unitarian minister of strong liberal views, attempted to put his hand up Dorothy Wordsworth's skirt.

All Except the Bastard, 'Bohemia'

2 The Act of God designation on all insurance policies; which means, roughly, that you cannot be insured for the accidents that are most likely to happen to you.

The Lady from Stalingrad Mansions, 'A Short History of Insurance'

3 They are short, blue-vested people who carry their own onions when cycling abroad, and have a yard which is 3.37 inches longer than other people's.
The Sanity Inspector, 'All You Need to Know about Europe'

4 Apart from cheese and tulips, the main product of the country is advocaat, a drink made from lawyers.
Referring to Holland
The Sanity Inspector, 'All You Need to Know about Europe'

5 Since both its national products, snow and chocolate, melt, the cuckoo clock was invented solely in order to give tourists something solid to remember it by.
Referring to Switzerland
The Sanity Inspector, 'And Though They Do Their Best'

6 Television is more interesting than people. If it were not, we should have people standing in the corners of our rooms.
In *The Times*

Corneille, Pierre (1606–84) French dramatist; a pioneer of such French tragedies as *Le Cid* (1636–37), *Horace* (1640), *Cinna* (1641), and *Polyeucte* (1641–42).

1 Do your duty and leave the rest to the Gods.
Horace, II:8

2 We triumph without glory when we conquer without danger.
Le Cid, II:2

3 The manner of giving is worth more than the gift.
Le Menteur, I:1

4 A good memory is needed after one has lied.
Le Menteur, IV:5

5 One often calms one's grief by recounting it.
Polyeucte, I:3

Cornford, F. M. (1886–1960) British poet, best known for the poem 'To a Fat Lady Seen from a Train'.

1 O fat white woman whom nobody loves,
Why do you walk through the fields in gloves . . .
Missing so much and so much?
To a Fat Lady Seen from a Train

2 Propaganda is that branch of the art of lying which consists in nearly deceiving your friends without quite deceiving your enemies.
New Statesman, 15 Sept 1978

Cornuel, Anne-Marie Bigot de (1605–94) French society hostess and courtier of Louis XIV. Her salon was frequented by the most influential people in France.

1 No man is a hero to his valet.
Lettres de Mlle Aïssé, 13 Aug 1728

Cory, William Johnson (1823–92) British schoolmaster and poet. His verse collections include *Ionica* (1858).

1 Jolly boating weather,
And a hay harvest breeze,
Blade on the feather,
Shade off the trees
Swing, swing together
With your body between your knees.
Eton Boating Song

Coubertin, Pierre de, Baron (1863–1937) French educator and sportsman. He revived the Olympic Games in 1894 and was president of the International Olympic Committee (1894–1925). The first modern Games were held in 1896 at Athens.

1 The most important thing in the Olympic Games is not winning but taking part . . . The essential thing in life is not conquering but fighting well.
Speech, Banquet to Officials of Olympic Games, London, 24 July 1908

Coué, Emile (1857–1920) French doctor and advocate of autosuggestion. Originally a pharmacist, he studied hypnotism and developed the psychotherapy known as Couéism.

1 Every day, in every way, I am getting better and better.
Formula for a cure by autosuggestion

Cousin, Victor (1792–1867) French philosopher. He was director of the École Normale and minister of public instruction (from 1840); his books include studies of Pascal and Kant.

1 Art for art's sake.
Lecture, Sorbonne, 1818

Coward, Sir Noël (1899–1973) British actor, dramatist, and songwriter. After his first success, *The Vortex* (1924), he wrote a number of comedies, including *Blithe Spirit* (1941) and *Brief Encounter* (1946), both made into films. His songs include *Mad Dogs and Englishmen*.

Quotations about Coward

1 He was his own greatest invention.
John Osborne (1929–) British dramatist. Attrib.

2 He was once Slightly in *Peter Pan*, and has been wholly in Peter Pan ever since.
Kenneth Tynan (1927–80) British theatre critic. Attrib.

Quotations by Coward

3 We have no reliable guarantee that the afterlife will be any less exasperating than this one, have we?
Blithe Spirit, I

4 Never mind, dear, we're all made the same, though some more than others.
The Café de la Paix

5 There's always something fishy about the French.
Conversation Piece, I:6

6 Dance, dance, dance little lady.
Title of song

7 Don't let's be beastly to the Germans.
Title of song

8 Don't put your daughter on the stage, Mrs Worthington.

Title of song

9 Everybody was up to something, especially, of course, those who were up to nothing.

Future Indefinite

10 Sunburn is very becoming – but only when it is even – one must be careful not to look like a mixed grill.

The Lido Beach

11 Mad about the boy.

Title of song

12 Mad dogs and Englishmen go out in the mid-day sun.

Title of song

13 And though the Van Dycks have to go
And we pawn the Bechstein grand,
We'll stand by the Stately Homes of England.

Operette, 'The Stately Homes of England'

14 The Stately Homes of England
How beautiful they stand,
To prove the upper classes
Have still the upper hand.

Operette, 'The Stately Homes of England'

15 Poor Little Rich Girl.

Title of song

16 Very flat, Norfolk.

Private Lives

17 Strange how potent cheap music is.

Private Lives

18 Certain women should be struck regularly, like gongs.

Private Lives

19 She refused to begin the 'Beguine'
Tho' they besought her to
And with language profane and obscene
She curs'd the man who taught her to
She curs'd Cole Porter too!

Sigh No More, 'Nina'

20 Twentieth-Century Blues.

Title of song

21 I've over-educated myself in all the things I shouldn't have known at all.

Wild Oats

22 Work is much more fun than fun.

The Observer, 'Sayings of the Week', 21 June 1963

23 Dear 338171 (May I call you 338?).

Starting a letter to T. E. Lawrence who had retired from public life to become Aircraftsman Brown, 338171
Letters to T. E. Lawrence

24 I never realized before that Albert married beneath him.

After seeing a certain actress in the role of Queen Victoria
Tynan on Theatre (K. Tynan)

25 Dear Mrs A., hooray hooray,
At last you are deflowered
On this as every other day
I love you. Noël Coward.

Telegram to Gertrude Lawrence on her marriage to Richard S. Aldrich

Cowley, Abraham (1618–67) English poet. A royalist secret agent in England, he wrote a metaphysical verse, which was published in *The Mistress* (1647) and other collections. He also published *Pindaric Odes* (1656).

1 God the first garden made, and the first city Cain.

The Garden

2 Life is an incurable disease.

To Dr Scarborough

Cowper, William (1731–1800) British poet. A lawyer and commissioner of bankrupts, his life was dogged by depression, bouts of insanity, and suicide attempts. His ballad *John Gilpin's Ride* (1783) and the long poem *The Task* (1785) established his reputation; he also translated Homer.

Quotations about Cowper

1 His taste lay in smiling, colloquial, good-natured humour; his melancholy was a black and diseased melancholy, not a grave and rich contemplativeness.

E. Brydges *Recollection of Foreign Travel*

2 That maniacal Calvinist and coddled poet.

Lord Byron (1788–1824) British poet. Attrib.

Quotations by Cowper

3 Regions Caesar never knew
Thy posterity shall sway,
Where his eagles never flew,
None invincible as they.

Boadicea

4 When the British warrior queen,
Bleeding from the Roman rods,
Sought, with an indignant mien,
Counsel of her country's gods.

Boadicea

5 Rome shall perish – write that word
In the blood that she has spilt.

Boadicea

6 We perish'd, each alone:
But I beneath a rougher sea,
And whelm'd in deeper gulphs than he.

The Castaway

7 He found it inconvenient to be poor.

Charity

8 Absence from whom we love is worse than death.

'Hope, like the Short-lived Ray'

9 John Gilpin was a citizen
Of credit and renown,
A train-band captain eke was he
Of famous London town.
John Gilpin

10 To-morrow is our wedding-day,
And we will then repair
Unto the Bell at Edmonton,
All in a chaise and pair.
John Gilpin

11 Now let us sing, Long live the king,
And Gilpin, long live he;
And when he next doth ride abroad,
May I be there to see!
John Gilpin

12 My hat and wig will soon be here,
They are upon the road.
John Gilpin

13 Says John, It is my wedding-day,
And all the world would stare,
If wife should dine at Edmonton,
And I should dine at Ware.
John Gilpin

14 What peaceful hours I once enjoyed!
How sweet their memory still!
But they have left an aching void
The world can never fill.
Olney Hymns, 1

15 Prayer makes the Christian's armour bright;
And Satan trembles when he sees
The weakest saint upon his knees.
Olney Hymns, 29

16 I seem forsaken and alone,
I hear the lion roar;
And every door is shut but one,
And that is Mercy's door.
Olney Hymns, 33

17 God moves in a mysterious way
His wonders to perform;
He plants his footsteps in the sea,
And rides upon the storm.
Olney Hymns, 35

18 The bud may have a bitter taste,
But sweet will be the flower.
Olney Hymns, 35

19 The poplars are felled, farewell to the shade,
And the whispering sound of the cool colonnade!
The Poplar Field

20 Mortals, whose pleasures are their only care,
First wish to be imposed on, and then are.
The Progress of Error

21 For 'tis a truth well known to most,
That whatsoever thing is lost –
We seek it, ere it come to light,
In every cranny but the right.
The Retired Cat

22 God made the country, and man made the town.
The Task

23 England, with all thy faults, I love thee still,
My country.
The Task

24 Variety's the very spice of life
That gives it all its flavour.
The Task

25 While the bubbling and loud-hissing urn
Throws up a steamy column, and the cups,
That cheer but not inebriate, wait on each,
So let us welcome peaceful evening in.
The Task

26 Nature is but a name for an effect
Whose cause is God.
The Task

27 Oh for a lodge in some vast wilderness,
Some boundless contiguity of shade,
Where rumour of oppression and deceit,
Of unsuccessful or successful war,
Might never reach me more!
The Task

28 Mountains interposed
Make enemies of nations, who had else,
Like kindred drops, been mingled into one.
The Task

29 Slaves cannot breathe in England; if their lungs
Receive our air, that moment they are free;
They touch our country, and their shackles fall.
A situation resulting from a judicial decision in 1772
The Task

30 Riches have wings, and grandeur is a dream.
The Task

31 Detested sport,
That owes its pleasures to another's pain.
The Task

32 Knowledge dwells
In heads replete with thoughts of other men;
Wisdom in minds attentive to their own.
The Task

33 Society, friendship, and love,
Divinely bestowed upon man,
Oh, had I the wings of a dove,
How soon would I taste you again!
Verses supposed to be written by Alexander Selkirk

34 I am monarch of all I survey,
My right there is none to dispute;
From the centre all round to the sea
I am lord of the fowl and the brute.
Oh, solitude! where are the charms
That sages have seen in thy face?
Better dwell in the midst of alarms,
Than reign in this horrible place.
Verses supposed to be written by Alexander Selkirk

Crabbe, George (1754–1832) British poet and clergyman.
His reputation was established by *The Village* (1783); other
writings, include *The Borough* (1810).

1 Books cannot always please, however good;
Minds are not ever craving for their food.

The Borough, 'Schools'

2 The ring so worn, as you behold,
So thin, so pale, is yet of gold.

His Mother's Wedding Ring

3 Oh! rather give me commentators plain,
Who with no deep researches vex the brain;
Who from the dark and doubtful love to run,
And hold their glimmering tapers to the sun.

The Parish Register, 'Baptisms'

Craig, Sir (Edward Henry) Gordon (1872–1966)
British actor and stage designer. The son of Ellen Terry, he
joined Henry Irving's company at the Lyceum as a child actor. He
opened an acting school in Florence and founded the theatrical
magazine *The Mask*.

1 Farce is the essential theatre. Farce refined becomes high comedy: farce brutalized becomes
tragedy.

The Story of my Days, Index

Crane, Stephen (1871–1900) US writer. His *Maggie, A Girl
of the Streets* (1893) was followed by the successful war novel *The
Red Badge of Courage* (1895).

1 The Red Badge of Courage.

Title of novel

Cranmer, Thomas (1489–1556) English churchman. For
supporting Henry VIII in his divorce dispute with the pope, he was
made Archbishop of Canterbury, in which position he introduced an
English Bible (1538) and two Prayer Books (1549 and 1552).
However, under Queen Mary he was burnt at the stake as a
heretic.

1 This hand hath offended.

Memorials of Cranmer (Strype)

Creighton, Mandell (1843–1901) British churchman. First
editor of the *English Historical Review* (1886–91), he became
Bishop of Peterborough (1891) and then of London (1897).

1 No people do so much harm as those who go
about doing good.

Life

Crick, Francis Harry Compton (1916–) British
biophysicist. He became famous for his work with James D.
Watson on the molecular structure of DNA.

1 We have discovered the secret of life!

On entering a Cambridge pub with James Watson to celebrate
the fact that they had unravelled the structure of DNA
The Double Helix (J. D. Watson)

Crisp, Quentin (?1910–) British model, publicist, and
writer. He first attracted attention with his book *The Naked Civil
Servant* (1968).

1 If any reader of this book is in the grip of some
habit of which he is deeply ashamed, I advise
him not to give way to it in secret but to do it
on television. No-one will pass him with
averted gaze on the other side of the street.
People will cross the road at the risk of losing
their own lives in order to say 'We saw you on
the telly'.

How to Become a Virgin

2 The young always have the same problem –
how to rebel and conform at the same time.
They have now solved this by defying their parents and copying one another.

The Naked Civil Servant

3 Keeping up with the Joneses was a full-time job
with my mother and father. It was not until
many years later when I lived alone that I realized how much cheaper it was to drag the
Joneses down to my level.

The Naked Civil Servant

4 There was no need to do any housework at all.
After the first four years the dirt doesn't get
any worse.

The Naked Civil Servant

5 Tears were to me what glass beads are to African traders.

The Naked Civil Servant

6 Vice is its own reward.

The Naked Civil Servant

7 I became one of the stately homos of England.

The Naked Civil Servant

8 I don't hold with abroad and think that foreigners
speak English when our backs are turned.

The Naked Civil Servant

9 The . . . problem which confronts homosexuals is
that they set out to win the love of a 'real' man.
If they succeed, they fail. A man who 'goes
with' other men is not what they would call a
real man.

The Naked Civil Servant

10 The idea that He would take his attention away
from the universe in order to give me a bicycle
with three speeds is just so unlikely I can't go
along with it.

The Sunday Times, 18 Dec 1977

Croce, Benedetto (1866–1952) Italian philospher. His
system was published in *Philosophy of Mind* (1910) and several
other books. He became minister of public instruction (1920–21).

1 Art is ruled uniquely by the imagination.

Esthetic, Ch. 1

Croker, John Wilson (1780–1857) British Tory politician,
born in Ireland. He attacked Keats' *Endymion* in the *Quarterly
Review* and edited Boswell's *Life of Johnson* (1831).

1 A game which a sharper once played with a
dupe, entitled 'Heads I win, tails you lose.'

Croker Papers

2 We now are, as we always have been, decidedly and conscientiously attached to what is called the Tory, and which might with more propriety be called the Conservative, party.

The first use of the term 'Conservative Party'
In *Quarterly Review*, Jan 1830

Crompton, Richmal (Richmal Crompton Lamburn; 1890–1969) British writer of children's books. Her first of many William books, *Just William*, appeared in 1922.

1 Violet Elizabeth dried her tears. She saw that they were useless and she did not believe in wasting her effects. 'All right,' she said calmly, 'I'll thcream then. I'll thcream, an' thcream, an' thcream till I'm thick.'

Violet Elizabeth Bott, a character in the *William* books, had both a lisp and an exceptional ability to get her own way
Just William

Cromwell, Oliver (1599–1658) English soldier and statesman. As a leader of the parliamentary army, he was largely responsible for Charles I's defeat in the Civil War. After the king's execution, as Lord Protector of England (1653–58), he failed to find a constitutional basis for ruling the country.

Quotations about Cromwell

1 Cromwell was a man in whom ambition had not wholly suppressed, but only suspended, the sentiments of religion.

Edmund Burke (1729–97) British politician. Letter, 1791

2 He will be looked upon by posterity as a brave, bad man.

Earl of Clarendon. *History of the rebellion* 1704

3 Whilst he was cautious of his own words, (not putting forth too many lest they should betray his thoughts) he made others talk until he had, as it were, sifted them, and known their most intimate designs.

Sir William Waller. *Recollections*

Quotations by Cromwell

4 Mr Lely, I desire you would use all your skill to paint my picture truly like me, and not flatter me at all; but remark all these roughnesses, pimples, warts, and everything as you see me, otherwise I will never pay a farthing for it.

The origin of the expression 'warts and all'
Anecdotes of Painting (Horace Walpole), Ch. 12

5 I beseech you, in the bowels of Christ, think it possible you may be mistaken.

Letter to the General Assembly of the Church of Scotland, 3 Aug 1650

6 What shall we do with this bauble? There, take it away.

Speech dismissing Parliament, 20 Apr 1653

7 It is not fit that you should sit here any longer! . . . you shall now give place to better men.

Speech to the Rump Parliament, 22 Jan 1655

8 The State, in choosing men to serve it, takes no notice of their opinions. If they be willing faithfully to serve it, that satisfies.

Said before the Battle of Marston Moor, 2 July 1644

9 The people would be just as noisy if they were going to see me hanged.

Referring to a cheering crowd

Cromwell, Thomas, Earl of Essex (c. 1485–1540) English chancellor of the exchequer. He drafted the legislation that made Henry VIII head of the English Church and thereby secured Henry's divorce from Catherine of Aragon, but was subsequently executed for arranging Henry's disastrous marriage to Anne of Cleves.

1 It much grieves me that I should be noted a traitor when I always had your laws on my breast, and that I should be a sacramentary. God he knoweth the truth, and that I am of the one and the other guiltless.

On being condemned to death for treason and heresy
Letter to Henry VIII, 30 June 1540

Crosby, Bing (Harry Lillis Crosby; 1904–77) US singer and crooner. Immensely popular, he made many films, often with Bob Hope.

1 There is nothing in the world I wouldn't do for Hope, and there is nothing he wouldn't do for me . . . We spend our lives doing nothing for each other.

Referring to Bob Hope
The Observer, 'Sayings of the Week', 7 May 1950

2 I think popular music in this country is one of the few things in the twentieth century that have made giant strides in reverse.

Interview, *This Week*

cummings, e(dward) e(stlin) (1894–1962) US poet. His verse relied to some extent on typographical devices. Collections include *Tulips and Chimneys* (1923) and *Eimi* (1933).

1 who knows if the moon's
a balloon, coming out of a keen city
in the sky – filled with pretty people?

Used for the title and epigraph of David Niven's first volume of autobiography, *The Moon's a Balloon*, about his experiences in the film industry
&

2 a pretty girl who naked is
is worth a million statues

Collected Poems, 133

3 a politician is an arse upon which everyone has sat except a man

A Politician

Curie, Marie (1867–1934) Polish chemist, who emigrated to France in 1891 and pioneered research into radioactivity. With her husband Pierre Curie she also discovered radium and polonium; she won the Nobel Prize in 1903 and 1911.

Quotations about Marie Curie

1 Women cannot be part of the Institute of France.

Emile Hilaire Amagat (1841–1915) French physicist. Comment following the rejection of Marie Curie by the Académie des Sciences, for which she had been nominated in 1910. She was rejected by one vote, and refused to allow her name to be submitted again or, for ten years, to allow her work to be published by the Académie.

2 Marie Curie is, of all celebrated beings, the only one whom fame has not corrupted.

Albert Einstein (1879–1955) German-born US physicist. *Madame Curie* (Eve Curie)

3 That one must do some work seriously and must be independent and not merely amuse oneself in life – this our mother has told us always, but never that science was the only career worth following.

Irene Joliot-Curie (1897–1956) French scientist. Recalling the advice of her mother, Marie Curie *A Long Way from Missouri* (Mary Margaret McBride), Ch. 10

Quotations by Marie Curie

4 After all, science is essentially international, and it is only through lack of the historical sense that national qualities have been attributed to it.

Memorandum, 'Intellectual Co-operation'

5 All my life through, the new sights of Nature made me rejoice like a child.

Pierre Curie

6 I have no dress except the one I wear every day. If you are going to be kind enough to give me one, please let it be practical and dark so that I can put it on afterwards to go to the laboratory.

Referring to a wedding dress
Letter to a friend, 1849

7 One never notices what has been done; one can only see what remains to be done. . . .

Letter to her brother, 18 Mar 1894

Curran, John Philpot (1750–1817) Irish judge. A Protestant, he sought Catholic emancipation and defended the leaders of the insurrection of 1798.

1 The condition upon which God hath given liberty to man is eternal vigilance.

Speech on the Right of Election of Lord Mayor of Dublin, 10 July 1790

Curtiz, Michael (1888–1962) Hungarian-born US film director. He made many films in Europe before settling in Hollywood, where he made a string of films ranging from *Mammy* (1930) to *Casablanca* (1942).

1 Bring on the empty horses!

Said during the filming of *The Charge of the Light Brigade*. Curtiz, who was not noted for his command of English grammar, meant 'riderless horses'. When people laughed at his order he became very angry, shouting, 'You think I know fuck-nothing, when I know fuck-all!' David Niven used the remark as the title of his second volume of autobiography about his experiences in the film industry.
Bring on the Empty Horses (David Niven)

Curzon, George Nathaniel, Marquess (1859–1925) British politician. He was viceroy of India (1898–1905) and became Lord Privy Seal in World War I. After the war he was foreign secretary (1919–20).

1 Not even a public figure. A man of no experience. And of the utmost insignificance.

Referring to Stanley Baldwin on his appointment as Prime Minister
Curzon: The Last Phase (Harold Nicolson)

2 Better send them a Papal Bull.

Written in the margin of a Foreign Office document. The phrase 'the monks of Mount Athos were violating their vows' had been misprinted as '. . . violating their cows'.
Life of Lord Curzon (Ronaldshay), Vol. III, Ch. 15

3 I hesitate to say what the functions of the modern journalist may be; but I imagine that they do not exclude the intelligent anticipation of facts even before they occur.

Speech, House of Commons, 29 Mar 1898

Cuvier, Georges Léopold, Baron (1769–1832) French zoologist, who pioneered the study of comparative anatomy and palaeontology.

1 Nurse, it was I who discovered that leeches have red blood.

On his deathbed when the nurse came to apply leeches
The Oxford Book of Death (D. Enright)

Cyrano de Bergerac, Savinien (1619–55) French writer and dramatist. Noted for his extraordinary nose and as a fighter of duels, he wrote a number of plays, including the comedy *Le Pédant Joué* (1654) and the tragedy *La Mort d'Agrippine* (1654).

1 Perish the Universe, provided I have my revenge.

La Mort d'Agrippine, IV

D

Dacre, Harry (19th century) British songwriter.

1 Daisy, Daisy, give me your answer, do!
I'm half crazy, all for the love of you!
It won't be a stylish marriage,
I can't afford a carriage,
But you'll look sweet upon the seat
Of a bicycle made for two!

Daisy Bell

Dahl, Roald (1916–90) British writer. His collections of short stories include *Kiss Kiss* (1959), *Switch Bitch* (1974), and *Tales of the Unexpected* (1979). He wrote several books for children, including *Charlie and the Chocolate Factory* (1964), *The Witches* (1983), and *Rhyme Stew* (1989).

1 Do you *know* what breakfast cereal is made of? It's made of all those little curly wooden shavings you find in pencil sharpeners!

Charlie and the Chocolate Factory, Ch. 27

Dali, Salvador (1904–1989) Spanish painter. From 1929 he produced startling works based on subconscious imagery and executed with photographic realism. After settling in New York (1940), he adopted other styles and also developed his talent for self-publicity.

1 It's either easy or impossible.
> Reply when asked if he found it hard to paint a picture
> Attrib.

Dalton, John (1766–1844) British scientist. His experients with gases led him to formulate Dalton's law of partial pressures and the foundations of modern atomic theory (1803).

1 This paper will no doubt be found interesting by those who take an interest in it.
> Said on many occasions when chairing scientific meetings
> Attrib.

Daly, Dan (20th century) Sergeant in the US Marines.

1 Come on, you sons of bitches! Do you want to live for ever?
> Remark during Allied resistance at Belleau Wood, June 1918. *See also* FREDERICK THE GREAT
> Attrib.

Damien, Father (Joseph de Veuster; 1840–89) Belgian Roman Catholic missionary, who died from leprosy after working in a leper colony in Hawaii.

1 What would you do with it? It is full of leprosy.
> When asked on his deathbed whether he would leave another priest his mantle, like Elijah
> *Memoirs of an Aesthete* (H. Acton)

Dana, Charles Anderson (1819–97) US newspaper editor, who both owned and edited the New York *Sun* (1868–97).

1 When a dog bites a man that is not news, but when a man bites a dog, that is news.
> New York *Sun*, 1882

Daniel, Samuel (c. 1562–1619) English poet and dramatist. He is best known for his sonnet *Delia* (1592) and his verse history *The Civil Wars* (1609).

1 Love is a sickness full of woes,
  All remedies refusing;
  A plant that with most cutting grows,
  Most barren with best using.
  Why so?
  More we enjoy it, more it dies;
  If not enjoyed, it sighing cries,
  Hey ho.
> *Hymen's Triumph*, I

Dante Alighieri (1265–1321) Italian poet. Born into a Guelf family, he was involved in the political struggles of the time, which forced him to leave his native Florence; he finally settled in Ravenna. His major works include *La vita nuova* (c. 1292) and *The Divine Comedy* (1307).

1 Abandon hope, all ye who enter here.
> The inscription at the entrance to Hell
> *Divine Comedy, Inferno*, III

2 There is no greater sorrow than to recall a time of happiness when in misery.
> *Divine Comedy, Inferno*, V

Danton, Georges Jacques (1759–94) French political activist and leader of the Cordeliers (a revolutionary club). He became minister of justice in the new republic but lost power in the Reign of Terror and was guillotined.

1 Boldness, and again boldness, and always boldness!
> Speech, French Legislative Committee, 2 Sept 1792

2 Thou wilt show my head to the people: it is worth showing.
> Said as he mounted the scaffold, 5 Apr 1794
> *French Revolution* (Carlyle), Bk. VI, Ch. 2

Darling, Charles John, Baron (1849–1936) British judge and writer.

1 If a man stays away from his wife for seven years, the law presumes the separation to have killed him; yet according to our daily experience, it might well prolong his life.
> *Scintillae Juris*

2 A timid question will always receive a confident answer.
> *Scintillae Juris*

3 Much truth is spoken, that more may be concealed.
> *Scintillae Juris*

4 Perjury is often bold and open. It is truth that is shamefaced – as, indeed, in many cases is no more than decent.
> *Scintillae Juris*

5 The Law of England is a very strange one; it cannot compel anyone to tell the truth. . . . But what the Law can do is to give you seven years for not telling the truth.
> *Lord Darling* (D. Walker-Smith), Ch. 27

6 The law-courts of England are open to all men, like the doors of the Ritz Hotel.
> Attrib.

Darrow, Clarence Seward (1857–1938) US lawyer.

1 I go to a better tailor than any of you and pay more for my clothes. The only difference is that you probably don't sleep in yours.
> Reply when teased by reporters about his appearance
> *2500 Anecdotes* (E. Fuller)

2 I do not consider it an insult but rather a compliment to be called an agnostic. I do not pretend to know where many ignorant men are sure.
> Remark during the trial (1925) of John Scopes for teaching the theory of evolution in school

Darwin, Charles Galton (1887–1962) British life scientist and great-grandson of the originator of the theory of evolution.

1 The evolution of the human race will not be accomplished in the ten thousand years of tame animals, but in the million years of wild animals, because man is and will always be a wild animal.
> *The Next Ten Million Years*, Ch. 4

Darwin, Charles Robert (1809–82) British life scientist, who originated the theory of evolution based on natural selection. The publication of his *Origin of Species by Means of Natural Selection* (1859) caused great controversy because it conflicted with the biblical account of creation. In *The Descent of Man* (1871), Darwin applied his theory to mankind.

Quotations about Darwin

1 I have no patience whatever with these gorilla damnifications of humanity.
Thomas Carlyle (1795–1881) Scottish historian and essayist. *Famous Sayings* (Edward Latham)

2 It is no secret that . . . there are many to whom Mr. Darwin's death is a wholly irreparable loss. And this not merely because of his wonderfully genial, simple, and generous nature; his cheerful and animated conversation, and the infinite variety and accuracy of his information; but because the more one knew of him, the more he seemed the incorporated ideal of a man of science.
T. H. Huxley (1825–95) British biologist. *Nature*, 1882

3 What Galileo and Newton were to the seventeenth century, Darwin was to the nineteenth.
Bertrand Russell (1872–1970) British philosopher. *History of Western Philosophy*

4 I never know whether to be more surprised at Darwin himself for making so much of natural selection, or at his opponents for making so little of it.
Robert Louis Stevenson (1850–94) Scottish writer.

Quotations by Darwin

5 I have tried lately to read Shakespeare, and found it so intolerably dull that it nauseated me.
Autobiography

6 The highest possible stage in moral culture is when we recognize that we ought to control our thoughts.
Descent of Man, Ch. 4

7 We must, however, acknowledge, as it seems to me, that man with all his noble qualities, still bears in his bodily frame the indelible stamp of his lowly origin.
Closing words
Descent of Man, Ch. 21

8 I have called this principle, by which each slight variation, if useful, is preserved, by the term of Natural Selection.
Origin of Species, Ch. 3

9 We will now discuss in a little more detail the struggle for existence.
Origin of Species, Ch. 3

10 The expression often used by Mr Herbert Spencer of the Survival of the Fittest is more accurate, and is sometimes equally convenient.
Origin of Species, Ch. 3

Darwin, Erasmus (1731–1802) British physician, biologist, and poet. The grandfather of Charles Darwin, his view of evolution was based on a concept later expounded by Lamarck. His books include *Economy of Vegetation*.

1 No, Sir, because I have time to think before I speak, and don't ask impertinent questions.
Reply when asked whether he found his stammer inconvenient
Reminiscences of My Father's Everyday Life (Sir Francis Darwin)

Davies, Sir John (1569–1626) English jurist and poet. The speaker of the Irish parliament, he was appointed lord chief justice of England but died before taking office. His verse includes *Orchestra* (1594) and *Hymns to Astraea* (1599).

1 Judge not the play before the play be done.
Respice Finem

Davies, W(illiam) H(enry) (1871–1940) British poet. For many years a tramp in both England and America, he first published his verse in 1905. His *Autobiography of a Super-Tramp* (1907) had a preface by G. B. Shaw.

1 It was the Rainbow gave thee birth,
And left thee all her lovely hues.
The Kingfisher

2 What is this life if, full of care,
We have no time to stand and stare?
Leisure

3 Sweet Stay-at-Home, sweet Well-content.
Sweet Stay-at-Home

4 I love thee for a heart that's kind –
Not for the knowledge in thy mind,
Sweet Stay-at-Home

da Vinci, Leonardo See Leonardo da Vinci.

Davis, Bette (Ruth Elizabeth Davis; 1908–89) US film star. Her films include *Of Human Bondage* (1934), *Jezebel* (1938), *The Little Foxes* (1941), and *All About Eve* (1950).

1 With the newspaper strike on I wouldn't consider it.
When told that a rumour was spreading that she had died
Book of Lists (I. Wallace)

2 I see – she's the original good time that was had by all.
Referring to a starlet of the time
The Filmgoer's Book of Quotes (Leslie Halliwell)

3 Pray to God and say the lines.
Advice to the actress Celeste Holm
Attrib.

Davis, Sammy, Jnr (1925–90) Black US singer and entertainer. He appeared in many films including *Porgy and Bess* (1959), *A Man Called Adam* (1966), and *The Cannonball Run* (1981).

1 Being a star has made it possible for me to get insulted in places where the average Negro could never hope to get insulted.
Yes I Can

2 I'm a coloured, one-eyed Jew.
When asked what his handicap was during a game of golf
Attrib.

Davy, Sir Humphry (1778–1829) British chemist. Best known as the inventor (1815) of the miner's safety lamp, he also discovered the use of nitrous oxide as an anaesthetic and identified several metallic elements.

1 The finest collection of frames I ever saw.
When asked what he thought of the Paris art galleries
Attrib.

Day, Clarence Shepard (1874–1935) US writer. His books include *This Simian World* (1920), *Life with Father* (1935), and *Life with Mother* (1937).

1 Imagine the Lord talking French! Aside from a few odd words in Hebrew, I took it completely for granted that God had never spoken anything but the most dignified English.
Life With Father, 'Father interferes'

2 'If you don't go to other men's funerals,' he told Father stiffly, 'they won't go to yours.'
Life With Father, 'Father plans'

Dayan, Moshe (1915–81) Israeli general and archaeologist. Chief of Israel's general staff (1953–58), he later became defence minister (1967; 1969–74), resigning after criticism that Israel was taken by surprise in the Yom Kippur War (1973–74).

1 Whenever you accept our views we shall be in full agreement with you.
Said to Cyrus Vance during Arab-Israeli negotiations
The Observer, 'Sayings of the Week', 14 Aug 1977

2 If we lose this war, I'll start another in my wife's name.
Attrib.

Day Lewis, C(ecil) (1904–72) British poet. A left-wing poet of the 1930s, his collections include *The Magnetic Mountain* (1933) and *Time to Dance* (1935). He was poet laureate (1968–72) and wrote detective stories as **Nicholas Blake**.

1 Now the peak of summer's past, the sky is overcast
And the love we swore would last for an age seems deceit.
Hornpipe

2 It is the logic of our times,
No subject for immortal verse –
That we who lived by honest dreams
Defend the bad against the worse.
Where are the War Poets?

de Blank, Joost (1908–68) Dutch-born British churchman. He became Bishop of Stepney and later Archbishop of Capetown. In this capacity his opposition to apartheid made him unpopular with the South African government.

1 Christ in this country would quite likely have been arrested under the Suppression of Communism Act.
Referring to South Africa
The Observer, 'Sayings of the Week', 27 Oct 1963

2 I suffer from an incurable disease – colour blindness.
Attrib.

Debs, Eugene Victor (1855–1926) US trade unionist, socialist, and pacifist.

1 It is the government that should ask me for a pardon.
When released from prison (1921) on the orders of President Harding after being jailed for sedition (1918)
The People's Almanac (D. Wallechinsky)

Debussy, Claude Achille (1862–1918) French composer. His opera *Pelléas et Mélisande* (1892–1902) and the three symphonic sketches *La Mer* (1903–05) are his best-known works. He also wrote much music for piano and for chamber ensembles.

1 Music is the arithmetic of sounds as optics is the geometry of light.
Attrib.

2 I love music passionately, and because I love it I try to free it from the barren conditions that stifle it.
Attrib.

3 The century of aeroplanes deserves its own music. As there are no precedents I must create anew.
Attrib.

Decatur, Stephen (1779–1820) US naval officer. He commanded the *United States* in the War of 1812, defeating the British *Macedonia*. He commanded the squadron which imposed peace on Algeria on American terms.

1 Our country! In her intercourse with foreign nations, may she always be in the right; but our country, right or wrong.
Speech, Norfolk, Virginia, Apr 1816

Deffand, Marquise du (Marie de Vichy-Chamrond; 1697–1780) French noblewoman whose friends included Voltaire and Walpole, with whom she corresponded.

1 The distance doesn't matter; it is only the first step that is difficult.
Referring to the legend of St Denis, who is traditionally believed to have carried his severed head for six miles after his execution
Letter to d'Alembert, 7 July 1763

Defoe, Daniel (1660–1731) British journalist and writer. Imprisoned for writing seditious pamphlets, he turned late in his life to fiction, achieving success with *Robinson Crusoe* (1719) and *Moll Flanders* (1722).

1 The good die early, and the bad die late.
Character of the late Dr. Annesley

2 Nature has left this tincture in the blood,
That all men would be tyrants if they could.
The Kentish Petition, Addenda

3 He bade me observe it, and I should always find, that the calamities of life were shared among the upper and lower part of mankind; but that the middle station had the fewest disasters.
Robinson Crusoe, Pt. I

4 I takes my man Friday with me.
Robinson Crusoe, Pt. I

5   Wherever God erects a house of prayer,
    The Devil always builds a chapel there;
    And 'twill be found, upon examination,
    The latter has the largest congregation.
    The True-Born Englishman, Pt. I

6   And of all plagues with which mankind are curst,
    Ecclesiastic tyranny's the worst.
    The True-Born Englishman, Pt. II

Degas, (Hilaire Germain) Edgar (1834–1917) French
artist. A master of the human figure in movement, some of his
best-known works are scenes of race meetings and ballet.

1   I feel as a horse must feel when the beautiful cup
    is given to the jockey.
    On seeing one of his pictures sold at auction
    Attrib.

de Gaulle, Charles André Joseph Marie (1890–
1970) French general and statesman. President (1958–69), he
became an international figure after World War II. He advocated
mechanized warfare in the 1930s, and became leader of the Free
French in London after the fall of France, taking over as head of
the provisional government after Germany's defeat.

Quotations about de Gaulle

1   Intelligent – brilliant – resourceful – he spoils
    his undoubted talents by his excessive assur-
    ance, his contempt for other people's point of
    view, and his attitude of a king in exile.
    Report, French War College, 1922

2   Just look at him! He might be Stalin with 200
    divisions.
    Winston Churchill (1874–1965) British statesman. Attrib.

3   An improbable creature, like a human giraffe,
    sniffing down his nostril at mortals beneath his
    gaze.
    Richard Wilson *The Second Book of Insults* (Nancy McPhee)

Quotations by de Gaulle

4   Deliberation is the work of many men. Action, of
    one alone.
    War Memoirs, Vol. 2

5   I myself have become a Gaullist only little by
    little.
    The Observer, 'Sayings of the Year', 29 Dec 1963

6   Now at last our child is just like all children.
    On the death of his retarded daughter Anne
    Ten First Ladies of the World (Pauline Frederick)

7   They really are bad shots.
    Remark after narrowly escaping death in an assassination attempt
    Ten First Ladies of the World (Pauline Frederick)

8   The French will only be united under the threat
    of danger. Nobody can simply bring together a
    country that has 265 kinds of cheese.
    Speech, 1951

9   *Changez vos amis.*
    Change your friends.
    Replying to the complaint by Jacques Soustelle that he was being
    attacked by his own friends
    Attrib.

10   One does not arrest Voltaire.
    Explaining why he had not arrested Jean-Paul Sartre for urging
    French soldiers in Algeria to desert
    Attrib.

11   Since a politician never believes what he says,
    he is surprised when others believe him.
    Attrib.

12   Treaties are like roses and young girls – they
    last while they last.
    Attrib.

13   In order to become the master, the politician
    poses as the servant.
    Attrib.

14   I have come to the conclusion that politics are
    too serious a matter to be left to the politicians.
    Attrib.

de Mille, Cecil B(lout) (1881–1959) US film producer and
director. His best-known films were such biblical epics as *The Ten
Commandments* (1923; remade in 1956), and *Samson and Delilah*
(1949).

1   Every time I make a picture the critics' estimate
    of American public taste goes down ten per
    cent.
    Halliwell's Filmgoer's and Video Viewer's Companion

2   I didn't write the Bible and didn't invent sin.
    Halliwell's Filmgoer's and Video Viewer's Companion

Dekker, Thomas (c. 1572–1632) English dramatist, his
best-known play being *The Shoemaker's Holiday* (1600). His
pamphlets, including *The Seven Deadly Sins of London* (1606),
were widely read.

1   Golden slumbers kiss your eyes,
    Smiles awake you when you rise.
    Patient Grissil, IV:2

2   The Englishman's dress is like a traitor's body
    that hath been hanged, drawn, and quartered,
    and is set up in various places; his cod-piece is in
    Denmark, the collar of his doublet and the belly
    in France; the wing and narrow sleeve in Ita-
    ly; the short waist hangs over a Dutch butcher's
    stall in Utrecht; his huge slops speak Spanish-
    ly. . . . And thus we that mock every nation
    for keeping of one fashion, yet steal patches
    from every one of them to piece out our pride.
    Seven Deadly Sins of London

De La Mare, Walter (1873–1956) British poet and
novelist. His verse collections include *Songs of Childhood* (1902)
and his novel *Memoirs of a Midget* (1921) is his best-known fiction
work.

1   It's a very odd thing –
    As odd as can be –
    That whatever Miss T eats
    Turns into Miss T.
    Miss T

2   Until we learn the use of living words we shall
    continue to be waxworks inhabited by
    gramophones.
    The Observer, 'Sayings of the Week', 12 May 1929

3 Too late for fruit, too soon for flowers.

On being asked, as he lay seriously ill, whether he would like some fruit or flowers
Attrib.

Delaney, Shelagh (1939–) British dramatist. Her first success was *A Taste of Honey* (1958), which was followed by *The Lion in Love* (1960). She has also written for radio and TV.

1 I'm not frightened of the darkness outside. It's the darkness inside houses I don't like.

A Taste of Honey, I:1

2 Women never have young minds. They are born three thousand years old.

A Taste of Honey, I:1

Delille, Jacques (1738–1813) French abbé and poet. He is remembered for his verse *Les Jardins* and his translations of Virgil and Milton.

1 Fate chooses your relations, you choose your friends.

Malheur et pitié, I

Denman, Thomas, Baron (1779–1854) British judge. Attorney general (1830) and lord chief justice (1832–50), he defended Queen Caroline before the House of Lords.

1 Trial by jury itself, instead of being a security to persons who are accused, will be a delusion, a mockery, and a snare.

Judgment in O'Connell v The Queen, 4 Sept 1844

Dennis, John (1657–1734) British critic and dramatist. His plays, including *Liberty Asserted* (1704), were less influential than his *Advancement and Reformation of Modern Poetry* (1701).

1 A man who could make so vile a pun would not scruple to pick a pocket.

The Gentleman's Magazine, 1781

Dennis, Nigel (Forbes) (1912–89) British writer and dramatist. *Cards of Identity* (1955) and *The Making of Moo* (1957) established him as a playwright. He was also a drama critic and columnist.

1 This man, she reasons, as she looks at her husband, is a poor fish. But he is the nearest I can get to the big one that got away.

Cards of Identity

2 But then one is always excited by descriptions of money changing hands. It's much more fundamental than sex.

Cards of Identity

De Quincey, Thomas (1785–1859) British writer. A friend of Wordsworth and Coleridge, he became addicted to opium as a consequence of taking it for toothache. His *Confessions of an Opium Eater* appeared in 1822.

1 Books, we are told, propose to *instruct* or to *amuse*. Indeed! . . . The true antithesis to knowledge, in this case, is not *pleasure*, but *power*. All that is literature seeks to communicate power; all that is not literature, to communicate knowledge.

Letters to a Young Man

2 Murder considered as one of the Fine Arts.

Essay title

3 Even imperfection itself may have its ideal or perfect state.

Murder considered as one of the Fine Arts

Descartes, René (1596–1650) French philosopher and mathematician. His *Le Discours de la Méthode* (1637) introduced his technique of analysis, while his work on analytical geometry resulted in the Cartesian system of coordinates.

1 *Cogito, ergo sum.*
I think, therefore I am.

Le Discours de la méthode

2 The reading of all good books is like a conversation with the finest men of past centuries.

Le Discours de la méthode

3 Travelling is almost like talking with men of other centuries.

Le Discours de la méthode

Deschamps, Eustache (c. 1340–c. 1407) French poet. He wrote many ballads and the poem *Le Miroir de mariage*.

1 Who will bell the cat?

Ballade: Le Chat et les souris

De Sica, Vittorio (1901–74) Italian film director. His films include *Shoeshine* (1946) and *Umberto D* (1952).

1 Moral indignation is in most cases 2 percent moral, 48 percent indignation and 50 percent envy.

The Observer, 1961

de Valois, Dame Ninette (Edris Stannus; 1898–) British ballet dancer and choreographer. She founded the Sadler's Wells (later Royal) Ballet in 1931, and directed it until 1963.

1 Ladies and gentleman, it takes more than one to make a ballet.

New Yorker

Devonshire, Spencer Compton Cavendish, 8th Duke of (1833–1908) Conservative politician. War secretary (1866) and secretary of state for India (1880–82).

1 I dreamt that I was making a speech in the House. I woke up, and by Jove I was!

Thought and Adventures (W. S. Churchill)

Devonshire, Edward William Spencer Cavendish, 10th Duke of (1895–1950) Conservative politician. He was an MP before inheriting his title and later a parliamentary undersecretary.

1 Good God, that's done it. He's lost us the tarts' vote.

Referring to Stanley BALDWIN's attack on newspaper proprietors; recalled by Harold Macmillan
Attrib.

De Vries, Peter (1910–) US novelist. His novels include *The Mackerel Plaza* (1958), *The Glory of the Hummingbird* (1975), *Slouching Towards Kalamazoo* (1983), and *Peckham's Marbles* (1986).

1 We know the human brain is a device to keep the ears from grating on one another.

Comfort me with Apples, Ch. 1

2 Gluttony is an emotional escape, a sign something is eating us.

Comfort me with Apples, Ch. 7

3 Probably a fear we have of facing up to the real issues. Could you say we were guilty of Noel Cowardice?

Comfort me with Apples, Ch. 8

4 I wanted to be bored to death, as good a way to go as any.

Comfort me with Apples, Ch. 17

5 Anyone informed that the universe is expanding and contracting in pulsations of eighty billion years has a right to ask, 'What's in it for me?'

The Glory of the Hummingbird, Ch. 1

6 It is the final proof of God's omnipotence that he need not exist in order to save us.

The Mackerel Plaza, Ch. 2

7 Let us hope . . . that a kind of Providence will put a speedy end to the acts of God under which we have been labouring.

The Mackerel Plaza, Ch. 3

8 Everybody hates me because I'm so universally liked.

The Vale of Laughter, Pt. I

De Wolfe, Elsie (1865–1950) US designer and leader of fashion.

1 It's beige! My color!

On first sighting the Acropolis
Elsie de Wolfe (J. Smith)

Díaz, Porfirio (1830–1915) Mexican general and statesman. He was President for seven terms but was finally forced to abdicate and he died in Paris in exile.

1 Poor Mexico, so far from God and so near to the United States!

Attrib.

Dibdin, Charles (1745–1814) British actor and dramatist. He wrote many plays including *The Waterman* (1774) and *The Quaker* (1775), as well as many songs for the theatre.

1 What argufies pride and ambition?
Soon or late death will take us in tow:
Each bullet has got its commission,
And when our time's come we must go.

Each Bullet has its Commission

2 Then trust me, there's nothing like drinking
So pleasant on this side the grave;
It keeps the unhappy from thinking,
And makes e'en the valiant more brave.

Nothing like Grog

Dickens, Charles (1812–70) British novelist. His career began with contributions to magazines using the pen name Boz, *Pickwick Papers* (1837) bringing him sudden fame. His many subsequent novels, all appearing in monthly instalments and depicting the poverty of the working classes in Victorian England, have remained immensely popular.

Quotations about Dickens

1 We were put to Dickens as children but it never quite took. That unremitting humanity soon had me cheesed off.

Alan Bennett (1934–) British playwright. *The Old Country*, II

2 It does not matter that Dickens' world is not life-like; it is alive.

Lord Cecil (1902–86) British writer and critic. *Early Victorian Novelists*

3 One would have to have a heart of stone to read the death of Little Nell without laughing.

Oscar Wilde (1854–1900) Irish-born British dramatist. Lecturing upon Dickens. *Lives of the Wits* (H. Pearson)

Quotations by Dickens

4 'There are strings', said Mr Tappertit, 'in the human heart that had better not be wibrated.'

Barnaby Rudge, Ch. 22

5 This is a London particular . . . A fog, miss.

Bleak House, Ch. 3

6 I expect a judgment. Shortly.

Bleak House, Ch. 3

7 'Old girl,' said Mr Bagnet, 'give him my opinion. You know it.'

Bleak House, Ch. 27

8 It is a melancholy truth that even great men have their poor relations.

Bleak House, Ch. 28

9 O let us love our occupations,
Bless the squire and his relations,
Live upon our daily rations,
And always know our proper stations.

The Chimes, '2nd Quarter'

10 'God bless us every one!' said Tiny Tim, the last of all.

A Christmas Carol

11 'I am a lone lorn creetur,' were Mrs Gummidge's words . . . 'and everythink goes contrary with me.'

David Copperfield, Ch. 3

12 Barkis is willin'.

David Copperfield, Ch. 5

13 Annual income twenty pounds, annual expenditure nineteen nineteen six, result happiness. Annual income twenty pounds, annual expenditure twenty pounds ought and six, result misery.

David Copperfield, Ch. 12

14 I am well aware that I am the 'umblest person going . . . .My mother is likewise a very 'umble person. We live in a numble abode.
Said by Uriah Heep
David Copperfield, Ch. 16

15 We are so very 'umble.
David Copperfield, Ch. 17

16 Uriah, with his long hands slowly twining over one another, made a ghastly writhe from the waist upwards.
David Copperfield, Ch. 17

17 Accidents will occur in the best-regulated families.
David Copperfield, Ch. 28

18 I'm Gormed – and I can't say no fairer than that.
David Copperfield, Ch. 63

19 When found, make a note of.
Dombey and Son, Ch. 15

20 There's a young man hid with me, in comparison with which young man I am a Angel. That young man hears the words I speak. That young man has a secret way pecooliar to himself, of getting at a boy, and at his heart, and at his liver.
Said by Magwitch
Great Expectations, Ch. 1

21 Now, what I want is Facts . . . Facts alone are wanted in life.
Hard Times, Bk. I, Ch. 1

22 Whatever was required to be done, the Circumlocution Office was beforehand with all the public departments in the art of perceiving – HOW NOT TO DO IT.
Little Dorrit, Bk. I, Ch. 10

23 In company with several other old ladies of both sexes.
Said by Mr Meagles
Little Dorrit, Bk. I, Ch. 17

24 It was not a bosom to repose upon, but it was a capital bosom to hang jewels upon.
Describing Mrs Merdle
Little Dorrit, Bk. I, Ch. 21

25 As she frequently remarked when she made any such mistake, it would be all the same a hundred years hence.
Said by Mrs Squeers
Martin Chuzzlewit, Ch. 9

26 Let us be moral. Let us contemplate existence.
Martin Chuzzlewit, Ch. 10

27 Here's the rule for bargains: 'Do other men, for they would do you.' That's the true business precept.
Martin Chuzzlewit, Ch. 11

28 Buy an annuity cheap, and make your life interesting to yourself and everybody else that watches the speculation.
Martin Chuzzlewit, Ch. 18

29 He'd make a lovely corpse.
Martin Chuzzlewit, Ch. 25

30 'She's the sort of woman now,' said Mould, . . . 'one would almost feel disposed to bury for nothing: and do it neatly, too!'
Martin Chuzzlewit, Ch. 25

31 He had but one eye, and the popular prejudice runs in favour of two.
Said by Mr Squeers
Nicholas Nickleby, Ch. 4

32 When he has learnt that bottinney means a knowledge of plants, he goes and knows 'em. That's our system, Nickleby; what do you think of it?
Said by Mr Squeers
Nicholas Nickleby, Ch. 8

33 Every baby born into the world is a finer one than the last.
Nicholas Nickleby, Ch. 36

34 All is gas and gaiters.
Nicholas Nickleby, Ch. 49

35 'Did you ever taste beer?' 'I had a sip of it once,' said the small servant. 'Here's a state of things!' cried Mr Swiveller . . . . 'She *never* tasted it – it can't be tasted in a sip!'
The Old Curiosity Shop, Ch. 57

36 Oliver Twist has asked for more.
Oliver Twist, Ch. 2

37 Known by the *sobriquet* of 'The artful Dodger.'
Oliver Twist, Ch. 8

38 'If the law supposes that,' said Mr Bumble . . . , 'the law is a ass – a idiot.'
Oliver Twist, Ch. 51

39 The question about everything was, would it bring a blush to the cheek of a young person?
Pondered by Mr Podsnap
Our Mutual Friend, Bk. I, Ch. 11

40 I think . . . that it is the best club in London.
Mr Tremlow describing the House of Commons
Our Mutual Friend, Bk. II, Ch. 3

41 He'd be sharper than a serpent's tooth, if he wasn't as dull as ditch water.
Our Mutual Friend, Bk. III, Ch. 10

42 Kent, sir – everybody knows Kent – apples, cherries, hops and women.
Pickwick Papers, Ch. 2

43 I wants to make your flesh creep.
Pickwick Papers, Ch. 8

44 'It's always best on these occasions to do what the mob do.'
'But suppose there are two mobs?' suggested Mr Snodgrass.
'Shout with the largest,' replied Mr Pickwick.
Pickwick Papers, Ch. 13

45 Take example by your father, my boy, and be very careful o' vidders all your life.
Pickwick Papers, Ch. 13

46 Poverty and oysters always seem to go together.
Pickwick Papers, Ch. 22

47 Wery glad to see you indeed, and hope our acquaintance may be a long 'un, as the gen'l'm'n said to the fi' pun' note.
Pickwick Papers, Ch. 25

48 Poetry's unnat'ral; no man ever talked poetry 'cept a beadle on boxin' day.
Pickwick Papers, Ch. 33

49 It's my opinion, sir, that this meeting is drunk.
Pickwick Papers, Ch. 33

50 I am afeered that werges on the poetical, Sammy.
Said by Sam Weller
Pickwick Papers, Ch. 33

51 Never sign a walentine with your own name.
Said by Sam Weller
Pickwick Papers, Ch. 33

52 Put it down a we, my lord, put it down a we!
Pickwick Papers, Ch. 34

53 Miss Bolo rose from the table considerably agitated, and went straight home, in a flood of tears and a Sedan chair.
Pickwick Papers, Ch. 35

54 Anythin' for a quiet life, as the man said wen he took the sitivation at the lighthouse.
Pickwick Papers, Ch. 43

55 A smattering of everything, and a knowledge of nothing.
Sketches by Boz, 'Tales', Ch. 3

56 It was the best of times, it was the worst of times, it was the age of wisdom, it was the age of foolishness, it was the epoch of belief, it was the epoch of incredulity, it was the season of Light, it was the season of Darkness, it was the spring of hope, it was the winter of despair, we had everything before us, we had nothing before us, we were all going direct to Heaven, we were all going direct the other way.
The opening words of the book
A Tale of Two Cities, Bk. I, Ch. 1

57 It is a far, far, better thing that I do, than I have ever done; it is a far, far, better rest that I go to, than I have ever known.
A Tale of Two Cities, Bk. II, Ch. 15

Dickinson, Emily (1830–86) US poet. Of her 1700 poems, only 7 were published during her lifetime. Six volumes were published posthumously.

1 Because I could not stop for Death,
He kindly stopped for me;
The carriage held but just ourselves
And Immortality.
The Chariot

2 Parting is all we know of heaven,
And all we need of hell.
My Life Closed Twice Before its Close

3 Our journey had advanced;
Our feet were almost come
To that odd fork in Being's road,
Eternity by term.
Our Journey had Advanced

4 Pain – has an Element of Blank –
It cannot recollect
When it begun – or if there were
A time when it was not –.
Pain

5 Success is counted sweetest
By those who ne'er succeed.
Success is Counted Sweetest

Diderot, Denis (1713–84) French writer and editor. With Voltaire he created the *Encyclopédie*, one of the chief works of the Enlightenment.

1 Wandering in a vast forest at night, I have only a faint light to guide me. A stranger appears and says to me: 'My friend, you should blow out your candle in order to find your way more clearly.' This stranger is a theologian.
Addition aux pensées philosophiques

2 It has been said that love robs those who have it of their wit, and gives it to those who have none.
Paradoxe sur le comédien

3 What a fine comedy this world would be if one did not play a part in it!
Letters to Sophie Volland

Dietrich, Marlene (Maria Magdalene von Losch; 1904–) German-born film star and singer. She made her name in the German version of *The Blue Angel* (1930); subsequently she went to Hollywood, where she made many films including *Destry Rides Again* (1939), *A Foreign Affair* (1948), *Judgement at Nuremberg* (1961), and *Just a Gigolo* (1978).

1 Once a woman has forgiven her man, she must not reheat his sins for breakfast.
Marlene Dietrich's ABC

2 Latins are tenderly enthusiastic. In Brazil they throw flowers at you. In Argentina they throw themselves.
Newsweek, 24 Aug 1959

3 The average man is more interested in a woman who is interested in him than he is in a woman – any woman – with beautiful legs.
News Item, 13 Dec 1954

4 Most women set out to try to change a man, and when they have changed him they do not like him.
Attrib.

Diller, Phyllis (1917–74) US writer, comedienne, and pianist.

1 Cleaning your house while your kids are still growing
Is like shoveling the walk before it stops snowing.
Phyllis Diller's Housekeeping Hints

2 Never go to bed mad. Stay up and fight.
Phyllis Diller's Housekeeping Hints

Dillingham, Charles Bancroft (1868–1934) US theatrical manager and producer. He managed the Globe Theatre in York, amongst others.

1 I bet you a hundred bucks he ain't in here.
Referring to the escapologist Harry Houdini; said at his funeral, while carrying his coffin
Attrib.

Diogenes (412–322 BC) Greek philosopher, who founded the Cynics. He is reputed to have lived in a tub in Athens and to have wandered the streets with a lamp, seeking an honest man.

1 Stand a little less between me and the sun.
When Alexander the Great asked if there was anything he wanted
Life of Alexander (Plutarch)

2 If only it were as easy to banish hunger by rubbing the belly as it is to masturbate.
Lives and Opinions of Eminent Philosophers (Diogenes Laertius)

3 I am a citizen of the world.
Replying to a question concerning his nationality
Attrib.

Dionysius of Halicarnassus (40–8 BC) Greek historian. He taught in Rome from 30 BC and compiled a 20-volume history of Rome.

1 History is philosophy teaching by examples.
Ars rhetorica, XI:2

Disney, Walt (1901–66) US film producer and animator. His most famous cartoon films include *Fantasia* (1940) and *Bambi* (1943); he opened the first Disneyland amusement park in California in 1955.

1 Too many people grow up. That's the real trouble with the world, too many people grow up. They forget. They don't remember what it's like to be 12 years old. They patronise, they treat children as inferiors. Well I won't do that.

2 Girls bored me – they still do. I love Mickey Mouse more than any woman I've ever known.
You Must Remember This (W. Wagner)

Disraeli, Benjamin, 1st Earl of Beaconsfield
(1804–81) British statesman of Italian-Jewish descent, who became Conservative prime minister (1868; 1874–80). He was supported by Queen Victoria, whom he made Empress of India. He also wrote novels including *Coningsby* (1844) and *Sybil* (1845).

Quotations about Disraeli

1 The soul of Dizzy was a chandelier.
Edmund Clerihew Bentley (1875–1956) British writer. *A Ballad of Souls*

2 He was without any rival whatever, the first comic genius who ever installed himself in Downing Street.
Michael Foot (1913–) British Labour politician and journalist. *Debts of Honour*

3 Disraeli lacked two qualities, failing which true eloquence is impossible. He was never quite in earnest, and he was not troubled by dominating conviction.
Henry Lucy (1843–1924) British journalist. *Sixty Years in the Wilderness*

Quotations by Disraeli

4 Youth is a blunder; manhood a struggle; old age a regret.
Coningsby, Bk. III, Ch. 1

5 Almost everything that is great has been done by youth.
Coningsby, Bk. III, Ch. 1

6 His Christianity was muscular.
Endymion, Bk. I, Ch. 14

7 'Sensible men are all of the same religion.' 'And pray what is that?' inquired the prince. 'Sensible men never tell.'
Endymion, Bk. I, Ch. 81

8 The blue ribbon of the turf.
Describing the Derby
Life of Lord George Bentinck, Ch. 26

9 When a man fell into his anecdotage it was a sign for him to retire from the world.
Lothair, Ch. 28

10 Every woman should marry – and no man.
Lothair, Ch. 30

11 'My idea of an agreeable person,' said Hugo Bohun, 'is a person who agrees with me.'
Lothair, Ch. 35

12 'Two nations; between whom there is no intercourse and no sympathy; who are as ignorant of each other's habits, thoughts, and feelings, as if they were dwellers in different zones, or inhabitants of different planets; who are formed by a different breeding are fed by a different food, are ordered by different manners, and are not governed by the same laws.'
'You speak of–' said Egremont, hesitatingly.
'THE RICH AND THE POOR.'
Sybil, Bk. II, Ch. 5

13 Little things affect little minds.
Sybil, Bk. III, Ch. 2

14 A majority is always the best repartee.
Tancred, Bk. II, Ch. 14

15 It destroys one's nerves to be amiable every day to the same human being.
The Young Duke

16 There are three kinds of lies: lies, damned lies and statistics.
Autobiography (Mark Twain)

17 I will not go down to posterity talking bad grammar.

Remark made when correcting proofs of his last parliamentary speech, 31 Mar 1881
Disraeli (Blake), Ch. 32

18 I know he is, and he adores his maker.

Replying to a remark made in defence of John Bright that he was a self-made man
The Fine Art of Political Wit (L. Harris)

19 Thank you for the manuscript; I shall lose no time in reading it.

His customary reply to those who sent him unsolicited manuscripts
Irreverent Social History (F. Muir)

20 I will sit down now, but the time will come when you will hear me.

Maiden Speech, House of Commons, 7 Dec 1837

21 The Continent will not suffer England to be the workshop of the world.

Speech, House of Commons, 15 Mar 1838

22 Thus you have a starving population, an absentee aristocracy, and an alien Church, and in addition the weakest executive in the world.
That is the Irish Question.

Speech, House of Commons, 16 Feb 1844

23 The right honourable gentleman caught the Whigs bathing, and walked away with their clothes.

Referring to Sir Robert Peel
Speech, House of Commons, 28 Feb 1845

24 A Conservative government is an organized hypocrisy.

Speech, 17 Mar 1845

25 A precedent embalms a principle.

Speech, House of Commons, 22 Feb 1848

26 He has to learn that petulance is not sarcasm, and that insolence is not invective.

Said of Sir C. Wood
Speech, House of Commons, 16 Dec 1852

27 I am myself a gentleman of the Press, and I bear no other scutcheon.

Speech, House of Commons, 18 Feb 1863

28 The question is this: Is man an ape or an angel? I, my lord, am on the side of the angels.

Speech, 25 Nov 1864

29 Assassination has never changed the history of the world.

Speech, House of Commons, 1 May 1865

30 An author who speaks about his own books is almost as bad as a mother who talks about her own children.

Speech, Glasgow, 19 Nov 1873

31 Lord Salisbury and myself have brought you back peace – but a peace I hope with honour.

Speech, House of Commons, 16 July 1878

32 A sophistical rhetorician inebriated with the exuberance of his own verbosity.

Referring to Gladstone
Speech, 27 July 1878

33 Your dexterity seems a happy compound of the smartness of an attorney's clerk and the intrigue of a Greek of the lower empire.

Speaking to Lord Palmerston
Attrib.

34 If a traveller were informed that such a man was leader of the House of Commons, he may well begin to comprehend how the Egyptians worshipped an insect.

Referring to Lord John Russell
Attrib.

35 Pray remember, Mr Dean, no dogma, no Dean.

Attrib.

36 Nobody is forgotten when it is convenient to remember him.

Attrib.

37 Her Majesty is not a subject.

Responding to Gladstone's taunt that Disraeli could make a joke out of any subject, including Queen Victoria
Attrib.

38 When I meet a man whose name I can't remember, I give myself two minutes; then, if it is a hopeless case, I aways say, And how is the old complaint?

Attrib.

39 She is an excellent creature, but she never can remember which came first, the Greeks or the Romans.

Referring to his wife
Attrib.

40 When I want to read a novel I write one.

Attrib.

41 I am dead: dead, but in the Elysian fields.

Said on his move to the House of Lords
Attrib.

42 No, it is better not. She will only ask me to take a message to Albert.

On his deathbed, declining an offer of a visit from Queen Victoria
Attrib.

Dix, Dom Gregory (1901–52) British monk. He was prior of Nashdom Abbey (1926–52). His books include *The Question of Anglican Orders* (1943).

1 It is no accident that the symbol of a bishop is a crook, and the sign of an archbishop is a double-cross.

Letter to *The Times*, 3 Dec 1977 (Francis Bown)

Dix, Dorothy (Elizabeth Meriwether Gilmer; 1861–1951) US journalist and writer. She wrote an agony aunt column for many years. Her books include *How to Win and Hold a Husband* (1939).

1 It is only the women whose eyes have been washed clear with tears who get the broad vision that makes them little sisters to all the world.

Dorothy Dix, Her Book, Introduction

2 I have learned to live each day as it comes, and not to borrow trouble by dreading tomorrow. It is the dark menace of the future that makes cowards of us.
Dorothy Dix, Her Book, Introduction

3 Now one of the great reasons why so many husbands and wives make shipwreck of their lives together is because a man is always seeking for happiness, while a woman is on a perpetual still hunt for trouble.
Dorothy Dix, Her Book, Ch. 1

4 The reason that husbands and wives do not understand each other is because they belong to different sexes.
News item

Dobrée, Bonamy (1891–1974) British scholar and writer. An authority on Restoration drama, his books include *Restoration Tragedy* (1929).

1 It is difficult to be humble. Even if you aim at humility, there is no guarantee that when you have attained the state you will not be proud of the feat.
John Wesley

Dodd, Ken (1931–) British comedian and entertainer.

1 The trouble with Freud is that he never played the Glasgow Empire Saturday night.
TV interview, 1965

Dodgson, Charles Lutwidge *See* Carroll, Lewis.

Donleavy, J(ames) P(atrick) (1926–) US novelist now living in Ireland. He made his name with *The Ginger Man* (1956). Other books include *The Onion Eaters* (1971), *Leila* (1983), and *Are You Listening Rabbi Löw?* (1987).

1 I got disappointed in human nature as well and gave it up because I found it too much like my own.
Fairy Tales of New York

Donne, John (1573–1631) English poet of the metaphysical school. He was ordained at the age of 43 and was appointed Dean of St Pauls (1621). His verse includes *Divine Poems* (1607) and *Epithalamium* (1613).

Quotations about Donne

1 With Donne, whose muse on dromedary trots,
Wreathe iron pokers into true-love knots.
Samuel Taylor Coleridge (1772–1834) British poet. *On Donne's Poetry*

2 Dr Donne's verses are like the peace of God; they pass all understanding.
James I (1566–1625) King of England.

Quotations by Donne

3 And new Philosophy calls all in doubt,
The Element of fire is quite put out;
The Sun is lost, and th' earth, and no man's wit
Can well direct him where to look for it.
An Anatomy of the World, 205

4 Come live with me, and be my love,
And we will some new pleasures prove
Of golden sands, and crystal brooks,
With silken lines, and silver hooks.
The Bait

5 For God's sake hold your tongue and let me love.
The Canonization

6 But I do nothing upon myself, and yet I am mine own Executioner.
Devotions, 12

7 No man is an Island, entire of itself; every man is a piece of the Continent, a part of the main.
Devotions, 17

8 Any man's death diminishes me, because I am involved in Mankind; And therefore never send to know for whom the bell tolls; it tolls for thee.
Devotions, 17

9 Love built on beauty, soon as beauty, dies.
Elegies, 2, 'The Anagram'

10 She, and comparisons are odious.
Elegies, 8, 'The Comparison'

11 Licence my roving hands, and let them go,
Before, behind, between, above, below.
Elegies, 18, 'Love's Progress'

12 O my America! my new-found-land,
My Kingdom, safeliest when with one man man'd.
Elegies, 19, 'Going To Bed'

13 Go, and catch a falling star,
Get with child a mandrake root,
Tell me, where all past years are,
Or who cleft the Devil's foot.
Go and Catch a Falling Star

14 Death be not proud, though some have called thee
Mighty and dreadful, for, thou art not so.
Holy Sonnets, 10

15 It comes equally to us all, and makes us all equal when it comes. The ashes of an Oak in the Chimney, are no epitaph of that Oak, to tell me how high or how large that was; It tells me not what flocks it sheltered while it stood, nor what men it hurt when it fell. The dust of great persons' graves is speechless too, it says nothing, it distinguishes nothing.
Speaking of Death
Sermons, XV

16 Busy old fool, unruly Sun,
Why dost thou thus,
Through windows and through curtains call on us?
The Sun Rising

17 I am two fools, I know,
For loving, and for saying so
In whining Poetry.

The Triple Fool

Dostoevsky, Anna (1846–1918) Russian diarist and writer. She was the wife of Fedor Dostoevsky.

1 From a timid, shy girl I had become a woman of resolute character, who could not longer be frightened by the struggle with troubles.

Dostoevsky Portrayed by His Wife

2 It seems to me that he has never loved, that he has only imagined that he has loved, that there has been no real love on his part. I even think that he is incapable of love; he is too much occupied with other thoughts and ideas to become strongly attached to anyone earthly.

Dostoevsky Portrayed by His Wife

Dostoevsky, Fedor Mikhailovich (1821–81) Russian novelist. His major works are *Crime and Punishment* (1866), *The Idiot* (1868–69), *The Possessed* (1869–72), and *The Brothers Karamazov* (1879–80).

1 The formula 'Two and two make five' is not without its attractions.

Notes from the Underground

Douglas, Lord Alfred (Bruce) (1870–1945) British writer and poet. At the centre of the Oscar Wilde scandal, he wrote *The City of the Soul* (1899) and a verse collection *Sonnets and Lyrics* (1935).

1 I am the Love that dare not speak its name.

Poem about homosexual love
Two Loves

Douglas, Archibald, 5th Earl of Angus (1449–1514) Scottish nobleman. He led the rebellion against James III. He was known as the 'Great Earl' and as 'Bell-the-Cat'.

1 I'll bell the cat.

Of his proposed capture of Robert Cochrane (executed 1482)

Douglas, James, 4th Earl of Morton (1525–81) Scottish nobleman. He was Lord High Chancellor of Scotland (1563) and helped to secure the abdication of Mary, Queen of Scots. He was regent in 1572 but was ousted and finally executed.

1 Here lies he who neither feared nor flattered any flesh.

Said of John Knox at his funeral, 26 Nov 1572
Life of John Knox (G. R. Preedy), VII

Douglas, Norman (1868–1952) British novelist. His novels include *South Wind* (1917); his travel books *Siren Land* (1911) and *Old Calabria* (1915) were also popular.

1 It is the drawback of all sea-side places that half the landscape is unavailable for purposes of human locomotion, being covered by useless water.

Alone, 'Mentone'

2 Bouillabaisse is only good because cooked by the French, who, if they cared to try, could produce an excellent and nutritious substitute out of cigar stumps and empty matchboxes.

Siren Land, 'Rain on the Hills'

3 Many a man who thinks to found a home discovers that he has merely opened a tavern for his friends.

South Wind, Ch. 24

Douglas, William (1672–1748) Scottish poet. He is remembered for his poem written for Anne, daughter of Sir Robert Laurie, called *Annie Laurie*.

1 And for bonnie Annie Laurie
I'll lay me doun and dee.

Annie Laurie

Douglas-Home, Sir Alec, Baron Home of the Hirsel (1903–) British statesman. Prime minister (1963–64). He was an MP before inheriting the Earldom of Home. He was then foreign secretary (1960–63) and renounced his title to succeed Macmillan as prime minister. He was made a life peer in 1974.

1 As far as the 14th Earl is concerned, I suppose Mr Wilson, when you come to think of it, is the 14th Mr Wilson.

On renouncing his peerage (as 14th Earl of Home) to become prime minister
TV interview, 21 Oct 1963

2 There are two problems in my life. The political ones are insoluble and the economic ones are incomprehensible.

Speech, Jan 1964

Douglas-Home, Lady Caroline (1937–) Daughter of Lord Home of the Hirsel. She has been a lady-in-waiting to the Duchess of Kent.

1 He is used to dealing with estate workers. I cannot see how anyone can say he is out of touch.

Referring to her father's suitability for his new role as prime minister
Daily Herald, 21 Oct 1963

Dow, Lorenzo (1777–1834) British churchman, who wrote *Reflections on the Love of God* (1836).

1 You will be damned if you do – And you will be damned if you don't.

Speaking of Calvinism
Reflections on the Love of God

Dowson, Ernest (Christopher) (1867–1900) British lyric poet. From 1894 he lived in France, where he died of tuberculosis and absinthe addiction.

1 I have been faithful to thee, Cynara! in my fashion.

Non Sum Qualis Eram Bonae Sub Regno Cynarae

2 I have forgot much, Cynara! gone with the wind, Flung roses, roses riotously with the throng.

Non Sum Qualis Eram Bonae Sub Regno Cynarae

3 And I was desolate and sick of an old passion.

Non Sum Qualis Eram Bonae Sub Regno Cynarae

4 They are not long, the days of wine and roses.

Vitae Summa Brevis Spem Nos Vetat Incohare Longam

Doyle, Sir Arthur Conan (1856–1930) British writer and creator of the detective Sherlock Holmes. Originally a doctor, he ceased to practise in 1890, devoting himself entirely to his writing. He also wrote books on spiritualism.

Quotations about Doyle

1 My contention is that Sherlock Holmes *is* literature on a humble but not ignoble level, whereas the mystery writers most in vogue now are not. The old stories are literature, not because of the conjuring tricks and the puzzles, not because of the lively melodrama, which they have in common with many other detective stories, but by virtue of imagination and style.

Edmund Wilson (1895–1972) US critic and writer. *Classics and Commercials*

2 Conan Doyle, a few words on the subject of. Don't you find as you age in the wood, as we are both doing, that the tragedy of life is that your early heroes lose their glamour? . . . Now, with Doyle I don't have this feeling. I still revere his work as much as ever. I used to think it swell, and I still think it swell.

P. G. Wodehouse (1881–1975) British humorous novelist. *Performing Flea*

Quotations by Doyle

3 It is an old maxim of mine that when you have excluded the impossible, whatever remains, however improbable, must be the truth.

The Beryl Coronet

4 You know my method. It is founded upon the observance of trifles.

The Boscombe Valley Mystery

5 The husband was a teetotaller, there was no other woman, and the conduct complained of was that he had drifted into the habit of winding up every meal by taking out his false teeth and hurling them at his wife.

A Case of Identity

6 It has long been an axiom of mine that the little things are infinitely the most important.

A Case of Identity

7 Depend upon it, there is nothing so unnatural as the commonplace.

A Case of Identity

8 It is my belief, Watson, founded upon my experience, that the lowest and vilest alleys of London do not present a more dreadful record of sin than does the smiling and beautiful countryside.

Copper Beeches

9 'Excellent!' I cried. 'Elementary,' said he.

Watson talking to Sherlock Holmes; Holmes's reply is often misquoted as 'Elementary my dear Watson'
The Crooked Man

10 'It is my duty to warn you that it will be used against you,' cried the Inspector, with the magnificent fair play of the British criminal law.

The Dancing Men

11 He is the Napoleon of crime.

Referring to Professor Moriarty
The Final Problem

12 A man should keep his little brain attic stocked with all the furniture that he is likely to use, and the rest he can put away in the lumber room of his library, where he can get it if he wants it.

Five Orange Pips

13 It is quite a three-pipe problem.

The Red-Headed League

14 An experience of women which extends over many nations and three continents.

The Sign of Four

15 'Is there any point to which you would wish to draw my attention?'
'To the curious incident of the dog in the night-time.'
'The dog did nothing in the night-time.'
'That was the curious incident,' remarked Sherlock Holmes.

The Silver Blaze

16 London, that great cesspool into which all the loungers of the Empire are irresistibly drained.

A Study in Scarlet

17 Mediocrity knows nothing higher than itself, but talent instantly recognizes genius.

The Valley of Fear

Drabble, Margaret (1939–) British novelist and writer. Her novels, which explore the emotional and moral dilemmas of women in contemporary society, include *The Waterfall* (1969), *The Needle's Eye* (1972), *The Middle Ground* (1980), *The Radiant Way* (1987), and *A Natural Curiosity* (1989).

1 Poverty, therefore, was comparative. One measured it by a sliding scale. One was always poor, in terms of those who were richer.

The Radiant Way

2 And there isn't any way that one can get rid of the guilt of having a nice body by saying that one can serve society with it, because that would end up with oneself as what? There simply doesn't seem to be any moral place for flesh.

A Summer Bird-Cage, Ch. 10

Drake, Sir Francis (1540–96) British navigator and admiral, who was the first Englishman to circumnavigate the globe, bringing back potatoes and tobacco from Virginia. He later helped to defeat the Spanish Armada.

1 I have singed the Spanish king's beard.

Referring to the raid on Cadiz harbour, 1587
Attrib.

2 There is plenty of time to win this game, and to thrash the Spaniards too.

Referring to the sighting of the Armada during a game of bowls, 20 July 1588
Attrib.

Drayton, Michael (1563–1631) English poet, whose *England's Heroical Epistles* (1597) and *Polyolbion* (1612–22), sang the praises of England.

1 Fair stood the wind for France
When we our sails advance.

Agincourt

2 Since there's no help, come let us kiss and part –
Nay, I have done, you get no more of me;
And I am glad, yea glad with all my heart
That thus so cleanly I myself can free.

Sonnets, 61

Dreiser, Theodore (1871–1945) US novelist. He made his reputation with *Sister Carrie* (1900). Subsequent successes included *An American Tragedy* (1925).

1 Shakespeare, I come!

His intended last words
The Constant Circle (S. Mayfield)

Drummond, Thomas (1797–1840) British engineer and statesman, whose limelight apparatus facilitated the 1820s survey of Britain. He was later appointed undersecretary of state for Ireland.

1 Property has its duties as well as its rights.

Letter to the Earl of Donoughmore, 22 May 1838

Dryden, John (1631–1700) British poet and dramatist. His play *Marriage à la Mode* (1673) and the verse satire *Absalom and Achitophel* (1681) were highly regarded. He was made poet laureate by Charles II in 1668, but having become a Catholic in 1685, he was deprived of the office on the accession of William of Orange.

Quotations about Dryden

1 He never heartily and sincerely praised any human being, or felt any real enthusiasm for any subject he took up.

John Keble (1792–1866) British poet and clergyman. *Lectures on Poetry*

2 Ev'n copious Dryden wanted, or forgot
The last and greatest art – the art to blot.

Alexander Pope (1688–1744) British poet. *Imitations of Horace*

Quotations by Dryden

3 In pious times, e'r Priest-craft did begin,
Before Polygamy was made a Sin.

Absalom and Achitophel, I

4 What e'r he did was done with so much ease,
In him alone, 'twas Natural to please.

Absalom and Achitophel, I

5 Great Wits are sure to Madness near alli'd
And thin Partitions do their Bounds divide.

Absalom and Achitophel, I

6 Bankrupt of Life, yet Prodigal of Ease.

Absalom and Achitophel, I

7 For Politicians neither love nor hate.

Absalom and Achitophel, I

8 But far more numerous was the Herd of such,
Who think too little, and who talk too much.

Absalom and Achitophel, I

9 A man so various, that he seem'd to be
Not one, but all Mankind's Epitome.
Stiff in Opinions, always in the wrong;
Was Everything by starts, and Nothing long.

Absalom and Achitophel, I

10 Did wisely from Expensive Sins refrain,
And never broke the Sabbath, but for Gain.

Absalom and Achitophel, I

11 During his Office, Treason was no Crime.
The Sons of Belial had a Glorious Time.

Absalom and Achitophel, I

12 Nor is the Peoples Judgment always true:
The Most may err as grossly as the Few.

Absalom and Achitophel, I

13 Beware the Fury of a Patient Man.

Absalom and Achitophel, I

14 The people's prayer, the glad diviner's theme,
The young men's vision, and the old men's dream!

Absalom and Achitophel, I

15 To die for faction is a common evil,
But to be hanged for nonsense is the Devil.

Absalom and Achitophel, II

16 None but the Brave deserves the Fair.

Alexander's Feast

17 Errors, like Straws, upon the surface flow;
He who would search for Pearls must dive below.

All for Love, Prologue

18 Men are but children of a larger growth;
Our appetites as apt to change as theirs,
And full as craving too, and full as vain.

All for Love, IV

19 So sicken waning moons too near the sun,
And blunt their crescents on the edge of day.

Annus Mirabilis

20 By viewing Nature, Nature's handmaid, art,
Makes mighty things from small beginnings grow.

Annus Mirabilis

21 Here lies my wife; here let her lie!
Now she's at rest, and so am I.

Epitaph Intended for Dryden's Wife

22 He was the man who of all modern, and perhaps ancient poets had the largest and most comprehensive soul.

Referring to Shakespeare
Essay of Dramatic Poesy

23 He was naturally learned; he needed not the spectacles of books to read nature; he looked inwards, and found her there.

Referring to Shakespeare
Essay of Dramatic Poesy

24 If by the people you understand the multitude, the *hoi polloi*, 'tis no matter what they think; they are sometimes in the right, sometimes in the wrong; their judgement is a mere lottery.

Essay of Dramatic Poesy

25 For present joys are more to flesh and blood Than a dull prospect of a distant good.

The Hind and the Panther, III

26 All humane things are subject to decay, And, when Fate summons, Monarchs must obey.

Mac Flecknoe

27 I am resolved to grow fat and look young till forty, and then slip out of the world with the first wrinkle and the reputation of five-and-twenty.

The Maiden Queen, III

28 I am to be married within these three days; married past redemption.

Marriage à la Mode, I

29 For, Heaven be thanked, we live in such an age, When no man dies for love, but on the stage.

Mithridates, Epilogue

30 A man is to be cheated into passion, but to be reasoned into truth.

Religio Laici, Preface

31 Happy the Man, and happy he alone, He who can call today his own: He who, secure within, can say, Tomorrow do thy worst, for I have liv'd today.

Translation of Horace, III

Dubček, Alexander (1921–) Czech statesman. A resistance fighter in World War II, he became leader of the Communist Party in 1968. His liberal reforms led to the Soviet invasion in 1968, shortly after which he was ousted from power. He re-emerged as a popular leader in 1989 and was subsequently elected chairman of the new Czech parliament.

1 Socialism with a human face.

A resolution by the party group in the Ministry of Foreign Affairs in 1968 referred to Czechoslovakian policy acquiring 'its own defined face'; the quotation is usually attributed to Dubček

2 Socialism with a human face must function again for a new generation. We have lived in the darkness for long enough.

Speech, Wenceslas Square, Prague, 24 Nov 1989

Dubin, Al (20th century) US songwriter.

1 Tiptoe through the tulips with me.

From the musical, *Gold Diggers of Broadway*
Tiptoe Through the Tulips

2 You may not be an angel
'Cause angels are so few,
But until the day that one comes along
I'll string along with you.

Twenty Million Sweethearts

Duhamel, Georges (1884–1966) French writer and physician. His books include *Des Légendes, des Batailles* (verse; 1907), *La Lumière* (play; 1911), *Civilisation* (war experiences; 1918), and many others.

1 Courtesy is not dead – it has merely taken refuge in Great Britain.

The Observer, 'Sayings of Our Times', 31 May 1953

Dulles, John Foster (1888–1959) US politician and diplomat. Eisenhower made him secretary of state (1953–59) and he was delegate to the UN, which he helped to form.

1 Yes, once – many, many years ago. I thought I had made a wrong decision. Of course, it turned out that I had been right all along. But I was wrong to have *thought* that I was wrong.

On being asked whether he had ever been wrong
Facing the Music (H. Temianka)

Dumas, Alexandre, Fils (1824–95) French writer. The illegitimate son of Dumas (Père), he is best known for *La Dame aux camélias* (1848), which Verdi used as the basis of his opera *La Traviata*. His plays include *Le Demi-monde* (1853) and *Le Fils naturel* (1858).

1 If God were suddenly condemned to live the life which he has inflicted on men, He would kill Himself.

Pensées d'album

2 All generalizations are dangerous, even this one.

Attrib.

3 It is only rarely that one can see in a little boy the promise of a man, but one can almost always see in a little girl the threat of a woman.

Attrib.

Dumas, Alexandre, Père (1802–70) French novelist and dramatist. His early melodramas were less successful than such novels as *The Three Musketeers* (1844) and *The Count of Monte Cristo* (1845).

1 All for one, and one for all.

The Three Musketeers

Du Maurier, Dame Daphne (1907–89) British novelist. Her books, often set in her native Cornwall, include *Rebecca* (1938), *My Cousin Rachel* (1951), and *The Flight of the Falcon* (1965).

1 Last night I dreamt I went to Manderley again.

Rebecca, Ch. 1

2 It . . . was full of dry rot. An unkind visitor said the only reason Menabilly still stood was that the woodworm obligingly held hands.

Interview – referring to her own house in Cornwall upon which Manderley in *Rebecca* was based

Duncan, Isadora (1878–1927) US dancer, who lived in Europe for most of her life. Her innovative dancing and her flamboyant lifestyle attracted considerable attention.

1 I have discovered the dance. I have discovered the art which has been lost for two thousand years.
My Life

2 People do not live nowadays – they get about ten percent out of life.
This Quarter Autumn, 'Memoirs'

3 America has all that Russia has not. Russia has things America has not. Why will America not reach out a hand to Russia, as I have given my hand?
Speaking in support of Russia following the 1917 Revolution
Speech, Symphony Hall, Boston, 1922

4 So that ends my first experience with matrimony, which I always thought a highly overrated performance.
The New York Times, 1923

5 Goodbye, my friends, I go on to glory.
She was strangled when her long scarf became entangled in the wheel of a sports car
Attrib.

Dunning, John, Baron Ashburton (1731–83) British lawyer and politician, who is remembered for his defence of The East India Company.

1 The influence of the Crown has increased, is increasing, and ought to be diminished.
Motion passed by the House of Commons, 1780

Duport, James (1606–79) English classicist. He is remembered for his collection of aphorisms *Homeri Gnomologia* (1660).

1 Whom God would destroy He first sends mad.
Homeri Gnomologia

Durocher, Leo (1905–) US baseball player and manager of the Brooklyn team (1951–54).

1 Nice guys finish last.
Attrib.

Durrell, Gerald Malcolm (1925–) British naturalist and writer. Brother of Lawrence Durrell, he wrote the autobiographical *My Family and Other Animals* (1956), about his childhood on Corfu, as well as such books as *The Stationary Ark* (1976), which concerns his zoo and wildlife conservation trust in Jersey.

1 . . . the important thing was that we devoted some of our time to natural history, and George meticulously and carefully taught me how to observe and how to note down observations in a diary. At once my enthusiastic but haphazard interest in nature became focused . . . The only mornings that I was ever on time for my lessons were those which were given up to natural history.
My Family and Other Animals

2 Every evening Mother would go for a walk with the dogs, and the family would derive much amusement from watching her progress down the hill. Roger, as senior dog, would lead the procession, followed by Widdle and Puke.

Then came Mother, wearing an enormous straw hat, which made her look like an animated mushroom, clutching in one hand a large trowel with which to dig any interesting wild plants she found. Dodo would waddle behind, eyes protruding and tongue flapping, and Sophia would bring up the rear, pacing along solemnly, carrying the imperial puppy on its cushion. Mother's Circus, Larry called it.
My Family and Other Animals

3 The sneeze in English is the harbinger of misery, even death. I sometimes think the only pleasure an Englishman has is in passing on his cold germs.
The Picnic

Durrell, Lawrence (1912–90) British novelist and poet. His Alexandria Quartet – *Justine* (1957), *Balthazar* (1958), *Mountolive* (1958), and *Clea* (1960) – established his reputation. Later books include *Tunc* (1968), *Nunquam* (1970), and the Avignon Quintet – *Monsieur* (1974), *Livia* (1978), *Constance* (1982), *Sebastian* (1983), and *Quinx* (1985).

1 No one can go on being a rebel too long without turning into an autocrat.
Balthazar, II

2 No more about sex, it's too boring.
Tunc

3 History is an endless repetition of the wrong way of living.
The Listener, 1978

Dyer, John (1700–58) British poet. He is remembered for *Grongar Hill* (1726) and *The Fleece* (1757).

1 Ever charming, ever new,
When will the landscape tire the view?
Grongar Hill

2 A little rule, a little sway,
A sunbeam in a winter's day,
Is all the proud and mighty have
Between the cradle and the grave.
Grongar Hill

Dylan, Bob (Robert Allen Zimmerman; 1941–) US popular singer and songwriter. Originally a member of the 1960s protest movement, producing such albums as *The Times They Are A-changin'* (1964), in the late 1970s his conversion to Christianity led to such religious albums as *Saved* (1980), and *Oh Mercy* (1989).

1 How many roads must a man walk down
Before you call him a man?
Blowin' in the Wind

2 Yes, 'n' how many years can some people exist
Before they're allowed to be free?
Yes, 'n' how many times can a man turn his head,
Pretending he just doesn't see?
The answer, my friend, is blowin' in the wind.
Blowin' in the Wind

3 She takes just like a woman, yes, she does
She makes love just like a woman, yes, she does
And she aches just like a woman
But she breaks just like a little girl.

Just Like a Woman

4 How does it feel
To be without a home
Like a complete unknown
Like a rolling stone?

Like a Rolling Stone

5 She knows there's no success like failure
And that failure's no success at all.

Love Minus Zero No Limit

6 Hey! Mr Tambourine Man, play a song for me.
I'm not sleepy and there is no place I'm going to.

Mr Tambourine Man

7 Come mothers and fathers
Throughout the land
And don't criticize
What you can't understand.

The Times They Are A-Changin'

8 Yeah, some of them are about ten minutes long,
others five or six.

On being asked, during an interview, if he would say something
about his songs

9 A Hard Rain's A-Gonna Fall.

Song title

E

Eames, Emma (1865–1952) US opera singer. She wrote an
autobiography *Some Memoirs and Reflections.*

1 I would rather be a brilliant memory than a
curiosity.

Referring to her retirement at the age of 47
The Elephant that Swallowed a Nightingale (C. Galtey)

Earhart, Amelia (1898–1937) US flyer; the first woman to
fly solo over both the Atlantic (1932) and Pacific (1935).

1 Courage is the price that Life exacts for granting
peace.

Courage

2 Of course I realized there was a measure of danger. Obviously I faced the possibility of not returning when first I considered going. Once
faced and settled there really wasn't any good
reason to refer to it.

Referring to her flight in the 'Friendship'
20 Hours: 40 Minutes – Our Flight in the Friendship, Ch. 5

Eban, Abba (1915–) Israeli politician.

1 History teaches us that men and nations behave
wisely once they have exhausted all other
alternatives.

The Observer, 'Sayings of the Week', 20 Dec 1970

Eccles, David McAdam, Viscount (1904–) British
politician. An MP (1943–62), he became minister of education
(1954–57; 1959–62) and paymaster general (1970–73).

1 A small acquaintance with history shows that all
Governments are selfish and the French Governments more selfish than most.

The Observer, 'Sayings of the Year', 29 Dec 1962

Eco, Umberto (1932–) Italian novelist and semiologist. His
historical mysteries include *The Name of the Rose* (1981) and
Foucault's Pendulum (1989).

1 The girl is lost; she is burnt flesh.

Referring to a suspected witch
The Name of the Rose

2 But laughter is weakness, corruption, the foolishness of our flesh.

The Name of the Rose

Eddington, Sir Arthur (1882–1944) British astronomer and
popularizer of science. His books include *The Nature of the
Physical World* (1928) and *The Expanding Universe* (1933).

1 Electrical force is defined as something which
causes motion of electrical charge; an electrical
charge is something which exerts electric
force.

The Nature of the Physical World

2 We used to think that if we knew one, we knew
two, because one and one are two. We are
finding that we must learn a great deal more
about 'and'.

The Harvest of a Quiet Eye (A. L. Mackay)

Eddy, Mary Baker (1821–1910) US religious leader who
founded the Church of Christ, Scientist, in Boston (1879).

1 The prayer that reforms the sinner and heals the
sick is an absolute faith that all things are possible to God – a spiritual understanding of Him,
an unselfed love.

Science and Health, with Key to the Scriptures

2 Christian Science explains all cause and effect as
mental, not physical.

Science and Health, with Key to the Scriptures

3 Sin brought death, and death will disappear with
the disappearance of sin.

Science and Health, with Key to the Scriptures

4 Sickness, sin and death, being inharmonious, do
not originate in God, nor belong to His
government.

Science and Health, with Key to the Scriptures

5 Disease can carry its ill-effects no farther than mortal mind maps out the way ... Disease is an image of thought externalized ... We classify disease as error, which nothing but Truth or Mind can heal ... Disease is an experience of so-called mortal mind. It is fear made manifest on the body.

Science and Health, with Key to the Scriptures

Eden, Sir (Robert) Anthony, 1st Earl of Avon (1897–1977) British statesman. He resigned as foreign secretary in 1938 in protest against Chamberlain's policy of appeasement, but was reappointed by Churchill, whom he succeeded as prime minister in 1955. He resigned in 1957 after the Suez debacle.

1 REPORTER: If Mr Stalin dies, what will be the effect on international affairs?
EDEN: That is a good question for you to ask, not a wise question for me to answer.

Interview on board the *Queen Elizabeth*, 4 Mar 1953

2 Everybody is always in favour of general economy and particular expenditure.

The Observer, 'Sayings of the Week', 17 June 1956

3 We are not at war with Egypt. We are in an armed conflict.

Speech, House of Commons, 4 Nov 1956

Eden, Clarissa, Countess of Avon (1920–85) Wife of the Earl of Avon (Sir Anthony Eden).

1 During the last few weeks I have felt that the Suez Canal was flowing through my drawing room.

Said during the Suez crisis of 1956
Attrib.

Edison, Thomas Alva (1847–1931) US inventor. A very prolific inventor, he produced the filament light bulb, the microphone, the gramophone, the alkaline accumulator, and some thousand other devices.

1 Genius is one per cent inspiration and ninety-nine per cent perspiration.

Attrib.

Edward III (1312–77) King of England (1327–77). Through his mother, Isabella of France, he claimed the French throne, thus starting the Hundred Years' War.

1 Let the boy win his spurs.

Replying to a suggestion that he should send reinforcements to his son, the Black Prince, during the Battle of Crécy, 1346
Attrib.

Edward VII (1841–1910) King of the United Kingdom (1901–10).

1 My good man, I'm not a strawberry.

Rebuking a footman who had spilt cream on him
The Last Country Houses (C. Aslat)

Edward VIII (1894–1972) King of the United Kingdom who abdicated in 1936 because of his relationship with the American divorcée Wallis Simpson, whom he subsequently married. He became the Duke of Windsor.

1 I have found it impossible to carry the heavy burden of responsibility and to discharge my duties as King as I would wish to do without the help and support of the woman I love.

Radio broadcast, 11 Dec 1936

2 Perhaps one of the only positive pieces of advice that I was ever given was that supplied by an old courtier who observed: 'Only two rules really count. Never miss an opportunity to relieve yourself; never miss a chance to sit down and rest your feet.'

A King's Story

3 Now what do I do with *this*?

On being handed the bill after a lengthy stay in a luxury hotel
Attrib.

4 Something must be done.

Said while visiting areas of high unemployment in South Wales during the 1930s
Attrib.

5 Of course, I do have a slight advantage over the rest of you. It helps in a pinch to be able to remind your bride that you gave up a throne for her.

Discussing the maintenance of happy marital relations
Attrib.

Einstein, Albert (1879–1955) German physicist who became a Swiss citizen (1901) and later a US citizen (1940). His theory of relativity revolutionized scientific thought. He was persuaded to write to President Roosevelt to warn him that Germany could possibly make an atomic bomb.

Quotations about Einstein

1 Einstein – the greatest Jew since Jesus. I have no doubt that Einstein's name will still be remembered and revered when Lloyd George, Foch and William Hohenzollern share with Charlie Chaplin that ineluctable oblivion which awaits the uncreative mind.

J. B. S. Haldane (1892–1964) British genetist. *Daedalus or Science and the Future*

2 The genius of Einstein leads to Hiroshima.

Pablo Picasso (1881–1973) Spanish painter. *Life with Picasso* (Françoise Gilot and Carlton Lake)

Quotations by Einstein

3 Science without religion is lame, religion without science is blind.

Out of My Later Years

4 We should take care not to make the intellect our god; it has, of course, powerful muscles, but no personality.

Out of My Later Life, 51

5 If you want to find out anything from the theoretical physicists about the methods they use, I advise you to stick closely to one principle: Don't listen to their words, fix your attention on their deeds.

The World As I See It

6 God is subtle but he is not malicious.

Inscribed over the fireplace in the Mathematical Institute, Princeton. It refers to Einstein's objection to the quantum theory.
Albert Einstein (Carl Seelig), Ch. 8

7 God does not play dice.

Einstein's objection to the quantum theory, in which physical events can only be known in terms of probabilities. It is sometimes quoted as 'God does not play dice with the Universe'.
Albert Einstein, Creator and Rebel (B. Hoffman), Ch. 10

8 When you are courting a nice girl an hour seems like a second. When you sit on a red-hot cinder a second seems like an hour. That's relativity.

News Chronicle, 14 Mar 1949

9 If only I had known, I should have become a watchmaker.

Reflecting on his role in the development of the atom bomb
New Statesman, 16 Apr 1965

10 Common sense is the collection of prejudices acquired by age eighteen.

Scientific American, Feb 1976

11 A theory can be proved by experiment; but no path leads from experiment to the birth of a theory.

The Sunday Times, 18 July 1976

12 As far as the laws of mathematics refer to reality, they are not certain, and as far as they are certain, they do not refer to reality.

The Tao of Physics (F. Capra), Ch. 2

13 I never think of the future. It comes soon enough.

Interview, 1930

Eisenhower, Dwight D(avid) (1890–1969) US general and statesman. President (1953–61) during the Cold War and the period of anticommunist witch hunts led by Senator McCarthy. In World War II he became supreme commander and was responsible for the D-day invasion of Europe.

Quotations about Eisenhower

1 Roosevelt proved a man could be president for life; Truman proved anybody could be president; and Eisenhower proved we don't need a president.

Anonymous

2 As an intellectual he bestowed upon the games of golf and bridge all the enthusiasm and perseverance that he withheld from books and ideas.

Emmet John Hughes *The Ordeal of Power*

3 The best clerk I ever fired.

Douglas Macarthur (1880–1964) US general. Attrib

Quotations by Eisenhower

4 The eyes of the world are upon you. The hopes and prayers of liberty-loving people everywhere march with you.

Order to his troops, 6 June 1944 (D-Day)

5 Whatever America hopes to bring to pass in this world must first come to pass in the heart of America.

Inaugural address, 1953

6 There is one thing about being President – nobody can tell you when to sit down.

The Observer, 'Sayings of the Week', 9 Aug 1953

7 You have a row of dominoes set up; you knock over the first one, and what will happen to the last one is that it will go over very quickly.

The so-called 'domino effect'; said during the Battle of Dien Bien Phu, in which the French were defeated by the communist Viet-Minh
Press conference, 7 Apr 1954

8 Your business is to put me out of business.

Addressing a graduating class at a university
Procession (J. Gunther)

9 The day will come when the people will make so insistent their demand that there be peace in the world that the Governments will get out of the way and let them have peace.

Attrib.

Elgar, Sir Edward (1857–1934) British composer, violinist, and conductor. His most famous works include the *Enigma Variations* (1899), the *Dream of Gerontius* (1900) and the *Pomp and Circumstance* marches (1901–30).

1 If I write a tune you all say it's commonplace – if I don't, you all say it's rot.

Letter to A. J. Jaeger, 20 Oct 1898

2 Lovely day: sun – zephyr – view – window open – liver – pills – proofs – bills – weedkiller – yah!

Letter to A. J. Jaeger, 20 May 1900

Eliot, George (Mary Ann Evans; 1819–80) British woman novelist who concealed her identity behind a man's name. Her novels, including *Adam Bede* (1854), *The Mill on the Floss* (1860), and *Silas Marner* (1861), were highly acclaimed.

1 A patronizing disposition always has its meaner side.

Adam Bede

2 It's but little good you'll do a-watering the last year's crop.

Adam Bede

3 He was like a cock who thought the sun had risen to hear him crow.

Adam Bede

4 A different taste in jokes is a great strain on the affections.

Daniel Deronda

5 Errors look so very ugly in persons of small means – one feels they are taking quite a liberty in going astray; whereas people of fortune may naturally indulge in a few delinquencies.

Janet's Repentance, Ch. 25

6 I should like to know what is the proper function of women, if it is not to make reasons for husbands to stay at home, and still stronger reasons for bachelors to go out.
The Mill on the Floss, Ch. 6

7 Animals are such agreeable friends – they ask no questions, they pass no criticisms.
Scenes of Clerical Life, 'Mr Gilfil's Love Story', Ch. 7

Eliot, T(homas) S(tearns) (1888–1965) US-born British poet and dramatist. He worked as a bank clerk before publication of his *Prufrock and Other Observations* (1917). *The Waste Land* (1922) established his reputation, which was confirmed by his *Four Quartets* (1935–41). His verse dramas include *Murder in the Cathedral* (1935) and *The Cocktail Party* (1949).

Quotations about Eliot

1 He likes to look on the bile when it is black.
Aldous Huxley (1894–1964) British novelist and essayist. *Ambrosia and Small Beer* (E. Marsh)

2 He is very yellow and glum. Perfect manners. Dyspeptic, ascetic, eclectic. Inhibitions. Yet obviously a nice man and a great poet.
Harold Nicolson (1886–1968) British writer. *Diary*, 2 May 1932

Quotations by Eliot

3 Because I do not hope to turn again
Because I do not hope
Because I do not hope to turn.
Ash-Wednesday

4 We can say of Shakespeare, that never has a man turned so little knowledge to such great account.
The Classics and the Man of Letters (lecture)

5 Hell is oneself;
Hell is alone, the other figures in it
Merely projections. There is nothing to escape from
And nothing to escape to. One is always alone.
The Cocktail Party, I:3

6 Time present and time past
Are both perhaps present in time future,
And time future contained in time past.
Four Quartets, 'Burnt Norton'

7 Human kind
Cannot bear very much reality.
Four Quartets, 'Burnt Norton'

8 Here I am, an old man in a dry month,
Being read to by a boy, waiting for rain.
Gerontion

9 We are the hollow men
We are the stuffed men
Leaning together
Headpiece filled with straw.
The Hollow Men

10 This is the way the world ends
Not with a bang but a whimper.
The Hollow Men

11 Let us go then, you and I,
When the evening is spread out against the sky
Like a patient etherized upon a table.
The Love Song of J. Alfred Prufrock

12 In the room the women come and go
Talking of Michelangelo.
The Love Song of J. Alfred Prufrock

13 I have measured out my life with coffee spoons.
The Love Song of J. Alfred Prufrock

14 I grow old . . . I grow old . . .
I shall wear the bottoms of my trousers rolled.
The Love Song of J. Alfred Prufrock

15 Shall I part my hair behind? Do I dare to eat a peach?
I shall wear white flannel trousers, and walk upon the beach.
I have heard the mermaids singing, each to each.
The Love Song of J. Alfred Prufrock

16 Macavity, Macavity, there's no one like Macavity,
There never was a Cat of such deceitfulness and suavity.
He always has an alibi, and one or two to spare:
At whatever time the deed took place – MACAVITY WASN'T THERE!
Macavity: The Mystery Cat

17 I am aware of the damp souls of the housemaids
Sprouting despondently at area gates.
Morning at the Window

18 The last temptation is the greatest treason:
To do the right deed for the wrong reason.
Murder in the Cathedral, I

19 The winter evening settles down
With smell of steaks in passageways.
Preludes

20 'Put your shoes at the door, sleep, prepare for life.'
The last twist of the knife.
Rhapsody on a Windy Night

21 Birth, and copulation, and death.
That's all the facts when you come to brass tacks.
Sweeney Agonistes, 'Fragment of an Agon'

22 The host with someone indistinct
Converses at the door apart,
The nightingales are singing near
The Convent of the Sacred Heart.
Sweeney among the Nightingales

23 No poet, no artist of any sort, has his complete meaning alone. His significance, his appreciation is the appreciation of his relation to the dead poets and artists.
Tradition and the Individual Talent

24 Poetry is not a turning loose of emotion, but an escape from emotion; it is not the expression of personality, but an escape from personality.
Tradition and the Individual Talent

25 April is the cruellest month, breeding
Lilacs out of the dead land, mixing
Memory and desire, stirring
Dull roots with spring rain.

The Waste Land, 'The Burial of the Dead'

26 I read, much of the night, and go south in the winter.

The Waste Land, 'The Burial of the Dead'

27 And I will show you something different from either
Your shadow at morning striding behind you,
Or your shadow at evening rising to meet you
I will show you fear in a handful of dust.

The Waste Land, 'The Burial of the Dead'

28 The years between fifty and seventy are the hardest. You are always being asked to do things, and you are not yet decrepit enough to turn them down.

Time, 23 Oct 1950

Elizabeth I (1533–1603) Queen of England. The daughter of Henry VIII and Anne Boleyn, she established the Protestant Church in England and had her Catholic cousin, Mary, Queen of Scots, beheaded. The Elizabethan age was one of greatness for England.

Quotations about Elizabeth I

1 The queen did fish for men's souls, and had so sweet a bait that no one could escape her network.

Christopher Hatton Attrib.

2 As just and merciful as Nero and as good a Christian as Mahomet.

John Wesley (1703–91) British religious leader. *Journal*. 29 Apr 1768

Quotations by Elizabeth I

3 Though God hath raised me high, yet this I count the glory of my crown: that I have reigned with your loves.

The Golden Speech, 1601

4 Madam I may not call you; mistress I am ashamed to call you; and so I know not what to call you; but howsoever, I thank you.

Writing to the wife of the Archbishop of Canterbury, expressing her disapproval of married clergy
Brief View of the State of the Church (Harington)

5 God may pardon you, but I never can.

To the Countess of Nottingham
History of England under the House of Tudor (Hume), Vol. II, Ch. 7

6 Good-morning, gentlemen both.

When addressing a group of eighteen tailors
Sayings of Queen Elizabeth (Chamberlin)

7 I will make you shorter by a head.

Sayings of Queen Elizabeth (Chamberlin)

8 I am your anointed Queen. I will never be by violence constrained to do anything. I thank God that I am endued with such qualities that if I were turned out of the Realm in my petticoat I were able to live in any place in Christome.

Sayings of Queen Elizabeth (Chamberlin)

9 Must! Is *must* a word to be addressed to princes? Little man, little man! thy father, if he had been alive, durst not have used that word.

Said to Robert Cecil, on her death bed
A Short History of the English People (J. R. Green), Ch. 7

10 If thy heart fails thee, climb not at all.

Written on a window in reply to Sir Walter RALEIGH's line.
Worthies of England (Fuller), Vol. I

11 I know I have the body of a weak and feeble woman, but I have the heart and stomach of a King, and of a King of England too.

Speech at Tilbury on the approach of the Spanish Armada

12 All my possessions for a moment of time.

Last words

Elizabeth II (1926–) Queen of the United Kingdom (since 1952) and head of the British Commonwealth. She married Prince Philip (1947).

1 I should like to be a horse.

When asked about her ambitions when a child
Attrib.

2 I think that everyone will conceed that – today of all days – I should begin by saying, 'My husband and I.'

On her silver-wedding
Speech, Guildhall, 1972

Elizabeth the Queen Mother (1900–) The wife of King George VI and mother of Elizabeth II. Formerly Lady Elizabeth Bowes-Lyon.

1 Now we can look the East End in the face.

Surveying the damage caused to Buckingham Palace by a bomb during the Blitz in World War II
Attrib.

Ellerton, John (1826–93) British churchman. He is remembered for his *Liturgy for Missionary Meetings*.

1 The day Thou gavest, Lord, is ended,
The darkness falls at Thy behest.

A Liturgy for Missionary Meetings

Ellis, (Henry) Havelock (1859–1939) British sexologist. His seven-volume *Studies in the Psychology of Sex* was a landmark in the open discussion of sexual problems.

1 The whole religious complexion of the modern world is due to the absence from Jerusalem of a lunatic asylum.

Impressions and Comments

2 There is, however, a pathological conditions which occurs so often, in such extreme forms, and in men of such pre-eminent intellectual ability, that it is impossible not to regard it as having a real association with such ability. I refer to gout.

A Study of British Genius, Ch. 8

3 What we call progress is the exchange of one nuisance for another nuisance.

Attrib.

Eluard, Paul (Eugène Grindel; 1895–1952) French surrealist poet. After becoming a communist in 1942 he adopted a more realistic style and his poetry was circulated secretly among Resistance fighters in World War II.

1 *Adieu tristesse*
Bonjour tristesse
Tu es inscrite dans les lignes du plafond.
Farewell sadness
Good day sadness
You are written in the lines of the ceiling.

La Vie

Emerson, Ralph Waldo (1803–82) US poet and essayist. Ordained in 1829, his book *Nature* (1836) contained his transcendental philosophy. He expressed his optimistic humanism in *Representative Men* (1850) and the *Conduct of Life* (1860).

Quotations about Emerson

1 I could readily see in Emerson a gaping flaw. It was the insinuation that had he lived in those days when the world was made, he might have offered some valuable suggestions.

Herman Melville (1819–91) US novelist. Attrib.

2 Emerson is one who lives instinctively on ambrosia – and leaves everything indigestible on his plate.

Friedrich Nietzsche (1844–1900) German philosopher. Attrib.

Quotations by Emerson

3 A person seldom falls sick, but the bystanders are animated with a faint hope that he will die.

Conduct of Life, 'Considerations by the Way'

4 Art is a jealous mistress.

Conduct of Life, 'Wealth'

5 The louder he talked of his honour, the faster we counted our spoons.

Conduct of Life, 'Worship'

6 The religions we call false were once true.

Essays, 'Character'

7 Nothing great was ever achieved without enthusiasm.

Essays, 'Circles'

8 A Friend may well be reckoned the masterpiece of Nature.

Essays, 'Friendship'

9 There is properly no history; only biography.

Essays, 'History'

10 All mankind love a lover.

Essays, 'Love'

11 The reward of a thing well done is to have done it.

Essays, 'New England Reformers'

12 Every man is wanted, and no man is wanted much.

Essays, 'Nominalist and Realist'

13 In skating over thin ice, our safety is in our speed.

Essays, 'Prudence'

14 Whoso would be a man must be a nonconformist.

Essays, 'Self-Reliance'

15 A foolish consistency is the hobgoblin of little minds, adored by little statesmen and philosophers and divines. With consistency a great soul has simply nothing to do.

Essays, 'Self-reliance'

16 To be great is to be misunderstood.

Essays, 'Self-Reliance'

17 What is a weed? A plant whose virtues have not been discovered.

Fortune of the Republic

18 Talent alone cannot make a writer. There must be a man behind the book.

Goethe

19 I pay the schoolmaster, but 'tis the schoolboys that educate my son.

Journal

20 The book written against fame and learning has the author's name on the title-page.

Journal

21 Old age brings along with its uglinesses the comfort that you will soon be out of it, – which ought to be a substantial relief to such discontented pendulums as we are.

Journal

22 Every hero becomes a bore at last.

Representative Men, 'Uses of Great Men'

23 Hitch your wagon to a star.

Society and Solitude, 'Civilization'

24 We boil at different degrees.

Society and Solitude, 'Eloquence'

25 America is a country of young men.

Society and Solitude, 'Old Age'

26 If a man make a better mouse-trap than his neighbour, though he build his house in the woods, the world will make a beaten path to his door.

Attrib.

Engels, Friedrich (1820–95) German socialist. A supporter of Karl Marx, he collaborated with him in many of his writings.

1 The state is not 'abolished', it withers away.

Anti-Dühring

English, Thomas Dunn (1819–1902) US lawyer, physician, and writer. He wrote many novels, plays, and songs, including the well-known *Ben Bolt*.

1　Oh! don't you remember sweet Alice, Ben Bolt,
Sweet Alice, whose hair was so brown,
Who wept with delight when you gave her a
smile,
And trembled with fear at your frown?

Ben Bolt

Epictetus (c. 60–110 AD) Stoic philosopher. His teaching was recorded by his pupil Arrian in *Discourses* and in the *Enchiridon*.

1　If you hear that someone is speaking ill of you, instead of trying to defend yourself you should say: 'He obviously does not know me very well, since there are so many other faults he could have mentioned'.

Enchiridion

Epicurus (341–270 BC) Greek philosopher who established the school of epicureanism in Athens, teaching that the greatest good was pleasure attained by tranquility and detachment.

1　It is not so much our friends' help that helps us as the confident knowledge that they will help us.

2　So death, the most terrifying of ills, is nothing to us, since so long as we exist, death is not with us; but when death comes, then we do not exist. It does not then concern either the living or the dead, since for the former it is not, and the latter are no more.

Letter to Menoeceus

Erasmus, Desiderius (1466–1536) Dutch humanist, scholar, and writer, one of the leading Renaissance thinkers. His works include *The Praise of Folly* (1511) and a translation of the Greek New Testament.

1　I have a Catholic soul, but a Lutheran stomach.

Replying to criticism of his failure to fast during Lent
Dictionnaire Encyclopédique

Eschenbach, Marie Ebner von (1830–1916) Austrian writer.

1　Whenever two good people argue over principles, they are both right.

Aphorism

2　We don't believe in rheumatism and true love until after the first attack.

Aphorism

3　We are so vain that we even care for the opinion of those we don't care for.

Aphorism

4　'Good heavens!' said he, 'if it be our clothes alone which fit us for society, how highly we should esteem those who make them.'

The Two Countesses

Estienne, Henri (1528–98) French scholar and printer. He ran the family printing business in Geneva, where he compiled the *Thesaurus Linguae Graecae* (1572).

1　*Si jeunesse savait; si vieillesse pouvait.*
If only youth knew, if only age could.

Les Prémices

Euclid (c. 300 BC) Greek mathematician who compiled his book *Elements*, containing all the geometry then known, from a few basic axioms.

1　*Quod erat demonstrandum.*
Which was to be proved.

Hence, of course, Q.E.D.
Elements, I:5

2　There is no 'royal road' to geometry.

Said to Ptolemy I when asked if there were an easier way to solve theorems
Comment on Euclid (Proclus)

Euripides (c. 480–406 BC) Greek dramatist. Of his 90 plays, only 19 survive, including *Medea* (431), *Hippolytus* (428), and *Electra* (415).

1　Those whom God wishes to destroy, he first makes mad.

Fragment

Evans, Abel (1679–1737) English writer.

1　Under this stone, Reader, survey
Dead Sir John Vanbrugh's house of clay.
Lie heavy on him, Earth! for he
Laid many heavy loads on thee!

Epitaph on Sir John Vanbrugh, Architect of Blenheim Palace

Evans, Dame Edith (1888–1976) British actress. She is remembered for her many Shakespearean roles, as well as her classic performance as Lady Bracknell in *The Importance of Being Earnest*.

1　When a woman behaves like a man, why doesn't she behave like a nice man?

The Observer, 'Sayings of the Week', 30 Sept 1956

2　Death is my neighbour now.

Said a week before her death
BBC radio interview, 14 Oct 1976

Evans, Harold (1928–　) British journalist; a former editor of *The Sunday Times*.

1　The camera cannot lie. But it can be an accessory to untruth.

Pictures on a Page

Evarts, William M(axwell) (1818–1901) US lawyer and statesman; secretary of state (1877–81).

1　It was a brilliant affair; water flowed like champagne.

Describing a dinner given by US President Rutherford B. Hayes (1877–81), an advocate of temperance
Attrib.

Evelyn, John (1620–1706) English diarist. His *Diary*, first published in 1818, covers the years 1641–1706.

1 His *Majestie* began first to Touch for the Evil according to costome: Thus, his Majestie sitting under his State in the *Banqueting* house: The *Chirurgeons* cause the sick to be brought or led up to the throne, who kneeling, the King strokes their faces or cheeks with both his hands at once: at which instant a *Chaplaine* in his formalities, says, *He put his hands upon them, & he healed them.*
Diary, 6 July 1660

2 The Plague still increasing . . .
Diary, 28 July 1665

3 This fatal night about ten, began that deplorable fire near Fish Street in London . . . all the sky were of a fiery aspect, like the top of a burning Oven, and the light seen above 40 miles round about for many nights.
The Fire of London (2–5 Sept 1666) began in a bakehouse in Pudding Lane and spread to two thirds of the city
Diary, 2/3 Sept 1666

Ewer, William Norman (1885–1976) British writer and humorist.

1 How odd
Of God
To choose
The Jews.
For a reply, *see* ANONYMOUS
How Odd

F

Fadiman, Clifton (1904–) US writer and broadcaster.

1 We prefer to believe that the absence of inverted commas guarantees the originality of a thought, whereas it may be merely that the utterer has forgotten its source.
Any Number Can Play

2 Experience teaches you that the man who looks you straight in the eye, particularly if he adds a firm handshake, is hiding something.
Enter, Conversing

Faraday, Michael (1791–1867) British scientist. He discovered the laws of electrolysis and the connection between electricity and magnetism. He also showed how electromagnetic induction could be used in the generator and transformer.

1 Tyndall, I must remain plain Michael Faraday to the last; and let me now tell you, that if I accepted the honour which the Royal Society desires to confer upon me, I would not answer for the integrity of my intellect for a single year.
Said when Faraday was offered the Presidency of the Royal Society
Faraday as a Discoverer (J. Tyndall), 'Illustrations of Character'

Farjeon, Herbert (1887–1945) British writer and dramatist. With his sister, Eleanor Farjeon, he wrote the plays *Kings and Queens* (1932) and *An Elephant in Arcady* (1938).

1 I've danced with a man, who's danced with a girl, who's danced with the Prince of Wales.
Picnic

Farmer, Edward (1809–76) British writer.

1 I have no pain, dear mother, now;
But oh! I am so dry:
Just moisten poor Jim's lips once more;
And, mother, do not cry!
A typical sentimental verse of the time. For a typical parody, *see* ANONYMOUS
The Collier's Dying Child

Farouk I (1920–65) The last king of Egypt. After the first Arab–Israeli War (1948–49) he was ousted and went into exile in Monaco (1952).

1 There will soon be only five kings left – the Kings of England, Diamonds, Hearts, Spades and Clubs.
Remark made to Lord Boyd-Orr

Farquhar, George (1678–1707) Irish dramatist. He achieved fame in London with his first play, *Love and a Bottle* (1699). *The Recruiting Officer* (1706) and *The Beaux' Stratagem* (1707) were subsequent successes.

1 There's no scandal like rags, nor any crime so shameful as poverty.
The Beaux' Stratagem, I:1

2 Lady Bountiful.
The Beaux' Stratagem, I:1

3 Spare all I have, and take my life.
The Beaux' Stratagem, V:2

Faulkner, William (1897–1962) US novelist. His first verse collection *The Marble Faun* (1924) was followed by the novels *Sartoris* (1929), *The Sound and the Fury* (1929), *Absalom, Absalom!* (1936), and *The Reivers* (1966).

1 The Swiss who are not a people so much as a neat clean quite solvent business.
Intruder in the Dust, Ch. 7

2 The writer's only responsibility is to his art . . . If a writer has to rob his mother, he will not hesitate; the 'Ode on a Grecian Urn' is worth any number of old ladies.
Attrib.

Fawkes, Guy (1570–1606) English conspirator. He was executed for his role in the Gunpowder Plot against James I, an event commemorated annually on 5 November with the burning of his effigy.

1 A desperate disease requires a dangerous remedy.

In justification of the Gunpowder Plot; said when questioned by the King and council immediately after his arrest, 5 Nov 1605
Dictionary of National Biography

2 ... to blow the Scots back again into Scotland.

One of his professed objectives for the Gunpowder Plot, referring to the Scottish-born King James I; said when questioned by the King and council immediately after his arrest, 5 Nov 1605
Dictionary of National Biography

Feather, Vic, Baron (1908–76) British trade-union leader. He was general secretary of the TUC (1969–73).

1 Industrial relations are like sexual relations. It's better between two consenting parties.
Guardian Weekly, 8 Aug 1976

Feiffer, Jules (1929–   ) US writer, cartoonist, and humorist.

1 At sixteen I was stupid, confused, insecure and indecisive. At twenty-five I was wise, self-confident, prepossessing and assertive. At forty five I am stupid, confused, insecure and indecisive. Who would have supposed that maturity is only a short break in adolescence?
The Observer, 3 Feb 1974

Feldman, Marty (1933–83) British comedian. He was originally a scriptwriter, but became a TV comedian and made a number of films, including *High Anxiety* (1978) and *Sex with a Smile* (1979).

1 Comedy, like sodomy, is an unnatural act.
The Times, 9 June 1969

Fénelon, François de Salignac de La Mothe (1651–1715) French writer and prelate. Archbishop of Cambrai, he wrote *Maximes des Saints*, which was condemned by the Pope.

1 Nothing is more despicable than a professional talker who uses his words as a quack uses his remedies.
Letter to M. Dacier

2 A good historian is timeless; although he is a patriot, he will never flatter his country in any respect.
Letter to M. Dacier

Ferber, Edna (1887–1968) US writer. She wrote such novels as *Gigolo* (1922), *Show Boat* (1926), and *Come and Get It* (1935), many of which were filmed.

1 Being an old maid is like death by drowning, a really delightful sensation after you cease to struggle.
Wit's End (R. E. Drennan), 'Completing the Circle'

Ferdinand I (1503–64) Holy Roman Emperor (1558–64). In 1526 he became King of Bohemia and of Hungary.

1 Let justice be done, though the world perish.
Attrib.

Ferdinand I (1793–1875) Emperor of Austria (1835–48). Of unsound mind, he abdicated during the 1848 revolution.

1 I am the emperor, and I want dumplings.
The Fall of the House of Habsburg (E. Crankshaw)

Fermi, Enrico (1901–54) Italian-born US physicist. He worked on particle physics and nuclear fission, and constructed the first atomic pile at the University of Chicago in 1942. He received the 1938 Nobel prize for physics.

1 Whatever Nature has in store for mankind, unpleasant as it may be, men must accept, for ignorance is never better than knowledge.
Atoms in the Family (Laura Fermi)

Fern, Fanny (1811–72) US writer.

1 The way to a man's heart is through his stomach.
Willis Parton

Ferrier, Kathleen (1912–53) British contralto, who died of cancer at the peak of her career.

1 Now I'll have *eine kleine Pause*.
Said shortly before her death
Am I Too Loud? (Gerald Moore)

Field, Eugene (1850–95) US poet and journalist. His work consisted mainly of verses for children and humorous articles. Books include *Trumpet and Drum* (1892) and *Echoes from the Sabine Farm* (1892).

1 He played the King as though under momentary apprehension that someone else was about to play the ace.
Referring to Creston Clarke's performance in the role of King Lear
Attrib.

Fielding, Henry (1707–54) British novelist and dramatist. He wrote some 25 plays and the novels *Joseph Andrews* (1742), *Jonathan Wild* (1743), and *Tom Jones* (1749).

1 It hath been often said, that it is not death, but dying, which is terrible.
Amelia, Bk. III, Ch. 4

2 These are called the pious frauds of friendship.
Amelia, Bk. III, Ch. 4

3 When widows exclaim loudly against second marriages, I would always lay a wager, that the man, if not the wedding-day, is absolutely fixed on.
Amelia, Bk. VI, Ch. 8

4 One fool at least in every married couple.
Amelia, Bk. IX, Ch. 4

5 I am as sober as a Judge.
Don Quixote in England, III:14

6 Oh! The roast beef of England. And old England's roast beef.
The Grub Street Opera, III:3

7 Never trust the man who hath reason to suspect that you know he hath injured you.
Jonathan Wild, Bk III, Ch. 4

8 He in a few minutes ravished this fair creature, or at least would have ravished her, if she had not, by a timely compliance, prevented him.
Jonathan Wild, Bk. III, Ch. 7

9 For clergy are men as well as other folks.
Joseph Andrews, Bk. II, Ch. 6

10 Public schools are the nurseries of all vice and immorality.
Joseph Andrews, Bk. III, Ch. 5

11 What is commonly called love, namely the desire of satisfying a voracious appetite with a certain quantity of delicate white human flesh.
Tom Jones, Bk. VI, Ch. 1

12 His designs were strictly honourable, as the phrase is; that is, to rob a lady of her fortune by way of marriage.
Tom Jones, Bk. XI, Ch. 4

13 Composed that monstrous animal a husband and wife.
Tom Jones, Bk. XV, Ch. 9

14 All Nature wears one universal grin.
Tom Thumb the Great, I:1

Fields, W(illiam) C(laude) (1880–1946) US actor. After starting in vaudeville, he began making film comedies in the 1920s.

1 It ain't a fit night out for man or beast.
The Fatal Glass of Beer

2 Fish fuck in it.
His reason for not drinking water
Attrib.

3 Anybody who hates children and dogs can't be all bad.
Attrib.

4 I am free of all prejudice. I hate everyone equally.
Attrib.

5 I have spent a lot of time searching through the Bible for loopholes.
Said during his last illness
Attrib.

Firbank, Ronald (1886–1926) British novelist. Best-known novels were *Caprice* (1917), *Valmouth* (1919), and *The Flower Beneath the Foot* (1922).

1 It is said, I believe, that to behold the Englishman at his *best* one should watch him play tip-and-run.
The Flower Beneath the Foot, Ch. 14

2 The world is disgracefully managed, one hardly knows to whom to complain.
Vainglory

3 To be sympathetic without discrimination is so very debilitating.
Vainglory

Firmont, Abbé Edgeworth de (1745–1807) Irish-born confessor to Louis XVI. He later became chaplain to the future Louis XVIII.

1 Son of Saint Louis, ascend to heaven.
Said to Louis XVI as he climbed up to the guillotine
Attrib.

Fitzgerald, Edward (1809–83) British poet and translator. His translation of *The Rubáiyát of Omar Khayyám* was a free adaption of the 12th-century Persian original.

1 Taste is the feminine of genius.
Letter to J. R. Lowell, Oct 1877

2 Awake! for Morning in the Bowl of Night
Has flung the Stone that puts the Stars to Flight:
And Lo! the Hunter of the East has caught
The Sultan's Turret in a Noose of Light.
The Rubáiyát of Omar Khayyám (1st edn.), I

3 Come, fill the Cup, and in the Fire of Spring
The Winter Garment of Repentance fling:
The Bird of Time has but a little way
To fly – and Lo! the Bird is on the Wing.
The Rubáiyát of Omar Khayyám (1st edn.), VII

4 The Wine of Life keeps oozing drop by drop,
The Leaves of Life keep falling one by one.
The Rubáiyát of Omar Khayyám (4th edn.), VIII

5 Here with a Loaf of Bread beneath the Bough,
A Flask of Wine, a Book of Verse – and Thou
Beside me singing in the Wilderness –
And Wilderness is Paradise enow.
The Rubáiyát of Omar Khayyám (1st edn.), XI

6 Ah, take the Cash in hand and waive the Rest;
Oh, the brave Music of a *distant* Drum!
The Rubáiyát of Omar Khayyám (1st edn.), XII

7 The Worldly Hope men set their Hearts upon
Turns Ashes – or it prospers; and anon,
Like Snow upon the Desert's dusty face,
Lighting a little Hour or two – is gone.
The Rubáiyát of Omar Khayyám (1st edn.), XIV

8 I sometimes think that never blows so red
The Rose as where some buried Caesar bled;
That every Hyacinth the Garden wears
Dropt in her Lap from some once lovely Head.
The Rubáiyát of Omar Khayyám (1st edn.), XVIII

9 Ah, my Belovéd, fill the Cup that clears
TO-DAY of past Regrets and Future Fears:
To-morrow! – Why, To-morrow I may be
Myself with Yesterday's Sev'n thousand Years.
The Rubáiyát of Omar Khayyám (1st edn.), XX

10 One thing is certain, that Life flies;
One thing is certain, and the Rest is Lies;
The Flower that once has blown for ever dies.
The Rubáiyát of Omar Khayyám (1st edn.), XXVI

11 I came like Water, and like Wind I go.
The Rubáiyát of Omar Khayyám (1st edn.), XXVIII

12 Ah, fill the Cup: – what boots it to repeat
How Time is slipping underneath our Feet:
Unborn TOMORROW, and dead YESTERDAY,
Why fret about them if TODAY be sweet!
The Rubáiyát of Omar Khayyám (1st edn.), XXXVII

13 'Tis all a Chequer-board of Nights and Days
Where Destiny with Men for Pieces plays:
Hither and thither moves, and mates, and slays,
And one by one back in the Closet lays.
The Rubáiyát of Omar Khayyám (1st edn.), XLIX

14 The Moving Finger writes; and, having writ,
Moves on: nor all thy Piety nor Wit
Shall lure it back to cancel half a Line,
Nor all thy Tears wash out a Word of it.
The Rubáiyát of Omar Khayyám (1st edn.), LI

15 And that inverted Bowl we call The Sky,
Whereunder crawling coop't we live and die,
Lift not thy hands to *It* for help – for It
Rolls impotently on as Thou or I.
The Rubáiyát of Omar Khayyám (1st edn.), LII

16 'Who *is* the Potter, pray, and who the Pot?'
The Rubáiyát of Omar Khayyám (1st edn.), LX

17 Strange, is it not? that of the myriads who
Before us pass'd the door of Darkness through,
Not one returns to tell us of the Road,
Which to discover we must travel too.
The Rubáiyát of Omar Khayyám (4th edn.), LXIV

18 Drink! for you know not whence you came, nor why:
Drink! for you know not why you go, nor where.
The Rubáiyát of Omar Khayyám (4th edn.), LXXIV

Fitzgerald, F(rancis) Scott (Key) (1896–1940) US novelist. His first successful novel was the autobiographical *This Side of Paradise* (1920). This was followed by *The Great Gatsby* (1925) and *Tender is the Night* (1934) before he declined into alcoholism.

Quotations about Fitzgerald

1 Fitzgerald was an alcoholic, a spendthrift and a superstar playboy possessed of a beauty and a glamour that only a Byron could support without artistic ruination.
Anthony Burgess (1917–) British novelist and critic. *The Observer*, 7 Feb 1982

2 The poor son-of-a-bitch!
Dorothy Parker (1893–1967) US writer. Quoting from *The Great Gatsby* on paying her last respects to Fitzgerald. *Thalberg: Life and Legend* (B. Thomas)

Quotations by Fitzgerald

3 In the real dark night of the soul it is always three o'clock in the morning.
See ST JOHN OF THE CROSS
The Crack-Up

4 Though the Jazz Age continued, it became less and less an affair of youth. The sequel was like a children's party taken over by the elders.
The Crack-Up

5 FITZGERALD. The rich are different from us.
HEMINGWAY. Yes, they have more money.
The Crack-Up, 'Notebooks, E'

6 I entertained on a cruising trip that was so much fun that I had to sink my yacht to make my guests go home.
The Crack-Up, 'Notebooks, K'

7 One of those men who reach such an acute limited excellence at twenty-one that everything afterward savours of anti-climax.
The Great Gatsby, Ch. 1

8 I was one of the few guests who had actually been invited. People were not invited – they went there.
The Great Gatsby, Ch. 3

9 One girl can be pretty – but a dozen are only a chorus.
The Last Tycoon

10 He differed from the healthy type that was essentially middle-class – he never seemed to perspire.
This Side of Paradise, Bk. I, Ch. 2

11 Beware of the artist who's an intellectual also. The artist who doesn't fit.
This Side of Paradise, Bk. II, Ch. 5

12 'I know myself,' he cried, 'but that is all.'
This Side of Paradise, Bk. II, Ch. 5

13 A big man has no time really to do anything but just sit and be big.
This Side of Paradise, Bk. III, Ch. 2

14 First you take a drink, then the drink takes a drink, then the drink takes you.
Ackroyd (Jules Feiffer), '1964, May 7'

15 Sometimes I don't know whether Zelda and I are real or whether we are characters in one of my novels.
Said of himself and his wife
A Second Flowering (Malcolm Cowley)

16 All good writing is *swimming under water* and holding your breath.
Letter to Frances Scott Fitzgerald

Fitzgerald, Zelda (1900–48) US writer. The wife of F. Scott Fitzgerald, she suffered increasingly from schizophrenia and was confined to an asylum from 1930.

1 I don't want to live – I want to love first, and live incidentally.
Letter to F. Scott Fitzgerald, 1919

2 Don't you think I was made for you? I feel like you had me ordered – and I was delivered to you – to be worn – I want you to wear me, like a watch-charm or a button hole boquet – to the world.
Zelda actually wrote 'boquet', not 'bouquet'
Letter to F. Scott Fitzgerald, 1919

3 A vacuum can only exist, I imagine, by the things which enclose it.

Journal, 1932

Fitzsimmons, Bob (Robert Prometheus Fitzsimmons; 1862–1917) British-born New Zealand boxer, who was world heavyweight champion (1897–99).

1 The bigger they come the harder they fall.

Remark before a fight, San Francisco, 9 June 1899

Flanagan, Bud (Robert Winthrop; 1896–1968) British comedian who formed part of a double-act with Chesney Allen, within the six-strong Crazy Gang. His songs include *Hometown, Underneath the Arches,* and *Umbrella Man.*

1 Underneath the arches
We dream our dreams away.

Underneath the Arches

Flanders, Michael (1922–75) British comedian and songwriter. Confined to a wheelchair by polio, he performed in a double-act with Donald Swann. *At the Drop of a Hat* (1956) was the forerunner of many other similar revues. He also wrote a number of songs.

1 Eating people is wrong.

The Reluctant Cannibal

Flaubert, Gustave (1821–80) French novelist. He made his name with *Madame Bovary* (1856), which was followed by *Salammbô* (1862), and *La Tentation de Saint Antoine* (1874).

1 All one's inventions are true, you can be sure of that. Poetry is as exact a science as geometry.

Letter to Louise Colet, 14 Aug 1853

2 Books are made not like children but like pyramids . . . and they're just as useless! and they stay in the desert! . . . Jackals piss at their foot and the bourgeois climb up on them.

Letter to Ernest Feydeau, 1857

Flecker, James Elroy (1884–1915) British poet, best known for his poem *The Golden Journey to Samarkand* (1913) and the verse drama *Hassan,* produced posthumously in 1922 with music by Delius.

1 For lust of knowing what should not be known,
We take the Golden Road to Samarkand.

Hassan, V:2

Fleming, Sir Alexander (1881–1955) British microbiologist. He shared a Nobel prize in 1945 for his discovery of the antibiotic penicillin.

Quotations about Fleming

1 'Pain in the mind' was not the spur that drove him to do research . . . but rather an urge to do a job better than the next man. Competition was the breath of life to him.

Leonard Colebrook (1883–1967) British medical researcher. *Biographical Memoirs of Fellows of the Royal Society*

2 The catalogue of Fleming's published work leaves little room for doubt that he had to an unusual degree the almost intuitive faculty for original observation coupled with a high degree of technical inventiveness and skill. He had in fact most of the qualities that make a great scientist: an innate curiosity and perceptiveness regarding natural phenomena, insight into the heart of a problem, technical ingenuity, persistence in seeing a job through and that physical and mental toughness that is essential to the top-class investigator.

R. Cruickshank. *Journal of Pathology and Bacteriology,* 1956

Quotations by Fleming

3 I have been trying to point out that in our lives chance may have an astonishing influence and, if I may offer advice to the young laboratory worker, it would be this – never to neglect an extraordinary appearance or happening. It may be – usually is, in fact – a false alarm that leads to nothing, but it may on the other hand be the clue provided by fate to lead you to some important advance.

Lecture at Harvard

4 A good gulp of hot whisky at bedtime – it's not very scientific, but it helps.

When asked about a cure for colds
News summary, 22 Mar 1954

Fleming, Ian Lancaster (1908–64) British journalist and writer. His tough romantic hero James Bond, secret agent 007, appeared in 12 novels and 7 short stories, most of them filmed, beginning with *Casino Royale* (1953).

1 Older women are best because they always think they may be doing it for the last time.

Life of Ian Fleming (John Pearson)

Fletcher, John (1579–1625) English dramatist, who collaborated with Francis Beaumont, Philip Massinger, and others on many plays.

1 Best while you have it use your breath,
There is no drinking after death.

With Jonson and others
The Bloody Brother, II:2

2 And he that will go to bed sober,
Falls with the leaf still in October.

The Bloody Brother, II:2

3 Death hath so many doors to let out life.

With Massinger
The Custom of the Country, II:2

Florian, Jean-Pierre Claris de (1755–94) French writer of fables.

1 *Plaisir d'amour ne dure qu'un moment,
Chagrin d'amour dure toute la vie.*
Love's pleasure lasts but a moment; love's sorrow lasts all through life.

Celestine

Florio, John (c. 1553–1625) English lexicographer and translator, who published an Italian–English dictionary (1598) and an English translation of Montaigne's *Essays* (1603).

1 England is the paradise of women, the purgatory of men, and the hell of horses.
Second Fruits

Foch, Ferdinand, Marshal (1851–1929) French soldier. He played a dominant part in World War I, being appointed supreme commander of all allied forces in 1918.

1 My centre is giving way, my right is in retreat; situation excellent. I shall attack.
Message sent during the second battle of the Marne, 1918
Biography of Foch (Aston), Ch. 13

2 What a marvellous place to drop one's mother-in-law!
Remark on being shown the Grand Canyon
Attrib.

3 None but a coward dares to boast that he has never known fear.
Attrib

Fontenelle, Bernard de (1657–1757) French philosopher, whose writings helped to popularize the theories of Descartes and Newton.

1 It is high time for me to depart, for at my age I now begin to see things as they really are.
Remark on his deathbed, at the age of 99
Anekdotenschatz (H. Hoffmeister)

2 I feel nothing, apart from a certain difficulty in continuing to exist.
Remark made on his deathbed, at the age of 99
Famous Last Words (B. Conrad)

Foot, Michael (Mackintosh) (1913–) British Labour politician and journalist. Leader of the Labour Party (1980–83). He has been editor of *Tribune* and political columnist in the *Daily Herald*. His many books include *Trial of Mussolini* (1943), *Parliament in Danger* (1959), and a two-volume biography of Aneurin Bevan (1962–73).

1 A Royal Commission is a broody hen sitting on a china egg.
Speech, House of Commons, 1964

Foote, Samuel (1720–77) British actor and dramatist. He built the Haymarket Theatre, where he presented some of his own plays, including *The Englishman in Paris* (1753) and *The Nabob* (1772).

1 So she went into the garden to cut a cabbage-leaf; to make an apple-pie; and at the same time a great she-bear, coming up the street, pops its head into the shop. 'What! no soap?' So he died, and she very imprudently married the barber; and there were present the Picninnies, and the Joblillies, and the Garyalies, and the grand Panjandrum himself, with the little round button at top, and they all fell to playing the game of catch as catch can, till the gun powder ran out at the heels of their boots.
Nonsense composed to test the actor Charles Macklin's claim that he could memorize anything

2 He is not only dull in himself, but the cause of dullness in others.
Parody of a line from Shakespeare's *Henry IV, Part 2*
Life of Johnson (J. Boswell)

Forbes, C. F. (1817–1911) British writer.

1 The sense of being well-dressed gives a feeling of inward tranquillity which religion is powerless to bestow.
Social Aims (Emerson)

Ford, Gerald R(udolph) (1913–) US statesman. Following Nixon's resignation, he became the first President of the USA not to have been elected to the office (1974–77).

Quotations about Ford

1 He looks like the guy in the science fiction movie who is the first to see 'The Creature'.
David Frye Attrib.

2 Jerry Ford is so dumb that he can't fart and chew gum at the same time.
Lyndon B. Johnson (1908–73) US statesman. Sometimes quoted as '. . . can't walk and chew gum'. *A Ford, Not a Lincoln* (R. Reeves), Ch. 1

Quotations by Ford

3 I guess it proves that in America anyone can be President.
Referring to his own appointment as president
A Ford Not a Lincoln (Richard Reeves), Ch. 4

Ford, Henry (1863–1947) US car manufacturer, who founded the Ford Motor Company in 1903 and introduced assembly-line production.

1 History is more or less bunk. It's tradition. We don't want tradition. We want to live in the present and the only history that is worth a tinker's damn is the history we make today.
Chicago Tribune, 25 May 1916

2 A business that makes nothing but money is a poor kind of business.
Interview

3 Exercise is bunk. If you are healthy, you don't need it: if you are sick, you shouldn't take it.
Attrib.

4 Any colour, so long as it's black.
Referring to the colour options offered for the Model-T Ford car
Attrib.

Ford, John (c. 1586–c. 1640) English dramatist. The tragedies *The Broken Heart* (1630) and *'Tis Pity She's a Whore* (1632) are still performed.

1 Tempt not the stars, young man, thou canst not play
With the severity of fate.
The Broken Heart, I:3

2 He hath shook hands with time.
The Broken Heart, V:2

3 'Tis Pity She's a Whore.
Play title

Ford, John (Sean O'Feeney; 1895–1973) US film director. Best known for westerns, including *Stagecoach* (1939) and *How The West Was Won* (1962), his other films include *The Grapes of Wrath* (1940).

1 It is easier to get an actor to be a cowboy than to get a cowboy to be an actor.

Attrib.

Forgy, Howell Maurice (1908–83) US naval captain.

1 Praise the Lord and pass the ammunition!

Remark made during the Japanese attack on Pearl Harbor, 7 Dec 1941
Attrib. in *The Los Angeles Times*

Formby, George (1905–61) British comedian. He was popular in music halls and in such films as *Keep Your Seats Please* (1936) and *Let George Do It* (1940), invariably featuring his comic songs accompanied by his ukelele.

1 I'm leaning on a lamp-post at the corner of the street,
In case a certain little lady walks by.

Leaning on a Lamp-post

2 With my little stick of Blackpool rock,
Along the Promenade I stroll.
It may be sticky but I never complain,
It's nice to have a nibble at it now and again

With My Little Stick of Blackpool Rock

Forrest, Nathan Bedford (1821–77) Confederate general in the US Civil War.

1 I got there fustest with the mostest.

Popular misquotation of his explanation of his success in capturing Murfreesboro; his actual words were, 'I just took the short cut and got there first with the most men'
A Civil War Treasury (B. Botkin)

2 Ah, colonel, all's fair in love and war, you know.

Remark to a captured enemy officer who had been tricked into surrendering
A Civil War Treasury (B. Botkin)

Forster, E(dward) M(organ) (1879–1970) British novelist. His books include *Where Angels Fear to Tread* (1905), *A Room with a View* (1908), *Howard's End* (1910), and *A Passage to India* (1924).

1 The historian must have . . . some conception of how men who are not historians behave. Otherwise he will move in a world of the dead.

Abinger Harvest, 'Captain Edward Gibbon'

2 It is not that the Englishman can't feel – it is that he is afraid to feel. He has been taught at his public school that feeling is bad form. He must not express great joy or sorrow, or even open his mouth too wide when he talks – his pipe might fall out if he did.

Abinger Harvest, 'Notes on the English Character'

3 They go forth into it with well-developed bodies, fairly developed minds, and undeveloped hearts.

Referring to public schoolboys going into the world
Abinger Harvest, 'Notes on the English Character'

4 Works of art, in my opinion, are the only objects in the material universe to possess internal order, and that is why, though I don't believe that only art matters, I do believe in Art for Art's sake.

Art for Art's Sake

5 Yes – oh dear, yes – the novel tells a story.

Aspects of the Novel, Ch. 2

6 Creative writers are always greater than the causes that they represent.

Gide and George

7 Beethoven's Fifth Symphony is the most sublime noise that has ever penetrated into the ear of man.

Howards End, Ch. 5

8 Death destroys a man, the idea of Death saves him.

Howards End, Ch. 27

9 Only connect!

Howards End, Epigraph

10 The so-called white races are really pinko-gray.

A Passage to India, Ch. 7

11 I hate the idea of causes, and if I had to choose between betraying my country and betraying my friend, I hope I should have the guts to betray my country.

Two Cheers for Democracy, 'What I Believe'

12 Spoon feeding in the long run teaches us nothing but the shape of the spoon.

The Observer, 'Sayings of the Week', 7 Oct 1951

Fosdick, Harry Emerson (1878–1969) US baptist minister. His books include *The Second Mile* (1908) and *On Being a Real Person* (1943).

1 An atheist is a man who has no invisible means of support.

Attrib.

Foster, S(tephen) C(ollins) (1826–64) US composer of popular songs, including *My Old Kentucky Home, The Old Folks at Home*, and *O, Susanna*. A big earner, but a bigger spender, he died in poverty.

1 Gwine to run all night!
Gwine to run all day!
I bet my money on the bob-tail nag.
Somebody bet on the bay.

Camptown Races

2 Weep no more, my lady,
Oh! weep no more today!
We will sing one song for the old Kentucky Home,
For the old Kentucky Home far away.

My Old Kentucky Home

3 'Way down upon de Swanee Ribber,
Far, far away,
Dere's where my heart is turning ebber:
Dere's where de old folks stay.
All up and down de whole creation
Sadly I roam,
Still longing for de old plantation,
And for de old folks at home.

The Old Folks at Home

4 O, Susanna! O, don't you cry for me,
I've come from Alabama, wid my banjo on my
knee.

O, Susanna

5 I'm coming, I'm coming,
For my head is bending low
I hear their gentle voices calling, 'Poor old Joe'

Poor Old Joe

6 Dere's no more work for poor old Ned,
He's gone whar de good niggers go.

Uncle Ned

Fourier, (François Marie) Charles (1772–1837)
French social scientist. His *Théorie des Quatre Mouvements* (1808)
advocated a reorganization of society known as Fourierism.

1 The extension of women's rights is the basic
principle of all social progress.

Théorie des Quatre Mouvements

Fowles, John (1926–) British novelist. He made his name
with such books as *The Collector* (1963), *The Magus* (1966), and
The French Lieutenant's Woman (1969), all of which have been
filmed. Later books include *Mantissa* (1982) and *A Maggot* (1985).

1 The most odious of concealed narcissisms –
prayer.

The Aristos

2 In essence the Renaissance was simply the
green end of one of civilization's hardest winters.

The French Lieutenant's Woman, Ch. 10

3 We all write poems; it is simply that poets are
the ones who write in words.

The French Lieutenant's Woman, Ch. 19

4 There are many reasons why novelists write,
but they all have one thing in common – a need
to create an alternative world.

The Sunday Times Magazine, 2 Oct 1977

Fox, Charles James (1749–1806) British Whig politician.
He became foreign secretary twice (1782; 1806); a supporter of
the French Revolution, he was dismissed from the privy council
for opposing war with France after the Revolution.

1 He was uniformly of an opinion which, though
not a popular one, he was ready to aver, that the
right of governing was not property but a trust.

Referring to William Pitt's plans for parliamentary reform
C.J. Fox (J. L. Hammond)

2 No man could be so wise as Thurlow looked.

Lives of the Lord Chancellors (Campbell), Vol. V

3 How much the greatest event it is that ever happened in the world! and how much the best!

Referring to the fall of the Bastille, 14 July 1789
Letter to Fitzpatrick, 30 July 1789

4 Kings govern by means of popular assemblies
only when they cannot do without them.

Attrib.

5 I die happy.

His last words
Life and Times of C. J. Fox (Russell), Vol. III

Fox, George (1624–91) English religious leader, who founded
the Quakers. He was frequently imprisoned for his beliefs; his
best-known work is his *Journal* (1674).

1 When the Lord sent me forth into the world, He
forbade me to put off my hat to any high or
low.

Journal

Fox, Henry Stephen (1791–1846) British diplomat.

1 I am so changed that my oldest creditors would
hardly know me.

Remark after an illness
Letter from Byron to John Murray, 8 May 1817

France, Anatole (Jacques Anatole François Thibault; 1844–
1924) French poet, novelist, and critic. His verse collection
Poèmes Dorés (1873) was followed by a number of novels,
including *La Révolte des Anges* (1914). His *Histoire Contemporaine*
comprises a series of books ending with *La Vie en Fleur* (1922).

1 It is only the poor who are forbidden to beg.

Crainquebille

2 To disarm the strong and arm the weak would
be to change the social order which it's my job
to preserve. Justice is the means by which established injustices are sanctioned.

Crainquebille

3 Man is so made that he can only find relaxation
from one kind of labour by taking up another.

The Crime of Sylvestre Bonnard

4 The Arab who builds himself a hut out of the
marble fragments of a temple in Palmyra is more
philosophical than all the curators of the museums in London, Munich or Paris.

The Crime of Sylvestre Bonnard

5 The wonder is, not that the field of the stars is
so vast, but that man has measured it.

The Garden of Epicurus

6 Christianity has done a great deal for love by
making a sin of it.

The Garden of Epicurus

7 A good critic is one who narrates the adventures
of his mind among masterpieces.

The Literary Life, Preface

8 It was in the barbarous, gothic times when
words had a meaning; in those days, writers expressed thoughts.

The Literary Life, 'M. Charles Morice'

9 The majestic egalitarianism of the law, which forbids rich and poor alike to sleep under bridges, to beg in the streets, and to steal bread.
The Red Lily, Ch. 7

10 It is only the poor who pay cash, and that not from virtue, but because they are refused credit.
A Cynic's Breviary (J. R. Solly)

Francis I (1494–1547) King of France (1515–47). His reign was dominated by conflict with Charles V, Holy Roman Emperor. At Pavia (1525) he was defeated by Charles and taken prisoner. He was released after agreeing to give up Burgundy and his claims to other lands – promises that he did not keep.

1 Of all I had, only honour and life have been spared.
Referring to his defeat at the Battle of Pavia, 24 Feb 1525; usually misquoted as 'All is lost save honour.'
Letter to Louise of Savoy (his mother), 1525

Frank, Anne (1929–45) German-Jewish girl, who fled with her family from Germany in 1933. While in hiding in a room in Amsterdam she wrote a diary covering the year 1942–43. The family were betrayed and she died in Belsen concentration camp.

1 It was a terrible time through which I was living. The war raged about us, and nobody knew whether or not he would be alive the next hour.
Tales from the Secret Annexe, 'Fear', 25 Mar 1944

2 I felt nothing, nothing but fear; I could neither eat nor sleep – fear clawed at my mind and body and shook me.
Tales from the Secret Annexe, 'Fear', 25 Mar 1944

3 I must indeed, try hard to control the talking habit, but I'm afraid that little can be done, as my case is hereditary. My mother, too, is fond of chatting, and has handed this weakness down to me.
Tales from the Secret Annexe, 'A Geometry Lesson', 12 Aug 1943

Franklin, Benjamin (1706–90) US scientist and statesman. His experiments with a kite established the electrical nature of thunderstorms and enabled him to invent lightning conductors. As a diplomat in Paris he negotiated peace with Britain in 1783.

Quotations about Franklin

1 I succeed him; no one can replace him.
Thomas Jefferson (1743–1826) US statesman. Replying to the questions 'Is it you, sir, who replaces Dr Franklin?' Letter, 1791

2 A philosophical Quaker full of mean and thrift maxims.
John Keats (1795–1821) British poet. Letter, 14 Oct 1818

Quotations by Franklin

3 Remember that time is money.
Advice to a Young Tradesman

4 No nation was ever ruined by trade.
Essays, 'Thoughts on Commercial Subjects'

5 A little neglect may breed mischief, . . . for want of a nail, the shoe was lost; for want of a shoe the horse was lost; and for want of a horse the rider was lost.
Poor Richard's Almanack

6 Some are weather-wise, some are otherwise.
Poor Richard's Almanack

7 Three may keep a secret, if two of them are dead.
Poor Richard's Almanack

8 At twenty years of age, the will reigns; at thirty, the wit; and at forty, the judgement.
Poor Richard's Almanack

9 Dost thou love life? Then do not squander time, for that's the stuff life is made of.
Poor Richard's Almanack

10 Many a long dispute among divines may be thus abridged: It is so. It is not so. It is so. It is not so.
Poor Richard's Almanack

11 What is the use of a new-born child?
Response when asked the same question of a new invention
Life and Times of Benjamin Franklin (J. Parton), Pt. IV

12 Man is a tool-making animal.
Life of Johnson (J. Boswell), 7 Apr 1778

13 A lonesome man on a rainy day who does not know how to read.
On being asked what condition of man he considered the most pitiable
Wit, Wisdom, and Foibles of the Great (C. Shriner)

14 Here Skugg
Lies snug
As a bug
In a rug.
An epitaph for a squirrel, 'skug' being a dialect name for the animal
Letter to Georgiana Shipley, 26 Sept 1772

15 We must indeed all hang together, or most assuredly, we shall all hang separately.
Remark on signing the Declaration of Independence, 4 July 1776

16 There never was a good war or a bad peace.
Letter to Josiah Quincy, 11 Sept 1783

17 In this world nothing is certain but death and taxes.
Letter to Jean-Baptiste Leroy, 13 Nov 1789

18 The body of
Benjamin Franklin, printer,
(Like the cover of an old book,
Its contents worn out,
And stript of its lettering and gilding)
Lies here, food for worms!
Yet the work itself shall not be lost,
For it will, as he believed, appear once more
In a new
And more beautiful edition,
Corrected and amended
By its Author!
Suggestion for his own epitaph

Franks, Oliver, Baron (1905–) British philosopher and administrator. British ambassador to the USA (1948–52), he was Provost of Worcester College, Oxford (1962–76), and has held many other academic offices.

1 It is a secret in the Oxford sense: you may tell it to only one person at a time.
Sunday Telegraph, 30 Jan 1977

Frayn, Michael (1933–) British journalist, novelist, and dramatist. His plays include *The Sandboy* (1971), *Noises Off* (1982), and *Look, Look* (1990). *The Tin Men* (1965) is his best-known novel.

1 No woman so naked as one you can see to be naked underneath her clothes.
Constructions

2 For hundreds of pages the closely-reasoned arguments unroll, axioms and theorems interlock. And what remains with us in the end? A general sense that the world can be expressed in closely-reasoned arguments, in interlocking axioms and theorems.
Constructions

3 To be absolutely honest, what I feel really bad about is that I don't feel worse. There's the ineffectual liberal's problem in a nutshell.
The Observer, 8 Aug 1965

Frederick the Great (1712–86) King of Prussia. A writer and composer himself, he gathered a distinguished circle of writers and musicians at his palace of Sans Souci near Potsdam.

1 Rascals, would you live for ever?
Addressed to reluctant soldiers at the Battle of Kolin, 18 June 1757. *See also* DALY

2 My people and I have come to an agreement which satisfies us both. They are to say what they please, and I am to do what I please.
Attrib.

3 A crown is merely a hat that lets the rain in.
Attrib.

Freed, Arthur (1894–1973) US film producer and songwriter. He made several musicals featuring his own lyrics.

1 I'm singing in the rain, just singing in the rain;
What a wonderful feeling, I'm happy again.
From the musical, *Hollywood Revue of 1929*
Singing in the Rain

Freud, Sir Clement (1924–) British Liberal politician, writer, broadcaster, and caterer. His books include *Freud on Food* (1978) and *The Book of Hangovers* (1981).

1 If you resolve to give up smoking, drinking and loving, you don't actually live longer; it just seems longer.
The Observer, 27 Dec 1964

2 I find it hard to say, because when I was there it seemed to be shut.
On being asked for his opinion of New Zealand. Similar remarks have been attributed to others.
BBC radio, 12 Apr 1978

Freud, Sigmund (1856–1939) Austrian psychoanalyst. As a physician in Vienna he studied hypnosis but moved on to develop psychoanalysis and the theory that many neuroses were caused by suppressed sexual desires. His works include *The Interpretation of Dreams* (1899) and *Totem and Taboo* (1913).

1 The voice of the intellect is a soft one, but it does not rest till it has gained a hearing.
The Future of an Illusion

2 The psychic development of the individual is a short repetition of the course of development of the race.
Leonardo da Vinci

3 Religion is an illusion and it derives its strength from the fact that it falls in with our instinctual desires.
New Introductory Lectures on Psychoanalysis, 'A Philosophy of Life'

4 Conscience is the internal perception of the rejection of a particular wish operating within us.
Totem and Taboo

5 At bottom God is nothing more than an exalted father.
Totem and Taboo

6 The great question which I have not been able to answer, despite my thirty years of research into the feminine soul, is 'What does a woman want'?
Psychiatry in American Life (Charles Rolo)

7 What progress we are making. In the Middle Ages they would have burned me. Now they are content with burning my books.
Referring to the public burning of his books in Berlin
Letter to Ernest Jones, 1933

Frisch, Max (1911–) Swiss dramatist and novelist. His plays include *The Fire Raisers* (1958) and *Andorra* (1961); among his novels are *Stiller* (1954), *Homo Faber* (1957), and *Man in the Holocene* (1979).

1 He cannot bear old men's jokes. That is not new. But now he begins to think of them himself.
Sketchbook 1966–71

Frost, David (1939–) British television personality.

1 Television is an invention that permits you to be entertained in your living room by people you wouldn't have in your home.
Remark, CBS television, 1971

Frost, Robert Lee (1875–1963) US poet, whose collections *Boy's Will* (1913) and *North of Boston* (1914) brought him considerable acclaim.

1 Most of the change we think we see in life
Is due to truths being in and out of favour.
The Black Cottage

2 No tears in the writer, no tears in the reader.
Collected Poems, Preface

3 Home is the place where, when you have to go there,
They have to take you in.
The Death of the Hired Man

4 Forgive, O Lord, my little jokes on Thee
And I'll forgive Thy great big one on me.
In the Clearing, 'Cluster of Faith'

5 Something there is that doesn't love a wall.
North of Boston, 'Mending Wall'

6 My apple trees will never get across
And eat the cones under his pines, I tell him.
He only says, 'Good fences make good
neighbours.'
North of Boston, 'Mending Wall'

7 Two roads diverged in a wood, and I –
I took the one less traveled by,
And that has made all the difference.
The Road Not Taken

8 The woods are lovely, dark, and deep,
But I have promises to keep,
And miles to go before I sleep,
And miles to go before I sleep.
Stopping by Woods on a Snowy Evening

9 Writing free verse is like playing tennis with the
net down.
Speech, Milton Academy, 17 May 1935

10 A diplomat is a man who always remembers a
woman's birthday but never remembers her age.
Attrib.

11 Poetry is what gets lost in translation.
Attrib.

Froude, J(ames) A(nthony) (1818–94) British historian.
His *History of England* (1856–70) established his reputation.

1 Wild animals never kill for sport. Man is the only
one to whom the torture and death of his fellow-creatures is amusing in itself.
Oceana, Ch. 5

2 Men are made by nature unequal. It is vain,
therefore, to treat them as if they were equal.
Short Studies on Great Subjects, 'Party Politics'

3 Fear is the parent of cruelty.
Short Studies on Great Subjects, 'Party Politics'

Fry, Christopher (1907–   ) British dramatist. His verse
drama *The Lady's Not for Burning* (1948) brought him considerable
popularity. Other plays include *Venus Observed* (1950), *A Sleep of
Prisoners* (1951), and *Gurtmantle* (1962).

1 Why so shy, my pretty Thomasina?
Thomasin, O Thomasin,
Once you were so promisin'.
The Dark Is Light Enough, II

2 I sometimes think
His critical judgement is so exquisite
It leaves us nothing to admire except his opinion.
The Dark is Light Enough, II

3 Religion
Has made an honest woman of the supernatural,
And we won't have it kicking over the traces
again.
The Lady's Not for Burning, II

4 Where in this small-talking world can I find
A longitude with no platitude?
The Lady's Not for Burning, III

5 Try thinking of love, or something.
Amor vincit insomnia.
A Sleep of Prisoners

Fry, Elizabeth (1780–1845) British prison reformer. A
Quaker, she campaigned for improvements in prison conditions
throughout Europe.

1 Does capital punishment tend to the security of
the people? By no means. It hardens the hearts
of men, and makes the loss of life appear light
to them; and it renders life insecure, inasmuch
as the law holds out that property is of greater
value than life.
Biography of Distinguished Women (Sarah Josepha Hale)

2 Punishment is not for revenge, but to lessen
crime and reform the criminal.
Biography of Distinguished Women (Sarah Josepha Hale)

Fuller, Richard Buckminster (1895–1983) US architect
and inventor. His Dymaxion house (1928) never achieved success
but his geodesic dome is widely used. Writings include *Operating
Manual for Spaceship Earth* (1969).

1 I am a passenger on the spaceship, Earth.
Operating Manual for Spaceship Earth

Fuller, Roy (Broadbent) (1912–   ) British poet and
novelist. As well as such volumes of poetry as *Poems* (1939) and
The Reign of Sparrows (1980) he has also published several novels,
including *Image of a Society* (1956), and three volumes of memoirs.

1 A ghost has made uneasy every bed.
You are not you without me and *The dead
Only are pleased to be alone* it said.
Royal Naval Air Station (1944)

2 Short, big-nosed men with nasty conical caps,
Occasionally leering but mostly glum,
Retroussé shoes and swords at oblong hips.

Or so the stone reliefs depicted them.
The Hittites

Fuller, Thomas (1608–61) English historian. His best-known
work is the *History of Worthies of England* (1662) – a biographical
dictionary.

1 There is a great difference between painting a
face and not washing it.
Church History, Bk. VII

2 A proverb is much matter decorated into few
words.
The History of the Worthies of England, Ch. 2

3 Fame is sometimes like unto a kind of mushroom, which Pliny recounts to be the greatest
miracle in nature, because growing and having
no root.
The Holy State and the Profane State

4 Many have been the wise speeches of fools, though not so many as the foolish speeches of wise men.
The Holy State and the Profane State

5 Anger is one of the sinews of the soul.
The Holy State and the Profane State

6 Learning hath gained most by those books by which the printers have lost.
The Holy State and the Profane State

Furber, Douglas (1885–1961) British songwriter; author and co-author of many musicals and songs.

1 Any time you're Lambeth way,
Any evening, any day,
You'll find us all doin' the Lambeth walk.
Doin' the Lambeth Walk

Fyleman, Rose (1877–1957) British writer of children's books.

1 There are fairies at the bottom of our garden.
Fairies and Chimneys

G

Gabor, Zsa Zsa (1919–) Hungarian-born US film star. Her films include *Moulin Rouge* (1953) and *Touch of Evil* (1958). In 1961 she published her autobiography *My Story*.

1 Husbands are like fires. They go out when unattended.
Newsweek, 28 Mar 1960

2 A man in love is incomplete until he has married. Then he's finished.
Newsweek, 28 Mar 1960

3 I never hated a man enough to give him diamonds back.
The Observer, 'Sayings of the Week', 28 Aug 1957

Gainsborough, Thomas (1727–88) British portrait and landscape painter.

1 We are all going to Heaven, and Vandyke is of the company.
Last words
Thomas Gainsborough (Boulton), Ch. 9

Gaisford, Thomas (1799–1855) British classicist and clergyman. He was dean of Christ Church, Oxford and edited many classical texts.

1 Nor can I do better, in conclusion, than impress upon you the study of Greek literature which not only elevates above the vulgar herd, but leads not infrequently to positions of considerable emolument.
Christmas Day Sermon at Oxford
Reminiscences of Oxford (Revd W. Tuckwell)

Gaitskell, Hugh (1906–63) British Labour politician. He was chancellor of the exchequer (1950–51) in Attlee's government and succeeded him as party leader. He reunited the party before his untimely death.

1 Surely the right course is to test the Russians, not the bombs.
Observer, 'Sayings of the Week', 23 June 1957

2 All terrorists, at the invitation of the Government, end up with drinks at the Dorchester.
Letter to *The Guardian*, 23 Aug 1977 (Dora Gaitskell)

3 There are some of us . . . who will fight, fight, fight, and fight again to save the party we love.
After his policy for a nuclear deterrent had been defeated
Speech, Labour Party conference, Scarborough, 3 Oct 1960

Galbraith, John Kenneth (1908–) US economist in the Keynesian tradition; he was US ambassador (1961–63) to India and adviser to President Kennedy. His books include *The Affluent Society* (1958), *Economics and the Public Purpose* (1973), and an autobiography, *A Life In Our Times* (1981).

1 Wealth is not without its advantages, and the case to the contrary, although it has often been made, has never proved widely persuasive.
The Affluent Society, Ch. 1

2 Wealth has never been a sufficient source of honour in itself. It must be advertised, and the normal medium is obtrusively expensive goods.
The Affluent Society, Ch. 7

3 Few things are as immutable as the addiction of political groups to the ideas by which they have once won office.
The Affluent Society, Ch. 13

4 In the affluent society no useful distinction can be made between luxuries and necessaries.
The Affluent Society, Ch. 21

5 All races have produced notable economists, with the exception of the Irish who doubtless can protest their devotion to higher arts.
The Age of Uncertainty, Ch. 1

6 Much of the world's work, it has been said, is done by men who do not feel quite well. Marx is a case in point.
The Age of Uncertainty, Ch. 3

7 Money differs from an automobile, a mistress or cancer in being equally important to those who have it and those who do not.
Attrib.

8 The salary of the chief executive of the large corporation is not a market award for achievement. It is frequently in the nature of a warm personal gesture by the individual to himself.
Annals of an Abiding Liberal

Galilei, Galileo (1564–1642) Italian scientist. He made a number of major discoveries in mechanics and astronomy. Using the newly invented telescope he showed that Copernicus' heliocentric model of the universe was vastly superior to the Ptolomaic system favoured by the Roman Catholic Church. The Inquisition, however, forced him to recant and held him under house arrest for some 25 years.

1 In my studies of astronomy and philosophy I hold this opinion about the universe, that the Sun remains fixed in the centre of the circle of heavenly bodies, without changing its place; and the Earth, turning upon itself, moves round the Sun.
   Letter to Cristina di Lorena, 1615

2 *Eppur si muove*
   Yet it moves
   Referring to the Earth. Remark supposedly made after his recantation (1632) of belief in the Copernican system. Attrib.

Galsworthy, John (1867–1933) British novelist and dramatist. His series of novels, *The Forsyte Saga*, made his name. Plays include *The Silver Box* (1906).

Quotations about Galsworthy

1 Galsworthy had not quite enough of the superb courage of his satire. He faltered, and gave in to the Forsytes. It is a thousand pities. He might have been the surgeon the modern soul needs so badly, to cut away the proud flesh of our Forsytes from the living body of men who are fully alive. Instead, he put down the knife and laid on a soft sentimental poultice, and helped to make the corruption worse.
   D. H. Lawrence (1885–1930) British novelist. *Phoenix*

2 He has the gift of becoming, as it were, a statesman of literature.
   Robert Lynd (1879–1949) Irish essayist and critic. *John o'London's weekly*, 8 Dec 1928

3 Galsworthy was a bad writer, and some inner trouble, sharpening his sensitiveness, nearly made him into a good one; his discontent healed itself, and he reverted to type.
   George Orwell (Eric Blair; 1905–50) British novelist. *New Statesman and Nation*, 12 Mar 1938

Quotations by Galsworthy

4 Oh, your precious 'lame ducks'!
   The Man of Property, Pt. II, Ch. 12

Gandhi, Indira (1917–84) Indian stateswoman. The daughter of Jawaharla Nehru, she was prime minister twice (1966–67; 1980–84). She was assassinated by Sikh extremists.

1 To bear many children is considered not only a religious blessing but also an investment. The greater their number, some Indians reason, the more alms they can beg.
   New York Review of Books, 'Indira's Coup' (Oriana Fallaci)

2 There exists no politician in India daring enough to attempt to explain to the masses that cows can be eaten.
   New York Review of Books, 'Indira's Coup' (Oriana Fallaci)

3 You cannot shake hands with a clenched fist.
   Remark at a press conference, New Delhi, 19 Oct 1971

4 There are moments in history when brooding tragedy and its dark shadows can be lightened by recalling great moments of the past.
   Letter to Richard Nixon, 16 Dec 1971

5 I don't mind if my life goes in the service of the nation. If I die today every drop of my blood will invigorate the nation.
   Said the night before she was assassinated by Sikh militants, 30 Oct 1984
   The Sunday Times, 3 Dec 1989

Gandhi, Mahatma (Mohandas Karamchand Gandhi; 1869–1948) Indian national leader who used civil disobedience to achieve political aims. He became leader of the Indian National Congress and was treated as a saint in his own country. He was influential in the achievement of Indian independence, but his advocacy of cooperation between Hindus and Muslims led to his assassination by a Hindu fanatic.

Quotations about Gandhi

1 A dear old man with his bald pate and spectacles, beaky nose and birdlike lips and benign but somewhat toothless smile.
   Rodney Bennett. *Teacher's World*, 7 May 1930

2 It is nauseating to see Mr Gandhi, a seditious Middle Temple lawyer, now posing as a fakir of a type well known in the East, striding half naked up the steps of the Viceregal Palace, while he is still organising and conducting a defiant campaign of civil disobedience, to parley on equal terms with the representative of the King Emperor.
   Winston Churchill (1874–1965) British statesman. Speech, 23 Feb 1931

3 Gandhi was very keen on sex. He renounced it when he was 36, so thereafter it was never very far from his thoughts.
   Woodrow Wyatt (1918–) British politician. *Sunday Times*, 27 Nov 1977

Quotations by Gandhi

4 It is better to be violent, if there is violence in our hearts, than to put on the cloak of nonviolence to cover impotence.
   Non-Violence in Peace and War

5 I think it would be a good idea.
   On being asked for his view on Western civilization
   Attrib.

6 I eat to live, to serve, and also, if it so happens, to enjoy, but I do not eat for the sake of enjoyment.
   Attrib.

Garbo, Greta (1905–90) Swedish-born US film star, whose films include *Grand Hotel* (1932), *Camille* (1936), and *Ninotchka* (1939). She retired in 1941 into an enigmatic private life.

1 I want to be alone.
   Words spoken by Garbo in the film *Grand Hotel*, and associated with her for the rest of her career. *See below.*

2 I never said, 'I want to be alone.' I only said, 'I want to be *left* alone.' There is all the difference.

Garbo (John Bainbridge)

Garfield, James A(bram) (1831–81) US statesman. He became Republican President (1881) after a military career. He was assassinated.

1 My fellow citizens, the President is dead, but the Government lives and God Omnipotent reigns.

Speech following the assassination of Lincoln

Garibaldi, Giuseppe (1807–82) Italian general and political leader, who was active in the campaign for Italian unification.

1 Anyone who wants to carry on the war against the outsiders, come with me. I can't offer you either honours or wages; I offer you hunger, thirst, forced marches, battles and death. Anyone who loves his country, follow me.

Garibaldi (Guerzoni)

Garland, Judy (Frances Gumm; 1922–69) US film star and singer. She established herself as a child star in *The Wizard of Oz* (1939). Later films, such as *Easter Parade* (1948) and *A Star Is Born* (1954) also brought success, but addiction caused her premature death.

1 I was born at the age of twelve on a Metro-Goldwyn-Mayer lot.

The Observer, 'Sayings of the Week', 18 Feb 1951

Garner, Alan (1934–) British children's writer. His fantasy novels which cross the bridge between children's and adult fiction, include *The Weirdstone of Brisingamen* (1960), *Elidor* (1965), *The Owl Service* (1967), *Red Shift* (1973), and *A Bag of Moonshine* (1986).

1 Possessive parents rarely live long enough to see the fruits of their selfishness.

The Owl Service

Garrick, David (1717–79) British actor and manager, who ran the Drury Lane Theatre (1747–76), where he introduced many innovations.

1 Prologues precede the piece – in mournful verse;
As undertakers – walk before the hearse.

Apprentice, Prologue

2 Come cheer up, my lads! 'tis to glory we steer,
To add something more to this wonderful year;
To honour we call you, not press you like slaves,
For who are so free as the sons of the waves?
Heart of oak are our ships,
Heart of oak are our men:
We always are ready;
Steady, boys, steady;
We'll fight and we'll conquer again and again.

Heart of Oak

Garrison, William Lloyd (1805–79) US abolitionist. He founded *The Liberator* (1831), the antislavery journal.

1 Our country is the world – our countrymen are all mankind.

The Liberator, 15 Dec 1837

2 The compact which exists between the North and the South is a covenant with death and an agreement with hell.

Resolution, Massachusetts Anti-Slavery Society, 27 Jan 1843

Garrod, Heathcote William (1878–1960) British classical scholar and literary critic.

1 Madam, I am the civilization they are fighting to defend.

Replying to criticism that he was not fighting to defend civilization, during World War I
Oxford Now and Then (D. Balsdon)

Gaskell, Elizabeth Cleghorn (1810–65) British novelist. Her novels include *Mary Barton* (1848) and *Cranford* (1853).

1 A man . . . is *so* in the way in the house!

Cranford, Ch. 1

2 'It is very pleasant dining with a bachelor,' said Miss Matty, softly, as we settled ourselves in the counting-house. 'I only hope it is not improper; so many pleasant things are!'

Cranford, Ch. 4

3 That kind of patriotism which consists in hating all other nations.

Sylvia's Lovers, Ch. 1

Gautier, Théophile (1811–72) French poet and critic. Verse collections include *Poésies* (1830) and *Émaux et camées* (1852).

1 I am a man for whom the outside world exists.

Journal des Goncourt, 1 May 1857

2 Yes, the work comes out more beautiful from a material that resists the process, verse, marble, onyx, or enamel.

L'Art

Gavarni, Paul (1801–66) French illustrator best known for his sketches of Parisian life.

1 *Les enfants terribles.*
The embarrassing young.

Title of a series of prints

Gay, John (1685–1732) English poet and dramatist. A member of the Scriblerus Club with Pope and Swift, his *Fables* (1727) were his best-known poems but he is now remembered for his ballad opera *The Beggar's Opera* (1728).

1 A moment of time may make us unhappy for ever.

The Beggar's Opera

2 How, like a moth, the simple maid
Still plays about the flame!

The Beggar's Opera

3 If with me you'd fondly stray,
Over the hills and far away.

The Beggar's Opera

4 Do you think your mother and I should have liv'd comfortably so long together, if ever we had been married?

The Beggar's Opera

5 She who has never loved has never lived.

Captives

6 In every age and clime we see,
Two of a trade can ne'er agree.

Fables

7 'While there is life, there's hope,' he cried;
'Then why such haste?' so groaned and died.

Fables

8 'Tis a gross error, held in schools,
That Fortune always favours fools.

Fables

9 Fools may our scorn, not envy raise,
For envy is a kind of praise.

Fables

10 Life is a jest; and all things show it.
I thought so once; but now I know it.

My Own Epitaph

11 No sir, tho' I was born and bred in England, I can dare to be poor, which is the only thing now-a-days men are asham'd of.

Polly

12 We only part to meet again.
Change, as ye list, ye winds; my heart shall be
The faithful compass that still points to thee.

Sweet William's Farewell

Geddes, Sir Eric Campbell (1875–1937) British politician. First Lord of the Admiralty (1917–18), he later became minister of transport (1919–21).

1 The Germans, if this Government is returned, are going to pay every penny; they are going to be squeezed, as a lemon is squeezed – until the pips squeak. My only doubt is not whether we can squeeze hard enough, but whether there is enough juice.

Speech, Cambridge, 10 Dec 1918

Geldof, Bob (1952–) Irish rock musician. Singer with The Boom Town Rats, he played a leading role in the fund raising organisation Band Aid, which was created in 1984 to raise millions of pounds for the starving in Africa. In 1986 he received an honorary knighthood.

1 I'm not interested in the bloody system! Why has he no food? Why is he starving to death?

The Observer, 'Sayings of the Week', 27 Oct 1985

2 I'm into pop because I want to get rich, get famous and get laid.

Attrib.

George, Dan (1899–1982) Canadian Indian chief, who acted in a number of films, including *Little Big Man* (1970).

1 When the white man came we had the land and they had the Bibles; now they have the land and we have the Bibles.

Attrib.

George II (1683–1760) King of Britain and Elector of Hanover. He was a considerable patron of music.

1 No, I shall have mistresses.

Reply to Queen Caroline's suggestion, as she lay on her death-bed, that he should marry again after her death.
Memoirs of George the Second (Hervey), Vol. II

2 Oh! he is mad, is he? Then I wish he would bite some other of my generals.

Replying to advisors who told him that General James Wolfe was mad
Attrib.

George IV (1762–1830) King of the United Kingdom and Hanover (1820–30). His treatment of Queen Caroline and secret marriage to Maria Fitzherbert undermined his authority.

1 Harris, I am not well; pray get me a glass of brandy.

On seeing Caroline of Brunswick for the first time
Diaries (Earl of Malmesbury)

George V (1865–1936) King of the United Kingdom (1910–36), who, with his consort, Mary of Teck, reigned throughout World War I and during the preparations for World War II.

1 I have many times asked myself whether there can be more potent advocates of peace upon earth through the years to come than this massed multitude of silent witnesses to the desolation of war.

Referring to the massed World War I graves in Flanders, 1922
Silent Cities (ed. Gavin Stamp)

2 Is it possible that my people live in such awful conditions? . . . I tell you, Mr Wheatley, that if I had to live in conditions like that I would be a revolutionary myself.

On being told Mr Wheatley's life story
The Tragedy of Ramsay MacDonald (L. MacNeill Weir), Ch. 16

3 How is the Empire?

Last words.
The Times, 21 Jan 1936

4 Bugger Bognor

His alleged last words, when his doctor promised him he would soon be well enough to visit Bognor Regis
Attrib.

George VI (1895–1952) King of the United Kingdom.

1 We're not a family; we're a firm.

Our Future King (Peter Lane)

2 It is not the walls that make the city, but the people who live within them. The walls of London may be battered, but the spirit of the Londoner stands resolute and undismayed.

Radio broadcast to the Empire, 23 Sept 1940

Getty, J(ean) Paul (1892–1976) US oil magnate, who retired to live in England and founded an art museum in California.

1 If you can actually count your money you are not really a rich man.
Gossip (A. Barrow)

2 The meek shall inherit the earth but not the mineral rights.
Attrib.

Gibbon, Edward (1737–94) British historian whose monumental *The History of the Decline and Fall of the Roman Empire* (1776–88) caused considerable controversy for its treatment of Christianity.

Quotations about Gibbon

1 Gibbon is an ugly, affected, disgusting fellow, and poisons our literary club for me. I class him among infidel wasps and venomous insects.
James Boswell (1740–95) Scottish lawyer and writer. *Diary*, 1779

2 Johnson's style was grand, Gibbon's elegant. Johnson marched to kettle-drums and trumpets. Gibbon moved to flutes and hautboys.
George Colman the Younger (1762–1836) British dramatist. *Ramdom Records*

Quotations by Gibbon

3 To the University of Oxford I acknowledge no obligation; and she will as cheerfully renounce me for a son, as I am willing to disclaim her for a mother. I spent fourteen months at Magdalen College: they proved the fourteen months the most idle and unprofitable of my whole life.
Autobiography

4 Crowds without company, and dissipation without pleasure.
Referring to London
Autobiography

5 The romance of *Tom Jones*, that exquisite picture of human manners, will outlive the palace of the Escurial and the imperial eagle of the house of Austria.
Autobiography

6 The various modes of worship, which prevailed in the Roman world, were all considered by the people as equally true; by the philosopher, as equally false; and by the magistrate, as equally useful. And thus toleration produced not only mutual indulgence, but even religious concord.
Decline and Fall of the Roman Empire, Ch. 2

7 The principles of a free constitution are irrecoverably lost, when the legislative power is nominated by the executive.
Decline and Fall of the Roman Empire, Ch. 3

8 His reign is marked by the rare advantage of furnishing very few materials for history; which is, indeed, little more than the register of the crimes, follies, and misfortunes of mankind.
Referring to the reign of Antoninus Pius
Decline and Fall of the Roman Empire, Ch. 3

9 Corruption, the most infallible symptom of constitutional liberty.
Decline and Fall of the Roman Empire, Ch. 21

10 All that is human must retrograde if it does not advance.
Decline and Fall of the Roman Empire, Ch. 71

Gibbons, Stella (1902–89) British poet and novelist, whose books include *The Mountain Beast* (poetry; 1930) and *Cold Comfort Farm* (novel; 1932).

1 Something nasty in the woodshed.
Cold Comfort Farm

Gibran, Kahlil (1883–1931) Lebanese mystic, painter, and poet. Known for combining Christian and Arabic ideas in such works as *The Prophet* (1923), he inspired a new school of Arabic poetry.

1 You may give them your love but not your thoughts.
For they have their own thoughts.
You may house their bodies but not their souls,
For their souls dwell in the house of tomorrow, which
you cannot visit, not even in your dreams.
The Prophet, 'On Children'

2 No human relation gives one possession in another – every two souls are absolutely different. In friendship or in love, the two side by side raise hands together to find what one cannot reach alone.
Beloved Prophet (Virginia Hilu)

Gide, André (1869–1951) French novelist and critic. Novels include *Fruits of the Earth* (1897), *The Vatican Cellars* (1914), and *The Counterfeiters* (1926).

1 *L'acte gratuite.*
The unmotivated action.
Les Caves du Vatican

2 One does not discover new lands without consenting to lose sight of the shore for a very long time.
The Counterfeiters

3 Fish die belly-upward and rise to the surface; it is their way of falling.
Journals

4 *Hugo – hélas!*
Replying to an inquiry as to whom he considered the finest poet of the 19th century.
André Gide–Paul Valéry Correspondence 1890–1942

Gilbert, Fred (1850–1903) British songwriter.

1 As I walk along the Bois Bou-long,
With an independent air,
You can hear the girls declare,
'He must be a millionaire',
You can hear them sigh and wish to die,
You can see them wink the other eye
At the man who broke the Bank at Monte Carlo.
The Bois de Boulogne was a fashionable recreational area on the outskirts of Paris
The Man who Broke the Bank at Monte Carlo (song)

Gilbert, Sir Humphrey (c. 1539–83) English navigator. Half-brother of Sir Walter Raleigh, he failed to reach America on his first voyage, but on his second (1583) reached Newfoundland, which he claimed for Britain.

1 We are as near to heaven by sea as by land.
   Remark made shortly before he went down with his ship Squirrel
   A Book of Anecdotes (D. George)

Gilbert, Sir William Schwenk (1836–1911) British dramatist and comic writer. His comic verse published as *Bab Ballads* (1896) preceded his libretti for 14 comic operas written for Arthur Sullivan's music.

1 He led his regiment from behind
   He found it less exciting.
   The Gondoliers, I

2 Of that there is no manner of doubt –
   No probable, possible shadow of doubt –
   No possible doubt whatever.
   The Gondoliers, I

3 A taste for drink, combined with gout,
   Had doubled him up for ever.
   The Gondoliers, I

4 All shall equal be.
   The Earl, the Marquis, and the Dook,
   The Groom, the Butler, and the Cook,
   The Aristocrat who banks with Coutts,
   The Aristocrat who cleans the boots.
   The Gondoliers, I

5 When every blessed thing you hold
   Is made of silver, or of gold,
   You long for simple pewter.
   When you have nothing else to wear
   But cloth of gold and satins rare,
   For cloth of gold you cease to care –
   Up goes the price of shoddy.
   The Gondoliers, I

6 I'm called Little Buttercup – dear Little
   Buttercup,
   Though I could never tell why.
   HMS Pinafore, I

7 I am the Captain of the *Pinafore*;
   And a right good captain too!
   HMS Pinafore, I

8 CAPTAIN. I'm never, never sick at sea!
   ALL. What never?
   CAPTAIN. No, never!
   ALL. What, *never*?
   CAPTAIN. Hardly ever!
   HMS Pinafore, I

9 And so do his sisters, and his cousins and his
   aunts!
   His sisters and his cousins,
   Whom he reckons up by dozens,
   And his aunts!
   HMS Pinafore, I

10 I always voted at my party's call,
   And I never thought of thinking for myself at all.
   HMS Pinafore, I

11 Stick close to your desks and never go to sea,
   And you all may be Rulers of the Queen's
   Navee!
   HMS Pinafore, I

12 When I was a lad I served a term
   As office boy to an Attorney's firm.
   I cleaned the windows and I swept the floor,
   And I polished up the handle of the big front
   door.
   I polished up that handle so carefullee
   That now I am the Ruler of the Queen's Navee!
   HMS Pinafore, I

13 For he might have been a Roosian,
   A French, or Turk, or Proosian,
   Or perhaps Ital-ian!
   But in spite of all temptations
   To belong to other nations,
   He remains an Englishman!
   HMS Pinafore, II

14 I see no objection to stoutness, in moderation.
   Iolanthe, I

15 Bow, bow, ye lower middle classes!
   Bow, bow, ye tradesmen, bow, ye masses!
   Iolanthe, I

16 When I went to the Bar as a very young man,
   (Said I to myself – said I),
   I'll work on a new and original plan,
   (Said I to myself – said I).
   Iolanthe, I

17 The prospect of a lot
   Of dull MPs in close proximity,
   All thinking for themselves is what
   No man can face with equanimity.
   Iolanthe, I

18 The Law is the true embodiment
   Of everything that's excellent.
   It has no kind of fault or flaw,
   And I, my lords, embody the Law.
   Iolanthe, I

19 I often think it's comical
   How Nature always does contrive
   That every boy and every gal
   That's born into the world alive
   Is either a little Liberal
   Or else a little Conservative!
   Iolanthe, II

20 The House of Peers, throughout the war,
   Did nothing in particular,
   And did it very well.
   Iolanthe, II

21 For you dream you are crossing the Channel,
   and tossing about in a steamer from Harwich –
   Which is something between a large bathing machine and a very small second-class carriage.
   Iolanthe, II

22 Pooh-Bah (Lord High Everything Else)
   The Mikado, Dramatis Personae

23 A wandering minstrel I –
A thing of shreds and patches,
Of ballads, songs and snatches,
And dreamy lullaby!

The Mikado, I

24 I can trace my ancestry back to a protoplasmal
primordial atomic globule. Consequently, my
family pride is something in-conceivable. I can't
help it. I was born sneering.

The Mikado, I

25 As some day it may happen that a victim must
be found
I've got a little list – I've got a little list
Of society offenders who might well be
underground,
And who never would be missed – who never
would be missed!

The Mikado, I

26 The idiot who praises, with enthusiastic tone,
All centuries but this, and every country but his
own.

The Mikado, I

27 Three little maids from school are we,
Pert as a school-girl well can be,
Filled to the brim with girlish glee.

The Mikado, I

28 Ah, pray make no mistake,
We are not shy;
We're very wide awake,
The moon and I.

The Mikado, II

29 My object all sublime
I shall achieve in time –
To let the punishment fit the crime –
The punishment fit the crime.

The Mikado, II

30 The billiard sharp whom any one catches,
His doom's extremely hard –
He's made to dwell –
In a dungeon cell
On a spot that's always barred.
And there he plays extravagant matches
In fitless finger-stalls
On a cloth untrue
With a twisted cue
And elliptical billiard balls.

The Mikado, II

31 I have a left shoulder-blade that is a miracle of
loveliness. People come miles to see it. My
right elbow has a fascination that few can resist.

The Mikado, II

32 Something lingering, with boiling oil in it, I fancy.

The Mikado, II

33 The flowers that bloom in the spring,
Tra la,
Have nothing to do with the case.
I've got to take under my wing,
Tra la,
A most unattractive old thing,
Tra la,
With a caricature of a face.

The Mikado, II

34 On a tree by a river a little tom-tit
Sang 'Willow, titwillow, titwillow!'

The Mikado, II

35 If this young man expresses himself in terms too
deep for *me*,
Why, what a very singularly deep young man
this deep young man must be!

Patience, I

36 Poor wandering one!
Though thou hast surely strayed,
Take heart of grace,
Thy steps retrace,
Poor wandering one!

The Pirates of Penzance, I

37 I am the very model of a modern Major-General,
I've information vegetable, animal and mineral,
I know the kings of England, and I quote the
fights historical,
From Marathon to Waterloo, in order
categorical.

The Pirates of Penzance, I

38 About binomial theorems I'm teeming with a lot
of news,
With many cheerful facts about the square on the
hypoteneuse.

The Pirates of Penzance, I

39 When the foeman bares his steel,
Tarantara! tarantara!
We uncomfortable feel.

The Pirates of Penzance, II

40 When constabulary duty's to be done –
A policeman's lot is not a happy one.

The Pirates of Penzance, II

41 He combines the manners of a Marquis with the
morals of a Methodist.

Ruddigore, I

42 Is life a boon?
If so, it must befall
That Death, whene'er he call,
Must call too soon.

The lines are written on Arthur Sullivan's memorial in the Embankment gardens
The Yeoman of the Guard, I

43 I have a song to sing O!
Sing me your song, O!

The Yeoman of the Guard, I

44 It's a song of a merryman, moping mum,
Whose soul was sad, and whose glance was glum,
Who sipped no sup, and who craved no crumb,
As he sighed for the love of a ladye.
The Yeoman of the Guard, I

45 She may very well pass for forty-three
In the dusk, with a light behind her!
Trial by Jury

46 Sir, I view the proposal to hold an international exhibition at San Francisco with an equanimity bordering on indifference.
Gilbert, His Life and Strife (Hesketh Pearson)

47 My dear chap! Good isn't the word!
Speaking to an actor after he had given a poor performance
Attrib.

48 Funny without being vulgar.
Referring to Sir Henry Irving's *Hamlet*
Attrib.

Gilman, Charlotte Perkins (1860–1935) US writer and lecturer on sociology, economics, and feminism.

1 However, one cannot put a quart in a pint cup.
The Living of Charlotte Perkins Gilman

2 New York . . . that unnatural city where every one is an exile, none more so than the American.
The Living of Charlotte Perkins Gilman

3 Where young boys plan for what they will achieve and attain, young girls plan for whom they will achieve and attain.
Women and Economics, Ch. 5

Ginsberg, Allen (1926–)
US poet. His first work *Howl* (1956), an attack on contemporary America, earned him a place in the Beat movement of the 1950s. Later works include *The Change* (1963), *The Fall of America* (1973), and *The White Shroud: Poems 1980–85* (1985).

1 I saw the best minds of my generation destroyed by madness, starving hysterical naked.
Howl

Giraudoux, Jean (1882–1944) French dramatist and writer. His novels, including *Elpénor* (1919), and *Adorable Clio* (1920), established his reputation. His later plays include *Ondine* (1939) and *The Madwoman of Chaillot* (1949).

1 It's odd how people waiting for you stand out far less clearly than people you are waiting for.
Tiger at the Gates, I

2 There's no better way of exercising the imagination than the study of law. No poet ever interpreted nature as freely as a lawyer interprets truth.
Tiger at the Gates, I

3 Only the mediocre are always at their best.
Attrib.

Gladstone, William Ewart (1809–98) British statesman. He became Liberal prime minister (1868–74; 1880–85; 1886; 1892–94), dominating British politics in opposition to Disraeli for much of the second half of the 19th century.

1 You cannot fight against the future. Time is on our side.
Advocating parliamentary reform
Speech, 1866

2 All the world over, I will back the masses against the classes.
Speech, Liverpool, 28 June 1886

3 We are part of the community of Europe, and we must do our duty as such.
Speech, Caenarvon, 10 Apr 1888

Glasse, Hannah (18th century) English writer, especially on cookery.

1 Take your hare when it is cased . . .
The saying 'First catch your hare' has often been attributed incorrectly to Mrs Glasse.
The Art of Cookery Made Plain and Easy, Ch. 1

Gloucester, William, Duke of (1743–1805) The brother of George III.

1 Another damned, thick, square book! Always scribble, scribble, scribble! Eh! Mr Gibbon?
Literary Memorials (Best)

Glover-Kind, John A. (19th century) US songwriter.

1 I do Like to be Beside the Seaside.
Song title

Godard, Jean-Luc (1930–) French film director. His new wave films include *Week-End* (1967), *Tout va bien* (1972), and *Je vous salue, Marie* (1985).

1 Photography is truth. And cinema is truth twenty-four times a second.
Le Petit Soldat

2 I like a film to have a beginning, a middle and an end, but not necessarily in that order.
Attrib.

Goebbels, Joseph (1897–1945) German politician. As Hitler's minister of propaganda he established a system for disseminating whatever 'information' the Nazis considered appropriate. Having murdered his six children, he committed suicide after the German collapse.

1 The Iron Curtain.
Das Reich

2 This was the Angel of History! We felt its wings flutter through the room. Was that not the fortune we awaited so anxiously?
Referring to Roosevelt's death
Diary

3 The English do not treat very kindly the men who conduct their wars for them.
Diaries

Goering, Hermann (1893–1946) German leader, who commanded the Brownshirts (1922) and established the Gestapo (1933). He developed the air force and became Hitler's successor in 1939. He committed suicide after being condemned to hang at the Nuremburg trials.

1 They entered the war to prevent us from going into the East, not to have the East come to the Atlantic.

Referring to the war aims of the British in World War II
Nuremberg Diary (G. M. Gilbert)

2 I herewith commission you to carry out all preparations with regard to . . . a *total solution* of the Jewish question, in those territories of Europe which are under German influence.

The Rise and Fall of the Third Reich (William Shirer)

3 Guns will make us powerful; butter will only make us fat.

Radio broadcast, 1936

4 When I hear anyone talk of Culture, I reach for my revolver.

Attrib. to Goering but probably said by Hanns JOHST

Goethe, Johann Wolfgang von (1749–1832) German poet, dramatist, and scientist. His novel *The Sorrows of Young Werther* (1774) brought him international fame, which was enhanced by *Faust* (1808), a poetic drama.

1 I do not know myself, and God forbid that I should.

Conversations with Eckermann, 10 Apr 1829

2 Dear friend, theory is all grey,
And the golden tree of life is green.

Faust, Pt. I

3 Two souls dwell, alas! in my breast.

Faust, Pt. I

4 I am the spirit that always denies.

Faust, Pt. I

5 A useless life is an early death.

Iphegenie, I:2

6 Superstition is the poetry of life.

Sprüche in Prosa, III

7 Talent develops in quiet places, character in the full current of human life.

Torquato Tasso, I

8 God could cause us considerable embarrassment by revealing all the secrets of nature to us: we should not know what to do for sheer apathy and boredom.

Memoirs (Riemer)

9 From today and from this place there begins a new epoch in the history of the world.

On witnessing the victory of the French at the battle of Valmy
The Story of Civilization (W. Durant), Vol. II

10 I was not unaware that I had begotten a mortal.

On learning of his son's death
The Story of Civilization (W. Durant), Vol. X

11 *Mehr Licht!*
More light!

Attrib. last words. In fact he asked for the second shutter to be opened, to allow more light in

Golding, Sir William (1911–) British novelist. He made his name with *Lord of the Flies* (1954). Subsequent books include *Free Fall* (1959), *The Spire* (1964), *A Moving Target* (1982), and a trilogy comprising *Rites of Passage* (1980), *Close Quarters* (1987), and *Fire Down Below* (1989). He won a Nobel Prize in 1983.

1 Philip is a living example of natural selection. He was as fitted to survive in this modern world as a tapeworm in an intestine.

Free Fall, Ch. 2

2 Ralph wept for the end of innocence, the darkness of man's heart, and the fall through the air of the true, wise friend called Piggy.

Lord of the Flies, Ch. 12

3 With lack of sleep and too much understanding I grow a little crazy, I think, like all men at sea who live too close to each other and too close thereby to all that is monstrous under the sun and moon.

Rites of Passage, (&)

Goldsmith, Oliver (1728–74) Irish-born British writer, dramatist, and poet. He is remembered for his novel *The Vicar of Wakefield* (1776) and the play *She Stoops to Conquer* (1773) in addition to a considerable amount of verse.

Quotations about Goldsmith

1 No man was more foolish when he had not a pen in his hand, or more wise when he had.

Samuel Johnson (1709–84) British lexicographer. *The Life of Johnson* (J. Boswell)

2 An inspired idiot.

Horace Walpole (1717–97) British writer. Attrib.

Quotations by Goldsmith

3 True genius walks along a line, and, perhaps, our greatest pleasure is in seeing it so often near falling, without being ever actually down.

The Bee, 'The Characteristics of Greatness'

4 As writers become more numerous, it is natural for readers to become more indolent.

The Bee, 'Upon Unfortunate Merit'

5 To a philosopher no circumstance, however trifling, is too minute.

The Citizen of the World

6 Ill fares the land, to hast'ning ills a prey,
Where wealth accumulates, and men decay;
Princes and lords may flourish, or may fade;
A breath can make them, as a breath has made;
But a bold peasantry, their country's pride,
When once destroy'd, can never be supplied.

The Deserted Village

7 In arguing too, the parson own'd his skill,
For e'en though vanquish'd, he could argue still;
While words of learned length, and thund'ring sound
Amazed the gazing rustics rang'd around,
And still they gaz'd, and still the wonder grew,
That one small head could carry all he knew.

The Deserted Village

8 Man wants but little here below,
Nor wants that little long.

Edwin and Angelina, or the Hermit

9 The doctor found, when she was dead,
Her last disorder mortal.

Elegy on Mrs. Mary Blaize

10 The dog, to gain some private ends,
Went mad and bit the man.

Elegy on the Death of a Mad Dog

11 The man recovered of the bite,
The dog it was that died.

Elegy on the Death of a Mad Dog

12 I hate the French because they are all slaves,
and wear wooden shoes.

Essays, 'Distresses of a Common Soldier'

13 The true use of speech is not so much to express our wants as to conceal them.

Essays, 'The Use of Language'

14 Friendship is a disinterested commerce between equals; love, an abject intercourse between tyrants and slaves.

The Good-Natured Man, I

15 We must touch his weaknesses with a delicate hand. There are some faults so nearly allied to excellence, that we can scarce weed out the fault without eradicating the virtue.

The Good-Natured Man, I

16 LEONTINE. An only son, sir, might expect more indulgence.
CROAKER. An only father, sir, might expect more obedience.

The Good-Natured Man, I

17 I am told he makes a very handsome corpse, and becomes his coffin prodigiously.

The Good-Natured Man, I

18 Silence is become his mother tongue.

The Good-Natured Man, II

19 I love everything that's old: old friends, old times, old manners, old books, old wine.

She Stoops to Conquer, I

20 In my time, the follies of the town crept slowly among us, but now they travel faster than a stagecoach.

She Stoops to Conquer, I

21 Let schoolmasters puzzle their brain,
With grammar, and nonsense, and learning,
Good liquor, I stoutly maintain,
Gives genius a better discerning.

She Stoops to Conquer, I

22 This is Liberty-Hall, gentlemen.

She Stoops to Conquer, II

23 Where wealth and freedom reign, contentment fails,
And honour sinks where commerce long prevails.

The Traveller

24 Laws grind the poor, and rich men rule the law.

The Traveller

25 A book may be amusing with numerous errors, or it may be very dull without a single absurdity.

The Vicar of Wakefield, Advertisement

26 I . . . chose my wife, as she did her wedding gown, not for a fine glossy surface, but such qualities as would wear well.

The Vicar of Wakefield, Preface

27 I was ever of opinion, that the honest man who married and brought up a large family, did more service than he who continued single and only talked of population.

The Vicar of Wakefield, Ch. 1

28 Let us draw upon content for the deficiencies of fortune.

The Vicar of Wakefield, Ch. 3

29 When lovely woman stoops to folly,
And finds too late that men betray,
What charm can soothe her melancholy,
What art can wash her guilt away?

The Vicar of Wakefield, Ch. 9

30 Conscience is a coward, and those faults it has not strength enough to prevent it seldom has justice enough to accuse.

The Vicar of Wakefield, Ch. 13

31 There is no arguing with Johnson; for when his pistol misses fire, he knocks you down with the butt end of it.

Life of Johnson (J. Boswell)

32 As I take my shoes from the shoemaker, and my coat from the tailor, so I take my religion from the priest.

Life of Johnson (J. Boswell)

Goldwater, Barry (1904–) US politician. An unsuccessful Republican candidate for the presidency, he served as a senator for Arizona.

1 A government that is big enough to give you all you want is big enough to take it all away.

Bachman's Book of Freedom Quotations (M. Ivens and R. Dunstan)

2 I would remind you that extremism in the defence of liberty is no vice. And let me remind you also that moderation in the pursuit of justice is no virtue!
Speech, San Francisco, 17 July 1964

3 You've got to forget about this civilian. Whenever you drop bombs, you're going to hit civilians.
Speech, New York, 23 Jan 1967

Goldwyn, Samuel (Samuel Goldfish; 1882–1974) Polish-born US film producer, whose own company merged with others to form Metro-Goldwyn-Mayer (MGM) in 1924 – a company that made many Hollywood successes. He is noted for his so-called 'Goldwynisms', most of which are apocryphal.

1 Let's have some new clichés.
The Observer, 'Sayings of the Week', 24 Oct 1948

2 Why should people go out and pay money to see bad films when they can stay at home and see bad television for nothing?
The Observer, 'Sayings of the Week', 9 Sept 1956

3 Too caustic? To hell with cost; we'll make the picture anyway.
Attrib.

4 We're overpaying him but he's worth it.
Attrib.

5 What we want is a story that starts with an earthquake and works its way up to a climax.
Attrib.

6 I am willing to admit that I may not always be right, but I am never wrong.
Attrib.

7 Chaplin is no business man – all he knows is that he can't take anything less.
Attrib.

8 I don't care if it doesn't make a nickel, I just want every man, woman, and child in America to see it!
Referring to his film The Best Years of Our Lives
Attrib.

9 A wide screen just makes a bad film twice as bad.
Attrib.

10 For years I have been known for saying 'Include me out'; but today I am giving it up for ever.
Address, Balliol College, Oxford, 1 Mar 1945

11 In two words: im - possible.
Attrib.

12 Anybody who goes to see a psychiatrist ought to have his head examined.
Attrib.

13 Every director bites the hand that lays the golden egg.
Attrib.

14 I'll give you a definite maybe.
Attrib.

15 A verbal contract isn't worth the paper it's written on.
Attrib.

16 You ought to take the bull between the teeth.
Attrib.

17 We have all passed a lot of water since then.
Attrib.

18 I read part of it all the way through.
Attrib.

19 If Roosevelt were alive he'd turn in his grave.
Attrib.

20 It's more than magnificent – it's mediocre.
Attrib.

21 'Why only twelve?' 'That's the original number.' 'Well, go out and get thousands.'
Referring to the number of disciples whilst filming a scene for The Last Supper
Attrib.

22 Yes, I'm going to have a bust made of them.
Replying to an admiring comment about his wife's hands
Attrib.

23 Tell me, how did you love my picture?
Attrib. in Colombo's Hollywood (J. R. Colombo)

Goncourt, Edmond de (1822–96) French novelist who collaborated with his brother, **Jules de Goncourt** (1830–70), in such books as Sœur Philomène (1861). He left his money to found the coveted Prix Goncourt.

1 Historians tell the story of the past, novelists the story of the present.
Journal

Gorbachov, Mikhail Sergeevich (1931–) Soviet statesman. He became general secretary of the Soviet Communist party in 1985 and president in 1988. His glasnost (openness) and perestroika (progress) policies aimed at radical reform of Soviet society and promoted better relations with the West.

1 And if the Russian word 'perestroika' has easily entered the international lexicon, this is due to more than just interest in what is going on in the Soviet Union. Now the whole world needs restructuring i.e. progressive development, a fundamental change.
Perestroika

2 Our rockets can find Halley's comet and fly to Venus with amazing accuracy, but side by side with these scientific and technical triumphs is an obvious lack of efficiency in using scientific achievements for economic needs, and many Soviet household appliances are of poor quality.
Perestroika

3 The Soviet people want full-blooded and unconditional democracy.
Speech, July 1988

Gordon, Adam Lindsay (1833–70) Australian poet. Collections include Sea Spray and Smoke Drift (1867) and Bush Ballads and Galloping Rhymes (1870).

1 Life is mostly froth and bubble;
Two things stand like stone,
Kindness in another's trouble,
Courage in your own.
Ye Wearie Wayfarer, Fytte 8

Gorky, Maxim (Aleksei Maksimovich Peshkov; 1868–1936)
Russian novelist, dramatist, and short-story writer. Novels include
Mother (1907); *The Lower Depths* (1903) is his best-known play.
Autobiographical writings include *Fragments from My Diary* (1924)
and *Reminiscences of My Youth* (1924).

1 You must write for children in the same way as
you do for adults, only better.
Attrib.

Gosse, Sir Edmund (1849–1928) British writer and critic.
Best known for his translations and biography of Ibsen and his
autobiographical *Father and Son* (1907).

1 We were as nearly bored as enthusiasm would
permit.
Referring to a play by Swinburne
Biography of Edward Marsh (C. Hassall)

2 A sheep in sheep's clothing.
Referring to T. Sturge Moore. Sometimes attributed to Winston
Churchill, referring to Clement Attlee.
Under the Bridge (Ferris Greenslet), Ch. 12

Gournay, Jean Claude Vincent de (1712–59) French
economist and advocate of free trade.

1 *Laissez faire, laissez passer.*
Liberty of action, liberty of movement.
Speech, Sept 1758

Grace, W(illiam) G(ilbert) (1848–1915) British doctor
and cricketer. He was captain of Gloucestershire (1871–98) and
England in 13 Test matches. He is regarded as England's greatest
cricketer.

1 They came to see me bat not to see you bowl.
Refusing to leave the crease after being bowled first ball in front
of a large crowd
Attrib.

Gracián, Baltasar (1601–58) Spanish writer and Jesuit. He
is remembered for his philosophical novel *El Criticón* (1651–57).

1 Good things, when short, are twice as good.
The Art of Worldly Wisdom

Grade, Lew, Baron (Lewis Winogradsky; 1906–) British
film and TV producer and impresario. Films include *The Legend of
the Lone Ranger* (1980), *Raise the Titanic* (1980), *On Golden Pond*
(1981), and *Sophie's Choice* (1982).

1 All my shows are great. Some of them are bad.
But they are all great.
The Observer, 'Sayings of the Week', 14 Sept 1975

2 What about it? Do you want to crucify the boy?
Referring to the revelation that an actor portraying Christ on
television was living with a woman to whom he was not married
Attrib.

Grafton, Richard (d. c. 1572) English chronicler and printer.
Printed the *Great Bible* (1539) and *Book of Common Prayer*
(1549). Also compiled two sets of historical chronicles (1562,
1568).

1 Thirty days hath November,
April, June and September,
February hath twenty-eight alone,
And all the rest have thirty-one.
Abridgement of the Chronicles of England, Introduction

Graham, Clementina Stirling (1782–1877) British
writer.

1 The best way to get the better of temptation is
just to yield to it.
Mystifications, 'Soirée at Mrs Russel's'

Graham, Harry (1874–1936) British writer, poet, and
dramatist. Verse collections include *Ruthless Rhymes for Heartless
Homes* (1899).

1 'There's been an accident' they said,
'Your servant's cut in half; he's dead!'
'Indeed!' said Mr Jones, 'and please
Send me the half that's got my keys.'
Ruthless Rhymes for Heartless Homes, 'Mr. Jones'

2 Billy, in one of his nice new sashes,
Fell in the fire and was burnt to ashes;
Now, although the room grows chilly,
I haven't the heart to poke poor Billy.
Ruthless Rhymes for Heartless Homes, 'Tender-Heartedness'

Graham, James, Marquis of Montrose (1612–50)
Scottish general. He fought for Charles I in the Civil War but his
army of highlanders was defeated (1645). He returned from exile
on the continent in 1650 but was captured and executed by the
parliamentarians.

1 Let them bestow on every airth a limb;
Then open all my veins, that I may swim
To thee, my Maker! in that crimson lake;
Then place my parboiled head upon a stake –
Scatter my ashes – strew them in the air; –
Lord! since thou know'st where all these atoms
are,
I'm hopeful thou'lt recover once my dust,
And confident thou'lt raise me with the just.
*Lines written on the Window of his Jail the Night before his
Execution*

Grahame, Kenneth (1859–1932) Scottish writer of
children's books, including *The Wind in the Willows* (1908), which
was later adapted by A. A. Milne as the play *Toad of Toad Hall*
(1929).

1 There is nothing – absolutely nothing – half so
much worth doing as simply messing about in
boats.
The Wind in the Willows, Ch. 1

2 The clever men at Oxford
Know all that there is to be knowed.
But they none of them know one half as much
As intelligent Mr Toad.
The Wind in the Willows, Ch. 10

Grandma Moses (Anna Mary Robertson Moses; 1860–
1961) US primitive painter. A farmer's wife, she took up painting
aged 67 and was entirely self-taught.

1 What a strange thing is memory, and hope; one looks backward, the other forward. The one is of today, the other is the Tomorrow. Memory is history recorded in our brain, memory is a painter, it paints pictures of the past and of the day.

Grandma Moses, My Life's History (ed. Aotto Kallir), Ch. 1

2 If I didn't start painting, I would have raised chickens.

Grandma Moses, My Life's History (ed. Aotto Kallir), Ch. 3

3 I don't advise any one to take it up as a business proposition, unless they really have talent, and are crippled so as to deprive them of physical labor.

Referring to painting
The New York Times 'How Do I Paint?', 11 May 1947

Grant, Cary (Archibald Leach; 1904–86) British-born US film star. Films include *Born to be Bad* (1934), *Topper* (1937), *The Philadelphia Story* (1940), *To Catch a Thief* (1955), and *Indiscreet* (1958).

1 'Old Cary Grant fine. How you?'

Replying to a telegram sent to his agent inquiring: 'How old Cary Grant?'
The Filmgoer's Book of Quotes (Leslie Halliwell)

Grant, Sir Robert (1779–1838) British hymn writer.

1 O worship the King, all glorious above!
O gratefully sing his power and his love!
Our Shield and Defender – the Ancient of Days,
Pavilioned in splendour, and girded with praise.

Hymn

Grant, Ulysses Simpson (1822–85) US general who became a Republican President (1869–77). As supreme commander of the Federal armies he defeated the Confederates.

Quotations about Grant

1 When Grant once gets possession of a place, he holds on to it as if he had inherited it.

Abraham Lincoln (1809–65) US statesman. Letter, 22 June 1864

2 Grant stood by me when I was crazy and I stood by him when he was drunk.

William Sherman (1820–91) US general and president. *Abraham Lincoln: The War Years* (Carl Sandburg)

Quotations by Grant

3 No terms except unconditional and immediate surrender can be accepted. I propose to move immediately upon your works.

Message to opposing commander, Simon Bolivar Buckner, during siege of Fort Donelson, 16 Feb 1862

4 I purpose to fight it out on this line, if it takes all summer.

Dispatch to Washington, 11 May 1864

5 Let us have peace.

On accepting nomination
Letter, 29 May 1868

6 I know no method to secure the repeal of bad or obnoxious laws so effective as their stringent execution.

Inaugural address, 4 Mar 1869

7 Let no guilty man escape, if it can be avoided . . . No personal considerations should stand in the way of performing a public duty.

Referring to the Whiskey Ring
Endorsement of a letter, 29 July 1875

Granville-Barker, Harley (1877–1946) British actor and dramatist. As co-manager of the Royal Court Theatre in London he was responsible for the first productions of several of Shaw's plays. His own plays included *The Madras House* (1910).

1 Rightly thought of there is poetry in peaches . . . even when they are canned.

The Madras House, I

2 But oh, the farmyard world of sex!

The Madras House, IV

3 What is the prose for God?

Waste, I

Graves, John Woodcock (1795–1886) British poet, huntsman, and songwriter, who is best remembered for his song 'D'ye Ken John Peel', about his Cumberland friend of this name, who was master of foxhounds at Caldbeck for nearly 50 years.

1 D'ye ken John Peel with his coat so gay?
D'ye ken John Peel at the break of the day?
D'ye ken John Peel when he's far far away
With his hounds and his horn in the morning?

'Twas the sound of his horn called me from my bed,
And the cry of his hounds has me oft-times led;
For Peel's view-hollo would waken the dead,
Or a fox from his lair in the morning.

John Peel

Graves, Robert (1895–1985) British poet and novelist. His World War I autobiography *Goodbye to All That* (1929) made his name and enabled him to publish several editions of his collected poems. His historical novels included *I Claudius* (1934) and *Claudius the God* (1934).

1 Goodbye to All That.

Book title

2 As for the Freudian, it is a very low, Central European sort of humour.

Occupation: Writer

3 In love as in sport, the amateur status must be strictly maintained.

Occupation: Writer

4 To be a poet is a condition rather than a profession.

Horizon

5 The remarkable thing about Shakespeare is that he is really very good – in spite of all the people who say he is very good.

The Observer, 'Sayings of the Week', 6 Dec 1964

Gray, Thomas (1716–71) British poet. He published several odes but is best known for his *Elegy Written in a Country Churchyard* (1751), written at Stoke Poges in Buckinghamshire.

1 The Curfew tolls the knell of parting day,
The lowing herd winds slowly o'er the lea,
The plowman homeward plods his weary way,
And leaves the world to darkness and to me.
Elegy Written in a Country Churchyard

2 Let not Ambition mock their useful toil,
Their homely joys, and destiny obscure;
Nor Grandeur hear with a disdainful smile,
The short and simple annals of the poor.
Elegy Written in a Country Churchyard

3 The boast of heraldry, the pomp of pow'r,
And all that beauty, all that wealth e'er gave,
Awaits alike th' inevitable hour,
The paths of glory lead but to the grave.
Elegy Written in a Country Churchyard

4 Can storied urn or animated bust
Back to its mansion call the fleeting breath?
Can honour's voice provoke the silent dust,
Or flatt'ry soothe the dull cold ear of death?
Elegy Written in a Country Churchyard

5 Full many a gem of purest ray serene,
The dark unfathom'd caves of ocean bear:
Full many a flower is born to blush unseen,
And waste its sweetness on the desert air.
Elegy Written in a Country Churchyard

6 Some village-Hampden, that with dauntless breast
The little Tyrant of his fields withstood;
Some mute inglorious Milton here may rest,
Some Cromwell guiltless of his country's blood.
Elegy Written in a Country Churchyard

7 Far from the madding crowd's ignoble strife,
Their sober wishes never learn'd to stray;
Along the cool sequester'd vale of life
They kept the noiseless tenor of their way.
Elegy Written in a Country Churchyard

8 Here rests his head upon the lap of Earth
A youth to fortune and to fame unknown.
Fair Science frown'd not on his humble birth,
And Melancholy mark'd him for her own.
Elegy Written in a Country Churchyard

9 Alas, regardless of their doom,
The little victims play!
Ode on a Distant Prospect of Eton College

10 To each his suff'rings, all are men,
Condemn'd alike to groan;
The tender for another's pain,
Th' unfeeling for his own.
Yet ah! why should they know their fate?
Since sorrow never comes too late,
And happiness too swiftly flies.
Thought would destroy their paradise.
No more; where ignorance is bliss,
'Tis folly to be wise.
Ode on a Distant Prospect of Eton College

11 What female heart can gold despise?
What cat's averse to fish?
Ode on the Death of a Favourite Cat

12 A fav'rite has no friend.
Ode on the Death of a Favourite Cat

13 Not all that tempts your wand'ring eyes
And heedless hearts, is lawful prize;
Nor all, that glisters, gold.
Ode on the Death of a Favourite Cat

Greeley, Horace (1811–72) US politician and journalist. He founded the *New Yorker* (1834) and the *Tribune* (1841). He later became an unsuccessful presidential candidate.

1 Go West, young man, and grow up with the country.
Hints toward Reform

Greene, Graham (1904–) British novelist. After the success of *The Man Within* (1929), he subsequently published *Brighton Rock* (1938), *The Power and the Glory* (1940), *The Heart of the Matter* (1948), *The Human Factor* (1978), *Monsignor Quixote* (1982), *The Captain and the Enemy* (1988), and others. His 'entertainments' (literary thrillers) include *The Third Man* (1950) and *Our Man in Havana* (1958).

1 Those who marry God . . . can become domesticated too – it's just as humdrum a marriage as all the others.
A Burnt-Out Case, Ch. 1

2 I have often noticed that a bribe . . . has that effect – it changes a relation. The man who offers a bribe gives away a little of his own importance; the bribe once accepted, he becomes the inferior, like a man who has paid for a woman.
The Comedians, Pt. I, Ch. 4

3 Catholics and Communists have committed great crimes, but at least they have not stood aside, like an established society, and been indifferent. I would rather have blood on my hands than water like Pilate.
The Comedians, Pt. III, Ch. 4

4 He gave the impression that very many cities had rubbed him smooth.
A Gun for Sale, Ch. 4

5 Against the beautiful and the clever and the successful, one can wage a pitiless war, but not against the unattractive.
The Heart of the Matter

6 They had been corrupted by money, and he had been corrupted by sentiment. Sentiment was the more dangerous, because you couldn't name its price. A man open to bribes was to be relied upon below a certain figure, but sentiment might uncoil in the heart at a name, a photograph, even a smell remembered.
The Heart of the Matter

7 That whisky priest, I wish we had never had him in the house.
The Power and the Glory, Pt. I

8 Of course, before we *know* he is a saint, there will have to be miracles.
The Power and the Glory, Pt. IV

9 Perhaps if I wanted to be understood or to understand I would bamboozle myself into belief, but I am a reporter; God exists only for leader-writers.
The Quiet American

10 Fame is a powerful aphrodisiac.
Radio Times, 10 Sept 1964

Greer, Germaine (1939–) Australian-born British writer and feminist. She made her reputation with *The Female Eunuch* (1970). Subsequent books include *Sex and Destiny* (1984).

1 Probably the only place where a man can feel really secure is in a maximum security prison, except for the imminent threat of release.
The Female Eunuch

2 Mother is the dead heart of the family, spending father's earnings on consumer goods to enhance the environment in which he eats, sleeps and watches the television.
The Female Eunuch

3 Love, love, love – all the wretched cant of it, masking egotism, lust, masochism, fantasy under a mythology of sentimental postures, a welter of self-induced miseries and joys, blinding and masking the essential personalities in the frozen gestures of courtship, in the kissing and the dating and the desire, the compliments and the quarrels which vivify its barrenness.
The Female Eunuch

Gregory I (540–604) Pope and saint. He sponsored Augustine's mission to England and introduced the Gregorian plainchant into the Catholic liturgy.

1 *Non Angli sed Angeli*
Not Angles, but angels.
Attrib.

Grellet, Stephen (1773–1855) French-born US missionary, who was responsible for many prison and almshouse reforms.

1 I expect to pass through this world but once; any good thing therefore that I can do, or any kindness that I can show to any fellow-creature, let me do it now; let me not defer or neglect it, for I shall not pass this way again.
Attrib.
Treasure Trove (John o'London)

Greville, Fulke, Baron Brooke (1554–1628) English poet and politician, who was chancellor of the exchequer (1614–22). His sonnets *Caelica* (1633) and biography *The Life of the Renowned Sir Philip Sidney* (1652) were widely read.

1 Oh wearisome condition of humanity!
Born under one law, to another bound.
Mustapha, V:6

Grey, Edward, Viscount (1862–1933) British statesman. He was Liberal foreign secretary (1905–16).

1 The United States is like a gigantic boiler. Once the fire is lighted under it there is no limit to the power it can generate.
Their Finest Hour (Winston S. Churchill), Ch. 32

2 The lamps are going out over all Europe; we shall not see them lit again in our lifetime.
Remark made on 3 Aug 1914, the eve of World War I

Griffith-Jones, Mervyn (1909–78) British lawyer. A prosecuting counsel at the Nuremberg War Trials (1945–46), he became a counsel to the Crown and later Common Serjeant in the City of London.

1 Would you allow your wife or your servant to read this book?
As counsel for the prosecution in the *Lady Chatterley's Lover* trial

2 It is a perfectly ordinary little case of a man charged with indecency with four or five guardsmen.
Attrib. in *This England* (Michael Bateman)

Grimké, Angelina (1805–79) US writer, abolitionist, and reformer.

1 I know you do not make the laws but I also know that you are the wives and mothers, the sisters and daughters of those who do . . .
The Anti-Slavery Examiner (Sep 1836), 'Appeal to the Christian Women of the South'

Gromyko, Andrei (1909–89) Soviet politician. He was ambassador to the US (1943–46), to the UK (1952–53), and Soviet representative to the UN (1946–49). He became foreign minister in 1957 and remained so until 1985, when he became president. He was replaced by Mikhail Gorbachov in 1988.

1 This man has a nice smile, but he has got iron teeth.
In proposing Mikhail Gorbachov for the post of Soviet Communist Party leader
Speech, 1985

Grossmith, George (1847–1912) British singer and comedian. With his brother Walter Weedon Grossmith (1854–1919) he wrote the highly successful *Diary of a Nobody* (1892).

1 What's the good of a home, if you are never in it?
The Diary of a Nobody, Ch. 1

Grossmith the Younger, George (1874–1935) British singer, actor, and songwriter. The son of George Grossmith, he appeared in many musical comedies and a few films.

1 If you were the only girl in the world,
And I were the only boy.
The Bing Boys, 'If you were the Only Girl' (with Fred Thompson; 1884–1949)

Guedalla, Philip (1889–1944) British writer. His books include *The Second Empire* (1922), *Conquistador* (1927), and *Argentine Tango* (1932).

1 The work of Henry James has always seemed divisible by a simple dynastic arrangement into three reigns: James I, James II, and the Old Pretender.
Collected Essays, 'Men of Letters: Mr. Henry James'

2 The little ships, the unforgotten Homeric catalogue of *Mary Jane* and *Peggy IV*, of *Folkestone Belle, Boy Billy*, and *Ethel Maud*, of *Lady Haig* and *Skylark* . . . the little ships of England brought the Army home.

Referring to the evacuation of Dunkirk
Mr. Churchill

3 Any stigma will do to beat a dogma.

Attrib.

4 History repeats itself; historians repeat each other.

Attrib.

Guevara, Che (Ernesto Guevara; 1928–67) Argentine revolutionary. Originally trained as a doctor, he became one of Castro's chief lieutenants after the invasion of Cuba in 1956. He was captured and killed by government troops in 1967 while trying to create a revolution in Bolivia.

1 I believe in the armed struggle as the only solution for those people who fight to free themselves, and I am consistent with my beliefs. Many will call me an adventurer – and that I am, only one of a different sort: one of those who risks his skin to prove his platitudes.

On leaving Cuba to join guerrillas in the Bolivian jungle
Last letter to his parents, 1965

Guitry, Sacha (1885–1957) French actor and dramatist. He wrote several light comedies and appeared in numerous films, including *Napoléon* (1955).

1 The others were only my wives. But you, my dear, will be my widow.

Allaying his fifth wife's jealousy of his previous wives
Speaker's and Toastmaster's Handbook (J. Brawle)

Gulbenkian, Nubar (1896–1972) Turkish oil magnate.

1 The best number for a dinner party is two – myself and a dam' good head waiter.

Attrib.

Gurney, Dorothy (1858–1932) British poet.

1 The kiss of sun for pardon,
The song of the birds for mirth –
One is nearer God's Heart in a garden
Than anywhere else on earth.
The Lord God Planted a Garden

Guthrie, Woody (Woodrow Wilson Guthrie; 1912–67) US folksinger and songwriter. His songs protesting against the social injustice of the Depression include 'The Old Grand Cooley Dan' and 'This Land is Your Land'.

1 They called me everything from a rambling honky-tonk hitter to a waterlogged harmonica player. One paper down in Kentucky said what us Okies needed next to three good square meals a day was some good music lessons.
Music on My Beat: An Intimate Volume of Shop Talk (Howard Taubman)

2 When Oklahoma talks to New York, New York hadn't ought to get restless and nervous, and when Chicago says something to Arizona, that ought not to cause trouble. I ain't mad at nobody that don't get mad at me. Looks like whatever you try to do, somebody jumps up and hollers and raises cain – then the feller next to him jumps up and hollers how much he likes it.
Music on My Beat: An Intimate Volume of Shop Talk (Howard Taubman)

3 This land is your land this land is my land,
From California to New York Island,
From the redwood forest to the Gulfstream waters,
This land was made for you and me.
This Land Is Your Land

Gwyn, Nell (1650–87) English actress. Originally an orange seller in Drury Lane, she became the mistress of Charles II.

1 Pray, good people, be civil. I am the Protestant whore.

On being surrounded in her coach by an angry mob in Oxford at the time of the Popish Terror
Nell Gwyn (Bevan), Ch. 13

H

Haggard, Sir Henry Rider (1856–1925) British novelist. *King Solomon's Mines* (1885) was his best-known work. His later books include *She* (1887).

1 She-who-must-be-obeyed.
She

Haig, Douglas, Earl (1861–1928) British general. He commanded the British Expeditionary Force in World War I; under Foch, he directed the assault on the Hindenberg Line.

1 Every position must be held to the last man: there must be no retirement. With our backs to the wall, and believing in the justice of our cause, each one of us must fight on to the end.
Order to the British Army, 12 Apr 1918

Haile Selassie (1892–1975) Emperor of Ethiopia (1930–36; 1941–74). After the Italian invasion (1936) he fled to Britain, but returned in 1941 with the authority of the Allies. He was deposed by a military coup and died shortly afterwards.

1 We have finished the job, what shall we do with the tools?

Telegram sent to Winston Churchill, mimicking his 'Give us the tools, and we will finish the job'
Ambrosia and Small Beer, Ch. 4 (Edward Marsh)

Hailsham, Quintin Hogg, Baron (1907–) British Conservative politician. He relinquished his hereditary peerage to contest (1963), unsuccessfully, the leadership of the Conservative party. He became lord chancellor (1970–74; 1979–87).

1 Some of the worst men in the world are sincere and the more sincere they are the worse they are.
The Observer, 'Sayings of the Week', 7 Jan 1968

2 You ought not to be ashamed of being bored. What you ought to be ashamed of is being boring.
The Observer, 'Sayings of the Week', 12 Oct 1975

3 A great party is not to be brought down because of a scandal by a woman of easy virtue and a proved liar.
Referring to the Profumo affair, in BBC interview, 13 June 1963
The Pendulum Years, Ch. 3 (Bernard Levin)

4 If the British public falls for this, I say it will be stark, staring bonkers.
Referring to Labour policy in the 1964 general-election campaign
Press conference, Conservative Central Office, 12 Oct 1964

Haldane, J(ohn) B(urdon) S(anderson) (1892–1964) British geneticist. A Marxist, he edited the *Daily Worker* in the 1930s. In 1957 he emigrated to India. His books include *Science and Ethics* (1928), *The Inequality of Man* (1932), and *Science and Everyday Life* (1939).

1 Einstein – the greatest Jew since Jesus. I have no doubt that Einstein's name will still be remembered and revered when Lloyd George, Foch and William Hohenzollern share with Charlie Chaplin that ineluctable oblivion which awaits the uncreative mind.
Daedalus or Science and the Future

2 Shelley and Keats were the last English poets who were at all up to date in their chemical knowledge.
Daedalus or Science and the Future

3 If human beings could be propagated by cutting, like apple trees, aristocracy would be biologically sound.
The Inequality of Man, title essay

4 My own suspicion is that the universe is not only queerer than we suppose, but queerer than we *can* suppose.
Possible Worlds, 'On Being the Right Size'

5 An inordinate fondness for beetles.
Reply when asked what inferences could be drawn about the nature of God from a study of his works
Reader's Digest, Feb 1979

Hale, Edward Everett (1822–1909) US author and clergyman. His books include *A New England Boyhood* (1893).

1 'Do you pray for the senators, Dr Hale?' 'No, I look at the senators and I pray for the country.'
New England Indian Summer (Van Wyck Brooks)

Hale, Sir Matthew (1609–76) English judge. He became lord chief justice (1671); his *History of the Common Law of England* (1713) was an important reference work.

1 Christianity is part of the Common Law of England.
Historia Placitorum Coronae (ed. Sollom Emlyn)

Hale, Nathan (1755–76) US revolutionary hero. Captured by the British as a spy, he was subsequently hanged.

1 I only regret that I have but one life to lose for my country.
Speech before his execution, 22 Sept 1776

Hale, Sarah Josepha (1788–1879) US writer and editor. Her books include *Poems for our Children* (1830).

1 Mary had a little lamb,
Its fleece was white as snow,
And everywhere that Mary went
The lamb was sure to go.
Poems for Our Children, 'Mary's Little Lamb'

Halifax, George Saville, Marquis of (1633–95) English statesman. Dismissed from offices he had held by James II, he supported the Glorious Revolution.

1 Men are not hanged for stealing horses, but that horses may not be stolen.
Political, Moral and Miscellaneous Thoughts and Reflections

2 It is a general mistake to think the men we like are good for everything, and those we do not, good for nothing.
Political, Moral and Miscellaneous Thoughts and Reflections

3 It is flattering some men to endure them.
Political, Moral and Miscellaneous Thoughts and Reflections

4 Our virtues and vices couple with one another, and get children that resemble both their parents.
Political, Moral and Miscellaneous Thoughts and Reflections

5 Popularity is a crime from the moment it is sought; it is only a virtue where men have it whether they will or no.
Political, Moral and Miscellaneous Thoughts and Reflections

6 When the People contend for their Liberty, they seldom get anything by their Victory but new masters.
Political, Moral and Miscellaneous Thoughts and Reflections

7 Power is so apt to be insolent and Liberty to be saucy, that they are seldom upon good Terms.
Political, Moral and Miscellaneous Thoughts and Reflections

8 Most men make little use of their speech than to give evidence against their own understanding.
Political, Moral and Miscellaneous Thoughts and Reflections

9 He had said he had known many kicked down stairs, but he never knew any kicked up stairs before.
Original Memoirs (Burnet)

Hall, Charles Sprague (19th century) US songwriter.

1 John Brown's body lies a-mouldering in the grave,
His soul is marching on!
The song commemorates the American hero who died in the cause of abolishing slavery
John Brown's Body

Halsey, Margaret (1910–) US writer.

1 . . . it takes a great deal to produce ennui in an Englishman and if you do, he only takes it as convincing proof that you are well-bred.
With Malice Toward Some

2 The attitude of the English . . . toward English history reminds one a good deal of the attitude of a Hollywood director toward love.
With Malice Toward Some

3 Living in England, provincial England, must be like being married to a stupid but exquisitely beautiful wife.
With Malice Toward Some

4 . . . the English think of an opinion as something which a decent person, if he has the misfortune to have one, does all he can to hide.
With Malice Toward Some

5 All of Stratford, in fact, suggests powdered history – add hot water and stir and you have a delicious, nourishing Shakespeare.
With Malice Toward Some

Hamilton, Sir William (1788–1856) Scottish philosopher. His books include edited lectures on metaphysics and logic.

1 Truth, like a torch, the more it's shook it shines.
Discussions on Philosophy, title page

2 On earth there is nothing great but man; in man there is nothing great but mind.
Lectures on Metaphysics

Hamilton, William (Willie) Winter (1917–) Scottish MP and Labour politician. An active antimonarchist, his publications include *My Queen and I* (1975).

1 The tourists who come to our island take in the Monarchy along with feeding the pigeons in Trafalgar Square.
My Queen and I, Ch. 9

2 Britain is not a country that is easily rocked by revolution . . . In Britain our institutions evolve. We are a Fabian Society writ large.
My Queen and I, Ch. 9

Hammarskjöld, Dag (1905–61) Swedish diplomat, who became secretary general of the UN. He was killed in a plane crash. His diaries, *Markings*, were published in 1964.

1 Pray that your loneliness may spur you into finding something to live for, great enough to die for.
Diaries, 1951

Hammerstein, Oscar (1895–1960) US lyricist and librettist. With Richard Rogers he wrote many successful musicals, including *Oklahoma* (1943), *South Pacific* (1949), and *The Sound of Music* (1959).

1 Hello, Young Lovers, Wherever You Are.
From the musical *The King and I*
Song title

2 I Whistle a Happy Tune.
From the musical *The King and I*
Song title

3 Oh, what a beautiful morning!
Oh, what a beautiful day!
From the musical *Oklahoma*
Oh, What a Beautiful Morning

4 Ol' man river, dat ol' man river,
He must know sumpin', but don't say nothin',
He just keeps rollin', he keeps on rollin' along.
From the musical *Show Boat*
Ol' Man River

5 The hills are alive with the sound of music
With the songs they have sung
For a thousand years.
The Sound of Music, title song

Hampton, Christopher (1946–) British writer and dramatist. Plays include *The Philanthropist* (1970), *Savages* (1973), *Treats* (1976), and *Les Liaisons Dangereuses* (1985).

1 You know very well that unless you're a scientist, it's much more important for a theory to be shapely, than for it to be true.
The Philanthropist, Sc. 1

2 You see, I always divide people into two groups. Those who live by what they know to be a lie, and those who live by what they believe, falsely, to be the truth.
The Philanthropist, Sc. 6

3 If I had to give a definition of capitalism I would say: the process whereby American girls turn into American women.
Savages, Sc. 16

4 It's possible to disagree with someone about the ethics of non-violence without wanting to kick his face in.
Treats, Sc. 4

5 Asking a working writer what he thinks about critics is like asking a lamp-post how it feels about dogs.
The Sunday Times Magazine, 16 Oct 1977

Hancock, John (1737–93) US revolutionary. President of congress (1775–77), and the first to sign the Declaration of Independence, he became governor of Massachusetts (1780–85; 1787–93).

1 There, I guess King George will be able to read that.
Referring to his signature, written in a bold hand, on the US Declaration of Independence.
The American Treasury (C. Fadiman)

Hankey, Katherine (1834–1911) British hymn writer.

1 Tell me the old, old story
Of unseen things above,
Of Jesus and His glory
Of Jesus and His love.
Tell Me the Old, Old Story

Hanrahan, Brian (1949–) British television journalist.

1 I'm not allowed to say how many planes joined the raid but I counted them all out and I counted them all back.

Reporting a British air attack in the opening phase of the Falklands War
BBC broadcast, 1 May 1982

Harback, Otto (1873–1963) US dramatist and librettist. His musical comedies included *Girl of My Dreams* (1910), *No! No! Nannette* (with Frank Mandel; 1924), and *The Desert Song* (1926).

1 Tea for Two, and Two for Tea.

From the musical *No! No! Nanette*
Song title

Harbord, James Guthrie (1866–1947) US general. He rose from the ranks to become chief of staff of the American Expeditionary Force in France during World War I.

1 I met the great little man, the man who can be silent in several languages.

Referring to Colonel House
Mr Wilson's War (John Dos Passos), Ch. 3

Harburg, E(dgar) Y(ip) (1896–1981) US songwriter.

1 It's only a paper moon,
Sailing over a cardboard sea,
But it wouldn't be make-believe
If you believed in me.

The Great Magoo, 'It's Only a Paper Moon'

2 Once I built a rail-road,
Now it's done.
Brother, can you spare a dime?

Often quoted as 'Buddy can you spare a dime'
New Americana, 'Brother Can You Spare a Dime'

3 Someday I'll wish upon a star.

From the musical *The Wizard of Oz*
Over the Rainbow

4 Somewhere over the rainbow,
Way up high:
There's a land that I heard of
Once in a lullaby.

From the musical *The Wizard of Oz*
Over the Rainbow

Harcourt, Sir William (1827–1904) British statesman. He was home secretary (1880–85) and later chancellor of the exchequer (1886; 1892–95).

1 We are all Socialists now.

Attrib.

Harding, Gilbert (1907–60) British broadcaster.

1 If, sir, I possessed the power of conveying unlimited sexual attraction through the potency of my voice, I would not be reduced to accepting a miserable pittance from the BBC for interviewing a faded female in a damp basement.

Said to Mae West's manager, who suggested that he should be more 'sexy' when interviewing her
Gilbert Harding by His Friends

Hardwicke, Philip Yorke, Earl of (1690–1764) English judge. He became attorney general (1724) and lord chancellor (1737).

1 His doubts are better than most people's certainties.

Referring to Dirleton's *Doubts*
Life of Johnson (J. Boswell)

Hardy, Thomas (1840–1928) British novelist and poet. His novels include *The Mayor of Casterbridge* (1886), *Tess of the D'Urbervilles* (1891), and *Jude the Obscure* (1895). His poetry was collected in *Wessex Poems* (1898) and he wrote an epic drama *The Dynasts* (1903–08).

Quotations about Hardy

1 Hardy became a sort of village atheist brooding and blaspheming over the village idiot.

G. K. Chesterton (1874–1936) British writer. *The Victorian Age in Literature*

2 The work of Thomas Hardy represents an interesting example of a powerful personality uncurbed by any institutional attachment or by submission to any objective beliefs . . . He seems to me to have written as nearly for the sake of 'self-expression' as a man well can; and the self which he had to express does not strike me as a particularly wholesome or edifying matter of communication.

T. S. Eliot (1888–1965) US-born British poet and dramatist. *After Strange Gods*

3 What a commonplace genius he has; or a genius for the commonplace, I don't know which. He doesn't rank so terribly high, really. But better than Bernard Shaw, even then.

D. H. Lawrence (1885–1930) British novelist. Letter to Martin Secker, 24 July 1928

4 No one has written worse English than Mr Hardy in some of his novels – cumbrous, stilted, ugly, and inexpressive – yes, but at the same time so strangely expressive of something attractive to us in Mr Hardy himself that we would not change it for the perfection of Sterne at his best. It becomes coloured by its surroundings; it becomes literature.

Virginia Woolf (1882–1941) British novelist. *The Moment*

Quotations by Hardy

5 A local cult called Christianity.

The Dynasts, I:6

6 My argument is that War makes rattling good history; but Peace is poor reading.

The Dynasts, II:5

7 A lover without indiscretion is no lover at all.

The Hand of Ethelberta, Ch. 20

8 Life's Little Ironies.

Title of book of stories

9 Dialect words – those terrible marks of the beast to the truly genteel.

The Mayor of Casterbridge, Ch. 20

10 Good, but not religious-good.

Under the Greenwood Tree, Ch. 2

11 That man's silence is wonderful to listen to.

Under the Greenwood Tree, Ch. 14

12 This is the weather the cuckoo likes,
And so do I;
When showers betumble the chestnut spikes,
And nestlings fly:
And the little brown nightingale bills his best,
And they sit outside at 'The Travellers' Rest'.

Weathers

13 This is the weather the shepherd shuns,
And so do I.

Weathers

14 If Galileo had said in verse that the world
moved, the Inquisition might have let him alone.

The Later Years of Thomas Hardy (F. E. Hardy)

Hargreaves, W. F. (1846–1919) British songwriter.

1 I'm Burlington Bertie:
I rise at ten-thirty.

Burlington Bertie

2 I walk down the Strand
With my gloves on my hand,
And I walk down again
With them off.

Burlington Bertie

Harington, Sir John (1561–1612) English writer. He
translated Ariosto's *Orlando Furioso* and his own collected
epigrams were published in 1618.

1 Treason doth never prosper: what's the reason?
For if it prosper, none dare call it treason.

Epigrams, 'Of Treason'

Harlow, Jean (Harlean Carpentier; 1911–37) US film actress.
Known as the 'Blonde Bombshell', she appeared in such films as
Platinum Blonde (1931), and *Bombshell* (1933) before her career
was cut short when she died from kidney failure, while making
Saratoga.

1 Would you be shocked if I put on something
more comfortable?

Hell's Angels

Harold II (c.1022–66) King of England (1066). He claimed to
have been designated heir to the throne by the childless Edward
the Confessor but was killed at the Battle of Hastings, when the
future William the Conqueror invaded.

1 He will give him seven feet of English ground, or
as much more as he may be taller than other
men.

Offer to Harald Hardraade, King of Norway, who invaded England immediately before William the Conqueror (1066)

Heimskringla (Snorri Sturluson)

Harris, George (1844–1922) US congressman; president of
Amherst college (1899–1912).

1 I intended to give you some advice but now I
remember how much is left over from last year
unused.

Said when addressing students at the start of a new academic
year

Braude's Second Encyclopedia (J. Braude)

Hart, Lorenz (1895–1943) US songwriter. He wrote the
lyrics for many musicals, including *Babes in Arms* (1937) and *The
Boys from Syracuse* (1938), for which Richard Rogers wrote the
music.

1 Bewitched, Bothered and Bewildered.

From the musical *Babes in Arms*
Song title

2 That's Why the Lady Is a Tramp.

From the musical *Babes in Arms*
Song title

Hartley, L(esley) P(oles) (1895–1972) British novelist.
His early trilogy, starting with *The Shrimp and the Anemone*
(1944), established his reputation. Later books include *The Boat*
(1949) and *The Go-Between* (1953).

1 Uniformity isn't bad, as some people still think,
because if the quality is good, it satisfies. People are never happy who want change.

Facial Justice, Ch. 13

2 The past is a foreign country: they do things differently there.

The Go-Between

Haskell, Arnold (1903–80) English writer on ballet.

1 Unlike so many who find success, she remained
a 'dinkum hard-swearing Aussie' to the end.

Referring to Dame Nellie Melba
Waltzing Matilda

Haskins, Minnie Louise (1875–1957) US writer.

1 And I said to the man who stood at the gate of
the year: 'Give me a light that I may tread safely into the unknown'. And he replied: 'Go out
into the darkness and put your hand into the
hand of God. That shall be to you better than
light and safer than a known way.'

Remembered because it was quoted by George VI in his Christmas broadcast, 1939
The Desert, Introduction

Hastings, Lady Flora (1806–39) British poet.

1 Grieve not that I die young. Is it not well
To pass away ere life hath lost its brightness?

Swan Song

Haughey, Charles (1925–) Irish statesman. He was
prime minister of Ireland (1979–81; 1982; and 1987–). He
became president of the Fianna Fail party in 1979.

1 It seems that the historic inability in Britain to
comprehend Irish feelings and sensitivities still
remains.

Speech, Feb 1988

Haw-Haw, Lord (William Joyce; 1906–46) Radio broadcaster of Nazi propaganda from Germany throughout World War II. Born in the USA of Irish parents, he was tried and executed for treason after the war.

1 Germany calling, Germany calling.
Radio broadcasts to Britain, during World War II

Hawker, R(obert) S(tephen) (1803–75) British poet. An Anglican clergyman, he later became a Roman Catholic priest. His verse collections include *Cornish Ballads and Other Poems* (1864).

1 And have they fixed the where and when?
And shall Trelawny die?
Here's twenty thousand Cornish men
Will know the reason why!
Referring to the imprisonment (1688) of Trelawny, Bishop of Bristol, by James II
Song of the Western Men

Hawthorne, Nathaniel (1804–64) US novelist and writer. His best-known novels, *The Scarlet Letter* (1850) and *The House of Seven Gables* (1851), were followed by a period in England as US consul in Liverpool, after which he lived in Italy.

1 We sometimes congratulate ourselves at the moment of waking from a troubled dream; it may be so the moment after death.
American Notebooks

2 Dr Johnson's morality was as English an article as a beefsteak.
Our Old Home, 'Lichfield and Uttoxeter'

Hay, Lord Charles (d. 1760) British soldier.

1 Gentlemen of the French Guard, fire first!
Said at the Battle of Fontenoy, 1745
Attrib.

Hay, Ian (John Hay Beith; 1876–1952) British novelist and dramatist. His novels include *Pip* (1907), *The Last Million* (1918), and *Paid, With Thanks* (1925). He also wrote the successful play *The Housemaster* (1930).

1 Funny peculiar, or funny ha-ha?
The Housemaster, III

Hay, Will (1888–1949) British comedian. After years in the music halls, he made a number of films, including *Oh, Mr Porter!* (1937).

1 MASTER. They split the atom by firing particles at it, at 5,500 miles a second.
BOY. Good heavens. And they only split it?
The Fourth Form at St Michael's

Hayes, J. Milton (1884–1940) British writer.

1 There's a one-eyed yellow idol to the north of Khatmandu,
There's a little marble cross below the town;
There's a broken-hearted woman tends the grave of Mad Carew
And the Yellow God forever gazes down.
The Green Eye of the Yellow God

Hazlitt, William (1778–1830) British essayist and journalist. His collections of writings include *Lectures on the English Poets* (1818) and *The Spirit of the Age* (1825).

Quotations about Hazlitt

1 He is your only good damner, and if I am ever damned I should like to be damned by him.
John Keats (1795–1821) British poet. Attrib.

2 He is not a proper person to be admitted into respectable society, being the most perverse and malevolent creature that ill-luck has thrown my way.
William Wordsworth (1770–1850) British poet. Letter to B. R. Haydon, Apr 1817

Quotations by Hazlitt

3 The least pain in our little finger gives us more concern and uneasiness than the destruction of millions of our fellow-beings.
American Literature, 'Dr Channing'

4 If the world were good for nothing else, it is a fine subject for speculation.
Characteristics

5 Man is an intellectual animal, and therefore an everlasting contradiction to himself. His senses centre in himself, his ideas reach to the ends of the universe; so that he is torn in pieces between the two, without a possibility of its ever being otherwise.
Characteristics

6 His sayings are generally like women's letters; all the pith is in the postscript.
Referring to Charles Lamb
Conversations of Northcote

7 He writes as fast as they can read, and he does not write himself down.
English Literature, Ch. XIV, 'Sir Walter Scott'

8 His worst is better than any other person's best.
English Literature, Ch. XIV, 'Sir Walter Scott'

9 So have I loitered my life away, reading books, looking at pictures, going to plays, hearing, thinking, writing on what pleased me best. I have wanted only one thing to make me happy, but wanting that have wanted everything.
English Literature, Ch. XVII, 'My First Acquaintance with Poets'

10 You will hear more good things on the outside of a stagecoach from London to Oxford than if you were to pass a twelvemonth with the undergraduates, or heads of colleges, of that famous university.
The Ignorance of the Learned

11 He talked on for ever; and you wished him to talk on for ever.
Referring to Coleridge
Lectures on the English Poets, Lecture VIII, 'On the Living Poets'

12 A nickname is the heaviest stone that the devil can throw at a man.
Nicknames

13 There is nothing good to be had in the country, or, if there is, they will not let you have it.
Observations on Wordsworth's 'Excursion'

14 The greatest offence against virtue is to speak ill of it.
On Cant and Hypocrisy

15 Those who make their dress a principal part of themselves, will, in general, become of no more value than their dress.
On the Clerical Character

16 The English (it must be owned) are rather a foul-mouthed nation
On Criticism

17 We can scarcely hate any one that we know.
On Criticism

18 There is an unseemly exposure of the mind, as well as of the body.
On Disagreeable People

19 No young man believes he shall ever die.
On the Feeling of Immortality in Youth

20 One of the pleasantest things in the world is going on a journey; but I like to go by myself.
On Going a Journey

21 When I am in the country I wish to vegetate like the country.
On Going a Journey

22 To great evils we submit; we resent little provocations.
On Great and Little Things

23 There is not a more mean, stupid, dastardly, pitiful, selfish, spiteful, envious, ungrateful animal than the public. It is the greatest of cowards, for it is afraid of itself.
On Living to Oneself

24 The art of pleasing consists in being pleased.
On Manner

25 A person may be indebted for a nose or an eye, for a graceful carriage or a voluble discourse, to a great-aunt or uncle, whose existence he has scarcely heard of.
On Personal Character

26 The dupe of friendship, and the fool of love; have I not reason to hate and to despise myself? Indeed I do; and chiefly for not having hated and despised the world enough.
On the Pleasure of Hating

27 We never do anything well till we cease to think about the manner of doing it.
On Prejudice

28 The most fluent talkers or most plausible reasoners are not always the justest thinkers.
On Prejudice

29 Rules and models destroy genius and art.
On Taste

30 The love of liberty is the love of others; the love of power is the love of ourselves.
The Times, 1819

31 Spleen can subsist on any kind of food.
On Wit and Humour

32 Well, I've had a happy life.
Last words

Healey, Denis Winston (1917–) British Labour politician. He became chancellor of the exchequer (1974–79) and was deputy leader of the Labour Party (1981–83). His books include *The Curtain Falls* (1951), *Labour Britain and the World* (1963), and *Healey's Eye* (1980).

1 Like being savaged by a dead sheep.
Referring to the attack launched by Geoffrey Howe upon his Budget proposals
The Listener, 21 Dec 1978

2 Their Europeanism is nothing but imperialism with an inferiority complex.
Referring to the policies of the Conservative party
The Observer, 'Sayings of the Week', 7 Oct 1962

3 I am the Gromyko of the Labour party.
Alluding to Andrei Gromyko (1909–), Soviet statesman who was foreign minister from 1957 to 1985
Attrib.

Hearst, William Randolph (1863–1951) US newspaper owner, who built up the vast newspaper empire that inspired Orson Welles' film *Citizen Kane* (1941).

1 Stop running those dogs on your page. I wouldn't have them peeing on my cheapest rug.
Referring to the publication of Thurber's drawings by one of his editors
The Years with Ross (James Thurber)

Heath, Edward (1916–) British statesman. He was Conservative prime minister (1970–74) when the UK joined the EEC. After losing two elections in 1975 he resigned the party leadership and was succeeded by Margaret Thatcher.

1 We may be a small island, but we are not a small people.
The Observer, 'Sayings of the Week', 21 June 1970

2 It is the unpleasant and unacceptable face of capitalism but one should not suggest that the whole of British industry consists of practices of this kind.
Referring to the Lonrho Affair
Speech, House of Commons, 15 May 1973

Heber, Reginald (1783–1826) British bishop and hymn writer.

1 From Greenland's icy mountains,
From India's coral strand,
Where Afric's sunny fountains
Roll down their golden sand.
From Greenland's Icy Mountains

2 What though the spicy breezes
Blow soft o'er Ceylon's isle;
Though every prospect pleases,
And only man is vile . . .
From Greenland's Icy Mountains

3 Holy, holy, holy, Lord God Almighty!
Early in the morning our song shall rise to thee.
Holy, Holy, Holy

Hegel, Georg Wilhelm Friedrich (1770–1831) German
philosopher. His works include *The Phenomenology of Mind* (1807)
and the *Encyclopedia of the Philosophical Sciences* (1817).

1 What experience and history teach is this – that
people and governments never have learned
anything from history, or acted on principles de-
duced from it.
Philosophy of History, Introduction

2 Only one man ever understood me. . . . And he
didn't understand me.
Said on his deathbed
Famous Last Words (B. Conrad)

Heifetz, Jascha (1901–87) Russian-born US violinist.

1 If the Almighty himself played the violin, the
credits would still read 'Rubinstein, God, and
Piatigorsky', in that order.
Whenever Heifitz played in trios with Arthur Rubinstein (piano)
and Gregor Piatigorsky (cello), Rubinstein always got top
billing
Los Angeles Times, 29 Aug 1982

Heine, Heinrich (1797–1856) German poet and writer. His
early collection *Buch der Lieder* (1827) preceded his move to Paris
(1831), where he remained until his death.

1 Whenever books are burned men also in the end
are burned.
Almansor

2 Sleep is good, death is better; but of course, the
best thing would be never to have been born at
all.
Morphine

3 I just met X in the street, I stopped for a moment to exchange ideas, and now I feel like a
complete idiot.
Autant en apportent les mots (Pedrazzini)

4 It is extremely difficult for a Jew to be converted, for how can he bring himself to believe in
the divinity of – another Jew?
Attrib.

5 God will pardon me. It is His trade.
Last words
Journal (Edmond and Charles Goncourt), 23 Feb 1863

Heisenberg, Werner (1901–76) German physicist, who
made great contributions to quantum theory and discovered the
uncertainty principle. He was one of the few physicists to remain
in Germany during the Nazi period.

1 An expert is someone who knows some of the
worst mistakes that can be made in his subject, and how to avoid them.
Physics and Beyond

2 Natural science does not simply describe and explain nature, it is part of the interplay between
nature and ourselves.
Physics and Philosophy

Heller, Joseph (1923–) US novelist. He made his name
with the war novel *Catch-22* (1961); subsequent books include
Good as Gold (1979), *God Knows* (1984), and *Picture This* (1988).

1 He was a self-made man who owed his lack of
success to nobody.
Catch-22, Ch. 3

2 He had decided to live for ever or die in the
attempt.
Catch-22, Ch. 3

3 There was only one catch and that was Catch-
22, which specified that a concern for one's
own safety in the face of dangers that were real
and immediate was the process of a rational
mind.
Catch-22, Ch. 5

4 He knew everything about literature except how
to enjoy it.
Catch-22, Ch. 8

5 Some men are born mediocre, some men
achieve mediocrity, and some men have mediocrity thrust upon them. With Major Major it had
been all three.
Catch-22, Ch. 9

6 Hungry Joe collected lists of fatal diseases and
arranged them in alphabetical order so that he
could put his finger without delay on any one
he wanted to worry about.
Catch-22, Ch. 17

7 Prostitution gives her an opportunity to meet
people. It provides fresh air and wholesome exercise, and it keeps her out of trouble.
Catch-22, Ch. 33

Hellman, Lillian (1905–84) US dramatist. Her plays include
The Little Foxes (1939) and *Watch on the Rhine* (1941), which
were made into films using her own screenplays. She also wrote
several books of memoirs.

1 Cynicism is an unpleasant way of saying the
truth.
The Little Foxes, I

2 I cannot and will not cut my conscience to fit this
year's fashions, even though I long ago came to
the conclusion that I was not a political person
and could have no comfortable place in any political group.
Letter to the US House of Representatives Committee on Un-
American Activities, *The Nation*, 31 May 1952

3 It makes me feel masculine to tell you that I do
not answer questions like this without being
paid for answering them.
When asked by *Harper's* magazine when she felt most masculine;
this question had already been asked of several famous men
Reader's Digest, July 1977

Helps, Sir Arthur (1813–75) British historian. Works include
Conquerors of the New World (1848) and *Friends in Council*
(1847–53).

1 Reading is sometimes an ingenious device for avoiding thought.
Friends in Council

2 What a blessing this smoking is! perhaps the greatest that we owe to the discovery of America.
Friends in Council

3 There is one statesman of the present day, of whom I always say that he would have escaped making the blunders that he has made if he had only ridden more in omnibuses.
Friends in Council

Helvétius, Claude-Adrien (1715–71) French philosopher. *De l'esprit* (1758), his major work, was publicly denounced by the Sorbonne.

1 Education made us what we are.
Discours XXX, Ch. 30

Hemans, Felicia Dorothea (1793–1835) British poet. Her lyrics include *Casabianca* and *The Homes of England.*

1 The boy stood on the burning deck
Whence all but he had fled;
The flame that lit the battle's wreck
Shone round him o'er the dead.
Casabianca

2 The stately homes of England,
How beautiful they stand!
Amidst their tall ancestral trees,
O'er all the pleasant land.
The Homes of England

Hemingway, Ernest (1898–1961) US novelist, who lived for much of his life in Paris. His first successful novel was *The Sun Also Rises* (1926); subsequent novels include *A Farewell to Arms* (1929) and *For Whom the Bell Tolls* (1940). He was a keen sportsman and admirer of bullfighting.

Quotations about Hemingway

1 He is the bully on the Left Bank, always ready to twist the milksop's arm.
Cyril Connolly (1903–74) British journalist. *The Observer,* 24 May 1964

2 He has never been known to use a word that might send the reader to the dictionary.
William Faulkner (1897–1962) US novelist. Attrib.

3 He has a capacity for enjoyment so vast that he gives away great chunks to those about him, and never even misses them. . . . He can take you to a bicycle race and make it raise your hair.
Dorothy Parker (1893–1967) US writer. *New Yorker,* 30 Nov 1929

Quotations by Hemingway

4 Bullfighting is the only art in which the artist is in danger of death and in which the degree of brilliance in the performance is left to the fighter's honour.
Death in the Afternoon, Ch. 9

5 But did thee feel the earth move?
For Whom the Bell Tolls, Ch. 13

6 If you are lucky enough to have lived in Paris as a young man, then wherever you go for the rest of your life, it stays with you, for Paris is a moveable feast.
A Moveable Feast, Epigraph

7 A man can be destroyed but not defeated.
The Old Man and the Sea

8 Because I am a bastard.
When asked why he had deserted his wife for another woman
Americans in Paris (B. Morton)

9 Poor Faulkner. Does he really think big emotions come from big words? He thinks I don't know the ten-dollar words. I know them all right. But there are older and simpler and better words, and those are the ones I use.
In response to Faulkner's jibe (see above)
Attrib.

Henley, William Ernest (1849–1903) British writer. An editor of various weekly journals, his verse collections include *Book of Verses* (1888) and *For England's Sake* (1900). He collaborated with Robert Louis Stevenson on several plays.

1 In the fell clutch of circumstance,
I have not winced nor cried aloud;
Under the bludgeonings of chance
My head is bloody, but unbowed.
Echoes, IV, 'Invictus. In Mem. R.T.H.B.'

2 It matters not how strait the gate,
How charged with punishments the scroll,
I am the master of my fate:
I am the captain of my soul.
Echoes, IV, 'Invictus. In Mem. R.T.H.B.'

Henri IV (1553–1610) The first Bourbon King of France. In 1594 he became a Roman Catholic, granting Huguenots freedom of worship by the Edict of Nantes (1598).

1 I want there to be no peasant in my kingdom so poor that he is unable to have a chicken in his pot every Sunday.
Hist. de Henry le Grand (Hardouin de Péréfixe)

2 Paris is worth a mass.
Said on entering Paris (March 1594), having secured its submission to his authority by becoming a Roman Catholic
Attrib.

3 The wisest fool in Christendom.
Referring to James I of England
Attrib.

Henry, Matthew (1662–1714) English nonconformist minister. His *Exposition of the Old and New Testaments* was completed by thirteen of his colleagues.

1 The better day, the worse deed.
Exposition of the Old and New Testaments

2 They that die by famine die by inches.
Exposition of the Old and New Testaments

3 All this and heaven too.
Life of Philip Henry

Henry, O. (William Sidney Porter; 1862–1910) US short-story writer. His pseudonym was invented while serving a prison sentence for embezzlement. His first collection, *Cabbages and Kings*, was published in 1904.

1 Life is made up of sobs, sniffles and smiles, with sniffles predominating.

The Gifts of the Magi

2 If men knew how women pass the time when they are alone, they'd never marry.

Memoirs of a Yellow Dog

3 Turn up the lights, I don't want to go home in the dark.

His last words, quoting a popular song of the time
O. Henry (C. A. Smith), Ch. 9

Henry, Patrick (1736–99) US statesman. The first governor of Virginia, he mobilized a Virginia militia on the eve of the American Revolution.

1 Caesar had his Brutus – Charles the First, his Cromwell – and George the Third – ('Treason,' cried the Speaker) . . . *may profit by their example.* If *this* be treason, make the most of it.

Speech, Virginia Convention, May 1765

2 I know not what course others may take; but as for me, give me liberty or give me death.

Speech, Virginia Convention, 23 Mar 1775

Henry II (1133–89) King of England. Married to Eleanor of Aquitaine, his empire stretched to the Pyrenees. He was unintentionally responsible for the murder of Thomas Becket.

1 Will no one rid me of this turbulent priest?

Referring to Thomas Becket, Archbishop of Canterbury; four of Henry's household knights took these words literally, hurried to Canterbury, and killed Becket in the cathedral (Dec 1170)
Attrib.

Henry VIII (1491–1547) King of England. Six times married, his divorce from his first wife, Catherine of Aragon, on her failure to produce a male heir, precipitated the Reformation in England.

1 You have sent me a Flanders mare.

Said on meeting his fourth wife, Anne of Cleves, for the first time
Attrib.

Hepworth, Dame Barbara (1903–75) British sculptor, whose typical works were massive abstract shapes in stone or wood, pierced by holes.

1 . . . I rarely draw what I see. I draw what I feel in my body.

World of Art Series (A. M. Hammersmith)

Heraclitus (c. 535–c. 475 BC) Greek philosopher. An early metaphysician, his major work was *On Nature*.

1 Everything flows and nothing stays.

Cratylus (Plato), 402a

2 You can't step into the same river twice.

Cratylus (Plato), 402a

Herbert, Sir A(lan) P(atrick) (1890–1971) British writer and politician. His novels include *The Secret Battle* (1919) and *Holy Deadlock* (1934). He also wrote the libretti for a number of musical comedies, of which the most successful was *Bless the Bride* (1947). As an MP, he helped to reform the divorce law and was the prime mover in the act to pay royalties to authors on library books.

1 Other people's babies –
That's my life!
Mother to dozens,
And nobody's wife.

A Book of Ballads, 'Other People's Babies'

2 Let's find out what everyone is doing,
And then stop everyone from doing it.

Let's Stop Somebody

3 The Common Law of England has been laboriously built about a mythical figure – the figure of 'The Reasonable Man'.

Uncommon Law

4 People must not do things for fun. We are not here for fun. There is no reference to fun in any Act of Parliament.

Uncommon Law

5 The critical period in matrimony is breakfast-time.

Uncommon Law

6 The Englishman never enjoys himself except for a noble purpose.

Uncommon Law

7 For any ceremonial purposes the otherwise excellent liquid, water, is unsuitable in colour and other respects.

Uncommon Law

8 An Act of God was defined as *something which no reasonable man could have expected.*

Uncommon Law

Herbert, George (1593–1633) English poet. His religious lyrics were collected in *The Temple* (1633).

1 I struck the board, and cried, 'No more;
I will abroad.'
What, shall I ever sigh and pine?
My lines and life are free; free as the road,
Loose as the wind, as large as store.

The Collar

2 But as I rav'd and grew more fierce and wild
At every word,
Methought I heard one calling, 'Child';
And I replied, 'My Lord.'

The Collar

3 Oh that I were an orange-tree,
That busy plant!
Then I should ever laden be,
And never want
Some fruit for Him that dressed me.

Employment

4 And now in age I bud again,
After so many deaths I live and write;
I once more smell the dew and rain,
And relish versing; O, my only Light,
It cannot be
That I am he
On whom Thy tempests fell all night.

The Flower

5 Death is still working like a mole,
And digs my grave at each remove.

Grace

6 Love bade me welcome; yet my soul drew back,
Guilty of dust and sin.

Love

7 'You must sit down,' says Love, 'and taste My meat,'
So I did sit and eat.

Love

8 He that makes a good war makes a good peace.

Outlandish Proverbs, 420

9 Sweet day, so cool, so calm, so bright,
The bridal of the earth and sky.

Virtue

10 Only a sweet and virtuous soul,
Like season'd timber, never gives;
But though the whole world turn to coal,
Then chiefly lives.

Virtue

Herford, Oliver (1863–1935) British-born US humorist, writer, and illustrator.

1 I would like to throw an egg into an electric fan.

When asked if he really had no ambition beyond making people laugh
Attrib.

Herrick, Robert (1591–1674) English poet. Ordained in 1623, his religious and secular verse is collected in *Hesperides* (1648).

1 Cherry ripe, ripe, ripe, I cry.
Full and fair ones; come and buy.

See also CAMPION
Hesperides, 'Cherry Ripe'

2 A sweet disorder in the dress
Kindles in clothes a wantonness.

Hesperides, 'Delight in Disorder'

3 'Twixt kings and tyrants there's this difference known;
Kings seek their subjects' good: tyrants their own.

Hesperides, 'Kings and Tyrants'

4 Fair daffodils, we weep to see
You haste away so soon:
As yet the early-rising sun
Has not attain'd his noon.
Stay, stay,
Until the hasting day
Has run
But to the even-song;
And, having pray'd together, we
Will go with you along.

We have short time to stay, as you,
We have as short a Spring;
As quick a growth to meet decay,
As you or any thing.

Hesperides, 'To Daffodils'

5 Gather ye rosebuds while ye may,
Old time is still a-flying:
And this same flower that smiles today
Tomorrow will be dying.

Hesperides, 'To the Virgins, to Make Much of Time'

6 Then be not coy, but use your time;
And while ye may, go marry:
For having lost but once your prime,
You may for ever tarry.

Hesperides, 'To the Virgins, to Make Much of Time'

7 Whenas in silks my Julia goes
Then, then (methinks) how sweetly flows
That liquefaction of her clothes.

Hesperides, 'Upon Julia's Clothes'

Hesse, Hermann (1877–1962) German novelist and poet. His novels include *Peter Camenzind* (1904) and *Steppenwolf* (1927). He lived in Switzerland from 1911.

1 If you hate a person, you hate something in him that is part of yourself. What isn't part of ourselves doesn't disturb us.

Demian, Ch. 6

2 Knowledge can be communicated but not wisdom.

Siddhartha

3 I believe that the struggle against death, the unconditional and self-willed determination to life, is the motive power behind the lives and activities of all outstanding men.

Steppenwolf, 'Treatise on the Steppenwolf'

Hewart, Gordon, Baron (1870–1943) British lawyer and politician. He became attorney general (1919–22) and lord chief justice (1922–40).

1 Justice should not only be done, but should manifestly and undoubtedly be seen to be done.

The Chief (R. Jackson)

Heywood, Thomas (c. 1574–1641) English dramatist and actor. He wrote numerous comedies and tragedies.

1 Seven cities warr'd for Homer, being dead,
Who, living, had no roof to shroud his head.

The Hierarchy of the Blessed Angels

2 A Woman Killed with Kindness.

Play title

Hicks, Sir (Edward) Seymour (1871–1949) British actor-manager. He was a comedian in the Gaiety company and specialized in musical comedies.

1 You will recognize, my boy, the first sign of old age: it is when you go out into the streets of London and realize for the first time how young the policemen look.

They Were Singing (C. Pulling)

Hickson, William Edward (1803–70) British educationalist and writer.

1 If at first you don't succeed,
Try, try again.

Try and Try Again

Higley, Brewster (19th century) US songwriter.

1 Oh give me a home where the buffalo roam,
Where the deer and the antelope play,
Where seldom is heard a discouraging word
And the skies are not cloudy all day.

Home on the Range

Hill, Aaron (1685–1750) British poet and dramatist. He wrote the words for Handel's *Rinaldo* and translated Voltaire's plays.

1 Tender-handed stroke a nettle,
And it stings you for your pains;
Grasp it like a man of mettle,
And it soft as silk remains.

Verses Written on Window

Hill, Geoffrey (William) (1932–) British poet. His publications include *For the Unfallen* (1959), *Mercian Hymns* (1971), and *Collected Poems* (1985).

1 I love my work and my children. God
Is distant, difficult. Things happen.
Too near the ancient troughs of blood
Innocence is no earthly weapon.

King Log, 'Ovid in the Third Reich'

2 As estimated, you died. Things marched, sufficient, to that end.
Just so much Zyklon and leather, patented terror, so many routine cries.

Zyklon B was the name of the poison gas used in the Nazi extermination camps during World War II
King Log, 'September Song'

3 King of the perennial holly-groves, the riven sandstone: overlord of the M5: architect of the historic rampart and ditch, the citadel at Tamworth, the summer hermitage in Holy Cross: guardian of the Welsh Bridge and the Iron Bridge: contractor to the desirable new estates: saltmaster: money-changer: commissioner for oaths: martyrologist: the friend of Charlemagne. 'I liked that,' said Offa, 'sing it again.'

Mercian Hymns, I, 'The Naming of Offa'

4 Fortified in their front parlours, at Yuletide men are the more murderous. Drunk, they defy battle-axes, bellow of whale-bone and dung.

Mercian Hymns, XXVI, 'Offa's Bestiary'

Hill, Rowland (1744–1833) British clergyman.

1 I do not see any reason why the devil should have all the good tunes.

Attrib.

Hillary, Sir Edmund (1919–) New Zealand mountaineer. With Tenzing Norgay he was the first to climb Everest. He became New Zealand's High Commissioner to India in 1984.

1 As far as I knew, he had never taken a photograph before, and the summit of Everest was hardly the place to show him how.

Referring to Tenzing Norgay, his companion on the conquest of Mt Everest (1953)
High Adventure

2 Well, we knocked the bastard off!

On first climbing Mount Everest (with Tenzing Norgay), 29 May 1953
Nothing Venture, Nothing Win

3 There is precious little in civilization to appeal to a Yeti.

The Observer, 'Sayings of the Week', 3 June 1960

Hilton, James (1900–54) British novelist. His novels *Lost Horizon* (1933) and *Good-bye, Mr Chips* (1934) were made into films and he subsequently worked as a scriptwriter in Hollywood.

1 Anno domini – that's the most fatal complaint of all in the end.

Good-bye, Mr Chips, Ch. 1

Hippocrates (c. 460–c. 377 BC) Greek physician, who founded the Hippocratic school of medicine, where students were required to take an oath (the Hippocratic oath) to observe a code of practice putting the patient's interest above all others.

1 The life so short, the craft so long to learn.

Describing medicine. It is often quoted in Latin as *Ars longa, vita brevis*, and interpreted as 'Art lasts, life is short'. *See also* CHAUCER
Aphorisms, I

2 Extreme remedies are most appropriate for extreme diseases.

Aphorisms, I

3 Sometimes give your services for nothing. . . .
And if there be an opportunity of serving one who is a stranger in financial straits, give full assistance to all such. For where there is love of man, there is also love of the art.

Precepts, Sect. VI

Hitchcock, Sir Alfred (1889–1980) British film director, working mainly in the USA from 1940. His films – mostly sophisticated thrillers – include *Vertigo* (1958), *North by Northwest* (1959), *Psycho* (1960), and *The Birds* (1963).

1 I made a remark a long time ago. I said I was very pleased that television was now showing murder stories, because it's bringing murder back into its rightful setting – in the home.

The Observer, 'Sayings of the Week', 17 Aug 1969

2 Actors should be treated like cattle.

Said in clarification of a remark attributed to him, 'Actors are like cattle'
Quote, Unquote (N. Rees)

Hitler, Adolf (1889–1945) German dictator, who became president of the Nazi party in 1921 and chancellor of Germany in 1933. His campaign of world conquest led to World War II, defeat and disgrace for Germany, and his own suicide.

Quotations about Hitler

1 The people Hitler never understood, and whose actions continued to exasperate him to the end of his life, were the British.

Allan Bullock (1914–) British academic and historian. *Hitler, A Study in Tyranny*, Ch. 8

2 Hitler showed surprising loyalty to Mussolini, but it never extended to trusting him.

Alan Bullock *Hitler, A Study in Tyranny*, Ch. II

3 I have only one purpose, the destruction of Hitler, and my life is much simplified thereby. If Hitler invaded Hell I would make at least a favourable reference to the Devil in the House of Commons.

Winston Churchill (1874–1965) British statesman. *The Grand Alliance*

4 The Italians will laugh at me; every time Hitler occupies a country he sends me a message.

Benito Mussolini (1883–1945) Italian dictator. *Hitler* (Alan Bullock), Ch. 8

5 That garrulous monk.

Benito Mussolini. *The Second World War* (W. Churchill)

6 I wouldn't believe Hitler was dead, even if he told me so himself.

Hjalmar Schacht (1877–1970) German banker. Attrib.

7 A racing tipster who only reached Hitler's level of accuracy would not do well for his clients.

A. J. P. Taylor (1906–) British historian. *The Origins of The Second World War*, Ch. 7

8 Germany was the cause of Hitler just as much as Chicago is responsible for the *Chicago Tribune.*

Alexander Woolcott (1887–1943) US writer and critic. Woollcott died after the broadcast. Radio broadcast, 1943

Quotations by Hitler

9 All those who are not racially pure are mere chaff.

Mein Kampf, Ch. 2

10 Only constant repetition will finally succeed in imprinting an idea on the memory of the crowd.

Mein Kampf, Ch. 6

11 The broad mass of a nation . . . will more easily fall victim to a big lie than to a small one.

Mein Kampf, Ch. 10

12 Germany will be either a world power or will not be at all.

Mein Kampf, Ch. 14

13 In starting and waging a war it is not right that matters, but victory.

The Rise and Fall of the Third Reich (W. L. Shirer), Ch. 16

14 The essential thing is the formation of the political will of the nation: that is the starting point for political action.

Speech, Düsseldorf, 27 Jan 1932

15 I go the way that Providence dictates with the assurance of a sleepwalker.

Referring to his successful re-occupation of the Rhineland, despite advice against the attempt
Speech, Munich, 15 Mar 1936

16 When Barbarossa commences, the world will hold its breath and make no comment.

Referring to the planned invasion of the USSR, Operation Barbarossa, which began on 22 June 1941
Attrib.

17 Is Paris burning?

Referring to the liberation of Paris, 1944

Hobbes, Thomas (1588–1679) English philosopher and political thinker. His *Leviathan* (1651) set out his political philosophy.

1 The condition of man . . . is a condition of war of everyone against everyone.

Leviathan, Pt. I, Ch. 4

2 True and False are attributes of speech, not of things. And where speech is not, there is neither Truth nor Falsehood.

Leviathan, Pt. I, Ch. 4

3 They that approve a private opinion, call it opinion; but they that mislike it, heresy: and yet heresy signifies no more than private opinion.

Leviathan, Pt. I, Ch. 11

4 No arts; no letters; no society; and which is worst of all, continual fear and danger of violent death; and the life of man, solitary, poor, nasty, brutish, and short.

Leviathan, Pt. I, Ch. 13

5 The only way to erect such a common power, as may be able to defend them from the invasion of foreigners, and the injuries of one another . . . is, to confer all their power and strength upon one man, or upon one assembly of men, that may reduce all their wills, by plurality of voices, unto one will . . . This is the generation of that great Leviathan, or rather (to speak more reverently) of that *Mortal God*, to which we owe under the *Immortal God*, our peace and defence.

Leviathan, Pt. II, Ch. 17

6 They that are discontented under *monarchy*, call it *tyranny*; and they that are displeased with *aristocracy,* call it *oligarchy* : so also, they which find themselves grieved under a *democracy*, call it *anarchy*, which signifies the want of government; and yet I think no man believes, that want of government, is any new kind of government.

Leviathan, Pt. II, Ch. 19

7 The Papacy is not other than the Ghost of the deceased Roman Empire, sitting crowned upon the grave thereof.

Leviathan, Pt. IV, Ch. 37

8 I am about to take my last voyage, a great leap in the dark.

Last words

Hobhouse, John Cam, Baron Broughton de Gyfford (1786–1869) British politician. He became secretary of war (1832–33) and secretary for Ireland (1833). He was a friend of Byron, advising that his *Memoirs* be destroyed. His own autobiography, *Recollections of a Long Life,* were published in 1865.

1 When I invented the phrase 'His Majesty's Opposition' he paid me a compliment on the fortunate hit.

Speaking about Canning
Recollections of a Long Life, II, Ch. 12

Hobson, Sir Harold (1904–) British theatre critic and writer. His books include *The Theatre Now* (1953) and the autobiography *Indirect Journey* (1978).

1 The United States, I believe, are under the impression that they are twenty years in advance of this country; whilst, as a matter of actual verifiable fact, of course, they are just about six hours behind it.

The Devil in Woodford Wells, Ch. 8

Hodgson, Ralph (1871–1962) British poet. His poems include *The Bells of Heaven, The Bull, Eve,* and *Last Blackbird.*

1 'Twould ring the bells of Heaven
The wildest peal for years,
If Parson lost his senses
And people came to theirs,
And he and they together
Knelt down with angry prayers
For tamed and shabby tigers
And dancing dogs and bears,
And wretched, blind, pit ponies,
And little hunted hares.

The Bells of Heaven

Hoffer, Eric (1902–83) US writer. Working as a docker on the Pacific Coast for many years, he was the author of several philosophical works.

1 When people are free to do as they please, they usually imitate each other.

The Passionate State of Mind

2 We have rudiments of reverence for the human body, but we consider as nothing the rape of the human mind.

Bartlett's Unfamiliar Quotations (Leonard Louis Levinson)

3 It is the malady of our age that the young are so busy teaching us that they have no time left to learn.

Attrib.

Hoffman, Heinrich (1809–74) German writer and illustrator.

1 But one day, one cold winter's day,
He screamed out, 'Take the soup away!'

Struwwelpeter, 'Augustus'

2 Look at little Johnny there,
Little Johnny Head-in-Air.

Struwwelpeter, 'Johnny Head-in-Air'

3 The door flew open, in he ran,
The great, long, red-legged scissor-man.

Struwwelpeter, 'The Little Suck-a-Thumb'

4 Anything to me is sweeter
Than to see Shock-headed Peter.

Struwwelpeter, 'Shock-headed Peter'

Hoffmann, Ernst Theodor Amadeus (1776–1822) German composer. His opera *Undine* (1816) was the basis for Offenbach's *Tales of Hoffmann.* He also wrote many romantic novels and stories.

1 He's a wicked man that comes after children when they won't go to bed and throws handfuls of sand in their eyes.

The Sandman

Hoffmann, Max (1869–1927) German general, who in World War I succeeded Ludendorff as chief of the general staff (1916).

1 LUDENDORFF. The English soldiers fight like lions.
HOFFMANN. True. But don't we know that they are lions led by donkeys.

Referring to the performance of the British army in World War I
The Donkeys (A. Clark)

Hoffmann von Fallersleben, Heinrich (1798–1876) German poet and scholar, author of the patriotic poem (1841) that was adopted as the German national anthem after World War I.

1 *Deutschland, Deutschland über alles.*
Germany, Germany before all else.

German national anthem

Hogg, James (1770–1835) Scottish poet and writer. Originally a shepherd (known as 'The Ettrick Shepherd'), he wrote many ballads and the novel *The Confessions of a Justified Sinner* (1824).

1 Where the pools are bright and deep,
Where the grey trout lies asleep,
Up the river and o'er the lea,
That's the way for Billy and me.

That's the Way for Billy and Me

2 My love she's but a lassie yet.

Title of song

Hokusai (1760–1849) Japanese painter and book illustrator, famous for his ukiyo-e colour prints. His best-known work is *Views of Mount Fuji* (1835).

1 If heaven had granted me five more years, I could have become a real painter.

Said on his deathbed
Famous Last Words (B. Conrad)

Holberg, Ludwig, Baron (1684–1754) Danish dramatist, poet, and historian, claimed as the founder of modern Danish and Norwegian literature. His works include the satirical epic poem *Peder Paas* (1719) and the comic play *The Political Tinker*.

1 Do you call that thing under your hat a head?

Reply to the jibe, 'Do you call that thing on your head a hat?'
Anekdotenschatz (H. Hoffmeister)

Holland, Henry Fox, Baron (1705–74) British politician. A Royalist, he accompanied Charles II to Holland. He became an MP, secretary of war (1746–54), and leader of the Commons (1755–56).

1 If Mr Selwyn calls again, shew him up: if I am alive I shall be delighted to see him; and if I am dead he would like to see me.

Said during his last illness. George Selwyn was known for his morbid fascination for dead bodies.
George Selwyn and his Contemporaries (J. H. Jesse), Vol. III

Holmes, John Haynes (1879–1964) US clergyman. His books include *Religion for Today* (1917) and *A Sensible Man's View of Religion* (1933).

1 The universe is not hostile, nor yet is it friendly. It is simply indifferent.

A Sensible Man's View of Religion

Holmes, Oliver Wendell (1809–94) US writer and physician. The dean of Harvard Medical School, he wrote several medical books as well as collections of verse and essays, including *Old Ironsides* (verse; 1830) and *The Autocrat of the Breakfast Table* (essays; 1857).

1 Man has his will, – but woman has her way.

The Autocrat of the Breakfast Table, Prologue

2 A thought is often original, though you have uttered it a hundred times.

The Autocrat of the Breakfast Table, Ch. 1

3 The world's great men have not commonly been great scholars, nor great scholars great men.

The Autocrat of the Breakfast Table, Ch. 6

4 The axis of the earth sticks out visibly through the centre of each and every town or city.

The Autocrat of the Breakfast Table, Ch. 6

5 Wisdom has taught us to be calm and meek, To take one blow, and turn the other cheek; It is not written what a man shall do If the rude caitiff smite the other too!

Non-Resistance

6 It is the province of knowledge to speak and it is the privilege of wisdom to listen.

The Poet at the Breakfast Table, Ch. 10

7 A moment's insight is sometimes worth a life's experience.

The Professor at the Breakfast Table, Ch. 10

8 It's giggle–gabble–gobble–'n' git.

Referring to afternoon tea
Attrib.

Holmes, Oliver Wendell, Jr. (1841–1935) US jurist. As a judge in the Supreme Court of Massachusetts and the US Supreme Court, he was known for his support of the individual rights of the private citizen. His best-known book is *The Common Law* (1881).

1 War? War is an organized bore.

Yankee from Olympus (C. Bowen)

2 Many ideas grow better when transplanted into another mind than in the one where they sprang up.

3 Oh, to be seventy again!

Said in his eighty-seventh year, while watching a pretty girl
The American Treasury (C. Fadiman)

Holst, Gustav (1874–1934) British composer. His best-known works are the choral *Hymn of Jesus* (1917) and the suite *The Planets*.

1 Never compose anything unless the not composing of it becomes a positive nuisance to you.

Letter to W. G. Whittaker

Homer (8th century) Greek epic poet. He is presumed to be the author of the *Iliad*, concerning the Trojan Wars, and the *Odyssey*, which records the adventures of Odysseus. Both poems have had a great influence on western culture.

1 For who could see the passage of a goddess unless she wished his mortal eyes aware?

Odyssey, Bk. X

2 Square in your ship's path are Seirênês, crying beauty to bewitch men coasting by; woe to the innocent who hears that sound!

Odyssey, Bk. XII

Hood, Thomas (1799–1845) British poet. His collection *Odes and Addresses* (1825) was followed by several volumes of humorous verse and such political poems as *The Story of the Shirt* (1843).

1 The sedate, sober, silent, serious, sad-coloured sect.

Referring to the Quakers
The Doves and the Crows

2 Ben Battle was a soldier bold, And used to war's alarms: But a cannon-ball took off his legs, So he laid down his arms!

Faithless Nelly Gray

3 For here I leave my second leg, And the Forty-second Foot!

Faithless Nelly Gray

4 The love that loves a scarlet coat Should be more uniform.

Faithless Nelly Gray

5 His death, which happen'd in his berth,
   At forty-odd befell:
   They went and told the sexton, and
   The sexton toll'd the bell.
   Faithless Sally Brown

6 I remember, I remember,
   The house where I was born,
   The little window where the sun
   Came peeping in at morn;
   He never came a wink too soon,
   Nor brought too long a day,
   But now, I often wish the night
   Had borne my breath away!
   I Remember

7 I remember, I remember,
   The fir trees dark and high;
   I used to think their slender tops
   Were close against the sky:
   It was a childish ignorance,
   But now 'tis little joy
   To know I'm farther off from heav'n
   Than when I was a boy.
   I Remember

8 But evil is wrought by want of thought,
   As well as want of heart!
   The Lady's Dream

9 For that old enemy the gout
   Had taken him in toe!
   Lieutenant Luff

10 No warmth, no cheerfulness, no healthful ease,
   No comfortable feel in any member –
   No shade, no shine, no butterflies, no bees,
   No fruits, no flowers, no leaves, no birds, –
   November!
   No!

11 O! men with sisters dear,
   O! men with mothers and wives!
   It is not linen you're wearing out,
   But human creatures' lives!
   The Song of the Shirt

12 Oh! God! that bread should be so dear,
   And flesh and blood so cheap!
   The Song of the Shirt

13 Holland . . . lies so low they're only saved by being dammed.
   Up the Rhine

14 What is a modern poet's fate?
   To write his thoughts upon a slate;
   The critic spits on what is done,
   Gives it a wipe – and all is gone.
   Alfred Lord Tennyson, A Memoir (Hallam Tennyson), Vol. II, Ch. 3

15 There are three things which the public will always clamour for, sooner or later: namely, Novelty, novelty, novelty.
   Announcement of *Comic Annual*, 1836

Hooker, Richard (c. 1554–1600) English theologian. His *On the Laws of Ecclesiastical Polity* (1594) influenced Anglican thought for several generations.

1 Change is not made without inconvenience, even from worse to better.
   English Dictionary (Johnson), Preface

Hoover, Herbert Clark (1874–1964) US statesman and Republican President (1929–33).

Quotations about Hoover

1 Facts to Hoovers' brain are as water to a sponge; they are absorbed into every tiny interstice.
   Bernard Baruch (1870–1965) US financier and presidential adviser. *Herbert Hoover: American Quaker* (D. Hinshaw)

2 Hoover, if elected, will do one thing that is almost incomprehensible to the human mind: he will make a great man out of Coolidge.
   Clarence Darrow (1857–1938) US lawyer. Remark during the presidential campaign, 1932

Quotations by Hoover

3 The American system of rugged individualism.
   Speech, New York, 22 Oct 1928

4 Older men declare war. But it is youth that must fight and die.
   Speech, Republican National Convention, Chicago, 27 June 1944

Hope, Anthony (Sir Anthony Hope Hawkins; 1863–1933) British novelist. After the success of *The Prisoner of Zenda* (1894), which was made into a film three times (1922, 1937, and 1952), he wrote many similar romances.

1 Unless one is a genius, it is best to aim at being intelligible.
   The Dolly Dialogues

2 He is very fond of making things which he does not want, and then giving them to people who have no use for them.
   The Dolly Dialogues

3 Economy is going without something you do want in case you should, some day, want something you probably won't want.
   The Dolly Dialogues

4 'You oughtn't to yield to temptation.'
   'Well, somebody must, or the thing becomes absurd.'
   The Dolly Dialogues

5 Boys will be boys – '
   'And even that . . . wouldn't matter if we could only prevent girls from being girls.'
   The Dolly Dialogues

6 *'Bourgeois,'* I observed, 'is an epithet which the riff-raff apply to what is respectable, and the aristocracy to what is decent'.
   The Dolly Dialogues

7 I wish you would read a little poetry sometimes. Your ignorance cramps my conversation.
   The Dolly Dialogues

8 Good families are generally worse than any others.

The Prisoner of Zenda, Ch. 1

9 His foe was folly and his weapon wit.

Written for the inscription on the memorial to W. S. Gilbert, Victoria Embankment, London

Hope, Laurence (Mrs M. H. Nicolson; 1804–1905) British poet and songwriter. A member of the British Raj, she wrote *The Garden of Kama and other Love Lyrics from India* (1901) under a male pseudonym. It contained the immensely popular song 'Pale Hands I Loved'.

1 Less than the dust beneath thy chariot wheel,
Less than the weed that grows beside thy door,
Less than the rust that never stained thy sword,
Less than the need thou hast in life of me,
Even less am I.

The Garden of Kama and other Love Lyrics from India, 'Less than the Dust'

2 Pale hands I loved beside the Shalimar,
Where are you now? Who lies beneath your spell?

The Garden of Kama and other Love Lyrics from India, 'Pale Hands I Loved'

Hopkins, Gerard Manley (1844–99) British Jesuit and poet. An innovator in poetry, he is remembered for his *Wreck of the Deutschland* and other verse.

1 Not, I'll not, carrion comfort, Despair, not feast on thee;
Not untwist – slack they may be – these last strands of man
In me or, most weary, cry *I can no more*. I can;
Can something, hope, wish day come, not choose not to be.

Carrion Comfort

2 That night, that year
Of now done darkness I wretch lay wrestling with (my God!) my God.

Carrion Comfort

3 The world is charged with the grandeur of God.

God's Grandeur

4 Glory be to God for dappled things –
For skies of couple-colour as a brinded cow;
For rose-moles all in stipple upon trout that swim.

Pied Beauty

5 Look at the stars! look, look up at the skies!
O look at all the fire-folk sitting in the air!
The bright boroughs, the circle-citadels there!

The Starlight Night

Hopper, Hedda (1890–1966) US writer. Originally an actress, she later became well known as a Hollywood gossip columnist.

1 At one time I thought he wanted to be an actor. He had certain qualifications, including no money and a total lack of responsibility.

From Under My Hat

Horace (Quintus Horatius Flaccus; 65–8 BC) Roman poet. His *Odes* and *Epistles* portray Roman life in considerable detail.

1 'Painters and poets alike have always had licence to dare anything.' We know that, and we both claim and allow to others in their turn this indulgence.

Ars Poetica

2 I strive to be brief, and I become obscure.

Ars Poetica

3 You will have written exceptionally well if, by skilful arrangement of your words, you have made an ordinary one seem original.

Ars Poetica

4 Many terms which have now dropped out of favour, will be revived, and those that are at present respectable will drop out, if usage so choose, with whom resides the decision and the judgement and the code of speech.

Ars Poetica

5 Scholars dispute, and the case is still before the courts.

Ars Poetica c. 8 BC

6 Mountains will heave in childbirth, and a silly little mouse will be born.

Ars Poetica

7 He always hurries to the main event and whisks his audience into the middle of things as though they knew already.

Ars Poetica

8 To the Greeks the Muse gave native wit, to the Greeks the gift of graceful eloquence.

Ars Poetica

9 I'm aggrieved when sometimes even excellent Homer nods.

Ars Poetica

10 Not gods, nor men, nor even booksellers have put up with poets being second-rate.

Ars Poetica

11 Let it be kept till the ninth year, the manuscript put away at home: you may destroy whatever you haven't published; once out, what you've said can't be stopped.

Ars Poetica

12 To save a man's life against his will is the same as killing him.

Ars Poetica

13 *Nullius addictus iurare in verba magistri,*
Quo me cumque rapit tempestas, deferor hospes.
Not bound to swear allegiance to any master, wherever the wind takes me I travel as a visitor.

Nullius in verba is the motto of the Royal Society
Epistles, I

14 The happy state of getting the victor's palm without the dust of racing.

Epistles, I

15 If possible honestly, if not, somehow, make money.
Epistles, I

16 Let me remind you what the wary fox said once upon a time to the sick lion: 'Because those footprints scare me, all directed your way, none coming back.'
Epistles, I

17 We are just statistics, born to consume resources.
Epistles, I

18 Believe each day that has dawned is your last. Some hour to which you have not been looking forward will prove lovely. As for me, if you want a good laugh, you will come and find me fat and sleek, in excellent condition, one of Epicurus' herd of pigs.
Epistles, I

19 To marvel at nothing is just about the one and only thing, Numicius, that can make a man happy and keep him that way.
Epistles, I

20 You may drive out nature with a pitchfork, yet she'll be constantly running back.
Epistles, I

21 They change their clime, not their frame of mind, who rush across the sea. We work hard at doing nothing: we look for happiness in boats and carriage rides. What you are looking for is here, is at Ulubrae, if only peace of mind doesn't desert you.
Epistles, I

22 For it is your business, when the wall next door catches fire.
Epistles, I

23 If you believe Cratinus from days of old, Maecenas, (as you must know) no verse can give pleasure for long, nor last, that is written by drinkers of water.
Epistles, I

24 And seek for truth in the groves of Academe.
Epistles, II

25 Hard to train to accept being poor.
Odes, I

26 And if you include me among the lyric poets, I'll hold my head so high it'll strike the stars.
Odes, I

27 Pale Death kicks his way equally into the cottages of the poor and the castles of kings.
Odes, I

28 Life's short span forbids us to enter on far-reaching hopes.
Odes, I

29 Drop the question what tomorrow may bring, and count as profit every day that Fate allows you.
Odes, I

30 Do not try to find out – we're forbidden to know – what end the gods have in store for me, or for you.
Odes, I

31 While we're talking, time will have meanly run on: pick today's fruits, not relying on the future in the slightest.
Odes, I

32 *Carpe diem*
Seize the day.
Odes, I

33 When things are steep, remember to stay level-headed.
Odes, II

34 *Dulce et decorum est pro patria mori.*
It is a sweet and seemly thing to die for one's country.
Odes, III

35 Force, if unassisted by judgement, collapses through its own mass.
Odes, III

36 Undeservedly you will atone for the sins of your fathers.
Odes, III

37 What do the ravages of time not injure? Our parents' age (worse than our grandparents') has produced us, more worthless still, who will soon give rise to a yet more vicious generation.
Odes, III

38 My life with girls has ended, though till lately I was up to it and soldiered on not ingloriously; now on this wall will hang my weapons and my lyre, discharged from the war.
Odes, III

39 I have executed a memorial longer lasting than bronze.
Odes, III

40 That I make poetry and give pleasure (if I give pleasure) are because of you.
Odes, IV

41 Not to hope for things to last for ever, is what the year teaches and even the hour which snatches a nice day away.
Odes, IV

42 Many brave men lived before Agamemnon's time; but they are all, unmourned and unknown, covered by the long night, because they lack their sacred poet.
Odes, IV

43 Not the owner of many possessions will you be right to call happy: he more rightly deserves the name of happy who knows how to use the gods' gifts wisely and to put up with rough poverty, and who fears dishonour more than death.

Odes, IV

44 Mix a little foolishness with your serious plans: it's lovely to be silly at the right moment.

Odes, IV

45 How is it, Maecenas, that no one lives contented with his lot, whether he has planned it for himself or fate has flung him into it, but yet he praises those who follow different paths?

Satires, I

46 An accomplished man to his finger-tips.

Satires, I

47 Strong enough to answer back to desires, to despise distinctions, and a whole man in himself, polished and well-rounded.

Satires, II

Horne, Richard Henry (*or* **Hengist**) (1803–84) English writer. A magistrate in Australia, his verse includes *Orion* (1843) and *Ballad Romances* (1846).

1 'Tis always morning somewhere in the world.

Orion, Bk III, Ch. 2

Horsley, Bishop Samuel (1733–1806) British bishop, who edited Newton's works.

1 In *this* country, my Lords, . . . the individual subject . . . 'has nothing to do with the laws but to obey them.'

House of Lords, 13 Nov 1795

Household, Geoffrey (Edward West) (1900–88) British writer and novelist. His novels include *Rogue Male* (1939), *A Time to Kill* (1952), and *Red Anger* (1975).

1 I have noticed that what cats most appreciate in a human being is not the ability to produce food which they take for granted – but his or her entertainment value.

Rogue Male

2 It's easy to make a man confess the lies he tells to himself; it's far harder to make him confess the truth.

Rogue Male

Housman, A(lfred) E(dward) (1859–1936) British scholar and poet. His own verse collections include *A Shropshire Lad* (1896) and *Last Poems* (1922).

Quotations about Housman

1 A prim, old-maidish, rather second-rate, rather tired, rather querulous person.

A. C. Benson (1862–1925) British writer. *Diaries*

2 The sad, compassionate, loving, romantic man.

Richard Graves. *A. E. Housman; The Scholar Poet*

Quotations by Housman

3 We'll to the woods no more,
The laurels all are cut.

Last Poems, Introductory

4 The candles burn their sockets,
The blinds let through the day,
The young man feels his pockets
And wonders what's to pay.

Last Poems, 'Eight O'Clock'

5 They say my verse is sad: no wonder;
Its narrow measure spans
Tears of eternity, and sorrow,
Not mine, but man's.

Last Poems, 'Fancy's Knell'

6 Even when poetry has a meaning, as it usually has, it may be inadvisable to draw it out . . . Perfect understanding will sometimes almost extinguish pleasure.

The Name and Nature of Poetry

7 Loveliest of trees, the cherry now
Is hung with bloom along the bough,
And stands about the woodland ride
Wearing white for Eastertide.

A Shropshire Lad, '1887'

8 They hang us now in Shrewsbury jail:
The whistles blow forlorn,
And trains all night groan on the rail
To men that die at morn.

A Shropshire Lad, 'Reveillé'

9 Look not in my eyes, for fear
They mirror true the sight I see,
And there you find your face too clear
And love it and be lost like me.

A Shropshire Lad, 'March'

10 Here of a Sunday morning
My love and I would lie,
And see the coloured counties,
And hear the larks so high
About us in the sky.

A Shropshire Lad, 'Bredon Hill'

11 Is my team ploughing,
That I was used to drive?

A Shropshire Lad, 'Bredon Hill'

12 The goal stands up, the keeper
Stands up to keep the goal.

A Shropshire Lad, 'Bredon Hill'

13 On Wenlock Edge the wood's in trouble;
His forest fleece the Wrekin heaves;
The gale, it plies the saplings double,
And thick on Severn snow the leaves.

A Shropshire Lad, 'The Welsh Marches'

14 East and west on fields forgotten
Bleach the bones of comrades slain,
Lovely lads and dead and rotten;
None that go return again.

A Shropshire Lad, 'The Welsh Marches'

15 Into my heart an air that kills
From yon far country blows:
What are those blue remembered hills,
What spires, what farms are those?

A Shropshire Lad, 'The Welsh Marches'

16 With rue my heart is laden
For golden friends I had,
For many a rose-lipt maiden
And many a lightfoot lad.

A Shropshire Lad, 'The Welsh Marches'

17 Malt does more than Milton can
To justify God's ways to man.

A Shropshire Lad, 'The Welsh Marches'

Howe, Julia Ward (1819–1910) US feminist and peace worker. She composed and published the *Battle Hymn of the Republic* (1862) and several books, including *Modern Society* (1881) and *At Sunset* (1910).

1 Mine eyes have seen the glory of the coming of the Lord:
He is trampling out the vintage where the grapes of wrath are stored.

Battle Hymn of the American Republic

Howitt, Mary (1799–1888) British writer. Her books, written with her husband William Howitt (1792–1879), include *The Literature and Romances of Northern Europe* (1852). She also wrote some verse.

1 'Will you walk into my parlour?' said a spider to a fly:
''Tis the prettiest little parlour that ever you did spy.'

The Spider and the Fly

Hoyle, Edmond (1672–1769) English writer on card games.

1 When in doubt, win the trick.

Hoyle's Games, 'Whist, Twenty-four Short Rules for Learners'

Hubbard, Elbert (1856–1915) US writer and editor.

1 One machine can do the work of fifty ordinary men. No machine can do the work of one extraordinary man.

Roycroft Dictionary and Book of Epigrams

2 Little minds are interested in the extraordinary; great minds in the commonplace.

Roycroft Dictionary and Book of Epigrams

3 Life is just one damned thing after another.

A Thousand and One Epigrams

Hughes, Ted (1930–) British poet; poet laureate (1984–), who married the poet Sylvia Plath in 1956. His poetry includes *The Hawk in the Rain* (1957), *Crow* (1970), *Cave Birds* (1975), and *River* (1983).

1 Death invented the phone it looks like the altar of death
Do not worship the telephone
It drags its worshippers into actual graves
With a variety of devices, through a variety of disguised voices

Selected Poems 1957–1981, 'Do not Pick up the Telephone'

2 And let her learn through what kind of dust
He has earned his thirst and the right to quench it
And what sweat he has exchanged for his money
And the blood-weight of money. He'll humble her

Selected Poems 1957–1981, 'Her Husband'

3 The war ended, the explosions stopped.
The men surrendered their weapons
And hung around limply.
Peace took them all prisoner.

Selected Poems 1957–1981, 'A Motorbike'

Hughes, Thomas (1822–96) British novelist. A Liberal MP, he is remembered for his novel *Tom Brown's Schooldays* (1857) based on Rugby School.

1 Life isn't all beer and skittles.

Tom Brown's Schooldays, Pt. I, Ch. 2

2 It's more than a game. It's an institution.

Referring to cricket
Tom Brown's Schooldays, Pt. II, Ch. 7

Hughes, William Morris (1864–1952) Australian statesman. He was prime minister first as leader of the Labour party (1915–16) and then as leader of the Nationalist Party (1916–23).

1 I'm waiting for the cock to crow.

Said in parliament, after being viciously critized by a member of his own party
The Fine Art of Political Wit (L. Harris)

Hugo, Victor (1802–85) French poet, novelist, and dramatist. His novels include *Notre Dame de Paris* (1831), *Le Roi s'amuse* (1832), and *Les Misérables* (1862). Verse collections include *Les Contemplations* (1856); at the age of 80 he wrote the play *Torquemada* (1882). He was regarded as a national hero and the foremost writer of 19th-century France.

Quotations about Hugo

1 In Victor Hugo we have the average sensual man impassioned and grandiloquent; in Zola we have the average sensual man going near the ground.

Matthew Arnold (1822–88) British poet and critic. *Discourses in America*

2 He will be eighty-one in February and walked upright without a stick. His white hair is as thick as his dark eyebrows, and his eyes are as bright and clear as a little child's. After dinner, he drank my health with a little speech of which – though I sat just opposite him – my accursed deafness prevented me hearing a single word.

Algernon Charles Swinburne (1837–1909) British poet. Letter to his mother, 26 Nov 1882

Quotations by Hugo

3 If suffer we must, let's suffer on the heights.

Contemplations, 'Les Malheureux'

4   A stand can be made against invasion by an
army; no stand can be made against invasion by
an idea.
Histoire d'un Crime, 'La Chute'

5   Symmetry is tedious, and tedium is the very basis of mourning. Despair yawns.
Les Misérables, Vol. II, Bk. IV, Ch. 1

6   The misery of a child is interesting to a mother,
the misery of a young man is interesting to a
young woman, the misery of an old man is interesting to nobody.
Les Misérables, 'Saint Denis'

7   Popularity? It's glory's small change.
Ruy Blas, III

8   ?
The entire contents of a telegram sent to his publishers asking
how *Les Misérables* was selling; the reply was '!'
The Literary Life (R. Hendrickson)

Hume, Basil George, Cardinal (1923–   ) British
Roman Catholic churchman. He became Archbishop of Westminster
in 1976; the first monk to hold this office.

1   Such persons are often good, conscientious and
faithful sons and daughters of the church.
Referring to Catholics who use contraceptives
The Observer, 'Sayings of the Week', 30 Mar 1980

2   There are times and occasions when it would be
marvellous to have a wife.
The Observer, 'Sayings of the Week', 6 Feb 1981

3   If you become holy, it is because God has made
you so. You will not know it anyway.
The Observer, 'Sayings of the Week,' 10 Jan 1984

Hume, David (1711–76) Scottish philosopher. His major
works were *A Treatise of Human Nature* (1739) and *An Enquiry
Concerning Human Understanding* (1748). He also wrote a *History
of England* (1754–62).

1   Custom, then, is the great guide of human life.
An Enquiry Concerning Human Understanding

2   If we take in our hand any volume; of divinity or
school metaphysics, for instance; let us ask,
*Does it contain any abstract reasoning concerning
quantity or number?* No. *Does it contain any experimental reasoning, concerning matter of fact
and existence?* No. Commit it then to the flames:
for it can contain nothing but sophistry and
illusion.
An Enquiry Concerning Human Understanding

3   The Christian religion not only was at first attended with miracles, but even at this day cannot
be believed by any reasonable person without
one. Mere reason is insufficient to convince us
of its veracity: and whoever is moved by faith
to assent to it, is conscious of a continued miracle in his own person, which subverts all the
principles of his understanding, and gives him a
determination to believe what is most contrary
to custom and experience.
Essays, 'Of Miracles'

4   Beauty in things exists in the mind which contemplates them.
Essays, 'Of Tragedy'

5   We never remark any passion or principle in
others, of which, in some degree or other, we
may not find a parallel in ourselves.
A Treatise of Human Nature

6   Everyone has observed how much more dogs
are animated when they hunt in a pack, than
when they pursue their game apart. We might,
perhaps, be at a loss to explain this phenomenon, if we had not experience of a similar in
ourselves.
A Treatise of Human Nature

7   Grief and disappointment give rise to anger, anger to envy, envy to malice, and malice to grief
again, till the whole circle be completed.
A Treatise of Human Nature

8   Philosophers never balance between profit and
honesty, because their decisions are general,
and neither their passions nor imaginations are
interested in the objects.
A Treatise of Human Nature

Hungerford, Margaret Wolfe (c. 1855–97) Irish
novelist. Her best-known book is *Molly Bawn* (1878).

1   Beauty is altogether in the eye of the beholder.
Molly Bawn

Hunt, George William (c. 1829–1904) British writer and
composer of music-hall songs.

1   We don't want to fight, but, by jingo if we do,
We've got the ships, we've got the men, we've
got the money too.
We've fought the Bear before, and while Britons
shall be true,
The Russians shall not have Constantinople.
We Don't Want to Fight

Hunt, (James Henry) Leigh (1784–1859) British poet
and journalist. A friend and supporter of Keats and other romantic
poets, he was imprisoned (1813) for attacks on the Prince Regent.
His books include *Imagination and Fancy* (1844) and *Autobiography*
(1850).

1   Abou Ben Adhem (may his tribe increase!)
Awoke one night from a deep dream of peace,
And saw, within the moonlight in his room,
Making it rich, and like a lily in bloom,
An angel writing in a book of gold: – . . .
Abou Ben Adhem and the Angel

2   'I pray thee then,
Write me as one that loves his fellow-men.'
Abou Ben Adhem and the Angel

3   And lo! Ben Adhem's name led all the rest.
Abou Ben Adhem and the Angel

4 Jenny kissed me when we met,
Jumping from the chair she sat in;
Time, you thief, who love to get
Sweets into your list, put that in:
Say I'm weary, say I'm sad,
Say that health and wealth have missed me,
Say I'm growing old, but add,
Jenny kissed me.

Writing about Jane Carlyle
Rondeau

5 Stolen sweets are always sweeter,
Stolen kisses much completer,
Stolen looks are nice in chapels,
Stolen, stolen, be your apples.

Song of Fairies Robbing an Orchard

Hupfeld, Herman (20th century) US songwriter.

1 You must remember this;
A kiss is just a kiss,
A sigh is just a sigh –
The fundamental things apply
As time goes by.

From the film *Casablanca*
As Time Goes By

Hurst, Sir Gerald (1877–1957) British writer and judge. His
books include *Closed Chapters* (1942) and *Lincoln's Inn Essays*
(1949).

1 One of the mysteries of human conduct is why
adult men and women all over England are
ready to sign documents which they do not read,
at the behest of canvassers whom they do not
know, binding them to pay for articles which
they do not want, with money which they have
not got.

Closed Chapters

Huss, John (Jan Hus; c. 1369–1415) Bohemian religious
reformer and priest. He was excommunicated (1410) for his
support of Wycliffe, tried for heresy, and burnt at the stake, which
led to the Hussite War (1419–34).

1 O holy simplicity!

On noticing a peasant adding a faggot to the pile at his execution.
Apophthegmata (Zincgreff-Weidner), Pt. III

Hutcheson, Francis (1694–1746) Scottish philosopher. His
various philosophical treatises include the posthumous *System of
Moral Philosophy* (1755).

1 That action is best, which procures the greatest
happiness for the greatest numbers.

Inquiry into the Original of our Ideas of Beauty and Virtue, Treatise II, 'Concerning Moral Good and Evil'

Huxley, Aldous (1894–1964) British novelist and essayist.
His novels include *Antic Hay* (1923), *Point Counter Point* (1928),
Brave New World (1932), and *Eyeless in Gaza* (1936). His non-
fiction includes *The Doors of Perception* (1954).

Quotations about Huxley

1 Mr. Huxley is perhaps one of those people who
have to perpetrate thirty bad novels before producing a good one.
T. S. Eliot (1888–1965) US-born British poet and dramatist.
Attrib.

2 Like a piece of litmus paper he has always been
quick to take the colour of his times.
The Observer, Profile, 27 Feb 1949

Quotations by Huxley

3 Thanks to words, we have been able to rise
above the brutes; and thanks to words, we have
often sunk to the level of the demons.
Adonis and the Alphabet

4 Since Mozart's day composers have learned the
art of making music throatily and palpitatingly
sexual.
Along the Road, 'Popular music'

5 Christlike in my behaviour,
Like every good believer,
I imitate the Saviour,
And cultivate a beaver.
Antic Hay, Ch. 4

6 He was only the Mild and Melancholy one foolishly disguised as a complete Man.
Antic Hay, Ch. 9

7 There are few who would not rather be taken in
adultery than in provincialism.
Antic Hay, Ch. 10

8 Mr Mercaptan went on to preach a brilliant sermon on that melancholy sexual perversion
known as continence.
Antic Hay, Ch. 18

9 Lady Capricorn, he understood, was still keeping
open bed.
Antic Hay, Ch. 21

10 Official dignity tends to increase in inverse ratio
to the importance of the country in which the
office is held.
Beyond the Mexique Bay

11 The time of our Ford.
Brave New World, Ch. 3

12 The proper study of mankind is books.
Chrome Yellow

13 We participate in a tragedy; at a comedy we only
look.
The Devils of Loudon, Ch. 11

14 Consistency is contrary to nature, contrary to
life. The only completely consistent people are
the dead.
Do What you Will

15 Thought must be divided against itself before it
can come to any knowledge of itself.
Do What You Will

16 People will insist . . . on treating the *mons Veneris* as though it were Mount Everest.

Eyeless in Gaza, Ch. 30

17 Death . . . It's the only thing we haven't succeeded in completely vulgarizing.

Eyeless in Gaza, Ch. 31

18 A million million spermatozoa,
All of them alive:
Out of their cataclysm but one poor Noah
Dare hope to survive.

Fifth Philosopher's Song

19 Christianity accepted as given a metaphysical system derived from several already existing and mutually incompatible systems.

Grey Eminence, Ch. 3

20 The quality of moral behaviour varies in inverse ratio to the number of human beings involved.

Grey Eminence, Ch. 10

21 'Bed,' as the Italian proverb succinctly puts it, 'is the poor man's opera.'

Heaven and Hell

22 I can sympathize with people's pains, but not with their pleasures. There is something curiously boring about somebody else's happiness.

Limbo, 'Cynthia'

23 She was a machine-gun riddling her hostess with sympathy.

Mortal Coils, 'The Gioconda Smile'

24 Most of one's life . . . is one prolonged effort to prevent oneself thinking.

Mortal Coils, 'Green Tunnels'

25 She was one of those indispensables of whom one makes the discovery, when they are gone, that one can get on quite as well without them.

Mortal Coils, 'Nuns at Luncheon'

26 Happiness is like coke – something you get as a by-product in the process of making something else.

Point Counter Point

27 There is no substitute for talent. Industry and all the virtues are of no avail.

Point Counter Point

28 Silence is as full of potential wisdom and wit as the unhewn marble of great sculpture.

Point Counter Point

29 A bad book is as much a labour to write as a good one; it comes as sincerely from the author's soul.

Point Counter Point

30 That all men are equal is a proposition to which, at ordinary times, no sane individual has ever given his assent.

Proper Studies

31 Those who believe that they are exclusively in the right are generally those who achieve something.

Proper Studies

32 Facts do not cease to exist because they are ignored.

Proper Studies

33 Most human beings have an almost infinite capacity for taking things for granted.

Themes and Variations

34 I'm afraid of losing my obscurity. Genuineness only thrives in the dark. Like celery.

Those Barren Leaves, Pt. I, Ch. 1

35 'It's like the question of the authorship of the *Iliad*,' said Mr Cardan. 'The author of that poem is either Homer or, if not Homer, somebody else of the same name.'

Those Barren Leaves, Pt. V, Ch. 4

36 How appallingly thorough these Germans always managed to be, how emphatic! In sex no less than in war – in scholarship, in science. Diving deeper than anyone else and coming up muddier.

37 Knowledge is proportionate to being. . . . You know in virtue of what you are.

Time Must Have a Stop, Ch. 26

38 The aristocratic pleasure of displeasing is not the only delight that bad taste can yield. One can love a certain kind of vulgarity for its own sake.

Vulgarity in Literature, Ch. 4

39 Defined in psychological terms, a fanatic is a man who consciously over-compensates a secret doubt.

Vulgarity in Literature, Ch. 4

Huxley, Sir Julian (1887–1975) British biologist. The first director general of UNESCO (1946–48), his books include *Essays of a Biologist* (1923) and *Evolution Restated* (1940).

1 We all know how the size of sums of money appears to vary in a remarkable way according as they are being paid in or paid out.

Essays of a Biologist, 5

2 Operationally, God is beginning to resemble not a ruler but the last fading smile of a cosmic Cheshire cat.

Religion without Revelation

Huxley, T(homas) H(enry) (1825–95) British biologist. A supporter of Darwin's theory of evolution, his books include *Science and Culture* (1881) and *Evolution and Ethics* (1893).

1 The great tragedy of Science – the slaying of a beautiful hypothesis by an ugly fact.

Collected Essays, 'Biogenesis and Abiogenesis'

2 Science is nothing but trained and organized common sense, differing from the latter only as a veteran may differ from a raw recruit: and its methods differ from those of common sense only as far as the guardsman's cut and thrust differ from the manner in which a savage wields his club.
Collected Essays, 'The Method of Zadig'

3 It is the customary fate of new truths to begin as heresies and to end as superstitions.
The Coming of Age of the Origin of Species

4 One of the unpardonable sins, in the eyes of most people, is for a man to go about unlabelled. The world regards such a person as the police do an unmuzzled dog, not under proper control.
Evolution and Ethics

5 I doubt if the philosopher lives, or ever has lived, who could know himself to be heartily despised by a street boy without some irritation.
Evolution and Ethics

6 The chess-board is the world; the pieces are the phenomena of the universe; the rules of the game are what we call the laws of Nature. The player on the other side is hidden from us. We know that his play is always fair, just, and patient. But also we know, to our cost, that he never overlooks a mistake, or makes the smallest allowance for ignorance.
Lay Sermons, 'A Liberal Education'

7 Some experience of popular lecturing had convinced me that the necessity of making things plain to uninstructed people was one of the very best means of clearing up the obscure corners in one's own mind.
Man's Place in Nature, Preface

8 If a little knowledge is dangerous, where is the man who has so much as to be out of danger?
On Elementary Instruction in Physiology

9 Logical consequences are the scarecrows of fools and the beacons of wise men.
Science and Culture, 'On the Hypothesis that Animals are Automata'

10 I am too much of a sceptic to deny the possibility of anything.
Letter to Herbert Spencer, 22 Mar 1886

11 I asserted – and I repeat – that a man has no reason to be ashamed of having an ape for his grandfather. If there were an ancestor whom I should feel shame in recalling it would rather be a *man* – a man of restless and versatile intellect – who, not content with an equivocal success in his own sphere of activity, plunges into scientific questions with which he has no real acquaintance, only to obscure them by an aimless rhetoric, and distract the attention of his hearers from the real point at issue by eloquent digressions and skilled appeals to religious prejudice.
Replying to Bishop WILBERFORCE in the debate on Darwin's theory of evolution at the meeting of the British Association at Oxford. No transcript was taken at the time; the version above is commonly quoted. After hearing Wilberforce's speech, and before rising himself, Huxley is said to have remarked, 'The Lord has delivered him into my hands!'
Speech, 30 June 1860

I

Ibarruri, Dolores (1895–1989) Spanish politician. A leading communist, known as 'La Pasionaria', she lived in the Soviet Union (1939–77), returning to Spain after the Communist party became legal.

1 They shall not pass!
The Spanish Civil War (H. Thomas), Ch. 16

2 It is better to die on your feet than to live on your knees.
Speech, Paris, 1936

3 It is better to be the widow of a hero than the wife of a coward.
Speech, Valencia, 1936

Ibsen, Henrik (1828–1906) Norwegian dramatist and poet. His initial successes came with *Brand* (1865) and *Peer Gynt* (1867). Subsequent works, such as *A Doll's House* (1879), *Ghosts* (1881), *An Enemy of the People* (1882), and *Hedda Gabler* (1890) established him a Europe's leading 19th-century playwright.

1 Fools are in a terrible, overwhelming majority, all the wide world over.
An Enemy of the People, IV

2 The majority has the might – more's the pity – but it hasn't right . . . The minority is always right.
An Enemy of the People, IV

3 The ‚worst enemy of truth and freedom in our society is the compact majority. Yes, the damned, compact, liberal majority.
An Enemy of the People, IV

4 A man should never put on his best trousers when he goes out to battle for freedom and truth.
An Enemy of the People, V

5 Ten o'clock . . . and back he'll come. I can just see him.
With vine leaves in his hair. Flushed and confident.
Hedda Gabler, II

6 Youth will come here and beat on my door, and force its way in.
The Master Builder, I

7 Castles in the air – they're so easy to take refuge in. So easy to build, too.

The Master Builder, III

8 What's a man's first duty? The answer's brief: To be himself.

Peer Gynt, IV:1

9 Take the life-lie away from the average man and straight away you take away his happiness.

The Wild Duck, V

10 On the contrary!

Ibsen's last words; his nurse had just remarked that he was feeling a little better
True Remarkable Occurrences (J. Train)

Icke, David (1952–) Green Party spokesperson.

1 Green politics is not about being far left or far right, but being far-sighted.

Speech, Green Party conference, Sept 1989

Ickes, Harold L(e Clair) (1874–1952) US Republican politician. He became Secretary of the Interior (1933–46).

1 I am against government by crony.

Comment on his resignation as Secretary of the Interior (1946) after a dispute with President Truman

2 The trouble with Senator Long is that he is suffering from halitosis of the intellect. That's presuming Emperor Long has an intellect.

The Politics of Upheaval (A. M. Schlesinger Jnr), Pt. II, Ch. 14

Illich, Ivan (1926–) Austrian sociologist. A former Catholic priest, he is critical of the consumer society. His books include *Deschooling Society* (1971) and *Tools for Conviviality* (1973).

1 Any attempt to reform the university without attending to the system of which it is an integral part is like trying to do urban renewal in New York City from the twelfth storey up.

Deschooling Society, Ch. 3

2 Man must choose whether to be rich in things or in the freedom to use them.

Deschooling Society, Ch. 4

3 We must rediscover the distinction between hope and expectation.

Deschooling Society, Ch. 7

4 In a consumer society there are inevitably two kinds of slaves: the prisoners of addiction and the prisoners of envy.

Tools for Conviviality

5 A just society would be one in which liberty for one person is constrained only by the demands created by equal liberty for another.

Tools for Conviviality

Inge, William Ralph (1860–1954) British churchman, who became Dean of St Pauls (1911–34) and wrote a number of books, including *Christian Mysticism* (1899).

1 What we know of the past is mostly not worth knowing. What is worth knowing is mostly uncertain. Events in the past may roughly be divided into those which probably never happened and those which do not matter.

Assessments and Anticipations, 'Prognostications'

2 The enemies of Freedom do not argue; they shout and they shoot.

The End of an Age, Ch. 4

3 The effect of boredom on a large scale in history is underestimated. It is a main cause of revolutions, and would soon bring to an end all the static Utopias and the farmyard civilization of the Fabians.

The End of an Age, Ch. 6

4 Many people believe that they are attracted by God, or by Nature, when they are only repelled by man.

More Lay Thoughts of a Dean

5 To become a popular religion, it is only necessary for a superstition to enslave a philosophy.

Outspoken Essays

6 It takes in reality only one to make a quarrel. It is useless for the sheep to pass resolutions in favour of vegetarianism while the wolf remains of a different opinion.

Outspoken Essays

7 Democracy is only an experiment in government, and it has the obvious disadvantage of merely counting votes instead of weighing them.

Possible Recovery?

8 Literature flourishes best when it is half a trade and half an art.

The Victorian Age

9 The proper time to influence the character of a child is about a hundred years before he is born.

The Observer, 21 June, 1929

10 A nation is a society united by a delusion about its ancestry and by a common hatred of its neighbours.

The Perpetual Pessimist (Sagittarius and George)

11 A man may build himself a throne of bayonets, but he cannot sit on it.

Wit and Wisdom of Dean Inge (ed. Marchant)

12 The nations which have put mankind and posterity most in their debt have been small states – Israel, Athens, Florence, Elizabethan England.

Wit and Wisdom of Dean Inge (ed. Marchant)

Ingersoll, Robert G(reen) (1833–99) US lawyer and agnostic. His books include *The Gods* (1876) and *Why I am an Agnostic* (1896).

1 An honest God is the noblest work of man.

The Gods

2 In nature there are neither rewards nor punishments – there are consequences.

Lectures & Essays, 'Some Reasons Why'

3 Many people think they have religion when they are troubled with dyspepsia.

Liberty of Man, Woman and Child, Section 3

4 Few rich men own their property. The property owns them.

Address to the McKinley League, New York. 29 Oct 1896

Ingrams, Richard (1937–) British editor and writer. Former editor of *Private Eye*, he has written a number of books, including *Mrs Wilson's Diary* (with John Wells; 1965), and *God's Apology* (1977).

1 I have come to regard the law courts not as a cathedral but rather as a casino.

The Guardian, 30 July 1977

2 My own motto is publish and be sued.

Referring to his editorship of *Private Eye*
BBC radio broadcast, 4 May 1977

Ionesco, Eugène (1912–) French dramatist. His 'theatre-of-the-absurd' plays include *The Bald Prima Donna* (1950), *Chairs* (1951), *Rhinoceros* (1960), and *Man with Bags* (1977).

1 Many people have delusions of grandeur but you're deluded by triviality.

Exit the King

Iphicrates (d. 353 BC) Athenian general who fought against Sparta during the Corinthian war (394–387 BC).

1 The difference between us is that my family begins with me, whereas yours ends with you.

Reply to a descendant of Harmodius (an Athenian hero), who had derided Iphicrates for being the son of a cobbler
Attrib.

Irving, Washington (1783–1859) US writer. His collection of short stories, *The Sketch Book* (1819), established his reputation, which was reinforced by his five-volume biography of George Washington.

1 Whenever a man's friends begin to compliment him about looking young, he may be sure that they think he is growing old.

Bracebridge Hall, 'Bachelors'

2 A tart temper never mellows with age, and a sharp tongue is the only edged tool that grows keener with constant use.

The Sketch Book, 'Rip Van Winkle'

3 There is a certain relief in change, even though it be from bad to worse; as I have found in travelling in a stage-coach, that it is often a comfort to shift one's position and be bruised in a new place.

Tales of a Traveller, 'To the Reader'

4 The almighty dollar, that great object of universal devotion throughout our land, seems to have no genuine devotees in these peculiar villages.

Wolfert's Roost, 'The Creole Village'

Isherwood, Christopher (1904–86) British novelist. He described pre-war Berlin in *Mr Norris Changes Trains* (1935) and *Goodbye to Berlin* (1939). Other books include *A Single Man* (1964) and the autobiographical *Christopher and His Kind* (1977).

1 I am a camera with its shutter open, quite passive, recording, not thinking.

Goodbye to Berlin

2 We live in stirring times – tea-stirring times.

Mr Norris Changes Trains

J

Jackson, Andrew (1767–1845) US statesman and soldier. A hero of the War of 1812, he served as US president from 1829 to 1937.

Quotations about Jackson

1 Where is there a chief magistrate of whom so much evil has been predicted, and from whom so much good has come?

Thomas H. Benton *30 Years in the U.S. Senate*, Vol. I

2 He was too generous to be frugal, too kind-hearted to be thrifty, too honest to live above his means.

Vernon Parrington (1871–1929) *Main Currents in American Thought*, Vol. I, Bk. II

Quotations by Jackson

3 Elevate them guns a little lower.

Order given whilst watching the effect of the US artillery upon the British lines at the battle of New Orleans
Attrib.

Jackson, F. J. Foakes (1855–1941) British academic.

1 It's no use trying to be *clever* – we are all clever here; just try to be *kind* – a little kind.

Advice given to a new don at Jesus College, Cambridge
Noted in A. C. Benson's Commonplace Book British academic.

Jackson, Jesse (1941–) US Black democrat politician. A Baptist preacher, he supported the civil rights leader Martin Luther King and ran for the presidential nomination in 1984 and 1988.

1 When people come together, flowers always flourish – the air is rich with the aroma of a new spring. Take New York, the dynamic metropolis. What makes New York so special? It's the invitation of the Statue of Liberty – give me your tired, your poor, your huddled masses who yearn to breathe free. Not restricted to English only.

Speech, Democratic Party Convention, Atlanta, July 1988

2 America is not a blanket woven from one thread, one color, one cloth.

Speech, Democratic Party Convention, Atlanta, July 1988

Jacobi, Karl Gustav Jacob (1804–51) German mathematician who made important discoveries in function theory, the theory of determinants, and mechanics.

1 Pardon me, madam, but *I* am my brother.

On being mistaken by a lady for his brother
Men of Mathematics (M. H. Jacobi)

Jacobs, Joe (1896–1940) US boxing manager.

1 We was robbed!

Complaining to the audience when the heavyweight title of Max Schmeling, whom he managed, was passed to Jack Sharkey
Attrib.

James, Alice (1848–92) US diarist; the sister of William and Henry James.

1 It is so comic to hear oneself called old, even at ninety I suppose!

Letter to William James, 14 June 1889
The Diary of Alice James (ed. Leon Edel)

2 Notwithstanding the poverty of my outside experience, I have always had a significance for myself, and every chance to stumble along my straight and narrow little path, and to worship at the feet of my Deity, and what more can a human soul ask for?

The Diary of Alice James (ed. Leon Edel)

3 I suppose one has a greater sense of intellectual degradation after an interview with a doctor than from any human experience.

The Diary of Alice James (ed. Leon Edel), 27 Sept 1890

James, Clive (Vivian Leopold (1939–) Australian writer and broadcaster. His publications include the autobiographical *May Week* (1990).

1 Even today, when some oaf who has confused rudeness with blunt speech tells me exactly what he thinks, I tend to stand there wondering what I have done to deserve it, instead of telling him exactly what I think right back.

Falling Towards England, Ch. 4

2 The owner of the business arrived in a Bentley to tour the shop-floor, his blazered school-age son in attendance. They paraded like royalty, with their hands behind their backs. Only the blunt-spoken supervisor got his hand shaken. It was because his hand was clean. In Australia the air would have been thick with first names. I really was in another country.

Falling Towards England, Ch. 8

James, Henry (1843–1916) US novelist, who spent much of his life in Europe (from 1876 in England). *Roderick Hudson* (1875), his first successful novel, was followed by *Washington Square* (1881), *The Bostonians* (1886), *The Turn of the Screw* (1898), *The Ambassadors* (1903), and several others.

Quotations about James

1 Henry James has a mind so fine that no idea could violate it.

T. S. Eliot (1888–1965) US-born British poet and dramatist.
Attrib.

2 Henry James was one of the nicest old ladies I ever met.

William Faulkner (1897–1962) US novelist. Attrib.

3 The work of Henry James has always seemed divisible by a simple dynastic arrangement into three reigns. James I, James II, and the Old Pretender.

Philip Guedalla (1889–1944) British writer. *Collected Essays*, 'Men of Letters: Mr. Henry James'

Quotations by James

4 Live all you can; it's a mistake not to. It doesn't so much matter what you do in particular, so long as you have your life. If you haven't had that what *have* you had?

The Ambassadors, Bk. V, Ch. 2

5 Experience was to be taken as showing that one might get a five-pound note as one got a light for a cigarette; but one had to check the friendly impulse to ask for it in the same way.

The Awkward Age

6 It takes a great deal of history to produce a little literature.

Life of Nathaniel Hawthorne, Ch. 1

7 He was unperfect, unfinished, inartistic; he was worse than provincial – he was parochial.

Referring to Thoreau
Life of Nathaniel Hawthorne, Ch. 4

8 To kill a human being is, after all, the least injury you can do him.

My Friend Bingham

9 The only obligation to which in advance we may hold a novel, without incurring the accusation of being arbitrary, is that it be interesting.

Partial Portraits, 'The Art of Fiction'

10 Experience is never limited, and it is never complete; it is an immense sensibility, a kind of huge spider-web of the finest silken threads suspended in the chamber of consciousness, and catching every air-borne particle in its tissue.

Partial Portraits, 'The Art of Fiction'

11 What is character but the determination of incident? What is incident but the illustration of character?

Partial Portraits, 'The Art of Fiction'

12 The superiority of one man's opinion over another's is never so great as when the opinion is about a woman.

The Tragic Muse, Ch. 9

13 Nurse, take away the candle and spare my blushes.

On being informed, whilst confined to his bed, that he had been awarded the Order of Merit
The American Treasury (C. Fadiman)

14 Summer afternoon – summer afternoon; to me those have always been the two most beautiful words in the English language.

A Backward Glance (Edith Wharton), Ch. 10

15 So it has come at last, the distinguished thing.
Referring to his own death
A Backward Glance (Edith Wharton), Ch. 14

James, William (1842–1910) US psychologist and philosopher. His most acclaimed works were *Varieties of Religious Experience* (1902) and *The Meaning of Truth* (1909).

1 Our civilization is founded on the shambles, and every individual existence goes out in a lonely spasm of helpless agony.
Varieties of Religious Experience

2 If merely 'feeling good' could decide, drunkenness would be the supremely valid human experience.
Varieties of Religious Experience

3 We are thinking beings, and we cannot exclude the intellect from participating in any of our functions.
Varieties of Religious Experience

4 The moral flabbiness born of the bitch-goddess Success.
Letter to H. G. Wells, 11 Sept 1906

James I (1566–1625) The first Stuart King of England and Ireland and, as James VI, King of Scotland. One of the achievements of his reign was the publication of the King James (Authorized) version of the Bible.

1 A custom loathsome to the eye, hateful to the nose, harmful to the brain, dangerous to the lungs, and in the black, stinking fume thereof, nearest resembling the horrible Stygian smoke of the pit that is bottomless.
Referring to smoking
A Counterblast to Tobacco

2 A branch of the sin of drunkenness, which is the root of all sins.
A Counterblast to Tobacco

3 I will govern according to the common weal, but not according to the common will.
History of the English People (J. R. Green)

4 These are rare attainments for a damsel, but pray tell me, can she spin?
On being introduced to a young girl proficient in Latin, Greek, and Hebrew
Attrib.

5 Dr Donne's verses are like the peace of God; they pass all understanding.
Attrib.

6 He was a bold man who first swallowed an oyster.
Attrib.

Jarrell, Randall (1914–65) US author and poet.

1 President Robbins was so well adjusted to his environment that sometimes you could not tell which was the environment and which was President Robbins.
Pictures from an Institution, Pt. I, Ch. 4

2 To Americans English manners are far more frightening than none at all.
Pictures from an Institution, Pt. I, Ch. 5

Jarry, Alfred (1873–1907) French surrealist dramatist. His *Ubu Roi* is a satire on bourgeois conventions.

1 Madame, I would have given you another!
On being reprimanded by a woman for firing his pistol in the vicinity of her child, who might have been killed
Recollections of a Picture Dealer (A. Vollard)

Jay, Peter (1937–   ) British economist and broadcaster. He is the son-in-law of the former Labour prime minister, James Callaghan.

1 As the Prime Minister put it to me . . . he saw his role as being that of Moses.
Referring to a conversation with James Callaghan
Guardian Weekly, 18 Sept 1977

Jeans, Sir James Hopwood (1877–1946) British scientist. He worked on the kinetic theory of gases but is best remembered for his books popularizing science, including *The Universe Around Us* (1930), *Through Space and Time* (1934), and *Science and Music* (1937).

1 Life exists in the universe only because the carbon atom possesses certain exceptional properties.
The Mysterious Universe, Ch. 1

2 Science should leave off making pronouncements: the river of knowledge has too often turned back on itself.
The Mysterious Universe, Ch. 5

Jefferson, Thomas (1743–1826) US statesman; the third President (1801–09). He was the chief author of the Declaration of Independence.

Quotations about Jefferson

1 His attachment to those of his friends whom he could make useful to himself was thoroughgoing and exemplary.
John Quincy Adams (1767–1848) Sixth president of the USA.
Diary, 29 July 1836

2 A gentleman of thirty-two who could calculate an eclipse, survey an estate, tie an artery, plan an edifice, try a cause, break a horse, dance a minuet, and play the violin.
James Parton *Life of Thomas Jefferson*, Ch. 19

Quotations by Jefferson

3 The whole commerce between master and slave is a perpetual exercise of the most boisterous passions, the most unremitting despotism on the one part, and degrading submissions on the other.
Notes on the State of Virginia

4 When in the course of human events, it becomes necessary for one people to dissolve the political bonds which have connected them with another, and to assume among the powers of the earth the separate and equal station to which the laws of nature and of Nature's God entitle them, a decent respect to the opinions of mankind requires that they should declare the causes which impel them to the separation.

Declaration of Independence, Preamble

5 We hold these truths to be sacred and undeniable; that all men are created equal and independent, that from that equal creation they derive rights inherent and inalienable, among which are the preservation of life, and liberty, and the pursuit of happiness.

Declaration of Independence (original draft)

6 We hold these truths to be self-evident: that all men are created equal; that they are endowed by their Creator with certain unalienable rights; that among these are life, liberty, and the pursuit of happiness.

Declaration of Independence, 4 July 1776

7 A little rebellion now and then is a good thing.

Letter to James Madison, 30 Jan 1787

8 The tree of liberty must be refreshed from time to time with the blood of patriots and tyrants. It is its natural manure.

Letter to W. S. Smith, 13 Nov 1787

Jellicoe, John Rushworth, Earl (1859–1935) British admiral. He was commander of the grand fleet in World War I.

1 I had always to remember that I could have lost the war in an afternoon.

Referring to the battle of Jutland

Jenkins, Roy (Harris), Baron (1920–   ) British statesman and historian. He was chancellor of the exchequer (1967–70), home secretary (1974–76), and president of the EEC commission (1977–81). Originally a member of the Labour Party he was one of the founders of the Social Democratic Party (1981).

1 The permissive society has been allowed to become a dirty phrase. A better phrase is the civilized society.

Speech, Abingdon, 19 July 1969

2 There are always great dangers in letting the best be the enemy of the good.

Speech, House of Commons, 1975

3 Breaking the mould of British politics.

Referring to the establishment of the Social Democratic Party

Jennings, Elizabeth (1926–   ) British poet and writer. Her collections include *Poems* (1953), *Song for a Birth or a Death* (1961), and *Moments of Grace* (1980).

1 Do not suppose that I do not fear death
Because I trust it is no end. You say
It must be a great comfort to live with
Such a faith, but you don't know the way
I battle on this earth

With faults of character I try to change
But they bound back on me like living things.
The Fear of Death

2 Now deep in my bed I turn
And the world turns on the other side.
In the Night

Jennings, Paul (1918–   ) British humorous writer.

1 Of all musicians, flautists are most obviously the ones who know something we don't know.
The Jenguin Pennings, 'Flautists Flaunt Afflatus'

2 Wembley, adj. Suffering from a vague *malaise*. 'I feel a bit w. this morning.'
The Jenguin Pennings, 'Ware, Wye, Watford'

Jerome, Jerome K(lapka) (1859–1927) British dramatist and humorist. His books include *The Idle Thoughts of an Idle Fellow* (1889), *Three Men in a Boat* (1889), and *The Passing of the Third Floor Buck* (1908).

1 Love is like the measles; we all have to go through with it.
Idle Thoughts of an Idle Fellow

2 Conceit is the finest armour a man can wear.
Idle Thoughts of an Idle Fellow

3 It is easy enough to say that poverty is no crime. No; if it were men wouldn't be ashamed of it. It is a blunder, though, and is punished as such. A poor man is despised the whole world over.
Idle Thoughts of an Idle Fellow

4 If you are foolish enough to be contented, don't show it, but grumble with the rest.
Idle Thoughts of an Idle Fellow

5 It is impossible to enjoy idling thoroughly unless one has plenty of work to do.
Idle Thoughts of an Idle Fellow

6 But there, everything has its drawbacks, as the man said when his mother-in-law died, and they came down upon him for the funeral expenses.
Three Men in a Boat, Ch. 3

7 I like work; it fascinates me. I can sit and look at it for hours. I love to keep it by me; the idea of getting rid of it nearly breaks my heart.
Three Men in a Boat, Ch. 15

Jerrold, Douglas William (1803–57) British dramatist. His plays include *Black-eyed Susan* (1829) and *Time Works Wonders* (1845).

1 Religion's in the heart, not in the knees.
The Devil's Ducat, I.2

2 The best thing I know between France and England is – the sea.
Wit and Opinions of Douglas Jerrold, 'The Anglo-French Alliance'

3 That fellow would vulgarize the day of judgment.
Wit and Opinions of Douglas Jerrold, 'A Comic Author'

4 Talk to him of Jacob's ladder, and he would ask the number of the steps.
Wit and Opinions of Douglas Jerrold, 'A Matter-of-fact Man'

5 Love's like the measles – all the worse when it comes late in life.
Wit and Opinions of Douglas Jerrold, 'A Philanthropist'

6 The ugliest of trades have their moments of pleasure. Now, if I were a grave-digger, or even a hangman, there are some people I could work for with a great deal of enjoyment.
Wit and Opinions of Douglas Jerrold, 'Ugly Trades'

7 The only athletic sport I ever mastered was backgammon.
Douglas Jerrold (W. Jerrold), Vol. I, Ch. I

8 Sir, you are like a pin, but without either its head or its point.
Speaking to a small thin man who was boring him
Attrib.

Jewel, John (1522–71) English bishop. His *Apologia pro Ecclesia Anglicana* (1562) was the first formal statement of Anglican theology.

1 In old time we had treen chalices and golden priests, but now we have treen priests and golden chalices.
Certain Sermons Preached Before the Queen's Majesty

Joad, Cyril (Edwin Mitchinson) (1891–1953) British writer and broadcaster.

1 Whenever I look inside myself I am afraid.
The Observer, 'Sayings of the Week', 8 Nov 1942

2 There was never an age in which useless knowledge was more important than in our own.
The Observer, 'Sayings of the Week', 30 Sept 1951

3 It will be said of this generation that it found England a land of beauty and left it a land of beauty spots.
The Observer, 'Sayings of Our Times', 31 May 1953

Joan of Arc, St (Jeanne d'Arc; c. 1412–31) French patriot. Known as the Maid of Orleans, she led an army against the English and won several victories before being captured and burned as a heretic.

1 Deliver the keys of all the good towns you have taken and violated in France to the Maid who has been sent by God the King of Heaven! Go away, for God's sake, back to your own country; otherwise, await news of the Maid, who will soon visit you to your great detriment.
Letter to the English, 1429, *Saint Joan of Arc* (Vita Sackville-West)

2 I was in my thirteenth year when God sent a voice to guide me. At first, I was very much frightened. The voice came towards the hour of noon, in summer, in my father's garden.
Said at her trial

3 If I said that God did not send me, I should condemn myself; truly God did send me.
Said at her trial

John III Sobieski (1624–96) King of Poland (1674–96).

1 I came; I saw; God conquered.
Announcing his victory over the Turks at Vienna to the pope (paraphrasing Caesar's 'veni, vidi, vici')
Attrib.

John XXIII (Angelo Roncalli; 1881–1963) Italian churchman, who was pope (1958–63) and called the 1962 Vatican Council. His diary, *The Journal of a Soul*, was published in 1965.

1 I am able to follow my own death step by step. Now I move softly towards the end.
Remark made two days before he died
The Guardian, 3 June 1963

John of the Cross, St (Juan de Yepes y Alvarez; 1542–91) Spanish churchman and poet. His mystical poems include *Noche oscura del alma*.

1 I die because I do not die.
Coplas del alma que pena por ver a dios

2 The dark night of the soul.
English translation of *Noche oscura del alma*, the title of a poem; *see also* FITZGERALD, F. SCOTT

John Paul II (Karol Wójtyla; 1920–) Polish pope (1978–); the first non-Italian pope since 1522.

1 It is unbecoming for a cardinal to ski badly.
Replying to the suggestion that it was inappropriate for him, a cardinal, to ski
John Paul II

2 We thus denounce the false and dangerous program of the arms race, of the secret rivalry between peoples for military superiority.
The Observer, 'Sayings of the Week', 19 Dec 1976

3 War should belong to the tragic past, to history: it should find no place on humanity's agenda for the future.
Speech, 1982

Johnson, Amy (1903–41) British flyer; she made record solo flights to Australia (1930), Tokyo (1932), and the Cape of Good Hope (1936). She flew the Atlantic in 1936 with her husband. She was killed in an air crash.

1 Had I been a man I might have explored the Poles or climbed Mount Everest, but as it was my spirit found outlet in the air. . . .
Myself When Young (ed. Margot Asquith)

Johnson, Hiram Warren (1866–1945) US politician. He was governor of California (1911–17) and a senator (1917).

1 The first casualty when war comes is truth.
Speech, US Senate, 1917

Johnson, Lyndon B(aines) (1908–73) US statesman. He became Democratic President from 1963 to 1969. His increased involvement in the Vietnam war made him unpopular.

Quotations about Johnson

1 An extraordinarily gifted president who was the wrong man from the wrong place at the wrong time under the wrong circumstances.

Eric F. Goldman *The Tragedy of Lyndon Johnson*, Ch. 18

2 Lyndon acts like there was never going to be a tomorrow.

Lady Bird Johnson (1912–) Wife of Lyndon B. Johnson. Attrib.

3 Kennedy promised, Johnson delivered.

Arthur Schlesinger Jnr (1917–) US historian, educator, and author. *The Observer*, 20 Nov 1983

Quotations by Johnson

4 Jerry Ford is so dumb that he can't fart and chew gum at the same time.

Sometimes quoted as '. . . can't walk and chew gum' *A Ford, Not a Lincoln* (R. Reeves), Ch. 1

5 If you're in politics and you can't tell when you walk into a room who's for you and who's against you, then you're in the wrong line of work.

The Lyndon Johnson Story (B. Mooney)

6 I am going to build the kind of nation that President Roosevelt hoped for, President Truman worked for and President Kennedy died for.

The Sunday Times, 27 Dec 1964

7 I'd much rather have that fellow inside my tent pissing out, than outside my tent pissing in.

When asked why he retained J. Edgar Hoover at the FBI *Guardian Weekly*, 18 Dec 1971

Johnson, Paul (1928–) British editor and writer. He was editor of the *New Statesman* (1965–70); his books include *The Suez War* (1957), *A History of Christianity* (1976), and *Ireland: Land of Troubles* (1980).

1 For me this is a vital litmus test: no intellectual society can flourish where a Jew feels even slightly uneasy.

The Sunday Times Magazine, 6 Feb 1977

Johnson, Samuel (1709–84) British lexicographer and writer. His *Dictionary of the English Language* appeared in 1755. The moral fable *Rasselas* (1759) was followed by *The Lives of the English Poets* (1781). His close friend James Boswell wrote his celebrated biography, *Boswell's Life of Johnson* (1791).

Quotations about Johnson

1 There is no arguing with Johnson, for when his pistol misses fire, he knocks you down with the butt of it.

Oliver Goldsmith (1728–74) Irish-born British writer. *Life of Johnson* (J. Boswell)

2 That great Cham of Literature, Samuel Johnson.

Tobias Smollett (1721–71) British novelist. Letter to John Wilkes, 16 Mar 1759

3 Johnson made the most brutal speeches to living persons; for though he was good-natured at bottom he was ill-natured at top.

Horace Walpole (1717–97) British writer. *Letters*

Quotations by Johnson

4 Every quotation contributes something to the stability or enlargement of the language.

Dictionary of the English Language

5 But these were the dreams of a poet doomed at last to wake a lexicographer.

Dictionary of the English Language

6 I am not yet so lost in lexicography, as to forget that words are the daughters of earth, and that things are the sons of heaven. Language is only the instrument of science, and words are but the signs of ideas: I wish, however, that the instrument might be less apt to decay, and that signs might be permanent, like the things which they denote.

Dictionary of the English Language

7 I have protracted my work till most of those whom I wished to please have sunk into the grave; and success and miscarriage are empty sounds.

Dictionary of the English Language

8 *Dull.* 8. To make dictionaries is dull work.

Dictionary of the English Language

9 *Excise.* A hateful tax levied upon commodities.

Dictionary of the English Language

10 *Lexicographer.* A writer of dictionaries, a harmless drudge.

Dictionary of the English Language

11 *Net.* Anything reticulated or decussated at equal distances, with interstices between the intersections.

Dictionary of the English Language

12 *Oats.* A grain, which in England is generally given to horses, but in Scotland supports the people.

Dictionary of the English Language

13 *Patron.* Commonly a wretch who supports with insolence, and is paid with flattery.

Dictionary of the English Language

14 When the messenger who carried the last sheet to Millar returned, Johnson asked him, 'Well, what did he say?' – 'Sir (answered the messenger), he said, thank God I have done with him.' – 'I am glad (replied Johnson, with a smile) that he thanks God for anything.'

After the final page of his *Dictionary* had been delivered

15 When two Englishmen meet, their first talk is of the weather.

The Idler

16 Pleasure is very seldom found where it is sought; our brightest blazes of gladness are commonly kindled by unexpected sparks.
The Idler

17 We are inclined to believe those whom we do not know because they have never deceived us.
The Idler

18 A Scotchman must be a very sturdy moralist who does not love Scotland better than truth.
Journey to the Western Islands of Scotland, 'Col'

19 The reciprocal civility of authors is one of the most risible scenes in the farce of life.
Life of Sir Thomas Browne

20 The true genius is a mind of large general powers, accidentally determined to some particular direction.
Lives of the English Poets, 'Cowley'

21 I am disappointed by that stroke of death, which has eclipsed the gaiety of nations and impoverished the public stock of harmless pleasure.
Epitaph on David Garrick
Lives of the English Poets, 'Edmund Smith'

22 We are perpetually moralists, but we are geometricians only by chance. Our intercourse with intellectual nature is necessary; our speculations upon matter are voluntary, and at leisure.
Lives of the English Poets, 'Milton'

23 There are minds so impatient of inferiority that their gratitude is a species of revenge, and they return benefits, not because recompense is a pleasure, but because obligation is a pain.
The Rambler

24 I have laboured to refine our language to grammatical purity, and to clear it from colloquial barbarisms, licentious idioms, and irregular combinations.
The Rambler

25 The love of life is necessary to the vigorous prosecution of any undertaking.
The Rambler

26 Almost every man wastes part of his life in attempts to display qualities which he does not possess, and to gain applause which he cannot keep.
The Rambler

27 There is a certain race of men that either imagine it their duty, or make it their amusement, to hinder the reception of every work of learning or genius, who stand as sentinels in the avenues of fame, and value themselves upon giving Ignorance and Envy the first notice of a prey.
The Rambler

28 Human life is everywhere a state in which much is to be endured, and little to be enjoyed.
Rasselas, Ch. 11

29 Marriage has many pains, but celibacy has no pleasures.
Rasselas, Ch. 26

30 Integrity without knowledge is weak and useless, and knowledge without integrity is dangerous and dreadful.
Rasselas, Ch. 41

31 Madam, before you flatter a man so grossly to his face, you should consider whether or not your flattery is worth his having.
Diary and Letters (Mme D'Arblay), Vol. I, Ch. 2

32 Every man has, some time in his life, an ambition to be a wag.
Diary and Letters (Mme D'Arblay), Vol. III, Ch. 46

33 If the man who turnips cries,
Cry not when his father dies,
'Tis a proof that he had rather
Have a turnip than his father.
Johnsonian Miscellanies (ed. G. B. Hill), Vol. I

34 GOLDSMITH. Here's such a stir about a fellow that has written one book, and I have written many.
JOHNSON. Ah, Doctor, there go two-and-forty sixpences you know to one guinea.
Referring to Beattie's *Essay on Truth*
Johnsonian Miscellanies (ed. G. B. Hill), Vol. I

35 It is very strange, and very melancholy, that the paucity of human pleasures should persuade us ever to call hunting one of them.
Johnsonian Miscellanies (ed. G. B. Hill), Vol. I

36 Was there ever yet anything written by mere man that was wished longer by its readers, excepting *Don Quixote, Robinson Crusoe,* and the *Pilgrim's Progress?*
Johnsonian Miscellanies (ed. G. B. Hill), Vol. I

37 A man is in general better pleased when he has a good dinner upon his table, than when his wife talks Greek.
Johnsonian Miscellanies (ed. G. B. Hill), Vol. II

38 A tavern chair is the throne of human felicity.
Johnsonian Miscellanies (ed. G. B. Hill), Vol. II

39 The only sensual pleasure without vice.
Referring to music
Johnsonian Miscellanies (ed. G. B. Hill), Vol. II

40 Difficult do you call it, Sir? I wish it were impossible.
On hearing a famous violinist
Johnsonian Miscellanies (ed. G. B. Hill), Vol. II

41 What is written without effort is in general read without pleasure.
Johnsonian Miscellanies (ed. G. B. Hill), Vol. II

42 Love is the wisdom of the fool and the folly of the wise.
Johnsonian Miscellanies (ed. G. B. Hill), Vol. II

43 In my early years I read very hard. It is a sad reflection, but a true one, that I knew almost as much at eighteen as I do now.
Life of Johnson (J. Boswell), Vol. I

44 It is incident to physicians, I am afraid, beyond all other men, to mistake subsequence for consequence.
Life of Johnson (J. Boswell), Vol. I

45 He was a vicious man, but very kind to me. If you call a dog *Hervey*, I shall love him.
Life of Johnson (J. Boswell), Vol. I

46 I'll come no more behind your scenes, David; for the silk stockings and white bosoms of your actresses excite my amorous propensities.
Said to the actor-manager David Garrick
Life of Johnson (J. Boswell), Vol. I

47 A man may write at any time, if he will set himself doggedly to it.
Life of Johnson (J. Boswell), Vol. I

48 Is not a Patron, my Lord, one who looks with unconcern on a man struggling for life in the water, and, when he has reached ground, encumbers him with help? The notice which you have been pleased to take of my labours, had it been early, had been kind; but it has been delayed till I am indifferent, and cannot enjoy it; till I am solitary, and cannot impart it; till I am known, and do not want it.
Letter to Lord Chesterfield, 7 Feb 1755
Life of Johnson (J. Boswell), Vol. I

49 A fly, Sir, may sting a stately horse and make him wince; but one is but an insect, and the other is a horse still.
Referring to critics
Life of Johnson (J. Boswell), Vol. I

50 This man I thought had been a Lord among wits; but, I find, he is only a wit among Lords.
Referring to Lord Chesterfield
Life of Johnson (J. Boswell), Vol. I

51 They teach the morals of a whore, and the manners of a dancing master.
Referring to Lord Chesterfield's *Letters*
Life of Johnson (J. Boswell), Vol. I

52 There are two things which I am confident I can do very well: one is an introduction to any literary work, stating what it is to contain, and how it should be executed in the most perfect manner; the other is a conclusion, shewing from various causes why the execution has not been equal to what the author promised to himself and to the public.
Life of Johnson (J. Boswell), Vol. I

53 Ignorance, madam, pure ignorance.
His reply on being questioned, by a lady reader of his *Dictionary*, why he had defined 'pastern' as the 'knee' of a horse
Life of Johnson (J. Boswell), Vol. I

54 If a man does not make new acquaintance as he advances through life, he will soon find himself left alone. A man, Sir, should keep his friendship in constant repair.
Life of Johnson (J. Boswell), Vol. I

55 The booksellers are generous liberal-minded men.
Life of Johnson (J. Boswell), Vol. I

56 No man will be a sailor who has contrivance enough to get himself into a jail; for being in a ship is being in a jail, with the chance of being drowned . . . A man in a jail has more room, better food, and commonly better company.
Life of Johnson (J. Boswell), Vol. I

57 BOSWELL. I do indeed come from Scotland, but I cannot help it . . .
JOHNSON. That, Sir, I find, is what a very great many of your countrymen cannot help.
Life of Johnson (J. Boswell), Vol. I

58 Yes, Sir, many men, many women, and many children.
When asked by Dr Blair whether any man of their own time could have written the poems of Ossian
Life of Johnson (J. Boswell), Vol. I

59 You *may* abuse a tragedy, though you cannot write one. You may scold a carpenter who has made you a bad table, though you cannot make a table. It is not your trade to make tables.
Referring to the qualifications needed to indulge in literary criticism
Life of Johnson (J. Boswell), Vol. I

60 He is the richest author that ever grazed the common of literature.
Referring to Dr John Campbell
Life of Johnson (J. Boswell), Vol. I

61 Great abilities are not requisite for an Historian . . . Imagination is not required in any high degree.
Life of Johnson (J. Boswell), Vol. I

62 Norway, too, has noble wild prospects; and Lapland is remarkable for prodigious noble wild prospects. But, Sir, let me tell you, the noblest prospect which a Scotchman ever sees, is the high road that leads him to England!
Life of Johnson (J. Boswell), Vol. I

63 A man ought to read just as inclination leads him; for what he reads as a task will do him little good.
Life of Johnson (J. Boswell), Vol. I

64 But if he does really think that there is no distinction between virtue and vice, why, Sir, when he leaves our houses let us count our spoons.
Life of Johnson (J. Boswell), Vol. I

65 Truth, Sir, is a cow, which will yield such people no more milk, and so they are gone to milk the bull.
Referring to sceptics
Life of Johnson (J. Boswell), Vol. I

66 Your levellers wish to level *down* as far as themselves; but they cannot bear levelling *up* to themselves.
Life of Johnson (J. Boswell), Vol. I

67 It is no matter what you teach them first, any more than what leg you shall put into your breeches first.
Referring to the education of children
Life of Johnson (J. Boswell), Vol. I

68 It is burning a farthing candle at Dover, to shew light at Calais.
Referring to the impact of Sheridan's works upon the English language
Life of Johnson (J. Boswell), Vol. I

69 A woman's preaching is like a dog's walking on his hinder legs. It is not done well; but you are surprised to find it done at all.
Life of Johnson (J. Boswell), Vol. I

70 This was a good dinner enough, to be sure; but it was not a dinner to *ask* a man to.
Life of Johnson (J. Boswell), Vol. I

71 I refute it *thus*.
Replying to Boswell's contention that they were unable to refute Bishop Berkeley's theory of matter, by kicking a large stone with his foot
Life of Johnson (J. Boswell), Vol. I

72 A very unclubable man.
Referring to Sir John Hawkins
Life of Johnson (J. Boswell), Vol. I

73 That all who are happy, are equally happy, is not true. A peasant and a philosopher may be equally *satisfied*, but not equally *happy*. Happiness consists in the multiplicity of agreeable consciousness.
Life of Johnson (J. Boswell), Vol. II

74 Our tastes greatly alter. The lad does not care for the child's rattle, and the old man does not care for the young man's whore.
Life of Johnson (J. Boswell), Vol. II

75 Shakespeare never had six lines together without a fault. Perhaps you may find seven, but this does not refute my general assertion.
Life of Johnson (J. Boswell), Vol. II

76 Why, Sir, most schemes of political improvement are very laughable things.
Life of Johnson (J. Boswell), Vol. II

77 There is no idolatry in the Mass. They believe God to be there, and they adore him.
Life of Johnson (J. Boswell), Vol. II

78 It matters not how a man dies, but how he lives. The act of dying is not of importance, it lasts so short a time.
Life of Johnson (J. Boswell), Vol. II

79 That fellow seems to me to possess but one idea, and that is a wrong one.
Life of Johnson (J. Boswell), Vol. II

80 I do not care to speak ill of any man behind his back, but I believe the gentleman is an *attorney*.
Life of Johnson (J. Boswell), Vol. II

81 The triumph of hope over experience.
Referring to the hasty remarriage of an acquaintance following the death of his first wife, with whom he had been most unhappy
Life of Johnson (J. Boswell), Vol. II

82 Every man has a lurking wish to appear considerable in his native place.
Letter to Sir Joshua Reynolds
Life of Johnson (J. Boswell), Vol. II

83 I would not give half a guinea to live under one form of government rather than another. It is of no moment to the happiness of an individual.
Life of Johnson (J. Boswell), Vol. II

84 Sir, I perceive you are a vile Whig.
Speaking to Sir Adam Fergusson
Life of Johnson (J. Boswell), Vol. II

85 A man who is good enough to go to heaven, is good enough to be a clergyman.
Life of Johnson (J. Boswell), Vol. II

86 Much may be made of a Scotchman, if he be *caught* young.
Referring to Lord Mansfield
Life of Johnson (J. Boswell), Vol. II

87 ELPHINSTON. What, have you not read it through? . . .
JOHNSON. No, Sir, do *you* read books *through*?
Life of Johnson (J. Boswell), Vol. II

88 Read over your compositions, and where ever you meet with a passage which you think is particularly fine, strike it out.
Recalling the advice of a college tutor
Life of Johnson (J. Boswell), Vol. II

89 The woman's a whore, and there's an end on't.
Referring to Lady Diana Beauclerk
Life of Johnson (J. Boswell), Vol. II

90 The Irish are a fair people; – they never speak well of one another.
Life of Johnson (J. Boswell), Vol. II

91 There are few ways in which a man can be more innocently employed than in getting money.
Life of Johnson (J. Boswell), Vol. II

92 He was dull in a new way, and that made many people think him *great*.
Referring to the poet Thomas Gray
Life of Johnson (J. Boswell), Vol. II

93 I think the full tide of human existence is at Charing-Cross.
Life of Johnson (J. Boswell), Vol. II

94 A man will turn over half a library to make one book.
Life of Johnson (J. Boswell), Vol. II

95 Patriotism is the last refuge of a scoundrel.
Life of Johnson (J. Boswell), Vol. II

96 Their learning is like bread in a besieged town: every man gets a little, but no man gets a full meal.

Referring to education in Scotland
Life of Johnson (J. Boswell), Vol. II

97 Knowledge is of two kinds. We know a subject ourselves, or we know where we can find information upon it.

Life of Johnson (J. Boswell), Vol. II

98 Politics are now nothing more than a means of rising in the world.

Life of Johnson (J. Boswell), Vol. II

99 In lapidary inscriptions a man is not upon oath.

Life of Johnson (J. Boswell), Vol. II

100 There is now less flogging in our great schools than formerly, but then less is learned there; so that what the boys get at one end they lose at the other.

Life of Johnson (J. Boswell), Vol. II

101 When men come to like a sea-life, they are not fit to live on land.

Life of Johnson (J. Boswell), Vol. II

102 There is nothing which has yet been contrived by man, by which so much happiness is produced as by a good tavern or inn.

Life of Johnson (J. Boswell), Vol. II

103 Questioning is not the mode of conversation among gentlemen.

Life of Johnson (J. Boswell), Vol. II

104 Fine clothes are good only as they supply the want of other means of procuring respect.

Life of Johnson (J. Boswell), Vol. II

105 If a madman were to come into this room with a stick in his hand, no doubt we should pity the state of his mind; but our primary consideration would be to take care of ourselves. We should knock him down first, and pity him afterwards.

Life of Johnson (J. Boswell), Vol. III

106 Consider, Sir, how should you like, though conscious of your innocence, to be tried before a jury for a capital crime, once a week.

Life of Johnson (J. Boswell), Vol. III

107 We would all be idle if we could.

Life of Johnson (J. Boswell), Vol. III

108 No man but a blockhead ever wrote, except for money.

Life of Johnson (J. Boswell), Vol. III

109 It is better that some should be unhappy than that none should be happy, which would be the case in a general state of equality.

Life of Johnson (J. Boswell), Vol. III

110 A man who has not been in Italy, is always conscious of an inferiority, from his not having seen what it is expected a man should see. The grand object of travelling is to see the shores of the Mediterranean.

Life of Johnson (J. Boswell), Vol. III

111 Why Sir, it is much easier to say what it is not. We all *know* what light is; but it is not easy to *tell* what it is.

When asked, 'What is poetry'
Life of Johnson (J. Boswell), Vol. III

112 Nay, Madam, when you are declaiming, declaim; and when you are calculating, calculate.

Commenting on Mrs Thrales's discourse on the price of children's clothes
Life of Johnson (J. Boswell), Vol. III

113 Sir, it is not so much to be lamented that Old England is lost, as that the Scotch have found it.

Life of Johnson (J. Boswell), Vol. III

114 To Oliver Goldsmith, A Poet, Naturalist, and Historian, who left scarcely any style of writing untouched, and touched none that he did not adorn.

Epitaph on Goldsmith
Life of Johnson (J. Boswell), Vol. III

115 If I had no duties, and no reference to futurity, I would spend my life in driving briskly in a post-chaise with a pretty woman.

Life of Johnson (J. Boswell), Vol. III

116 Depend upon it, Sir, when a man knows he is to be hanged in a fortnight, it concentrates his mind wonderfully.

Life of Johnson (J. Boswell), Vol. III

117 When a man is tired of London, he is tired of life; for there is in London all that life can afford.

Life of Johnson (J. Boswell), Vol. III

118 He who praises everybody praises nobody.

Life of Johnson (J. Boswell), Vol. III

119 Round numbers are always false.

Life of Johnson (J. Boswell), Vol. III

120 All argument is against it; but all belief is for it.

Of the ghost of a dead person
Life of Johnson (J. Boswell), Vol. III

121 Seeing Scotland, Madam, is only seeing a worse England.

Life of Johnson (J. Boswell), Vol. III

122 A country governed by a despot is an inverted cone.

Life of Johnson (J. Boswell), Vol. III

123 I am willing to love all mankind, *except an American.*

Life of Johnson (J. Boswell), Vol. III

124 Sir, the insolence of wealth will creep out.

Life of Johnson (J. Boswell), Vol. III

125 All censure of a man's self is oblique praise. It is in order to shew how much he can spare.
Life of Johnson (J. Boswell), Vol. III

126 Were it not for imagination, Sir, a man would be as happy in the arms of a chambermaid as of a Duchess.
Life of Johnson (J. Boswell), Vol. III

127 There are innumerable questions to which the inquisitive mind can in this state receive no answer: Why do you and I exist? Why was this world created? Since it was to be created, why was it not created sooner?
Life of Johnson (J. Boswell), Vol. III

128 Claret is the liquor for boys; port for men; but he who aspires to be a hero must drink brandy.
Life of Johnson (J. Boswell), Vol. III

129 A man who exposes himself when he is intoxicated, has not the art of getting drunk.
Life of Johnson (J. Boswell), Vol. III

130 Worth seeing? yes; but not worth going to see.
Referring to the Giant's Causeway
Life of Johnson (J. Boswell), Vol. III

131 I have got no further than this: Every man has a right to utter what he thinks truth, and every other man has a right to knock him down for it. Martyrdom is the test.
Life of Johnson (J. Boswell), Vol. IV

132 They are forced plants, raised in a hot-bed; and they are poor plants; they are but cucumbers after all.
Referring to Gray's *Odes*
Life of Johnson (J. Boswell), Vol. IV

133 A Frenchman must be always talking, whether he knows anything of the matter or not; an Englishman is content to say nothing, when he has nothing to say.
Life of Johnson (J. Boswell), Vol. IV

134 Sir, your wife, under pretence of keeping a bawdy-house, is a receiver of stolen goods.
An example of the customary badinage between travellers on the Thames
Life of Johnson (J. Boswell), Vol. IV

135 Depend upon it that if a man talks of his misfortunes there is something in them that is not disagreeable to him; for where there is nothing but pure misery there never is any recourse to the mention of it.
Life of Johnson (J. Boswell), Vol. IV

136 Mrs Montagu has dropt me. Now, Sir, there are people whom one should like very well to drop, but would not wish to be dropped by.
Life of Johnson (J. Boswell), Vol. IV

137 Classical quotation is the *parole* of literary men all over the world.
Life of Johnson (J. Boswell), Vol. IV

138 I have two very cogent reasons for not printing any list of subscribers: – one, that I have lost all the names, – the other, that I have spent all the money.
Referring to subscribers to his *Dictionary of the English Language*
Life of Johnson (J. Boswell), Vol. IV

139 Always, Sir, set a high value on spontaneous kindness. He whose inclination prompts him to cultivate your friendship of his own accord, will love you more than one whom you have been at pains to attach to you.
Life of Johnson (J. Boswell), Vol. IV

140 Resolve not to be poor: whatever you have, spend less. Poverty is a great enemy to human happiness; it certainly destroys liberty, and it makes some virtues impracticable and others extremely difficult.
Life of Johnson (J. Boswell), Vol. IV

141 I hate a fellow whom pride, or cowardice, or laziness drives into a corner, and who does nothing when he is there but sit and *growl*; let him come out as I do, and *bark*.
Life of Johnson (J. Boswell), Vol. IV

142 How few of his friends' houses would a man choose to be at when he is sick.
Life of Johnson (J. Boswell), Vol. IV

143 There is a wicked inclination in most people to suppose an old man decayed in his intellects. If a young or middle-aged man, when leaving a company, does not recollect where he laid his hat, it is nothing; but if the same inattention is discovered in an old man, people will shrug up their shoulders, and say, 'His memory is going.'
Life of Johnson (J. Boswell), Vol. IV

144 Sir, there is no settling the point of precedency between a louse and a flea.
When Maurice Morgann asked him who he considered to be the better poet – Smart or Derrick
Life of Johnson (J. Boswell), Vol. IV

145 When I observed he was a fine cat, saying, 'why yes, Sir, but I have had cats whom I liked better than this'; and then as if perceiving Hodge to be out of countenance, adding, 'but he is a very fine cat, a very fine cat indeed.'
Life of Johnson (J. Boswell), Vol. IV

146 My dear friend, clear your *mind* of cant . . . You may *talk* in this manner; it is a mode of talking in Society: but don't *think* foolishly.
Life of Johnson (J. Boswell), Vol. IV

147 As I know more of mankind I expect less of them, and am ready now to call a man *a good man*, upon easier terms than I was formerly.
Life of Johnson (J. Boswell), Vol. IV

148 If a man were to go by chance at the same time with Burke under a shed, to shun a shower, he would say – 'this is an extraordinary man.'

Referring to Edmund Burke
Life of Johnson (J. Boswell), Vol. IV

149 It is as bad as bad can be: it is ill-fed, ill-killed, ill-kept, and ill-drest.

About the roast mutton at an inn
Life of Johnson (J. Boswell), Vol. IV

150 Milton, Madam, was a genius that could cut a Colossus from a rock; but could not carve heads upon cherry-stones.

When Miss Hannah More had wondered why Milton could write the epic *Paradise Lost* but only very poor sonnets
Life of Johnson (J. Boswell), Vol. IV

151 Sir, I have found you an argument; but I am not obliged to find you an understanding.

Life of Johnson (J. Boswell), Vol. IV

152 No man is a hypocrite in his pleasures.

Life of Johnson (J. Boswell), Vol. IV

153 Dublin, though a place much worse than London, is not so bad as Iceland.

Letter to Mrs Christopher Smart
Life of Johnson (J. Boswell), Vol. IV

154 Sir, I look upon every day to be lost, in which I do not make a new acquaintance.

Life of Johnson (J. Boswell), Vol. IV

155 I will be conquered; I will not capitulate.

Referring to his illness
Life of Johnson (J. Boswell), Vol. IV

156 A cow is a very good animal in the field; but we turn her out of a garden.

Responding to Boswell's objections to the expulsion of six Methodists from Oxford University
The Personal History of Samuel Johnson (C. Hibbert)

157 A lawyer has no business with the justice or injustice of the cause which he undertakes, unless his client asks his opinion, and then he is bound to give it honestly. The justice or injustice of the cause is to be decided by the judge.

Tour to the Hebrides (J. Boswell)

158 I have, all my life long, been lying till noon; yet I tell all young men, and tell them with great sincerity, that nobody who does not rise early will ever do any good.

Tour to the Hebrides (J. Boswell)

159 I am always sorry when any language is lost, because languages are the pedigree of nations.

Tour to the Hebrides (J. Boswell)

160 No, Sir; there were people who died of dropsies, which they contracted in trying to get drunk.

Scornfully criticizing the strength of the wine in Scotland before the Act of Union in response to Boswell's claim that there had been a lot of drunkenness
Tour to the Hebrides (J. Boswell)

161 A cucumber should be well sliced, and dressed with pepper and vinegar, and then thrown out, as good for nothing.

Tour to the Hebrides (J. Boswell)

162 Come, let me know what it is that makes a Scotchman happy!

Ordering for himself a glass of whisky
Tour to the Hebrides (J. Boswell)

163 I am sorry I have not learned to play at cards. It is very useful in life: it generates kindness and consolidates society.

Tour to the Hebrides (J. Boswell)

164 Fly fishing may be a very pleasant amusement; but angling or float fishing I can only compare to a stick and a string, with a worm at one end and a fool at the other.

Attrib. in *Instructions to Young Sportsmen* (Hawker)

Johst, Hanns (b. 1890) German novelist and dramatist.

1 Whenever I hear the word 'culture' . . . I reach for my gun.

Popularly attrib. to Herman GOERING
Schlageter, I:1

Joliot-Curie, Irène (1897–1956) French scientist. The daughter of Marie Curie, she worked with her husband Frédéric Joliot (1900–59). They were the first to produce artificial radioactivity and received the Nobel Chemistry prize in 1935.

1 That one must do some work seriously and must be independent and not merely amuse oneself in life – this our mother has told us always, but never that science was the only career worth following.

Recalling the advice of her mother, Marie Curie
A Long Way from Missouri (Mary Margaret McBride), Ch. 10

Jolson, Al (Asa Yoelson; 1886–1950) US actor and singer, born in Russia. A vaudeville singer, he became famous for his blacked-up face and the song *Mammy*. He appeared in the first full-length talkie *The Jazz Singer* (1927).

1 You ain't heard nothin' yet, folks.

In the film *The Jazz Singer*, July 1927; later adopted as a catch phrase by President Ronald Reagan
The Jazz Singer

Jones, John Paul (1747–92) Scottish-born US naval commander. He commanded the flagship *Bonhomme Richard* in the naval battle against the British in 1779 and later served in the Russian navy.

1 I have not yet begun to fight.

Retort when informed his ship was sinking
Life and Letters of J. P. Jones (De Koven), Vol. I

Jonson, Ben (1573–1637) English dramatist and poet. His plays include *Volpone* (1606), *The Alchemist* (1610), and *Bartholomew Fair* (1614); he published two collections of verse.

Quotations about Jonson

1 He invades authors like a monarch and what would be theft in other poets, is only victory in him.

John Dryden (1631–1700) British poet and dramatist. *Essay of Dramatic Poesy*

2 O Rare Ben Jonson.

John Young. Epitaph in Westminster Abbey.

Quotations by Jonson

3 Fortune, that favours fools.

The Alchemist, Prologue

4 Neither do thou lust after that tawney weed tobacco.

Bartholomew Fair, II:6

5 Alas, all the castles I have, are built with air, thou know'st.

Eastward Ho, II:2

6 Ods me, I marvel what pleasure or felicity they have in taking their roguish tobacco. It is good for nothing but to choke a man, and fill him full of smoke and embers.

Every Man in His Humour, III:5

7 Drink to me only with thine eyes,
And I will pledge with mine;
Or leave a kiss but in the cup,
And I'll not look for wine.
The thirst that from the soul doth rise
Doth ask a drink divine;
But might I of Jove's nectar sup,
I would not change for thine.

I sent thee late a rosy wreath,
Not so much honouring thee,
As giving it a hope that there
It could not wither'd be.

The Forest, IX, 'To Celia'

8 They say princes learn no art truly, but the art of horsemanship. The reason is, the brave beast is no flatterer. He will throw a prince as soon as his groom.

Timber, or Discoveries made upon Men and Matter

9 Talking and eloquence are not the same: to speak, and to speak well, are two things.

Timber, or Discoveries made upon Men and Matter

10 Thou hadst small Latin, and less Greek.

To the Memory of William Shakespeare

11 He was not of an age, but for all time!

To the Memory of William Shakespeare

12 Sweet Swan of Avon!

To the Memory of William Shakespeare

13 She is Venus when she smiles;
But she's Juno when she walks,
And Minerva when she talks.

The Underwood, 'Celebration of Charis, V. His Discourse with Cupid'

14 Good morning to the day: and, next, my gold! –
Open the shrine, that I may see my saint.

Volpone, I:1

15 Calumnies are answered best with silence.

Volpone, II:2

16 Come, my Celia, let us prove,
While we can, the sports of love,
Time will not be ours for ever,
He, at length, our good will sever.

Volpone, III:6

Joseph, Michael (1897–1958) British publisher.

1 Authors are easy to get on with – if you're fond of children.

The Observer, 1949

Joseph II (1741–90) Holy Roman Emperor (1765–90).

1 Here lies Joseph, who failed in everything he undertook.

Suggesting his own epitaph when reflecting upon the disappointment of his hopes for reform
Attrib.

Jowett, Benjamin (1817–93) British theologian and classicist. His *Epistles of St Paul* (1855) caused considerable protest. As Master of Balliol College, Oxford, he was known for his care of students.

1 My dear child, you must believe in God in spite of what the clergy tell you.

Autobiography (Asquith), Ch. 8

2 One man is as good as another until he has written a book.

Letters of B. Jowett (Abbott and Campbell)

3 Nowhere probably is there more true feeling, and nowhere worse taste, than in a churchyard – both as regards the monuments and the inscriptions. Scarcely a word of true poetry anywhere.

Letters of B. Jowett (Abbott and Campbell)

4 Young men make great mistakes in life; for one thing, they idealize love too much.

Letters of B. Jowett (Abbott and Campbell)

5 Research! A mere excuse for idleness; it has never achieved, and will never achieve any results of the slightest value.

Unforgotten Years (Logan Pearsall Smith)

6 The way to get things done is not to mind who gets the credit of doing them.

Attrib.

7 If you don't find a God by five o'clock this afternoon you must leave the college.

Responding to a conceited young student's assertion that he could find no evidence for a God
Attrib.

Joyce, James (1882–1941) Irish novelist and poet. His short stories *The Dubliners* (1914) brought him to public notice, but it was his controversial stream-of-consciousness novel *Ulysses* (1922) that made him famous. *Finnegans Wake* (1939) was his last book.

Quotations about Joyce

1 My God, what a clumsy olla putrida James Joyce is! Nothing but old fags and cabbage-stumps of quotations from the Bible and the rest, stewed in the juice of deliberate, journalistic dirty-mindedness.

D. H. Lawrence (1885–1930) British novelist. Letter to Aldous Huxley, 15 Aug 1928

2 There are passages of *Ulysses* that can be read only in the toilet if one wants to extract the full flavour from them.

Henry Miller (1891–1980) US novelist. *Black Spring*

3 *Ulysses* . . . I rather wish I had never read it. It gives me an inferiority complex. When I read a book like that and then come back to my own work, I feel like a eunuch who has taken a course in voice production and can pass himself off fairly well as a bass or a baritone, but if you listen closely you can hear the good old squeak just the same as ever.

George Orwell (Eric Blair; 1903–50) British novelist. Letter to Brenda Salkeld, Sept 1934

4 He was not only the greatest literary stylist of his time. He was also the only living representative of the European tradition of the artist who carries on with his creative work unaffected by the storm which breaks around him in the world outside his study.

Stephen Spender (1909–) British poet. *Listener*, 23 Jan 1941

Quotations by Joyce

5 Three quarks for Muster Mark!

The word quark has since been adopted by physicists for hypothetical elementary particles
Finnegans Wake

6 Ireland is the old sow that eats her farrow.

A Portrait of the Artist as a Young Man, Ch. 5

7 'When I makes tea I makes tea,' as old mother Grogan said. 'And when I makes water I makes water'.

Ulysses

8 'History', Stephen said, 'is a nightmare from which I am trying to awake'.

Ulysses

9 Greater love than this, he said, no man hath that a man lay down his wife for a friend. Go thou and do likewise. Thus, or words to that effect, saith Zarathustra, sometime regius professor of French letters to the University of Oxtail.

Ulysses

10 The snotgreen sea. The scrotumtightening sea.

Ulysses

11 It is a symbol of Irish art. The cracked looking glass of a servant.

Ulysses

12 The desire of the moth for the star.

Commenting on the interruption of a music recital when a moth flew into the singer's mouth
James Joyce (R. Ellmann)

13 Never mind about my soul, just make sure you get my tie right.

Responding to the painter Patrick Tuohy's assertion that he wished to capture Joyce's soul in his portrait of him
James Joyce (R. Ellmann)

14 We have met too late. You are too old for me to have any effect on you.

On meeting W. B. Yeats
James Joyce (R. Ellmann)

Juang-zu (4th century BC) Chinese Taoist philosopher.

1 Above ground I shall be food for kites; below I shall be food for mole-crickets and ants. Why rob one to feed the other?

Deciding against interment when asked on his deathbed what his wishes were regarding the disposal of his body
Famous Last Words (B. Conrad)

Julia (39 BC – AD 14) Daughter of Augustus. She was notorious for her extravagance and licentious behaviour.

1 Today I dressed to meet my father's eyes; yesterday it was for my husband's.

On being complimented by her father, the emperor Augustus, on her choice of a more modest dress than the one she had worn the previous day
Saturnalia (Macrobius)

2 He sometimes forgets that he is Caesar, but I always remember that I am Caesar's daughter.

Replying to suggestions that she should live in the simple style of her father, which contrasted with her own extravagance
Saturnalia (Macrobius)

Jung, Carl Gustav (1875–1961) Swiss psychoanalyst. He collaborated with Freud until 1912, subsequently elaborated his own theory of analysis, described in such books as *The Psychology of the Unconscious* (1916) and *Modern Man in Search of a Soul* (1933).

1 Fortunately, in her kindness and patience, Nature has never put the fatal question as to the meaning of their lives into the mouths of most people. And where no one asks, no one needs to answer.

The Development of Personality

2 The pendulum of the mind oscillates between sense and nonsense, not between right and wrong.

Memories, Dreams, Reflections, Ch. 5

3 A man who has not passed through the inferno of his passions has never overcome them.

Memories, Dreams, Reflections, Ch. 9

4 As far as we can discern, the sole purpose of human existence is to kindle a light in the darkness of mere being.

Memories, Dreams, Reflections, Ch. 11

5 Every form of addiction is bad, no matter whether the narcotic be alcohol or morphine or idealism.
Memories, Dreams, Reflections, Ch. 12

6 Among all my patients in the second half of life . . . there has not been one whose problem in the last resort was not that of finding a religious outlook on life.
Modern Man in Search of a Soul

7 The least of things with a meaning is worth more in life than the greatest of things without it.
Modern Man in Search of a Soul

8 Sentimentality is a superstructure covering brutality.
Reflections

9 Show me a sane man and I will cure him for you.
The Observer, 19 July 1975

10 Wherever an inferiority complex exists, there is a good reason for it. There is always something inferior there, although not just where we persuade ourselves that it is.
Interview, 1943

11 We need more understanding of human nature, because the only real danger that exists is man himself . . . We know nothing of man, far too little. His psyche should be studied because we are the origin of all coming evil.
BBC television interview

Junius An unidentified writer of letters (1769–72) to the *London Public Advertiser*, criticizing the government of George III. Sir Philip Francis (1740–1818) was possibly the author.

1 The Liberty of the press is the *Palladium* of all the civil, political and religious rights of an Englishman.
Letters, 'Dedication'

2 There is a holy, mistaken zeal in politics, as well as religion. By persuading others we convince ourselves.
Letter, 19 Dec 1769

Junot, Andoche, Duc d'Abrantes (1771–1813) French general. He served under Napoleon and became governor of Paris (1806). Having captured Lisbon (1807), he was defeated by Wellesley and had to evacuate Portugal.

1 I am my own ancestor.
Said on being made a duke
Attrib.

Justinian I (482–565 AD) Byzantine emperor. He codified Roman Law in the Justinian Code and, as a Christian, built the church of St Sophia in Constantinople.

1 Justice is the constant and perpetual wish to render to every one his due.
Institutes, I

Juvenal (Decimus Junius Juvenalis; 60–130 AD) Roman satirist. His *Satires* (c. 100 AD) savagely attack Roman society.

1 It's hard not to write satire.
Satires, I

2 No one ever suddenly became depraved.
Satires, II

3 The misfortunes of poverty carry with them nothing harder to bear than that it exposes men to ridicule.
Satires, III

4 It's not easy for people to rise out of obscurity when they have to face straitened circumstances at home.
Satires, III

5 *Quis custodiet ipsos custodes?*
Who is to guard the guards themselves?
Satires, VI

6 I will have this done, so I order it done; let my will replace reasoned judgement.
Satires, VI

7 Many suffer from the incurable disease of writing, and it becomes chronic in their sick minds.
Satires, VII

8 The people long eagerly for just two things – bread and circuses.
Satires, X

9 Travel light and you can sing in the robber's face.
Satires, X

10 *Orandum est ut sit mens sana in corpore sano.*
Your prayer must be for a sound mind in a sound body.
Satires, X

11 No one delights more in vengeance than a woman.
Satires, XIII

12 A child deserves the maximum respect; if you ever have something disgraceful in mind, don't ignore your son's tender years.
Satires, XIV

K

Kafka, Franz (1883–1924) Czech novelist, many of whose books were published posthumously against his wish by Max Brod, his literary executor. His novels include *Metamorphosis* (1912), *The Trial* (1925), and *The Castle* (1926).

1 Don't despair, not even over the fact that you don't despair.
Diary

2 I have the true feeling of myself only when I am unbearably unhappy.

Diary

3 It's often safer to be in chains than to be free.

The Trial, Ch. 8

4 Let me remind you of the old maxim: people under suspicion are better moving than at rest, since at rest they may be sitting in the balance without knowing it, being weighed together with their sins

The Trial, Ch. 8

Kant, Immanuel (1724–1804) German philosopher. His *Critique of Pure Reason* (1781), *Critique of Practical Reason* (1788), and *Critique of Judgment* (1790) summarize his powerful theories.

1 Two things fill the mind with ever new and increasing wonder and awe, the more often and the more seriously reflection concentrates upon them: the starry heaven above me and the moral law within me.

Critique of Practical Reason, Conclusion

2 Finally, there is an imperative which commands a certain conduct immediately . . . This imperative is Categorical . . . This imperative may be called that of Morality.

Grundlegung zur Metaphysik der Sitten, II

3 . . . because happiness is not an ideal of reason but of imagination.

Grundlegung zur Metaphysik der Sitten, II

4 Out of the crooked timber of humanity no straight thing can ever be made.

Idee zu einer allgemeinen Geschichte in weltbürgerlicher Absicht

Karr, Alphonse (1808–90) French writer and editor of *Figaro* (1839). He founded the satirical review *Les Guêpes*. His books include *Voyage autour de mon jardin* (1845) and *Le Credo du jardinier* (1875).

1 *Plus ça change, plus c'est la même chose.*
   The more things change, the more they stay the same.

Les Guêpes, Jan 1849

2 If we are to abolish the death penalty, I should like to see the first step taken by our friends the murderers.

Les Guêpes, Jan 1849

Kaufman, George S(imon) (1889–1961) US dramatist and journalist. He collaborated with Moss Hart on *Bandwagon* (1931) and many other Broadway comedies and with George Gershwin on *Of Thee I Sing* (1932).

1 Over my dead body!

On being asked to suggest his own epitaph
The Algonquin Wits (R. Drennan)

2 God finally caught his eye.

Referring to a dead waiter
George S. Kaufman and the Algonquin Round Table (S. Meredith)

Kavanagh, Ted (1892–1958) British radio scriptwriter, mainly remembered for his wartime radio comedy series, *ITMA*.

1 Can I do you now, sir?

Said by Mrs Mop
ITMA, BBC Radio

2 I don't mind if I do.

Said by Colonel Chinstrap
ITMA, BBC Radio

3 It's that man again.

ITMA, BBC Radio

4 It has been discovered experimentally that you can draw laughter from an audience anywhere in the world, of any class or race, simply by walking on to a stage and uttering the words 'I am a married man'.

News Review, 10 July 1947

Kearney, Denis (1847–1907) US Labor leader.

1 Horny-handed sons of toil.

Speech, San Francisco, c. 1878

Keats, John (1795–1821) British poet. Trained as a doctor, he devoted most of his short life to poetry. *Endymion* (1818) was attacked by the critics but he eventually established his reputation with *La Belle Dame Sans Merci* (1820), *Ode to a Nightingale* (1820), and other works. He died in Rome of tuberculosis.

Quotations about Keats

1 What harm he has done in English Poetry. As Browning is a man with a moderate gift passionately desiring movement and fulness, and obtaining but a confused multitudinousness, so Keats with a very high gift, is yet also consumed with this desire: and cannot produce the truly living and moving, as his conscience keeps telling him.

Matthew Arnold (1822–88) British poet and critic. Letter to A. H. Clough, 1848

2 Such writing is a sort of mental masturbation – he is always f--gg--g his *Imagination*. I don't mean he is *indecent*, but viciously soliciting his own ideas into a state, which is neither poetry nor any thing else but a Bedlam vision produced by raw pork and opium.

Lord Byron (1788–1824) British poet. Letter to John Murray, 9 Nov 1820

3 Here is Johnny Keats' piss-a-bed poetry. No more Keats, I entreat; flay him alive; if some of you don't I must skin him myself; there is no bearing the idiotism of the Mankin.

Lord Byron (1788–1824) British poet. Letter to John Murray, 12 Oct 1821

4 In what other English poet (however superior to him in other respects) are you so *certain* of never opening a page without lighting upon the loveliest imagery and the most eloquent expressions? Name one.

Leigh Hunt (1784–1859) British poet. *Imagination and Fancy*

5 I see a schoolboy when I think of him. With face
and nose pressed to a sweetshop window.
W. B. Yeats (1865–1939) Irish poet.

Quotations by Keats

6 Bright star, would I were steadfast as thou art.
Bright Star

7 A thing of beauty is a joy for ever:
Its loveliness increases; it will never
Pass into nothingness; but still will keep
A bower quiet for us, and a sleep
Full of sweet dreams, and health, and quiet
breathing.
Endymion, I

8 Their smiles,
Wan as primroses gather'd at midnight
By chilly finger'd spring.
Endymion, IV

9 St Agnes' Eve – Ah, bitter chill it was!
The owl, for all his feathers, was a-cold;
The hare limp'd trembling through the frozen
grass,
And silent was the flock in woolly fold.
The Eve of Saint Agnes, I

10 The Beadsman, after thousand aves told,
For aye unsought-for slept among his ashes cold.
The Eve of Saint Agnes, I

11 Soft adorings from their loves receive
Upon the honey'd middle of the night.
The Eve of Saint Agnes, VI

12 The music, yearning like a God in pain.
The Eve of Saint Agnes, VII

13 He play'd an ancient ditty, long since mute,
In Provence call'd, 'La belle dame sans mercy'.
The Eve of Saint Agnes, XXXIII

14 And they are gone: aye, ages long ago
These lovers fled away into the storm.
The Eve of Saint Agnes, XLII

15 Fanatics have their dreams, wherewith they
weave
A paradise for a sect.
The Fall of Hyperion, I

16 The poet and the dreamer are distinct,
Diverse, sheer opposite, antipodes.
The one pours out a balm upon the world,
The other vexes it.
The Fall of Hyperion, I

17 Ever let the fancy roam,
Pleasure never is at home.
Fancy, I

18 Where's the cheek that doth not fade,
Too much gaz'd at? Where's the maid
Whose lip mature is ever new?
Fancy, I

19 Four seasons fill the measure of the year;
There are four seasons in the mind of men.
Four Seasons

20 O aching time! O moments big as years!
Hyperion, I

21 As when, upon a trancèd summer-night,
Those green-rob'd senators of mighty woods,
Tall oaks, branch-charmèd by the earnest stars,
Dream, and so dream all night without a stir.
Hyperion, I

22 Oh what can ail thee, knight at arms
Alone and palely loitering;
The sedge has wither'd from the lake,
And no birds sing.
La Belle Dame Sans Merci

23 'La belle Dame sans Merci
Hath thee in thrall!'
La Belle Dame Sans Merci

24 Love in a hut, with water and a crust,
Is – Love, forgive us! – cinders, ashes, dust;
Love in a palace is perhaps at last
More grievous torment than a hermit's fast.
Lamia, II

25 Do not all charms fly
At the mere touch of cold philosophy?
Lamia, II

26 Souls of poets dead and gone,
What Elysium have ye known,
Happy field or mossy cavern,
Choicer than the Mermaid Tavern?
Have ye tippled drink more fine
Than mine host's Canary wine?
Lines on the Mermaid Tavern

27 Thou still unravish'd bride of quietness,
Thou foster-child of silence and slow time.
Ode on a Grecian Urn

28 Heard melodies are sweet, but those unheard
Are sweeter; therefore, ye soft pipes, play on.
Ode on a Grecian Urn

29 Thou, silent form, dost tease us out of thought
As doth eternity: Cold Pastoral!
Ode on a Grecian Urn

30 'Beauty is truth, truth beauty,' – that is all
Ye know on earth, and all ye need to know.
Ode on a Grecian Urn

31 For ever warm and still to be enjoy'd,
For ever panting and for ever young;
All breathing human passion far above,
That leaves a heart high-sorrowful and cloy'd,
A burning forehead, and a parching tongue.
Ode on a Grecian Urn

32 No, no, go not to Lethe, neither twist
Wolf's-bane, tight-rooted, for its poisonous wine.
Ode on Melancholy

33 Nor let the beetle, nor the death-moth be
Your mournful Psyche.

Ode on Melancholy

34 Ay, in the very temple of delight
Veil'd Melancholy has her sovran shrine.
Though seen of none save him whose strenuous tongue
Can burst Joy's grape against his palate fine.

Ode on Melancholy

35 My heart aches, and a drowsy numbness pains
My sense.

Ode to a Nightingale

36 O, for a draught of vintage! that hath been
Cool'd a long age in the deep-delved earth.

Ode to a Nightingale

37 O for a beaker full of the warm South,
Full of the true, the blushful Hippocrene,
With beaded bubbles winking at the brim,
And purple-stained mouth.

Ode to a Nightingale

38 Fade far away, dissolve, and quite forget
What thou among the leaves hast never known,
The weariness, the fever, and the fret,
Here, where men sit and hear each other groan.

Ode to a Nightingale

39 Thou wast not born for death, immortal Bird!
No hungry generations tread thee down;
The voice I hear this passing night was heard
In ancient days by emperor and clown:
Perhaps the self-same song that found a path
Through the sad heart of Ruth, when sick for home,
She stood in tears amid the alien corn;
The same that oft-times hath
Charm'd magic casements, opening on the foam
Of perilous seas, in faery lands forlorn.

Ode to a Nightingale

40 Darkling I listen; and, for many a time
I have been half in love with easeful Death,
Call'd him soft names in many a mused rhyme,
To take into the air my quiet breath;
Now more than ever seems it rich to die,
To cease upon the midnight with no pain,
While thou art pouring forth thy soul abroad
In such an ecstasy!

Ode to a Nightingale

41 Much have I travell'd in the realms of gold,
And many goodly states and kingdoms seen.

On first looking into Chapman's Homer

42 Then felt I like some watcher of the skies
When a new planet swims into his ken;
Or like stout Cortez when with eagle eyes
He star'd at the Pacific – and all his men
Look'd at each other with a wild surmise –
Silent, upon a peak in Darien.

On first looking into Chapman's Homer

43 It keeps eternal whisperings around
Desolate shores, and with its mighty swell
Gluts twice ten thousand Caverns.

On the Sea

44 A drainless shower
Of light is poesy; 'tis the supreme of power;
'Tis might half slumb'ring on its own right arm.

Sleep and Poetry

45 Season of mists and mellow fruitfulness,
Close bosom-friend of the maturing sun;
Conspiring with him how to load and bless
With fruit the vines that round the thatch-eaves run.

To Autumn

46 Where are the songs of Spring? Ay, where are they?

To Autumn

47 O soft embalmer of the still midnight.

To Sleep

48 Turn the key deftly in the oiled wards,
And seal the hushed casket of my soul.

To Sleep

49 Here lies one whose name was writ in water.

Suggesting his own epitaph (recalling a line from *Philaster* by Beaumont and Fletcher)
Life of Keats (Lord Houghton), Ch. 2

50 A long poem is a test of invention which I take to be the Polar star of poetry, as fancy is the sails, and imagination the rudder.

Letter to Benjamin Bailey, 8 Oct 1817

51 I am certain of nothing but the holiness of the heart's affections and the truth of imagination – what the imagination seizes as beauty must be truth – whether it existed before or not.

Letter to Benjamin Bailey, 22 Nov 1817

52 O for a life of sensations rather than of thoughts!

Letter to Benjamin Bailey, 22 Nov 1817

53 Negative Capability, that is, when a man is capable of being in uncertainties, mysteries, doubts, without any irritable reaching after fact and reason.

Letter to G. and T. Keats, 21 Dec 1817

54 The excellence of every art is its intensity, capable of making all disagreeables evaporate, from their being in close relationship with beauty and truth.

Letter to G. and T. Keats, 21 Dec 1817

55 There is an old saying 'well begun is half done' – 'tis a bad one. I would use instead – Not begun at all until half done.

Letter, 1817

56 We hate poetry that has a palpable design upon us – and if we do not agree, seems to put its hand in its breeches pocket. Poetry should be great and unobtrusive, a thing which enters into one's soul, and does not startle or amaze it with itself, but with its subject.

Letter to J. H. Reynolds, 3 Feb 1818

57 If poetry comes not as naturally as leaves to a tree it had better not come at all.

Letter to John Taylor, 27 Feb 1818

58 Scenery is fine – but human nature is finer.

Letter to Benjamin Bailey, 13 Mar 1818

59 Axioms in philosophy are not axioms until they are proved upon our pulses; we read fine things but never feel them to the full until we have gone the same steps as the author.

Letter to J. H. Reynolds, 3 May 1818

60 I am in that temper that if I were under water I would scarcely kick to come to the top.

Letter to Benjamin Bailey, 21 May 1818

61 I do think better of womankind than to suppose they care whether Mister John Keats five feet high likes them or not.

Letter to Benjamin Bailey, 18 July 1818

62 I think I shall be among the English Poets after my death.

Letter to George and Georgiana Keats, 14 Oct 1818

63 I never can feel certain of any truth but from a clear perception of its beauty.

Letter to George and Georgiana Keats, 16 Dec 1818 – 4 Jan 1819

64 Nothing ever becomes real till it is experienced – even a proverb is no proverb to you till your life has illustrated it.

Letter to George and Georgiana Keats, 19 Mar 1819

65 My friends should drink a dozen of Claret on my Tomb.

Letter to Benjamin Bailey, 14 Aug 1819

66 Give me books, fruit, French wine and fine weather and a little music out of doors, played by somebody I do not know.

Letter to Fanny Keats, 29 Aug 1819

67 Love is my religion – I could die for that.

Letter to Fanny Brawne, 13 Oct 1819

68 Though a quarrel in the streets is a thing to be hated, the energies displayed in it are fine; the commonest man shows a grace in his quarrel.

Letter

69 I go among the fields and catch a glimpse of a stoat or a fieldmouse peeping out of the withered grass – the creature hath a purpose and its eyes are bright with it. I go amongst the buildings of a city and I see a man hurrying along – to what? the Creature has a purpose and his eyes are bright with it.

Letter, 1819

70 Upon the whole I dislike mankind: whatever people on the other side of the question may advance, they cannot deny that they are always surprised at hearing of a good action and never of a bad one.

Letter, 1820

71 Is there another life? Shall I awake and find all this a dream? There must be, we cannot be created for this sort of suffering.

Letter, 1820

72 I shall soon be laid in the quiet grave – thank God for the quiet grave – O! I can feel the cold earth upon me – the daisies growing over me – O for this quiet – it will be my first.

In a letter to John Taylor by Joseph Severn, 6 Mar 1821

Keble, John (1792–1866) British poet and clergyman. His sermon on national apostasy (1833) led to the formation of the Oxford Movement. His hymns were published as *The Christian Year* (1827).

1 The trivial round, the common task,
Would furnish all we ought to ask;
Room to deny ourselves; a road
To bring us, daily, nearer God.

The Christian Year, 'Morning'

Keller, Helen (Adams) (1880–1968) US writer and lecturer. Blind and deaf from infancy, she learnt to speak, read, and write, graduating from Radcliffe College in 1904. Her lectures raised money for educating the handicapped, and her books include the autobiographical *The Story of My Life* (1902).

1 . . . militarism . . . is one of the chief bulwarks of capitalism, and the day that militarism is undermined, capitalism will fail.

The Story of My Life

2 . . . we could never learn to be brave and patient, if there were only joy in the world.

Atlantic Monthly (May 1890)

3 How reconcile this world of fact with the bright world of my imagining? My darkness has been filled with the light of intelligence, and behold, the outer day-light world was stumbling and groping in social blindness.

The Cry for Justice (ed. Upton Sinclair)

Kelvin, William Thomson, 1st Baron (1824–1907) British physicist, famous for his work in thermodynamics. He devised the Kelvin temperature scale, with a zero point of absolute zero. The unit of thermodynamic temperature is named after him.

1 At what time does the dissipation of energy begin?

On realizing that his wife was planning an afternoon excursion
Memories of a Scientific Life (A. Fleming)

Kemble, Charles (1775–1854) British actor, specializing in comic roles. Father of the actress Fanny Kemble and brother of Sarah Siddons, he managed the Covent Garden Theatre from 1822.

1 Sir, I now pay you this exorbitant charge, but I must ask you to explain to her Majesty that she must not in future look upon me as a source of income.

On being obliged to hand over his income tax to the tax collector
Humour in the Theatre (J. Aye)

Kemble, John Philip (1757–1823) British tragic actor, brother of Charles Kemble. He managed the Drury Lane and Covent Garden theatres.

1 Ladies and gentlemen, unless the play is stopped, the child cannot possibly go on.

Announcement to the audience when the play he was in was continually interrupted by a child crying
A Book of Anecdotes (D. George)

Kempis, Thomas à (Thomas Hemmerken; c. 1380–1471) German monk and writer. He is reputed to be the author of the religious treatise *The Imitation of Christ*.

1 *Sic transit gloria mundi.*
Thus the glory of the world passes away.
The Imitation of Christ, I

2 It is much safer to obey than to rule.
The Imitation of Christ, I

3 If you cannot mould yourself as you would wish, how can you expect other people to be entirely to your liking?
The Imitation of Christ, I

4 Man proposes but God disposes.
The Imitation of Christ, I

5 Would to God that we might spend a single day really well!
The Imitation of Christ, I

Ken, Thomas (1637–1711) English bishop. He was deprived of his see after refusing to take the oath of allegiance to William and Mary. He was also the author of many hymns.

1 Teach me to live, that I may dread
The grave as little as my bed.
An Evening Hymn

2 Redeem thy mis-spent time that's past;
Live this day, as if 'twere thy last.
A Morning Hymn

Keneally, Thomas (1935–) Australian novelist. His books include *The Chant of Jimmie Blacksmith* (1972), the award-winning *Schindler's Ark* (1982), *A Family Madness* (1985), and *The Playmaker* (1987).

1 Pass a law to give every single wingeing bloody Pommie his fare home to England. Back to the smoke and the sun shining ten days a year and shit in the streets. Yer can have it.
The Chant of Jimmy Blacksmith

Kennedy, John Fitzgerald (1917–63) US statesman; the first Roman Catholic President (1961–63). His liberal New Frontier policies were cut short by his assassination.

Quotations about Kennedy

1 The enviably attractive nephew who sings an Irish ballad for the company and then winsomely disappears before the table-clearing and dishwashing begin.

Lyndon B. Johnson (1908–73) US statesman. *A Political Education* (H. McPherson)

2 Kennedy the politician exuded that musk odour which acts as an aphrodisiac to many women.

Theodore H. White (1906–64) British novelist. *In Search of History*

Quotations by Kennedy

3 It was involuntary. They sank my boat.

Responding to praise of his courage whilst serving in the US navy against the Japanese in World War II
Nobody Said It Better (M. Ringo)

4 I can't see that it's wrong to give him a little legal experience before he goes out to practice law.

On being criticized for making his brother Robert attorney general
Nobody Said It Better (M. Ringo)

5 I guess this is the week I earn my salary.

Comment made during the Cuban missile crisis
Nobody Said It Better (M. Ringo)

6 We must use time as a tool, not as a couch.
The Observer, 'Sayings of the Week', 10 Dec 1961

7 The United States has to move very fast to even stand still.
The Observer, 'Sayings of the Week', 21 July 1963

8 The worse I do, the more popular I get.

Referring to his popularity following the failure of the US invasion of Cuba
The People's Almanac (D. Wallechinsky)

9 Do you realize the responsibility I carry? I'm the only person standing between Nixon and the White House.

Said to Arthur Schlesinger, 13 Oct 1960; Richard Nixon was the Republican candidate in the 1960 US Presidential election
A Thousand Days (Arthur M. Schlesinger, Jnr)

10 We stand today on the edge of a new frontier.

Said on his nomination as Presidential candidate
Speech, Democratic Party Convention, 15 July 1960

11 And so, my fellow Americans: ask not what your country can do for you – ask what you can do for your country. My fellow citizens of the world: ask not what America will do for you, but what together we can do for the freedom of man.

Inaugural address, 20 Jan 1961

12 I think it's the most extraordinary collection of talent, of human knowledge, that has ever been gathered together at the White House – with the possible exception of when Thomas Jefferson dined alone.

Said at a dinner for Nobel Prizewinners, 29 Apr 1962

13 The war against hunger is truly mankind's war of liberation.

Speech, World Food Congress, 4 June 1963

14 If we cannot now end our differences, at least we can help make the world safe for diversity.

Speech, American University (Washington, DC), 10 June 1963

15 All free men, wherever they may live, are citizens of Berlin. And therefore, as a free man, I take pride in the words *Ich bin ein Berliner.*

Speech, City Hall, West Berlin, 26 June 1963

16 When power narrows the areas of man's concern, poetry reminds him of the richness and diversity of his existence.

Address at Dedication of the Robert Frost Library, 26 Oct 1963

17 In free society art is not a weapon . . . Artists are not engineers of the soul.

Address at Dedication of the Robert Frost Library, 26 Oct 1963

18 Victory has a thousand fathers but defeat is an orphan.

Attrib.

Kennedy, Joseph Patrick (1888–1969) US businessman and diplomat. Ambassador to the UK (1937–40), he was the father of John, Robert, and Edward Kennedy.

1 I think the primary notion back of most gambling is the excitement of it. While gamblers naturally want to win, the majority of them derive pleasure even if they lose. The desire to win, rather than the excitement involved, seems to me the compelling force behind speculation.

The Kennedys, Ch. 2 (Peter Collier and David Horowitz)

Kennedy, Robert (1925–68) US politician. Attorney general (1961–64) in his brother's administration, he became a senator in 1965 and was campaigning for the Democratic presidential nomination in 1968 when he was assassinated.

1 What is objectionable, what is dangerous about extremists is not that they are extreme but that they are intolerant.

The Pursuit of Justice

2 I was the seventh of nine children. When you come from that far down you have to struggle to survive.

The Kennedy Neurosis (B. G. Clinch)

3 One fifth of the people are against everything all the time.

The Observer, 'Sayings of the Week', 10 May 1964

Kerouac, Jack (1922–69) US novelist. His novel *On the Road* (1957) introduced the beat movement; subsequent books include *Big Sur* (1962) and *Desolation Angels* (1965).

1 You can't teach the old maestro a new tune.

On the Road, Pt. I

2 We're really all of us bottomly broke. I haven't had time to work in weeks.

On the Road, Pt. I

3 I had nothing to offer anybody except my own confusion.

On the Road, Pt. II

4 The beat generation.

Expression

Kerr, Jean (1923–) US dramatist, screenwriter, and humorist. Her works include the screenplay for *Please Don't Eat the Daisies* (1960).

1 Man is the only animal that learns by being hypocritical. He pretends to be polite and then, eventually, he *becomes* polite.

Finishing Touches

2 You don't seem to realize that a poor person who is unhappy is in a better position than a rich person who is unhappy. Because the poor person has hope. He thinks money would help.

Poor Richard

3 Even though a number of people have tried, no one has yet found a way to drink for a living.

Poor Richard

4 I feel about airplanes the way I feel about diets. It seems to me that they are wonderful things for other people to go on.

The Snake Has All the Lines, 'Mirror, Mirror, on the Wall'

Key, Ellen (Karolina Sofia Key; 1849–1926) Swedish writer and feminist. After teaching and lecturing in Sweden, she made a number of lecture tours abroad.

1 . . . the emancipation of women is practically the greatest egoistic movement of the nineteenth century, and the most intense affirmation of the right of the self that history has yet seen . . .

The Century of the Child, Ch. 2

2 At every step the child should be allowed to meet the real experiences of life; the thorns should never be plucked from his roses.

The Century of the Child, Ch. 3

3 Nothing would more effectively further the development of education than for all flogging pedagogues to learn to educate with the head instead of with the hand.

The Century of the Child, Ch. 3

4 Corporal punishment is as humiliating for him who gives it as for him who receives it; it is ineffective besides. Neither shame nor physical pain have any other effect than a hardening one . . .

The Century of the Child, Ch. 8

5 Love is moral even without legal marriage, but marriage is immoral without love.

The Morality of Woman and Other Essays, 'The Morality of Woman'

6 Formerly, a nation that broke the peace did not trouble to try and prove to the world that it was done solely from higher motives . . . *Now war has a bad conscience.* Now every nation assures us that it is bleeding for a human cause, the fate of which hangs in the balance of its victory. . . . No nation dares to admit the guilt of blood before the world.

War, Peace, and the Future, Preface

7 Everything, everything in war is barbaric . . . But the worst barbarity of war is that it forces men collectively to commit acts against which individually they would revolt with their whole being.

War, Peace, and the Future, Ch. 6

Key, Francis Scott (1779–1843) US lawyer and writer of *The Star Spangled Banner,* first published in the Baltimore paper *American* in 1814.

1 'Tis the star-spangled banner; O long may it wave
O'er the land of the free, and the home of the brave!

The Star-Spangled Banner

Keynes, John Maynard, Baron (1883–1946) British economist. His *General Theory of Employment, Interest and Money* (1936), which supports increased public spending as a means of reducing unemployment, still has its advocates.

1 In the long run we are all dead.

Collected Writings, 'A Tract on Monetary Reform'

2 I do not know which makes a man more conservative – to know nothing but the present, or nothing but the past.

The End of Laisser-Faire, I

3 Marxian Socialism must always remain a portent to the historians of Opinion – how a doctrine so illogical and so dull can have exercised so powerful and enduring an influence over the minds of men, and, through them, the events of history.

The End of Laisser-Faire, III

4 This goat-footed bard, this half-human visitor to our age from the hag-ridden magic and enchanted woods of Celtic antiquity.

Referring to Lloyd George
Essays and Sketches in Biography

5 Worldly wisdom teaches that it is better for the reputation to fail conventionally than to succeed unconventionally.

The General Theory of Employment, Interest and Money, Bk. IV, Ch. 12

6 It is better that a man should tyrannize over his bank balance than over his fellow citizens.

The General Theory of Employment, Interest and Money, Bk. VI, Ch. 24

7 Practical men, who believe themselves to be quite exempt from any intellectual influences, are usually the slaves of some defunct economist. Madmen in authority, who hear voices in the air, are distilling their frenzy from some academic scribbler of a few years back.

The General Theory of Employment, Interest and Money, Bk. VI, Ch. 24

8 I will not be a party to debasing the currency.

On refusing to pay more than a small tip on having his shoes polished, whilst on a visit to Africa
John Maynard Keynes (C. Hession)

9 Does that mean that because Americans won't listen to sense, you intend to talk nonsense to them?

Said before a monetary conference, 1944 or 1945

10 No, I don't know his telephone number. But it was up in the high numbers.

Attrib.

11 The avoidance of taxes is the only pursuit that still carries any reward.

Attrib.

Khayyam, Omar see **Fitzgerald, Edward**

Khomeini, Ayatollah Ruholla (1902–89) Iranian Shiite Muslim leader. In 1979 he returned from exile to lead an Islamic revolution and headed a repressive regime strictly based on Islamic principles.

1 A learned man who is not cleansed is more dangerous than an ignorant man.

Speech, 6 July 1980

2 The author of the Satanic Verses book, which is against Islam, the Prophet and the Koran, and all those involved in its publication who were aware of its content, are sentenced to death. I ask all Moslems to execute them wherever they find them.

Announcing a death sentence against the British author Salman RUSHDIE, whose novel *The Satanic Verses,* had offended Islamic fundamentalists
Speech, 14 Feb 1989

Khrushchev, Nikita (1894–1971) Soviet statesman. Stalin's successor, he became prime minister (1958–64). As a result of his unsuccessful confrontation with Kennedy over the attempted installation of missiles in Cuba he was ousted from office.

1 We had no use for the policy of the Gospels: if someone slaps you, just turn the other cheek. We had shown that anyone who slapped us on our cheek would get his head kicked off.

Khrushchev Remembers, Vol. II

2 When you are skinning your customers, you should leave some skin on to grow so that you can skin them again.

Said to British businessmen
The Observer, 'Sayings of the Week', 28 May 1961

3 They talk about who won and who lost. Human reason won. Mankind won.

Referring to the Cuban missiles crisis
The Observer, 'Sayings of the Week', 11 Nov 1962

4 If you start throwing hedgehogs under me, I shall throw two porcupines under you.

The Observer, 'Sayings of the Week', 10 Nov 1963

5 Every year humanity takes a step towards Communism. Maybe not you, but at all events your grandson will surely be a Communist.

Said to Sir William Hayter, June 1956

6 We will bury you.

Said at a reception at the Kremlin, 26 Nov 1956

7 Politicians are the same all over. They promise to build a bridge even where there's no river.

Said to journalists while visiting the USA, Oct 1960

8 If you feed people just with revolutionary slogans they will listen today, they will listen tomorrow, they will listen the day after tomorrow, but on the fourth day they will say 'To hell with you!'

Attrib.

Kierkegaard, Søren (1813–55) Danish philosopher. His books, *The Concept of Irony* (1841), *Either-Or* (1843), and *Works of Love* (1847), influenced existentialism.

1 Job endured everything – until his friends came to comfort him, then he grew impatient.

Journal

2 That is the road we all have to take – over the Bridge of Sighs into eternity.

Kierkegaard Anthology (Auden)

Kilmer, Alfred Joyce (1886–1918) US poet, who was killed in action in World War I. His verse collections include *Summer of Love* (1911) and *Trees and Other Poems* (1914).

1 I think that I shall never see
A poem lovely as a tree.

Trees

2 Poems are made by fools like me,
But only God can make a tree.

Trees

Kilvert, Francis (1840–79) British diarist and clergyman. His diary, written in the Welsh marches in the 1870s, was published in 1938.

1 Of all noxious animals, too, the most noxious is a tourist. And of all tourists the most vulgar, ill-bred, offensive and loathsome is the British tourist.

Diary, 5 Apr 1870

2 It is a fine thing to be out on the hills alone. A man can hardly be a beast or a fool alone on a great mountain.

Diary, 29 May 1871

King, Benjamin Franklin (1857–94) American humorist.

1 Nothing to do but work,
Nothing to eat but food,
Nothing to wear but clothes,
To keep one from going nude.

The Pessimist

King, Martin Luther (1929–68) US Black clergyman and civil-rights leader. His nonviolent demonstrations led to the Civil Rights Act (1964). He was awarded the Nobel Peace Prize in 1964 and assassinated four years later.

1 A riot is at bottom the language of the unheard.

Chaos or Community, Ch. 4

2 I want to be the white man's brother, not his brother-in-law.

New York Journal-American, 10 Sept 1962

3 If a man hasn't discovered something that he would die for, he isn't fit to live.

Speech, Detroit, 23 June 1963

4 I have a dream that one day this nation will rise up, live out the true meaning of its creed: we hold these truths to be self-evident, that all men are created equal.

He used the words 'I have a dream' in a number of speeches
Speech, Washington, 27 Aug 1963

Kingsley, Charles (1819–75) British writer and clergyman. A chaplain to Queen Victoria, he is remembered for his novels, including *Westward Ho!* (1855) and the children's book *The Water Babies* (1863).

1 Be good, sweet maid, and let who can be clever;
Do lovely things, not dream them, all day long;
And so make Life, and Death, and that For Ever,
One grand sweet song.

A Farewell. To C. E. G.

2 To be discontented with the divine discontent, and to be ashamed with the noble shame, is the very germ and first upgrowth of all virtue.

Health and Education

3 We have used the Bible as if it was a constable's handbook – an opium-dose for keeping beasts of burden patient while they are being overloaded.

Letters to the Chartists, 2

4 'O Mary, go and call the cattle home,
And call the cattle home,
And call the cattle home,
Across the sands of Dee.'
The western wind was wild and dank with foam,
And all alone went she.

The Sands of Dee

5 The western tide crept up along the sand,
And o'er and o'er the sand,
And round and round the sand,
As far as eye could see.
The rolling mist came down and hid the land:
And never home came she.

The Sands of Dee

6 When all the world is young, lad,
And all the trees are green;
And every goose a swan, lad,
And every lass a queen;
Then hey for boot and horse, lad,
And round the world away:
Young blood must have its course, lad,
And every dog his day.
Songs from The Water Babies, 'Young and Old'

7 For men must work, and women must weep,
And there's little to earn, and many to keep,
Though the harbour bar be moaning.
The Three Fishers

8 He did not know that a keeper is only a poacher
turned outside in, and a poacher a keeper
turned inside out.
The Water Babies, Ch. 1

9 The loveliest fairy in the world; and her name is
Mrs Doasyouwouldbedoneby.
The Water Babies, Ch. 5

10 More ways of killing a cat than choking her with
cream.
Westward Ho!, Ch. 20

11 Some say that the age of chivalry is past, that
the spirit of romance is dead. The age of chivalry
is never past, so long as there is a wrong left
unredressed on earth.
Life (Mrs C. Kingsley), Vol. II, Ch. 28

Kinnock, Neil (1942–) British politician; leader of the
Labour Party since 1983.

1 It is inconceivable that we could transform this
society without a major extension of public
ownership.
Marxism Today, 1983

2 Proportional Representation, I think, is fundamentally counter-democratic.
Marxism Today, 1983

3 You cannot fashion a wit out of two half-wits.
The Times, 1983

4 We cannot remove the evils of capitalism without
taking its source of power: ownership.
Tribune, 1975

5 I'm prepared to take advice on leisure from
Prince Philip. He's a world expert on leisure.
He's been practising for most of his adult life.
Western Mail, 1981

6 Compassion is not a sloppy, sentimental feeling
for people who are underprivileged or sick . . .
it is an absolutely practical belief that, regardless of a person's background, ability or ability to
pay, he should be provided with the best that
society has to offer.
Maiden speech, House of Commons, 1970

7 Like Brighton pier, all right as far as it goes, but
inadequate for getting to France.
Speech, House of Commons, 1981

8 Those who prate about Blimpish patriotism in
the mode of Margaret Thatcher are also the
ones who will take millions off the caring services of this country.
Speech, Labour Party Conference, Brighton, 1983

9 The grotesque chaos of a Labour council – a *Labour* council – hiring taxis to scuttle around a
city handing out redundancy notices to its own
workers.
Attacking militant members in Liverpool
Speech, Labour Party Conference, Bournemouth, 1985

10 Political renegades always start their career of
treachery as 'the best men of all parties' and end
up in the Tory knackery.
Speech, Welsh Labour Party Conference, 1985

11 The idea that there is a model Labour voter, a
blue-collar council house tenant who belongs to
a union and has 2.4 children, a five-year-old car
and a holiday in Blackpool, is patronizing and
politically immature.
Speech, 1986

12 I would die for my country . . . but I would not
let my country die for me.
Speech on nuclear disarmament, 1987

Kipling, (Joseph) Rudyard (1865–1936) Indian-born
British writer and poet. His verse collection *Barrack Room
Ballads and Other Verses* (1892) included the well-known poems 'If'
and 'Gunga Din'. Other works were the *Jungle Books* (1894,
1895), *Kim* (1901) and the children's books *Just So Stories* (1902)
and *Puck of Pook's Hill* (1906).

Quotations about Kipling

1 I doubt that the infant monster has any more to
give.
Henry James (1843–1916) US novelist. *Letters*, Vol. 3

2 Kipling has done more than any other since Disraeli to show the world that the British race is
sound to the core and that rust and dry rot are
strangers to it.
Cecil Rhodes (1853–1902) South African statesman. *Rhodes: A
Life* (J. G. MacDonald)

Quotations by Kipling

3 Oh, East is East, and West is West, and never
the twain shall meet.
The Ballad of East and West

4 And a woman is only a woman, but a good cigar
is a smoke.
The Betrothed

5 Teach us delight in simple things,
And mirth that has no bitter springs;
Forgiveness free of evil done,
And love to all men 'neath the sun!
The Children's Song

6 But the Devil whoops, as he whooped of old:
'It's clever, but is it art?'
The Conundrum of the Workshops

7 'For they're hangin' Danny Deever, you can hear
the Dead March play,
The Regiment's in 'ollow square – they're
hangin' 'im to-day;
They've taken of 'is buttons off an' cut 'is stripes
away,
An' they're hangin' Danny Deever in the
mornin'.'

Danny Deever

8 Winds of the World, give answer! They are
whimpering to and fro –
And what should they know of England who only
England know?

The English Flag

9 When the Himalayan peasant meets the he-bear
in his pride,
He shouts to scare the monster, who will often
turn aside.
But the she-bear thus accosted rends the peasant tooth and nail
For the female of the species is more deadly
than the male.

The Female of the Species

10 So 'ere's to you, Fuzzy-Wuzzy, at your 'ome in
the Soudan;
You're a pore benighted 'eathen but a first-class
fightin' man;
An' 'ere's to you, Fuzzy-Wuzzy, with your
'ayrick 'ead of 'air –
You big black boundin' beggar – for you broke a
British square!

Fuzzy-Wuzzy

11 We're poor little lambs who've lost our way,
Baa! Baa! Baa!
We're little black sheep who've gone astray,
Baa-aa-aa!
Gentleman-rankers out on the spree,
Damned from here to Eternity,
God ha' mercy on such as we,
Baa! Yah! Bah!

Gentleman-Rankers

12 Oh, Adam was a gardener, and God who made
him sees
That half a proper gardener's work is done upon
his knees,
So when your work is finished, you can wash
your hands and pray
For the Glory of the Garden, that it may not
pass away!

The Glory of the Garden

13 The uniform 'e wore
Was nothin' much before,
An' rather less than 'arf o' that be'ind.

Gunga Din

14 An' for all 'is dirty 'ide
'E was white, clear white, inside
When 'e went to tend the wounded under fire!

Gunga Din

15 Though I've belted you an' flayed you,
By the livin' Gawd that made you,
You're a better man than I am, Gunga Din!

Gunga Din

16 If you can keep your head when all about you
Are losing theirs and blaming it on you,
If you can trust yourself when all men doubt
you,
But make allowance for their doubting too;
. . .
If you can meet with Triumph and Disaster
And treat those two imposters just the same.

If

17 If you can talk with crowds and keep your
virtue,
Or walk with Kings – nor lose the common
touch,
If neither foes nor loving friends can hurt you,
If all men count with you, but none too much;
If you can fill the unforgiving minute
With sixty seconds' worth of distance run,
Yours is the Earth and everything that's in it,
And – which is more – you'll be a Man my son!

If

18 Asia is not going to be civilized after the methods of the West. There is too much Asia and
she is too old.

Life's Handicap, 'The Man Who Was'

19 The Light that Failed.

Novel title

20 The Saxon is not like us Normans. His manners
are not so polite.
But he never means anything serious till he talks
about justice and right,
When he stands like an ox in the furrow with his
sullen set eyes on your own,
And grumbles, 'This isn't fair dealing,' my son,
leave the Saxon alone.

Norman and Saxon

21 The silliest woman can manage a clever man; but
it needs a very clever woman to manage a fool.

Plain Tales from the Hills, 'Three and – an Extra'

22 If, drunk with sight of power, we loose
Wild tongues that have not Thee in awe,
Such boastings as the Gentiles use,
Or lesser breeds without the Law.

Recessional

23 On the road to Mandalay
Where the flyin'-fishes play.

The Road to Mandalay

24 I am sick o' wastin' leather on these gritty pavin'-stones,
An' the blasted English drizzle wakes the fever in my bones;
Tho' I walks with fifty 'ousemaids outer Chelsea to the Strand,
An' they talks a lot o' lovin', but wot do they understand?
Beefy face an' grubby 'and –
Law! Wot do they understand?
I've a neater, sweeter maiden in a cleaner, greener land!

The Road to Mandalay

25 Ship me somewheres east of Suez, where the best is like the worst,
Where there aren't no Ten Commandments, an' a man can raise a thirst:
For the temple-bells are callin', an' it's there that I would be –
By the old Moulmein Pagoda, looking lazy at the sea.

The Road to Mandalay

26 Being kissed by a man who didn't wax his moustache was – like eating an egg without salt.

Soldiers Three, 'The Gadsbys, Poor Dear Mamma'

27 No one thinks of winter when the grass is green!

A St Helena Lullaby

28 Oh, it's Tommy this, an' Tommy that, an' 'Tommy, go away';
But it's 'Thank you, Mister Atkins,' when the band begins to play.

Tommy

29 It's Tommy this, an' Tommy that, an' 'Chuck him out, the brute!'
But it's 'Saviour of 'is country' when the guns begin to shoot.

Tommy

30 They shut the road through the woods
Seventy years ago.
Weather and rain have undone it again,
And now you would never know
There was once a road through the woods.

The Way Through the Woods

31 Take up the White Man's burden –
And reap his old reward:
The blame of those ye better,
The hate of those ye guard.

The White Man's Burden

32 I've just read that I am dead. Don't forget to delete me from your list of subscribers.

Writing to a magazine that had mistakenly published an announcement of his death
Anekdotenschatz (H. Hoffmeister)

33 A Soldier of the Great War Known unto God.

The words he selected to be inscribed on the headstones of the graves of unknown soldiers when he was literary adviser for the Imperial War Graves Commission, 1919
Silent Cities (ed. Gavin Stamp)

34 Words are, of course, the most powerful drug used by mankind.

Speech, 14 Feb 1923

35 Power without responsibility – the prerogative of the harlot throughout the ages.

Better known for its subsequent use by BALDWIN
Attrib.

Kissinger, Henry (1923–) German-born US politician and diplomat. Secretary of State (1973–76), he helped to negotiate an end to the Vietnam war and, with his shuttle diplomacy, a truce between Syria and Israel (1974). His books include *Nuclear Weapons and Foreign Policy* (1956) and *Years of Upheaval* (1982).

1 The conventional army loses if it does not win. The guerrilla wins if he does not lose.

Foreign Affairs, XIII (Jan 1969), 'The Vietnam Negotiations'

2 Power is the ultimate aphrodisiac.

The Guardian, 28 Nov 1976

3 Moderation is a virtue only in those who are thought to have an alternative.

The Observer, 24 Jan 1982

4 We are all the President's men.

Said regarding the invasion of Cambodia, 1970
The Sunday Times Magazine, 4 May 1975

5 Even a paranoid can have enemies.

Time, 24 Jan 1977

Kitchener (of Khartoum), Horatio Herbert, Earl (1850–1916) British field marshal. He reconquered the Sudan (1898) and became its governor general (1899). In World War I he became war secretary; he initiated a successful recruitment campaign but did not achieve effective power.

1 I don't mind your being killed, but I object to your being taken prisoner.

Said to the Prince of Wales (later Edward VIII) when he asked to go to the Front
Journal (Viscount Esher), 18 Dec 1914

Klinger, Friedrich Maximilian von (1752–1831) German dramatist and novelist. His best-known play is *Sturm und Drang* (1776).

1 *Sturm und Drang.*
Storm and stress.

Used to designate a late 18th-century literary movement in Germany
Play title

Knox, John (c. 1514–72) Scottish religious reformer. A Protestant, he became chaplain to Edward VI of England. After Mary I's accession he returned to Scotland and became the leading Protestant reformer there.

1 A man with God is always in the majority.

Inscription, Reformation Monument, Geneva, Switzerland

2 The First Blast of the Trumpet Against the Monstrous Regiment of Women.

Title of Pamphlet, 1558

Knox, Philander Chase (1853–1921) US lawyer and politician. He served as attorney general (1901–04) and secretary of state (1909–13).

1 Oh, Mr. President, do not let so great an achievement suffer from any taint of legality.

Responding to Theodore Roosevelt's request for legal justification of his acquisition of the Panama Canal Zone
Violent Neighbours (T. Buckley)

Knox, Ronald (Arbuthnot) (1888–1957) British Roman Catholic priest and writer. He is remembered for his translation of the Vulgate (1945–49) and *A Spiritual Aeneid* (1918).

1 It is so stupid of modern civilization to have given up believing in the devil when he is the only explanation of it.

Let Dons Delight

2 The baby doesn't understand English and the Devil knows Latin.

Said when asked to conduct a baptism service in English
Ronald Knox (Evelyn Waugh), Pt. I, Ch. 5

3 A loud noise at one end and no sense of responsibility at the other.

Definition of a baby
Attrib.

4 There once was a man who said 'God
Must think it exceedingly odd
If he find that this tree
Continues to be
When there's no one about in the Quad.'

For a reply, *see* ANONYMOUS
Attrib.

Knox, Vicesimus (1752–1821) British essayist and supporter of feminism.

1 Can anything be more absurd than keeping women in a state of ignorance, and yet so vehemently to insist on their resisting temptation?

Liberal Education, Vol. I, 'On the Literary Education of Women'

Koestler, Arthur (1905–83) Hungarian-born British writer and novelist. His novels include *Darkness at Noon* (1940), *Thieves in the Night* (1946), and *The Call Girls* (1972). Nonfiction concerned politics, as in *The Yogi and the Commissar* (1945), or scientific creativity, as in *The Act of Creation* (1964) and *The Ghost in the Machine* (1967). He and his wife committed suicide when his Parkinson's disease became intolerable.

1 In my youth I regarded the universe as an open book, printed in the language of physical equations, whereas now it appears to me as a text written in invisible ink, of which in our rare moments of grace we are able to decipher a small fragment.

Bricks to Babel, Epilogue

2 One may not regard the world as a sort of metaphysical brothel for emotions.

Darkness at Noon, 'The Second Hearing'

3 If the creator had a purpose in equipping us with a neck, he surely meant us to stick it out.

Encounter, May 1970

4 Two half-truths do not make a truth, and two half-cultures do not make a culture.

The Ghost in the Machine, Preface

5 The most persistent sound which reverberates through men's history is the beating of war drums.

Janus: A Summing Up, Prologue

6 A writer's ambition should be to trade a hundred contemporary readers for ten readers in ten years' time and for one reader in a hundred years' time.

New York Times Book Review, 1 Apr 1951

7 Hitherto man had to live with the idea of death as an individual; from now onward mankind will have to live with the idea of its death as a species.

Referring to the development of the atomic bomb
Peter's Quotations (Laurence J. Peter)

Kollwitz, Käthe (1867–1945) German sculptor and graphic artist. Deeply concerned about social injustice, many of her works depicted victims of urban poverty, war, and fascism.

1 I do not want to die . . . until I have faithfully made the most of my talent and cultivated the seed that was placed in me until the last small twig has grown.

Diaries and Letters, 15 Feb 1915

Koran (or Queran) Islamic bible. One of the prime sources of Islamic law, the Koran is a compilation of revelations said to have been given to the prophet Mohammed.

1 Praise be to God, the Lord of all creatures; the most merciful, the king of the day of judgment. Thee do we worship, and of thee do we beg assistance. Direct us in the right way, in the way of those to whom thou hast been gracious; not of those against whom thou art incensed, nor of those who go astray.

Opening words of the *Koran*

2 But the Jews will not be pleased with thee, neither the Christians, until thou follow their religion; say, The Direction of God is the true direction. And verily if thou follow their desires, after the knowledge which hath been given thee, thou shalt find no patron or protector against God. They to whom we have given the book of the Koran, and who read it with its true reading, they believe therein; and whoever believeth not therin, they shall perish.

Koran, Ch. II

3 War is enjoined you against the Infidels . . . They will ask thee concerning the sacred month, whether they may war therein: Answer, To war therein is grievous; but to obstruct the way of God, and infidelity towards him, and to keep men from the holy temple, and to drive out his people from thence, is more grievous in the sight of God, and the temptation to idolatry is more grievous than to kill in the sacred months.

Koran, Ch. II

4 The month of Ramadan shall ye fast, in which the Koran was sent down from heaven, a direction unto men, and declarations of direction, and the distinction between good and evil.

Ch. II

5 Ye are forbidden to eat that which dieth of itself, and blood, and swine's flesh, and that on which the name of any besides God hath been invocated; and that which hath been strangled, or killed by a blow, or by a fall, or by the horns of another beast, and that which hath been eaten by a wild beast, except what ye shall kill yourselves; and that which hath been sacrificed unto idols.

Ch. V

6 Marry those who are single among you, and such as are honest of your men-servants and your maid-servants: if they be poor, God will enrich them of his abundance; for God is bounteous and wise.

Ch. XXIV

7 The whore, and the whoremonger, shall ye scourge with a hundred stripes.

Ch. XXIV

8 Suffer the women whom ye divorce to dwell in some part of the houses wherein ye dwell; according to the room and conveniences of the habitations which ye possess; and make them not uneasy, that ye may reduce them to straits.

Ch. LXV

9 Verily the life to come shall be better for thee than this present life: and thy Lord shall give thee a reward wherewith thou shalt be well pleased. Did he not find thee an orphan, and hath he not taken care of thee? And did he not find thee wandering in error, and hath he not guided thee into the truth? And did he not find thee needy, and hath he not enriched thee?

Ch. XCIII

Korda, Sir Alexander (Sandor Kellner; 1893–1956) Hungarian-born British film director and producer. His successes include *The Scarlet Pimpernel* (1934) and *Anna Karenina* (1948).

1 It's not enough to be Hungarian, you must have talent too.

Alexander Korda (K. Kulik)

Kristofferson, Kris (1936–) US film actor and pop singer.

1 Freedom's just another word for nothing left to lose.

Me and Bobby McGee

Kubrick, Stanley (1928–) US film director and writer. His leading films include *Dr Strangelove* (1963), *2001: A Space Odyssey* (1968), *A Clockwork Orange* (1971), *The Shining* (1980), and *Full Metal Jacket* (1987).

1 The great nations have always acted like gangsters, and the small nations like prostitutes.

The Guardian, 5 June 1963

2 The very meaninglessness of life forces man to create his own meaning. If it can be written or thought, it can be filmed.

Halliwell's Filmgoer's and Video Viewer's Companion

L

Labouchère, Henry, Baron Taunton (1798–1869) British statesman. He was president of the Board of Trade (1839–41; 1847–52) and colonial secretary (1855–58).

1 I do not object to Gladstone's always having the ace of trumps up his sleeve, but only to his pretence that God had put it there.

Attrib.

La Bruyère, Jean de (1645–96) French satirist. He served in the household of Louis II and wrote one book of lasting merit *Les Caractères de Théophraste* (1688).

1 A pious man is one who would be an atheist if the king were.

Les Caractères

2 The majority of men devote the greater part of their lives to making their remaining years unhappy.

Les Caractères

3 There are some who speak one moment before they think.

Les Caractères

4 The pleasure of criticizing robs us of the pleasure of being moved by some very fine things.

Les Caractères

5 Liberality lies less in giving liberally than in the timeliness of the gift.

Les Caractères

6 There are only three events in a man's life; birth, life, and death; he is not conscious of being born, he dies in pain, and he forgets to live.

Les Caractères

7 Women run to extremes; they are either better or worse than men.

Les Caractères

8 One must laugh before one is happy, or one may die without ever laughing at all.

Les Caractères

9 Party loyalty lowers the greatest of men to the petty level of the masses.

Les Caractères

10 There exist some evils so terrible and some misfortunes so horrible that we dare not think of them, whilst their very aspect makes us shudder; but if they happen to fall on us, we find ourselves stronger than we imagined, we grapple with our ill luck, and behave better than we expected we should.
Les Caractères

11 If poverty is the mother of crime, stupidity is its father.
Les Caractères

12 'There is a report that Piso is dead; it is a great loss; he was an honest man, who deserved to live longer; he was intelligent and agreeable, resolute and courageous, to be depended upon, generous and faithful.' Add: 'provided he is really dead'.
Les Caractères

13 If we heard it said of Orientals that they habitually drank a liquor which went to their heads, deprived them of reason and made them vomit, we should say: 'How very barbarous!'
Les Caractères

14 To endeavour to forget anyone is a certain way of thinking of nothing else.
Les Caractères

15 A slave has but one master; an ambitious man has as many masters as there are people who may be useful in bettering his position.
Les Caractères

16 The shortest and best way to make your fortune is to let people see clearly that it is in their interests to promote yours.
Les Caractères

Laclos, Pierre (-Ambrose-François) Choderlos
(1741–1803) French soldier and writer. His scandalous novel *Les Liaisons dangereuses* (1782) reached a wider audience in the 1980s as a stage play and film.

1 How lucky we are that women defend themselves so poorly! We should, otherwise, be no more to them than timid slaves.
Les Liaisons Dangereuses, Letter 4

2 Prudence is, it seems to me, the virtue which must be preferred above the rest when one is determining the fate of others; and especially when it is a case of sealing that fate with sacred and indissoluble promises, such as those of marriage.
Les Liaisons Dangereuses, Letter 104

3 Have you not as yet observed that pleasure, which is undeniably the sole motive force behind the union of the sexes, is nevertheless not enough to form a bond between them? And that, if it is preceded by desire which impels, it is succeeded by disgust which repels? That is a law of nature which love alone can alter.
Les Liaisons Dangereuses, Letter 131

4 Who would not shudder to think of the misery that may be caused by a single dangerous intimacy? And how much suffering could be avoided if it were more often thought of!
Les Liaisons Dangereuses, Letter 175

La Fontaine, Jean de (1621–95) French poet. His *Fables* (1668–94) was his major work. He repudiated his somewhat bawdy *Contes* (1664) after his religious conversion in 1692.

1 Rather suffer than die is man's motto.
Fables, I, 'La Mort et le Bûcheron'

2 Be advised that all flatterers live at the expense of those who listen to them.
Fables, I, 'Le Corbeau et le Renard'

3 One should oblige everyone to the extent of one's ability. One often needs someone smaller than oneself.
Fables, II, 'Le Lion et le Rat'

4 Patience and passage of time do more than strength and fury.
Fables, II, 'Le Lion et le Rat'

5 This fellow did not see further than his own nose.
Fables, III, 'Le Renard et le Bouc'

6 A mountain in labour shouted so loud that everyone, summoned by the noise, ran up expecting that she would be delivered of a city bigger than Paris; she brought forth a mouse.
Fables, V, 'La Montagne qui accouche'

7 He told me never to sell the bear's skin before one has killed the beast.
Fables, V, 'L'Ours et les deux Compagnons'

8 People must help one another; it is nature's law.
Fables, VIII, 'L'Âne et le Chien'

9 A hungry stomach has no ears.
Fables, IX, 'Le Milan et le Rossignol'

10 What God does, He does well.
Fables, IX, 'Le Gland et la Citrouille'

11 But the shortest works are always the best.
Fables, X, 'Les Lapins'

Laing, R(onald) D(avid) (1927–89) British psychiatrist. His radical views on schizophrenia were set out in his books *The Divided Self* (1960), *The Politics of Experience* (1967), and *The Politics of the Family* (1971). *Knots* (1970) is a collection of his poetry.

1 The statesmen of the world who boast and threaten that they have Doomsday weapons are far more dangerous, and far more estranged from 'reality', than many of the people on whom the label 'psychotic' is affixed.
The Divided Self, Preface

2 Schizophrenia cannot be understood without understanding despair.
The Divided Self, Ch. 2

3 Few books today are forgivable.
The Politics of Experience, Introduction

4 We are effectively destroying ourselves by violence masquerading as love.
The Politics of Experience, Ch. 13

5 Madness need not be all breakdown. It may also be break-through. It is potential liberation and renewal as well as enslavement and existential death.
The Politics of Experience, Ch. 16

Lamb, A. J. (1870–1928) British songwriter.

1 She's only a bird in a gilded cage.
Song title

Lamb, Lady Caroline (1785–1828) The wife of William Lamb (who became the Whig prime minister, Viscount Melbourne). She had a much publicized affair with Lord Byron and wrote a novel, *Glenarvon* (1816), containing idealized portraits of herself and Byron. She died insane.

1 Mad, bad, and dangerous to know.
Said of Byron
Journal

Lamb, Charles (1775–1834) British essayist. He is best remembered for his *Essays of Elia* (1822).

Quotations about Lamb

1 Charles Lamb I sincerely believe to be in some considerable degree insane. A more pitiful, rickety, gasping, staggering, stammering tomfool I do not know.
Thomas Carlyle (1795–1881) Scottish historian and essayist. Attrib.

2 Charles Lamb, a clever fellow certainly, but full of villainous and abortive puns when he miscarries of every minute.
Thomas Moore (1779–1852) Irish poet. *Diary*, 4 Apr 1823

Quotations by Lamb

3 Nothing is to me more distasteful than that entire complacency and satisfaction which beam in the countenances of a new-married couple.
Essays of Elia, 'A Bachelor's Complaint of Married People'

4 We are nothing; less than nothing, and dreams. We are only what might have been, and must wait upon the tedious shores of Lethe millions of ages before we have existence, and a name.
In Greek mythology, Lethe was a river in the underworld, whose waters were drunk by souls about to be reborn in order to forget their past lives
Essays of Elia, 'Dream Children'

5 I hate a man who swallows it, affecting not to know what he is eating. I suspect his taste in higher matters.
Referring to food
Essays of Elia, 'Grace before Meat'

6 I have been trying all my life to like Scotchmen, and am obliged to desist from the experiment in despair.
Essays of Elia, 'Imperfect Sympathies'

7 Man is a gaming animal. He must always be trying to get the better in something or other.
Essays of Elia, 'Mrs Battle's Opinions on Whist'

8 In everything that relates to science, I am a whole Encyclopaedia behind the rest of the world.
Essays of Elia, 'The Old and the New Schoolmaster'

9 Boys are capital fellows in their own way, among their mates; but they are unwholesome companions for grown people.
Essays of Elia, 'The Old and the New Schoolmaster' people

10 The human species, according to the best theory I can form of it, is composed of two distinct races, the men who borrow, and the men who lend.
Essays of Elia, 'The Two Races of Men'

11 Borrowers of books – those mutilators of collections, spoilers of the symmetry of shelves, and creators of odd volumes.
Essays of Elia, 'The Two Races of Men'

12 Credulity is the man's weakness, but the child's strength.
Essays of Elia, 'Witches and other Night Fears'

13 I love to lose myself in other men's minds. When I am not walking, I am reading; I cannot sit and think. Books think for me.
Last Essays of Elia, 'Detached Thoughts on Books and Reading'

14 Newspapers always excite curiosity. No one ever lays one down without a feeling of disappointment.
Last Essays of Elia, 'Detached Thoughts on Books and Reading'

15 A poor relation – is the most irrelevant thing in nature.
Last Essays of Elia, 'Poor Relations'

16 It is a pistol let off at the ear; not a feather to tickle the intellect.
Referring to the nature of a pun
Last Essays of Elia, 'Popular Fallacies'

17 How sickness enlarges the dimensions of a man's self to himself.
Last Essays of Elia, 'The Convalescent'

18 The greatest pleasure I know, is to do a good action by stealth, and to have it found out by accident.
The Athenaeum, 'Table Talk by the late Elia', 4 Jan 1834

19 I have had playmates, I have had companions In my days of childhood, in my joyful schooldays –

All, all are gone, the old familiar faces.
The Old Familiar Faces

20 Riddle of destiny, who can show What thy short visit meant, or know What thy errand here below?
On an Infant Dying as soon as Born

21 Damn the age. I'll write for antiquity.
Referring to his lack of payment for the *Essays of Elia*
English Wits (L. Russell)

22 DR PARR. How have you acquired your power of smoking at such a rate?
LAMB. I toiled after it, sir, as some men toil after virtue.

Memoirs of Charles Lamb (Talfourd)

23 I came home . . . hungry as a hunter.

Letter to Coleridge, Apr 1800

24 Separate from the pleasure of your company, I don't much care if I never see another mountain in my life.

Letter to William Wordsworth, 30 Jan 1801

25 A little thin, flowery border, round, neat, not gaudy.

Letter to Wordsworth, June 1806

26 This very night I am going to leave off tobacco! Surely there must be some other world in which this unconquerable purpose shall be realized. The soul hath not her generous aspirings implanted in her in vain.

Letter to Thomas Manning, 26 Dec 1815

Lamb, Mary (1764–1847) Sister of Charles Lamb. She killed her mother in a fit of insanity and was looked after by her brother until he, himself, became insane.

1 A child's a plaything for an hour.

Parental Recollections

Lampton, William James (1859–1917) British writer.

1 Same old slippers,
Same old rice,
Same old glimpse of
Paradise.

June Weddings

Lancaster, Osbert (1908–86) British cartoonist and writer of many books on architecture, including *Pillar to Post* (1938).

1 'Fan vaulting' . . . an architectural device which arouses enormous enthusiasm on account of the difficulties it has all too obviously involved but which from an aesthetic standpoint frequently belongs to the 'Last-supper-carved-on-a-peach-stone' class of masterpiece.

Pillar to Post, 'Perpendicular'

2 A hundred and fifty accurate reproductions of Anne Hathaway's cottage, each complete with central heating and garage.

Pillar to Post, 'Stockbrokers Tudor'

Lanchester, Elsa (1902–86) British-born US actress, married to Charles Laughton. Her many films include *The Bride of Frankenstein* (1935), *Bell, Book, and Candle* (1957), and *Mary Poppins* (1964).

1 She looked as though butter wouldn't melt in her mouth – or anywhere else.

Referring to Maureen O'Hara
Attrib.

Landon, Letitia (1802–38) British poet and novelist. She sometimes used the initials L.E.L. as a pen name. Her verse collections include *The Venetian Bracelet* (1829); her best-known novel is *Ethel Churchill* (1837).

1 Were it not better to forget
Than but remember and regret?

Despondency

2 Few, save the poor, feel for the poor.

The Poor

3 We might have been – These are but common words,
And yet they make the sum of life's bewailing.

Three Extracts from the Diary of a Week

Landor, Walter Savage (1775–1864) British poet and writer. His collections include *Imaginary Conversations of Literary Men and Statesmen* (1824–29), *Hellenics* (1847), and *Dry Sticks, Fagoted* (1858).

1 Stand close around, ye Stygian set,
With Dirce in one boat conveyed!
Or Charon, seeing, may forget
That he is old and she a shade.

In Greek mythology, Dirce, a follower of Dionysius, was killed by her great-nephews Amphion and Zethus because of her mistreatment of their mother Antiope; Charon was the ferryman who transported dead souls across the River Styx to the underworld
Dirce

2 Prose on certain occasions can bear a great deal of poetry: on the other hand, poetry sinks and swoons under a moderate weight of prose.

Imaginary Conversations, 'Archdeacon Hare and Walter Landor'

3 Goodness does not more certainly make men happy than happiness makes them good.

Imaginary Conversations, 'Lord Brooke and Sir Philip Sidney'

4 States, like men, have their growth, their manhood, their decrepitude, their decay.

Imaginary Conversations, 'Pollio and Calvus'

5 Clear writers, like clear fountains, do not seem so deep as they are; the turbid look the most profound.

Imaginary Conversations, 'Southey and Porson'

6 Fleas know not whether they are upon the body of a giant or upon one of ordinary size.

Imaginary Conversations, 'Southey and Porson'

7 I strove with none; for none was worth my strife;
Nature I loved, and, next to Nature, Art;
I warmed both hands before the fire of life;
It sinks, and I am ready to depart.

I Strove with None

8 Good God, I forgot the violets!

Having thrown his cook out of an open window onto the flowerbed below
Irreverent Social History (F. Muir)

Landseer, Sir Edwin Henry (1802–73) British painter and sculptor. His Highland paintings were popular with Queen Victoria; his four bronze lions stand at the foot of Nelson's column in Trafalgar Square, London.

1 If people only knew as much about painting as I do, they would never buy my pictures.

Said to W. P. Frith
Landseer the Victorian Paragon (Campbell Lennie), Ch. 12

Lang, Andrew (1844–1912) Scottish writer and poet. His historical writings include *A History of Scotland* (1900–07) and *John Knox and the Reformation* (1905). His *Custom and Myth* (1884) was an important work of literary mythology and his poetry included the popular collection *Grass of Parnassus* (1888).

1 He uses statistics as a drunken man uses lamp-posts – for support rather than illumination.

Treasury of Humorous Quotations

Lang, Julia S. (1921–) British broadcaster who presented the BBC children's radio series *Listen With Mother*.

1 Are you sitting comfortably? Then I'll begin.

Introduction to the story in *Listen with Mother*

Langbridge, Frederick (1849–1923) British religious writer.

1 Two men look out through the same bars: One sees the mud, and one the stars.

A Cluster of Quiet Thoughts

Langland, William (c. 1330–c. 1400) English poet. He was the reputed author of the allegorical poem *The Vision of Piers Plowman*.

1 In a somer season, when soft was the sonne.

The Vision of Piers Plowman, Prologue

2 Dowel, Dobet and Dobest.

Do well, Do better, and Do Best: three concepts central to the search for Truth in *Piers Plowman*, in which they appear as allegorical characters
The Vision of Piers Plowman

Laplace, Pierre-Simon, Marquis de (1749–1827) French mathematician and astronomer. His major work *Mécanique céleste* (1799–1825) reported work he did with Lagrange (although Lagrange was not credited).

1 I have no need of that hypothesis.

On being asked by Napoleon why he had made no mention of God in his book about the universe, *Mécanique céleste*. See also
BONHOEFFER
Men of Mathematics (E. Bell)

Lardner, Ring, Jnr (1885–1933) American humorist and writer of short stories. His books include *Gullible's Travels* (1917), *The Big Town* (1921), and *What of It?* (1925).

1 He looked at me as if I was a side dish he hadn't ordered.

Referring to W. H. Taft, US president (1909–13)
The Home Book of Humorous Quotations (A. K. Adams)

2 How do you look when I'm sober?

Speaking to a flamboyantly dressed stranger who walked into the club where he was drinking
Ring (J. Yardley)

3 Frenchmen drink wine just like we used to drink water before Prohibition.

Wit's End (R. E. Drennan)

Larkin, Philip (1922–85) British poet. Collections include *The Whitsun Weddings* (1964) and *High Windows* (1974). He also edited *The Oxford Book of Twentieth Century Verse* (1973) and wrote two novels.

1 Clearly money has something to do with life – In fact, they've a lot in common, if you enquire: You can't put off being young until you retire.

Money

2 Perhaps being old is having lighted rooms Inside your head, and people in them, acting. People you know, yet can't quite name.

The Old Fools

3 Get stewed: Books are a load of crap.

A Study of Reading Habits

4 They fuck you up, your mum and dad. They may not mean to, but they do. They fill you with the faults they had And add some extra, just for you.

This be the Verse

5 Far too many relied on the classic formula of a beginning, a muddle, and an end.

Referring to modern novels
New Fiction, 15 (January 1978)

Laski, H(arold) J(oseph) (1893–1950) British political theorist. A socialist and teacher at the London School of Economics, he became leader of the Labour Party during Attlee's administration, although his Marxist leanings failed to influence the parliamentary party.

1 The meek do not inherit the earth unless they are prepared to fight for their meekness.

Attrib.

Latimer, Hugh (1485–1555) English churchman, who became an advisor to Henry VIII after showing his Protestant inclinations. On the accession of the Roman Catholic Queen Mary, he was imprisoned and burnt at the stake with Nicholas Ridley for refusing to acknowledge Catholic doctrines.

1 The drop of rain maketh a hole in the stone, not by violence, but by oft falling.

See also LUCRETIUS; OVID
Sermon preached before Edward VI

2 Be of good comfort, Master Ridley, and play the man; we shall this day light such a candle, by God's grace, in England as I trust shall never be put out.

Said to Nicholas Ridley as they were about to be burnt at the stake for heresy
Famous Last Words (B. Conrad)

Lauder, Sir Harry (Hugh MacLennon; 1870–1950) Scottish music-hall artist. His famous songs included 'I Love a Lassie' and 'Roamin' in the Gloamin'.

1 Just a wee deoch-an-duoris Before we gang awa' . . . If y' can say It's a braw brecht moonlecht necht, Yer a' recht, that's a'.

Song

2　O! it's nice to get up in the mornin',
　　But it's nicer to stay in bed.
　　Song

3　Roamin' in the gloamin',
　　By the bonny banks of Clyde.
　　Song

4　I love a lassie.
　　Song title

5　Keep right on to the end of the road.
　　Song title

Laurence, William L. (1888–1977) US journalist.

1　At first it was a giant column that soon took the shape of a supramundane mushroom.
　　Referring to the explosion of the first atomic bomb, over Hiroshima, 6 Aug 1945
　　The New York Times, 26 Sept 1945

Law, (Andrew) Bonar (1858–1923) British statesman. He became Conservative prime minister (1922–23) after Lloyd George's resignation from the coalition, in which Bonar Law had been chancellor of the exchequer.

1　I must follow them; I am their leader.
　　Mr Balfour (E. T. Raymond), Ch. 15

2　If, therefore, war should ever come between these two countries, which Heaven forbid! it will not, I think, be due to irresistible natural laws, it will be due to the want of human wisdom.
　　Referring to the UK and Germany
　　Speech, House of Commons, 27 Nov 1911

3　We have heard of people being thrown to the wolves, but never before have we heard of a man being thrown to the wolves with a bargain on the part of the wolves that they would not eat him.
　　Referring to the fact that the then war minister, Col Seely, had offered his resignation
　　Speech, House of Commons, Mar 1914

4　If I am a great man, then a good many of the great men of history are frauds.
　　Attrib.

5　Look at that man's eyes. You will hear more of him later.
　　Referring to Mussolini
　　Attrib.

Lawrence, D(avid) H(erbert) (1885–1930) British novelist. The son of a coalminer, he earned his reputation with the autobiographical *Sons and Lovers* (1913). Subsequent novels include *Women in Love* (1921), *Kangaroo* (1923), and *Lady Chatterley's Lover* (1928).

Quotations about Lawrence

1　Interesting, but a type I could not get on with. Obsessed with self. Dead eyes and a red beard, long narrow face. A strange bird.
　　John Galsworthy (1867–1933) British novelist. *Life and Letters* (edited by H. V. Marriot)

2　For Lawrence, existence was one long convalescence, it was as though he were newly reborn from a mortal illness every day of his life.
　　Aldous Huxley (1894–1964) British novelist. *The Olive Tree*

Quotations by Lawrence

3　You must always be a-waggle with LOVE.
　　Bibbles

4　The English people on the whole are surely the *nicest* people in the world, and everyone makes everything so easy for everybody else, that there is almost nothing to resist at all.
　　Dull London

5　To the Puritan all things are impure, as somebody says.
　　Etruscan Places, 'Cerveteri'

6　The Romans and Greeks found everything human. Everything had a face, and a human voice. Men spoke, and their fountains piped an answer.
　　Fantasia of the Unconscious, Ch. 4

7　The refined punishments of the spiritual mode are usually much more indecent and dangerous than a good smack.
　　Fantasia of the Unconscious, Ch. 4

8　Morality which is based on ideas, or on an ideal, is an unmitigated evil.
　　Fantasia of the Unconscious, Ch. 7

9　When Eve ate this particular apple, she became aware of her own womanhood, mentally. And mentally she began to experiment with it. She has been experimenting ever since. So has man. To the rage and horror of both of them.
　　Fantasia of the Unconscious, Ch. 7

10　O pity the dead that are dead, but cannot make the journey, still they moan and beat against the silvery adamant walls of life's exclusive city.
　　The Houseless Dead

11　How beastly the bourgeois is especially the male of the species.
　　How beastly the bourgeois is

12　You may be the most liberal Liberal Englishman, and yet you cannot fail to see the categorical difference between the responsible and the irresponsible classes.
　　Kangaroo, Ch. 1

13　And all lying mysteriously within the Australian underdark, that peculiar, lost weary aloofness of Australia. There was the vast town of Sydney. And it didn't seem to be real, it seemed to be sprinkled on the surface of a darkness into which it never penetrated.
　　Kangaroo, Ch. 1

14 The very best that is in the Jewish blood: a faculty for pure disinterestedness, and warm, physically warm love, that seems to make the corpuscles of the blood glow.
Kangaroo, Ch. 6

15 We have all lost the war. All Europe.
The Ladybird, 'The Ladybird'

16 The young Cambridge group, the group that stood for 'freedom' and flannel trousers and flannel shirts open at the neck, and a well-bred sort of emotional anarchy, and a whispering, murmuring sort of voice, and an ultra-sensitive sort of manner.
Lady Chatterley's Lover, Ch. 1

17 It's all this cold-hearted fucking that is death and idiocy.
Lady Chatterley's Lover, Ch. 14

18 But tha mun dress thysen, an' go back to thy stately homes of England, how beautiful they stand. Time's up! Time's up for Sir John, an' for little Lady Jane! Put thy shimmy on, Lady Chatterley!
Lady Chatterley's Lover, Ch. 15

19 Water is H_2O, hydrogen two parts, oxygen one, but there is also a third thing, that makes it water
and nobody knows what that is.
Pansies, 'The Third Thing'

20 It always seemed to me that men wore their beards, like they wear their neckties, for show. I shall always remember Lewis for saying his beard was part of him.
St Mawr

21 The modern pantheist not only sees the god in everything, he takes photographs of it.
St Mawr

22 It was one of those places where the spirit of aboriginal England still lingers, the old savage England, whose last blood flows still in a few Englishmen, Welshmen, Cornishmen.
St Mawr

23 Ideal mankind would abolish death, multiply itself million upon million, rear up city upon city, save every parasite alive, until the accumulation of mere existence is swollen to a horror.
St Mawr

24 And suddenly she craved again for the more absolute silence of America. English stillness was so soft, like an inaudible murmur of voices, of presences.
St Mawr

25 You may have my husband, but not my horse. My husband won't need emasculating, and my horse I won't have you meddle with. I'll preserve one last male thing in the museum of this world, if I can.
St Mawr

26 There's nothing so artificial as sinning nowadays. I suppose it once was real.
St Mawr

27 One realizes with horror, that the race of men is almost extinct in Europe. Only Christ-like heroes and woman-worshipping Don Juans, and rabid equality-mongrels.
Sea and Sardinia, Ch. 3

28 A snake came to my water-trough
On a hot, hot day, and I in pyjamas for the heat,
To drink there.
Snake

29 And so, I missed my chance with one of the lords
Of life.
And I have something to expiate;
A pettiness.
Snake

30 When I read Shakespeare I am struck with wonder
That such trivial people should muse and thunder
In such lovely language.
When I Read Shakespeare

31 Be a good animal, true to your animal instincts.
The White Peacock, Pt. II, Ch. 2

32 No absolute is going to make the lion lie down with the lamb unless the lamb is inside.
The Later D. H. Lawrence

33 Away with all ideals. Let each individual act spontaneously from the for ever incalculable prompting of the creative wellhead within him. There is no universal law.
Phoenix, Preface to 'All Things are Possible' by Leo Shostov

34 Russia will certainly inherit the future. What we already call the greatness of Russia is only her pre-natal struggling.
Phoenix, Preface to 'All Things are Possible' by Leo Shostov

35 Pornography is the attempt to insult sex, to do dirt on it.
Phoenix, 'Pornography and Obscenity'

36 It is no good casting out devils. They belong to us, we must accept them and be at peace with them.
Phoenix, 'The Reality of Peace'

37 Neither can you expect a revolution, because there is no new baby in the womb of our society. Russia is a collapse, not a revolution.
Phoenix, 'The Good Man'

38 I am a man, and alive . . . For this reason I am a novelist. And being a novelist, I consider myself superior to the saint, the scientist, the philosopher, and the poet, who are all great masters of different bits of man alive, but never get the whole hog.
Phoenix, 'Why the Novel Matters'

39 We know these new English Catholics. They are the last words in Protest. They are Protestants protesting against Protestantism.

Phoenix, 'Review of Eric Gill, *Art Nonsense*'

40 To every man who struggles with his own soul in mystery, a book that is a book flowers once, and seeds, and is gone.

Phoenix, 'A Bibliography of D.H.L.'

41 I like to write when I feel spiteful: it's like having a good sneeze.

Letter to Lady Cynthia Asquith, Nov 1913

42 They are great parables, the novels, but false art. They are only parables. All the people are *fallen angels* – even the dirtiest scrubs. This I cannot stomach. People are not fallen angels, they are merely people.

Referring to the novels of Dostoyevsky
Letter to J. Middleton Murry and Katherine Mansfield, 17 Feb 1916

43 I am only half there when I am ill, and so there is only half a man to suffer. To suffer in one's whole self is so great a violation, that it is not to be endured.

Letter to Catherine Carswell, 16 Apr 1916

44 The dead don't die. They look on and help.

Letter

45 I'm not sure if a mental relation with a woman doesn't make it impossible to love her. To know the *mind* of a woman is to end in hating her. Love means the pre-cognitive flow . . . it is the honest state before the apple.

Letter to Dr Trigant Burrow, 3 Aug 1927

Lawrence, James (1781–1813) US naval officer. He commanded the *Hornet* on its raids against British shipping and was later transferred to the *Chesapeake*.

1 Don't give up the ship.

Last words as he lay dying in his ship, the US frigate *Chesapeake*, during the battle with the British frigate *Shannon*
Attrib.

Lawrence, T(homas) E(dward) (1888–1935) British soldier and writer, known as Lawrence of Arabia. He became famous after leading a successful Arab revolt against the Turks (1917–18). He wrote *The Seven Pillars of Wisdom* (1926) and *The Mint* (1955).

Quotations about Lawrence

1 Arabian Lawrence, who, whatever his claims as a man, was surely a sonorous fake as a writer.

Kingsley Amis (1922–) British novelist. *What Became of Jane Austen?*

2 . . . a bore and a bounder and a prig. He was intoxicated with his own youth, and loathed any milieu which he couldn't dominate. Certainly he had none of a gentleman's instincts, strutting about Peace Conferences in Arab dress.

Sir Henry Channon (1897–1958) US-born British politician. *Diary*, 25 May 1935

3 There are those who have tried to dismiss his story with a flourish of the Union Jack, a psychoanalytical catchword, or a sneer. It should move our deepest admiration and pity. Like Shelley and like Baudelaire it may be said of him that he suffered, in his own person, the neurotic ills of an entire generation.

Christopher Isherwood (1904–86) British novelist. *Exhumations*

4 He was retiring and yet craved to be seen, he was sincerely shy and naively exhibitionist. He had to rise above others and then humble himself, and in his self-inflicted humiliation demonstrate his superiority.

Lewis B. Namier (1888–1960) Polish educator and historian. *T. E. Lawrence by His Friends* (A. W. Lawrence)

5 He had a genius for backing into the limelight.

Lowell Thomas. *Lawrence of Arabia*

Quotations by Lawrence

6 Many men would take the death-sentence without a whimper to escape the life-sentence which fate carries in her other hand.

The Mint, Pt. I, Ch. 4

7 All men dream: but not equally. Those who dream by night in the dusty recesses of their minds wake in the day to find that it was vanity: but the dreamers of the day are dangerous men, for they may act their dream with open eyes, to make it possible.

Seven Pillars of Wisdom, Ch. 1

8 I fancy, for myself, that they are rather out of touch with reality; by reality I mean shops like Selfridges, and motor buses, and the *Daily Express*.

Referring to expatriate authors living in Paris, such as James Joyce
Letter to W. Hurley, 1 Apr 1929

9 I'm re-reading it with a slow deliberate carelessness.

Letter to Edward Marsh, 18 Apr 1929

Lazarus, Emma (1849–87) US poet and philanthropist. Her collections include *Admetus and Other Poems* (1871) and *Songs of a Semite* (1882). She organized relief for Jews persecuted in Russia (1879–83).

1 Give me your tired, your poor,
Your huddled masses yearning to breathe free,
The wretched refuse of your teeming shore,
Send these, the homeless, tempest-tossed to me,
I lift my lamp beside the golden door!

Used as an inscription on the Statue of Liberty
The New Colossus

Leach, Sir Edmund (1910–89) British social anthropologist and author of *Rethinking Anthropology* (1961), *Genesis as Myth* (1970), *Social Anthropology* (1982), and many other books and articles.

1 Far from being the basis of the good society, the family, with its narrow privacy and tawdry secrets, is the source of all our discontents.

In the BBC Reith Lectures for 1967. Lecture reprinted in *The Listener*

Leacock, Stephen (Butler) (1869–1944) English-born Canadian economist and humorist. His *Literary Lapses* (1910) and *Nonsense Novels* (1911) were two of some 30 humorous books.

1 If every day in the life of a school could be the last day but one, there would be little fault to find with it.

College Days, 'Memories and Miseries of a Schoolmaster'

2 The classics are only primitive literature. They belong in the same class as primitive machinery and primitive music and primitive medicine.

Homer and Humbug

3 I detest life-insurance agents; they always argue that I shall some day die, which is not so.

Literary Lapses, 'Insurance. Up to Date'

4 Get your room full of good air, then shut up the windows and keep it. It will keep for years. Anyway, don't keep using your lungs all the time. Let them rest.

Literary Lapses, 'How to Live to be 200'

5 Astronomy teaches the correct use of the sun and the planets.

Literary Lapses, 'A Manual of Education'

6 The landlady of a boarding-house is a parallelogram – that is, an oblong angular figure, which cannot be described, but which is equal to anything.

Literary Lapses, 'Boarding-House Geometry'

7 Any two meals at a boarding-house are together less than two square meals.

Literary Lapses, 'Boarding-House Geometry'

8 It takes a good deal of physical courage to ride a horse. This, however, I have. I get it at about forty cents a flask, and take it as required.

Literary Lapses, 'Reflections on Riding'

9 The great man . . . walks across his century and leaves the marks of his feet all over it, ripping out the dates on his goloshes as he passes.

Literary Lapses, 'The Life of John Smith'

10 Lord Ronald said nothing; he flung himself from the room, flung himself upon his horse and rode madly off in all directions.

Nonsense Novels, 'Gertrude the Governess'

11 Golf may be played on Sunday, not being a game within the view of the law, but being a form of moral effort.

Other Fancies, 'Why I refuse to play Golf'

12 A 'Grand Old Man'. That means on our continent any one with snow white hair who has kept out of jail till eighty.

The Score and Ten

13 The general idea, of course, in any first-class laundry is to see that no shirt or collar ever comes back twice.

Winnowed Wisdom, Ch. 6

Lear, Edward (1812–88) British artist and writer. His *Book of Nonsense* (1846) was the forerunner of several others, such as *Laughable Lyrics* (1876).

1 There was an Old Man with a beard,
Who said, 'It is just as I feared! –
Two Owls and a Hen,
Four Larks and a Wren,
Have all built their nests in my beard!'

Book of Nonsense

2 On the Coast of Coromandel
Where the early pumpkins blow,
In the middle of the woods
Lived the Yonghy-Bonghy-Bò.

The Courtship of the Yonghy-Bonghy-Bò

3 The Dong! – the Dong!
The wandering Dong through the forest goes!
The Dong! – the Dong!
The Dong with a luminous Nose!

The Dong with a Luminous Nose

4 They went to sea in a sieve, they did
In a sieve they went to sea.

The Jumblies

5 Far and few, far and few,
Are the lands where the Jumblies live;
Their heads are green, and their hands are blue,
And they went to sea in a sieve.

The Jumblies

6 Serve up in a clean dish, and throw the whole out of the window as fast as possible.

To make an Amblongus Pie

7 He has many friends, laymen and clerical.
Old Foss is the name of his cat:
His body is perfectly spherical,
He weareth a runcible hat.

Nonsense Songs, Preface

8 The Owl and the Pussy-Cat went to sea
In a beautiful pea-green boat,
They took some honey, and plenty of money,
Wrapped up in a five-pound note.

The Owl and the Pussy-Cat

9 They dined on mince, and slices of quince,
Which they ate with a runcible spoon;
And hand in hand, on the edge of the sand,
They danced by the light of the moon.

The Owl and the Pussy-Cat

Leavis, F(rank) R(aymond) (1895–1978) British literary critic, who stressed the moral value of the study of literature. He edited the journal *Scrutiny* (1932–53) and wrote *The Great Tradition* (1948), as well as studies of Dickens and D. H. Lawrence.

1 His verse exhibits . . . something that is rather like Keats's vulgarity with a Public School accent.

Referring to Rupert Brooke
New Bearings in English Poetry, Ch. 2

Lebowitz, Fran (1950–) US writer and columnist. Her collected essays *Metropolitan Life* (1978) established her reputation as a humorous writer.

1 Never judge a cover by its book.

Metropolitan Life

2 Food is an important part of a balanced diet.

Metropolitan Life, 'Food for Thought and Vice Versa'

3 Life is something to do when you can't get to sleep.

The Observer, 21 Jan 1979

Leboyer, Frédérick (1918–) French obstetrician.

1 Birth may be a matter of a moment. But it is a unique one.

Birth Without Violence

2 Making love is the sovereign remedy for anguish.

Birth without Violence

3 There must be love
Without love you will be merely skilful.

Entering the World (M. Odent)

Le Corbusier (Charles-Édouard Jeanneret; 1887–1965) Swiss-born French architect. He progressed from cubist-style houses to more innovative ideas, such as the *unité d'habitation* at Marseilles. The city of Chandigarh was his most ambitious town-planning project.

1 A house is a machine for living in.

Towards a New Architecture

2 'A great epoch has begun. There exists a new spirit.'

Towards a New Architecture

3 If you want to see bad taste, go into the houses of the rich.

Attrib.

Ledru-Rollin, Alexandre Auguste (1807–74) French lawyer and politician. An advocate of universal suffrage, he was largely responsible for its adoption in France.

1 Let me pass, I have to follow them, I am their leader.

Trying to force his way through a mob during the Revolution of 1848, of which he was one of the chief instigators
The Fine Art of Political Wit (L. Harris)

Lee, Harper (1926–) US writer. Her only novel *To Kill a Mockingbird* (1960) was made into a film in 1963.

1 Being Southerners, it was a source of shame to some members of the family that we had no recorded ancestors on either side of the Battle of Hastings.

To Kill a Mockingbird, Pt. I, Ch. 1

2 Shoot all the bluejays you want, if you can hit 'em, but remember it's a sin to kill a mockingbird.

To Kill a Mockingbird, Pt. II, Ch. 10

Lee, Laurie (1914–) British novelist and poet. His most famous publication is the novel *Cider with Rosie* (1959), about his rural childhood; other works include *As I Walked Out One Midsummer Morning* (1969) and *I Can't Stay Long* (1976).

1 As the drought continued, prayer was abandoned and more devilish steps adopted. Finally soldiers with rifles marched to the tops of the hills and began shooting at passing clouds.

Cider With Rosie, 'First Names'

2 Being so recently born, birth had no meaning, it was the other extreme that enthralled me. Death was absorbing, and I saw much of it; it was my childhood's continuous fare.

Cider With Rosie, 'Public Death, Private Murder'

3 The old couple were shocked and terrified, and lay clutching each other's hands. 'The Workhouse' – always a word of shame, grey shadow falling on the close of life, most feared by the old (even when called The Infirmary); abhorred more than debt, or prison, or beggary, or even the stain of madness.

Cider with Rosie, 'Public Death, Private Murder'

4 Myself, my family, my generation, were born in a world of silence; a world of hard work and necessary patience . . . Man and horse were all the power we had – abetted by levers and pulleys. But the horse was king, and almost everything grew around him . . . This was what we were born to, and all we knew at first. Then, to the scream of the horse, the change began. The brass-lamped motor-car came coughing up the road.

Cider With Rosie, 'Last Days'

Lee, Robert E(dward) (1807–70) US general. An outstanding leader, he was a Confederate commander in the US Civil War and defended Virginia against Federal attacks.

1 It is well that war is so terrible; else we would grow too fond of it.

Speaking to another general during the battle of Fredericksburg
The American Treasury (C. Fadiman)

2 I should be trading on the blood of my men.

Refusing to write his memoirs
Nobody Said It Better (M. Ringo)

Lefèvre, Théo (1914–73) Belgian prime minister (1961–65). A lawyer, he became a member of the underground after the German occupation in 1940. He entered parliament as a Christian Democrat in 1946.

1 In Western Europe there are now only small countries – those that know it and those that don't know it yet.

The Observer, 'Sayings of the Year', 1963

Lehman, Ernest (1920–) US screenwriter and author.

1 Sweet Smell of Success.
Novel and film title

Lehrer, Tom (1928–) US university teacher and songwriter. He has taught physics, business administration, and psychology. His humorous songs are collected in *Tom Lehrer's Song Book* (1954) and others.

1 It is sobering to consider that when Mozart was my age he had already been dead for a year.
An Encyclopedia of Quotations about Music (N. Shapiro)

Leigh, Fred W. (19th century) British songwriter.

1 There was I, waiting at the church,
Waiting at the church, waiting at the church,
When I found he'd left me in the lurch,
Lor', how it did upset me! . . .
Can't get away to marry you today –
My wife won't let me.
Waiting at the Church

Lenclos, Ninon de (1620–1705) French courtesan whose salon was popular with many writers and politicians, including her lovers La Rochefoucauld and Sévigné.

1 Old age is woman's hell.
Attrib.

Lenin, Vladimir Ilich (Vladimir Ilich Ulyanov; 1870–1924) Russian revolutionary leader, who led the Bolsheviks to victory, establishing the Soviet of People's Commissars and the Third International. He died after a series of strokes resulting from an assassination attempt; his embalmed body is on permanent exhibition in Moscow.

1 If it were necessary to give the briefest possible definition of imperialism we should have to say that imperialism is the monopoly stage of capitalism.
Imperialism, the Highest Stage of Capitalism, Ch. 7

2 One step forward, two steps back . . . It happens in the lives of individuals, and it happens in the history of nations and in the development of parties.
One Step Forward, Two Steps Back

3 Under capitalism we have a state in the proper sense of the word, that is, a special machine for the suppression of one class by another.
The State and Revolution, Ch. 5

4 So long as the state exists there is no freedom. When there is freedom there will be no state.
The State and Revolution, Ch. 5

5 Under socialism *all* will govern in turn and will soon become accustomed to no one governing.
The State and Revolution, Ch. 6

6 A Social-Democrat must never forget that the proletariat will inevitably have to wage a class struggle for Socialism even against the most democratic and republican bourgeoisie and petty bourgeoisie.
The State and Revolution, Ch. 10

7 Any cook should be able to run the country.
The First Circle (Alexander Solzhenitsyn)

8 When a liberal is abused, he says: Thank God they didn't beat me. When he is beaten, he thanks God they didn't kill him. When he is killed, he will thank God that his immortal soul has been delivered from its mortal clay.
Lenin heard this characterization at a meeting, and repeated it with approval
The Government's Falsification of the Duma and the Tasks of the Social-Democrats, 'Proletary', Dec 1906

9 Communism is Soviet power plus the electrification of the whole country.
Political slogan of 1920, promoting the programme of electrification

10 A good man fallen among Fabians.
Referring to Bernard Shaw
Attrib.

11 It is true that liberty is precious – so precious that it must be rationed.
Attrib.

Lennon, John (1940–80) British rock musician and member of the Beatles. His most distinctive solo recording was *Imagine* (1971). He was assassinated in 1980.

1 Life is what happens to you while you're busy making other plans.
Beautiful Boy

2 For I don't care too much for money,
For money can't buy me love.
Can't Buy Me Love (with Paul McCartney)

3 Waits at the window, wearing the face that she keeps in a jar by the door
Who is it for? All the lonely people, where do they all come from?
All the lonely people, where do they all belong?
Eleanor Rigby (with Paul McCartney)

4 If there's anything that you want,
If there's anything I can do,
Just call on me,
And I'll send it along with love from me to you.
From Me to You (with Paul McCartney)

5 I've got to admit it's getting better.
It's a little better all the time.
Getting Better (with Paul McCartney)

6 It's been a hard day's night.
A Hard Day's Night (with Paul McCartney)

7 Picture yourself in a boat on a river with tangerine trees and marmalade skies.
Somebody calls you, you answer quite slowly a girl with kaleidoscope eyes.
Lucy in the Sky with Diamonds (with Paul McCartney)

8 He's a real Nowhere Man,
Sitting in his Nowhere Land,
Making all his nowhere plans for nobody.
Doesn't have a point of view,
Knows not where he's going to,
Isn't he a bit like you and me?
Nowhere Man (with Paul McCartney)

9 Sergeant Pepper's Lonely Hearts Club Band.
Song title (with Paul McCartney)

10 She loves you, yeh, yeh, yeh,
And with a love like that you know you should be glad.
She Loves You (with Paul McCartney)

11 She's leaving home after living alone for so many years.
She's Leaving Home (with Paul McCartney)

12 I get by with a little help from my friends.
With a Little Help from My Friends (with Paul McCartney)

13 We're more popular than Jesus Christ now. I don't know which will go first. Rock and roll or Christianity.
The Beatles Illustrated Lyrics

Lenthall, William (1591–1662) English parliamentarian and speaker of the Long Parliament.

1 I have neither eye to see, nor tongue to speak here, but as the House is pleased to direct me.
Said on 4 Jan 1642 in the House of Commons when asked by Charles I if he had seen five MPs whom the King wished to arrest. It was a succinct restatement of the Speaker's traditional role
Historical Collections (Rushworth)

Leo X (Giovanni de' Medici; 1475–1521) Pope (1513–21). The son of Lorenzo the Magnificent, he was a lavish patron of the arts. He gave France control over its own church appointments (Concordat of Boulogne; 1516).

1 Since God has given us the papacy, let us enjoy it.
Men of Art (T. Craven)

Léon, Luis Ponce de (1527–91) Spanish monk, Thomist theologian, and vicar-general of the Augustinian order. His works include lyrics and translations of classical and biblical texts.

1 As I was saying the other day.
Said on resuming a lecture interrupted by five years' imprisonment

Leonard, Hugh (1926–) Irish dramatist whose plays include *A Leap in the Dark* (1957), *Da* (1973), and *Scorpions* (1983). He has also written plays for television.

1 The problem with Ireland is that it's a country full of genius, but with absolutely no talent.
Said during an interview
The Times, Aug 1977

Leonardo da Vinci 1452–1519) Italian artist, engineer, and scientist. His best-known paintings are the *Last Supper* and the *Mona Lisa*. His *Notebooks* (1508–18) cover a wide range of subjects.

Quotations about Leonardo da Vinci

1 He was the most relentlessly curious man in history. Everything he saw made him ask how and why. Why does one find sea-shells in the mountains? How do they build locks in Flanders? How does a bird fly? What accounts for cracks in walls? What is the origin of winds and clouds? Find out; write it down; if you can see it, draw it.
Sir Kenneth Clark (1938–69) British art historian and writer. *Civilisation*

2 Of all these questions the one he asks most insistently is about man. How does he walk. How does the heart pump blood. What happens when he yawns and sneezes? How does a child live in the womb. Why does he die of old age? Leonardo discovered a centenarian in a hospital in Florence and waited gleefully for his demise so that he could examine his veins.
Sir Kenneth Clark (1938–69) British art historian and writer. *Civilisation*

3 He bores me. He ought to have stuck to his flying machines.
Pierre Auguste Renoir (1841–1919) French impressionist painter.

4 Leonardo undertook for Francesco Zanobi del Giocondo the portrait of his wife Mona Lisa. She was very beautiful and while he was drawing her portrait he engaged people to play and sing, and jesters to keep her merry, and remove that melancholy which painting usually gives to portraits. This figure of Leonardo's has such a pleasant smile that it seems rather divine than human, and was considered marvellous, an exact copy of Nature.
Giorgio Vasari (1511–74) Italian art historian. *Lives of Painters, Architects and Sculptors*

Quotations by Leonardo da Vinci

5 A man with wings large enough and duly attached might learn to overcome the resistance of the air, and conquering it succeed in subjugating it and raise himself upon it.
Flight of Birds

6 While I thought that I was learning how to live, I have been learning how to die.
Notebooks

7 Those who are enamoured of practice without science are like a pilot who goes into a ship without rudder or compass and never has any certainty where he is going.
Practice should always be based upon a sound knowledge of theory.
Notebooks

Leonidas (died 480 BC) King of Sparta (490–480 BC). He defended the pass of Thermopylae, against an enormous Persian army, with a small force all of which was lost.

1 Go, stranger, and tell the Lacedaemonians that here we lie, obedient to their commands.

Epitaph over the tomb in which he and his followers were buried after their defeat at Thermopylae

Leopold II (1835–1909) King of the Belgians (1865–1909). He sponsored Stanley's exploration of the Congo and obtained Belgian sovereignty over it in 1885.

1 A constitutional king must learn to stoop.

Instructing Prince Albert, the heir apparent, to pick up some papers that had fallen onto the floor
The Mistress (Betty Kelen)

Lerner, Alan Jay (1918–86) US songwriter and librettist, who collaborated with Frederick Loewe in such musicals as *My Fair Lady* (1956) and *Camelot* (1960).

1 An Englishman's way of speaking absolutely classifies him
The moment he talks he makes some other Englishman despise him.

My Fair Lady, I:1

2 All I want is a room somewhere,
Far away from the cold night air;
With one enormous chair . . .
Oh, wouldn't it be lovely?

My Fair Lady, I:1

3 I'd be equally as willing
For a dentist to be drilling
Than to ever let a woman in my life.

My Fair Lady, I:2

4 Oozing charm from every pore,
He oiled his way around the floor.

My Fair Lady, II:1

5 I'm getting married in the morning!
Ding dong! the bells are gonna chime.
Pull out the stopper!
Let's have a whopper!
But get me to the church on time!

My Fair Lady, II:3

6 Why can't a woman be more like a man?
Men are so honest, so thoroughly square;
Eternally noble, historically fair.

My Fair Lady, II:4

7 I've grown accustomed to the trace
Of something in the air,
Accustomed to her face.

My Fair Lady, II:6

Lesage, Alain-René (1668–1747) French writer. He is remembered for his novel *Gil Blas* (1715–35), *Le Diable boiteux* (1707), and the play *Crispin rival de son maître* (1707).

1 Justice is such a fine thing that we cannot pay too dearly for it.

Crispin rival de son maître, IX

2 They made peace between us; we embraced, and we have been mortal enemies ever since.

Le Diable boiteux, Ch. 3

Lessing, Doris (1919–) British novelist, brought up in Rhodesia. Her works include the five-novel sequence *Children of Violence* (1952–69), *The Golden Notebook* (1962), *Memoirs of a Survivor* (1974), *The Good Terrorist* (1985), and *The Fifth Child* (1988).

1 . . . that is what learning is. You suddenly understand something you've understood all your life, but in a new way.

The Four-Gated City

2 When old settlers say 'One has to understand the country', what they mean is, 'You have to get used to our ideas about the native.' They are saying, in effect, 'Learn our ideas, or otherwise get out; we don't want you.'

Referring specifically to South Africa
The Grass is Singing, Ch. 1

3 When a white man in Africa by accident looks into the eyes of a native and sees the human being (which it is his chief preoccupation to avoid), his sense of guilt, which he denies, fumes up in resentment and he brings down the whip.

The Grass is Singing, Ch. 8

4 If people dug up the remains of this civilization a thousand years hence, and found Epstein's statues and that man Ellis, they would think we were just savages.

Martha Quest, Pt. I, Ch. 1

5 In university they don't tell you that the greater part of the law is learning to tolerate fools.

Martha Quest, Pt. III, Ch. 2

6 If a fish is the movement of water embodied, given shape, then cat is a diagram and pattern of subtle air.

Particularly Cats, Ch. 2

Lessing, Gotthold Ephraim (1729–81) German dramatist. His plays include *Minna von Barnhelm* (1763), *Miss Sara Sampson* (1755), and *Emilia Galotti* (1772). In his *Hamburgische Dramaturgie* (1767–69) he expounded his theories of drama.

1 A man who does not lose his reason over certain things has none to lose.

Emilia Galotti, IV:7

L'Estrange, Sir Roger (1616–1704) English journalist and writer. His writings include the *Observator* (1681–87) and translations of Seneca, Cicero, and Josephus, as well as *Aesop's Fables* (1692).

1 It is with our passions as it is with fire and water, they are good servants, but bad masters.

Aesop's Fables, 38

2 Though this may be play to you, 'tis death to us.

Aesop's Fables, 398

Lethaby, W(illiam) R(ichard) (1857–1931) British architect whose work was characteristic of the Arts and Crafts movement at the beginning of the 20th century.

1 Art is not a special sauce applied to ordinary cooking; it is the cooking itself if it is good.

Form in Civilization, 'Art and Workmanship'

Leverson, Ada Beddington (1862–1933) British writer.

1 It is an infallible sign of the second-rate in nature and intellect to make use of everything and everyone.
The Limit

2 Thou canst not serve both cod and salmon.
Reply when offered a choice of fish at dinner
The Times, 7 Nov 1970

3 The last gentleman in Europe.
Said of Oscar Wilde
Letters to the Sphinx (Wilde), 'Reminiscences', 2

4 I'm sure he had a fork in the other.
Reply when told by Oscar Wilde of a devoted *apache* (Parisian gangster) who used to follow him with a knife in one hand
Attrib.

Levin, Bernard (1928–) British journalist and author. A columnist in *The Times*, television personality, and music critic, he has written several books including *Taking Sides* (1979) and *Enthusiasms* (1983).

1 Inflation in the Sixties was a nuisance to be endured, like varicose veins or French foreign policy.
The Pendulum Years, 'Epilogue'

2 Once, when a British Prime Minister sneezed, men half a world away would blow their noses. Now when a British Prime Minister sneezes nobody else will even say 'Bless You'.
The Times, 1976

3 What has happened to architecture since the second world war that the only passers-by who can contemplate it without pain are those equipped with a white stick and a dog?
The Times, 1983

Lévis, Gaston Pierre Marc, Duc de (1764–1830) French writer and soldier. His books include *Maximes et Réflexions* (1808).

1 *Noblesse oblige.*
Nobility has its own obligations.
Maximes et Réflexions

Lévi-Strauss, Claude (1908–) French anthropologist and leading exponent of structuralism. His works include *The Elementary Structures of Kinship* (1949), *Structural Anthropology* (1958), *From Honey to Ashes* (1967), *The Way of the Masks* (1975), and *The Jealous Potter* (1985).

1 The anthropologist respects history, but he does not accord it a special value. He conceives it as a study complementary to his own: one of them unfurls the range of human societies in time, the other in space.
The Savage Mind

Lewes, G(eorge) H(enry) (1817–78) British philosopher and writer. He was the common-law husband of Marian Evans (George Eliot). His books include a *Life of Goethe* (1855), *The History of Philosophy from Thales to Comte* (1845–46), *Physiology of Common Life* (1859), and *The Problems of Life and Mind* (1874–79).

1 Murder, like talent, seems occasionally to run in families.
The Physiology of Common Life, Ch. 12

Lewis, C(live) S(taples) (1898–1963) British academic and writer. An Oxford professor, his books on Christianity include *The Problem of Pain* (1940) and *The Screwtape Letters* (1942). He also wrote children's books and science fiction.

1 Friendship is unnecessary, like philosophy, like art . . . . It has no survival value; rather it is one of those things that give value to survival.
The Four Loves, Friendship

2 The coarse joke proclaims that we have here an animal which finds its own animality either objectionable or funny.
Miracles

3 There is wishful thinking in Hell as well as on earth.
The Screwtape Letters, Preface

4 There must be several young women who would render the Christian life intensely difficult to him if only you could persuade him to marry one of them.
The Screwtape Letters

5 The Future is something which everyone reaches at the rate of sixty minutes an hour, whatever he does, whoever he is.
The Screwtape Letters

6 She's the sort of woman who lives for others – you can always tell the others by their hunted expression.
The Screwtape Letters

Lewis, D(ominic) B(evan) Wyndham (1891–1969) British journalist and writer, especially of biographies. He wrote *François Villon* (1928) and *Emperor of the West, Charles V* (1932) among others.

1 I am one of those unfortunates to whom death is less hideous than explanations.
Welcome to All This

Lewis, Sir George Cornewall (1806–63) British statesman and writer. He became chancellor of the exchequer (1855–58), home secretary under Lord Palmerston (1859–61), and secretary for war (1861–63).

1 Life would be tolerable, were it not for its amusements.
The Perpetual Pessimist (Sagittarius and George)

Lewis, John Llewellyn (1880–1969) US labour leader and president of the United Mine Workers of America for 40 years; he organized mass-production workers into industrial unions.

1 I'm not interested in classes . . . Far be it from me to foster inferiority complexes among the workers by trying to make them think they belong to some special class. That has happened in Europe but it hasn't happened here yet.
The Coming of the New Deal (A. M. Schlesinger, Jnr), Pt. 7, Ch. 25

Lewis, (Percy) Wyndham (1882–1957) British novelist and painter. He helped to found the Vorticist movement in 1913; his novels include *The Apes of God* (1930) and the trilogy *The Human Age* (1928–55).

1 The soul started at the knee-cap and ended at the navel.
The Apes of God, Pt. XII

2 'Dying for an idea,' again, sounds well enough, but why not let the idea die instead of you?
The Art of Being Ruled, Pt. I, Ch. 1

3 I believe that (in one form or another) castration may be the solution. And the feminization of the white European and American is already far advanced, coming in the wake of the war.
The Art of Being Ruled, Pt. II, Ch. 2

4 The 'homo' is the legitimate child of the 'suffragette'.
The Art of Being Ruled, Pt. VIII, Ch. 4

5 You persisted for a certain number of years like a stammer. You were a *stammer*, if you like, of Space-Time.
The Human Age, 'The Childermass'

6 The revolutionary simpleton is everywhere.
Time and Western Man, Bk. I, Ch. 6

Lewis, Sinclair (1885–1951) US novelist. The first US writer to win the Nobel prize (1930), he is remembered for *Main Street* (1920), *Babbitt* (1922), and *Elmer Gantry* (1927).

1 In fact there was but one thing wrong with the Babbitt house; it was not a home.
Babbitt, Ch. 2

2 In other countries, art and literature are left to a lot of shabby bums living in attics and feeding on booze and spaghetti, but in America the successful writer or picture-painter is indistinguishable from any other decent business man.
Babbitt, Ch. 14

3 She did her work with the thoroughness of a mind that reveres details and never quite understands them.
Babbitt, Ch. 18

4 Our American professors like their literature clear and cold and pure and very dead.
Speech, on receiving the Nobel Prize, 1930

Ley, Robert (1890–1945) German Nazi. He was head of the Labour Front (from 1933) and committed suicide awaiting trial as a war criminal.

1 *Kraft durch Freude.*
Strength through joy.
German Labour Front slogan

Leybourne, George (?–1884) British songwriter.

1 O, he flies through the air with the greatest of ease,
This daring young man on the flying trapeze.
The Man on the Flying Trapeze

Liberace (Wladzin Valentino Liberace; 1919–87) US pianist and showman. He made a number of films and was highly successful on TV.

1 I cried all the way to the bank.
Said when asked whether he minded being criticized
Liberace: An Autobiography, Ch. 2

Lichtenberg, Georg Christoph (1742–99) German physicist and writer. He wrote satirical books on several subjects and published a collection of *Aphorisms* (1764–99).

1 Probably no invention came more easily to man than Heaven.
Aphorisms

2 There can hardly be a stranger commodity in the world than books. Printed by people who don't understand them; sold by people who don't understand them; bound, criticized and read by people who don't understand them; and now even written by people who don't understand them.
Aphorisms

3 Just as the meanest and most vicious deeds require spirit and talent, so even the greatest deeds require a certain insensitiveness which on other occasions is called stupidity.
Aphorisms

Lie, Trygve (1896–1968) Norwegian lawyer, who became the first secretary-general of the United Nations (1946–53). Formerly foreign minister of Norway, he presided over the commission that drafted the UN charter.

1 Now we are in a period which I can characterize as a period of cold peace.
The Observer, 'Sayings of the Week', 21 Aug 1949

Liebermann, Max (1847–1935) German painter and etcher, who specialized in portraits and genre scenes, such as *Women Plucking Geese* (1872) and *The Flax Spinners* (1887).

1 I can piss the old boy in the snow.
Remark to an artist who said he could not draw General Paul von Hindenburg's face
Conversations with Stravinsky (Igor Stravinsky and Robert Craft)

Lillie, Beatrice (Constance Sylvia Muston, Lady Peel; 1898–1989) Canadian-born British actress, who was a star of revues between the wars. She also made a few films, including *Exit Smiling* (1926) and *On Approval* (1943).

1 I'll simply say here that I was born Beatrice Gladys Lillie at an extremely tender age because my mother needed a fourth at meals.
Every Other Inch a Lady, Ch. 1

2 Heard there was a party. Came.
On arriving breathlessly at a friend's house seeking help after a car crash
Attrib.

Lillo, George (1693–1739) English dramatist. His plays include *The Christian Hero* (1735) and *Fatal Curiosity* (1736), as well as the ballad opera *Silvia, or the Country Burial* (1730).

1 There's sure no passion in the human soul,
But finds its food in music.
Fatal Curiosity, I:2

Lincoln, Abraham (1809–65) US statesman and Republican president (1861–65). He achieved freedom for slaves and the prohibition of slavery. He was assassinated a few days after the surrender of the South in the Civil War.

Quotations about Lincoln

1   Mr. Lincoln is like a waiter in a large eating house where all the bells are ringing at once; he cannot serve them all at once and so some grumblers are to be expected.
John Bright (1811–89) British radical politician. Cincinnati Gazette, 1864

2   My heart burned within me with indignation and grief; we could think of nothing else. All night long we had but little sleep, waking up perpetually to the sense of a great shock and grief. Everyone is feeling the same. I never knew such a universal feeling.
Elizabeth Gaskell (1810–65) British novelist. Letter to C. E. Norton, 28 Apr 1865

3   Lincoln had faith in time, and time has justified his faith.
Benjamin Harrison (1833–92) US president. Lincoln Day Address, 1898

4   Mr Lincoln's soul seems made of leather, and incapable of any grand or noble emotion. . . . He lowers, he never elevates you.
New York Post, 1863

Quotations by Lincoln

5   So you're the little woman who wrote the book that made this great war!
Said on meeting Harriet Beecher Stowe, the author of *Uncle Tom's Cabin* (1852), which stimulated opposition to slavery before the US Civil War
Abraham Lincoln: The War Years (Carl Sandburg), Vol. II, Ch. 39

6   The Lord prefers common-looking people. That is why he makes so many of them.
Our President (James Morgan), Ch. 6

7   Die when I may, I want it said of me by those who know me best, that I have always plucked a thistle and planted a flower where I thought a flower would grow.
Presidential Anecdotes (P. Boller)

8   I intend no modification of my oft-expressed personal wish that all men everywhere could be free.
Letter to Horace Greeley, 22 Aug 1862

9   If you don't want to use the army, I should like to borrow it for a while. Yours respectfully, A. Lincoln.
Letter to General George B. McClellan, whose lack of activity during the US Civil War irritated Lincoln

10 No man is good enough to govern another man without that other's consent.
Speech, 1854

11 The ballot is stronger than the bullet.
Speech, 19 May 1856

12 Those who deny freedom to others, deserve it not for themselves.
Speech, 19 May 1856

13 It is not our frowning battlements . . . or the strength of our gallant and disciplined army. These are not our reliance against a resumption of tyranny in our fair land. . . . Our defense is in the preservation of the spirit which prizes liberty as the heritage of all men, in all lands, everywhere.
Speech, 11 Sept 1858

14 What is conservatism? Is it not adherence to the old and tried, against the new and untried?
Speech, 27 Feb 1860

15 This country, with its institutions, belongs to the people who inhabit it. Whenever they shall grow weary of the existing government, they can exercise their constitutional right of amending it, or their revolutionary right to dismember or overthrow it.
First Inaugural Address, 4 Mar 1861

16 An old Dutch farmer, who remarked to a companion once that it was not best to swap horses in mid-stream.
Speech, 9 June 1864

17 In a larger sense we cannot dedicate, we cannot consecrate, we cannot hallow this ground. The brave men, living and dead, who struggled here, have consecrated it far above our power to add or detract. The world will little note, nor long remember, what we say here, but it can never forget what they did here. It is for us, the living, rather to be dedicated here to the unfinished work which they who fought here have thus far so nobly advanced. It is rather for us to be here dedicated to the great task remaining before us . . . that we here highly resolve that the dead shall not have died in vain, that this nation, under God, shall have a new birth of freedom; and that government of the people, by the people, and for the people, shall not perish from the earth.
Report of Lincoln's address at the dedication (19 Nov 1863) of the national cemetery on the site of the Battle of Gettysburg

18 You can fool some of the people all the time and all the people some of the time; but you can't fool all the people all the time.
Attrib.

19 People who like this sort of thing will find this is the sort of thing they like.
A comment on a book
Attrib.

20 I can't spare this man; he fights.
Resisting demands for the dismissal of Ulysses Grant
Attrib.

21 Well, he looks like a man.
On catching sight of Walt Whitman for the first time
Attrib.

22 I don't know who my grandfather was; I am much more concerned to know what his grandson will be.

Taking part in a discussion on ancestry
Attrib.

Lindsay, (Nicholas) Vachel (1879–1931) US poet, who recited his poetry before audiences in return for food and shelter. His best-known volumes are *General Booth Enters into Heaven and Other Poems* (1913) and *The Congo and Other Poems* (1914).

1 And who will bring white peace
That he may sleep upon his hill again?

Abraham Lincoln Walks at Midnight

2 Booth died blind and still by faith he trod,
Eyes still dazzled by the ways of God.

General William Booth Enters Heaven

Linklater, Eric (1889–1974) Scottish novelist, who lived in the USA for many years. His books include *Juan in America* (1931) and *Judas* (1939).

1 With a heavy step Sir Matthew left the room and spent the morning designing mausoleums for his enemies.

Juan in America, Prologue

2 I've been married six months. She looks like a million dollars, but she only knows a hundred and twenty words and she's only got two ideas in her head. The other one's hats.

Juan in America, Pt. II, Ch. 5

3 There won't be any revolution in America . . . The people are too clean. They spend all their time changing their shirts and washing themselves. You can't feel fierce and revolutionary in a bathroom.

Juan in America, Pt. V, Ch. 3

4 All I've got against it is that it takes you so far from the club house.

Referring to golf
Poet's Pub, Ch. 3

Linton, W(illiam) J(ames) (1812–97) British writer and wood engraver. An active Chartist, his books include *To the Future* (1848), *The Plaint of Freedom* (1852), and *Claribel and Other Poems* (1865).

1 For he's one of Nature's Gentlemen, the best of every time.

Nature's Gentleman

Lippman, Walter (1889–1974) US editor and writer. A columnist in the *New York Herald-Tribune*, he wrote the influential book *Public Opinion* (1922).

1 In a free society the state does not administer the affairs of men. It administers justice among men who conduct their own affairs.

An Enquiry into the Principles of a Good Society

Livermore, Mary Ashton (c. 1820–1905) US writer, lecturer, feminist, and social reformer. Her most popular book was *What Shall We Do with Our Daughters* (1883).

1 Other books have been written by men physicians . . . One would suppose in reading them that women possess but one class of physical organs, and that these are always diseased. Such teaching is pestiferous, and tends to cause and perpetuate the very evils it professes to remedy.

What Shall We Do with Our Daughters?, Ch. 2

2 Above the titles of wife and mother, which, although dear, are transitory and accidental, there is the title human being, which precedes and out-ranks every other.

What Shall We Do with Our Daughters?, Ch. 7

Livy (Titus Livius; 59 BC–17 AD) Roman historian. Of his monumental 142-volume history of Rome, only 35 books survive.

1 Woe to the vanquished.

History, V:48

Lloyd, Harold (1893–1971) US silent-film comedian. He usually took the part of a bespectacled little man who ultimately triumphed over adversity.

1 I am just turning forty and taking my time about it.

Reply when, aged 77, he was asked his age
The Times, 23 Sept 1970

Lloyd, Marie (1870–1922) British music-hall singer, who specialized in cockney humour.

1 Oh, mister porter, what shall I do?
I wanted to go to Birmingham, but they've carried me on to Crewe.

Oh, Mister Porter

2 A little of what you fancy does you good.

Song title

3 I'm one of the ruins that Cromwell knocked about a bit.

Song title

Lloyd, Robert (1733–64) British poet. His books include *The Actor* (1760) and a comic opera *Capricious Lovers* (1764).

1 Slow and steady wins the race.

The Hare and the Tortoise

Lloyd George, David, Earl of Dwyfor (1863–1945) British Liberal statesman. As prime minister (1916–22), he replaced Asquith as leader of a coalition government during World War I and for four years after it.

Quotations about Lloyd George

1 He couldn't see a belt without hitting below it.

Margot Asquith (1865–1945) The second wife of Herbert Asquith. *Autobiography*

2 He spent his whole life in plastering together the true and the false and therefrom extracting the plausible.

Stanley Baldwin (1867–1947) British statesman. *The Fine Art of Political Wit* (Leon Harris)

3 He did not care in which direction the car was travelling, so long as he remained in the driver's seat.

Lord Beaverbrook (1879–1964) Canadian-born British newspaper proprietor. *New Statesman*, 14 June 1963

4 My one ardent desire is that after the war he should be publicly castrated in front of Nurse Cavell's statue.

Lytton Strachey (1880–1932) British writer. *The Times*, 15 Jan 1972

Quotations by Lloyd George

5 He saw foreign policy through the wrong end of a municipal drainpipe.

Referring to Neville Chamberlain
The Fine Art of Political Wit (Harris), Ch. 6

6 Poor Bonar can't bear being called a liar. Now I don't mind.

Referring to Bonar Law, prime minister 1922–23
Stanley Baldwin (G. M. Young)

7 You cannot feed the hungry on statistics.

Advocating Tariff Reform
Speech, 1904

8 Mr Balfour's Poodle.

Referring to the House of Lords and its in built Conservative majority; said in reply to a claim that it was 'the watchdog of the nation'
Remark, House of Commons, 26 June 1907

9 There are no credentials. They do not even need a medical certificate. They need not be sound either in body or mind. They only require a certificate of birth – just to prove that they are first of the litter. You would not choose a spaniel on these principles.

Budget Speech, 1909

10 A fully equipped Duke costs as much to keep up as two Dreadnoughts, and Dukes are just as great a terror, and they last longer.

Speech, Limehouse, 30 July 1909

11 What is our task? To make Britain a fit country for heroes to live in.

Speech, 24 Nov 1918

12 Every man has a House of Lords in his own head. Fears, prejudices, misconceptions – those are the peers, and they are hereditary.

Speech, Cambridge, 1927

13 If we are going in without the help of Russia we are walking into a trap.

Speech, House of Commons, 3 Apr 1939

14 The Right Hon. gentleman has sat so long on the fence that the iron has entered his soul.

Referring to Sir John Simon
Attrib.

15 When they circumcised Herbert Samuel they threw away the wrong bit.

Attrib. in *The Listener*, 7 Sept 1978

16 Like a cushion, he always bore the impress of the last man who sat on him.

Referring to Lord Derby
Attrib. in *The Listener*, 7 Sept 1978. This remark is also credited to Earl Haig

17 Well, I find that a change of nuisances is as good as a vacation.

On being asked how he maintained his cheerfulness when beset by numerous political obstacles
Attrib.

18 This war, like the next war, is a war to end war.

Referring to the popular opinion that World War I would be the last major war

19 The world is becoming like a lunatic asylum run by lunatics.

The Observer, 'Sayings of Our Times', 31 May 1953

20 A politician is a person with whose politics you don't agree; if you agree with him he is a statesman.

Attrib.

Locke, John (1632–1704) English philosopher. His best-known work was the *Essay Concerning Human Understanding* (1690). His book *Of Government* (1690) was also influential.

1 New opinions are always suspected, and usually opposed, without any other reason but because they are not already common.

An Essay Concerning Human Understanding, dedicatory epistle

2 It is one thing to show a man that he is in an error, and another to put him in possession of truth.

An Essay Concerning Human Understanding, Bk. IV, Ch. 7

Lockier, Francis (1667–1740) English writer.

1 In all my travels I never met with any one Scotchman but what was a man of sense. I believe everybody of that country that has any, leaves it as fast as they can.

Anecdotes (Joseph Spence)

Lodge, David John (1935–) British author and critic whose novels include *The British Museum is Falling Down* (1965), *Changing Places* (1975), *Small World* (1984), and *Nice Work* (1988).

1 Literature is mostly about having sex and not much about having children; life is the other way round.

The British Museum is Falling Down, Ch. 4

2 Rummidge . . . had lately suffered the mortifying fate of most English universities of its type (civic redbrick): having competed strenuously for fifty years with two universities chiefly valued for being old, it was, at the moment of drawing level, rudely overtaken in popularity and prestige by a batch of universities chiefly valued for being new.

Changing Places, Ch. 1

3 Four times, under our educational rules, the human pack is shuffled and cut – at eleven-plus, sixteen-plus, eighteen-plus and twenty-plus – and happy is he who comes top of the deck on each occasion, but especially the last. This is called Finals, the very name of which implies that nothing of importance can happen after it. The British postgraduate student is a lonely for-lorn soul . . . for whom nothing has been real since the Big Push.

Changing Places, Ch. 1

4 The British, he thought, must be gluttons for satire: even the weather forecast seemed to be some kind of spoof, predicting every possible combination of weather for the next twenty-four hours without actually committing itself to anything specific.

Changing Places, Ch. 2

5 Walt Whitman who laid end to end words never seen in each other's company before outside of a dictionary.

Changing Places, Ch. 5

6 It was difficult to decide whether the system that produced the kettle was a miracle of human in-genuity and co-operation or a colossal waste of resources, human and natural. Would we all be better off boiling our water in a pot hung over an open fire? Or was it the facility to do things at the touch of a button that freed men, and more particularly women, from servile labour and made it possible for them to become literary critics?

Nice Work, V

Loesser, Frank (1910–69) US songwriter. His film scores included *Hans Christian Andersen* (1952) and *Guys and Dolls* (1955).

1 I'd like to get you
On a slow boat to China.

Slow Boat to China

Logau, Friedrich von, Baron (1604–55) German poet and writer. His best-known collection is *Deutscher Sinngedichte Dreitausend* (1654).

1 Though the mills of God grind slowly, yet they grind exceeding small;
Though with patience He stands waiting, with exactness grinds He all.

Sinngedichte, III

Logue, Christopher (1926–) British poet, journalist, dramatist, and actor. His verse collections include *Songs* (1959) and *Twelve Cards* (1972). His play *The Lilywhite Boys* (with Hugo Claus; 1959) was successful and he has written several screenplays.

1 Said Marx: 'Don't be snobbish, we seek to abolish
The 3rd Class, not the 1st.'

Christopher Logue's ABC, 'M'

Lombardi, Vince (1913–70) US football coach.

1 Winning isn't everything, but wanting to win is.

Lombroso, Cesare (1853–1909) Italian criminologist. His book *L'uomo delinquente* (1876) put forward the view that there is a criminal type.

1 The ignorant man always adores what he cannot understand.

The Man of Genius, Pt. III, Ch. 3

London, Jack (1876–1916) US novelist. *The Call of the Wild* (1903) was written after his experience of the Klondike gold rush (1897). Other books include *The Sea Wolf* (1902) and *Martin Eden* (1909).

1 In an English ship, they say, it is poor grub, poor pay, and easy work; in an American ship, good grub, good pay, and hard work. And this is applicable to the working populations of both countries.

The People of the Abyss, Ch. 20

Longfellow, Henry Wadsworth (1807–82) US poet. A professor of modern languages, he travelled widely in Europe. His narrative poems, including *Evangeline* (1847) and *The Song of Hiawatha* (1855), achieved great popularity.

Quotations about Longfellow

1 Longfellow is to poetry what the barrel-organ is to music.

Van Wyck Brooks *The Flowering of New England*

2 The gentleman was a sweet, beautiful soul, but I have entirely forgotten his name.

Ralph Waldo Emerson (1803–82) US poet and essayist. Attend-ing Longfellow's funeral. Attrib.

Quotations by Longfellow

3 I shot an arrow into the air,
It fell to earth, I knew not where.

The Arrow and the Song

4 I stood on the bridge at midnight,
As the clocks were striking the hour.

The Bridge

5 If you would hit the mark, you must aim a little above it;
Every arrow that flies feels the attraction of earth.

Elegiac Verse

6 Sorrow and silence are strong, and patient en-durance is godlike.

Evangeline

7 The shades of night were falling fast,
As through an Alpine village passed
A youth, who bore, 'mid snow and ice,
A banner with the strange device,
Excelsior!

Opening of a poem best known as a Victorian drawing-room bal-lad, and the butt of many music hall jokes. Excelsior means 'higher' (Latin)

Excelsior

8 Know how sublime a thing it is
To suffer and be strong.

The Light of Stars

9 You would attain to the divine perfection,
And yet not turn your back upon the world.

Michael Angelo

10 Art is long, and Time is fleeting,
And our hearts, though stout and brave,
Still, like muffled drums, are beating
Funeral marches to the grave.

See also HIPPOCRATES
A Psalm of Life

11 There is a Reaper whose name is Death,
And, with his sickle keen,
He reaps the bearded grain at a breath,
And the flowers that grow between.

The Reaper and the Flowers

12 'Wouldst thou' – so the helmsman answered –
'Learn the secret of the sea?
Only those who brave its dangers
Comprehend its mystery!'

The Secret of the Sea

13 Onaway! Awake, beloved!

Opening of the song sung by Chibiabos at Hiawatha's wedding
feast; best known in the setting by Coleridge-Taylor
The Song of Hiawatha, XI, 'Hiawatha's Wedding-feast'

14 Our ingress into the world
Was naked and bare;
Our progress through the world
Is trouble and care.

Tales of A Wayside Inn, 'The Student's Tale'

15 Ships that pass in the night, and speak each
other in passing;
Only a signal shown and a distant voice in the
darkness;
So on the ocean of life we pass and speak one
another,
Only a look and a voice; then darkness again and
a silence.

Tales of a Wayside Inn, 'The Theologian's Tale. Elizabeth'

16 Under the spreading chestnut tree
The village smithy stands;
The smith, a mighty man is he,
With large and sinewy hands;
And the muscles of his brawny arms
Are strong as iron bands.

The Village Blacksmith

17 Looks the whole world in the face,
For he owes not any man.

The Village Blacksmith

18 It was the schooner Hesperus,
That sailed the wintry sea;
And the skipper had taken his little daughter,
To bear him company.

The Wreck of the Hesperus

Longford, Francis Aungier Pakenham, Earl of
(1905–) British politician and social reformer. His books include
Born to Believe (1953), *The Idea of Punishment* (1961), *St Francis
of Assisi* (1978), and *Saints* (1987), as well as several biographies.

1 No sex without responsibility.

The Observer, 'Sayings of the Week', 3 May 1954

2 On the whole I would not say that our Press is
obscene. I would say that it trembles on the
brink of obscenity.

The Observer, 'Sayings of the Year', 1963

Longworth, Alice Roosevelt (1884–1980) US hostess.
She was a daughter of Theodore Roosevelt.

1 He looks as if he had been weaned on a pickle.

Referring to John Calvin Coolidge, US President 1923–29
Crowded Hours

Loos, Anita (1891–1981) US novelist and scriptwriter. She
worked in Hollywood for many years and is best remembered for
Gentlemen Prefer Blondes (1928).

1 Gentlemen always seem to remember blondes.

Gentlemen Prefer Blondes, Ch. 1

2 So this gentleman said a girl with brains ought to
do something else with them besides think.

Gentlemen Prefer Blondes, Ch. 1

3 Kissing your hand may make you feel very very
good but a diamond and safire bracelet lasts
forever.

Gentlemen Prefer Blondes, Ch. 4

4 Any girl who was a lady would not even think of
having such a good time that she did not remember to hang on to her jewelry.

Gentlemen Prefer Blondes, Ch. 4

5 I'm furious about the Women's Liberationists.
They keep getting up on soapboxes and proclaiming that women are brighter than men.
That's true, but it should be kept very quiet or it
ruins the whole racket.

The Observer, 'Sayings of the Year', 30 Dec 1973

Lorenz, Konrad (1903–89) Austrian zoologist and pioneer of
ethology. His books include *King Solomon's Ring* (1949), *Man
Meets Dog* (1950), *On Aggression* (1963), *Behind the Mirror*
(1973), and *The Foundations of Ethology* (1981). He won a Nobel
Prize in 1973.

1 It is a good morning exercise for a research scientist to discard a pet hypothesis every day
before breakfast. It keeps him young.

On Aggression, Ch. 2

Louis, Joe (Joseph Louis Barrow; 1914–81) US boxer. He has
been regarded as one of the best boxers of all time, having been
world heavyweight champion from 1937 to 1948.

1 He can run, but he can't hide.

Referring to the speed for which his coming opponent, Billy
Conn, was renowned
Attrib.

Louis Philippe (1773–1850) King of the French (1830–48), described as the 'Citizen King'. He supported the French Revolution until 1793, when he deserted to Austria. Returning to France after the Restoration, he became king after the July Revolution had ousted Charles X. He abdicated in the 1848 Revolution and died in exile in England.

1 *La cordiale entente qui existe entre mon gouvernement et le sien.*
   The friendly understanding that exists between my government and hers.
   Queen Victoria's: referring to an informal understanding reached between Britain and France in 1843. The more familiar phrase, 'entente cordiale', was first used in 1844
   Speech, 27 Dec 1843

Louis XIV (1638–1715) French king. He believed in the divine right of kings, held a lavish court at Versailles, and was a generous patron of the arts.

1 How could God do this to me after all I have done for him?
   On receiving news of the French army's defeat at the battle of Blenheim
   Saint-Simon at Versailles (L. Norton)

2 Has God then forgotten what I have done for him?
   Reportedly said after Marlborough's pyrrhic victory over the French at the Battle of Malplaquet, 11 Sept 1709

3 First feelings are always the most natural.
   First impressions at the Battle of Malplaquet, 11 Sept 1709
   Recorded by Mme de Sévigné,

4 *L'État c'est moi.*
   I am the State.
   Attrib.

5 The Pyrenees have ceased to exist.
   On the accession of his grandson to the Spanish throne (1700); attributed by Voltaire

6 Ah, if I were not king, I should lose my temper.
   Attrib.

7 Why are you weeping? Did you imagine that I was immortal?
   Noticing as he lay on his deathbed that his attendants were crying
   Louis XIV (V. Cronin)

Louis XVI (1754–93) King of France (1774–93). He and his family fled to Varennes during the French Revolution, but were captured and subsequently guillotined' Married to Queen Marie Antoinette.

1 *Rien.*
   Nothing.
   Diary, 14 July 1789 – the day the Bastille fell

Louis XVIII (1755–1824) French king, who ruled after Napoleon's overthrow, fled from Paris when Napoleon returned from Elba, and ruled again with diminished prestige after Waterloo.

1 Punctuality is the politeness of kings.
   Attrib.

Lovelace, Richard (1618–58) English poet. Twice imprisoned during the Civil War as a royalist, he wrote his famous poem 'To Althea, from Prison'. His best poems are collected in *Lucasta* (1649).

1 Stone walls do not a prison make,
   Nor iron bars a cage.
   To Althea, from Prison

Lovell, Maria (1803–77) British actress and dramatist.

1 Two souls with but a single thought,
   Two hearts that beat as one.
   Ingomar the Barbarian, II (transl. of Friedrich Halm)

Lover, Samuel (1797–1868) Irish novelist and portrait painter. Novels include *Rory O'More* (1837) and *Handy Andy* (1842).

1 When once the itch of literature comes over a man, nothing can cure it but the scratching of a pen.
   Handy Andy, Ch. 36

Low, David (Alexander Cecil) (1871–1963) New-Zealand-born newspaper cartoonist. Working in *The Star*, *Evening Standard*, and *The Guardian*, he created world-famous characters, notably Colonel Blimp.

1 I do not know whether he draws a line himself. But I assume that his is the direction . . . It makes Disney the most significant figure in graphic art since Leonardo.
   Walt Disney (R. Schickel), Ch. 20

Lowe, Robert, Viscount Sherbrooke (1811–92) British lawyer and politician. He became chancellor of the exchequer (1868–73) and home secretary (1873–74) under Gladstone.

1 The Chancellor of the Exchequer is a man whose duties make him more or less of a taxing machine. He is intrusted with a certain amount of misery which it is his duty to distribute as fairly as he can.
   Speech, House of Commons, 11 Apr 1870

Lowell, Robert (1917–77) US poet. Imprisoned as a conscientious objector (1943), he became involved in left-wing politics in the 1960s. His last book was *Day by Day* (1977).

1 The man is killing time – there's nothing else.
   The Drinker

2 The monument sticks like a fishbone
   in the city's throat.
   For the Union Dead

3 But I suppose even God was born
   too late to trust the old religion –
   all those setting out
   that never left the ground,
   beginning in wisdom, dying in doubt.
   Tenth Muse

Lowry, Malcolm (1909–57) British novelist, who lived in Canada from 1940. *Ultramarine* (1933) was based on his experiences as a sailor and *Under the Volcano* (1947) reflects his stay in Mexico.

1 Where are the children I might have had? You may suppose I might have wanted them. Drowned to the accompaniment of the rattling of a thousand douche bags.
Under the Volcano, Ch. 10

2 How alike are the groans of love to those of the dying.
Under the Volcano, Ch. 12

3 Malcolm Lowry
Late of the Bowery
His prose was flowery
And often glowery
He lived, nightly, and drank, daily,
And died playing the ukulele.
'Epitaph'

Loyola, St Ignatius (1491–1556) Spanish priest, who founded the Society of Jesus (Jesuits) in 1540. His *Spiritual Exercises* (1548) is still highly regarded.

1 To give and not to count the cost;
To fight and not to heed the wounds;
To toil and not to seek for rest;
To labour and not ask for any reward
Save that of knowing that we do Thy will.
Prayer for Generosity

2 To arrive at the truth in all things, we ought always to be ready to believe that what seems to us white is black if the hierarchical Church so defines it.
Spiritual Exercises

Lucan (Marcus Annaeus Lucanus; 39–65 AD) Roman poet. The nephew of Seneca, he committed suicide after his plot against Nero was discovered. *Pharsalia*, an epic poem about the civil war between Pompey and Caesar, is his main surviving work.

1 I have a wife, I have sons: all of them hostages given to fate.
See also BACON (1521–1626)
Works, VII

Lucas, George (1945–) US film director and producer whose films include *American Graffiti* (1973), *Star Wars* (1977), *Raiders of the Lost Ark* (1981), and *Return of the Jedi* (1983).

1 May the Force be with you.
Star Wars

Lucretius (Titus Lucretius Carus; c. 99–55 BC) Roman philosopher and poet. His six-volume *On the Nature of the Universe* gives a complete account of the philosophy of Epicurus.

1 Nothing can be created out of nothing.
On the Nature of the Universe, I

2 Constant dripping hollows out a stone.
On the Nature of the Universe, I. *See also* LATIMER; OVID

3 *Inque brevi spatio mutantur saecla animantum Et quasi cursores vitai lampada tradunt.*
The generations of living things pass in a short time, and like runners hand on the torch of life.
On the Nature of the Universe, II

4 What is food to one man is bitter poison to others.
On the Nature of the Universe, IV

Luther, Martin (1483–1546) German Protestant and founder of Lutheranism. Incensed by the sale of indulgences to swell papal funds, he nailed his thesis to the door of the Wittenberg church, and was subsequently excommunicated. After the Augsburg Confession (1530) he gave up his hope of reforming the church and set up the separate Protestant church.

Quotations about Luther

1 The Diet of Worms. Luther's appearing there on 17th April 1521 may be considered as the greatest scene in Modern European history, the point, indeed, from which the whole subsequent history of civilisation takes its rise.
Thomas Carlyle (1795–1881) Scottish historian and essayist. *Heroes and Heroworship*

2 A single friar who goes counter to all Christianity for a thousand years must be wrong.
Charles V (1500–58) Holy Roman Emperor. Diet of Worms

3 Luther was guilty of two great crimes – he struck the Pope in his crown and the monks in their bellies.
Erasmus (1466–1536) Dutch humanist, scholar and writer. *Colloquies*

Quotations by Luther

4 Here stand I. I can do no other. God help me. Amen.
Speech at the Diet of Worms, 18 Apr 1521

5 Who loves not wine, woman and song, Remains a fool his whole life long.
Attrib.

Lutyens, Sir Edwin Landseer (1869–1944) British architect who was responsible for the viceregal palace in New Delhi (1912–30).

1 The answer is in the plural and they bounce.
Attrib.

2 This piece of cod passes all understanding.
Comment made in a restaurant
Attrib.

Lyndhurst, John Singleton Copley, Baron (1772–1863) US-born British lawyer who became lord chancellor (1827–30; 1834–35; 1841–46).

1 Campbell has added another terror to death.
Referring to Lord Campbell's controversial *Lives of the Lord Chancellors* (1845–47), from which Lyndhurst was excluded because he was still alive

Lyte, Henry Francis (1793–1847) British hymn writer and Anglican clergyman.

1 Abide with me; fast falls the eventide;
The darkness deepens; Lord, with me abide;
When other helpers fail, and comforts flee,
Help of the helpless, O, abide with me.
Abide with Me

Lytton, Lady Constance (1869–1923) British suffragette, daughter of the Earl of Lytton. She was imprisoned, went on a hunger strike, and was released – but was rearrested posing as a working-class woman. As home secretary, Churchill refused a public enquiry into the difference in her treatment on these occasions.

1 The first time you meet Winston you see all his faults and the rest of your life you spend in discovering his virtues.
Referring to Churchill
Edward Marsh (Christopher Hassall), Ch. 7

Lytton, 1st Earl of *See* Meredith, Owen

M

Macarthur, Douglas (1880–1964) US general. As allied commander, he recaptured the south-west Pacific in World War II and commanded the occupation of Japan. The commander of UN forces in the Korean War, he advocated active operations against China, for which he was dismissed by Truman.

1 I shall return.
Message (11 Mar 1942) on leaving for Australia from Corregidor Island (Philippines), which he had been defending against the Japanese

2 There is no security in this life. There is only opportunity.
MacArthur, His Rendezvous with History (Courtney Whitney)

Macaulay, Dame Rose (1889–1958) British writer. She wrote many novels, including *Dangerous Ages* (1921) and *The Towers of Trebizond* (1956).

1 Gentlemen know that fresh air should be kept in its proper place – out of doors – and that, God having given us indoors and out-of-doors, we should not attempt to do away with this distinction.
Crewe Train, Pt. I, Ch. 5

2 Decades have a delusive edge to them. They are not, of course, really periods at all, except as any other ten years would be. But we, looking at them, are caught by the different name each bears, and give them different attributes, and tie labels on them, as if they were flowers in a border.
Told by an Idiot, Pt. II, Ch. 1

3 A group of closely related persons living under one roof; it is a convenience, often a necessity, sometimes a pleasure, sometimes the reverse; but who first exalted it as admirable, an almost religious ideal?
The World My Wilderness, Ch. 20

4 Poem me no poems.
Poetry Review, Autumn 1963

5 The great and recurrent question about abroad is, is it worth getting there?
Attrib.

6 It was a book to kill time for those who like it better dead.
Attrib.

Macaulay, Thomas Babington, Baron (1800–59) British historian and writer. An MP for many years, he is remembered for his five-volume *History of England* (1849–61).

1 The English Bible, a book which, if everything else in our language should perish, would alone suffice to show the whole extent of its beauty and power.
Essays and Biographies, 'John Dryden'. *Edinburgh Review*

2 His imagination resembled the wings of an ostrich. It enabled him to run, though not to soar.
Essays and Biographies, 'John Dryden'. *Edinburgh Review*

3 Knowledge advances by steps, and not by leaps.
Essays and Biographies, 'History'. *Edinburgh Review*

4 The gallery in which the reporters sit has become a fourth estate of the realm.
Referring to the press gallery in the House of Commons
Historical Essays Contributed to the 'Edinburgh Review', 'Hallam's "Constitutional History"'

5 The reluctant obedience of distant provinces generally costs more than it is worth.
Historical Essays Contributed to the 'Edinburgh Review', 'Lord Mahon's War of the Succession'

6 The highest intellects, like the tops of mountains, are the first to catch and to reflect the dawn.
Historical Essays Contributed to the 'Edinburgh Review', 'Sir James Mackintosh'

7 He . . . felt towards those whom he had deserted that peculiar malignity which has, in all ages, been characteristic of apostates.
History of England, Vol. I, Ch. 1

8 The Puritan hated bear-baiting, not because it gave pain to the bear, but because it gave pleasure to the spectators.
History of England, Vol. I, Ch. 2

9 There were gentlemen and there were seamen in the navy of Charles the Second. But the seamen were not gentlemen; and the gentlemen were not seamen.
History of England, Vol. I, Ch. 3

10 In every age the vilest specimens of human nature are to be found among demagogues.
History of England, Vol. I, Ch. 5

11 Then out spake brave Horatius,
The Captain of the Gate:
'To every man upon this earth
Death cometh soon or late.
And how can man die better
Than facing fearful odds,
For the ashes of his fathers,
And the temples of his Gods?'
Lays of Ancient Rome, 'Horatius', 27

12 The dust and silence of the upper shelf.
Literary Essays Contributed to the 'Edinburgh Review', 'Milton'

13 As civilization advances, poetry almost necessarily declines.
Literary Essays Contributed to the 'Edinburgh Review', 'Milton'

14 Perhaps no person can be a poet, or can even enjoy poetry, without a certain unsoundness of mind.
Literary Essays Contributed to the 'Edinburgh Review', 'Milton'

15 Many politicians of our time are in the habit of laying it down as a self-evident proposition, that no people ought to be free till they are fit to use their freedom. The maxim is worthy of the fool in the old story, who resolved not to go into the water till he had learnt to swim. If men are to wait for liberty till they become wise and good in slavery, they may indeed wait for ever.
Literary Essays Contributed to the 'Edinburgh Review', 'Milton'

16 We know no spectacle so ridiculous as the British public in one of its periodical fits of morality.
Literary Essays Contributed to the 'Edinburgh Review', 'Moore's 'Life of Lord Byron''

17 His writing bears the same relation to poetry which a Turkey carpet bears to a picture. There are colours in the Turkey carpet out of which a picture might be made. There are words in Mr Montgomery's writing which, when disposed in certain orders and combinations, have made, and will make again, good poetry. But, as they now stand, they seem to be put together on principle in such a manner as to give no image of anything 'in the heavens above, or in the earth beneath, or in the waters under the earth'.
Literary Essays Contributed to the 'Edinburgh Review', 'Mr. Robert Montgomery's Poems'

18 Thank you, madam, the agony is abated.
Replying, aged four, to a lady who asked if he had hurt himself
Life and Letters of Macaulay (Trevelyan), Ch. 1

19 Ye diners-out from whom we guard our spoons.
Letter to Hannah Macaulay, 29 June 1831

20 I shall not be satisfied unless I produce something that shall for a few days supersede the last fashionable novel on the tables of young ladies.
Letter to Macvey Napier, 5 Nov 1841

21 A broken head in Cold Bath Fields produces a greater sensation among us than three pitched battles in India.
Speech, 10 July 1833

MacCarthy, Sir Desmond (1877–1952) British writer and theatre critic.

1 When I meet those remarkable people whose company is coveted, I often wish they would show off a little more.
Theatre, 'Good Talk'

2 You understand *Epipsychidion* best when you are in love; *Don Juan* when anger is subsiding into indifference. Why not Strindberg when you have a temperature?
Theatre, 'Miss Julie and the Pariah'

3 The whole of art is an appeal to a reality which is not without us but in our minds.
Theatre, 'Modern Drama'

MacDiarmid, Hugh (Christopher Murray Grieve; 1892–1978) Scottish poet. A Marxist and Scottish nationalist, he wrote his early verse, such as *A Drunken Man Looks at the Thistle* (1926), in a Scots language but later used English.

1 Killing
Is the ultimate simplification of life.
England's Double Knavery

2 It is very rarely that a man loves
And when he does it is nearly always fatal.
The International Brigade

3 Our principal writers have nearly all been fortunate in escaping regular education.
The Observer, 'Sayings of the Week', 29 Mar 1953

MacDonald, Betty (1908–58) US writer. Her books include *The Egg and I* (1945).

1 In high school and college my sister Mary was very popular with the boys, but I had braces on my teeth and got high marks.
The Egg and I, Ch. 2

MacDonald, (James) Ramsey (1866–1937) British statesman. He was the first Labour prime minister (1924; 1929–31; 1931–35). His first (minority) administration was defeated after a vote of no confidence. His second administration was broadened into a coalition in which he was replaced by Baldwin in 1935.

1 Let them especially put their demands in such a way that Great Britain could say that she supported both sides.
Referring to France and Germany
The Origins of the Second Word War (A. J. P. Taylor), Ch. 3

2 Society goes on and on and on. It is the same with ideas.
Speech, 1935

Machiavelli, Niccolò (1469–1527) Italian statesman, diplomat, and political theorist. In his best-known book, *The Prince* (1532; written 1513), he argues that all means are justified in achieving a stable political state.

1 It is the nature of men to be bound by the benefits they confer as much as by those they receive.
The Prince

MacInnes, Colin (1914–76) British novelist and journalist. His best-known novels are *City of Spades* (1957) and *Absolute Beginners* (1957).

1 In England, pop art and fine art stand resolutely back to back.
England, Half English, 'Pop Songs and Teenagers'

2 England is . . . a country infested with people who love to tell us what to do, but who very rarely seem to know what's going on.
England, Half English, 'Pop Songs and Teenagers'

3 A coloured man can tell, in five seconds dead, whether a white man likes him or not. If the white man *says* he does, he is instantly – and usually quite rightly – mistrusted.
England, Half English, 'A Short Guide for Jumbles'

Mackenzie, Sir Compton (1883–1972) British writer. He made his reputation with the semiautobiographical *Sinister Street* (1913). Later novels include *The Parson's Progress* (1923) and *Whisky Galore* (1947). He also wrote some verse and several plays.

1 Women do not find it difficult nowadays to behave like men; but they often find it extremely difficult to behave like gentlemen.
On Moral Courage

Mackintosh, Sir James (1765–1832) Scottish lawyer, philosopher, and historian, who became a judge in India. His best-known philosophical work is the *Dissertation on the Progress of Ethical Philosophy* (1830); he also wrote a number of historical books and articles.

1 The Commons, faithful to their system, remained in a wise and masterly inactivity.
Vindiciae Gallicae

MacLeish, Archibald (1892–1982) US poet and dramatist. *Collected Poems* (1952) was followed by the plays *JB* (1958) and *Six Plays* (1980).

1 We have learned the answers, all the answers: It is the question that we do not know.
The Hamlet of A. Macleish

Macleod, Fiona (William Sharp; 1856–1905) Scottish poet and writer. He published several collections of verse under his own name, including *Earth's Voices* (1884) and *Romantic Ballads and Poems of Fantasy* (1888). As Fiona Macleod he published a number of works on the Celtic world, including *Green Fire* (1896), *The Immortal Hour* (1900), and *Deirdre* (1903).

1 My heart is a lonely hunter that hunts on a lonely hill.
The Lonely Hunter

Macleod, Iain (1913–70) British politician. After various ministerial posts in the 1950s and 1960s, he became chancellor of the exchequer in 1970, but died in office. He was also a bridge theorist who, with Jack Marx, invented the Acol system.

1 History is too serious to be left to historians.
The Observer, 'Sayings of the Week', 16 July 1961

Macmillan, (Maurice) Harold, Earl of Stockton (1894–1986) British statesman and publisher; Conservative prime minister (1957–63). His last year in office was notorious for the Profumo scandal.

Quotations about Macmillan

1 By far the most radical man I've known in politics wasn't on the labour side at all – Harold Macmillan. If it hadn't been for the war he'd have joined the Labour party. If that had happened Macmillan would have been Labour Prime Minister, and not me.
Clement Attlee (1883–1967) British statesman and Labour prime minister. *The Abuse of Power* (James Margach)

2 One can never escape the suspicion, with Mr Macmillan, that all his life was a preparation for elder statesmanship.
Frank Johnson. *The Times*, 30 Mar 1981

3 Harold Macmillan was the first person to recognise that in the modern world of media exposure a Prime Minister has to be something of a showman, equally at home in the theatre spotlight or the sawdust of the circus ring.
James Margach. *The Abuse of Power*

4 What a pity it is that now we have the most intelligent Prime Minister of the century, he has to conceal his intelligence from the public for fear they will suspect it.
Harold Nicolson (1886–1968) British diplomat and literary critic. Diary, 9 Feb 1957

Quotations by Macmillan

5 Most of our people have never had it so good.
Speech, Bedford Football Ground, 20 July 1957

6 I thought the best thing to do was to settle up these little local difficulties, and then turn to the wider vision of the Commonwealth.
Referring to resignation of ministers
Remark, London Airport, 7 Jan 1958

7 When you're abroad you're a statesman: when you're at home you're just a politician.
Speech, 1958

8 The wind of change is blowing through the continent. Whether we like it or not, this growth of national consciousness is a political fact.
Speech, South African Parliament, 3 Feb 1960

9 Selling the family silver.
Referring to privatization of profitable nationalized industries
Speech, House of Lords, 1986

10 There are three groups that no prime minister should provoke: the Treasury, the Vatican, and the National Union of Mineworkers.
First used by Stanley BALDWIN
Attrib.

11 Power? It's like a dead sea fruit; when you achieve it, there's nothing there.
Attrib.

MacNally, Leonard (1752–1820) Irish dramatist, poet, and political informer. He betrayed the revolutionaries, whom he had supposedly joined, to the government. His work includes the song *The Lass of Richmond Hill*.

1   On Richmond Hill there lives a lass,
     More sweet than May day morn,
     Whose charms all other maids surpass,
     A rose without a thorn.
     The Lass of Richmond Hill

MacNeice, Louis (1907–63) Irish-born British poet. His
verse publications include *Blind Fireworks* (1929), *Autumn Journal*
(1939), and *The Burning Perch* (1963). He also wrote radio plays
and worked for the BBC.

1   It's no go the picture palace, it's no go the
     stadium,
     It's no go the country cot with a pot of pink
     geraniums,
     It's no go the Government grants, it's no go the
     elections,
     Sit on your arse for fifty years and hang your hat
     on a pension.
     Bagpipe Music

2   Time was away and somewhere else,
     There were two glasses and two chairs
     And two people with one pulse.
     Meeting Point

3   That the world will never be quite – what a
     cliché – the same again
     Is what we only learn by the event
     When a friend dies out on us and is not there
     To share the periphery of a remembered scent
     Tam Cari Capitis

Madariaga y Rogo, Salvador de (1886–1978) Spanish
diplomat and writer. The Spanish ambassador to the USA (1931)
and France (1932–34), he also wrote a number of historical books
and biographies.

1   First the sweetheart of the nation, then the
     aunt, woman governs America because America
     is a land of boys who refuse to grow up.
     The Perpetual Pessimist (Sagitarius and George)

2   In politics, as in grammar, one should be able to
     tell the substantives from the adjectives. Hitler
     was a substantive; Mussolini only an adjective.
     Hitler was a nuisance. Mussolini was bloody.
     Together a bloody nuisance.
     Attrib.

Madden, Samuel (1686–1765) Irish writer, best
remembered for his poem *Boulter's Monument* (1745).

1   Words are men's daughters, but God's sons are
     things.
     See also Samuel JOHNSON
     Boulter's Monument

Magee, William Connor (1821–91) British clergyman.
He became Bishop of Peterborough (1868–91) and Archbishop of
York (1891).

1   It would be better that England should be free
     than that England should be compulsorily
     sober.
     Speech on the Intoxicating Liquor Bill, House of Lords, 2 May
     1872

Magidson, Herb (20th century) US songwriter.

1   Music, Maestro, Please.
     Song title

Mailer, Norman (1923–) US writer. His books include the
novels *The Naked and the Dead* (1948), *The American Dream*
(1965), *The Executioner's Song* (1979), *Tough Guys Don't Dance*
(1984), and *Why Are We In Vietnam* (1988).

1   Growth is a greater mystery than death. All of
     us can understand failure, we all contain failure
     and death within us, but not even the successful
     man can begin to describe the impalpable ela-
     tions and apprehensions of growth.
     Advertisements for Myself

2   Once a newspaper touches a story, the facts are
     lost forever, even to the protagonists.
     The Presidential Papers

Maistre, Joseph de (1753–1821) French monarchist, who
opposed the Revolution. He had faith in the divine right of kings
and a belief, expressed in *Du Pape* (1819), in the infallibility of the
pope.

1   Every country has the government it deserves.
     Lettres et Opuscules Inédits, 15 Aug 1811

2   Scratch the Russian and you will find the Tartar.
     Attributed also to Napoleon and Prince de Ligne

Major, John (1943–) British Conservative politician; prime
minister (1990–).

1   The Conservative Party is constantly changing,
     like the British . . . though it retains the same
     basic concerns and philosophy.
     Remark, Dec 1989

Malcolm X (1925–65) US Black leader. An advocate of violent
means of achieving racial equality, he was assassinated while
addressing a rally of the Organization of Afro-American Unity,
which he founded in 1964.

1   It's just like when you've got some coffee that's
     too black, which means it's too strong. What do
     you do? You integrate it with cream, you
     make it weak . . . It used to wake you up, now it
     puts you to sleep.
     Referring to Black Power and the Civil Rights movement
     Malcolm X Speaks, Ch. 14

**Malesherbes, Chrétien Guillaume de
Lamoignonde** (1721–94) French statesman, noted for his
liberalism as director of censorship. Banned from court in 1771 for
criticizing the monarchy, he was nevertheless executed as a
royalist during the Revolution.

1   A new maxim is often a brilliant error.
     Pensées et maximes

Malherbe, François de (1555–1628) French poet. Court
poet to Henry IV, his poetry is mostly devoted to religious and
political themes.

1 But she was of the world where the fairest things have the worst fate. Like a rose, she has lived as long as roses live, the space of one morning.
Consolation à M. du Périer

Mallaby, Sir (Howard) George (1902–78) British diplomat and writer. His books include memoirs and literary criticism.

1 Never descend to the ways of those above you.
From My Level

Mallet, Robert (1915–) French writer and academic. Rector of the University of Paris (1969–80), he is the author of poetry, plays, and novels.

1 How many pessimists end up by desiring the things they fear, in order to prove that they are right.
Apostilles

Mallory, George Leigh (1886–1924) British mountaineer.

1 Because it is there.
Answer to the question 'Why do you want to climb Mt. Everest?'
George Mallory (D. Robertson)

Malory, Sir Thomas (1400–71) English writer. Probably a Warwickshire knight and MP, he is remembered as the author of *Morte d'Arthur*, an account of the legendary court of King Arthur, based on French sources.

1 For, as I suppose, no man in this world hath lived better than I have done, to achieve that I have done.
Morte d'Arthur, Bk. XVII, Ch. 16

2 For love that time was not as love is nowadays.
Morte d'Arthur, Bk. XX, Ch. 3

3 And much more am I sorrier for my good knights' loss than for the loss of my fair queen; for queens I might have enough, but such a fellowship of good knights shall never be together in no company.
Morte d'Arthur, Bk. XX, Ch. 9

4 Then Sir Launcelot saw her visage, but he wept not greatly, but sighed!
Morte d'Arthur, Bk. XXI, Ch. 11

Malthus, Thomas Robert (1766–1834) British clergyman and economist. His *Essays on the Principle of Population* (1798–1803) warns that the geometrical increase in population, if unrestrained, will quickly outstrip the arithmetical growth of food production.

1 Population, when unchecked, increases in a geometrical ratio. Subsistence only increases in an arithmetical ratio.
Essays on the Principle of Population

2 The perpetual struggle for room and food.
Essays on the Principle of Population

Mancroft, Stormont Samuel, Baron (1917–87) British businessman and writer. A well-known after-dinner speaker, he also wrote *Booking the Cooks* (1969) and *Bees in Some Bonnets* (1979).

1 Happy is the man with a wife to tell him what to do and a secretary to do it.
The Observer, 'Sayings of the Week', 18 Dec 1966

Mandela, Nelson (1918–) Black South African lawyer and politician. An active member of the African National Congress, he was charged with treason, acquitted in 1961, retried in 1963–64, and sentenced to life imprisonment. He was released in 1990 after an international campaign and travelled widely as deputy president of the ANC.

1 The soil of our country is destined to be the scene of the fiercest fight and the sharpest struggles to rid our continent of the last vestiges of white minority rule.
Observer, 'Sayings of the Eighties', 15 June 1980

2 I cannot and will not give any undertaking at a time when I, and you, the people, are not free. Your freedom and mine cannot be separated.
Message read by his daughter to a rally in Soweto, 10 Feb 1985

3 I have cherished the ideal of a democratic and free society in which all persons live together in harmony and with equal opportunities . . . if needs be, it is an ideal for which I am prepared to die.
Speech, 11 Feb 1990, after his release from prison. Mandela was reiterating his words at his trial in 1964.

4 It indicates the deadly weight of the terrible tradition of a dialogue between master and servant which we have to overcome.
Referring to the first meeting between the government and the ANC
The Independent, 'Quote Unquote', 5 May 1990

Mandelstam, Osip (1891–1938) Russian poet. His verse collections include *Tristia* (1922). He was arrested as a political dissident (1934) and is presumed to have died in a labour camp.

1 No, I am no one's contemporary – ever. That would have been above my station . . . How I loathe that other with my name. He certainly never was me.
Poems, No. 141

2 Now I'm dead in the grave with my lips moving And every schoolboy repeating my words by heart.
Poems, No. 306

Manikan, Ruby (20th century) Indian Church leader.

1 If you educate a man you educate a person, but if you educate a woman you educate a family.
The Observer, 'Sayings of the Week', 30 Mar 1947

Mankeiwicz, Herman J. (1897–1953) US journalist, screenwriter, and wit. His films include *Citizen Kane* (with Orson Welles; 1941), *Christmas Holiday* (1944), and *Pride of St Louis* (1952).

1 It is the only disease you don't look forward to being cured of.
Referring to death
Citizen Kane

2 There, but for the Grace of God, goes God.

Said of Orson Welles in the making of *Citizen Kane*. Also attributed to others
The Citizen Kane Book

3 You know it's hard to hear what a bearded man is saying. He can't speak above a whisker.

Wit's End (R. E. Drennan)

Mann, Thomas (1875–1955) German novelist. His books include *Buddenbrooks* (1901), *The Magic Mountain* (1924), *Doctor Faustus* (1947), and the four novels *Joseph and His Brothers* (1933–44). His novella *Death in Venice* (1912) became a film and an opera. He went to the USA in the 1930s to escape the Nazis.

1 What we call mourning for our dead is perhaps not so much grief at not being able to call them back as it is grief at not being able to want to do so.

The Magic Mountain

2 Every intellectual attitude is latently political.

The Observer, 11 Aug 1974

Mansfield, Katherine (1888–1923) New-Zealand-born British short-story writer and poet. She married (1918) John Middleton Murry and lived abroad on account of her tuberculosis. Her collections include *In a German Pension* (1911), *Bliss* (1920), and *The Garden Party* (1922). Her *Poems* (1923), *Journal* (1927), and *Letters* (1928) were published after her premature death.

1 How idiotic civilization is! Why be given a body if you have to keep it shut up in a case like a rare, rare fiddle?

Bliss and Other Stories, 'Bliss'

2 Whenever I prepare for a journey I prepare as though for death. Should I never return, all is in order. This is what life has taught me.

The Journal of Katherine Mansfield, 1922

Mansfield, William Murray, Earl of (1705–93) British judge and politician. He was chief justice of the Kings Bench (1756–88).

1 Consider what you think justice requires, and decide accordingly. But never give your reasons; for your judgement will probably be right, but your reasons will certainly be wrong.

Advice given to a new colonial governor
Lives of the Chief Justices (Campbell), Ch. 40

Mao Tse-Tung (1893–1976) Chinese communist leader. As chairman of the Communist Party, in 1949 he proclaimed the People's Republic of China and in 1966–68 launched the Cultural Revolution. He developed the form of communism known as Maoism.

Quotations about Mao Tse-Tung

1 No Chinese thinker in the period since Confucius has attained the degree of acceptance and authority which Mao has acquired.

C. P. Fitzgerald *Mao Tse-Tung and China*

2 He dominated the room as I have never seen any person do except Charles de Gaulle.

Henry Kissinger (1923–) German-born US politician and diplomat. *Memoirs*

Quotations by Mao Tse-Tung

3 'War is the continuation of politics'. In this sense war is politics and war itself is a political action.

See also CHOW EN-LAI; CLAUSEWITZ
Quotations from Chairman Mao Tse-Tung, Ch. 5

4 We are advocates of the abolition of war, we do not want war; but war can only be abolished through war, and in order to get rid of the gun it is necessary to take up the gun.

Quotations from Chairman Mao Tse-Tung, Ch. 5

5 All reactionaries are paper tigers.

Quotations from Chairman Mao Tse-Tung, Ch. 6

6 Letting a hundred flowers blossom and a hundred schools of thought contend is the policy for promoting the progress of the arts and the sciences.

Quotations from Chairman Mao Tse-Tung, Ch. 32

7 Every Communist must grasp the truth, 'Political power grows out of the barrel of a gun.'

Selected Works, Vol II, 'Problems of War and Strategy', 6 Nov 1938

8 To read too many books is harmful.

The New Yorker, 7 Mar 1977

9 The atom bomb is a paper tiger which the United States reactionaries use to scare people.

Interview, Aug 1946

10 The government burns down whole cities while the people are forbidden to light lamps.

Attrib.

Map, Walter (c. 1140–c. 1209) Welsh clergyman and writer. He became Archdeacon of Oxford (from 1197). His *De Nugis Curialium* (c. 1182) is a miscellany of gossip, theological argument, diary, etc. He was also involved in the formulation of parts of the Arthurian legend.

1 If die I must, let me die drinking in an inn.

De Nugis Curialium

Marco Polo (c. 1254–1324) Venetian traveller. Having spent many years in the service of the Mongol emperor Kublai Khan, he fought for the Venetians against the Genoese and was captured. In prison he dictated an account of his travels.

1 I have not told half of what I saw.

Last words
The Story of Civilization (W. Durant), Vol. I

Marcus Aurelius Antoninus (121–180 AD) Roman emperor (161–180). He is remembered for his *Meditations*, 12 books of Stoic aphorisms.

1 Whatever this is that I am, it is a little flesh and breath, and the ruling part.

Meditations, Bk. II, Ch. 2

2 And thou wilt give thyself relief, if thou doest every act of thy life as if it were the last.

Meditations, Bk. II, Ch. 5

3 Remember that no man loses any other life than this which he now lives, nor lives any other than this which he now loses.

Meditations, Bk. II, Ch. 14

4 All things from eternity are of like forms and come round in a circle.
Meditations, Bk. II, Ch. 14

5 The universe is transformation; our life is what our thoughts make it.
Meditations, Bk. IV, Ch. 3

6 Everything that happens happens as it should, and if you observe carefully, you will find this to be so.
Meditations, Bk. IV, Ch. 10

7 Everything is only for a day, both that which remembers and that which is remembered.
Meditations, Bk. IV, Ch. 35

8 Time is like a river made up of the events which happen, and its current is strong; no sooner does anything appear than it is swept away, and another comes in its place, and will be swept away too.
Meditations, Bk. IV, Ch. 43

9 Nothing happens to any man that he is not formed by nature to bear.
Meditations, Bk. V, Ch. 18

10 Live with the gods. And he does so who constantly shows them that his soul is satisfied with what is assigned to him.
Meditations, Bk. V, Ch. 27

11 Remember that to change your mind and follow him who sets you right is to be none the less free than you were before.
Meditations, Bk. VIII, Ch. 16

12 Whatever may happen to you was prepared for you from all eternity; and the implication of causes was from eternity spinning the thread of your being.
Meditations, Bk. X, Ch. 5

Marcuse, Herbert (1898–1979) German-born US philosopher, noted for his radical anti-authoritarian views. His books include *The Ethics of Revolution* (1966).

1 Not every problem someone has with his girlfriend is necessarily due to the capitalist mode of production.
The Listener

Marie-Antoinette (1755–93) Queen of France, as wife of Louis XVI. Her extravagance contributed to the unpopularity of the monarchy and after the Revolution, like her husband, she was guillotined.

1 Let them eat cake.
On being told that the people had no bread to eat; in fact she was repeating a much older saying
Attrib.

Marlborough, Sarah, Duchess of (1660–1744) Wife of John Churchill, 1st Duke of Marlborough. A trusted friend of Princess (later Queen) Anne, she exercised control over the Whig ministry after Anne's accession. However, she eventually fell from favour and lived in retirement.

1 The Duke returned from the wars today and did pleasure me in his top-boots.
Attributed to her in various forms; a more ambitious version goes '. . . pleasure me three times in his top-boots'
Attrib.

Marlowe, Christopher (1564–93) English dramatist and poet. His plays include *Tamburlaine the Great* (1587), *The Jew of Malta* (1590), *Doctor Faustus* (1592), and *Edward II* (1592). He was killed in a fight in a Deptford tavern.

1 When all the world dissolves,
And every creature shall be purified,
All place shall be hell that is not heaven.
Doctor Faustus, II:1

2 Was this the face that launch'd a thousand ships
And burnt the topless towers of Ilium?
Sweet Helen, make me immortal with a kiss.
Doctor Faustus, V:1

3 Oh, thou art fairer than the evening air
Clad in the beauty of a thousand stars.
Doctor Faustus, V:1

4 Now hast thou but one bare hour to live,
And then thou must be damn'd perpetually!
Stand still, you ever-moving spheres of heaven,
That time may cease, and midnight never come.
Doctor Faustus, V:2

5 Ugly hell, gape not! come not, Lucifer!
I'll burn my books!
Doctor Faustus, V:2

6 Cut is the branch that might have grown full straight,
And burned is Apollo's laurel-bough,
That sometime grew within this learned man.
Doctor Faustus, Epilogue

7 My men, like satyrs grazing on the lawns,
Shall with their goat-feet dance an antic hay.
Edward II, I:1

8 Who ever loved, that loved not at first sight?
Hero and Leander, I

9 I count religion but a childish toy,
And hold there is no sin but ignorance.
The Jew of Malta, Prologue

10 And, as their wealth increaseth, so enclose
Infinite riches in a little room.
The Jew of Malta, I:1

11 FRIAR BARNARDINE. Thou hast committed –
BARABAS. Fornication: but that was in another country;
And beside the wench is dead.
The Jew of Malta, IV:1

12 I'm arm'd with more than complete steel –
The justice of my quarrel.
Play also attributed to others
Lust's Dominion, IV:3

13 Come live with me, and be my love;
And we will all the pleasures prove
That hills and valleys, dales and fields,
Woods or steepy mountain yields.

The Passionate Shepherd to his Love

14 And I will make thee beds of roses
And a thousand fragrant posies.

The Passionate Shepherd to his Love

Marquis, Don(ald Robert) (1878–1937) US journalist and writer. His column in the *New York Sun* (1912–22) introduced mehitabel (a cat) and archy (a cockroach). Books include *archy and mehitabel* (1927) and *The Old Soak* (1921).

1 An idea isn't responsible for the people who believe in it.

New York Sun

2 To stroke a platitude until it purrs like an epigram.

New York Sun

Marryat, Captain Frederick (1792–1848) British novelist. His books deriving from his experience in the navy include *Mr. Midshipman Easy* (1836) and *Masterman Ready* (1841).

1 If you please, ma'am, it was a very little one.

Said by the nurse to excuse the fact that she had had an illegitimate baby
Mr. Midshipman Easy, Ch. 3

2 I never knows the children. It's just six of one and half-a-dozen of the other.

The Pirate, Ch. 4

3 I think it much better that . . . every man paddle his own canoe.

Settlers in Canada, Ch. 8

Marsh, Sir Edward Howard (1872–1953) British civil servant, writer, and wit. Private secretary to Winston Churchill (1917–22; 1924–29) and others, he wrote several books including *Minima* (1947).

1 Dear Roger Fry whom I love as a man but detest as a movement.

Roger Fry (1866–1934) was an artist and art critic, who championed the postimpressionists
Edward Marsh (Christopher Hassall), Ch. 11

Martineau, Harriet (1802–76) British writer. She wrote novels and books on history, religion, and economics.

1 I am in truth very thankful for not having married at all.

Harriet Martineau's Autobiography, Vol. I

2 If there is any country on earth where the course of true love may be expected to run smooth, it is America.

Society in America, Vol. III, 'Marriage'

3 . . . the early marriages of silly children . . . where . . . every woman is married before she well knows how serious a matter human life is.

Society in America, Vol. III, 'Marriage'

4 In no country, I believe, are the marriage laws so iniquitous as in England, and the conjugal relation, in consequence, so impaired.

Society in America, Vol. III, 'Marriage'

5 Any one must see at a glance that if men and women marry those whom they do not love, they must love those whom they do not marry.

Society in America, Vol. III, 'Marriage'

6 . . . is it to be understood that the principles of the Declaration of Independence bear no relation to half of the human race?

Society in America, Vol. III, 'Marriage'

Marvell, Andrew (1621–78) English poet. MP for Hull for nearly 20 years, he published many pamphlets attacking corruption in the government. His poetry, much of which was published posthumously, includes 'To His Coy Mistress' and 'The Garden'.

1 How vainly men themselves amaze
To win the palm, the oak, or bays.

The Garden

2 Annihilating all that's made
To a green thought in a green shade.

The Garden

3 So restless Cromwell could not cease
In the inglorious arts of peace.

An Horatian Ode upon Cromwell's Return from Ireland

4 He nothing common did or mean
Upon that memorable scene,
But with his keener eye
The axe's edge did try.

Referring to the execution of Charles I
An Horatian Ode upon Cromwell's Return from Ireland

5 Ye living lamps, by whose dear light
The nightingale does sit so late,
And studying all the summer night,
Her matchless songs does meditate.

The Mower to the Glow-worms

6 I have a garden of my own,
But so with roses overgrown,
And lilies, that you would it guess
To be a little wilderness.

The Nymph Complaining for the Death of her Fawn

7 Who can foretell for what high cause
This darling of the Gods was born?

The Picture of Little T.C. in a Prospect of Flowers

8 Gather the flowers, but spare the buds.

The Picture of Little T.C. in a Prospect of Flowers

9 Had we but world enough, and time,
This coyness, lady, were no crime.

To His Coy Mistress

10 But at my back I always hear
Time's winged chariot hurrying near;
And yonder all before us lie
Deserts of vast eternity.

To His Coy Mistress

11 Let us roll all our strength and all
Our sweetness up into one ball,
And tear our pleasures with rough strife
Thorough the iron gates of life:
Thus, though we cannot make our sun
Stand still, yet we will make him run.
To His Coy Mistress

12 The grave's a fine and private place,
But none, I think, do there embrace.
To His Coy Mistress

Marx, Groucho (Julius Marx; 1895–1977) US comedian and film actor; the member of the Marx brothers team who specialized in wisecracks. Their films included *Monkey Business* (1931), *Horse Feathers* (1932), *A Night at the Opera* (1935), and *A Night in Casablanca* (1945).

1 You're the most beautiful woman I've ever seen, which doesn't say much for you.
Animal Crackers

2 One morning I shot an elephant in my pajamas. How he got into my pajamas I'll never know.
Animal Crackers

3 What's a thousand dollars? Mere chicken feed. A poultry matter.
The Cocoanuts

4 Your eyes shine like the pants of my blue serge suit.
The Cocoanuts

5 Either he's dead or my watch has stopped.
A Day at the Races

6 A child of five would understand this. Send somebody to fetch a child of five.
Duck Soup

7 My husband is dead.
 – I'll bet he's just using that as an excuse.
I was with him to the end.
 – No wonder he passed away.
I held him in my arms and kissed him.
 – So it was murder!
Duck Soup

8 Go, and never darken my towels again!
Duck Soup

9 Remember, men, we're fighting for this woman's honour; which is probably more than she ever did.
Duck Soup

10 There's a man outside with a big black moustache.
 – Tell him I've got one.
Horse Feathers

11 You're a disgrace to our family name of Wagstaff, if such a thing is possible.
Horse Feathers

12 You've got the brain of a four-year-old boy, and I bet he was glad to get rid of it.
Horse Feathers

13 Look at me: I worked my way up from nothing to a state of extreme poverty.
Monkey Business

14 I want to register a complaint. Do you know who sneaked into my room at three o'clock this morning? . . .
 – Who? . . .
Nobody, and that's my complaint.
Monkey Business

15 Do you suppose I could buy back my introduction to you?
Monkey Business

16 Sir, you have the advantage of me.
 – Not yet I haven't, but wait till I get you outside.
Monkey Business

17 Do they allow tipping on the boat?
 – Yes, sir.
Have you got two fives?
 – Oh, yes, sir.
Then you won't need the ten cents I was going to give you.
A Night at the Opera

18 The strains of Verdi will come back to you tonight, and Mrs Claypool's cheque will come back to you in the morning.
A Night at the Opera

19 Send two dozen roses to Room 424 and put 'Emily, I love you' on the back of the bill.
A Night in Casablanca

20 I never forget a face, but I'll make an exception in your case.
The Guardian, 18 June 1965

21 I was so long writing my review that I never got around to reading the book.
Attrib.

22 Time wounds all heels.
Attrib.

23 Please accept my resignation. I don't want to belong to any club that will accept me as a member.
Resigning from the Friar's Club in Hollywood; *see also* BENCHLEY
Attrib.

24 No, Groucho is not my real name. I'm breaking it in for a friend.
Attrib.

25 Whoever named it necking was a poor judge of anatomy.
Attrib.

26 A man is only as old as the woman he feels.
Attrib.

Marx, Karl (1818–83) German philosopher and revolutionary. *The Communist Manifesto* (1848), *A Contribution to the Critique of Political Economy* (1859), and *Das Kapital* (1867) are some of his books on the theory of communism. He became leader of the First International and lived abroad (in London from 1849) for much of his life.

1 The history of all hitherto existing society is the history of class struggles.

The Communist Manifesto, 1

2 The workers have nothing to lose but their chains. They have a world to gain. Workers of the world, unite.

The Communist Manifesto, 4

3 From each according to his abilities, to each according to his needs.

Criticism of the Gotha Programme

4 Religion . . . is the opium of the people.

Criticism of the Hegelian Philosophy of Right, Introduction

5 Capitalist production begets, with the inexorability of a law of nature, its own negation.

Das Kapital, Ch. 15

6 Hegel says somewhere that all great events and personalities in world history reappear in one fashion or another. He forgot to add: the first time as tragedy, the second as farce.

The Eighteenth Brumaire of Louis Napoleon

7 The dictatorship of the proletariat.

Attrib.

Mary I (1516–58) Queen of England, the daughter of Henry VIII and Catherine of Aragon. Resolutely attempting to reestablish Catholicism in England, she had nearly 300 citizens burnt at the stake, which earned her the nickname 'Bloody Mary'.

1 When I am dead and opened, you shall find 'Calais' lying in my heart.

Chronicles (Holinshed), III

Maschwitz, Eric (20th century) British songwriter.

1 A Nightingale Sang in Berkeley Square.

Song title

Masefield, John (1878–1967) British poet. His poetry includes *Salt-Water Ballads* (1902) and *Reynard the Fox* (1919). He also wrote several novels of which *Sard Harker* (1924) is the best known. He was poet laureate from 1930 to 1967.

1 He was one of those born neither to obey nor to command, but to be evil to the commander and the obeyer alike. Perhaps there was nothing in life that he had much wanted to do, except to shoot rabbits and hit his father on the jaw, and both these things he had done.

The Bird of Dawning

2 Quinquireme of Nineveh from distant Ophir
Rowing home to haven in sunny Palestine,
With a cargo of ivory,
And apes and peacocks,
Sandalwood, cedarwood, and sweet white wine.

Cargoes

3 Dirty British coaster with a salt-caked smoke stack,
Butting through the Channel in the mad March days,
With a cargo of Tyne coal,
Road-rail, pig-lead,
Firewood, iron-ware, and cheap tin trays.

Cargoes

4 The stars grew bright in the winter sky,
The wind came keen with a tang of frost,
The brook was troubled for new things lost,
The copse was happy for old things found,
The fox came home and he went to ground.

Reynard the Fox

5 I must down to the seas again, to the lonely sea and the sky,
And all I ask is a tall ship and a star to steer her by,
And the wheel's kick and the wind's song and the white sail's shaking,
And a grey mist on the sea's face and a grey dawn breaking.

Often quoted using 'sea' rather than 'seas'
Sea Fever

Mason, Walt (1862–1939) Canadian poet and humorous writer. His books include *Uncle Walt* (1910) and *Terse Verse* (1917).

1 He's the Man Who Delivers the Goods.

The Man Who Delivers the Goods

Massinger, Philip (1583–1640) English dramatist. His most popular plays were *A New Way to Pay Old Debts* (1621) and *The City Madam* (1632). In 1625 he became chief dramatist for the King's Men.

1 He that would govern others, first should be The master of himself.

The Bondman, I

Mathew, Sir James (1830–1908) British judge, who became a Lord Justice of Appeal.

1 In England, Justice is open to all, like the Ritz hotel.

Miscellany-at-Law (R. E. Megarry)

Matthews, Brander (1852–1929) US writer and professor of literature. His plays include *On Probation* and he wrote several books on drama.

1 A gentleman need not know Latin, but he should at least have forgotten it.

Attrib.

Maudling, Reginald (1917–77) British politician. He became Conservative chancellor of the exchequer (1962–64) and home secretary (1970–72).

1 There comes a time in every man's life when he must make way for an older man.

Remark made on being replaced in the shadow cabinet by John Davies, his elder by four years
The Guardian, 20 Nov 1976

Maugham, W(illiam) Somerset (1874–1965) British novelist and doctor. After practising medicine, he became a full-time writer with the success of *Liza of Lambeth* (1896). *Of Human Bondage* (1915), *The Moon and Sixpence* (1919), and *The Razor's Edge* (1944) were among his most successful books.

1 You know, of course, that the Tasmanians, who never committed adultery, are now extinct.
The Bread-Winner

2 Hypocrisy is the most difficult and nerve-racking vice that any man can pursue; it needs an unceasing vigilance and a rare detachment of spirit. It cannot, like adultery or gluttony, be practised at spare moments; it is a whole-time job.
Cakes and Ale, Ch. 1

3 From the earliest times the old have rubbed it into the young that they are wiser than they, and before the young had discovered what nonsense this was they were old too, and it profited them to carry on the imposture.
Cakes and Ale, Ch. 9

4 You can't learn too soon that the most useful thing about a principle is that it can always be sacrificed to expediency.
The Circle, III

5 A woman will always sacrifice herself if you give her the opportunity. It is her favourite form of self-indulgence.
The Circle, III

6 When married people don't get on they can separate, but if they're not married it's impossible. It's a tie that only death can sever.
The Circle, III

7 She's too crafty a woman to invent a new lie when an old one will serve.
The Constant Wife, II

8 The mystic sees the ineffable, and the psychopathologist the unspeakable.
The Moon and Sixpence, Ch. 1

9 Impropriety is the soul of wit.
The Moon and Sixpence, Ch. 4

10 Because women can do nothing except love, they've given it a ridiculous importance.
The Moon and Sixpence, Ch. 41

11 Like all weak men he laid an exaggerated stress on not changing one's mind.
Of Human Bondage, Ch. 37

12 People ask you for criticism, but they only want praise.
Of Human Bondage, Ch. 50

13 Money is like a sixth sense without which you cannot make a complete use of the other five.
Of Human Bondage, Ch. 51

14 The degree of a nation's civilization is marked by its disregard for the necessities of existence.
Our Betters, I

15 The right people are rude. They can afford to be.
Our Betters, II

16 It was such a lovely day I thought it was a pity to get up.
Our Betters, II

17 For to write good prose is an affair of good manners. It is, unlike verse, a civil art . . . . Poetry is baroque.
The Summing Up

18 I would sooner read a time-table or a catalogue than nothing at all. They are much more entertaining than half the novels that are written.
The Summing Up

19 Life is too short to do anything for oneself that one can pay others to do for one.
The Summing Up

20 There is an impression abroad that everyone has it in him to write one book; but if by this is implied a good book the impression is false.
The Summing Up

21 I'll give you my opinion of the human race . . . Their heart's in the right place, but their head is a thoroughly inefficient organ.
The Summing Up

22 Casting my mind's eye over the whole of fiction, the only absolutely original creation I can think of is Don Quixote.
10 Novels and Their Authors, Ch. 1

23 Music-hall songs provide the dull with wit, just as proverbs provide them with wisdom.
A Writer's Notebook

24 I recognize that I am made up of several persons and that the person that at the moment has the upper hand will inevitably give place to another. But which is the real one? All of them or none?
A Writer's Notebook

25 Sentimentality is only sentiment that rubs you up the wrong way.
A Writer's Notebook

26 Dying is a very dull, dreary affair. And my advice to you is to have nothing whatever to do with it.
Escape from the Shadows (Robin Maugham)

27 I am sick of this way of life. The weariness and sadness of old age make it intolerable. I have walked with death in hand, and death's own hand is warmer than my own. I don't wish to live any longer.
Said on his ninetieth birthday
Familiar Medical Quotations (M. B. Strauss)

28 I've always been interested in people, but I've never liked them.
The Observer, 'Sayings of the Week', 28 Aug 1949

29 The trouble with our younger authors is that they are all in the sixties.
The Observer, 'Sayings of the Week', 14 Oct 1951

Maurois, André (Émile Herzog; 1885–1967) French writer. Having served in the British army in World War I he wrote several biographies of British people, including Disraeli, Shelley, and Byron. He also wrote biographies of Voltaire, Proust, and Victor Hugo.

1 If men could regard the events of their own lives with more open minds they would frequently discover that they did not really desire the things they failed to obtain.
The Art of Living

2 In England there is only silence or scandal.
Attrib.

Maxton, James (1885–1946) Scottish Labour leader. He became an MP in 1922. His books include *Lenin* (1932) and *If I were Dictator* (1935).

1 Sit down, man. You're a bloody tragedy.
Said to Ramsay MacDonald when he made his last speech in Parliament
Attrib.

Mayakovsky, Vladimir (1893–1930) Soviet poet. His collections include *Mystery Bouffe* (1918) and *150 Million* (1920). An active member of the Bolsheviks, he committed suicide.

1 Art is not a mirror to reflect the world, but a hammer with which to shape it.
The Guardian, 11 Dec 1974

Mayer, Louis B(urt) (1885–1957) Russian-born US film producer. With Samuel Goldwyn he founded Metro-Goldwyn-Mayer, which perpetuated the star system in Hollywood.

1 The number one book of the ages was written by a committee, and it was called The Bible.
Comment to writers who had objected to changes in their work
The Filmgoer's Book of Quotes (Leslie Halliwell)

Maynard, Sir John (1602–90) English judge and politician. He was imprisoned briefly (1655) for criticizing Cromwell's government.

1 I have forgotten more law than you ever knew, but allow me to say, I have not forgotten much.
Replying to Judge Jeffreys' suggestion that he was so old he had forgotten the law

Mayo, William James (1861–1934) US surgeon, who, with his brother Charles, founded the Mayo Clinic.

1 Specialist – A man who knows more and more about less and less.
Also attributed to Nicholas Butler

McCarthy, Joseph (20th century) US lyricist, who usually worked with composer Harry Tierney.

1 In my sweet little Alice blue gown,
When I first wandered out in the town.
Alice Blue Gown

McCarthy, Joseph R(aymond) (1908–57) US senator, notorious as the instigator of investigations of supposed communists (1950–54).

1 McCarthyism is Americanism with its sleeves rolled.
Speech, 1952

2 It looks like a duck, walks like a duck, and quacks like a duck.
Suggested method of identifying a communist
Attrib.

McCarthy, Mary (1912–89) US novelist. Her books include *Groves of Academe* (1952), *The Group* (1963), and *Cannibals and Missionaries* (1979).

1 If someone tells you he is going to make 'a realistic decision', you immediately understand that he has resolved to do something bad.
On the Contrary

2 There are no new truths, but only truths that have not been recognized by those who have perceived them without noticing.
On the Contrary

3 When an American heiress wants to buy a man, she at once crosses the Atlantic. The only really materialistic people I have ever met have been Europeans.
On the Contrary

4 The immense popularity of American movies abroad demonstrates that Europe is the unfinished negative of which America is the proof.
On the Contrary

5 An interviwer asked me what book I thought best represented the modern American woman. All I could think of to answer was: *Madame Bovary*.
On the Contrary

6 And I don't feel the attraction of the Kennedys at all . . . I don't think they are Christians; they may be Catholics but they are not Christians, in my belief anyway.
The Observer, 14 Oct 1979

McCartney, Paul (1943–) British rock musician and composer. Formerly a member of the Beatles, he wrote many songs with John Lennon. He later formed the band Wings and released such hit albums as *Band on the Run* (1973) before launching a new solo career. See Lennon, John.

1 The issues are the same. We wanted peace on earth, love, and understanding between everyone around the world. We have learned that change comes slowly.
The Observer, 'Sayings of the Week', 7 June 1987

McCrae, John (1872–1918) Canadian poet and doctor. He was killed at the end of World War I, in which he worked as a medical officer. He is remembered for his war poem *In Flanders Fields*.

1 In Flanders fields the poppies blow
Between the crosses, row on row,
That mark our place.
In Flanders Fields, 'Ypres Salient', 3 May 1915

McCullers, Carson Smith (1917–67) US writer and playwright. Her novels include *The Heart is a Lonely Hunter* (1940) and *The Member of the Wedding* (1946); her other work includes *The Ballad of the Sad Cafe* (1951), *Clock without Hands* (1961), and *The Mortgaged Heart* (1971).

1 I suppose my central theme is the theme of spiritual isolation. Certainly I have always felt alone.

The World We Imagine (Mark Shorer)

McEnroe, John (Patrick Jnr) (1959–) US tennis player. A temperamental but brilliant player, he was Wimbledon singles champion in 1981, 1983, and 1984.

1 I've never tolerated phoneyness in anyone and there's a lot of it at Wimbledon.

The Observer, 'Sayings of the Eighties', 16 Aug 1981

2 You are the pits.

To an umpire at Wimbledon, 1981.
The Sunday Times, 24 June 1984

McGonagall, William (1830–1902) Scottish poet. His naive doggerel has earned him the title of the world's worst poet. His *Poetic Gems* were published in 1890, including the unbelievable 'The Tay Bridge Disaster'.

1 Alas! Lord and Lady Dalhousie are dead, and buried at last,
Which causes many people to feel a little downcast.

The Death of Lord and Lady Dalhousie

2 Beautiful Railway Bridge of the Silv'ry Tay!
Alas, I am very sorry to say
That ninety lives have been taken away
On the last Sabbath day of 1879,
Which will be remember'd for a very long time.

The Tay Bridge Disaster

McGough, Roger (1937–) British poet. Publications include *Watchword* (1969), *Gig* (1972), *Waving at Trains* (1982), *The Stowaways* (1986), and *An Imaginary Menagerie* (1988).

1 You will put on a dress of guilt
and shoes with broken high ideals.

Comeclose and Sleepnow

McLuhan, Marshall (1911–81) Canadian sociologist and writer on the impact of technology on society. His books include *The Medium is the Message* (1967) and *The City as Classroom* (1977).

1 The new electronic interdependence recreates the world in the image of a global village.

The Gutenberg Galaxy

2 For tribal man space was the uncontrollable mystery. For technological man it is time that occupies the same role.

The Mechanical Bride, 'Magic that Changes Mood'

3 If the nineteenth century was the age of the editorial chair, ours is the century of the psychiatrist's couch.

Understanding Media, Introduction

4 The medium is the message. This is merely to say that the personal and social consequences of any medium . . . result from the new scale that is introduced into our affairs by each extension of ourselves or by any new technology.

Understanding Media, Ch. 1

5 The car has become the carapace, the protective and aggressive shell, of urban and suburban man.

Understanding Media, Ch. 22

6 Television brought the brutality of war into the comfort of the living room. Vietnam was lost in the living rooms of America – not on the battlefields of Vietnam.

Montreal *Gazette*, 16 May 1975

Mead, Margaret (1901–78) US anthropologist, working mainly in New Guinea and the Pacific Islands. Her books include *Coming of Age in Samoa* (1929) and various works on education and science.

1 We are living beyond our means. As a people we have developed a life-style that is draining the earth of its priceless and irreplaceable resources without regard for the future of our children and people all around the world.

Redbook, 'The Energy Crisis – Why Our World Will Never Again Be the Same'

2 Women want mediocre men, and men are working to be as mediocre as possible.

Quote Magazine, 15 May 1958

Mearns, Hughes (1875–1965) US writer and educationalist. His books include *Creative Power* (1929) and *Creative Adult* (1940), as well as several novels.

1 As I was going up the stair
I met a man who wasn't there.
He wasn't there again to-day.
I wish, I wish he'd stay away.

The Psychoed

Medawar, Sir Peter Brian (1915–87) British immunologist, who shared a Nobel Prize with Sir Macfarlane Burnet for his work on the immune system. His general books include *The Art of the Soluble* (1967), *Induction and Intuition* (1969), and *The Limits of Science* (1984).

1 Scientific discovery is a private event, and the delight that accompanies it, or the despair of finding it illusory does not travel.

Hypothesis and Imagination

Meir, Golda (1898–1978) Russian-born Israeli stateswoman, who was brought up in the USA. A founder of the Israeli Workers' Party, she became minister of Labour (1949–56) and foreign minister (1956–66), before becoming prime minister (1969–74).

1 A leader who doesn't hesitate before he sends his nation into battle is not fit to be a leader.

As Good as Golda (ed. Israel and Mary Shenker)

2 I can honestly say that I was never affected by the question of the success of an undertaking. If I felt it was the right thing to do, I was for it regardless of the possible outcome.
Golda Meir: Woman with a Cause (Marie Syrkin)

3 . . . there's no difference between one's killing and making decisions that will send others to kill. It's exactly the same thing, or even worse.
L'Europeo (Oriana Fallaci)

4 Pessimism is a luxury that a Jew never can allow himself.
The Observer, 'Sayings of the Year', 29 Dec 1974

5 Being seventy is not a sin.
Reader's Digest (July 1971), 'The Indestructible Golda Meir'

6 We intend to remain alive. Our neighbors want to see us dead. This is not a question that leaves much room for compromise.
Reader's Digest (July 1971), 'The Indestructible Golda Meir'

7 There are not enough prisons and concentration camps in Palestine to hold all the Jews who are ready to defend their lives and property.
Speech, 2 May 1940

Melba, Dame Nellie (Helen Porter Mitchell; 1861–1931) Australian soprano.

1 The first rule in opera is the first rule in life: see to everything yourself.
Melodies and Memories

2 Music is not written in red, white and blue. It is written in the heart's blood of the composer.
Melodies and Memories

3 One of the drawbacks of Fame is that one can never escape from it.
Melodies and Memories

4 So you're going to Australia! Well, I made twenty thousand pounds on my tour there, but of course *that* will never be done again. Still, it's a wonderful country, and you'll have a good time. What are you going to sing? All I can say is – sing 'em muck! It's all they can understand!
Speaking to Clara Butt
Clara Butt: Her Life Story (W. H. Ponder)

Melbourne, William Lamb, Viscount (1779–1848) British statesman. Whig prime minister (1934; 1835–41). His marriage to Lady Caroline Ponsonby (1805) ended in divorce after her affair with Lord Byron.

Quotations about Melbourne

1 He is nothing more than a sensible, honest man who means to do his duty to the Sovereign and his country, instead of the ignorant man he pretends to be.
Sydney Smith (1771–1845) British clergyman and essayist
Attrib.

2 He is the person who makes us feel safe and comfortable.
Victoria (1819–1901) Queen of the United Kingdom. *Journal*, 4 July 1838

Quotations by Melbourne

3 Now, is it to lower the price of corn, or isn't it? It is not much matter which we say, but mind, we must all say *the same*.
Said at a cabinet meeting
The English Constitution (Bagehot), Ch. 1

4 What I want is men who will support me when I am in the wrong.
Replying to someone who said he would support Melbourne as long as he was in the right
Lord M. (Lord David Cecil)

5 For God's sake, ma'am, let's have no more of that. If you get the English people into the way of making kings, you'll get them into the way of *unmaking* them.
Advising Queen Victoria against granting Prince Albert the title of King Consort
Lord M. (Lord David Cecil)

6 I like the Garter; there is no damned merit in it.
Lord Melbourne (H. Dunckley), 'On the Order of the Garter'

7 I wish I was as cocksure of anything as Tom Macaulay is of everything.
Preface to Lord Melbourne's Papers (Earl Cowper)

8 Nobody ever did anything very foolish except from some strong principle.
The Young Melbourne (Lord David Cecil)

9 Damn it all, another Bishop dead, – I verily believe they die to vex me.
Attrib.

10 While I cannot be regarded as a pillar, I must be regarded as a buttress of the church, because I support it from the outside.
Attrib.

11 Things have come to a pretty pass when religion is allowed to invade the sphere of private life.
Attrib.

Mellon, Andrew William (1855–1937) US financier and art collector. Ambassador to the UK (1932–33), he donated his art collection to the National Gallery of Art in Washington, DC.

1 A nation is not in danger of financial disaster merely because it owes itself money.
Attrib.

Melville, Herman (1819–91) US novelist. After sailing in a whaler to the South Seas, he wrote *Typee* (1846), *Redburn* (1849), and his best known book, *Moby Dick* (1851). His *Billy Budd*, posthumously published in 1924, was used by Benjamin Britten as the libretto of an opera.

1 Better sleep with a sober cannibal than a drunken Christian.
Moby Dick, Ch. 3

2 A whale ship was my Yale College and my Harvard.
Moby Dick, Ch. 24

Menander (c. 341–c. 290 BC) Greek dramatist. He wrote many comedies, of which *Dyscolus* is the only one to survive, although others are known from their Roman adaptations.

1 Whom the gods love dies young.
Dis Exapaton

Mencken, H(enry) L(ouis) (1880–1956) US journalist and editor. His collected essays were published in *Prejudices* (6 vols; 1919–27).

1 Puritanism – The haunting fear that someone, somewhere, may be happy.
A Book of Burlesques

2 Conscience is the inner voice that warns us somebody may be looking.
A Mencken Chrestomathy

3 We must respect the other fellow's religion, but only in the sense and to the extent that we respect his theory that his wife is beautiful and his children smart.
Notebooks, 'Minority Report'

4 It is now quite lawful for a Catholic woman to avoid pregnancy by a resort to mathematics, though she is still forbidden to resort to physics and chemistry.
Notebooks, 'Minority Report'

5 War will never cease until babies begin to come into the world with larger cerebrums and smaller adrenal glands.
Notebooks, 'Minority Report'

6 One of the things that makes a Negro unpleasant to white folk is the fact that he suffers from their injustice. He is thus a standing rebuke to them.
Notebooks, 'Minority Report'

7 The chief contribution of Protestantism to human thought is its massive proof that God is a bore.
Notebooks, 'Minority Report'

8 The worst government is the most moral. One composed of cynics is often very tolerant and human. But when fanatics are on top there is no limit to oppression.
Notebooks, 'Minority Report'

9 God is the immemorial refuge of the incompetent, the helpless, the miserable. They find not only sanctuary in His arms, but also a kind of superiority, soothing to their macerated egos; He will set them above their betters.
Notebooks, 'Minority Report'

10 It takes a long while for a naturally trustful person to reconcile himself to the idea that after all God will not help him.
Notebooks, 'Minority Report'

11 A society made up of individuals who were all capable of original thought would probably be unendurable. The pressure of ideas would simply drive it frantic.
Notebooks, 'Minority Report'

12 Poetry is a comforting piece of fiction set to more or less lascivious music.
Prejudices, 'The Poet and his Art'

13 No man is genuinely happy, married, who has to drink worse gin than he used to drink when he was single.
Prejudices, 'Reflections on Monogamy'

14 Faith may be defined briefly as an illogical belief in the occurrence of the improbable.
Prejudices, 'Types of Men'

15 He is the only man who is for ever apologizing for his occupation.
Referring to businessmen
Prejudices, 'Types of Men'

16 An idealist is one who, on noticing that a rose smells better than a cabbage, concludes that it will also make better soup.
Sententiae

17 Opera in English, is, in the main, just about as sensible as baseball in Italian.
The Frank Muir Book (Frank Muir)

18 I've made it a rule never to drink by daylight and never to refuse a drink after dark.
New York Post, 18 Sept 1945

Menuhin, Sir Yehudi (1916–) US-born British violinist of Russian-Jewish parents. A former director of the Bath Festival, he founded a school for musically gifted children.

1 Music creates order out of chaos; for rhythm imposes unanimity upon the divergent, melody imposes continuity upon the disjointed, and harmony imposes compatibility upon the incongruous.
The Sunday Times, 10 Oct 1976

Mercer, Johnny (1909–76) US lyricist and composer, who wrote many hit tunes in Hollywood in the 1930s.

1 Jeepers Creepers – where'd you get them peepers?
Jeepers Creepers

2 That old black magic has me in its spell.
That Old Black Magic

Meredith, George (1828–1909) British novelist and poet. His poem *Modern Love* (1862) was partly based on his own unhappy marriage; his novels included *The Egoist* (1879) and *The Tragic Comedians* (1880).

1 I expect that Woman will be the last thing civilized by Man.
The Ordeal of Richard Feverel, Ch. 1

2 Kissing don't last: cookery do!
The Ordeal of Richard Feverel, Ch. 28

3 Much benevolence of the passive order may be traced to a disinclination to inflict pain upon oneself.
Vittoria, Ch. 42

Meredith, Owen (Robert Bulmer-Lytton, 1st Earl of Lytton; 1831–91) British statesman and poet. He became Viceroy of India in 1876. As Owen Meredith he published several volumes of poetry.

1 Genius does what it must, and Talent does what it can.
Last Words of a Sensitive Second-rate Poet

Merrill, Bob (Robert Merrill; 1890–1977) US lyricist and composer. His chief film score was for *Funny Girl* (1968).

1 People who need people are the luckiest people in the world.
People Who Need People

Meynell, Alice (1847–1922) British poet and literary critic.

1 My heart shall be thy garden.
The Garden

Michelet, Jules (1798–1874) French historian. His main works are his 17 volume *History of France* (1833–67) and *The French Revolution* (1847–53).

1 You are one of the forces of nature.
From a letter received by Dumas
Memoirs, Vol. VI, Ch. 138 (Alexandre Dumas)

Middleton, Thomas (1580–1627) English dramatist. His best-known plays are *A Game at Chess* (1624), *Women Beware Women* (c. 1621), and *The Changeling* (in collaboration with William Rowley; 1622).

1 Though I be poor, I'm honest.
The Witch, III:2

Midlane, Albert (1825–1909) British hymn writer.

1 There's a Friend for little children
Above the bright blue sky,
A Friend who never changes,
Whose love will never die.
Hymn

Mikes, George (1912–87) Hungarian-born British writer and humorist.

1 On the Continent people have good food; in England people have good table manners.
How to be an Alien

2 An Englishman, even if he is alone, forms an orderly queue of one.
How to be an Alien

3 Continental people have sex life; the English have hot-water bottles.
How to be an Alien

4 It was twenty-one years ago that England and I first set foot on each other. I came for a fortnight; I have stayed ever since.
How to be Inimitable

5 The one class you do *not* belong to and are not proud of at all is the lower-middle class. No one ever describes himself as belonging to the lower-middle class.
How to be Inimitable

Mill, John Stuart (1806–73) British philosopher and social reformer. His works include *On Liberty* (1859), *Utilitarianism* (1863), and *Subjection of Women* (1869).

1 Ask yourself whether you are happy, and you cease to be so.
Autobiography, Ch. 5

2 He who knows only his own side of the case knows little of that.
On Liberty, Ch. 2

3 All good things which exist are the fruits of originality.
On Liberty, Ch. 3

4 The liberty of the individual must be thus far limited; he must not make himself a nuisance to other people.
On Liberty, Ch. 3

5 The worth of a State in the long run is the worth of the individuals composing it.
On Liberty, Ch. 5

6 The most important thing women have to do is to stir up the zeal of women themselves.
Letter to Alexander Bain, 14 July 1869

Millard, Emma (1787–1870) British songwriter.

1 Rocked in the cradle of the deep.
Song

Millay, Edna St Vincent (1892–1950) US poet. Her verse collections include *A Few Figs from Thistles* (1920), *The Buck in the Snow* (1928), and *Huntsman, What Quarry?* (1939). She also wrote the play *The Lamp and the Bell* (1921) and an opera libretto.

1 My candle burns at both ends;
It will not last the night;
But ah, my foes, and oh my friends –
It gives a lovely light!
A Few Figs from Thistles, 'First Fig'

Miller, Arthur (1915–) US dramatist. His plays include *Death of a Salesman* (1947), *The Crucible* (1953), *After the Fall* (1964), based on the life of his late wife, Marilyn Monroe, *The Price* (1968), and *Two Way Mirror* (1985).

1 There are many who stay away from church these days because you hardly ever mention God any more.
The Crucible, I

2 He's liked, but he's not well liked.
Death of a Salesman, I

3 Years ago a person, he was unhappy, didn't know what to do with himself – he'd go to church, start a revolution – *something*. Today you're unhappy? Can't figure it out? What is the salvation? Go shopping.
The Price, I

4 I am inclined to notice the ruin in things, perhaps because I was born in Italy.
A View from the Bridge, I

5 A good newspaper, I suppose, is a nation talking to itself.
The Observer, 'Sayings of the Week', 26 Nov 1961

6 Why should I go? She won't be there.

When asked if he would attend Marilyn Monroe's funeral
Attrib.

Miller, Henry (1891–1980) US novelist. He lived in Paris in the 1930s and established his reputation with the sexually explicit novels *Tropic of Cancer* (1934) and *Tropic of Capricorn* (1939). His later books include *My Life and Times* (1972).

1 Sex is one of the nine reasons for reincarnation . . . The other eight are unimportant.

Big Sur and the Oranges of Hieronymus Bosch

2 Every man with a belly full of the classics is an enemy of the human race.

Tropic of Cancer, 'Dijon'

Miller, Jonathan (1934–) British doctor and television and stage director. Co-author of *Beyond the Fringe* (1961–64), he has produced plays, operas, and the television series *The Body in Question* (1978).

1 I'm not really a Jew; just Jew-ish, not the whole hog.

Beyond the Fringe

2 They do those little personal things people sometimes do when they think they are alone in railway carriages; things like smelling their own armpits.

Beyond the Fringe

Miller, Max (Harold Sargent; 1895–1963) British music-hall comedian, known for his vulgar clothes and suggestive act.

1 There was a little girl
Who had a little curl
Right in the middle of her forehead,
When she was good she was very very good
And when she was bad she was very very popular.

The Max Miller Blue Book

Milligan, Spike (1918–) British comic actor and author, best known as co-author of and performer in the BBC radio series *The Goon Show*.

1 I shook hands with a friendly Arab . . . I still have my right hand to prove it.

A Dustbin of Milligan, 'Letters to Harry Secombe'

2 I have for instance among my purchases . . . several original Mona Lisas and all painted (according to the Signature) by the great artist Kodak.

A Dustbin of Milligan, 'Letters to Harry Secombe'

3 – 'Do you come here often?'
'Only in the mating season.'

The Goon Show

4 I don't like this game.

The Goon Show

5 I'm walking backwards till Christmas.

The Goon Show

6 MORIARTY. How are you at Mathematics?
HARRY SECOMBE. I speak it like a native.

The Goon Show

7 You silly twisted boy.

The Goon Show

8 Contraceptives should be used on every conceivable occasion.

The Last Goon Show of All

9 Policemen are numbered in case they get lost.

The Last Goon Show of All

10 Money can't buy friends, but you can get a better class of enemy.

Puckoon, Ch. 6

11 One day the don't-knows will get in, and then where will we be?

Attributed remark made about a pre-election poll

Mills, Hugh (1913–71) British screenwriter. His films include *Knave of Hearts* (1952) and *Prudence and the Pill* (1968).

1 Nothing unites the English like war. Nothing divides them like Picasso.

Prudence and the Pill

Milman, Henry Hart (1791–1868) British poet and historian. As dean of St Paul's he is known for his historical works, including *History of the Jews* (1830) and *History of Latin Christianity* (1854–55). He also wrote poetry, including *Samor* (1818) and the tragedy *Fazio* (1815).

1 Ride on! ride on in majesty!
In lowly pomp ride on to die.

Ride On

Milne, A(lan) A(lexander) (1882–1956) British writer, best known for his books for and about his son Christopher Robin, including *When We Were Very Young* (1924), *Winnie-the-Pooh* (1926), and *Now We Are Six* (1927).

1 I am old enough to be – in fact am – your mother.

Belinda

2 If the English language had been properly organized . . . then there would be a word which meant both 'he' and 'she', and I could write, 'If John or Mary comes heesh will want to play tennis,' which would save a lot of trouble.

The Christopher Robin Birthday Book

3 For one person who dreams of making fifty thousand pounds, a hundred people dream of being left fifty thousand pounds.

If I May, 'The Future'

4 They're changing guard at Buckingham Palace –
Christopher Robin went down with Alice.
Alice is marrying one of the guard.
'A soldier's life is terrible hard,'
Says Alice.

When We Were Very Young, 'Buckingham Palace'

5 And some of the bigger bears try to pretend
That they came round the corner to look for a friend;
And they'll try to pretend that nobody cares
Whether you walk on the lines or the squares.

When We Were Young, 'Lines and Squares'

6 I am a Bear of Very Little Brain, and long words
Bother me.
Winnie-the-Pooh, Ch. 4

7 Time for a little something.
Winnie-the-Pooh, Ch. 6

Milton, John (1608–74) English poet. His poems include
L'Allegro and *Il Penseroso* (1632) and the great epics *Paradise Lost*
(1667) and *Paradise Regained* (1671).

Quotations about Milton

1 Our Language sunk under him, and was unequal
to that greatness of soul which furnished him
with such glorious conceptions.
Joseph Addison (1672–1719) British essayist. *The Spectator*

2 Milton the prince of poets – so we say
A little heavy but no less divine
An independent being in his day –
Learn'd, pious, temperate in love and wine.
Lord Byron (1788–1824) British poet. *Don Juan*

3 The whole of Milton's poem, *Paradise Lost*, is
such barbarous trash, so outrageously offensive
to reason and to common sense that one is
naturally led to wonder how it can have been
tolerated by a people amongst whom astronomy, navigation and chemistry are understood.
William Cobbett (1763–1835) British journalist and writer. *A
Year's Residence in The United States*

4 As a poet, Milton seems to me the greatest of
eccentrics. His work illustrates no general
principles of good writing; the only principles of
writing that it illustrates are such as are valid
only for Milton himself to observe.
T. S. Eliot (1888–1965) US-born British poet and dramatist.
Essays: Milton

5 Milton, Madam, was a genius that could cut a
Colossus from a rock; but could not carve heads
upon cherry-stones.
Samuel Johnson (1709–84) British lexicographer. *Life of Johnson*
(James Boswell)

Quotations by Milton

6 Who kills a man kills a reasonable creature,
God's image; but he who destroys a good book,
kills reason itself, kills the image of God, as it
were in the eye.
Areopagitica

7 A good book is the precious life-blood of a
master spirit, embalmed and treasured up on
purpose to a life beyond life.
Areopagitica

8 Let her and Falsehood grapple; who ever knew
Truth put to the worse, in a free and open
encounter?
Areopagitica

9 Blest pair of Sirens, pledges of Heaven's joy,
Sphere-born harmonious sisters, Voice and
Verse.
At a Solemn Music

10 Wrapt in a pleasing fit of melancholy.
Comus

11 Hence, vain deluding Joys,
The brood of Folly without father bred!
Il Penseroso

12 And looks commercing with the skies,
Thy rapt soul sitting in thine eyes.
Il Penseroso

13 Sweet bird, that shunn'st the noise of folly,
Most musical, most melancholy!
Referring to the nightingale
Il Penseroso

14 Where glowing embers through the room
Teach light to counterfeit a gloom,
Far from all resort of mirth,
Save the cricket on the hearth.
Il Penseroso

15 Where more is meant than meets the ear.
Il Penseroso

16 Come, and trip it as you go
On the light fantastic toe.
L'Allegro

17 To hear the lark begin his flight,
And singing startle the dull night,
From his watch-tower in the skies,
Till the dappled dawn doth rise.
L'Allegro

18 Then to the spicy nut-brown ale.
L'Allegro

19 Or sweetest Shakespeare, Fancy's child,
Warble his native wood-notes wild.
L'Allegro

20 The melting voice through mazes running;
Untwisting all the chains that tie
The hidden soul of harmony.
L'Allegro

21 Yet once more, O ye laurels, and once more,
Ye myrtles brown, with ivy never sere,
I come to pluck your berries harsh and crude,
And with forced fingers rude
Shatter your leaves before the mellowing year.
Lycidas

22 Under the opening eye-lids of the morn.
Lycidas

23 As killing as the canker to the rose.
Lycidas

24 To sport with Amaryllis in the shade,
Or with the tangles of Neaera's hair.
Lycidas

25 Fame is the spur that the clear spirit doth raise
(That last infirmity of noble mind)
To scorn delights, and live laborious days.
Lycidas

26 The hungry sheep look up, and are not fed,
But, swoln with wind and the rank mist they
draw,
Rot inwardly, and foul contagion spread.
Lycidas

27 At last he rose, and twitched his mantle blue:
To-morrow to fresh woods, and pastures new.
Lycidas

28 Rhyme being no necessary adjunct or true ornament of poem or good verse, in longer works
especially, but the invention of a barbarous age,
to set off wretched matter and lame metre.
Paradise Lost, The Verse. Preface to 1668 ed.

29 The troublesome and modern bondage of
Rhyming.
Paradise Lost, The Verse. Preface to 1668 ed.

30 Of Man's first disobedience, and the fruit
Of that forbidden tree, whose mortal taste
Brought death into the World, and all our woe
. . .
Paradise Lost, Bk. I

31 What in me is dark
Illumine, what is low raise and support;
That, to the height of this great argument,
I may assert Eternal Providence,
And justify the ways of God to men.
Paradise Lost, Bk. I

32 What though the field be lost?
All is not lost – the unconquerable will,
And study of revenge, immortal hate,
And courage never to submit or yield:
And what is else not to be overcome?
Paradise Lost, Bk. I

33 A mind not to be changed by place or time.
The mind is its own place, and in itself
Can make a Heaven of Hell, a Hell of Heaven.
Paradise Lost, Bk. I

34 To reign is worth ambition, though in Hell:
Better to reign in Hell than serve in Heaven.
Paradise Lost, Bk. I

35 Care
Sat on his faded cheek.
Paradise Lost, Bk. I

36 Tears such as angels weep, burst forth.
Paradise Lost, Bk. I

37 Who overcomes
By force, hath overcome but half his foe.
Paradise Lost, Bk. I

38 From morn
To noon he fell, from noon to dewy eve,
A summer's day, and with the setting sun
Dropped from the zenith, like a falling star.
Paradise Lost, Bk. I

39 High on a throne of royal state, which far
Outshone the wealth of Ormus and of Ind,
Or where the gorgeous East with richest hand
Showers on her kings barbaric pearl and gold,
Satan exalted sat, by merit raised
To that bad eminence.
Paradise Lost, Bk. II

40 Long is the way
And hard, that out of hell leads up to light.
Paradise Lost, Bk. II

41 Vain wisdom all, and false philosophy.
Paradise Lost, Bk. II

42 For neither man nor angel can discern
Hypocrisy, the only evil that walks
Invisible, except to God alone.
Paradise Lost, Bk. III

43 Which way I fly is Hell; myself am Hell;
And, in the lowest deep, a lower deep
Still threat'ning to devour me opens wide,
To which the Hell I suffer seems a Heaven.
Paradise Lost, Bk. IV

44 Farewell remorse! All good to me is lost;
Evil, be thou my Good.
Paradise Lost, Bk. IV

45 A heav'n on earth.
Paradise Lost, Bk. IV

46 Now came still Evening on, and Twilight grey
Had in her sober livery all things clad.
Paradise Lost, Bk. IV

47 Abashed the devil stood,
And felt how awful goodness is.
Paradise Lost, Bk. IV

48 Midnight brought on the dusky hour
Friendliest to sleep and silence.
Paradise Lost, Bk. V

49 In solitude
What happiness? who can enjoy alone,
Or, all enjoying, what contentment find?
Paradise Lost, Bk. VIII

50 Accuse not Nature, she hath done her part;
Do thou but thine.
Paradise Lost, Bk. VIII

51 Revenge, at first though sweet,
Bitter ere long back on itself recoils.
Paradise Lost, Bk. IX

52 The world was all before them, where to choose
Their place of rest, and Providence their guide:
They, hand in hand, with wandering steps and
slow,
Through Eden took their solitary way.
Paradise Lost, Bk. XII

53 Most men admire
Virtue, who follow not her lore.
Paradise Regained, Bk. I

54 Beauty stands
  In the admiration only of weak minds
  Led captive.
  Paradise Regained, Bk. II

55 Let us with a gladsome mind
  Praise the Lord, for he is kind,
  For his mercies ay endure,
  Ever faithful, ever sure.
  Psalm

56 A little onward lend thy guiding hand
  To these dark steps, a little further on.
  Samson Agonistes

57 Ask for this great deliverer now, and find him
  Eyeless in Gaza at the mill with slaves.
  Samson Agonistes

58 O dark, dark, dark, amid the blaze of noon,
  Irrecoverably dark, total eclipse,
  Without all hope of day!
  Samson Agonistes

59 How soon hath Time, the subtle thief of youth,
  Stolen on his wing my three-and-twentieth year!
  Sonnet: 'On Being Arrived at the Age of Twenty-three'

60 When I consider how my light is spent
  Ere half my days in this dark world and wide,
  And that one talent which is death to hide
  Lodged with me useless.
  Sonnet: 'On his Blindness'

61 God doth not need
  Either man's work or his own gifts. Who best
  Bear his mild yoke, they serve him best: his state
  Is kingly; thousands at his bidding speed,
  And post o'er land and ocean without rest;
  They also serve who only stand and wait.
  Sonnet: 'On his Blindness'

62 New Presbyter is but old Priest writ large.
  Sonnet: 'On the New Forcers of Conscience under the Long Parliament'

63 Peace hath her victories
  No less renowned than war.
  Sonnet: 'To the Lord General Cromwell, May 1652'

64 None can love freedom heartily, but good men;
  the rest love not freedom, but licence.
  Tenure of Kings and Magistrates

65 One tongue is sufficient for a woman.
  On being asked whether he would allow his daughters to learn foreign languages
  Attrib.

Mirabeau, Honoré Gabriel Riquetti, Comte de
(1749–91) French statesman. A revolutionary leader, who visited England and Germany, he wrote *De la monarchie prussienne sous Frédéric le Grand* (1788). An influential speaker in the National Assembly, he argued for a constitutional monarchy. He was elected president of the Assembly but died before taking office.

1 War is the national industry of Prussia.
  Attrib.

Mitchell, Adrian
(1932–) British writer and dramatist. Plays include *Tyger* (1971), *The White Deer* (1978), *The Wild Animal Song Contest* (1983), and *Love Songs of World War Three* (1987). Novels include *The Bodyguard* (1970) and *Wartime* (1973). He has also written several verse collections and children's books.

1 I want to be a movement
  But there's no one on my side.
  Loose Leaf Poem

Mitchell, Joni
(1943–) Singer and songwriter. Her albums include *Clouds* (1969), *Blue* (1971), *The Hissing of Summer Lawns* (1975), and *Wild Things Run Fast* (1982).

1 I've looked at life from both sides now
  From win and lose and still somehow
  It's life's illusions I recall
  I really don't know life at all.
  Both Sides Now

Mitchell, Julian
(1935–) British writer and dramatist. His novels include *As Far as You Can Go* (1963) and *The Undiscovered Country* (1968). The plays *Half-Life* (1977), *Another Country* (1981), and *After Aida* (1986) have been successful.

1 The sink is the great symbol of the bloodiness of family life. All life is bad, but family life is worse.
  As Far as You Can Go, Pt. I, Ch. 1

Mitchell, Margaret
(1909–49) US novelist, whose single success was *Gone with the Wind* (1936, filmed 1939).

1 Until you've lost your reputation, you never realize what a burden it was or what freedom really is.
  Gone with the Wind

2 Fighting is like champagne. It goes to the heads of cowards as quickly as of heroes. Any fool can be brave on a battle field when it's be brave or else be killed.
  Gone with the Wind

3 Death and taxes and childbirth! There's never any convenient time for any of them!
  Gone with the Wind

4 After all, tomorrow is another day.
  The closing words of the book
  Gone with the Wind

5 Gone With the Wind.
  From the poem *Non Sum Qualis Eram* (Ernest Dowson): 'I have forgotten much, Cynara! Gone with the wind...'
  Book title

Mitford, Jessica Lucy
(1917–) British writer, sister of Nancy Mitford, who settled in the USA. *Hons and Rebels* (1960) gives an account of her eccentric family; her other books include *The American Way of Death* (1965).

1 I have nothing against undertakers personally. It's just that I wouldn't want one to bury my sister.
  Attrib. in *Saturday Review*, 1 Feb 1964

Mitford, Nancy
(1904–73) British writer, sister of Jessica Mitford. Her best-known novels are *The Pursuit of Love* (1945), *Love in a Cold Climate* (1949), and *The Blessing* (1951). She has also written historical biographies.

1 An aristocracy in a republic is like a chicken whose head has been cut off: it may run about in a lively way, but in fact it is dead.
Noblesse Oblige

2 English women are elegant until they are ten years old, and perfect on grand occasions.
The Wit of Women (L. and M. Cowan)

Mizner, Wilson (1876–1933) US writer and wit.

1 Be nice to people on your way up because you'll meet 'em on your way down.
Also attributed to Jimmy Durante
A Dictionary of Catch-Phrases (Eric Partridge)

Molière (Jean Baptiste Poquelin; 1622–73) French dramatist. In his plays, such as *Tartuffe* (1664), *Le Bourgeois Gentilhomme* (1670), and *Le Malade imaginaire* (1673), he satirized contemporary society.

1 He who lives without tobacco is not worthy to live.
Don Juan, I:1

2 One should eat to live, not live to eat.
L'Avare, III:2

3 Good heavens! I have been talking prose for over forty years without realizing it.
Le Bourgeois Gentilhomme, II:4

4 One dies only once, and it's for such a long time!
Le Dépit amoureux, V:3

5 He must have killed a lot of men to have made so much money.
Le Malade imaginaire, I:5

6 It is a stupidity second to none, to busy oneself with the correction of the world.
Le Misanthrope, I:1

7 One should examine oneself for a very long time before thinking of condemning others.
Le Misanthrope, III:4

8 Age will bring all things, and everyone knows, Madame, that twenty is no age to be a prude.
Le Misanthrope, III:4

9 Grammar, which can govern even kings.
Les Femmes savantes, II:6

10 It is a public scandal that gives offence, and it is no sin to sin in secret.
Tartuffe, IV:5

Monmouth, James Scott, Duke of (1649–85) An illegitimate son of Charles II, and the focus of the Protestant opposition to the Catholic James II. After James' accession he landed at Lyme Regis from exile in France to raise a rebellion, but was defeated at Sedgemoor and beheaded.

1 Do not hack me as you did my Lord Russell.
Said to the headsman before his execution
History of England (Macaulay), Vol. I, Ch. 5

Monroe, Harriet (1860–1936) US poet and editor.

1 . . . poetry, 'The Cinderella of the Arts.'
Famous American Women (Hope Stoddard), 'Harriet Monroe'

Monroe, Marilyn (Norma-Jean Baker; 1926–62) US film star. A comedienne and sex symbol, her films include *Gentlemen Prefer Blondes* (1953) and *The Misfits* (1961), written by her third husband, Arthur Miller. She died of a barbiturate overdose.

1 JOURNALIST. Didn't you have anything on?
M. M. I had the radio on.
Attrib.

Monsell, John (1811–75) British hymn writer.

1 Fight the good fight with all thy might,
Christ is thy strength and Christ thy right,
Lay hold on life, and it shall be
Thy joy and crown eternally.
Hymn

Montagu, Lady Mary Wortley (1689–1762) English writer. The wife of the English ambassador to Turkey, she is remembered especially for her letters written from Constantinople, published as *Letters from the East*.

1 Satire should, like a polished razor keen,
Wound with a touch that's scarcely felt or seen.
To the Imitator of the First Satire of Horace, Bk. II

Montague, C(harles) E(dward) (1867–1928) British editor, writer, and critic. His novels include *Rough Justice* (1926); he also wrote *Disenchantment* (1922) about his experiences in World War I.

1 War hath no fury like a non-combatant.
Disenchantment, Ch. 15

2 To be amused at what you read – that is the great spring of happy quotation
A Writer's Notes on his Trade

Montaigne, Michel de (1533–92) French essayist. His *Essais* (1580 and 1588) started a new literary genre, in which he expressed his philosophy of humanism.

1 The greatest thing in the world is to know how to be self-sufficient.
Essais, I

2 A man must keep a little back shop where he can be himself without reserve. In solitude alone can he know true freedom.
Essais, I

3 Unless a man feels he has a good enough memory, he should never venture to lie.
Essais, I

4 The daughter-in-law of Pythagoras said that a woman who goes to bed with a man ought to lay aside her modesty with her skirt, and put it on again with her petticoat.
Essais, I

5 When I play with my cat, who knows whether she is not amusing herself with me more than I with her?
Essais, II

6 Man is quite insane. He wouldn't know how to create a maggot and he creates Gods by the dozen.
Essais, II

7 Marriage is like a cage; one sees the birds outside desperate to get in, and those inside equally desperate to get out.
Essais, III

8 Many a man has been a wonder to the world, whose wife and valet have seen nothing in him that was even remarkable. Few men have been admired by their servants.
Essais, III

9 The world is but a school of inquiry.
Essais, III

10 Poverty of goods is easily cured; poverty of soul, impossible.
Essais, III

11 A man who fears suffering is already suffering from what he fears.
Essais, III

Montesquieu, Charles Louis de Secondat, Baron de (1688–1755) French writer and historian. He is remembered for his influential *Considérations sur les causes de la grandeur et de la décadence des romains* (1734) and *Esprit des lois* (1748).

1 An empire founded by war has to maintain itself by war.
Considérations sur les causes de la grandeur et de la décadence des romains, Ch. 8

2 A really intelligent man feels what other men only know.
Essai sur les causes qui peuvent affecter les esprits et les caractères

3 Liberty is the right to do everything which the laws allow.
L'Esprit des lois

4 There is a very good saying that if triangles invented a god, they would make him three-sided.
Lettres persanes

5 No kingdom has ever had as many civil wars as the kingdom of Christ.
Lettres persanes

6 Great lords have their pleasures, but the people have fun.
Pensées diverses

7 The English are busy; they don't have time to be polite.
Pensées diverses

8 I suffer from the disease of writing books and being ashamed of them when they are finished.
Pensées diverses

Montessori, Maria (1870–1952) Italian doctor and educationalist. She devised the Montessori system for educating young children.

1 And if education is always to be conceived along the same antiquated lines of a mere transmission of knowledge, there is little to be hoped from it in the bettering of man's future. For what is the use of transmitting knowledge if the individual's total development lags behind?
The Absorbent Mind

2 We teachers can only help the work going on, as servants wait upon a master.
The Absorbent Mind

Montgomery of Alamein, Bernard Law, Viscount (1887–1976) British field marshal, who commanded the Eighth Army in Africa in World War II, which defeated Rommel. He became chief of the land forces in the Normandy invasion and after victory over Germany was deputy commander of NATO forces (1951–58).

1 The U.S. has broken the second rule of war. That is, don't go fighting with your land army on the mainland of Asia. Rule One is don't march on Moscow. I developed these two rules myself.
Referring to the Vietnam war
Montgomery of Alamein (Chalfont)

2 This sort of thing may be tolerated by the French, but we are British — thank God.
Comment on a bill to relax the laws against homosexuals
Daily Mail, 27 May 1965

Montherlant, Henry de (1896–1972) French novelist and dramatist. His work includes the four-novel cycle, *Les Jeunes Filles* (1936), *Pitié pour les femmes* (1936), *Le Démon du bien* (1937), and *Les Lépreuses* (1939).

1 A lot of people, on the verge of death, utter famous last words or stiffen into attitudes, as if the final stiffening in three days' time were not enough; they will have ceased to exist three days' hence, yet they still want to arouse admiration and adopt a pose and tell a lie with their last gasp.
Explicit Mysterium

2 Stupidity does not consist in being without ideas. Such stupidity would be the sweet, blissful stupidity of animals, molluscs and the gods. Human Stupidity consists in having lots of ideas, but stupid ones.
Notebooks

Montrose, Percy (19th century) US songwriter.

1 In a cavern, in a canyon,
Excavating for a mine
Dwelt a miner, Forty-niner,
And his daughter, Clementine.
Oh, my darling, Oh, my darling, Oh, my darling Clementine!
Thou art lost and gone for ever, dreadful sorry, Clementine.
Clementine

2 But I kissed her little sister,
And forgot my Clementine.
Clementine

Moore, Clement Clarke (1779–1863) US writer. He is remembered for his Hebrew lexicon and the ballad 'A Visit from St. Nicholas'.

1 'Twas the night before Christmas, when all through the house
Not a creature was stirring, not even a mouse;
The stockings were hung by the chimney with care,
In hopes that St Nicholas soon would be there.

In Troy Sentinel, 23 Dec 1823, 'A Visit from St. Nicholas'

Moore, Edward (1712–57) British dramatist. His works include *Fables of the Female Sex* (1744) as well as the tragedies *The Foundling* (1747–48) and *The Gamester* (1753).

1 This is adding insult to injuries.
The Foundling, V

2 I am rich beyond the dreams of avarice.
The Gamester, II

Moore, George (1852–1933) Irish writer and art critic. His best-known works are the novels *Esther Waters* (1894) and *The Brook Kerith* (1916). He also wrote plays, poetry, short stories, and an autobiography.

1 A man travels the world over in search of what he needs and returns home to find it.
The Brook Kerith, Ch. 11

2 Acting is therefore the lowest of the arts, if it is an art at all.
Mummer-Worship

3 To be aristocratic in Art one must avoid polite society.
Enemies of Promise (Cyril Connolly), Ch. 15

Moore, Thomas (1779–1852) Irish poet. His most popular works are the collection *Irish Melodies* (1807–34) and the oriental romance *Lalla Rookh* (1817).

1 Yet, who can help loving the land that has taught us
Six hundred and eighty-five ways to dress eggs?
The Fudge Family in Paris

2 The harp that once through Tara's halls
The soul of music shed,
Now hangs as mute on Tara's walls
As if that soul were fled. –
So sleeps the pride of former days,
So glory's thrill is o'er;
And hearts, that once beat high for praise,
Now feel that pulse no more.
Irish Melodies, 'The Harp that Once'

3 The Minstrel Boy to the war has gone,
In the ranks of death you'll find him;
His father's sword he has girded on,
And his wild harp slung behind him.
Irish Melodies, 'The Minstrel Boy'

4 She is far from the land where her young hero sleeps,
And lovers are round her, sighing:
But coldly she turns from their gaze, and weeps,
For her heart in his grave is lying.
Irish Melodies, 'She is Far'

5 'Tis the last rose of summer
Left blooming alone;
All her lovely companions
Are faded and gone.
Irish Melodies, ''Tis the Last Rose'

6 I never nurs'd a dear gazelle,
To glad me with its soft black eye
But when it came to know me well,
And love me, it was sure to die!
See also PAYN
Lalla Rookh

7 Oft in the stilly night,
Ere Slumber's chain has bound me,
Fond Memory brings the light
Of other days around me;
The smiles, the tears,
Of boyhood's years,
The words of love then spoken;
The eyes that shone,
Now dimmed and gone,
The cheerful hearts now broken!
National Airs, 'Oft in the Stilly Night'

Moravia, Alberto (Alberto Pincherle; 1907–90) Italian novelist. His books include *The Time of Indifference* (1929), *Roman Tales* (1954), *The Lie* (1966), *1934* (1983), and *Erotic Tales* (1985).

1 The ratio of literacy to illiteracy is constant, but nowadays the illiterates can read and write.
The Observer, 14 Oct 1979

More, Sir Thomas (1478–1535) English lawyer, scholar, and saint. As chancellor to Henry VIII (1529–32), he opposed the king's assumption of the headship of the English Church; he was subsequently imprisoned, tried, and beheaded for treason.

1 Yea, marry, now it is somewhat, for now it is rhyme; before, it was neither rhyme nor reason.
On reading an unremarkable book recently rendered into verse by a friend of his
Apophthegms (Bacon), 287

2 I cumber you goode Margaret muche, but I woulde be sorye, if it shoulde be any lenger than to morrowe, for it is S. Thomas evin and the vtas of Sainte Peter and therefore to morowe longe I to goe to God, it were a daye very meete and conveniente for me. I neuer liked your maner towarde me better then when you kissed me laste for I loue when doughterly loue and deere charitie hathe no laisor to looke to worldely curtesye. Fare well my deere childe and praye for me, and I shall for you and all your friendes that we maie merily meete in heaven.
Last letter to Margaret Roper, his daughter, on the eve of his execution on 6 July 1535

3 I pray you, Master Lieutenant, see me safe up, and for coming down let me shift for myself.
On climbing onto the scaffold prior to his execution
Life of Sir Thomas More (William Roper)

4 Pluck up thy spirits, man, and be not afraid to do thine office; my neck is very short; take heed therefore thou strike not awry, for saving of thine honesty.

Said to the headsman at his execution
Life of Sir Thomas More (Roper)

5 This hath not offended the king.

Said as he drew his beard aside before putting his head on the block

Morell, Thomas (1703–84) British classicist, who edited the works of Chaucer and Spenser. He wrote the librettos for Handel's oratorios *Judas Maccabaeus* (1746) and *Joshua* (1748).

1 See, the conquering hero comes!
Sound the trumpets, beat the drums!

The libretto for Handel's oratorio
Joshua, Pt. III

Morgan, Augustus de (1806–71) British mathematician and logician. He developed a new system of nomenclature for logical expression, formulated 'de Morgan's theorem', and advocated decimal coinage.

1 Great fleas have little fleas upon their backs to bite 'em,
And little fleas have lesser fleas, and so *ad infinitum.*

A Budget of Paradoxes

Morgan, Elaine (1920–) British writer and educator. She has written a number of plays and television scripts.

1 The trouble with specialists is that they tend to think in grooves.

The Descent of Woman, Ch. 1

2 . . . the rumblings of women's liberation are only one pointer to the fact that you already have a discontented work force. And if conditions continue to lag so far behind the industrial norm and the discomfort increases, you will find . . . that you will end up with an inferior product.

The Descent of Woman, Ch. 11

Morgenstern, Christian (1871–1914) German poet. His collections include *Ich und die Welt* (1898) and *Ich und Du* (1911).

1 There is a ghost
That eats handkerchiefs;
It keeps you company
On all your travels.

Der Gingganz, 'Gespenst'

Morley, Christopher Darlington (1890–1957) US writer and journalist. His books include *Parnassus on Wheels* (1917), *Kathleen* (1920), *Where The Blue Begins* (1922) and *Thunder on the Left* (1925).

1 There are three ingredients in the good life: learning, earning and yearning.

Parnassus on Wheels, Ch. 10

2 Why do they put the Gideon Bibles only in the bedrooms where it's usually too late?

Quotations for Speakers and Writers

Morley, Robert (1908–) British actor. His many films include *Major Barbara* (1940), *Oscar Wilde* (1960), *The Blue Bird* (1976), and *High Road to China* (1982).

1 Beware of the conversationalist who adds 'in other words'. He is merely starting afresh.

The Observer, 'Sayings of the Week', 6 Dec 1964

2 There's no such thing in Communist countries as a load of old cod's wallop, the cod's wallop is always fresh made.

Punch, 20 Feb 1974

Morpurgo, J(ack) E(ric) (1918–) British writer and academic. Professor of American Literature at Sussex University (1969–83), he has written books on history, travel, and literary criticism.

1 Austria is Switzerland speaking pure German and with history added.

The Road to Athens

Morris, Desmond (1928–) British biologist and writer. His books, including *The Naked Ape* (1967), *Manwatching* (1977), and *Bodywatching* (1985), draw parallels between human and animal behaviour.

1 Clearly, then, the city is not a concrete jungle, it is a human zoo.

The Human Zoo, Introduction

2 Observe diners arriving at any restaurant and you will see them make a bee-line for the wall-seats. No one ever voluntarily selects a centre table in an open space. Open seating positions are only taken when all the wall-seats are already occupied. This dates back to a primeval feeding practice of avoiding sudden attack during the deep concentration involved in consuming food.

Manwatching, 'Feeding Behaviour'

3 There are one hundred and ninety-three living species of monkeys and apes. One hundred and ninety-two of them are covered with hair. The exception is a naked ape self-named *Homo sapiens.*

The Naked Ape, Introduction

4 He is proud that he has the biggest brain of all the primates, but attempts to conceal the fact that he also has the biggest penis.

The Naked Ape, Introduction

Morris, George Pope (1802–64) US journalist. He edited several papers and published a volume of collected verse containing the poems 'Woodman, Spare That Tree' and 'My Mother's Bible'.

1 Woodman, spare that tree!
Touch not a single bough!
In youth it sheltered me,
And I'll protect it now.

Woodman, Spare That Tree

Morris, William (1834–96) British designer, artist, and poet. Associated with the Pre-Raphaelite Brotherhood, he designed stained glass, carpets, wallpaper, and furniture and founded the Kemoscott Press in 1890; his ideas influenced both the Arts and Crafts movement and the development of British socialism.

1 It is not this or that tangible steel or brass machine which we want to get rid of, but the great intangible machine of commercial tyrrany which oppresses the lives of us all.
Arts and Crafts Movement

2 Nothing should be made by man's labour which is not worth making or which must be made by labour degrading to the makers.
Arts and Crafts Movement

3 I don't want art for a few, any more than education for a few, or freedom for a few.
Arts and Crafts Movement

4 Art will make our streets as beautiful as the woods, as elevating as the mountain-side: it will be a pleasure and a rest, and not a weight upon the spirits to come from the open country into a town. Every man's house will be fair and decent, soothing to his mind and helpful to his work.
Arts and Crafts Movement

Mortimer, John Clifford (1923–) British lawyer, novelist, and dramatist. Best-known for his TV series about Horace Rumpole, a fictional barrister, his plays include *The Dock Brief* (1958); among his novels are *Paradise Postponed* (1985) and *Summer's Lease* (1988).

1 Eddy was a tremendously tolerant person, but he wouldn't put up with the Welsh. He always said, surely there's enough English to go round.
Two Stars for Comfort, I:2

2 No brilliance is needed in the law. Nothing but common sense, and relatively clean finger nails.
A Voyage Round My Father, I

Morton, J. B. (1893–1979) British journalist and story writer, who for many years wrote a newspaper column under the name 'Beachcomber'.

1 She has a Rolls body and a Balham mind.
The Best of Beachcomber, 'A Foul Innuendo'

2 SIXTY HORSES WEDGED IN A CHIMNEY
The story to fit this sensational headline has not turned up yet.
The Best of Beachcomber, 'Mr Justice Cocklecarrot: Home Life'

3 Vegetarians have wicked, shifty eyes, and laugh in a cold and calculating manner. They pinch little children, steal stamps, drink water, favour beards . . . wheeze, squeak, drawl and maunder.
By the Way, '4 June'

4 Dr Strabismus (Whom God Preserve) of Utrecht is carrying out research work with a view to crossing salmon with mosquitoes. He says it will mean a bite every time for fishermen.
By the Way, 'January Tail-piece'

5 Wagner is the Puccini of music.
Attrib.

Mosley, Sir Oswald (1896–1980) British politician and founder of the British Union of Fascists (1932). His second wife (from 1936) was Diana Mitford.

1 Before the organization of the Blackshirt movement free speech did not exist in this country.
Selections from the *New Statesman, This England*, Pt. I

2 I am not and never have been, a man of the right. My position was on the left and is now in the centre of politics.
The Times, 26 Apr 1968

3 'Can't' will be the epitaph of the British Empire – unless we wake up in time.
Speech, Manchester, 9 Dec 1937

Motley, John Lothrop (1814–77) US historian and diplomat. His particular interest was the history of the Netherlands from 1847. He served as ambassador to Austria (1861–67) and Great Britain (1869–70).

1 Give us the luxuries of life, and we will dispense with its necessities.
The Autocrat of the Breakfast Table (O. W. Holmes), Ch. 6

Mountbatten of Burma, Louis, 1st Earl (1900–79) British admiral and diplomat. After active service in World War II, he was appointed the last Viceroy of India in 1947 and was governor general (1947–48). He was killed in Ireland by an IRA bomb.

Quotations about Mountbatten

1 When he finally retired as Chief of Defence Staff in 1965 there was a sigh of relief among the professionals. One can see why and understand, but his departure was the eclipse of a genius – maddening, unveracious, and arrogant, but a genius nevertheless.
Lord Blake. *The Times*, 14 Mar 1985

2 Not everyone liked him. He was too successful, too rich, too vain, and not quite clever enough to compensate for his faults, but surely no one would deny that he was a hero.
David Holloway (1924–) Literary editor. *The Daily Telegraph*, 20 Aug 1980

3 I am sure that Dickie has done marvellously. But it is curious that we should regard as a hero the man who liquidated the Empire which other heroes such as Clive, Warren Hastings, and Napier won for us. Very odd indeed.
Harold Nicolson (1886–1968) British writer. Diary, 3 June 1947

Quotations by Mountbatten

4 You can divide my life into two. During the first part of my life I was an ordinary conventional naval officer, trying not to be different in the sense of being royal, trying not to show myself off as being rich and ostentatious – like always using a small car to drive to the dockyard instead of my Rolls Royce.
Mountbatten, Hero of Our Time, Ch. 9 (Richard Hough)

5 Do you really think the IRA would think me a worthwhile target?
Mountbatten, Hero of Our Time, Ch. 11 (Richard Hough)

6 As a military man who has given half a century of active service, I say in all sincerity that the nuclear arms race has no military purpose. Wars cannot be fought with nuclear weapons; their existence only adds to our perils because of the illusions which they have generated.

Speech, Strasbourg, 11 May 1979

7 Actually I vote Labour, but my butler's a Tory.

Said to a Tory canvasser during the 1945 election

Muggeridge, Malcolm (1903–90) British writer and editor. The editor of *Punch* (1953–57), he wrote a number of books including *The Thirties* (1940), *Affairs of the Heart* (1949), and *Jesus Rediscovered* (1969), as well as an autobiography and diaries.

1 An orgy looks particularly alluring seen through the mists of righteous indignation.

The Most of Malcolm Muggeridge, 'Dolce Vita in a Cold Climate'

2 The orgasm has replaced the Cross as the focus of longing and the image of fulfilment.

The Most of Malcolm Muggeridge, 'Down with Sex'

3 Macmillan seemed, in his very person, to embody the national decay he supposed himself to be confuting. He exuded a flavour of mothballs.

Tread Softly For You Tread on My Jokes, 'England, whose England'

4 A ready means of being cherished by the English is to adopt the simple expedient of living a long time. I have little doubt that if, say, Oscar Wilde had lived into his nineties, instead of dying in his forties, he would have been considered a benign, distinguished figure suitable to preside at a school prize-giving or to instruct and exhort scoutmasters at their jamborees. He might even have been knighted.

Tread Softly for you Tread on my Jokes

5 Its avowed purpose is to excite sexual desire, which, I should have thought, it unnecessary in the case of the young, inconvenient in the case of the middle aged, and unseemly in the old.

Tread Softly For You Tread On My Jokes

6 He is not only a bore but he bores for England.

Referring to Sir Anthony Eden
In *Newstatesmanship* (E. Hyams), 'Boring for England'

Muir, Frank (1920–) British writer and broadcaster. With Dennis Norden he wrote many well-known comedy scripts. His books include *Frank Muir on Children* (1980) and *A Book at Bathtime* (1982).

1 I've examined your son's head, Mr Glum, and there's nothing there.

Take It from Here (Frank Muir and Dennis Norden), 1957

2 It has been said that a bride's attitude towards her betrothed can be summed up in three words: Aisle. Altar. Hymn.

Upon My Word! (Frank Muir and Dennis Norden), 'A Jug of Wine'

3 Another fact of life that will not have escaped you is that, in this country, the twenty-four-hour strike is like the twenty-four-hour flu. You have to reckon on it lasting at least five days.

You Can't Have Your Kayak and Heat It (Frank Muir and Dennis Norden), 'Great Expectations'

4 Dogs, like horses, are quadrupeds. That is to say, they have four rupeds, one at each corner, on which they walk.

You Can't Have Your Kayak and Heat It (Frank Muir and Denis Norden), 'Ta-ra-ra-boom-de-ay!'

Munro, Hector Hugh *See* Saki.

Münster, Ernst Friedrich Herbert (1766–1839) Hanovarian statesman. Ambassador to Russia (1801–04) and minister in London (1805–31), he was partly responsible for the entente between Russia and England.

1 Absolutism tempered by assassination.

Referring to the Russian Constitution
Letter

Murdoch, Dame Iris (1919–) Irish-born British novelist and philosophy teacher. Her novels include *The Bell* (1958), *A Severed Head* (1961), *The Sea, The Sea* (1978), *The Good Apprentice* (1985), and *The Message to the Planet* (1989).

1 All art deals with the absurd and aims at the simple. Good art speaks truth, indeed *is* truth, perhaps the only truth.

The Black Prince, 'Bradley Pearson's Foreword'

2 Writing is like getting married. One should never commit oneself until one is amazed at one's luck.

The Black Prince, 'Bradley Pearson's Foreword'

3 'What are you famous *for*?'
'For nothing. I am just famous.'

The Flight from the Enchanter

4 He led a double life. Did that make him a liar? He did not feel a liar. He was a man of two truths.

The Sacred and Profane Love Machine

5 Only lies and evil come from letting people off.

A Severed Head

Murphy, Arthur (1727–1805) Irish dramatist, writer, and actor. His plays include *The Apprentice* (1756) and *The Upholsterer* (1757). He also translated Sallust and Tacitus.

1 Above the vulgar flight of common souls.

Zenobia, V

Murphy, C. W. (19th century) British songwriter.

1 Has anybody here seen Kelly?
Kelly from the Isle of Man?

Has Anybody Here Seen Kelly?

Murray, David (1888–1962) British journalist and writer, editor of the *Times Literary Supplement* (1938–44).

1 A reporter is a man who has renounced everything in life but the world, the flesh, and the devil.

The Observer, 'Sayings of the Week', 5 July 1931

Musset, Alfred de (1810–57) French dramatist and poet. His *Contes d'Espagne et d'Italie* (1830) established his reputation; subsequent poems included 'La Nuit de mai' and 'L'Espoir en dieu'. *Barberine* (1835) and *Un Caprice* (1837) are his best-remembered plays. He had an affair with George Sand.

1 I cannot help it; – in spite of myself, infinity torments me.

L'Espoir en Dieu

2 Great artists have no country.

Lorenzaccio, I:5

Mussolini, Benito (1883–1945) Italian dictator, responsible for the organization and spread of fascism in Italy. In World War II he formed the Axis with Germany (1940); after the Allied invasion of Italy, he was deposed (1943) and murdered.

1 I should be pleased, I suppose, that Hitler has carried out a revolution on our lines. But they are Germans. So they will end by ruining our idea.

Benito Mussolini (C. Hibbert), Pt. II, Ch. 1

2 The Italians will laugh at me; every time Hitler occupies a country he sends me a message.

Hitler (Alan Bullock), Ch. 8

3 We cannot change our policy now. After all, we are not political whores.

Hitler (Alan Bullock), Ch. 8

4 Fascism is a religion; the twentieth century will be known in history as the century of Fascism.

On Hitler's seizing power
Sawdust Caesar (George Seldes), Ch. 24

5 Fascism is not an article for export.

Report in the German press, 1932

N

Nabokov, Vladimir (1899–1977) Russian-born US novelist. He was educated at Cambridge but emigrated to the USA in 1945. Of his many novels *Lolita* (1955) is the best known.

1 Lolita, light of my life, fire of my loins. My sin, my Soul.

Lolita

2 Life is a great surprise. I do not see why death should not be an even greater one.

Pale Fire, 'Commentary'

3 Like so many ageing college people, Pnin had long ceased to notice the existence of students on the campus.

Pnin, Ch. 3

4 Discussion in class, which means letting twenty young blockheads and two cocky neurotics discuss something that neither their teacher nor they know.

Pnin, Ch. 6

5 Poor Knight! he really had two periods, the first – a dull man writing broken English, the second – a broken man writing dull English.

The Real Life of Sebastian Knight, Ch. 1

6 Spring and summer did happen in Cambridge almost every year.

The Real Life of Sebastian Knight, Ch. 5

7 A novelist is, like all mortals, more fully at home on the surface of the present than in the ooze of the past.

Strong Opinions, Ch. 20

8 Literature and butterflies are the two sweetest passions known to man.

Radio Times, Oct 1962

Nairne, Carolina, Baroness (1766–1845) Scottish songwriter.

1 Better lo'ed ye canna be,
Will ye no come back again?

Referring to Bonnie Prince Charlie
Bonnie Charlie's now awa!

2 Charlie is my darling, my darling, my darling,
Charlie is my darling, the young Chevalier.

Referring to Bonnie Prince Charlie
Charlie is my Darling

3 Wi' a hundred pipers an' a', an' a'.

A romantic glorification of the 1745 Jacobite Rebellion
The Hundred Pipers

Napoleon I (Napoleon Bonaparte; 1769–1821) French emperor. Having extended his power into most of Europe, the disastrous invasion of Russia (1812) marked a turning point; after his defeat at Waterloo (1815) he was exiled to St Helena, where he died.

Quotations about Napoleon

1 That infernal creature who is the curse of all the human race becomes every day more and more abominable.

Alexander I (1777–1825) Tsar of Russia. Letter to his sister Catherine, 5 Jan 1812

2 Napoleon is a dangerous man in a free country. He seems to me to have the makings of a tyrant, and I believe that were he to be king he would be fully capable of playing such a part, and his name would become an object of detestation to posterity and every right-minded patriot.

Lucien Bonaparte (1775–1840) Younger brother of Napoleon. Letter to his brother Joseph, 1790

3 Napoleon – mighty somnambulist of a vanished dream.

Victor Hugo (1802–85) French writer. *Les Miserables*

4 Bonaparte's whole life, civil, political and military, was a fraud. There was not a transaction, great or small, in which lying and fraud were not introduced.
Duke of Wellington (1769–1852) British general and statesman.
Letter, 29 Dec 1835

Quotations by Napoleon

5 I still love you, but in politics there is no heart, only head.
Referring to his divorce, for reasons of state, from the Empress Josephine (1809)
Bonaparte (C. Barnett)

6 Maybe it would have been better if neither of us had been born.
Said while looking at the tomb of the philosopher Jean-Jacques Rousseau, whose theories had influenced the French Revolution
The Story of Civilization (W. Durant), Vol. II

7 There rises the sun of Austerlitz.
Said at the Battle of Borodino (7 Sept 1812), near Moscow; the Battle of Austerlitz (2 Dec 1805) was Napoleon's great victory over the Russians and Austrians

8 It's the most beautiful battlefield I've ever seen.
Referring to carnage on the field of Borodino, near Moscow, after the battle (7 Sept 1812)
Attrib.

9 It is only a step from the sublime to the ridiculous.
Remark following the retreat from Moscow, 1812
Attrib.

10 France has more need of me than I have need of France.
Speech, 31 Dec 1813

11 The bullet that is to kill me has not yet been moulded.
In reply to his brother Joseph, King of Spain, who had asked whether he had ever been hit by a cannonball
Attrib.

12 Oh well, no matter what happens, there's always death.
Attrib.

13 England is a nation of shopkeepers.
Attrib.

14 An army marches on its stomach.
Attrib.

15 *Tête d'Armée.*
Chief of the Army.
Last words
Attrib.

Napoleon III (1808–73) French emperor. The nephew of Napoleon I, he ruled for 20 years before being driven into exile during the Franco-Prussian War.

1 This vice brings in one hundred million francs in taxes every year. I will certainly forbid it at once – as soon as you can name a virtue that brings in as much revenue.
Reply when asked to ban smoking
Anekdotenschatz (H. Hoffmeister)

2 I don't care for war, there's far too much luck in it for my liking.
Said after the narrow but bloody French victory at Solferino (24 June 1859)
The Fall of the House of Habsburg (E. Crankshaw)

Narváez, Ramón Maria (1800–68) Spanish general and political leader, several times prime minister under Isabella II.

1 I do not have to forgive my enemies, I have had them all shot.
Said on his deathbed, when asked by a priest if he forgave his enemies.
Famous Last Words (B. Conrad)

Nash, Ogden (1902–71) US poet. He wrote many books of satirical verse, including *I'm a Stranger Here Myself* (1938) and *Collected Verse* (1961).

1 The cow is of the bovine ilk;
One end is moo, the other, milk.
The Cow

2 A door is what a dog is perpetually on the wrong side of.
A Dog's Best Friend Is His Illiteracy

3 To be an Englishman is to belong to the most exclusive club there is.
England Expects

4 Women would rather be right than reasonable.
Frailty, Thy Name Is a Misnomer

5 Home is heaven and orgies are vile
But you need an orgy, once in a while.
Home, 99.44 100% Sweet Home

6 Beneath this slab
John Brown is stowed.
He watched the ads
And not the road.
Lather as You Go

7 Do you think my mind is maturing late,
Or simply rotted early?
Lines on Facing Forty

8 Children aren't happy with nothing to ignore,
And that's what parents were created for.
The Parents

9 I prefer to forget both pairs of glasses and pass my declining years saluting strange women and grandfather clocks.
Peekaboo, I Almost See You

10 I think that I shall never see
A billboard lovely as a tree.
Perhaps unless the billboards fall,
I'll never see a tree at all.
Song of the Open Road

Neale, John Mason (1818–66) British churchman and hymn writer. His *Introduction to the History of the Holy Eastern Church* (1850) is less well-known than his hymn 'Jerusalem the Golden' and his carol 'Good King Wenceslas'.

1 Art thou weary, art thou languid,
Art thou sore distressed?
Art thou Weary?

2 Good King Wenceslas looked out,
On the Feast of Stephen;
When the snow lay round about,
Deep and crisp and even.

Good King Wenceslas

3 Jerusalem the golden,
With milk and honey blest,
Beneath thy contemplation
Sink heart and voice opprest.

Jerusalem the Golden

Needham, Joseph (1900–) British biochemist, who lived and worked in China. His books include *The Sceptical Biologist* (1929), *Science and Civilisation in China* (1954–), and *Celestial Lancets* (1980).

1 *Laboratorium est oratorium.* The place where we do our scientific work is a place of prayer.

The Harvest of a Quiet Eye (A. L. Mackay)

Nehru, Jawaharlal (1889–1964) Indian statesman; the first Prime Minister of independent India (1947–64). He abandoned his legal career to follow Gandhi in 1929 and was subsequently elected president of the Indian National Congress; he was the father of Indira Gandhi.

1 I do not know how to tell you and how to say it. Our beloved leader is no more.

Broadcast to the Indian nation telling them of Gandhi's assassination, Jan 1948.

Nelson, Horatio, Viscount (1758–1805) British admiral. Hero of many naval battles, he defeated the French at Trafalgar (1805) but was killed during the battle. His affair with Lady Hamilton caused a considerable scandal.

1 The Nelson touch.

Diary, 9 Oct 1805

2 You must hate a Frenchman as you hate the devil.

Life of Nelson (Southey), Ch. 3

3 I have only one eye: I have a right to be blind sometimes: I really do not see the signal.

Remark, Battle of Copenhagen, 2 Apr 1801; Nelson ignored Admiral Parker's order to disengage by placing his telescope to his blind eye; an hour later, he was victorious

Life of Nelson Ch. 7 (Robert Southey)

4 England expects every man will do his duty.

Signal hoisted prior to the Battle of Trafalgar, 1805

5 In case signals can neither be seen nor perfectly understood, no captain can do very wrong if he places his ship alongside that of an enemy.

Memorandum before Trafalgar, 9 Oct 1805

6 Kiss me, Hardy.

Last words, spoken to Sir Thomas Hardy, captain of the *Victory*, during the Battle of Trafalgar, 1805

Nevins, Allan (1890–1971) US historian. His books include *Grover Cleveland – A Study in Courage* (1932) and *The Gateway to History* (1938).

1 The former allies had blundered in the past by offering Germany too little, and offering even that too late, until finally Nazi Germany had become a menace to all mankind.

Current History, May 1935

Newbolt, Sir Henry John (1862–1938) British poet. An authority on the British navy, many of his poems are about the sea and his *Songs of the Sea* (1904) and *Songs of the Fleet* (1910) were set to music by Stanford.

1 He clapped the glass to his sightless eye,
And 'I'm damned if I see it', he said.

Referring to Lord Nelson at the battle of Copenhagen
Admirals All

2 'Take my drum to England, hang et by the shore,
Strike et when your powder's runnin' low;
If the Dons sight Devon, I'll quit the port o' Heaven,
An' drum them up the Channel as we drummed them long ago.'

Drake's Drum

3 Drake he's in his hammock till the great Armadas come.
(Capten, art tha sleepin' there below?)
Slung atween the round shot, listenin' for the drum,
An dreamin' arl the time o' Plymouth Hoe.

Drake's Drum

4 Now the sunset breezes shiver,
And she's fading down the river,
But in England's song for ever
She's the Fighting Téméraire.

The Fighting Téméraire

5 But cared greatly to serve God and the King,
And keep the Nelson touch.

See NELSON
Minora Sidera

6 There's a breathless hush in the Close tonight –
Ten to make and the match to win –
A bumping pitch and a blinding light,
An hour to play and the last man in.

Vitaï Lampada

7 The sand of the desert is sodden red, –
Red with the wreck of a square that broke; –
The gatling's jammed and the colonel dead,
And the regiment blind with the dust and smoke.
The river of death has brimmed its banks
And England's far and honour a name.
But the voice of a schoolboy rallies the ranks:
'Play up! play up! and play the game!'

Vitaï Lampada

Newcastle, Margaret, Duchess of (1624–74) Second wife of William Cavendish, 1st Duke of Newcastle, the Royalist leader and patron of the arts. She wrote several volumes of poems, letters, and plays.

1 For all the Brothers were valiant, and all the Sisters virtuous.

Epitaph, in Westminster Abbey

Newley, Anthony (1931–) British actor, composer, singer, and comedian.

1 Stop the World, I Want to Get Off.

With Leslie Bricusse
Title of musical

Newman, Ernest (1868–1959) British music critic and writer. He wrote studies of several composers, including Wagner and Elgar.

1 I sometimes wonder which would be nicer – an opera without an interval, or an interval without an opera.

Berlioz, Romantic and Classic, (ed. Peter Heyworth)

2 The higher the voice the smaller the intellect.

Attrib.

Newman, John Henry, Cardinal (1801–90) British theologian. His *Tracts for the Times* (from 1833) gave their name to the Tractarian Movement. He published many theological works, including the hymn *Lead, Kindly Light* (1833).

1 It is very difficult to get up resentment towards persons whom one has never seen.

Apologia pro Vita Sua (1864), 'Mr Kingsley's Method of Disputation'

2 It is almost a definition of a gentleman to say that he is one who never inflicts pain.

The Idea of a University, 'Knowledge and Religious Duty'

3 Lead, kindly Light, amid the encircling gloom,
Lead thou me on;
The night is dark, and I am far from home,
Lead thou me on.

Lead Kindly Light

4 She holds that it were better for sun and moon to drop from heaven, for the earth to fail, and for all the many millions who are upon it to die of starvation in extremest agony, as far as temporal affliction goes, than that one soul, I will not say, should be lost, but should commit one single venial sin, should tell one wilful untruth, . . . or steal one poor farthing without excuse.

Referring to the Roman Catholic Church
Lectures on Anglican Difficulties, VIII

5 *We can believe what we choose.* We are answerable for what we choose to believe.

Letter to Mrs Froude, 27 June 1848

6 When men understand what each other mean, they see, for the most part, that controversy is either superfluous or hopeless.

Sermon, Oxford, Epiphany 1839

Newton, Sir Isaac (1642–1727) British scientist, one of the greatest of all time, who discovered gravitation, recognized that white light is a mixture of coloured lights, invented calculus, and laid the foundations of dynamics with his laws of motion. His principal publications were the *Principia Mathematica* (1686–87) and *Optiks* (1704).

Quotations about Newton

1 He lived the life of a solitary, and like all men who are occupied with profound meditation, he acted strangely. Sometimes, in getting out of bed, an idea would come to him, and he would sit on the edge of the bed, half dressed, for hours at a time.

Louis Figuier (1819–94) French writer. *Vies des Savants* (translated by B.H. Clark)

2 Sir Isaac Newton, though so deep in algebra and fluxions, could not readily make up a common account; and whilst he was Master of the Mint, used to get someone to make up the accounts for him.

Alexander Pope (1688–1744) British poet. *Observations, Anecdotes and characters* (Rev. Joseph Spence)

3 He was a highly neurotic young don at Trinity College, Cambridge, who became the most revolutionary mathematician in Europe at the age of 24.

Michael Ratcliffe *The Times,* 26 Mar 1981

Quotations by Newton

4 Nature is very consonant and conformable with herself.

Opticks, Bk. III

5 I do not know what I may appear to the world, but to myself I seem to have been only like a boy playing on the sea-shore, and diverting myself in now and then finding a smoother pebble or a prettier shell than ordinary, whilst the great ocean of truth lay all undiscovered before me.

Isaac Newton (L. T. More)

6 O Diamond! Diamond! thou little knowest the mischief done!

Said to a dog that set fire to some papers, representing several years' work, by knocking over a candle
Wensley-Dale . . . a Poem (Thomas Maude)

7 If I have seen further it is by standing on the shoulders of giants.

Letter to Robert Hooke, 5 Feb 1675

Newton, John (1725–1807) British hymn writer and clergyman. After several years as a naval midshipman, and then a slave trader, he was ordained and became a curate at Olney. He became friendly with Cowper and joint writer with him of the *Olney Hymns* (1779).

1 Glorious things of thee are spoken,
Zion, city of our God.

Glorious Things

2 How sweet the name of Jesus sounds.
In a believer's ear!

The Name of Jesus

Nicholas I (1796–1855) Tsar of Russia. A notorious autocrat, his attempts to take Constantinople instigated war with Turkey, which led to the Crimean War.

1 We have on our hands a sick man – a very sick man.

Referring to Turkey, the 'sick man of Europe'; said to Sir G. H. Seymour, British envoy to St Petersburg, Jan 1853
Attrib.

2 Russia has two generals in whom she can confide – Generals Janvier and Février.

Referring to the Russian winter. Nicholas himself succumbed to a February cold in 1855 – the subject of the famous *Punch* Cartoon, 'General Février turned traitor', 10 Mar 1855
Attrib.

Niebuhr, Reinhold (1892–1971) US churchman. He wrote a number of books, including *Does Civilization Need Religion* (1927) and *Beyond Tragedy* (1937).

1 Man's capacity for evil makes democracy necessary and man's capacity for good makes democracy possible.

Quoted by Anthony Wedgwood Benn in *The Times*, 18 July 1977

Niemöller, Martin (1892–1984) German pastor. He was a U-boat commander in World War I, ordained in 1924, dismissed from his post by the Nazis in 1934, and sent to a concentration camp in 1937. He survived to become a bishop in the Evangelical Church.

1 In Germany, the Nazis came for the Communists and I didn't speak up because I was not a Communist. Then they came for the Jews and I didn't speak up because I was not a Jew. Then they came for the trade unionists and I didn't speak up because I was not a trade unionist. Then they came for the Catholics and I was a Protestant so I didn't speak up. Then they came for me . . . By that time there was no one to speak up for anyone.

Concise Dictionary of Religious Quotations (W. Neil)

Nietzsche, Friedrich Wilhelm (1844–1900) German philosopher. His rejection of all religion and his glorification of the superman in *Thus Spake Zarathustra* (1883–92) influenced Nazi philosophy in Germany.

Quotations about Nietzsche

1 Nietzsche . . . was a confirmed Life Force worshipper. It was he who raked up the Superman, who is as old as Prometheus.

George Bernard Shaw (1856–1950) Irish dramatist and critic.
Man and Superman, III

Quotations by Nietzsche

2 When a man is in love he endures more than at other times; he submits to everything.

The Antichrist

3 God created woman. And boredom did indeed cease from that moment – but many other things ceased as well! Woman was God's *second* mistake.

The Antichrist

4 I call Christianity the one great curse, the one enormous and innermost perversion, the one great instinct of revenge, for which no means are too venomous, too underhand, too underground and too petty – I call it the one immortal blemish of mankind.

The Antichrist

5 God is dead: but considering the state the species Man is in, there will perhaps be caves, for ages yet, in which his shadow will be shown.

Die Fröhliche Wissenschaft, Bk. III

6 Believe me! The secret of reaping the greatest fruitfulness and the greatest enjoyment from life is to *live dangerously!*

Die Fröhliche Wissenschaft, Bk. IV

7 As an artist, a man has no home in Europe save in Paris.

Ecce Homo

8 My time has not yet come either; some are born posthumously.

Ecce Homo

9 My doctrine is: Live that thou mayest desire to live again – that is thy duty – for in any case thou wilt live again!

Eternal Recurrence

10 Do you really believe that the sciences would ever have originated and grown if the way had not been prepared by magicians, alchemists, astrologers and witches whose promises and pretensions first had to create a thirst, a hunger, a taste for *hidden* and *forbidden* powers? Indeed, infinitely more had to be *promised* than could ever be fulfilled in order that anything at all might be fulfilled in the realms of knowledge.

The Gay Science

11 The thought of suicide is a great source of comfort: with it a calm passage is to be made across many a bad night.

Jenseits von Gut und Böse

12 Morality in Europe today is herd-morality.

Jenseits von Gut und Böse

13 Is not life a hundred times too short for us to bore ourselves?

Jenseits von Gut und Böse

14 In the philosopher there is nothing whatever impersonal; and, above all, his morality bears decided and decisive testimony to *who he is* – that is to say, to the order of rank in which the innermost drives of his nature stand in relation to one another.

Jenseits von Gut und Böse

15 Insects sting, not from malice, but because they want to live. It is the same with critics – they desire our blood, not our pain.

Miscellaneous Maxims and Reflections

16 He who does not need to lie is proud of not being a liar.

Nachgelassene Fragmente

17 I teach you the Superman. Man is something that is to be surpassed.

Thus Spake Zarathustra

18 To show pity is felt as a sign of contempt because one has clearly ceased to be an object of *fear* as soon as one is pitied.

The Wanderer and His Shadow

Nightingale, Florence (1820–1910) British nurse. She worked under appalling conditions in the Crimean War, becoming known as 'The Lady with the Lamp'. Later she founded the Nightingale School of Nurses at St Thomas's Hospital, London.

1 It may seem a strange principle to enunciate as the very first requirement in a Hospital that it should do the sick no harm.

Notes on Hospitals, Preface

2 No *man*, not even a doctor, ever gives any other definition of what a nurse should be than this – "devoted and obedient." This definition would do just as well for a porter. It might even do for a horse. It would not do for a policeman.

Notes on Nursing

3 To understand God's thoughts we must study statistics, for these are the measure of his purpose.

Life . . . of Francis Galton (K. Pearson), Vol. II, Ch. 13

4 The first possibility of rural cleanliness lies in *watersupply*.

Letter to Medical Officer of Health, Nov 1891

Niven, David (1909–83) British film actor. His films include *The Prisoner of Zenda* (1937), *The Guns of Navarone* (1961), *Paper Tiger* (1975), and *Candleshoe* (1977). His two volumes of autobiography, *The Moon's a Balloon* (1972) and *Bring on the Empty Horses* (1975) became bestsellers.

1 The Moon's a Balloon.

From e. e. cummings, '&': 'Who knows if the moon's a balloon, coming out of a keen city in the sky – filled with pretty people?'
Book title

2 Volunteers usually fall into two groups. There are the genuinely courageous who are itching to get at the throat of the enemy, and the restless who will volunteer for anything in order to escape from the boredom of what they are presently doing.

The Moon's a Balloon, Ch. 12

3 War is a great accelerator of events so ten days later, we were married in the tiny Norman church of Huish village at the foot of the Wiltshire Downs. Trubshawe, now in the uniform of the Royal Sussex Regiment, was best man, and friends from far and near came by train, by bicycle or by blowing their petrol rations for a month – some came on horseback.

The Moon's a Balloon, Ch. 12

Niven, Larry (1938–) US science-fiction writer. His works include *Ringworld* (1970) and, with Jerry Pournelle, *The Mote in God's Eye* (1974), *Lucifer's Hammer* (1977), and *Footfall* (1985).

1 On my twenty-first birthday my father said, 'Son, here's a million dollars. Don't lose it.'

When asked 'What is the best advice you have ever been given?'
Attrib.

Nixon, Richard Milhous (1913–) US president. A republican, he became president in 1969 and was responsible for ending the US commitment in Vietnam (1973). He was forced to resign after the Watergate scandal (1974), but was pardoned by his successor, President Ford.

Quotations about Nixon

1 President Nixon's motto was, if two wrongs don't make a right, try three.

Norman Cousins *Daily Telegraph*, 17 July 1969

2 Nixon is the kind of politician who would cut down a redwood tree and then mount the stump to make a speech for conservation.

Adlai Stevenson (1900–65) US statesman. Attrib.

Quotations by Nixon

3 There can be no whitewash at the White House.

Referring to the Watergate scandal
The Observer, 'Sayings of the Week', 30 Dec 1973

4 I let down my friends, I let down my country. I let down our system of government.

The Observer, 'Sayings of the Week', 8 May 1977

5 You won't have Nixon to kick around any more, gentlemen. This is my last Press Conference.

Press conference for governorship of California, 2 Nov 1962

6 Let us begin by committing ourselves to the truth, to see it like it is and to tell it like it is, to find the truth, to speak the truth and live with the truth. That's what we'll do.

Nomination acceptance speech, Miami, 8 Aug 1968

7 It is time for the great silent majority of Americans to stand up and be counted.

Election speech, Oct 1970

8 This is the greatest week in the history of the world since the creation.

Said when men first landed on the moon
Attrib., 24 July 1969

9 I don't give a shit what happens. I want you all to stonewall it, let them plead the Fifth Amendment, cover-up or anything else, if it'll save it, save the plan.

Referring to the Watergate cover-up
In conversation, 22 Mar 1973 (tape transcript)

10 I am not a crook.

Attrib., 17 Nov 1973

Norden, Dennis (1922–) British scriptwriter and broadcaster. With Frank Muir he wrote many comedy radio scripts. His books include *Upon My Word* (1974) and *Oh, My Word!* (1980).
See Muir, Frank.

Norman, Barry (1933–) British cinema critic and broadcaster.

1 Perhaps at fourteen every boy should be in love with some ideal woman to put on a pedestal and worship. As he grows up, of course, he will put her on a pedestal the better to view her legs.

The Listener

Norman, Frank (1931–80) British dramatist and novelist. His low-life musicals include *Fings Ain't Wot They Used T'Be* (1959) and *A Kayf Up West* (1964).

1 Fings Ain't Wot They Used T'Be.

Title of musical

North, Christopher (John Wilson; 1785–1854) Scottish poet, essayist, and critic. His works include poetry, fiction, and *Noctes Ambrosianae* (1822–35), a collection of articles on literature, politics, and philosophy.

1 His Majesty's dominions, on which the sun never sets.

Noctes Ambrosianae, 20 Apr 1829

2 Laws were made to be broken.

Noctes Ambrosianae, 24 May 1830

Northcliffe, Alfred Charles William Harmsworth, Viscount (1865–1922) Irish-born British newspaper proprietor, who, with his brother, who became Lord Rothermere, bought the *Evening News* (1894). He later founded the *Daily Mail* and the *Daily Mirror* and acquired control of *The Times*.

1 They are only ten.

Rumoured to have been a notice to remind his staff of his opinion of the mental age of the general public
Attrib.

2 When I want a peerage, I shall buy one like an honest man.

Attrib.

Northcote, Sir Stafford, 1st Earl of Iddesleigh (1818–87) British statesman. An MP, he became chancellor of the exchequer (1874–80) in Disraeli's administration and foreign secretary (1886) under Gladstone.

1 Argue as you please, you are nowhere, that grand old man, the Prime Minister, insists on the other thing.

Referring to Gladstone; the phrase, and its acronym GOM, became his nickname – temporarily reversed to MOG ('Murderer of Gordon') in 1885, after the death of General Gordon at Khartoum
Speech, Liverpool, 12 Apr 1882

Norton, Caroline Elizabeth Sarah (1808–77) British poet and writer. She wrote a pamphlet on divorce reform but is remembered for her poetry.

1 I do not love thee! – no! I do not love thee!
And yet when thou art absent I am sad.

I do Not Love Thee

Norworth, Jack (1879–1959) US vaudeville comedian and songwriter.

1 Oh! shine on, shine on, harvest moon
Up in the sky.
I ain't had no lovin'
Since April, January, June or July.

Shine On, Harvest Moon (song)

Nostradamus (Michel de Notredame; 1503–66) French astrologer and physician. His famous prophecies were composed in rhyming quotations and first appeared in 1555.

1 At night they will think they have seen the sun, when they see the half pig man: Noise, screams, battle seen fought in the skies. The brute beasts will be heard to speak.

Thought to prophecy a 20th-century air-battle
The Prophecies of Nostradamus, Century I, 64

2 The blood of the just will be demanded of London burnt by fire in three times twenty plus six. The ancient lady will fall from her high position, and many of the same denomination will be killed.

Believed to refer to the Great Fire of London, 1666. The 'ancient lady' is interpreted as the Cathedral of St. Paul's, which was destroyed in the fire
The Prophecies of Nostradamus, Century II, 51

Novello, Ivor (David Ivor Davies; 1893–1951) British actor, composer, and dramatist. In World War I he wrote 'Keep the Home Fires Burning' and later wrote a number of musicals, including *Careless Rapture* (1936) and *The Dancing Years* (1939).

1 And Her Mother Came Too.

Title of song

2 There's something Vichy about the French.

Ambrosia and Small Beer (Edward Marsh), Ch. 4

Noyes, Alfred (1880–1958) British poet. His epic narrative poems include *Drake* (1906–08) and *The Torchbearers* (1922–30).

1 The wind was a torrent of darkness among the gusty trees,
The moon was a ghostly galleon tossed upon cloudy seas,
The road was a ribbon of moonlight over the purple moor,
And the highwayman came riding –
Riding – riding –
The highwayman came riding, up to the old inn-door.

The Highwayman

2 Look for me by moonlight;
Watch for me by moonlight;
I'll come to thee by moonlight, though hell should bar the way!

The Highwayman

Nursery Rhymes A selection of nursery rhymes is given here. The wording used is the one most commonly used today; not the form in the form in the original publication.

1   A frog he would a-wooing go,
    Heigh ho! says Rowley,
    A frog he would a-wooing go,
    Whether his mother would let him or no.
    With a rowley, powley, gammon and spinach,
    Heigh ho! says Anthony Rowley.
    Melismata (Thomas Ravenscroft)

2   All the birds of the air
    Fell a-sighing and a-sobbing,
    When they heard the bell toll
    For poor Cock Robin.
    Tommy Thumb's Pretty Song Book

3   As I was going to St Ives,
    I met a man with seven wives.
    Each wife had seven sacks
    Each sack had seven cats,
    Each cat had seven kits,
    How many were going to St Ives?
    Mother Goose's Quarto

4   Baa, baa, black sheep,
    Have you any wool?
    Yes, sir, yes, sir,
    Three bags full;
    One for the master,
    And one for the dame,
    And one for the little boy
    Who lives down the lane.
    Tommy Thumb's Pretty Song Book

5   Bobby Shafto's gone to sea,
    Silver buckles on his knee;
    He'll come back and marry me,
    Bonny Bobby Shafto!
    Songs for the Nursery

6   Boys and girls come out to play,
    The moon doth shine as bright as day.
    Useful Transactions in Philosophy (William King)

7   Come, let's to bed
    Says Sleepy-head;
    Tarry a while, says Slow;
    Put on the pan;
    Says Greedy Nan,
    Let's sup before we go.
    Gammer Gurton's Garland (R. Christopher)

8   Curly locks, Curly locks,
    Wilt thou be mine?
    Thou shalt not wash dishes
    Nor yet feed the swine,
    But sit on a cushion
    And sew a fine seam,
    And feed upon strawberries,
    Sugar and cream
    Infant Institutes

9   Ding dong, bell,
    Pussy's in the well.
    Who put her in?
    Little Johnny Green.
    Who pulled her out?
    Little Tommy Stout.
    Mother Goose's Melody

10 Doctor Foster went to Gloucester
    In a shower of rain:
    He stepped in a puddle,
    Right up to his middle,
    And never went there again.
    The Nursery Rhymes of England (J. O. Halliwell)

11 Eena, meena, mina, mo,
    Catch a nigger by his toe;
    If he hollers, let him go,
    Eena, meena, mina, mo.
    Games and Songs of American Children (Newell)

12 Georgie Porgie, pudding and pie,
    Kissed the girls and made them cry;
    When the boys came out to play,
    Georgie Porgie ran away.
    The Nursery Rhymes of England (J. O. Halliwell)

13 Goosey, goosey gander,
    Whither shall I wander?
    Upstairs and downstairs
    And in my lady's chamber
    Gammer Gurton' Garland

14 Hey diddle diddle,
    The cat and the fiddle,
    The cow jumped over the moon;
    The little dog laughed
    To see such sport,
    And the dish ran away with the spoon.
    Mother Goose's Melody

15 Hickory, dickory, dock,
    The mouse ran up the clock.
    The clock struck one,
    The mouse ran down,
    Hickory, dickory, dock.
    Tommy Thumb's Pretty Song Book

16 Hot cross buns!
    Hot cross buns!
    One a penny, two a penny,
    Hot cross buns!
    Christmas Box

17 How many miles to Babylon?
    Three score miles and ten.
    Can I get there by candle-light?
    Yes, and back again.
    If your heels are nimble and light,
    You may get there by candle-light.
    Songs for the Nursery

18 Humpty Dumpty sat on a wall,
    Humpty Dumpty had a great fall.
    All the king's horses,
    And all the king's men,
    Couldn't put Humpty together again.
    Gammer Gurton's Garland

19 Hush-a-bye, baby, on the tree top,
    When the wind blows the cradle will rock;
    When the bough breaks the cradle will fall,
    Down will come baby, cradle, and all.
    Mother Goose's Melody

20 I had a little nut tree,
Nothing would it bear
But a silver nutmeg
And a golden pear;
The King of Spain's daughter
Came to visit me,
And all for the sake
Of my little nut tree.

Newest Christmas Box

21 I had a little pony,
His name was Dapple Grey;
I lent him to a lady
To ride a mile away.
She whipped him, she lashed him,
She rode him through the mire;
I would not lend my pony now,
For all the lady's hire.

Poetical Alphabet

22 I love sixpence, jolly little sixpence,
I love sixpence better than my life;
I spent a penny of it, I lent a penny of it,
And I took fourpence home to my wife.

Gammer Gurton's Garland

23 I'm the king of the castle,
Get down you dirty rascal.

Brand's Popular Antiquities

24 I see the moon,
And the moon sees me;
God bless the moon,
And God bless me.

Gammer Gurton's Garland

25 Jack and Jill went up the hill
To fetch a pail of water;
Jack fell down and broke his crown,
And Jill came tumbling after.

Mother Goose's Melody

26 Jack Sprat could eat no fat,
His wife could eat no lean,
And so between them both you see,
They licked the platter clean.

Paroemiologia Anglo-Latina (John Clark)

27 Ladybird, ladybird,
Fly away home,
Your house is on fire
And your children all gone.

Tommy Thumb's Pretty Song Book

28 Little Bo-peep has lost her sheep,
And can't tell where to find them;
Leave them alone, and they'll come home,
Bringing their tails behind them.

Gammer Gurton's Garland

29 Little Boy Blue,
Come blow your horn,
The sheep's in the meadow,
The cow's in the corn.

Famous Tommy Thumb's Little Story Book

30 Little Jack Horner
Sat in the corner,
Eating a Christmas pie;
He put in his thumb,
And pulled out a plum,
And said, What a good boy am I!

Namby Pamby (Henry Carey)

31 Little Miss Muffet
Sat on a tuffet,
Eating her curds and whey;
There came a big spider,
Who sat down beside her
And frightened Miss Muffet away.

Songs for the Nursery

32 Little Tommy Tucker,
Sings for his supper:
What shall we give him?
White bread and butter
How shall he cut it
Without a knife?
How will be be married
Without a wife?

Tommy Thumb's Pretty Song Book

33 London Bridge is broken down,
My fair lady.

Namby Pamby (Henry Carey)

34 Mary, Mary, quite contrary,
How does your garden grow?
With silver bells and cockle shells,
And pretty maids all in a row.

Tommy Thumb's Pretty Song Book

35 Monday's child is fair of face,
Tuesday's child is full of grace,
Wednesday's child is full of woe,
Thursday's child has far to go,
Friday's child is loving and giving,
Saturday's child works hard for his living,
And the child that is born on the Sabbath day
Is bonny and blithe, and good and gay.

Traditions of Devonshire (A. E. Bray)

36 My mother said that I never should
Play with the gypsies in the wood;
If I did, she would say,
Naughty girl to disobey.

Come Hither (Walter de la Mare)

37 Oh! the grand old Duke of York
He had ten thousand men;
He marched them up to the top of the hill,
And he marched them down again.
And when they were up they were up,
And when they were down they were down,
And when they were only half way up,
They were neither up nor down.

Traditional

38 Old King Cole
Was a merry old soul,
And a merry old soul was he;
He called for his pipe,
And he called for his bowl,
And he called for his fiddlers three.

Useful Transactions in Philosophy (William King)

39 Old Mother Hubbard
Went to the cupboard,
To fetch her poor dog a bone;
But when she got there
The cupboard was bare
And so the poor dog had none.

The Comic Adventures of Old Mother Hubbard and Her Dog

40 One, two,
Buckle my shoe;
Three, four,
Knock at the door.

Songs for the Nursery

41 Oranges and lemons,
Say the bell of St Clement's.
You owe me five farthings,
Say the bells of St Martin's.
When will you pay me?
Say the bells of Old Bailey.
When I grow rich,
Say the bells of Shoreditch.
When will that be?
Say the bells of Stepney.
I'm sure I don't know,
Says the great bell at Bow.
Here comes a candle to light you to bed,
Here comes a chopper to chop off your head.

Tommy Thumb's Pretty Song Book

42 Pat-a-cake, pat-a-cake, baker's man,
Bake me a cake as fast as you can;
Pat it and prick it, and mark it with B,
Put it in the oven for baby and me.

The Campaigners (Tom D'Urfey)

43 Peter Piper picked a peck of pickled pepper;
A peck of pickled pepper Peter Piper picked;
If Peter Piper picked a peck of pickled pepper,
Where's the peck of pickled pepper Peter Piper
picked?

*Peter Piper's Practical Principles of Plain and Perfect
Pronunciation*

44 Polly put the kettle on,
Polly put the kettle on,
Polly put the kettle on,
We'll all have tea.

Sukey take it off again,
Sukey take it off again,
Sukey take it off again,
They've all gone away.

Traditional

45 Pussy cat, pussy cat, where have you been?
I've been to London to look at the queen.
Pussy cat, pussy cat, what did you there?
I frightened a little mouse under her chair.

Songs for the Nursery

46 Ride a cock-horse to Banbury Cross,
To see a fine lady upon a white horse;
Rings on her fingers and bells on her toes,
And she shall have music wherever she goes.

Gammer Gurton's Garland

47 Ring-a-ring o'roses,
A pocket full of posies,
A-tishoo! A-tishoo!
We all fall down.

Mother Goose (Kate Greenway)

48 Round and round the garden
Like a teddy bear;
One step, two step,
Tickle you under there!

Traditional

49 Rub-a-dub-dub,
Three men in a tub,
And who do you think they be?
The butcher, the baker,
The candlestick-maker,
And they all sailed out to sea.

Christmas Box

50 See-saw, Margery Daw,
Jacky shall have a new master;
He shall have but a penny a day,
Because he can't work any faster.

Mother Goose's Melody

51 Simple Simon met a pieman,
Going to the fair;
Says Simple Simon to the pieman,
Let me taste your ware.
Says the pieman to Simple Simon,
Show me first your penny;
Says Simple Simon to the pieman,
Indeed I have not any.

Simple Simon (Chapbook Advertisement)

52 Sing a song of sixpence,
A pocket full of rye;
Four and twenty blackbirds,
Baked in a pie.
When the pie was opened,
The birds began to sing;
Was not that a dainty dish,
To set before the king?

The king was in his counting-house,
Counting out his money;
The queen was in the parlour,
Eating bread and honey.
The maid was in the garden,
Hanging out the clothes,
When down came a blackbird,
And pecked off her nose.

Tommy Thumb's Pretty Song Book

53 Solomon Grundy,
Born on a Monday,
Christened on Tuesday,
Married on Wednesday,
Took ill on Thursday,
Worse on Friday,
Died on Saturday,
Buried on Sunday.
This is the end
Of Solomon Grundy.

The Nursery Rhymes of England (J. O. Halliwell)

54 The first day of Christmas,
My true love sent to me
A partridge in a pear tree.

Mirth without Mischief

55 The lion and the unicorn
Were fighting for the crown;
The lion beat the unicorn
All round about the town.

Useful Transactions in Philosophy (William King)

56 The Queen of Hearts
She made some tarts,
All on a summer's day;
The Knave of Hearts
He stole the tarts,
And took them clean away.

The European Magazine

57 There was a crooked man, and he walked a crooked mile,
He found a crooked sixpence against a crooked stile:
He bought a crooked cat, which caught a crooked mouse,
And they all lived together in a little crooked house.

The Nursery Rhymes of England (J. O. Halliwell)

58 There was an old woman
Lived under a hill,
And if she's not gone
She lives there still.

Academy of Complements

59 There was an old woman who lived in a shoe,
She had so many children she didn't know what to do;
She gave them some broth without any bread;
She whipped them all soundly and put them to bed.

Gammer Gurton's Garland

60 The twelfth day of Christmas,
My true love sent to me
Twelve lords a-leaping,
Eleven ladies dancing,
Ten pipers piping,
Nine drummers drumming,
Eight maids a-milking,
Seven swans a-swimming,
Six geese a-laying,
Five gold rings,
Four colly birds,
Three French hens,
Two turtle doves, and
A partridge in a pear tree.

Mirth without Mischief

61 Thirty days hath September,
April, June, and November;
All the rest have thirty-one,
Excepting February alone
And that has twenty-eight days clear
And twenty-nine in each leap year.

Abridgement of the Chronicles of England (Richard Grafton)

62 This is the farmer sowing his corn,
That kept the cock that crowed in the morn,
That waked the priest all shaven and shorn,
That married the man all tattered and torn,
That kissed the maiden all forlorn,
That milked the cow with the crumpled horn,
That tossed the dog,
That worried the cat,
That killed the rat,
That ate the corn,
That lay in the house that Jack built.

Nurse Truelove's New-Year-Gift

63 This little piggy went to market,
This little piggy stayed at home,
This little piggy had roast beef,
This little piggy had none,
And this little piggy cried, Wee-wee-wee-wee-wee,
I can't find my way home.

The Famous Tommy Thumb's Little Story Book

64 Three blind mice, see how they run!
They all run after the farmer's wife,
Who cut off their tails with a carving knife,
Did you ever see such a thing in your life,
As three blind mice?

Deuteromelia (Thomas Ravenscroft)

65 Tinker,
Tailor,
Soldier,
Sailor,
Rich man,
Poor man,
Beggarman,
Thief.

Popular Rhymes and Nursery Tales (J. O. Halliwell)

66 Tom, he was a piper's son,
He learnt to play when he was young,
And all the tune that he could play
Was 'Over the hills and far away'.

Tom, The Piper's Son

67 Tom, Tom, the piper's son,
Stole a pig and away he run;
The pig was eat
And Tom was beat,
And Tom went howling down the street.

Tom, The Piper's Son

68 Two little dicky birds,
Sitting on a wall;
One named Peter,
The other named Paul,
Fly away, Peter!
Fly away, Paul!
Come back, Peter!
Come back, Paul!

Mother Goose's Melody

69 Wee Willie Winkie runs through the town
Upstairs and downstairs and in his nightgown,
Rapping at the window, crying through the lock,
Are the children all in bed? It's past eight
o'clock.

In *Whistle-Binkie* (W. Miller)

70 What are little boys made of?
Frogs and snails
And puppy-dogs' tails,
That's what little boys are made of.
What are little girls made of?
Sugar and spice
And all that's nice,
That's what little girls are made of.

Nursery Rhymes (J. O. Halliwell)

71 What is your fortune, my pretty maid?
My face is my fortune, sir, she said.
Then I can't marry you, my pretty maid.
Nobody asked you, sir, she said.

Archaeologia Cornu-Britannica (William Pryce)

72 Where are you going to, my pretty maid?
I'm going a-milking, sir, she said.

Archaeologia Cornu-Britannica (William Pryce)

73 Who killed Cock Robin?
I, said the Sparrow,
With my bow and arrow,
I killed Cock Robin.
Who saw him die?
I, said the Fly,
With my little eye,
I saw him die.

Tommy Thumb's Pretty Song Book

74 Yankee Doodle came to town,
Riding on a pony;
He stuck a feather in his cap
And called it macaroni.

Gammer Gurton's Garland

O

Oakeley, Frederick (1802–80) British churchman, who became Roman Catholic canon of Westminster. He translated the Latin hymn *Adeste Fideles* (1841).

1 O come all ye faithful,
Joyful and triumphant,
O come ye, O come ye to Bethlehem.

Translated from the Latin hymn, *Adeste Fideles*
O Come All Ye Faithful

Oates, Lawrence Edward Grace (1880–1912) British soldier and explorer. He was a member of Scott's expedition to the Antarctic (1910–12) and reached the South Pole. Afraid that his lameness on the return journey would slow down the others, he heroically walked out into the blizzard to die.

1 I am just going outside and may be some time.

Last words before leaving the tent and vanishing into the blizzard.
Journal (R. F. Scott), 17 Mar 1912

O'Brien, Conor Cruise (1917–) Irish diplomat and writer. He became UN representative in the Congo (1961) and later a minister (1973–77) in the Irish government. He was then a senator (1977–79) before becoming editor (1979–81) of *The Observer* newspaper in London. His books include *United Nation: Sacred Drama* (1967), *Camus* (1969), *States of Ireland* (1972), and *Passion and Cunning* (1988).

1 It is a city where you can see a sparrow fall to the ground, and God watching it.

Referring to Dublin
Attrib.

O'Brien, Edna (1936–) Irish novelist. Her books include *The Country Girls* (1960), *Night* (1972), *Returning* (1982), and *Lantern Slides* (1990). She has also written plays and filmscripts.

1 To Crystal, hair was the most important thing on earth. She would never get married because you couldn't wear curlers in bed.

Winter's Tales, 8, 'Come into the Drawing Room, Doris'

2 The vote, I thought, means nothing to women. We should be armed.

Quoted as epigraph to *Fear of Flying* (Erica Jong), Ch. 16

O'Brien, Flann (Brian O'Nolan; 1911–66) Irish novelist and journalist. His books include *At Swim-Two-Birds* (1939) and *The Third Policeman* (1967). As "Myles na Gopaleen" he wrote a satirical column in the *Irish Times*.

1 A thing of duty is a boy for ever.

About policemen always seeming to be young-looking
The Listener, 24 Feb 1977

O'Casey, Sean (1884–1964) Irish dramatist. Formerly a labourer, his plays give a starkly realistic picture of Irish life. They include *Juno and the Paycock* (1924) and *The Silver Tassie* (1928).

1 I ofen looked up at the sky an' assed meself the question – what is the stars, what is the stars?

Juno and the Paycock, I

2 He's an oul' butty o' mine – oh, he's a darlin' man, a daarlin' man.

Juno and the Paycock, I

3 There's no reason to bring religion into it. I think we ought to have as great a regard for religion as we can, so as to keep it out of as many things as possible.

The Plough and the Stars, I

4 English literature's performing flea.

Referring to P. G. Wodehouse
Attrib.

Ochs, Adolph Simon (1858–1935) US newspaper publisher. His newspapers included the Chattanooga, New York, and Philadelphia *Times*.

1   All the news that's fit to print.

The motto of the *New York Times*

O'Connell, Daniel (1775–1847) Irish politician. A Roman Catholic, he succeeded in forcing Catholic emancipation, becoming an MP at Westminster himself. He agitated for repeal of the union of Ireland and Britain and became Lord Mayor of Dublin (1841).

1   Peel's smile: like the silver plate on a coffin.

Referring to Sir Robert Peel; quoting J. P. Curran (1750–1817)
Hansard, 26 Feb 1835

O'Hara, Geoffrey (1882–1967) Canadian-born US songwriter and composer. His operettas include *Riding Down the Sky* (1928) and *Harmony Hall* (1933).

1   K-K-Katy, beautiful Katy,
You're the only g-g-g-girl that I adore,
When the m-m-m-moon shines over the cow-shed,
I'll be waiting at the k-k-k-kitchen door.

K-K-Katy (song)

O'Keefe, Patrick (1872–1934) US advertising agent.

1   Say it with flowers.

Slogan for Society of American Florists

Okham, William of (c. 1280–1349) English philosopher. A pupil of Duns Scotus, he is remembered for the proposition known as 'Okham's Razor'.

1   Entities should not be multiplied unnecessarily. No more things should be presumed to exist than are absolutely necessary.

'Okham's Razor'. Despite its attribution to William of Okham, it was in fact a repetition of an ancient philosophical maxim.

Olivier, Laurence, Baron (1907–89) British actor and manager. With the Old Vic Theatre he played many leading Shakespearean roles and later made several films of Shakespeare's plays. He was director of the National Theatre Company (1961–73). The Olivier Theatre at the National Theatre is named after him.

1   Shakespeare – the nearest thing in incarnation to the eye of God.

Kenneth Harris Talking To: 'Sir Laurence Olivier'

O'Neill, Eugene (1888–1953) US dramatist. His plays include *Emperor Jones* (1920), *Mourning Becomes Electra* (1931), *The Iceman Cometh* (1946), and *Long Day's Journey into Night* (1956).

1   Life is for each man a solitary cell whose walls are mirrors.

Lazarus Laughed

2   Life is perhaps best regarded as a bad dream between two awakenings.

Marco Millions

3   Our lives are merely strange dark interludes in the electric display of God the Father.

Strange Interlude

Opie, John (1761–1807) British painter, known as the 'Cornish Wonder'. He painted many portraits of writers, including Dr Johnson, Burke, and Southey.

1   I mix them with my brains, sir.

When asked what he mixed his colours with
Self-Help (Samuel Smiles), Ch. 4

Oppenheimer, J. Robert (1904–67) US physicist. He contributed to quantum mechanics and was in charge of the development of the atom bomb at Los Alamos. His opposition to the H-bomb resulted in his dismissal as chairman of the Atomic Energy Commission and his investigation as a security risk.

1   We knew the world would not be the same.

After the first atomic test
The Decision to Drop the Bomb

2   The physicists have known sin; and this is a knowledge which they cannot lose.

Lecture, Massachusetts Institute of Technology, 25 Nov 1947

3   I am become death, the destroyer of worlds.

Quoting Vishnu from the *Gita*, at the first atomic test in New Mexico, 16 July 1945
Attrib.

Orczy, Emmusca, Baroness (1865–1947) British novelist, born in Hungary. Her books include *The Scarlet Pimpernel* (1905).

1   We seek him here, we seek him there,
Those Frenchies seek him everywhere.
Is he in heaven? – Is he in hell?
That damned elusive Pimpernel?

The Scarlet Pimpernel, Ch. 12

2   The weariest nights, the longest days, sooner or later must perforce come to an end.

The Scarlet Pimpernel, Ch. 22

Ortega y Gasset, José (1883–1955) Spanish philosopher and writer. His best-known book is *The Revolt of the Masses* (1930).

1   The uprising of the masses implies a fabulous increase of vital possibilities; quite the contrary of what we hear so often about the decadence of Europe.

The Revolt of the Masses, Ch. 2

2   Revolution is not the uprising against pre-existing order, but the setting-up of a new order contradictory to the traditional one.

The Revolt of the Masses, Ch. 6

Orton, Joe (1933–67) British dramatist. His black comedies include *Entertaining Mr Sloane* (1964), *Loot* (1965), and *What the Butler Saw* (1969). He was battered to death by his homosexual lover.

1   I'd the upbringing a nun would envy and that's the truth. Until I was fifteen I was more familiar with Africa than my own body.

Entertaining Mr Sloane, I

2   It's all any reasonable child can expect if the dad is present at the conception.

Entertaining Mr Sloane, III

3   The humble and meek are thirsting for blood.

Funeral Games, I

4 Every luxury was lavished on you – atheism, breast-feeding, circumcision. I had to make my own way.
Loot, I

5 Reading isn't an occupation we encourage among police officers. We try to keep the paper work down to a minimum.
Loot, II

6 God is a gentleman. He prefers blondes.
Loot, II

7 You were born with your legs apart. They'll send you to the grave in a Y-shaped coffin.
What the Butler Saw, I

Orwell, George (Eric Blair; 1903–50) British novelist. His books include *The Road to Wigan Pier* (1937), *Animal Farm* (1945), and *Nineteen Eighty-Four* (1949).

Quotations about Orwell

1 He could not blow his nose without moralising on the state of the handkerchief industry.
Cyril Connolly (1903–74) British journalist. *The Evening Colonnade*

2 He was a kind of saint, and in that character, more likely in politics to chastise his own side than the enemy.
V. S. Pritchett (1900–) British short-story writer. *New Statesman*, 1950

Quotations by Orwell

3 Man is the only creature that consumes without producing.
An allegory of the Marxist analysis of capitalism, with man representing the capitalist
Animal Farm, Ch. 1

4 Four legs good, two legs bad.
Animal Farm, Ch. 3

5 War is war. The only good human being is a dead one.
Animal Farm, Ch. 4

6 He intended, he said, to devote the rest of his life to learning the remaining twenty-two letters of the alphabet.
Animal Farm, Ch. 9

7 All animals are equal but some animals are more equal than others.
Animal Farm, Ch. 10

8 The high sentiments always win in the end, the leaders who offer blood, toil, tears and sweat always get more out of their followers than those who offer safety and a good time. When it comes to the pinch, human beings are heroic.
The Art of Donald McGill

9 I'm fat, but I'm thin inside. Has it ever struck you that there's a thin man inside every fat man, just as they say there's a statue inside every block of stone?
Coming Up For Air, Pt. I, Ch. 3

10 Before the war, and especially before the Boer War, it was summer all the year round.
Coming Up for Air, Pt. II, Ch. 1

11 Prolonged, indiscriminate reviewing of books involves constantly *inventing* reactions towards books about which one has no spontaneous feelings whatever.
Confessions of a Book Reviewer

12 He was an embittered atheist (the sort of atheist who does not so much disbelieve in God as personally dislike Him).
Down and Out in Paris and London, Ch. 30

13 Probably the Battle of Waterloo *was* won on the playing-fields of Eton, but the opening battles of all subsequent wars have been lost there.
The Lion and the Unicorn, 'England, Your England'

14 A family with the wrong members in control – that, perhaps, is as near as one can come to describing England in a phrase.
The Lion and the Unicorn, 'The Ruling Class'

15 Who controls the past controls the future. Who controls the present controls the past.
Nineteen Eighty-Four

16 If you want a picture of the future, imagine a boot stamping on a human face – for ever.
Nineteen Eighty-Four

17 Big Brother is watching you.
Nineteen Eighty-Four

18 War is Peace, Freedom is Slavery, Ignorance is Strength.
Nineteen Eighty-Four

19 Doublethink means the power of holding two contradictory beliefs in one's mind simultaneously, and accepting both of them.
Nineteen Eighty-Four

20 In our time, political speech and writing are largely the defence of the indefensible.
Politics and the English Language

21 The books one reads in childhood, and perhaps most of all the bad and good bad books, create in one's mind a sort of false map of the world, a series of fabulous countries into which one can retreat at odd moments throughout the rest of life, and which in some cases can even survive a visit to the real countries which they are supposed to represent.
Riding Down from Bangor

22 It is brought home to you . . . that it is only because miners sweat their guts out that superior persons can remain superior.
The Road to Wigan Pier, Ch. 2

23 I sometimes think that the price of liberty is not so much eternal vigilance as eternal dirt.
The Road to Wigan Pier, Ch. 4

24 We may find in the long run that tinned food is a deadlier weapon than the machine-gun.

The Road to Wigan Pier, Ch. 6

25 There can hardly be a town in the South of England where you could throw a brick without hitting the niece of a bishop.

The Road to Wigan Pier, Ch. 7

26 As with the Christian religion, the worst advertisement for Socialism is its adherents.

The Road to Wigan Pier, Ch. 11

27 To the ordinary working man, the sort you would meet in any pub on Saturday night, Socialism does not mean much more than better wages and shorter hours and nobody bossing you about.

The Road to Wigan Pier, Ch. 11

28 The higher-water mark, so to speak, of Socialist literature is W. H. Auden, a sort of gutless Kipling.

The Road to Wigan Pier, Ch. 11

29 We have nothing to lose but our aitches.

Referring to the middle classes
The Road to Wigan Pier, Ch. 13

30 The quickest way of ending a war is to lose it.

Second Thoughts on James Burnham

31 Most people get a fair amount of fun out of their lives, but on balance life is suffering and only the very young or the very foolish imagine otherwise.

Shooting an Elephant

32 Serious sport has nothing to do with fair play. It is bound up with hatred, jealousy, boastfulness, disregard of all rules and sadistic pleasure in witnessing violence; in other words it is war minus the shooting.

The Sporting Spirit

33 To a surprising extent the war-lords in shining armour, the apostles of the martial virtues, tend not to die fighting when the time comes. History is full of ignominious getaways by the great and famous.

Who Are the War Criminals?

34 He is pretty certain to come back into favour. One of the surest signs of his genius is that women dislike his books.

Referring to Conrad
New English Weekly, 23 July 1936

35 Each generation imagines itself to be more intelligent than the one that went before it, and wiser than the one that comes after it.

Book Review

36 At 50, everyone has the face he deserves.

Last words in his manuscript notebook, 17 Apr 1949

Osborne, John (1929–) British dramatist. He made his reputation as one of the Angry Young Men with *Look Back in Anger* (1956). His subsequent plays include *The Entertainer* (1957), *Luther* (1960), *Inadmissible Evidence* (1964), *West of Suez* (1971), and *A Better Class of Person* (1981).

1 Don't clap too hard – it's a very old building.

The Entertainer

2 Well, there are only two posh papers on a Sunday – the one you're reading and this one.

Look Back in Anger, I

3 He really deserves some sort of decoration . . . a medal inscribed 'For Vaguery in the Field'.

Look Back in Anger, I

4 I don't think one 'comes down' from Jimmy's university. According to him, it's not even red brick, but white tile.

Look Back in Anger, II:1

5 They spend their time mostly looking forward to the past.

Look Back in Anger, II:1

6 Poor old Daddy – just one of those sturdy old plants left over from the Edwardian Wilderness, that can't understand why the sun isn't shining any more.

Look Back in Anger, II:2

7 She's like the old line about justice – not only must be done but must be seen to be done.

Time Present, I

8 I never deliberately set out to shock, but when people don't walk out of my plays I think there is something wrong.

The Observer, 'Sayings of the Week', 19 Jan 1975

O'Sullivan, John L. (1813–95) US writer.

1 A torchlight procession marching down your throat.

Referring to whisky
Collections and Recollections (G. W. E. Russell), Ch. 19

Otis, James (1725–83) US political activist, who defended the legal rights of American colonists.

1 Taxation without representation is tyranny.

As 'No taxation without representation' this became the principal slogan of the American Revolution
Generally attributed to Otis

Ouida (Marie Louise de la Ramée; 1839–1908) British novelist. Her adventure stories included *Under Two Flags* (1867).

1 Christianity has made of death a terror which was unknown to the gay calmness of the Pagan.

The Failure of Christianity

2 . . . with peaches and women, it's only the side next the sun that's tempting.

Strathmore

3 The song that we hear with our ears is only the song that is sung in our hearts.

Wisdom, Wit and Pathos, 'Ariadne'

4 A cruel story runs on wheels, and every hand oils the wheels as they run.

Wisdom, Wit and Pathos, 'Moths'

Ouspensky, P. D. (1878–1947) Russian-born occultist. His writings include *Tertium Organum* (1912) and *A New Model of the Universe* (1914).

1 Man, as he is, is not a genuine article. He is an imitation of something, and a very bad imitation.

The Psychology of Man's Possible Evolution, Ch. 2

Overbury, Sir Thomas (1581–1613) English poet. Imprisoned in the Tower for disrespect to the monarch, he was poisoned by the agents of Lady Essex, whose marriage to Viscount Rochester he had opposed. His best-known poem is *A Wife* (1614).

1 He disdains all things above his reach, and preferreth all countries before his own.

Miscellaneous Works, 'An Affectate Traveller'

Ovid (Publius Ovidius Naso; 43 BC–17 AD) Roman poet. He is remembered for his love poems, including the *Amores* and *Heroides*, and his *Metamorphoses*, a collection of mythical and historical tales.

Quotations about Ovid

1 Ovid had nothing in common with the older Roman poets; their dignity, virility and piety were entirely lacking in him. But he possessed an exquisite sensitiveness to beauty, and abounding imaginative power, which they lacked.

Concise Universal Biography (J.A. Hammerton)

2 The true cause of Ovid's sudden exile is not known; some attribute it to a shameful amour with Livia, wife of Augustus; others support that it arose from the knowledge which Ovid had of the unpardonable incest of the emperor with his daughter Julia; these reasons are indeed merely conjectural; the cause was of a private and secret nature of which Ovid himself was afraid to speak.

John Lemprière (1765–1824) British scholar. *Classical Dictionary*

Quotations by Ovid

3 Whether a pretty woman grants or withholds her favours, she always likes to be asked for them.

Ars Amatoria

4 Dripping water hollows out a stone, a ring is worn away by use.

See also LATIMER; LUCRETIUS
Epistulae Ex Ponto, Bk. IV

5 Now there are fields where Troy once was.

Heroides, Bk. I

6 *Tu quoque.*
You also.

Tristia

7 All things can corrupt perverted minds.

Tristia, Bk. II

Owen, David (1938–) British doctor and politician. He became Labour foreign secretary (1977–79) but resigned from the Labour party in 1983 to cofound the Social Democratic Party. With David Steel he headed the SDP-Liberal Alliance; when the Liberals and the SDP merged in 1988, he led a reduced SDP until it was disbanded in 1990.

1 It was on this issue, the nuclear defence of Britain, on which I left the Labour Party, and on this issue I am prepared to stake my entire political career.

The Observer, 'Sayings of the Week', 9 Nov 1986

2 No general in the midst of battle has a great discussion about what he is going to do if defeated.

The Observer, 'Sayings of the Week', 6 June 1987

Owen, Robert (1771–1858) British social reformer. He advocated 'villages of cooperation' run on Socialist lines, modelled on the New Lanark mill, which he managed. He was also active in the trades-union movement.

1 All the world is queer save thee and me, and even thou art a little queer.

Referring to William Allen, his partner in business
Attrib., 1828

Owen, Wilfred (1893–1918) British poet. Written during World War I, his poetry expresses the horror of war and includes 'Strange Meeting' and 'Anthem for Doomed Youth'. He was killed in action.

1 The pallor of girls' brows shall be their pall;
Their flowers the tenderness of patient minds,
And each slow dusk a drawing-down of blinds.

Anthem for Doomed Youth

2 And in the happy no-time of his sleeping
Death took him by the heart.

Asleep

3 The old Lie: *Dulce et decorum est*
Pro patria mori.

Dulce et decorum est

4 Red lips are not so red
As the stained stones kissed by the English dead.

Greater Love

5 Above all I am not concerned with Poetry. My subject is War, and the pity of War. The Poetry is in the pity.

Poems, Preface

Oxenstierna, Axel, Count (1583–1654) Swedish statesman, who was chancellor of Sweden (1612–54). After the death of Gustavus II Adolphus, he led Sweden into the Thirty Years' War.

1 Do you not know, my son, with how little wisdom the world is governed?

Letter to his son, 1648

P

Paine, Thomas (1737–1809) British writer and political philosopher. His pamphlets include *Common Sense* (1776), which influenced the move towards American Independence.

1   It is necessary to the happiness of man that he be mentally faithful to himself. Infidelity does not consist in believing, or in disbelieving, it consists in professing to believe what one does not believe.
The Age of Reason, Pt. I

2   The sublime and the ridiculous are often so nearly related that it is difficult to class them separately. One step above the sublime makes the ridiculous; and one step above the ridiculous makes the sublime again.
The Age of Reason, Pt. 2

3   Government, even in its best state, is but a necessary evil; in its worst state, an intolerable one.
Common Sense, Ch. 1

4   As to religion, I hold it to be the indispensable duty of government to protect all conscientious professors thereof, and I know of no other business which government hath to do therewith.
Common Sense, Ch. 4

5   The summer soldier and the sunshine patriot will, in this crisis, shrink from the service of their country.
Pennsylvania Journal, 'The American Crisis'

Paisley, Ian (1926–) Northern Irish churchman and politician. A staunch defender of Protestant unionism, he entered the House of Commons as an MP in 1974.

1   We are reasonable. We have always been reasonable. We are noted for our sweet reasonableness.
The Observer, 'Sayings of the Week', 11 May 1975

2   I would rather be British than just.
The Sunday Times, 12 Dec 1971

Palmer, Samuel (1805–81) British landscape painter. He was influenced by William Blake in his early mystical paintings, but became more conventional as he grew older and more successful.

1   A picture has been said to be something between a thing and a thought.
Life of Blake (Arthur Symons)

Palmerston, Henry John Temple, Viscount (1784–1865) British statesman. Changing from Tory to Whig (1830), he became prime minister (1855–58; 1859–65).

1   Accidental and fortuitous concurrence of atoms.
Speech, House of Commons, 1857

2   Die, my dear Doctor, that's the last thing I shall do!
Last words
Attrib.

Pankhurst, Dame Christabel (1880–1958) British suffragette. The daughter of Emmeline Pankhurst, she was arrested for assaulting the policeman who removed her from an election meeting.

1   Never lose your temper with the Press or the public is a major rule of political life.
Unshackled

2   We are not ashamed of what we have done, because, when you have a great cause to fight for, the moment of greatest humiliation is the moment when the spirit is proudest.
Speech, Albert Hall, London, 19 Mar 1908

3   We are here to claim our rights as women, not only to be free, but to fight for freedom. It is our privilege, as well as our pride and our joy, to take some part in this militant movement, which, as we believe, means the regeneration of all humanity.
Speech, 23 Mar 1911

4   What we suffragettes aspire to be when we are enfranchised is ambassadors of freedom to women in other parts of the world, who are not so free as we are.
Speech, Carnegie Hall, New York, 25 Oct 1915

Pankhurst, Emmeline (1858–1928) British suffragette. She founded, in Manchester, the Women's Social and Political Union (1903). She was frequently imprisoned for destroying property, but during World War I abandoned her campaign and encouraged women to do industrial war work.

1   . . . if civilisation is to advance at all in the future, it must be through the help of women, women freed of their political shackles, women with full power to work their will in society. It was rapidly becoming clear to my mind that men regarded women as a servant class in the community, and that women were going to remain in the servant class until they lifted themselves out of it.
My Own Story

2   Women had always fought for men, and for their children. Now they were ready to fight for their own human rights. Our militant movement was established.
My Own Story

3   I have no sense of guilt. I look upon myself as a prisoner of war. I am under no moral obligation to conform to, or in any way accept, the sentence imposed upon me.
Speech in court, Apr 1913
The Fighting Pankhursts (David Mitchell)

4 We have taken this action, because as women . . . we realize that the condition of our sex is so deplorable that it is our duty even to break the law in order to call attention to the reasons why we do so.

Speech in court, 21 Oct 1908
Shoulder to Shoulder (ed. Midge Mackenzie)

Pankhurst, Sylvia (1882–1960) British suffragette. The daughter of Emmeline Pankhurst, she wrote a biography of her mother.

1 I could not give my name to aid the slaughter in this war, fought on both sides for grossly material ends, which did not justify the sacrifice of a single mother's son. Clearly I must continue to oppose it, and expose it, to all whom I could reach with voice or pen.

The Home Front, Ch. 25

2 I have gone to war too . . . I am going to fight capitalism even if it kills me. It is wrong that people like you should be comfortable and well fed while all around you people are starving.

The Fighting Pankhursts (David Mitchell)

Park, Mungo (1771–1806) Scottish explorer. He twice explored the River Niger and wrote *Travels in the Interior Districts of Africa* (1797). In a subsequent expedition his party was attacked by Africans and he died.

1 The sight of it gave me infinite pleasure, as it proved that I was in a civilized society.

Remark on finding a gibbet in an unexplored part of Africa
Attrib.

Parker, Charlie (Christopher) (1920–55) US black jazz saxophonist and composer, at the peak of his fame during the 1950s. He was known as 'Bird' or 'Yardbird'.

1 Music is your own experience, your thoughts, your wisdom. If you don't live it, it won't come out of your horn.

Hear Me Talkin' to Ya (Nat Shapiro and Nat Hentoff)

Parker, Clarke Ross (1914–74) British songwriter, who with Hughie Charles (1907–) wrote 'There'll Always Be an England'.

1 There'll always be an England
While there's a country lane,
Wherever there's a cottage small
Beside a field of grain.

There'll Always Be an England

Parker, Dorothy (Rothschild) (1893–1967) US writer and wit. Her New York circle in the 1920s included Ogden Nash and James Thurber. She is best known for her short stories, sketches, and poems; her books include *Not So Deep As a Well* (1936).

Quotations about Parker

1 She has put into what she has written a voice, a state of mind, an era, a few moments of human experience that nobody else has conveyed.

Edmund Wilson (1895–1972) US critic and writer. Attrib.

2 She is a combination of Little Nell and Lady Macbeth.

Alexander Woollcott (1887–1943) US journalist. *While Rome Burns*

Quotations by Parker

3 Razors pain you
Rivers are damp;
Acids stain you;
And drugs cause cramp.
Guns aren't lawful;
Nooses give;
Gas smells awful;
You might as well live.

Enough Rope, 'Resumé'

4 He lies below, correct in cypress wood,
And entertains the most exclusive worms.

Epitaph for a Very Rich Man

5 All I say is, nobody has any business to go around looking like a horse and behaving as if it were all right. You don't catch horses going around looking like people, do you?

Horsie

6 How do people go to sleep? I'm afraid I've lost the knack. I might try busting myself smartly over the temple with the nightlight. I might repeat to myself, slowly and soothingly, a list of quotations beautiful from minds profound; if I can remember any of the damn things.

The Little Hours

7 I'm never going to be famous . . . I don't do anything. Not one single thing. I used to bite my nails, but I don't even do that any more.

The Little Hours

8 Why is it no one ever sent me yet
One perfect limousine, do you suppose?
Ah no, it's always just my luck to get
One perfect rose.

One Perfect Rose

9 Sorrow is tranquillity remembered in emotion.

Sentiment

10 It costs me never a stab nor squirm
To tread by chance upon a worm.
"Aha, my little dear," I say,
"Your clan will pay me back one day."

Sunset Gun, 'Thought for a Sunshiny Morning'

11 By the time you swear you're his,
Shivering and sighing,
And he vows his passion is
Infinite, undying –
Lady, make a note of this:
One of you is lying.

Unfortunate Coincidence

12 That should assure us of at least forty-five minutes of undisturbed privacy.

Pressing a button marked NURSE during a stay in hospital
The Algonquin Wits (R. Drennan)

13 The poor son-of-a-bitch!

Quoting from *The Great Gatsby* on paying her last respects to F. Scott Fitzgerald
Thalberg: Life and Legend (B. Thomas)

14 If all the young ladies who attended the Yale promenade dance were laid end to end, no one would be the least surprised.

While Rome Burns (Alexander Woollcott)

15 Brevity is the soul of lingerie.

While Rome Burns (Alexander Woollcott)

16 This is not a novel to be tossed aside lightly. It should be thrown with great force.

Book review
Wit's End (R. E. Dremman)

17 A list of authors who have made themselves most beloved and therefore, most comfortable financially, shows that it is our national joy to mistake for the first-rate, the fecund rate.

Wit's End (R. E. Drennan)

18 You can't teach an old dogma new tricks.

Wit's End (R. E. Drennan)

19 I was fired from there, finally, for a lot of things, among them my insistence that the Immaculate Conception was spontaneous combustion.

Writers at Work, First Series (Malcolm Cowley)

20 This is on me.

Suggesting words for tombstone
You Might As Well Live (J. Keats), Pt. I, Ch. 5

21 It serves me right for putting all my eggs in one bastard.

Said on going into hospital to get an abortion
You Might as Well Live (J. Keats), Pt. II, Ch. 3

22 Oh, don't worry about Alan . . . Alan will always land on somebody's feet.

Said of her husband on the day their divorce became final
You Might As Well Live (J. Keats), Pt. IV, Ch. 1

23 How could they tell?

Reaction to news of the death of Calvin Coolidge, US President 1923–29; also attributed to H. L. Mencken
You Might As Well Live (J. Keats)

24 Dear Mary, We all knew you had it in you.

Telegram sent to a friend on the successful outcome of her much-publicized pregnancy

25 You can lead a whore to culture but you can't make her think.

Speech to American Horticultural Society

26 You know, she speaks eighteen languages. And she can't say 'No' in any of them.

Speaking of an acquaintance
Attrib.

27 Men seldom make passes
At girls who wear glasses.

Attrib.

28 Check enclosed.

Giving her version of the two most beautiful words in the English language
Attrib.

29 She ran the whole gamut of the emotions from A to B.

Referring to a performance by Katharine Hepburn on Broadway
Attrib.

30 Excuse my dust.

Her own epitaph

Parker, Henry Taylor (1867–1934) US music critic.

1 Those people on the stage are making such a noise I can't hear a word you're saying.

Rebuking some talkative members of an audience, near whom he was sitting
The Humor of Music (L. Humphrey)

Parker, Hubert Lister (1900–72) Lord Chief Justice of England (1958–71).

1 A judge is not supposed to know anything about the facts of life until they have been presented in evidence and explained to him at least three times.

The Observer, 'Sayings of the Week', 12 Mar 1961

Parker, John (1729–75) US general. In the American Revolution he commanded the Minutemen at Lexington.

1 Stand your ground. Don't fire unless fired upon, but if they mean to have a war, let it begin here!

Command given at the start of the Battle of Lexington
Familiar Quotations (J. Bartlett)

Parkinson, Cyril Northcote (1919–) British historian and writer. He is best known for his book *Parkinson's Law* (1958), a study of business administration.

1 Work expands so as to fill the time available for its completion.

Parkinson's Law, Ch. 1

2 The rise in the total of those employed is governed by Parkinson's Law and would be much the same whether the volume of work were to increase, diminish or even disappear.

Parkinson's Law, Ch. 1

3 The British, being brought up on team games, enter their House of Commons in the spirit of those who would rather be doing something else. If they cannot be playing golf or tennis, they can at least pretend that politics is a game with very similar rules.

Parkinson's Law, Ch. 2

4 It is now known . . . that men enter local politics solely as a result of being unhappily married.

Parkinson's Law, Ch. 10

Parnell, Charles Stewart (1846–91) Irish politician. In 1880 he became leader of the Home Rule Party but lost support after being cited in Katherine O'Shea's divorce case; later he married her.

1 When a man takes a farm from which another has been evicted, you must show him . . . by leaving him severely alone, by putting him into a moral Coventry, by isolating him from his kind as if he were a leper of old – you must show him your detestation of the crimes he has committed.

The first person to be treated was a Captain Boycott – hence the verb, 'to boycott'
Speech, Ennis, 19 Sept 1880

2 No man has a right to fix the boundary of the march of a nation; no man has a right to say to his country – thus far shalt thou go and no further.

Speech, Cork, 21 Jan 1885

Parr, Samuel (1747–1825) British writer and scholar. A learned but querulous man, he published *Characters of Fox* in 1809.

1 Now that the old lion is dead, every ass thinks he may kick at him.

Referring to Dr Johnson
Life of Johnson (J. Boswell)

Pascal, Blaise (1623–62) French philosopher and mathematician. At the age of 18 he invented the first calculating machine. His works include *Lettres provinciales* (1656), a defence of Jansenist doctrine, and *Pensées sur la religion* (1669).

1 I have made this letter longer than usual, only because I have not had the time to make it shorter.

Lettres provinciales, XVI

2 Not to care for philosophy is to be a true philosopher.

Pensées, I

3 The more intelligence one has the more people one finds original. Commonplace people see no difference between men.

Pensées, I

4 If you want people to think well of you, do not speak well of yourself.

Pensées, I

5 I cannot forgive Descartes; in all his philosophy he did his best to dispense with God. But he could not avoid making Him set the world in motion with a flip of His thumb; after that he had no more use for God.

Pensées, II

6 Had Cleopatra's nose been shorter, the whole face of the world would have changed.

Pensées, II

7 The heart has its reasons which reason does not know.

Pensées, IV

Pasternak, Boris (1890–1960) Russian Jewish poet and novelist. His book *Dr Zhivago* was banned in Russia, but was an international success after its publication in Italy in 1957.

1 And yet the order of the acts is planned, The way's end destinate and unconcealed. Alone. Now is the time of Pharisees. *To live is not like walking through a field.*

Hamlet (trans. Henry Kamen)

Pasteur, Louis (1822–95) French scientist. He developed the process of pasteurization to kill microorganisms in milk and invented vaccination to induce immunity against viral diseases. He founded, and was first director of, the Pasteur Institute in Paris.

Quotations about Pasteur

1 Some years after his death it was decided by a popular vote conducted in his country that Louis Pasteur was the greatest Frenchman of all time. The success of his method might be explained as being due to the exercise of three fundamental rules, keen observation, precise tests, and the drawing of irrefutable conclusions from critical premises.

Piers Compton (1903–) British writer. *The Genius of Louis Pasteur*

2 The victory over rabies, that most dreaded of diseases, lifted Pasteur into indisputable fame. He had risen by progressive steps, by studies which were all, despite their diversity, connected and supported by one another.

L. Descour *Pasteur and His Work*

Quotations by Pasteur

3 Wine is the most healthful and most hygienic of beverages.

Études sur le vin, Pt. I, Ch. 2

4 There are no such things as applied sciences, only applications of science.

Address, 11 Sept 1872

5 When meditating over a disease, I never think of finding a remedy for it, but, instead, a means of preventing it.

Address to the Fraternal Association of Former Students of the École Centrale des Arts et Manufactures, Paris, 15 May 1884

Pater, Walter (Horatio) (1839–94) British critic. His books include *Studies in the History of the Renaissance* (1873) and *Marius the Epicurean* (1885), in which he supported 'art for art's sake'.

1 She is older than the rocks among which she sits.

Referring to the *Mona Lisa*
The Renaissance, 'Leonardo da Vinci'

2 All art constantly aspires towards the condition of music.

The Renaissance, 'The School of Giorgione'

Paterson, Andrew Barton (1864–1941) Australian journalist and poet. His books include a verse collection, *The Animals Noah Forgot* (1933), the personal recollections *Happy Despatches* (1934), and the racing story *The Shearer's Colt* (1936). He also wrote the words of Australia's national song *Waltzing Matilda*.

1 Once a jolly swagman camped by a billy-bong,
Under the shade of a coolibah tree,
And he sang as he sat and waited for his billy-
boil,
'You'll come a-waltzing, Matilda, with me.'
Waltzing Matilda

Patmore, Coventry (1823–96) British poet. An associate of
the Pre-Raphaelite Brotherhood, he wrote a poetic treatment of
marriage in four volumes, *The Angel in the House* (1854–62).
After becoming a Catholic in 1864 he wrote primarily on religious
themes.

1 Love's perfect blossom only blows
Where noble manners veil defect.
Angels may be familiar; those
Who err each other must respect.
The Angel in the House, Bk. I, Prelude 2

2 It was not like your great and gracious ways!
Do you, that have nought other to lament,
Never, my Love, repent
Of how, that July afternoon,
You went,
With sudden, unintelligible phrase, – And fright-
ened eye,
Upon your journey of so many days,
Without a single kiss or a good-bye?
The Unknown Eros, Bk. I, 'Departure'

Patton, George S(mith), Jr. (1885–1945) US general.
In World War II he commanded the Third Army in France, in its
spectacular defeat of the Germans.

1 Dear Ike, Today I spat in the Seine.
Message sent to Eisenhower reporting his crossing of the Seine
in World War II
The American Treasury (C. Fadiman)

Paul, Leslie (Allen) (1905–85) British writer. His books
include *Annihilation of Man* (1944), *Son of Man* (1961), and *First
Love* (1971).

1 Angry Young Man.
Book title

Pavese, Cesare (1908–50) Italian novelist and poet. His
books include *Il Compagno* (1947) and *La luna e i falò* (1950).
His diaries were published after his suicide as *The Business of
Living* (1952).

1 One stops being a child when one realizes that
telling one's trouble does not make it better.
The Business of Living: Diaries 1935–50

2 No one ever lacks a good reason for suicide.
The Savage God (A. Alvarez)

Pavlov, Ivan Petrovich (1849–1936) Russian physiologist.
He became famous for his studies with dogs on the conditioned
reflex and its implications on human learning, he won the Nobel
prize in 1904.

1 School yourself to demureness and patience.
Learn to innure yourself to drudgery in science.
Learn, compare, collect the facts.
Bequest to the Academic Youth of Soviet Russia, 27 Feb 1936

2 Experiment alone crowns the efforts of medicine, experiment limited only by the natural
range of the powers of the human mind. Observation discloses in the animal organism numerous phenomena existing side by side, and
interconnected now profoundly, now indirectly,
or accidentally. Confronted with a multitude of
different assumptions the mind must *guess* the
real nature of this connection.
Experimental Psychology and Other Essays, Pt. X

Pavlova, Anna (1881–1931) Russian ballet dancer. She
joined Diaghilev's company in Paris in 1909 and later formed her
own company.

1 . . . although one may fail to find happiness in
theatrical life, one never wishes to give it up after having once tasted its fruits. To enter the
School of the Imperial Ballet is to enter a convent whence frivolity is banned, and where
merciless discipline reigns.
Pavlova: A Biography (ed. A. H. Franks), 'Pages of My Life'

2 As is the case in all branches of art, success depends in a very large measure upon individual
initiative and exertion, and cannot be achieved
except by dint of hard work.
Pavlova: A Biography (ed. A. H. Franks), 'Pages of My Life'

3 When a small child . . . I thought that success
spelled happiness. I was wrong. Happiness is
like a butterfly which appears and delights us for
one brief moment, but soon flits away.
Pavlova: A Biography (ed. A. H. Franks), 'Pages of My Life'

Payn, James (1830–98) British writer and editor. He was
editor of *Chambers's Journal* (1859–74) and the *Cornhill Magazine*
(1883–96). His novels include *Carlyon's Year* (1868) and *Another's
Burden* (1897).

1 I had never had a piece of toast
Particularly long and wide,
But fell upon the sanded floor,
And always on the buttered side.
See also Thomas MOORE
Chambers's Journal, 2 Feb 1884

Payne, John Howard (1791–1852) US actor and dramatist.
His play *Brutus, or the Fall of Tarquin* (1818) was a success in
New York but failed in London and he was imprisoned for debt.
His opera *Clari, or the Maid of Milan* (1823) contains 'Home,
Sweet Home', the song for which he is remembered.

1 Mid pleasures and palaces though we may roam,
Be it ever so humble, there's no place like
home;

. . .

Home, home, sweet, sweet home!
There's no place like home! there's no place like
home!
Clari, or the Maid of Milan

Peabody, Elizabeth (1804–94) US educationalist. She
opened the first American kindergarten.

1 I saw it, but I did not realize it.

Giving a Transcendentalist explanation for her accidentally walking into a tree
The Peabody Sisters of Salem (L. Tharp)

Peacock, Thomas Love (1785–1866) British novelist. His satirical novels include *Nightmare Abbey* (1818) and *Gryll Grange* (1860).

1 Respectable means rich, and decent means poor. I should die if I heard my family called decent.

Crotchet Castle, Ch. 3

2 Ancient sculpture is the true school of modesty. But where the Greeks had modesty, we have cant; where they had poetry, we have cant; where they had patriotism, we have cant; where they had anything that exalts, delights, or adorns humanity, we have nothing but cant, cant, cant.

Crotchet Castle, Ch. 7

3 A book that furnishes no quotations is, *me judice*, no book – it is a plaything.

Crotchet Castle, Ch. 9

4 Nothing can be more obvious than that all animals were created solely and exclusively for the use of man.

Headlong Hall, Ch. 2

5 Marriage may often be a stormy lake, but celibacy is almost always a muddy horse-pond.

Melincourt

6 There are two reasons for drinking; one is, when you are thirsty, to cure it; the other, when you are not thirsty, to prevent it . . . Prevention is better than cure.

Melincourt

7 The mountain sheep are sweeter,
But the valley sheep are fatter;
We therefore deemed it meeter
To carry off the latter.

The Misfortunes of Elphin, Ch. 11, 'The War-Song of Dinas Vawr'

8 He was sent, as usual, to a public school, where a little learning was painfully beaten into him, and from thence to the university, where it was carefully taken out of him.

Nightmare Abbey, Ch. 1

9 Laughter is pleasant, but the exertion is too much for me.

Said by the Hon. Mr Listless
Nightmare Abbey, Ch. 5

10 Sir, I have quarrelled with my wife; and a man who has quarrelled with his wife is absolved from all duty to his country.

Nightmare Abbey, Ch. 11

Peake, Mervyn (1911–68) British novelist, poet, and artist. He is most famous for his gothic trilogy *Titus Groan* (1946), *Gormenghast* (1950), and *Titus Alone* (1959).

1 EQUALITY . . . is the thing. It is the only true and central premise from which constructive ideas can radiate freely and be operated without prejudice.

Titus Groan, 'The Sun Goes Down Again'

Peary, Robert Edwin (1856–1920) US explorer, who was the first man to reach the North Pole (1909).

1 The Eskimo had his own explanation. Said he: 'The devil is asleep or having trouble with his wife, or we should never have come back so easily.'

The North Pole

2 Nothing easier. One step beyond the pole, you see, and the north wind becomes a south one.

Explaining how he knew he had reached the North Pole
Attrib.

Peck, Gregory (1916–) US film star. His films include *The Keys of the Kingdom* (1944), *Twelve O'Clock High* (1949), *Mirage* (1965), *Shootout* (1971), *The Omen* (1976), *The Sea Wolves* (1980), and *Old Gringo* (1988).

1 If you have to tell them who you are, you aren't anybody.

Remarking upon the failure of anyone in a crowded restaurant to recognize him
Pieces of Eight (S. Harris)

Peel, Arthur Wellesley, Viscount (1829–1912) British politician and son of Sir Robert Peel, who created the Irish constabulary. Arthur Peel became Speaker of the House of Commons (1884–95).

1 My father didn't create you to arrest me.

Protesting against his arrest by the police, recently established by his father
Attrib.

Pegler, (James) Westbrook (1894–1969) US journalist who was a war correspondent and later a sports commentator.

1 He will go from resort to resort getting more tanned and more tired.

On the abdication of Edward VIII
Six Men (Alistair Cooke), Pt. II

Péguy, Charles Pierre (1873–1914) French writer. He wrote several biographies of such notable Frenchmen as Victor Hugo and Henri Bergson. He was killed in World War I.

1 It is impossible to write ancient history because we do not have enough sources, and impossible to write modern history because we have far too many.

Clio

Peirce, C. S. (1839–1914) US physicist and logician. He founded pragmatism and wrote many papers on mathematics and logic.

1 The universe ought to be presumed too vast to have any character.

Collected Papers, VI

Pembroke, Henry Herbert, 10th Earl of (1734–94) British general.

1 Dr Johnson's sayings would not appear so extraordinary, were it not for his *bow-wow way*.
Life of Johnson (J. Boswell)

Penn, William (1644–1718) English preacher and campaigner. He joined the Society of Friends in 1664 and was imprisoned in the Tower for his political writings in 1668. Here he wrote *No Cross, No Crown* (1669) outlining Quaker practices. In 1682 he went to America to set up Quaker settlements, and founded and drew up the constitution for Pennsylvania.

1 No pain, no palm; no thorns, no throne; no gall, no glory; no cross, no crown.
No Cross, No Crown

2 Men are generally more careful of the breed of their horses and dogs than of their children.
Some Fruits of Solitude, in Reflections and Maxims relating to the conduct of Humane Life, Pt. I, No 52

Pepys, Samuel (1633–1703) English diarist. His *Diary* (1660–1669) includes detailed descriptions of the Plague and the Fire of London.

Quotations about Pepys

1 A vain, silly, transparent coxcomb without either solid talents or a solid nature.
J.G. Lockhart (1794–1854) Scottish biographer and critic.

2 Matter-of-fact, like the screech of a sash window being thrown open, begins one of the greatest texts in our history and our literature.
Richard Ollard *Pepys*

3 Obliged to give up writing today – read Pepys instead.
Walter Scott (1771–1832) Scottish novelist. Journal, 5 Jan 1826

4 He had a kind of idealism in pleasure; like the princess in the fairy story, he was conscious of a rose-leaf out of place.
Robert Louis Stevenson (1850–94) Scottish writer. *Samuel Pepys*

Quotations by Pepys

5 And so to bed.
Diary, 6 May 1660 and *passim*

6 I went out to Charing Cross, to see Major-general Harrison hanged, drawn, and quartered; which was done there, he looking as cheerful as any man could do in that condition.
Diary, 13 Oct 1660

7 But Lord! to see the absurd nature of Englishmen, that cannot forbear laughing and jeering at everything that looks strange.
Diary, 27 Nov 1662

8 My wife, who, poor wretch, is troubled with her lonely life.
Diary, 19 Dec 1662

9 Went to hear Mrs Turner's daughter . . . play on the harpsichon; but, Lord! it was enough to make any man sick to hear her; yet was I forced to commend her highly.
Diary, 1 May 1663

10 Most of their discourse was about hunting, in a dialect I understand very little.
Diary, 22 Nov 1663

11 Pretty witty Nell.
Referring to Nell Gwynne
Diary, 3 Apr 1665

12 Thence I walked to the Tower; but Lord! how empty the streets are and how melancholy, so many poor sick people in the streets full of sores . . . in Westminster, there is never a physician and but one apothecary left, all being dead.
Written during the Great Plague – the last major outbreak of bubonic plague in England, and the worse since the Black Death of 1348
Diary, 16 Sept 1665

13 Strange to say what delight we married people have to see these poor fools decoyed into our condition.
Diary, 25 Dec 1665

14 Music and women I cannot but give way to, whatever my business is.
Diary, 9 Mar 1666

15 To church; and with my mourning, very handsome, and new periwig, make a great show.
Diary, 31 Mar 1667

16 My wife hath something in her gizzard, that only waits an opportunity of being provoked to bring up.
Diary, 17 June 1668

17 And so I betake myself to that course, which is almost as much as to see myself go into my grave – for which, and all the discomforts that will accompany my being blind, the good God prepare me!
The closing words of Pepys's Diary; he lived another 34 years and did not go blind
Diary, 31 May 1669

Perelman, S(idney) J(oseph) (1904–79) US humorous writer, who began contributing to the *New Yorker* in the 1930s. He published numerous collections, including *Crazy Like a Fox* (1944) and *Baby, It's Cold Inside* (1970).

1 For years I have let dentists ride roughshod over my teeth: I have been sawed, hacked, chopped, whittled, bewitched, bewildered, tattooed, and signed on again; but this is cuspid's last stand.
Crazy Like a Fox, 'Nothing but the Tooth'

2 I'll dispose of my teeth as I see fit, and after they've gone, I'll get along. I started off living on gruel, and by God, I can always go back to it again.
Crazy Like a Fox, 'Nothing but the Tooth'

3 I tried to resist his overtures, but he plied me with symphonies, quartettes, chamber music and cantatas.
Crazy Like a Fox, 'The Love Decoy'

4 He bit his lip in a manner which immediately awakened my maternal sympathy, and I helped him bite it.

Crazy Like a Fox, 'The Love Decoy'

5 A case of the tail dogging the wag.

Having escaped with some difficulty from the persistent attentions of some prostitutes in the street
Another Almanac of Words at Play (W. Epsy)

6 Love is not the dying moan of a distant violin – it's the triumphant twang of a bedspring.

Quotations for Speakers and Writers (A. Andrews)

Pericles (c. 495–429 BC) Greek statesman, who dominated Athens during its golden age by means of his oratory and honesty. He built the Parthenon and encouraged Sophocles, Anaxagoras, and Phidias in their various arts. He lost office due to his unsuccessful strategy in the Peloponnesian War.

1 Our love of what is beautiful does not lead to extravagance; our love of the things of the mind does not make us soft.

Part of the funeral oration, 430 BC, for the dead of the first year of the Peloponnesian War
Attrib. in *Histories* Bk. II, Ch. 40 (Thucydides)

Perkins, Francis (1882–1965) US social worker and politician. She became secretary of labor (1933–45).

1 Call me madame.

Deciding the term of address she would prefer when made the first woman to hold a cabinet office in the USA
Familiar Quotations (J. Bartlett)

Perlman, Itzhak (1945–) Israeli violinist. He lost the use of his legs through polio at the age of four and plays from a wheelchair.

1 You see, our fingers are circumcised, which gives it a very good dexterity, you know, particularly in the pinky.

Responding to an observation that many great violinists are Jewish
Close Encounters (M. Wallace)

Perón, Evita (Maria Eva Duarte de Perón; 1919–52) Argentine leader. Second wife of President Juan Perón, she was adored by the people for her charitable work.

1 Our president has declared that the only privileged persons in our country are the children.

Speech, American Congress of Industrial Medicine, 5 Dec 1949

2 Almsgiving tends to perpetuate poverty; and does away with it once and for all. Almsgiving leaves a man just where he was before. Aid restores him to society as an individual worthy of all respect and not as a man with a grievance. Almsgiving is the generosity of the rich; social aid levels up social inequalities. Charity separates the rich from the poor; and raises the needy and sets him on the same level with the rich.

Speech, American Congress of Industrial Medicine, 5 Dec 1949

Perón, Juan Domingo (1895–1974) Argentine statesman. He rose to power by a military coup in 1943 and was elected president in 1946. His wife Eva (known as 'Evita'; 1919–52) was idolized by the poor and Perón lost popularity after her death. However, he returned to power in 1973, died in office, and was succeeded by his third wife Isabel (1930–).

1 If I had not been born Perón, I would have liked to be Perón.

The Observer, 'Sayings of the Week', 21 Feb 1960

Perronet, Edward (1726–92) British hymn writer.

1 All hail, the power of Jesus' name!
Let angels prostrate fall.

Hymn

Porry, Olivor Hazard (1785–1819) US naval officer. In the War of 1812 he contested British control of Lake Erie.

1 We have met the enemy, and they are ours.

Message sent reporting his victory in a naval battle on Lake Erie
Familiar Quotations (J. Bartlett)

Perugino, Pietro (1446–1523) Italian painter. He painted the fresco *Delivery of the Keys to St Peter* in the Sistine Chapel and *Entombment* in the Pitti Palace.

1 I am curious to see what happens in the next world to one who dies unshriven.

Giving his reasons for refusing to see a priest as he lay dying
Attrib.

Pétain, Henri Philippe (1856–1951) French marshal. He became prime minister in 1940, signed an armistice with Germany, and moved his government to Vichy. After the war he was accused of collaboration with the Germans and died in prison.

1 To make a union with Great Britain would be fusion with a corpse.

On hearing Churchill's suggestion for an Anglo-French union, 1940
Their Finest Hour (Winston S. Churchill), Ch. 10

2 *Ils ne passeront pas.*
They shall not pass.

Attrib; probably derived from General R. G. Nivelle's Order of the Day, '*Vous ne les laisserez pas passer*' (June 1916)

Peter, Laurence J. (1919–90) Canadian writer. He is best known for his book *The Peter Principle*.

1 *Papyromania* – compulsive accumulation of papers . . .
Papyrophobia – abnormal desire for 'a clean desk'.

The Peter Principle, Glossary

2 Work is accomplished by those employees who have not yet reached their level of incompetence.

The Peter Principle

3 A pessimist is a man who looks both ways before crossing a one-way street.

Peter's Quotations

Peterborough, Charles Mordaunt, 3rd Earl of (1658–1735) English military and naval commander. On the accession of William III he became first lord of the treasury (1689). Under George I he was appointed chief of the navy.

1 In the first place, I have only five guineas in my pocket; and in the second, they are very much at your service.

Persuading an angry mob that he was not the Duke of Marlborough, notorious for his meanness
Dictionary of National Biography

Petrarch (Francesco Petrarca; 1304–74) Italian lyric poet and scholar. He is mainly remembered for his series of love poems addressed to Laura, the *Canzoniere*. Other works include *Secretum Meum* and *Africa*.

1 It may be only glory that we seek here, but I persuade myself that, as long as we remain here, that is right. Another glory awaits us in heaven and he who reaches there will not wish even to think of earthly fame. So this is the natural order, that among mortals the care of things mortal should come first; to the transitory will then succeed the eternal; from the first to the second is the natural progression.

Secretum Meum

2 She closed her eyes; and in sweet slumber lying, her spirit tiptoed from its lodging-place.
It's folly to shrink in fear, if this is dying;
for death looked lovely in her lovely face.

Triumphs

Petronius Arbiter (1st century AD) Roman satirist. A companion of Nero, he wrote the *Satyricon*, a licentious and satirical romance.

1 A huge dog, tied by a chain, was painted on the wall and over it was written in capital letters 'Beware of the dog.'

Latin, *Cave canem*
Satyricon: Cena Trimalchionis, 29

2 He's gone to join the majority.

Referring to a dead man
Satyricon: Cena Trimalchionis, 42

Pevsner, Sir Nikolaus (Bernhard Leon; 1902–83) German-born British art historian. His best-known works are *An Outline of European Architecture* (1942) and *The Buildings of England* (1951–74).

1 No part of the walls is left undecorated. From everywhere the praise of the Lord is drummed into you.

London, except the Cities of London and Westminster

Phelps, Edward John (1822–1900) US lawyer and diplomat. He was US minister to Great Britain (1855–89).

1 The man who makes no mistakes does not usually make anything.

Speech, Mansion House, London, 24 Jan 1899

Philip, John Woodward (1840–1900) US naval officer. He commanded the *Texas* in the battle off Santiago in 1898.

1 Don't cheer, boys; the poor devils are dying.

Restraining his victorious crew during the naval battle off Santiago in the Spanish-American War
Attrib.

Philip, Prince, Duke of Edinburgh (1921–) The consort of Queen Elizabeth II. The son of Prince Andrew of Greece, he assumed his uncle's name, Mountbatten, when he became a British citizen.

1 I include 'pidgin-English' . . . even though I am referred to in that splendid language as 'Fella belong Mrs Queen'.

Speech, English-Speaking Union Conference, Ottawa, 29 Oct 1958

2 I think it is about time we pulled our fingers out . . . The rest of the world most certainly does not owe us a living.

Speech, London, 17 Oct 1961

3 The biggest waste of water in the country by far. You spend half a pint and flush two gallons.

Speech, 1965

4 Simply having a convention which says you must not make species extinct does not make a blind bit of difference.

Referring to the UN treaty on world conservation, Mar 1989
The Sunday Correspondent, 31 Dec, 1989

5 I'm self-employed.

Answering a query as to what nature of work he did
Attrib.

6 I declare this thing open – whatever it is.

Opening a new annex at Vancouver City Hall
Attrib.

7 A man can be forgiven a lot if he can quote Shakespeare in an economic crisis.

Attrib.

Philippe, Charles-Louis (1874–1909) French novelist. His books include *Bubu de Montparnasse* (1901).

1 One always has the air of someone who is lying when one speaks to a policeman.

Les Chroniques du canard sauvage

Phillips, Wendell (1811–84) US reformer. He advocated the abolition of slavery, prohibition, and women's suffrage.

1 We live under a government of men and morning newspapers.

Address: The Press

2 One on God's side is a majority.

Speech, Brooklyn, 1 Nov 1859

3 Every man meets his Waterloo at last.

Speech, Brooklyn, 1 Nov 1859

Phillpotts, Eden (1862–1960) British novelist and dramatist. His novels include *Lying Prophets* (1896) and *Widecombe Fair* (1913). *The Farmer's Wife* (1917) was his first play.

1 His father's sister had bats in the belfry and was put away.

Peacock House, 'My First Murder'

Picasso, Pablo (1881–1973) Spanish painter, sculptor, and stage designer. An exceptionally versatile artist, his work was influenced by cubism, surrealism, African sculpture, and classicism.

Quotations about Picasso

1 A Catalan wizard who fools with shapes.

Bernhard Berenson (1865–1959) US art critic and writer. *Berenson: A Biography* (Sylvia Sprigge)

2 His sickness has created atrocities that are repellent. Every one of his paintings deforms man, his body and his face.

V. Kemenov Soviet art critic.

3 Nothing unites the English like war. Nothing divides them like Picasso.

Hugh Mills (1913–71) British screenwriter. *Prudence and The Pill*

4 If my husband would ever meet a woman on the street who looked like the women in his paintings he would fall over in a dead faint.

Mme Picasso

Quotations by Picasso

5 There's no such thing as a bad Picasso, but some are less good than others.

Come to Judgment (A. Whitman)

6 Painting is a blind man's profession. He paints not what he sees, but what he feels, what he tells himself about what he has seen.

Journals (Jean Cocteau), 'Childhood'

7 God is really only another artist. He invented the giraffe, the elephant, and the cat. He has no real style, He just goes on trying other things.

Life with Picasso (Françoise Gilot and Carlton Lake), Ch. 1

8 I hate that aesthetic game of the eye and the mind, played by these connoisseurs, these mandarins who 'appreciate' beauty. What *is* beauty, anyway? There's no such thing. I never 'appreciate', any more than I 'like'. I love or I hate.

Life with Picasso (Françoise Gilot and Carlton Lake), Ch. 2

9 Age only matters when one is ageing. Now that I have arrived at a great age, I might just as well be twenty.

The Observer, *Shouts and Murmurs*, 'Picasso in Private' (John Richardson)

10 When I was their age, I could draw like Raphael, but it took me a lifetime to learn to draw like them.

Visiting an exhibition of drawings by children
Picasso: His Life and Work (Ronald Penrose)

11 It's better like that, if you want to kill a picture all you have to do is to hang it beautifully on a nail and soon you will see nothing of it but the frame. When it's out of place you see it better.

Explaining why a Renoir in his apartment was hung crooked
Picasso: His Life and Work (Ronald Penrose)

Pickles, Wilfred (1904–78) British radio personality and character actor. He presented the series *Have a Go* with his wife Mabel in the 1940s and 1950s.

1 Give him the money, Barney.

Said to Barney Colehan
Have a Go (BBC radio programme), *passim*

Pinero, Sir Arthur (1855–1934) British dramatist. His early farces included *The Magistrate* (1885) and *Dandy Dick* (1887). *The Second Mrs Tanqueray* (1893) dealt with serious social problems.

1 From forty to fifty a man is at heart either a stoic or a satyr.

The Second Mrs Tanqueray, I

Pinter, Harold (1930–) British dramatist. His well-known plays include *The Birthday Party* (1958), *The Caretaker* (1960), *Family Voices* (1981), and *Mountain Language* (1988). He has also written film scripts and directed plays.

1 If only I could get down to Sidcup! I've been waiting for the weather to break. He's got my papers, this man I left them with, it's got it all down there, I could prove everything.

The Caretaker, I

2 In other words, apart from the known and the unknown, what else is there?

The Homecoming, II

3 The earth's about five thousand million years old. Who can afford to live in the past?

The Homecoming

4 The weasel under the cocktail cabinet.

Reply when asked what his plays were about.
Anger and After (J. Russell Taylor)

Piron, Alexis (1689–1773) French poet and dramatist. He is also known for his epigrams.

1 I think you would have been very glad if I had written it.

Discussing Voltaire's *Sémiramis* with him after its poor reception on the first night
Cyclopaedia of Anecdotes (K. Arvine)

Pirsig, Robert T. (1928–) US writer, best-known for his book *Zen and the Art of Motorcycle Maintenance* (1974).

1 You are never dedicated to something you have complete confidence in. No one is fanatically shouting that the sun is going to rise tomorrow. They *know* it's going to rise tomorrow. When people are fanatically dedicated to political or religious faiths or any other kind of dogmas or goals, it's always because these dogmas or goals are in doubt.

Zen and the Art of Motorcycle Maintenance, Pt. II, Ch. 13

2 One geometry cannot be more true than another; it can only be more convenient. Geometry is not true, it is advantageous.

Zen and the Art of Motorcycle Maintenance, Pt. III, Ch. 22

3 Traditional scientific method has always been at the very *best*, 20-20 hindsight. It's good for seeing where you've been.

Zen and the Art of Motorcycle Maintenance, Pt. III, Ch. 24

4 We keep passing unseen through little moments of other people's lives.

Zen and the Art of Motorcycle Maintenance, Pt. III, Ch. 24

5 That's the classical mind at work, runs fine inside but looks dingy on the surface.

Zen and the Art of Motorcycle Maintenance, Pt. III, Ch. 25

Pitter, Ruth (1897–) British poet. Her published works include *A Trophy of Arms* (1936), *The Ermine* (1953), and *End of Drought* (1975).

1 The seldom female in a world of males!
The Kitten's Eclogue, IV

Pitts, William Ewart (1900–) Chief Constable, Derbyshire County Police (1953–67).

1 It is the overtakers who keep the undertakers busy.
The Observer, 'Sayings of the Week', 22 Dec 1963

Pitt the Elder, William, 1st Earl of Chatham (1708–78) British statesman. An outstanding orator, he entered parliament in 1735, becoming paymaster general (1746–55) and secretary of state in 1756. He was in charge of foreign affairs during the Seven Years' War. Pitt resigned in 1761, returning to form a new ministry (1766–68) as Earl of Chatham.

1 The poorest man may in his cottage bid defiance to all the forces of the Crown. It may be frail – its roof may shake – the wind may blow through it – the storm may enter – the rain may enter – but the King of England cannot enter! – all his force dares not cross the threshold of the ruined tenement!
Statesmen in the Time of George III (Lord Brougham), Vol. I

2 The atrocious crime of being a young man . . . I shall neither attempt to palliate nor deny.
Speech, House of Commons, 27 Jan 1741

3 Unlimited power is apt to corrupt the minds of those who possess it.
See also Lord ACTON
Speech, House of Lords, 9 Jan 1770

4 Where laws end, tyranny begins.
Speech, House of Lords, referring to the Wilkes case, 9 Jan 1770

5 There is something behind the throne greater than the King himself.
Speech, House of Lords, 2 Mar 1770

6 If I were an American, as I am an Englishman, while a foreign troop was landed in my country, I never would lay down my arms, – never – never – never!
Speech, House of Lords, 18 Nov 1777

Pitt the Younger, William (1759–1806) British statesman, Britain's youngest prime minister at the age of 24 (1783–1801). He resigned following George III's refusal to accept Catholic emancipation, but returned to office (1804–06) for a second administration.

1 Necessity is the plea for every infringement of human freedom. It is the argument of tyrants; it is the creed of slaves.
Speech, House of Commons, 18 Nov 1783

2 Roll up that map: it will not be wanted these ten years.
On learning that Napoleon had won the Battle of Austerlitz
Attrib.

3 I think I could eat one of Bellamy's veal pies.
Last words
Attrib.

4 Oh, my country! How I leave my country!
Last words
Attrib.

Plath, Sylvia (1932–63) US poet and novelist. She married Ted Hughes in 1956; her only novel, *The Bell Jar*, was published less than a month after she committed suicide. Other works include *Ariel* (1965), *Crossing the Water* (1971), *Winter Trees* (1971), and *Collected Poems* (1981).

1 Dying
is an art, like everything else.
I do it exceptionally well.
Lady Lazarus

2 The surgeon is quiet, he does not speak.
He has seen too much death, his hands are full of it.
Winter Trees, 'The Courage of Shutting-Up'

3 I am no shadow
Though there is a shadow starting from my feet.
I am a wife.
The city waits and aches. The little grasses
Crack through stone, and they are green with life.
Winter Trees, 'The Three Women'

Plato (429–347 BC) Greek philosopher. A disciple of Socrates and teacher of Aristotle, he founded the first university (the Academy) in Athens. His works include the *Phaedo* (on immortality), *Symposium* (on love), and *Republic* (on government).

1 The good is the beautiful.
Lysis

2 Our object in the construction of the state is the greatest happiness of the whole, and not that of any one class.
Republic, Bk. 4

3 I wonder if we could contrive . . . some magnificent myth that would in itself carry conviction to our whole community.
Republic, Bk. 5

4 There will be no end to the troubles of states, or indeed, my dear Glaucon, of humanity itself, till philosophers become kings in this world, or till those we now call kings and rulers really and truly become philosophers.
Republic, Bk. 5

5 Democracy passes into despotism.
Republic, Bk. 8

6 Let no one ignorant of mathematics enter here.
Inscription written over the entrance to the Academy
Biographical Encyclopedia (I. Asimov)

Plautus, Titus Maccius (254–184 BC) Roman dramatist. His 21 surviving plays were adapted from Greek New Comedy writers and have influenced both Shakespeare and Moliere.

1 He whom the gods favour dies young.
Bacchides IV

Pliny the Elder (Gaius Plinius Secundus; 23–79 AD) Roman scholar. His *Natural History* was a major source of knowledge until the 17th century. He died while closely observing an eruption of Vesuvius.

1 Attic wit.

Natural History, II

2 Amid the miseries of our life on earth, suicide is God's best gift to man.

Natural History, II

3 It is far from easy to determine whether she has proved a kind parent to man or a merciless step-mother.

Referring to Nature
Natural History, VII

4 There is always something new out of Africa.

Natural History, VIII

5 *In vino veritas.*
Truth comes out in wine.

Natural History, XIV

Plomer, William (1903–73) South African poet and novelist. His published works include *Taste and Remember* (1966) and *Celebrations* (1972). He also wrote several libretti for operas by Benjamin Britten.

1 A pleasant old buffer, nephew to a lord,
Who believed that the bank was mightier than the sword,
And that an umbrella might pacify barbarians abroad:
Just like an old liberal
Between the wars.

Father and Son: 1939

2 With first-rate sherry flowing into second-rate whores,
And third-rate conversation without one single pause:
Just like a couple
Between the wars.

Father and Son: 1939

3 On a sofa upholstered in panther skin
Mona did researches in original sin.

Mews Flat Mona

Plotinus (205–270 AD) Egpytian-born Greek philosopher. He developed Plato's mysticism and founded neoplatonism.

1 It is bad enough to be condemned to drag around this image in which nature has imprisoned me. Why should I consent to the perpetuation of the image of this image?

Refusing to have his portrait painted
Attrib.

Poe, Edgar Allan (1809–49) US poet and writer. His many prose tales and horror stories include *The Fall of the House of Usher* (1839) and the first detective story, *The Murders in the Rue Morgue* (1841).

1 Once upon a midnight dreary, while I pondered, weak and weary,
Over many a quaint and curious volume of forgotten lore,
While I nodded, nearly napping, suddenly there came a tapping,
As of some one gently rapping, rapping at my chamber door.

The Raven

2 Take thy beak from out my heart, and take thy form from off my door!
Quoth the Raven, 'Nevermore.'

The Raven

Pompadour, Madame de (1721–64) The mistress of Louis XV of France. She exerted great influence in political affairs and was blamed for the Seven Years' War.

1 *Après nous le déluge.*
After us the deluge.

After the Battle of Rossbach, 1757

Pompidou, Georges (Jean Raymond) (1911–74) French statesman. He was four times prime minister, and followed de Gaulle as president (1969–74).

1 A statesman is a politician who places himself at the service of the nation. A politician is a statesman who places the nation at his service.

The Observer, 'Sayings of the Year', 30 Dec 1973

Pope, Alexander (1688–1744) British poet. His witty and satirical poems include the mock-heroic *The Rape of the Lock* (1712), the mock epic *The Dunciad* (1728), and the philosophical *An Essay on Man* (1733).

Quotations about Pope

1 The wicked asp of Twickenham.

Lady Mary Wortley Montague (1689–1762) English writer. Attrib.

2 In Pope I cannot read a line,
But with a sigh I wish it mine;
When he can in one couplet fix
More sense than I can do in six:
It gives me such a jealous fit,
I cry, 'Pox take him and his wit!'

Jonathan Swift (1667–1745) Irish-born Anglican priest and writer. *On the Death of Dr. Swift*

Quotations by Pope

3 Ye gods! annihilate but space and time.
And make two lovers happy.

The Art of Sinking in Poetry, 11

4 The right divine of kings to govern wrong.

The Dunciad, IV

5 When man's whole frame is obvious to a flea.

The Dunciad, IV

6 I mount! I fly!
O grave! where is thy victory?
O death! where is thy sting?

The Dying Christian to his Soul

7 A heap of dust alone remains of thee;
'Tis all thou art, and all the proud shall be!
Elegy to the Memory of an Unfortunate Lady

8 Line after line my gushing eyes o'erflow,
led through a sad variety of woe.
Eloisa to Abelard

9 You beat your pate, and fancy wit will come;
Knock as you please, there's nobody at home.
Epigram

10 Do good by stealth, and blush to find it fame.
Epilogue to the Satires, Dialogue I

11 Ask you what provocation I have had?
The strong antipathy of good to bad.
Epilogue to the Satires, Dialogue II

12 Yes; I am proud, I must be proud to see
Men not afraid of God, afraid of me.
Epilogue to the Satires, Dialogue II

13 The Muse but serv'd to ease some friend, not Wife,
To help me through this long disease, my life.
Epistle to Dr. Arbuthnot

14 Damn with faint praise, assent with civil leer,
And, without sneering, teach the rest to sneer.
Epistle to Dr. Arbuthnot

15 Curst be the verse, how well so'er it flow,
That tends to make one worthy man my foe.
Epistle to Dr. Arbuthnot

16 Wit that can creep, and pride that licks the dust.
Epistle to Dr. Arbuthnot

17 No creature smarts so little as a fool.
Epistle to Dr. Arbuthnot

18 In wit a man; simplicity a child.
Epitaph on Mr. Gay

19 Nature, and Nature's laws lay hid in night:
God said, *Let Newton be!* and all was light.
For a reply, *see* SQUIRE
Epitaphs, 'Intended for Sir Isaac Newton'

20 'Tis hard to say, if greater want of skill
Appear in writing or in judging ill.
An Essay on Criticism

21 'Tis with our judgments as our watches, none
Go just alike, yet each believes his own.
An Essay on Criticism

22 Of all the causes which conspire to blind
Man's erring judgment, and misguide the mind,
What the weak head with strongest bias rules,
Is Pride, the never-failing vice of fools.
An Essay on Criticism

23 A little learning is a dangerous thing;
Drink deep, or taste not the Pierian spring:
There shallow draughts intoxicate the brain,
And drinking largely sobers us again.
An Essay on Criticism

24 Whoever thinks a faultless piece to see,
Thinks what ne'er was, nor is, nor e'er shall be.
An Essay on Criticism

25 True wit is nature to advantage dress'd;
What oft was thought, but ne'er so well express'd.
An Essay on Criticism

26 True ease in writing comes from art, not chance,
As those move easiest who have learn'd to dance.
'Tis not enough no harshness gives offence,
The sound must seem an echo to the sense.
An Essay on Criticism

27 Fondly we think we honour merit then,
When we but praise ourselves in other men.
An Essay on Criticism

28 To err is human, to forgive, divine.
An Essay on Criticism

29 For fools rush in where angels fear to tread.
An Essay on Criticism

30 Words are like leaves; and where they most abound,
Much fruit of sense beneath is rarely found.
An Essay on Criticism

31 Nor in the critic let the man be lost.
An Essay on Criticism

32 Hope springs eternal in the human breast;
Man never is, but always to be blest.
An Essay on Man, I

33 Created half to rise, and half to fall;
Great lord of all things, yet a prey to all;
Sole judge of truth, in endless error hurl'd;
The glory, jest, and riddle of the world!
An Essay on Man, II

34 Know then thyself, presume not God to scan,
The proper study of Mankind is Man.
An Essay on Man, II

35 And hence one master-passion in the breast,
Like Aaron's serpent, swallows up the rest.
An Essay on Man, II

36 That true self-love and social are the same;
That virtue only makes our bliss below;
And all our knowledge is, ourselves to know.
An Essay on Man, IV

37 Order is heaven's first law.
An Essay on Man, IV

38 Not to admire, is all the art I know
To make men happy, and to keep them so.
Imitations of Horace, 'To Mr. Murray'

39 To observations which ourselves we make.
We grow more partial for th' observer's sake.
Moral Essays, I

40 'Tis education forms the common mind,
Just as the twig is bent, the tree's inclined.
Moral Essays, I

41 Most women have no characters at all.
Moral Essays, II

42 Men, some to business, some to pleasure take;
But every woman is at heart a rake.
Moral Essays, II

43 Woman's at best a contradiction still.
Moral Essays, II

44 See how the world its veterans rewards!
A youth of frolics, an old age of cards.
Moral Essays, II

45 The ruling passion, be it what it will
The ruling passion conquers reason still.
Moral Essays, III

46 Who shall decide when doctors disagree?
Moral Essays, III

47 Where'er you walk, cool gales shall fan the glade,
Trees, where you sit, shall crowd into a shade:
Where'er you tread, the blushing flow'rs shall rise,
And all things flourish where you turn your eyes.
Pastorals, 'Summer'

48 What dire offence from am'rous causes springs,
What mighty contests rise from trivial things.
The Rape of the Lock, I

49 Here thou great Anna! whom three realms obey,
Dost sometimes counsel take – and sometimes Tea.
The Rape of the Lock, III

50 Not louder shrieks to pitying heav'n are cast,
When husbands, or when lap-dogs breathe their last.
The Rape of the Lock, III

51 The hungry judges soon the sentence sign,
And wretches hang that jury-men may dine.
The Rape of the Lock, III

52 Coffee which makes the politician wise,
And see through all things with his half-shut eyes.
The Rape of the Lock, III

53 The vulgar boil, the learned roast an egg.
Satires and Epistles of Horace Imitated, Bk II

54 A man should never be ashamed to own he has been in the wrong, which is but saying, in other words, that he is wiser to-day than he was yesterday.
Thoughts on Various Subjects

55 It is with narrow-souled people as with narrow-necked bottles: the less they have in them, the more noise they make in pouring it out.
Thoughts on Various Subjects

56 When men grow virtuous in their old age, they only make a sacrifice to God of the devil's leavings.
Thoughts on Various Subjects

57 I never knew any man in my life who could not bear another's misfortunes perfectly like a Christian.
Thoughts on Various Subjects

58 The vanity of human life is like a river, constantly passing away, and yet constantly coming on.
Thoughts on Various Subjects

59 Here am I, dying of a hundred good symptoms.
Anecdotes by and about Alexander Pope (Joseph Spence)

60 'Blessed is the man who expects nothing, for he shall never be disappointed' was the ninth beatitude.
Letter to Fortescue, 23 Sept 1725

61 How often are we to die before we go quite off this stage? In every friend we lose a part of ourselves, and the best part.
Letter to Jonathan Swift, 5 Dec 1732

62 I am His Highness' dog at Kew;
Pray tell me sir, whose dog are you?
On the collar of a dog given to Frederick, Prince of Wales

Popper, Sir Karl (1902–) Austrian-born British philosopher. Interested in science and politics, he has written *The Logic of Scientific Discovery* (1935), *The Open Society and its Enemies* (1945), *The Poverty of Historicism* (1957), and *Of Clouds and Clocks* (1966), among many other books.

1 Our knowledge can only be finite, while our ignorance must necessarily be infinite.
Conjectures and Refutations

2 Our civilization . . . has not yet fully recovered from the shock of its birth – the transition from the tribal or 'closed society', with its submission to magical forces, to the 'open society' which sets free the critical powers of man.
The Open Society and Its Enemies

3 There is no history of mankind, there are only many histories of all kinds of aspects of human life. And one of these is the history of political power. This is elevated into the history of the world.
The Open Society and Its Enemies

4 We must plan for freedom, and not only for security, if for no other reason than that only freedom can make security secure.
The Open Society and Its Enemies

5 Science must begin with myths, and with the criticism of myths.
British Philosophy in the Mid-Century (ed. C. A. Mace)

6 We may become the makers of our fate when we have ceased to pose as its prophets.
The Observer, 28 Dec 1975

Porson, Richard (1759–1808) British classicist. He edited many classical plays and became known for his *Letters to Archdeacon Travis* (1788–89).

1 Life is too short to learn German.
Gryll Grange (T. L. Peacock), Ch. 3

2 Your works will be read after Shakespeare and Milton are forgotten – and not till then.

Giving his opinion of the poems of Robert Southey
Quotable Anecdotes (L. Meissen)

Porter, Cole (1893–1964) American songwriter and composer, noted for his witty lyrics. He wrote scores for such musicals as *Kiss Me Kate* (1953), *High Society* (1956), and *Can-Can* (1959).

1 Now: heaven knows, anything goes.

Anything Goes, title song

2 I've Got You Under My Skin.

Born to Dance, song title

3 I love Paris in the springtime.

Can-Can, 'I Love Paris'

4 Night and day, you are the one,
Only you beneath the moon and under the sun.

The Gay Divorcee, 'Night and Day'

5 Miss Otis regrets she's unable to lunch today.

Hi Diddle Diddle, Miss Otis Regrets

6 HE. Have you heard it's in the stars
Next July we collide with Mars?
SHE. Well, did you evah! What a swell party this is.

High Society 'Well, Did You Evah!'

7 And we suddenly know, what heaven we're in,
When they begin the beguine.

Jubilee, 'Begin the Beguine'

8 But I'm always true to you, darlin', in my fashion,
Yes, I'm always true to you, darlin', in my way.

Kiss Me, Kate, 'Always True to You in My Fashion'

9 Let's Do It; Let's Fall in Love.

Paris, song title

10 Who Wants to Be a Millionaire? I don't.

Who Wants to be a Millionaire?, title song

Porter, Sir George (1920–   ) British chemist who developed the technique of flash photolysis. He won the Nobel prize for chemistry in 1967.

1 If sunbeams were weapons of war, we would have had solar energy long ago.

The Observer, 'Sayings of the Week', 26 Aug 1973

2 Should we force science down the throats of those that have no taste for it? Is it our duty to drag them kicking and screaming into the twenty-first century? I am afraid that it is.

Speech, Sept 1986

Portland, William John Arthur Charles James Cavendish-Bentinck, 6th Duke of (1857–1943) British peer.

1 What! Can't a fellow even enjoy a biscuit any more?

On being informed that as one of several measures to reduce his own expenses he would have to dispense with one of his two Italian pastry cooks
Their Noble Lordships (S. Winchester)

Post, Emily (1873–1960) US writer and columnist. She is remembered for her book *Etiquette* (1922).

1 Ideal conversation must be an exchange of thought, and not, as many of those who worry most about their shortcomings believe, an eloquent exhibition of wit or oratory.

Etiquette, Ch. 6

2 To the old saying that man built the house but woman made of it a 'home' might be added the modern supplement that woman accepted cooking as a chore but man has made of it a recreation.

Etiquette, Ch. 34

Potter, Beatrix (1866–1943) British children's writer and illustrator. *The Tale of Peter Rabbit* (1900) was the first of many books.

1 I shall tell you a tale of four little rabbits whose names were Flopsy, Mopsy, Cottontail and Peter.

The Tale of Peter Rabbit

2 Don't go into Mr McGregor's garden: your Father had an accident there; he was put in a pie by Mrs McGregor.

The Tale of Peter Rabbit

Potter, Stephen (1900–70) British writer and critic. He is best known for his humorous studies on how to outwit an opponent, including *Gamesmanship* (1947), *Lifemanship* (1950), and *One-Upmanship* (1952).

1 Gamesmanship or The Art of Winning Games Without Actually Cheating.

Book title

2 *How to be one up* – how to make the other man feel that something has gone wrong, however slightly.

Lifemanship, Introduction

3 It is an important general rule always to refer to your friend's country establishment as a 'cottage'.

Lifemanship, Ch. 2

4 There is no doubt that basic weekendmanship should contain some reference to Important Person Play.

Lifemanship, Ch. 2

5 Donsmanship . . . 'the art of criticizing without actually listening'.

Lifemanship, Ch. 6

6 It is WRONG to do what everyone else does – namely, to hold the wine list just out of sight, look for the second cheapest claret on the list, and say, 'Number 22, please'.

One-Upmanship, Ch. 14

7 A good general rule is to state that the bouquet is better than the taste, and vice versa.

One-Upmanship, Ch. 14

Pound, Ezra (1885–1972) US poet and critic. His poetry includes *Hugh Selwyn Mauberly* (1920) and *The Pisan Cantos* (1925–69). His support for Mussolini led to his confinement in a US mental hospital (1946–58).

Quotations about Pound

1 To me Pound remains the exquisite showman minus the show.

Ben Hecht *Pounding Ezra*

2 I confess I am seldom interested in what he is saying, but only in the way he says it.

T. S. Eliot (1888–1965) US born British poet and dramatist. *The Dial*, 'Isolated superiority'

Quotations by Pound

3 Music begins to atrophy when it departs too far from the dance; . . . poetry begins to atrophy when it gets too far from music.

ABC of Reading, 'Warning'

4 One of the pleasures of middle age is to *find out* that one WAS right, and that one was much righter than one knew at say 17 or 23.

ABC of Reading, Ch. 1

5 Literature is news that STAYS news.

ABC of Reading, Ch. 2

6 Any general statement is like a cheque drawn on a bank. Its value depends on what is there to meet it.

ABC of Reading, Ch. 2

7 Winter is icummen in,
Lhude sing Goddamm,
Raineth drop and staineth slop
And how the wind doth ramm!
Sing: Goddamm.

Ancient Music

8 And even I can remember
A day when the historians left blanks in their writings,
I mean for things they didn't know.

Cantos, XIII

9 Bah! I have sung women in three cities,
But it is all the same;
And I will sing of the sun.

Cino

10 The difference between a gun and a tree is a difference of tempo. The tree explodes every spring.

Criterion, July 1937

11 Great Literature is simply language charged with meaning to the utmost possible degree.

How to Read

12 For three years, out of key with his time,
He strove to resuscitate the dead art
Of poetry to maintain 'the sublime'
In the old sense. Wrong from the start.

Pour l'élection de son sépulcre

Powell, Anthony (1905–) British novelist. His satirical *A Dance to the Music of Time* comprises twelve volumes published between 1951 and 1975; later novels include *The Fisher King* (1986).

1 He fell in love with himself at first sight and it is a passion to which he has always remained faithful. Self-love seems so often unrequited.

A Dance to the Music of Time: The Acceptance World, Ch. 1

2 Dinner at the Huntercombes' possessed 'only two dramatic features – the wine was a farce and the food a tragedy'.

A Dance to the Music of Time: The Acceptance World, Ch. 4

3 All men are brothers, but, thank God, they aren't all brothers-in-law.

A Dance to the Music of Time: At Lady Molly's, Ch. 4

4 It must be generations since anyone but highbrows lived in this cottage . . . I imagine most of the agricultural labourers round here commute from London.

A Dance to the Music of Time: The Kindly Ones, Ch. 2

5 One of the worst things about life is not how nasty the nasty people are. You know that already. It is how nasty the nice people can be.

A Dance to the Music of Time: The Kindly Ones, Ch. 4

6 Growing old is like being increasingly penalized for a crime you haven't committed.

A Dance to the Music of Time: Temporary Kings, Ch. 1

7 People think that because a novel's invented, it isn't true. Exactly the reverse is the case. Biography and memoirs can never be wholly true, since they cannot include every conceivable circumstance of what happened. The novel can do that.

A Dance to the Music of Time: Hearing Secret Harmonies, Ch. 3

Powell, (John) Enoch (1912–) British politician. In 1974 he left the Conservative Party after his dismissal from the shadow cabinet, following a controversial speech on immigration, which he has always opposed.

1 As I look ahead, I am filled with foreboding. Like the Roman, I seem to see 'the River Tiber foaming with much blood'.

Talking about immigration
Speech in Birmingham, 20 Apr 1968

2 Above any other position of eminence, that of Prime Minister is filled by fluke.

The Observer, 'Sayings of the Week', 8 Mar 1987

Powell, Sir John (1645–1713) English judge.

1 Let us consider the reason of the case. For nothing is law that is not reason.

Coggs v. Bernard, 2 Lord Raymond, 911

Powys, John Cowper (1872–1963) British novelist bestknown for such West-Country stories as *Wolf Solent* (1929) and *A Glastonbury Romance* (1932).

1 He combined scepticism of everything with credulity about everything . . . and I am convinced
this is the true Shakespearean way wherewith
to take life.
Autobiography

2 Who has not watched a mother stroke her child's
cheek or kiss her child *in a certain way* and felt
a nervous shudder at the possessive outrage
done to a free solitary human soul?
The Meaning of Culture

Prescott, William (1726–95) US revolutionary soldier. He
was colonel of a regiment in the War of Independence (1775) and
fought in the battle of Bunker Hill.

1 Don't fire until you see the whites of their eyes.
Command given at the Battle of Bunker Hill

Previn, André (1929–) German-born conductor, pianist,
and composer who has become a US citizen. He was conductor of
the London Symphony Orchestra (1969–79) and the Royal
Philharmonic Orchestra (1987–).

1 The basic difference between classical music and
jazz is that in the former the music is always
greater than its performance – whereas the
way jazz is performed is always more important
than what is being played.
An Encyclopedia of Quotations about Music (Nat Shapiro)

Priestley, J(ohn) B(oynton) (1894–1984) British novelist
and dramatist, who also published books of criticism and memoirs.
His many successful works include *The Good Companions* (1929)
and *Dangerous Corner* (1932). He was a popular radio broadcaster
during World War II.

1 Comedy, we may say, is society protecting itself
– with a smile.
George Meredith

2 They will review a book by a writer much older
than themselves as if it were an over-ambitious
essay by a second-year student . . . It is the
little dons I complain about, like so many corgis
trotting up, hoping to nip your ankles.
Outcries and Asides

3 A number of anxious dwarfs trying to grill a
whale.
Referring to politicians
Outcries and Asides

4 The greater part of critics are parasites, who, if
nothing had been written, would find nothing to
write.
Outcries and Asides

5 If there was a little room somewhere in the British Museum that contained only about twenty
exhibits and good lighting, easy chairs, and a notice imploring you to smoke, I believe I
should become a museum man.
Self-Selected Essays, 'In the British Museum'

6 Our trouble is that we drink too much tea. I see
in this the slow revenge of the Orient, which
has diverted the Yellow River down our throats.
The Observer, 'Sayings of the Week', 15 May 1949

7 It is hard to tell where MCC ends and the
Church of England begins.
New Statesman, 20 July 1962, 'Topside Schools'

8 God can stand being told by Professor Ayer and
Marghanita Laski that He doesn't exist.
The Listener, 1 July 1965, 'The BBC's Duty to Society'

9 A novelist who writes nothing for 10 years finds
his reputation rising. Because I keep on producing books they say there must be something
wrong with this fellow.
The Observer, 'Sayings of the Week', 21 Sept 1969

10 Our great-grandchildren, when they learn how
we began this war by snatching glory out of defeat . . . may also learn how the little holiday
steamers made an excursion to hell and came
back glorious.
Referring to the British Expeditionary Force's evacuation from
Dunkirk
Broadcast, 5 June 1940

Prior, Matthew (1664–1721) British poet and politician. He
served as a diplomat in France and Holland; on the death of
Queen Anne he was imprisoned and while in prison wrote *Alma,
or the Progress of the Mind* (1718). Many of his brief epigrammatic
poems are collected in *Poems on Several Occasions* (1709).

1 Cur'd yesterday of my disease,
I died last night of my physician.
The Remedy Worse than the Disease

2 For hope is but the dream of those that wake.
Solomon, II

3 From ignorance our comfort flows,
The only wretched are the wise.
To the Hon. Charles Montague

Pritchett, Sir V(ictor) S(awden) (1900–) British
short-story writer and critic, who has also written frequently about
Spain. His books include two acclaimed autobiographical works, *A
Cab at the Door* (1968) and *Midnight Oil* (1971).

1 The detective novel is the art-for-art's-sake of
yawning Philistinism.
Books in General, 'The Roots of Detection'

Procter, Adelaide Anne (1825–64) British poet and
writer. She wrote *Legends and Lyrics* (1858), which included 'The
Lost Chord', and several hymns. She also wrote verse under the
pseudonym 'Mary Berwick'.

1 Seated one day at the organ,
I was weary and ill at ease,
And my fingers wandered idly
Over the noisy keys.
    . . .
But I struck one chord of music,
Like the sound of a great Amen.
Better known in the setting by Sir Arthur Sullivan
Legends and Lyrics, 'A Lost Chord'

Proudhon, Pierre Joseph (1809–65) French socialist.
Founder and editor of radical journals, he played an active part in
the socialist movement in Paris (1848) and is regarded as the
father of anarchism.

1 Property is theft.
Qu'est-ce que la Propriété?, Ch. 1

Proust, Marcel (1871–1922) French novelist. His masterpiece was a series of partly autobiographical novels, *À la recherche du temps perdu* (1913–27), which give a detailed portrait of the life of his time.

Quotations about Proust

1 Reading Proust is like bathing in someone else's dirty water.
Alexander Woollcott Attrib.

Quotations by Proust

2 The taste was that of the little crumb of madeleine which on Sunday mornings at Combray . . . , when I used to say good-day to her in her bedroom, my aunt Léonie used to give me, dipping it first in her own cup of real or of lime-flower tea.
À la recherche du temps perdu: Du côté de chez Swann

3 People often say that, by pointing out to a man the faults of his mistress, you succeed only in strengthening his attachment to her, because he does not believe you; yet how much more so if he does!
À la recherche du temps perdu: Du côté de chez Swann

4 The human face is indeed, like the face of the God of some Oriental theogony, a whole cluster of faces, crowded together but on different surfaces so that one does not see them all at once.
À la recherche du temps perdu: À l'ombre des jeunes filles en fleurs

5 There can be no peace of mind in love, since the advantage one has secured is never anything but a fresh starting-point for further desires.
À la recherche du temps perdu: À l'ombre des jeunes filles en fleurs

6 As soon as one is unhappy one becomes moral.
À la recherche du temps perdu: À l'ombre des jeunes filles en fleurs

7 A PUSHING LADY. What are your views on love? MME LEROI. Love? I make it constantly but I never talk about it.
À la recherche du temps perdu: Le Côté de Guermantes

8 It has been said that the highest praise of God consists in the denial of Him by the atheist, who finds creation so perfect that he can dispense with a creator.
À la recherche du temps perdu: Le Côté de Guermantes

9 A doctor who doesn't say too many foolish things is a patient half-cured, just as a critic is a poet who has stopped writing verse and a policeman a burglar who has retired from practice.
À la recherche du temps perdu: Le Côté de Guermantes

10 Neurosis has an absolute genius for malingering. There is no illness which it cannot counterfeit perfectly . . . If it is capable of deceiving the doctor, how should it fail to deceive the patient?
À la recherche du temps perdu: Le Côté de Guermantes

11 As soon as he ceased to be mad he became merely stupid. There are maladies we must not seek to cure because they alone protect us from others that are more serious.
À la recherche du temps perdu: Le Côté de Guermantes

12 His hatred of snobs was a derivative of his snobbishness, but made the simpletons (in other words, everyone) believe that he was immune from snobbishness.
À la recherche du temps perdu: Le Côté de Guermantes

13 There is nothing like desire for preventing the thing one says from bearing any resemblance to what one has in mind.
À la recherche du temps perdu: Le Côté de Guermantes

14 Good-bye, I've barely said a word to you, it is always like that at parties, we never see the people, we never say the things we should like to say, but it is the same everywhere in this life. Let us hope that when we are dead things will be better arranged.
À la recherche du temps perdu: Sodome et Gomorrhe

15 I have sometimes regretted living so close to Marie . . . because I may be very fond of her, but I am not quite so fond of her company.
À la recherche du temps perdu: Sodome et Gomorrhe

16 I have a horror of sunsets, they're so romantic, so operatic.
À la recherche du temps perdu: Sodome et Gomorrhe

17 It is seldom indeed that one parts on good terms, because if one were on good terms one would not part.
À la recherche du temps perdu: La Prisonnière

18 One of those telegrams of which M. de Guermantes had wittily fixed the formula: 'Cannot come, lie follows'.
À la recherche du temps perdu: Le Temps retrouvé

19 Happiness is beneficial for the body, but it is grief that develops the powers of the mind.
À la recherche du temps perdu: Le Temps retrouvé

20 Everything great in the world is done by neurotics; they alone founded our religions and created our masterpieces.
The Perpetual Pessimist (Sagittarius and George)

Proverbs A selection of the commonest proverbs and other sayings is given here. The proverbs are arranged in alphabetical order.

1 A bad penny always turns up.

2 A bad workman always blames his tools.

3 A bird in the hand is worth two in the bush.

4 Absence makes the heart grow fonder.

5 A cask of wine works more miracles than a church full of saints.
Italian proverb

6 A cat has nine lives.

7 A cat may look at a king.

8 Accidents will happen in the best regulated families.

9 A chain is no stronger than its weakest link.

10 A constant guest is never welcome.

11 Actions speak louder than words.

12 Adam's ale is the best brew.

13 A dimple in the chin, a devil within.

14 A drowning man will clutch at a straw.

15 A fool and his money are soon parted.

16 A fool at forty is a fool indeed.

17 A fool believes everything.

18 A friend in need is a friend indeed.

19 After a storm comes a calm.

20 After shaking hands with a Greek, count your fingers.

21 A good dog deserves a good bone.

22 A good drink makes the old young.

23 A good face is a letter of recommendation.

24 A good friend is my nearest relation.

25 A good scare is worth more than good advice.

26 A hedge between keeps friendship green.

27 A judge knows nothing unless it has been explained to him three times.

28 A lawyer never goes to law himself.

29 A lawyer's opinion is worth nothing unless paid for.

30 A liar is worse than a thief.

31 All are not saints that go to church.

32 All cats are grey in the dark.

33 All good things must come to an end.

34 All is fair in love and war.

35 All men are mortal.

36 All roads lead to Rome.

37 All's grist that comes to the mill.

38 All's well that ends well.

39 All that glitters is not gold.

40 All the world loves a lover.

41 All work and no play makes Jack a dull boy.

42 Although there exist many thousand subjects for elegant conversation, there are persons who cannot meet a cripple without talking about feet.
Chinese proverb

43 A man can die but once.

44 A man is as old as he feels, and a woman as old as she looks.

45 A man of straw is worth a woman of gold.

46 A meal without flesh is like feeding on grass.
Indian proverb

47 A miss is as good as a mile.

48 An apple a day keeps the doctor away.

49 An apple-pie without some cheese is like a kiss without a squeeze.

50 An atheist is one point beyond the devil.

51 An Englishman's home is his castle.

52 An Englishman's word is his bond.

53 An honest man's word is as good as his bond.

54 An hour in the morning is worth two in the evening.

55 A nod is as good as a wink to a blind horse.

56 Any port in a storm.

57 Any publicity is good publicity.

58 A penny saved is a penny earned.

59 A piece of churchyard fits everybody.

60 Appearances are deceptive.

61 A priest sees people at their best, a lawyer at their worst, but a doctor sees them as they really are.

62 A rainbow in the morning is the shepherd's warning; a rainbow at night is the shepherd's delight.

63 Ask a silly question and you'll get a silly answer.

64 Ask no questions and hear no lies.

65 A spur in the head is worth two in the heel.

66 As soon as man is born he begins to die.

67 A still tongue makes a wise head.

68 A stitch in time saves nine.

69 A tale never loses in the telling.

70 A trouble shared is a trouble halved.

71 A truly great man never puts away the simplicity of a child.
Chinese proverb

72 Attack is the best form of defence.

73 A watched pot never boils.

74 A woman's place is in the home.

75 A woman's work is never done.

76 A young physician fattens the churchyard.

77 Bad news travels fast.

78 Barking dogs seldom bite.

79 Beauty is in the eye of the beholder.

80 Beauty is only skin-deep.

81 Beauty is potent but money is omnipotent.

82 Beggars can't be choosers.

83 Believe nothing of what you hear, and only half of what you see.

84 Benefits make a man a slave.
Arabic proverb

85 Better a lie that heals than a truth that wounds.

86 Better an egg today than a hen tomorrow.

87 Better a thousand enemies outside the house than one inside.
Arabic proverb

88 Better be a fool than a knave.

89 Better be an old man's darling than a young man's slave.

90 Better be envied than pitied.

91 Better be safe than sorry.

92 Better late than never.

93 Birds of a feather flock together.

94 Blood is thicker than water.

95 Books and friends should be few but good.

96 Borrowed garments never fit well.

97 Bread is the staff of life.

98 Caesar's wife must be above suspicion.

99 Charity begins at home.

100 Christmas comes but once a year.

101 Civility costs nothing.

102 Cold hands, warm heart.

103 Constant dripping wears away the stone.

104 Curiosity killed the cat.

105 Cut your coat according to your cloth.

106 Dead men tell no tales.

107 Death defies the doctor.

108 Death is the great leveller.

109 Desperate cuts must have desperate cures.

110 Divide and rule.

111 Do as I say, not as I do.

112 Do as you would be done by.

113 Dog does not eat dog.

114 Doing is better than saying.

115 Don't count your chickens before they are hatched.

116 Don't cross the bridge till you get to it.

117 Don't cut off your nose to spite your face.

118 Don't meet troubles half-way.

119 Don't put all your eggs in one basket.

120 Don't spoil the ship for a ha'porth of tar.

121 Don't teach your grandmother to suck eggs.

122 Don't throw the baby out with the bathwater.

123 Don't wash your dirty linen in public.

124 Early to bed and early to rise, makes a man healthy, wealthy and wise.

125 Easier said than done.

126 East, west, home's best.

127 Easy come, easy go.

128 Eat to live and not live to eat.

129 Empty vessels make the greatest sound.

130 Even a worm will turn.

131 Every book must be chewed to get out its juice.
Chinese proverb

132 Every cloud has a silver lining.

133 Every dog has his day.

134 Every dog is allowed one bite.

135 Every family has a skeleton in the cupboard.

136 Every little helps.

137 Every man after his fashion.

138 Every man for himself, and the devil take the hindmost.

139 Every man is his own worst enemy.

140 Every man to his trade.

141 Every one is innocent until he is proved guilty.

142 Every one to his taste.

143 Every picture tells a story.

144 Everything comes to him who waits.

145 Experience is the best teacher.

146 Experience is the mother of wisdom.

147 Faith will move mountains.

148 Familiarity breeds contempt.

149 Fear of death is worse than death itself.

150 Fight fire with fire.

151 Finders keepers, losers seekers.

152 Fine feathers make fine birds.

153 Fine words butter no parsnips.

154 Fingers were made before forks, and hands before knives.

155 First come, first served.

156 First impressions are the most lasting.

157 First things first.

158 Fish and guests smell in three days.

159 Fools build houses, and wise men buy them.

160 Fools live poor to die rich.

161 Footprints on the sands of time are not made by sitting down.

162 Forbidden fruit is sweet.

163 Forewarned is forearmed.

164 Forgive and forget.

165 Fortune favours fools.

166 For want of a nail the shoe was lost; for want of a shoe the horse was lost; for want of a horse the rider was lost.

167 From clogs to clogs is only three generations.

168 From small beginnings come great things.

169 From the sublime to the ridiculous is only a step.

170 Garbage in, garbage out.

171 Genius is an infinite capacity for taking pains.

172 Give a dog a bad name and hang him.

173 Give a thief enough rope and he'll hang himself.

174 Give him an inch and he'll take a yard.

175 Give me a child for the first seven years, and you may do what you like with him afterwards.

176 God defend me from my friends; from my enemies I can defend myself.

177 God helps them that help themselves.

178 God is always on the side of the big battalions.

179 Good fences make good neighbours.

180 Go to bed with the lamb, and rise with the lark.

181 Great minds think alike.

182 Great oaks from little acorns grow.

183 Grey hairs are death's blossoms.

184 Half a loaf is better than no bread.

185 Handsome is as handsome does.

186 Haste makes waste.

187 Health is better than wealth.

188 He helps little that helps not himself.

189 He that fights and runs away, may live to fight another day.

190 He that has no children brings them up well.

191 He that has no wife, beats her oft.

192 He that is his own lawyer has a fool for a client.

193 He that knows little, often repeats it.

194 He that knows nothing, doubts nothing.

195 He that lives long suffers much.

196 He travels fastest who travels alone.

197 He was a bold man that first ate an oyster.

198 He who drinks a little too much drinks much too much.

199 He who hesitates is lost.

200 He who lives by the sword dies by the sword.

201 He who pays the piper calls the tune.

202 He who rides a tiger is afraid to dismount.

203 He who sups with the devil should have a long spoon.

204 History repeats itself.

205 Hoist your sail when the wind is fair.

206 Home is home, though it be never so homely.

207 Home is where the heart is.

208 Honesty is the best policy.

209 Hope for the best.

210 Hunger is the best sauce.

211 If a job's worth doing, it's worth doing well.

212 If anything can go wrong, it will.

213 If at first you don't succeed, try, try, try again.

214 If ifs and ans were pots and pans, there'd be no trade for tinkers.

215 If the mountain will not come to Mahomet, Mahomet must go to the mountain.

216 If wishes were horses, beggars would ride.

217 If you can't be good, be careful.

218 If you don't like the heat, get out of the kitchen.

219 If you play with fire you get burnt.

220 If you trust before you try, you may repent before you die.

221 If you want a thing well done, do it yourself.

222 Imitation is the sincerest form of flattery.

223 In for a penny, in for a pound.

224 In the country of the blind, the one-eyed man is king.

225 It is a long lane that has no turning.

226 It is better to be born lucky than rich.

227 It is easy to bear the misfortunes of others.

228 It is easy to be wise after the event.

229 It is no use crying over spilt milk.

230 It never rains but it pours.

231 It's an ill wind that blows nobody any good.

232 It's a small world.

233 It's too late to shut the stable door after the horse has bolted.

234 It takes all sorts to make a world.

235 It takes two to make a quarrel.

236 It takes two to tango.

237 It will all come right in the wash.

238 It will be all the same in a hundred years.

239 Jack of all trades, master of none.

240 Keep something for a rainy day.

241 Keep your mouth shut and your eyes open.

242 Keep your weather-eye open.

243 Kill not the goose that lays the golden egg.

244 Knowledge is power.

245 Knowledge is the mother of all virtue; all vice proceeds from ignorance.

246 Know thyself.

247 Laugh and grow fat.

248 Laugh before breakfast, you'll cry before supper.

249 Laughter is the best medicine.

250 Learning is a treasure which accompanies its owner everywhere.
Chinese proverb

251 Least said soonest mended.

252 Leave well alone.

253 Lend only that which you can afford to lose.

254 Let bygones be bygones.

255 Let sleeping dogs lie.

256 Let the cobbler stick to his last.

257 Life begins at forty.

258 Life is just a bowl of cherries.

259 Life is not all beer and skittles.

260 Life is sweet.

261 Like breeds like.

262 Like father, like son.

263 Listeners never hear good of themselves.

264 Live and learn.

265 Long absent, soon forgotten.

266 Look after number one.

267 Look before you leap.

268 Look on the bright side.

269 Love conquers all.

270 Love is blind.

271 Love laughs at locksmiths.

272 Love makes the world go round.

273 Love me, love my dog.

274 Love will find a way.

275 Love your neighbour, yet pull not down your hedge.

276 Lucky at cards, unlucky in love.

277 Mackerel sky and mares' tails make lofty ships carry low sails.

278 Make hay while the sun shines.

279 Manners maketh man.

280 Man proposes, God disposes.

281 Many a mickle makes a muckle.

282 Many a true word is spoken in jest.

283 Many hands make light work.

284 Many irons in the fire, some must cool.

285 March comes in like a lion and goes out like a lamb.

286 March winds and April showers bring forth May flowers.

287 Marriages are made in heaven.

288 Marry in haste, and repent at leisure.

289 Marry in Lent, and you'll live to repent.

290 Marry in May, rue for aye.

291 Meet on the stairs and you won't meet in heaven.

292 Mind your own business.

293 Moderation in all things.

294 Monday's child is fair of face, Tuesday's child is full of grace; Wednesday's child is full of woe, Thursday's child has far to go; Friday's child is loving and giving, Saturday's child works hard for its living; and the child that's born on the Sabbath day, is fair and wise and good and gay.

295 More haste, less speed.

296 Music helps not the toothache.

297 Music is the food of love.

298 Necessity is the mother of invention.

299 Needs must when the devil drives.

300 Ne'er cast a clout till May be out.

301 Never do things by halves.

302 Never judge from appearances.

303 Never look a gift horse in the mouth.

304 Never put off till tomorrow what you can do today.

305 Never say die.

306 Never speak ill of the dead.

307 Never too late to learn.

308 Ninety per cent of inspiration is perspiration.

309 No bees, no honey; no work, no money.

310 No love like the first love.

311 No man is a hero to his valet.

312 No man is infallible.

313 No names, no pack-drill.

314 No news is good news.

315 No pleasure without pain.

316 Nothing is certain but death and taxes.

317 Nothing so bad but it might have been worse.

318 Nothing succeeds like success.

319 Nothing ventured, nothing gained.

320 No time like the present.

321 Old habits die hard.

322 Old sins cast long shadows.

323 Old soldiers never die, they simply fade away.

324 Once a parson always a parson.

325 One for sorrow, two for mirth; three for a wedding, four for a birth; five for silver, six for gold; seven for a secret, not to be told; eight for heaven, nine for hell; and ten for the devil's own sel.
Referring to magpies or crows; there are numerous variants

326 One good turn deserves another.

327 One hour's sleep before midnight, is worth two after.

328 One joy scatters a hundred griefs.
Chinese proverb

329 One man's meat is another man's poison.

330 One swallow does not make a summer.

331 Opportunity seldom knocks twice.

332 Out of debt, out of danger.

333 Out of sight, out of mind.

334 Patience is a virtue.

335 Penny wise, pound foolish.

336 Pigs might fly, if they had wings.

337 Possession is nine points of the law.

338 Poverty is not a crime.

339 Practice makes perfect.

340 Practise what you preach.

341 Prevention is better than cure.

342 Promises are like pie-crust, made to be broken.

343 Punctuality is the politeness of princes.

344 Put an Irishman on the spit, and you can always get another Irishman to baste him.

345 Put off the evil hour as long as you can.

346 Rain before seven: fine before eleven.

347 Rain, rain, go away, come again another day.

348 Red sky at night, shepherd's delight; red sky in the morning, shepherd's warning.

349 Revenge is a dish that tastes better cold.

350 Revenge is sweet.

351 Rome was not built in a day.

352 Sailors have a port in every storm.

353 Salt water and absence wash away love.

354 Save your breath to cool your porridge.

355 Saying is one thing, and doing another.

356 Scratch my back and I'll scratch yours.

357 See a pin and pick it up, all the day you'll have good luck; see a pin and let it lie, you'll want a pin before you die.

358 Seeing is believing.

359 See Naples and die.

360 Self-praise is no recommendation.

361 Send a fool to the market and a fool he will return again.

362 Silence is golden.

363 Slow but sure wins the race.

364 Small is beautiful.

365 Soon learnt, soon forgotten.

366 Spare the rod and spoil the child.

367 Speak when you are spoken to.

368 Speech is silver, silence is golden.

369 Sticks and stones may break my bones, but words will never hurt me.

370 Still waters run deep.

371 Strike while the iron is hot.

372 St. Swithin's Day, if thou dost rain, for forty days it will remain; St. Swithin's Day, if thou be fair, for forty days 'twill rain no more.

373 Take a hair of the dog that bit you.

374 Take care of the pence, and the pounds will take care of themselves.

375 Take things as they come.

376 Talk of the devil, and he is bound to appear.

377 Tell the truth and shame the devil.

378 The best of friends must part.

379 The best things come in small parcels.

380 The best things in life are free.

381 The better the day, the better the deed.

382 The cuckoo comes in April, and stays the month of May; sings a song at midsummer, and then goes away.

383 The darkest hour is just before the dawn.

384 The devil finds work for idle hands to do.

385 The devil is not so black as he is painted.

386 The devil looks after his own.

387 The early bird catches the worm.

388 The end justifies the means.

389 The exception proves the rule.

390 The eye is bigger than the belly.

391 The eyes are the window of the soul.

392 The family that prays together stays together.

393 The first day a guest, the second day a guest, the third day a calamity.
Indian proverb

394 The first step is the hardest.

395 The first wife is matrimony, the second company, the third heresy.

396 The good die young.

397 The guest who outstays his fellow-guests loses his overcoat.
Chinese proverb

398 The hand that rocks the cradle rules the world.

399 The last straw breaks the camel's back.

400 The law does not concern itself about trifles.

401 The more the merrier; the fewer the better fare.

402 The nearer the bone, the sweeter the flesh.

403 The north wind does blow, and we shall have snow.

404 The old man has his death before his eyes; the young man behind his back.

405 There are more old drunkards than old doctors.

406 There are only twenty-four hours in the day.

407 There is a time and place for everything.

408 There is honour among thieves.

409 There is more than one way to skin a cat.

410 There is no accounting for tastes.

411 There is safety in numbers.

412 There's a black sheep in every flock.

413 There's always room at the top.

414 There's many a good tune played on an old fiddle.

415 There's many a slip 'twixt the cup and the lip.

416 There's no fool like an old fool.

417 There's no place like home.

418 There's no smoke without fire.

419 There's nowt so queer as folk.

420 There's one law for the rich, and another for the poor.

421 There's only one pretty child in the world, and every mother has it.

422 There will be sleeping enough in the grave.

423 The road to hell is paved with good intentions.

424 The shoemaker's son always goes barefoot.

425 The streets of London are paved with gold.

426 The style is the man.

427 The way to a man's heart is through his stomach.

428 The weakest goes to the wall.

429 Things are not always what they seem.

430 Third time lucky.

431 Throw dirt enough, and some will stick.

432 Throw out a sprat to catch a mackerel.

433 Time and tide wait for no man.

434 Time is a great healer.

435 Time will tell.

436 To deceive oneself is very easy.

437 To err is human.

438 Tomorrow is another day.

439 Tomorrow never comes.

440 Too many cooks spoil the broth.

441 Travel broadens the mind.

442 True love never grows old.

443 Truth fears no trial.

444 Truth is stranger than fiction.

445 Truth will out.

446 Two heads are better than one.

447 Two wrongs do not make a right.

448 Union is strength.

449 United we stand, divided we fall.

450 Vice is often clothed in virtue's habit.

451 Walls have ears.

452 Waste not, want not.

453 We must learn to walk before we can run.

454 What can't be cured, must be endured.

455 What must be, must be.

456 What's done cannot be undone.

457 What you don't know can't hurt you.

458 What you lose on the swings you gain on the roundabouts.

459 When one door shuts, another opens.

460 When poverty comes in at the door, love flies out of the window.

461 When the cat's away, the mice will play.

462 When the wine is in, the wit is out.

463 Where there's a will there's a way.

464 While there's life there's hope.

465 Whom the gods love dies young.

466 Who spits against the wind, it falls in his face.

467 Why buy a cow when milk is so cheap?

468 Why keep a dog and bark yourself?

469 You can have too much of a good thing.

470 You can lead a horse to the water, but you can't make him drink.

471 You cannot run with the hare and hunt with the hounds.

472 You can't get a quart into a pint pot.

473 You can't get blood out of a stone.

474 You can't make an omelette without breaking eggs.

475 You can't make bricks without straw.

476 You can't please everyone.

477 You can't take it with you when you go.

478 You can't teach an old dog new tricks.

479 You can't tell a book by its cover.

Pryce-Jones, David (1936–) British author and critic. His novels include *Owls and Satyrs* (1960), *The Sands of Summer* (1963), and *Quondam* (1965).

1 When you're bored with yourself, marry and be bored with someone else.
Owls and Satyrs

Psalms The version of the Psalms included here is the more familiar Coverdale version taken from The Book of Common Prayer, rather than that from the Authorized Version of the Bible.

1 Blessed is the man that hath not walked in the counsel of the ungodly, nor stood in the way of sinners, and hath not sat in the seat of the scornful.

But his delight is in the law of the Lord; and in his law will he exercise himself day and night.
And he shall be like a tree planted by the waterside, that will bring forth his fruit in due season.
His leaf also shall not wither; and look, whatsoever he doeth shall prosper.
1:1–4

2 All mine enemies shall be confounded, and sore vexed: they shall be turned back, and put to shame suddenly.
6:10

3 Out of the mouth of very babes and sucklings hast thou ordained strength, because of thine enemies, that thou mightest still the enemy, and the avenger.
For I will consider thy heavens, even the works of thy fingers, the moon and the stars, which thou hast ordained.
What is man, that thou art mindful of him? and the son of man, that thou visitest him?
Thou madest him lower than the angels, to crown him with glory and worship.
8:2–5

4 In the Lord put I my trust: how say ye then to my soul, that she should flee as a bird unto the hill?
For lo, the ungodly bend their bow, and make ready their arrows within the quiver that they may privily shoot at them which are true of heart.
11:1–2

5 Upon the ungodly he shall rain snares, fire and brimstone, storm and tempest: this shall be their portion to drink.
11:7

6 Keep me as the apple of an eye; hide me under the shadow of thy wings.
17:8

7 Thou also shalt light my candle: the Lord my God shall make my darkness to be light.
For in thee I shall discomfit an host of men; and with the help of my God I shall leap over the wall.
18:28–29

8 In them hath he set a tabernacle for the sun, which cometh forth as a bridegroom out of his chamber, and rejoiceth as a giant to run his course.
19:5

9 The fear of the Lord is clean, and endureth for ever: the judgments of the Lord are true, and righteous altogether.
More to be desired are they than gold, yea, than much fine gold: sweeter also than honey, and the honey-comb.
19:9–10

10 Let the words of my mouth, and the meditation of my heart, be alway acceptable in thy sight, O Lord, my strength, and my redeemer.

19:14–15

11 The Lord is my shepherd; therefore can I lack nothing.
He shall feed me in a green pasture: and lead me forth beside the waters of comfort.
He shall convert my soul: and bring me forth in the paths of righteousness, for his Name's sake.
Yea, though I walk through the valley of the shadow of death, I will fear no evil: for thou art with me; thy rod and thy staff comfort me.
Thou shalt prepare a table before me against them that trouble me: thou hast anointed my head with oil, and my cup shall be full.
But thy loving-kindness and mercy shall follow me all the days of my life: and I will dwell in the house of the Lord for ever.

23:1–6

12 The Lord is my shepherd; I shall not want.
He maketh me to lie down in green pastures: he leadeth me beside the still waters.

Authorised Version 23:1–2

13 Thou preparest a table before me in the presence of mine enemies: thou anointest my head with oil; my cup runneth over.
Surely goodness and mercy shall follow me all the days of my life: and I will dwell in the house of the Lord for ever.

Authorised Version 23:5–6

14 Lift up your heads, O ye gates, and be ye lift up, ye everlasting doors; and the King of glory shall come in.
Who is the King of glory? it is the Lord strong and mighty, even the Lord mighty in battle.

24:7–8

15 The Lord is my light, and my salvation; whom then shall I fear? the Lord is the strength of my life; of whom then shall I be afraid?

27:1

16 The voice of the Lord breaketh the cedar-trees; yea, the Lord breaketh the cedars of Libanus.

29:5

17 For his wrath endureth but the twinkling of an eye, and in his pleasure is life: heaviness may endure for a night, but joy cometh in the morning.
And in my prosperity I said, I shall never be removed; thou, Lord, of thy goodness hast made my hill so strong.

30:5–6

18 In thee, O Lord, have I put my trust: let me never be put to confusion; deliver me in thy righteousness.

31:1

19 Into thy hands I commend my spirit: for thou hast redeemed me, O Lord, thou God of truth.

31:6

20 I am clean forgotten, as a dead man out of mind: I am become like a broken vessel.

31:14

21 He loveth righteousness and judgment: the earth is full of the goodness of the Lord.

33:5

22 I will alway give thanks unto the Lord: his praise shall ever be in my mouth.

34:1

23 When thou with rebukes dost chasten man for sin, thou makest his beauty to consume away, like as it were a moth fretting a garment: every man therefore is but vanity.

39:12

24 As for me, I am poor and needy; but the Lord careth for me.
Thou art my helper and redeemer; make no long tarrying, O my God.

40:20–21

25 Yea, even mine own familiar friend, whom I trusted, who did also eat of my bread, hath laid great wait for me.

41:9

26 Like as the hart desireth the water-brooks, so longeth my soul after thee, O God.
My soul is athirst for God, yea, even for the living God: when shall I come to appear before the presence of God?

42:1–2

27 God is in the midst of her, therefore shall she not be removed God shall help her, and that right early.
The heathen make much ado, and the kingdoms are moved: but God hath shewed his voice, and the earth shall melt away.

46:5–6

28 He maketh wars to cease in all the world; he breaketh the bow, and knappeth the spear in sunder, and burneth the chariots in the fire.
Be still then, and know that I am God: I will be exalted among the heathen, and I will be exalted in the earth.
The Lord of hosts is with us; the God of Jacob is our refuge.

46:9–11

29 Man being in honour hath no understanding: but is compared unto the beasts that perish.

49:20

30 Wash me throughly from my wickedness, and cleanse me from my sin.
For I acknowledge my faults: and my sin is ever before me.

51:2–3

31 Behold, I was shapen in wickedness: and in sin hath my mother conceived me.

But lo, thou requirest truth in the inward parts: and shalt make me to understand wisdom secretly.

Thou shalt purge me with hyssop, and I shall be clean: thou shalt wash me, and I shall be whiter than snow.

Thou shalt make me hear of joy and gladness: that the bones which thou hast broken may rejoice.

Turn thy face from my sins: and put out all my misdeeds.

Make me a clean heart, O God: and renew a right spirit within me.

51:5–10

32 For thou desirest no sacrifice, else would I give it thee: but thou delightest not in burnt-offerings.

The sacrifice of God is a troubled spirit: a broken and contrite heart, O God, shalt thou not despise.

51:16–17

33 And I said, O that I had wings like a dove: for then would I flee away, and be at rest.

55:6

34 We took sweet counsel together, and walked in the house of God as friends.

55:15

35 For thou hast delivered my soul from death, and my feet from falling, that I may walk before God in the light of the living.

56:13

36 God shall send forth his mercy and truth: my soul is among lions.

And I lie even among the children of men, that are set on fire: whose teeth are spears and arrows, and their tongue a sharp sword.

57:4–5

37 O set me up upon the rock that is higher than I: for thou hast been my hope, and a strong tower for me against the enemy.

I will dwell in thy tabernacle for ever; and my trust shall be under the covering of thy wings.

61:3–4

38 Then shall the earth bring forth her increase; and God, even our own God, shall give us his blessing.

67:6

39 Let them be wiped out of the book of the living, and not be written among the righteous.

69:29

40 Let them for their reward be soon brought to shame, that cry over me, There, there.

70:3

41 They that dwell in the wilderness shall kneel before him; his enemies shall lick the dust.

72:9

42 So man did eat angels' food: for he sent them meat enough.

78:26

43 So the Lord awaked as one out of sleep, and like a giant refreshed with wine.

78:66

44 O how amiable are thy dwellings, thou Lord of hosts!

My soul hath a desire and longing to enter into the courts of the Lord: my heart and my flesh rejoice in the living God.

Yea, the sparrow hath found her an house, and the swallow a nest where she may lay her young, even thy altars, O Lord of hosts, my King and my God.

84:1–3

45 For one day in thy courts is better than a thousand.

I had rather be a door-keeper in the house of my God, than to dwell in the tents of ungodliness.

84:10–11

46 Mercy and truth are met together; righteousness and peace have kissed each other.

Truth shall flourish out of the earth; and righteousness hath looked down from heaven.

85:10–11

47 Her foundations are upon the holy hills; the Lord loveth the gates of Sion more than all the dwellings of Jacob.

Very excellent things are spoken of thee, thou city of God.

87:1–2

48 Lord, thou hast been our refuge from one generation to another.

Before the mountains were brought forth, or ever the earth and the world were made, thou art God from everlasting, and world without end.

90:1–2

49 For a thousand years in thy sight are but as yesterday, seeing that is past as a watch in the night.

As soon as thou scatterest them they are even as a sleep; and fade away suddenly like the grass.

In the morning it is green, and groweth up; but in the evening it is cut down, dried up, and withered.

90:4–6

50 For when thou art angry all our days are gone: we bring our years to an end, as it were a tale that is told.

The days of our age are threescore years and ten; and though men be so strong that they come to fourscore years, yet is their strength then but labour and sorrow; so soon passeth it away, and we are gone.

90:9–10

51 For he shall deliver thee from the snare of the hunter, and from the noisome pestilence.

He shall defend thee under his wings, and thou shalt be safe under his feathers: his faithfulness and truth shall be thy shield and buckler.

Thou shalt not be afraid for any terror by night; nor for the arrow that flieth by day;

For the pestilence that walketh in darkness; nor for the sickness that destroyeth in the noonday.

A thousand shall fall beside thee, and ten thousand at thy right hand; but it shall not come nigh thee.

91:3-7

52 The righteous shall flourish like a palm-tree: and shall spread abroad like a cedar in Libanus.

92:11

53 He that planted the ear, shall he not hear? or he that made the eye, shall he not see?

94:9

54 O come, let us sing unto the Lord: let us heartily rejoice in the strength of our salvation.

Let us come before his presence with thanksgiving, and shew ourselves glad in him with psalms.

For the Lord is a great God, and a great King above all gods.

In his hand are all the corners of the earth: and the strength of the hills is his also.

The sea is his, and he made it: and his hands prepared the dry land.

95:1-5

55 Venite, exultemus

Vulgate 95:1

56 For he is the Lord our God; and we are the people of his pasture, and the sheep of his hand.

To-day if ye will hear his voice, harden not your hearts; as in the provocation, and as in the day of temptation in the wilderness.

95:7-8

57 Whoso hath also a proud look and high stomach, I will not suffer him.

101:7

58 The days of man are but as grass: for he flourisheth as a flower of the field.

For as soon as the wind goeth over it, it is gone; and the place thereof shall know it no more.

103:15-16

59 O give thanks unto the Lord, for he is gracious: and his mercy endureth for ever.

106:1

60 They that go down to the sea in ships, and occupy their business in great waters;

These men see the works of the Lord, and his wonders in the deep.

For at his word the stormy wind ariseth, which lifteth up the waves thereof.

They are carried up to the heaven, and down again to the deep: their soul melteth away because of the trouble.

They reel to and fro, and stagger like a drunken man, and are at their wit's end.

107:23-27

61 The Lord said unto my Lord, Sit thou on my right hand, until I make thine enemies thy footstool.

110:1

62 The fear of the Lord is the beginning of wisdom; a good understanding have all they that do thereafter; the praise of it endureth for ever.

111:10

63 The sea saw that, and fled: Jordan was driven back.

The mountains skipped like rams, and the little hills like young sheep.

114:3-4

64 Their idols are silver and gold, even the work of men's hands.

They have mouths, and speak not; eyes have they, and see not.

They have ears, and hear not; noses have they, and smell not.

They have hands, and handle not; feet have they, and walk not; neither speak they through their throat.

115:4-7

65 The snares of death compassed me round about; and the pains of hell gat hold upon me.

116:3

66 And why? thou hast delivered my soul from death, mine eyes from tears, and my feet from falling.

I will walk before the Lord in the land of the living.

I believed, and therefore will I speak; but I was sore troubled: I said in my haste, All men are liars.

116:8-10

67 I will lift up mine eyes unto the hills, from whence cometh my help.

121:1

68 The Lord himself is thy keeper: the Lord is thy defence upon thy right hand;

So that the sun shall not burn thee by day, neither the moon by night.

The Lord shall preserve thee from all evil: yea, it is even he that shall keep thy soul.

The Lord shall preserve thy going out, and thy coming in, from this time forth for evermore.

121:5-8

69 Turn our captivity, O Lord, as the rivers in the south.
They that sow in tears shall reap in joy.
He that now goeth on his way weeping, and beareth forth good seed, shall doubtless come again with joy, and bring his sheaves with him.
126:5-7

70 By the waters of Babylon we sat down and wept, when we remembered thee, O Sion.
As for our harps, we hanged them up upon the trees that are therein.
For they that led us away captive required of us then a song, and melody, in our heaviness: Sing us one of the songs of Sion.
How shall we sing the Lord's song in a strange land?
If I forget thee, O Jerusalem, let my right hand forget her cunning.
If I do not remember thee, let my tongue cleave to the roof of my mouth; yea, if I prefer not Jerusalem in my mirth.
137:1-6

71 Such knowledge is too wonderful and excellent for me: I cannot attain unto it.
139:5

72 Man is like a thing of nought: his time passeth away like a shadow.
144:4

73 O put not your trust in princes, nor in any child of man; for there is no help in them.
For when the breath of man goeth forth he shall turn again to his earth; and then all his thoughts perish.
146:2-3

74 The Lord looseth men out of prison: the Lord giveth sight to the blind.
The Lord helpeth them that are fallen: the Lord careth for the righteous.
The Lord careth for the strangers: he defendeth the fatherless and widow; as for the way of the ungodly, he turneth it upside down.
146:7-9

75 The Lord doth build up Jerusalem, and gather together the out-casts of Israel.
He healeth those that are broken in heart, and giveth medicine to heal their sickness.
He telleth the number of the stars, and calleth them all by their names.
147:2-4

76 Let the saints be joyful with glory: let them rejoice in their beds.
Let the praises of God be in their mouth, and a two-edged sword in their hands.
149:5-6

77 Praise him in the cymbals and dances: praise him upon the strings and pipe.
Praise him upon the well-tuned cymbals: praise him upon the loud cymbals.
150:4-5

Pudney, John Sleigh (1909-77) British poet and writer. His poetry collections include *Ten Summers* (1944) and *Collected Poems* (1957); novels include *Jacobson's Ladder* (1938), *The Net* (1952), and *Thin Air* (1961). He has written many other books, plays, and film scripts.

1 Do not despair
For Johnny head-in-air;
He sleeps as sound
As Johnny underground.
For Johnny

2 Better by far
For Johnny-the-bright-star,
To keep your head
And see his children fed.
For Johnny

Pyrrhus (319-272 BC) King of Epirus. An expansionist, he built an empire that was based on victories incurring heavy loss of life, especially at Asculum. Hence the expression 'Pyrrhic victory'.

1 Such another victory and we are ruined.
Commenting upon the costliness of his victory at the Battle of Asculum, 279 BC
Life of Pyrrhus (Plutarch)

Q

Quarles, Francis (1592-1644) English poet. A Royalist, he wrote pamphlets in defence of Charles I. His verse collections include *Divine Poems* (1633) and *Emblems* (1635).

1 I wish thee as much pleasure in the reading, as I had in the writing.
Emblems, 'To the Reader'

2 My soul; sit thou a patient looker-on;
Judge not the play before the play is done:
Her plot hath many changes, every day
Speaks a new scene; the last act crowns the play.
Epigram, Respice Finem

Quayle, Dan (James Danforth Quayle; 1947-) US politician; vice-president (1989-).

1 Space is almost infinite. As a matter of fact we think it is infinite.
The Sunday Times, 31 Dec 1989

Queensberry, William Douglas, 4th Duke of (1724-1810) British peer, known for his extravagance. Known as 'Old Q', he became vice-admiral of Scotland (1767-76).

1 What is there to make so much of in the Thames? I am quite tired of it. Flow, flow, flow, always the same.
Century of Anecdote (J. Timbs)

Quesnay, François (1694-1774) French economist. Originally physician to Louis XV, he concentrated on economics after 1756; his books include *Tableau économique* (1758).

1 *Laissez faire, laissez passer.*
Let it be, let it pass.
Attrib.

Quincy, Josiah (1772–1864) US statesman and lawyer. A member of the House of Representatives (1805–13), he became mayor of Boston (1823–29) and president of Harvard (1829–45). His books include *A History of Harvard University* (1840).

1 As it will be the right of all, so it will be the duty of some, definitely to prepare for a separation, amicably if they can, violently if they must.
Abridgement of Debates of Congress, Vol. IV, 14 Jan 1811

R

Rabelais, François (1483–1553) French humanist and satirist. He is best known for his *Pantagruel* (1532) and *Gargantua* (1534), which are renowned for their bawdiness.

Quotations about Rabelais

1 Rabelais is the wondrous mask of ancient comedy . . . henceforth a human living face, remaining enormous and coming among us to laugh at us and with us.
Victor Hugo (1802–85) French writer. Attrib.

Quotations by Rabelais

2 I drink for the thirst to come.
Gargantua, Bk. I, Ch. 5

3 Appetite comes with eating.
Gargantua, Bk. I, Ch. 5

4 In their rules there was only one clause: Do what you will.
Referring to the fictional Abbey of Thélème
Gargantua, Bk. I, Ch. 57

5 Man never found the deities so kindly
As to assure him that he'd live tomorrow.
Pantagruel, Bk. III, Ch. 2

6 Not everyone is a debtor who wishes to be; not everyone who wishes makes creditors.
Pantagruel, Bk. III, Ch. 3

7 Nature abhors a vacuum.
Attrib.

8 I owe much; I have nothing; the rest I leave to the poor.
Last words
Attrib.

9 Ring down the curtain, the farce is over.
Last words
Attrib.

10 I am going in search of a great perhaps.
Last words
Attrib.

Rachmaninov, Sergei (1873–1943) Russian composer, pianist, and conductor, living mostly in the USA after 1917. His works include operas, symphonies, and piano concertos.

1 My dear hands. Farewell, my poor hands.
On being informed that he was dying from cancer
The Great Pianists (H. Schonberg)

Racine, Jean (1639–99) French dramatist. His classical verse tragedies include *Andromaque* (1667), *Bérénice* (1670), and *Phèdre* (1677). His last religious dramas were *Esther* (1689) and *Athalie* (1691).

1 Oh, I have loved him too much to feel no hate for him.
Andromaque, II:1

2 Now my innocence begins to weigh me down.
Andromaque, III:1

3 I loved you when you were inconstant. What should I have done if you had been faithful?
Andromaque, IV:5

4 Crime, like virtue, has its degrees.
Phèdre, IV:2

Radcliffe, Ann (Ward) (1764–1823) British novelist. Her popular gothic novels include *A Sicilian Romance* (1790), *The Mysteries of Udolpho* (1794), and *The Italian* (1797).

1 Fate sits on these dark battlements, and frowns;
And as the portals open to receive me,
Her voice, in sullen echoes, through the courts,
Tells of a nameless deed.
The Mysteries of Udolpho

2 At first a small line of inconceivable splendour emerged on the horizon, which, quickly expanding, the sun appeared in all of his glory, unveiling the whole face of nature, vivifying every colour of the landscape, and sprinkling the dewy earth with glittering light.
The Romance of the Forest

Rae, John (1931–) British schoolmaster and writer. His books include *The Custard Boys* (1960), *Christmas is Coming* (1976), *The Public School Revolution 1964–79* (1981), and *Letters from School* (1987).

1 War is, after all, the universal perversion. We are all tainted: if we cannot experience our perversion at first hand we spend our time reading war stories, the pornography of war; or seeing war films, the blue films of war; or titillating our senses with the imagination of great deeds, the masturbation of war.
The Custard Boys, Ch. 6

Raglan, FitzRoy James Henry Somerset, 1st Baron (1788–1855) British field marshal. He served with distinction in the Napoleonic Wars but was criticized for his strategy as commander in the Crimean War.

1 Don't carry away that arm till I have taken off my ring.

Request immediately after his arm had been amputated following the battle of Waterloo
Dictionary of National Biography

Raleigh, Sir Walter (1554–1618) English explorer and writer. A favourite of Elizabeth I, he introduced the potato and tobacco plant from America into England. Under James I he was imprisoned for treason and eventually executed.

1 If all the world and love were young,
And truth in every shepherd's tongue,
These pretty pleasures might me move
To live with thee, and be thy love.

Answer to Marlow

2 Fain would I climb, yet fear I to fall.

Written on a window pane. For the reply *see* ELIZABETH I
Attrib.

3 Even such is Time, that takes in trust
Our youth, our joys, our all we have,
And pays us but with age and dust;
Who in the dark and silent grave,
When we have wandered all our ways,
Shuts up the story of our days;
But from this earth, this grave, this dust,
My God shall raise me up, I trust.

Written on the night before his execution
Attrib.

4 The world itself is but a large prison, out of which some are daily led to execution.

Said after his trial for treason, 1603
Attrib.

5 'Tis a sharp remedy, but a sure one for all ills.

Referring to the executioner's axe just before he was beheaded
Attrib.

6 So the heart be right, it is no matter which way the head lies.

On laying his head on the executioner's block
Attrib.

7 I have a long journey to take, and must bid the company farewell.

Last words
Sir Walter Raleigh (Edward Thompson), Ch. 26

Raleigh, Sir Walter Alexander (1861–1922) British scholar and critic. He wrote several books on English literature and the first volume of a history of the RAF (1922).

1 We could not lead a pleasant life,
And 'twould be finished soon,
If peas were eaten with the knife,
And gravy with the spoon.
Eat slowly: only men in rags
And gluttons old in sin
Mistake themselves for carpet bags
And tumble victuals in.

Laughter from a Cloud, 'Stans puer ad mensam'

2 I wish I loved the Human Race;
I wish I loved its silly face;
I wish I liked the way it walks;
I wish I liked the way it talks;
And when I'm introduced to one
I wish I thought *What Jolly Fun!*

Laughter from a Cloud, 'Wishes of an Elderly Man'

3 An anthology is like all the plums and orange peel picked out of a cake.

Letter to Mrs Robert Bridges, 15 Jan 1915

Ramanujan, Srinivasa (1887–1920) Indian mathematician, who went to England in 1914 to carry out research. He is known for his theories of numbers and continued fractions.

1 No, it is a very interesting number, it is the smallest number expressible as a sum of two cubes in two different ways.

The mathematician G. H. Hardy had referred to the number – 1729 – on the back of a taxi cab, as 'dull'. The two ways are $1^3 + 12^3$ and $9^3 + 10^3$.
Collected Papers of Srinivasa Ramanujan

Raphael, Frederic (1931–) British author of novels, short stories, and screenplays. His books include *A Wild Surmise* (1961), *The Glittering Prizes* (1976), and *After the War* (1988); he wrote the screenplays for *Darling* (1965), *Far From the Madding Crowd* (1967), *Rogue Male* (1976), and other films.

1 This is the city of perspiring dreams.

Referring to Cambridge
The Glittering Prizes: An Early Life, III

2 We thought philosophy ought to be patient and unravel people's mental blocks. Trouble with doing that is, once you've unravelled them, their heads fall off.

The Glittering Prizes: A Double Life, III:2

3 I come from suburbia, Dan, personally, I don't ever want to go back. It's the one place in the world that's further away than anywhere else.

The Glittering Prizes: A Sex Life, I:3

4 Great restaurants are, of course, nothing but mouth-brothels. There is no point in going to them if one intends to keep one's belt buckled.

The Sunday Times Magazine, 25 Sept 1977

Rattigan, Sir Terence (1911–77) British dramatist. His popular plays include *French Without Tears* (1936), *The Deep Blue Sea* (1952), and *Ross* (1960).

1 A nice respectable, middle-class, middle-aged maiden lady, with time on her hands and the money to help her pass it . . . Let us call her Aunt Edna . . . Aunt Edna is universal, and to those who feel that all the problems of the modern theatre might be saved by her liquidation, let me add that . . . She is also immortal.

Collected Plays, Vol II, Preface

2 You can be in the Horse Guards and still be common, dear.

Separate Tables: 'Table Number Seven'

Reade, Charles (1814–84) British novelist and dramatist. Of his many novels the best known is *The Cloister and the Hearth* (1861), a historical romance.

1 Make 'em laugh; make 'em cry; make 'em wait.

Advice to an aspiring writer
Attrib.

Reagan, Ronald (1911–) US Republican president (1981–89). He entered politics as governor of California (1966–74) after a career as a film actor.

Quotations about Reagan

1 That youthful sparkle in his eyes is caused by his contact lenses, which he keeps highly polished.

Sheilah Graham *The Times*, 22 Aug 1981

2 As the age of television progresses the Reagans will be the rule, not the exception. To be perfect for television is all a President has to be these days

Gore Vidal (1925–) US novelist. Attrib.

3 A triumph of the embalmer's art.

Gore Vidal Attrib.

4 Ask him the time, and he'll tell you how the watch was made.

Jane Wyman (1914–) US film actress and the first wife of Reagan. Attrib.

Quotations by Reagan

5 Please assure me that you are all Republicans!

Addressing the surgeons on being wheeled into the operating theatre for an emergency operation after an assassination attempt
Presidential Anecdotes (P. Boller)

6 No one can kill Americans and brag about it. No one.

The Observer, 'Sayings of the Week', 27 Apr 1986

7 You know, by the time you reach my age, you've made plenty of mistakes if you've lived your life properly.

The Observer, 'Sayings of the Week', 8 Mar 1987

8 I used to say that politics was the second lowest profession and I have come to know that it bears a great similarity to the first.

The Observer, 13 May 1979

9 Honey, I forgot to duck.

Said to his wife, Nancy, after an assassination attempt by John Hinckley III, 30 Mar 1981
The Sunday Times, 3 Dec 1989

10 They say hard work never hurt anybody, but I figure why take the chance.

Attrib.

Reed, Henry (1914–86) British poet and dramatist. His collected poems appeared in *A Map of Verona* (1946) and *The Lessons of the War* (1970). He wrote many plays for radio.

1 And the various holds and rolls and throws and breakfalls
Somehow or other I always seemed to put
In the wrong place. And as for war, my wars
Were global from the start.

A Map of Verona, 'Lessons of the War', III

2 Today we have naming of parts. Yesterday,
We had daily cleaning. And tomorrow morning
We shall have what to do after firing. But today,
Today we have naming of parts.

Naming of Parts

3 They call it easing the Spring: it is perfectly easy
If you have any strength in your thumb: like the bolt,
And the breech, and the cocking-piece, and the point of balance,
Which in our case we have not got.

Naming of Parts

4 In a civil war, a general must know – and I'm afraid it's a thing rather of instinct than of practice – he must know exactly when to move over to the other side.

Not a Drum was Heard: The War Memoirs of General Gland

5 If one doesn't get birthday presents it can remobilize very painfully the persecutory anxiety which usually follows birth.

The Primal Scene, as it were

6 I have known her pass the whole evening without mentioning a single book, or *in fact anything unpleasant* at all.

A Very Great Man Indeed

Reed, Rex (1938–) US columnist and actor. He appeared in the film of *Myra Breckinridge* and also wrote a showbiz column. His collections include *Do You Really Sleep in the Nude?*

1 In Hollywood, if you don't have happiness you send out for it.

Colombo's Hollywood (J. R. Colombo), 'Hollywood the Bad'

2 Cannes is where you lie on the beach and stare at the stars – or vice versa.

Attrib.

Reedy, George Edward (1917–) US government official and writer. He held various appointments as aide and consultant to President Lyndon Johnson. His books include *The Twilight of the Presidency* (1970).

1 You know that nobody is strongminded around a President . . . it is always: 'yes sir', 'no sir' (the 'no sir' comes when he asks whether you're dissatisfied).

The White House (ed. R. Gordon Hoxie)

Reich, Wilhelm (1897–1957) Austrian-born US psychiatrist, who became known for his theory that a universal energy is released during sexual intercourse.

1 The few bad poems which occasionally are created during abstinence are of no great interest.

The Sexual Revolution

Reinhardt, Gottfried (1911–) Austrian film producer, living in the USA. His films include *The Red Badge of Courage* (1951) and *Town without Pity* (1961).

1 Money is good for bribing yourself through the inconveniences of life.

Picture (Lillian Ross), 'Looks Like We're Still in Business'

Reith, John Charles Walsham, Baron (1889–1971) British administrator. He became the first general manager of the BBC and subsequently director general (1927–38). The annual Reith lectures were named after him.

1 You can't think rationally on an empty stomach, and a whole lot of people can't do it on a full one either.
Attrib.

Remarque, Erich Maria (1898–1970) German novelist. After being wounded in World War I he wrote *All Quiet on the Western Front* (1929), which became a bestseller. It was banned by the Nazis, and he lived abroad after 1932, eventually becoming a US citizen. Other books include *Three Comrades* (1937) and *Flotsam* (1941).

1 All Quiet on the Western Front
Title of novel

Renard, Jules (1894–1910) French writer. His works include the autobiographical *Poil de carotte* (1894) and *Journal* (1925–27) as well as accounts of animal and rural life.

1 Be modest! It is the kind of pride least likely to offend.
Journal

2 The profession of letters is, after all, the only one in which one can make no money without being ridiculous.
Journal

3 There is false modesty, but there is no false pride.
Journal

Rendall, Montague John (1862–1950) British schoolmaster. He became headmaster of Winchester College (1911–24) and then vice-president of the BBC (1927–33).

1 Nation shall speak peace unto nation.
Motto of BBC, 1927

Renoir, Pierre Auguste (1841–1919) French impressionist painter. An influential figure in the early years of the movement, he abandoned impressionism after 1882, his later paintings being mostly of nudes.

1 The pain passes, but the beauty remains.
Explaining why he still painted when his hands were twisted with arthritis
Attrib.

2 I just keep painting till I feel like pinching. Then I know it's right.
Explaining how he achieved such lifelike flesh tones in his nudes
Attrib.

Revson, Charles (1906–75) US business tycoon, cofounder and president of the cosmetic firm Revlon.

1 In the factory we make cosmetics. In the store we sell hope.
Fire and Ice (A. Tobias)

Rexford, Eben (1848–1916) British songwriter.

1 Darling, I am growing old,
Silver threads among the gold.
Silver Threads Among the Gold

Reynolds, Sir Joshua (1723–92) British portrait painter. The most fashionable portraitist of his day, he painted Dr Johnson, Gibbon, Garrick, and the Duchess of Devonshire.

1 If you have great talents, industry will improve them: if you have but moderate abilities, industry will supply their deficiency.
Discourse to Students of the Royal Academy, 11 Dec 1769

2 A mere copier of nature can never produce anything great.
Discourse to Students of the Royal Academy, 14 Dec 1770

3 He who resolves never to ransack any mind but his own, will be soon reduced, from mere barrenness, to the poorest of all imitations; he will be obliged to imitate himself, and to repeat what he has before often repeated.
Discourse to Students of the Royal Academy, 10 Dec 1774

4 I should desire that the last words which I should pronounce in this Academy, and from this place, might be the name of – Michael Angelo.
Discourse to Students of the Royal Academy, 10 Dec 1790

Reynolds, Malvina (1900–78) US folksinger and songwriter.

1 They're all made out of ticky-tacky, and they all look just the same.
Little Boxes, song describing a housing scheme built in the hills south of San Francisco.

Rhodes, Cecil John (1853–1902) South African financier and statesman. Prime minister of Cape Colony (1890–96), he helped to found Rhodesia, which was named in his honour.

1 The real fact is that I could no longer stand their eternal cold mutton.
Explaining why he had left his friends in England and come to South Africa
Cecil Rhodes (G. le Sueur)

2 Remember that you are an Englishman, and have consequently won first prize in the lottery of life.
Dear Me (Peter Ustinov), Ch. 4

3 How can I possibly dislike a sex to which Your Majesty belongs?
Replying to Queen Victoria's suggestion that he disliked women
Rhodes (Lockhart)

4 So little done, so much to do.
Last words

Rhys, Jean (1894–1979) Dominican-born British novelist. Her books include *Voyage in the Dark* (1934), *Good Morning, Midnight* (1939), and *The Wide Sargasso Sea* (1966).

1 Next week, or next month, or next year I'll kill myself. But I might as well last out my month's rent, which has been paid up, and my credit for breakfast in the morning.
Good Morning, Midnight, Pt. II

2 I often want to cry. That is the only advantage women have over men – at least they can cry.
Good Morning, Midnight, Pt. II

3 The feeling of Sunday is the same everywhere, heavy, melancholy, standing still. Like when they say, 'As it was in the beginning, is now, and ever shall be, world without end.'
Voyage in the Dark, Ch. 4

Rice, Grantland (1880–1954) US sportswriter, known widely as 'Granny'.

1 For when the One Great Scorer comes
To write against your name,
He marks – not that you won or lost –
But how you played the game.
Alumnus Football

Rice, Sir Stephen (1637–1715) English politician.

1 I will drive a coach and six horses through the Act of Settlement.
State of the Protestants of Ireland (W. King), Ch. 3

Rice-Davies, Mandy (1944–) British call girl, who was involved, with Christine Keeler, in the Profumo scandal and the trial of Dr Stephen Ward.

1 He would, wouldn't he?
Of Lord Astor, when told that he had repudiated her evidence at the trial of Stephen Ward, 29 June 1963

Richards, Sir Gordon (1904–86) British champion jockey and later horse trainer.

1 Mother always told me my day was coming, but I never realized that I'd end up being the shortest knight of the year.
Referring to his diminutive size, on learning of his knighthood
Attrib.

Richards, I(vor) A(rmstrong) (1893–1979) British critic, linguist, and poet. His publications include *Principles of Literary Criticism* (1924) and *Tomorrow Morning Faustus!* (1962).

1 It is a perfectly possible means of overcoming chaos.
Referring to poetry
Science and Poetry

Richardson, Sir Ralph (1902–83) British actor who rose to fame during the 1930s. He appeared in many Shakespearean and classical roles as well as in films.

1 The art of acting consists in keeping people from coughing.
The Observer

2 In music, the punctuation is absolutely strict, the bars and the rests are absolutely defined. But our punctuation cannot be quite strict, because we have to relate it to the audience. In other words, we are continually changing the score.
The Observer Magazine, 'Tynan on Richardson', 18 Dec 1977

3 The most precious things in speech are pauses.
Attrib.

Richelieu, Armand Jean du Plessis, Cardinal de (1585–1642) French statesman. He was advisor to Louis XIII's mother and became the king's chief minister in 1629. He suppressed the Huguenots and planned France's strategy in the Thirty Years' War.

1 Secrecy is the first essential in affairs of the State.
Testament Politique, Maxims

2 Not least among the qualities in a great King is a capacity to permit his ministers to serve him.
Testament Politique, Maxims

3 If you give me six lines written by the most honest man, I will find something in them to hang him.
Exact wording uncertain
Attrib.

Richelieu, Armand-Emmanuel du Plessis, Duc de (1766–1822) French statesman. A monarchist, he fled to Russia during the French Revolution, returning in 1815 to become prime minister under Louis XVIII.

1 Madame, you must really be more careful. Suppose it had been someone else who found you like this.
Discovering his wife with her lover
The Book of Lists (D. Wallechinsky)

Richler, Mordecai (1931–) Canadian novelist now living in England. His novels include *The Apprenticeship of Duddy Kravitz* (1959), *St Urbain's Horseman* (1971), *Joshua Then and Now* (1980), and *Home Sweet Home* (1984).

1 Remember this, Griffin. The revolution eats its own. Capitalism re-creates itself.
Cocksure, Ch. 22

2 And furthermore did you know that behind the discovery of America there was a Jewish financier?
Cocksure, Ch. 24

Richter, Jean Paul (Johann Paul Friedrich Richter; 1763–1825) German novelist. His novels include *Hesperus* (1795), *Titan* (1800–03), and *Der Komet* (1820–22). He used the pseudonym 'Jean Paul'.

1 Providence has given to the French the empire of the land, to the English that of the sea, and to the Germans that of the air.
Quoted by Thomas Carlyle

Ridge, William Pett (1860–1930) British novelist and dramatist. His novels include *Love at Paddington Green* and *Aunt Bertha*.

1 When you take the bull by the horns . . . what happens is a toss up.
Love at Paddington Green, Ch. 4

2 'How did you think I managed at dinner, Clarence?' 'Capitally!' 'I had a knife and two forks left at the end,' she said regretfully.
Love at Paddington Green, Ch. 6

Rilke, Rainer Maria (1875–1926) Austrian poet. His collections include *Das Stunden Buch* (1905), *Duineser Elegien* (1923), and *Die Sonette an Orpheus* (1923).

1 Spring has returned. The earth is like a child that knows poems.
Die Sonette an Orpheus, I, 21

2 The machine threatens all achievement.
Die Sonette an Orpheus, II, 10

3 The hero is strangely akin to those who die young.
Duineser Elegien, VI

4 Stuck with placards for 'Deathless', that bitter beer that tastes sweet to its drinkers.
Duineser Elegien, X

5 I never read anything concerning my work. I feel that criticism is a letter to the public which the author, since it is not directed to him, does not have to open and read.
Letters

Rimsky-Korsakov, Nikolai (1844–1908) Russian composer. One of the 'Mighty Five' nationalist composers, his works include the tone poem *Scheherazade* (1880) and the operas *The Snow Maiden* (1880) and *The Golden Cockerel* (1906).

1 I have already heard it. I had better not go: I will start to get accustomed to it and finally like it.
Referring to music by Debussy
Conversations with Stravinsky (Robert Craft and Igor Stravinsky)

Ripley, R. L. (1893–1949) US writer and journalist.

1 Believe it or not.
Title of newspaper column

Rivarol, Antoine de (1753–1801) French writer and wit.

1 Very good, but it has its *longueurs*.
Giving his opinion of a couplet by a mediocre poet
Das Buch des Lachens (W. Scholz)

Rivera, Antonio (d. 1936) Spanish Nationalist hero.

1 Fire – without hatred.
Giving the order to open fire at the siege of the Alcázar
The Siege of the Alcázar (C. Eby)

Robbins, Tom (1936–) US novelist and short-story writer. His books include *Another Roadside Attraction* (1971) and *Still Life with Woodpecker* (1980).

1 Human beings were invented by water as a device for transporting itself from one place to another.
Another Roadside Attraction

Robespierre, Maximilien François Marie Isidore de (1758–94) French lawyer and revolutionary. He became a leader of the Jacobins at the beginning of the French Revolution; after Louis XVI's execution he wielded total power on the Committee of Public Safety. Public opinion turned against his Reign of Terror, however, and he was guillotined.

1 Any institution which does not suppose the people good, and the magistrate corruptible, is evil.
Déclaration des Droits de l'homme, 24 Apr 1793

Robin, Leo (1899–1984) US songwriter and lyricist.

1 Thanks For the Memory.
Song title

2 Diamonds Are A Girl's Best Friend.
Song title

Robinson, Edwin Arlington (1869–1935) US poet. He made his name with the verse novel *Captain Craig* (1902). Other poems include *Man Against the Sky* (1916) and *Tristam* (1927).

1 I shall have more to say when I am dead.
John Brown

Robinson, James Harvey (1863–1936) US historian and educator. A pioneer in new teaching methods, his books include *The Development of Modern Europe* (1907) and *The Ordeal of Civilization* (1926).

1 Partisanship is our great curse. We too readily assume that everything has two sides and that it is our duty to be on one or the other.
The Mind in the Making

Robinson, Robert (1927–) British writer and broadcaster. His books include *Landscape with Dead Dons* (1956) and *Robinson Country* (1983).

1 The national dish of America is menus.
BBC TV programme, *Robinson's Travels*, Aug 1977

2 Certain people are born with natural false teeth.
BBC radio programme, *Stop the Week*, 1977

Roche, Sir Boyle (1743–1807) British politician.

1 What has posterity done for us?
Speech, Irish Parliament, 1780

2 Mr Speaker, I smell a rat; I see him forming in the air and darkening the sky; but I'll nip him in the bud.
Attrib.

Rochefort, (Victor) Henri, Marquis de Rochefort-Luçay (1830–1913) French journalist, noted for his radical views.

1 My scribbling pays me zero francs per line – not including the white spaces.
Referring to his salary as a writer
Autant en apportent les mots (Pedrazzini)

Rochefoucauld, François, Duc de la (1613–80) French writer. His literary circle included Mme de Sévigné and the Comtesse de La Fayette. He is best known for his *Maximes*, published in five editions between 1665 and 1678.

1 Self-love is the greatest of all flatterers.
Maximes, 2

2 We are all strong enough to bear the misfortunes of others.
Maximes, 19

3 We need greater virtues to sustain good fortune than bad.
Maximes, 25

4 If we had no faults of our own, we would not take so much pleasure in noticing those of others.
Maximes, 31

5 Self-interest speaks all sorts of tongues, and plays all sorts of roles, even that of disinterestedness.
Maximes, 39

6 We are never so happy nor so unhappy as we imagine.
Maximes, 49

7 To succeed in the world, we do everything we can to appear successful.
Maximes, 50

8 There are very few people who are not ashamed of having been in love when they no longer love each other.
Maximes, 71

9 If one judges love by its visible effects, it looks more like hatred than like friendship.
Maximes, 72

10 The love of justice in most men is simply the fear of suffering injustice.
Maximes, 78

11 Silence is the best tactic for him who distrusts himself.
Maximes, 79

12 It is more shameful to distrust one's friends than to be deceived by them.
Maximes, 84

13 Everyone complains of his memory, but no one complains of his judgement.
Maximes, 89

14 In the misfortune of our best friends, we always find something which is not displeasing to us.
Maximes, 99

15 The intellect is always fooled by the heart.
Maximes, 102

16 One gives nothing so freely as advice.
Maximes, 110

17 One had rather malign oneself than not speak of oneself at all.
Maximes, 138

18 To refuse praise reveals a desire to be praised twice over.
Maximes, 149

19 Hypocrisy is the homage paid by vice to virtue.
Maximes, 218

20 The height of cleverness is to be able to conceal it.
Maximes, 245

21 There is scarcely a single man sufficiently aware to know all the evil he does.
Maximes, 269

22 We only confess our little faults to persuade people that we have no large ones.
Maximes, 327

23 The accent of one's birthplace lingers in the mind and in the heart as it does in one's speech.
Maximes, 342

24 We seldom attribute common sense except to those who agree with us.
Maximes, 347

25 Nothing prevents us from being natural so much as the desire to appear so.
Maximes, 431

26 Quarrels would not last so long if the fault were on only one side.
Maximes, 496

27 Most usually our virtues are only vices in disguise.
Maximes, added to the 4th edition

Rochester, John Wilmot, Earl of (1647–80) English courtier and poet. One of the most dissolute companions of Charles II, he wrote many short love poems and longer satirical poems, such as *A Satire against Mankind*.

1 Here lies our sovereign lord the King,
Whose word no man relies on;
He never said a foolish thing,
Nor ever did a wise one.
See CHARLES II for a reply
Epitaph on Charles II

Rogers, Samuel (1763–1855) British poet. He established his reputation with *The Pleasures of Memory* (1792), later collections including *Human Life* (1819). He declined to become poet laureate on Wordsworth's death.

1 It doesn't much signify whom one marries, for one is sure to find next morning that it was someone else.
Table Talk (ed. Alexander Dyce)

2 When a new book is published, read an old one.
Attrib.

Rogers, Will (1879–1935) US actor and humorist. He starred in many films and contributed daily articles to the *New York Times* (from 1926). He also wrote several books.

1 You can't say civilization don't advance, however, for in every war they kill you a new way.
Autobiography, Ch. 12

2 England elects a Labour Government. When a man goes in for politics over here, he has no time to labour, and any man that labours has no time to fool with politics. Over there politics is an obligation; over here it's a business.
Autobiography, Ch. 14

3 Communism is like prohibition, it's a good idea but it won't work.
Autobiography, Nov 1927

4 Everything is funny, as long as it's happening to somebody else.
The Illiterate Digest

5 Being a hero is about the shortest-lived profession on earth.
Saturday Review, 'A Rogers Thesaurus', 25 Aug 1962

6 Coolidge is a better example of evolution than either Bryan or Darrow, for he knows when not to talk, which is the biggest asset the monkey possesses over the human.
Saturday Review, 'A Rogers Thesaurus', 25 Aug 1962

7 I don't make jokes – I just watch the government and report the facts.
Saturday Review, 'A Rogers Thesaurus', 25 Aug 1962

8 It has made more liars out of the American people than Golf.
Referring to income tax
Saturday Review, 'A Rogers Thesaurus', 25 Aug 1962

9 The more you read about politics, you got to admit that each party is worse than the other.
Saturday Review, 'A Rogers Thesaurus', 25 Aug 1962

10 A comedian can only last till he either takes himself serious or his audience takes him serious.
Newspaper article, 1931

11 See what will happen to you if you don't stop biting your fingernails.
Message written on a postcard of the Venus de Milo that he sent to his young niece

12 So live that you wouldn't be ashamed to sell the family parrot to the town gossip.
Attrib.

Roland, Madame Marie Jeanne Philipon (1754–93) French revolutionary. Her Paris salon was the meeting place for the Girondists (1791–93). After their fall she was tried and guillotined.

1 *O liberté! O liberté! Que de crimes on commet en ton nom!*
Oh liberty! Oh liberty! What crimes are committed in thy name!
Said as she mounted the steps of the guillotine at her execution
Attrib.

Rolleston, Sir Humphrey (1862–1944) British physician and medical writer.

1 First they get *on*, then they get *honour*, then they get *honest*.
Referring to physicians
Confessions of an Advertising Man (David Ogilvy)

Rolmaz, James (19th century) British songwriter.

1 Where did you get that hat?
Where did you get that tile?
Where Did You Get That Hat?

Roosevelt, Eleanor (1884–1962) US writer and lecturer, wife of Franklin D. Roosevelt.

1 No one can make you feel inferior without your consent.
This is My Story

2 I think if the people of this country can be reached with the truth, their judgment will be in favor of the many, as against the privileged few.
Ladies' Home Journal

3 I used to tell my husband that, if he could make *me* understand something, it would be clear to all the other people in the country.
Newspaper column, 'My Day', 12 Feb 1947

4 ... I have spent many years of my life in opposition and I rather like the role.
Letter to Bernard Baruch, 18 Nov 1952

Roosevelt, Franklin D(elano) (1882–1945) US Democratic president. Although partially paralysed by polio (from 1921), he was re-elected three times and became an effective war leader.

Quotations about Roosevelt

1 A chameleon on plaid.
Herbert Hoover (1874–1964) US statesman. Attrib.

2 The man who started more creations since Genesis – and finished none.
Hugh Johnson Attrib.

Quotations by Roosevelt

3 I murdered my grandmother this morning.
His habitual greeting to any guest at the White House he suspected of paying no attention to what he said
Ear on Washington (D. McClellan)

4 It is fun to be in the same decade with you.
After Churchill had congratulated him on his 60th birthday
The Hinge of Fate (Winston S. Churchill), Ch. 4

5 Stalin hates the guts of all your top people. He thinks he likes me better, and I hope he will continue to do so.
The Hinge of Fate (Winston S. Churchill), Ch. 11

6 Defeat of Germany means the defeat of Japan, probably without firing a shot or losing a life.
The Hinge of Fate (Winston S. Churchill), Ch. 25

7 The best immediate defence of the United States is the success of Great Britain defending itself.
At press conference, 17 Dec 1940
Their Finest Hour (Winston S. Churchill), Ch. 28

8 The forgotten man at the bottom of the economic pyramid.
Speech on radio, 7 Apr 1932

9 I pledge you, I pledge myself, to a new deal for the American people.
Speech accepting nomination for presidency, Chicago, 2 July 1932

10 Let me assert my firm belief that the only thing we have to fear is fear itself.
First Inaugural Address, 4 Mar 1933

11 In the field of world policy; I would dedicate this nation to the policy of the good neighbor.
First Inaugural Address, 4 Mar 1933

12 A radical is a man with both feet firmly planted in air.
Broadcast, 26 Oct 1939

13 We must be the great arsenal of democracy.
Broadcast address to Forum on Current Problems, 29 Dec 1940

14 We look forward to a world founded upon four essential human freedoms. The first is freedom of speech and expression – everywhere in the world. The second is freedom of every person to worship God in his own way – everywhere in the world. The third is freedom from want . . . everywhere in the world. The fourth is freedom from fear . . . anywhere in the world.

Speech to Congress, 6 Jan 1941

15 Never before have we had so little time in which to do so much.

Radio address, 23 Feb 1942

16 We all know that books burn – yet we have the greater knowledge that books cannot be killed by fire. People die, but books never die. No man and no force can abolish memory . . . In this war, we know, books are weapons.

Message to American Booksellers Association, 23 Apr 1942

17 More than an end to war, we want an end to the beginnings of all wars.

Speech broadcast on the day after his death (13 Apr 1945)

Roosevelt, Theodore (1858–1919) US Republican president. His presidency (1901–09) is remembered for his Square Deal programme for social reform and the construction of the Panama Canal.

Quotations about Roosevelt

1 I always enjoy his society, he is so hearty, so straightforward, outspoken and, for the moment, so absolutely sincere.

Mark Twain (Samuel Langhorne Clemens; 1835–1910) US writer. *Autobiography*

2 Father always wanted to be the bride at every wedding and the corpse at every funeral.

Nicholas Roosevelt *A Front Row Seat*

Quotations by Roosevelt

3 No man is justified in doing evil on the ground of expediency.

The Strenuous Life

4 Kings and such like are just as funny as politicians.

Mr Wilson's War (John Dos Passos), Ch. 1

5 A man who will steal *for* me will steal *from* me.

Firing a cowboy who had applied Roosevelt's brand to a steer belonging to a neighbouring ranch
Roosevelt in the Bad Lands (Herman Hagedorn)

6 I wish to preach, not the doctrine of ignoble ease, but the doctrine of the strenuous life.

Speech, Chicago, 10 Apr 1899

7 There is a homely adage which runs 'Speak softly and carry a big stick, you will go far'.

Speech, Minnesota State Fair, 2 Sept 1901

8 A man who is good enough to shed his blood for the country is good enough to be given a square deal afterwards. More than that no man is entitled to, and less than that no man shall have.

Speech at the Lincoln Monument, Springfield, Illinois, 4 June 1903

9 There is no room in this country for hyphenated Americanism.

Speech, New York, 12 Oct 1915

10 There can be no fifty-fifty Americanism in this country. There is room here for only one hundred per cent Americanism.

Speech, Saratoga, 19 July 1918

Roscommon, Wentworth Dillon, Earl of (1633–85) Irish-born English poet. His reputation rests on his translation of Horace's *Ars Poetica* (1680) and an *Essay on Translated Verse* (1684).

1 But words once spoke can never be recall'd.

Art of Poetry

2 The multitude is always in the wrong.

Essay on Translated Verse

Rose, Billy (1899–1966) US songwriter and nightclub owner.

1 Does the Spearmint Lose Its Flavour on the Bedpost Overnight?

Song title

2 Me and My Shadow.

Song title

Rosebery, Archibald Philip Primrose, Earl of (1847–1929) British statesman. Liberal prime minister after Gladstone (1894–95), he was also a well-known racehorse owner and biographer.

1 The Empire is a Commonwealth of Nations.

Speech, Adelaide, 18 Jan 1884

2 Before Irish Home Rule is conceded by the Imperial Parliament, England as the predominant member of the three kingdoms will have to be convinced of its justice and equity.

Speech, House of Lords, 11 Mar 1894

3 It is beginning to be hinted that we are a nation of amateurs.

Rectorial Address, Glasgow, 16 Nov 1900

4 You have to clean your plate.

Said to the Liberal Party
Speech, Chesterfield, 16 Dec 1901

Ross, Alan Strode Campbell (1907–78) British professor of linguistics. His books include *Noblesse Oblige* and *What are U*.

1 U and Non-U, An Essay in Sociological Linguistics.

Essay title, *Noblesse Oblige*, 1956

Ross, Harold W. (1892–1951) US journalist. He founded, and for many years edited, *The New Yorker*.

1 I've never been in there... but there are only three things to see, and I've seen colour reproductions of all of them.
Referring to the Louvre
A Farewell to Arms (Ernest Hemingway)

2 I don't want you to think I'm not incoherent.
The Years with Ross (James Thurber)

Rossetti, Christina (1830–74) British poet and supporter of the Pre-Raphaelite Brotherhood founded by her brother, Dante Gabriel Rossetti. Her collections include *Goblin Market* (1862), *The Prince's Progress* (1866), and *New Poems* (1896). Twice refusing offers of marriage, she lived a solitary, sickly, and religious life.

1 Come to me in the silence of the night;
Come in the speaking silence of a dream;
Come with soft rounded cheeks and eyes as bright
As sunlight on a stream;
Come back in tears,
O memory, hope, love of finished years.
Echo

2 For there is no friend like a sister
In calm or stormy weather;
To cheer one on the tedious way,
To fetch one if one goes astray,
To lift one if one totters down,
To strengthen whilst one stands.
Goblin Market

3 In the bleak mid-winter
Frosty wind made moan,
Earth stood hard as iron,
Water like a stone;
Snow had fallen, snow on snow,
Snow on snow,
In the bleak mid-winter,
Long ago.
Mid-Winter

4 Remember me when I am gone away,
Gone far away into the silent land.
Remember

5 Better by far you should forget and smile
Than that you should remember and be sad.
Remember

6 Does the road wind up-hill all the way?
Yes, to the very end.
Will the day's journey take the whole long day?
From morn to night, my friend.
Up-Hill

7 Will there be beds for me and all who seek?
Yea, beds for all who come.
Up-Hill

8 When I am dead, my dearest,
Sing no sad songs for me;
Plant thou no roses at my head,
Nor shady cypress tree:
Be the green grass above me
With showers and dewdrops wet;
And if thou wilt, remember,
And if thou wilt, forget.
When I am Dead

9 Who has seen the wind?
Neither you nor I:
But when the trees bow down their heads,
The wind is passing by.
Who Has Seen the Wind?

Rossetti, Dante Gabriel (1828–82) British painter and poet. With Millais and Holman Hunt he founded the Pre-Raphaelite Brotherhood. His poetic works include *Poems* (1870) and *Ballads and Sonnets* (1881).

1 A sonnet is a moment's monument, –
Memorial from the Soul's eternity
To one dead deathless hour.
The House of Life, Introduction

2 Look in my face; my name is Might-have-been.
I am also called No-more, Too-late, Farewell.
The House of Life, 'A Superscription'

3 I have been here before.
But when or how I cannot tell:
I know the grass beyond the door,
The sweet keen smell,
The sighing sound, the lights around the shore.
Sudden Light

4 The Stealthy School of Criticism.
Letter to the *Athenaeum*, 1871

Rossini, Gioacchino (1792–1868) Italian operatic composer. His works include *Tancredi* (1813), *The Barber of Seville* (1816), *The Thieving Magpie* (1817), and *William Tell* (1829).

1 Wagner has lovely moments but awful quarters of an hour.
Remark made to Emile Naumann, April 1867
Italienische Tondichter (Naumann)

2 Give me a laundry-list and I'll set it to music.
Attrib.

Rostand, Edmond (1868–1918) French poet and dramatist. His verse collection *Les Musardises* (1890) established his reputation as a poet but he then wrote for the theatre, his plays including *La Samaritaine* (1897), *Cyrano de Bergerac* (1898), *L'Aiglon* (1900), and *Chantecler* (1910).

1 My nose is huge! Vile snub-nose, flat-nosed ass, flat-head, let me inform you that I am proud of such an appendage, since a big nose is the proper sign of a friendly, good, courteous, witty, liberal, and brave man, such as I am.
Cyrano de Bergerac, I:1

Rostand, Jean (1894–1977) French biologist and writer, son of Edmond Rostand. His books include *Pensées d'un biologiste* (1955).

1 A married couple are well suited when both partners usually feel the need for a quarrel at the same time.
Le Mariage

2 Never feel remorse for what you have thought about your wife; she has thought much worse things about you.
Le Mariage

3 Kill a man, and you are a murderer. Kill millions of men, and you are a conqueror. Kill everyone, and you are a god.

Pensées d'un biologiste

Roth, Philip (1933–) US novelist. His books include *Goodbye, Columbus* (1959), *Portnoy's Complaint* (1969), *The Ghost Writer* (1979), *The Anatomy Lesson* (1983), and *The Prague Orgy* (1985).

1 Doctor, my doctor, what do you say – let's put the id back in yid!

Portnoy's Complaint

2 A Jewish man with parents alive is a fifteen-year-old boy, and will remain a fifteen-year-old boy till they die.

Portnoy's Complaint

Rouget de Lisle, Claude Joseph (1760–1836) French military engineer and composer. He wrote the words and music of *La Marseillaise* in 1792.

1 *Allons, enfants, de la patrie,*
Le jour de gloire est arrivé.
Come, children of our native land,
The day of glory has arrived.

La Marseillaise (French national anthem)

Rourke, M. E. (20th century) US songwriter and lyricist.

1 And when I told them how beautiful you are
They didn't believe me! They didn't believe me!

They Didn't Believe Me

Rousseau, Jean Jacques (1712–78) French philosopher and writer. His most influential work was *Du Contrat social* (1762). Other works include *La Nouvelle Héloïse* (1760) and *Émile* (1762).

1 Man was born free and everywhere he is in chains.

Du Contrat social, Ch. 1

2 He who pretends to look on death without fear lies. All men are afraid of dying, this is the great law of sentient beings, without which the entire human species would soon be destroyed.

Julie, ou la Nouvelle Héloïse

3 Everything is good when it leaves the Creator's hands; everything degenerates in the hands of man.

Attrib.

Routh, Martin Joseph (1755–1854) British scholar. He edited a collection of ecclesiastical writings from the second and third centuries in his *Reliquiae Sacrae* (1814–48).

1 Always verify your references.

Attrib.

Rowe, Nicholas (1674–1718) English dramatist. His plays include *The Fair Penitent* (1703) and *The Tragedy of Jane Shore* (1714). He became poet laureate in 1715.

1 At length the morn and cold indifference came.

The Fair Penitent, I:1

Rowland, Edward (20th century) British songwriter, known as 'Red Rowley'.

1 A mademoiselle from Armenteers,
She hasn't been kissed for forty years,
Hinky, dinky, par-lee-voo.

Armentières was completely destroyed (1918) in World War I
Mademoiselle from Armentières

Rowland, Helen (1876–1950) US writer, journalist, and humorist.

1 When you see what some girls marry, you realize how they must hate to work for a living.

Reflections of a Bachelor Girl

2 The follies which a man regrets most in his life are those which he didn't commit when he had the opportunity.

Reflections of a Bachelor Girl

3 It takes a woman twenty years to make a man of her son, and another woman twenty minutes to make a fool of him.

Reflections of a Bachelor Girl

4 Never trust a husband too far, nor a bachelor too near.

The Rubaiyat of a Bachelor

Rowse, A(lfred) L(eslie) (1903–) British historian and critic. *The Elizabethan Renaissance* (1971) is his best-known book. He has identified The Dark Lady of Shakespeare's sonnets.

1 Burnings of people and (what was more valuable) works of art.

Historical Essays (H. R. Trevor-Roper)

Rubens, Paul Alfred (1875–1917) British dramatist and songwriter.

1 We Don't Want To Lose You But We Think You Ought To Go.

Title of song

Rubinstein, Helena (1882–1965) Polish-born US cosmetics manufacturer and business woman, whose products are famous throughout the world.

1 I have always felt that a woman has the right to treat the subject of her age with ambiguity until, perhaps, she passes into the realm of over ninety. Then it is better she be candid with herself and with the world.

My Life for Beauty, Pt. I, Ch. 1

2 There are no ugly women, only lazy ones.

My Life for Beauty, Pt. II, Ch. 1

Rue, Danny La (Daniel Patrick Carroll; 1928–) British entertainer and female impersonator.

1 The essence of any blue material is timing. If you sit on it, it becomes vulgar.

Attrib.

Runcie, Robert Alexander Kennedy (1921–) British churchman; Archbishop of Canterbury (1980–91).

1 We must reject a privatization of religion which results in its reduction to being simply a matter of personal salvation.

The Observer, 'Sayings of the Week', 17 Apr 1988

2 My advice was delicately poised between the cliché and the indiscretion.

Comment to the press concerning his advice to the Prince of Wales and Lady Diana Spencer on their approaching wedding, 13 July 1981

Runciman, Sir Steven (1903–) British academic and diplomat. His books include *Byzantine Civilization* (1933), *A History of the Crusades* (1951–54), and *Mistra* (1980).

1 Unlike Christianity, which preached a peace that it never achieved, Islam unashamedly came with a sword.

A History of the Crusades, 'The First Crusade'

Runyon, (Alfred) Damon (1884–1946) US writer and journalist. His works include *Rhymes of the Firing Line* (1912), the collection of short stories *Guys and Dolls* (1932), and the play *A Slight Case of Murder* (1935).

1 All she has to do is to walk around and about Georgie White's stage with only a few light bandages on, and everybody considers her very beautiful, especially from the neck down.

Furthermore, 'A Very Honourable Guy'

2 My boy . . . always try to rub up against money, for if you rub up against money long enough, some of it may rub off on you.

Furthermore, 'A Very Honourable Guy'

3 More than Somewhat.

Title of a collection of stories

4 And you cannot tell by the way a party looks or how he lives in this town, if he has any scratch, because many a party who is around in automobiles, and wearing good clothes, and chucking quite a swell is nothing but a phonus bolonus and does not have any real scratch whatever.

More than Somewhat, 'The Snatching of Bookie Bob'

5 She is a smart old broad. It is a pity she is so nefarious.

Runyon à la carte, 'Broadway Incident'

6 At such an hour the sinners are still in bed resting up from their sinning of the night before, so they will be in good shape for more sinning a little later on.

Runyon à la carte, 'The Idyll of Miss Sarah Brown'

7 I once knew a chap who had a system of just hanging the baby on the clothes line to dry and he was greatly admired by his fellow citizens for having discovered a wonderful innovation on changing a diaper.

Short Takes, 'Diaper Dexterity'

8 A free-loader is a confirmed guest. He is the man who is always willing to come to dinner.

Short Takes, 'Free-Loading Ethics'

9 He is without strict doubt a Hoorah Henry, and he is generally figured as nothing but a lob as far as doing anything useful in this world is concerned.

Short Takes, 'Tight Shoes'

10 These citizens are always willing to bet that what Nicely-Nicely dies of will be over-feeding and never anything small like pneumonia, for Nicely-Nicely is known far and wide as a character who dearly loves to commit eating.

Take it Easy, 'Lonely Heart'

Rushdie, Salman (1947–) Indian-born British novelist. His novels include *Grimus* (1975), *Midnight's Children* (1981), *Shame* (1983), *The Satanic Verses* (1988), which caused offence to Muslim fundamentalists and prompted the Ayatollah Khomeini to issue a death warrant, forcing Rushdie into hiding, and *Haroun and the Sea* (1990).

1 Mahound shakes his head, 'Your blasphemy, Salman, can't be forgiven. Did you think I wouldn't work it out? To set your words against the Words of God.'

The Satanic Verses

2 I call upon the intellectual community in this country and abroad to stand up for freedom of the imagination, an issue much larger than my book or indeed my life.

Press statement, 14 Feb 1989

Ruskin, John (1819–1900) British art critic and writer on sociology and economics. His books include *Modern Painters* (1843–60), *The Seven Lamps of Architecture* (1849), and *Munera Pulveris* (1862).

Quotations about Ruskin

1 A certain girlish petulance of style that distinguishes Ruskin was not altogether a defect. It served to irritate and fix attention where a more evenly judicial writer might have remained unread.

W. R. Sickert (1860–1942) British impressionist painter. *New Age*, 'The Spirit of the Hive'

2 I doubt that art needed Ruskin any more than a moving train needs one of its passengers to shove it.

Tom Stoppard (1937–) Czech-born British dramatist. *Times Literary Supplement*, 3 June 1977

Quotations by Ruskin

3 No person who is not a great sculptor or painter can be an architect. If he is not a sculptor or painter, he can only be a *builder*.

Lectures on Architecture and Painting

4 Life without industry is guilt, and industry without art is brutality.

Lectures on Art, 'The Relation of Art to Morals', 23 Feb 1870

5 What is poetry? The suggestion, by the imagination, of noble grounds for the noble emotions.

Modern Painters, Vol. III

6 Mountains are the beginning and the end of all natural scenery.

Modern Painters, Vol. IV

7 If a book is worth reading, it is worth buying.

Sesame and Lilies, 'Of Kings' Treasuries'

8 All books are divisible into two classes, the books of the hour, and the books of all time.

Sesame and Lilies, 'Of Kings' Treasuries'

9 How long most people would look at the best book before they would give the price of a large turbot for it!

Sesame and Lilies, 'Of Kings' Treasuries'

10 When we build let us think that we build for ever.

The Seven Lamps of Architecture, 'The Lamp of Memory'

11 Remember that the most beautiful things in the world are the most useless, peacocks and lilies for instance.

The Stones of Venice, Vol. I, Ch. 2

12 To make your children *capable of honesty* is the beginning of education.

Time and Tide, Letter VIII

13 Fine art is that in which the hand, the head, and the heart of man go together.

The Two Paths, Lecture II

14 Nobody cares much at heart about Titian, only there is a strange undercurrent of everlasting murmur about his name, which means the deep consent of all great men that he is greater than they.

The Two Paths, Lecture II

15 No human being, however great, or powerful was ever so free as a fish.

The Two Paths, Lecture V

16 Whereas it has long been known and declared that the poor have no right to the property of the rich, I wish it also to be known and declared that the rich have no right to the property of the poor.

Unto this Last, Essay III

17 I have seen, and heard, much of Cockney impudence before now; but never expected to hear a coxcomb ask two hundred guineas for flinging a pot of paint in the public's face.

On Whistler's painting 'Nocturne in Black and Gold'
Letter, 18 June 1877

18 What have we to say to India?

Referring to the completion of the British-Indian cable
Attrib.

Russell, Bertrand Arthur William, Earl (1872–1970)

British philosopher. His many books include *Principia Mathematica* (with A. N. Whitehead; 1910) and *Our Knowledge of the External World* (1914). He was an ardent pacifist and campaigner for nuclear disarmament.

Quotations about Russell

1 In trying to recall his face I am able to see it only in profile – the sharp, narrow silhouette of an aggressive jester.

Arthur Koestler (1905–83) Hungarian-born British writer.
Stranger on the Square

2 The beauty of Bertrand Russell's beautiful mathematical mind is absolute, like the third movement of Beethoven's A Minor Quartet.

Ethel Mannin *Confessions and Impressions*

Quotations by Russell

3 I have a certain hesitation in starting my biography too soon for fear of something important having not yet happened. Suppose I should end my days as President of Mexico; the biography would seem incomplete if it did not mention this fact.

Letter to Stanley Unwin, Nov 1930

4 Three passions, simple but overwhelmingly strong, have governed my life: the longing for love, the search for knowledge, and unbearable pity for the suffering of mankind.

The Autobiography of Bertrand Russell, Prologue

5 I was told that the Chinese said they would bury me by the Western Lake and build a shrine to my memory. I have some slight regret that this did not happen, as I might have become a god, which would have been very *chic* for an atheist.

The Autobiography of Bertrand Russell, Vol. II, Ch. 3

6 One of the symptoms of approaching nervous breakdown is the belief that one's work is terribly important. If I were a medical man, I should prescribe a holiday to any patient who considered his work important.

The Autobiography of Bertrand Russell, Vol. II, Ch. 5

7 ... the nuns who never take a bath without wearing a bathrobe all the time. When asked why, since no man can see them, they reply 'Oh, but you forget the good God.'

The Basic Writings, Pt. II, Ch. 7

8 The megalomaniac differs from the narcissist by the fact that he wishes to be powerful rather than charming, and seeks to be feared rather than loved. To this type belong many lunatics and most of the great men of history.

The Conquest of Happiness

9 There are two motives for reading a book: one, that you enjoy it, the other that you can boast about it.

The Conquest of Happiness

10 Man is not a solitary animal, and so long as social life survives, self-realization cannot be the supreme principle of ethics.

History of Western Philosophy, 'Romanticism'

11 The more you are talked about, the more you will wish to be talked about. The condemned murderer who is allowed to see the account of his trial in the Press is indignant if he finds a newspaper which has reported it inadequately. . . . Politicians and literary men are in the same case.
Human Society in Ethics and Politics

12 Of all forms of caution, caution in love is perhaps the most fatal to true happiness.
Marriage and Morals

13 Mathematics may be defined as the subject in which we never know what we are talking about, nor whether what we are saying is true.
Mysticism and Logic, Ch. 4

14 Pure mathematics consists entirely of assertions to the effect that, if such and such a proposition is true of *anything*, then such and such another proposition is true of that thing. It is essential not to discuss whether the first proposition is really true, and not to mention what the anything is, of which it is supposed to be true.
Mysticism and Logic, Ch. 5

15 Organic life, we are told, has developed gradually from the protozoon to the philosopher, and this development, we are assured, is indubitably an advance. Unfortunately it is the philosopher, not the protozoon, who gives us this assurance.
Mysticism and Logic, Ch. 6

16 Brief and powerless is Man's life; on him and all his race the slow, sure doom falls pitiless and dark.
Mysticism and Logic, 'A Free Man's Worship'

17 No one gossips about other people's secret virtues.
On Education

18 Matter . . . a convenient formula for describing what happens where it isn't.
An Outline of Philosophy

19 It is undesirable to believe a proposition when there is no ground whatever for supposing it true.
Sceptical Essays

20 We have, in fact, two kinds of morality side by side; one which we preach but do not practise, and another which we practise but seldom preach.
Sceptical Essays

21 Mathematics possesses not only truth, but supreme beauty – a beauty cold and austere, like that of sculpture.
The Study of Mathematics

22 In America everybody is of the opinion that he has no social superiors, since all men are equal, but he does not admit that he has no social inferiors.
Unpopular Essays

23 People don't seem to realize that it takes time and effort and preparation to think. Statesmen are far too busy making speeches to think.
Kenneth Harris Talking To: 'Bertrand Russell' (Kenneth Harris)

24 There's a Bible on that shelf there. But I keep it next to Voltaire – poison and antidote.
Kenneth Harris Talking To: 'Bertrand Russell' (Kenneth Harris)

25 Obscenity is what happens to shock some elderly and ignorant magistrate.
Look magazine

26 The collection of prejudices which is called political philosophy is useful provided that it is not called philosophy.
The Observer, 'Sayings of the Year', 1962

27 Not a gentleman; dresses too well.
Referring to Anthony Eden
Six Men (A. Cooke)

28 Many people would sooner die than think. In fact they do.
Thinking About Thinking (A. Flew)

29 You may reasonably expect a man to walk a tightrope safely for ten minutes; it would be unreasonable to do so without accident for two hundred years.
On the subject of nuclear war between the USA and the Soviets
The Tightrope Men (D. Bagley)

30 Few people can be happy unless they hate some other person, nation or creed.
Attrib.

31 Patriots always talk of dying for their country, and never of killing for their country.
Attrib.

32 Of course not. After all, I may be wrong.
On being asked whether he would be prepared to die for his beliefs
Attrib.

33 Every time I talk to a savant I feel quite sure that happiness is no longer a possibility. Yet when I talk with my gardener, I'm convinced of the opposite.
Attrib.

Russell, George William (1867–1935) Irish poet and dramatist, writing under the pseudonym 'AE'. His works include the play *Deirdre* (1902).

1 No, thank you, I was born intoxicated.
Refusing a drink that was offered him
10,000 Jokes, Toasts, and Stories (L. Copeland)

Russell, John, Earl (1792–1878) British statesman. He became an MP in 1813 and was appointed home secretary (1835–39) by Lord Melbourne. He was twice prime minister (1846–52; 1865–66). He resigned as prime minister after the defeat of the second parliamentary reform bill.

1 Two mothers-in-law.
His answer when asked what he would consider a proper punishment for bigamy
Anekdotenschatz (H. Hoffmeister)

2 A proverb is one man's wit and all men's wisdom.

Attrib.

Russell, Sir William Howard (1820–1907) British journalist. As war correspondent for *The Times* he reported the Crimean War, his dispatches being collected in *The War* (1855–56).

1 They dashed on towards that *thin red line tipped with steel*.

Description of the Russian charge against the British at the battle of Balaclava, 1854
The British Expedition to the Crimea

Rutherford, Ernest, Baron (1871–1937) British physicist, born in New Zealand. As director of the Cavendish Laboratory at Cambridge he elucidated the nature of radioactivity, discovered the atomic nucleus, and put forward the Rutherford model of the atom.

1 When we have found how the nucleus of atoms are built-up we shall have found the greatest secret of all – except life. We shall have found the basis of everything – of the earth we walk on, of the air we breathe, of the sunshine, of our physical body itself, of everything in the world, however great or however small – except life.

Passing Show 24

2 We haven't the money, so we've got to think.

Attrib.

Ryle, Gilbert (1900–76) British philosopher. The editor of *Mind* (1947–71), he summarized his own work in *The Concept of Mind* (1949).

1 Philosophy is the replacement of category-habits by category-disciplines.

The Concept of Mind, Introduction

2 A myth is, of course, not a fairy story. It is the presentation of facts belonging to one category in the idioms appropriate to another. To explode a myth is accordingly not to deny the facts but to re-allocate them.

The Concept of Mind, Introduction

3 The dogma of the Ghost in the Machine.

The Concept of Mind, Ch. 1

S

Sackville-West, Vita (Victoria Sackville-West; 1892–1962) British poet and novelist. She established her reputation as a poet with *The Land* (1926); her novels include *The Edwardians* (1930), *All Passion Spent* (1931), and *Grand Canyon* (1942).

1 Among the many problems which beset the novelist, not the least weighty is the choice of the moment at which to begin his novel.

The Edwardians, Ch. 1

2 The country habit has me by the heart,
For he's bewitched for ever who has seen,
Not with his eyes but with his vision, Spring
Flow down the woods and stipple leaves with sun.

The Land, 'Winter'

3 Travel is the most private of pleasures. There is no greater bore than the travel bore. We do not in the least want to hear what he has seen in Hong-Kong.

Passenger to Tehran, Ch. 1

4 For observe, that to hope for Paradise is to live in Paradise, a very different thing from actually getting there.

Passenger to Tehran, Ch. 1

5 Those who have never dwelt in tents have no idea either of the charm or of the discomfort of a nomadic existence. The charm is purely romantic, and consequently very soon proves to be fallacious.

Twelve Days, Ch. 6

Saddam Hussein (1937–) Iraqi leader; president (1979–).

1 They will drown in their own blood.

Speech referring to the coalition forces at the start of the Gulf conflict, 1990

2 The mother of battles will be our battle of victory and martyrdom.

Speech referring to the Gulf War, 1991

Sade, Donatien Alphonse François, Marquis de (1740–1814) French novelist, who wrote whilst in prison for sexual offences. Sadism was named after him; he died in a mental asylum.

1 All universal moral principles are idle fancies.

The 120 Days of Sodom

Sadleir, Michael (1888–1957) British author and publisher, best-known for his novel *Fanny by Gaslight* (1940).

1 Fanny by Gaslight.

Book title

Sagan, Françoise (1935–) French writer, whose works include the novels *Bonjour Tristesse* (1954), *La femme fardée* (1981), and *With Fondest Regards* (1986) as well as several plays.

1 Every little girl knows about love. It is only her capacity to suffer because of it that increases.

Daily Express

Sahl, Mort (1926–) US political comedian popular in the early 1960s. He also appeared in a few films, such as *All the Young Men* (1960) and *Don't Make Waves* (1967).

1 Would you buy a second-hand car from this man?

Referring to President Nixon
Attrib.

Saint-Exupéry, Antoine de (1900–44) French novelist and aviator, whose books are based on his flying experiences. He also wrote *The Little Prince* (1943), a children's story. He failed to return from a mission during World War II.

1 It is such a secret place, the land of tears.

The Little Prince, Ch. 7

2 You become responsible, forever, for what you have tamed. You are responsible for your rose.
The Little Prince, Ch. 21

3 Man's 'progress' is but a gradual discovery that his questions have no meaning.
The Wisdom of the Sands

Saint-Lambert, Jean François, Marquis de (1716–1803) French poet and philosopher.

1 Often I am still listening when the song is over.
Les Saisons, 'Le Printemps'

Saintsbury, George Edward Bateman (1845–1933) British writer and critic. He wrote many books on the history of English literature and on wines.

1 It is the unbroken testimony of all history that alcoholic liquors have been used by the strongest, wisest, handsomest, and in every way best races of all times.
Notes on a Cellar-Book

Sakharov, Andrei Dimitrievich (1921–1989) Soviet nuclear physicist. His opposition to nuclear weapons and defence of free speech won him a Nobel peace prize in 1975; he was exiled to Gorkii (1980–86) but was elected to the Soviet parliament in 1989, shortly before his death.

1 There'll be a hard fight tomorrow.
Said to a friend shortly before his death

Saki (Hector Hugh Munro; 1870–1916) British writer. He is best-known for his collections of humorous short stories, including *Reginald* (1904), *The Chronicles of Clovis* (1911), and *Beasts and Super-Beasts* (1914).

1 By insisting on having your bottle pointing to the north when the cork is being drawn, and calling the waiter Max, you may induce an impression on your guests which hours of laboured boasting might be powerless to achieve. For this purpose, however, the guests must be chosen as carefully as the wine.
The Chaplet

2 Addresses are given to us to conceal our whereabouts.
Cross Currents

3 'I believe I take precedence,' he said coldly; 'you are merely the club Bore: I am the club Liar.'
A Defensive Diamond

4 Waldo is one of those people who would be enormously improved by death.
Referring to Ralph Waldo Emerson
The Feast of Nemesis

5 Children with Hyacinth's temperament don't know better as they grow older; they merely know more.
Hyacinth

6 The people of Crete unfortunately make more history than they can consume locally.
The Jesting of Arlington Stringham

7 To say that anything was a quotation was an excellent method, in Eleanor's eyes, for withdrawing it from discussion.
The Jesting of Arlington Stringham

8 He's simply got the instinct for being unhappy highly developed.
The Match-Maker

9 All decent people live beyond their incomes nowadays, and those who aren't respectable live beyond other people's. A few gifted individuals manage to do both.
The Match-Maker

10 Oysters are more beautiful than any religion . . . There's nothing in Christianity or Buddhism that quite matches the sympathetic unselfishness of an oyster.
The Match-Maker

11 His socks compelled one's attention without losing one's respect.
Ministers of Grace

12 The young have aspirations that never come to pass, the old have reminiscences of what never happened.
Reginald at the Carlton

13 There may have been disillusionments in the lives of the medieval saints, but they would scarcely have been better pleased if they could have foreseen that their names would be associated nowadays chiefly with racehorses and the cheaper clarets.
Reginald at the Carlton

14 The Western custom of one wife and hardly any mistresses.
Reginald in Russia

15 But, good gracious, you've got to educate him first.
You can't expect a boy to be vicious till he's been to a good school.
Reginald in Russia

16 The cook was a good cook, as cooks go; and as cooks go she went.
Reginald on Besetting Sins

17 People may say what they like about the decay of Christianity; the religious system that produced green Chartreuse can never really die.
Reginald on Christmas Presents

18 Even the Hooligan was probably invented in China centuries before we thought of him.
Reginald on House-Parties

19 Every reformation must have its victims. You can't expect the fatted calf to share the enthusiasm of the angels over the prodigal's return.
Reginald on the Academy

20 I think she must have been very strictly brought up, she's so desperately anxious to do the wrong thing correctly.
Reginald on Worries

21 I always say beauty is only sin deep.

Reginald's Choir Treat

22 In baiting a mouse-trap with cheese, always leave room for the mouse.

The Square Egg

23 Sherard Blaw, the dramatist who had discovered himself, and who had given so ungrudgingly of his discovery to the world.

The Unbearable Bassington, Ch. 13

Salinger, J(erome) D(avid) (1919–) US novelist who achieved success with *The Catcher in the Rye* (1951); later books include *Franny and Zooey* (1961), *Seymour, An Introduction* (1963), and *Raise High the Roof Beam, Carpenters* (1963).

1 If you really want to hear about it, the first thing you'll probably want to know is where I was born and what my lousy childhood was like, and how my parents were occupied and all before they had me, and all that David Copperfield kind of crap.

The opening words of the book
The Catcher in the Rye

2 Sex is something I really don't understand too hot. You never know *where* the hell you are. I keep making up these sex rules for myself, and then I break them right away.

The Catcher in the Rye, Ch. 9

3 They didn't act like people and they didn't act like actors. It's hard to explain. They acted more like they knew they were celebrities and all. I mean they were good, but they were *too* good.

The Catcher in the Rye, Ch. 17

Salisbury, Robert Arthur Talbot Gascoyne-Cecil, Marquess of (1830–1903) British statesman; Conservative prime minister (1885–86; 1886–92; 1895–1902). He was elected an MP in 1853, later becoming Disraeli's foreign secretary (1878).

1 Written by office boys for office boys.

Reaction to the launch of the *Daily Mail*, 1896
Northcliffe, an Intimate Biography (Hamilton Fyfe), Ch. 4

2 We are part of the community of Europe and we must do our duty as such.

Speech, Caernarvon, 11 Apr 1888

Salk, Jonas E. (1914–) US virologist, who developed the first antipolio vaccine.

1 The people – could you patent the sun?

On being asked who owned the patent on his antipolio vaccine
Famous Men of Science (S. Bolton)

Sallust (Gaius Sallustius Crispus; c. 86–c. 34 BC) Roman historian and politician. He supported Caesar against Pompey and was appointed governor of Numidia, but retired from politics after being accused of corruption. He is remembered for his *Bellum Catilinae* and *Bellum Jugurthinum*.

1 To like and dislike the same things, that is indeed true friendship.

Bellum Catilinae

Salvandy, Comte de (1795–1856) French nobleman.

1 We are dancing on a volcano.

A remark made before the July Revolution in 1830

Sampson, Anthony (1926–) British writer and journalist. He has written several surveys of Britain, including *The Changing Anatomy of Britain* (1982).

1 Members rise from CMG (known sometimes in Whitehall as 'Call me God') to the KCMG ('Kindly Call me God') to . . . The GCMG ('God Calls me God').

Anatomy of Britain, Ch. 18

Samuel, Herbert (Louis), Viscount (1870–1963) British Liberal statesman and philosopher. He was high commissioner for Palestine (1920–25) and home secretary (1916 and 1931). His books include *Philosophy and the Ordinary Man* (1932).

1 It takes two to make a marriage a success and only one a failure.

A Book of Quotations

2 A truism is on that account none the less true.

A Book of Quotations

3 A library is thought in cold storage.

A Book of Quotations

4 Hansard is history's ear, already listening.

The Observer, 'Sayings of the Week', 18 Dec 1949

5 Without doubt the greatest injury . . . was done by basing morals on myth, for sooner or later myth is recognized for what it is, and disappears. Then morality loses the foundation on which it has been built.

Romanes Lecture, 1947

6 A difficulty for every solution.

Referring to the Civil Service
Attrib.

Sand, George (Aurore Dupin, Baronne Dudevant; 1804–76) French novelist, whose lovers included Alfred de Musset and Chopin.

1 One is happy as a result of one's own efforts, once one knows the necessary ingredients of happiness – simple tastes, a certain degree of courage, self denial to a point, love of work, and, above all, a clear conscience. Happiness is no vague dream, of that I now feel certain.

Correspondence, Vol. V

2 Liszt said to me today that God alone deserves to be loved. It may be true, but when one has loved a man it is very different to love God.

Intimate Journal

Sandburg, Carl (1878–1967) US author and poet, who wrote mostly in free verse. His *Complete Poems* were published in 1951. He also wrote books for children and a two-volume biography of Abraham Lincoln (1926, 1939).

1 Sometime they'll give a war and nobody will come.

The People, Yes

Sanders, George (1906–72) British film actor, who specialized in playing villains and cads. His films include *Rebecca* (1940) and *All About Eve* (1950).

1 Dear World, I am leaving you because I am bored. I am leaving you with your worries. Good luck.
Suicide note

Santayana, George (1863–1952) US philosopher and poet. His books include *Realms of Being* (1927–40), *Background of my Life* (1945), several volumes of poetry, and a novel.

Quotations about Santayana

1 He stood on the flat road to heaven and buttered slides to hell for all the rest.
Oliver Wendell Holmes (1809–94) US writer. Letter, 5 Dec 1913

Quotations by Santayana

2 The working of great institutions is mainly the result of a vast mass of routine, petty malice, self interest, carelessness, and sheer mistake. Only a residual fraction is thought.
The Crime of Galileo

3 The young man who has not wept is a savage, and the old man who will not laugh is a fool.
Dialogues in Limbo, Ch. 3

4 The Bible is literature, not dogma.
Introduction to the Ethics of Spinoza

5 Happiness is the only sanction of life; where happiness fails, existence remains a mad and lamentable experiment.
The Life of Reason

6 Progress, far from consisting in change, depends on retentiveness. Those who cannot remember the past are condemned to repeat it.
The Life of Reason

7 Because there's no fourth class.
On being asked why he always travelled third class
Living Biographies of the Great Philosophers (H. Thomas)

8 Life is not a spectacle or a feast; it is a predicament.
The Perpetual Pessimist (Sagittarius and George)

9 England is the paradise of individuality, eccentricity, heresy, anomalies, hobbies, and humours.
Soliloquies in England, 'The British Character'

10 Trust the man who hesitates in his speech and is quick and steady in action, but beware of long arguments and long beards.
Soliloquies in England, 'The British Character'

11 There is no cure for birth and death save to enjoy the interval.
Soliloquies in England, 'War Shrines'

12 It is a great advantage for a system of philosophy to be substantially true.
The Unknowable

13 For an idea ever to be fashionable is ominous, since it must afterwards be always old-fashioned.
Winds of Doctrine, 'Modernism and Christianity'

14 If all the arts aspire to the condition of music, all the sciences aspire to the condition of mathematics.
The Observer, 'Sayings of the Week', 4 Mar 1928

Sarasate (y Navascués), Pablo (1844–1908) Spanish violinist and composer.

1 A genius! For thirty-seven years I've practised fourteen hours a day, and now they call me a genius!
On being hailed as a genius by a critic
Attrib.

Sargent, Epes (1813–80) US writer and dramatist.

1 A life on the ocean wave,
A home on the rolling deep.
A Life on the Ocean Wave

Sargent, John Singer (1856–1925) US portrait painter who lived in England, but visited the US annually. As an American citizen he refused a knighthood.

1 Every time I paint a portrait I lose a friend.
Attrib.

Sargent, Sir Malcolm (1895–1967) British conductor. He was chief conductor of the London Promenade Concerts from 1957 to 1967.

1 Just a little more reverence, please, and not so much astonishment.
Rehearsing the female chorus in 'For Unto Us a Child is Born' from Handel's *Messiah*
2500 Anecdotes (E. Fuller)

Saroyan, William (1908–81) US dramatist and writer. His writings include the play *The Time of Your Life* (1939) and the novel *The Human Comedy* (1943).

1 Everybody has got to die, but I have always believed an exception would be made in my case. Now what?
Last words
Time, 16 Jan 1984

Sartre, Jean-Paul (1905–80) French philosopher, dramatist, and novelist. The principal exponent of existentialism, he wrote a number of books on this subject, including *Critique de la raison dialectique* (1960). His novels include the trilogy *The Roads to Freedom* (1945–49), and *The Respectable Prostitute* (1946) is the best known of his plays.

Quotations about Sartre

1 His adult life resembled his childhood in the sense that he lorded it over admiring women.
James Fenton (1949–) British writer and editor. *The Times*, 22 Nov 1984

2 He is a philosopher remarkable for the force, one might almost say the animal vigour, of his thought; a novelist of great fecundity and a sumptuous flow of words, mixed a little too carefully with vulgar expressions and low-class slang; a playwright able to sustain themes apparently void of dramatic interest; and a political journalist with a word to say on all contemporary problems.
The Observer, 7 Mar 1947

3 The ineptitude of M. Sartre's political performance has tempted some British critics to dismiss him as a phoney, particularly as he rarely hesitates to adapt the facts to fit the cause for which he currently cares.
The Observer, 4 Dec 1960

Quotations by Sartre

4 I hate victims who respect their executioners.
Altona

5 An American is either a Jew, or an anti-Semite, unless he is both at the same time.
Altona

6 Man is condemned to be free.
Existentialism is a Humanism

7 Three o'clock is always too late or too early for anything you want to do.
Nausea

8 Things are entirely what they appear to be and *behind them* . . . there is nothing.
Nausea

9 My thought is *me*: that is why I can't stop. I exist by what I think . . . and I can't prevent myself from thinking.
Nausea

10 I know perfectly well that I don't want to do anything; to do something is to create existence – and there's quite enough existence as it is.
Nausea

11 I don't think the profession of historian fits a man for psychological analysis. In our work we have to deal only with simple feelings to which we give generic names such as Ambition and Interest.
Nausea

12 I think they do that to pass the time, nothing more. But time is too large, it refuses to let itself be filled up.
Nausea

13 You get the impression that their normal condition is silence and that speech is a slight fever which attacks them now and then.
Nausea

14 The poor don't know that their function in life is to exercise our generosity.
Words

15 A kiss without a moustache, they said then, is like an egg without salt; I will add to it: and it is like Good without Evil.
Words

16 She believed in nothing; only her scepticism kept her from being an atheist.
Words

17 There is no such thing as psychological. Let us say that one can improve the biography of the person.
The Divided Self (R. D. Laing), Ch. 8

18 In the first days of the revolt you must kill: to shoot down a European is to kill two birds with one stone, to destroy an oppressor and the man he oppresses at the same time: there remain a dead man, and a free man.
The Wretched of the Earth (F. Fanon), Preface

Sassoon, Siegfried (1886–1967) British poet and writer. After serving in World War I he published several collections of anti-war verse, including *The Old Huntsman* (1917) and *Counter Attack* (1918). His autobiographical prose work, *Memoirs of George Sherston*, included the well-known *Memoirs of a Fox-Hunting Man* (1928).

1 If I were fierce and bald and short of breath,
I'd live with scarlet Majors at the Base,
And speed glum heroes up the line to death.
Base Details

2 And when the war is done and youth stone dead
I'd toddle safely home and die – in bed.
Base Details

3 Soldiers are citizens of death's grey land,
Drawing no dividend from time's tomorrows.
Dreamers

4 'Good morning; good morning!' the general said
When we met him last week on our way to the line.
Now the soldiers he smiled at are most of 'em dead,
And we're cursing his staff for incompetent swine.
The General

5 Man, it seemed, had been created to jab the life out of Germans.
Memoirs of an Infantry Officer, Pt. I, Ch. 1

6 I am making this statement as a wilful defiance of military authority because I believe that the War is being deliberately prolonged by those who have the power to end it.
Memoirs of an Infantry Officer, Pt. X, Ch. 3

7 Safe with his wound, a citizen of life,
He hobbled blithely through the garden gate,
And thought: 'Thank God they had to amputate!'
The One-Legged Man

Sassoon, Vidal (1928–) British hair stylist whose clientele includes many rich and famous people.

1   The only place where success comes before work is a dictionary.
Quoting one of his teachers in a BBC radio broadcast

Satie, Erik (1866–1925) French composer. He composed chiefly piano works, such as *Trois Gymnopédies* (1888), *Pièces froides* (1897), and *Trois morceaux en forme de poire* (1903).

1   My doctor has always told me to smoke. He even explains himself: 'Smoke, my friend. Otherwise someone else will smoke in your place.'
Mémoires d'un amnésique

2   When I was young, I was told: 'You'll see, when you're fifty'. I am fifty and I haven't seen a thing.
From a letter to his brother
Erik Satie (Pierre-Daniel Templier), Ch. 1

3   To be played with both hands in the pocket.
Direction on one of his piano pieces
The Unimportance of Being Oscar (O. Levant)

Savile, George, Marquis of Halifax (1633–95) *See* Halifax.

Sayers, Dorothy L(eigh) (1893–1957) British writer of detective stories, featuring Lord Peter Wimsey as the detective. She also wrote plays on religious themes.

1   I can't see that she could have found anything nastier to say if she'd thought it out with both hands for a fortnight.
Busman's Holiday, 'Prothalamion'

2   As I grow older and older,
And totter towards the tomb,
I find that I care less and less
Who goes to bed with whom.
That's Why I Never Read Modern Novels

Scanlon, Hugh, Baron (1913–) British trade-union leader. He was president of the Amalgamated Union of Engineering Workers (1968–78) and a member of the TUC General Council.

1   Here we are again with both feet firmly planted in the air.
Referring to his union's attitude to the Common Market
The Observer, 'Sayings of the Year', 30 Dec 1973

Scarron, Paul (1610–60) French poet, dramatist, and satirist. He was paralysed from the age of 30.

1   At last I am going to be well!
As he lay dying
Attrib.

Schelling, Friedrich Wilhelm Joseph von (1775– 1854) German philosopher. His metaphysical philosophy is expounded in his *System of Transcendental Idealism* (1800).

1   Architecture in general is frozen music.
Philosophie der Kunst

Schiller, Friedrich von (1759–1805) German dramatist and writer. His early plays included *Die Rauber* (1781) and *Don Carlos* (1787), while his later dramas included the *Wallenstein* trilogy (1798–99), *Die Jungfrau von Orleans* (1801), and *Wilhelm Tell* (1804). Beethoven used Schiller's *An die Freude* (Ode to Joy; 1786) in his choral symphony.

1   Against stupidity the gods themselves struggle in vain.
Die Jungfrau von Orleans, III:6

2   The sun does not set in my dominions.
Said by Philip II
Don Carlos, I:6

Schlegel, Friedrich von (1772–1829) German diplomat, writer, and critic. Many of his philosophical and literary articles appeared in the journal *Das Athenäum*, which he published with his brother. He also wrote the novel *Lucinde* (1799) and various philosophical books, such as *Philosophie des Lebens* (1828).

1   A historian is a prophet in reverse.
Das Athenäum

Schlieffen, Alfred, Graf von (1833–1913) German general. His strategy for defeating France was adopted by Germany at the start of World War I, but was unsuccessful.

1   When you march into France, let the last man on the right brush the Channel with his sleeve.
Referring to the Schlieffen plan
August 1914 (Barbara Tuchman), Ch. 2

Schliemann, Heinrich (1822–90) German archaeologist, who excavated many cities of the Mycenaean civilization.

1   I have looked upon the face of Agamemnon.
On discovering a gold death mask at an excavation in Mycenae
The Story of Civilization (W. Durant), Vol. 2

Schnabel, Artur (1882–1951) Austrian concert pianist, famous for his performances of Beethoven. He also composed music for the piano and for orchestra.

1   I know two kinds of audience only – one coughing and one not coughing.
See also AGATE
My Life and Music, Pt. II, Ch. 10

2   The notes I handle no better than many pianists. But the pauses between the notes – ah, that is where the art resides.
Chicago Daily News, 11 June 1958

3   The sonatas of Mozart are unique; they are too easy for children, and too difficult for artists.
An Encyclopedia of Quotations about Music (Nat Shapiro)

4   When a piece gets difficult make faces.
Advice given to the pianist Vladimir Horowitz
The Unimportance of Being Oscar (O. Levant)

Schneckenburger, Max (1819–49) German poet. His song *Die Wacht am Rhein* (1840), set to music by Karl Wilhelm, became a patriotic song.

1   *Die Wacht am Rhein*
The Watch on the Rhine
Song title

Schopenhauer, Arthur (1788–1860) German philosopher. His books include *Die Welt als Wille und Vorstellung* (1819) and *Die Beiden Grundprobleme der Ethik* (1841).

1   To be alone is the fate of all great minds – a fate deplored at times, but still always chosen as the less grievous of two evils.
Aphorismen zur Lebensweisheit

2 Intellect is invisible to the man who has none.

Aphorismen zur Lebensweisheit

3 Every parting gives a foretaste of death; every coming together again a foretaste of the resurrection.

Gedanken über vielerlei Gegenstände, XXVI

4 The fundamental fault of the female character is that it has no sense of justice.

Gedanken über vielerlei Gegenstände, XXVII

5 The thing-in-itself, the will-to-live, exists whole and undivided in every being, even in the tiniest; it is present as completely as in all that ever were, are, and will be, taken together.

Parerga and Paralipomena

6 To expect a man to retain everything that he has ever read is like expecting him to carry about in his body everything that he has ever eaten.

Parerga and Paralipomena

7 After your death you will be what you were before your birth.

Parerga and Paralipomena

8 Wealth is like sea-water; the more we drink, the thirstier we become; and the same is true of fame.

Parerga and Paralipomena

Schulz, Charles M. (1922–) US cartoonist, who created the *Peanuts* strip cartoon.

1 I love mankind – it's people I can't stand.

Go Fly a Kite, Charlie Brown

Schumacher, E. F. (1911–77) German-born economist and conservationist.

1 The heart of the matter, as I see it, is the stark fact that world poverty is primarily a problem of two million villages, and thus a problem of two thousand million villagers.

Small is Beautiful, A Study of Economics as if People Mattered Ch. 13

2 After all, for mankind as a whole there are no exports. We did not start developing by obtaining foreign exchange from Mars or the moon. Mankind is a closed society.

Small is Beautiful, A Study of Economics as if People Mattered Ch. 14

Schwarzkopf, Norman (1934–) US general, who led the coalition forces during the Gulf conflict (1990–91)

1 We're going around, over, through, on top, underneath.

Press conference, 24 Feb 1991, describing his tactics for attacking the Iraqi army.

Schwarzenberg, Felix, Prince (1800–52) Austrian statesman. As prime minister he successfully restricted Prussian influence over German states.

1 Austria will astound the world with the magnitude of her ingratitude.

On being asked whether Austria was under any obligation to Russia for help received previously
The Fall of the House of Habsburg (E. Crankshaw)

Schweitzer, Albert (1875–1965) French Protestant theologian, philosopher, physician, and musician. He is remembered for his medical missionary work in Lambaréné, Gabon (1913–65), and his recordings of Bach organ music.

1 The purpose of human life is to serve and to show compassion and the will to help others.

The Schweitzer Album

2 I too had thoughts once of being an intellectual, but I found it too difficult.

Remark made to an African who refused to perform a menial task on the grounds that he was an intellectual
Attrib.

3 Here, at whatever hour you come, you will find light and help and human kindness.

Inscribed on the lamp outside his jungle hospital at Lambaréné

Scott, C(harles) P(restwich) (1846–1932) British journalist. He became editor of the *Manchester Guardian* (1872) and later its owner. He was also an MP (1895–1906).

1 Its primary office is the gathering of news. At the peril of its soul it must see that the supply is not tainted. Neither in what it gives, nor in what it does not give, nor in the mode of presentation, must the unclouded face of truth suffer wrong. Comment is free but facts are sacred.

Manchester Guardian, 6 May 1926

2 Television? No good will come of this device. The word is half Greek and half Latin.

Attrib.

Scott, Paul Mark (1920–78) British novelist. He is best remembered for the Raj Quartet, consisting of *Jewel in the Crown* (1966), *The Day of the Scorpion* (1968), *The Towers of Silence* (1971), and *A Division of the Spoils* (1975).

1 Our Eastern Empire, I mean. It was, you know, what *made* the English middle class. It taught us the hitherto upper-class secrets of government and civil administration. Now we must largely be content again with commerce and science.

The Bender

2 I have been in the houses of very rich people who are rich because they have talents or vital statistics and in such places you have but definitely to wet your finger and hold it up and you may then go like without hesitation following the wind blowing from looward and presently drop anchor. But in the houses of people who have both money and class it is like of no use to wet your finger and hold it up because someone will simply stick upon it a canapé filled with *pâté de foie*.

The Bender

3 There were people in Mayapore who said I only kept up with Lady Manners for snob reasons, *Indian* snob reasons, like calling an English person by his Christian name.

The Jewel in the Crown

Scott, Robert Falcon, Captain (1868–1912) British
explorer. He led two expeditions to the Antarctic, the first in
Discovery (1900–04) and the second in *Terra Nova* (1910–12), in
which he was beaten to the pole by Amundsen and perished on
the return journey.

1 Great God! this is an awful place.
Referring to the South Pole
Journal, 17 Jan 1912

2 Had we lived, I should have had a tale to tell of
the hardihood, endurance, and courage of my
companions which would have stirred the heart
of every Englishman. These rough notes and
our dead bodies must tell the tale.
Message to the Public

Scott, Sir Walter (1771–1832) Scottish novelist. Originally a
lawyer, he turned to writing for a living after the success of his
narrative poem, *The Lay of the Last Minstrel* (1805). *Waverley*
(1814) was the first of many successful historical novels, including
Rob Roy (1817), *The Heart of Midlothian* (1818), *The Bride of
Lammermoor* (1818), *Ivanhoe* (1819), and *The Talisman* (1825).

Quotations about Scott

1 It can be said of him, when he departed he took
a Man's life with him. No sounder piece of British manhood was put together in that eighteenth century of time.
Thomas Carlyle (1795–1881) Scottish historian and essayist.
Essays, 'Lockhart's Life of Scott'

2 Sir Walter Scott, when all is said and done, is an
inspired butler.
William Hazlitt (1778–1830) British essayist. *Mrs Siddons*

Quotations by Scott

3 Look back, and smile at perils past.
The Bridal of Triermain, Introduction

4 It's ill taking the breeks aff a wild Highlandman.
The Fair Maid of Perth, Ch. 5

5 The Big Bow-Wow strain I can do myself like
any now going; but the exquisite touch, which
renders ordinary commonplace things and characters interesting, from the truth of the
description and the sentiment, is denied to me.
In praise of Jane Austen
Journal, 14 Mar 1826

6 For ne'er
Was flattery lost on poet's ear:
A simple race! they waste their toil
For the vain tribute of a smile.
The Lay of the Last Minstrel, IV

7 True love's the gift which God has given
To man alone beneath the heaven.
The Lay of the Last Minstrel, V

8 Breathes there the man, with soul so dead,
Who never to himself hath said,
This is my own, my native land!
Whose heart hath ne'er within him burn'd,
As home his footsteps he hath turn'd
From wandering on a foreign strand!
The Lay of the Last Minstrel, VI

9 O Caledonia! stern and wild,
Meet nurse for a poetic child!
Land of brown heath and shaggy wood,
Land of the mountain and the flood,
Land of my sires! what mortal hand
Can e'er untie the filial band
That knits me to thy rugged strand!
The Lay of the Last Minstrel, VI

10 His morning walk was beneath the elms in the
churchyard; 'for death,' he said, 'had been his
next-door neighbour for so many years, that he
had no apology for dropping the acquaintance.'
The Legend of Montrose, Introduction

11 There is a Southern proverb, – fine words butter no parsnips.
The Legend of Montrose, Ch. 3

12 To that dark inn, the grave!
The Lord of the Isles, VI

13 But search the land of living men,
Where wilt thou find their like agen?
Marmion, I

14 O, young Lochinvar is come out of the west,
Through all the wide Border his steed was the
best.
Marmion, V

15 So faithful in love, and so dauntless in war,
There never was knight like the young
Lochinvar.
Marmion, V

16 The stubborn spear-men still made good
Their dark impenetrable wood,
Each stepping where his comrade stood,
   The instant that he fell.
Marmion, VI

17 Ridicule often checks what is absurd, and fully as
often smothers that which is noble.
Quentin Durward

18 But with the morning cool repentance came.
Rob Roy, Ch. 12

19 See yon pale stripling! when a boy,
A mother's pride, a father's joy!
Rokeby, III

20 O, Brignal banks are wild and fair,
   And Gretna woods are green,
And you may gather garlands there
   Would grace a summer queen.
Rokeby, III

21 My heart's in the Highlands, my heart is not
here,
My heart's in the Highlands a-chasing the deer.
Waverley, Ch. 28

22 No, this right hand shall work it all off.
Refusing offers of help following his bankruptcy in 1826
Century of Anecdote (J. Timbs)

23 All health is better than wealth.
Familiar Letters, Letter to C. Carpenter, 4 Aug 1812

Scott, William, Baron Stowell (1745–1836) British jurist. A friend of Dr Johnson, he was the highest authority on maritime and international law. He became Advocate-General for the Lord High Admiral.

1 A dinner lubricates business.
Life of Johnson (J. Boswell), 1791

2 A precedent embalms a principle.
An opinion given while Advocate-General
Attrib.

Searle, Ronald William Fordham (1920–) British cartoonist, who worked for the *Sunday Express* and *Punch* magazine. He created the notorious schoolgirls of St Trinian's.

1 Though loaded firearms were strictly forbidden at St Trinian's to all but Sixth-Formers . . . one or two of them carried automatics acquired in the holidays, generally the gift of some indulgent relative.
The Terror of St Trinian's, Ch. 3

2 In the spring . . . your lovely Chloë lightly turns to one mass of spots.
The Terror of St Trinian's, Ch. 7

Sears, E(dmund) H(amilton) (1810–76) US clergyman and hymn writer.

1 It came upon the midnight clear,
That glorious song of old,
From Angels bending near the earth
To touch their harps of gold;
'Peace on the earth; good will to man
From Heaven's all gracious King.'
The world in solemn stillness lay
To hear the angels sing.
That Glorious Song of Old

Sébastiani, Horace François, Comte (1772–1851) French general and diplomat.

1 At the moment of writing, calm reigned in Warsaw.
After the defeat of the military insurrection in Warsaw

Secombe, Sir Harry (1921–) Welsh singer, actor, and comedian. He performed in BBC radio's 'Goon Show' (1949–60) and has made many appearances on stage and television. His films include *Oliver!* (1968).

1 My advice if you insist on slimming: Eat as much as you like – just don't swallow it.
Daily Herald, 5 Oct 1962

2 At last God caught his eye.
Suggested epitaph for a head waiter.
Punch, May 1962

Sedgwick, Catharine Maria (1789–1867) US writer.

1 I expect no very violent transition.
Comparing heaven with her home-town of Stockbridge, Massachussetts
Edie (Jean Stein)

Sedgwick, John (1813–64) US general in the Union army during the US Civil War.

1 Nonsense, they couldn't hit an elephant at this dist –
His last words, in response to a suggestion that he should not show himself over the parapet during the Battle of the Wilderness
Attrib.

Seeger, Alan (1888–1916) US poet. He came to Europe in 1912, enlisted in the French Foreign Legion in World War I, and was killed on active service. His collections of verse include *Juvenilia* and *Later Poems*.

1 I have a rendezvous with Death
At some disputed barricade.
I Have a Rendezvous with Death

Seeger, Pete (1919–) US folksinger and songwriter, who wrote 'Where Have All the Flowers Gone?' and 'Kisses Sweeter than Wine'.

1 Where have all the flowers gone?
Young girls picked them every one.
Where Have All the Flowers Gone?

Seeley, Sir John Robert (1834–95) British historian and writer. His *Ecce Homo* (1865) and *Natural Religion* (1882) caused considerable controversy; *The Expansion of England* (1883) and *The Growth of British Policy* (1895) were his best-known historical works.

1 We the English seem, as it were, to have conquered and peopled half the world in a fit of absence of mind.
The Expansion of England, I

2 History is past politics, and politics present history.
Quoting the historian E. A. Freeman
The Growth of British Policy

Segal, Erich (1937–) US writer, author of the novel upon which the film *Love Story* (1970) was based.

1 What can you say about a 25-year-old girl who died? That she was beautiful? And brilliant. That she loved Mozart and Bach. And the Beatles. And me.
Love Story

2 Love means never having to say you're sorry.
Love Story

Selden, John (1584–1654) English historian, jurist, antiquary, and statesman. He wrote many erudite works but is best remembered for *Table Talk* (1689), a posthumously published collection of his sayings.

1 A king is a thing men have made for their own sakes, for quietness' sake. Just as if in a family one man is appointed to buy the meat.
Table Talk

2 Every law is a contract between the king and the people and therefore to be kept.
Table Talk

3 Ignorance of the law excuses no man; not that all men know the law, but because 'tis an excuse every man will plead, and no man can tell how to confute him.
Table Talk

4 Pleasure is nothing else but the intermission of pain.
Table Talk

5 Preachers say, Do as I say, not as I do. But if the physician had the same disease upon him that I have, and he should bid me do one thing, and himself do quite another, could I believe him?
Table Talk

6 For a priest to turn a man when he lies a-dying, is just like one that has a long time solicited a woman, and cannot obtain his end; at length makes her drunk, and so lies with her.
Table Talk

7 Pleasures are all alike simply considered in themselves . . . He that takes pleasure to hear sermons enjoys himself as much as he that hears plays.
Table Talk

8 'Tis not the drinking that is to be blamed, but the excess.
Table Talk

9 Marriage is nothing but a civil contract.
Table Talk

Selfridge, H(arry) Gordon (1857–1947) US-born businessman who became a British subject. He came to London in 1906 and established Selfridge's, making it one of the largest department stores in Europe.

1 The customer is always right.
Slogan adopted at his shops

2 This famous store needs no name on the door.
Slogan

Sellar, Walter Carruthers (1898–1951) British humorous writer who collaborated with Robert Julius Yeatman (1897–1968).

1 For every person wishing to teach there are thirty not wanting to be taught.
And Now All This

2 To confess that you are totally Ignorant about the Horse, is social suicide: you will be despised by everybody, especially the horse.
Horse Nonsense

3 1066 And All That.
Book title

4 The Roman Conquest was, however, a *Good Thing*, since the Britons were only natives at the time.
1066 And All That

5 The Cavaliers (Wrong but Wromantic) and the Roundheads (Right but Repulsive).
1066 And All That

6 Napoleon's armies used to march on their stomachs, shouting: 'Vive l'intérieur!'
1066 And All That

7 America became top nation and history came to a full stop.
1066 And All That

8 Do not on any account attempt to write on both sides of the paper at once.
1066 And All That, Test Paper 5

Sellers, Peter (1925–80) British comic actor. After success as one of the *Goons* radio comedy team (1952–60), he starred in such films as *I'm All Right Jack* (1959), *The Millionairess* (1961), *Dr Strangelove* (1963), the hugely successful Pink Panther series (1963–77), in which he played the bumbling detective Clouseau, and *Being There* (1980).

1 If you ask me to play myself, I will not know what to do. I do not know who or what I am.
Halliwell's Filmgoer's and Video Viewer's Companion

2 There used to be a me behind the mask, but I had it surgically removed.
Halliwell's Filmgoer's and Video Viewer's Companion

Selznick, David O(liver) (1902–65) US film producer. His films include *A Star is Born* (1937), *Gone with the Wind* (1939), and *A Farewell to Arms* (1957).

1 I have no middle name. I briefly used my mother's maiden name, Sachs. I had an uncle, whom I greatly disliked, who was also named David Selznick, so in order to avoid the growing confusion between the two of us, I decided to take a middle initial and went through the alphabet to find one that seemed to me to give the best punctuation, and decided on 'O'.
Memo From David O. Selznick (Rudy Behlmer)

Seneca (c. 4 BC–65 AD) Roman author and statesman, author of nine tragedies, 13 philosophical treatises, and many essays. Tutor to Nero, he was later forced by the emperor to commit suicide.

1 Live among men as if God beheld you; speak to God as if men were listening.
Epistles

2 Conversation has a kind of charm about it, an insinuating and insidious something that elicits secrets from us just like love or liquor.
Epistles

3 The body is not a permanent dwelling, but a sort of inn (with a brief sojourn at that) which is to be left behind when one perceives that one is a burden to the host.
Epistulae ad Lucilium, CXX

Servetus, Michael (1511–53) Spanish physician and theologian, who was burnt at the stake for attacking the doctrine of the Trinity. He also made discoveries concerning the circulation of blood.

1 I will burn, but this is a mere incident. We shall continue our discussion in eternity.
Comment to the judges of the Inquisition after being condemned to be burned at the stake as a heretic
Borges: A Reader (E. Monegal)

Service, Robert William (1874–1958) Canadian poet. His best-known ballads, including 'The Shooting of Dan McGrew' (1907), were based on his experience of the Yukon gold rush.

1 A promise made is a debt unpaid.
   The Cremation of Sam McGee

2 Ah! the clock is always slow;
   It is later than you think.
   It is Later than You Think

3 This is the Law of the Yukon, that only the
   strong shall thrive;
   That surely the weak shall perish, and only the
   Fit survive.
   The Law of the Yukon

4 When we, the Workers, all demand: 'What are
   we fighting for?' . . .
   Then, then we'll end that stupid crime, that devil's madness – War.
   Michael

Sévigné, Marie de Rabutin-Chantal, Marquise de (1626–96) French writer. She left some 1500 letters, mostly written to her children after her husband's death.

1 I have been dragged against my will to the fatal
   period when *old age* must be endured; I see it,
   I have attained it; and I would, at least, contrive not to go beyond it, not to advance in the
   road of infirmities, pain, loss of memory, *disfig-
   urements*, which are ready to lay hold of me.
   Letter to her daughter, 30 Nov 1689

2 The more I see of men, the more I admire dogs.
   Attrib.

Shadwell, Thomas (1642–92) English dramatist. His works include comedies such as *The Virtuoso* (1676) and *Bury Fair* (1689); his best-known opera is *The Enchanted Isle* (1674).

1 Words may be false and full of art,
   Sighs are the natural language of the heart.
   Psyche, III

2 'Tis the way of all flesh.
   The Sullen Lovers, V:2

3 Every man loves what he is good at.
   A True Widow, V:1

Shaffer, Peter (1926–) British dramatist who established his reputation with the play *Five-Finger Exercise* (1958); he subsequently wrote such plays as *The Royal Hunt of the Sun* (1964), *Equus* (1973), *Amadeus* (1979), and *Lettice and Lovage* (1987).

1 All my wife has ever taken from the Mediterranean – from that whole vast intuitive culture –
   are four bottles of Chianti to make into lamps,
   and two china condiment donkeys labelled Sally
   and Peppy.
   Equus, I:18

2 Passion, you see, can be destroyed by a doctor.
   It cannot be created.
   Equus, II:35

3 Rehearsing a play is making the word flesh. Publishing a play is reversing the process.
   Equus, Note

Shaftesbury, Anthony Ashley Cooper, 7th Earl of (1801–85) British reformer and philanthropist, who became an MP in 1826. He obtained reform of the lunacy laws (1845) and did much for factory reform, achieving the ten-hour working day, as well as ending the employment of children in mines and as chimney sweeps.

1 . . . *fully resolved never to do or accept anything*,
   however pressed by the strong claims of public
   necessity and public usefulness, which should,
   in the least degree, limit my opportunity or control my free action in respect of the Ten Hours
   Bill.
   Diary, 17 April 1844.

2 My habits are formed on metropolitan activity,
   and I must ever be groping where there is the
   most mischief.
   Diary, 1847.

Shah, Idries (1924–) British author, born in India.

1 A certain person may have, as you say, a wonderful presence: I do not know. What I do
   know is that he has a perfectly delightful
   absence.
   Reflections, 'Presence and Absence'

Shahn, Ben (1898–1969) US artist, born in Lithuania.

1 An amateur is an artist who supports himself
   with outside jobs which enable him to paint. A
   professional is someone whose wife works to enable him to paint.
   Outlining the difference between professional and amateur painters
   Attrib.

Shakespeare, William (1564–1616) English dramatist and poet, universally acknowledged to be the greatest English writer of historical plays, comedies, and tragedies. His sonnets have love and friendship as their themes.

Quotations about Shakespeare

1 Others abide our question, Thou art free,
   We ask and ask: Thou smilest and art still,
   Out-topping knowledge.
   Matthew Arnold (1822–88) British poet and critic. *Shakespeare*

2 When he killed a calf he would do it in a high
   style, and make a speech.
   John Aubrey (1626–1697) English antiquary. *Brief Lives*, 'William Shakespeare'

3 Our myriad-minded Shakespeare.
   Samuel Taylor Coleridge (1772–1834) British poet. *Biographia
   Literaria*, Ch. 15

4 I have tried lately to read Shakespeare, and
   found it so intolerably dull that it nauseated me.
   Charles Darwin (1809–82) British life scientist. *Autobiography*

5 He was the man who of all modern, and perhaps ancient poets had the largest and most comprehensive soul.

John Dryden (1631–1700) British poet and dramatist. *Essay of Dramatic Poesy*

6 He was naturally learned; he needed not the spectacles of books to read nature; he looked inwards, and found her there.

John Dryden *Essay of Dramatic Poesy*

7 We can say of Shakespeare, that never has a man turned so little knowledge to such great account.

T. S. Elliot (1888–1965) US-born British poet and dramatist. *The Classics and the Man of Letters* (lecture)

8 The remarkable thing about Shakespeare is that he is really very good – in spite of all the people who say he is very good.

Robert Graves (1895–1985) British poet and novelist. *The Observer*, 'Sayings of the Week', 6 Dec 1964

9 Shakespeare never had six lines together without a fault. Perhaps you may find seven, but this does not refute my general assertion.

Samuel Johnson (1709–84) British lexicographer. *Life of Johnson* (J. Boswell), Vol. II

10 He was not of an age, but for all time!

Ben Jonson (1573–1637) English dramatist. *To the Memory of William Shakespeare*

11 Sweet Swan of Avon!

Ben Jonson *To the Memory of William Shakespeare*

12 When I read Shakespeare I am struck with wonder
That such trivial people should muse and thunder
In such lovely language.

D. H. Lawrence (1885–1930) British novelist. *When I Read Shakespeare*

13 Or sweetest Shakespeare, Fancy's child,
Warble his native wood-notes wild.

John Milton (1608–74) English poet. *L'Allegro*

14 Shakespeare – The nearest thing in incarnation to the eye of God.

Laurence Olivier (1907–89) British actor. *Kenneth Harris Talking To*, 'Sir Laurence Olivier'

15 A man can be forgiven a lot if he can quote Shakespeare in an economic crisis.

Prince Philip (1921–) The consort of Queen Elizabeth II. Attrib.

16 Brush Up Your Shakespeare.

Cole Porter (1891–1964) US composer and lyricist. *Kiss Me Kate*

17 With the single exception of Homer, there is no eminent writer, not even Sir Walter Scott, whom I can despise so entirely as I despise Shakespeare when I measure my mind against his... It would positively be a relief to me to dig him up and throw stones at him.

George Bernard Shaw (1856–1950) Irish dramatist and critic. *Dramatic Opinions and Essays*, Vol. 2

18 Wonderful women! Have you ever thought how much we all, and women especially, owe to Shakespeare for his vindication of women in these fearless, high-spirited, resolute and intelligent heroines?

Ellen Terry (1847–1928) British actress. *Four Lectures on Shakespeare*, 'The Triumphant Women'

19 One of the greatest geniuses that ever existed, Shakespeare, undoubtedly wanted taste.

Horace Walpole (1717–97) British writer. Letter to Wren, 9 Aug 1764

Quotations by Shakespeare

The quotations by William Shakespeare are arranged in alphabetical order of his plays. These are followed by the poems and sonnets.

All's Well that Ends Well

20 Our remedies oft in ourselves do lie,
Which we ascribe to heaven.

I:1

21 A young man married is a man that's marred.

II:3

22 The web of our life is of a mingled yarn, good and ill together.

IV:3

23 Th' inaudible and noiseless foot of Time.

V:3

Antony and Cleopatra

24 The triple pillar of the world transform'd
Into a strumpet's fool.

I:1

25 There's beggary in the love that can be reckon'd.

I:1

26 In time we hate that which we often fear.

I:3

27 Where's my serpent of old Nile?

I:5

28 My salad days,
When I was green in judgment, cold in blood,
To say as I said then!

I:5

29 The barge she sat in, like a burnish'd throne,
Burn'd on the water. The poop was beaten gold;
Purple the sails, and so perfumed that
The winds were love-sick with them; the oars were silver,
Which to the tune of flutes kept stroke and made
The water which they beat to follow faster,
As amorous of their strokes. For her own person,
It beggar'd all description.

II:2

30 Age cannot wither her, nor custom stale
Her infinite variety. Other women cloy
The appetites they feed, but she makes hungry
Where most she satisfies.
II:2

31 I will praise any man that will praise me.
II:6

32 Celerity is never more admir'd
Than by the negligent.
III:7

33 To business that we love we rise betime,
And go to't with delight.
IV:4

34 Unarm, Eros; the long day's task is done,
And we must sleep.
IV:12

35 I am dying, Egypt, dying; only
I here importune death awhile, until
Of many thousand kisses the poor last
I lay upon thy lips.
IV:13

36 The crown o' the earth doth melt. My lord!
O, wither'd is the garland of the war,
The soldier's pole is fall'n! Young boys and girls
Are level now with men. The odds is gone,
And there is nothing left remarkable
Beneath the visiting moon.
IV:13

37 The bright day is done,
And we are for the dark.
V:2

38 Dost thou not see my baby at my breast
That sucks the nurse asleep?
Holding the asp to her breast
V:2

39 She shall be buried by her Antony!
No grave upon the earth shall clip in it
A pair so famous.
V:2

As You Like It

40 Well said; that was laid on with a trowel.
I:2

41 O, how full of briers is this working-day world!
I:3

42 And this our life, exempt from public haunt,
Finds tongues in trees, books in the running brooks,
Sermons in stones and good in everything.
II:1

43 I had rather bear with you than bear you.
II:4

44 If thou rememb'rest not the slightest folly
That ever love did make thee run into,
Thou hast not lov'd.
II:4

45 Under the greenwood tree
Who loves to lie with me,
And turn his merry note
Unto the sweet bird's throat,
Come hither, come hither, come hither.
Here shall he see
No enemy
But winter and rough weather.
II:5

46 And so, from hour to hour, we ripe and ripe,
And then, from hour to hour, we rot and rot;
And thereby hangs a tale.
II:7

47 All the world's a stage,
And all the men and women merely players;
They have their exits and their entrances;
And one man in his time plays many parts,
His acts being seven ages.
II:7

48 Last scene of all,
That ends this strange eventful history,
Is second childishness and mere oblivion;
Sans teeth, sans eyes, sans taste, sans every thing.
II:7

49 Blow, blow, thou winter wind,
Thou art not so unkind
As man's ingratitude.
II:7

50 Most friendship is feigning, most loving mere folly.
II:7

51 He that wants money, means, and content, is without three good friends.
III:2

52 Do you not know I am a woman? When I think, I must speak.
III:2

53 I do desire we may be better strangers.
III:2

54 The truest poetry is the most feigning.
III:3

55 Men have died from time to time, and worms have eaten them, but not for love.
IV:1

56 Your If is the only peace-maker; much virtue in If.
V:4

57 If it be true that good wine needs no bush, 'tis true that a good play needs no epilogue.
Epilogue

Coriolanus

58 Custom calls me to't.
What custom wills, in all things should we do't,
The dust on antique time would lie unswept,
And mountainous error be too highly heap'd
For truth to o'erpeer.
II:3

59 Like a dull actor now
I have forgot my part and I am out,
Even to a full disgrace.
V:3

Cymbeline

60 O, this life
Is nobler than attending for a check,
Richer than doing nothing for a bribe,
Prouder than rustling in unpaid-for silk.
III:3

61 Society is no comfort
To one not sociable.
IV:2

62 Fear no more the heat o' th' sun
Nor the furious winter's rages;
Thou thy worldly task hast done,
Home art gone, and ta'en thy wages.
Golden lads and girls all must,
As chimney-sweepers, come to dust.
IV:2

63 Every good servant does not all commands.
V:1

Hamlet

64 For this relief much thanks. 'Tis bitter cold,
And I am sick at heart.
I:1

65 A little more than kin, and less than kind.
I:2

66 But I have that within which passes show –
these but the trappings and the suits of woe.
I:2

67 O! that this too too solid flesh would melt,
Thaw, and resolve itself into a dew.
Or that the Everlasting had not fix'd
His canon 'gainst self-slaughter! O God! O God!
How weary, stale, flat, and unprofitable,
Seem to me all the uses of this world!
I:2

68 Frailty, thy name is woman!
I:2

69 It is not, nor it cannot come to good.
I:2

70 'A was a man, take him for all in all,
I shall not look upon his like again.
I:2

71 Foul deeds will rise,
Though all the earth o'erwhelm them, to men's eyes.
I:2

72 Do not, as some ungracious pastors do,
Show me the steep and thorny way to heaven,
Whiles, like a puff'd and reckless libertine,
Himself the primrose path of dalliance treads
And recks not his own rede.
I:3

73 Costly thy habit as thy purse can buy,
But not express'd in fancy; rich, not gaudy;
For the apparel oft proclaims the man.
I:3

74 Neither a borrower nor a lender be;
For loan oft loses both itself and friend,
And borrowing dulls the edge of husbandry.
This above all: to thine own self be true,
And it must follow, as the night the day,
Thou canst not then be false to any man.
I:3

75 But to my mind, though I am native here
And to the manner born, it is a custom
More honour'd in the breach than the observance.
I:4

76 Something is rotten in the state of Denmark.
I:4

77 Murder most foul, as in the best it is;
But this most foul, strange, and unnatural.
I:5

78 There are more things in heaven and earth, Horatio,
Than are dreamt of in your philosophy.
I:5

79 The time is out of joint; O cursed spite,
That ever I was born to set it right!
I:5

80 Brevity is the soul of wit.
II:2

81 To be honest, as this world goes, is to be one man pick'd out of ten thousand.
II:2

82 Though this be madness, yet there is method in't.
II:2

83 There is nothing either good or bad, but thinking makes it so.
II:2

84 What a piece of work is a man! How noble in reason! how infinite in faculties! in form and moving, how express and admirable! in action, how like an angel! in apprehension, how like a god! the beauty of the world! the paragon of animals! And yet, to me, what is this quintessence of dust? Man delights not me – no, nor woman neither.
II:2

85 I am but mad north-north-west; when the wind is southerly, I know a hawk from a handsaw.
II:2

86 The play, I remember, pleas'd not the million; 'twas caviare to the general.
II:2

87 Use every man after his desert, and who shall scape whipping?
II:2

88 The play's the thing
Wherein I'll catch the conscience of the King.
II:2

89 To be, or not to be – that is the question;
Whether 'tis nobler in the mind to suffer
The slings and arrows of outrageous fortune,
Or to take arms against a sea of troubles,
And by opposing end them? To die, to sleep –
No more; and by a sleep to say we end
The heart-ache and the thousand natural shocks
That flesh is heir to, 'tis a consummation
Devoutly to be wish'd. To die, to sleep;
To sleep, perchance to dream. Ay, there's the rub;
For in that sleep of death what dreams may come,
When we have shuffled off this mortal coil,
Must give us pause.
III:1

90 The dread of something after death –
The undiscover'd country, from whose bourn
No traveller returns.
III:1

91 Thus conscience does make cowards of us all;
And thus the native hue of resolution
Is sicklied o'er with the pale cast of thought.
III:1

92 Get thee to a nunnery: why wouldst thou be a breeder of sinners?
III:1

93 Madness in great ones must not unwatch'd go.
III:1

94 It out-herods Herod.
III:2

95 Suit the action to the word, the word to the action; with this special observance, that you o'erstep not the modesty of nature.
III:2

96 The lady doth protest too much, methinks.
III:2

97 Very like a whale.
III:2

98 A king of shreds and patches.
III:4

99 How all occasions do inform against me,
And spur my dull revenge! What is a man,
If his chief good and market of his time
Be but to sleep and feed? a beast, no more.
IV:4

100 Some craven scruple
Of thinking too precisely on th' event.
IV:4

101 When sorrows come, they come not single spies,
But in battalions!
IV:5

102 There's such divinity doth hedge a king
That treason can but peep to what it would.
IV:5

103 There's rosemary, that's for remembrance;
pray, love, remember: and there is pansies,
that's for thoughts.
IV:5

104 Too much of water hast thou, poor Ophelia,
And therefore I forbid my tears.
IV:7

105 Alas, poor Yorick! I knew him, Horatio: a fellow of infinite jest, of most excellent fancy.
V:1

106 There's a divinity that shapes our ends,
Rough-hew them how we will.
V:2

107 If thou didst ever hold me in thy heart,
Absent thee from felicity awhile,
And in this harsh world draw thy breath in pain,
To tell my story.
V:2

108 The rest is silence.
V:2

Henry IV, Part One

109 If all the year were playing holidays, To sport would be as tedious as to work.
I:2

110 Falstaff sweats to death
And lards the lean earth as he walks along.
II:2

111 Out of this nettle, danger, we pluck this flower, safety.
II:3

112 I have more flesh than another man, and therefore more frailty.
III:3

113 Honour pricks me on. Yea, but how if honour prick me off when I come on? How then? Can honour set to a leg? No. Or an arm? No. Or take away the grief of a wound? No. Honour hath no skill in surgery, then? No. What is honour? A word. What is in that word? Honour. What is that honour? Air.
V:1

114 But thoughts, the slaves of life, and life, time's fool,
And time, that takes survey of all the world,
Must have a stop.
V:4

115 The better part of valour is discretion; in the which better part I have saved my life.
V:4

Henry IV, Part Two

116 I am not only witty in myself, but the cause that wit is in other men. I do here walk before thee like a sow that hath overwhelm'd all her litter but one.
I:2

117 Well, I cannot last ever; but it was always yet the trick of our English nation, if they have a good thing, to make it too common.
I:2

118 I can get no remedy against this consumption of the purse; borrowing only lingers and lingers it out, but the disease is incurable.
I:2

119 He hath eaten me out of house and home.
II:1

120 Is it not strange that desire should so many years outlive performance?
II:4

121 Uneasy lies the head that wears a crown.
III:1

122 We have heard the chimes at midnight.
III:2

123 I care not; a man can die but once; we owe God a death.
III:2

124 Care I for the limb, the thews, the stature, bulk, and big assemblance of a man! Give me the spirit.
III:2

Henry V

125 I dare not fight; but I will wink and hold out mine iron.
II:1

126 Though patience be a tired mare, yet she will plod.
II:1

127 His nose was as sharp as a pen, and 'a babbl'd of green fields.
Referring to Falstaff on his deathbed
II:3

128 Once more unto the breach, dear friends, once more;
Or close the wall up with our English dead.
III:1

129 But when the blast of war blows in our ears,
Then imitate the action of the tiger;
Stiffen the sinews, summon up the blood,
Disguise fair nature with hard-favoured rage;
Then lend the eye a terrible aspect.
III:1

130 The game's afoot:
Follow your spirit; and, upon this charge
Cry 'God for Harry! England and Saint George!'
III:1

131 Men of few words are the best men.
III:2

132 I think the King is but a man as I am: the violet smells to him as it doth to me.
IV:1

133 Every subject's duty is the King's; but every subject's soul is his own.
IV:1

134 Old men forget; yet all shall be forgot,
But he'll remember, with advantages,
What feats he did that day.
IV:3

135 And gentlemen in England, now a-bed
Shall think themselves accurs'd they were not here,
And hold their manhoods cheap whiles any speaks
That fought with us upon Saint Crispin's day.
IV:3

136 There is occasions and causes why and wherefore in all things.
V:1

Henry VIII

137 Heat not a furnace for your foe so hot
That it do singe yourself. We may outrun
By violent swiftness that which we run at,
And lose by over-running.
I:1

138 I would not be a queen
For all the world.
II:3

139 Farewell, a long farewell, to all my greatness!
This is the state of man: to-day he puts forth

The tender leaves of hopes: to-morrow
blossoms
And bears his blushing honours thick upon him;
The third day comes a frost, a killing frost,
And when he thinks, good easy man, full
surely
His greatness is a-ripening, nips his root,
And then he falls, as I do.
III:2

140 Had I but serv'd my God with half the zeal
I serv'd my King, he would not in mine age
Have left me naked to mine enemies.
III:2

141 Men's evil manners live in brass: their virtues
We write in water.
IV:2

Julius Caesar

142 Beware the ides of March.
I:2

143 Why, man, he doth bestride the narrow world
Like a Colossus; and we petty men
Walk under his huge legs, and peep about
To find ourselves dishonourable graves.
Men at some time are masters of their fates:
The fault, dear Brutus, is not in our stars,
But in ourselves, that we are underlings.
I:2

144 Let me have men about me that are fat;
Sleek-headed men, and such as sleep o' nights.
Yond Cassius has a lean and hungry look;
He thinks too much. Such men are dangerous.
I:2

145 For mine own part, it was Greek to me.
I:2

146 Cowards die many times before their deaths:
The valiant never taste of death but once.
II:2

147 *Et tu, Brute?*
III:1

148 Why, he that cuts off twenty years of life
Cuts off so many years of fearing death.
III:1

149 O mighty Caesar! dost thou lie so low?
Are all thy conquests, glories, triumphs,
spoils,
Shrunk to this little measure?
III:1

150 O, pardon me, thou bleeding piece of earth,
That I am meek and gentle with these
butchers!
Thou art the ruins of the noblest man
That ever lived in the tide of times.
III:1

151 Cry 'Havoc!' and let slip the dogs of war.
III:1

152 Not that I lov'd Caesar less, but that I lov'd
Rome more.
III:2

153 Friends, Romans, countrymen, lend me your
ears
I come to bury Caesar, not to praise him.
The evil that men do lives after them;
The good is oft interred with their bones.
III:2

154 For Brutus is an honourable man;
So are they all, all honourable men.
III:2

155 Ambition should be made of sterner stuff.
III:2

156 If you have tears, prepare to shed them now.
III:2

157 For I have neither wit, nor words, nor worth,
Action, nor utterance, nor the power of
speech,
To stir men's blood; I only speak right on.
III:2

158 A friend should bear his friend's infirmities,
But Brutus makes mine greater than they are.
IV:3

159 There is a tide in the affairs of men
Which, taken at the flood, leads on to fortune;
Omitted, all the voyage of their life
Is bound in shallows and in miseries.
On such a full sea are we now afloat,
And we must take the current when it serves,
Or lose our ventures.
IV:3

160 This was the noblest Roman of them all.
All the conspirators save only he
Did that they did in envy of great Caesar.
V:5

161 His life was gentle; and the elements
So mix'd in him that Nature might stand up
And say to all the world 'This was a man!'
Referring to Brutus
V:5

King John

162 Well, whiles I am a beggar, I will rail
And say there is no sin but to be rich;
And being rich, my virtue then shall be
To say there is no vice but beggary.
II:1

163 Bell, book, and candle, shall not drive me
back,
When gold and silver becks me to come on.
III:3

164 Life is as tedious as a twice-told tale
Vexing the dull ear of a drowsy man.
III:4

165 To gild refined gold, to paint the lily,
To throw a perfume on the violet,

To smooth the ice, or add another hue
Unto the rainbow, or with taper-light
To seek the beauteous eye of heaven to
garnish,
Is wasteful and ridiculous excess.
IV:2

166 How oft the sight of means to do ill deeds
Makes ill deeds done!
IV:2

167 I beg cold comfort.
V:7

King Lear

168 Nothing will come of nothing. Speak again.
I:1

169 This is the excellent foppery of the world,
that, when we are sick in fortune, often the
surfeits of our own behaviour, we make guilty
of our disasters the sun, the moon, and stars.
I:2

170 Ingratitude, thou marble-hearted fiend,
More hideous when thou show'st thee in a
child
Than the sea-monster!
I:4

171 How sharper than a serpent's tooth it is
To have a thankless child!
I:4

172 O, let me not be mad, not mad, sweet heaven!
Keep me in temper; I would not be mad!
I:5

173 Thou whoreson zed! thou unnecessary letter!
II:2

174 Down, thou climbing sorrow,
Thy element's below.
II:4

175 O, reason not the need! Our basest beggars
Are in the poorest thing superfluous.
Allow not nature more than nature needs,
Man's life is cheap as beast's.
II:4

176 Blow, winds, and crack your cheeks; rage,
blow.
You cataracts and hurricanoes, spout
Till you have drench'd our steeples, drown'd
the cocks.
III:2

177 Rumble thy bellyful. Spit, fire; spout rain.
Nor rain, wind, thunder, fire, are my
daughters
I tax not you, you elements, with unkindness.
III:2

178 I am a man
More sinn'd against than sinning.
III:2

179 O! that way madness lies; let me shun that.
III:4

180 Poor naked wretches, wheresoe'er you are,
That bide the pelting of this pitiless storm,
How shall your houseless heads and unfed
sides,
Your loop'd and window'd raggedness, defend
you
From seasons such as these?
III:4

181 Take physic, pomp;
Expose thyself to feel what wretches feel.
III:4

182 Out vile jelly!
Where is thy lustre now?
Spoken by Cornwall as he puts out Gloucester's remaining eye
III:7

183 I have no way, and therefore want no eyes;
I stumbled when I saw.
IV:1

184 The worst is not
So long as we can say 'This is the worst'.
IV:1

185 As flies to wanton boys are we to th' gods –
They kill us for their sport.
IV:1

186 Ay, every inch a king.
IV:6

187 The wren goes to't, and the small gilded fly
Does lecher in my sight.
IV:6

188 Through tatter'd clothes small vices do appear;
Robes and furr'd gowns hide all.
IV:6

189 Get thee glass eyes,
And, like a scurvy politician, seem
To see the things thou dost not.
IV:6

190 When we are born, we cry that we are come
To this great stage of fools.
IV:6

191 Thou art a soul in bliss; but I am bound
Upon a wheel of fire, that mine own tears
Do scald like molten lead.
IV:7

192 Men must endure
Their going hence, even as their coming
hither:
Ripeness is all.
V:2

193 The gods are just, and of our pleasant vices
Make instruments to plague us.
V:3

194 And my poor fool is hang'd! No, no, no life!
Why should a dog, a horse, a rat have life,

And thou no breath at all? Thou'lt come no more,
Never, never, never, never.
V:3

Love's Labour's Lost

195 At Christmas I no more desire a rose
Than wish a snow in May's newfangled shows.
I:1

196 He hath never fed of the dainties that are bred in a book; he hath not eat paper, as it were; he hath not drunk ink; his intellect is not replenished.
IV:2

197 For where is any author in the world
Teaches such beauty as a woman's eye?
Learning is but an adjunct to oneself.
IV:3

198 A jest's prosperity lies in the ear
Of him that hears it, never in the tongue
Of him that makes it.
V:2

199 When icicles hang by the wall,
And Dick the shepherd blows his nail,
And Tom bears logs into the hall,
And milk comes frozen home in pail,
When blood is nipp'd, and ways be foul,
Then nightly sings the staring owl:
'Tu-who;
Tu-whit, Tu-who' – A merry note,
While greasy Joan doth keel the pot.
V:2

Macbeth

200 When shall we three meet again
In thunder, lightning, or in rain?
I:1

201 So foul and fair a day I have not seen.
I:3

202 This supernatural soliciting
Cannot be ill; cannot be good.
I:3

203 Come what come may,
Time and the hour runs through the roughest day.
I:3

204 Nothing in his life
Became him like the leaving it: he died
As one that had been studied in his death
To throw away the dearest thing he ow'd
As 'twere a careless trifle.
I:4

205 Yet do I fear thy nature;
It is too full o' th' milk of human kindness
To catch the nearest way.
I:5

206 The raven himself is hoarse

That croaks the fatal entrance of Duncan
Under my battlements.
I:5

207 If it were done when 'tis done, then 'twere well
It were done quickly.
I:7

208 That but this blow
Might be the be-all and the end-all here –
But here upon this bank and shoal of time –
We'd jump the life to come.
I:7

209 I have no spur
To prick the sides of my intent, but only
Vaulting ambition, which o'er-leaps itself,
And falls on th' other.
I:7

210 False face must hide what the false heart doth know.
I:7

211 Is this a dagger which I see before me,
The handle toward my hand? Come, let me clutch thee:
I have thee not, and yet I see thee still.
II:1

212 Methought I heard a voice cry, 'Sleep no more!'
Macbeth doth murder sleep,' the innocent sleep,
Sleep that knits up the ravell'd sleave of care,
The death of each day's life, sore labour's bath,
Balm of hurt minds, great nature's second course,
Chief nourisher in life's feast.
II:2

213 It provokes the desire, but it takes away the performance. Therefore much drink may be said to be an equivocator with lechery.
II:3

214 I had else been perfect,
Whole as the marble, founded as the rock,
As broad and general as the casing air,
But now I am cabin'd, cribb'd, confin'd, bound in
To saucy doubts and fears.
II:4

215 Nought's had, all's spent,
Where our desire is got without content.
'Tis safer to be that which we destroy,
Than by destruction dwell in doubtful joy.
III:2

216 Stand not upon the order of your going,
But go at once.
III:4

217 I am in blood
Stepp'd in so far that, should I wade no more,

Returning were as tedious as go o'er.
III:4

218 Eye of newt, and toe of frog,
Wool of bat, and tongue of dog,
Adder's fork, and blind-worm's sting,
Lizard's leg, and howlet's wing,
For a charm of powerful trouble,
Like a hell-broth boil and bubble.
IV:2

219 Be bloody bold, and resolute, laugh to scorn
The power of man, for none of woman born
Shall harm Macbeth.
IV:1

220 Out, damned spot! out, I say!
V:1

221 Yet who would have thought the old man to
have had so much blood in him?
V:1

222 Here's the smell of the blood still. All the perfumes of Arabia will not sweeten this little
hand.
V:1

223 I have liv'd long enough.
My way of life
Is fall'n into the sear, the yellow leaf;
And that which should accompany old age,
As honour, love, obedience, troops of friends,
I must not look to have.
V:3

224 I have supp'd full with horrors.
V:5

225 Tomorrow, and tomorrow, and tomorrow,
Creeps in this petty pace from day to day
To the last syllable of recorded time,
And all our yesterdays have lighted fools
The way to dusty death. Out, out, brief
candle!
Life's but a walking shadow, a poor player,
That struts and frets his hour upon the stage,
And then is heard no more; it is a tale
Told by an idiot, full of sound and fury,
Signifying nothing.
V:5

226 I gin to be aweary of the sun,
And wish th' estate o' th' world were now
undone.
V:5

227 MACBETH. I bear a charmed life, which must
not yield
To one of woman born.
MACDUFF. Despair thy charm;
And let the angel whom thou still hast serv'd
Tell thee Macduff was from his mother's womb
Untimely ripp'd.
V:8

Measure for Measure

228 But man, proud man

Dress'd in a little brief authority,
Most ignorant of what he's most assur'd,
His glassy essence, like an angry ape,
Plays such fantastic tricks before high heaven
As makes the angels weep.
II:2

229 That in the captain's but a choleric word
Which in the soldier is flat blasphemy.
II:2

230 The miserable have no other medicine
But only hope.
III:1

231 Thou hast nor youth nor age;
But, as it were, an after-dinner's sleep,
Dreaming on both.
III:1

232 Ay, but to die, and go we know not where;
To lie in cold obstruction, and to rot;
This sensible warm motion to become
A kneaded clod; and the delighted spirit
To bathe in fiery floods or to reside
In thrilling region of thick-ribbed ice.
III:1

233 I am a kind of burr; I shall stick.
IV:3

234 Haste still pays haste, and leisure answers
leisure;
Like doth quit like, and Measure still for
Measure.
V:1

235 They say best men are moulded out of faults
And, for the most, become much more the
better
For being a little bad.
V:1

The Merchant of Venice

236 As who should say 'I am Sir Oracle,
And when I ope my lips let no dog bark'.
I:1

237 If to do were as easy as to know what were
good to do, chapels had been churches, and
poor men's cottages princes' palaces.
I:2

238 How like a fawning publican he looks!
I hate him for he is a Christian.
But more for that in low simplicity
He lends out money gratis, and brings down
The rate of usance here with us in Venice.
I:3

239 The devil can cite Scripture for his purpose.
I:3

240 You call me misbeliever, cut-throat dog,
And spit upon my Jewish gaberdine,
And all for use of that which is mine own.
I:3

241 It is a wise father that knows his own child.
II:2

242 But love is blind, and lovers cannot see
The pretty follies that themselves commit.
II:6

243 My daughter! O my ducats! O my daughter!
Fled with a Christian! O my Christian ducats!
Justice! the law! my ducats, and my daughter!
II:8

244 The ancient saying is no heresy:
Hanging and wiving goes by destiny.
II:9

245 Hath not a Jew eyes? Hath not a Jew hands,
organs, dimensions, senses, affections, pas
sions, fed with the same food, hurt with the
same weapons, subject to the same diseases,
healed by the same means, warmed and
cooled by the same winter and summer, as a
Christian is? If you prick us, do we not
bleed? If you tickle us, do we not laugh? If
you poison us, do we not die? And if you
wrong us, shall we not revenge?
III:1

246 The quality of mercy is not strain'd;
It droppeth as the gentle rain from heaven
Upon the place beneath. It is twice blest;
It blesseth him that gives and him that takes.
IV:1

247 A Daniel come to judgment! yea, a Daniel!
IV:1

248 The moon shines bright: in such a night as
this,
. . . in such a night
Troilus methinks mounted the Troyan walls,
And sigh'd his soul toward the Grecian tents,
Where Cressid lay that night.
V:1

249 How sweet the moonlight sleeps upon this
bank!
Here will we sit, and let the sounds of music
Creep in our ears; soft stillness and the night
Become the touches of sweet harmony.
V:1

250 I am never merry when I hear sweet music.
V:1

251 The man that hath no music in himself,
Nor is not mov'd with concord of sweet
sounds,
Is fit for treasons, stratagems, and spoils.
V:1

252 How far that little candle throws his beams!
So shines a good deed in a naughty world.
V:1

253 For a light wife doth make a heavy husband.
V:1

The Merry Wives of Windsor

254 Why, then the world's mine oyster,
Which I with sword will open.
II:2

255 O, what a world of vile ill-favour'd faults
Looks handsome in three hundred pounds a
year!
III:4

256 They say there is divinity in odd numbers, either in nativity, chance, or death.
V:1

A Midsummer Night's Dream

257 For aught that I could ever read,
Could ever hear by tale or history,
The course of true love never did run smooth.
I:1

258 Love looks not with the eyes, but with the
mind;
And therefore is wing'd Cupid painted blind.
I:1

259 I am slow of study.
I:2

260 Ill met by moonlight, proud Titania.
II:1

261 A lion among ladies is a most dreadful thing;
for there is not a more fearful wild-fowl than
your lion living.
III:1

262 Lord, what fools these mortals be!
III:2

263 The lunatic, the lover, and the poet,
Are of imagination all compact.
V:1

264 The poet's eye, in a fine frenzy rolling,
Doth glance from heaven to earth, from earth
to heaven;
And as imagination bodies forth
The forms of things unknown, the poet's pen
Turns them to shapes, and gives to airy
nothing
A local habitation and a name.
V:1

265 If we shadows have offended,
Think but this, and all is mended, That you
have but slumber'd here While these visions
did appear.
V:2

Much Ado About Nothing

266 Would you have me speak after my custom, as
being a professed tyrant to their sex?
I:1

267 Friendship is constant in all other things
Save in the office and affairs of love.
II:1

268 Silence is the perfectest herald of joy: I were but little happy if I could say how much.
II:1

269 Doth not the appetite alter? A man loves the meat in his youth that he cannot endure in his age.
II:3

270 To be a well-favoured man is the gift of fortune; but to write and read comes by nature.
III:3

271 I thank God I am as honest as any man living that is an old man and no honester than I.
III:5

272 Comparisons are odorous.
III:5

273 Our watch, sir, have indeed comprehended two aspicious persons.
III:5

274 Write down that they hope they serve God; and write God first; for God defend but God should go before such villains!
IV:2

275 For there was never yet philosopher
That could endure the toothache patiently.
V:1

Othello

276 To mourn a mischief that is past and gone
Is the next way to draw new mischief on.
I:3

277 Put money in thy purse.
I:3

278 There are many events in the womb of time which will be delivered.
I:3

279 For I am nothing if not critical.
II:1

280 To suckle fools and chronicle small beer.
II:1

281 Reputation, reputation, reputation! O, I have lost my reputation! I have lost the immortal part of myself, and what remains is bestial.
II:3

282 Good name in man and woman, dear my lord,
Is the immediate jewel of their souls:
Who steals my purse steals trash; 'tis something, nothing;
'Twas mine, 'tis his, and has been slave to thousands;
But he that filches from me my good name
Robs me of that which not enriches him
And makes me poor indeed.
III:3

283 O, beware, my lord, of jealousy;
It is the green-ey'd monster which doth mock
The meat it feeds on.
III:3

284 O curse of marriage,
That we can call these delicate creatures ours,
And not their appetites! I had rather be a toad,
And live upon the vapour of a dungeon,
Than keep a corner in the thing I love
For others' uses.
III:3

285 He that is robb'd, not wanting what is stol'n,
Let him not know't, and he's not robb'd at all.
III:3

286 Farewell the neighing steed and the shrill trump,
The spirit-stirring drum, th'ear piercing fife,
The royal banner, and all quality,
Pride, pomp, and circumstance, of glorious war!
III:3

287 Put out the light, and then put out the light.
If I quench thee, thou flaming minister,
I can again thy former light restore,
Should I repent me; but once put out thy light,
Thou cunning'st pattern of excelling nature,
I know not where is that Promethean heat
That can thy light relume.
V:2

288 Then must you speak
Of one that lov'd not wisely, but too well;
Of one not easily jealous, but, being wrought,
Perplexed in the extreme; of one whose hand,
Like the base Indian, threw a pearl away
Richer than all his tribe.
V:2

Pericles

289 Kings are earth's gods; in vice their law's their will.
I:1

290 3RD FISHERMAN. Master, I marvel how the fishes live in the sea.
1ST FISHERMAN. Why, as men do a-land – the great ones eat up the little ones.
II:1

291 O you gods!
Why do you make us love your goodly gifts
And snatch them straight away?
III:1

Richard II

292 The purest treasure mortal times afford
Is spotless reputation; that away,
Men are but gilded loam or painted clay.
I:1

293 Things sweet to taste prove in digestion sour.
I:3

294 Teach thy necessity to reason thus:
There is no virtue like necessity.
I:3

295 This royal throne of kings, this sceptred isle,
This earth of majesty, this seat of Mars,
This other Eden, demi-paradise,
This fortress built by Nature for herself
Against infection and the hand of war,
This happy breed of men, this little world,
This precious stone set in the silver sea,
Which serves it in the office of a wall,
Or as a moat defensive to a house,
Against the envy of less happier lands;
This blessed plot, this earth, this realm, this
England,
This nurse, this teeming womb of royal kings,
Fear'd by their breed, and famous by their
birth.
II:1

296 Not all the water in the rough rude sea
Can wash the balm from an anointed king;
The breath of worldly men cannot depose
The deputy elected by the Lord.
III:2

297 The worst is death, and death will have his
day.
III:2

298 For God's sake let us sit upon the ground
And tell sad stories of the death of kings:
How some have been depos'd, some slain in
war,
Some haunted by the ghosts they have
depos'd,
Some poison'd by their wives, some sleeping
kill'd,
All murder'd – for within the hollow crown
That rounds the mortal temples of a king
Keeps Death his court.
III:2

299 How sour sweet music is
When time is broke and no proportion kept!
So is it in the music of men's lives.
V:5

Richard III

300 Now is the winter of our discontent
Made glorious summer by this sun of York.
I:1

301 O Lord, methought what pain it was to drown,
What dreadful noise of waters in my ears,
What sights of ugly death within my eyes!
I:4

302 Woe to the land that's govern'd by a child!
II:3

303 A horse! a horse ! my kingdom for a horse.
V:4

Romeo and Juliet

304 From forth the fatal loins of these two foes
A pair of star-cross'd lovers take their life.
Prologue

305 O! then, I see, Queen Mab hath been with
you.
She is the fairies' midwife . . .
And in this state she gallops night by night
Through lovers' brains, and then they dream of
love.
I:4

306 O! she doth teach the torches to burn bright
It seems she hangs upon the cheek of night
Like a rich jewel in an Ethiop's ear;
Beauty too rich for use, for earth too dear.
I:5

307 My only love sprung from my only hate!
Too early seen unknown, and known too late!
I:5

308 He jests at scars, that never felt a wound.
But, soft! what light through yonder window
breaks?
It is the east, and Juliet is the sun.
II:2

309 O Romeo, Romeo! wherefore art thou Romeo?
II:2

310 What's in a name? That which we call a rose
By any other name would smell as sweet.
II:2

311 O, swear not by the moon, th' inconstant
moon,
That monthly changes in her circled orb,
Lest that thy love prove likewise variable.
II:2

312 Good night, good night! Parting is such sweet
sorrow
That I shall say good night till it be morrow.
II:2

313 Wisely and slow; they stumble that run fast.
II:3

314 Therefore love moderately: long love doth so;
Too swift arrives as tardy as too slow.
II:6

315 A plague o' both your houses!
They have made worms' meat of me.
III:1

316 Thank me no thankings, nor proud me no
prouds.
III:5

317 'Tis an ill cook that cannot lick his own fingers.
IV:2

The Taming of the Shrew

318 No profit grows where is no pleasure ta'en;
In brief, sir, study what you most affect.
I:1

319 This is a way to kill a wife with kindness.
IV:1

320 Our purses shall be proud, our garments poor;
For 'tis the mind that makes the body rich;
And as the sun breaks through the darkest
clouds,
So honour peereth in the meanest habit.
IV:3

The Tempest

321 Full fathom five thy father lies;
Of his bones are coral made;
Those are pearls that were his eyes;
Nothing of him that doth fade
But doth suffer a sea-change
Into something rich and strange.
I:2

322 When they will not give a doit to relieve a lame
beggar, they will lay out ten to see a dead
Indian.
II:2

323 Misery acquaints a man with strange
bedfellows.
II:2

324 He that dies pays all debts.
III:2

325 Our revels now are ended. These our actors,
As I foretold you, were all spirits, and
Are melted into air, into thin air;
And, like the baseless fabric of this vision,
The cloud-capp'd towers, the gorgeous
palaces,
The solemn temples, the great globe itself,
Yea, all which it inherit, shall dissolve,
And, like this insubstantial pageant faded,
Leave not a rack behind. We are such stuff
As dreams are made on; and our little life
Is rounded with a sleep.
IV:1

326 I'll break my staff,
Bury it certain fathoms in the earth,
And deeper than did ever plummet sound
I'll drown my book.
V:1

327 How beauteous mankind is! O brave new world
That has such people in't!
V:1

Troilus and Cressida

328 That she belov'd knows nought that knows not
this:
Men prize the thing ungain'd more than it is.
I:2

329 O, when degree is shak'd,
Which is the ladder of all high designs,
The enterprise is sick!
I:3

330 To be wise and love
Exceeds man's might.
III:2

331 Time hath, my lord, a wallet at his back,
Wherein he puts alms for oblivion,
A great-siz'd monster of ingratitudes.
III:3

332 The end crowns all,
And that old common arbitrator, Time,
Will one day end it.
IV:5

333 Lechery, lechery! Still wars and lechery! Nothing else holds fashion.
V:2

Twelfth Night

334 If music be the food of love, play on,
Give me excess of it, that, surfeiting,
The appetite may sicken and so die.
I:1

335 Is it a world to hide virtues in?
I:3

336 Many a good hanging prevents a bad marriage.
I:5

337 Not to be abed after midnight is to be up
betimes.
II:3

338 What is love? 'Tis not hereafter;
Present mirth hath present laughter;
What's to come is still unsure.
In delay there lies no plenty,
Then come kiss me, sweet and twenty;
Youth's a stuff will not endure.
II:3

339 Dost thou think, because thou art virtuous,
there shall be no more cakes and ale?
II:3

340 She never told her love,
But let concealment, like a worm i' th' bud,
Feed on her damask cheek. She pin'd in
thought;
And with a green and yellow melancholy
She sat like Patience on a monument,
Smiling at grief.
II:4

341 Some are born great, some achieve greatness,
and some have greatness thrust upon 'em.
II:5

342 Love sought is good, but given unsought is
better.
III:1

343 If this were play'd upon a stage now, I could
condemn it as an improbable fiction.
III:4

344 Still you keep o' th' windy side of the law.
III:4

345 I hate ingratitude more in a man
Than lying, vainness, babbling drunkenness,
Or any taint of vice whose strong corruption
Inhabits our frail blood.
III:4

The Two Gentlemen of Verona

346 Home-keeping youth have ever homely wits.
I:1

347 I have no other but a woman's reason:
I think him so, because I think him so.
I:2

348 Who is Silvia? What is she,
That all our swains commend her?
Holy, fair, and wise is she.
IV:2

The Winter's Tale

349 What's gone and what's past help
Should be past grief.
III:2

350 I would there were no age between ten and
three and twenty, or that youth would sleep
out the rest; for there is nothing in the between but getting wenches with child, wrong-
ing the ancientry, stealing, fighting.
III:3

351 *Exit, pursued by a bear.*
Stage direction
III:3

352 A snapper-up of unconsidered trifles.
IV:2

353 Though I am not naturally honest, I am so
sometimes by chance.
IV:3

354 Though authority be a stubborn bear, yet he is
oft led by the nose with gold.
IV:3

Poems and Sonnets

355 Crabbed age and youth cannot live together:
Youth is full of pleasure, age is full of care;
Youth like summer morn, age like winter
weather;
Youth like summer brave, age like winter bare.
The Passionate Pilgrim, XII

356 Beauty itself doth of itself persuade
The eyes of men without an orator.
The Rape of Lucrece, I

357 From fairest creatures we desire increase,
That thereby beauty's rose might never die.
Sonnet 1

358 Shall I compare thee to a summer's day?
Thou art more lovely and more temperate.
Rough winds do shake the darling buds of
May,
And summer's lease hath all too short a date.
Sonnet 18

359 A woman's face, with Nature's own hand
painted,
Hast thou, the Master Mistress of my passion.
Sonnet 20

360 When in disgrace with fortune and men's eyes
I all alone beweep my outcast state,
And trouble deaf heaven with my bootless
cries,
And look upon myself, and curse my fate,
Wishing me like to one more rich in hope
Featur'd like him, like him with friends
possess'd,
Desiring this man's art, and that man's scope,
With what I most enjoy contented least.
Sonnet 29

361 When to the sessions of sweet silent thought
I summon up remembrance of things past,
I sigh the lack of many a thing I sought,
And with old woes new wail my dear time's
waste.
Sonnet 30

362 Not marble, nor the gilded monuments
Of princes, shall outlive this powerful rhyme.
Sonnet 55

363 Like as the waves make towards the pebbled
shore,
So do our minutes hasten to their end.
Sonnet 60

364 That time of year thou mayst in me behold
When yellow leaves, or none, or few, do hang
Upon those boughs which shake against the
cold,
Bare ruin'd choirs, where late the sweet birds
sang.
Sonnet 73

365 Farewell! thou art too dear for my possessing,
And like enough thou know'st thy estimate:
The charter of thy worth gives thee releasing;
My bonds in thee are all determinate.
Sonnet 87

366 For sweetest things turn sourest by their
deeds:
Lilies that fester smell far worse than weeds.
Sonnet 94

367 When in the chronicle of wasted time
I see descriptions of the fairest wights.
Sonnet 106

368 Let me not to the marriage of true minds
Admit impediments. Love is not love
Which alters when it alteration finds,
Or bends with the remover to remove.
O, no! it is an ever-fixed mark,
That looks on tempests and is never shaken.
Sonnet 116

369 Love alters not with his brief hours and weeks,
But bears it out even to the edge of doom.
If this be error, and upon me prov'd,
I never writ, nor no man ever lov'd.
Sonnet 116

370 Th' expense of spirit in a waste of shame
Is lust in action; and till action, lust
Is perjur'd, murd'rous, bloody, full of blame,
Savage, extreme, rude, cruel, not to trust;
Enjoy'd no sooner but despised straight.
Sonnet 129

371 My mistress' eyes are nothing like the sun;
Coral is far more red than her lips' red.
Sonnet 130

372 And yet, by heaven, I think my love as rare
As any she belied with false compare.
Sonnet 130

373 Two loves I have, of comfort and despair,
Which like two spirits do suggest me still;
The better angel is a man right fair,
The worser spirit a woman colour'd ill.
Sonnet 144

Sharpe, Tom (1928–) British novelist, author of such humorous works as *Indecent Exposure* (1973), *Porterhouse Blue* (1974), *Blott on the Landscape* (1975), and *Vintage Stuff* (1982).

1 The South African Police would leave no stone unturned to see that nothing disturbed the even terror of their lives.
Indecent Exposure, Ch. 1

2 Skullion had little use for contraceptives at the best of times. Unnatural, he called them, and placed them in the lower social category of things along with elastic-sided boots and made-up bow ties. Not the sort of attire for a gentleman.
Porterhouse Blue, Ch. 9

3 His had been an intellectual decision founded on his conviction that if a little knowledge was a dangerous thing, a lot was lethal.
Porterhouse Blue, Ch. 18

Shaw, George Bernard (1856–1950) Irish dramatist and critic. His plays, with their long prefaces, established him as the leading British playwright of his time. Included among his prose works are *The Intelligent Woman's Guide to Socialism and Capitalism* (1928) and *The Black Girl in Search of God* (1932).

Quotations about Shaw

1 Shaw's works make me admire the magnificent tolerance and broadmindedness of the English.
James Joyce (1882–1941) Irish novelist. *The Wild Geese* (Gerald Griffin)

2 He writes like a Pakistani who has learned English when he was twelve years old in order to become a chartered accountant.
John Osborne (1929–) British dramatist. Attrib.

Quotations by Shaw

3 Whether you think Jesus was God or not, you must admit that he was a first-rate political economist.
Androcles and the Lion, Preface, 'Jesus as Economist'

4 All great truths begin as blasphemies.
Annajanska

5 You are a very poor soldier: a chocolate cream soldier!
Arms and the Man, I

6 Silence is the most perfect expression of scorn.
Back to Methuselah

7 When a stupid man is doing something he is ashamed of, he always declares that it is his duty.
Caesar and Cleopatra, III

8 A man of great common sense and good taste, – meaning thereby a man without originality or moral courage.
Referring to Julius Caesar
Caesar and Cleopatra, Notes

9 The British soldier can stand up to anything except the British War Office.
The Devil's Disciple, II

10 I never expect a soldier to think.
The Devil's Disciple, III

11 With the single exception of Homer, there is no eminent writer, not even Sir Walter Scott, whom I can despise so entirely as I despise Shakespeare when I measure my mind against his . . . It would positively be a relief to me to dig him up and throw stones at him.
Dramatic Opinions and Essays, Vol. 2

12 Physically there is nothing to distinguish human society from the farm-yard except that children are more troublesome and costly than chickens and women are not so completely enslaved as farm stock.
Getting Married, Preface

13 My way of joking is to tell the truth. It's the funniest joke in the world.
John Bull's Other Island, II

14 Cusins is a very nice fellow, certainly: nobody would ever guess that he was born in Australia.
Major Barbara, I

15 Nobody can say a word against Greek: it stamps a man at once as an educated gentleman.
Major Barbara, I

16 Alcohol is a very necessary article . . . It enables Parliament to do things at eleven at night that no sane person would do at eleven in the morning.
Major Barbara, II

17 He never does a proper thing without giving an improper reason for it.
Major Barbara, III

18 He knows nothing; and he thinks he knows everything. That points clearly to a political career.
Major Barbara, III

19 CUSINS. Do you call poverty a crime?
UNDERSHAFT. The worst of all crimes. All the other crimes are virtues beside it.
Major Barbara, IV

20 Give women the vote, and in five years there will be a crushing tax on bachelors.
Man and Superman, Preface

21 A lifetime of happiness: no man alive could bear it: it would be hell on earth.
Man and Superman, I

22 Very nice sort of place, Oxford, I should think, for people that like that sort of place.
Man and Superman, II

23 It is a woman's business to get married as soon as possible, and a man's to keep unmarried as long as he can.
Man and Superman, II

24 There are two tragedies in life. One is to lose your heart's desire. The other is to gain it.
Man and Superman, IV

25 In heaven an angel is nobody in particular.
Man and Superman, 'Maxims for Revolutionists'

26 Beware of the man who does not return your blow: he neither forgives you nor allows you to forgive yourself.
Man and Superman, 'Maxims for Revolutionists'

27 Do not love your neighbour as yourself. If you are on good terms with yourself it is an impertinence; if on bad, an injury.
Man and Superman, 'Maxims for Revolutionists'

28 Titles distinguish the mediocre, embarrass the superior, and are disgraced by the inferior.
Man and Superman, 'Maxims for Revolutionists'

29 Self-denial is not a virtue; it is only the effect of prudence on rascality.
Man and Superman, 'Maxims for Revolutionists'

30 If you strike a child, take care that you strike it in anger, even at the risk of maiming it for life. A blow in cold blood neither can nor should be forgiven.
Man and Superman, 'Maxims for Revolutionists'

31 The golden rule is that there are no golden rules.
Man and Superman, 'Maxims for Revolutionists'

32 He who can, does. He who cannot, teaches.
Man and Superman, 'Maxims for Revolutionists'

33 Optimistic lies have such immense therapeutic value that a doctor who cannot tell them convincingly has mistaken his profession.
Misalliance, Preface

34 Heaven, as conventionally conceived, is a place so inane, so dull, so useless, so miserable, that nobody has ever ventured to describe a whole day in heaven, though plenty of people have described a day at the seaside.
Misalliance, Preface

35 The secret of being miserable is to have leisure to bother about whether you are happy or not.
Misalliance, Preface

36 The English have no respect for their language, and will not teach their children to speak it . . . It is impossible for an Englishman to open his mouth, without making some other Englishman despise him.
Pygmalion, Preface

37 They all thought she was dead; but my father he kept ladling gin down her throat till she came to so sudden that she bit the bowl off the spoon.
Pygmalion, III

38 Gin was mother's milk to her.
Pygmalion, III

39 Assassination is the extreme form of censorship.
The Shewing-Up of Blanco Posnet, 'The Limits of Toleration'

40 It is the sexless novel that should be distinguished: the sex novel is now normal.
Table-Talk of G.B.S.

41 It does not follow . . . that the right to criticize Shakespeare involves the power of writing better plays. And in fact . . . I do not profess to write better plays.
Three Plays for Puritans, Preface

42 We're from Madeira, but perfectly respectable, so far.
You Never Can Tell, I

43 Well, sir, you never can tell. That's a principle in life with me, sir, if you'll excuse my having such a thing, sir.
You Never Can Tell, II

44 I've been offered titles, but I think they get one into disreputable company.
Gossip (A. Barrow)

45 The thought of two thousand people crunching celery at the same time horrified me.
Explaining why he had turned down an invitation to a vegetarian gala dinner
The Greatest Laughs of All Time (G. Lieberman)

46 It's a funny thing about that bust. As time goes on it seems to get younger and younger.
Referring to a portrait bust sculpted for him by Rodin
More Things I Wish I'd Said (K. Edwards)

47 The trouble, Mr Goldwyn is that you are only interested in art and I am only interested in money.
Turning down Goldwyn's offer to buy the screen rights of his plays
The Movie Moguls (Philip French), Ch. 4

48 I quite agree with you, sir, but what can two do against so many?

Responding to a solitary hiss heard amongst the applause at the first performance of *Arms and the Man* in 1894
Oxford Book of Literary Anecdotes

49 Certainly, there is nothing else here to enjoy.

Said at a party when his hostess asked him whether he was enjoying himself
Pass the Port (Oxfam)

50 Far too good to waste on children.

Reflecting upon youth
10,000 Jokes, Toasts, and Stories (L. Copeland)

51 Better never than late.

Responding to an offer by a producer to present one of Shaw's plays, having earlier rejected it
The Unimportance of Being Oscar (Oscar Levant)

52 LORD NORTHCLIFFE. The trouble with you, Shaw, is that you look as if there were famine in the land.
G.B.S. The trouble with you, Northcliffe, is that you look as if you were the cause of it.

Attrib.

53 If all economists were laid end to end, they would not reach a conclusion.

Attrib.

Shawcross, Hartley (William), Lord (1902–)
British Labour politician and lawyer, who was Attorney-General (1945–51).

1 We are the masters at the moment – and not only for the moment, but for a very long time to come.

Sometimes quoted as, 'We are the masters now!'
House of Commons, 2 Apr 1946

Sheen, J(ohn) Fulton (1895–1979) US Roman Catholic
archbishop. He was a broadcaster and prolific writer of books and pamphlets.

1 Every child should have an occasional pat on the back, as long as it is applied low enough, and hard enough.

US Roman Catholic archbishop. *On Children* (Frank Muir)

2 The big print giveth and the fine print taketh away.

Referring to his contract for a televison appearance
Attrib.

Shelley, Percy Bysshe (1792–1822) British poet. Most of
his poetry was written in Italy, including *Prometheus Unbound* (1818–19), *Adonais* (1821), and much lyrical poetry.

Quotations about Shelley

1 In his poetry as well as in his life Shelley was indeed 'a beautiful and ineffectual angel', beating in the void his luminous wings in vain.

Matthew Arnold (1822–88) British poet and critic. *Literature and Drama*, 'Shelley'

2 Poor Shelley always was, and is, a kind of ghastly object; colourless, pallid, tuneless, without health or warmth or vigour.

Thomas Carlyle (1795–1881) Scottish historian and essayist. *Reminiscences*

Quotations by Shelley

3 I weep for Adonais – he is dead!
O, weep for Adonais! though our tears
Thaw not the frost which binds so dear a head!

Prompted by the death of Keats
Adonais, I

4 He hath awakened from the dream of life –
'Tis we, who lost in stormy visions, keep
With phantoms an unprofitable strife,
And in mad trance, strike with our spirit's knife
Invulnerable nothings.

Adonais, XXXIX

5 I wield the flail of the lashing hail,
And whiten the green plains under,
And then again I dissolve it in rain,
And laugh as I pass in thunder.

The Cloud

6 I am the daughter of Earth and Water,
And the nursling of the Sky;
I pass through the pores of the ocean and shores;
I change, but I cannot die,
For after the rain when with never a stain
The pavilion of Heaven is bare,
And the winds and sunbeams with their convex gleams
Build up the blue dome of air,
I silently laugh at my own cenotaph,
And out of the caverns of rain,
Like a child from the womb, like a ghost from the tomb,
I arise and unbuild it again.

The Cloud

7 Poetry is the record of the best and happiest moments of the happiest and best minds.

A Defence of Poetry

8 Life may change, but it may fly not;
Hope may vanish, but can die not;
Truth be veiled, but still it burneth;
Love repulsed, – but still it returneth!

Hellas, I

9 Let there be light! said Liberty,
And like sunrise from the sea,
Athens arose!

Hellas, I

10 London, that great sea, whose ebb and flow
At once is deaf and loud, and on the shore
Vomits its wrecks, and still howls on for more.

Letter to Maria Gisborne, I

11 Have you not heard
When a man marries, dies, or turns Hindoo,
His best friends hear no more of him?

Referring to Thomas Love Peacock, who worked for the East
India Company and had recently married
Letter to Maria Gisborne, I

12 Lift not the painted veil which those who live
Call life.

Lift not the Painted Veil

13 I met Murder on the way –
He had a mask like Castlereagh.

Viscount Castlereagh (1769–1822) was British foreign secretary
(1812–22); he was highly unpopular and became identified with
such controversial events as the Peterloo massacre of 1819
The Mask of Anarchy, 5

14 O Wild West Wind, thou breath of Autumn's
being,
Thou, from whose unseen presence the leaves
dead
Are driven, like ghosts from an enchanter
fleeing,
Yellow, and black, and pale, and hectic red,
Pestilence-stricken multitudes.

Ode to the West Wind

15 If Winter comes, can Spring be far behind?

Ode to the West Wind

16 I met a traveller from an antique land
Who said: Two vast and trunkless legs of stone
Stand in the desert.

Referring to the legs of a broken statue of the Pharaoh Rameses
II (1301–1234 BC; Greek name, Ozymandias)
Ozymandias

17 'My name is Ozymandias, king of kings:
Look on my works, ye Mighty, and despair!'

Ozymandias

18 Sometimes
The Devil is a gentleman.

Peter Bell the Third

19 Teas,
Where small talk dies in agonies.

Peter Bell the Third

20 'Twas Peter's drift
To be a kind of moral eunuch.

Peter Bell the Third

21 Hell is a city much like London –
A populous and smoky city.

Peter Bell the Third

22 Death is the veil which those who live call life:
They sleep, and it is lifted.

Prometheus Unbound, III

23 It is a modest creed, and yet
Pleasant if one considers it,
To own that death itself must be,
Like all the rest, a mockery.

The Sensitive Plant, III

24 Hail to thee, blithe Spirit!
Bird thou never wert,
That from Heaven, or near it,
Pourest thy full heart
In profuse strains of unpremeditated art.

To a Skylark

25 Music, when soft voices die,
Vibrates in the memory –
Odours, when sweet violets sicken,
Live within the sense they quicken.

Rose leaves, when the rose is dead,
Are heaped for the beloved's bed;
And so thy thoughts, when thou art gone,
Love itself shall slumber on.

To

26 For she was beautiful – her beauty made
The bright world dim, and everything beside
Seemed like the fleeting image of a shade.

The Witch of Atlas, XII

Shenstone, William (1714–63) British poet. His works
include *The Schoolmistress* (1737) and *Pastoral Ballad* (1755).

1 Laws are generally found to be nets of such a
texture, as the little creep through, the great
break through, and the middle-sized are alone
entangled in.

Similar remarks have been made by others; *see* SOLON; SWIFT
Essays on Men, Manners, and Things, 'On Politics'

Sheridan, Philip H(enry) (1831–88) US general. He
commanded the Army of the Shenandoah and led a number of
raids into Confederate territory.

1 The only good Indians I ever saw were dead.

The People's Almanac 2 (D. Wallechinsky)

Sheridan, Richard Brinsley (1751–1816) British
dramatist. His best-known comedies are *The Rivals* (1775) and
School for Scandal (1777). He was manager of the Drury Lane
Theatre and a Whig MP (1780–1812).

Quotations about Sheridan

1 Good at a fight, but better at a play
God-like in giving, but the devil to pay.

Lord Byron (1788–1824) British poet. *On a Cast of Sheridan's
Hand*

2 He could not make enemies. If anyone came to
request the payment of a loan from him he borrowed more. A cordial shake of his hand was
a receipt in full for all demands.

William Hazlitt (1778–1830) British essayist. *New Monthly Magazine*, Jan 1824

Quotations by Sheridan

3 If it is abuse – why one is always sure to hear of
it from one damned good-natured friend or
other!

The Critic, I

4 A progeny of learning.

The Rivals, I

5 Illiterate him, I say, quite from your memory.
The Rivals, II

6 It gives me the hydrostatics to such a degree.
The Rivals, III

7 As headstrong as an allegory on the banks of the Nile.
The Rivals, III

8 He is the very pine-apple of politeness!
The Rivals, III

9 If I reprehend any thing in this world, it is the use of my oracular tongue, and a nice derangement of epitaphs!
The Rivals, III

10 You had no taste when you married me.
The School for Scandal, I

11 I'm called away by particular business. But I leave my character behind me.
The School for Scandal, II

12 Well, then, my stomach must just digest in its waistcoat.
On being warned that his drinking would destroy the coat of his stomach
The Fine Art of Political Wit (L. Harris)

13 What His Royal Highness most particularly prides himself upon, is the excellent harvest.
Lampooning George IV's habit of taking credit for everything good in England
The Fine Art of Political Wit (L. Harris)

14 My dear fellow, be reasonable; the sum you ask me for is a very considerable one, whereas I only ask you for twenty-five pounds.
On being refused a further loan of £25 from a friend to whom he already owed £500
Literary and Scientific Anecdotes (W. Keddie)

15 Whatsoever might be the extent of the private calamity, I hope it will not interfere with the public business of the country.
On learning, whilst in the House of Commons, that his Drury Lane Theatre was on fire
Memoirs of Life of the R. Hon. Richard Brinsley Sheridan (T. Moore)

16 A man may surely be allowed to take a glass of wine by his own fireside.
As he sat in a coffeehouse watching his Drury Lane Theatre burn down
Memoirs of the Life of the Rt. Hon. Richard Brinsley Sheridan (T. Moore)

17 Thank God, that's settled.
Handing one of his creditors an IOU
Wit, Wisdom, and Foibles of the Great (C. Shriner)

18 Won't you come into the garden? I would like my roses to see you.
Said to a young lady
Attrib. in *The Perfect Hostess*

19 It is not my interest to pay the principal, nor my principle to pay the interest.
To his tailor when he requested the payment of a debt, or of the interest on it at least
Attrib.

20 The Right Honourable gentleman is indebted to his memory for his jests, and to his imagination for his facts.
Replying to a speech in the House of Commons
Attrib.

21 Mr. Speaker, I said the honorable member was a liar it is true and I am sorry for it. The honourable member may place the punctuation where he pleases.
On being asked to apologize for calling a fellow MP a liar
Attrib.

Sheridan, Tom (1775–1817) Son of the playwright Richard Brinsley Sheridan; he was colonial treasurer to the Cape of Good Hope.

1 I'm sorry to hear that, sir, you don't happen to have the shilling about you now, do you?
To his father, on learning that he was to be cut off in his will with a shilling
The Fine Art of Political Wit (L. Harris)

Sherman, William Tecumseh, General (1820–91) US general. One of the great Civil War generals, he fought in Georgia and the Carolinas (1864–65), contributing to the Confederate defeat.

1 I will not accept if nominated, and will not serve if elected.
Replying to a request that he accept the Republican presidential nomination
Attrib.

2 I am tired and sick of war. Its glory is all moonshine . . . War is hell.
Attrib. in address, Michigan Military Academy, 19 June 1879

Sherrington, Sir Charles Scott (1857–1952) British physiologist, who shared the Nobel Prize in 1932 for his study of the nervous system.

1 If it is for mind that we are seaching the brain, then we are supposing the brain to be much more than a telephone-exchange. We are supposing it a telephone-exchange along with the subscribers as well.
Man on his Nature

Sherwood, Robert Emmet (1896–1955) US writer and dramatist. He wrote *Waterloo Bridge* (1930), *The Petrified Forest* (1934), and *Idiot's Delight* (1936). He also wrote a novel, *The Virtuous Knight* (1931).

1 The trouble with me is, I belong to a vanishing race. I'm one of the intellectuals.
The Petrified Forest

2 It is disappointing to report that George Bernard Shaw appearing as George Bernard Shaw is sadly miscast in the part. Satirists should be heard and not seen.
Reviewing a Shaw play

Shorter, Clement King (1857–1926) British journalist and literary critic. He founded and edited *The Sketch* (1893–1900), and was editor of *The Sphere* (1900–26). He wrote *Charlotte Brontë and her Circle* (1896), *Sixty Years of Victorian Literature* (1897), and *Napoleon's Fellow Travellers* (1909).

1   The latest definition of an optimist is one who fills up his crossword puzzle in ink.
The Observer, 'Sayings of the Week', 22 Feb 1925

Shuter, Edward (1728–76) British actor, who excelled in plays by Goldsmith, Sheridan, Farquhar, and others.

1   A hole is the accident of a day, while a darn is premeditated poverty.
Explaining why he did not mend the holes in his stocking
Dictionary of National Biography

Sickert, Walter Richard (1860–1942) British impressionist painter and etcher, who painted scenes of Venice and Dieppe, and subjects from music hall and domestic life.

1   Nothing links man to man like the frequent passage from hand to hand of cash.
A Certain World (W. H. Auden)

Siddons, Sarah (Sarah Kemble; 1755–1831) English actress. Her most famous role was Lady Macbeth.

1   . . . sorry am I to say I have often observed, that I have performed worst when I most ardently wished to do better than ever.
Letter to Rev. Whalley, 16 July 1781

2   I am, as you may observe, acting again . . . Our theatre is going on, to the astonishment of everybody. Very few of the actors are paid, and all are vowing to withdraw themselves: yet still we go on. Sheridan is certainly omnipotent.
Letter, 9 Nov 1796

Sidney, Algernon (1622–83) English statesman. A prominent Whig politician, he was beheaded for his involvement in the Rye House Plot against Charles II and James, Duke of York.

1   'Tis not necessary to light a candle to the sun.
Discourses concerning Government, Ch. 2

Sidney, Sir Philip (1554–86) English poet and courtier. His works include *Astrophel and Stella* (1591) and the first work of English literary criticism, *The Defence of Poesy* (1595).

1   Biting my truant pen, beating myself for spite: 'Fool!' said my Muse to me, 'look in thy heart and write.'
Sonnet, *Astrophel and Stella*

2   There have been many most excellent poets that have never versified, and now swarm many versifiers that need never answer to the name of poets.
The Defence of Poesy

3   Love of honour and honour of love.
Referring to the ideal of chivalry
English Literature: Mediaeval (W. P. Ker)

4   Thy need is yet greater than mine.
Giving his own water bottle to a humble wounded soldier after he had himself been wounded
Attrib.

Sieyès, Emmanuel-Joseph, Abbé de (1748–1836) French churchman, a major figure during the Revolution who also played a key role in the rise of Napoleon.

1   *J'ai vécu.*
I survived.
Replying to an enquiry concerning what he had done during the Terror
Dictionnaire Encyclopédique (E. Guérard)

Sigismund (1368–1437) Holy Roman Emperor (1411–37), King of Hungary (1387–1437), and King of Bohemia (1419–37). He conducted two unsuccessful crusades agains the Turks.

1   Only do always in health what you have often promised to do when you are sick.
His advice on achieving happiness
Biographiana, Vol. I

2   I am the Roman Emperor, and am above grammar.
Responding to criticism of his Latin
Attrib.

Simon, Paul (1941–) US singer and songwriter, who has written such successful songs as 'The Boxer', 'Bridge Over Troubled Water', and 'Sound of Silence'. For many years he collaborated with Art Garfunkel. His most recent albums include *Graceland* (1986).

1   Like a bridge over troubled water, I will ease your mind.
Bridge Over Troubled Water

2   Here's to you, Mrs Robinson, Jesus loves you more than you will know.
Mrs Robinson

3   People talking without speaking, People listening without hearing, People writing songs that voices never shared.
Sound of Silence

Simpson, N(orman) F(rederick) (1919–) British dramatist. His work, influenced by the Theatre of the Absurd, includes the plays *A Resounding Tinkle* (1956) and *One-Way Pendulum* (1959).

1   Knocked down a doctor? With an ambulance? How could she? It's a contradiction in terms.
One-Way Pendulum, I

Singer, Isaac Bashevis (1904–) Polish-born US novelist and short-story writer. His novels are written in Yiddish; they include *Gimple the Fool* (1957), *The Slave* (1960), *Old Love* (1979), and *The King of the Fields* (1989).

1   Children . . . have no use for psychology. They detest sociology. They still believe in God, the family, angels, devils, witches, goblins, logic, clarity, punctuation, and other such obsolete stuff . . . When a book is boring, they yawn openly. They don't expect their writer to redeem humanity, but leave to adults such childish illusions.
Speech on receiving the Nobel Prize for Literature
The Observer, 17 Dec 1978

2   We have to believe in free will. We've got no choice.
The Times, 21 June 1982

Sitting Bull (c. 1834–90) US Sioux Indian chief, who defeated General Custer at the massacre of Little Big Horn in 1876. He was killed during a later outbreak of hostilities.

1 The white man knows how to make everything, but he does not know how to distribute it.
Attrib.

Sitwell, Dame Edith (1887–1964) British poet and writer, sister of Osbert Sitwell. *Façade* (1923) was set to music by William Walton; her other collections include *Gold Coast Customs* (1929).

1 My poems are hymns of praise to the glory of life.
Collected Poems, 'Some Notes on My Poetry'

2 Who dreamed that Christ has died in vain?
He walks again on the Seas of Blood,
He comes in the terrible Rain.
The Shadow of Cain

3 A lady asked me why, on most occasions, I wore black. 'Are you in mourning?'
'Yes.'
'For whom are you in mourning?'
'For the world.'
Taken Care Of, Ch. 1

4 A pompous woman of his acquaintance, complaining that the head-waiter of a restaurant had not shown her and her husband immediately to a table, said, 'We had to tell him who we were.' Gerald, interested, enquired, 'And who were you?'
Taken Care Of, Ch. 15

5 I have often wished I had time to cultivate modesty . . . But I am too busy thinking about myself.
The Observer, 'Sayings of the Week', 30 Apr 1950

6 I enjoyed talking to her, but thought *nothing* of her writing. I considered her 'a beautiful little knitter'.
Referring to Virginia Woolf
Letter to G. Singleton

Sitwell, Sir Osbert (1892–1969) British writer of short stories, novels, and poetry, best-known for his nostalgic memoirs. His sister was Dame Edith Sitwell.

1 In reality, *killing time*
Is only the name for another of the multifarious ways
By which Time kills us.
Milordo Inglese

2 But He was never, well,
What I call
A Sportsman;
For forty days
He went out into the desert
– And never shot anything.
Old Fashioned Sportsmen

Skelton, Red (Richard Bernard Skelton; 1913–) US actor and comedian; he made more than 45 films and was the star of a long-running TV show until his retirement in 1970.

1 It proves what they say, give the public what they want to see and they'll come out for it.
Said while attending the funeral in 1958 of Hollywood producer Harry Cohn. It has also been attributed to Samuel Goldwyn while attending Louis B. Mayer's funeral in 1957

Skelton, Robin (1925–) British academic and author of many books on poetry.

1 A man does not write poems about what he knows, but about what he does not know.
Teach Yourself Poetry

Skinner, B(urrhus) F(rederic) (1904–90) US psychologist. He investigated learning ability in animals by means of carefully controlled experiments and advocated behaviourism in his books, including *The Behaviour of Organisms* (1938), *Beyond Freedom and Dignity* (1971), and *Notebooks* (1980).

1 Indeed one of the ultimate advantages of an education is simply coming to the end of it.
The Technology of Teaching

2 Education is what survives when what has been learnt has been forgotten.
New Scientist, 21 May 1964, 'Education in 1984'

Skinner, Cornelia Otis (1901–79) US stage actress. She made a few films, including *The Uninvited* (1944) and *The Swimmer* (1967).

1 Woman's virtue is man's greatest invention.
Attrib.

Slezak, Leo (1873–1946) Czechoslovakian-born tenor, noted for his performances in Wagnerian operas. He also appeared in several films.

1 What time is the next swan?
When the mechanical swan left the stage without him during a performance of *Lohengrin*
What Time Is the Next Swan? (Walter Slezak)

Slocombe, George Edward (1894–1963) British journalist. He worked for the *Daily Herald* (1920–31), the *Evening Standard* (1932–34), and the *Sunday Express* (from 1940). He also wrote several books including *A History of Poland* (1916) and *Crisis in Europe* (1934).

1 He was the Messiah of the new age, and his crucifixion was yet to come.
Referring to Woodrow Wilson and his visit to the Versailles conference
Mirror to Geneva

Smiles, Samuel (1812–1904) British writer. He wrote several biographies and was a railway journalist. He is remembered for his book *Self-Help* (1859).

1 We often discover what *will* do, by finding out what will not do; and probably he who never made a mistake never made a discovery.
Self-Help, Ch. 11

2 A place for everything, and everything in its place.
Thrift, Ch. 5

Smith, Adam (1723–90) Scottish economist. He lectured on logic and moral philosophy (1752–63) and wrote *An Enquiry into the Nature and Causes of the Wealth of Nations* (1776).

1 People of the same trade seldom meet together but the conversation ends in a conspiracy against the public, or in some diversion to raise prices.
The Wealth of Nations

2 With the great part of rich people, the chief employment of riches consists in the parade of riches.
The Wealth of Nations

3 There is no art which one government sooner learns of another than that of draining money from the pockets of the people.
The Wealth of Nations

4 Science is the great antidote to the poison of enthusiasm and supersition.
The Wealth of Nations

Smith, Sir Cyril (1928–) British Liberal politician, noted for his bulk and outspoken manner. His autobiography is entitled *Big Cyril* (1977).

1 If ever there's any emergence of a fourth party in this country, the task of the Liberal party is to strangle it at birth.
The Guardian, 1981

2 Parliament is the longest running farce in the West End.
The Times, 23 Sept 1977

Smith, Ian (Douglas) (1919–) Rhodesian (Zimbabwe) politician and prime minister (1964–79). In 1965 he made a unilateral declaration of independence (UDI) from Britain, and was for many years opposed to black majority rule in Zimbabwe.

1 I don't believe in black majority rule ever in Rhodesia . . . not in a thousand years.
Speech, Mar 1976

Smith, Logan Pearsall (1865–1946) US writer. He spent most of his life in England and is best known for his collections *Trivia* (1902) and *Afterthoughts* (1931) as well as his books on language, such as *The English Language* (1912).

1 A best-seller is the gilded tomb of a mediocre talent.
Afterthoughts, 'Art and Letters'

2 It is the wretchedness of being rich that you have to live with rich people.
Afterthoughts, 'In the World'

3 People say that life is the thing, but I prefer reading.
Afterthoughts, 'Myself'

4 Married women are kept women, and they are beginning to find it out.
Afterthoughts, 'Other people'

5 I might give my life for my friend, but he had better not ask me to do up a parcel.
Trivia

6 I am one of the unpraised, unrewarded millions without whom Statistics would be a bankrupt science. It is we who are born, who marry, who die, in constant ratios.
Trivia

7 I cannot forgive my friends for dying: I do not find these vanishing acts of theirs at all amusing.
Trivia

8 Thank heavens the sun has gone in and I don't have to go out and enjoy it.
Attrib.

9 Yes there is a meaning; at least for me, there is one thing that matters – to set a chime of words tinkling in the minds of a few fastidious people.
Contemplating whether life has any meaning, shortly before his death
Attrib.

Smith, Stevie (Florence Margaret Smith; 1902–71) British poet and novelist. She worked as a secretary and lived in her aunt's home in Palmer's Green, London, all her adult life. Her novel *Novel on Yellow Paper* (1936) was followed by her first verse collection *A Good Time Was Had by All* (1937). Her *Collected Poems* (1975) were published posthumously.

1 A Good Time Was Had by All.
Book title

2 Nobody heard him, the dead man,
But still he lay moaning:
I was much further out than you thought
And not waving but drowning.
Not Waving But Drowning

3 Private Means is dead,
God rest his soul,
Officers and fellow-rankers said.
Private Means is Dead

4 This Englishwoman is so refined
She has no bosom and no behind.
This Englishwoman

5 I do really think that death will be marvellous . . . If there wasn't death, I think you couldn't go on.
The Observer, 9 Nov 1969

Smith, Sydney (1771–1845) British clergyman, essayist, and wit. He helped to found the *Edinburgh Review* (1802), and published many of his sermons, essays, speeches, and letters.

1 Mankind are always happy for having been happy, so that if you make them happy now, you make them happy twenty years hence by the memory of it.
Elementary Sketches of Moral Philosophy

2 The moment the very name of Ireland is mentioned, the English seem to bid adieu to common feeling, common prudence, and common sense, and to act with the barbarity of tyrants, and the fatuity of idiots.
The Letters of Peter Plymley

3 They are written as if sin were to be taken out of man like Eve out of Adam – by putting him to sleep.
Referring to boring sermons
Anecdotes of the Clergy (J. Larwood)

4 Heat, madam! It was so dreadful that I found there was nothing for it but to take off my flesh and sit in my bones.
Discussing the hot weather with a lady acquaintance
Lives of the Wits (H. Pearson)

5 You never expected justice from a company, did you? They have neither a soul to lose nor a body to kick.
Memoir (Lady Holland)

6 What you don't know would make a great book.
Memoir (Lady Holland)

7 That knuckle-end of England – that land of Calvin, oat-cakes, and sulphur.
Memoir (Lady Holland)

8 How can a bishop marry? How can he flirt? The most he can say is, 'I will see you in the vestry after service'.
Memoir (Lady Holland)

9 You find people ready enough to do the Samaritan, without the oil and twopence.
Memoir (Lady Holland)

10 My definition of marriage . . . it resembles a pair of shears, so joined that they cannot be separated; often moving in opposite directions, yet always punishing anyone who comes between them.
Memoir (Lady Holland)

11 He has occasional flashes of silence, that make his conversation perfectly delightful.
Referring to Lord Macaulay
Memoir (Lady Holland)

12 Minorities . . . are almost always in the right.
The Smith of Smiths (H. Pearson), Ch. 9

13 I am just going to pray for you at St Paul's, but with no very lively hope of success.
On meeting an acquaintance
The Smith of Smiths (H. Pearson), Ch. 13

14 I look upon Switzerland as an inferior sort of Scotland.
Letter to Lord Holland, 1815

15 He who drinks a tumbler of London water has literally in his stomach more animated beings than there are men, women and children on the face of the globe.
Letter

16 You must not think me necessarily foolish because I am facetious, nor will I consider you necessarily wise because you are grave.
Letter to Bishop Blomfield

17 No furniture so charming as books.
Attrib.

18 He rose by gravity; I sank by levity.
Comparing his career with that of his brother, Robert Percy Smith
Attrib.

Smith, Thorne (1892–1934) US humorist and writer. His books include *Topper* (1926) and *The Night Life of the Gods* (1931).

1 Steven's mind was so tolerant that he could have attended a lynching every day without becoming critical.
The Jovial Ghosts, Ch. 11

Smollett, Tobias George (1721–71) British novelist and journalist. His novels include *Roderick Random* (1748) and *Peregrine Pickle* (1751). He also wrote a *Complete History of England* (1757–58).

1 I think for my part one half of the nation is mad – and the other not very sound.
Referring to the English
The Adventures of Sir Launcelot Greaves, Ch. 6

2 True patriotism is of no party.
The Adventures of Sir Launcelot Greaves

3 Hark ye, Clinker, you are a most notorious offender. You stand convicted of sickness, hunger, wretchedness, and want.
Humphrey Clinker, Letter to Sir Watkin Phillips, 24 May

4 Some folk are wise, and some are otherwise.
Roderick Random, Ch. 6

5 He was formed for the ruin of our sex.
Roderick Random, Ch. 22

6 That great Cham of literature, Samuel Johnson.
Letter to John Wilkes, 16 Mar 1759

Snow, C(harles) P(ercy), Baron (1905–80) British novelist. A scientific civil servant, he wrote the 11-novel series *Strangers and Brothers* (1940–70), which included *The Masters* (1951) and *Corridors of Power* (1964). His lecture *The Two Cultures and the Scientific Revolution* (1959) created considerable controversy.

1 'I grant you that he's not two-faced,' I said. 'But what's the use of that when the one face he has got is so peculiarly unpleasant?'
The Affair, Ch. 4

2 The official world, the corridors of power, the dilemmas of conscience and egotism – she disliked them all.
Homecomings, Ch. 22

3 Jam today, and men aren't at their most exciting: Jam tomorrow, and one often sees them at their noblest.
The Two Cultures and the Scientific Revolution, 4

Snowden, Philip, 1st Viscount (1864–1937) British politician. He became chancellor of the exchequer in the 1924 and 1929 Labour governments.

1 It would be desirable if every government, when it comes to power, should have its old speeches burned.

Socrates (469–399 BC) Athenian philosopher. Although he wrote nothing himself, much is known of his philosophy from the writings of his pupils, especially Plato. Charged with corrupting youth and atheism, he was condemned to death.

Quotations about Socrates

1   Socrates was the first to call philosophy down from the heavens and to place it in cities, and even to introduce it into homes and compel it to enquire about life and standards and good and ill.
Cicero (106–43 BC) Roman orator and statesman. *Tusculanae Disputationes*

2   He was so orderly in his way of life that on several occasions when pestilence broke out in Athens he was the only man who escaped infection.
Diogenes Laertius (fl. 3rd century AD) Greek author. *Lives of Eminent Philosophers*

3   Socrates is a doer of evil, who corrupts the youth; and who does not believe in the gods of the state, but has other new divinities of his own. Such is the charge.
Plato (429–347 BC) Greek Philosopher. *Dialogue*

Quotations by Socrates

4   Nothing can harm a good man, either in life or after death.
Apology (Plato)

5   The unexamined life is not worth living.
Apology (Plato)

6   But already it is time to depart, for me to die, for you to go on living; which of us takes the better course, is concealed from anyone except God.
Apology (Plato)

7   How many things I can do without!
Examining the range of goods on sale at a market
Lives of the Eminent Philosophers (Diogenes Laertius), II

8   I am not an Athenian or a Greek, but a citizen of the world.
Of Banishment (Plutarch)

9   Crito, we owe a cock to Aesculapius; please pay it and don't let it pass.
Last words before his execution by drinking hemlock
Phaedo (Plato), 118

Solon (6th century BC) Athenian statesman who founded Athenian democracy and instituted a new constitution based on a lenient legal code.

1   Wrongdoing can only be avoided if those who are not wronged feel the same indignation at it as those who are.
Greek Wit (F. Paley)

2   Laws are like spider's webs: if some poor weak creature come up against them, it is caught; but a bigger one can break through and get away.
Similar remarks have been made by others; *see* SHENSTONE; SWIFT
Lives of the Eminent Philosophers (Diogenes Laertius), I

Solzhenitsyn, Alexander (1918–) Soviet novelist. Imprisoned for political dissent, he left the Soviet Union in 1974 and now lives in the USA. His books include *One Day in the Life of Ivan Denisovich* (1962), *Cancer Ward* (1968), *Gulag Archipelago* (1974–78), and *October 1916* (1985).

Quotations about Solzhenitsyn

1   What is there about the Gulag Archipelago that made it a kind of last straw and that drove the politburo to arbitrary arrest and expulsion of its author?
Robert Conquest (1917–) British literary editor.

2   Solzhenitsyn's novel is one of the steps in the completion of the literature of the Twenties and Thirties.
F.D. Reeve (1928–) US editor and translator.

3   Solzhenitsyn's analysis of the butcher-like amorality of contemporary men absorbed in the niceties of trimming a carcass whose former life they thought they did not need and therefore undervalued is couched in a superbly artful fiction. Like Tolstoy, he is a man of great talent and of stupendous moral dignity.
F.D. Reeve (1928–) US editor and translator.

Quotations by Solzhenitsyn

4   The whole of his life had prepared Podduyev for living, not for dying.
Cancer Ward, Pt. I, Ch. 8

5   Nowadays we don't think much of a man's love for an animal; we laugh at people who are attached to cats. But if we stop loving animals, aren't we bound to stop loving humans too?
Cancer Ward, Pt. I, Ch. 20

6   When truth is discovered by someone else, it loses something of its attractiveness.
Candle in the Wind, 3

7   You took my freedom away a long time ago and you can't give it back because you haven't got it yourself.
The First Circle, Ch. 17

8   You only have power over people so long as you don't take *everything* away from them. But when you've robbed a man of everything he's no longer in your power – he's free again.
The First Circle, Ch. 17

9   Their teacher had advised them not to read Tolstoy novels, because they were very long and would easily confuse the clear ideas which they had learned from reading critical studies of him.
The First Circle, Ch. 40

10   No regime has ever loved great writers, only minor ones.
The First Circle, Ch. 57

11 This universal, obligatory force-feeding with lies is now the most agonizing aspect of existence in our country – worse than all our material miseries, worse than any lack of civil liberties.
Letter to Soviet Leaders, 6

12 Forget the outside world. Life has different laws in here. This is Campland, an invisible country. It's not in the geography books, or the psychology books or the history books. This is the famous country where ninety-nine men weep while one laughs.
The Love-Girl and the Innocent, I:3

13 For us in Russia communism is a dead dog, while, for many people in the West, it is still a living lion.
The Listener, 15 Feb 1979

14 In our country the lie has become not just a moral category but a pillar of the State.
The Observer, 'Sayings of the Year', 29 Dec 1974

15 The salvation of mankind lies only in making everything the concern of all.
Nobel Lecture, 1970

Somerville, E(dith) Œ(none) (1858–1949) Irish writer. In collaboration with Martin Ross (Violet Martin; 1862–1915) she wrote *Some Experiences of an Irish R.M.* (1899), which became an international success.

1 It is an ancient contention of my wife that I, in common with all other men, in any dispute between a female relative and a tradesman, side with the tradesman, partly from fear, partly from masculine clannishness, and most of all from a desire to stand well with the tradesman.
Some Experiences of an Irish R.M., 'The Pug-nosed Fox'

2 I have endured the Sandhurst riding-school, I have galloped for an impetuous general, I have been steward at regimental races, but none of these feats have altered my opinion that the horse, as a means of locomotion is obsolete.
Some Experiences of an Irish R.M., 'Great-Uncle McCarthy'

3 Neither principalities nor powers should force me into the drawing-room, where sat the three unhappy women of my party, being entertained within an inch of their lives by Mrs McRory.
Further Experiences of an Irish R.M., 'Sharper than a Ferret's Tooth'

Sondheim, Stephen Joshua (1930–) US composer and lyricist, noted for such musicals as *West Wide Story* (1957), *A Funny Thing Happened on the Way to the Forum* (1962), *Sweeney Todd* (1979), and *Into The Woods* (1990).

1 Everything's Coming Up Roses.
Song title

2 Send in the Clowns.
Song title

Sontag, Susan (1933–) US novelist and essayist. Her writings include *Against Interpretation* (1966), *Styles of Radical Will* (1969), *Illness as Metaphor* (1978), and *AIDS and Its metaphors* (1988).

1 Illness is the night-side of life, a more onerous citizenship. Everyone who is born holds dual citizenship, in the kingdom of the well and in the kingdom of the sick. Although we all prefer to use only the good passport, sooner or later each of us is obliged, at least for a spell, to identify ourselves as citizens of that other place.
Illness as Metaphor

2 A photograph is not only an image (as a painting is an image), an interpretation of the real; it is also a trace, something directly stencilled off the real, like a footprint or a death mask.
On Photography

Sophocles (c. 496–406 BC) Greek dramatist. Only 7 of his 123 plays survive; the best-known are *Electra*, *Oedipus Rex*, *Oedipus at Colonus*, and *Antigone*.

1 Sleep's the only medicine that gives ease.
Philoctetes, 766

2 I depict men as they ought to be, but Euripides portrays them as they are.
Poetics (Aristotle)

3 Someone asked Sophocles, 'How do you feel now about sex? Are you still able to have a woman?' He replied, 'Hush, man; most gladly indeed am I rid of it all, as though I had escaped from a mad and savage master.'
Republic (Plato), Bk. I

Soule, John Babsone Lane (1815–91) US writer and editor.

1 Go West, young man, go West!
Terre Haute (Indiana) *Express*, 1851

Southey, Robert (1774–1843) British poet and writer. A friend of Wordsworth, his epics include *Thalaba* (1801) and *Madoc* (1805); shorter poems include *The Battle of Blenheim* and *The Inchcape Rock*. He also wrote a *Life of Nelson* (1813) and became poet laureate in 1813.

1 'And everybody praised the Duke,
Who this great fight did win.'
'But what good came of it at last?'
Quoth little Peterkin.
'Why that I cannot tell,' said he,
'But 'twas a famous victory.'
The Battle of Blenheim

2 Curses are like young chickens, they always come home to roost.
The Curse of Kehama, Motto

3 Live as long as you may, the first twenty years are the longest half of your life.
The Doctor, Ch. 130

4 You are old, Father William, the young man cried,
The few locks which are left you are grey;
You are hale, Father William, a hearty old man,
Now tell me the reason, I pray.
See also Lewis CARROLL
The Old Man's Comforts, and how he Gained them

5 In the days of my youth I remembered my God!
And He hath not forgotten my age.
The Old Man's Comforts, and how he Gained them

Spaak, Paul Henri (1899–1972) Belgian statesman. He
became prime minister of Belgium (1938–39; 1947–50), secretary
general of NATO (1957–61), and first president of the United
Nations (1946).

1 Our agenda is now exhausted. The secretary
general is exhausted. All of you are exhausted. I
find it comforting that, beginning with our very
first day, we find ourselves in such complete
unanimity.
*Concluding the first General Assembly meeting of the United
Nations*

Spark, Muriel (1918–) British novelist, born in Edinburgh.
Her popular novels include *The Prime of Miss Jean Brodie* (1961),
The Abbess of Crewe (1974), *Territorial Rights* (1979), *The Only
Problem* (1984), and *A Far Cry From Kensington* (1988).

1 A short neck denotes a good mind . . . You see,
the messages go quicker to the brain because
they've shorter to go.
The Ballad of Peckham Rye, Ch. 7

2 Parents learn a lot from their children about cop-
ing with life.
The Comforters, Ch. 6

3 Every communist has a fascist frown, every fascist a communist smile.
The Girls of Slender Means, Ch. 4

4 Selwyn Macgregor, the nicest boy who ever
committed the sin of whisky.
The Go-Away Bird, 'A Sad Tale's Best for Winter'

5 Being over seventy is like being engaged in a
war. All our friends are going or gone and we
survive amongst the dead and the dying as on a
battlefield.
Memento Mori, Ch. 4

6 Give me a girl at an impressionable age, and she
is mine for life.
The Prime of Miss Jean Brodie, Ch. 1

7 One's prime is elusive. You little girls, when you
grow up, must be on the alert to recognize
your prime at whatever time of your life it may
occur. You must then live it to the full.
The Prime of Miss Jean Brodie, Ch. 1

8 If you had been mine when you were seven you
would have been the crème de la crème.
The Prime of Miss Jean Brodie, Ch. 2

9 Art and religion first; then philosophy; lastly science. That is the order of the great subjects of
life, that's their order of importance.
The Prime of Miss Jean Brodie, Ch. 2

10 To me education is a leading out of what is already there in the pupil's soul. To Miss Mackay it is a putting in of something that is not
there, and that is not what I call education, I call
it intrusion.
The Prime of Miss Jean Brodie, Ch. 2

11 But I did not remove my glasses, for I had not
asked for her company in the first place, and
there is a limit to what one can listen to with
the naked eye.
Voices at Play, 'The Dark Glasses'

12 Do you think it pleases a man when he looks into
a woman's eyes and sees a reflection of the
British Museum Reading Room?
The Wit of Women (L. and M. Cowan)

Sparrow, John Hanbury Angus (1906–) British
lawyer and academic. He became Warden of All Souls College,
Oxford (1952–77). His books include *Controversial Essay* (1966),
Grave Epigrams and Other Verses (1981), and *Leaves from a
Victorian Diary* (1985).

1 That indefatigable and unsavoury engine of pollution, the dog.
Letter to The Times, 30 Sep 1975

Speight, Johnny (1920–) British television scriptwriter,
best known for his creation of the character Alf Garnett in *Till
Death Do Us Part*.

1 You silly moo.
Till Death Do Us Part

2 If Her Majesty stood for Parliament – if the Tory Party had any sense and made Her its leader
instead of that grammar school twit Heath –
us Tories, mate, would win every election we
went in for.
Till Death Do Us Part

3 Don't be daft. You don't get any pornography on
there, not on the telly. Get filth, that's all. The
only place you get pornography is in yer Sunday papers.
Till Death Do Us Part

4 Have you noticed, the last four strikes we've
had, it's pissed down? It wouldn't be a bad idea
to check the weather reports before they pull
us out next time.
Till Death Do Us Part

Spencer, Herbert (1820–1903) British philosopher and
supporter of Darwinism. His *First Principles* (1862) was the first
of a multivolume treatise *System of Synthetic Philosophy* (1860–96).

1 The Republican form of Government is the highest form of government; but because of this it
requires the highest type of human nature – a
type nowhere at present existing.
Essays, 'The Americans'

2 It was remarked to me by the late Mr Charles
Roupell . . . that to play billiards well was a sign
of an ill-spent youth.
Life and Letters of Spencer (Duncan), Ch. 20

3 Survival of the fittest.
Principles of Biology

Spencer, Sir Stanley (1891–1959) British artist, noted for
his paintings of scenes from World War I and of religious subjects.
His best-known works include *The Resurrection: Cookham* and the
series *Resurrection: Port Glasgow*.

1 I no more like people personally than I like dogs. When I meet them I am only apprehensive whether they will bite me, which is reasonable and sensible.
Stanley Spencer, a Biography (Maurice Collis), Ch. 17

2 Beautifully done.
Said to the nurse who had injected him, just before he died
Stanley Spencer, a Biography (Maurice Collis), Ch. 19

Spender, Sir Stephen (1909–) British poet, who became famous as one of the left wing poets of the 1930s. His *Collected Poems* was published in 1985, other publications include *The Temple* (1988).

1 Pylons, those pillars
Bare like nude giant girls that have no secret.
The Pylons

2 Moving thought the silent crowd
Who stand behind dull cigarettes,
These men who idle in the road,
I have the sense of falling light.

They lounge at corners of the street
And greet friends with a shrug of the shoulder
And turn their empty pockets out,
The cynical gestures of the poor.
Unemployed

3 Who live under the shadow of a war,
What can I do that matters?
Who live under the Shadow

4 People sometimes divide others into those you laugh at and those you laugh with. The young Auden was someone you could laugh-at-with.
Address, W. H. Auden's memorial service, Oxford, 27 Oct 1973

Spenser, Edmund (1552–99) English poet. His *Faerie Queene*, an allegory in six volumes, was dedicated to Elizabeth I.

1 Sleep after toil, port after stormy seas,
Ease after war, death after life does greatly please.
The Faerie Queene, I:9

2 Sweet Thames! run softly, till I end my Song.
Prothalamion, 18

3 And he that strives to touch the stars,
Oft stumbles at a straw.
The Shepherd's Calendar, 'July'

Spiel, Hilde (1911–) Austrian writer; her works include *Kati auf der Bruche* (1933).

1 Malice is like a game of poker or tennis; you don't play it with anyone who is manifestly inferior to you.
The Darkened Room

Spinoza, Benedict (Baruch de Spinoza; 1632–77) Dutch philosopher and theologian of Jewish parents. His *Tractatus Theologico-Politicus* (1670) enraged both Jewish and Christian scholars. His *Ethics* (1677) was published posthumously.

1 Nature abhors a vacuum.
Ethics

2 Man is a social animal.
Ethics

3 We feel and know that we are eternal.
Ethics

4 Desire is the very essence of man.
Ethics

5 I have striven not to laugh at human actions, not to weep at them, nor to hate them, but to understand them.
Tractatus Theologico-Politicus, Ch. 1

Spock, Dr Benjamin McLane (1903–) US pediatrician and psychiatrist, author of *The Commonsense Book of Baby and Child Care* (1946); later books include *Dr Spock talks with Mothers* (1961) and *Raising Children in a Difficult Time* (1974). Subsequently he became associated with the peace movement and was a candidate for the US presidency (1972).

1 To win in Vietnam, we will have to exterminate a nation.
Dr Spock on Vietnam, Ch.7

2 There are only two things a child will share willingly – communicable diseases and his mother's age.
Attrib.

Spooner, William Archibald (1844–1930) British clergyman and academic, remembered for his 'spoonerisms', phrases in which the first letters of words are transposed.

1 You will find as you grow older that the weight of rages will press harder and harder on the employer.
Spooner (Sir W. Hayter), Ch. 6

2 I remember your name perfectly, but I just can't think of your face.
Attrib.

3 Kinquering Congs their titles take.
A scrambled announcement of the hymn in New College Chapel, (probably apocryphal)

4 Let us drink to the queer old Dean.
Attrib.

5 Sir, you have tasted two whole worms; you have hissed all my mystery lectures and have been caught fighting a liar in the quad; you will leave Oxford by the town drain.
Attrib.

Spring-Rice, Sir Cecil Arthur (1859–1918) British diplomat, who became ambassador to the USA (1913–18).

1 I vow to thee, my country – all earthly things above –
Entire and whole and perfect, the service of my love.
I Vow to Thee, My Country

2 I am the Dean of Christ Church, Sir:
There's my wife; look well at her.
She's the Broad and I'm the High;
We are the University.
The Masque of Balliol

Spyri, Johanna (1827–1901) Swiss writer, best known for her story for children *Heidi* (1880–81).

1 Oh, I wish that God had not given me what I prayed for! It was not so good as I thought.
Heidi, Ch. 11

2 Anger has overpowered him, and driven him to a revenge which was rather a stupid one, I must acknowledge, but anger makes us all stupid.
Heidi, Ch. 23

Squire, Sir John Collings (1884–1958) British journalist and dramatist, a leading member of the Georgian school of pastoral poetry.

1 But I'm not so think as you drunk I am.
Ballade of Soporific Absorption

2 But Shelley had a hyper-thyroid face.
Ballade of the Glandular Hypothesis

3 It did not last: the Devil howling 'Ho!
Let Einstein be!' restored the status quo.
Answer to POPE's Epitaph for Newton
Epigrams, 'The Dilemma'

4 God heard the embattled nations shout
Gott strafe England and God save the King.
Good God, said God,
I've got my work cut out.
1914

Stacpoole, H(enry) de Vere (1863–1931) Irish-born novelist and ship's doctor, best known for his romance *The Blue Lagoon* (1908).

1 In home-sickness you must keep moving – it is the only disease that does not require rest.
The Bourgeois

Stalin, Joseph (J. Dzhugashvili; 1879–1953) Soviet statesman. A Bolshevik under Lenin, he became supreme dictator in 1929. In the 1930s he eliminated his rivals in various purges, but led the Soviet Union to victory in World War II. After the war his autocratic rule was intensified and he built up an empire of Eastern European Communist countries.

1 The Pope! How many divisions has *he* got?
When urged by Pierre Laval to tolerate Catholicism in the USSR to appease the Pope, 13 May 1935
The Second World War (W. S. Churchill), Vol. I, Ch. 8

2 The state is an instrument in the hands of the ruling class for suppressing the resistance of its class enemies.
Stalin's Kampf (ed. M. R. Werner)

3 The tasks of the party are . . . to be cautious and not allow our country to be drawn into conflicts by warmongers who are accustomed to have others pull the chestnuts out of the fire for them.
Speech, 8th Congress of the Communist Party, 6 Jan 1941

4 The party is the rallying-point for the best elements of the working class.
Attrib.

5 Gaiety is the most outstanding feature of the Soviet Union.
Attrib.

6 A single death is a tragedy; a million is a statistic.
Attrib.

Stanley, Sir Henry Morton (1841–1904) British explorer. While working as a journalist in the USA he was sent to search for Dr Livingstone in Africa. He made several subsequent expeditions into Africa.

1 Dr Livingstone, I presume?
On finding David Livingstone at Ujiji on Lake Tanganyika, Nov 1871
How I found Livingstone, Ch. 11

Stanton, C. E. (1859–1933) US colonel who fought in World War I.

1 Lafayette, we are here!
The Marquis de Lafayette (1757–1834) aided the colonists in the US War of Independence
Address at Lafayette's grave, Paris, 4 July 1917

Stanton, Elizabeth (1815–1902) US suffragette.

1 I have been into many of the ancient cathedrals – grand, wonderful, mysterious. But I always leave them with a feeling of indignation because of the generations of human beings who have struggled in poverty to build these altars to the unknown god.
Diary

2 . . . we still wonder at the stolid incapacity of all men to understand that woman feels the invidious distinctions of sex exactly as the black man does those of color, or the white man the more transient distinctions of wealth, family, position, place, and power; that shefeels as keenly as man the injustice of disfranchisement.
History of Woman Suffrage (with Susan B. Anthony and Mathilda Gage), Vol. I

3 It is impossible for one class to appreciate the wrongs of another.
History of Woman Suffrage (with Susan B. Anthony and Mathilda Gage), Vol. I

4 The prolonged slavery of women is the darkest page in human history.
History of Woman Suffrage (with Susan B. Anthony and Mathilda Gage), Vol. I

5 Womanhood is the great fact in her life; wifehood and motherhood are but incidental relations.
History of Woman Suffrage (with Susan B. Anthony and Mathilda Gage), Vol. I

6 *Declaration of Sentiments:* . . . We hold these truths to be self-evident: that all men and women are created equal . . .
History of Woman Suffrage (with Susan B. Anthony and Mathilda Gage), Vol. I

Stanton, Frank L(ebby) (1857–1927) US journalist and poet. He published *Songs of a Day and Songs of the Soil* (1892) and *Up From Georgia* (1902); he has been called the poet laureate of Georgia.

1 Sweetes' li'l' feller,
Everybody knows;
Dunno what to call 'im,
But he's mighty lak' a rose!

Sweetes' Li'l' Feller

Stapledon, Olaf (1886–1950) British philosopher and science-fiction writer, whose influential novels include *Last and First Men* (1930) and *Star Maker* (1937).

1 That strange blend of the commercial traveller, the missionary, and the barbarian conqueror, which was the American abroad.

Last and First Men, Ch. 3

2 At the close of this period I, the communal mind, emerged re-made, as from a chrysalis; and for a brief moment, which was indeed the supreme moment of the cosmos, I faced the Star Maker.

Star Maker, Ch. 13

Stark, John (1728–1822) US general in the American War of Independence.

1 Yonder are the Hessians. They were bought for seven pounds and tenpence a man. Are you worth more? Prove it. Tonight the American flag floats from yonder hill or Molly Stark sleeps a widow!

Urging on his troops at the battle of Bennington in 1777
The American Treasury (C. Fadiman)

Stead, Christina (1902–83) Australian novelist. Her best-known novels are *The Man Who Loved Children* (1940) and *For Love Alone* (1944).

1 A self-made man is one who believes in luck and sends his son to Oxford.

House of All Nations, 'Credo'

Steel, Sir David (1938–) British politician. He became leader of the Liberal Party in 1976. With David Owen he headed the SDP-Liberal Alliance.

1 Go back to your constituencies and prepare for government!

Speech to party conference, 1985

2 I sense that the British electorate is now itching to break out once and for all from the discredited straight-jacket of the past.

The Times, 2 June 1987

Steele, Sir Richard (1672–1729) Dublin-born British essayist and dramatist. With Joseph Addison he founded, and wrote for, the magazines *The Tatler* and *Spectator*. He wrote a number of theatrical comedies, including *The Funeral* (1701).

1 Reading is to the mind what exercise is to the body.

The Tatler, 147

2 A little in drink, but at all times yr faithful husband.

Letter to his wife, 27 Sept 1708

Steffens, (Joseph) Lincoln (1866–1936) US journalist. His books include *The Struggle for Self-Government* (1906) and an autobiography (1931).

1 I have seen the future and it works.

Speaking to Bernard Baruch after visiting the Soviet Union, 1919
Autobiography, Ch. 18

Stein, Gertrude (1874–1946) US writer, who lived in Paris from 1903. Her books include *Tender Buttons* (1914) and *The Autobiography of Alice B. Toklas* (1933).

1 She always says she dislikes the abnormal, it is so obvious. She says the normal is so much more simply complicated and interesting.

The Autobiography of Alice B. Toklas

2 In the United States there is more space where nobody is than where anybody is. That is what makes America what it is.

The Geographical History of America

3 Rose is a rose is a rose is a rose.

Sacred Emily

4 Besides Shakespeare and me, who do you think there is?

Speaking to a friend she considered knew little about literature
Charmed Circle (J. Mellow)

5 The Jews have produced only three originative geniuses: Christ, Spinoza, and myself.

Charmed Circle (J. Mellow)

6 That's what you are. That's what you all are. All of you young people who served in the war. You are a lost generation.

A Moveable Feast (E. Hemingway)

Steinbeck, John (1902–68) US novelist. Many of his novels are set in the mid-West of America during the Depression; they include *Of Mice and Men* (1937), *The Grapes of Wrath* (1939), and *East of Eden* (1952).

1 The American Standard translation *orders* men to triumph over sin, and you can call sin ignorance. The King James translation makes a promise in 'Thou shalt', meaning that men will surely triumph over sin. But the Hebrew word, the word *timshel* – 'Thou mayest' – that gives a choice. It might be the most important word in the world. That says the way is open. That throws it right back on a man. For if 'Thou mayest' – it is also true that 'Thou mayest not'.

Referring to Genesis 4:7
East of Eden, Ch. 24

2 Man, unlike any other thing organic or inorganic in the universe, grows beyond his work, walks up the stairs of his concepts, emerges ahead of his accomplishments.

The Grapes of Wrath, Ch. 14

3 Okie use' to mean you was from Oklahoma. Now it means you're scum. Don't mean nothing itself, it's the way they say it.
The Grapes of Wrath, Ch. 18

Stekel, Wilhelm (1868–1940) Viennese psychiatrist, who was a noted disciple of Freud.

1 The mark of the immature man is that he wants to die nobly for a cause, while the mark of the mature man is that he wants to live humbly for one.
The Catcher in the Rye (J. D. Salinger), Ch. 24

Stendhal (Henri Beyle; 1783–1842) French novelist and writer. He is remembered for his novels *Le Rouge et le noir* (1830) and *La Chartreuse de Parme* (1839). He also wrote several biographies and popular romances.

1 A novel is a mirror walking along a main road.
Le Rouge et le noir, Ch. 49

2 Romanticism is the art of presenting people with the literary works which are capable of affording them the greatest possible pleasure, in the present state of their customs and beliefs. Classicism, on the other hand, presents them with the literature that gave the greatest possible pleasure to their great-grandfathers.
Racine et Shakespeare, Ch. 3

Stephens, James (1882–1950) Irish novelist and poet. His novel *The Crock of Gold* (1912) was adapted as the musical *Finian's Rainbow*.

1 Finality is death. Perfection is finality. Nothing is perfect. There are lumps in it.
The Crock of Gold

2 Curiosity will conquer fear even more than bravery will.
The Crock of Gold

3 Men come of age at sixty, women at fifteen.
The Observer, 'Sayings of the Week', 1 Oct 1944

Stern, Richard G. (1928–) US writer. His books include *Golk* (1960) and *In Any Case* (1962).

1 Anybody can shock a baby, or a television audience. But it's too easy, and the effect is disproportionate to the effort.
Golk, Ch. 4

Sterne, Laurence (1713–68) Irish-born British writer and clergyman. *Tristram Shandy* (1759) established his reputation and was followed by *A Sentimental Journey* (1768). He also published books of sermons.

1 He gave a deep sigh – I saw the iron enter into his soul!
A Sentimental Journey, 'The Captive. Paris'

2 They are a loyal, a gallant, a generous, an ingenious, and good-temper'd people as is under heaven – if they have a fault, they are too *serious*.
Referring to the French
A Sentimental Journey, 'The Character. Versailles'

3 I am positive I have a soul; nor can all the books with which materialists have pestered the world ever convince me of the contrary.
A Sentimental Journey, 'Maria, Moulines'

4 I wish either my father or my mother, or indeed both of them, as they were in duty both equally bound to it, had minded what they were about when they begot me.
Tristram Shandy

5 So long as a man rides his hobby-horse peaceably and quietly along the king's highway, and neither compels you or me to get up behind him, – pray, Sir, what have either you or I to do with it?
Tristram Shandy

6 'Tis known by the name of perseverance in a good cause, – and of obstinacy in a bad one.
Tristram Shandy

7 Writing, when properly managed, (as you may be sure I think mine is) is but a different name for conversation.
Tristram Shandy

8 Whenever a man talks loudly against religion, – always suspect that it is not his reason, but his passions which have got the better of his creed.
Tristram Shandy

9 A man should know something of his own country, too, before he goes abroad.
Tristram Shandy

10 An ounce of a man's own wit is worth a ton of other people's.
Tristram Shandy

Stevenson, Adlai E(wing) (1900–65) US statesman. Governor of Illinois (1949–53), he twice stood unsuccessfully for the presidency (1952; 1956) as Democratic candidate.

1 An editor is one who separates the wheat from the chaff and prints the chaff.
The Stevenson Wit

2 A politician is a statesman who approaches every question with an open mouth.
Also attrib. to Arthur Goldberg
The Fine Art of Political Wit (L. Harris)

3 Power corrupts, but lack of power corrupts absolutely.
The Observer, Jan 1963

4 Let's talk sense to the American people. Let's tell them the truth, that there are no gains without pains.
Speech, Chicago, 26 July 1952

5 There is no evil in the atom; only in men's souls.
Speech, Hartford, Connecticut, 18 Sept 1952

6 My definition of a free society is a society where it is safe to be unpopular.
Speech, Detroit, Oct 1952

7 He said that he was too old to cry, but it hurt too much to laugh.

Said after losing an election, quoting a story told by Abraham Lincoln
Speech, 5 Nov 1952

8 She would rather light candles than curse the darkness, and her glow has warmed the world.

Referring to Eleanor Roosevelt
Address, United Nations General Assembly, 9 Nov 1962

Stevenson, Robert Louis (1850–94) Scottish writer. His books include *Treasure Island* (1883), *Kidnapped* (1886), and *The Strange Case of Dr Jekyll and Mr Hyde* (1886).

Quotations about Stevenson

1 Stevenson seemed to pick the right word up on the point of his pen, like a man playing spillikins.

G. K. Chesterton (1874–1936) British writer. *The Victorian Age in Literature*

2 I think of Mr Stevenson as a consumptive youth weaving garlands of sad flowers with pale, weak hands.

George Moore (1852–1933) Irish writer and art critic. *Confessions of a Young Man*

Quotations by Stevenson

3 If your morals make you dreary, depend upon it, they are wrong.

Across the Plains

4 Politics is perhaps the only profession for which no preparation is thought necessary.

Familiar Studies of Men and Books, 'Yoshida-Torajiro'

5 Vanity dies hard; in some obstinate cases it outlives the man.

Prince Otto

6 Wealth I ask not; hope nor love,
Nor a friend to know me;
All I seek, the heaven above
And the road below me.

Songs of Travel, 'The Vagabond'

7 For my part, I travel not to go anywhere, but to go. I travel for travel's sake. The great affair is to move.

Travels with a Donkey, 'Cheylard and Luc'

8 Fifteen men on the dead man's chest
Yo-ho-ho, and a bottle of rum!
Drink and the devil had done for the rest –
Yo-ho-ho, and a bottle of rum!

Treasure Island, Ch. 1

9 Pieces of eight!

Treasure Island, Ch. 10

10 Many's the long night I've dreamed of cheese – toasted, mostly.

Treasure Island, Ch. 15

11 Of all my verse, like not a single line;
But like my title, for it is not mine.
That title from a better man I stole;
Ah, how much better, had I stol'n the whole!

Underwoods, Foreword

12 Under the wide and starry sky
Dig the grave and let me lie.
Glad did I live and gladly die,
 – And I laid me down with a will.
This is the verse you grave for me:
'Here he lies where he longed to be;
Home is the sailor, home from sea,
 And the hunter home from the hill.'

Underwoods, Bk. I, 'Requiem'

13 Even if we take matrimony at its lowest, even if we regard it as no more than a sort of friendship recognized by the police.

Virginibus Puerisque

14 Man is a creature who lives not upon bread alone, but principally by catchwords; and the little rift between the sexes is astonishingly widened by simply teaching one set of catchwords to the girls and another to the boys.

Virginibus Puerisque

15 The cruellest lies are often told in silence.

Virginibus Puerisque

16 When the torrent sweeps a man against a boulder, you must expect him to scream, and you need not be surprised if the scream is sometimes a theory.

Virginibus Puerisque

17 Old and young, we are all on our last cruise.

Virginibus Puerisque

18 Books are good enough in their own way, but they are a mighty bloodless substitute for life.

Virginibus Puerisque

19 Extreme *busyness*, whether at school or college, kirk or market, is a symptom of deficient vitality.

Virginibus Puerisque

20 There is no duty we so much underrate as the duty of being happy.

Virginibus Puerisque

21 Give me the young man who has brains enough to make a fool of himself!

Virginibus Puerisque

22 Lastly (and this is, perhaps, the golden rule), no woman should marry a teetotaller, or a man who does not smoke.

Virginibus Puerisque

23 Marriage is a step so grave and decisive that it attracts light-headed, variable men by its very awfulness.

Virginibus Puerisque

24 In marriage, a man becomes slack and selfish and undergoes a fatty degeneration of his moral being.

Virginibus Puerisque

25 Marriage is like life in this – that it is a field of battle, and not a bed of roses.

Virginibus Puerisque

26 To travel hopefully is a better thing than to arrive, and the true success is to labour.

Virginibus Puerisque

27 It's deadly commonplace, but, after all, the commonplaces are the great poetic truths.

Weir of Hermiston, Ch. 6

Stocks, Mary, Baroness (1891–1975) British politician, writer, and broadcaster. She was noted for her concern with the social aspects of economic policy.

1 It is clearly absurd that it should be possible for a woman to qualify as a saint with direct access to the Almighty while she may not qualify as a curate.

Still More Commonplace

2 The House of Lords is a perfect eventide home.

The Observer, 'Sayings of the Week', 4 Oct 1970

Stockwood, Mervyn (Arthur) (1913–) British churchman, Bishop of Southwark (1959–80). He is noted for his outspokenness on both moral and political issues.

1 A psychiatrist is a man who goes to the Folies-Bergère and looks at the audience.

The Observer, 'Sayings of the Week', 15 Oct 1961

Stoddard, Elizabeth Drew (Barstow) (1823–1902) US novelist and poet.

1 A woman despises a man for loving her, unless she returns his love.

Two Men, Ch. 32

Stoker, Bram (Abraham Stoker; 1847–1912) Irish author. He is mainly remembered for his gothic horror story *Dracula* (1897), subsequently made into many films.

1 The mouth . . . was fixed and rather cruel-looking, with peculiarly sharp white teeth; these protruded over the lips, whose remarkable ruddiness showed astonishing vitality in a man of his years.

Referring to Count Dracula
Dracula, Ch. 2

2 His eyes flamed red with devilish passion; the great nostrils of the white aquiline nose opened wide and quivered at the edges; and the white sharp teeth, behind the full lips of the blood-dripping mouth; champed together like those of a wild beast. . . . Further and further back he cowered, as we, lifting our crucifixes, advanced.

Dracula, Ch. 21

Stone, I(sidor) F(einstein) (1907–89) US writer and publisher, noted for his left wing views. As publisher of *I. F. Stone's Weekly* (1953–71) he condemned McCarthyism, the war in Vietnam, and racism.

1 If you live long enough, the venerability factor creeps in; you get accused of things you never did and praised for virtues you never had.

Peter's Quotations (Laurence J. Peter)

Stone, Samuel. J. (1839–1901) US hymn writer.

1 The Church's one foundation
Is Jesus Christ her Lord;
She is His new creation
By water and the Word.

Hymn

Stopes, Marie Charlotte Carmichael (1880–1958) British campaigner for birth control. She opened the first birth control clinic in Holloway in 1921; her books include *Married Love* (1918), *Wise Parenthood* (1918) and *Contraception: Its Theory, History and Practice* (1923).

Quotations about Stopes

1 A fascinating combination of scientist and would-be poet, of mystic and crank, of propagandist and neurotic, Marie Stopes splendidly embraced the challenge of society and set up her first birth-control clinic in London in 1921, but she completely failed to write a poem of any consequence.

Keith Briant *Marie Stopes*

2 Her frontal attacks on old taboos, her quasi-prophetic tone, her flowery fervour, aroused strong opposition from those who disagreed with her for religious reasons or felt that she had overstepped the bounds of good taste.

The Daily Telegraph, Obituary, 3 Oct 1958

3 Dr Marie Stopes made contraceptive devices respectable in a somewhat gushing book, *Married Love*. For this she deserves to be remembered among the great benefactors of the age.

A.J.P. Taylor (1906–90) British historian. *English History 1914–45*

Quotations by Stopes

4 An impersonal and scientific knowledge of the structure of our bodies is the surest safeguard against prurient curiosity and lascivious gloating.

Married Love, Ch. 5

5 . . . each coming together of man and wife, even if they have been mated for many years, should be a fresh adventure; each winning should necessitate a fresh wooing.

Married Love, Ch. 10

6 We are not much in sympathy with the typical hustling American business man, but we have often felt compunction for him, seeing him nervous and harassed, sleeplessly, anxiously hunting dollars and all but overshadowed by his overdressed, extravagant and idle wife, who sometimes insists that her spiritual development necessitates that she shall have no children . . . Yet such wives imagine that they are upholding women's emancipation.
The Fighting Pankhursts (David Mitchell)

Stoppard, Tom (1937–) Czech-born British dramatist. He achieved notice with his play *Rosencrantz and Guildenstern Are Dead* (1967), subsequently building on this success with *Jumpers* (1972), *Travesties* (1975), *Night and Day* (1978), *The Real Thing* (1983), and *Hapgood* (1988).

1 Skill without imagination is craftsmanship and gives us many useful objects such as wickerwork picnic baskets. Imagination without skill gives us modern art.
Artist Descending a Staircase

2 This is a British murder inquiry and some degree of justice must be seen to be more or less done.
Jumpers, II

3 Socialists treat their servants with respect and then wonder why they vote Conservative.
Lord Malquist and Mr Moon, Pt. V, Ch. 1

4 The House of Lords, an illusion to which I have never been able to subscribe – responsibility without power, the prerogative of the eunuch throughout the ages.
See Lord ACTON
Lord Malquist and Mr Moon, Pt. VI, Ch. 1

5 He's someone who flies around from hotel to hotel and thinks the most interesting thing about any story is the fact that he has arrived to cover it.
Referring to foreign correspondents
Night and Day, I

6 The media. It sounds like a convention of spiritualists.
Night and Day, I

7 MILNE. No matter how imperfect things are, if you've got a free press everything is correctable, and without it everything is conceivable. RUTH. I'm with you on the free press. It's the newspapers I can't stand.
Night and Day, I

8 Eternity's a terrible thought. I mean, where's it going to end?
Rosencrantz and Guildenstern Are Dead, II

9 The bad end unhappily, the good unluckily. That is what tragedy means.
Rosencrantz and Guildenstern Are Dead, II

10 Life is a gamble, at terrible odds – if it was a bet, you wouldn't take it.
Rosencrantz and Guildenstern Are Dead, III

11 What is an artist? For every thousand people there's nine hundred doing the work, ninety doing well, nine doing good, and one lucky bastard who's the artist.
Travesties, I

12 It's better to be quotable than to be honest.
The Guardian

13 I doubt that art needed Ruskin any more than a moving train needs one of its passengers to shove it.
The Times Literary Supplement, 3 June 1977

Stout, Rex Todhunter (1886–1975) US writer of detective stories, including *Death of a Doxy* and *Three Witnesses*, in which the detective was Nero Wolfe.

1 There are two kinds of statistics, the kind you look up and the kind you make up.
Death of a Doxy, Ch. 9

2 I like to walk around Manhattan, catching glimpses of its wild life, the pigeons and cats and girls.
Three Witnesses, 'When a Man Murders'

Stowe, Harriet Beecher (1811–96) US novelist. She achieved fame with *Uncle Tom's Cabin* (1852), which greatly helped the antislavery lobby. Her other books include *The Minister's Wooing* (1859) and *Oldtown Folks* (1864). Her article accusing Lord Byron of incest with his sister caused great controversy.

1 The bitterest tears shed over graves are for words left unsaid and deeds left undone.
Little Foxes, Ch. 3

2 'Do you know who made you?' 'Nobody, as I knows on,' said the child, with a short laugh . . . 'I 'spect I grow'd.'
Uncle Tom's Cabin, Ch. 20

3 Whipping and abuse are like laudanum: You have to double the dose as the sensibilities decline.
Uncle Tom's Cabin, Ch. 20

4 I did not write it. God wrote it. I merely did his dictation.
Referring to *Uncle Tom's Cabin*
Attrib.

Stowell, William Scott, Baron (1745–1836) *See* Scott, William.

Strachey, (Evelyn) John St Loe (1901–63) British politician and Labour theorist. He became minister of food in Attlee's post-war government. His books include *The Menace of Fascism* (1933) and *The Economics of Progress* (1939).

1 Becoming an Anglo-Catholic must surely be a sad business – rather like becoming an amateur conjurer.
The Coming Struggle for Power, Pt. III, Ch. 11

2 Fascism means war.
Slogan, 1930s

Strachey, (Giles) Lytton (1880–1932) British writer. A member of the Bloomsbury group, he wrote biographies of Queen Victoria, Elizabeth I, and others, as well as a perceptive volume, *Eminent Victorians* (1918).

1 Yet her conception of God was certainly not orthodox. She felt towards Him as she might have felt towards a glorified sanitary engineer; and in some of her speculations she seems hardly to distinguish between the Deity and the Drains.
Eminent Victorians, 'Florence Nightingale'

2 It should not merely be useful and ornamental; it should preach a high moral lesson.
Referring to Prince Albert's plans for the Great Exhibition
Queen Victoria, Ch. 4

3 Albert was merely a young foreigner, who suffered from having no vices, and whose only claim to distinction was that he had happened to marry the Queen of England.
Queen Victoria, Ch. 5

4 If this is dying, I don't think much of it.
Last words
Lytton Strachey (Michael Holroyd), Pt. V, Ch. 17

Stratton, Eugene (1861–1918) British music-hall singer.

1 I know she likes me,
'Cause she says so.
The Lily of Laguna

2 Little Dolly Daydream, pride of Idaho.
Little Dolly Daydream

Stravinsky, Igor (1882–1971) Russian-born US composer. His early ballet scores, commissioned by Diaghilev, include *The Firebird* (1910), *Petrushka* (1911), and *The Rite of Spring* (1913). His later work includes a piano concerto (1924), the oratorio *Oedipus Rex* (1927) and the opera *The Rake's Progress* (1951).

1 Rachmaninov's immortalizing totality was his scowl. He was a six-and-a-half-foot-tall scowl.
Conversations with Igor Stravinsky (Igor Stravinsky and Robert Craft)

2 He was the only pianist I have ever seen who did not grimace. That is a great deal.
Referring to Rachmaninov
Conversations with Igor Stravinsky (Igor Stravinsky and Robert Craft)

3 I had another dream the other day about music critics. They were small and rodent-like with padlocked ears, as if they had stepped out of a painting by Goya.
The Evening Standard, 29 Oct 1969

4 My music is best understood by children and animals.
The Observer, 'Sayings of the Week', 8 Oct 1961

5 A good composer does not imitate; he steals.
Twentieth Century Music (Peter Yates)

6 I don't write modern music. I only write good music.
To journalists on his first visit to America, 1925

7 Hurry! I never hurry. I have no time to hurry.
Responding to his publisher's request that he hurry his completion of a composition
Attrib.

Streatfield, Sir Geoffrey Hugh Benbow (1897–1978) British lawyer. During World War II he became Assistant Judge Advocate-General and later a high-court judge.

1 Facts speak louder than statistics.
The Observer, 'Sayings of the Week', 19 Mar 1950

Strindberg, August (1849–1912) Swedish dramatist. His plays include *The Father* (1887), *The Dance of Death* (1900), and *The Ghost Sonata* (1907).

1 I loathe people who keep dogs. They are cowards who haven't got the guts to bite people themselves.
A Madman's Diary

Strunsky, Simeon (1879–1948) Russian-born US editor and essayist. His books include *The Patient Observer* (1911) and *No Mean City* (1917).

1 Famous remarks are seldom quoted correctly.
No Mean City

Sullivan, Annie (1866–1936) US teacher of the handicapped; her most famous pupil was Helen Keller.

1 It's queer how ready people always are with advice in any real or imaginary emergency, and no matter how many times experience has shown them to be wrong, they continue to set forth their opinions, as if they had received them from the Almighty!
Letter, 12 June 1887

2 She likes stories that make her cry – I think we all do, it's so nice to feel sad when you've nothing particular to be sad about.
Referring to Helen Keller
Letter, 12 Dec 1887

3 Language grows out of life, out of its needs and experiences . . . *Language* and *knowledge* are indissolubly connected; they are interdependent. Good work in language presupposes and depends on a real knowledge of things.
Speech, American Association to Promote the Teaching of Speech to the Deaf, July 1894

Sully, Maximilien de Béthune, Duc de (1560–1641) French statesman. Henry IV's chief minister, he retired after Henry's assassination.

1 The English take their pleasures sadly after the fashion of their country.
Memoirs

Svevo, Italo (Ettore Schmitz; 1861–1928) Italian writer. His novels include *Una Vita* (1883), *Senilità* (1898), and *La Coscienza di Zeno* (1923).

1 The really original woman is the one who first imitates a man.
A Life, Ch. 8

Swaffer, Hannen (1879–1962) British journalist.

1 Freedom of the press in Britain is freedom to print such of the proprietor's prejudices as the advertisers don't object to.
Attrib.

Swift, Jonathan (1667–1745) Irish-born Anglican priest who became a poet and satirist in London. He is remembered for his *Journal to Stella* (1710–13) and *A Tale of A Tub* (1704), but best of all for *Gulliver's Travels* (1726), written after his return to Dublin as dean of St Patrick's.

Quotations about Swift

1 He delivered Ireland from plunder and oppression; and showed that wit, confederated with truth, had such force as authority was unable to resist.
Samuel Johnson (1709–84) British lexicographer. Attrib.

2 A monster gibbering, shrieking and gnashing imprecations against mankind.
William Makepeace Thackeray (1811–63) British novelist. Attrib.

Quotations by Swift

3 Satire is a sort of glass, wherein beholders do generally discover everybody's face but their own.
The Battle of the Books, 'Preface'

4 'Tis an old maxim in the schools,
That flattery's the food of fools;
Yet now and then your men of wit
Will condescend to take a bit.
Cadenus and Vanessa

5 It is folly of too many to mistake the echo of a London coffee-house for the voice of the kingdom.
The Conduct of the Allies

6 I have heard of a man who had a mind to sell his house, and therefore carried a piece of brick in his pocket, which he shewed as a pattern to encourage purchasers.
The Drapier's Letters, 2 (4 Aug 1724)

7 I cannot but conclude the bulk of your natives to be the most pernicious race of little odious vermin that nature ever suffered to crawl upon the surface of the earth.
Referring to the English
Gulliver's Travels, 'Voyage to Brobdingnag', Ch. 6

8 Whoever could make two ears of corn or two blades of grass to grow upon a spot of ground where only one grew before would deserve better of mankind and do more essential service to his country than the whole race of politicians put together.
Gulliver's Travels, 'Voyage to Brobdingnag', Ch. 7

9 So, naturalist observe, a flea
Hath smaller fleas that on him prey,
And these have smaller fleas to bite 'em.
And so proceed *ad infinitum*.
On Poetry

10 Promises and pie-crust are made to be broken.
Polite Conversation, Dialogue 1

11 Bachelor's fare; bread and cheese, and kisses.
Polite Conversation, Dialogue 1

12 He was a bold man that first eat an oyster.
Polite Conversation, Dialogue 2

13 I never saw, heard, nor read, that the clergy were beloved in any nation where Christianity was the religion of the country. Nothing can render them popular, but some degree of persecution.
Thoughts on Religion

14 When a true genius appears in the world, you may know him by this sign, that the dunces are all in confederacy against him.
Thoughts on Various Subjects

15 What they do in heaven we are ignorant of; what they do *not* we are told expressly, that they neither marry, nor are given in marriage.
Thoughts on Various Subjects

16 I never wonder to see men wicked, but I often wonder to see them not ashamed.
Thoughts on Various Subjects

17 Most sorts of diversion in men, children, and other animals, are an imitation of fighting.
Thoughts on Various Subjects

18 Laws are like cobwebs, which may catch small flies, but let wasps and hornets break through.
Similar remarks have been made by others; *see* SHENSTONE; SOLON
A Tritical Essay upon the Faculties of the Mind

19 For God's sake, madam, don't say that in England for if you do, they will surely tax it.
Responding to Lady Carteret's admiration for the quality of the air in Ireland
Lives of the Wits (H. Pearson)

20 I shall be like that tree; I shall die from the top.
Predicting his own mental decline on seeing a tree with a withered crown
Lives of the Wits (H. Pearson)

21 If Heaven had looked upon riches to be a valuable thing, it would not have given them to such a scoundrel.
Letter to Miss Vanhomrigh, 12–13 Aug 1720

22 Ah, a German and a genius! a prodigy, admit him!
Learning of the arrival of Handel: Swift's last words
Attrib.

Swinburne, Algernon Charles (1837–1909) British poet. He made his name with *Poems and Ballads* (1866). Later works included *A Song of Italy* (1867), *Erechteus* (1876), and *Tristam of Lyonesse* (1882).

1 When the hounds of spring are on winter's
   traces,
   The mother of months in meadow or plain
   Fills the shadows and windy places
   With lisp of leaves and ripple of rain . . .
   Atlanta in Calydon

2 Here, where the world is quiet;
   Here, where all trouble seems
   Dead winds' and spent waves' riot
   In doubtful dreams of dreams.
   The Garden of Proserpine

3 Glory to Man in the highest! for Man is the
   master of things.
   Hymn of Man

Symonds, John Addington (1840–93) British art
historian. His major work was the seven-volume *Renaissance in
Italy* (1875–86). He also wrote poetry and literary biography.

1 These things shall be! A loftier race
   Than e'er the world hath known shall rise,
   With flame of freedom in their souls,
   And light of knowledge in their eyes.
   Hymn

Symons, Arthur (William) (1865–1945) British poet. His
works include *Days and Nights* (1889), *Amoris Victima* (1897), the
influential *The Symbolist Movement in Literature* (1899), and other
volumes of verse and criticism.

1 As a perfume doth remain
   In the folds where it hath lain,
   So the thought of you, remaining
   Deeply folded in my brain,
   Will not leave me: all things leave me:
   You remain.
   Memory

Synge, John Millington (1871–1909) Anglo-Irish
dramatist. His plays include *The Shadow of the Glen* (1903), *Riders
to the Sea* (1904), *The Playboy of the Western World* (1907), and
Deirdre of the Sorrows (1910).

1 I've lost the only playboy of the western world.
   The closing words
   The Playboy of the Western World, III

Syrus, Publilius (1st century BC) Roman dramatist. He was
the author of several mime plays and an anthology of stoic maxims.

1 They live ill who expect to live always.
   Moral Sayings, 457

2 The madman thinks the rest of the world crazy.
   Moral Sayings, 386

3 Pain of mind is worse than pain of body.
   Sententiae

4 He gives twice who gives promptly.
   Attrib.

5 Necessity knows no law.
   Attrib.

Szasz, Thomas (1920–) US psychiatrist and writer. His
writings include *Pain and Pleasure* (1957) and *The Second Sin*
(1974).

1 Men are rewarded and punished not for what
   they do, but rather for how their acts are defined. This is why men are more interested in
   better justifying themselves than in better behaving themselves.
   The Second Sin

2 Traditionally, sex has been a very private, secretive activity. Herein perhaps lies its powerful
   force for uniting people in a strong bond. As
   we make sex less secretive, we may rob it of
   its power to hold men and women together.
   The Second Sin

3 Formerly, when religion was strong and science
   weak, men mistook magic for medicine, now,
   when science is strong and religion weak, men
   mistake medicine for magic.
   The Second Sin

4 A child becomes an adult when he realizes that
   he has a right not only to be right but also to
   be wrong.
   The Second Sin

5 Happiness is an imaginary condition, formerly often attributed by the living to the dead, now
   usually attributed by adults to children, and by
   children to adults.
   The Second Sin

6 The stupid neither forgive nor forget; the naive
   forgive and forget; the wise forgive but do not
   forget.
   The Second Sin

7 Psychiatrists classify a person as neurotic if he
   suffers from his problems in living, and a
   psychotic if he makes others suffer.
   The Second Sin

8 If you talk to God, you are praying; if God talks
   to you, you have schizophrenia. If the dead talk
   to you, you are a spiritualist; if God talks to
   you, you are a schizophrenic.
   The Second Sin

9 Masturbation: the primary sexual activity of
   mankind. In the nineteenth century it was a disease; in the twentieth, it's a cure.
   The Second Sin

Szent-Györgyi, Albert (1893–1986) Hungarian-born US
biochemist. He discovered the role of vitamin C and interpreted in
biochemical terms the method by which muscles contract.

1 Discovery consists of seeing what everybody has
   seen and thinking what nobody has thought.
   The Scientist Speculates (I. J. Good)

T

Taber, Robert (20th century) US writer. A merchant seaman (1942–45), he was the only American among Castro's defending forces at Playa Giron.

1 The guerrilla fights the war of the flea, and his military enemy suffers the dog's disadvantages: too much to defend; too small, ubiquitous, and agile an enemy to come to grips with.
The War of the Flea, Ch. 2

Tabrar, Joseph (20th century) US songwriter.

1 Daddy wouldn't buy me a bow-wow, bow-wow.
I've got a little cat
And I'm very fond of that.
Daddy Wouldn't Buy Me A Bow-wow (song)

Tacitus, Cornelius (c. 55–c. 120 AD) Roman historian. He became governor of Asia (112–13 AD). His major works were the *Histories* and the *Annals*, surveying Roman history in the periods 69–96 AD and 14–68 AD, respectively.

1 They make a wilderness and call it peace.
Agricola, 30

2 It is part of human nature to hate the man you have hurt.
Agricola, 42

3 Love of fame is the last thing even learned men can bear to be parted from.
Histories, IV, 6

Taft, William Howard (1857–1930) US statesman. He became president (1909–13), having been a judge and the secretary of war (1904–08). After his defeat for a second term as president he became professor of law at Yale.

1 Well, I have one consolation, No candidate was ever elected ex-president by such a large majority!
Referring to his disastrous defeat in the 1912 presidential election
Attrib.

Taine, Hippolyte Adolphe (1828–93) French writer and philosopher. His works include *Essais de critique et d'histoire* (1855), *Idéalisme anglais* (1864), and *De l'intelligence* (1870).

1 Vice and virtues are products like sulphuric acid and sugar.
Histoire de la littérature anglaise, Introduction

Talleyrand (Charles Maurice de Talleyrand-Périgord; 1754–1838) French politician. During the French Revolution he attempted to reform the church, but was excommunicated by the pope. He was foreign minister (1797–1807) and ambassador to Britain (1830–34).

1 I found there a country with thirty-two religions and only one sauce.
Referring to America
Autant en apportent les mots (Pedrazzini)

2 Accidentally.
Replying, during the reign of Louis Philippe, to the query 'How do you think this government will end?'
The Wheat and the Chaff (F. Mitterrand)

3 It is the beginning of the end.
Referring to Napoleon's defeat at Borodino, 1813
Attrib.

4 Speech was given to man to disguise his thoughts.
Attrib.

5 Not too much zeal.
Attrib.

6 War is much too serious a thing to be left to military men.
Attrib.

7 Mistrust first impulses; they are nearly always good.
Sometimes attrib. to Count Montrond
Attrib.

8 Well, you might try getting crucified and rising again on the third day.
Giving his opinion upon what action might impress the French peasantry
Attrib.

Tarkington, Booth (1869–1946) US novelist. His books, many of which were made into films, include *Monsieur Beaucaire* (1900), *Penrod* (1914), *The Magnificent Ambersons* (1918), and *Alice Adams* (1921).

1 Mystics always hope that science will some day overtake them.
Looking Forward to the Great Adventure

2 There are two things that will be believed of any man whatsoever, and one of them is that he has taken to drink.
Penrod, Ch. 10

Tate, Allen (1899–1979) US poet and critic. His collected poems were published in 1978, including 'Ode to the Confederate Dead' (1926). He also wrote a novel, *The Fathers* (1938).

1 Row upon row with strict impunity
The headstones yield their names to the element.
Ode to the Confederate Dead

Tate, Nahum (1652–1715) Irish-born English poet and dramatist. His plays were mostly adaptations of Shakespeare. With Nicholas Brady (1659–1726) he wrote the *New Version of the Psalms of David* (1696). He was poet laureate from 1692.

1 As pants the hart for cooling streams
When heated in the chase.
New Version of the Psalms, 'As Pants the Hart'

2 Through all the changing scenes of life.
New Version of the Psalms, 'Through all the Changing'

3 While shepherds watch'd their flocks by night,
All seated on the ground,
The Angel of the Lord came down,
And Glory shone around.

Supplement to the New Version of the Psalms, 'While Shepherds Watched'

Taupin, Bernie (1950–) British songwriter. His musical partnership with Elton John began in 1967. His solo album *Taupin* was released in 1971.

1 Goodbye Norma Jean
Though I never knew you at all
You had the grace to hold yourself
While those around you crawled.
They crawled out of the woodwork
And they whispered into your brain
Set you on the treadmill
And made you change your name.

Lyrics for a song by Elton John
Candle in the Wind (song)

Tawney, R(ichard) H(enry) (1880–1962) British economist and historian. His best-known books were *The Acquisitive Society* (1921) and *Religion and the Rise of Capitalism* (1926).

1 As long as men are men, a poor society cannot be too poor to find a right order of life, nor a rich society too rich to have need to seek it.

The Acquisitive Society

Taylor, A(lan) J(ohn) P(ercivale) (1906–90) British historian. His best-known book is *The Origins of the Second World War* (1961).

1 History gets thicker as it approaches recent times.

English History, 1914–1945, Bibliography

2 He aspired to power instead of influence, and as a result forfeited both.

Referring to Lord Northcliffe
English History, 1914–1945, Ch. 1

3 Communism continued to haunt Europe as a spectre – a name men gave to their own fears and blunders. But the crusade against Communism was even more imaginary than the spectre of Communism.

The Origins of the Second World War, Ch. 2

4 Lenin was the first to discover that capitalism 'inevitably' caused war; and he discovered this only when the First World War was already being fought. Of course he was right. Since every great state was capitalist in 1914, capitalism obviously 'caused' the First World War; but just as obviously it had 'caused' the previous generation of Peace.

The Origins of the Second World War, Ch. 6

5 A racing tipster who only reached Hitler's level of accuracy would not do well for his clients.

The Origins of the Second World War, Ch. 7

6 Psychoanalysts believe that the only 'normal' people are those who cause no trouble either to themselves or anyone else.

The Trouble Makers

7 He was what I often think is a dangerous thing for a statesman to be – a student of history; and like most of those who study history, he learned from the mistakes of the past how to make new ones.

Referring to Napoleon III
The Listener, 6 June 1963

8 They say that men become attached even to Widnes.

The Observer, 15 Sept 1963

Taylor, Bert Leston (1866–1921) US journalist. He was a regular columnist in the Chicago *Daily Tribune*.

1 A bore is a man who, when you ask him how he is, tells you.

Attrib.

Taylor, Elizabeth (1912–75) British writer. Her books include the novels *A View of the Harbour* (1949), *A Wreath of Roses* (1950), and *The Devastating Boys* (1972).

1 She shrank from words, thinking of the scars they leave, which she would be left to tend when he had gone. If he spoke the truth, she could not bear it; if he tried to muffle it with tenderness, she would look upon it as pity.

The Blush

2 It is very strange . . . that the years teach us patience; that the shorter our time, the greater our capacity for waiting.

A Wreath of Roses, Ch. 10

Taylor, Jane (1783–1824) British writer, who, with her sister Ann Taylor, wrote *Original Poems for Infant Minds* and *Rhymes for the Nursery* (1806).

1 Twinkle, twinkle, little star,
How I wonder what you are!
Up above the world so high,
Like a diamond in the sky!

Rhymes for the Nursery (with Ann Taylor), 'The Star'

Taylor, Jeremy (1613–67) English Anglican theologian, who became Bishop of Down and Connor at the Restoration. He wrote *The Rule and Exercise of Holy Dying* (1651) and *The Rule of Conscience* (1660).

1 As our life is very short, so it is very miserable, and therefore it is well it is short.

The Rule and Exercise of Holy Dying, Ch. 1

2 He that loves not his wife and children, feeds a lioness at home and broods a nest of sorrows.

Sermons, 'Married Love'

Taylor, John (20th century) The editor of the *Tailor and Cutter*.

1 The only man who really needs a tail coat is a man with a hole in his trousers.
The Observer, 'Shouts and Murmurs'

Tebbitt, Norman (Beresford) (1931–) British Conservative politician noted for his abrasive debating style. He was secretary of state for employment (1981–83), trade and industry secretary (1983–85), and chairman of the Conservative Party (1985–87).

1 My father did not wait around . . . he got on his bike and went out looking for work.
Speech

2 I hope Mrs Thatcher will go until the turn of the century looking like Queen Victoria.
The Observer, 'Sayings of the Week', 17 May 1987

Teilhard de Chardin, Pierre (1881–1955) French Jesuit and palaeontologist. His books, which were suppressed by the Catholic Church during his lifetime, included *The Phenomenon of Man* (1955) and *Le Milieu divin* (1957).

1 From an evolutionary point of view, man has stopped moving, if he ever did move.
The Phenomenon of Man, Postscript

Temple, Frederick (1821–1902) British churchman. He became headmaster of Rugby (1857–69), Bishop of London (1885–96), and Archbishop of Canterbury (1896–1902).

1 'My aunt was suddenly prevented from going a voyage in a ship what went down –
would you call that a case of Providential interference?'
'Can't tell: didn't know your aunt.'
Memoirs of Archbishop Temple (Sandford), Vol. II

2 There is a certain class of clergyman whose mendicity is only equalled by their mendacity.
Remark at a meeting of the Ecclesiastical Commissioners
Years of Endeavour (Sir George Leveson Gower)

Temple, William (1881–1944) British churchman. Son of Frederick Temple, he too was a headmaster (of Repton; 1910–14), who became Archbishop of Canterbury (1942–44). He wrote *Nature, Man, and God* (1934).

1 Christianity is the most materialistic of all great religions.
Reading in St John's Gospel, Vol. I, Introduction

2 It is a mistake to assume that God is interested only, or even chiefly, in religion.
Concise Dictionary of Religious Quotations (W. Neil)

3 'Are you not,' a Rugby master had asked him in discussing one of his essays, 'a little out of your depth here?' 'Perhaps, Sir,' was the confident reply, 'but I can swim.'
William Temple (F. A. Iremonger)

4 Personally, I have always looked on cricket as organized loafing.
Remark to parents when headmaster of Repton School

5 It is not the ape, nor the tiger in man that I fear, it is the donkey.
Attrib.

6 The Church exists for the sake of those outside it.
Attrib.

7 I believe in the Church, One Holy, Catholic and Apostolic, and I regret that it nowhere exists.
Attrib.

Tenniel, Sir John (1820–1914) British illustrator and cartoonist. He is best known for his illustrations for *Alice in Wonderland* (1865). He worked on *Punch* from 1851 to 1901.

1 Dropping the pilot.
Caption of a cartoon. The cartoon refers to Bismarck's resignation portraying him as a ship's pilot walking down the gangway of the ship while Wilhelm II watches from the deck.
Punch, 29 Mar 1890

Tennyson, Alfred, Baron (1809–92) British poet. He established his reputation with *Morte d'Arthur* (1842). Of his many other works, *In Memoriam* (1850), *The Charge of the Light Brigade* (1854), *Maud* (1855), and *The Idylls of the King* (1859) are outstanding. He became poet laureate in 1850.

Quotations about Tennyson

1 . . . there was little about melancholia that he didn't know; there was little else that he did.
W. H. Auden (1907–73) British poet. *Selected Poems of Tennyson*, Introduction

2 Let school-miss Alfred vent her chaste delight
On 'darling little rooms so warm and bright.'
Edward Bulwer-Lytton (1803–73) British novelist and politician. Attrib.

3 Alfred is always carrying a bit of chaos round with him, and turning it into cosmos.
Thomas Carlyle (1795–1881) Scottish historian and essayist.

4 Tennyson was not Tennysonian.
Henry James (1843–1916) US novelist. *The Middle Years*

Quotations by Tennyson

5 And the stately ships go on
To their haven under the hill;
But O for the touch of a vanish'd hand,
And the sound of a voice that is still!
Break, Break, Break

6 For men may come and men may go
But I go on for ever.
The Brook

7 I come from haunts of coot and hern,
I make a sudden sally
And sparkle out among the fern,
To bicker down a valley.
The Brook

8 Half a league, half a league,
Half a league onward,
All in the valley of Death
Rode the six hundred.
The Charge of the Light Brigade

9 'Forward the Light Brigade!'
Was there a man dismay'd?
Not tho' the soldier knew
Some one had blunder'd:
Their's not to make reply,
Their's not to reason why,
Their's but to do and die:
Into the valley of Death
Rode the six hundred.
The Charge of the Light Brigade

10 Into the jaws of Death,
Into the mouth of Hell.
The Charge of the Light Brigade

11 Come not, when I am dead,
To drop thy foolish tears upon my grave,
To trample round my fallen head,
And vex the unhappy dust thou wouldst not
save.
Come Not, When I Am Dead

12 Sunset and evening star,
And one clear call for me!
And may there be no moaning of the bar
When I put out to sea.
Crossing the Bar

13 God made the woman for the man,
And for the good and increase of the world.
Edwin Morris

14 Half light, half shade,
She stood, a sight to make an old man young.
The Gardener's Daughter

15 That a lie which is all a lie may be met and
fought with outright,
But a lie which is part a truth is a harder matter
to fight.
The Grandmother

16 Dreams are true while they last, and do we not
live in dreams?
The Higher Pantheism

17 His honour rooted in dishonour stood,
And faith unfaithful kept him falsely true.
Idylls of the King, 'Lancelot and Elaine'

18 He makes no friend who never made a foe.
Idylls of the King, 'Lancelot and Elaine'

19 For man is man and master of his fate.
Idylls of the King, 'The Marriage of Geraint'

20 An arm
Rose up from out the bosom of the lake,
Clothed in white samite, mystic, wonderful.
Idylls of the King, 'The Passing of Arthur'

21 Authority forgets a dying king.
Idylls of the King, 'The Passing of Arthur'

22 For now I see the true old times are dead,
When every morning brought a noble chance,
And every chance brought out a noble knight.
Idylls of the King, 'The Passing of Arthur'

23 And slowly answer'd Arthur from the barge:
'The old order changeth, yielding place to new,
And God fulfils himself in many ways.'
Idylls of the King, 'The Passing of Arthur'

24 If thou shouldst never see my face again,
Pray for my soul. More things are wrought by
prayer
Than this world dreams of.
Idylls of the King, 'The Passing of Arthur'

25 I am going a long way
With these thou seest – if indeed I go
(For all my mind is clouded with a doubt) –
To the island-valley of Avilion;
Where falls not hail, or rain, or any snow,
Nor ever wind blows loudly; but it lies
Deep-meadow'd, happy, fair with orchard lawns
And bowery hollows crown'd with summer sea,
Where I will heal me of my grievous wound.
Idylls of the King, 'The Passing of Arthur'

26 Our little systems have their day;
They have their day and cease to be.
In Memoriam A.H.H., Prologue

27 For words, like Nature, half reveal
And half conceal the Soul within.
In Memoriam A.H.H., V

28 I hold it true, whate'er befall;
I feel it, when I sorrow most;
'Tis better to have loved and lost
Than never to have loved at all.
In Memoriam A.H.H., XXVII

29 And so the Word had breath, and wrought
With human hands the creed of creeds
In loveliness of perfect deeds,
More strong than all poetic thought.
In Memoriam A.H.H., XXXVI

30 But what am I?
An infant crying in the night:
An infant crying for the light:
And with no language but a cry.
In Memoriam A.H.H., LIV

31 Are God and Nature then at strife
That Nature lends such evil dreams?
So careful of the type she seems,
So careless of the single life.
In Memoriam A.H.H., LV

32 Sleep, Death's twin-brother, knows not Death,
Nor can I dream of thee as dead.
In Memoriam A.H.H., LXVIII

33 I dreamed there would be Spring no more,
That Nature's ancient power was lost.
In Memoriam A.H.H., LXIX

34 So many worlds, so much to do,
So little done, such things to be.
In Memoriam A.H.H., LXXIII

35 Ring out, wild bells, to the wild sky,
The flying cloud, the frosty light:
The year is dying in the night;
Ring out, wild bells, and let him die.
In Memoriam A.H.H., CVI

36 'Tis held that sorrow makes us wise.
In Memoriam A.H.H., CXIII

37 My regret
Becomes an April violet,
And buds and blossoms like the rest.
In Memoriam A.H.H., CXV

38 One God, one law, one element,
And one far-off divine event,
To which the whole creation moves.
In Memoriam A.H.H., CXXXI

39 A simple maiden in her flower
Is worth a hundred coats-of-arms.
Lady Clara Vere de Vere, II

40 Kind hearts are more than coronets,
And simple faith than Norman blood.
Lady Clara Vere de Vere, VI

41 On either side the river lie
Long fields of barley and of rye,
That clothe the wold and meet the sky;
And thro' the field the road runs by
To many-tower'd Camelot.
The Lady of Shalott, Pt. I

42 Willows whiten, aspens quiver,
Little breezes dusk and shiver.
The Lady of Shalott, Pt. I

43 Or when the moon was overhead,
Came two young lovers lately wed;
'I am half sick of shadows,' said
The Lady of Shalott.
The Lady of Shalott, Pt. II

44 She has heard a whisper say,
A curse is on her if she stay
To look down to Camelot.
The Lady of Shalott, Pt. II

45 A bow-shot from her bower-eaves,
He rode between the barley-sheaves,
The sun came dazzling thro' the leaves
And flamed upon the brazen graves
Of bold Sir Lancelot.
The Lady of Shalott, Pt. III

46 'The curse is come upon me,' cried
The Lady of Shalott.
The Lady of Shalott, Pt. III

47 But Lancelot mused a little space;
He said, 'She has a lovely face;
God in his mercy lend her grace,
The Lady of Shalott.'
The Lady of Shalott, Pt. IV

48 Ah God! the petty fools of rhyme
That shriek and sweat in pigmy wars.
Literary Squabbles

49 Nourishing a youth sublime
With the fairy tales of science, and the long re-
sult of Time.
Locksley Hall

50 In the Spring a young man's fancy lightly turns to
thoughts of love.
Locksley Hall

51 Such a one do I remember, whom to look at was
to love.
Locksley Hall

52 So I triumphed ere my passion, sweeping thro'
me, left me dry,
Left me with the palsied heart, and left me with
the jaundiced eye.
Locksley Hall

53 Not with blinded eyesight poring over miserable
books.
Locksley Hall

54 Time driveth onward fast,
And in a little while our lips are dumb.
Let us alone. What is it that will last?
All things are taken from us, and become
Portions and parcels of the dreadful Past.
The Lotos-Eaters, 'Choric Song'

55 Music that gentlier on the spirit lies,
Than tir'd eyelids upon tir'd eyes.
The Lotos-Eaters, 'Choric Song'

56 Come into the garden, Maud,
For the black bat, night, has flown,
Come into the garden, Maud,
I am here at the gate alone.
Maud, I

57 The rose was awake all night for your sake,
Knowing your promise to me;
The lilies and roses were all awake,
They sighed for the dawn and thee.
Maud, I

58 I embrace the purpose of God and the doom
assigned.
Maud, III

59 But the churchmen fain would kill their church,
As the churches have kill'd their Christ.
Maud, V

60 You must wake and call me early, call me early,
mother dear;
To-morrow 'ill be the happiest time of all the
glad New-year;
Of all the glad New-year, mother, the maddest
merriest day;
For I'm to be Queen o' the May, mother, I'm to
be Queen o' the May.
The May Queen

61 The splendour falls on castle walls
And snowy summits old in story.
The Princess, III

62 Tears, idle tears, I know not what they mean,
Tears from the depth of some divine despair.
The Princess, IV

63 Dear as remembered kisses after death,
And sweet as those by hopeless fancy feign'd
On lips that are for others: deep as love,
Deep as first love, and wild with all regret;
O Death in Life, the days that are no more.
The Princess, IV

64 O tell her, brief is life but love is long.
The Princess, IV

65 Man is the hunter; woman is his game:
The sleek and shining creatures of the chase,
We hunt them for the beauty of their skins.
The Princess, V

66 Man for the field and woman for the hearth:
Man for the sword and for the needle she:
Man with the head and woman with the heart:
Man to command and woman to obey;
All else confusion.
The Princess, V

67 Home they brought her warrior dead.
She nor swoon'd, nor utter'd cry:
All her maidens, watching said,
'She must weep or she will die.'
The Princess, VI

68 The moans of doves in immemorial elms,
And murmuring of innumerable bees.
The Princess, VII

69 Revolts, republics, revolutions, most
No graver than a schoolboy's barring out.
The Princess, Conclusion

70 And they blest him in their pain, that they were
not left to Spain,
To the thumbscrew and the stake, for the glory
of the Lord.
The Revenge, III

71 A day less or more
At sea or ashore,
We die – does it matter when?
The Revenge, XI

72 My strength is as the strength of ten,
Because my heart is pure.
Sir Galahad

73 How sweet are looks that ladies bend
On whom their favours fall!
Sir Galahad

74 Battering the gates of heaven with storms of
prayer.
St Simeon Stylites

75 The woods decay, the woods decay and fall,
The vapours weep their burthen to the ground,
Man comes and tills the field and lies beneath,
And after many a summer dies the swan.
Tithonus

76 The Gods themselves cannot recall their gifts.
Tithonus

77 A life that moves to gracious ends
Thro' troops of unrecording friends,
A deedful life, a silent voice.
To – , after reading a Life and Letters

78 God gives us love. Something to love
He lends us; but, when love is grown
To ripeness that on which it throve
Falls off, and love is left alone.
To J.S.

79 A still small voice spake unto me,
'Thou art so full of misery,
Were it not better not to be?'
The Two Voices

80 All experience is an arch wherethro'
Gleams that untravelled world, whose margin
fades
For ever and for ever when I move.
Ulysses

81 We are not now that strength which in old days
Moved earth and heaven; that which we are, we
are;
One equal temper of heroic hearts,
Made weak by time and fate, but strong in will
To strive, to seek, to find, and not to yield.
Ulysses

82 Every moment dies a man,
Every moment one is born.
For a parody, *see* BABBAGE
The Vision of Sin

Terence (Publius Terentius Afer; c. 190–159 BC) Roman poet.

1 Nothing has yet been said that's not been said
before.
Eunuchus, Prologue

2 I am a man, I count nothing human foreign to
me.
Heauton Timorumenos

3 Fortune favours the brave.
Phormio

4 So many men, so many opinions.
Phormio

Teresa, Mother (Agnes Gonxha Bojaxhui; 1910–)
Yugoslav-born nun of Albanian parents. She founded the Order of
the Missionaries of Charity in Calcutta, her nuns helping lepers,
cripples, and the aged throughout the world.

1 . . . the poor are our brothers and sisters . . .
people in the world who need love, who need
care, who have to be wanted.
Time, 'Saints Among Us', 29 Dec 1975

2 Loneliness and the feeling of being unwanted is
the most terrible poverty.
Time, 'Saints Among Us', 29 Dec 1975

3 To keep a lamp burning we have to keep putting oil in it.

Time, 'Saints Among Us', 29 Dec 1975

4 This is not for me. The honour is for the poor.

Said on receiving the Order of Merit, 24 Nov 1983
The Sunday Times, 3 Dec 1989

Teresa of Ávila, St (1515–82) Spanish mystic and nun. She reformed the Carmelite order in Ávila and described her mystical experiences in *The Way of Perfection* (1565) and *The Interior Castle* (1577).

1 Alas, O Lord, to what a state dost Thou bring those who love Thee!

The Interior Castle, VI

Terry, Dame Ellen (1847–1928) British actress. She performed with Sir Henry Irving at the Lyceum Theatre and later managed the Imperial Theatre.

1 Wonderful women! Have you ever thought how much we all, and women especially, owe to Shakespeare for his vindication of women in these fearless, high-spirited, resolute and intelligent heroines?

Four Lectures on Shakespeare, 'The Triumphant Women'

2 Imagination! imagination! I put it first years ago, when I was asked what qualities I thought necessary for success upon the stage.

The Story of My Life, Ch. 2

3 What is a diary as a rule? A document useful to the person who keeps it, dull to the contemporary who reads it, invaluable to the student, centuries afterwards, who treasures it!

The Story of My Life, Ch. 14

4 How Henry would have loved it!

Referring to Sir Henry Irving's funeral
Yesterdays (Robert Hitchens)

Tertullian, Quintus Septimius Florens (c. 160–225 AD) Carthaginian father of the church. He was converted to Christianity (190 AD) but withdrew from the church in 207 to form a Montanist group. His many works include *Apologeticus* and *De Baptismo*.

1 The blood of the martyrs is the seed of the Church.

Traditional misquotation: more accurately, 'Our numbers increase as often as you cut us down: the blood of Christians is the seed.'
Apologeticus, L

2 See how these Christians love one another.

Apologeticus, XXXIX

3 I believe because it is impossible.

The usual misquotation of 'It is certain because it is impossible.'
De Carne Christi, V

Thackeray, William Makepeace (1811–63) British novelist. He became a full-time writer after the success of *Vanity Fair* (1847). Later novels include *Pendennis* (1848), *Henry Esmond* (1852), and *The Newcomes* (1853).

1 He who meanly admires mean things is a Snob.

The Book of Snobs, Ch. 2

2 It is impossible, in our condition of society, not to be sometimes a Snob.

The Book of Snobs, Ch. 3

3 'Tis not the dying for a faith that's so hard, Master Harry – every man of every nation has done that – 'tis the living up to it that is difficult.

Henry Esmond, Ch. 6

4 'Tis strange what a man may do, and a woman yet think him an angel.

Henry Esmond, Ch. 7

5 Remember, it is as easy to marry a rich woman as a poor woman.

Pendennis, Ch. 28

6 The *Pall Mall Gazette* is written by gentlemen for gentlemen.

Pendennis, Ch. 32

7 There are some meannesses which are too mean even for man – woman, lovely woman alone, can venture to commit them.

A Shabby-Genteel Story, Ch. 3

8 Oh, Vanity of vanities!
How wayward the decrees of Fate are;
How very weak the very wise,
How very small the very great are!

Vanitas Vanitatum

9 This I set down as a positive truth. A woman with fair opportunities and without a positive hump, may marry whom she likes.

Vanity Fair, Ch. 4

10 Whenever he met a great man he grovelled before him, and my-lorded him as only a freeborn Briton can do.

Vanity Fair, Ch. 13

11 If a man's character is to be abused, say what you will, there's nobody like a relation to do the business.

Vanity Fair, Ch. 19

12 I think I could be a good woman if I had five thousand a year.

Vanity Fair, Ch. 36

Thales (c. 624–547 BC) Greek philosopher and astronomer. He predicted the solar eclipse of 585 BC from observations made by the Babylonians.

1 Because there is no difference.

His reply when asked why he chose to carry on living after saying there was no difference between life and death
The Story of Civilization (W. Durant), Vol. 2

Thatcher, Denis (1915–) British businessman, married to Mrs Margaret Thatcher.

1 I do, and I also wash and iron them.

Replying to the question 'Who wears the pants in this house?'
Times (Los Angeles), 21 Apr 1981

Thatcher, Margaret (1925–) British politician, prime minister (1979–90). Trained as a chemist and a barrister, she became a Conservative MP in 1959 and minister of education and science (1970–74).

Quotations about Thatcher

1 Mrs Thatcher is a woman of common views but uncommon abilities.
Julian Critchley (1930–) British Conservative politician. *The Times*, Profile: Margaret Thatcher

2 Attila the Hen.
Clement Freud (1924–) British Liberal politician and broadcaster. BBC Radio program, *The News Quiz*

3 She approaches the problems of our country with all the one-dimensional subtlety of a comic-strip.
Denis Healey (1917–) British Labour politician. Speech, House of Commons, 22 May 1979

Quotations by Thatcher

4 I'm not hard – I'm frightfully soft. But I will not be hounded.
Daily Mail, 1972

5 Let our children grow tall, and some taller than others if they have it in them to do so.
Speech, US tour, 1975

6 Britain is no longer in the politics of the pendulum, but of the ratchet.
Speech, Institute of Public Relations, 1977

7 I love argument, I love debate. I don't expect anyone just to sit there and agree with me, that's not their job.
The Times, 1980

8 If a woman like Eva Peron with no ideals can get that far, think how far I can go with all the ideals that I have.
The Sunday Times, 1980

9 U-turn if you want to. The lady's not for turning.
Speech, Conservative Conference, 1980

10 There is no easy popularity in that but I believe people accept there is no alternative.
The oft-used phrase 'There is no alternative' led to the acronymic nickname 'TINA'
Speech, Conservative Women's Conference, 21 May 1980

11 No one would have remembered the Good Samaritan if he'd only had good intentions. He had money as well.
Television interview, 1980

12 The battle for women's rights has been largely won.
The Guardian, 1982

13 Pennies do not come from heaven. They have to be earned here on earth.
Sunday Telegraph, 1982

14 Victorian values . . . were the values when our country became great.
Television interview, 1982

15 Oh. I have got lots of human weaknesses, who hasn't?
The Times, 1983

16 State socialism is totally alien to the British character.
The Times, 1983

17 I am painted as the greatest little dictator, which is ridiculous – you always take some consultations.
The Times, 1983

18 We are the true peace movement.
The Times, 1983

19 And what a prize we have to fight for: no less than the chance to banish from our land the dark divisive clouds of Marxist socialism.
Speech, Scottish Conservative Conference, 1983

20 Young people ought not to be idle. It is very bad for them.
The Times, 1984

21 I love being at the centre of things.
Reader's Digest, 1984

22 This was the day I was meant not to see.
On her feelings the Sunday after she had escaped death in the IRA bomb explosion at the Grand Hotel, Brighton. TV interview, Oct 1984

23 I am certain that we will win the election with a good majority. Not that I am ever over-confident.
Evening Standard, 1987

24 I don't mind how much my ministers talk – as long as they do what I say.
The Times, 1987

25 I wasn't lucky. I deserved it.
Said after receiving school prize, aged nine
Attrib.

26 It's a funny old world!
Said to her ministers at the cabinet meeting at which she resigned as Conservative leader, 22 Nov, 1990

Themistocles (c. 528–462 BC) Athenian statesman. He built up Athenian naval power and fortifications, but was ostracized in 471 and died in Asia.

1 Athens holds sway over all Greece; I dominate Athens; my wife dominates me; our newborn son dominates her.
Explaining an earlier remark to the effect that his young son ruled all Greece
Attrib.

Theodoric (c. 445–526) King of the Ostrogoths and of Italy (493–526). His capital was at Ravenna.

1 If this man is not faithful to his God, how can he be faithful to me, a mere man?
Explaining why he had had a trusted minister, who had said he would adopt his master's religion, beheaded
Dictionnaire Encyclopédique (E. Guérard)

Theroux, Paul (1941–) US-born writer. His novels include *Girls at Play* (1969), *Saint Jack* (1973), *The Mosquito Coast* (1981), and *Chicago Loop* (1990). Other books include *The Great Railway Bazaar* (1975).

1 Ever since childhood, when I lived within earshot of the Boston and Maine, I have seldom heard a train go by and not wished I was on it.
The Great Railway Bazaar

2 The Japanese have perfected good manners and made them indistinguishable from rudeness.
The Great Railway Bazaar, Ch. 2

3 They say that if the Swiss had designed these mountains they'd be rather flatter.
Referring to the Alps
The Great Railway Bazaar, Ch. 28

4 The ship follows Soviet custom: it is riddled with class distinctions so subtle, it takes a trained Marxist to appreciate them.
The Great Railway Bazaar, Ch. 30

5 A foreign swear-word is practically inoffensive except to the person who has learnt it early in life and knows its social limits.
Saint Jack, Ch. 12

Thiers, Louis Adolphe (1797–1877) French statesman and historian. He became the first president of the Third Republic (1870–73). His books include the 10-volume *History of the French Revolution* (1823–27).

1 The king reigns, and the people govern themselves.
In an unsigned article attributed to Thiers
Le National, 20 Jan 1830

2 Everything must be taken seriously, nothing tragically.
Speech, French National Assembly, 24 May 1873

3 She was – but I assure you that she was a very bad cook.
Defending his social status after someone had remarked that his mother had been a cook
Attrib.

Thomas, Brandon (1856–1914) British actor and dramatist. His best-known play is the farce *Charley's Aunt* (1892).

1 I'm Charley's aunt from Brazil, where the nuts come from.
Charley's Aunt, I

Thomas, Dylan (1914–53) Welsh poet. His collections include *18 Poems* (1934) and *Deaths and Entrances* (1946). His radio play *Under Milk Wood* (1954) is also well known. His early death resulted from alcoholism.

Quotations about Thomas

1 The first time I saw Dylan Thomas I felt as if Rubens had suddenly taken it into his head to paint a youthful Silenus.
Edith Sitwell (1887–1964) British poet and writer. *Taken Care of: An Autobiography*

2 He was a detestable man. Men pressed money on him, and women their bodies. Dylan took both with equal contempt. His great pleasure was to humiliate people.
A. J. P. Taylor (1906–90) British historian. *Autobiography*

Quotations by Thomas

3 Though they go mad they shall be sane,
Though they sink through the sea they shall rise again.
Though loves be lost love shall not;
And death shall have no dominion.
And death shall have no dominion

4 I, born of flesh and ghost, was neither
A ghost nor man, but mortal ghost.
And I was struck down by death's feather.
Before I knocked

5 These poems, with all their crudities, doubts, and confusions, are written for the love of Man and in praise of God, and I'd be a damn' fool if they weren't.
Collected Poems, Note

6 When *I* take up assassination, I shall start with the surgeons in this city and work *up* to the gutter.
The Doctor and the Devils, 88

7 Do not go gentle into that good night,
Old age should burn and rave at close of day;
Rage, rage, against the dying of the light.
Do not go gentle into that good night

8 Now as I was young and easy under the apple boughs
About the lilting house and happy as the grass was green.
Fern Hill

9 Time held me green and dying
Though I sang in my chains like the sea.
Fern Hill

10 The force that through the green fuse drives the flower
Drives my green age.
The force that through the green fuse drives the flower

11 The hand that signed the treaty bred a fever,
And famine grew, and locusts came;
Great is the hand that holds dominion over
Man by a scribbled name.
The hand that signed the paper

12 The hunchback in the park
A solitary mister
Propped between trees and water.
The hunchback in the park

13 And the wild boys innocent as strawberries.
The hunchback in the park

14 Light breaks where no sun shines;
Where no sea runs, the waters of the heart
Push in their tides.
Light breaks where no sun shines

15 I missed the chance of a lifetime, too. Fifty love-lies in the rude and I'd left my Bunsen burner home.
Portrait of the Artist as a Young Dog, 'One Warm Saturday'

16 After the first death, there is no other.
A Refusal to Mourn the Death, by Fire, of a Child in London

17 This bread I break was once the oat,
This wine upon a foreign tree
Plunged in its fruit;
Man in the day or wind at night
Laid the crops low, broke the grape's joy.
This bread I break

18 MR PRITCHARD. I must dust the blinds and then I must raise them.
MRS OGMORE PRITCHARD. And before you let the sun in, mind it wipes its shoes.
Under Milk Wood

19 Gomer Owen who kissed her once by the pig-sty when she wasn't looking and never kissed her again although she was looking all the time.
Under Milk Wood

20 Sleeping as quiet as death, side by wrinkled side, toothless, salt and brown, like two old kippers in a box.
Under Milk Wood

21 The hands of the clock have stayed still at half past eleven for fifty years. It is always opening time in the Sailors Arms.
Under Milk Wood

22 Chasing the naughty couples down the grass-green gooseberried double bed of the wood.
Under Milk Wood

23 Every night of her married life she has been late for school.
Under Milk Wood

24 Oh, isn't life a terrible thing, thank God?
Under Milk Wood

25 Oh I'm a martyr to music.
Under Milk Wood

26 . . . his nicotine eggyellow weeping walrus Victorian moustache worn thick and long in memory of Doctor Crippen.
Under Milk Wood

27 Portraits of famous bards and preachers, all fur and wool from the squint to the kneecaps.
Under Milk Wood

28 It is a winter's tale
That the snow blind twilight ferries over the lakes
And floating fields from the farm in the cup of the vales.
A Winter's Tale

29 The land of my fathers. My fathers can have it.
Referring to Wales
Dylan Thomas (John Ackerman)

30 Somebody's boring me, I think it's me.
Remark made after he had been talking continuously for some time
Four Absentees (Rayner Heppenstall)

31 Too many of the artists of Wales spend too much time about the position of the artist of Wales. There is only one position for an artist anywhere: and that is, upright.
New Statesman, 18 Dec 1964

Thomas, Edward (1878–1917) British poet. His early naturalist books, such as *The Woodland Life* (1897), were succeeded by poetry after meeting Robert Frost. Collections include *Poems* (1917), the year in which he was killed in action in World War I.

1 Yes. I remember Adlestrop –
The name, because one afternoon
Of heat the express train drew up there
Unwontedly. It was late June.
Adlestrop

2 The past is the only dead thing that smells sweet.
Early One Morning

3 There is not any book
Or face of dearest look
That I would not turn from now
To go into the unknown
I must enter, and leave, alone,
I know not how.
Lights Out

4 Now all roads lead to France
And heavy is the tread
Of the living; but the dead
Returning lightly dance.
Roads

5 Make me content
With some sweetness
From Wales
Whose nightingales
Have no wings.
Words

Thomas, Gwyn (1913–81) British writer and dramatist. His novels include *The Dark Philosophers* (1946), *Now Lead Us Home* (1952), and *The Sky of Our Lives* (1972). His best-known plays are *The Keep* (1961) and *Jackie the Jumper* (1962).

1 I wanted a play that would paint the full face of sensuality, rebellion and revivalism. In South Wales these three phenomena have played second fiddle only to the Rugby Union which is a distillation of all three.
Jackie the Jumper (Introduction), 'Plays and Players' 19 Jan 1963

2 My life's been a meeting, Dad, one long meeting. Even on the few committees I don't yet belong to, the agenda winks at me when I pass.
The Keep, I

3 A bit like God in his last years, the Alderman.
The Keep, I

4 Her first economic drive will be to replace X-ray by hearsay.

The Keep, II

5 There are still parts of Wales where the only concession to gaiety is a striped shroud.

Punch, 18 June 1958

Thomas, Irene (1920–) British writer and broadcaster.

1 Protestant women may take the Pill. Roman Catholic women must keep taking the *Tablet*.

Attrib.

2 It should be a very happy marriage – they are both so much in love with *him*.

Attrib.

3 It was the kind of show where the girls are not auditioned – just measured.

Attrib.

4 The cello is not one of my favourite instruments. It has such a lugubrious sound, like someone reading a will.

Attrib.

Thomas, Lewis (1913–) US pathologist. His books include *Notes of a Biology Watcher* (1974), *More Notes of a Biology Watcher* (1979), and *Late Night Thoughts on Listening to Mahler's Ninth Symphony* (1983).

1 Worrying is the most natural and spontaneous of all human functions. It is time to acknowledge this, perhaps even to learn to do it better.

More Notes of a Biology Watcher, 'The Medusa and the Snail'

Thomas, Norman M. (1884–1968) US politician. He was socialist candidate for the presidency (1928–1948).

1 While I'd rather be right than president, at any time I'm ready to be both.

Referring to his lack of success in presidential campaigns
Come to Judgment (A. Whitman)

Thomas, R(onald) S(tuart) Welsh poet and clergyman. His collections of verse include *The Stones of the Field* (1946), *Song at the Year's Turning* (1955), and *Pietà* (1966).

1 What was it Chaucer
Said once about the long toil
That goes like blood to the poem's making?
Leave it to nature and the verse sprawls,
Limp as bindweed, if it break at all
Life's iron crust.

Poetry for Supper, 'Poetry for Supper'

2 We live in our own world,
A world that is too small
For you to stoop and enter
Even on hands and knees,
The adult subterfuge.

Song at the Year's Turning, 'Children's Song'

3 . . . an impotent people,
Sick with inbreeding,
Worrying the carcase of an old song.

Welsh Landscape

Thompson, E(dward) P(almer) (1924–) British historian. His best-known book is *The Making of the English Working Class* (1963).

1 This going into Europe will not turn out to be the thrilling mutual exchange supposed. It is more like nine middle-aged couples with failing marriages meeting in a darkened bedroom in a Brussels hotel for a Group Grope.

On the Europe debate, *Sunday Times*, 27 Apr 1975

Thompson, Francis (1859–1907) British poet. An opium addict, he was befriended by Wilfred Meynell and attained a critical success with his *Poems* (1893), which included 'The Hound of Heaven'. As a Roman Catholic, much of his work had religious themes.

1 I fled Him, down the nights and down the days;
I fled Him, down the arches of the years;
I fled Him, down the labyrinthine ways
Of my own mind; and in the mist of tears
I hid from Him, and under running laughter.

The Hound of Heaven

2 Shall shine the traffic of Jacob's ladder
Pitched between Heaven and Charing Cross.

The Kingdom of God

3 Spring is come home with her world-wandering feet.
And all the things are made young with young desires.

The Night of Forebeing, 'Ode to Easter'

Thompson, William Hepworth (1810–86) British academic who became master of Trinity College, Cambridge.

1 We are none of us infallible – not even the youngest of us.

Referring to G. W. Balfour, who was a junior fellow of Trinity College at the time
Collections and Recollections (G. W. E. Russell), Ch. 18

2 What time he can spare from the adornment of his person he devotes to the neglect of his duties.

Referring to the Cambridge Professor of Greek, Sir Richard Jebb
With Dearest Love to All (M. R. Bobbit), Ch. 7

Thomson, James (1700–48) British poet born in Scotland. His works include *The Seasons* (1730), the song 'Rule Britannia' (1740), and *The Castle of Indolence* (1748), an allegory.

1 When Britain first, at heaven's command,
Arose from out the azure main,
This was the charter of the land,
And guardian angels sung this strain:
'Rule, Britannia, rule the waves;
Britons never will be slaves.'

Alfred: a Masque, Act II, Scene the last

2 Oh! Sophonisba! Sophonisba! oh!

Sophonisba, III

Thomson, James (1834–82) British poet. Trained as an army schoolmaster, he was discharged, possibly for alcoholism, in 1862. His best known poem is *The City of Dreadful Night* (1874).

1 For life is but a dream whose shapes return,'
Some frequently, some seldom, some by night
And some by day.
The City of Dreadful Night, I

2 I find no hint throughout the universe
Of good or ill, of blessing or of curse;
I find alone Necessity Supreme.
The City of Dreadful Night, XIV

Thomson, Joseph (1858–95) Scottish explorer. A geologist,
he led several expeditions to central Africa, discovered Lake
Rukwa, and gained part of Sudan for Britain.

1 Crossing Piccadilly Circus.
His reply when asked by J. M. Barrie what was the most hazard-
ous part of his expedition to Africa
J. M. Barrie (D. Dunbar)

Thomson of Fleet, Roy Herbert, Baron (1894–
1976) Canadian-born British newspaper proprietor, who acquired
The Sunday Times (1959) and *The Times* (1966).

1 It's just like having a licence to print your own
money.
Speaking about commercial television
Attrib.

Thoreau, Henry David (1817–62) US writer. He is best
known for *Walden* (1854), an account of his year spent as a
recluse in the Walden woods in Massachusetts. He also wrote
poetry and many essays, including one on *Civil Disobedience*.

Quotations about Thoreau

1 Whatever question there may be of his talent,
there can be none I think of his genius. It was a
slim and crooked one, but it was eminently
personal.
Henry James (1843–1916) US novelist. *Hawthorne*

2 I love Henry, but I cannot like him; and as for
taking his arm, I should as soon think of taking
the arm of an elm tree.
Remark by an unknown friend

Quotations by Thoreau

3 Under a government which imprisons any unjust-
ly, the true place for a just man is also a prison.
Civil Disobedience

4 The most attractive sentences are not perhaps
the wisest, but the surest and soundest.
Journal, 1842

5 Whatever sentence will bear to be read twice,
we may be sure was thought twice.
Journal, 1842

6 Some circumstantial evidence is very strong, as
when you find a trout in the milk.
Journal, 1850

7 What men call social virtues, good fellowship, is
commonly but the virtue of pigs in a litter,
which lie close together to keep each other
warm. It brings men together in crowds and
mobs in bar-rooms and elsewhere, but it does
not deserve the name of virtue.
Journal, 1852

8 As if you could kill time without injuring eternity.
Walden, 'Economy'

9 The mass of men lead lives of quiet desperation.
Walden, 'Economy'

10 I have lived some thirty years on this planet, and
I have yet to hear the first syllable of valuable
or even earnest advice from my seniors.
Walden, 'Economy'

11 There are now-a-days professors of philosophy
but not philosophers.
Walden, 'Economy'

12 As for doing good, that is one of the professions
which are full
Walden, 'Economy'

13 Beware of all enterprises that require new
clothes.
Walden, 'Economy'

14 I never found the companion that was so companionable as solitude.
Walden, 'Solitude'

15 The three-o'-clock in the morning courage,
which Bonaparte thought was the rarest.
Walden, 'Sounds'

16 Our life is frittered away by detail . . . Simplify,
simplify.
Walden, 'Where I Lived, and What I Lived For'

17 Time is but the stream I go a-fishing in.
Walden, 'Where I Lived, and What I Lived For'

18 I once had a sparrow alight upon my shoulder for
a moment while I was hoeing in a village garden, and I felt that I was more distinguished by
that circumstance than I should have been by
any epaulet I could have worn.
Walden, 'Winter Visitors'

19 It takes two to speak the truth – one to speak,
and another to hear.
A Week on the Concord and Merrimack Rivers

20 Not that the story need be long, but it will take a
long while to make it short.
Letter, 16 Nov 1867

21 One world at a time.
On being asked his opinion of the hereafter
Attrib.

22 I did not know that we had ever quarrelled.
On being urged to make his peace with God
Attrib.

23 Yes – around Concord.
On being asked whether he had travelled much
Attrib.

Thorndike, Dame Sybil (1882–1976) British actress. She played many Shakespearean roles and the title role in Shaw's *St Joan*. She was married to the actor Sir Lewis Casson.

1 Divorce? Never. But murder often!

Replying to a query as to whether she had ever considered divorce during her long marriage to Sir Lewis Casson
Attrib.

Thorpe, Jeremy (1929–) British politician and lawyer. He was leader of the Liberal Party (1967–76) until he was charged with incitement to murder a man with whom he was alleged to have had a homosexual relationship. He was acquitted of the charge.

1 Greater love hath no man than this, that he lay down his friends for his life.

After Macmillan's 1962 Cabinet reshuffle
The Pendulum Years (Bernard Levin), Ch. 12

Thorpe, Rose Hartwick (1850–1939) US poet and novelist. She is remembered for her poem *Curfew Shall Not Ring Tonight* (1866).

1 And her face so sweet and pleading, yet with sorrow pale and worn,
Touched his heart with sudden pity – lit his eye with misty light;
'Go, your lover lives!' said Cromwell; 'Curfew shall not ring tonight!'

Curfew Shall Not Ring Tonight

Thucydides (c. 460–c. 400 BC) Greek historian and general. An Athenian general in the Peloponnesian War, he was banished for 20 years for his failure at Amphipolis, providing him with the opportunity to write his eight-volume *History of the Peloponnesian War*.

1 To famous men all the earth is a sepulchre.

History of the Peloponnesian War, Bk. II, Ch. 43

2 It is a great glory in a woman to show no more weakness than is natural to her sex, and not be talked of, either for good or evil by men.

History of the Peloponnesian War, Bk. II, Ch. 45

Thurber, James (1894–1961) US writer, humorist, and cartoonist. A contributor to the *New Yorker*, he published a number of collected writings, including *The Thurber Carnival* (1945).

Quotations about Thurber

1 A tall, thin, spectacled man with the face of a harassed rat.

Russell Maloney *Saturday Review*, 'Tilley the Toiler'

Quotations by Thurber

2 'Joe,' I said, 'was perhaps the first great nonstop literary drinker of the American nineteenth century. He made the indulgences of Coleridge and De Quincey seem like a bit of mischief in the kitchen with the cooking sherry.'

Alarms and Diversions, 'The Moribundant Life . . . '

3 I was seized by the stern hand of Compulsion, that dark, unseasonable Urge that impels women to clean house in the middle of the night.

Alarms and Diversions, 'There's a Time for Flags'

4 It is better to have loafed and lost than never to have loafed at all.

Fables for Our Time, 'The Courtship of Arthur and Al'

5 You can fool too many of the people too much of the time.

Fables for Our Time, 'The Owl Who Was God'

6 Early to rise and early to bed makes a male healthy and wealthy and dead.

Fables for Our Time, 'The Shrike and the Chipmunks'

7 Old Nat Burge sat . . . He was . . . watching the moon come up lazily out of the old cemetery in which nine of his daughters were lying, and only two of them were dead.

Let Your Mind Alone, 'Bateman Comes Home'

8 No man . . . who has wrestled with a self-adjusting card table can ever quite be the man he once was.

Let Your Mind Alone, 'Sex ex Machina'

9 I suppose that the high-water mark of my youth in Columbus, Ohio, was the night the bed fell on my father.

My Life and Hard Times, Ch. 1

10 Her own mother lived the latter years of her life in the horrible suspicion that electricity was dripping invisibly all over the house.

My Life and Hard Times, Ch. 2

11 Then, with that faint fleeting smile playing about his lips, he faced the firing squad; erect and motionless, proud and disdainful, Walter Mitty, the undefeated, inscrutable to the last.

My World and Welcome to It, 'The Secret Life of Walter Mitty'

12 A man should not insult his wife publicly, at parties. He should insult her in the privacy of the home.

Thurber Country

13 The difference between our decadence and the Russians' is that while theirs is brutal, ours is apathetic.

The Observer, 'Sayings of the Week', 5 Feb 1961

14 The War between Men and Women.

Title of a series of cartoons

15 Well, if I called the wrong number, why did you answer the phone?

Cartoon caption

16 You wait here and I'll bring the etchings down.

Cartoon caption

17 I said the hounds of spring are on winter's traces – but let it pass, let it pass!

Cartoon caption

18 Why do you have to be a nonconformist like everybody else?

Attrib. Actually a cartoon caption by Stan Hunt in the *New Yorker*

19 Surely you don't mean by unartificial insemination!

On being accosted at a party by a drunk woman who claimed she would like to have a baby by him
Attrib.

20 It had only one fault. It was kind of lousy.

Remark made about a play
Attrib.

21 God bless . . . God damn.

His last words
Attrib.

Thurlow, Edward, Baron (1731–1806) British lawyer, who became lord chancellor (1778–83). He presided at the trial of Warren Hastings, favoured coercion of the American colonies, upheld the interests of slave traders, and defended royal prerogatives.

1 When I forget my sovereign, may God forget me!

Speech, House of Lords, 15 Dec 1778

2 As guardian of His Majesty's conscience.

Speech, House of Lords, 1779

Tillich, Paul (1886–1965) German-born US theologian. A Lutheran pastor, he went to the USA when the Nazis came to power and became a university lecturer. His major work is *Systematic Theology* (1950–63).

1 Neurosis is the way of avoiding non-being by avoiding being.

The Courage to Be

Tilzer, Harry (Albert von Tilzer; 1878–1956) British songwriter.

1 Come, Come, Come and have a drink with me Down at the old 'Bull and Bush'.

The Old Bull and Bush

Tintoretto (Jacopo Robusti; 1518–94) Venetian painter. Many of his famous religious paintings hang in Venice.

1 Grant me paradise in this world; I'm not so sure I'll reach it in the next.

Arguing that he be allowed to paint the *Paradiso* at the doge's palace in Venice, despite his advanced age
Attrib.

Tocqueville, Alexis de (1805–59) French writer, historian, and politician. He wrote *Démocratie en Amérique* (1833) after visiting the USA. Elected to the Chamber of Deputies (1839), he was briefly foreign minister (1844). When Louis Napoleon came to power he retired to write *L'Ancien Régime et la révolution* (1856).

1 The French want no-one to be their *superior*. The English want *inferiors*. The Frenchman constantly raises his eyes above him with anxiety. The Englishman lowers his beneath him with satisfaction. On either side it is pride, but understood in a different way.

Voyage en Angleterre et en Irlande de 1835, 18 May

Tolkien, J(ohn) R(onald) R(euel) (1892–1973) British writer. While professor of English literature at Oxford he wrote *The Lord of the Rings* (1954–55). Related works include *The Hobbit* (1937) and *The Silmarillion* (1977).

Quotations about Tolkien

1 Though Tolkien lived in the twentieth century he can scarcely be called a modern writer. His roots were buried deep in early literature, and the major names in twentieth-century writing meant little or nothing to him.

Humphrey Carpenter *The Inklings*

2 He is a smooth, pale, fluent little chap – can't read Spenser because of the forms – thinks all literature is written for the amusement of *men* between thirty and forty . . . His pet abomination is the idea of 'liberal studies'. Technical hobbies are more in his line. No harm in him; only needs a smack or so.

C.S. Lewis (1898–1963) British academic and writer. Diary, May 1926

3 All who love that kind of children's book that can be read and re-read by adults should take note that a new star has appeared in this constellation. To the trained eye some of the characters will seem almost mythopoeic.

C.S. Lewis (1898–1963) British academic and writer. *The Times*, 7 Oct 1937

Quotations by Tolkien

4 In a hole in the ground there lived a hobbit.

The Hobbit, Ch. 1

5 One Ring to rule them all, One Ring to find them,
One Ring to bring them all and in the darkness bind them.

The Lord of the Rings, Pt. I: *The Fellowship of the Ring*, Ch. 2

6 . . . he willed that the hearts of Men should seek beyond the world and should find no rest therein; but they should have a virtue to shape their life, amid the powers and chances of the world, beyond the Music of the Ainur, which is a fate to all things else.

'He' is Ilúvatar, the Creator
The Silmarillion, Ch. 1

7 Nearly all marriages, even happy ones, are mistakes: in the sense that almost certainly (in a more perfect world, or even with a little more care in this very imperfect one) both partners might be found more suitable mates. But the real soul-mate is the one you are actually married to.

Letter to Michael Tolkien, 6–8 Mar 1941

Tolstoy, Leo (Nikolaevich), Count (1828–1910) Russian writer. His fame rests on his two epic novels *War and Peace* (1865–69) and *Anna Karenina* (1875–77). In 1876 he was converted to a form of Christian mysticism, about which he wrote copiously.

Quotations about Tolstoy

1 Tolstoy towered above his age as Dante and Michelangelo and Beethoven had done. His novels are marvels of sustained imagination, but his life was full of inconsistencies. He wanted to be one with the peasants, yet he continued to live like an aristocrat. He preached universal love, yet he quarrelled so painfully with his poor demented wife that at the age of 82 he ran away from her.
Sir Kenneth Clark (1938–69) British art historian and writer. *Civilisation*

2 I like Leo Tolstoy enormously, but in my opinion he won't write much of anything else. (I could be wrong.)
Fedor Mikhailovich Dostoevsky (1821–81) Russian novelist.

3 It has been said that a careful reading of *Anna Karenina*, if it teaches you nothing else, will teach you how to make strawberry jam.
Julian Mitchell (1935–) British writer. *Radio Times*, 30 Oct 1976

4 Tolstoy, like myself, wasn't taken in by superstitions like science and medicine.
George Bernard Shaw (1856–1950) Irish dramatist and critic.

Quotations by Tolstoy

5 All happy families resemble one another, each unhappy family is unhappy in its own way.
Anna Karenina, Pt. I, Ch. 1

6 If you want to be happy, be.
Kosma Prutkov

7 I am always with myself, and it is I who am my tormentor.
Memoirs of a Madman

8 The highest wisdom has but one science – the science of the whole – the science explaining the whole creation and man's place in it.
War and Peace, Bk.V, Ch. 2

9 The chief attraction of military service has consisted and will consist in this compulsory and irreproachable idleness.
War and Peace, Bk. VII, Ch. 1

10 All, everything that I understand, I understand only because I love.
War and Peace, Bk. VII, Ch. 16

11 Our body is a machine for living. It is organized for that, it is its nature. Let life go on in it unhindered and let it defend itself, it will do more than if you paralyse it by encumbering it with remedies.
War and Peace, Bk. X, Ch. 29

12 Pure and complete sorrow is as impossible as pure and complete joy.
War and Peace, Bk. XV, Ch. 1

13 Art is not a handicraft, it is the transmission of feeling the artist has experienced.
What is Art?, Ch. 19

14 I sit on a man's back, choking him and making him carry me, and yet assure myself and others that I am very sorry for him and wish to ease his lot by all possible means – except by getting off his back.
What Then Must We Do?, Ch. 16

15 Historians are like deaf people who go on answering questions that no one has asked them.
A Discovery of Australia, 'Being an Historian' (Manning Clark)

16 Even in the valley of the shadow of death, two and two do not make six.
Refusing to reconcile himself with the Russian Orthodox Church as he lay dying
Attrib.

Tolstoy, Sophie (1844–1919) Russian writer. The wife of Leo Tolstoy, she kept a revealing diary of her life with him.

1 One can't live on love alone; and I am so stupid that I can do nothing but think of him.
A Diary of Tolstoy's Wife, 1860–1891

2 I am a source of satisfaction to him, a nurse, a piece of furniture, a *woman* – nothing more.
A Diary of Tolstoy's Wife, 1860–1891

3 He would like to destroy his old diaries and to appear before his children and the public only in his patriarchal robes. His vanity is immense!
A Diary of Tolstoy's Wife, 1860–1891

Tomaschek, Rudolphe (20th century) German scientist.

1 Modern Physics is an instrument of Jewry for the destruction of Nordic science . . . True physics is the creation of the German spirit.
The Rise and Fall of the Third Reich (W. L. Shirer), Ch. 8

Tooke, John Horne (1736–1812) British clergyman, politician, and etymologist. While imprisoned for supporting the Americans in the American Revolution, he wrote a treatise on etymology.

1 With all my heart. Whose wife shall it be?
Replying to the suggestion that he take a wife
Attrib.

Toplady, Augustus Montague (1740–78) British hymn writer and clergyman. He was a supporter of Calvinism and opponent of Methodism.

1 Rock of ages, cleft for me,
Let me hide myself in Thee.
Rock of Ages

Toscanini, Arturo (1867–1957) Italian conductor. Originally a cellist, he became famous as a conductor of opera at the Scala, Milan, and at the Metropolitan Opera in New York. He was conductor of the NBC Symphony Orchestra (1937–57).

1 They are for prima donnas or corpses – I am neither.
Refusing a floral wreath at the end of a performance
The Elephant that Swallowed a Nightingale (C. Galtey)

2 It's too late to apologize.
Retort to the insult 'Nuts to you!' shouted at him by a player he had just ordered from the stage during rehearsal
The Humor of Music (L. Humphrey)

3 After I die, I shall return to earth as a gatekeeper of a bordello and I won't let any of you – not a one of you – enter!

Rebuking an incompetent orchestra
The Maestro: The Life of Arturo Toscanini (Howard Taubman)

4 Can't you read? The score demands *con amore*, and what are you doing? You are playing it like married men!

Criticizing the playing of an Austrian orchestra during rehearsal
Attrib.

5 Madame, there you sit with that magnificent instrument between your legs, and all you can do is *scratch* it!

Rebuking an incompetent woman cellist
Attrib.

Tourneur, Cyril (1575–1626) English dramatist. His poems include *The Transformed Metamorphosis* (1600). The *Revenger's Tragedy* (1607) and *The Atheist's Tragedy* (1611) are his best-known plays.

1 Were't not for gold and women, there would be no damnation.

The Revenger's Tragedy, II:1

Toynbee, Arnold (1889–1975) British historian. His *Study of History* (12 volumes; 1934–61) was his major work.

1 No annihilation without representation.

Urging the need for a greater British influence in the UNO, 1947

2 America is a large, friendly dog in a very small room. Every time it wags its tail it knocks over a chair.

Broadcast news summary, 14 July 1954

Tracy, Spencer (1900–67) US film star. After playing gangster roles he costarred with Katherine Hepburn in a number of films, including *Woman of the Year* (1942) and *Guess Who's Coming to Dinner* (1967). He also made *Inherit the Wind* (1960) and *Judgement at Nuremberg* (1961).

1 There were times my pants were so thin I could sit on a dime and tell if it was heads or tails.

Of leaner times in his life
Spencer Tracy (L. Swindell)

2 Days off.

Explaining what he looked for in a script
Attrib.

3 This is a movie, not a lifeboat.

Defending his demand for equal billing with Katherine Hepburn
Attrib.

Trapp, Joseph (1679–1747) English churchman and academic.

1 The King, observing with judicious eyes
The state of both his universities,
To Oxford sent a troop of horse, and why?
That learned body wanted loyalty;
To Cambridge books, as very well discerning
How much that loyal body wanted learning.

Written after George I donated the Bishop of Ely's library to Cambridge
Literary Anecdotes (Nichols), Vol. III

Tree, Sir Herbert Beerbohm (1853–1917) British actor and theatre manager. He managed both the Haymarket Theatre and Her Majesty's Theatre and founded RADA.

1 I was born old and get younger every day. At present I am sixty years young

Beerbohm Tree (Hesketh Pearson)

2 My poor fellow, why not carry a watch?

Remark made to a man carrying a grandfather clock
Beerbohm Tree (Hesketh Pearson)

3 He is an old bore; even the grave yawns for him.

Referring to Israel Zangwill
Beerbohm Tree (Hesketh Pearson)

4 The only man who wasn't spoilt by being lionized was Daniel.

Beerbohm Tree (Hesketh Pearson)

5 A whipper-snapper of criticism who quoted dead languages to hide his ignorance of life.

Refering to A. B. Walleley
Beerbohm Tree (Hesketh Pearson)

6 The national sport of England is obstacle-racing. People fill their rooms with useless and cumbersome furniture, and spend the rest of their lives in trying to dodge it.

Beerbohm Tree (Hesketh Pearson)

7 Oh my God! Remember you're in Egypt. The *skay* is only seen in Kensington.

To a leading lady
Beerbohm Tree (Hesketh Pearson)

8 When I pass my name in such large letters I blush, but at the same time instinctively raise my hat.

Beerbohm Tree (Hesketh Pearson)

9 Take that black box away. I can't act in front of it.

Objecting to the presence of the camera while performing in a silent film
Hollywood: The Pioneers (K. Brownlow)

10 Ladies, just a little more virginity, if you don't mind.

Directing a group of sophisticated actresses
Smart Aleck (H. Teichmann)

Trevelyan, George Macaulay (1876–1962) British historian, best known for his popular *English Social History* (1942).

1 Disinterested intellectual curiosity is the life blood of real civilisation.

English Social History, Preface

2 Education . . . has produced a vast population able to read but unable to distinguish what is worth reading.

English Social History, Ch. 18

3 Nelson, born in a fortunate hour for himself and for his country, was always in his element and always on his element.

History of England, Bk. V, Ch. 5

Trinder, Tommy (1909–89) British cockney music-hall, radio, and film comedian. His best-known film was *The Foreman Went to France* (1942).

1 They're overpaid, overfed, oversexed and over here.

Referring to the G.I.s
Attrib.

Trollope, Anthony (1815–82) British novelist. He established his reputation with the Barsetshire series of novels, including *The Warden* (1855) and *Barchester Towers* (1857). Later books include *Phineas Finn* (1869).

Quotations about Trollope

1 He has a gross and repulsive face but appears *bon enfant* when you talk to him. But he is the dullest Briton of them all.

Henry James (1843–1916) US novelist. Letter to his family, 1 Nov 1875

Quotations by Trollope

2 He must have known me had he seen me as he was wont to see me, for he was in the habit of flogging me constantly. Perhaps he did not recognize me by my face.

Autobiography, Ch. 1

3 Three hours a day will produce as much as a man ought to write.

Autobiography, Ch. 15

4 No man thinks there is much ado about nothing when the ado is about himself.

The Bertrams, Ch. 27

5 Those who have courage to love should have courage to suffer.

The Bertrams, Ch. 27

6 In these days a man is nobody unless his biography is kept so far posted up that it may be ready for the national breakfast-table on the morning after his demise.

Doctor Thorne, Ch. 25

7 The comic almanacs give us dreadful pictures of January and February; but, in truth, the months which should be made to look gloomy in England are March and April. Let no man boast himself that he has got through the perils of winter till at least the seventh of May.

Doctor Thorne, Ch. 47

8 It's dogged as does it. It ain't thinking about it.

Last Chronicle of Barset, Ch. 61

9 With many women I doubt whether there be any more effectual way of touching their hearts than ill-using them and then confessing it. If you wish to get the sweetest fragrance from the herb at your feet, tread on it and bruise it.

Miss Mackenzie, Ch. 10

10 We cannot bring ourselves to believe it possible that a foreigner should in any respect be wiser than ourselves. If any such point out to us our follies, we at once claim those follies as the special evidences of our wisdom.

Orley Farm, Ch. 18

11 It is because we put up with bad things that hotel-keepers continue to give them to us.

Orley Farm, Ch. 18

12 As for conceit, what man will do any good who is not conceited? Nobody holds a good opinion of a man who has a low opinion of himself.

Orley Farm, Ch. 22

13 Mr Turnbull had predicted evil consequences . . . and was now doing the best in his power to bring about the verification of his own prophecies.

Phineas Finn, Ch. 25

14 I doubt whether any girl would be satisfied with her lover's mind if she knew the whole of it.

The Small House at Allington, Ch. 4

15 And, above all things, never think that you're not good enough yourself. A man should never think that. My belief is that in life people will take you very much at your own reckoning.

The Small House at Allington, Ch. 32

16 Those who offend us are generally punished for the offence they give; but we so frequently miss the satisfaction of knowing that we are avenged!

The Small House at Allington, Ch. 50

Trotsky, Leon (Lev Davidovich Bronstein; 1879–1940) Russian revolutionary. Originally a Menshevik, he returned from exile to become a Bolshevik and played a major role in the October (1917) Revolution. After Lenin's death he was exiled by Stalin and murdered in Mexico (possibly by a Soviet agent).

1 Revolution by its very nature is sometimes compelled to take in more territory than it is capable of holding. Retreats are possible – when there is territory to retreat from.

Diary in Exile, 15 Feb 1935

2 Old age is the most unexpected of all the things that happen to a man.

Diary in Exile, 8 May 1935

3 The 23rd of February was International Woman's Day . . . It had not occurred to anyone that it might become the first day of the revolution.

History of the Russian Revolution, Pt. I, Ch. 7

4 The revolution does not choose its paths: it made its first steps towards victory under the belly of a Cossack's horse.

History of the Russian Revolution, Pt. I, Ch. 7

5 Revolutions are always verbose.

History of the Russian Revolution, Pt. II, Ch. 12

6 Insurrection is an art, and like all arts it has its laws.

History of the Russian Revolution, Pt. III, Ch. 6

7 The fundamental premise of a revolution is that the existing social structure has become incapable of solving the urgent problems of development of the nation.

History of the Russian Revolution, Pt. III, Ch. 6

8 From being a patriotic myth, the Russian people have become an awful reality.
History of the Russian Revolution, Pt. III, Ch. 7

9 For us, the tasks of education in socialism were closely integrated with those of fighting. Ideas that enter the mind under fire remain there securely and for ever.
My Life, Ch. 35

10 It was the supreme expression of the mediocrity of the apparatus that Stalin himself rose to his position.
My Life, Ch. 40

11 Lenin's method leads to this: the party organization at first substitutes itself for the party as a whole. Then the central committee substitutes itself for the party organization, and finally a single dictator substitutes himself for the central committee.
The Communist Parties of Western Europe (N. McInnes), Ch. 3

12 Patriotism to the Soviet State is a revolutionary duty, whereas patriotism to a bourgeois State is treachery.
Disputed Barricade (Fitzroy Maclean)

13 An ally has to be watched just like an enemy.
Expansion and Coexistence (A. Ulam)

Troubridge, Sir T. St Vincent (1895–1963) British army officer.

1 There is an iron curtain across Europe.
Sunday Empire News, 21 Oct 1945

Truman, Harry S. (1884–1972) US statesman. He became president (1945–53) after the death of Roosevelt and ordered the dropping of the atom bombs on Hiroshima and Nagasaki. His administration also established NATO.

Quotations about Truman

1 The captain with the mighty heart.
Dean Acheson (1893–1971) US lawyer and statesman. *Present at the Creation.*

2 Truman is short, square, simple, and looks one straight in the face.
Harold Nicolson (1886–1968) British writer. *Diaries*, 8 Aug 1945

Quotations by Truman

3 If you can't stand the heat, get out of the kitchen.
Perhaps proverbial in origin, possibly echoes the expression 'kitchen cabinet'
Mr Citizen, Ch. 15

4 If we see that Germany is winning the war we ought to help Russia, and if Russia is winning we ought to help Germany, and in that way let them kill as many as possible.
New York Times, 24 July 1941, when Russia was invaded by Germany

5 A politician is a man who understands government, and it takes a politician to run a government. A statesman is a politician who's been dead ten or fifteen years.
New York World Telegram and Sun, 12 Apr 1958

6 The President spends most of his time kissing people on the cheek in order to get them to do what they ought to do without getting kissed.
The Observer, 'Sayings of the Week', 6 Feb 1949

7 It's a recession when your neighbour loses his job; it's a depression when you lose your own.
The Observer, 'Sayings of the Week', 6 Apr 1958

8 I didn't fire him because he was a dumb son of a bitch, although he was, but that's not against the law for generals. If it was, half to three-quarters of them would be in gaol.
Referring to General MacArthur
Plain Speaking (Merle Miller)

9 Give me a one-handed economist! All my economists say, 'on the one hand . . . on the other'.
Presidential Anecdotes (P. Boller)

10 The buck stops here.
Sign kept on his desk during his term as president
Presidential Anecdotes (P. Boller)

11 You don't set a fox to watching the chickens just because he has a lot of experience in the hen house.
Referring to Vice-President Nixon's nomination for President
Speech, 30 Oct 1960

Tuchman, Barbara W. (1912–89) US editor and writer. Her books include *The Lost British Policy* (1938), and *August 1914* (1962).

1 Dead battles, like dead generals, hold the military mind in their dead grip.
August 1914, Ch. 2

Tucker, Sophie (Sophia Abuza; 1884–1966) Russian-born US popular singer and vaudeville star.

1 The Last of the Red Hot Mamas.
Description of herself. *Dictionary of Biographical Quotation* (J. Wintle and R. Kenin)

2 Life begins at forty.
Attrib.

3 From birth to age eighteen, a girl needs good parents. From eighteen to thirty-five, she needs good looks. From thirty-five to fifty-five, she needs a good personality. From fifty-five on, she needs good cash.
Attrib.

4 Keep breathing.
Her reply, at the age of 80, when asked the secret of her longevity
Attrib.

Tupper, Martin Farquhar (1810–89) British writer. His *Proverbial Philosophy* (1838) was an international success. He also wrote ballads and a novel.

1 A good book is the best of friends, the same to-day and for ever.
Proverbial Philosophy, 'Of Reading'

2 It is well to lie fallow for a while.
Proverbial Philosophy, 'Of Recreation'

Turenne, Henri de la Tour d'Auvergne, Vicomte de (1611–75) French marshal, who made his name in the Thirty Years' War and commanded the French armies that invaded the Spanish Netherlands and in the war against Holland.

1 God is always on the side of the big battalions.

Attrib.

Turgenev, Ivan (1818–83) Russian novelist. A critic of the Russian system in *Sportsman's Sketches* (1852), he was briefly imprisoned. The novels *Fathers and Sons* (1862) and *The Torrents of Spring* (1872) established his reputation, but he is best known for the play *A Month in the Country* (1870).

1 I agree with no man's opinion. I have some of my own.

Fathers and Sons, Ch. 13

2 The temerity to believe in nothing.

Fathers and Sons, Ch. 14

3 Go and try to disprove death. Death will disprove you, and that's all!

Fathers and Sons, Ch. 27

4 Whatever a man prays for, he prays for a miracle. Every prayer reduces itself to this: 'Great God grant that twice two be not four.'

Prayer

Turgot, Anne-Robert-Jacques, Baron de l'Aulne (1727–81) French economist and advocate of laissez-faire. One of the Physiocrats, he became comptroller general in 1774.

1 He snatched the lightning shaft from heaven, and the sceptre from tyrants.

An inscription for a bust of Benjamin Franklin, alluding both to Franklin's invention of the lightning conductor and to his role in the American Revolution
Vie de Turgot (A. N. de Condorcet)

Turk, Roy (20th century) US songwriter.

1 Walking My Baby Back Home.

Title of song

Turnbull, Margaret (fl. 1920s–1942) US writer and dramatist of Scottish origin.

1 No man is responsible for his father. That is entirely his mother's affair.

Alabaster Lamps

2 When a man confronts catastrophe on the road, he looks in his purse – but a woman looks in her mirror.

The Left Lady

Turner, Joseph Mallord William (1775–1851) British landscape and seascape painter, who anticipated the French impressionists.

1 My business is to paint not what I know, but what I see.

Responding to a criticism of the fact that he had painted no portholes on the ships in a view of Plymouth
Proust: The Early Years (G. Painter)

2 I've lost one of my children this week.

His customary remark following the sale of one of his paintings
Sketches of Great Painters (E. Chubb)

Tusser, Thomas (1524–80) English farmer and writer. His *Five Hundred Points of Good Husbandry* (1557), written in verse, was a source of many proverbs.

1 February, fill the dyke
With what thou dost like.

Five Hundred Points of Good Husbandry, 'February's Husbandry'

2 Sweet April showers
Do spring May flowers.

Five Hundred Points of Good Husbandry, 'April's Husbandry'

3 At Christmas play and make good cheer,
For Christmas comes but once a year.

Five Hundred Points of Good Husbandry, 'The Farmer's Daily Diet'

4 Seek home for rest,
For home is best.

Five Hundred Points of Good Husbandry, 'Instructions to Housewifery'

Tutu, Desmond, Archbishop (1931–) South African clergyman noted for his campaign against apartheid. He became Archbishop of Johannesburg in 1984.

1 We don't want apartheid liberalized. We want it dismantled. You can't improve something that is intrinsically evil.

The Observer, 'Sayings of the Week', 10 Mar 1985

2 It seems that the British Government sees black people as expendable.

Speech, June 1986

3 Beware when you take on the Church of God. Others have tried and have bitten the dust.

Speech, Apr 1987

Tuwim, Julian (1894–1954) Polish writer and poet.

1 There are two kinds of blood, the blood that flows in the veins and the blood that flows out of them.

We, the Polish Jews

Twain, Mark (Samuel Langhorne Clemens; 1835–1910) US writer. A steamboat pilot, he wrote a novel, *The Adventures of Huckleberry Finn* (1884), which established his reputation as a writer.

Quotations about Twain

1 The average American loves his family. If he has any love left over for some other person, he generally selects Mark Twain.

Thomas Edison (1847–1931) US inventor. Attrib.

2 Mark Twain and I are in the same position. We have to put things in such a way as to make people, who would otherwise hang us, believe that we are joking.

George Bernard Shaw (1856–1950) Irish dramatist and critic. Attrib.

Quotations by Twain

3 There was things which he stretched, but mainly he told the truth.

The Adventures of Huckleberry Finn, Ch. 1

4 There are three kinds of lies: lies, damned lies, and statistics.

Autobiography

5 Soap and education are not as sudden as a massacre, but they are more deadly in the long run.
The Facts concerning the Recent Resignation

6 It takes your enemy and your friend, working together, to hurt you to the heart; the one to slander you and the other to get the news to you.
Following the Equator

7 It is by the goodness of God that in our country we have those three unspeakably precious things: freedom of speech, freedom of conscience, and the prudence never to practise either of them.
Following the Equator, heading of Ch. 20

8 Man is the only animal that blushes. Or needs to.
Following the Equator, heading of Ch. 27

9 I must have a prodigious quantity of mind; it takes me as much as a week, sometimes, to make it up.
The Innocents Abroad, Ch. 7

10 They spell it Vinci and pronounce it Vinchy; foreigners always spell better than they pronounce.
The Innocents Abroad, Ch. 19

11 The radical invents the views. When he has worn them out, the conservative adopts them.
Notebooks

12 Familiarity breeds contempt – and children.
Notebooks

13 When people do not respect us we are sharply offended; yet deep down in his heart no man much respects himself.
Notebooks

14 Good breeding consists in concealing how much we think of ourselves and how little we think of other persons.
Notebooks

15 Adam was but human – this explains it all. He did not want the apple for the apple's sake, he wanted it only because it was forbidden.
Pudd'nhead Wilson's Calendar, Ch. 2

16 There ain't no way to find out why a snorer can't hear himself snore.
Tom Sawyer Abroad, Ch. 10

17 Something that everybody wants to have read and nobody wants to read.
Definition of a classic of literature
Speech at Nineteenth Century Club, New York, 20 Nov 1900

18 Reports of my death are greatly exaggerated.
On learning that his obituary had been published
Cable to the Associated Press

19 That's right. 'Taint yours, and 'taint mine.
Agreeing with a friend's comment that the money of a particular rich industrialist was 'tainted'.
Attrib.

20 Scarce, sir. Mighty scarce.
Responding to the question 'In a world without women what would men become?'
Attrib.

21 To cease smoking is the easiest thing I ever did. I ought to know because I've done it a thousand times.
Referring to giving up smoking. Attrib.

Tynan, Kenneth (1927–80) British theatre critic and producer. He became literary manager of the National Theatre. His books inlcude *He That Plays the King* (1950) and *Curtains* (1961).

1 A novel is a static thing that one moves through; a play is a dynamic thing that moves past one.
Curtains

2 William Congreve is the only sophisticated playwright England has produced; and like Shaw, Sheridan, and Wilde, his nearest rivals, he was brought up in Ireland.
Curtains, 'The Way of the World'

3 A good drama critic is one who perceives what is happening in the theatre of his time. A great drama critic also perceives what is not happening.
Tynan Right and Left, Foreword

4 A good many inconveniences attend play-going in any large city, but the greatest of them is usually the play itself.
New York Herald Tribune

5 A critic is a man who knows the way but can't drive the car.
New York Times Magazine, 9 Jan 1966

6 What, when drunk, one sees in other women, one sees in Garbo sober.
The Sunday Times, 25 Aug 1963

Tyrrell, George (1861–1909) Irish Catholic theologian. Dismissed by the Jesuits for his modernism he was later excommunicated. His books include *Christianity at the Cross-Roads* (1909) and *Immortality* (1914). He also wrote an autobiography.

1 I never quite forgave Mahaffy for getting himself suspended from preaching in the College Chapel. Ever since his sermons were discontinued, I suffer from insomnia in church.
As I Was Going Down Sackville Street (Oliver St John Gogarty), Ch. 25

U

Uccello, Paolo (1397–1475) Italian painter. His paintings, including *A Hunt in a Forest* and *St George and the Dragon*, show his concern with the problems of perspective.

1 What a delightful thing this perspective is!
Men of Art (T. Craven)

Unamuno y Jugo, Miguel de (1864–1936) Spanish writer and philosopher. His major philosophical work is *The Tragic Sense of Life* (1913).

1 All right, my lord creator, Don Miguel, you too will die and return to the nothing whence you came. God will cease to dream you!
Mist

2 Man, by the very fact of being man, by possessing consciousness, is, in comparison with the ass or the crab, a disease animal. Consciousness is a disease.
The Tragic Sense of Life, 1

3 May God deny you peace but give you glory!
Closing words
The Tragic Sense of Life

4 They will conquer, but they will not convince.
Referring to the Franco rebels
Attrib.

Updike, John (1932–) US novelist and writer. His novels include *Rabbit, Run* (1960), *Couples* (1968), *Marry Me* (1976), *Rabbit is Rich* (1981), and *The Witches of Eastwick* (1984).

1 A healthy male adult bore consumes each year one and a half times his own weight in other people's patience.
Assorted Prose, 'Confessions of a Wild Bore'

2 In general the churches, visited by me too often on weekdays . . . bore for me the same relation to God that billboards did to Coca-Cola: they promoted thirst without quenching it.
A Month of Sundays, Ch. 2

3 Americans have been conditioned to respect newness, whatever it costs them.
A Month of Sundays, Ch. 18

4 He is a man of brick. As if he was born as a baby literally of clay and decades of exposure have baked him to the colour and hardness of brick.
Rabbit, Run

Ure, Mary (1933–75) British actress. She was married to the actor Robert Shaw.

1 I have a big house – and I hide a lot.
Explaining how she coped with her large family of children
Attrib.

Ustinov, Sir Peter (1921–) British actor, director, and dramatist. His plays include *The Love of Four Colonels* (1951), *Romanoff and Juliet* (1956), and *Beethoven's Tenth* (1983). He is also a well-known impersonator and raconteur.

1 Thanks to the movies, gunfire has always sounded unreal to me, even when being fired at.
Dear Me, Ch. 7

2 And here is the lesson I learned in the army. If you want to do a thing badly, you have to work at it as though you want to do it well.
Dear Me, Ch. 8

3 I am an optimist, unrepentant and militant. After all, in order not to be a fool an optimist must know how sad a place the world can be. It is only the pessimist who finds this out anew every day.
Dear Me, Ch. 9

4 There are no old men any more. *Playboy* and *Penthouse* have between them made an ideal of eternal adolescence, sunburnt and saunaed, with the grey dorianed out of it.
Dear Me, Ch. 18

5 I believe that the Jews have made a contribution to the human condition out of all proportion to their numbers: I believe them to be an immense people. Not only have they supplied the world with two leaders of the stature of Jesus Christ and Karl Marx, but they have even indulged in the luxury of following neither one nor the other.
Dear Me, Ch. 19

6 This is a free country, madam. We have a right to share your privacy in a public place.
Romanoff and Juliet, I

7 As for being a General, well, at the age of four with paper hats and wooden swords we're all Generals. Only some of us never grow out of it.
Romanoff and Juliet, I

8 A diplomat these days is nothing but a headwaiter who's allowed to sit down occasionally.
Romanoff and Juliet, I

9 If Botticelli were alive today he'd be working for *Vogue*.
The Observer, 'Sayings of the Week', 21 Oct 1962

10 People at the top of the tree are those without qualifications to detain them at the bottom.
Attrib.

V

Vachell, Horace Annesley (1861–1955) British writer. His novels include *Quinney's* (1914) and *Vicar's Walk* (1933). *Plus Fours* (1923) was his best-known play.

1 In nature there are no rewards or punishments; there are consequences.
The Face of Clay, Ch. 10

Vail, Amanda (Warren Miller; 1921–66) US writer, author of the novels *Love Me Little* (1957) and *The Bright Young Things* (1958).

1 Sometimes I think if there was a third sex men wouldn't get so much as a glance from me.
Love Me Little, Ch. 6

Valéry, Paul (1871–1945) French poet and writer. His verse includes *La Jeune Parque* (1917) and *Aurore* (1917); *L'Âme et la danse* (1924) and *Regards sur le monde actuel* (1931) are his best-known prose books.

1 God made everything out of nothing. But the nothingness shows through.
Mauvaises Pensées et autres

2 The term Science should not be given to anything but the aggregate of the recipes that are always successful. All the rest is literature.
Moralités

3 Liberty is the hardest test that one can inflict on a people. To know how to be free is not given equally to all men and all nations.
Reflections on the World Today, 'On the Subject of Dictatorship'

4 Politics is the art of preventing people from taking part in affairs which properly concern them.
Tel quel

Vanburgh, Sir John (1664–1726) English architect and dramatist. His plays include *The Relapse* (1696) and *The Provok'd Wife* (1697), written before his most successful work as an architect, which includes Castle Howard (begun 1699) and Blenheim Palace (begun 1705).

1 The want of a thing is perplexing enough, but the possession of it is intolerable.
The Confederacy, I:2

2 As if a woman of education bought things because she wanted 'em.
The Confederacy, II:1

3 Much of a muchness.
The Provok'd Husband, I:1

4 Thinking is to me the greatest fatigue in the world.
The Relapse, II:1

5 Once a woman has given you her heart you can never get rid of the rest of her.
The Relapse, II:1

6 No man worth having is true to his wife, or can be true his wife, or ever was, or ever will be so.
The Relapse, III:2

Vanderbilt, William Henry (1821–85) US railway chief. Having inherited a fortune from his father, he became president of the New York Central Railroad.

1 The public be damned. I am working for my stockholders.
Refusing to speak to a reporter, who was seeking to find out his views on behalf of the public

2 I have had no real gratification or enjoyment of any sort more than my neighbor on the next block who is worth only half a million.
Famous Last Words (B. Conrad)

Van der Post, Sir Laurens (1906–) South African novelist resident in England. His books include *The Hunter and the Whale* (1967), *A Story Like the Wind* (1972), and *Testament to the Bushmen* (with Jane Taylor; 1984). *Venture to the Interior* (1952) and *The Lost World of the Kalahari* (1958) were earlier travel books.

1 'The story is like the wind', the Bushman prisoner said. 'It comes from a far off place, and we feel it.'
A Story Like the Wind

2 Organized religion is making Christianity political rather than making politics Christian.
The Observer, 'Sayings of the Week', 9 Nov 1986

Varah, Rev Chad (1911–) British churchman. He founded a nonreligious charity, the Samaritans, in 1953 to provide a nonprofessional, free, confidential, and anonymous service to anyone in distress.

1 I am the only man in the world who cannot commit suicide.
Attrib.

Vaughan Williams, Ralph (1872–1958) British composer. He wrote nine symphonies, including the choral *A Sea Symphony,* and *Sinfonia Antarctica;* other works include the ballet *Job* (1931) and the opera *The Pilgrim's Progress* (1951).

1 Music. But in the next world I shan't be doing music, with all the striving and disappointments. I shall be being it.
In reply to a question, two weeks before his death, asking him what he would like to be if he were reincarnated
Letter (Sylvia Townsend Warner)

Vauvenargues, Luc de Clapiers, Marquis de (1715–47) French soldier and writer, remembered for his *Introduction à la connaissance de l'esprit humain suivie de réflexions et de maximes* (1746).

1 Great thoughts come from the heart.
Réflexions et maximes

2 To achieve great things we must live as though we were never going to die.
Réflexions et maximes

3 We should expect the best and the worse from mankind, as from the weather.
Réflexions et maximes

Veblen, Thorstein Bunde (1857–1929) US social scientist. His books include *The Theory of the Leisure Class* (1899) and *The Higher Learning in America* (1918).

1 All business sagacity reduces itself in the last analysis to a judicious use of sabotage.
The Nature of Peace

2 The outcome of any serious research can only be to make two questions grow where only one grew before.
The Place of Science in Modern Civilization

3 Conspicuous consumption of valuable goods is a means of reputability to the gentleman of leisure.
The Theory of the Leisure Class

Vega Carpio, Lope Félix de (1562–1635) Spanish dramatist and poet. Most of his plays were based on Spanish history.

1 All right, then, I'll say it: Dante makes me sick.
On being informed he was about to die
Attrib.

Vegetius (Flavius Vegetius Renatus; 4th century AD) Roman writer, remembered for his military treatise *Epitoma Rei Militaris*.

1 Let him who desires peace, prepare for war.
Epitoma Rei Militaris, 3, 'Prologue'

Verne, Jules (1828–1905) French writer. His most celebrated works include *Journey to the Centre of the Earth* (1864), *20,000 Leagues Under the Sea* (1873), and *Round the World in Eighty Days* (1873).

1 My curiosity was aroused to fever-pitch, and my uncle tried in vain to restrain me. When he saw that my impatience was likely to do me more harm than the satisfaction of my curiosity, he gave way.
Journey to the Centre of the Earth

2 But from the final orders given him by his master when he left the *Mongolia* Passepartout realized that the same thing would happen in Bombay as had happened in Suez and Paris. And he began to wonder if that bet of Mr. Fogg's was not a serious business after all and if fate would not drag him round the world in eighty days in spite of his desire for a quiet life.
Round the World in Eighty Days

Verrall, Arthur Woollgar (1851–1912) British classicist. He edited the works of Aeschylus and Euripides.

1 Oh, quite easy! The Septuagint minus the Apostles.
Reply to a person who thought the number 58 difficult to remember

Vespasian (9–79 AD) Roman emperor (69–79). He ended the civil war and was deified after his death.

1 Dear me, I believe I am becoming a god. An emperor ought at least to die on his feet.
Last words
Lives of the Caesars (Suetonius)

Vicky (Victor Weisz; 1913–66) German-born British cartoonist. His work appeared in the *Evening Standard* and *The New Statesman and Nation*.

1 Introducing Super-Mac.
Cartoon caption depicting Harold Macmillan as Superman
Evening Standard, 6 Nov 1958

Victoria (1819–1901) Queen of the United Kingdom (1837–1901). She succeeded her uncle William IV and married her cousin Prince Albert of Saxe-Coburg-Gotha. Disraeli, her close ally after Albert's death in 1861, made her Empress of India.

Quotations about Victoria

1 Victoria has greatly improved, and has become very reasonable and good-natured.
Prince Albert (1819–61) The consort of Queen Victoria. Letter to his brother Ernst, 1843

2 Queen Victoria in her eighties was more known, more revered, and a more important part of the life of the country than she had ever been. Retirement, for a monarch, is not a good idea.
Charles, Prince of Wales (1948–) Eldest son of Elizabeth II

3 She's more of a man than I expected.
Henry James (1843–1916) US novelist. *Diary* (E.M. Forster)

4 Nowadays a parlourmaid as ignorant as Queen Victoria was when she came to the throne would be classed as mentally defective.
George Bernard Shaw (1856–1950) Irish dramatist and critic.

Quotations by Victoria

5 I sat between the King and Queen. We left supper soon. My health was drunk. I then danced one more quadrille with Lord Paget. . . . I was *very* much amused.
Journal, 16 June 1833

6 . . . I *too well* know its truth, from experience, that whenever any poor Gipsies are encamped anywhere and crimes and robberies &c. occur, it is invariably laid to their account, which is shocking; and if they are always looked upon as vagabonds, how *can* they become good people?
Journal, 29 Dec 1836

7 The Queen is most anxious to enlist every one who can speak or write to join in checking this mad, wicked folly of 'Woman's Rights', with all its attendant horrors, on which her poor feeble sex is bent, forgetting every sense of womanly feeling and propriety.
Letter to Sir Theodore Martin, 29 May 1870

8 The danger to the country, to Europe, to her vast Empire, which is involved in having all these great interests entrusted to the shaking hand of an old, wild, and incomprehensible man of 82½, is very great!
Reaction to Gladstone's fourth and last appointment as prime minister, 1892
Letter to Lord Lansdowne, 12 Aug 1892

9 He speaks to Me as If I was a public meeting.
Referring to Gladstone
Collections and Recollections (G. W. E. Russell), Ch. 14

10 A strange, horrible business, but I suppose good enough for Shakespeare's day.
Giving her opinion of *King Lear*
Living Biographies of Famous Rulers (H. Thomas)

11 Move Queen Anne? Most certainly not! Why it might some day be suggested that *my* statue should be moved, which I should much dislike.

Said at the time of her Diamond Jubilee (1897), when it was suggested that the statue of Queen Anne should be moved from outside St. Paul's
Men, Women and Things (Duke of Portland), Ch. 5

12 We are not amused!

Attrib.

Vidal, Gore (1925–) US novelist. His books include *Myra Breckinridge* (1968), *Burr* (1974), and *Lincoln* (1984).

1 The novel being dead, there is no point to writing made-up stories. Look at the French who will not and the Americans who cannot.

Myra Breckinridge, Ch. 2

2 American writers want to be not good but great; and so are neither.

Two Sisters

3 The astronauts! . . . Rotarians in outer space.

Two Sisters

4 Never have children, only grandchildren.

Two Sisters

5 It is not enough to succeed. Others must fail.

Antipanegyric for Tom Driberg (G. Irvine)

6 Whenever a friend succeeds, a little something in me dies.

The Sunday Times Magazine, 16 Sept 1973

7 I'm all for bringing back the birch, but only between consenting adults.

Said when asked by David Frost in a TV interview for his views about corporal punishment

Viera Gallo, José Antonio (1943–) Chilean politician.

1 Socialism can only arrive by bicycle.

Compare Norman TEBBIT
Energy and Equity (Ivan Illich)

Vigny, Alfred de (1797–1863) French poet, novelist, and dramatist. He established his reputation with the novel *Cinq-Mars* (1826), but the play *Chatterton* (1835) is regarded as his most important work. His poetry collections include *Destinées* (1867).

1 The true God, the mighty God, is the God of ideas.

La Bouteille à la mer

2 Alas, Lord, I am powerful but alone. Let me sleep the sleep of the earth.

Moïse

3 An army is a nation within a nation; it is one of the vices of our age.

Servitude et grandeur militaire, 1

Villiers, Alan John (1903–) Australian naval commander and writer. His books include *Vanished Fleets* (1931) and *The Making of a Sailor* (1938).

1 Only fools and passengers drink at sea.

The Observer, 'Sayings of the Week', 28 Apr 1957

Villon, François (1431–85) French poet. He became a vagrant and criminal, for which he was banished from Paris in 1463. His works include *Le Petit Testament* (1456) and *Le Grand Testament* (1461).

1 *Mais où sont les neiges d'antan?*
But where are the snows of yesteryear?

Ballade des dames du temps jadis

Virchow, Rudolph (1821–1902) German pathologist. His book *Cellular Pathology* (1858) established the foundations of this science.

1 Marriages are not normally made to avoid having children.

Bulletin of the New York Academy of Medicine, 4:995, 1928
(F. H. Garrison)

2 Human beings, yes, but not surgeons.

Answering a query as to whether human beings could survive appendectomy, which had recently become a widespread practice
Anekdotenschatz (H. Hoffmeister)

Virgil (Publius Vergilius Maro; 70–19 BC) Roman poet. His *Eclogues* (42–37 BC) were followed by the *Georgics* (36–29 BC), works that expressed his pastoral and agricultural interests. His national epic in 12 books, the *Aeneid*, led to his veneration by subsequent generations.

Quotations about Virgil

1 A crawling and disgusting parasite, a base scoundrel, and pander to unnatural passions.

William Cobbett (1763–1835) British journalist and writer.

2 Thou are my master and my author, thou art he from whom alone I took the style whose beauty has done me honour.

Dante (1265–1321) Italian poet. *Divine Comedy*, 'Inferno', I

3 Virgil's great judgement appears in putting things together, and in his picking gold out of the dunghills of old Roman writers.

Alexander Pope (1688–1744) British poet. *Observations, Anecdotes and Characters* (Rev. Joseph Spence)

Quotations by Virgil

4 Anger supplies the arms.

Aeneid, Bk. I

5 I sing of arms and the man who first from the shores of Troy came destined an exile to Italy and the Lavinian beaches, much buffeted he on land and on the deep by force of the gods because of fierce Juno's never-forgetting anger.

Referring to Aeneas
Aeneid, Bk. I

6 O you who have borne even heavier things, God will grant an end to these too.

Aeneid, Bk. I

7 Maybe one day we shall be glad to remember even these hardships.

Aeneid, Bk. I

8 A grief too much to be told, O queen, you bid me renew.

The opening words of Aeneas' account to Dido of the fall of Troy
Aeneid, Bk. II

9 *Equo ne credite, Teucri.*
Quidquid id est timeo Danaos et dona ferentis.
Do not trust the horse, Trojans. Whatever it is, I fear the Greeks even when they bring gifts.
Aeneid, Bk. II

10 It was the time when first sleep begins for weary mortals and by the gift of the gods creeps over them most welcomely.
Aeneid, Bk. II

11 What do you not drive human hearts into, cursed craving for gold!
Aeneid, Bk. III

12 Woman is always fickle and changing.
Aeneid, Bk. IV

13 The way down to Hell is easy.
Aeneid, Bk. VI

14 I see wars, horrible wars, and the Tiber foaming with much blood.

Part of the Sibyl's prophecy to Aeneas, foretelling his difficulties in winning a home in Italy
Aeneid, Bk. VI

15 Fear lent wings to his feet.
Aeneid, Bk. VIII

16 Everyone is dragged on by their favourite pleasure.
Eclogue, Bk. II

17 There's a snake hidden in the grass.
Eclogue, Bk. III

18 Love conquers all things: let us too give in to Love.
Eclogue, Bk. X

19 But meanwhile it is flying, irretrievable time is flying.
Georgics, Bk. III

Vizinczey, Stephen (1933–) Hungarian-born British writer. His works include the novels *In Praise of Older Women* (1965) and *An Innocent Millionaire* (1983).

1 Don't let anybody tell you you're wasting your time when you're gazing into space. There is no other way to conceive an imaginary world. I never sit down in front of a bare page to invent something. I daydream about my characters, their lives and their struggles, and when a scene has been played out in my imagination and I think I know what my characters felt, said and did, I take pen and paper and try to *report* what I've witnessed.
Truth and Lies in Literature

2 Rejection, derision, poverty, failure, the constant struggle against one's own limitations – these are the chief events in the lives of most great artists.
Truth and Lies in Literature

3 I was told I am a true cosmopolitan. I am unhappy everywhere.
The Guardian, 7 Mar 1968

Voltaire (François-Marie Arouet; 1694–1778) French writer and philosopher. A fearless campaigner against injustice, he was imprisoned in the Bastille, exiled to England, Germany, and Switzerland, and later became a hero of French culture. His works include *Lettres philosophiques* (1734), the fable *Candide* (1759), and the *Dictionnaire philosophique* (1764).

Quotations about Voltaire

1 He does not inflame his mind with grand hopes of the immortality of the soul. He says it may be, but he knows nothing of it. And his mind is in perfect tranquillity.

James Boswell (1740–95) Scottish lawyer and writer. *Boswell on the Grand Tour* (F.A. Pottle)

2 When he talked our language he was animated with the soul of a Briton. He had bold fights. He had humour. He had an extravagance.

James Boswell (1740–95) Scottish lawyer and writer. *Boswell on the Grand Tour* (ed. by F. A. Pottle)

3 I have done but very little but read Voltaire since I saw you. He is an exquisite fellow. One thing in him is peculiarly striking – his clear knowledge of the limits of human understanding.

Dr J. Currie (1756–1805) Scottish physician and writer. Letter to Thomas Creevey, 17 Dec 1798

4 I was born much too soon, but I do not regret it; I have seen Voltaire.

Frederick the Great (1712–86) King of Prussia. Attrib.

5 Here lies the child spoiled by the world which he spoiled.

Baronne de Montolieu. Epitaph on Voltaire

Quotations by Voltaire

6 If we do not find anything pleasant, at least we shall find something new.
Candide, Ch. 17

7 *Dans ce pay-ci, il est bon de tuer de temps en temps un amiral pour encourager les autres.*
In this country it is good to kill an admiral from time to time, to encourage the others.

Referring to England: Admiral Byng was executed for failing to defeat the French at Minorca (1757)
Candide, Ch. 23

8 All is for the best in the best of all possible worlds.
Candide, Ch. 30

9 'That is well said,' replied Candide, 'but we must cultivate our garden.'
Candide, Ch. 30

10 Work banishes those three great evils, boredom, vice, and poverty.
Candide, Ch. 30

11 . . . use thought only to justify their injustices, and speech only to conceal their thoughts.
Referring to men
Dialogue, 'Le Chapon et la poularde'

12 The best is the enemy of the good.
Dictionnaire philosophique, 'Art dramatique'

13 Superstition sets the whole world in flames; philosophy quenches them.
Dictionnaire philosophique, 'Superstition'

14 If God did not exist, it would be necessary to invent Him.
Épîtres, 'À l'auteur du livre des trois' Imposteurs'

15 The secret of the arts is to correct nature.
Épîtres, 'À M. de Verrière'

16 This agglomeration which was called and which still calls itself the Holy Roman Empire was neither holy, nor Roman, nor an empire.
Essai sur les moeurs et l'esprit des nations, LXX

17 All our ancient history, as one of our wits remarked, is no more than accepted fiction.
Jeannot et Colin

18 All styles are good except the tiresome sort.
L'Enfant prodigue, Preface

19 If God made us in His image, we have certainly returned the compliment.
Le Sottisier

20 Indeed, history is nothing more than a tableau of crimes and misfortunes.
L'Ingénu, Ch. 10

21 It is one of the superstitions of the human mind to have imagined that virginity could be a virtue.
Notebooks

22 Governments need to have both shepherds and butchers.
Notebooks

23 God is on the side not of the heavy battalions, but of the best shots.
Notebooks

24 We owe respect to the living; to the dead we owe only truth.
Oeuvres, 'Première lettre sur Oedipe'

25 Faith consists in believing when it is beyond the power of reason to believe. It is not enough that a thing be possible for it to be believed.
Questions sur l'encyclopédie

26 Marriage is the only adventure open to the cowardly.
Thoughts of a Philosopher

27 Never having been able to succeed in the world, he took his revenge by speaking ill of it.
Zadig, Ch. 4

28 There are two things for which animals are to be envied: they know nothing of future evils, or of what people say about them.
Letter, 1739

29 Men will always be mad and those who think they can cure them are the maddest of all.
Letter, 1762

30 The great consolation in life is to say what one thinks.
Letter, 1765

31 Once the people begin to reason, all is lost.
Letter to Damilaville, 1 Apr 1766

32 I am not like a lady at the court of Versailles, who said: 'What a dreadful pity that the bother at the tower of Babel should have got language all mixed up, but for that, everyone would always have spoken French.'
French was the dominant language in the educated circles of 18th-century Europe
Letter to Catherine the Great, Empress of Russia, 26 May 1767

33 The man who leaves money to charity in his will is only giving away what no longer belongs to him.
Letter, 1769

34 Men of England! You wish to kill me because I am a Frenchman. Am I not punished enough in not being born an Englishman?
Addressing an angry London mob who desired to hang him because he was a Frenchman
Attrib.

35 I think it must be so, for I have been drinking it for sixty-five years and I am not dead yet.
On learning that coffee was considered a slow poison
Attrib.

36 He was a great patriot, a humanitarian, a loyal friend – provided, of course, that he really is dead.
Giving a funeral oration
Attrib.

37 I do not think this poem will reach its destination.
Reviewing Rousseau's poem 'Ode to Posterity'
Attrib.

38 Once: a philosopher; twice: a pervert!
Turning down an invitation to an orgy, having attended one the previous night for the first time
Attrib.

39 I disapprove of what you say, but I will defend to the death your right to say it.
Attrib.

Vorster, John (Balthazar Johannes Vorster; 1915–83) South African politician. He became prime minister (1966–78) after Verwoerd's assassination. An extreme right winger, he retired over financial irregularities.

1 As far as criticism is concerned, we don't resent that unless it is absolutely biased, as it is in most cases.
The Observer, 'Sayings of the Week', 9 Nov 1969

Voznesensky, Andrei (1933–) Soviet poet. His translated poetry includes *Selected Poems* (1964), *Antiworlds* (1967), and *Temptation* (1978).

1 The art of creation
is older than the art of killing.
Poem with a Footnote

Vukovich, Bill (1918–55) US motor-racing driver.

1 There's no secret. You just press the accelerator to the floor and steer left.
Explaining his success in the Indianapolis 500
Attrib.

W

Wain, John (1925–) British novelist and poet. His books include the novels *Hurry on Down* (1953), *The Contenders* (1958), *Young Shoulders* (1982) and the biographies *Samuel Johnson* (1974) and *Dear Shadows* (1985). His verse is collected in *Poems 1949–79* (1981).

1 Poetry is to prose as dancing is to walking.
Talk, BBC radio, 13 Jan 1976

Walesa, Lech (1943–) Polish politician and trade unionist. He became leader of Solidarity on its formation in 1980 and was awarded the Nobel peace prize in 1983; in 1989 he helped form Poland's first noncommunist government since World War II.

1 I've never worked for prizes . . . I'm as ready to receive prizes as I am to be thrown into prison, not that I'm ungrateful for this honor; it's just that neither the one nor the other could ever divert me from the course I've set myself.
Walesa's response when awarded the Nobel Peace Prize, 1983
A Path of Hope, 'Private Citizen'

2 SOLIDARITY was born at that precise moment when the shipyard strike evolved from a local success in the shipyard, to a strike in support of other factories and business enterprises, large and small, in need of our protection: moral reasons impelled us toward solidarity with our neighbors and our co-workers in every line of endeavor.
A Path of Hope, 'The Strike and the August Agreements'

3 The hungry hare has no frontiers and doesn't follow ideologies. The hungry hare goes where it finds the food. And the other hares don't block its passage with the tanks.
Interview, 1981

Waley, Arthur (David) (1889–1966) British poet and translator of Chinese and Japanese poetry.

1 Keep off your thoughts from things that are past and done;
For thinking of the past wakes regret and pain.
Translation from the Chinese of Po-Chü-I
Resignation

Wall, Max (1908–90) British comedian.

1 Wall is the name – Max Wall. My father was the Great Wall of China. He was a brick.
Opening line of one of his acts

2 To me Adler will always be Jung.
Telegram to Larry Adler on his 60th birthday

Wallace, Edgar (1875–1932) British thriller and detective-story writer. He became a Hollywood scriptwriter having written some 170 popular novels.

1 A writer of crook stories ought never to stop seeking new material.
Said when a candidate for Parliament
The Long Weekend (Alan Hodge)

2 What is a highbrow? It is a man who has found something more interesting than women.
Interview

Wallace, Henry (1888–1965) US economist and politician. The secretary of agriculture (1933–40), he became vice-president of the USA (1941–45). His books include *New Frontiers* (1934) and *The American Choice* (1940).

1 The century on which we are entering – the century which will come out of this war – can be and must be the century of the common man.
Speech, 'The Price of Free World Victory', 8 May 1942

Wallace, Lew (1827–1905) US soldier, lawyer, and writer. He became a Federal general in the Civil War and governor of New Mexico (1878–81). His books include *The Fair God* (1873), *Ben Hur* (1880), and *The Prince of India* (1893).

1 Beauty is altogether in the eye of the beholder.
The Prince of India

Wallace, William Ross (1819–81) US poet and songwriter.

1 The hand that rocks the cradle
Is the hand that rules the world.
John o'London's Treasure Trove

Wallach, Eli (1915–) US actor and film star. An advocate of 'the method', he has appeared in many films including *Baby Doll* (1956), *Lord Jim* (1965), *The Salamander* (1980), and *Tough Guys* (1986).

1 There's something about a crowd like that that brings a lump to my wallet.
Remarking upon the long line of people at the box office before one of his performances
Attrib.

Walpole, Horace, 4th Earl of Orford (1717–97) British writer and fourth son of Robert Walpole. He is remembered for his gothic novel *The Castle of Otranto* (1765) and his gothic-revival villa at Twickenham, Strawberry Hill.

1 I am, sir for the last time in my life, Your Humble Servant Horace Walpole.
Ending a letter written to an uncle with whom he had recently quarrelled
Horace Walpole (R. Ketton-Cremes)

2 I have led a life of business so long that I have lost my taste for reading, and now – what shall I do?
Thraliana (K. Balderston)

3 Our supreme governors, the mob.

Letter to Sir Horace Mann, 7 Sept 1743

4 One of the greatest geniuses that ever existed, Shakespeare, undoubtedly wanted taste.

Letter to Wren, 9 Aug 1764

5 It is charming to totter into vogue.

Letter to G. A. Selwyn, 1765

6 The world is a comedy to those who think, a tragedy to those who feel.

Letter to Sir Horace Mann, 1769

7 By the waters of Babylon we sit down and weep, when we think of thee, O America!

On the eve of the American Revolution
Letter to Mason, 12 June 1775

8 When people will not weed their own minds, they are apt to be overrun with nettles.

Letter to Lady Ailesbury, 10 July 1779

9 I do not dislike the French from the vulgar antipathy between neighbouring nations, but for their insolent and unfounded airs of superiority.

Letter to Hannah More, 14 Oct 1787

10 Come, Robert, you shall drink twice while I drink once, for I cannot permit the son in his sober senses to witness the intoxication of his father.

Explaining why he filled his son's glass twice for every glass he drank himself
Attrib.

Walpole, Sir Robert, 1st Earl of Orford (1676–1745) British statesman. A Whig MP, he became secretary for war (1708–10) and chancellor of the exchequer (1715). He then became Britain's first prime minister (1721–42), maintaining his power by skilful management of parliament.

1 Anything but history, for history must be false.

Walpoliana

2 They now *ring* the bells, but they will soon *wring* their hands.

Said when war declared in 1739 with Spain, against Walpole's wishes
Memoirs of Sir Robert Walpole (W. Coxe)

3 All those men have their price.

Memoirs of Sir Robert Walpole (W. Coxe)

4 My Lord Bath, you and I are now two as insignificant men as any in England.

Said to William Pulteney, Earl of Bath, when they were promoted to the peerage (1742)
Political & Literary Anecdotes (W. King)

5 The balance of power.

Speech, House of Commons

Walton, Izaak (1593–1683) English writer, remembered for his treatise on fishing, *The Compleat Angler* (1653).

1 Angling may be said to be so like the mathematics, that it can never be fully learnt.

The Compleat Angler, Epistle to the Reader

2 Angling is somewhat like poetry, men are to be born so.

The Compleat Angler, Ch. 1

3 I remember that a wise friend of mine did usually say, 'that which is everybody's business is nobody's business'.

The Compleat Angler, Ch. 2

4 We may say of angling as Dr Boteler said of strawberries, 'Doubtless God could have made a better berry, but doubtless God never did.'

The Compleat Angler, Ch. 5

5 I love such mirth as does not make friends ashamed to look upon one another next morning.

The Compleat Angler, Ch. 5

6 Let the blessing of St Peter's Master be . . . upon all that are lovers of virtue; and dare trust in His providence; and be quiet; and go a-Angling.

The Compleat Angler, Ch. 21

7 Of this blest man, let his just praise be given, Heaven was in him, before he was in heaven.

Referring to Dr Richard Sibbes
Written in a copy of Returning Backslider by Richard Sibbes

Warburton, William (1698–1779) British churchman. He became chaplain (1754) to George II and Bishop of Gloucester (1759). He was a friend and literary executor of Alexander Pope.

1 Orthodoxy is my doxy; heterodoxy is another man's doxy.

Said to Lord Sandwich
Memoirs (Priestley), Vol. I

Ward, Artemus (Charles Farrar Browne; 1834–67) US humorous writer. He wrote for the Cleveland *Plain Dealer* and New York *Vanity Fair*, later publishing *Artemus Ward, His Book* (1862) and *Artemus Ward, His Travels* (1865).

1 I prefer temperance hotels – although they sell worse kinds of liquor than any other kind of hotels.

Artemus Ward's Lecture

2 Why is this thus? What is the reason of this thusness?

Artemus Ward's Lecture

3 I am happiest when I am idle. I could live for months without performing any kind of labour, and at the expiration of that time I should feel fresh and vigorous enough to go right on in the same way for numerous more months.

Pyrotechny

4 Why care for grammar as long as we are good?

Pyrotechny

5 Let us all be happy, and live within our means, even if we have to borrer the money to do it with.

Science and Natural History

Ware, George (19th century) British songwriter.

1 The boy I love is up in the gallery,
The boy I love is looking now at me.
The Boy in the Gallery

Warhol, Andy (Andrew Warhola; 1926–87) US pop artist and film producer, who made his reputation with paintings of soup cans and film stars. His films include *Sleep* (1963) and *The Chelsea Girls* (1966).

1 An artist is someone who produces things that people don't need to have but that he – for *some reason* – thinks it would be a good idea to give them.
From A to B and Back Again, 'Atmosphere'

2 Sex is the biggest nothing of all time.
Halliwell's Filmgoer's and Video Viewer's Companion

3 In the future, everyone will be famous for 15 minutes.
Attrib.

Warner, Susan (1819–85) US novelist. Her successful novels include *The Wide, Wide World* (1850), *Queechy* (1852), *Daisy* (1868), and *Nobody* (1882). Some books were written in collaboration with her sister Anna Bartlett Ward (1827–1915).

1 Jesus loves me – this I know,
For the Bible tells me so.
The Love of Jesus

Warren, Earl (1891–1971) US lawyer. Attorney general (1939–43) and governor (1943–53) of California, he became chief justice of the USA in 1953, ending racial segregation in US schools.

1 Many people consider the things which government does for them to be social progress, but they consider the things government does for others as socialism.
Peter's Quotations (Laurence J. Peter)

Washington, George (1732–99) US statesman and first president of the USA (1789–97). Commander in chief of the American forces in the American Revolution, he presided over the Constitutional Convention (1787) and was elected president of the new republic.

Quotations about Washington

1 First in war, first in peace, first in the hearts of his countrymen.
Henry Lee Addressing the House of Representatives, Dec 1799

2 The crude commercialism of America, its materializing spirit are entirely due to the country having adopted for its natural hero a man who could not tell a lie.
Oscar Wilde (1854–1900) Irish-born British dramatist. *The Decay of Lying*

Quotations by Washington

3 Associate yourself with men of good quality if you esteem your own reputation; for 'tis better to be alone than in bad company.
Rules of Civility

4 I heard the bullets whistle, and believe me, there is something charming in the sound.
Referring to a recent skirmish in the French and Indian War
Presidential Anecdotes (P. Boller)

5 Father, I cannot tell a lie. I did it with my little hatchet.
Attrib.

Watson, James Dewey (1928–) US geneticist. With Francis Crick he discovered the double-helical structure of the DNA molecule. His book *The Double Helix* (1968) gave a popular account of the discovery.

1 The thought could not be avoided that the best home for a feminist was in another person's lab.
The Double Helix, Ch. 2

2 Already for thirty-five years he had not stopped talking and almost nothing of fundamental value had emerged.
Referring to Francis Crick
The Double Helix, Ch. 8

Watts, Isaac (1674–1748) English theologian and hymn writer. His 600 hymns include 'O God, our help in ages past' and 'There is a land of pure delight'.

1 For Satan finds some mischief still
For idle hands to do.
Divine Songs for Children, 'Against Idleness and Mischief'

2 How doth the little busy bee
Improve each shining hour,
And gather honey all the day
From every opening flower!
Divine Songs for Children, 'Against Idleness and Mischief'

3 Let dogs delight to bark and bite,
For God hath made them so;
Let bears and lions growl and fight,
For 'tis their nature too.
Divine Songs for Children, 'Against Quarrelling'

4 Lord, I ascribe it to Thy grace,
And not to chance, as others do,
That I was born of Christian race,
And not a Heathen, or a Jew.
Divine Songs for Children, 'Praise for the Gospel'

5 There's no repentance in the grave.
Divine Songs for Children, 'Solemn Thoughts of God and Death'

6 Our God, our help in ages past,
Our hope for years to come,
Our shelter from the stormy blast,
And our eternal home.
Our God, Our Help in Ages Past

7 'Tis the voice of the sluggard, I heard him complain:
'You have waked me too soon, I must slumber again.'
The Sluggard

8 When I survey the wondrous Cross,
On which the Prince of Glory died,
My richest gain I count but loss
And pour contempt on all my pride.

When I Survey the Wondrous Cross

Waugh, Auberon (1939–) British novelist and critic. His
publications include the novel *Consider the Lilies* (1968) and
Another Voice (1986).

1 The English are growing demented about children. When I was a boy the classroom had icicles inside every window at this time of year.
We were savagely beaten three times a week
and made to run half-naked in the snow. But the
toughest NUPE mass-murderer starts blubbing
if you suggest that one little kiddie might have
to queue a little longer for its dins-dins as a result of NUPE's just action.

The Diaries of Auberon Waugh 1976–1985, 'January 25, 1979'

2 Politicians can forgive almost anything in the way
of abuse; they can forgive subversion, revolution, being contradicted, exposed as liars, even
ridiculed, but they can never forgive being
ignored.

The Observer, 11 Oct 1981

Waugh, Evelyn (1903–66) British novelist. He established
his reputation with *Decline and Fall* (1928) and *Vile Bodies* (1930).
Later books, after his conversion to Catholicism, include
Brideshead Revisited (1945) and the war trilogy *Sword of Honour*
(1952–61).

Quotations about Waugh

1 I expect you know my friend Evelyn Waugh,
who, like you, your Holiness, is a Roman
Catholic.

Randolph Churchill (1911–68) British political journalist. Remark
made during an audience with the Pope

2 Mr. Waugh, I always feel, is an antique in search
of a period, a snob in search of a class, perhaps
even a mystic in search of a beatific vision.

Malcolm Muggeridge (1903–) British writer. *The Most of Malcolm Muggeridge*

Quotations by Waugh

3 I expect you'll be becoming a schoolmaster sir.
That's what most of the gentlemen does sir,
that gets sent down for indecent behaviour.

Decline and Fall, Prelude

4 The sound of the English county families baying
for broken glass.

Decline and Fall, Prelude

5 We class schools you see, into four grades:
Leading School, First-rate School, Good School,
and School.

Decline and Fall, Pt. I, Ch. 1

6 We schoolmasters must temper discretion with
deceit.

Decline and Fall, Pt. I, Ch. 1

7 Very hard for a man with a wig to keep order.

Decline and Fall, Pt. I, Ch. 3

8 That's the public-school system all over. They
may kick you out, but they never let you down.

Decline and Fall, Pt. I, Ch. 3

9 Meanwhile you will write an essay on 'self-indulgence'. There will be a prize of half a crown for
the longest essay, irrespective of any possible
merit.

Decline and Fall, Pt. I, Ch. 5

10 I can't quite explain it, but I don't believe one
can ever be unhappy for long provided one does
just exactly what one wants to and when one
wants to.

Decline and Fall, Pt. I, Ch. 5

11 Nonconformity and lust stalking hand in hand
through the country, wasting and ravaging.

Decline and Fall, Pt. I, Ch. 5

12 For generations the British bourgeoisie have
spoken of themselves as gentlemen, and by that
they have meant, among other things, a self-
respecting scorn of irregular perquisites. It is
the quality that distinguishes the gentleman
from both the artist and the aristocrat.

Decline and Fall, Pt. I, Ch. 6

13 There aren't many left like him nowadays, what
with education and whisky the price it is.

Decline and Fall, Pt. I, Ch. 7

14 'The Welsh,' said the Doctor, 'are the only nation in the world that has produced no graphic
or plastic art, no architecture, no drama. They
just sing,' he said with disgust, 'sing and blow
down wind instruments of plated silver.'

Decline and Fall, Pt. I, Ch. 8

15 We can trace almost all the disasters of English
history to the influence of Wales.

Decline and Fall, Pt. I, Ch. 8

16 I have noticed again and again since I have been
in the Church that lay interest in ecclesiastical
matters is often a prelude to insanity.

Decline and Fall, Pt. I, Ch. 8

17 I have often observed in women of her type a
tendency to regard all athletics as inferior forms
of fox-hunting.

Decline and Fall, Pt. I, Ch. 10

18 I haven't been to sleep for over a year. That's
why I go to bed early. One needs more rest if
one doesn't sleep.

Decline and Fall, Pt. II, Ch. 3

19 There is a species of person called a 'Modern
Churchman' who draws the full salary of a bene-
ficed clergyman and need not commit himself to
any religious belief.

Decline and Fall, Pt. II, Ch. 4

20 I came to the conclusion many years ago that almost all crime is due to the repressed desire for aesthetic expression.
Decline and Fall, Pt. III, Ch. 1

21 He stood twice for Parliament, but so diffidently that his candidature passed almost unnoticed.
Decline and Fall, Pt. III, Ch. 1

22 Anyone who has been to an English public school will always feel comparatively at home in prison.
Decline and Fall, Pt. III, Ch. 4

23 He was greatly pained at how little he was pained by the events of the afternoon.
Decline and Fall, Pt. III, Ch. 4

24 Instead of this absurd division into sexes they ought to class people as static and dynamic.
Decline and Fall, Pt. III, Ch. 7

25 We are all American at puberty; we die French.
Diaries, 'Irregular Notes', 18 July 1961

26 Punctuality is the virtue of the bored.
Diaries, 'Irregular Notes', 26 Mar 1962

27 Assistant masters came and went . . . . Some liked little boys too little and some too much.
A Little Learning

28 You never find an Englishman among the underdogs – except in England of course.
The Loved One

29 In the dying world I come from quotation is a national vice. It used to be the classics, now it's lyric verse.
The Loved One

30 Enclosing every thin man, there's a fat man demanding elbow-room.
Similar sentiments have been expressed by others. *See* AMIS; CONNOLLY; ORWELL
Officers and Gentlemen, Interlude

31 Feather-footed through the plashy fen passes the questing vole.
Scoop, Bk. I, Ch. 1

32 '*The Beast* stands for strong mutually antagonistic governments everywhere', he said. 'Self-sufficiency at home, self-assertion abroad.'
Scoop, Bk. I, Ch. 1

33 Yes, cider and tinned salmon are the staple diet of the agricultural classes.
Scoop, Bk. I, Ch. 1

34 Pappenhacker says that every time you are polite to a proletarian you are helping to bolster up the capitalist system.
Scoop, Bk. I, Ch. 5

35 'I will not stand for being called a woman in my own house,' she said.
Scoop, Bk. I, Ch. 5

36 News is what a chap who doesn't care much about anything wants to read. And it's only news until he's read it. After that it's dead.
Scoop, Bk. I, Ch. 5

37 As there was no form of government common to the peoples thus segregated, nor tie of language, history, habit, or belief, they were called a Republic.
Scoop, Bk. II, Ch. 1

38 The better sort of Ishmaelites have been Christian for many centuries and will not publicly eat human flesh uncooked in Lent, without special and costly dispensation from their bishop.
Scoop, Bk. II, Ch. 1

39 Other nations use 'force'; we Britons alone use 'Might'.
Scoop, Bk. II, Ch. 5

40 Up to a point, Lord Copper.
A euphemism for 'No'
Scoop, passim

41 Particularly against books the Home Secretary is. If we can't stamp out literature in the country, we can at least stop it being brought in from outside.
Vile Bodies, Ch. 2

42 When the war broke out she took down the signed photograph of the Kaiser and, with some solemnity, hung it in the menservants' lavatory; it was her one combative action.
Vile Bodies, Ch. 3

43 She had heard someone say something about an Independent Labour Party, and was furious that she had not been asked.
Vile Bodies, Ch. 4

44 All this fuss about sleeping together. For physical pleasure I'd sooner go to my dentist any day.
Vile Bodies, Ch. 6

45 Lady Peabury was in the morning room reading a novel; early training gave a guilty spice to this recreation, for she had been brought up to believe that to read a novel before luncheon was one of the gravest sins it was possible for a gentlewoman to commit.
Work Suspended, 'An Englishman's Home'

46 I wouldn't give up writing about God at this stage, if I was you. It would be like P. G. Wodehouse dropping Jeeves half-way through the Wooster series.
Said to Grahame Greene, who proposed to write a political novel
Evelyn Waugh (Christopher Sykes)

47 Simply a radio personality who outlived his prime.
Referring to Winston Churchill
Evelyn Waugh (Christopher Sykes)

48 Manners are especially the need of the plain. The pretty can get away with anything.
The Observer, 'Sayings of the Year,' 1962

49 No writer before the middle of the 19th century wrote about the working classes other than as grotesque or as pastoral decoration. Then when they were given the vote certain writers started to suck up to them.

Interview
Paris Review, 1963

50 Nurse unupblown.

Cable sent after he had failed, while a journalist serving in Ethiopia, to substantiate a rumour that an English nurse had been blown up in an Italian air raid
Our Marvelous Native Tongue (R. Claiborne)

51 A typical triumph of modern science to find the only part of Randolph that was not malignant and remove it.

Remarking upon the news that Randolph Churchill had had a non-cancerous lung removed
Attrib.

52 Like German opera, too long and too loud.

Giving his opinions of warfare after the battle of Crete, 1941
Attrib.

53 I put the words down and push them a bit.

Obituary, *New York Times*, 11 Apr 1966

Wavell, Archibald Percival, Earl (1883–1950) British field marshal. He became chief of staff in Palestine after service in World War I. In World War II he defeated the Italians in Africa. He was viceroy of India (1943–47). A poet himself, he edited an anthology.

1 It is like a cigar. If it goes out, you can light it again but it never tastes quite the same.

Giving his opinion of love
Attrib.

Wayne, John (Marion Michael Morrison; 1907–79) US film actor. He played numerous heroic roles in such adventure films as *Stagecoach* (1939), *Rio Bravo* (1959), *The Green Berets* (1968), and *True Grit* (1969).

1 I play John Wayne in every picture regardless of the character, and I've been doing all right, haven't I?
I never had a goddam artistic problem in my life, never, and I've worked with the best of them.

Halliwell's Filmgoer's and Video Viewer's Companion

Weatherly, Frederic Edward (1848–1929) British lawyer and songwriter. His successes include 'London Bridge', 'Danny Boy', and 'Roses of Picardy'.

1 Where are the boys of the Old Brigade?

The Old Brigade

2 Roses are flowering in Picardy,
But there's never a rose like you.

Roses of Picardy

Webb, Beatrice (1858–1943) British economist and writer. The wife of Sidney Webb, Baron Passfield, she collaborated with him on several books, including *The History of Trade Unionism* (1894) and *Industrial Democracy* (1897).

1 Religion is love; in no case is it logic.

My Apprenticeship, Ch. 2

2 If I ever felt inclined to be timid as I was going into a room full of people, I would say to myself, 'You're the cleverest member of one of the cleverest families in the cleverest class of the cleverest nation in the world, why should you be frightened?'

Portraits from Memory (Bertrand Russell), 'Sidney and Beatrice Webb'

Webb, Sydney, Baron Passfield (1859–1947) British economist. An ardent socialist, he was a founder of the Fabian Society and the London School of Economics. He was a member of the London County Council and an MP. He wrote several books, some with his wife Beatrice Webb.

1 Old people are always absorbed in something, usually themselves; we prefer to be absorbed in the Soviet Union.

The Webbs and Their Work (Kingsley Martin)

2 The inevitability of gradualness.

Presidential Address to Labour Party Conference, 1923

Webster, Daniel (1782–1852) US statesman. A senator and renowned orator, he became secretary of state (1841–43; 1850–52) and an unsuccessful presidential candidate.

Quotations about Webster

1 Daniel Webster struck me much like a steam engine in trousers.

Sydney Smith (1771–1845) British clergyman and essayist. *A Memoir of the Reverend Sydney Smith* (Lady Holland)

2 God is the only president of the day, and Webster is his orator.

Henry David Thoreau (1817–62) US writer. Attrib.

Quotations by Webster

3 Age cannot wither her, nor custom stale her infinite virginity.

Paraphrasing a line from Shakespeare's *Antony and Cleopatra* on hearing of Andrew Jackson's steadfast maintenance that his friend Peggy Eaton did not deserve her scandalous reputation
Presidential Anecdotes (P. Boller)

4 The people's government, made for the people, made by the people, and answerable to the people.

Second speech on Foote's resolution, Jan 26 1830

5 The past, at least, is secure.

Speech, US Senate, 26 Jan 1830

6 I was born an American; I will live an American; I shall die an American.

Speech, US Senate, 17 July 1850

7 There is always room at the top.

When advised not to become a lawyer because the profession was overcrowded
Attrib.

Webster, John (1580–1625) English dramatist. His plays include *The White Devil* (1612) and *The Duchess of Malfi* (1613). He also collaborated with other dramatists, including Thomas Dekker.

1 Other sins only speak; murder shrieks out.

The Duchess of Malfi, IV:2

2 Physicians are like kings, – they brook no contradiction.

The Duchess of Malfi, V:2

3 We are merely the stars' tennis-balls, struck and bandied
Which way please them.

The Duchess of Malfi, V:4

4 I saw him even now going the way of all flesh, that is to say towards the kitchen.

Westward Hoe, II:2

5 We think caged birds sing, when indeed they cry.

The White Devil, V:4

Webster, Noah (1758–1843) US lexicographer and writer. His *American Dictionary of the English Language* (1828) did much to standardize US spellings.

1 No, my dear, it is *I* who am surprised; you are merely astonished.

Responding to his wife's comment that she had been surprised to find him embracing their maid
Attrib.

Weil, Simone (1909–43) French philosopher and religious mystic. An active socialist in the 1930s, she became a Roman Catholic in 1938. Her books include *Waiting for God* (1951) and *The Need for Roots* (1952).

1 Culture is an instrument wielded by professors to manufacture professors, who when their turn comes will manufacture professors.

The Need for Roots

2 The word 'revolution' is a word for which you kill, for which you die, for which you send the labouring masses to their death, but which does not possess any content.

Oppression and Liberty, 'Reflections Concerning the Causes of Liberty and Social Oppression'

3 But not even Marx is more precious to us than the truth.

Oppression and Liberty, 'Revolution Proletarienne'

4 The future is made of the same stuff as the present.

On Science, Necessity, and the Love of God (ed. Richard Rees), 'Some Thoughts on the Love of God'

Weiss, Peter (1916–82) German novelist and dramatist. He left Nazi Germany for Sweden in 1939. His plays include *Marat/Sade* (1964) and *The Investigation* (1965).

1 We invented the Revolution
but we don't know how to run it.

Marat/Sade, 15

Weissmuller, Johnny (1904–84) US swimmer and film actor. The winner of five Olympic gold medals, he later became the first Tarzan in sound films.

1 Me? Tarzan?

Reacting to an invitation to play Tarzan
Attrib.

Welch, Raquel (Raquel Tejada; 1940–) US film star, who became a sex symbol in the 1960s. Her later films include *Myra Breckinridge* (1970) and *The Prince and the Pauper* (1977).

1 The mind can also be an erogenous zone.

Colombo's Hollywood (J. R. Colombo)

Welles, Orson (1915–85) US film actor, director, and writer. He established his film reputation with *Citizen Kane* (1941), which he followed with *The Magnificent Ambersons* (1942). He featured, as an actor, in the title role of *The Third Man* (1949).

1 In Italy for thirty years under the Borgias they had warfare, terror, murder, bloodshed – they produced Michelangelo, Leonardo da Vinci and the Renaissance. In Switzerland they had brotherly love, five hundred years of democracy and peace, and what did they produce . . . ? The cuckoo clock.

The Third Man

2 I started at the top and worked my way down.

The Filmgoer's Book of Quotes (Leslie Halliwell)

3 There are only two emotions in a plane: boredom and terror.

The Observer, 'Sayings of the Week', 12 May 1985

4 I would just like to mention Robert Houdin who in the eighteenth century invented the vanishing bird-cage trick and the theater matinée – may he rot and perish. Good afternoon.

Addressing the audience at the end of a matinée performance
Great Theatrical Disasters (G. Brandreth)

Wellington, Arthur Wellesley, Duke of (1769– 1852) British general and statesman. He defeated the French in the Peninsular War and Napoleon at Waterloo. Known as the 'Iron Duke', he became Tory prime minister (1828–30). Under Peel he served as foreign secretary (1834–35).

Quotations about Wellington

1 He accepted peace as if he had been defeated.

Napoleon I (Napoleon Bonaparte; 1769–1821) French emperor.
Attrib.

2 The Duke of Wellington has exhausted nature and exhausted glory. His career was one unclouded longest day.

The Times, Obituary, 16 Sept 1852

Quotations by Wellington

3 It all depends upon that article there.

Indicating a passing infantryman when asked if he would be able to defeat Napoleon
The Age of Elegance (A. Bryant)

4 Yes, and they went down very well too.

Replying to the observation that the French cavalry had come up very well during the Battle of Waterloo
The Age of Elegance (A. Bryant)

5 In my situation as Chancellor of the University of Oxford, I have been much exposed to authors.

Collections and Recollections (G. W. E. Russell)

6 Not upon a man from the colonel to the private in a regiment – both inclusive. We may pick up a marshal or two perhaps; but not worth a damn.
Said during the Waterloo campaign, when asked whether he anticipated any desertions from Napoleon's army
Creevey Papers, Ch. X

7 It has been a damned serious business – Blücher and I have lost 30,000 men. It has been a damned nice thing – the nearest run thing you ever saw in your life . . . By God! I don't think it would have done if I had not been there.
Referring to the Battle of Waterloo
Creevey Papers, Ch. X

8 I always say that, next to a battle lost, the greatest misery is a battle gained.
Diary (Frances, Lady Shelley)

9 I see no reason to suppose that these machines will ever force themselves into general use.
Referring to steam locomotives
Geoffrey Madan's Notebooks (J. Gere)

10 I hate the whole race . . . There is no believing a word they say – your professional poets, I mean – there never existed a more worthless set than Byron and his friends for example.
Lady Salisbury's diary, 26 Oct 1833

11 I used to say of him that his presence on the field made the difference of forty thousand men.
Referring to Napoleon
Notes of Conversations with the Duke of Wellington (Stanhope), 2 Nov 1831

12 The next greatest misfortune to losing a battle is to gain such a victory as this.
Recollections (S. Rogers)

13 The greatest tragedy in the world, Madam, except a defeat.
In reply to the remark, 'What a glorious thing must be a victory'
Recollections (S. Rogers)

14 You must build your House of Parliament upon the river: so . . . that the populace cannot exact their demands by sitting down round you.
Words on Wellington (Sir William Fraser)

15 I don't know what effect these men will have on the enemy, but, by God, they frighten me.
Referring to his generals
Attrib.

16 I have got an infamous army, very weak and ill-equipped, and a very inexperienced staff.
Written at the beginning of the Waterloo campaign
Letter to Lord Stewart, 8 May 1815

17 It is not the business of generals to shoot one another.
Refusing an artillery officer permission to fire upon Napoleon himself during the Battle of Waterloo, 1815
Attrib.

18 Up, Guards, and at 'em.
Order given at the battle of Waterloo, 18 June 1815
Attrib.

19 The battle of Waterloo was won on the playing fields of Eton.
Attrib.

20 Yes, about ten minutes.
Responding to a vicar's query as to whether there was anything he would like his forthcoming sermon to be about
Attrib.

21 Very well, then I shall not take off my boots.
Responding to the news, as he was going to bed, that the ship in which he was travelling seemed about to sink
Attrib.

22 Ours is composed of the scum of the earth.
Of the British army
Remark, 4 Nov 1831

23 Publish and be damned!
On being offered the chance to avoid mention in the memoirs of Harriette Wilson by giving her money
Attrib.

24 I don't care a twopenny damn what becomes of the ashes of Napoleon Bonaparte.
Attrib.

25 Don't quote Latin; say what you have to say, and then sit down.
Advice to a new Member of Parliament
Attrib.

26 A battle of giants.
Referring to the Battle of Waterloo; said to Samuel Rogers
Attrib.

27 Sparrowhawks, Ma'am.
Advice when asked by Queen Victoria how to remove sparrows from the Crystal Palace
Attrib.

Wells, H(erbert) G(eorge) (1866–1946) British writer.
After studying science, he won a literary reputation with *The Time Machine* (1895) and *Kipps* (1905). His other books included *An Outline of History* (1920) and *The Shape of Things to Come* (1933).

Quotations about Wells

1 Whatever Wells writes is not only alive, but kicking.
Henry James (1843–1916) US novelist. Attrib.

2 I doubt whether in the whole course of our history, any one individual has explored as many avenues, turned over so many stones, ventured along so many culs-de-sac. Science, history, politics, all were within his compass.
Malcolm Muggeridge (1903–) British writer. *The Observer*, 11 Sept 1966

Quotations by Wells

3 The cat is the offspring of a cat and the dog of a dog, but butlers and lady's maids do not reproduce their kind. They have other duties.
Bealby, Pt I, Ch. 1

4 He was quite sure that he had been wronged. Not to be wronged is to forgo the first privilege of goodness.
Bealby, Pt. IV, Ch. 1

5 Miss Madeleine Philips was making it very manifest to Captain Douglas that she herself was a career; that a lover with any other career in view need not – as the advertisements say – apply.
Bealby, Pt. V, Ch. 5

6 He began to think the tramp a fine, brotherly, generous fellow. He was also growing accustomed to something – shall I call it an olfactory bar – that had hitherto kept them apart.
Bealby, Pt. VI, Ch. 3

7 The army ages men sooner than the law and philosophy; it exposes them more freely to germs, which undermine and destroy, and it shelters them more completely from thought, which stimulates and preserves.
Bealby, Pt. VIII, Ch. 1

8 He had one peculiar weakness; he had faced death in many forms but he had never faced a dentist. The thought of dentists gave him just the same sick horror as the thought of Socialism.
Bealby, Pt. VIII, Ch. 1

9 In the Country of the Blind the One-eyed Man is King.
The Country of the Blind

10 '*Language*, man!' roared Parsons; 'why, it's LITERATURE!'
The History of Mr Polly, Pt. I, Ch. 3

11 'You're a Christian?' 'Church of England,' said Mr Polly. 'Mm,' said the employer, a little checked. 'For good all round business work, I should have preferred a Baptist.'
The History of Mr Polly, Pt. III, Ch. 1

12 Arson, after all, is an artificial crime . . . A large number of houses deserve to be burnt.
The History of Mr Polly, Pt. X, Ch. 1

13 'It's giving girls names like that', said Buggins, 'that nine times out of ten makes 'em go wrong. It unsettles 'em. If ever I was to have a girl, if ever I was to have a dozen girls, I'd call 'em all Jane.'
Referring to the name Euphemia
Kipps, Bk. I, Ch. 4

14 It's 'aving 'ouses built by men, I believe, makes all the work and trouble.
Kipps, Bk. III, Ch. 1

15 Everybody hates house-agents because they have everybody at a disadvantage. All other callings have a certain amount of give and take; the house-agent simply takes.
Kipps, Bk. III, Ch. 1

16 We were taught as the chief subjects of instruction Latin and Greek. We were taught very badly because the men who taught us did not habitually use either of these languages.
The New Machiavelli, Bk. I., Ch. 3

17 Cynicism is humour in ill-health.
Short Stories, 'The Last Trump'

18 He doubted the existence of the Deity but accepted Carnot's cycle, and he had read Shakespeare and found him weak in chemistry.
Short Stories, 'The Lord of the Dynamos'

19 Bricklayers kick their wives to death, and dukes betray theirs; but it is among the small clerks and shopkeepers nowadays that it comes most often to the cutting of throats.
Short Stories, 'The Purple Pileus'

20 The War to End War.
Book title

21 If Max gets to Heaven he won't last long. He will be chucked out for trying to pull off a merger between Heaven and Hell . . . after having secured a controlling interest in key subsidiary companies in both places, of course.
Referring to Lord Beaverbrook
Beaverbrook (A. J. P. Taylor)

22 One thousand years more. That's all *Homo sapiens* has before him.
Diary (Harold Nicolson)

Wesker, Arnold (1932–) British dramatist. His early socialist plays on Jewish themes, *Chicken Soup with Barley* (1958), *Roots* (1959), and *I'm Talking About Jerusalem* (1960), were followed by *Chips with Everything* (1962), *The Merchant* (1978), and *Shoeshine* (1988) among other plays.

1 You breed babies and you eat chips with everything.
Chips with Everything, I:2

2 Every place I look at I work out the cubic feet, and I say it will make a good warehouse or it won't. Can't help myself. One of the best warehouses I ever see was the Vatican in Rome.
Chips with Everything, I:6

3 Don't you sit there and sigh gal like you was Lady Nevershit.
Roots, III

Wesley, Charles (1707–88) British religious leader, who founded Methodism with his brother John Wesley. He composed a large number of hymns.

1 Gentle Jesus, meek and mild,
Look upon a little child;
Pity my simplicity,
Suffer me to come to thee.
Hymns and Sacred Poems

Wesley, John (1703–91) British religious leader, who founded Methodism with his brother Charles Wesley.

1 I look upon all the world as my parish.
Journal, 11 June 1739

2 Beware you be not swallowed up in books! An ounce of love is worth a pound of knowledge.
Life of Wesley (R. Southey), Ch. 16

3 We should constantly use the most common, little, easy words (so they are pure and proper) which our language affords.

Advice for preaching to 'plain people'
Attrib.

West, Mae (1892–1980) US actress, sex symbol, and comedienne. She made her reputation in the theatre with *Diamond Lil* (1928). Her films included *She Done Him Wrong* (1933) and *I'm No Angel* (1933).

Quotations about West

1 In a non-permissive age, she made remarkable inroads against the taboos of her day, and did so without even lowering her neckline.

Leslie Halliwell (1929–) British journalist and author. *The Filmgoer's Book of Quotes*

2 She stole everything but the cameras.

George Raft (1895–1980) US actor. Attrib.

Quotations by West

3 A man in the house is worth two in the street.

Belle of the Nineties, film 1934

4 My goodness those diamonds are lovely! Goodness had nothing whatever to do with it.

Used in 1959 as the title of the first volume of her autobiography
Diamond Lil, film 1932

5 I have a lot of respect for that dame. There's one lady barber that made good.

Referring to Delilah
Going to Town, film 1934

6 Beulah, peel me a grape.

I'm No Angel, film 1933

7 A gold rush is what happens when a line of chorus girls spot a man with a bank roll.

Klondike Annie, film 1936

8 I always did like a man in uniform. And that one fits you grand. Why don't you come up sometime and see me?

Often misquoted as 'Come up and see me some time'
She Done Him Wrong, film 1933

9 You're a fine woman, Lou. One of the finest women that ever walked the streets.

She Done Him Wrong, film 1933

10 You can say what you like about long dresses, but they cover a multitude of shins.

Peel Me a Grape (J. Weintraub)

11 It's hard to be funny when you have to be clean.

The Wit and Wisdom of Mae West (ed. J. Weintraub)

12 It is better to be looked over than overlooked.

The Wit and Wisdom of Mae West (ed. J. Weintraub)

13 I used to be Snow White . . . but I drifted.

The Wit and Wisdom of Mae West (ed. J. Weintraub)

14 When women go wrong, men go right after them.

The Wit and Wisdom of Mae West (ed. J. Weintraub)

15 I'm glad you like my Catherine. I like her too. She ruled thirty million people and had three thousand lovers. I do the best I can in two hours.

After her performance in *Catherine the Great*
Speech from the stage

16 Everything.

When asked what she wanted to be remembered for
Attrib.

17 When I'm good I'm very good, but when I'm bad I'm better.

Attrib.

18 Whenever I'm caught between two evils, I take the one I've never tried.

Attrib.

19 I've been in *Who's Who*, and I know what's what, but this is the first time I ever made the dictionary.

On having a life-jacket named after her
Attrib.

West, Nathaniel (Nathan Weinstein; 1903–40) US novelist and scriptwriter. His novels include *Miss Lonelyhearts* (1933) and *The Day of the Locust* (1939).

1 Are you in trouble? Do you need advice? Write to Miss Lonelyhearts and she will help.

Miss Lonelyhearts

West, Dame Rebecca (Cicely Isabel Fairfield; 1892–1983) British novelist and journalist. Novels include *The Thinking Reed* (1936) and *The Birds Fall Down* (1966). Other books, such as *The Meaning of Treason* (1949) and *A Train of Powder*, are essays in political journalism.

1 But there are other things than dissipation that thicken the features. Tears, for example.

Black Lamb and Grey Falcon, 'Serbia'

2 . . . any authentic work of art must start an argument between the artist and his audience.

The Court and the Castle, Pt. I, Ch. 1

3 The point is that nobody likes having salt rubbed into their wounds, even if it is the salt of the earth.

The Salt of the Earth, Ch. 2

4 God forbid that any book should be banned. The practice is as indefensible as infanticide.

The Strange Necessity, 'The Tosh Horse'

5 There is no such thing as conversation. It is an illusion. There are intersecting monologues, that is all.

There Is No Conversation, Ch. 1

6 Margaret Thatcher's great strength seems to be the better people know her, the better they like her. But, of course, she has one great disadvantage – she is a daughter of the people and looks trim, as the daughters of the people desire to be. Shirley Williams has such an advantage over her because she's a member of the upper-middle class and can achieve that kitchen-sink-revolutionary look that one cannot get unless one has been to a really good school.

Said in an interview with Jilly Cooper
The Sunday Times, 25 July 1976

7 My dear – the people we should have been seen dead with.

Cable sent to Noël Coward after learning they had both been on a Nazi death list
Times Literary Supplement, 1 Oct 1982

8 Just how difficult it is to write biography can be reckoned by anybody who sits down and considers just how many people know the real truth about his or her love affairs.

Vogue magazine

Weston, R. P. (20th century) British songwriter.

1 Good-bye-ee! – good-bye-ee!
Wipe the tear, baby dear, from your eye-ee.
Tho' it's hard to part, I know,
I'll be tickled to death to go.
Don't cry-ee! – don't sigh-ee!
There's a silver lining in the sky-ee! –
Bonsoir, old thing! cheerio! chin-chin!
Nahpoo! Toodle-oo! Good-bye-ee!

Good-bye-ee! (with Bert Lee)

2 Some soldiers send epistles, say they'd sooner sleep in thistles
Than the saucy, soft, short shirts for soldiers, sister Susie sews.

Sister Susie's Sewing Shirts for Soldiers

Wetherell, Sir Charles (1770–1846) British lawyer and judge.

1 Then there is my noble and biographical friend who has added a new terror to death.

Referring to Lord Campbell
Misrepresentations in Campbell's Lives of Lyndhurst and Brougham (Lord St. Leonards)

Weygand, Maxime (1867–1965) French general. He was the chief of Foch's general staff in World War I. In World War II he was in command during the 1940 retreat and subsequently the Vichy government's commander in North Africa.

1 In three weeks England will have her neck wrung like a chicken.

Said at the fall of France; see CHURCHILL
Their Finest Hour (Winston S. Churchill)

Wharton, Edith (1862–1937) US novelist. Her books include *The Valley of Decision* (1902), *The Age of Innocence* (1920), and *Certain People* (1930).

1 An unalterable and unquestioned law of the musical world required that the German text of French operas sung by Swedish artists should be translated into Italian for the clearer understanding of English speaking audiences.

The Age of Innocence, Bk. I, Ch. 1

2 She keeps on being Queenly in her own room with the door shut.

The House of Mirth, Bk. II, Ch. 1

3 Another unsettling element in modern art is that common symptom of immaturity, the dread of doing what has been done before.

The Writing of Fiction, Ch. 1

4 Mrs Ballinger is one of the ladies who pursue Culture in bands, as though it were dangerous to meet it alone.

Xingu, Ch. 1

Whately, Richard (1787–1863) British churchman, theologian, and logician. He became Archbishop of Dublin (1831–63) and wrote a number of religious books but is remembered for his *Logic* (1826) and *Rhetoric* (1828).

1 Happiness is no laughing matter.

Apophthegms

2 Honesty is the best policy; but he who is governed by that maxim is not an honest man.

Apophthegms

Wheeler, Hugh (1912–87) British-born US novelist and dramatist. His plays include *A Little Night Music* (1974), adapted from an Ingmar Bergman film, and *Sweeny Todd* (1979).

1 To lose a lover or even a husband or two during the course of one's life can be vexing. But to lose one's teeth is a catastrophe.

A Little Night Music

Whewell, William (1794–1866) British philosopher and mathematician, who became master of Trinity College (1841–66) and vice-chancellor of Cambridge University (1843; 1856). His books include *History of the Inductive Sciences* (1837) and *Plurality of Worlds* (1853).

1 Hence no force however great can stretch a cord however fine into an horizontal line which is accurately straight: there will always be a bending downwards.

An example of unintentional versification
Elementary Treatise on Mechanics (1819 edition), Ch. 4

Whistler, James Abbott McNeill (1834–1903) US painter. Living mostly in Europe, he established his reputation with *The Artist's Mother* and *Nocturne in Blue and Gold*. He was also the author of *The Gentle Art of Making Enemies* (1890).

Quotations about Whistler

1 I have seen, and heard, much of cockney impudence before now, but never expected to hear a coxcomb ask two hundred guineas for flinging a pot of paint in the public's face.

John Ruskin (1819–1900) British art critic and writer. *Fors Clavigera*, 2 July 1877

2 That he is indeed one of the very greatest master of painting, is my opinion. And I may add that in this opinion Mr. Whistler himself entirely concurs.

Oscar Wilde (1854–1900) Irish-born British dramatist. *Pall Mall Gazette*, 21 Feb 1885

Quotations by Whistler

3 I am not arguing with you – I am telling you.

The Gentle Art of Making Enemies

4 Nature is usually wrong.

The Gentle Art of Making Enemies

5 No, no, Oscar, you forget. When you and I are together we never talk about anything except me.

Cable replying to Oscar Wilde's message: 'When you and I are together we never talk about anything except ourselves'
The Gentle Art of Making Enemies

6 If silicon had been a gas I should have been a major-general.

Referring to his failure in a West Point chemistry examination
English Wits (L. Russell)

7 No, I ask it for the knowledge of a lifetime.

Replying to the taunt, during the Ruskin trial, that he was asking a fee of 200 guineas for two days' painting.
Lives of the Wits (H. Pearson)

8 Isn't it? I know in my case I would grow intolerably conceited.

Replying to the pointed observaton that it was as well that we do not not see ourselves as others see us
The Man Whistler (H. Pearson)

9 A LADY. I only know of two painters in the world: yourself and Velasquez.
WHISTLER. Why drag in Velasquez?

Whistler Stories (D. Seitz)

10 You shouldn't say it is not good. You should say you do not like it; and then, you know, you're perfectly safe.

Whistler Stories (D. Seitz)

11 A LADY. This landscape reminds me of your work.
WHISTLER. Yes madam, Nature is creeping up.

Whistler Stories (D. Seitz)

12 Perhaps not, but then you can't call yourself a great work of nature.

Responding to a sitter's complaint that his portrait was not a great work of art
Whistler Stories (D. Seitz)

13 I cannot tell you that, madam. Heaven has granted me no offspring.

Replying to a lady who had inquired whether he thought genius hereditary
Whistler Stories (D. Seitz)

14 It has none, your Highness. Its history dates from today.

Replying to a query from the Prince of Wales about the history of the Society of British Artists, which he was visiting for the first time.
Whistler Stories (D. Seitz)

15 It is very simple. The artists retired. The British remained.

Explaining his resignation as president of the Royal Society of British Artists
Whistler Stories (D. Seitz)

16 Well, not bad, but there are decidedly too many of them, and they are not very well arranged. I would have done it differently.

His reply when asked if he agreed that the stars were especially beautiful one night.
Attrib.

17 You will, Oscar, you will.

Replying to Oscar Wilde's exclamation 'I wish I had said that!'
Attrib.

18 The explanation is quite simple. I wished to be near my mother.

Explaining to a snobbish lady why he had been born in such an unfashionable place as Lowell, Massachusetts
Attrib.

19 Listen! There never was an artistic period. There never was an Art-loving nation.

Attrib.

White, Andrew Dickson (1832–1918) US educationalist and diplomat. He helped to found Cornell University and was its first president (1868–85). He was also US ambassador to Germany (1897–1902).

1 I will not permit thirty men to travel four hundred miles to agitate a bag of wind.

Refusing to allow the Cornell football team to visit Michigan to play a match
The People's Almanac (D. Wallechinsky)

White, Elwyn Brooks (1899–1985) US journalist and humorous writer. A regular contributor to *The New Yorker*, he wrote many books including *One Man's Meat* (1942), *The Second Tree from the Corner* (1954), and *Points of my Compass* (1962).

1 Commuter – one who spends his life
In riding to and from his wife;
A man who shaves and takes a train,
And then rides back to shave again.

The Commuter

2 As in the sexual experience, there are never more than two persons present in the act of reading – the writer who is the impregnator, and the reader who is the respondent.

The Second Tree from the Corner

3 To perceive Christmas through its wrapping becomes more difficult with every year.

The Second Tree from the Corner

White, Henry Kirke (1785–1806) British poet. He is remembered for his verse collection *Clifton Grove* (1803) and for several hymns.

1 Much in sorrow, oft in woe,
Onward, Christians, onward go.

A hymn, better known in its later form, 'Oft in danger, oft in woe'

White, Patrick (1912–90) British-born Australian novelist. His novels include *The Tree of Man* (1955), *Voss* (1957), *The Solid Mandala* (1966), and *Memoirs of Many in One* (1986).

1 But bombs *are* unbelievable until they actually fall.
Riders in the Chariot, I:4

2 'I dunno,' Arthur said. 'I forget what I was taught. I only remember what I've learnt.'
The Solid Mandala, Ch. 2

3 All my novels are an accumulation of detail. I'm a bit of a bower-bird.
Southerly, 139

4 Well, good luck to you, kid! I'm going to write the Great Australian Novel.
The Vivisector, 112

White, T(erence) H(anbury) (1906–64) British novelist. His best-known books are on Arthurian legend and include *The Once and Future King* (1958).

1 The Victorians had not been anxious to go away for the weekend. The Edwardians, on the contrary, were nomadic.
Farewell Victoria, Ch. 4

White, William Allen (1868–1944) US writer. His books include *In Our Town* (1906), *In the Heart of a Fool* (1918), and *The Changing West* (1939). He was editor and owner of the *Emporia Gazette*.

1 All dressed up, with nowhere to go.
Referring to the Progressive Party, after Theodore Roosevelt's withdrawal from the 1916 US Presidential election

Whitehead, A(lfred) N(orth) (1861–1947) British philosopher and mathematician. With Bertrand Russell he wrote *Principia Mathematica* (1910–13). Other books include *The Principles of Natural Knowledge* (1919) and *The Concept of Nature* (1920).

1 Where are no whole truths; all truths are half-truths. It is trying to treat them as whole truths that plays the devil.
Dialogues, 16

2 Intelligence is quickness to apprehend as distinct from ability, which is capacity to act wisely on the thing apprehended.
Dialogues, 135

3 Art is the imposing of a pattern on experience, and our aesthetic enjoyment is recognition of the pattern.
Dialogues, 228

4 Philosophy is the product of wonder.
Nature and Life, Ch. 1

5 A science which hesitates to forget its founders is lost.
Attrib.

6 The history of Western philosophy is, after all, no more than a series of footnotes to Plato's philosophy.
Attrib.

Whitehorn, Katherine (1926–) British journalist and writer. She has written a column in *The Observer* since 1960. Her books include *Only on Sundays* (1966), *How to Survive Children* (1975), and *View from a Column* (1981).

1 Hats divide generally into three classes: offensive hats, defensive hats, and shrapnel.
Shouts and Murmurs, 'Hats'

2 And what would happen to my illusion that I am a force for order in the home if I wasn't married to the only man north of the Tiber who is even untidier than I am?
Sunday Best, 'Husband-Swapping'

3 The Life and Soul, the man who will never go home while there is one man, woman or glass of anything not yet drunk.
Sunday Best, 'Husband-Swapping'

4 It is a pity, as my husband says, that more politicians are not bastards by birth instead of vocation.
The Observer, 1964

5 Have you ever taken anything out of the clothes basket because it had become, relatively, the cleaner thing?
The Observer, 'On Shirts', 1964

6 The best careers advice to give to the young is 'Find out what you like doing best and get someone to pay you for doing it.'
The Observer, 1975

7 A good listener is not someone who has nothing to say. A good listener is a good talker with a sore throat.
Attrib.

Whitelaw, William (Stephen Ian), Viscount (1918–) British politician. He became home secretary in Mrs Thatcher's administration and subsequently lord president of the council and leader of the House of Lords.

1 It is never wise to try to appear to be more clever than you are. It is sometimes wise to appear slightly less so.
The Observer, 'Sayings of the Year', 1975

2 I do not intend to prejudge the past.
Said on arriving in Ulster as Minister for Northern Ireland
The Times, 3 Dec 1973

3 I am not prepared to go about the country stirring up apathy.
Attrib.

Whiting, William (1825–78) British hymn writer.

1 O hear us when we cry to Thee
For those in peril on the sea.
Eternal Father Strong to Save

Whitlam, Gough (1916–) Australian statesman. He became Labor leader in 1967 and then prime minister (1972–75). He was dismissed by the governor, Sir John Kerr, and resigned the leadership of the Labor Party in 1977.

1 I do not mind the Liberals, still less do I mind the Country Party, calling me a bastard. In some circumstances I am only doing my job if they do. But I hope you will not publicly call me a bastard, as some bastards in the Caucus have.
Speech to the Australian Labor Party, 9 June 1974

Whitman, Walt (1819–92) US poet. His first verse collection, *Leaves of Grass* (1855), was poorly received at first, although it went through nine editions in his lifetime. Other books include *Democratic Vistas* (1871), *November Boughs* (1888), and *Goodbye, My Fancy* (1891).

Quotations about Whitman

1 Walt Whitman who laid end to end words never seen in each other's company before outside of a dictionary.

David Lodge (1935–) British author. *Changing Places*, Ch. 5

2 He is a writer of something occasionally like English, and a man of something occasionally like genius.

Algernon Charles Swinburne (1837–1909) British poet. *Whitmania*

Quotations by Whitman

3 No one will ever get at my verses who insists upon viewing them as a literary performance.

A Backward Glance O'er Travel'd Roads

4 I hear it was charged against me that I sought to destroy institutions,
But really I am neither for nor against institutions.

I Hear It was Charged against Me

5 If anything is sacred the human body is sacred.

I Sing the Body Electric, 8

6 I celebrate myself, and sing myself,
And what I assume you shall assume.

Song of Myself, 1

7 I think I could turn and live with animals, they're so placid and self-contained,
I stand and look at them long and long.

Song of Myself, 32

8 Behold, I do not give lectures or a little charity,
When I give I give myself.

Song of Myself, 40

9 I have said that the soul is not more than the body,
And I have said that the body is not more than the soul,
And nothing, but God, is greater to one than one's self is.

Song of Myself, 48

10 Do I contradict myself?
Very well then I contradict myself,
(I am large, I contain multitudes).

Song of Myself, 51

11 Where the populace rise at once against the never-ending audacity of elected persons.

Song of the Broad Axe, 5

12 A great city is that which has the greatest men and women.

Song of the Broad-Axe, 5

13 After you have exhausted what there is in business, politics, conviviality, and so on – have found that none of these finally satisfy, or permanently wear – what remains? Nature remains.

Specimen Days, 'New Themes Entered Upon'

14 The earth does not argue,
Is not pathetic, has no arrangements,
Does not scream, haste, persuade, threaten, promise,
Makes no discriminations, has no conceivable failures,
Closes nothing, refuses nothing, shuts none out.

To the sayers of words

Whittier, John Greenleaf (1807–92) US poet. A Quaker and an abolitionist, his books include *Legends of New England in Prose and Verse* (1831), *Songs of Labor* (1850), *Snow-Bound* (1866), and *At Sundown* (1890). His best-known poem is 'Barbara Frietchie'.

1 Up from the meadows rich with corn,
Clear in the cool September morn,

The clustered spires of Frederick stand
Green-walled by the hills of Maryland.

Barbara Frietchie

2 'Shoot, if you must, this old gray head,
But spare your country's flag,' she said.

A shade of sadness, a blush of shame,
Over the face of the leader came.

Barbara Frietchie

Whittington, Robert (16th century) English writer.

1 As time requireth, a man of marvellous mirth and pastimes, and sometimes of as sad gravity, as who say: a man for all seasons.

Referring to Sir Thomas More; after Erasmus
Vulgaria, Pt. II, 'De constructione nominum'

Whorf, Benjamin Lee (1897–1941) US linguist. His best-known work is *Language, Thought, and Reality* (1956). He earned his living as an insurance inspector.

1 We dissect nature along lines laid down by our native language . . . Language is not simply a reporting device for experience but a defining framework for it.

New Directions in the Study of Language (ed. Hoyer), 'Thinking in Primitive Communities'

Wigg, George Edward Cecil, Baron (1900–76) British politician. He was paymaster general (1964–67) and became President of the Betting Office Licensees' Association.

1 For Hon. Members opposite the deterrent is a phallic symbol. It convinces them that they are men.

The Observer, 'Sayings of the Week', 8 Mar 1964

Wilberforce, Samuel (1805–73) British churchman. He became Bishop of Oxford (1845) and of Winchester (1869). His books include *Agathos* (1840).

1 And, in conclusion, I would like to ask the gentleman . . . whether the ape from which he is descended was on his grandmother's or his grandfather's side of the family.
See T. H. HUXLEY
Speech, 30 June 1960

2 If I were a cassowary
On the plains of Timbuctoo,
I would eat a missionary,
Cassock, band, and hymn-book too.
Also attrib. to W. M. Thackeray
Attrib.

Wilberforce, William (1759–1833) British philanthropist. As an MP he fought to end the slave trade.

1 God Almighty has set me two great objects, the suppression of the Slave Trade and the reformation of manners.
Diary, 1787

2 They charge me with fanaticism. If to be feelingly alive to the sufferings of my fellow-creatures is to be a fanatic, I am one of the most incurable fanatics ever permitted to be at large.
Speech, House of Commons, 19 June 1816

Wilcox, Ella Wheeler (1850–1919) US poet. Her verse collections include *Drops of Water* (1872), *Poems of Passion* (1873), and *The Art of Being Alive* (1914).

1 We flatter those we scarcely know,
We please the fleeting guest,
And deal full many a thoughtless blow
To those who love us best.
Life's Scars

2 No question is ever settled
Until it is settled right.
Settle the Question Right

3 Laugh, and the world laughs with you;
Weep, and you weep alone,
For the sad old earth must borrow its mirth,
But has trouble enough of its own.
Solitude

4 So many gods, so many creeds,
So many paths that wind and wind,
While just the art of being kind
Is all the sad world needs.
The World's Need

Wilde, Oscar Fingal O'Flahertie Wills (1856–1900) Irish-born British poet and dramatist. His comedies *Lady Windermere's Fan* (1892), *An Ideal Husband* (1895), and *The Importance of Being Earnest* (1895) made him a leading figure in London society. However he was ruined by a trial (1895) arising from his homosexual relationships, especially with Lord Alfred Douglas. During his imprisonment he wrote *De Profundis* (1905) and the *The Ballad of Reading Gaol* (1898).

Quotations about Wilde

1 From the beginning Wilde performed his life and continued to do so even after fate had taken the plot out of his hands.
W. H. Auden (1907–73) British poet. *Forwards and Afterwards*

2 If with the literate I am
Impelled to try an epigram
I never seek to take the credit
We all assume that Oscar said it.
Dorothy Parker (1893–1967) US writer. Attrib.

3 He was over-dressed, pompous, snobbish, sentimental and vain. But he had an undeniable *flair* for the possibilities of commercial theatre.
Evelyn Waugh (1903–66) British novelist. *Harper's Bazaar*, Nov 1930

Quotations by Wilde

4 I never saw a man who looked
With such a wistful eye
Upon that little tent of blue
Which prisoners call the sky.
The Ballad of Reading Gaol, I:3

5 Yet each man kills the thing he loves,
By each let this be heard,
Some do it with a bitter look,
Some with a flattering word.
The coward does it with a kiss,
The brave man with a sword!
The Ballad of Reading Gaol, I:7

6 The Governor was strong upon
The Regulations Act:
The Doctor said that Death was but
A scientific fact:
And twice a day the Chaplain called,
And left a little tract.
The Ballad of Reading Gaol, III:3

7 Something was dead in each of us,
And what was dead was Hope.
The Ballad of Reading Gaol, III:31

8 For he who lives more lives than one
More deaths than one must die.
The Ballad of Reading Gaol, III:37

9 I know not whether Laws be right,
Or whether Laws be wrong;
All that we know who lie in gaol
Is that the wall is strong;
And that each day is like a year,
A year whose days are long.
The Ballad of Reading Gaol, V:1

10 As long as war is regarded as wicked, it will always have its fascination. When it is looked upon as vulgar, it will cease to be popular.
The Critic as Artist, Pt. 2

11 The man who sees both sides of a question is a man who sees absolutely nothing at all.
The Critic as Artist, Pt. 2

12 A little sincerity is a dangerous thing, and a great deal of it is absolutely fatal.
The Critic as Artist, Pt. 2

13 Ah! don't say you agree with me. When people agree with me I always feel that I must be wrong.
The Critic as Artist, Pt. 2

14 There is no sin except stupidity.
The Critic as Artist, Pt. 2

15 There is much to be said in favour of modern journalism. By giving us the opinions of the uneducated, it keeps us in touch with the ignorance of the community.
The Critic as Artist, Pt. 2

16 Art never expresses anything but itself.
The Decay of Lying

17 To love oneself is the beginning of a lifelong romance.
An Ideal Husband, III

18 Other people are quite dreadful. The only possible society is oneself.
An Ideal Husband, III

19 Really, if the lower orders don't set us a good example, what on earth is the use of them?
The Importance of Being Earnest, I

20 I have invented an invaluable permanent invalid called Bunbury, in order that I may be able to go down into the country whenever I choose.
The Importance of Being Earnest, I

21 All women become like their mothers. That is their tragedy. No man does. That's his.
The Importance of Being Earnest, I

22 The amount of women in London who flirt with their own husbands is perfectly scandalous. It looks so bad. It is simply washing one's clean linen in public.
The Importance of Being Earnest, I

23 The old-fashioned respect for the young is fast dying out.
The Importance of Being Earnest, I

24 In married life three is company and two is none.
The Importance of Being Earnest, I

25 Ignorance is like a delicate exotic fruit; touch it, and the bloom is gone.
The Importance of Being Earnest, I

26 To lose one parent, Mr Worthing, may be regarded as a misfortune; to lose both looks like carelessness.
The Importance of Being Earnest, I

27 I hope you have not been leading a double life, pretending to be wicked and being really good all the time. That would be hypocrisy.
The Importance of Being Earnest, II

28 On an occasion of this kind it becomes more than a moral duty to speak one's mind. It becomes a pleasure.
The Importance of Being Earnest, II

29 CECILY. When I see a spade I call it a spade. GWENDOLEN. I am glad to say I have never seen a spade. It is obvious that our social spheres have been widely different.
The Importance of Being Earnest, II

30 I never travel without my diary. One should always have something sensational to read in the train.
The Importance of Being Earnest, II

31 In matters of grave importance, style, not sincerity, is the vital thing.
The Importance of Being Earnest, III

32 Three addresses always inspire confidence, even in tradesmen.
The Importance of Being Earnest, III

33 Never speak disrespectfully of Society, Algernon. Only people who can't get into it do that.
The Importance of Being Earnest, III

34 No woman should ever be quite accurate about her age. It looks so calculating.
The Importance of Being Earnest, III

35 This suspense is terrible. I hope it will last.
The Importance of Being Earnest, III

36 It is a terrible thing for a man to find out suddenly that all his life he has been speaking nothing but the truth.
The Importance of Being Earnest, III

37 Please do not shoot the pianist. He is doing his best.
Impressions of America, 'Leadville'

38 I can resist everything except temptation.
Lady Windermere's Fan, I

39 It is absurd to divide people into good and bad. People are either charming or tedious.
Lady Windermere's Fan, I

40 I am the only person in the world I should like to know thoroughly.
Lady Windermere's Fan, II

41 We are all in the gutter, but some of us are looking at the stars.
Lady Windermere's Fan, III

42 There is nothing in the whole world so unbecoming to a woman as a Nonconformist conscience.
Lady Windermere's Fan, III

43 A man who knows the price of everything and the value of nothing.
A cynic
Lady Windermere's Fan, III

44 There is no such thing as a moral or an immoral book. Books are well written, or badly written.
The Picture of Dorian Gray, Preface

45 All Art is quite useless.
The Picture of Dorian Gray, Preface

46 There is only one thing in the world worse than being talked about, and that is not being talked about.
The Picture of Dorian Gray, Ch. 1

47 The only way to get rid of a temptation is to yield to it.
The Picture of Dorian Gray, Ch. 2

48 It is only shallow people who do not judge by appearances.

The Picture of Dorian Gray, Ch. 2

49 I can sympathize with everything, except suffering.

The Picture of Dorian Gray, Ch. 3

50 Women represent the triumph of matter over mind, just as men represent the triumph of mind over morals.

The Picture of Dorian Gray, Ch. 4

51 A cigarette is the perfect type of a perfect pleasure. It is exquisite, and it leaves one unsatisfied. What more can one want?

The Picture of Dorian Gray, Ch. 6

52 Anybody can be good in the country.

The Picture of Dorian Gray, Ch. 19

53 As for the virtuous poor, one can pity them, of course, but one cannot possibly admire them.

The Soul of Man under Socialism

54 Democracy means simply the bludgeoning of the people by the people for the people.

See LINCOLN
The Soul of Man under Socialism

55 Art is the most intense mode of individualism that the world has known.

The Soul of Man Under Socialism

56 Twenty years of romance makes a woman look like a ruin; but twenty years of marriage make her something like a public building.

A Woman of No Importance, I

57 MRS ALLONBY. They say, Lady Hunstanton, that when good Americans die they go to Paris.
LADY HUNSTANTON. Indeed? And when bad Americans die, where do they go to?
LORD ILLINGWORTH. Oh, they go to America.

See APPLETON, Thomas Gold
A Woman of No Importance, I

58 The English country gentleman galloping after a fox – the unspeakable in full pursuit of the uneatable.

A Woman of No Importance, I

59 One should never trust a woman who tells one her real age. A woman who would tell one that, would tell one anything.

A Woman of No Importance, I

60 LORD ILLINGWORTH. The Book of Life begins with a man and a woman in a garden.
MRS ALLONBY. It ends with Revelations.

A Woman of No Importance, I

61 Moderation is a fatal thing, Lady Hunstanton. Nothing succeeds like excess.

A Woman of No Importance, III

62 Ah, every day dear Herbert becomes *de plus en plus Oscarié*. It is a wonderful case of nature imitating art.

Referring to Beerbohm Tree's unconscious adoption of some of the mannerisms of a character he was playing in one of Wilde's plays
Great Theatrical Disasters (G. Brandreth)

63 I suppose that I shall have to die beyond my means.

When told that an operation would be expensive. He is also believed to have said 'I am dying beyond my means' on accepting a glass of champagne as he lay on his deathbed
Life of Wilde (Sherard)

64 One would have to have a heart of stone to read the death of Little Nell without laughing.

Lecturing upon Dickens
Lives of the Wits (H. Pearson)

65 A thing is not necessarily true because a man dies for it.

Oscariana

66 He hasn't an enemy in the world, and none of his friends like him.

Said of G. B. Shaw
Sixteen Self Sketches (Shaw), Ch. 17

67 With our James vulgarity begins at home, and should be allowed to stay there.

Referring to the artist James Whistler
Letter to the *World*

68 The man who can dominate a London dinner-table can dominate the world.

Attrib. by R. Aldington in his edition of Wilde

69 The gods bestowed on Max the gift of perpetual old age.

Referring to Max Beerbohm
Attrib.

70 The play was a great success, but the audience was a disaster.

Referring to a play that had recently failed
Attrib.

71 Who am I to tamper with a masterpiece?

Refusing to make alterations to one of his own plays
Attrib.

72 It requires one to assume such indecent postures.

Explaining why he did not play cricket
Attrib.

73 If this is the way Queen Victoria treats her prisoners, she doesn't deserve to have any.

Complaining at having to wait in the rain for transport to take him to prison
Attrib.

74 Grief has turned her fair.

Referring to the fact that a recently-bereaved lady friend had dyed her hair blonde
Attrib.

75 Work is the curse of the drinking classes.

Attrib.

76 Nothing, except my genius.

Replying to a US customs official on being asked if he had anything to declare
Attrib.

77 I should be like a lion in a cave of savage Daniels.

Explaining why he would not be attending a function at a club whose members were hostile to him
Attrib.

78 Dear Frank, we believe you; you have dined in every house in London – *once*.

Interrupting Frank Harris's interminable account of the houses he had dined at
Attrib.

79 Either that wall paper goes, or I do.

Last words, as he lay dying in a drab Paris bedroom
Time, 16 Jan 1984

Wilder, Billy (Samuel Wilder; 1906–) Austrian-born US film director. His films include *The Lost Weekend* (1945), *Some Like it Hot* (1959), and *Buddy, Buddy* (1981).

1 I've met a lot of hardboiled eggs in my time, but you're twenty minutes.

Ace in the Hole

2 It was like going to the dentist making a picture with her. It was hell at the time, but after it was all over, it was wonderful.

Referring to Marilyn Monroe
The Show Business Nobody Knows (E. Wilson)

3 France is a country where the money falls apart in your hands and you can't tear the toilet paper.

Attrib.

4 You have Van Gogh's ear for music.

Said to Cliff Osmond
Attrib.

Wilder, Thornton (1897–1975) US novelist and dramatist. His works include the novel *The Bridge of San Luis Rey* (1927) and the plays *Our Town* (1938) and *The Skin of Our Teeth* (1942).

1 A living is made, Mr Kemper, by selling something that everybody needs at least once a year. Yes, sir! And a million is made by producing something that everybody needs every day. You artists produce something that nobody needs at any time.

The Matchmaker, II

2 The best part of married life is the fights. The rest is merely so-so.

The Matchmaker, II

3 Never support two weaknesses at the same time. It's your combination sinners – your lecherous liars and your miserly drunkards – who dishonour the vices and bring them into bad repute.

The Matchmaker, III

4 But there comes a moment in everybody's life when he must decide whether he'll live among human beings or not – a fool among fools or a fool alone.

The Matchmaker, IV

5 My advice to you is not to inquire why or whither, but just enjoy your ice-cream while it's on your plate, – that's my philosophy.

The Skin of Our Teeth, I

6 When you're at war you think about a better life; when you're at peace you think about a more comfortable one.

The Skin of Our Teeth, III

7 Literature is the orchestration of platitudes.

Time magazine

Wilhelm I (1797–1888) King of Prussia (1861–88) and Emperor of Germany (1871–88). He led the German armies in the Franco-Prussian War and supported Bismark in strengthening Prussian control of Germany.

1 I haven't got time to be tired.

Said during his last illness

Wilhelm II (1859–1941) King of Prussia and Emperor of Germany (1888–1918). After Germany's defeat in World War I (in which he was known as 'Kaiser Bill') he was forced to abdicate.

1 You will be home before the leaves have fallen from the trees.

Said to troops leaving for the Front, Aug 1914
August 1914 (Barbara Tuchman), Ch. 9

2 I would have liked to go to Ireland, but my grandmother would not let me. Perhaps she thought I wanted to take the little place.

Queen Victoria was his grandmother
Carson (H. Montgomery Hyde), Ch. 9

3 The Admiral of the Atlantic salutes the Admiral of the Pacific.

Telegram sent to Czar Nicholas II during a naval exercise
The Shadow of the Winter Palace (E. Crankshaw)

4 It is my Royal and Imperial Command that you . . . exterminate first the treacherous English, and . . . walk over General French's contemptible little Army.

Referring to the British Expeditionary Force; veterans of this force are known as 'Old Contemptibles'
The Times, 1 Oct 1914

5 The machine is running away with *him* as it ran away with *me*.

Referring to Hitler
Remark to Sir Robert Bruce-Lockhart and Sir John Wheeler-Bennett, 27 Aug 1939

Wilhelmina (1880–1962) Queen of the Netherlands (1890–1948).

1 And when we open our dykes, the waters are ten feet deep.

Replying to a boast by Wilhelm II that his guardsmen were all seven feet tall
Attrib.

Wilkes, John (1725–97) British politician. A member of the Hellfire Club, who had led a profligate life, he became an MP in 1757. In 1764 he was expelled from Parliament for libel, failed to stand trial, and was outlawed. He was re-elected MP in 1768 and re-expelled from the House, being finally allowed back in 1774, when he also became Lord Mayor of London.

1 LORD SANDWICH. You will die either on the gallows, or of the pox.
WILKES. That must depend on whether I embrace your lordship's principles or your mistress.
Sometimes attrib. to Samuel Foote
Portrait of a Patriot (Charles Chenevix-Trench), Ch. 3

2 The chapter of accidents is the longest chapter in the book.
Attrib. in *The Doctor* (Southey), Vol. IV

Wilkinson, Ellen Cicely (1891–1947) British feminist and politician. She was active in the Labour movement and the suffragettes, becoming an MP in 1924 and minister of education in 1945.

1 I should like to help Britain to become a Third Programme country.
The Observer, 'Sayings of the Week', 2 Feb 1947

William (I) the Conqueror (1027–87) King of England (1066–87). As Duke of Normandy, he successfully invaded England, killing Harold II at the battle of Hastings, to become the first Norman King.

1 By the splendour of God I have taken possession of my realm; the earth of England is in my two hands.
Said after falling over when coming ashore at Pevensey with his army of invasion
Attrib.

William III (1650–1702) King of Great Britain (1689–1702) as joint sovereign with his wife, Mary II. Known as William of Orange, he defeated James II, the former king, at the battle of the Boyne (1690).

1 There is one certain means by which I can be sure never to see my country's ruin; I will die in the last ditch.
History of England (Hume)

2 Every bullet has its billet.
Journal (John Wesley), 6 June 1765

William of Wykeham (1324–1404) English churchman. Appointed Bishop of Winchester in 1366, he became Lord Chancellor (1367–71; 1389–91). Between his two chancellorships he founded New College, Oxford (1379), and Winchester College (1382).

1 Manners maketh man.
Motto of Winchester College and New College, Oxford

Williams, Harry (1874–1924) British songwriter.

1 Good-bye Piccadilly, Farewell Leicester Square;
It's a long, long way to Tipperary, but my heart's right there!
Written with Jack Judge (1878–1938)
It's a Long Way to Tipperary

Williams, Kenneth (1926–88) British comic actor who appeared in films (notably the 'Carry On' series), on stage and TV, and in radio programmes.

1 The nicest thing about quotes is that they give us a nodding acquaintance with the originator which is often socially impressive.
Acid Drops

Williams, Raymond Henry (1921–88) British academic and writer. His books include *Culture and Society* (1958), *The Country and the City* (1973), and *Writing in Society* (1983).

1 A very large part of English middle-class education is devoted to the training of servants . . .
In so far as it is, by definition, the training of upper servants, it includes, of course, the instilling of that kind of confidence which will enable the upper servants to supervise and direct the lower servants.
Culture and Society, Ch. 3

Williams, Tennessee (1911–83) US dramatist. He established his reputation with *The Glass Menagerie* (1945). Subsequent successes include *A Streetcar Named Desire* (1947) and *Cat on a Hot Tin Roof* (1955).

1 My suit is pale yellow. My nationality is French, and my normality has been often subject to question.
Camino Real, Block 4

2 You can be young without money but you can't be old without it.
Cat on a Hot Tin Roof, I

3 That Europe's nothin' on earth but a great big auction, that's all it is.
Cat on a Hot Tin Roof, I

4 A vacuum is a hell of a lot better than some of the stuff that nature replaces it with.
Cat On A Hot Tin Roof

5 I can't stand a naked light bulb, any.more than I can a rude remark or a vulgar action.
A Streetcar Named Desire, II:3

6 I have always depended on the kindness of strangers.
A Streetcar Named Desire, II:3

7 If people behaved in the way nations do they would all be put in straitjackets.
BBC interview

8 He was meddling too much in my private life.
Explaining why he had given up visiting his psychoanalyst
Attrib.

Williams, William Carlos (1883–1963) US poet. His collections include *Collected Poems* (1934) and *Pictures from Brueghel* (1963). *Paterson* (1946–58) used various experimental techniques.

1 Minds like beds always made up,
(more stony than a shore)
unwilling or unable.
Patterson, I, Preface

Willkie, Wendell Lewis (1892–1944) US lawyer and businessman. He became Republican nominee for the president of the USA (1940). He wrote an autobiographical book *One World* (1943).

1 The constitution does not provide for first and second class citizens.
An American Programme, Ch. 2

2 There exists in the world today a gigantic reservoir of good will toward us, the American people.
One World, Ch. 10

3 Freedom is an indivisible word. If we want to enjoy it, and fight for it, we must be prepared to extend it to everyone, whether they are rich or poor, whether they agree with us or not, no matter what their race or the colour of their skin.
One World, Ch. 13

Wilson, Sir Angus (1913–) British novelist. His books include *Hemlock and After* (1952), *Anglo Saxon Attitudes* (1956), *Setting the World on Fire* (1980), and *The Collected Stories of Angus Wilson* (1987).

1 She was more than ever proud of the position of the bungalow, so almost in the country.
A Bit Off the Map, 'A Flat Country Christmas'

2 I have no concern for the common man except that he should not be so common.
No Laughing Matter

3 'God knows how you Protestants can be expected to have any sense of direction,' she said. 'It's different with us. I haven't been to mass for years, I've got every mortal sin on my conscience, but I know when I'm doing wrong. I'm still a Catholic.'
The Wrong Set, 'Significant Experience'

Wilson, Charles Erwin (1890–1961) US engineer. He was president of General Motors (1941) and became secretary of defense (1953–57).

1 For many years I thought what was good for our country was good for General Motors, and vice versa.
Said in testimony to the Senate Armed Services Committee, Jan 1953
Attrib.

Wilson, Edmund (1895–1972) US critic and writer. His books include *Axel's Castle* (1931), *The Wound and the Bow* (1941), and *The Scrolls from the Dead Sea* (1955).

1 Of all the great Victorian writers, he was probably the most antagonistic to the Victorian age itself.
Referring to Dickens
The Wound and the Bow, 'The Two Scrooges'

Wilson of Rievaulx, Harold, Baron (1916–) British Labour statesman. He became prime minister (1964–70; 1974–76), after succeeding Gaitskell as leader of the Labour Party in 1963.

1 Hence the practised performances of latter-day politicians in the game of musical daggers: never be left holding the dagger when the music stops.
The Governance of Britain, Ch. 2

2 If I had the choice between smoked salmon and tinned salmon, I'd have it tinned. With vinegar.
The Observer, 'Sayings of the Week,' 11 Nov 1962

3 Everybody should have an equal chance – but they shouldn't have a flying start.
The Observer, 'Sayings of the Year', 1963

4 One man's wage rise is another man's price increase.
The Observer, 'Sayings of the Week', 11 Jan 1970

5 The monarchy is a labour-intensive industry.
The Observer, 'Sayings of the Week', 13 Feb 1977

6 All these financiers, all the little gnomes of Zürich and the other financial centres, about whom we keep on hearing.
Speech, House of Commons, 12 Nov 1956

7 There is something utterly nauseating about a system of society which pays a harlot 25 times as much as it pays its Prime Minister, 250 times as much as it pays its Members of Parliament, and 500 times as much as it pays some of its ministers of religion.
Referring to the case of Christine Keeler
Speech, House of Commons, June 1963

8 We are redefining and we are restating our socialism in terms of the scientific revolution . . . the Britain that is going to be forged in the white heat of this revolution will be no place for restrictive practices or out-dated methods on either side of industry.
Speech, Labour Party Conference, 1 Oct 1963

9 After half a century of democratic advance, the whole process has ground to a halt with a 14th Earl.
Speech, Manchester, 19 Oct 1963

10 From now, the pound is worth 14 per cent or so less in terms of other currencies. It does not mean, of course, that the pound here in Britain, in your pocket or purse or in your bank, has been devalued.
Speech after devaluation of the pound, 20 Nov 1967

11 A week is a long time in politics.
First said in 1965 or 1966, and repeated on several occasions
Attrib.

12 I believe the greatest asset a head of state can have is the ability to get a good night's sleep.
The World Tonight, BBC Radio, 16 Apr 1975

Wilson, Harriette (1789–1846) British writer and courtesan, whose *Memoirs* were widely read.

1 I shall not say why and how I became, at the age of fifteen, the mistress of the Earl of Craven.
Memoirs, Opening

Wilson, (Thomas) Woodrow (1856–1925) US statesman. He became Democratic president in 1913 and declared war on Germany in 1917. He negotiated the peace treaty in 1918, making the League of Nations a part of the treaty. For this measure he received no support in the Senate.

Quotations about Wilson

1 The spacious philanthropy which he exhaled upon Europe stopped quite sharply at the coasts of his own country.

Winston Churchill (1874–1965) British statesman. *World Crisis*

2 Like Odysseus, he looked wiser when seated.

John Maynard Keynes (1883–1946) British economist. *The Worldly Philosophers* (R. Heilbron)

Quotations by Wilson

3 Never murder a man who is committing suicide.

Mr Wilson's War (John Dos Passos), Pt. II, Ch. 10

4 Once lead this people into war and they'll forget there ever was such a thing as tolerance.

Mr Wilson's War (John Dos Passos), Pt. III, Ch. 2

5 America . . . is the prize amateur nation of the world. Germany is the prize professional nation.

Speech, Aug 1917
Mr Wilson's War (John Dos Passos), Pt. III, Ch. 13

6 The war we have just been through, though it was shot through with terror, is not to be compared with the war we would have to face next time.

Mr Wilson's War (John Dos Passos), Pt. V, Ch. 22

7 Right is more precious than peace.

Radio Times, 10 Sept 1964

8 Business underlies everything in our national life, including our spiritual life. Witness the fact that in the Lord's Prayer the first petition is for daily bread. No one can worship God or love his neighbour on an empty stomach.

Speech, New York, 1912

9 No nation is fit to sit in judgement upon any other nation.

Address, Apr 1915

10 There is such a thing as a man being too proud to fight.

Address to foreign-born citizens, 10 May 1915

11 The world must be made safe for democracy.

Address to Congress, asking for a declaration of war, 2 Apr 1917

12 Sometimes people call me an idealist. Well, that is the way I know I am an American. America is the only idealistic nation in the world.

Speech, Sioux Falls, 8 Sept 1919

Wimperis, Arthur (1874–1953) British screenwriter and songwriter.

1 My dear fellow a unique evening! I wouldn't have left a turn unstoned.

Replying when asked his opinion of a vaudeville show
Fifty Years of Vaudeville (E. Short)

Winchell, Walter (1879–1972) US journalist and broadcaster, pioneer of modern gossip-writing.

1 I saw it at a disadvantage – the curtain was up.

Referring to a show starring Earl Carroll
Come to Judgment (A. Whiteman)

Windsor, Duchess of (Wallis Warfield Simpson; 1896–1986) The wife of the Duke of Windsor (formerly Edward VIII) who abdicated in order to marry her.

1 I don't remember any love affairs. One must keep love affairs quiet.

Los Angeles Times, 11 Apr 1974

2 One can never be too thin or too rich.

Attrib.

Wittgenstein, Ludwig (1889–1951) Austrian philosopher, who studied with Bertrand Russell and G. E. Moore at Cambridge. His major works are *Tractatus Logico-Philosophicus* (1921) and *Philosophical Investigations* (1953).

1 Philosophy, as we use the word, is a fight against the fascination which forms of expression exert upon us.

The Blue Book

2 In order to draw a limit to thinking, we should have to be able to think both sides of this limit.

Tractatus Logico-Philosophicus, Preface

3 The world is everything that is the case.

Tractatus Logico-Philosophicus, Ch. 1

4 Philosophy is not a theory but an activity.

Tractatus Logico-Philosophicus, Ch. 4

5 Logic must take care of itself.

Tractatus Logico-Philosophicus, Ch. 5

6 Whereof one cannot speak, thereon one must remain silent.

Tractatus Logico-Philosophicus, Ch. 7

7 If there were a verb meaning 'to believe falsely', it would not have any significant first person, present indicative.

A Certain World (W. H. Auden)

Wodehouse, Sir P(elham) G(renville) (1881–1975) British humorous novelist. His books feature the 1920s upper-class bachelor Bertie Wooster and his immaculate manservant Jeeves. He lived abroad, becoming a US citizen in 1955.

Quotations about Wodehouse

1 P. G. Wodehouse, whose works I place a little below Shakespeare's and any distance you like above anybody else's.

James Agate (1877–1947) British theatre critic. *P. G. Wodehouse* (David A. Jensen)

2 English Literature's performing flea.

Sean O'Casey (1884–1964) Irish dramatist. Attrib.

Quotations by Wodehouse

3 All the unhappy marriages come from the husbands having brains. What good are brains to a man? They only unsettle him.
The Adventures of Sally

4 It is no use telling me that there are bad aunts and good aunts. At the core they are all alike. Sooner or later, out pops the cloven hoof.
The Code of the Woosters

5 He spoke with a certain what-is-it in his voice, and I could see that, if not actually disgruntled, he was far from being gruntled.
The Code of the Woosters

6 Big chap with a small moustache and the sort of eye that can open an oyster at sixty paces.
The Code of the Woosters

7 Jeeves coughed one soft, low, gentle cough like a sheep with a blade of grass stuck in its throat.
The Inimitable Jeeves, Ch. 13

8 It was my Uncle George who discovered that alcohol was a food well in advance of modern medical thought.
The Inimitable Jeeves, Ch. 16

9 It is a good rule in life never to apologize. The right sort of people do not want apologies, and the wrong sort take a mean advantage of them.
The Man Upstairs

10 New York is a small place when it comes to the part of it that wakes up just as the rest is going to bed.
My Man Jeeves, 'The Aunt and the Sluggard'

11 His ideas of first-aid stopped short at squirting soda-water.
My Man Jeeves, 'Doing Clarence a Bit of Good'

12 I don't owe a penny to a single soul – not counting tradesmen, of course.
My Man Jeeves, 'Jeeves and the Hard-Boiled Egg'

13 She fitted into my biggest armchair as if it had been built round her by someone who knew they were wearing armchairs tight about the hips that season.
My Man Jeeves, 'Jeeves and the Unbidden Guest'

14 I spent the afternoon musing on Life. If you come to think of it, what a queer thing Life is! So unlike anything else, don't you know, if you see what I mean.
My Man Jeeves, 'Rallying Round Old George'

15 If I had had to choose between him and a cockroach as a companion for a walking-tour, the cockroach would have had it by a short head.
My Man Jeeves, 'The Spot of Art'

16 There is only one cure for grey hair. It was invented by a Frenchman. It is called the guillotine.
The Old Reliable

17 I can honestly say that I always look on Pauline as one of the nicest girls I was ever engaged to.
Thank You Jeeves, Ch. 6

18 The Right Hon. was a tubby little chap who looked as if he had been poured into his clothes and had forgotten to say 'When!'
Very Good Jeeves!, 'Jeeves and the Impending Doom'

19 The stationmaster's whiskers are of a Victorian bushiness and give the impression of having been grown under glass.
Wodehouse at Work to the End (Richard Usborne), Ch. 2

20 Like so many substantial Americans, he had married young and kept on marrying, springing from blonde to blonde like the chamois of the Alps leaping from crag to crag.
Wodehouse at Work to the End (Richard Usborne), Ch. 2

21 Unlike the male codfish which, suddenly finding itself the parent of three million five hundred thousand little codfish, cheerfully resolves to love them all, the British aristocracy is apt to look with a somewhat jaundiced eye on its younger sons.
Wodehouse at Work to the End (Richard Usborne), Ch. 5

22 He was either a man of about a hundred and fifty who was rather young for his years or a man of about a hundred and ten who had been aged by trouble.
Wodehouse at Work to the End (Richard Usborne), Ch. 6

23 It is never difficult to distinguish between a Scotsman with a grievance and a ray of sunshine.
Wodehouse at Work to the End (Richard Usborne), Ch. 8

Wolfe, Charles (1791–1823) Irish poet and churchman. He is remembered for his poem *The Burial of Sir John Moore at Corunna*.

1 Not a drum was heard, not a funeral note,
As his corse to the rampart we hurried.
The Burial of Sir John Moore at Corunna, I

2 We carved not a line, and we raised not a stone –
But we left him alone with his glory.
The Burial of Sir John Moore at Corunna, VIII

Wolfe, Humbert (1886–1940) British poet. His collections include *Lampoons* (1925), *News of the Devil* (1926), and *The Blind Rose* (1928).

1 You cannot hope
to bribe or twist,
thank God! the
British journalist.

But, seeing what
the man will do
unbribed, there's
no occasion to.
The Uncelestial City, Bk. I, 'Over the Fire'

Wolfe, James (1727–59) British general. He fought at Dettingen and Culloden Moor; in Canada, under Amherst, he played a significant part in the capture of Louisburg from the French. In 1759 he commanded at the siege of Quebec, his forces scaling the Heights of Abraham and routing the French, completing their conquest in North America. He died in the battle.

1 I would rather have written those lines than take Quebec.

Referring to Gray's Elegy, on the eve of the Battle of Quebec, 1759
Attrib.

2 Now God be praised, I will die in peace.

His last words, after being mortally wounded at the Battle of Quebec, 1759
Historical Journal of Campaigns, 1757–60 (J. Knox), Vol. II

Wolfe, Thomas (1900–38) US novelist. His best-known book is *Look Homeward, Angel* (1929), one of four autobiographical novels.

1 Most of the time we think we're sick, it's all in the mind.

Look Homeward, Angel, Pt. I, Ch. 1

2 One belongs to New York instantly. One belongs to it as much in five minutes as in five years.

The Web and the Rock

Wolff, Charlotte (1904–86) German-born British psychiatrist and writer. Her books include *On the Way to Myself* (1969).

1 Women have always been the guardians of wisdom and humanity which makes them natural, but usually secret, rulers. The time has come for them to rule openly, but together with and not against men.

Bisexuality: A Study, Ch. 2

Wollstonecraft, Mary (1759–97) British writer and feminist. She is remembered for *A Vindication of the Rights of Women* (1792). The wife of William Goodwin, the social philosopher, she died giving birth to her daughter Mary, who married the poet Shelley.

1 The *divine right* of husbands, like the divine right of kings, may, it is hoped, in this enlightened age, be contested without danger.

A Vindication of the Rights of Woman, Ch. 3

2 I do not wish them to have power over men; but over themselves.

Referring to women
A Vindication of the Rights of Woman, Ch. 4

Wolsey, Thomas (1475–1530) English churchman and statesman. Henry VIII made him Bishop of Lincoln (1514), Archbishop of York and a cardinal (1515), and Lord Chancellor (1515–29). After failing to obtain the pope's agreement to Henry's divorce from Catharine of Aragon, he fell from power and died before his trial came to court.

1 Had I but served God as diligently as I have served the king, he would not have given me over in my gray hairs.

Remark to Sir William Kingston
Negotiations of Thomas Wolsey (Cavendish)

Wood, Mrs Henry (1814–87) British novelist, best remembered for her novel *East Lynne* (1861).

1 Dead! and . . . never called me mother.

East Lynne (dramatized version; the words do not occur in the novel)

Woodroofe, Thomas (1899–1978) British radio broadcaster. A naval lieutenant-commander, he broadcast on behalf of the Admiralty during World War II.

1 The Fleet's lit up. It is like fairyland; the ships are covered with fairy lights.

Said during commentary at the Coronation Review of the Royal Navy, May 1937

Woolf, Virginia (1882–1941) British novelist and writer, a member of the Bloomsbury Group, with her husband Leonard Woolf, the writer and publisher. She suffered from clinical depression and eventually drowned herself. Her novels include *Mrs Dalloway* (1925), *To the Lighthouse* (1927), *Orlando* (1928), and *The Waves* (1931).

1 The poet gives us his essence, but prose takes the mould of the body and mind entire.

The Captain's Death Bed, 'Reading'

2 *Middlemarch*, the magnificent book which with all its imperfections is one of the few English novels for grown up people.

The Common Reader, 'George Eliot'

3 Trivial personalities decomposing in the eternity of print.

The Common Reader, 'Jane Eyre'

4 Those comfortably padded lunatic asylums which are known, euphemistically, as the stately homes of England.

The Common Reader, 'Lady Dorothy Nevill'

5 Fraser . . . left his children unbaptized – his wife did it secretly in the washing basin.

Jacob's Room, Ch. 9

6 There is in the British Museum an enormous mind. Consider that Plato is there cheek by jowl with Aristotle; and Shakespeare with Marlowe. This great mind is hoarded beyond the power of any single mind to possess it.

Jacob's Room, Ch. 9

7 If you do not tell the truth about yourself you cannot tell it about other people.

The Moment and Other Essays

8 The older one grows the more one likes indecency.

Monday or Tuesday

9 Women have served all these centuries as looking-glasses possessing the magic and delicious power of reflecting the figure of man at twice its natural size.

A Room of One's Own

10 Why are women . . . so much more interesting to men than men are to women?

A Room of One's Own

11 I would venture to guess that Anon, who wrote so many poems without signing them, was often a woman.

A Room of One's Own

12 Literature is strewn with the wreckage of men who have minded beyond reason the opinions of others.

A Room of One's Own

Woollcott, Alexander (1887–1943) US journalist and writer. The drama critic of the *New York Times* (1914–22), he also wrote *Shouts and Murmurs* (1923), *Going to Pieces* (1928), and *While Rome Burns* (1934).

1 Subjunctive to the last, he preferred to ask, 'And that, sir, would be the Hippodrome?'

While Rome Burns, 'Our Mrs Parker'

2 I must get out of these wet clothes and into a dry Martini.

Reader's Digest

3 Just what God would have done if he had the money.

On being shown round Moss Hart's elegant country house and grounds
Attrib.

4 All the things I really like to do are either immoral, illegal, or fattening.

Attrib.

Wordsworth, Dorothy (1771–1855) British diarist and sister of William Wordsworth, with whom she lived in the Lake District. Her *Journals* have been widely read.

1 But as we went along there were more and yet more and at last under the boughs of the trees, we saw that there was a long belt of them along the shore, about the breadth of a country turnpike road. I never saw daffodils so beautiful they grew among the mossy stones about and about them, some rested their heads upon these stones as on pillow for weariness and the rest tossed and reeled and danced and seemed as if they verily laughed with the wind that blew upon them over the lake.

The Grasmere Journals, 15 Apr 1802

Wordsworth, Mary (1770–1850) Wife of William Wordsworth.

1 Mr Wordsworth is never interrupted.

Rebuking John Keats for interrupting a long monologue by William Wordsworth
Attrib.

Wordsworth, William (1770–1850) British poet. His reputation was based on his *Lyrical Ballads* (1798), written with Samuel Taylor Coleridge. After settling in the Lake District with his wife and sister he produced *The Prelude*, a verse autobiography published posthumously, and much other verse.

Quotations about Wordsworth

1 Time may restore us in his course Goethe's sage mind and Byron's force:
But where will Europe's latter hour
Again find Wordsworth's healing power?

Matthew Arnold (1822–88) British poet and critic. *Memorial Verses*

2 Wordsworth went to the Lakes, but he never was a lake poet. He found in stones the sermons he had already put there.

Oscar Wilde (1854–1900) Irish-born British dramatist. *The Decay of Lying*

Quotations by Wordsworth

3 Strongest minds
Are often those of whom the noisy world
Hears least.

The Excursion

4 The good die first,
And they whose hearts are dry as summer dust
Burn to the socket.

The Excursion

5 The wiser mind
Mourns less for what age takes away
Than what it leaves behind.

The Fountain

6 I travelled among unknown men
In lands beyond the sea;
Nor, England! did I know till then
What love I bore to thee.

I Travelled among Unknown Men

7 I wandered lonely as a cloud
That floats on high o'er vales and hills,
When all at once I saw a crowd,
A host, of golden daffodils.

I Wandered Lonely as a Cloud

8 For oft, when on my couch I lie
In vacant or in pensive mood,
They flash upon that inward eye
Which is the bliss of solitude.

I Wandered Lonely as a Cloud

9 That best portion of a good man's life,
His little, nameless, unremembered acts
Of kindness and of love.

Lines composed a few miles above Tintern Abbey

10 That blessed mood,
In which the burthen of the mystery,
In which the heavy and the weary weight
Of all this unintelligible world,
Is lightened.

Lines composed a few miles above Tintern Abbey

11 We are laid asleep
In body, and become a living soul:
While with an eye made quiet by the power
Of harmony, and the deep power of joy,
We see into the life of things.

Lines composed a few miles above Tintern Abbey

12 I have learned
To look on nature, not as in the hour
Of thoughtless youth; but hearing often-times
The still, sad music of humanity.

Lines composed a few miles above Tintern Abbey

13 Nature never did betray
The heart that loved her.

Lines composed a few miles above Tintern Abbey

14 Nor greetings where no kindness is, nor all
The dreary intercourse of daily life,
Shall e'er prevail against us, or disturb
Our cheerful faith, that all which we behold
Is full of blessings.

Lines composed a few miles above Tintern Abbey

15 A power is passing from the earth
To breathless Nature's dark abyss;
But when the great and good depart,
What is it more than this –

That Man who is from God sent forth,
Doth yet again to God return? –
Such ebb and flow must ever be,
Then wherefore should we mourn?

Referring to Charles James Fox, the hero of the liberal Whigs,
who died in 1806
Lines on the Expected Dissolution of Mr. Fox

16 If this belief from heaven be sent,
If such be Nature's holy plan,
Have I not reason to lament
What man has made of man?

Lines written in Early Spring

17 The sweetest thing that ever grew
Beside a human door!

Lucy Gray

18 There neither is, nor can be, any *essential* difference between the language of prose and metri-
cal composition.

Lyrical Ballads, Preface

19 Poetry is the spontaneous overflow of powerful
feelings: it takes its origin from emotion recol-
lected in tranquillity.

Lyrics Ballads, Preface

20 Every great and original writer, in proportion as
he is great and original, must himself create the
taste by which he is to be relished.

Lyrical Ballads, Preface

21 There is a comfort in the strength of love;
'Twill make a thing endurable, which else
Would overset the brain, or break the heart.

Michael, 448

22 Why art thou silent! Is thy love a plant
Of such weak fibre that the treacherous air
Of absence withers what was once so fair?

Miscellaneous Sonnets, III

23 My heart leaps up when I behold
A rainbow in the sky:
So was it when my life began;
So is it now I am a man;
So be it when I shall grow old,
Or let me die!
The Child is Father of the Man;
And I could wish my days to be
Bound each to each by natural piety.

My Heart Leaps Up

24 There was a time when meadow, grove, and
stream,
The earth, and every common sight,
To me did seem
Apparelled in celestial light,
The glory and the freshness of a dream.

Ode. Intimations of Immortality, I

25 Whither is fled the visionary gleam?
Where is it now, the glory and the dream?

Our birth is but a sleep and a forgetting:
The Soul that rises with us, our life's Star,
Hath had elsewhere its setting,
And cometh from afar;
Not in entire forgetfulness,
And not in utter nakedness,
But trailing clouds of glory do we come
From God, who is our home:
Heaven lies about us in our infancy!
Shades of the prison-house begin to close
Upon the growing boy.

Ode. Intimations of Immortality, IV

26 Earth fills her lap with pleasures of her own:
Yearnings she hath in her own natural kind.

Ode. Intimations of Immortality, VI

27 Provoke
The years to bring the inevitable yoke.

Ode. Intimations of Immortality, VIII

28 Hence in a season of calm weather
Though inland far we be,
Our souls have sight of that immortal sea
Which brought us hither . . .

Ode. Intimations of Immortality, IX

29 Though nothing can bring back the hour
Of splendour in the grass, of glory in the flower;
We will grieve not, rather find
Strength in what remains behind . . .

Ode. Intimations of Immortality, IX

30 Another race hath been, and other palms are
won.
Thanks to the human heart by which we live,
Thanks to its tenderness, its joys and fears,
To me the meanest flower that blows can give
Thoughts that do often lie too deep for tears.

Ode. Intimations of Immortality, IX

31 Those obstinate questionings
Of sense and outward things,
Fallings from us, vanishings;
Blank misgivings of a Creature
Moving about in worlds not realised,
High instincts before which our mortal nature
Did tremble like a guilty thing surprised.

Ode. Intimations of Immortality, IX

32 The clouds that gather round the setting sun
Do take a sober colouring from an eye
That hath kept watch o'er man's mortality.

Ode. Intimations of Immortality, XI

33 Me this unchartered freedom tires;
 I feel the weight of chance-desires:
 My hopes no more must change their name,
 I long for a repose that ever is the same.
 Ode to Duty

34 O Nightingale, thou surely art
 A creature of a 'fiery heart'.
 O Nightingale

35 Fair seed-time had my soul, and I grew up
 Fostered alike by beauty and by fear.
 The Prelude, I

36 When the deed was done
 I heard among the solitary hills
 Low breathings coming after me, and sounds
 Of undistinguishable motion, steps
 Almost as silent as the turf they trod.
 The Prelude, I

37 The grim shape
 Towered up between me and the stars, and still,
 For so it seemed, with purpose of its own
 And measured motion like a living thing,
 Strode after me.
 The Prelude, I

38 I was taught to feel, perhaps too much,
 The self-sufficing power of Solitude.
 The Prelude, II

39 We were brothers all
 In honour, as in one community,
 Scholars and gentlemen.
 The Prelude, IX

40 Bliss was it in that dawn to be alive,
 But to be young was very heaven!
 Referring to the French Revolution
 The Prelude, XI

41 That which sets
 ... The budding rose above the rose full
 blown.
 Referring to the French Revolution
 The Prelude, XI

42 Not in Utopia, – subterranean fields, –
 Or some secreted island, Heaven knows where!
 But in the very world, which is the world
 Of all of us, – the place where, in the end,
 We find our happiness, or not at all!
 Referring to the French Revolution
 The Prelude, XI

43 There is
 One great society alone on earth:
 The noble living and the noble dead.
 The Prelude, XI

44 The pious bird with the scarlet breast,
 Our little English robin.
 The Redbreast chasing the Butterfly

45 Still glides the Stream, and shall for ever glide;
 The Form remains, the Function never dies.
 The River Duddon, 'After-Thought'

46 The good old rule
 Sufficeth them, the simple plan,
 That they should take, who have the power,
 And they should keep who can.
 Rob Roy's Grave

47 A youth to whom was given
 So much of earth – so much of heaven,
 And such impetuous blood.
 Ruth

48 She dwelt among the untrodden ways
 Beside the springs of Dove,
 A maid whom there were none to praise
 And very few to love . . .
 She Dwelt Among the Untrodden Ways

49 A slumber did my spirit seal;
 I had no human fears:
 She seemed a thing that could not feel
 The touch of earthly years.

 No motion has she now, no force;
 She neither hears nor sees;
 Rolled round in earth's diurnal course,
 With rocks, and stones, and trees.
 A Slumber did my Spirit seal

50 Behold her, single in the field,
 Yon solitary Highland lass!
 The Solitary Reaper

51 Another year! – another deadly blow!
 Another mighty empire overthrown!
 And we are left, or shall be left, alone.
 Napoleon defeated Prussia at the Battles of Jena and Anerstädt,
 14 Oct 1806
 Sonnets, 'Another year!'

52 Earth has not anything to show more fair:
 Dull would he be of soul who could pass by
 A sight so touching in its majesty:
 The City now doth, like a garment, wear
 The beauty of the morning; silent, bare,
 Ships, towers, domes, theatres, and temples lie
 Open unto the fields, and to the sky;
 All bright and glittering in the smokeless air.
 Sonnets, 'Composed upon Westminster Bridge'

53 Dear God! the very houses seem asleep;
 And all that mighty heart is lying still!
 Sonnets, 'Composed upon Westminster Bridge'

54 We must be free or die, who speak the tongue
 That Shakspeare spake; the faith and morals
 hold
 Which Milton held.
 Sonnets, 'It is not to be thought of'

55 Milton! thou shouldst be living at this hour:
 England hath need of thee; she is a fen
 Of stagnant waters: altar, sword, and pen,
 Fireside, the heroic wealth of hall and bower,
 Have forfeited their ancient English dower
 Of inward happiness.
 Sonnets, 'Milton! thou shouldst'

56 Thy soul was like a star, and dwelt apart.
 Sonnets, 'Milton! thou shouldst'

57 Plain living and high thinking are no more.
Sonnets, 'O friend! I know not'

58 Once did she hold the gorgeous east in fee;
And was the safeguard of the west.
Sonnets, 'Once did she hold'

59 Venice, the eldest Child of Liberty.
She was a maiden City, bright and free.
Venice, a republic since the Middle Ages, was conquered by Napoleon in 1797 and absorbed into his Kingdom of Italy in 1805
Sonnets, 'Once did she hold'

60 When she took unto herself a mate,
She must espouse the everlasting sea.
Sonnets, 'Once did she hold'

61 Men are we, and must grieve when even the shade
Of that which once was great is passed away.
Sonnets, 'Once did she hold'

62 Thou hast great allies;
Thy friends are exultations, agonies,
And love, and man's unconquerable mind.
Sonnets, 'Toussaint, the most unhappy man'

63 Two voices are there; one is of the sea,
One of the mountains; each a mighty voice:
In both from age to age thou didst rejoice,
They were thy chosen music, Liberty!
Sonnets, 'Two voices are there'

64 The world is too much with us; late and soon,
Getting and spending, we lay waste our powers:
Little we see in Nature that is ours.
Sonnets, 'The world is too much with us'

65 I'd rather be
A Pagan suckled in a creed outworn;
So might I, standing on this pleasant lea,
Have glimpses that would make me less forlorn;
Have sight of Proteus rising from the sea;
Or hear Old Triton blow his wreathed horn.
Sonnets, 'The world is too much with us'

66 Strange fits of passion have I known:
And I will dare to tell,
But in the lover's ear alone,
What once to me befell.
Strange Fits of Passion

67 Come forth into the light of things,
Let Nature be your Teacher.
The Tables Turned

68 One impulse from a vernal wood
May teach you more of man,
Of moral evil and of good,
Than all the sages can.
The Tables Turned

69 Three years she grew in sun and shower,
Then Nature said, 'A lovelier flower
On earth was never sown;
This child I to myself will take;
She shall be mine, and I will make
A Lady of my own.'
Three Years she Grew

70 'Tis said that some have died for love.
'Tis Said that some have Died

71 Sweet childish days, that were as long
As twenty days are now.
To a Butterfly, I've Watched you now

72 Small service is true service, while it lasts.
To a Child, Written in her Album

73 Ethereal minstrel! pilgrim of the sky!
Dost thou despise the earth where cares abound?
To a Skylark

74 Thrice welcome, darling of the spring!
Even yet thou art to me
No bird, but an invisible thing,
A voice, a mystery.
To the Cuckoo

75 Thou unassuming common-place
Of Nature.
To the Daisy

76 Pleasures newly found are sweet
When they lie about our feet.
To the Small Celandine

77 Like an army defeated
The snow hath retreated.
Written in March

Work, Henry Clay (1832–84) US songwriter. His most popular songs were 'Come Home, Father' and 'Marching Through Georgia'.

1 Father, dear father, come home with me now,
The clock in the steeple strikes one.
A temperance song
Come Home, Father

2 My grandfather's clock was too large for the shelf.
So it stood ninety years on the floor.
Grandfather's Clock

3 But it stopped short – never to go again –
When the old man died.
Grandfather's Clock

4 'Hurrah! hurrah! we bring the Jubilee!
Hurrah! hurrah! the flag that makes you free!'
So we sang the chorus from Atlanta to the sea
As we were marching through Georgia.
Commemorating the march (Nov–Dec 1864) by a Union army under General Sherman through Confederate Georgia
Marching Through Georgia

Wotton, Sir Henry (1568–1639) English poet and diplomat. James I's ambassador to Venice, his poems include *On his Mistress, the Queen of Bohemia*.

1 In *Architecture* as in all other *Operative* Arts, the *end* must direct the *Operation*. The *end* is to build well. Well building hath three Conditions. *Commodity, Firmness*, and *Delight*.
Elements of Architecture, Pt. I

2   The itch of disputing will prove the scab of churches.

A Panegyric to King Charles

3   An ambassador is an honest man sent to lie abroad for the good of his country.

Life (Izaak Walton)

4   Take heed of thinking. *The farther you go from the church of Rome, the nearer you are to God.*

Reliquiae Wottonianae (Izaak Walton)

Wren, Sir Christopher (1632–1723) English architect. Professor of astronomy at London and Oxford, he later abandoned astronomy for architecture. His plan for rebuilding London after the Great Fire (1667) was rejected but he built 51 churches, 36 company halls, and St Paul's Cathedral. Later buildings include Greenwich Hospital (1694) and some additions to Hampton Court.

1   Architecture has its political use; public buildings being the ornament of a country; it establishes a nation, draws people and commerce; makes the people love their native country, which passion is the original of all great actions in a commonwealth.

Parentalia

2   *Si monumentum requiris, circumspice.*
    If you seek my monument, look around you.

Inscription in St Paul's Cathedral, London

Wright, Frank Lloyd (1869–1959) US architect. One of the most individual architects of the modern movement, he designed the Guggenheim Museum in New York.

1   The physician can bury his mistakes, but the architect can only advise his client to plant vines.

New York Times Magazine, 4 Oct 1953

2   Give me the luxuries of life and I will willingly do without the necessities.

Attrib.

3   The tall modern office building is the machine pure and simple . . . the engine, the motor and the battleship are the works of art of the century.

Attrib.

Wright, Orville (1871–1948) US aviator. With his brother, Wilbur (1867–1912), he made the first powered flight in 1903, in North Carolina.

1   The airplane stays up because it doesn't have the time to fall.

Explaining the principles of powered flight
Attrib.

Wycherley, William (1640–1716) English dramatist. His Restoration comedies include *The Country Wife* (1675) and *The Plain Dealer* (1676).

1   A mistress should be like a little country retreat near the town, not to dwell in constantly, but only for a night and away.

The Country Wife, I:1

2   Well, a widow, I see, is a kind of sinecure.

The Plain Dealer, V:3

Wycliffe, John (1329–84) English religious reformer. As an Oxford student and, later, lecturer in philosophy, he supervised the first English translation of the Bible; his followers, the Lollards, were early protestants.

1   I believe that in the end the truth will conquer.

Said to John of Gaunt, duke of Lancaster, 1381
Short History of the English People (J. R. Green)

Wyndham, John (John (Wyndham Parkes Lucas) Benyon Harris; 1903–69) British science-fiction writer, whose novels include *The Day of the Triffids* (1951), *The Kraken Wakes* (1953), and *The Chrysalids* (1955).

1   Wondering why one's friends chose to marry the people they did is unprofitable, but recurrent. One could so often have done so much better for them.

The Kraken Wakes

2   Man's arrogance is boastful, woman's is something in the fibre . . . Men may build and destroy and play with all their toys; they are uncomfortable nuisances, ephemeral conveniences, mere scamperers-about, while woman, in mystical umbilical connexion with the great tree of life itself, *knows* that she is indispensable.

The Midwich Cuckoos, 'Interview with a Child'

Wynne-Tyson, Esme (1898–) British writer. Her works include plays, novels, and some nonfiction.

1   Scheherazade is the classical example of a woman saving her head by using it.

See ARABIAN NIGHTS
Attrib.

Wynne-Tyson, Jon (1924–) British humorous writer, son of Esme Wynne-Tyson.

1   The wrong sort of people are always in power because they would not be in power if they were not the wrong sort of people.

The Times Literary Supplement

XYZ

Xenophanes (c. 560 BC–c. 478 BC) Greek poet and philosopher; fragments of his writings, elegies, and a poem on nature survive.

1   The Ethiopians say that their gods are snub-nosed and black, the Thracians that theirs have light blue eyes and red hair.

Fragment 15

Xenophon (430–354 BC) Greek historian and soldier. His writings include *Memorabilia*, *Apology*, and *Symposium*, as well as his best-known work *Anabasis*.

1   The sea! the sea!

Anabasis, IV:7

Xerxes (d. 465 BC) King of Persia (486–465). He invaded Greece in 480 but was forced to retreat after defeats at Salamis (480), Plataea (479), and Mycale (479); he was subsequently assassinated.

1 I am moved to pity, when I think of the brevity of human life, seeing that of all this host of men not one will still be alive in a hundred years' time.

On surveying his army

Yamamoto, Isoroku (1884–1943) Japanese admiral. He became commander in chief of the combined fleet and was killed in action in the southwest Pacific.

1 I fear we have only awakened a sleeping giant, and his reaction will be terrible.

Said after the Japanese attack on Pearl Harbor, 1941

Yankwich, Léon R. US lawyer and Californian judge.

1 There are no illegitimate children – only illegitimate parents.

Decision, State District Court, Southern District of California, June 1928, quoting columnist O. O. McIntyre

Ybarra, Thomas Russell (b. 1880) Venezuelan-born US writer. His books include *America Faces South* (1939) and the autobiographical *Young Man of Caracas* (1941).

1 A Christian is a man who feels
Repentance on a Sunday
For what he did on Saturday
And is going to do on Monday.

The Christian

Yeatman, Robert Julian (1897–1968) British humorous writer. *See* Sellar, Walter Carruthers.

Yeats, W(illiam) B(utler) (1865–1939) Irish poet and dramatist. His verse collections include *The Tower* (1928) and *The Winding Stair* (1929). With Lady Gregory, he founded the Abbey Theatre in Dublin, for which he wrote many plays.

Quotations about Yeats

1 Willie Yeats stood for enchantment.

G. K. Chesterton (1874–1936) British writer. Attrib.

2 Yeats is not a man of this world; and when you hurl an enormous, smashing chunk of it at him, he dodges it, small blame to him.

George Bernard Shaw (1856–1950) Irish dramatist and critic. Letter to Sean O'Casey

Quotations by Yeats

3 That William Blake
Who beat upon the wall
Till Truth obeyed his call.

An Acre of Grass

4 O chestnut tree, great rooted blossomer,
Are you the leaf, the blossom or the bole?
O body swayed to music; O brightening glance,
How can we know the dancer from the dance?

Among School Children

5 When I think of all the books I have read, and of the wise words I have heard spoken, and of the anxiety I have given to parents and grandparents, and of the hopes that I have had, all life weighed in the scales of my own life seems to me preparation for something that never happens.

Autobiography

6 Now that my ladder's gone
I must lie down where all the ladders start,
In the foul rag-and-bone shop of the heart.

The Circus Animals' Desertion

7 Though leaves are many, the root is one;
Through all the lying days of my youth
I swayed my leaves and flowers in the sun;
Now I may wither into the truth.

The Coming of Wisdom with Time

8 But Love has pitched his mansion in
The place of excrement.

Crazy Jane Talks with the Bishop

9 Wine comes in at the mouth
And love comes in at the eye;
That's all we shall know for truth
Before we grow old and die.

A Drinking Song

10 All changed, changed utterly:
A terrible beauty is born

Easter 1916

11 Out of the quarrel with others we make rhetoric; out of the quarrel with ourselves we make poetry.

Essay

12 When I play on my fiddle in Dooney,
Folk dance like a wave of the sea.

The Fiddler of Dooney

13 For the good are always the merry,
Save by an evil chance,
And the merry love the fiddle,
And the merry love to dance

The Fiddler of Dooney

14 One that is ever kind said yesterday:
'Your well-belovèd's hair has threads of grey,
And little shadows come about her eyes.'

The Folly of Being Comforted

15 I have drunk ale from the Country of the Young
And weep because I know all things now.

He Thinks of his Past Greatness

16 Nor law, nor duty bade me fight,
Nor public men, nor cheering crowds,
A lonely impulse of delight
Drove to this tumult in the clouds;
I balanced all, brought all to mind,
The years to come seemed waste of breath,
A waste of breath the years behind
In balance with this life, this death.

An Irish Airman Foresees his Death

17 I will arise and go now, and go to Innisfree,
  And a small cabin build there, of clay and wattles
  made;
  Nine bean rows will I have there, a hive for the
  honey bee,
  And live alone in the bee-loud glade.
  The Lake Isle of Innisfree

18 And I shall have some peace there, for peace
  comes dropping slow,
  Dropping from the veils of the morning to where
  the cricket sings.
  The Lake Isle of Innisfree

19 The wind blows out of the gates of the day,
  The wind blows over the lonely of heart,
  And the lonely of heart is withered away.
  The Land of Heart's Desire

20 I shudder and I sigh to think
  That even Cicero
  And many-minded Homer were
  Mad as the mist and snow.
  Mad as the Mist and Snow

21 Time drops in decay,
  Like a candle burnt out.
  The Moods

22 Never to have lived is best, ancient writers say;
  Never to have drawn the breath of life,
  never to have looked into the eye of day
  The second best's a gay goodnight and quickly
  turn away.
  Oedipus at Colonus

23 In dreams begins responsibility.
  Old Play, Epigraph, Responsibilities

24 Where, where but here have Pride and Truth,
  That long to give themselves for wage,
  To shake their wicked sides at youth
  Restraining reckless middle age?
  *On hearing that the Students of our New University have joined
  the Agitation against Immoral Literature*

25 A pity beyond all telling
  Is hid in the heart of love.
  The Pity of Love

26 An intellectual hatred is the worst.
  A Prayer for My Daughter

27 That is no country for old men. The young
  In one another's arms, birds in the trees
  – Those dying generations – at their song,
  The salmon-falls, the mackerel-crowded seas,
  Fish, flesh, or fowl, commend all summer long
  Whatever is begotten, born, and dies.
  Sailing to Byzantium, I

28 Things fall apart; the centre cannot hold;
  Mere anarchy is loosed upon the world,
  The blood-dimmed tide is loosed, and
  everywhere
  The ceremony of innocence is drowned;
  The best lack all conviction, while the worst
  Are full of passionate intensity.
  The Second Coming

29 A woman of so shining loveliness
  That men threshed corn at midnight by a tress,
  A little stolen tress.
  The Secret Rose

30 And pluck till time and times are done
  The silver apples of the moon
  The golden apples of the sun.
  The Song of Wandering Aengus

31 But was there ever dog that praised his fleas?
  *To a Poet, who would have me Praise certain Bad Poets, Imitators
  of His and Mine*

32 Under bare Ben Bulben's head
  In Drumcliff churchyard Yeats is laid . . .
  On limestone quarried near the spot
  By his command these words are cut: *Cast a
  cold eye On life, on death. Horseman, pass by!*
  Under Ben Bulben, VI

33 When you are old and gray and full of sleep,
  And nodding by the fire, take down this book,
  And slowly read, and dream of the soft look
  Your eyes had once, and of their shadows deep
  . . .
  When you are Old

34 Love fled
  And paced upon the mountains overhead
  And hid his face amid a crowd of stars.
  When you are Old

35 But I, being poor, have only my dreams;
  I have spread my dreams under your feet;
  Tread softly because you tread on my dreams.
  He Wishes for the Cloths of Heaven

36 It's not a writer's business to hold opinions.
  *Speaking to playwright, Denis Johnston
  The Guardian, 5 May 1977*

37 He is all blood, dirt and sucked sugar stick.
  *Referring to Wilfred Owen
  Letters on Poetry to Dorothy Wellesley, Letter, 21 Dec 1936*

38 O'CONNOR. How are you?
  W.B.Y. Not very well, I can only write prose
  today.
  Attrib.

Yellen, Jack (b. 1892) US lyricist and music publisher.

1 Happy Days Are Here Again.
  *Used by Roosevelt as a campaign song in 1932
  Song title*

Yevtushenko, Yevgeny (1933–) Soviet poet. His poem
Babi Yar (1961) made him popular both inside the Soviet Union
and abroad; later publications include the novel *Wild Berries* (1984)
and *Almost at the End* (1987).

1 No Jewish blood runs among my blood,
  but I am as bitterly and hardly hated
  by every anti-semite
  as if I were a Jew. By this
  I am a Russian.
  Babi Yar

2 Leaves – we cannot have,
sky – we cannot have,
But there is so much we can have –
to embrace tenderly in a darkened room.
Babi Yar

3 The hell with it. Who never knew the price of happiness will not be happy.
Lies

York and Albany, Frederick Augustus, Duke of
(1763–1827) The second son of George III of England. He commanded the expedition to the Netherlands against the French (1793–95).

1 Then the little man wears a shocking bad hat.
Referring to Horace Walpole; *compare* Wellington on House of Commons
Attrib.

Young, Andrew John (1885–1971) Scottish poet and minister of the Free Church. His *Collected Poems* appeared in 1936. The *Complete Poems* were revised in 1974.

1 For still I looked on that same star,
That fitful, fiery Lucifer,
Watching with mind as quiet as moss
Its light nailed to a burning cross.
The Evening Star

2 Stars lay like yellow pollen
That from a flower has fallen;
And single stars I saw
Crossing themselves in awe;
Some stars in sudden fear
Fell like a falling tear.
The Stars

3 There is a happy land,
Far, far away,
Where saints in glory stand,
Bright, bright as day.
There is a Happy Land

Young, Edward (1683–1765) British poet. His verse collection *Night Thoughts* (1742–45) gave rise to the 'graveyard poets'. His plays include *Busiris* (1719), *Revenge* (1721), and *The Brothers* (1726).

1 Some for renown, on scraps of learning dote,
And think they grow immortal as they quote.
Love of Fame, I

2 Be wise with speed,
A fool at forty is a fool indeed.
Love of Fame, II

3 All men think all men mortal, but themselves.
Night Thoughts

4 By night an atheist half believes a God.
Night Thoughts

5 Procrastination is the thief of time.
Night Thoughts

6 The bell strikes one. We take no note of time
But from its loss.
Night Thoughts

7 Time flies, death urges, knells call, heaven invites,
Hell threatens.
Night Thoughts

8 Man wants but little, nor that little long.
Night Thoughts

Young, G. W. (19th century) British writer.

1 Though in silence, with blighted affection, I pine,
Yet the lips that touch liquor must never touch mine!
The Lips That Touch Liquor

Young, Michael (1915–) British political writer.

1 The Rise of the Meritocracy.
Book title

Zamoyski, Jan (1541–1605) Grand chancellor of Poland (1575–1605). He commanded the Polish army that succeeded in defending Poland against Turks, Cossacks, and Swedes.

1 The king reigns, but does not govern.
Speech, Polish Parliament, 1605

Zangwill, Israel (1864–1926) British writer and dramatist. His early books, such as *Children of the Ghetto* (1892), established his reputation. Subsequent successes include *The Melting Pot* (1908), *The Next Religion* (1912), and *The Cockpit* (1921). His poetry includes *Blind Children* (1903).

1 No Jew was ever fool enough to turn Christian unless he was a clever man.
Children of the Ghetto, Ch. 1

2 America is God's Crucible, the great Melting-Pot where all the races of Europe are melting and re-forming!
The Melting Pot, I

3 The law of dislike for the unlike will always prevail. And whereas the unlike is normally situated at a safe distance, the Jews bring the unlike into the heart of *every milieu*, and must there defend a frontier line as large as the world.
Speeches, Articles and Letters, 'The Jewish Race'

Zanuck, Darryl F. (1902–79) US film producer. He cofounded 20th-Century Productions, which merged with Fox in 1935 to form 20th-Century Fox, of which he became president in 1962.

1 If two men on the same job agree all the time, then one is useless. If they disagree all the time, then both are useless.
The Observer, 'Sayings of the Week', 23 Oct 1949

Zola, Emile (1840–1902) French novelist. His first successful novel, *Thérèse Raquin* (1867), was followed by the 20-novel series *Les Rougon-Macquart* (1871–93). *Nana* (1880) and *Germinal* (1885) were later successes. His open letter *J'accuse* (1898), supporting Dreyfus, led to his exile in England followed by a hero's return after Dreyfus was cleared.

1 Don't go on looking at me like that, because you'll wear your eyes out.
La Bête Humaine, Ch. 5

2 *J'accuse.*
I accuse.

Title of an open letter to the French President, denouncing the
French army's conduct in the Dreyfus affair
L'Aurore, 13 Jan 1898

3 Truth is on the march; nothing can stop it now.

Referring to the Dreyfus scandal
Attrib.

•INDEX

INDEX

acts of God a kind of Providence will . . . end . . . the a.

DE VRIES, 7

Adam A.'s ale

PROVERBS, 12

A. was but human

TWAIN, 15

grant that the old A. in this Child BOOK OF COMMON PRAYER, 21

Oh, A. was a gardener

KIPLING, 12

When A. delved

BALL, 1

adamant the silvery a. walls of life's exclusive city

LAWRENCE, D, 10

addiction a. of political groups to ideas GALBRAITH, 3

Every form of a. is bad

JUNG, 5

prisoners of a. and . . . prisoners of envy

ILLICH, 4

the terminal point of a. is . . . damnation

AUDEN, 5

Addison give his days and nights to the volumes of A.

ADDISON, 1

addresses A. . . . conceal our whereabouts

SAKI, 2

Three a. always inspire confidence

WILDE, 32

adieu a., kind friends, a.

ANONYMOUS, 1

A.! my native shore

BYRON, 9

adjectives be able to tell the substantives from the a.

MADARIAGA Y ROGO, 2

Adler A. will always be Jung

WALL, 2

Adlestrop I remember A.

THOMAS, E, 1

admiral good to kill an a.

VOLTAIRE, 7

The A. of the Atlantic salutes the A. of the Pacific WILHELM II, 3

admiration Beauty stands In the a. . . . of weak minds

MILTON, 54

admire a greater fool to a. him

BOILEAU, 3

Not to a.

POPE, 38

one cannot possibly a. them

WILDE, 53

The English instinctively a.

AGATE, 2

admired Few men have been a. by their servants MONTAIGNE, 8

admiring the cure for a. the House of Lords BAGEHOT, 4

ado much a. about nothing when the a. is about himself

TROLLOPE, 4

the heathen make much a.

PSALMS, 27

adolescence a man suffering from petrified a. BEVAN, 3

maturity is only a short break in a.

FEIFFER, 1

Adonais I weep for A.

SHELLEY, 3

adores he a. his maker

DISRAELI, 18

The ignorant man always a.

LOMBROSO, 1

adorned as a bride a. for her husband

BIBLE, 473

adornment What time he can spare from the a. of his person

THOMPSON, W, 2

adrenal larger cerebrums and smaller a. glands MENCKEN, 5

ads He watched the a. And not the road

NASH, 6

adult A child becomes an a. when

SZASZ, 4

His a. life resembled his childhood

SARTRE, 1

What is an a.

BEAUVOIR, 1

adultery and gods a.

BYRON, 19

commit a. at one end

CARY, J, 1

rather be taken in a. than in provincialism HUXLEY, A, 7

the Tasmanians, who never committed a., are now extinct

MAUGHAM, 1

thou shalt not commit a.

BIBLE, 115

would have constituted a.

BENCHLEY, 4

advance if civilisation is to a. . . . it must be through . . . women

PANKHURST, E, 1

advantage him who desires his own a. not harm another

BUDDHA, 2

The a. of doing one's praising

BUTLER, S, 26

you have the a. of me

MARX, G, 16

advantages Wealth is not without its a. GALBRAITH, 1

adventure coming together of man and wife . . . should be a fresh a.

STOPES, 5

extravagance . . . thrift and a. seldom go hand in hand . . . .

CHURCHILL, J, 2

Marriage is the only a. open to the cowardly VOLTAIRE, 26

To die will be an awfully big a.

BARRIE, 5

adventures A good critic . . . narrates the a. of his mind

FRANCE, 7

adversity a. doth best discover virtue BACON, FRANCIS, 8

advertised Wealth . . . must be a. GALBRAITH, 2

advertisement the worst a. for Socialism is its adherents

ORWELL, 26

advertisers as the a. don't object to

SWAFFER, 1

advice A. is seldom welcome

CHESTERFIELD, 12

a. . . . poised between the cliché

RUNCIE, 2

how ready people always are with a.

SULLIVAN, 1

intended to give you some a.

HARRIS, 1

nothing so freely as a.

ROCHEFOUCAULD, 16

to hear . . . valuable or even earnest a. from my seniors

THOREAU, 10

woman seldom asks a.

ADDISON, 16

advocaat a., a drink made from lawyers

COREN, 4

advocate the soul of a martyr with the intellect of an a.

BAGEHOT, 10

aeroplanes century of a. deserves its own music DEBUSSY, 3

Aesculapius we owe a cock to A. SOCRATES, 9

Aesop prettily devised of A. BACON, FRANCIS, 58

aesthetic the degree of my a. emotion BELL, C, 2

afar a. and asunder

BOWEN, E. E., 1

affair The great a. is to move STEVENSON, R, 7

affairs tide in the a. of men SHAKESPEARE, 159

affectation Universities incline wits to sophistry and a.

BACON, FRANCIS, 65

affections A different taste in jokes is a . . . strain on the a.

ELIOT, G, 4

affluent the a. society

GALBRAITH, 4

afford purest treasure mortal times a. SHAKESPEARE, 292

afraid A. of Virginia Woolf

ALBEE, 1

be not a. to do thine office

MORE, 1

Englishman . . . is a. to feel

FORSTER, 2

Men not a. of God, a. of me

POPE, 12

thou shalt not be a. for any terror by night PSALMS, 11

Whenever I look inside myself I am a.

JOAD, 1

Afric Where A.'s sunny fountains

HEBER, 1

Africa more familiar with A. than my own body

ORTON, 1

something new out of A. PLINY THE ELDER, 4

after-dinner an a.'s sleep SHAKESPEARE, 231

afterlife that the a. will be any less exasperating than this one

COWARD, 3

afternoon could lose the war in an a. CHURCHILL, W, 36

I could have lost the war in an a.

JELLICOE, 1

Summer a. – summer a.

JAMES, H, 14

against A. whom

ADLER, 2

He said he was a. it

COOLIDGE, 5

If . . . you can't tell . . . who's for you and who's a. you

JOHNSON, L, 5

neither for nor a. institutions

WHITMAN, 4

Agamemnon I have looked upon the face of A. SCHLIEMANN, 1

Many brave men . . . before A.'s time HORACE, 42

age A child blown up by a.

BEAUVOIR, 1

A. cannot wither her

SHAKESPEARE, 244

A. . . . nor custom stale her infinite virginity WEBSTER, D, 3

a. of chivalry is gone

BURKE, E, 9

A. only matters when one is ageing PICASSO, 9

A. shall not weary them

BINYON, 3

A. will bring all things

MOLIÈRE, 8

A. will not be defied BACON, FRANCIS, 42

an a. in which useless knowledge was . . . important JOAD, 2

And now in a. I bud again

HERBERT, G, 4

an old a. of cards

POPE, 44

A tart temper never mellows with a.

IRVING, 2

At twenty years of a.

FRANKLIN, 8

a woman has the right to treat . . . her a. with ambiguity

RUBINSTEIN, 1

Cool'd a long a. in the deep-delved earth KEATS, 36

Crabbed a. and youth cannot live together SHAKESPEARE, 355

Damn the a. I'll write for antiquity LAMB, CHARLES, 21

Do you think at your a., it is right

CARROLL, 6

Drives my green a.

THOMAS, D, 10

gift of perpetual old a.

WILDE, 69

He hath not forgotten my a.

SOUTHEY, 5

He was the Messiah of the new a.

SLOCOMBE, 1

I summon a. To grant youth's heritage BROWNING, R, 49

It is . . . at my a. I now begin to see things as they really are

FONTENELLE, 1

lady of a certain a.

BYRON, 32

Lo, Hudled up, together Lye Gray A., Grene youth, White Infancy

ANONYMOUS, 53

no a. between ten and three and twenty SHAKESPEARE, 350

nothing in thy youth, how canst thou find any thing in thine a.

BIBLE, 87

not of an a., but for all time

JONSON, 11

No woman should ever be quite accurate about her a. WILDE, 34

Old a. . . . gives us what we have earned BRENAN, 3

Old a. is the most unexpected of all . . . things TROTSKY, 3

Our parents' a. . . . . has produced us, more worthless still

HORACE, 37

The a. of chivalry is never past KINGSLEY, 11

Thou has nor youth nor a. SHAKESPEARE, 231

what a. takes away

WORDSWORTH, W, 5

When men grow virtuous in their old a.   POPE, 56
when Mozart was my a.   LEHRER, 1
who tells one her real a.   WILDE, 59
Years hence, perhaps, may dawn an a.   ARNOLD, M, 20
aged a. diplomats . . . bored than for young men to die
   AUSTIN, W, 1
a man of about a hundred and ten who had been a.
   WODEHOUSE, 22
the beauty Of an a. face   CAMPBELL, JOSEPH, 1
ageing Age only matters when one is a.   PICASSO, 9
Like so many a. college people   NABOKOV, 3
agenda Our a. is now exhausted. . . . we find ourselves in such
complete unanimity   SPAAK, 1
the a. winks at me   THOMAS, G, 2
agent prime a. of all human perception   COLERIDGE, S, 5
ages His acts being seven a.   SHAKESPEARE, 47
Our God, our help in a. past   WATTS, 6
Rock of a., cleft for me   TOPLADY, 1
aggregate the a. of the recipes that are always successful
   VALÉRY, 2
aging A. . . . the only . . . way to live a long time   AUBER, 3
agitate I will not permit thirty men . . . to a. a bag of wind
   WHITE, A, 1
agnostic rather a compliment to be called an a.   DARROW, 2
agonies Thy friends are exultations, a., And love
   WORDSWORTH, W, 62
agony individual existence goes out in a lonely spasm of helpless
a.   JAMES, W, 1
agree colours will a. in the dark   BACON, FRANCIS, 57
don't say you a. with me   WILDE, 13
If two men on the same job a.   ZANUCK, 1
those who a. with us   ROCHEFOUCAULD, 24
Two of a trade can ne'er a.   GAY, 6
agreeable I do not want people to be very a.   AUSTEN, 30
My idea of an a. person   DISRAELI, 11
agreement My people and I have come to an a.
   FREDERICK THE GREAT, 2
Whenever you accept our views we shall be in full a.   DAYAN, 1
agrees a person who a. with me   DISRAELI, 11
agricultural labourers the a. round here commute from London
   POWELL, A, 4
Aids A. pandemic is a classic own-goal   ANNE, 4
ail what can a. thee, knight at arms   KEATS, 22
ain't bet you a hundred bucks he a. in here   DILLINGHAM, 1
air both feet firmly planted in the a.   SCANLON, 1
cat is a diagram and pattern of subtle a.   LESSING, D, 6
Get your room full of good a.   LEACOCK, 3
my spirit found outlet in the a.   JOHNSON, A, 1
the castles I have, are built with a.   JONSON, 5
to the Germans that of the a.   RICHTER, 1
waste its sweetness on the desert a.   GRAY, 5
airplane The a. stays up because it doesn't have the time to fall
   WRIGHT, O, 1
airplanes a. . . . are wonderful things for other people   KERR, 4
I feel about a. the way I feel about diets   KERR, 4
airth Let them bestow on every a. a limb   GRAHAM, J, 1
aisle A.. Altar. Hymn   MUIR, 2
aitches We have nothing to lose but our a.   ORWELL, 29
Alabama I've come from A.   FOSTER, 4
Alamein Before A. we never had a victory   CHURCHILL, W, 16
alarms confused a. of struggle and flight   ARNOLD, M, 11
albatross I shot the a.   COLERIDGE, S, 27
Albert A. was merely a young foreigner   STRACHEY, L, 3
ask me to take a message to A.   DISRAELI, 42
that A. married beneath him   COWARD, 24
alcohol A. . . . enables Parliament to do things at eleven
   SHAW, 16
A. is like love   CHANDLER, R, 3
my Uncle George . . . discovered that a. was a food
   WODEHOUSE, 8
alcoholic a. liquors have been used by the . . . best races
   SAINTSBURY, 1
Fitzgerald was an a.   FITZGERALD, F S, 1
ale a. from the Country of the Young   YEATS, 15
no more cakes and a.   SHAKESPEARE, 339
the spicy nut-brown a.   MILTON, 18
Alexander Some talk of A., and some of Hercules
   ANONYMOUS, 73
Alfred school-miss A. vent her chaste delight   TENNYSON, 2
algebra Sir Isaac Newton . . . deep in a. and fluxions
   NEWTON, I, 2
What is a. exactly   BARRIE, 6

Algerian Come in, you Anglo-Saxon swine And drink of my A.
wine   BEHAN, 9
Alice A. – Mutton; Mutton – A.   CARROLL, 37
In my sweet little A. blue gown   MCCARTHY, J, 1
Oh! don't you remember sweet A., Ben Bolt   ENGLISH, 1
alien amid the a. corn   KEATS, 39
State socialism is totally a.   THATCHER, M, 16
alike among so many million of faces, there should be none a.
   BROWNE, T, 6
alive Bliss was it in that dawn to be a.   WORDSWORTH, W, 40
he is no longer a.   BENTLEY, E, 3
he shall save his soul a.   BIBLE, 127
host of men not one will still be a. in a hundred years' time
   XERXES, 1
if I am a.   HOLLAND, 1
needst not strive . . . to keep a.   CLOUGH, 6
nobody knew whether . . . he would be a. the next hour   FRANK, 1
Not while I'm a., he ain't   BEVIN, 1
We intend to remain a.   MEIR, 6
Whatever Wells writes is not only a.   WELLS, 1
all A. for one, and one for a.   DUMAS, PÈRE, 1
A. good things   PROVERBS, 33
a. our yesterdays   SHAKESPEARE, 225
A.'s well   PROVERBS, 38
are you sure they are a. horrid   AUSTEN, 14
'A was a man, take him for a. in a.   SHAKESPEARE, 70
Christ is a., and in a.   BIBLE, 20
Ripeness is a.   SHAKESPEARE, 192
'Tis a. thou art   POPE, 1
allegiance Not bound to swear a. to any master   HORACE, 1
allegory headstrong as an a.   SHERIDAN, R, 7
alley she lives in our a.   CAREY, H, 3
allies former a. had blundered   NEVINS, 1
Thou hast great a.   WORDSWORTH, W, 62
all-round a wonderful a. man   BEERBOHM, 20
ally An a. has to be watched   TROTSKY, 13
Almighty If the A. himself played the violin   HEIFETZ, 1
almonds Don't eat too many a.   COLETTE, 5
alms a. for oblivion   SHAKESPEARE, 331
almsgiving A. tends to perpetuate poverty   PERÓN, E, 2
alone A., a., all, all a.   COLERIDGE, S, 31
A. and palely loitering   KEATS, 22
And we are left, or shall be left, a.   WORDSWORTH, W, 51
better to be a. than in bad company   WASHINGTON, 3
Hell is a.   ELIOT, T, 5
I am here at the gate a.   TENNYSON, 56
I am the cat that walks a.   BEAVERBROOK, 1
I hate to be a.   BANKHEAD, 4
I want to be a.   GARBO, 1
I want to be *left* a.   GARBO, 2
No poet . . . has . . . meaning a.   ELIOT, T, 23
powerful but a.   VIGNY, 2
The dead Only are pleased to be a.   FULLER, ROY, 1
To be a. is the fate of all great minds   SCHOPENHAUER, 1
We perish'd, each a.   COWPER, 6
woe to him that is a. when he falleth   BIBLE, 69
Alph Where A., the sacred river, ran   COLERIDGE, S, 14
Alpha A. and Omega   BIBLE, 459
alphabet the remaining twenty-two letters of the a.   ORWELL, 6
also You a.   OVID, 6
altar Aisle. A.. Hymn   MUIR, 2
altars generations . . . have struggled in poverty to build these a.
   STANTON, E, 1
alter I dare not a. these things   AUSTIN, A, 2
alternative a need to create an a. world   FOWLES, 4
I prefer old age to the a.   CHEVALIER, M, 2
there is no a.   THATCHER, M, 10
alway lo, I am with you a.   BIBLE, 433
always Minorities . . . are almost a. in the right   SMITH, SYDNEY, 12
am I A. THAT I A.   BIBLE, 107
in the infinite I A.   COLERIDGE, S, 5
I think therefore I a.   DESCARTES, 1
Amaryllis sport with A. in the shade   MILTON, 24
amateur America . . . is the prize a. nation   WILSON, W, 5
An a. is an artist who supports himself with outside jobs which
enable him to paint   SHAHN, 1
In love . . . the a. status   GRAVES, R, 3
the last time that I will take part as an a.   AUBER, 1
amateurs a disease that afflicts a.   CHESTERTON, 24
nation of a.   ROSEBERY, 3
amaze How vainly men themselves a.   MARVELL, 1

ambiguity a woman has the right to treat . . . her age with a.
RUBINSTEIN, 1

ambition A., Distraction, Uglification, and Derision CARROLL, 15
A. should be made of sterner stuff SHAKESPEARE, 155
A writer's a. should be KOESTLER, 6
Cromwell was a man in whom a. had . . . suspended . . . religion
CROMWELL, O, 1
Every man has . . . an a. to be a wag JOHNSON, S, 32
Let not A. mock GRAY, 2
Vaulting a., which o'er-leaps itself SHAKESPEARE, 209
What argufies pride and a. DIBDIN, 1

ambitious an a. man has as many masters as . . . may be useful
LA BRUYÈRE, 15

Amblongus A. Pie LEAR, 6
ambrosia Emerson is one who lives . . . on a. EMERSON, 2
ambulance Knocked down a doctor? With an a. SIMPSON, 4
amen sound of a great A. PROCTER, 4
America A. became top nation SELLAR, 7
A.! . . . God shed His grace on thee BATES, 1
A. . . . has gone directly from barbarism to degeneration
CLEMENCEAU, 1
A. is a country of young men EMERSON, 25
A. is a large, friendly dog TOYNBEE, 2
A. is just ourselves ARNOLD, M, 4
A. is . . . the great Melting-Pot ZANGWILL, 2
A. is the only idealistic nation WILSON, W, 12
A. . . . is the prize amateur nation WILSON, W, 5
A.'s really only a kind of Russia BURGESS, 1
ask not what A. will do for you KENNEDY, JOHN, 11
behind the discovery of A. RICHLER, 2
first come to pass in the heart of A. EISENHOWER, 5
in A. anyone can be President FORD, G, 3
my A.! my new-found-land DONNE, 12
The business of A. is business COOLIDGE, 3
The crude commercialism of A. WASHINGTON, 2
the greatest that we owe to the discovery of A. HELPS, 2
the more absolute silence of A. LAWRENCE, D, 24
The national dish of A. ROBINSON, R, 1
Vietnam was lost in the living rooms of A. MCLUHAN, 6
what makes A. what it is STEIN, 2
when we think of thee, O A. WALPOLE, H, 7
Why will A. not reach out . . . to Russia DUNCAN, 3
woman governs A. MADARIAGA Y ROGO, 1
American A. heiress wants to buy a man MCCARTHY, M, 3
A. system of rugged individualism HOOVER, 3
an A. citizen . . . attacking an ex-secretary of state
CHURCHILL, W, 1
An A. is either a Jew, or an anti-Semite SARTRE, 5
capitalism . . . the process whereby A. girls turn into A. women
HAMPTON, 3
I am willing to love all mankind, *except an A.* JOHNSON, S, 123
If I were an A., as I am an Englishman PITT THE ELDER, 6
It hasn't taken Winston long to get used to A. ways ACHESON, 3
I was born an A. WEBSTER, D, 6
Let's talk sense to the A. people STEVENSON, A, 4
the A. abroad STAPLEDON, 1
the feminization of the white European and A. is already far
advanced LEWIS, W, 3
the greatest A. friend we have ever known CHURCHILL, W, 26
We are all A. at puberty WAUGH, E, 25
Americanism hyphenated A. ROOSEVELT, T, 9
McCarthyism is A. MCCARTHY, J, R, 1
There can be no fifty-fifty A. ROOSEVELT, T, 10
Americans A. have been conditioned to respect newness
UPDIKE, 3
because A. won't listen to sense KEYNES, 9
Good A., when they die, go to Paris APPLETON, T, 1
No one can kill A. and brag REAGAN, 6
the matter with A. CHESTERTON, 42
when good A. die they go to Paris WILDE, 57
amiable how a. are thy dwellings PSALMS, 44
It destroys one's nerves to be a. every day DISRAELI, 15
amis *Changez vos a.* DE GAULLE, 9
ammunition Praise the Lord and pass the a. FORGY, 1
amo *Odi et a.* CATULLUS, 2
amor *A. vincit insomnia* FRY, C, 5
amorality the butcher-like a. of . . . men SOLZHENITSYN, 3
amorous the silk stockings and white bosoms of your actresses
excite my a. propensities JOHNSON, S, 46
amplified I'm being a. by the mike CHESTERTON, 45
amputate 'Thank God they had to a.!' SASSOON, S, 7
am'rous dire offence from a. causes springs POPE, 48

amused how to be a. rather than shocked BUCK, 3
I was *very* much a. VICTORIA, 5
one has to be very old before one learns how to be a. BUCK, 3
We are not a. VICTORIA, 12
amusement all literature is written for the a. of *men* TOLKIEN, 2
amusing Any a. deaths BOWRA, 2
analogy Though a. is often misleading BUTLER, S, 17
analysis the profession of historian fits a man for psychological a.
SARTRE, 2
anarchy a well-bred sort of emotional a. LAWRENCE, D, 16
they which find themselves grieved under a *democracy*, call it *a.*
HOBBES, 6
anathema A. Maranatha BIBLE, 43
ancestor I am my own a. JUNOT, 1
ancestors a. on either side of the Battle of Hastings LEE, H, 1
when his half-civilized a. were hunting the wild boar BENJAMIN, 1
ancestry I can trace my a. back to a . . . globule GILBERT, W, 24
nation is a society united by a delusion about its a. INGE, 10
ancient an a. Mariner COLERIDGE, S, 24
with the a. is wisdom BIBLE, 228
anecdotage man fell into his a. DISRAELI, 9
angel An a. writing in a book of gold HUNT, L, 1
A. of Death has been abroad BRIGHT, 1
A. of the Lord came down TATE, N, 3
in action, how like an a. SHAKESPEARE, 84
in comparison with which . . . I am a A. DICKENS, 20
In heaven an a. is nobody in particular SHAW, 1
Is man an ape or an a. DISRAELI, 28
This was the A. of History GOEBBELS, 2
woman yet think him an a. THACKERAY, 4
You may not be an a. DUBIN, 2
angels A. can fly CHESTERTON, 34
fools rush in where a. fear to tread POPE, 29
gave you manna . . . a.' bread BIBLE, 97
have entertained a. unawares BIBLE, 187
I . . . am on the side of the a. DISRAELI, 28
Its visits, Like those of a. BLAIR, R, 2
man did eat a.'s food PSALMS, 42
Not Angles, but a. GREGORY I, 1
One more devils'-triumph and sorrow for a. BROWNING, R, 32
People are not fallen a. LAWRENCE, D, 34
Tears such as a. weep MILTON, 36
the tongues of men and of a. BIBLE, 38
thou madest him lower than the a. PSALMS, 3
anger A. is one of the sinews of the soul FULLER, T, 5
a. makes us all stupid SPYRI, 1
A. supplies the arms VIRGIL, 4
fierce Juno's never-forgetting a. VIRGIL, 5
Grief and disappointment give rise to a. HUME, D, 7
he that is slow to a. is better than the mighty BIBLE, 452
Angles Not A., but angels GREGORY I, 1
angling A. is somewhat like poetry WALTON, 1
A. may be said to be . . . like the mathematics WALTON, 1
Let the blessing . . . be . . . upon all that are lovers of virtue; . . .
and go a-A. WALTON, 6
We may say of a. as Dr Boteler said of strawberries WALTON, 4
Anglo-Catholic Becoming an A. must . . . be a sad business
STRACHEY, J, 1
Anglo-Saxon Come in, you A. swine And drink of my Algerian
wine BEHAN, 9
those are A. attitudes CARROLL, 33
angry A Young Man PAUL, 1
The man who gets a . . . . in the right way . . . is commended
ARISTOTLE, 2
anguish drinking deep of that divinest a. BRONTË, E, 4
Making love is the sovereign remedy for a. LEBOYER, 6
angular an oblong a. figure LEACOCK, 6
animal 'Are you a. – or vegetable – or mineral?' CARROLL, 35
information vegetable, a. and mineral GILBERT, W, 37
Man is a gaming a. LAMB, CHARLES, 7
man is and will always be a wild a. DARWIN, C G, 1
Man is an intellectual a. HAZLITT, 5
Man is a noble a. BROWNE, T, 12
man is . . . a religious a. BURKE, E, 11
Man is a social a. SPINOZA, 1
Man is by nature a political a. ARISTOTLE, 6
Man is the only a. that can remain on friendly terms with the
victims . . . he eats BUTLER, S, 20
This a. is very bad ANONYMOUS, 100
true to your a. instincts LAWRENCE, D, 31
Whenever you observe an a. closely CANETTI, 1
animality its own a. either objectionable or funny LEWIS, C, 2

animals All a. are equal   ORWELL, 7
all a. were created . . . for the use of man   PEACOCK, 4
all there is to distinguish us from other a.   BEAUMARCHAIS, 2
A. are such agreeable friends   ELIOT, G, 7
a. . . . know nothing . . . of what people say about them
                                                            VOLTAIRE, 28
But if we stop loving a.   SOLZHENITSYN, 5
I could . . . live with a.   WHITMAN, 7
My music . . . understood by children and a.   STRAVINSKY, 4
paragon of a.   SHAKESPEARE, 84
some a. are more equal than others   ORWELL, 7
The a. went in one by one   ANONYMOUS, 78
There are two things for which a. are . . . envied   VOLTAIRE, 28
Wild a. never kill for sport   FROUDE, 1
animated a. with the soul of a Briton   VOLTAIRE, 2
Anna great A.! whom three realms obey   POPE, 49
annals short and simple a. of the poor   GRAY, 2
Anne Hathaway accurate reproductions of A.'s cottage
                                                           LANCASTER, 2
Annie Laurie for bonnie A.   DOUGLAS, W, 1
annihilating A. all that's made   MARVELL, 2
annihilation No a.   TOYNBEE, 1
anno domini A. . . . the most fatal complaint   HILTON, 1
annual A. income twenty pounds   DICKENS, 13
annuity Buy an a. cheap   DICKENS, 28
anomaly Poverty is an a. to rich people   BAGEHOT, 11
anon I would . . . guess that A. . . . was often a woman
                                                             WOOLF, 11
another A. year! – a. deadly blow   WORDSWORTH, W, 51
He who would do good to a.   BLAKE, W, 16
I would have given you a.   JARRY, 1
Life is just one damned thing after a.   HUBBARD, 3
No man can . . . condemn a.   BROWNE, T, 7
answer a. a fool according to his folly   BIBLE, 456
A timid question will . . . receive a confident a.   DARLING, 2
But a. came there none   CARROLL, 29
give a. as need requireth   BIBLE, 82
I do not a. questions like this without being paid   HELLMAN, 3
more than the wisest man can a.   COLTON, 4
The a. . . . is blowin' in the wind   DYLAN, 2
There are innumerable questions to which the inquisitive mind can
. . . receive no a.   JOHNSON, S, 127
where no one asks, no one needs to a.   JUNG, 1
would not stay for an a.   BACON, FRANCIS, 56
antagonistic the most a. to the Victorian age   WILSON, E, 1
antan les neiges d'a.   VILLON, 2
anthology a. is like all the plums and orange peel picked out of a
cake   RALEIGH, W A, 3
antic dance an a. hay   MARLOWE, 7
anticipation the intelligent a. of facts   CURZON, 3
anti-clerical it makes me understand a. things   BELLOC, 16
anti-climax everything afterward savours of a.   FITZGERALD, F S, 7
antidote the a. to desire   CONGREVE, 17
antipathy I do not dislike the French from . . . vulgar a.
                                                         WALPOLE, H, 9
strong a. of good to bad   POPE, 11
antiquity Damn the age. I'll write for a.   LAMB, CHARLES, 21
owes his celebrity merely to his a.   CHAUCER, 1
anti-Semite An American is either a Jew, or an a.   SARTRE, 5
hated by every a. as if I were a Jew   YEVTUSHENKO, 1
anvil My sledge and a. lie declined   ANONYMOUS, 60
anxious a. to do the wrong thing correctly   SAKI, 20
anybody If you have to tell them who you are, you aren't a.
                                                            PECK, 1
anyone a. here whom I have not insulted   BRAHMS, 1
anywhere go a. I damn well please   BEVIN, 3
apartheid We don't want a. liberalized   TUTU, 1
apathy God could cause us . . . sheer a. and boredom   GOETHE, 8
to go about the country stirring up a.   WHITELAW, 3
ape a man has no reason to be ashamed of having an a. for his
grandfather   HUXLEY, T, 11
Is man an a. or an angel   DISRAELI, 28
It is not the a., nor the tiger   TEMPLE, W, 5
the a. from which he is descended   WILBERFORCE, S, 1
The exception is a naked a.   MORRIS, D, 3
ape-like The a. virtues without which   CONNOLLY, 4
aphorisms The great writers of a.   CANETTI, 3
The hunter for a. . . . has to fish in muddy water   BRADLEY, F, 1
aphrodisiac Fame is a powerful a.   GREENE, 10
Power is the ultimate a.   KISSINGER, 2
apologize a good rule in life never to a.   WODEHOUSE, 9
It's too late to a.   TOSCANINI, 2

apology Never make a defence or a.   CHARLES I, 1
apostates that peculiar malignity . . . characteristic of a.
                                                         MACAULAY, T, 7
apostle great a. of the Philistines, Lord Macaulay   ARNOLD, M, 21
apostles The Septuagint minus the A.   VERRALL, 1
apparatus Brain, n. An a. with which we think   BIERCE, 4
apparel a. oft proclaims the man   SHAKESPEARE, 73
appeal The whole of art is an a. to a reality   MACCARTHY, 3
appealed hast thou a. unto Caesar   BIBLE, 17
appear Things are . . . what they a. to be   SARTRE, 8
appearances A. are deceptive   PROVERBS, 60
A. are not . . . a clue to the truth   COMPTON-BURNETT, 1
Keep up a.   CHURCHILL, C, 5
shallow people . . . do not judge by a.   WILDE, 48
appeaser An a. is one who feeds a crocodile   CHURCHILL, W, 70
appetite A. comes with eating   RABELAIS, 3
a. may sicken and so die   SHAKESPEARE, 334
the desire of satisfying a voracious a.   FIELDING, 11
apple An a. a day   PROVERBS, 48
as the a. of his eye   BIBLE, 59
I raised thee up under the a. tree   DIDLE, 500
keep me as the a. of an eye   PSALMS, 6
My a. trees will never . . . eat the cones   FROST, R, 6
want the a. for the a.'s sake   TWAIN, 15
When Eve ate this particular a.   LAWRENCE, D, 9
apple-pie An a. without some cheese   PROVERBS, 49
apples comfort me with a.   BIBLE, 487
The silver a. of the moon   YEATS, 30
applications only a. of science   PASTEUR, 4
applied sciences There are no such things as a.   PASTEUR, 4
appreciate I never 'a.'   PICASSO, 8
appreciation total dependence on the a. of others   CONNOLLY, 11
apprehend Intelligence is quickness to a.   WHITEHEAD, 2
apprehensions the impalpable elations and a. of growth
                                                          MAILER, 1
approve They that a. . . . call it opinion   HOBBES, 3
April And after A., when May follows   BROWNING, R, 26
A. is the cruellest month   ELIOT, T, 25
months . . . look gloomy in England are March and A.
                                                        TROLLOPE, 7
My regret Becomes an A. violet   TENNYSON, 37
Now that A.'s there   BROWNING, R, 25
Sweet A. showers   TUSSER, 2
Aprille Whan that A. with his shoures sote   CHAUCER, 3
Arab I shook hands with a friendly A.   MILLIGAN, 1
Arabia All the perfumes of A.   SHAKESPEARE, 222
Arabs The Jews and A. should . . . settle their differences
                                                         AUSTIN, W, 2
arch All experience is an a.   TENNYSON, 80
archaeologist An a. is the best husband   CHRISTIE, 6
archbishop the sign of an a. is a double-cross
                                                    DIX, DOM GREGORY, 1
arch-enemy love . . . has one a. – and that is life   ANOUILH, 1
arches Underneath the a.   FLANAGAN, 1
architect Each man the a. of his own fate   APPIUS CAECUS, 1
the a. can only advise   WRIGHT, F, 1
who is not a great sculptor or painter can be an a.   RUSKIN, 3
architecture A. has its political use   WREN, 1
A. in general is frozen music   SCHELLING, 1
Fashion is a.   CHANEL, 4
What has happened to a.   LEVIN, 2
ardua Per a. ad astra   ANONYMOUS, 68
arguing I am not a. with you   WHISTLER, 3
In a. too, the parson own'd his skill   GOLDSMITH, 7
argument All a. is against it   JOHNSON, S, 120
any authentic work of art must start an a.   WEST, R, 2
I have found you an a.   JOHNSON, S, 151
I love a., I love debate   THATCHER, M, 7
to get the best of an a.   CARNEGIE, 2
arguments beware of long a. and long beards   SANTAYANA, 10
the world can be expressed in . . . a.   FRAYN, 2
Arian In three sips the A. frustrate   BROWNING, R, 53
arise shall . . . a. with healing in his wings   BIBLE, 343
aristocracy an absentee a.   DISRAELI, 22
An a. in a republic is like a chicken whose head has been cut off
                                                       MITFORD, N, 1
a. . . . government by the badly educated   CHESTERTON, 43
If human beings could be propagated . . . a. would be . . . sound
                                                        HALDANE, 3
riff-raff apply to what is respectable . . . a. to what is decent
                                                          HOPE, 6
they that are displeased with a., call it oligarchy   HOBBES, 6

Unlike the male codfish . . . the British a. is   WODEHOUSE, 21
aristocrat the quality that distinguishes the gentleman from both
  the artist and the a.   WAUGH, E, 12
aristocratic To be a. in Art   MOORE, G, 3
  to distinguish . . . the a. class from the Philistines   ARNOLD, M, 8
arithmetic different branches of A.   CARROLL, 15
  Music is the a. of sounds   DEBUSSY, 1
ark an a. of bulrushes   BIBLE, 103
  into the a., two and two   BIBLE, 158
arm An a. Rose up from . . . the lake   TENNYSON, 20
  Don't carry away that a. till I have . . . my ring   RAGLAN, 1
  Human on my faithless a.   AUDEN, 20
  soon think of taking the a. of an elm tree   THOREAU, 2
Armageddon a place called . . . A.   BIBLE, 467
armchair She fitted into my biggest a.   WODEHOUSE, 13
arm'd a. with more than complete steel   MARLOWE, 12
Armenteers A mademoiselle from A.   ROWLAND, 1
armies ignorant a. clash by night   ARNOLD, M, 11
  not a. . . . but flocks of sheep   CERVANTES, 5
armistice a short a. with truth   BYRON, 25
armour a. of light   BOOK OF COMMON PRAYER, 4
  Conceit is the finest a.   JEROME, 2
  Prayer makes the Christian's a. bright   COWPER, 15
arms Anger supplies the a.   VIRGIL, 4
  For the theatre one needs long a.   BERNHARDT, 1
  I never would lay down my a.   PITT THE ELDER, 1
  I sing of a. and the man   VIRGIL, 5
  It is always opening time in the Sailors A.   THOMAS, D, 21
  So he laid down his a.   HOOD, 2
army An a. is a nation within a nation   VIGNY, 3
  An a. marches on its stomach   NAPOLEON I, 14
  Chief of the A.   NAPOLEON I, 15
  contemptible little A.   WILHELM II, 4
  If you don't want to use the a., I should like to borrow it   LINCOLN, 9
  terrible as an a. with banners   BIBLE, 496
  The a. ages men sooner than the law   WELLS, 7
  The conventional a. loses if it does not win   KISSINGER, 1
  the little ships of England brought the A. home   GUEDALLA, 2
Arnold A. is a dandy Isaiah   ARNOLD, M, 2
arrest arbitrary a. and expulsion   SOLZHENITSYN, 1
  My father didn't create you to a. me   PEEL, 1
  One does not a. Voltaire   DE GAULLE, 10
arrested Christ . . . would quite likely have been a.   DE BLANK, 1
arrive To travel hopefully is . . . better . . . than to a.   STEVENSON, R, 26
arrow Every a. . . . feels the attraction of earth   LONGFELLOW, 5
  I, said the Sparrow, With my bow and a.   NURSERY RHYMES, 73
  I shot an a. into the air   LONGFELLOW, 3
  the a. that flieth by day   PSALMS, 51
arrows whose teeth are spears and a.   PSALMS, 36
arse a politician is an a.   CUMMINGS, 2
  Sit on your a. for fifty years   MACNEICE, 1
arsenal a. of democracy   ROOSEVELT, F, 13
arson A., after all, is an artificial crime   WELLS, 12
art All a. deals with the absurd   MURDOCH, 1
  All A. is quite useless   WILDE, 45
  An a. can only be learned   BUTLER, S, 5
  any authentic work of a. must start an argument   WEST, R, 2
  A. and religion first; then philosophy   SPARK, 9
  A. . . . can go on mattering once it has stopped hurting   BOWEN, ELIZABETH, 2
  a. constantly aspires towards . . . music   PATER, 2
  A. for a.'s sake   COUSIN, 1; FORSTER, 4
  A. is a jealous mistress   EMERSON, 4
  A. is long, and Time is fleeting   LONGFELLOW, 10
  A. is not a mirror . . . but a hammer   MAYAKOVSKY, 1
  A. is not a special sauce   LETHABY, 1
  a. is not a weapon   KENNEDY, JOHN, 17
  A. is ruled . . . by the imagination   CROCE, 1
  A. is the imposing of a pattern on experience   WHITEHEAD, 2
  A. is the most intense mode of individualism   WILDE, 55
  A. is . . . the transmission of feeling   TOLSTOY, L, 13
  a. is to give life a shape   ANOUILH, 5
  A. never expresses anything   WILDE, 16
  a. of pleasing consists   HAZLITT, 24
  aspires . . . to the condition of a.   CONRAD, 5
  Bullfighting is the only a. in which the artist is in danger of death   HEMINGWAY, 4
  Desiring this man's a.   SHAKESPEARE, 360
  Dying is an a.   PLATH, 1
  excellence of every a. is its intensity   KEATS, 54

Fine a. is that in which the hand   RUSKIN, 13
great parables . . . but false a.   LAWRENCE, D, 42
half a trade and half an a.   INGE, 8
I don't want a. for a few   MORRIS, W, 3
I doubt that a. needed Ruskin   RUSKIN, 13
I have discovered the a. . . . lost for two thousand years   DUNCAN, 1
industry without a. is brutality   RUSKIN, 4
Insurrection is an a.   TROTSKY, 6
It's clever but is it a.   KIPLING, 6
Mr Goldwyn . . . you are only interested in a.   SHAW, 47
nature is the a. of God   BROWNE, T, 3
Nature's handmaid, a.   DRYDEN, 20
Politics is not a science . . . but an a.   BISMARCK, 7
Politics is the a. of the possible   BISMARCK, 3
Rules and models destroy genius and a.   HAZLITT, 29
sombre enemy of good a.   CONNOLLY, 10
the a. of the possible   BUTLER, R, 1
The last and greatest a. – the a. to blot   DRYDEN, 22
The whole of a. is an appeal to a reality   MACCARTHY, 3
They say princes learn no a. truly, but . . . horsemanship   JONSON, 8
To be aristocratic in A.   MOORE, G, 3
True ease in writing comes from a.   POPE, 26
wonderful case of nature imitating a.   WILDE, 62
writer's only responsibility is to his a.   FAULKNER, 2
artful The a. Dodger   DICKENS, 37
article It all depends upon that a. there   WELLINGTON, 3
articles to pay for a. . . . they do not want   HURST, 1
artificial All things are a.   BROWNE, T, 3
  nothing so a. as sinning nowadays   LAWRENCE, D, 26
artist An amateur is an a. who supports himself with outside jobs
  which enable him to paint   SHAHN, 1
  As an a., a man has no home   NIETZSCHE, 2
  Beware of the a. who's an intellectual   FITZGERALD, F S, 11
  distinguishes the gentleman from both the a. and the aristocrat   WAUGH, E, 12
  God is really only another a.   PICASSO, 7
  only one position for an a. anywhere   THOMAS, D, 31
  Remember I'm an a.   CARY, J, 2
  What is an a.   STOPPARD, 11
artistic temperament . . . afflicts amateurs   CHESTERTON, 24
  never had a goddam a. problem   WAYNE, 1
  There never was an a. period   WHISTLER, 19
artists A. are not engineers of the soul   KENNEDY, JOHN, 17
  Great a. have no country   MUSSET, 2
  The a. retired. The British remained   WHISTLER, 15
art-loving an A. nation   WHISTLER, 19
arts If all the a. aspire to the condition of music   SANTAYANA, 14
  Murder . . . one of the Fine A.   DE QUINCEY, 2
  secret of the a. is to correct nature   VOLTAIRE, 15
ashamed few people who are not a. of having been in love   ROCHEFOUCAULD, 8
I am a. of confessing   BURNEY, 1
some habit of which he is deeply a.   CRISP, 1
to see them not a.   SWIFT, 10
We are not a. of what we have done   PANKHURST, C, 2
ashes a. of Napoleon   WELLINGTON, 24
Asia There is too much A. and she is too old   KIPLING, 18
ask a., and it shall be given   BIBLE, 375
  A. a silly question   PROVERBS, 63
  A. no questions   PROVERBS, 64
  those things which we a. faithfully   BOOK OF COMMON PRAYER, 6
  To labour and not to a. for any reward   LOYOLA, 1
asks where no one a., no one needs to answer   JUNG, 1
asleep The devil is a.   PEARY, 1
asp wicked a. of Twickenham   POPE, 1
aspect Meet in her a.   BYRON, 40
aspens Willows whiten, a. quiver   TENNYSON, 42
aspicious two a. persons   SHAKESPEARE, 273
aspirations The young have a.   SAKI, 12
aspires art constantly a. towards . . . music   PATER, 2
  a. . . . to the condition of art   CONRAD, 5
aspirings The soul hath not her generous a. implanted in her in vain   LAMB, CHARLES, 26
ass a strong a.   BIBLE, 181
  every a. thinks he may kick at him   PARR, 1
  the law is a a.   DICKENS, 38
  the Lord opened the mouth of the a.   BIBLE, 438
assassination Absolutism tempered by a.   MÜNSTER, 1
  A. has never changed   DISRAELI, 29
  A. . . . the extreme form of censorship   SHAW, 39

assemblance   Care I for the . . . a. of a man   SHAKESPEARE, 124
assemblies   Kings govern by . . . a. only when   FOX, C, 4
assertions   Pure mathematics consists entirely of a.   RUSSELL, B, 14
assessment   not interested in making an a. of myself   BRANDO, 2
asset   the greatest a. a head of state can have   WILSON, HAROLD, 12
assigned   purpose of God and the doom a.   TENNYSON, 58
associate   good must a.   BURKE, E, 20
I . . . like to a. with . . . priests   BELLOC, 16
assure   a. him that he'd live tomorrow   RABELAIS, 5
astonished   a. at my own moderation   CLIVE, 1
it is *I* who am surprised; you are merely a.   WEBSTER, N, 1
astonishment   Dear Sir, Your a.'s odd   ANONYMOUS, 15
Just a little more reverence . . . , and not so much a.   SARGENT, M, 1
astound   Austria will a. the world with . . . her ingratitude   SCHWARZENBERG, 1
astronauts   The a.! . . . Rotarians in outer space   VIDAL, 3
astronomy   A. teaches the correct use   LEACOCK, 5
asunder   afar and a.   BOWEN, E. E., 1
let no man put a.   BOOK OF COMMON PRAYER, 29
what . . . God hath joined together, let not man put a.   BIBLE, 403
asylum   the absence from Jerusalem of a lunatic a.   ELLIS, 1
world is . . . like a lunatic a.   LLOYD GEORGE, 19
asylums   Those comfortably padded lunatic a. . . . the stately homes   WOOLF, 4
atheism   Every luxury . . . a., breast-feeding, circumcision   ORTON, 4
God never wrought miracle to convince a.   BACON, FRANCIS, 9
atheist   an a. half believes a God   YOUNG, E, 4
An a. is a man who has no invisible means of support   FOSDICK, 1
An a. is one point   PROVERBS, 50
A pious man . . . would be an a. if the king were   LA BRUYÈRE, 1
Hardy became a sort of village a.   HARDY, 1
He was an embittered a.   ORWELL, 12
I am an a. . . . thank God   BUÑUEL, 1
only her scepticism kept her from being an a.   SARTRE, 16
very *chic* for an a.   RUSSELL, B, 5
Athens   A. arose   SHELLEY, 9
A. holds sway over all Greece   THEMISTOCLES, 1
athirst   my soul is a. for God   PSALMS, 26
athletic   The only a. sport I ever mastered   JERROLD, 7
athletics   a. as inferior forms of fox-hunting   WAUGH, E, 17
Atlantic   The Admiral of the A. salutes the Admiral of the Pacific   WILHELM II, 3
to have the East come to the A.   GOERING, 1
A to B   She ran . . . emotions from A.   PARKER, D, 29
atom   The a. bomb is a paper tiger   MAO TSE-TUNG, 9
There is no evil in the a.   STEVENSON, A, 5
They split the a. by firing particles at it   HAY, W, 1
atomic   The way to win an a. war   BRADLEY, O, 1
atoms   Accidental and fortuitous concurrence of a.   PALMERSTON, 1
atone   a. for the sins of your fathers   HORACE, 36
atrocities   His sickness has created a. that are repellent   PICASSO, 2
atrophy   Music begins to a.   POUND, 3
attached   men become a. even to Widnes   TAYLOR, A, 8
attachment   His a. to . . . his friends . . . was thoroughgoing and exemplary   JEFFERSON, 1
attack   A. is the best form   PROVERBS, 72
don't believe in . . . true love until after the first a.   ESCHENBACH, 2
situation excellent. I shall a.   FOCH, 1
attacks   Her frontal a. on old taboos   STOPES, 2
attainments   These are rare a. . . . but . . . can she spin   JAMES I, 4
attention   a. to the inside . . . contempt for the outside   CHESTERFIELD, 14
He would take his a. away from the universe   CRISP, 10
Attic   A. wit   PLINY THE ELDER, 1
glory of the A. stage   ARNOLD, M, 42
attic   brain a. stocked with all the furniture that he is likely to use   DOYLE, 12
Attila   A. the Hen   THATCHER, M, 2
attitude   his a. of a king in exile   DE GAULLE, 1
the largest scope for change still lies in men's a. to women   BRITTAIN, 1
attitudes   Anglo-Saxon a.   CARROLL, 33
attorney   the gentleman is an *a.*   JOHNSON, S, 80
attraction   Every arrow . . . feels the a. of earth   LONGFELLOW, 5

The chief a. of military service   TOLSTOY, L, 9
attractive   if they are in the least a.   CAMPBELL, R, 2
The most a. sentences are not perhaps the wisest   THOREAU, 4
audacity   a. of elected persons   WHITMAN, 11
Auden   A. was someone you could laugh-at-with   SPENDER, 4
high watermark . . . of Socialist literature is W. H. A.   AUDEN, 2
to write like Tennyson . . . rather than Eliot or A.   BETJEMAN, 2
We have one poet of genius in A.   AUDEN, 1
W. H. A., a sort of gutless Kipling   ORWELL, 28
audience   a. was a disaster   WILDE, 70
I know two kinds of a.   SCHNABEL, 1
the a. want to be surprised . . . by things that they expect   BERNARD, T, 1
whether the a. thinks you are crying   BERGMAN, 2
auditioned   kind of show where the girls are not a.   THOMAS, I, 3
auld   a. acquaintance be forgot   BURNS, R, 4
for a. lang syne   BURNS, R, 5
aunt   Charley's a. from Brazil   THOMAS, B, 1
Aunt Edna   A. is universal   RATTIGAN, 1
aunts   bad a. and good a.   WODEHOUSE, 4
Aussie   a dinkum hard-swearing A   HASKELL, 1
Austen   Jane A.   SCOTT, WALTER, 5
Jane A.'s books, too, are absent from this library   AUSTEN, 3
More can be learnt from Miss A.   AUSTEN, 1
Austerlitz   There rises the sun of A.   NAPOLEON I, 7
Australia   A. the air would have been thick with first names   JAMES, C, 2
guess . . . he was born in A.   SHAW, 14
So you're going to A.   MORPURGO, 1
Australian   I'm going to write the Great A. Novel   WHITE, P, 4
Austria   A. is Switzerland . . . with history added   MORPURGO, 1
A. will astound the world with . . . her ingratitude   SCHWARZENBERG, 1
author   An a. who speaks about his own books   DISRAELI, 30
bad novel tells us . . . about its a.   CHESTERTON, 23
He is the richest a. that ever grazed   JOHNSON, S, 60
Thou are my master and my a.   VIRGIL, 2
authority   a. be a stubborn bear   SHAKESPEARE, 354
A. forgets a dying king   TENNYSON, 21
man Dress'd in a little brief a.   SHAKESPEARE, 228
No morality can be founded on a.   AYER, 1
Nothing destroyeth a. so much   BACON, FRANCIS, 22
The defiance of established . . . a.   ARENDT, 1
the degree of acceptance and a. which Mao has acquired   MAO TSE-TUNG, 1
the highest a. for believing that the meek shall inherit the Earth   BIRKENHEAD, 1
authors   A. are easy to get on with   JOSEPH, 1
much exposed to a.   WELLINGTON, 5
The faults of great a.   COLERIDGE, S, 20
their a. could not endure being wrong   CAMUS, 7
The reciprocal civility of a.   JOHNSON, S, 19
The trouble with our younger a. is   MAUGHAM, 29
automobile   Money differs from an a.   GALBRAITH, 7
avarice   rich beyond the dreams of a.   MOORE, E, 2
ave   *a. atque vale*   CATULLUS, 3
avenged   the satisfaction of knowing that we are a.   TROLLOPE, 16
average   a. American loves his family   TWAIN, 1
Take the life-lie away from the a. man   IBSEN, 9
aves   Beadsman, after thousand a. told   KEATS, 10
Avilion   To the island-valley of A.   TENNYSON, 25
avoidance   The a. of taxes . . . still carries . . . reward   KEYNES, 11
avoiding   Reading . . . ingenious device for a. thought   HELPS, 1
Avon   Sweet Swan of A.   JONSON, 11
a-waggle   You must always be a.   LAWRENCE, D, 3
awake   At last a.   BROWNING, R, 23
A.! for Morning in the Bowl of Night   FITZGERALD, E, 2
I dream when I am a.   CALDERÓN DE LA BARCA, 2
Onaway! A., beloved   LONGFELLOW, 13
The lilies and roses were all a.   TENNYSON, 57
We're very wide a., The moon and I   GILBERT, W, 28
away   Over the hills and far a.   GAY, 3
Take the soup a.   HOFFMAN, 1
the big one that got a.   DENNIS, N, 1
aweary   I gin to be a. of the sun   SHAKESPEARE, 226
awful   Abashed the devil . . . felt how a. goodness is   MILTON, 47
awfulness   by its very a.   STEVENSON, R, 23
awoke   I a. one morning   BYRON, 45
axe   his keener eye The a.'s edge did try   MARVELL, 4
Lizzie Borden took an a.   ANONYMOUS, 52
axioms   A. in philosophy are not a.   KEATS, 59

bars Nor iron b. a cage	LOVELACE, 1
barter All government . . . is founded on compromise and b.	
	BURKE, E, 14
base doing good to b. fellows	CERVANTES, 9
baseball as sensible as b. in Italian	MENCKEN, 17
based All progress is b.	BUTLER, S, 11
basement interviewing a faded female in a damp b.	HARDING, 1
basing b. morals on myth	SAMUEL, 5
bastard Because I am a b.	HEMINGWAY, 8
I hope you will not publicly call me a b.	WHITLAM, 1
one lucky b. who's the artist	STOPPARD, 1
putting all my eggs in one b.	PARKER, D, 21
we knocked the b. off	HILLARY, 2
bastards It is a pity . . . that more politicians are not b.	
	WHITEHORN, 4
bat black b., night, has flown	TENNYSON, 56
They came to see me b. not to see you bowl	GRACE, 1
Twinkle, twinkle, little b.	CARROLL, 10
Bath Oh! who can ever be tired of B.	AUSTEN, 15
bath B. . . . once a week to avoid being a public menace	
	BURGESS, 3
the nuns who never take a b.	RUSSELL, B, 7
bathing b. in someone else's dirty water	PROUST, 1
caught the Whigs b.	DISRAELI, 23
something between a large b. machine	GILBERT, W, 21
bathroom fierce and revolutionary in a b.	LINKLATER, 3
bats b. in the belfry	PHILLPOTTS, 1
battalions God is always on the side of the big b.	TURENNE, 1
God is on the side not of the heavy b., but of the best shots	
	VOLTAIRE, 23
battering B. the gates of heaven	TENNYSON, 74
battle A b. of giants	WELLINGTON, 26
b. to the strong	BIBLE, 74
greatest misery is a b. gained	WELLINGTON, 8
next greatest misfortune to losing a b.	WELLINGTON, 12
No general in the midst of b. has a great discussion . . . if	
defeated	OWEN, D, 2
Noise, screams, b. seen fought in the skies	NOSTRADAMUS, 1
The b. for women's rights	THATCHER, M, 12
The b. of Britain	CHURCHILL, W, 53
the B. of Waterloo *was* won on the playing-fields of Eton	
	ORWELL, 13
battlefield the most beautiful b.	NAPOLEON I, 8
we survive amongst the dead and the dying as on a b.	SPARK, 5
battles Dead b., like dead generals	TUCHMAN, 1
bauble What shall we do with this b.	CROMWELL, O, 6
baying b. for broken glass	WAUGH, E, 4
bayonets A man may build . . . a throne of b.	INGE, 11
boys To win the palm, the oak, or b.	MARVELL, 1
bc If you want to b. happy, b.	TOLSTOY, L, 6
To b., or not to b.	SHAKESPEARE, 89
What must b., must b.	PROVERBS, 455
beaches we shall fight on the b.	CHURCHILL, W, 51
beacons Logical consequences are the scarecrows of fools and	
the b. of wise men	HUXLEY, T, 9
beadle a b. on boxin' day	DICKENS, 48
beads what glass b. are to African traders	CRISP, 5
Beadsman The B., after thousand aves told	KEATS, 10
beak Take thy b. from out my heart	POE, 2
beaker a b. full of the warm South	KEATS, 37
Beale Miss Buss and Miss B. Cupid's darts do not feel	
	ANONYMOUS, 56
be-all b. and the end-all here	SHAKESPEARE, 208
bean The home of the b. and the cod	BOSSIDY, 1
bear a B. of Very Little Brain	MILNE, 6
any man . . . who could not b. another's misfortunes . . . like a	
Christian	POPE, 37
authority be a stubborn b.	SHAKESPEARE, 354
Exit, pursued by a b.	SHAKESPEARE, 351
Human kind cannot b.	ELIOT, T, 7
I had rather b. with you than b. you	SHAKESPEARE, 43
never . . . sell the b.'s skin	LA FONTAINE, 7
Round and round the garden Like a teddy b.	NURSERY RHYMES, 48
they think I shall be able to b. it best	CHURCHILL, W, 22
bear-baiting Puritan hated b.	MACAULAY, T, 8
beard Dead eyes and a red b.	LAWRENCE, D, 1
singed the Spanish king's b.	DRAKE, 1
There was an Old Man with a b.	LEAR, 1
bearded hard to hear what a b. man is saying	MANKEIWICZ, 1
He reaps the b. grain at a breath	LONGFELLOW, 11
beards beware of long arguments and long b.	SANTAYANA, 10
men wore their b., like they wear their neckties	LAWRENCE, D, 20

bears And dancing dogs and b.	HODGSON, 1
And some of the bigger b. try to pretend	MILNE, 5
b. and lions growl and fight	WATTS, 3
beast b. of the earth	BIBLE, 141
Dialect words – those terrible marks of the b.	HARDY, 9
Either a b. or a god	ARISTOTLE, 7
for man or b.	FIELDS, 1
hardly be a b. or a fool alone on a great mountain	KILVERT, 2
Man's life is cheap as b.'s	SHAKESPEARE, 175
The B. stands for strong mutually antagonistic governments	
	WAUGH, E, 32
the mark . . . of the b.	BIBLE, 466
beastie Wee, sleekit, cow'rin', tim'rous b.	BURNS, R, 21
beastly Don't let's be b. to the Germans	COWARD, 7
beasts man . . . compared unto the b. that perish	PSALMS, 29
beat make the b. keep time with short steps	ANDERSEN, 3
The b. generation	KEROUAC, 4
Two hearts that b. as one	LOVELL, 1
beaten I was b. up by Quakers	ALLEN, W, 5
public school, where . . . learning was painfully b. into him	
	PEACOCK, 8
beautiful Against the b. . . . one can wage a pitiless war	
	GREENE, 5
All things bright and b.	ALEXANDER, 1
b. . . . for someone who could not read	CHESTERTON, 48
light, shade, and perspective . . . make it b.	CONSTABLE, 1
many men, so b.	COLERIDGE, S, 32
most b. things . . . are the most useless	RUSKIN, 11
Our love of what is b. does not lead to extravagance	PERICLES, 1
Rich men's houses are seldom b.	ASQUITH, M, 2
The good is the b.	PLATO, 1
the most b. battlefield	NAPOLEON I, 8
the most b. woman I've ever seen	MARX, G, 1
the name of which was B.	BUNYAN, 4
the work comes out more b.	GAUTIER, 2
when a woman isn't b.	CHEKHOV, 12
beautifully B. done	SPENCER, S, 2
beauty A thing of b. is a joy for ever	KEATS, 7
B. and the lust for learning	BEERBOHM, 15
b. being the best of all we know	BRIDGES, 1
B. in distress	BURKE, E, 7
B. in things exists in the mind which contemplates them	
	HUME, D, 4
B. is in the eye	PROVERBS, 79
B. is . . . in the eye of the beholder HUNGERFORD, 1; WALLACE, L, 1
b. is only sin deep	SAKI, 21
B. is only skin-deep	PROVERBS, 80
B. is potent	PROVERBS, 81
B. is truth, truth b.	KEATS, 30
B. itself doth of itself persuade The eyes of men	
	SHAKESPEARE, 356
B. sat with me all the summer day	BRIDGES, 2
B. stands In the admiration . . . of weak minds	MILTON, 54
B. too rich for use	SHAKESPEARE, 306
better to be first with an ugly woman than the hundredth with a	
b.	BUCK, 5
But b.'s self she is, When all her robes are gone	ANONYMOUS, 58
Clad in the b. of a thousand stars	MARLOWE, 3
Exuberance is B.	BLAKE, W, 29
Fostered alike by b. and by fear	WORDSWORTH, W, 35
her b. made The bright world dim	SHELLEY, 26
Love built on b.	DONNE, 9
love permanence more than . . . b.	CASSON, 1
Mathematics possesses . . . b.	RUSSELL, B, 21
She walks in b.	BYRON, 40
Teaches such b. as a woman's eye	SHAKESPEARE, 197
the b. Of an aged face	CAMPBELL, JOSEPH, 1
the laws of poetic truth and poetic b.	ARNOLD, M, 15
The pain passes, but the b. remains	RENOIR, 1
There is no excellent b.	BACON, FRANCIS, 12
this generation . . . found England a land of b.	JOAD, 3
What *is* b., anyway? There's no such thing	PICASSO, 8
beaver And cultivate a b.	HUXLEY, A, 5
because B. it is there	MALLORY, 1
Becket Thomas B.	HENRY II, 1
become What's b. of Waring	BROWNING, R, 58
becoming I believe I am b. a god	VESPASIAN, 1
Sunburn is very b.	COWARD, 10
bed and die – in b.	SASSOON, S, 2
And so to b.	PEPYS, 5
B. . . . is the poor man's opera	HUXLEY, A, 21
Each within our narrow b.	CASWALL, 1

Culture, the acquainting ourselves with the b. ARNOLD, M, 22
For home is b. TUSSER, 4
His worst is better than any other person's b. HAZLITT, 8
It was the b. of times DICKENS, 56
letting the b. be the enemy of the good JENKINS, 2
look at the b. book . . . price of a turbot . . . RUSKIN, 9
Men of few words are the b. SHAKESPEARE, 131
Stolen sweets are b. CIBBER, 2
The b. is the enemy of the good VOLTAIRE, 12
The b. lack all conviction YEATS, 28
the b. of all possible worlds VOLTAIRE, 8
The b. of friends PROVERBS, 378
The b. things in life PROVERBS, 380
the b. which has been thought and said in the world
ARNOLD, M, 3
the shortest works are always the b. LA FONTAINE, 11
we live in the b. of all possible worlds CABELL, 2
we will do our b. CHURCHILL, W, 57
bestial what remains is b. SHAKESPEARE, 281
bestow Let them b. on every airth a limb GRAHAM, J, 1
bestride he doth b. the narrow world Like a Colossus
SHAKESPEARE, 143
best-seller A b. . . . because it was selling well BOORSTIN, 2
A b. is the gilded tomb of a mediocre talent SMITH, L, 1
bet I b. my money on the bob-tail nag FOSTER, 1
Bethlehem O come ye to B. OAKELEY, 1
O little town of B. BROOKS, P, 1
betimes to be up b. SHAKESPEARE, 337
betray Nature never did b. WORDSWORTH, W, 12
betrayed woe unto that man by whom the Son of man is b.
BIBLE, 423
betraying if I had to choose between b. my country and b. my
friend FORSTER, 1
betrothed a bride's attitude towards her b. MUIR, 2
better a far, far, b. thing DICKENS, 57
always . . . trying to get the b. LAMB, CHARLES, 7
b. is he . . . who hath not seen the evil work under the sun
BIBLE, 68
b. strangers SHAKESPEARE, 53
B. than a play CHARLES II, 5
b. to have loved and lost TENNYSON, 28
b. to have no opinion of God BACON, FRANCIS, 52
b. to marry than to burn BIBLE, 30
for b. for worse BOOK OF COMMON PRAYER, 27
He is no b. AUSTIN, A, 1
I am getting b. and b. COUÉ, 1
if you knows of a b. 'ole BAIRNSFATHER, 1
I've got to admit it's getting b. LENNON, 2
nae b. than he should be BURNS, R, 8
no b. than you should be BEAUMONT, 1
One could . . . have done so much b. for them WYNDHAM, 1
something b. than our brains to depend upon CHESTERFIELD, 20
the old is b. BIBLE, 321
when I'm bad I'm b. WEST, M, 14
When you meet someone b. . . . turn your thoughts to becoming
his equal CONFUCIUS, 1
You're a b. man than I am, Gunga Din KIPLING, 15
Beulah B., peel me a grape WEST, M, 6
bewailing the sum of life's b. LANDON, 3
beware all should cry, B. COLERIDGE, S, 17
B. of the artist who's an intellectual FITZGERALD, F S, 11
'B. of the dog.' PETRONIUS, 1
B. of the man who does not return your blow SHAW, 26
bewildered Bewitched, Bothered and B. HART, 1
I was b. once BOONE, 1
bewitch crying beauty to b. men HOMER, 1
bewitched B., Bothered and Bewildered HART, 1
bewitching the b. of naughtiness BIBLE, 519
beyond All decent people live b. their incomes nowadays SAKI, 9
Bible have used the B. as if it was a constable's handbook
KINGSLEY, 3
I didn't write the B. DE MILLE, 2
quotations from the B. and the rest JOYCE, 1
searching through the B. for loopholes FIELDS, 5
that book is the B. ARNOLD, M, 31
The B. is literature SANTAYANA, 4
the B. tells me so WARNER, 1
The English B. MACAULAY, T, 1
There's a B. on that shelf there RUSSELL, B, 24
Bibles they have the land and we have the B. GEORGE, 1
bicycle a b. made for two DACRE, 1
Socialism can only arrive by b. VIERA GALLO, 1

big A b. man has no time FITZGERALD, F S, 13
A government . . . b. enough to give you all you want
GOLDWATER, 1
b. emotions come from b. words HEMINGWAY, 9
he was too b. for them BULMER-THOMAS, 1
the b. one that got away DENNIS, N, 1
The b. print giveth and the fine print taketh away SHEEN, 2
Big Brother B. is watching you ORWELL, 17
bigger it's a great deal b. CARLYLE, T, 33
The b. they come FITZSIMMONS, 1
bike he got on his b. TEBBITT, 1
bile He likes . . . the b. when it is black ELIOT, T, 1
bill put 'Emily, I love you' on the back of the b. MARX, G, 19
billboard A b. lovely as a tree NASH, 10
billboards the churches . . . bore for me the same relation to God
that b. did to Coca-Cola UPDIKE, 2
billiard The b. sharp whom any one catches GILBERT, W, 30
billiards to play b. well SPENCER, H, 2
Billy B. . . . Fell in the fire GRAHAM, H, 2
That's the way for B. and me HOGG, 1
billy-bong Once a jolly swagman camped by a b. PATERSON, 1
biographies History is the essence of . . . b. CARLYLE, T, 6
biography a man is nobody unless his b. TROLLOPE, 6
hesitation in starting my b. too soon RUSSELL, B, 3
history . . . the b. of great men CARLYLE, T, 11
how difficult it is to write b. WEST, R, 8
no history; only b. EMERSON, 9
birch I'm all for bringing back the b. VIDAL, 7
bird A b. in the hand PROVERBS, 9
Lo! the B. is on the Wing FITZGERALD, E, 3
my soul . . . should flee as a b. PSALMS, 4
She's only a b. in a gilded cage LAMB, A, 1
The B. of Time FITZGERALD, E, 3
bird-cage a b. played with toasting-forks BEECHAM, 7
Robert Houdin who . . . invented the vanishing b. trick and the
theater matinée WELLES, 4
birds All the b. of the air NURSERY RHYMES, 2
B. of a feather PROVERBS, 93
no b. sing KEATS, 22
No fruits, no flowers, no leaves, no b. HOOD, 10
spring now comes unheralded by the return of the b. CARSON, 3
that make fine b. AESOP, 5
Two little dicky b., Sitting on a wall NURSERY RHYMES, 68
where late the sweet b. sang SHAKESPEARE, 364
Birmingham Am in B. CHESTERTON, 46
One has no great hopes from B. AUSTEN, 10
birth B., and copulation, and death ELIOT, T, 21
b. had no meaning LEE, L, 2
B. may be a matter of a moment LEBOYER, 1
From b. to age eighteen, a girl needs good parents TUCKER, 3
no credentials . . . not even . . . a certificate of b.
LLOYD GEORGE, 9
no cure for b. and death SANTAYANA, 11
what you were before your b. SCHOPENHAUER, 7
birthday A diplomat . . . always remembers a woman's b.
FROST, R, 10
If one doesn't get b. presents REED, H, 5
is it my b. or am I dying ASTOR, N, 4
birthplace accent of one's b. lingers ROCHEFOUCAULD, 23
biscuit Can't a fellow even enjoy a b. PORTLAND, 1
bishop a b. . . . must be blameless BIBLE, 507
another B. dead MELBOURNE, 9
blonde to make a b. kick a hole CHANDLER, R, 1
How can a b. marry SMITH, SYDNEY, 8
Make him a b., and you will silence him CHESTERFIELD, 21
May you be the mother of a b. BEHAN, 11
the symbol of a b. is a crook DIX, DOM GREGORY, 1
bisier he semed b. than he was CHAUCER, 10
bit He b. his lip in a manner PERELMAN, 4
The dog . . . Went mad and b. the man GOLDSMITH, 10
bitches Now we are all sons of b. BAINBRIDGE, 1
bite b. the hand that fed them BURKE, E, 19
would b. some other of my generals GEORGE II, 2
bites when a man b. a dog DANA, 1
when a man b. a dog that is news BOGART, J, 1
biting See what will happen . . . if you don't stop b. your
fingernails ROGERS, W, 11
black A lady asked me why . . . I wore b. SITWELL, E, 3
Any colour, so long as it's b. FORD, H, 4
coffee that's too b. . . . You integrate it with cream
MALCOLM X, 1
I am b., as if bereav'd of light BLAKE, W, 48
I don't believe in b. majority rule SMITH, I, 1

looking for a b. hat — BOWEN, C, 2
One b., and one white, and two khaki — ANONYMOUS, 95
sees b. people as expendable — TUTU, 2
Take that b. box away — TREE, 9
That old b. magic — MERCER, 2
The Ethiopians say that their gods are . . . b. — XENOPHANES, 1
The future is . . . b. — BALDWIN, J, 5
There's a b. sheep — PROVERBS, 412
Two lovely b. eyes — COBORN, 1
blackbirds Four and twenty b., Baked in a pie — NURSERY RHYMES, 52
Blackpool With my little stick of B. rock — FORMBY, 2
Blackshirt Before the organization of the B. movement — MOSLEY, 1
blame Everyone threw the b. on me — CHURCHILL, W, 22
blank Pain – has an Element of B. — DICKINSON, 4
Where were you fellows when the paper was b. — ALLEN, F, 2
blanket not a b. woven from one thread, one color, one cloth — JACKSON, J, 2
blanks historians left b. in their writings — POUND, 8
blasphemies All great truths begin as b. — SHAW, 4
blast b. of war — SHAKESPEARE, 129
bleed If you prick us, do we not b. — SHAKESPEARE, 245
blemish Christianity . . . the one immortal b. of mankind — NIETZSCHE, 4
lamb . . . without b. — BIBLE, 109
Blenheim I dine at B. once a week — ANONYMOUS, 59
bless B. relaxes — BLAKE, W, 28
God b. us, every one — DICKENS, 10
blessed all generations shall call me b. — BIBLE, 309
b. are the poor in spirit — BIBLE, 360
b. are they that have not seen, and yet have believed — BIBLE, 278
b. is he that cometh in the name of the Lord — BIBLE, 407
b. is the man that endureth temptation — BIBLE, 216
B. is the man who expects nothing — POPE, 60
blessing b. of God Almighty — BOOK OF COMMON PRAYER, 11
Let the b. . . . be . . . upon all that are lovers of virtue . . . and go a-Angling — WALTON, 7
blessings all which we behold Is full of b. — WORDSWORTH, W, 14
blest It is twice b. — SHAKESPEARE, 246
The bed be b. — ADY, 1
they b. him in their pain — TENNYSON, 70
this b. man, let his just praise be given — WALTON, 7
blind A b. man in a dark room — BOWEN, C, 2
Booth died b. — LINDSAY, 2
Country of the B. — WELLS, 9
for which, and all the discomforts that will accompany my being b., the good God prepare me — PEPYS, 17
I was eyes to the b. — BIBLE, 235
Lord giveth sight to the b. — PSALMS, 74
love is b. — SHAKESPEARE, 242
Painting is a b. man's profession — PICASSO, 6
union of a deaf man to a b. woman — COLERIDGE, S, 22
whereas I was b., now I see — BIBLE, 255
wing'd Cupid painted b. — SHAKESPEARE, 258
blinded with b. eyesight — TENNYSON, 53
blindness the . . . world was stumbling . . . in social b. — KELLER, 3
bliss B. was it in that dawn to be alive — WORDSWORTH, W, 40
where ignorance is b., 'Tis folly to be wise — GRAY, 10
blithe Hail to thee, b. Spirit — SHELLEY, 24
No lark more b. than he — BICKERSTAFFE, 1
blitz A b. of a boy is Timothy Winters — CAUSLEY, 1
block a chip off the old b. — BURKE, E, 27
there's a statue inside every b. of stone — ORWELL, 9
blockhead No man but a b. ever wrote — JOHNSON, S, 108
blonde A b. to make a bishop kick a hole — CHANDLER, R, 1
springing from b. to b. like the chamois of the Alps — WODEHOUSE, 20
blondes Gentlemen always seem to remember b. — LOOS, 1
blood b. and iron — BISMARCK, 1
B. is thicker — PROVERBS, 94
b., toil, tears and sweat — CHURCHILL, W, 49
critics . . . desire our b., not our pain — NIETZSCHE, 15
He is all b., dirt and sucked sugar stick — YEATS, 37
his b. be on us — BIBLE, 430
How does the heart pump b. — LEONARDO DA VINCI, 2
humble and meek are thirsting for b. — ORTON, 3
I am in b. Stepp'd in so far — SHAKESPEARE, 217
leeches have red b. — CUVIER, 1
my b. of the new testament — BIBLE, 424
. . . rather have b. on my hands . . . Pilate — GREENE, 3
Seas of B. — SITWELL, E, 2

shed his b. for the country — ROOSEVELT, T, 8
The b. of the martyrs is the seed of the Church — TERTULLIAN, 1
the b. that she has spilt — COWPER, 5
the old savage England, whose last b. flows still — LAWRENCE, D, 22
There are two kinds of b. — TUWIM, 1
'the River Tiber foaming with much b.' — POWELL, E, 1
thought the old man . . . had so much b. in him — SHAKESPEARE, 221
trading on the b. of my men — LEE, R, 2
white in the b. of the Lamb — BIBLE, 463
Who so sheddeth man's b. — BIBLE, 160
without shedding of b. is no remission — BIBLE, 188
You can't get b. — PROVERBS, 473
blood-dripping full lips of the b. mouth — STOKER, 2
bloodiness The sink is the great symbol of the b. of family life — MITCHELL, JULIAN, 1
bloody All the faces . . . seem to be b. Poms — CHARLES, PRINCE, 1
Be b. bold, and resolute — SHAKESPEARE, 219
My head is b., but unbowed — HENLEY, 1
bloom It's a sort of b. on a woman — BARRIE, 8
lilac is in b. — BROOKE, 2
blossom Love's perfect b. — PATMORE, 1
blot The last and greatest art – the art to b. — DRYDEN, 2
blow A b. in cold blood — SHAW, 30
Another year! – another deadly b. — WORDSWORTH, W, 51
Beware of the man who does not return your b. — SHAW, 26
B., b., thou winter wind — SHAKESPEARE, 49
b. his nose . . . state of the handkerchief industry — ORWELL, 2
b. the Scots back again into Scotland — FAWKES, 2
B. . . . till you burst — BROWNING, R, 44
B., winds, and crack your cheeks — SHAKESPEARE, 176
but a word and a b. — BUNYAN, 6
themselves must strike the b. — BYRON, 12
this b. Might be the be-all and the end-all here — SHAKESPEARE, 208
bludgeoning the b. of the people — WILDE, 54
blue In my sweet little Alice b. gown — MCCARTHY, J, 1
Little Boy B., Come blow your horn — NURSERY RHYMES, 29
that little tent of b. — WILDE, 4
The b. ribbon of the turf — DISRAELI, 8
The essence of any b. material — RUE, 1
What are those b. remembered hills — HOUSMAN, 15
blues Twentieth-Century B. — COWARD, 20
blue-vested short, b. people — COREN, 3
blunder . . . poverty . . . is a b. — JEROME, 3
worse than a crime, it is a b. — BOULAY DE LA MEURTHE, 1
Youth is a b. — DISRAELI, 4
blunders escaped making the b. that he has made — HELPS, 3
blunt oaf who has confused rudeness with b. speech — JAMES, C, 1
blush b. to the cheek of a young person — DICKENS, 39
b. to find it fame — POPE, 10
flower is born to b. unseen — GRAY, 5
blushes Man is the only animal that b. — TWAIN, 8
take away the candle and spare my b. — JAMES, H, 13
boar when his half-civilized ancestors were hunting the wild b. — BENJAMIN, 1
boarding-house Any two meals at a b. — LEACOCK, 7
boat a beautiful pea-green b. — LEAR, 8
Do they allow tipping on the b. — MARX, G, 17
It was involuntary. They sank my b. — KENNEDY, JOHN, 3
On a slow b. to China — LOESSER, 1
boating Jolly b. weather — CORY, 1
boats messing about in b. — GRAHAME, 1
we look for happiness in b. and carriage rides — HORACE, 21
Bobby B. Shafto's gone to sea — NURSERY RHYMES, 1
bob-tail I bet my money on the b. nag — FOSTER, 1
bodies many b. of the saints which slept arose — BIBLE, 432
our dead b. must tell the tale — SCOTT, R, 2
scientific knowledge of the structure of our b. — STOPES, 4
well-developed b., fairly developed minds, and undeveloped hearts — FORSTER, 3
You may house their b. but not their souls — GIBRAN, 1
body a sound mind in a sound b. — JUVENAL, 10
b. of a weak and feeble woman — ELIZABETH I, 11
company . . . have neither a soul to lose nor a b. to kick — SMITH, SYDNEY, 5
fear clawed at my mind and b. — FRANK, 2
fear made manifest on the b. — EDDY, 5
Happiness is beneficial for the b. — PROUST, 19
Man has no B. distinct from his Soul — BLAKE, W, 31
mind that makes the b. rich — SHAKESPEARE, 320
more familiar with Africa than my own b. — ORTON, 1
Our b. is a machine for living — TOLSTOY, L, 11
Over my dead b. — KAUFMAN, 1

Pain of mind is worse than pain of b. — SYRUS, 3
take, eat; this is my b. — BIBLE, 424
The b. is not a permanent dwelling — SENECA, 3
the human b. is sacred — WHITMAN, 5
the soul is not more than the b. — WHITMAN, 9
We have rudiments of reverence for the human b. — HOFFER, 2
Why be given a b. if you . . . keep it shut up — MANSFIELD, K, 1
your b. is the temple of the Holy Ghost — BIBLE, 28
Bogart The Humphrey B. of Absurdism — CAMUS, 3
Bognor Bugger B. — GEORGE V, 4
boil b. at different degrees — EMERSON, 24
boiler The United States is like a gigantic b. — GREY, 1
bold Be bloody b., and resolute — SHAKESPEARE, 219
b. man . . . swallowed an oyster — JAMES I, 6
He was a b. man — PROVERBS, 197
boldness B., and again b., and always b. — DANTON, 1
bombs *are* unbelievable until they . . . fall — WHITE, P, 1
Come, friendly b., and fall on Slough — BETJEMAN, 10
drop b. . . . hit civilians — GOLDWATER, 3
Ears like b. — CAUSLEY, 1
test the Russians, not the b. — GAITSKELL, 1
Bonaparte The three-o'-clock in the morning courage, which B. thought was the rarest — THOREAU, 15
Bonar Poor B. can't bear being called a liar — LLOYD GEORGE, 6
bone b. to his b. — BIBLE, 129
The nearer the b. — PROVERBS, 26
boneless the b. wonder — CHURCHILL, W, 45
bones East and west on fields forgotten Bleach the b. of comrades slain — HOUSMAN, 14
Heat, madam! . . . to take off my flesh and sit in my b. — SMITH, SYDNEY, 4
Of his b. are coral made — SHAKESPEARE, 321
O ye dry b. — BIBLE, 128
the b. which thou hast broken — PSALMS, 31
The healthy b. of a single Pomeranian grenadier — BISMARCK, 5
bonhomie Overcame his natural b. — BENTLEY, E, 5
bonjour *B. tristesse* — ELUARD, 1
bonkers If the British public falls for this . . . it will be . . . b. — HAILSHAM, 4
bon mot to produce an occasional *b.* — BALZAC, 6
bonnie By the b. milldams o' Binnorie — ANONYMOUS, 97
My B. lies over the ocean — ANONYMOUS, 57
bonny the child that is born on the Sabbath day Is b. and blithe, and good and gay — NURSERY RHYMES, 35
bono Cui b. — CICERO, 5
bonum Summum b. — CICERO, 3
Boojum Snark *was* a B. — CARROLL, 22
book A b. may be amusing — GOLDSMITH, 25
A b.'s a b., although there's nothing in't — BYRON, 37
a b. . . . sealed with seven seals — BIBLE, 460
A b. that furnishes no quotations is, . . . a plaything — PEACOCK, 3
a b. that is a b. flowers once — LAWRENCE, D, 40
a b. to kill time — MACAULAY, R, 6
A good b. is the best of friends — TUPPER, 1
A good b. is the precious life-blood — MILTON, 7
An angel writing in a b. of gold: – — HUNT, L, 1
Another damned, thick, square b. — GLOUCESTER, 1
any b. should be banned — WEST, R, 4
bad b. is as much a labour to write as a good one — HUXLEY, A, 2
Bell, b., and candle — SHAKESPEARE, 163
dainties that are bred in a b. — SHAKESPEARE, 196
do not throw this b. about — BELLOC, 2
Every b. must be chewed — PROVERBS, 131
go away and write a b. about it — BRABAZON OF TARA, 1
Go, litel b. — CHAUCER, 21
half a library to make one b. — JOHNSON, S, 94
he who destroys a good b., kills reason — MILTON, 6
If a b. is worth reading — RUSKIN, 7
I'll drown my b. — SHAKESPEARE, 326
little woman who wrote the b. that made this great war — LINCOLN, 5
moral or an immoral b. — WILDE, 44
never got around to reading the b. — MARX, G, 21
Never judge a cover by its b. — LEBOWITZ, 1
new b. is published, read an old one — ROGERS, S, 2
that everyone has it in him to write one b. — MAUGHAM, 20
the b. of the living — PSALMS, 39
The number one b. . . . was written by a committee — MAYER, 1
The possession of a b. — BURGESS, 5
There are two motives for reading a b. — RUSSELL, B, 9
There is not any b. Or face — THOMAS, E, 3
There must be a man behind the b. — EMERSON, 18

What is the use of a b. — CARROLL, 4
What you don't know would make a great b. — SMITH, SYDNEY, 6
When a b. is boring, they yawn openly — SINGER, 1
without mentioning a single b., or *in fact anything unpleasant* — REED, H, 6
Would you allow your wife . . . to read this b. — GRIFFITH-JONES, 1
You can't tell a b. — PROVERBS, 479
books against b. the Home Secretary is — WAUGH, E, 41
All b. are divisible into two classes — RUSKIN, 8
An author who speaks about his own b. — DISRAELI, 30
be not swallowed up in b. — WESLEY, J, 2
between a man of sense and his b. — CHESTERFIELD, 1
B. and friends — PROVERBS, 95
B. are a load of crap — LARKIN, 3
B. are . . . a mighty bloodless substitute for life — STEVENSON, R, 18
B. are made . . . like pyramids — FLAUBERT, 2
B. are well written, or badly written — WILDE, 44
b. by which the printers have lost — FULLER, T, 6
B. cannot always please — CRABBE, 1
b. cannot be killed by fire — ROOSEVELT, F, 16
b., . . . , criticized and read by people who don't understand them — LICHTENBERG, 2
B. must follow sciences — BACON, FRANCIS, 63
B. . . . propose to *instruct* or to *amuse* — DE QUINCEY, 1
B. think for me — LAMB, CHARLES, 13
Borrowers of b. — LAMB, CHARLES, 11
but b. never die — ROOSEVELT, F, 16
come not, Lucifer! I'll burn my b. — MARLOWE, 5
Few b. today are forgivable — LAING, 3
Give me b., fruit, French wine and fine weather — KEATS, 66
God has written all the b. — BUTLER, S, 13
His b. were read — BELLOC, 10
If my b. had been any worse — CHANDLER, R, 5
I keep my b. at the British Museum — BUTLER, S, 8
Morality's a gesture. . . . learnt from b. — BOLT, 1
No furniture so charming as b. — SMITH, SYDNEY, 17
of making many b. there is no end — BIBLE, 78
poring over miserable b. — TENNYSON, 53
Prolonged . . . reviewing of b. involves constantly *inventing* reactions — ORWELL, 11
proper study of mankind is b. — HUXLEY, A, 12
Some b. are to be tasted — BACON, FRANCIS, 50
Some b. are undeservedly forgotten — AUDEN, 10
the b. of the hour — RUSKIN, 8
The b. one reads in childhood . . . create in one's mind a . . . false map — ORWELL, 21
the disease of writing b. — MONTESQUIEU, 8
The reading of all good b. — DESCARTES, 2
To read too many b. — MAO TSE-TUNG, 8
true University . . . collection of b. — CARLYLE, T, 12
We all know that b. burn — ROOSEVELT, F, 16
Whenever b. are burned — HEINE, 1
When I think of all the b. I have read — YEATS, 5
women dislike his b. — ORWELL, 34
bookseller he once shot a b. — CAMPBELL, T, 7
booksellers b. are generous liberal-minded men — JOHNSON, S, 55
nor even b. have put up with poets being second-rate — HORACE, 1
boon Is life a b. — GILBERT, W, 42
boorish the opinionated, the ignorant, and the b. — ARISTOTLE, 3
boot imagine a b. stamping on a human face — ORWELL, 16
Booth B. died blind — LINDSAY, 2
boots before the truth has got its b. on — CALLAGHAN, 1
If ever he went to school without any b. — BULMER-THOMAS, 1
Very well, then I shall not take off my b. — WELLINGTON, 21
Bo-peep Little B. has lost her sheep — NURSERY RHYMES, 28
bordello After I die, I shall return to earth as a gatekeeper of a b. — TOSCANINI, 3
Border Through all the wide B. — SCOTT, WALTER, 14
bore a b. and a bounder and a prig — LAWRENCE, T, 2
A b. is a man who — TAYLOR, B, 1
A healthy male adult b. — UPDIKE, 1
B., n. A person who talks — BIERCE, 3
Every hero becomes a b. — EMERSON, 22
He is an old b. — TREE, 1
He is . . . decrepit and forgetful . . . a b. — BELLOC, 2
Is not life . . . too short . . . to b. ourselves — NIETZSCHE, 13
no greater b. than the travel b. — SACKVILLE-WEST, 3
proof that God is a b. — MENCKEN, 7
War is an organized b. — HOLMES, O, JR., 1
you are . . . the club B.: I am the club Liar — SAKI, 3
bored aged diplomats to be b. — AUSTIN, W, 1
Bores and B. — BYRON, 34

Dear World, I am leaving you because I am b.   SANDERS, 1
I wanted to be b. to death   DE VRIES, 4
Punctuality is the virtue of the b.   WAUGH, E, 26
We were as nearly b. as enthusiasm would permit   GOSSE, 1
When you're b. with yourself   PRYCE-JONES, 1
boredom God could cause us . . . sheer apathy and b.   GOETHE, 8
The effect of b. on a large scale   INGE, 3
three great evils, b., vice, and poverty   VOLTAIRE, 10
bores he b. for England   MUGGERIDGE, 6
the *B.* and *Bored*   BYRON, 34
boring curiously b. about . . . happiness   HUXLEY, A, 22
Somebody's b. me, I think it's me   THOMAS, D, 30
you ought to be ashamed of . . . being b.   HAILSHAM, 2
born a silly little mouse will be b.   HORACE, 6
As soon as man is b.   PROVERBS, 66
a time to be b., and a time to die   BIBLE, 67
best . . . never to have been b. at all   HEINE, 2
better if neither of us had been b.   NAPOLEON I, 6
b. again, not of corruptible seed   BIBLE, 440
b. to obey   COMPTON-BURNETT, 3
B. under one law   GREVILLE, 1
Every moment one is b.   TENNYSON, 82
except a man be b. again   BIBLE, 243
Fascism . . . future refusing to be b.   BEVAN, 2
he is not conscious of being b.   LA BRUYÈRE, 6
He was b. an Englishman   BEHAN, 3
I was b. . . . at an extremely tender age because my mother
  needed a fourth at meals   LILLIE, 1
I was b. at the age of twelve   GARLAND, 1
I was b. old   TREE, 1
I was free b.   BIBLE, 16
joy that a man is b. into the world   BIBLE, 263
let the day perish wherein I was b.   BIBLE, 225
Man that is b. of a woman . . . short time to live   BOOK OF
  COMMON PRAYER, 2
Man was b. free   ROUSSEAU, 1
natural to die as to be b.   BACON, FRANCIS, 19
none of woman b. Shall harm Macbeth   SHAKESPEARE, 219
No, thank you, I was b. intoxicated   RUSSELL, G, 1
One is not b. a woman   BEAUVOIR, 3
one of woman b.   SHAKESPEARE, 227
powerless to be b.   ARNOLD, M, 19
Some are b. great   SHAKESPEARE, 341
Some men are b. mediocre   HELLER, 5
sucker b. every minute   BARNUM, 1
that which is b. of the flesh is flesh   BIBLE, 244
that which is b. of the Spirit is spirit   BIBLE, 244
The house where I was b.   HOOD, 6
to have been b.   CALDERÓN DE LA BARCA, 1
to the manner b.   SHAKESPEARE, 75
We are all b. mad   BECKETT, 5
Whatever is begotten, b., and dies   YEATS, 27
boroughs The bright b., the circle-citadels there   HOPKINS, 5
borrow If you don't want to use the army, I should like to b. it
  LINCOLN, 9
the men who b., and the men who lend   LAMB, CHARLES, 10
borrowed B. garments   PROVERBS, 96
borrower Neither a b. nor a lender be   SHAKESPEARE, 74
borrowers B. of books   LAMB, CHARLES, 11
borrowing be not made a beggar by banqueting upon b.   BIBLE, 86
b. dulls the edge of husbandry   SHAKESPEARE, 74
bosom Abraham's b.   BIBLE, 333
not a b. to repose upon   DICKENS, 24
bosoms the silk stockings and white b. of your actresses excite
  my amorous propensities   JOHNSON, S, 46
Boston A B. man   APPLETON, T, 2
this is good old B.   BOSSIDY, 1
both Dreaming on b.   SHAKESPEARE, 231
said on b. sides   ADDISON, 13
bother long words B. me   MILNE, 7
bothered Bewitched, B. and Bewildered   HART, 1
Botticelli If B. were alive today   USTINOV, 9
bottinney b. means a knowledge of plants   DICKENS, 32
bottle Yo-ho-ho, and a b. of rum   STEVENSON, R, 8
bottles It is with . . . people as with . . . b.   POPE, 55
bottom b. of the economic pyramid   ROOSEVELT, F, 8
the best reasons . . . for remaining at the b.   COLBY, 2
bough Loaf of Bread beneath the B.   FITZGERALD, E, 5
boughs young and easy under the apple b.   THOMAS, D, 8
bought b. things because she wanted 'em   VANBURGH, 2
bouillabaisse B. is only good because cooked by the French
  DOUGLAS, N, 2

boulder When the torrent sweeps a man against a b.
  STEVENSON, R, 16
Boulogne There was an old man of B.   ANONYMOUS, 92
bound Tomorrow my hands will be b.   BAILLY, 1
boundary right to fix the b. of . . . a nation   PARNELL, 2
bounder a bore and a b. and a prig   LAWRENCE, T, 2
bountiful Lady B.   FARQUHAR, 2
bouquet the b. is better than the taste   POTTER, S, 7
bourgeois *B.* . . . is an epithet   HOPE, 6
How beastly the b. is   LAWRENCE, D, 11
bourgeoisie the British b. have spoken of themselves as
  gentlemen   WAUGH, E, 12
bourn from whose b. No traveller returns   SHAKESPEARE, 90
bovine The cow is of the b. ilk   NASH, 1
Bow I'm sure I don't know, Says the great bell at B.
  NURSERY RHYMES, 41
bow at the name of Jesus every knee should b.   BIBLE, 443
B., b., ye lower middle classes   GILBERT, W, 15
I, said the Sparrow, With my b. and arrow   NURSERY RHYMES, 73
bowels in the b. of Christ   CROMWELL, O, 5
my b. were moved for him   BIBLE, 494
bower-bird I'm a bit of a b.   WHITE, P, 3
bowl inverted B. we call The Sky   FITZGERALD, E, 15
love in a golden b.   BLAKE, W, 11
They came to see me bat not to see you b.   GRACE, 1
bow-wow Daddy wouldn't buy me a b.   TABRAR, 1
box 'B. about: 'twill come to my father anon'   AUBREY, 1
Take that black b. away   TREE, 9
boy And said, What a good b. am I   NURSERY RHYMES, 30
a secret way . . . of getting at a b.   DICKENS, 20
A thing of duty is a b. for ever   O'BRIEN, F, 1
every b. and every gal That's born into the world alive
  GILBERT, W, 19
If . . . I were the only b.   GROSSMITH THE YOUNGER, 1
Let the b. win his spurs   EDWARD III, 1
Love is a b.   BUTLER, S, 4
Mad about the b.   COWARD, 11
rarely . . . one can see in a little b. the promise of a man
  DUMAS, FILS, 3
Shades of the prison-house begin to close Upon the growing b.
  WORDSWORTH, W, 25
The b. I love is up in the gallery   WARE, 1
The b. stood on the burning deck   HEMANS, 1
the little b. Who lives down the lane   NURSERY RHYMES, 4
To know I'm farther off from heav'n Than when . . . a b.   HOOD, 7
boyhood The smiles, the tears, Of b.'s years   MOORE, T, 7
boys As flies to wanton b.   SHAKESPEARE, 185
B. and girls come out to play   NURSERY RHYMES, 6
B. are capital fellows in their own way   LAMB, CHARLES, 9
B. do not grow up gradually   CONNOLLY, 13
B. will be b.   HOPE, 5
Claret is the liquor for b.   JOHNSON, S, 128
Where are the b. of the Old Brigade   WEATHERLY, 1
Where . . . b. plan for what . . . young girls plan for whom
  GILMAN, 3
Written by office b. for office b.   SALISBURY, 1
bracelet diamond and safire b. lasts forever   LOOS, 3
braces Damn b.   BLAKE, W, 28
braes Ye banks and b.   BURNS, R, 24
brain a Bear of Very Little B.   MILNE, 9
b. attic stocked with all the furniture that he is likely to use
  DOYLE, 12
B., n. An apparatus with which we think   BIERCE, 4
If it is for mind that we are seaching the b.   SHERRINGTON, 1
Let schoolmasters puzzle their b.   GOLDSMITH, 4
the biggest b. of all the primates   MORRIS, D, 4
the human b. is a device to keep the ears from grating
  DEVRIES, 1
we are supposing the b. . . . more than a telephone-exchange
  SHERRINGTON, 1
with no deep researches vex the b.   CRABBE, 3
You've got the b. of a four-year-old boy   MARX, G, 12
brains a girl with b. ought to do something else   LOOS, 2
b. enough to make a fool of himself   STEVENSON, R, 21
gallops night by night Through lovers' b.   SHAKESPEARE, 305
I mix them with my b.   OPIE, 1
something better than our b. to depend upon   CHESTERFIELD, 20
What good are b. to a man   WODEHOUSE, 3
branch Cut is the b. that might have grown   MARLOWE, 6
brandy I am not well; pray get me . . . b.   GEORGE IV, 1
brass B. bands are all very well in their place   BEECHAM, 8
Men's evil manners live in b.   SHAKESPEARE, 141

sounding b.	BIBLE, 38
brave Any fool can be b. on a battle field	MITCHELL, M, 2
b. new world . . . such people in't	SHAKESPEARE, 327
Fortune favours the b.	TERENCE, 3
land of the free, and the home of the b.	KEY, F, 1
looked upon by posterity as a b., bad man	CROMWELL, O, 2
Many b. men . . . before Agamemnon's time; . . . are	
all, unmourned and unknown, . . . because they lack their sacred	
poet	HORACE, 42
the B. deserves the Fair	DRYDEN, 16
we could never learn to be b. . . . if there were only joy	
	KELLER, 2
braw a b. brecht moonlecht necht	LAUDER, 1
Brazil B., where the nuts come from	THOMAS, B, 1
breach a custom more honour'd in the b.	SHAKESPEARE, 75
Once more unto the b.	SHAKESPEARE, 128
bread b. and cheese, and kisses	SWIFT, 11
b. and circuses	JUVENAL, 8
b. eaten in secret is pleasant	BIBLE, 449
b. enough and to spare	BIBLE, 331
B. is the staff of life	PROVERBS, 97
cast thy b. upon the waters	BIBLE, 77
gave you manna . . . angels' b.	BIBLE, 97
I am the b. of life	BIBLE, 250
if his son ask b., will he give him a stone	BIBLE, 376
Jesus took b., and blessed it	BIBLE, 424
Loaf of B. beneath the Bough	FITZGERALD, E, 5
man shall not live by b. alone	BIBLE, 356
that b. should be so dear	HOOD, 12
Their learning is like b. in a besieged town	JOHNSON, S, 96
This b. I break was once the oat	THOMAS, D, 17
breakfast she must not reheat his sins for b.	DIETRICH, 1
breakfast-table ready for the national b.	TROLLOPE, 6
breakfast-time critical period in matrimony is b.	HERBERT, A, 5
breaking B. the mould	JENKINS, 3
breast charms to soothe a savage b.	CONGREVE, 8
my baby at my b.	SHAKESPEARE, 38
breast-feeding Every luxury . . . atheism, b., circumcision	
	ORTON, 4
breasts they add weight to the b.	COLETTE, 5
breath blow hot and cold with the same b.	AESOP, 2
Can storied urn . . . Back to its mansion call the fleeting b.	
	GRAY, 4
Competition was the b. of life to him	FLEMING, A, 1
He reaps the bearded grain at a b.	LONGFELLOW, 11
in this harsh world draw thy b. in pain	SHAKESPEARE, 107
The years to come seemed waste of b.	YEATS, 16
wish the night Had borne my b. away	HOOD, 6
world will hold its b.	HITLER, 16
breathed God . . . b. into his nostrils	BIBLE, 144
breathing Keep b.	TUCKER, 4
breathings heard among the solitary hills Low b.	
	WORDSWORTH, W, 36
brecht a braw b. moonlecht necht	LAUDER, 1
breed happy b. of men	SHAKESPEARE, 295
Men are . . . more careful of the b. of their horses and dogs than	
of their children	PENN, 2
breeder b. of sinners	SHAKESPEARE, 92
breeding Good b. consists in concealing how . . . we think of	
ourselves	TWAIN, 14
who are formed by a different b. . . . not governed by the same	
laws	DISRAELI, 12
breeks taking the b. aff a wild Highlandman	SCOTT, WALTER, 4
breeze The fair b. blew	COLERIDGE, S, 29
breezes spicy b. Blow soft o'er Ceylon's isle	HEBER, 2
brethren the least of these my b.	BIBLE, 422
brevity B. is the soul of lingerie	PARKER, D, 15
B. is the soul of wit	SHAKESPEARE, 80
brewery O take me to a b. And leave me there to die	
	ANONYMOUS, 43
bribe doing nothing for a b.	SHAKESPEARE, 60
The man who offers a b. gives away . . . his own importance	
	GREENE, 2
You cannot hope to b. or twist . . . the British journalist	
	WOLFE, H, 1
bribes How many b. he had taken	BENTLEY, E, 1
bribing Money is good for b. yourself	REINHARDT, 1
brick carried a . . . b. in his pocket	SWIFT, 6
He is a man of b.	UPDIKE, 1
I found it b.	AUGUSTUS, 1
bricklayers B. kick their wives to death	WELLS, 19
bricks You can't make b.	PROVERBS, 475

bride a b.'s attitude towards her betrothed	MUIR, 2
as a b. adorned for her husband	BIBLE, 473
It helps . . . to remind your b. that you gave up a throne for her	
	EDWARD VIII, 5
the b. at every wedding	ROOSEVELT, T, 2
unravish'd b. of quietness	KEATS, 27
bridegroom behold, the b. cometh	BIBLE, 416
the sun . . . cometh forth as a b.	PSALMS, 8
bridge Beautiful Railway B. of the Silv'ry Tay	MCGONAGALL, 2
he bestowed upon the games of golf and b.	EISENHOWER, 2
I stood on the b. at midnight	LONGFELLOW, 4
Like a b. over troubled water	SIMON, 1
London B. is broken down	NURSERY RHYMES, 33
over the B. of Sighs into eternity	KIERKEGAARD, 2
They promise to build a b. even where there's no river	
	KHRUSHCHEV, 7
brief I strive to be b., and I become obscure	HORACE, 2
Out, out, b. candle	SHAKESPEARE, 225
briers how full of b.	SHAKESPEARE, 41
brigade Where are the boys of the Old B.	WEATHERLY, 1
brigands B. demand your money	BUTLER, S, 99
bright All things b. and beautiful	ALEXANDER, 1
her beauty made The b. world dim	SHELLEY, 26
Look on the b. side	PROVERBS, 268
she doth teach the torches to burn b.	SHAKESPEARE, 306
the creature hath a purpose and its eyes are b. with it	KEATS, 69
Tiger! burning b.	BLAKE, W, 39
young lady named B.	BULLER, 1
brightening He died when his prospects seemed to be b.	
	ANONYMOUS, 27
brighter proclaiming that women are b. than men	LOOS, 5
brightness To pass away ere life hath lost its b.	HASTINGS, 1
Brighton Like B. pier . . . inadequate for getting to France	
	KINNOCK, 7
bright-star Johnny-the-b.	PUDNEY, 2
brilliance No b. is needed in the law	MORTIMER, 2
brilliant a far less b. pen than mine	BEERBOHM, 4
. . . b. men . . . will come to a bad end	BEERBOHM, 11
The dullard's envy of b. men	BEERBOHM, 11
brillig 'Twas b., and the slithy toves	CARROLL, 23
brimstone b. and fire	BIBLE, 167
bring thou knowest not what a day may b. forth	BIBLE, 457
Britain a time when B. had a savage culture	BANDA, 1
battle of B. is about to begin	CHURCHILL, W, 53
B. . . . Fabian Society writ large	HAMILTON, W, 2
B. fit country for heroes to live in	LLOYD GEORGE, 11
B. is no longer in the politics of the pendulum	THATCHER, M, 6
B. is not . . . easily rocked by revolution	HAMILTON, W, 2
to help B. to become a Third Programme	WILKINSON, 1
When B. first, at heaven's command	THOMSON, JAMES, 1
Britannia 'Rule, B., rule the waves; Britons never will be slaves.'	
	THOMSON, JAMES, 1
British but we are B. – thank God	MONTGOMERY OF ALAMEIN, 2
'Can't' will be the epitaph of the B. Empire	MOSLEY, 3
Hitler never understood . . . the B.	HITLER, 1
I would rather be B. than just	PAISLEY, 2
Kipling has done more . . . to show . . . that the B. race is sound	
to the core	KIPLING, 2
less known by the B. than these selfsame B. Islands	BORROW, 1
liquidation of the B. Empire	CHURCHILL, W, 61
socialism . . . alien to the B. character	THATCHER, M, 16
The artists retired. The B. remained	WHISTLER, 15
The B., being brought up on team games	PARKINSON, 3
The B. love permanence	CASSON, 1
the magnificent fair play of the B. criminal law	DOYLE, 10
when a B. Prime Minister sneezed	LEVIN, 2
you broke a B. square	KIPLING, 10
British Museum a little room somewhere in the B. that	
	PRIESTLEY, 5
a reflection of the B. Reading Room	SPARK, 12
I keep my books at the B.	BUTLER, S, 8
There is in the B. an enormous mind	WOOLF, 6
Briton animated with the soul of a B.	VOLTAIRE, 2
as only a free-born B. can do	THACKERAY, 10
dullest B. of them all	TROLLOPE, 1
Britons B. were only natives	SELLAR, 4
'Rule, Britannia, rule the waves; B. never will be slaves.'	
	THOMSON, JAMES, 1
broad She is a smart old b.	RUNYON, 5
She's the B. and I'm the High	SPRING-RICE, 2
broadmindedness magnificent tolerance and b. of the English	
	SHAW, 1

broke We're really all of us bottomly b.   KEROUAC, 2
broken A b. head in Cold Bath Fields   MACAULAY, T, 21
baying for b. glass   WAUGH, E, 4
healeth those that are b. in heart   PSALMS, 75
I am become like a b. vessel   PSALMS, 20
Laws were made to be b.   NORTH, 2
Like many of the upper class He liked the sound of b. glass   BELLOC, 14
peace has b. out   BRECHT, 10
the bones which thou hast b.   PSALMS, 31
broker An honest b.   BISMARCK, 6
bronchitis nobody goes to the theatre unless he . . . has b.   AGATE, 1
bronze executed a memorial longer lasting than b.   HORACE, 39
brook b. no contradiction   WEBSTER, J, 2
brothel a sort of metaphysical b. for emotions   KOESTLER, 2
brothels b. with bricks of Religion   BLAKE, W, 20
brother B., can you spare a dime   HARBURG, 2
am I my b.'s keeper   BIBLE, 154
I want to be the white man's b.   KING, M, 2
love God, and hateth his b.   BIBLE, 284
my b. Jonathan   BIBLE, 483
Pardon me, . . . *I* am my b.   JACOBI, 1
the same is my b.   BIBLE, 390
brotherhood Freedom! Equality! B.   ANONYMOUS, 50
brother-in-law not his b.   KING, M, 2
brotherly let b. love continue   BIBLE, 187
brothers All men are b.   POWELL, A, 3
all the B. were valiant   NEWCASTLE, 1
b. all In honour   WORDSWORTH, W, 39
the poor are our b. and sisters   TERESA, MOTHER, 1
brought b. nothing into this world   BIBLE, 510
never b. to min'   BURNS, R, 4
Brown John B.'s body   HALL, 1
Browning Robert B., you writer of plays   BROWNING, R, 30
bruise sweetest fragrance from the herb . . . tread on it and b. it   TROLLOPE, 9
bruised it is often a comfort to . . . be b. in a new place   IRVING, 3
Brunswick Hamelin Town's in B.   BROWNING, R, 41
brush B. Up Your Shakespeare   SHAKESPEARE, 16
Brussels meeting in a darkened bedroom in a B. hotel   THOMPSON, E, 1
brutality industry without art is b.   RUSKIN, 4
Sentimentality is a superstructure covering b.   JUNG, 8
brute I never saw a b. I hated so   BROWNING, R, 16
brutes Exterminate all b.   CONRAD, 1
Thanks to words, we have been able to rise above the b.   HUXLEY, A, 3
Brutus B. is an honourable man   SHAKESPEARE, 154
Caesar had his B. – Charles the First, his Cromwell   HENRY, P, 1
The fault, dear B., is not in our stars   SHAKESPEARE, 143
bubble Life is mostly froth and b.   GORDON, 1
Like a hell-broth boil and b.   SHAKESPEARE, 218
bubbles With beaded b. winking at the brim   KEATS, 37
buck The b. stops here   TRUMAN, 10
Buckingham changing guard at B. Palace   MILNE, 4
buckle One, two, B. my shoe   NURSERY RHYMES, 40
buckler his faithfulness and truth shall be thy shield and b.   PSALMS, 51
bucks bet you a hundred b. he ain't in here   DILLINGHAM, 1
bud And now in age I b. again   HERBERT, G, 4
Buddhism nothing in Christianity or B. that quite matches   SAKI, 10
budding That which sets . . . The b. rose above the rose full blown   WORDSWORTH, W, 41
buds Gather the flowers, but spare the b.   MARVELL, 8
the darling b. of May   SHAKESPEARE, 358
buffalo give me a home where the b. roam   HIGLEY, 1
bugger B. Bognor   GEORGE V, 4
build let us think that we b. for ever   RUSKIN, 10
The *end* is to b. well   WOTTON, 1
They promise to b. a bridge even where there's no river   KHRUSHCHEV, 7
builder he can only be a *b.*   RUSKIN, 3
building tall modern office b. is the machine   WRIGHT, F, 3
twenty years of marriage make her . . . like a public b.   WILDE, 56
Well b. hath three Conditions   WOTTON, 1
buildings I go amongst the b. of a city   KEATS, 69
Luftwaffe . . . knocked down our b.   CHARLES, PRINCE, 4
built till we have b. Jerusalem   BLAKE, W, 33
Bulben Under bare Ben B.'s head   YEATS, 32

Bull Better send them a Papal B.   CURZON, 2
Down at the old 'B. and Bush'   TILZER, 1
bull take the b. between the teeth   GOLDWYN, 16
When you take the b. by the horns . . .   RIDGE, 1
bullet ballot is stronger than the b.   LINCOLN, 11
Each b. has got its commission   DIBDIN, 1
Every b. has its billet   WILLIAM III, 2
The b. that is to kill me   NAPOLEON I, 11
bullets I heard the b. whistle . . . charming in the sound   WASHINGTON, 4
bullfighting B. is the only art   HEMINGWAY, 4
bully He is the b. . . . ready to twist the milksop's arm   HEMINGWAY, 5
bulrushes an ark of b.   BIBLE, 103
England may as well dam . . . the Nile with b.   CHILD, 3
bump And things that go b. in the night   ANONYMOUS, 19
bums art and literature are left to a lot of shabby b.   LEWIS, S, 2
Bunbury an invaluable permanent invalid called B.   WILDE, 10
bungalow proud of the position of the b. . . . in the country   WILSON, A, 1
bunk History is more or less b.   FORD, H, 1
buns Hot cross b.! . . . One a penny, two a penny   NURSERY RHYMES, 16
Bunsen burner and I'd left my B. home   THOMAS, D, 15
burden Take up the White Man's b.   KIPLING, 31
that one is a b. to the host   SENECA, 3
The dreadful b.   BOILEAU, 4
buried They all be b. at Wimble   ANONYMOUS, 29
Burlington I'm B. Bertie   HARGREAVES, 1
burn better to marry than to b.   BIBLE, 30
come not, Lucifer! I'll b. my books   MARLOWE, 5
He would b. your house down   CHAMFORT, 1
I will b., but . . . continue our discussion in eternity   SERVETUS, 1
sun shall not b. thee by day   PSALMS, 68
burned every government . . . should have its old speeches b.   SNOWDEN, 1
Whenever books are b.   HEINE, 1
burning The boy stood on the b. deck   HEMANS, 1
the b. of the leaves   BINYON, 1
The spirit b. but unbent   BYRON, 17
To keep a lamp b.   TERESA, MOTHER, 1
burnings B. of people and (what was more valuable)   ROWSE, 1
burnish'd Furnish'd and b. by Aldershot sun   BETJEMAN, 11
burnt lamb for a b.   BIBLE, 169
burnt-offerings but thou delightest not in b.   PSALMS, 32
burr kind of b.; I shall stick   SHAKESPEARE, 233
burst Blow your pipe there till you b.   BROWNING, R, 44
burthen the b. of the mystery . . . Is lightened   WORDSWORTH, W, 10
bury I come to b. Caesar, not to praise him   SHAKESPEARE, 153
let the dead b. their dead   BIBLE, 382
the sort of woman now . . . one would almost feel disposed to b. for nothing   DICKENS, 30
We will b. you   KHRUSHCHEV, 6
bus , Hitler has missed the b.   CHAMBERLAIN, N, 7
bush the b. burned with fire   BIBLE, 105
business A b. that makes nothing but money   FORD, H, 2
All b. sagacity reduces itself . . . to . . . sabotage   VEBLEN, 1
a woman's b. to get married   SHAW, 23
B. as usual   CHURCHILL, W, 43
B. . . . . may bring money . . . friendship hardly ever does   AUSTEN, 9
B. underlies everything in our national life   WILSON, W, 8
Chaplin is no b. man   GOLDWYN, 7
dinner lubricates b.   SCOTT, WILLIAM, 1
everybody's b. is nobody's b.   WALTON, 3
'For good all round b. work, I should have preferred a Baptist.'   WELLS, 11
If everybody minded their own b.   CARROLL, 7
I have led a life of b. so long that I have lost my taste for reading, and now – what shall I do   WALPOLE, H, 2
it is not only our fate but our b. to lose innocence   BOWEN, ELIZABETH, 1
That's the true b. precept   DICKENS, 27
The b. of America is b.   COOLIDGE, 3
There's No B. Like Show B.   BERLIN, 1
The Swiss . . . are not a people so much as a . . . b.   FAULKNER, 1
To b. that we love we rise betime   SHAKESPEARE, 33
Whatsoever . . . the private calamity, I hope it will not interfere with the public b. of the country   SHERIDAN, R, 15
Your b. is to put me out of b.   EISENHOWER, 8
Buss Miss B. and Miss Beale Cupid's darts do not feel   ANONYMOUS, 56

bust I'm going to have a b. made of them GOLDWYN, 22
It's a funny thing about that b. . . . seems to get younger and younger SHAW, 46
bustle the b. of man's worktime BROWNING, R, 24
busy How doth the little b. bee WATTS, 2
It is a stupidity . . . to b. oneself with the correction of the world MOLIÈRE, 6
The English are b. MONTESQUIEU, 7
thou knowest how b. I must be this day ASTLEY, 1
busyness Extreme b. STEVENSON, R, 19
butcher The b., the baker, The candlestick-maker NURSERY RHYMES, 49
butchers Governments need to have both shepherds and b. VOLTAIRE, 22
butler I vote Labour, but my b.'s a Tory MOUNTBATTEN, 7
Sir Walter Scott . . . is an inspired b. SCOTT, WALTER, 2
butlers b. and lady's maids do not reproduce their kind WELLS, 3
butter b. in a lordly dish BIBLE, 293
b. will only make us fat GOERING, 3
b. wouldn't melt in her mouth LANCHESTER, 1
fine words b. no parsnips SCOTT, WALTER, 11
Buttercup I'm called Little B. GILBERT, W, 6
buttered I had never had a piece of toast . . . But fell . . . on the b. side PAYN, 1
butterflies Literature and b. are the two sweetest passions NABOKOV, 8
No shade, no shine, no b., no bees HOOD, 10
butterfly a man dreaming I was a b. CHUANG TSE, 1
Float like a b. ALI, 2
Happiness is like a b. PAVLOVA, 3
buttress a b. of the church MELBOURNE, 10
buy American heiress wants to b. a man MCCARTHY, M, 3
I could b. back my introduction MARX, G, 15
would never b. my pictures LANDSEER, 1
bygones Let b. be b. PROVERBS, 254
Byron a more worthless set than B. WELLINGTON, 10
Goethe's sage mind and B.'s force WORDSWORTH, W, 1
the words: B. is dead CARLYLE, J, 3
When B.'s eyes were shut in death ARNOLD, M, 26

C

cabbages c. and kings CARROLL, 28
The c. are coming now BETJEMAN, 10
cabin'd c., cribb'd, confin'd, bound in SHAKESPEARE, 214
cabs busy driving c. and cutting hair BURNS, G, 1
Caesar Ave C., morituri te salutant ANONYMOUS, 9
C.! dost thou lie so low SHAKESPEARE, 140
C. had his Brutus – Charles the First, his Cromwell HENRY, P, 1
C.'s laurel crown BLAKE, W, 4
C.'s wife must be above suspicion CAESAR, 2
hast thou appealed unto C. BIBLE, 17
I always remember that I am C.'s daughter JULIA, 1
I come to bury C. SHAKESPEARE, 153
Not that I lov'd C. less SHAKESPEARE, 152
Regions C. never knew COWPER, 3
render . . . unto C. the things which are C.'s BIBLE, 410
Rose . . . where some buried C. bled FITZGERALD, E, 8
that C. might be great CAMPBELL, T, 5
cage Marriage is like a c. MONTAIGNE, 7
Nor iron bars a c. LOVELACE, 1
robin redbreast in a c. BLAKE, W, 10
She's only a bird in a gilded c. LAMB, A, 1
caged We think c. birds sing, when indeed they cry WEBSTER, J, 5
Cain the Lord set a mark upon C. BIBLE, 155
caitiff If the rude c. smite the other too HOLMES, O, 5
cake Bake me a c. as fast as you can NURSERY RHYMES, 42
Let them eat c. MARIE-ANTOINETTE, 1
cakes no more c. and ale SHAKESPEARE, 339
Calais 'C.' lying in my heart MARY I, 1
calamities the c. of life DEFOE, 3
calamity Whatsoever . . . the private c., I hope it will not interfere with the public business of the country SHERIDAN, R, 15
calculating political leader for the Labour Party is a desiccated c. machine BEVAN, 4
Caledonia C.! stern and wild SCOTT, WALTER, 9
calf a molten c. BIBLE, 120
but the c. won't get much sleep ALLEN, W, 8
killed a c. he would do it in a high style SHAKESPEARE, 2
the fatted c. BIBLE, 332
California From C. to New York Island GUTHRIE, 3

call one clear c. for me TENNYSON, 12
called c. a cold a cold BENNETT, ARNOLD, 3
calling Germany c. HAW-HAW, 1
calm c. reigned in Warsaw SÉBASTIANI, 1
sea is c. to-night ARNOLD, M, 10
Wisdom has taught us to be c. and meek HOLMES, O, 5
calumnies C. are answered best JONSON, 15
Calvary the place, which is called C. BIBLE, 338
Calvin land of C., oat-cakes, and sulphur SMITH, SYDNEY, 7
Calvinist That maniacal C. and coddled poet COWPER, 2
Cambridge Oxford is on the whole more attractive than C. BAEDEKER, 1
Spring and summer did happen in C. NABOKOV, 6
The young C. group LAWRENCE, D, 16
To C. books TRAPP, 1
came I c.; I saw; God conquered JOHN III SOBIESKI, 1
I c., I saw, I conquered CAESAR, 4
I c. like Water FITZGERALD, E, 11
camel easier for a c. to go through the eye of a needle BIBLE, 405
Camelot many tower'd C. TENNYSON, 41
To look down to C. TENNYSON, 44
camera I am a c. ISHERWOOD, 1
I love the c. BOGARDE, 2
The c. cannot lie. But . . . EVANS, H, 1
cameras She stole everything but the c. WEST, M, 2
Campbells The C. are comin' ANONYMOUS, 79
Campland This is C., an invisible country SOLZHENITSYN, 12
can Talent does what it c. MEREDITH, O, 1
cancel to c. half a Line FITZGERALD, E, 14
cancels debt which c. all others COLTON, 5
candid save me, from the c. friend CANNING, 1
candidates C. should not attempt more than six BELLOC, 18
candle a c. of understanding BIBLE, 100
Bell, book, and c. SHAKESPEARE, 163
blow out your c. . . . to find your way DIDEROT, 1
It is burning a farthing c. at Dover JOHNSON, S, 68
light a c., and put it under a bushel BIBLE, 361
light a c. to the sun SIDNEY, A, 1
Like a c. burnt out YEATS, 21
little c. throws his beams SHAKESPEARE, 252
My c. burns at both ends MILLAY, 1
Out, out, brief c. SHAKESPEARE, 225
take away the c. and spare my blushes JAMES, H, 13
thou . . . shalt light my c. PSALMS, 7
we shall this day light such a c. . . . as I trust shall never be put out LATIMER, 2
candle-light Can I get there by c. NURSERY RHYMES, 17
candles She would rather light c. than curse the darkness STEVENSON, A, 8
The c. burn their sockets HOUSMAN, 4
candlestick The butcher, the baker, The c.-maker NURSERY RHYMES, 49
canem Cave c. PETRONIUS, 1
canker killing as the c. to the rose MILTON, 23
Cannes C. . . . lie on the beach REED, R, 2
cannibal Better sleep with a sober c. than a drunken Christian MELVILLE, 1
cannon-ball c. took off his legs HOOD, 2
canoe every man paddle his own c. MARRYAT, 3
Canossa We will not go to C. BISMARCK, 4
can't 'C.' will be the epitaph of the British Empire MOSLEY, 3
cant clear your mind of c. JOHNSON, S, 146
love – all the wretched c. of it GREER, 3
where the Greeks had modesty, we have c. PEACOCK, 2
capability Negative C. KEATS, 53
capable c. of being well set to music ADDISON, 11
capital Boys are c. fellows in their own way LAMB, CHARLES, 9
capitalism C. re-creates RICHLER, 1
c. . . . : the process whereby American girls turn into American women HAMPTON, 3
I am going to fight c. PANKHURST, S, 2
imperialism is the monopoly stage of c. LENIN, 1
Lenin was the first to discover that c. 'inevitably' caused war TAYLOR, A, 4
militarism . . . is one of the chief bulwarks of c. KELLER, 1
unacceptable face of c. HEATH, 2
We cannot remove the evils of c. KINNOCK, 4
capitalist C. production begets . . . its own negation MARX, K, 5
Not every problem someone has with his girlfriend is . . . due to . . . c. . . . production MARCUSE, 1
capitulate I will be conquered; I will not c. JOHNSON, S, 155

Capricorn Lady C. . . . was . . . keeping open bed HUXLEY, A, 9
captain C. of the *Pinafore* GILBERT, W, 7
I am the c. of my soul HENLEY, 2
captains C. of industry CARLYLE, T, 22
Capten C., art tha sleepin' there below NEWBOLT, 3
captive Beauty stands . . . Led c. MILTON, 54
car always using a small c. to drive to the dockyard
 MOUNTBATTEN, 4
in which direction the c. was travelling LLOYD GEORGE, 3
I thought I told you to wait in the c. BANKHEAD, 12
The c. has become the carapace MCLUHAN, 5
carbon c. atom possesses certain exceptional properties JEANS, 1
carbuncle Like a c. on the face of an old and valued friend
 CHARLES, PRINCE, 3
cardinal unbecoming for a c. to ski badly JOHN PAUL II, 1
card wrestled with a self-adjusting c. table THURBER, 8
cards an old age of c. POPE, 44
cheat at c. BOSWELL, 2
I have not learned to play at c. JOHNSON, S, 163
care age is full of c. SHAKESPEARE, 355
Begone, dull c. ANONYMOUS, 10
C. Sat on his faded cheek MILTON, 35
I c. for nobody . . . If no one cares for me BICKERSTAFFE, 2
I don't c. for war NAPOLEON III, 2
Our progress . . . Is trouble and c. LONGFELLOW, 14
pleasures are their only c. COWPER, 20
Sleep that knits up the ravell'd sleave of c. SHAKESPEARE, 212
so vain . . . c. for the opinion of those we don't c. for
 ESCHENBACH, 3
take c. of the minutes CHESTERFIELD, 11
Take c. of the pence CHESTERFIELD, 10
what is past my help is past my c. BEAUMONT, 2
career a lover with any other c. in view WELLS, 5
having a c. of my own BALFOUR, 1
Miss Madeleine Philips . . . was a c. WELLS, 5
nothing which might damage his c. BARRIE, 10
science was the only c. worth following JOLIOT-CURIE, 1
careers The best c. advice to give to the young WHITEHORN, 6
careful be very c. o' vidders DICKENS, 45
careless first fine c. rapture BROWNING, R, 27
carelessness To lose one parent . . . a misfortune; to lose both
looks like c. WILDE, 26
with a slow deliberate c. LAWRENCE, T, 9
cares the earth where c. abound WORDSWORTH, W, 73
careth he that is married c. . . . how he may please his wife
 BIBLE, 31
cargo With a c. of ivory MASEFIELD, 2
With a c. of Tyne coal MASEFIELD, 2
caring take millions off the c. services KINNOCK, 8
carpe C. diem HORACE, 32
Carpenter Walrus and the C. CARROLL, 27
carpet a Turkey c. bears to a picture MACAULAY, T, 17
Eat slowly: only men in rags . . . Mistake themselves for c. bags
 RALEIGH, W A, 1
carriage Go together like a horse and c. CAHN, 1
very small second-class c. GILBERT, W, 21
we look for happiness in boats and c. rides HORACE, 21
carriages when they think they are alone in railway c.
 MILLER, J, 2
carry certain we can c. nothing out BIBLE, 510
Carthage C. must be destroyed CATO THE ELDER, 1
Cary Grant Old C. fine GRANT, C, 1
case If ever there was a c. of clearer evidence ARABIN, 1
in our c. we have not got REED, H, 3
the c. is still before the courts HORACE, 5
the reason of the c. POWELL, J, 1
there had been a lady in the c. BYRON, 29
The world is everything that is the c. WITTGENSTEIN, 3
casements Charm'd magic c. KEATS, 39
cash Nothing links man to man like . . . c. SICKERT, 1
only the poor who pay c. FRANCE, 10
take the C. in hand FITZGERALD, E, 6
cashiers c. of the Musical Banks BUTLER, S, 2
casino I have come to regard . . . courts . . . as a c. INGRAMS, 1
cask A c. of wine PROVERBS, 5
casket seal the hushed c. of my soul KEATS, 48
Cassius C. has a lean and hungry look SHAKESPEARE, 144
cassock C., band, and hymn-book too WILBERFORCE, S, 2
cassowary If I were a c. WILBERFORCE, S, 2
cast c. thy bread upon the waters BIBLE, 77
he that is without sin . . . let him first c. a stone BIBLE, 251
pale c. of thought SHAKESPEARE, 91

The die is c. CAESAR, 3
casteth perfect love c. out fear BIBLE, 283
casting It is no good c. out devils LAWRENCE, D, 36
castle A c. called Doubting C. BUNYAN, 7
The house of every one is to him as his c. COKE, E, 1
Castlereagh Murder . . . had a mask like C. SHELLEY, 13
castles C. in the air IBSEN, 7
Pale Death kicks his way equally into . . . the c. of kings
 HORACE, 27
the c. I have, are built with air JONSON, 5
castrated after the war he should be publicly c. LLOYD GEORGE, 4
casualty except the c. list of the World War CAPONE, 1
The first c. when war comes JOHNSON, H, 1
cat A c. has nine lives PROVERBS, 6
A c. may look PROVERBS, 7
a C. of such deceitfulness ELIOT, T, 16
c. is a diagram and pattern of subtle air LESSING, D, 6
God . . . a cosmic Cheshire c. HUXLEY, J, 2
Had Tiberius been a c. ARNOLD, M, 33
He bought a crooked c., which caught a crooked mouse
 NURSERY RHYMES, 57
he is a very fine c. JOHNSON, S, 145
Hey diddle diddle, The c. and the fiddle NURSERY RHYMES, 44
I am the c. that walks alone BEAVERBROOK, 1
I'll bell the c. DOUGLAS, ARCHIBALD, 1
More ways of killing a c. KINGSLEY, 10
That tossed the dog, That worried the c. NURSERY RHYMES, 62
The C., the Rat, and Lovell our dog COLLINGBOURNE, 1
What c.'s averse to fish GRAY, 11
When I play with my c. MONTAIGNE, 5
When the c.'s away PROVERBS, 461
Who will bell the c. DESCHAMPS, 1
cataclysm Out of their c. but one poor Noah HUXLEY, A, 18
catastrophe to lose one's teeth is a c. WHEELER, 1
When a man confronts a c. . . . a woman looks in her mirror
 TURNBULL, 2
catch Go, and c. a falling star DONNE, 5
only one c. and that was C.-22 HELLER, 3
catches it is your business, when the wall next door c. fire
 HORACE, 22
catchwords Man is a creature who lives . . . by c.
 STEVENSON, R, 14
categorical This imperative is C. KANT, 2
cathedrals the ancient c. – grand, wonderful, mysterious
 STANTON, J, 2
Catherine I'm glad you like my C. WEST, M, 15
Catholic Evelyn Waugh . . . is a Roman C. WAUGH, E, 1
he clings to the Roman C. Church BELLOC, 1
I am a C. . . . I go to Mass every day BELLOC, 17
I have a C. soul, but a Lutheran stomach ERASMUS, 2
I'm still a C. WILSON, A, 3
quite lawful for a C. woman to avoid pregnancy by . . .
mathematics MENCKEN, 4
who, like you, your Holiness, is a Roman C. CHURCHILL, R, 5
Catholics C. and Communists have committed great crimes
 GREENE, 3
they may be C. but they are not Christians MCCARTHY, M, 6
We know these new English C. LAWRENCE, D, 39
cats All c. are grey PROVERBS, 32
A lotta c. copy the Mona Lisa ARMSTRONG, L, 1
what c. most appreciate . . . is . . . entertainment value
 HOUSEHOLD, 1
cattle Actors should be treated like c. HITCHCOCK, 2
O Mary, go and call the c. home KINGSLEY, 4
thou art cursed above all c. BIBLE, 151
cause for what high c. This darling of the Gods MARVELL, 2
the name of perseverance in a good c. STERNE, 6
causes Home of lost c. ARNOLD, M, 13
they should declare the c. which impel them to . . . separation
 JEFFERSON, 4
caustic Too c.? To hell with cost GOLDWYN, 3
cautious he was c. of his own words CROMWELL, O, 3
cavaliero a perfect c. BYRON, 6
Cavaliers C. (Wrong but Wromantic) SELLAR, 5
cave C. canem PETRONIUS, 1
I should be like a lion in a c. of savage Daniels WILDE, 77
caverns Gluts twice ten thousand C. KEATS, 43
Through c. measureless to man COLERIDGE, S, 14
caves be c. . . . in which his shadow will be shown NIETZSCHE, 5
sunny pleasure-dome with c. of ice COLERIDGE, S, 15
caviare c. to the general SHAKESPEARE, 86
cavity John Brown is filling his last c. ANONYMOUS, 74

cease   have their day and c. to be   TENNYSON, 26
he maketh wars to c. in all the world   PSALMS, 28
I will not c. from mental fight   BLAKE, W, 33
restless Cromwell could not c.   MARVELL, 3
ceases   forbearance c. to be a virtue   BURKE, E, 5
cedar   spread abroad like a c. in Libanus   PSALMS, 52
cedars   the c. of Libanus   PSALMS, 16
celebrate   I c. myself   WHITMAN, 6
poetry cannot c. them   AUDEN, 8
celebrity   A c. . . . works hard . . . to become known, then wears
dark glasses   ALLEN, F, 1
owes his c. merely to his antiquity   CHAUCER, 1
The c. . . . known for his well-knownness   BOORSTIN, 1
celerity   C. is never more admir'd   SHAKESPEARE, 32
celery   Genuineness . . . Like c.   HUXLEY, A, 34
The thought of two thousand people crunching c.   SHAW, 45
Celia   Come, my C., let us prove   JONSON, 16
celibacy   c. is . . . a muddy horse-pond   PEACOCK, 5
cello   The c. is not one of my favourite instruments   THOMAS, I, 4
cells   These little grey c.   CHRISTIE, 3
cemetery   old c. in which nine of his daughters were lying   THURBER, 7
censor   Deleted by French c.   BENNETT, J, 1
censorship   Assassination . . . the extreme form of c.   SHAW, 39
censure   All c. of a man's self   JOHNSON, S, 125
centre   I love being at the c. of things   THATCHER, M, 21
the c. cannot hold   YEATS, 28
century   Mrs Thatcher will go until the turn of the c.   TEBBITT, 2
The c. on which we are entering . . . must be the c. of the
common man   WALLACE, H, 1
The great man . . . walks across his c.   LEACOCK, 9
the twentieth c. will be . . . the c. of Fascism   MUSSOLINI, 4
cereal   Do you *know* what breakfast c. is made of   DAHL, 1
cerebrums   larger c. and smaller adrenal glands   MENCKEN, 5
certain   I am c. that we will win the election with a good majority   THATCHER, M, 23
nothing is c. but death and taxes   FRANKLIN, 17
One thing is c.   FITZGERALD, E, 10
certainties   begin with c.   BACON, FRANCIS, 2
His doubts are better than . . . c.   HARDWICKE, 1
cesspool   London, that great c.   DOYLE, 16
Ceylon   spicy breezes Blow soft o'er C.'s isle   HEBER, 2
chaff   An editor . . . separates the wheat from the c.   STEVENSON, A, 1
chain   A c. is no stronger   PROVERBS, 9
the flesh to feel the c.   BRONTË, E, 3
chains   c. that tie The hidden soul of harmony   MILTON, 20
It's often safer to be in c.   KAFKA, 3
Man . . . everywhere he is in c.   ROUSSEAU, 1
nothing to lose but their c.   MARX, K, 2
chair   Give Dayrolles a c.   CHESTERFIELD, 23
the nineteenth century was the age of the editorial c.   MCLUHAN, 3
chairs   The c. are being brought in from the garden   AUDEN, 18
chaise   All in a c. and pair   COWPER, 10
chaise-longue   hurly-burly of the c.   CAMPBELL, MRS PATRICK, 2
chalices   In old time we had treen c. and golden priests   JEWEL, 1
Cham   That great C. of literature, Samuel Johnson   SMOLLETT, 6
chamber   rapping at my c. door   POE, 1
Upstairs and downstairs And in my lady's c.   NURSERY RHYMES, 13
chambermaid   a man would be as happy in the arms of a c.   JOHNSON, S, 126
chameleon   A c. on plaid   ROOSEVELT, F, 1
chamois   springing from blonde to blonde like the c. of the Alps   WODEHOUSE, 20
champagne   Fighting is like c.   MITCHELL, M, 2
like a glass of c. that has stood   ATTLEE, 3
water flowed like c.   EVARTS, 1
chance   every c. brought out a noble knight   TENNYSON, 22
in our lives c. may have an astonishing influence   FLEMING, A, 3
time and c. happeneth to them all   BIBLE, 74
Chancellor   C. of the Exchequer   LOWE, 1
chandelier   The soul of Dizzy was a c.   DISRAELI, 1
change   C. is not made without inconvenience   HOOKER, 4
I c., but I cannot die   SHELLEY, 6
If you leave a thing alone you leave it to a torrent of c.   CHESTERTON, 33
Most of the c. we think we see   FROST, R, 1
Most women set out to try to c. a man   DIETRICH, 4
Only c. enraged him   CAREY, J, 1
People are never happy who want c.   HARTLEY, 1
Plus ça c.   KARR, 1

the largest scope for c. still lies in men's attitude to women   BRITTAIN, 1
The more things c.   KARR, 1
There is a certain relief in c.   IRVING, 3
The wind of c.   MACMILLAN, 8
changed   All c., c. utterly   YEATS, 10
changeth   The old order c.   TENNYSON, 23
changez   C. *vos amis*   DE GAULLE, 9
changing   c. scenes of life   TATE, N, 2
Woman is always fickle and c.   VIRGIL, 12
Channel   dream you are crossing the C.   GILBERT, W, 21
let the last man . . . brush the C. with his sleeve   SCHLIEFFEN, 1
chaos   a perfectly possible means of overcoming c.   RICHARDS, I, 1
carrying a bit of c. round with him   TENNYSON, 3
The grotesque c. of a Labour council   KINNOCK, 6
chapel   Devil always builds a c. there   DEFOE, 5
Who lied in the c. Now lies in the Abbey   BYRON, 39
chapels   c. had been churches   SHAKESPEARE, 237
Chaplain   twice a day the C. called   WILDE, 6
Chaplin   C. is no business man   GOLDWYN, 7
chaps   Biography is about C.   BENTLEY, E, 3
chapter   c. of accidents   CHESTERFIELD, 18
c. of accidents is the longest . . . in the book   WILKES, 2
character   I had become a woman of . . . c.   DOSTOEVSKY, 1
I leave my c. behind   SHERIDAN, R, 11
proper time to influence the c. of a child   INGE, 9
What is c. but the determination of incident   JAMES, H, 11
characteristic   typically English c.   ADCOCK, 1
characters   c. in one of my novels   FITZGERALD, F S, 15
c. stand before me in my mind's eye   BLYTON, 1
Most women have no c.   POPE, 41
some of the c. will seem almost mythopoeic   TOLKIEN, 3
charge   Electrical force . . . causes motion of electrical c.   EDDINGTON, 1
charged   it was c. against me   WHITMAN, 4
Charing Cross   between Heaven and C.   THOMPSON, F, 2
I went out to C., to see Major-general Harrison hanged   PEPYS, 6
the full tide of human existence is at C.   JOHNSON, S, 93
chariot   a c. . . . of fire   BIBLE, 301
Swing low sweet c.   ANONYMOUS, 76
the dust beneath thy c. wheel   HOPE, 1
Time's winged c.   MARVELL, 10
charity   C. begins at home   DROWNE, T, 8
C. is the power of defending that which we know to be
indefensible   CHESTERTON, 21
c. never faileth   BIBLE, 38
C. separates the rich from the poor   PERÓN, E, 2
c. suffereth long, and is kind   BIBLE, 38
In c. there is no excess   BACON, FRANCIS, 27
knowledge puffeth up, but c. edifieth   BIBLE, 32
lectures or a little c.   WHITMAN, 8
now abideth faith, hope, c.   BIBLE, 38
the greatest of these is c.   BIBLE, 38
The living need c.   ARNOLD, G, 1
The man who leaves money to c. in his will   VOLTAIRE, 33
without c. are nothing worth   BOOK OF COMMON PRAYER, 8
Charles the First   Caesar had his Brutus – C., his Cromwell   HENRY, P, 1
Charles the Second   There were gentlemen and . . . seamen in
the navy of C.   MACAULAY, T, 9
Charley   I'm C.'s aunt from Brazil   THOMAS, B, 1
Charlie   C. is my darling   NAIRNE, 2
charm   Conversation has a kind of c.   SENECA, 2
Oozing c. . . . He oiled his way   LERNER, 4
the c. . . . of a nomadic existence   SACKVILLE-WEST, 5
charming   c. people have something to conceal   CONNOLLY, 11
I heard the bullets whistle . . . c. in the sound   WASHINGTON, 4
It is c. to totter into vogue   WALPOLE, H, 5
People are either c. or tedious   WILDE, 39
charms   Whose c. all other maids surpass   MACNALLY, 1
Charon   C., seeing, may forget   LANDOR, 1
Chartreuse   religious system that produced Green C.   SAKI, 17
chaste   godly poet must be c. himself   CATULLUS, 1
school-miss Alfred vent her c. delight   TENNYSON, 2
chastise   in politics to c. his own side than the enemy   ORWELL, 2
chastity   Give me c. and continence   AUGUSTINE OF HIPPO, 2
Chatterley   Put thy shimmy on, Lady C.   LAWRENCE, D, 18
cheap   flesh and blood so c.   HOOD, 12
cheat   c. at cards   BOSWELL, 2
cheating   *Peace*, n. . . . a period of c.   BIERCE, 10
check   C. enclosed   PARKER, D, 28
dreadful is the c.   BRONTË, E, 3

Got no c. books, got no banks — BERLIN, 1
cheek Care Sat on his faded c. — MILTON, 35
the c. that doth not fade — KEATS, 18
turn the other c. — HOLMES, O, 5
whosoever shall smite thee on thy right c. — BIBLE, 364
cheeks Blow, winds, and crack your c. — SHAKESPEARE, 176
cheer cups, That c. but not inebriate — COWPER, 25
Don't c., boys; the poor devils are dying — PHILIP, J, 1
cheerful God loveth a c. giver — BIBLE, 45
cheerfulness No warmth, no c., no healthful ease — HOOD, 10
cheese 265 kinds of c. — DE GAULLE, 8
bread and c., and kisses — SWIFT, 11
c. – toasted, mostly — STEVENSON, R, 10
when the c. is gone — BRECHT, 8
cheesed unremitting humanity soon had me c. off — DICKENS, 1
Cheltenham Here lie I . . . Killed by drinking C. waters — ANONYMOUS, 25
chemical c. barrage has been hurled against the fabric of life — CARSON, 2
Shelley and Keats were . . . up to date in . . . c. knowledge — HALDANE, 2
chemistry he had read Shakespeare and found him weak in c. — WELLS, 18
cheque Any general statement is like a c. — POUND, 6
Mrs Claypool's c. will come back to you — MARX, G, 18
chequer-board a C. of Nights and Days — FITZGERALD, E, 13
cherish to love and to c. — BOOK OF COMMON PRAYER, 27
cherry Before the c. orchard was sold — CHEKHOV, 6
c. ripe — ALISON, 1
C. ripe, ripe, ripe — HERRICK, 1
Loveliest of trees, the c. — HOUSMAN, 7
Till 'C. ripe' themselves do cry — CAMPION, 2
chess Life's too short for c. — BYRON, H, 1
the devil played at c. with me — BROWNE, T, 4
chess-board c. is the world; the pieces . . . the phenomena of the universe — HUXLEY, T, 6
chest Fifteen men on the dead man's c. — STEVENSON, R, 8
chestnut O c. tree — YEATS, 4
Under the spreading c. tree — LONGFELLOW, 16
chestnuts warmongers who . . . have others pull the c. out of the fire — STALIN, 3
chew he can't fart and c. gum at the same time — JOHNSON, L, 4
chewing c. little bits of String — BELLOC, 5
chic very c. for an atheist — RUSSELL, B, 5
chicken a c. in his pot every Sunday — HENRI IV, 1
England will have her neck wrung like a c. — WEYGAND, 1
Some c. — CHURCHILL, W, 59
chickens children are more troublesome and costly than c. — SHAW, 12
count their c. ere they're hatched — BUTLER, S, 3
Don't count your c. — AESOP, 8
If I didn't start painting, I would have raised c. — GRANDMA MOSES, 2
You don't set a fox to watching the c. — TRUMAN, 11
chief C. Defect of Henry King — BELLOC, 5
C. of the Army — NAPOLEON I, 15
child A c. becomes an adult when — SZASZ, 4
A c. deserves the maximum respect — JUVENAL, 12
A c.'s a plaything for an hour — LAMB, M, 1
all any reasonable c. can expect — ORTON, 2
better . . . a poor and a wise c. than an old and foolish king — BIBLE, 71
C.! do not throw this book about — BELLOC, 3
c. of five would understand this — MARX, G, 6
Every c. should have an occasional pat on the back — SHEEN, 1
flourish in a c. of six — BELLOC, 4
getting wenches with c. — SHAKESPEARE, 350
give her the living c. — BIBLE, 298
Give me a c. for the first seven years — PROVERBS, 175
grant that the old Adam in this C. — BOOK OF COMMON PRAYER, 21
He who shall teach the c. to doubt — BLAKE, W, 3
I just want every man, woman, and c. in America to see it — GOLDWYN, 8
If you strike a c. — SHAW, 30
nobody's c. — CASE, 1
Now at last our c. is just like all children — DE GAULLE, 6
One stops being a c. when . . . telling one's trouble does not make it better — PAVESE, 1
receive one such little c. in my name — BIBLE, 400
simplicity a c. — POPE, 18
spoil the c. — BUTLER, S, 4
sweetest Shakespeare, Fancy's c. — MILTON, 19

The C. is Father of the Man — WORDSWORTH, W, 23
There are only two things a c. will share willingly — SPOCK, 2
unless the play is stopped, the c. cannot . . . go on — KEMBLE, J, 1
unto us a c. is born — BIBLE, 201
What is the use of a new-born c. — FRANKLIN, 11
when I was a c., I spake as a c. — BIBLE, 38
wise father that knows his own c. — SHAKESPEARE, 241
Woe to the land that's govern'd by a c. — SHAKESPEARE, 302
childbirth Death and taxes and c. — MITCHELL, M, 3
Mountains will heave in c. — HORACE, 6
Childe C. Roland to the Dark Tower — BROWNING, R, 17
childhood His adult life resembled his c. — SARTRE, 1
his egotism was all but second c. — CARROLL, 2
The books one reads in c. . . . create in one's mind a . . . false map — ORWELL, 21
childish I put away c. things — BIBLE, 38
Sweet c. days — WORDSWORTH, W, 71
childishness second c. — SHAKESPEARE, 48
children a Friend for little c. Above the bright blue sky — MIDLANE, 1
Anybody who hates c. and dogs — FIELDS, 3
Are the c. all in bed? It's past eight o'clock — NURSERY RHYMES, 69
as c. fear to go in the dark — BACON, FRANCIS, 18
a wicked man that comes after c. — HOFFMANN, E, 1
c. are more troublesome and costly than chickens — SHAW, 12
C. aren't happy with nothing to ignore — NASH, 8
c. are true judges of character — AUDEN, 23
C. have never been very good at listening — BALDWIN, J, 4
C. . . . have no use for psychology. — SINGER, 1
c., obey your parents — BIBLE, 95
C. should acquire . . . heroes and villains from fiction — AUDEN, 4
C. sweeten labours — BACON, FRANCIS, 39
C. with Hyacinth's temperament . . . merely know more — SAKI, 5
Come dear c. — ARNOLD, M, 16
desire not a multitude of unprofitable c. — BIBLE, 85
Do you hear the c. weeping — BROWNING, E, 2
except ye . . . become as little c. — BIBLE, 399
Familiarity breeds . . . c. — TWAIN, 3
Far too good to waste on c. — SHAW, 50
He that has no c. — PROVERBS, 190
He that loves not his wife and c. — TAYLOR, JEREMY, 1
his wife is beautiful and his c. smart — MENCKEN, 3
I love all my c. — CARTER, L, 1
I've lost one of my c. this week — TURNER, 2
Let our c. grow tall — THATCHER, M, 5
like a c.'s party taken over by the elders — FITZGERALD, F S, 4
make your c. *capable of honesty* is the beginning of education — RUSKIN, 12
Men are but c. of a larger growth — DRYDEN, 18
Men are . . . more careful of the breed of their horses and dogs than of their c. — PENN, 2
Most of the people . . . will be c. — ANDERSEN, 3
My music . . . understood by c. and animals — STRAVINSKY, 4
Never have c. — VIDAL, 6
Now at last our child is just like all c. — DE GAULLE, 6
only privileged persons in our country are the c. — PERÓN, E, 1
Parents learn a lot from their c. — SPARK, 2
provoke not your c. — BIBLE, 22
She had so many c. she didn't know what to do — NURSERY RHYMES, 59
the c. I might have had — LOWRY, 1
the early marriages of silly c. — MARTINEAU, 3
The English are growing demented about c. — WAUGH, A, 1
They patronise, they treat c. as inferiors — DISNEY, 1
to avoid having c. — VIRCHOW, 1
To bear many c. is considered . . . an investment — GANDHI, I, 1
We have no c., except me — BEHAN, 10
when they started life as c. — AMIS, 2
write for c. . . . as you do for adults — GORKY, 1
chill St Agnes' Eve – Ah, bitter c. it was — KEATS, 9
chime to set a c. of words tinkling in . . . a few fastidious people — SMITH, L, 9
chimes c. at midnight — SHAKESPEARE, 122
chimney SIXTY HORSES WEDGED IN A C. — MORTON, 1
chimney-sweepers As c., come to dust — SHAKESPEARE, 62
China Even the Hooligan was probably invented in C. — SAKI, 18
On a slow boat to C. — LOESSER, 1
The infusion of a C. plant — ADDISON, 12
Chinese Nothing . . . can destroy the C. people — BUCK, 2
chip c. of the old block — BURKE, E, 27
chips You breed babies and you eat c. — WESKER, 1
chirche-dore Housbondes at c. — CHAUCER, 12

chivalry age of c. is gone   BURKE, E, 9
Cervantes laughed c. out of fashion   CERVANTES, 2
Chi Wen Tzu C. always thought three times before taking action   CONFUCIUS, 2
Chloë In the spring . . . your lovely C.   SEARLE, 2
chocolate a c. cream soldier   SHAW, 5
both its national products, snow and c., melt   COREN, 5
Venice is like eating . . . c. liqueurs   CAPOTE, 1
choice But . . . 'Thou mayest' – that gives a c.   STEINBECK, 1
choir Sweet singing in the c.   ANONYMOUS, 81
choirs Bare ruin'd c.   SHAKESPEARE, 364
choose *We can believe what we c.*   NEWMAN, J, 5
Chopin to bridge the awful gap between Dorothy and C.   ADE, 2
chord c. of music   PROCTER, 1
chorus a dozen are only a c.   FITZGERALD, F S, 9
chose *plus c'est la même c.*   KARR, 1
chosen a c. vessel   BIBLE, 8
but few are c.   BIBLE, 409
Christ C. is all, and in all   BIBLE, 20
C. . . . would quite likely have been arrested   DE BLANK, 1
churches have kill'd their C.   TENNYSON, 59
I beseech you, in the bowels of C.   CROMWELL, O, 5
The Jews have produced . . . C., Spinoza, and myself   STEIN, 5
We're more popular than Jesus C.   LENNON, 13
Who dreamed that C. has died in vain   SITWELL, E, 2
Christendom wisest fool in C.   HENRI IV, 3
Christian A C. . . . feels Repentance on a Sunday   YBARRA, 1
any man . . . who could not bear another's misfortunes . . . like a C.   POPE, 69
Better sleep with a sober cannibal than a drunken C.   MELVILLE, 1
C. Science explains all cause and effect as mental   EDDY, 2
good a C. as Mahomet   ELIZABETH I, 2
How very hard . . . To be a C.   BROWNING, R, 22
I die a C.   CHARLES I, 2
Indian snob reasons, like calling an English person by his C. name   SCOTT, P, 3
in what peace a C. can die   ADDISON, 19
I was born of C. race, And not a Heathen, or a Jew   WATTS, 4
No Jew was ever fool enough to turn C.   ZANGWILL, 1
object . . . to form C. men   ARNOLD, T, 1
Onward, C. soldiers   BARING-GOULD, 1
several young women . . . would render the C. life intensely difficult   LEWIS, C, 4
The C. religion not only was at first attended with miracles   HUME, D, 3
Christianity C. accepted as given a metaphysical system   HUXLEY, A, 19
C. . . . but why journalism   BALFOUR, 2
C. has done a great deal for love   FRANCE, 6
C. has made of death a terror   OUIDA, 1
C. is part of the Common Law of England   HALE, M, 1
C. is the most materialistic of all great religions   TEMPLE, W, 1
C. . . . says that they are all fools   CHESTERTON, 22
C. the one great curse   NIETZSCHE, 4
C. . . . the one immortal blemish of mankind   NIETZSCHE, 4
counter to all C. for a thousand years   LUTHER, 2
decay of C.   SAKI, 9
His C. was muscular   DISRAELI, 6
local cult called C.   HARDY, 5
loving C. better than Truth   COLERIDGE, S, 3
nothing in C. or Buddhism that quite matches   SAKI, 10
Rock and roll or C.   LENNON, 13
Christians C. awake, salute the happy morn   BYROM, 1
Onward, C., onward go   WHITE, H, 1
settle their differences like good C.   AUSTIN, W, 2
these C. love one another   TERTULLIAN, 2
they may be Catholics but they are not C.   MCCARTHY, M, 6
Christ-like C. heroes and woman-worshipping Don Juans   LAWRENCE, D, 27
Christmas At C. I no more desire a rose   SHAKESPEARE, 195
C. comes but once a year   PROVERBS, 100
C. should fall out in the Middle of Winter   ADDISON, 14
Eating a C. pie   NURSERY RHYMES, 30
For C. comes but once a year   TUSSER, 3
I'm walking backwards till C.   MILLIGAN, 5
perceive C. through its wrapping   WHITE, E, 2
The first day of C., My true love sent to me   NURSERY RHYMES, 54
'Twas the night before C.   MOORE, C, 1
Christopher Robin went down with Alice   MILNE, 5
chronicle c. small beer   SHAKESPEARE, 280
the c. of wasted time   SHAKESPEARE, 367
church an alien C.   DISRAELI, 22

Beware when you take on the C. of God   TUTU, 3
But get me to the c. on time   LERNER, 5
he'd go to c., start a revolution – *something*   MILLER, A, 3
I believe in the C.   TEMPLE, W, 7
straying away from the c.   BRUCE, 1
The blood of the martyrs is the seed of the C.   TERTULLIAN, 1
The C. exists   TEMPLE, W, 6
The C.'s one foundation   STONE, S, 1
The farther you go from the c. of Rome   WOTTON, 4
There are many who stay away from c.   MILLER, A, 1
There is no salvation outside the c.   AUGUSTINE OF HIPPO, 3
There was I, waiting at the c.   LEIGH, 1
where MCC ends and the C. of England begins   PRIESTLEY, 7
churches chapels had been c.   SHAKESPEARE, 237
c. have kill'd their Christ   TENNYSON, 59
the c. . . . bore for me the same relation to God that billboards did to Coca-Cola   UPDIKE, 2
The itch of disputing will prove the scab of c.   WOTTON, 2
churchman a species of person called a 'Modern C.'   WAUGH, E, 19
churchyard A piece of c. fits everybody   PROVERBS, 39
nowhere worse taste, than in a c.   JOWETT, 3
young physician fattens the c.   PROVERBS, 76
Cicero C. And . . . Homer were *Mad as the mist and snow*   YEATS, 20
cider c. and tinned salmon   WAUGH, E, 33
cigar a good c. is a smoke   KIPLING, 4
It is like a c. . . . it never tastes quite the same   WAVELL, 1
cigarette A c. is . . . a perfect pleasure   WILDE, 31
Cinderella poetry, 'The C. of the Arts.'   MONROE, H, 1
cinema c. is truth twenty-four times a second   GODARD, 1
circle All things from eternity . . . come round in a c.   MARCUS AURELIUS, 4
circumcised our fingers are c.   PERLMAN, 1
When they c. Herbert Samuel   LLOYD GEORGE, 15
circumcision Every luxury . . . atheism, breast-feeding, c.   ORTON, 4
circumlocution C. Office   DICKENS, 22
circumstance Pride, pomp, and c.   SHAKESPEARE, 286
To a philosopher no c. . . . is too minute   GOLDSMITH, 5
circumstances to face straitened c. at home   JUVENAL, 4
circumstantial Some c. evidence is very strong   THOREAU, 6
circuses bread and c.   JUVENAL, 8
cities I have sung women in three c.   POUND, 9
many c. had rubbed him smooth   GREENE, 4
The government burns down whole c.   MAO TSE-TUNG, 10
citizen a c. of the world   BACON, FRANCIS, 28; SOCRATES, 8
an American c. . . . attacking an ex-secretary of state   CHURCHILL, W, 1
I am a c. of the world   DIOGENES, 3
citizens All free men . . . are c. of Berlin   KENNEDY, JOHN, 15
city axis of the earth sticks out visibly through . . . every town or c.   HOLMES, O, 4
first c. Cain   COWLEY, 1
great c. . . . has the greatest men and women   WHITMAN, 12
hiring taxis to scuttle around a c.   KINNOCK, 9
I go amongst the buildings of a c.   KEATS, 69
It is a c. where you can see a sparrow fall   O'BRIEN, C, 1
the c. is not a concrete jungle, it is a human zoo   MORRIS, D, 1
the c. of perspiring dreams   RAPHAEL, 1
the holy c., new Jerusalem   BIBLE, 473
very excellent things are spoken of thee, thou c. of God   PSALMS, 47
civil In a c. war a general must know   REED, H, 4
civilians drop bombs . . . hit c.   GOLDWATER, 3
civilisation Disinterested intellectual curiosity . . . life blood of . . . c.   TREVELYAN, 1
if c. is to advance . . . it must be through . . . women   PANKHURST, E, 1
the whole subsequent history of c. takes its rise   LUTHER, 1
civility C. costs nothing   PROVERBS, 101
The reciprocal c. of authors   JOHNSON, S, 19
civilization As c. advances, poetry . . . declines   MACAULAY, T, 13
C. is . . . equal respect for all men   ADDAMS, 2
How idiotic c. is   MANSFIELD, K, 1
It is so stupid of modern c.   KNOX, R, 1
little in c. to appeal to a Yeti   HILLARY, 3
Madam, I am the c. they are fighting to defend   GARROD, 1
Our c. is founded on the shambles   JAMES, W, 1
The degree of a nation's c.   MAUGHAM, 14
the Renaissance was . . . the green end of one of c.'s hardest winters   FOWLES, 2

without the usual interval of c. — CLEMENCEAU, 1
You can't say c. don't advance — ROGERS, W, 1
civilized it proved that I was in a c. society — PARK, 1
Woman will be the last thing c. by Man — MEREDITH, G, 1
clap Don't c. too hard — OSBORNE, 1
clapped c. the glass to his sightless eye — NEWBOLT, 1
claret C. is the liquor for boys — JOHNSON, S, 128
drink a dozen of C. on my Tomb — KEATS, 65
look for the second cheapest c. . . . and say, 'Number 22 . . .' — POTTER, S, 6
said of c. — BENTLEY, R, 1
class a special machine for the suppression of one c. by another — LENIN, 3
Because there's no fourth c. — SANTAYANA, 7
Discussion in c. — NABOKOV, 1
Every c. is unfit to govern — ACTON, 1
for one c. to appreciate the wrongs of another — STANTON, E, 3
For this c. we have . . . the designation of Philistines — ARNOLD, M, 7
Like many of the upper c. He liked the sound of broken glass — BELLOC, 14
Mr. Waugh . . . is . . . a snob in search of a c. — WAUGH, E, 2
Poets and painters . . . constitute a special c. — BRENAN, 6
The constitution . . . first and second c. citizens — WILLKIE, 1
The history of all . . . society is the history of c. struggles — MARX, K, 1
The one c. you do *not* belong to — MIKES, 5
the proletariat will . . . wage a c. struggle for Socialism — LENIN, 6
Without c. differences . . . living theatre — BURGESS, 6
young Englishman of our upper c. — ARNOLD, M, 6
classes back the masses against the c. — GLADSTONE, 2
Hats divide generally into three c. — WHITEHORN, 1
I'm not interested in c. — LEWIS, J, 1
responsible and the irresponsible c. — LAWRENCE, D, 12
classical C. quotation is the *parole* of literary men — JOHNSON, S, 137
That's the c. mind at work — PIRSIG, 5
The basic difference between c. music and jazz — PREVIN, 1
classicism C. . . . presents . . . the literature that gave . . .
pleasure to their great-grandfathers — STENDHAL, 2
classics Every man with a belly full of the c. — MILLER, H, 2
The c. are only primitive literature — LEACOCK, 2
clay absorbs a c. After his labours — CALVERLEY, 2
clean Bath . . . once a day to be passably c. — BURGESS, 3
c. your plate — ROSEBERY, 4
hard to be funny when you have to be c. — WEST, M, 11
cleanliness The first possibility of rural c. lies in *water supply.* — NIGHTINGALE, 4
cleansed learned man who is not c. — KHOMEINI, 1
clear His right was c., his will was strong — ANONYMOUS, 102
if he could make *me* understand . . . it would be c. to all — ROOSEVELT, E, 3
clearing-house the C. of the World — CHAMBERLAIN, J, 1
cleft Rock of ages, c. for me — TOPLADY, 1
Clementine Dwelt a miner, Forty-niner, And his daughter, C. — MONTROSE, 1
clenched You cannot shake hands with a c. fist — GANDHI, I, 3
Cleopatra Had C.'s nose been shorter — PASCAL, 6
clergy c. are men — FIELDING, 1
I never saw . . . the c. were beloved in any nation — SWIFT, 13
clergyman c. whose mendicity is only equalled by their mendacity — TEMPLE, F, 2
good enough to be a c. — JOHNSON, S, 85
clerk C. ther was of Oxenford also — CHAUCER, 7
The best c. I ever fired — EISENHOWER, 3
the smartness of an attorney's c. — DISRAELI, 33
clever Be good, sweet maid, and let who can be c. — KINGSLEY, 1
Charles Lamb, a c. fellow certainly — LAMB, CHARLES, 4
c. man . . . came of . . . stupid people — CARLYLE, T, 32
it needs a very c. woman to manage a fool — KIPLING, 21
It's c., but is it art? — KIPLING, 4
never wise to try to appear . . . more c. — WHITELAW, 1
not quite c. enough to compensate for his faults — MOUNTBATTEN, 2
no use trying to be c. — JACKSON, F, 1
The silliest woman can manage a c. man — KIPLING, 21
To be c. enough to get . . . money, one must be stupid — CHESTERTON, 25
cleverest You're the c. member of . . . the c. nation in the world — WEBB, B, 2
cleverness height of c. is . . . to conceal it — ROCHEFOUCAULD, 20
cliché The c. is dead poetry — BRENAN, 4
clichés Let's have some new c. — GOLDWYN, 1

cliffs the chalk c. of Dover — BALDWIN, S, 6
climate common where the c.'s sultry — BYRON, 19
If it's heaven for c. — BARRIE, 1
climax a story that starts with an earthquake and . . . a c. — GOLDWYN, 5
climb Fain would I c., yet fear I to fall — RALEIGH, W, 2
clime change their c., not their frame of mind — HORACE, 21
Clive What I like about C. — BENTLEY, E, 3
clock c. in the steeple strikes one — WORK, 1
grandfather's c. — WORK, 2
Stands the Church c. at ten to three — BROOKE, 4
The c. struck one, The mouse ran down — NURSERY RHYMES, 15
The mouse ran up the c. — NURSERY RHYMES, 15
clocks hands of c. in railway stations — CONNOLLY, 13
pass my declining years saluting . . . grandfather c. — NASH, 4
the c. were striking the hour — LONGFELLOW, 4
clogs From c. to c. — PROVERBS, 167
cloke knyf under the c. — CHAUCER, 13
Clootie Satan, Nick, or C. — BURNS, R, 3
close a breathless hush in the C. tonight — NEWBOLT, 6
I have sometimes regretted living so c. to Marie — PROUST, 1
closed Mankind is a c. society — SCHUMACHER, 2
the transition from the . . . 'c.' . . . to the 'open society' — POPPER, 2
close-up Life is a tragedy . . . in c. — CHAPLIN, 9
closing c. time in the gardens of the West — CONNOLLY, 3
cloth not a blanket woven from one thread, one color, one c. — JACKSON, J, 2
clothes After that you just take the girl's c. off — CHANDLER, R, 3
as if she were taking off all her c. — COLETTE, 2
bought her wedding c. — ADDISON, 16
enterprises that require new c. — THOREAU, 13
Fine c. are good — JOHNSON, S, 104
hanging the baby on the c. line to dry — RUNYON, 7
Have you ever taken anything out of the c. basket — WHITEHORN, 3
if it be our c. alone which fit us for society — ESCHENBACH, 1
Nothing to wear but c. — KING, B, 1
No woman so naked as . . . underneath her c. — FRAYN, 1
walked away with their c. — DISRAELI, 23
wrapped him in swaddling c. — BIBLE, 313
cloud a c. received him out of their sight — BIBLE, 1
a pillar of a c. — BIBLE, 111
Every c. has a silver lining — PROVERBS, 132
fiend hid in a c. — BLAKE, 11
I wandered lonely as a c. — WORDSWORTH, W, 7
clouds But trailing c. of glory — WORDSWORTH, W, 25
c. that gather round the setting sun — WORDSWORTH, W, 32
clout Ne'er cast a c. — PROVERBS, 300
clown I remain . . . a c. — CHAPLIN, 8
clowns Send in the C. — SONDHEIM, 2
club I don't want to belong to any c. — MARX, G, 23
Mankind is a c. — CHESTERTON, 40
takes you so far from the c. house — LINKLATER, 1
the best c. in London — DICKENS, 40
the most exclusive c. there is — NASH, 3
cluster The human face is . . . a whole c. of faces — PROUST, 4
Clyde the bonny banks of C. — LAUDER, 3
CMG Members rise from C. . . . 'Call me God' — SAMPSON, 1
coach c. and six horses through the Act of Settlement — RICE, S, 1
indifference and a c. and six — COLMAN, THE ELDER, 1
coal though the whole world turn to c. — HERBERT, G, 10
coalitions period of c. . . . is now over — ASHDOWN, 1
coals heap c. of fire upon his head — BIBLE, 454
coaster Dirty British c. — MASEFIELD, 1
coat a c. of many colours — BIBLE, 174
cobbler Let the c. stick — PROVERBS, 256
cobwebs Laws are like c. — SWIFT, 15
laws were like c. — BACON, FRANCIS, 5
Coca-Cola the churches . . . bore for me the same relation to God
that billboards did to C. — UPDIKE, 2
cocaine C. isn't habit-forming — BANKHEAD, 7
cock before the c. crow, thou shalt deny me — BIBLE, 425
He was like a c. — ELIOT, G, 3
That kept the c. that crowed in the morn — NURSERY RHYMES, 62
waiting for the c. to crow — HUGHES, W, 1
we owe a c. to Aesculapius — SOCRATES, 9
cockles Crying, C. and mussels! alive, alive, O — ANONYMOUS, 47
cockroach to choose between him and a c. as a companion — WODEHOUSE, 15
cocksure as c. of anything — MELBOURNE, 7
cocktail weasel under the c. cabinet — PINTER, 4
cod piece of c. passes all understanding — LUTYENS, 2
serve both c. and salmon — LEVERSON, 2

Marriage, n. . . . a c. . . . making in all two   BIERCE, 8
the c. of Europe   SALISBURY, 2
We are part of the c. of Europe   GLADSTONE, 3
commute   the agricultural labourers round here c. from London   POWELL, A, 4
commuter   C. . . . riding to and from his wife   WHITE, E, 1
compact   the damned, c., liberal majority   IBSEN, 2
companion   to choose between him and a cockroach as a c.   WODEHOUSE, 15
companionable   so c. as solitude   THOREAU, 14
companions   Boys . . . are unwholesome c. for grown people   LAMB, CHARLES, 9
c. for middle age   BACON, FRANCIS, 34
company   better to be alone than in bad c.   WASHINGTON, 3
c. . . . have neither a soul to lose nor a body to kick   SMITH, SYDNEY, 5
Crowds without c.   GIBBON, 4
I've been offered titles . . . get one into disreputable c.   SHAW, 44
pleasure of your c.   LAMB, CHARLES, 24
Take the tone of the c.   CHESTERFIELD, 8
Tell me what c. thou keepest   CERVANTES, 22
You never expected justice from a c.   SMITH, SYDNEY, 5
comparative   progress is simply a c.   CHESTERTON, 18
compare   any she belied with false c.   SHAKESPEARE, 372
c. thee to a summer's day   SHAKESPEARE, 358
Learn, c., collect the facts   PAVLOV, 1
compared   The war we have just been through . . . is not to be c.   WILSON, W, 6
comparisons   c. are odious   DONNE, 10
C. are odorous   SHAKESPEARE, 272
compass   my heart shall be The faithful c.   GAY, 12
compassed   snares of death c. me round   PSALMS, 65
compassion   But a certain Samaritan . . . had c. on him   BIBLE, 325
C. is not a sloppy, sentimental feeling   KINNOCK, 6
The purpose of human life is to serve and to show c.   SCHWEITZER, 1
competition   C. was the breath of life to him   FLEMING, A, 1
complacency   c. and satisfaction . . . in . . . a new-married couple   LAMB, CHARLES, 3
complain   one hardly knows to whom to c.   FIRBANK, 2
complaint   Anno domini . . . the most fatal c.   HILTON, 1
how is the old c.   DISRAELI, 38
I want to register a c.   MARX, G, 14
complete   disguised as a C. Man   HUXLEY, A, 6
now I feel like a c. idiot   HEINE, 3
complex   Wherever an inferiority c. exists, there is . . . reason for it   JUNG, 10
compliance   by a timely c.   FIELDING, 8
compliment   returned the c.   VOLTAIRE, 19
compose   Never c. . . . unless . . . not composing . . . becomes a positive nuisance   HOLST, 1
composed   When I c. that, I was . . . inspired by God   BEETHOVEN, 2
composer   A good c. . . . steals   STRAVINSKY, 5
composition   difference between . . . prose and metrical c.   WORDSWORTH, W, 18
comprehended   c. two aspicious persons   SHAKESPEARE, 273
comprehensive   largest and most c. soul   SHAKESPEARE, 5
compromise   All government . . . is founded on c. and barter   BURKE, E, 14
C. used to mean that half a loaf   CHESTERTON, 39
not a question that leaves much room for c.   MEIR, 6
compulsion   seized by the stern hand of C.   THURBER, 4
compulsory   c. and irreproachable idleness   TOLSTOY, L, 9
comrade   stepping where his c. stood   SCOTT, WALTER, 16
comrades   East and west on fields forgotten Bleach the bones of c. slain   HOUSMAN, 14
walked willingly to his death . . . to . . . save his c.   ATKINSON, 1
conceal   Addresses . . . c. our whereabouts   SAKI, 2
height of cleverness is . . . to c. it   ROCHEFOUCAULD, 20
speech only to c. their thoughts   VOLTAIRE, 11
concealed   Much truth is spoken . . . more . . . c.   DARLING, 3
concealing   Good breeding consists in c. how . . . we think of ourselves   TWAIN, 14
concealment   c., like a worm i' th' bud   SHAKESPEARE, 340
conceit   C. is the finest armour   JEROME, 2
conceited   I would grow intolerably c.   WHISTLER, 8
what man will do any good who is not c.   TROLLOPE, 12
concept   If the c. of God has   BALDWIN, 1
conception   if the dad is present at the c.   ORTON, 2
concepts   walks up the stairs of his c.   STEINBECK, 2
concessions   The c. of the weak are the c. of fear   BURKE, E, 13

conclusions   Life is the art of drawing . . . c.   BUTLER, S, 10
concord   toleration produced . . . religious c.   GIBBON, 6
Yes – around C.   THOREAU, 23
concurrence   Accidental and fortuitous c. of atoms   PALMERSTON, 1
condemn   No man can justly censure or c. another   BROWNE, T, 7
condemned   If God were suddenly c. to live the life   DUMAS, FILS, 1
Man is c. to be free   SARTRE, 6
condemning   One should examine oneself . . . before . . . c. others   MOLIÈRE, 7
condition   hopes for the human c.   CAMUS, 16
The c. of man . . . is a c. of war   HOBBES, 1
the c. of our sex is so deplorable that it is our duty   PANKHURST, E, 4
To be a poet is a c.   GRAVES, R, 4
wearisome c. of humanity   GREVILLE, 1
what delight we married people have to see . . . fools decoyed into our c.   PEPYS, 13
conditioned   Americans have been c. to respect newness   UPDIKE, 3
conditions   my people live in such awful c.   GEORGE V, 2
conduct   C. . . . to the prejudice of good order and military discipline   ANONYMOUS, 14
conference   naked into the c. chamber   BEVAN, 11
confess   It's easy to make a man c. . . . lies   HOUSEHOLD, 2
Men will c.   COLBY, 1
only c. our little faults   ROCHEFOUCAULD, 22
We c. our bad qualities . . . out of fear   BRENAN, 7
confessing   I am ashamed of it   BURNEY, 1
women . . . ill-using them and then c. it   TROLLOPE, 9
confidence   never dedicated to something you have complete c. in   PIRSIG, 1
Three addresses always inspire c.   WILDE, 32
confident   There are two things which I am c. I can do very well   JOHNSON, S, 52
confin'd   cabin'd, cribb'd, c., bound in   SHAKESPEARE, 214
conflict   We are in an armed c.   EDEN, A, 3
conform   how to rebel and c. at the same time   CRISP, 2
conformable   Nature is very consonant and c.   NEWTON, I, 4
confounded   mine enemies shall be c.   PSALMS, 2
confusion   I had nothing to offer anybody except my own c.   KEROUAC, 3
let me never be put to c.   PSALMS, 18
Congreve   C. is the only sophisticated playwright   TYNAN, 2
Congs   Kinquering C. their titles take   SPOONER, 3
connect   Only c.   FORSTER, 9
conquer   in the end the truth will c.   WYCLIFFE, 1
They will c., but . . . not convince   UNAMUNO Y JUGO, 4
We'll fight and we'll c.   GARRICK, 2
when we c. without danger   CORNEILLE, 2
conquered   I came; I saw; God c.   JOHN III SOBIESKI, 1
I came, I saw, I c.   CAESAR, 1
I will be c.; I will not capitulate   JOHNSON, S, 155
the English seem . . . to have c. and peopled half the world   SEELEY, 1
conquering   C. kings   CHANDLER, J, 1
not c. but fighting well   COUBERTIN, 1
See, the c. hero comes   MORELL, 1
conquest   The Roman C. was, however, a *Good Thing*   SELLAR, 4
conscience   a Nonconformist c.   WILDE, 42
As guardian of His Majesty's c.   THURLOW, 2
c. does make cowards of us all   SHAKESPEARE, 88
C. is a coward   GOLDSMITH, 30
C. is . . . rejection of a particular wish   FREUD, S, 4
C. is the inner voice   MENCKEN, 2
dilemmas of c. and egotism   SNOW, 2
I cannot . . . cut my c. to fit this year's fashions   HELLMAN, 2
I'll catch the c. of the King   SHAKESPEARE, 88
Now war has a bad c.   KEY, E, 6
why is my liberty judged of another man's c.   BIBLE, 36
consciousness   man, by possessing c., is . . . a disease animal   UNAMUNO Y JUGO, 2
consent   No one can make you feel inferior without your c.   ROOSEVELT, E, 1
consequence   It is incident to physicians . . . to mistake subsequence for c.   JOHNSON, S, 44
consequences   men never violate the laws of God without suffering the c.   CHILD, 1
conservatism   c. . . . adherence to the old and tried   LINCOLN, 14
c. is based upon the idea   CHESTERTON, 33
Conservative   C. government is an organized hypocrisy   DISRAELI, 24

Or else a little C.   GILBERT, W, 19
to what is called the Tory, and which might . . . be called the
   C., party   CROKER, 2
conservative   The radical invents the views . . . the c. adopts them
    TWAIN, 11
which makes a man more c.   KEYNES, 2
consider   c. your ways   BIBLE, 184
When I c. how my light is spent   MILTON, 60
considerable   to appear c. in his native place   JOHNSON, S, 82
considered   hast thou c. my servant Job   BIBLE, 222
consistency   C. is contrary to nature   HUXLEY, A, 14
consonant   Nature is very c. and conformable   NEWTON, I, 4
conspiracy   not a Party, it is a c.   BEVAN, 1
People of the same trade seldom meet together but the
   conversation ends in a c.   SMITH, A, 1
conspirators   All the c.   SHAKESPEARE, 160
constabulary   When c. duty's to be done   GILBERT, W, 40
constant   A c. guest   PROVERBS, 10
C. dripping   PROVERBS, 103
Friendship is c. in all other things   SHAKESPEARE, 267
constitution   The c. . . . first and second class citizens   WILLKIE, 2
The principles of a free c.   GIBBON, 7
constitutional   A c. king must learn to stoop   LEOPOLD II, 1
c. right   LINCOLN, 15
definition of a c. statesman   BAGEHOT, 9
construction   Our object in the c. of the state   PLATO, 2
consultations   dictator . . . always take some c.   THATCHER, M, 17
consulted   the right to be c. . . . to encourage . . . to warn
    BAGEHOT, 7
consume   more history than they can c.   SAKI, 6
statistics, born to c. resources   HORACE, 17
consumed   is yet also c. with this desire   KEATS, 1
consumer   In a c. society there are . . . two kinds of slaves
    ILLICH, 4
consumes   Man . . . c. without producing   ORWELL, 3
consummation   a c. Devoutly to be wish'd   SHAKESPEARE, 89
consummatum   c. est   BIBLE, 272
consumption   Conspicuous c. . . . is a means of reputability
    VEBLEN, 3
this c. of the purse   SHAKESPEARE, 118
consumptive   c. youth weaving garlands of sad flowers
    STEVENSON, R, 2
contemplates   Beauty in things exists in the mind which c. them
    HUME, D, 4
contemplation   right mindfulness, right c.   BUDDHA, 4
contemporary   I am no one's c. – ever   MANDELSTAM, 1
to trade a hundred c. readers for   KOESTLER, 6
contempt   attention to the inside . . . c. for the outside
    CHESTERFIELD, 14
she was only an Object of C.   AUSTEN, 12
To show pity is felt as a sign of c.   NIETZSCHE, 18
contemptible   c. little Army   WILHELM II, 4
content   desire is got without c.   SHAKESPEARE, 215
Let us draw upon c. for the deficiencies of fortune   GOLDSMITH, 28
contented   How is it . . . that no one lives c. with his lot
    HORACE, 45
If you are foolish enough to be c., don't show it   JEROME, 4
With what I most enjoy c. least   SHAKESPEARE, 360
contentment   Where wealth and freedom reign, c. fails
    GOLDSMITH, 23
contests   mighty c. rise from trivial things   POPE, 48
continence   Give me chastity and c.   AUGUSTINE OF HIPPO, 2
that melancholy sexual perversion known as c.   HUXLEY, A, 8
continent   On the C. people have good food   MIKES, 1
continental   C. people have sex life   MIKES, 3
continual   c. state of inelegance   AUSTEN, 28
continuation   All diplomacy is a c. of war   CHOU EN LAI, 1
War is the c. of politics   CLAUSEWITZ, 1
contraception   a terrific story about oral c.   ALLEN, W, 11
contraceptive   Dr Marie Stopes made c. devices respectable
    STOPES, 3
It's like having a totally efficient c.   BURGESS, 6
contraceptives   C. should be used   MILLIGAN, 8
Skullion had little use for c.   SHARPE, 2
contract   A verbal c. isn't worth the paper   GOLDWYN, 15
Every law is a c.   SELDEN, 7
Marriage is . . . but a civil c.   SELDEN, 9
contradict   Do I c. myself   WHITMAN, 10
contradiction   brook no c.   WEBSTER, J, 2
Man is . . . an everlasting c. to himself   HAZLITT, 5
Woman's at best a c.   POPE, 43

contradictory   Doublethink means the power of holding two c.
   beliefs   ORWELL, 19
contrairy   everythink goes c. with me   DICKENS, 11
contraries   Without C. is no progression   BLAKE, W, 18
contrariwise   'C.,' continued Tweedledee   CARROLL, 26
contrary   Mary, Mary, quite c.   NURSERY RHYMES, 34
On the c.   IBSEN, 10
control   I must . . . try hard to c. the talking habit   FRANK, 3
we ought to c. our thoughts   DARWIN, C R, 6
controversy   born fool who voluntarily engages in c. with Mr.
   Adams   ADAMS, J, 1
that c. is either superfluous or hopeless   NEWMAN, J, 6
convalescence   For Lawrence, existence was one long c.
    LAWRENCE, D, 2
convenient   Nobody is forgotten when it is c. to remember him
    DISRAELI, 36
convent   C. of the Sacred Heart   ELIOT, T, 22
To enter the . . . Ballet is to enter a c.   PAVLOVA, 1
convention   c. which says you must not make species extinct
    PHILIP, PRINCE, 4
conventional   The c. army loses if it does not win   KISSINGER, 1
conventionally   to fail c.   KEYNES, 5
conversation   a c. with the finest men   DESCARTES, 2
And third-rate c.   PLOMER, 2
a proper subject of c.   CHESTERFIELD, 19
C. has a kind of charm   SENECA, 2
c. must be an exchange of thought   POST, 1
make his c. perfectly delightful   SMITH, SYDNEY, 11
Questioning is not the mode of c.   JOHNSON, S, 103
There is no such thing as c.   WEST, R, 5
Writing . . . is but a different name for c.   STERNE, 7
Your ignorance cramps my c.   HOPE, 1
conversationalist   the c. who adds 'in other words'   MORLEY, R, 1
converted   difficult for a Jew to be c.   HEINE, 4
conviction   The best lack all c.   YEATS, 28
convince   They will conquer, but . . . not c.   UNAMUNO Y JUGO, 4
cook   a good c., as cooks go   SAKI, 16
Any c. should be able to   LENIN, 7
C. is a little unnerved   BETJEMAN, 6
ill c. that cannot lick his own fingers   SHAKESPEARE, 317
she was a very bad c.   THIERS, 3
cookery   c. do   MEREDITH, G, 2
cooking   woman accepted c. . . . but man . . . made of it a
   recreation   POST, 2
cooks   Too many c.   PROVERBS, 440
Coolidge   C. is a better example of evolution   ROGERS, W, 6
copier   c. of nature can never produce anything great
    REYNOLDS, J, 2
copies   more c. of my works are left behind   BENCHLEY, 3
copulation   Birth, and c., and death   ELIOT, T, 21
copy   A lotta cats copy the Mona Lisa   ARMSTRONG, L, 1
copying   by defying their parents and c. one another   CRISP, 2
coral   C. is far more red   SHAKESPEARE, 371
Of his bones are c. made   SHAKESPEARE, 321
cord   a threefold c. is not quickly broken   BIBLE, 70
cordial   gold in phisik is a c.   CHAUCER, 11
cordiale   La c. entente   LOUIS PHILIPPE, 1
corn   amid the alien c.   KEATS, 39
That ate the c.   NURSERY RHYMES, 62
the meadows rich with c.   WHITTIER, 1
Whoever could make two ears of c. . . . grow . . . where only one
   grew before   SWIFT, 8
corner   a c. in the thing I love   SHAKESPEARE, 284
some c. of a foreign field   BROOKE, 6
corners   people standing in the c. of our rooms   COREN, 6
Cornish   twenty thousand C. men   HAWKER, 1
Coromandel   On the Coast of C.   LEAR, 2
coronets   Kind hearts are more than c.   TENNYSON, 40
corpse   He'd make a lovely c.   DICKENS, 29
he makes a very handsome c.   GOLDSMITH, 17
the c. at every funeral   ROOSEVELT, T, 2
the sort of greeting a c. would give to an undertaker
    BALDWIN, S, 5
corpses   They are for prima donnas or c.   TOSCANINI, 1
corpuscles   make the c. of the blood glow   LAWRENCE, D, 14
correct   Astronomy teaches the c. use   LEACOCK, 5
correction   It is a stupidity . . . to busy oneself with the c. of the
   world   MOLIÈRE, 6
correctly   anxious to do the wrong thing c.   SAKI, 20
corridors   c. of power   SNOW, 2
corroboration   c. . . . in the records of Somerset House
    BIRKENHEAD, 1

corrupt Among a people generally c. BURKE, E, 22
power is apt to c. PITT THE ELDER, 3
Power tends to c. ACTON, 2
corrupted one whom fame has not c. CURIE, 2
They had been c. by money GREENE, 6
corruptible born again, not of c. seed BIBLE, 440
corruption C., the most infallible symptom of constitutional liberty GIBBON, 9
I have said to c., thou art my father BIBLE, 232
corrupts Power c. STEVENSON, A, 3
Socrates is a doer of evil, who c. the youth SOCRATES, 3
corse As his c. to the rampart WOLFE, C, 1
cosmetics In the factory we make c. REVSON, 1
cosmopolitan I was told I am a true c. VIZINCZEY, 3
cosmos c. is about the smallest hole CHESTERTON, 30
cost To give and not to count the c. LOYOLA, 1
Too caustic? To hell with c. GOLDWYN, 3
cottage Love and a c. COLMAN, THE ELDER, 1
poorest man may in his c. bid defiance to . . . the Crown PITT THE ELDER, 1
to refer to your friend's country establishment as a 'c.' POTTER, S, 3
cottages Pale Death kicks his way equally into the c. of the poor and the castles of kings HORACE, 27
couch the century of the psychiatrist's c. MCLUHAN, 3
time as a tool not as a c. KENNEDY, JOHN, 6
when on my c. I lie WORDSWORTH, W, 8
cough Jeeves coughed one soft, low, gentle c. WODEHOUSE, 7
coughing The art of acting consists in keeping people from c. RICHARDSON, 1
council The grotesque chaos of a Labour c. – a *Labour* c. KINNOCK, 9
counsel C. of her country's gods COWPER, 4
sometimes c. take – and sometimes Tea POPE, 49
the c. of the ungodly PSALMS, 1
we took sweet c. together PSALMS, 34
count Don't c. your chickens AESOP, 115
If you can . . . c. your money you are not . . . rich man GETTY, 1
To give and not to c. the cost LOYOLA, 1
counted I c. them all out and I c. them all back HANRAHAN, 1
countenance the Lord lift up his c. upon thee BIBLE, 436
counter-democratic Proportional Representation . . . is fundamentally c. KINNOCK, 2
counterpoint Too much c.; what is worse, Protestant c. BEECHAM, 6
counties see the coloured c. HOUSMAN, 10
countries preferreth all c. before his own OVERBURY, 1
country absolved from all duty to his c. PEACOCK, 10
a c. diversion CONGREVE, 15
A c. governed by a despot JOHNSON, S, 122
a c. of young men EMERSON, 25
A man should know something of his own c. STERNE, 9
an honest man sent to lie abroad for . . . his c. WOTTON, 3
Anybody can be good in the c. WILDE, 52
Anyone who loves his c., follow me GARIBALDI, 1
Counsel of her c.'s gods COWPER, 4
c. from whose bourn no traveller returns SHAKESPEARE, 90
every time Hitler occupies a c. HITLER, 4
God made the c. COWPER, 22
go down into the c. WILDE, 20
good news from a far c. BIBLE, 455
Great artists have no c. MUSSET, 3
How I leave my c. PITT THE YOUNGER, 4
I have but one life to lose for my c. HALE, N, 1
I love thee still, My c. COWPER, 23
In the c. of the blind PROVERBS, 224
I vow to thee, my c. SPRING-RICE, 1
I would die for my c. KINNOCK, 12
loathe the c. CONGREVE, 15
My c., right or wrong CHESTERTON, 8
nothing good . . . in the c. HAZLITT, 13
Our c. is the world GARRISON, 1
our c., right or wrong DECATUR, 1
Patriots . . . talk of dying for their c. RUSSELL, B, 31
proud of the position of the bungalow . . . in the c. WILSON, A, 1
said things about my own c. that I . . . sweat to think of BUCHAN, 2
she is my c. still CHURCHILL, C, 2
soil of our c. is destined to be the scene of the fiercest fight MANDELA, 1
That is no c. for old men YEATS, 27
The history of every c. begins in the heart CATHER, 1

The idiot who praises . . . every c. but his own GILBERT, W, 26
The past is a foreign c. HARTLEY, 2
The undiscover'd c. SHAKESPEARE, 90
This c. . . . belongs to the people who inhabit it LINCOLN, 5
to leave his c. as good as he had found it COBBETT, 2
we can die but once to serve our c. ADDISON, 8
what was good for our c. WILSON, C, 1
When I am in the c. I wish to vegetate HAZLITT, 21
countrymen first in the hearts of his c. WASHINGTON, 1
countryside a more dreadful record of sin than . . . c. DOYLE, 8
county The sound of the English c. families WAUGH, E, 4
couple A married c. are well suited ROSTAND, J, 1
Splendid c. – slept with both BOWRA, 3
courage be strong and of a good c. BIBLE, 58
C. is the price . . . for granting peace EARHART, 2
c. to love . . . c. to suffer TROLLOPE, 5
good deal of physical c. to ride a horse LEACOCK, 8
not quite enough of the superb c. of his satire GALSWORTHY, 2
tale . . . of . . . c. of my companions SCOTT, R, 2
The Red Badge of C. CRANE, 1
three o'clock in the morning c. THOREAU, 12
Whistling aloud to bear his c. up BLAIR, R, 1
course c. of true love never did run smooth SHAKESPEARE, 257
courteous If a man be . . . c. to strangers BACON, FRANCIS, 28
courtesy C. is not dead DUHAMEL, 1
courtier Here lies a noble c. Who never kept his word ANONYMOUS, 28
courting When you are c. a nice girl EINSTEIN, 8
courts I have come to regard . . . c. . . . as a casino INGRAMS, 1
my soul hath a desire and longing to enter into the c. of the Lord PSALMS, 44
the case is still before the c. HORACE, 5
The law-c. of England are open to all men DARLING, 6
courtship C. to marriage CONGREVE, 11
covenant a c. between me and the earth BIBLE, 161
a c. with death GARRISON, 2
cover I . . . will c. thee with my hand BIBLE, 122
Never judge a c. by its book LEBOWITZ, 1
covet thou shalt not c. BIBLE, 115
cow A c. is a very good animal in the field JOHNSON, S, 156
That milked the c. with the crumpled horn NURSERY RHYMES, 4
The c. is of the bovine ilk NASH, 1
The c. jumped over the moon NURSERY RHYMES, 14
The c.'s in the corn NURSERY RHYMES, 29
Three acres and a c. COLLINGS, 1
till the c. comes home BEAUMONT, 12
Truth, Sir, is a c. JOHNSON, S, 65
Why buy a c. PROVERBS, 467
coward better to be the widow of a hero than the wife of a c. IBARRURI, 3
Conscience is a c. GOLDSMITH, 30
No c. soul is mine BRONTË, 4
None but a c. . . . has never known fear FOCH, 3
The c. does it with a kiss WILDE, 5
cowardice guilty of Noel C. DE VRIES, 3
cowardly Marriage is the only adventure open to the c. VOLTAIRE, 26
cowards C. die many times SHAKESPEARE, 146
the future . . . makes c. of us DIX, DOROTHY, 2
Thus conscience does make c. of us all SHAKESPEARE, 91
cowboy easier to get an actor to be a c. FORD, JOHN, 1
cows daring . . . to explain . . . that c. can be eaten GANDHI, I, 2
coxcomb A vain . . . c. without . . . solid talents PEPYS, 1
to hear a c. ask two hundred guineas RUSKIN, 17
coyness This c., lady, were no crime MARVELL, 5
cradle Between the c. and the grave DYER, 2
Rocked in the c. of the deep MILLARD, 1
The hand that rocks the c. WALLACE, W, 1
cradles bit the babies in the c. BROWNING, R, 42
craft the c. so long to lerne CHAUCER, 19
The life so short, the c. so long to learn HIPPOCRATES, 1
craftsmanship Skill without imagination is c. STOPPARD, 1
crafty too c. a woman to invent a new lie MAUGHAM, 7
cranny We seek . . . In every c. but the right COWPER, 21
crap Books are a load of c. LARKIN, 3
craven why and how I became . . . mistress of the Earl of C. WILSON, HARRIETTE, 1
crazy a little c. . . . like all men at sea GOLDING, 3
I was c. and . . . he was drunk GRANT, U, 2
cream coffee that's too black . . . You integrate it with c. MALCOLM X, 1

create meaninglessness of life forces man to c. his own meaning
KUBRICK, 2
My father didn't c. you to arrest me PEEL, 1
created God c. . . . the earth BIBLE, 137
man alone leaves traces of what he c. BRONOWSKI, 1
Man . . . had been c. to jab the life out of Germans SASSOON, S, 5
Thou hast c. us for Thyself AUGUSTINE OF HIPPO, 1
we cannot be c. for this sort of suffering KEATS, 71
creates he c. Gods by the dozen MONTAIGNE, 6
creation an ugly *woman* is a blot on the fair face of c.
BRONTË, C, 1
greatest week . . . since the c. NIXON, 8
Had I been present at the C. ALFONSO THE WISE, 1
The art of c. is older VOZNESENSKY, 1
creations The man who started more c. since Genesis
ROOSEVELT, F, 2
creator All right, my lord c., Don Miguel UNAMUNO Y JUGO, 1
Man . . . hasn't been a c., only a destroyer CHEKHOV, 10
creature every c. of God is good BIBLE, 508
No c. smarts . . . as a fool POPE, 17
the c. hath a purpose and its eyes are bright with it KEATS, 69
Who kills a man kills a reasonable c. MILTON, 6
creatures call these delicate c. ours SHAKESPEARE, 284
From fairest c. we desire increase SHAKESPEARE, 357
credentials no c. . . . not even . . . a certificate of birth
LLOYD GEORGE, 9
credit The way to get things done is not to mind who gets the c.
JOWETT, 6
creditors my oldest c. would hardly know me FOX, H, 1
not everyone who wishes makes c. RABELAIS, 6
credits c. would still read 'Rubinstein, God, and Piatigorsky'
HEIFETZ, 1
credulity C. is . . . the child's strength LAMB, CHARLES, 12
He combined scepticism . . . with c. POWYS, 1
creed got the better of his c. STERNE, 8
the c. of a second-rate man BAGEHOT, 9
wrought . . . the c. of creeds TENNYSON, 29
creeds So many gods, so many c. WILCOX, 43
Vain are the thousand c. BRONTË, E, 2
creep I wants to make your flesh c. DICKENS, 43
Wit that can c. POPE, 16
creepers Jeepers C. MERCER, 1
creetur lone lorn c. DICKENS, 11
crème you would have been the c. de la c. SPARK, 8
Crete The people of C. . . . make more history SAKI, 6
Cretians the C. are alway liars BIBLE, 515
cricket I do love c. – it's so very English BERNHARDT, 2
I have always looked on c. TEMPLE, W, 4
It's not in support of c. BEERBOHM, 19
the c. on the hearth MILTON, 14
where the c. sings YEATS, 18
Cricklewood Midland, bound for C. BETJEMAN, 8
cried I c. all the way to the bank LIBERACE, 1
crime all c. is due to the repressed desire for aesthetic
expression WAUGH, E, 20
Arson, after all, is an artificial c. WELLS, 12
C., like virtue, has its degrees RACINE, 4
Do you call poverty a c. SHAW, 19
If poverty is the mother of c., stupidity is its father
LABRUYÈRE, 11
man's greatest c. CALDERÓN DE LA BARCA, 1
no . . . c. so shameful as poverty FARQUHAR, 1
The atrocious c. of being a young man PITT THE ELDER, 2
the Napoleon of c. DOYLE, 11
The punishment fit the c. GILBERT, W, 29
This coyness, lady, were no c. MARVELL, 9
Treason was no C. DRYDEN, 11
worse than a c., it is a blunder BOULAY DE LA MEURTHE, 1
crimes Catholics and Communists have committed great c.
GREENE, 3
history is . . . a tableau of c. and misfortunes VOLTAIRE, 20
how many c. committed CAMUS, 7
Luther was guilty of two great c. LUTHER, 3
Oh liberty! . . . What c. are committed in thy name ROLAND, 1
cripple persons who cannot meet a c. without talking about feet
BRAMAH, 2
crippled I don't advise any one to take it up . . . unless they . . .
are c. GRANDMA MOSES, 3
crisp Deep and c. and even NEALE, 2
critic A c. is a man who TYNAN, 5
A good c. . . . narrates the adventures of his mind FRANCE, 7
c. spits on what is done HOOD, 14

Nor in the c. let the man be lost POPE, 31
the function of the c. BELL, C, 2
critical c. judgement is so exquisite FRY, C, 2
nothing if not c. SHAKESPEARE, 279
criticism A great deal of contemporary c. CHESTERTON, 4
As far as c. is concerned VORSTER, 1
c. is a letter to the public RILKE, 5
my own definition of c. ARNOLD, M, 14
People ask you for c. MAUGHAM, 12
The Stealthy School of C. ROSSETTI, D, 4
criticize don't c. What you can't understand DYLAN, 7
criticizing The pleasure of c. LA BRUYÈRE, 4
critics Asking a working writer . . . about c. HAMPTON, 5
c. all are ready made BYRON, 38
c. . . . desire our blood, not our pain NIETZSCHE, 15
The greater part of c. are parasites PRIESTLEY, 4
crocodile An appeaser is one who feeds a c. CHURCHILL, W, 70
crocodiles wisdom of the c. BACON, FRANCIS, 60
Cromwell Caesar had his Brutus – Charles the First, his C.
HENRY, P, 1
C. was a man in whom ambition had . . . suspended . . . religion
CROMWELL, O, 1
restless C. could not cease MARVELL, 3
ruins that C. knocked about a bit LLOYD, M, 3
Some C. guiltless GRAY, 6
crony government by c. ICKES, 1
crook A writer of c. stories WALLACE, E, 1
I am not a c. NIXON, 10
the symbol of a bishop is a c. DIX, DOM GREGORY, 1
crooked the c. timber of humanity KANT, 4
There was a c. man, and he walked a c. mile
NURSERY RHYMES, 57
crookedly so I started c. BLACKMORE, 1
crop watering the last year's c. ELIOT, G, 2
crops Man . . . Laid the c. low THOMAS, D, 17
cross Don't c. the bridge PROVERBS, 116
Hot c. buns! NURSERY RHYMES, 16
no c., no crown PENN, 1
The orgasm has replaced the C. MUGGERIDGE, 2
When I survey the wondrous C. WATTS, 8
cross-bow With my c. I shot COLERIDGE, S, 27
crossed a girl likes to be c. in love a little now and then
AUSTEN, 24
crossword an optimist . . . fills up his c. puzzle in ink SHORTER, 1
crow before the cock c., thou shalt deny me BIBLE, 425
sun had risen to hear him c. ELIOT, G, 3
waiting for the cock to c. HUGHES, W, 1
crowd a c. like that . . . brings a lump to my wallet WALLACH, 1
And hid his face amid a c. of stars YEATS, 34
Far from the madding c. GRAY, 7
crowds C. without company GIBBON, 4
If you can talk with c. and keep your virtue KIPLING, 17
It brings men together in c. and mobs in bar-rooms THOREAU, 7
crown c. o' the earth doth melt SHAKESPEARE, 36
no cross, no c. PENN, 1
poorest man may in his cottage bid defiance to . . . the C.
PITT THE ELDER, 1
the c. of life BIBLE, 216
The influence of the C. has increased DUNNING, 1
Uneasy lies the head that wears a c. SHAKESPEARE, 121
within the hollow c. SHAKESPEARE, 298
crucible America is God's C. ZANGWILL, 2
crucified preach Christ c. BIBLE, 24
Where the dear Lord was c. ALEXANDER, 3
you might try getting c. TALLEYRAND, 8
crucify Do you want to c. the boy GRADE, 1
cruel A c. story runs on wheels OUIDA, 4
C., but composed and bland ARNOLD, M, 8
cruellest April is the c. month ELIOT, T, 25
cruelty Fear is the parent of c. FROUDE, 3
cruise we are all on our last c. STEVENSON, R, 17
crumbs c. which fell from the rich man's table BIBLE, 333
cry don't you c. for me FOSTER, 4
I often want to c. RHYS, 2
let them . . . be soon brought to shame, that c. over me
PSALMS, 40
make 'em c. READE, 1
mother, do not c. FARMER, 1
She likes stories that make her c. SULLIVAN, 2
the c. of him that ruleth among fools BIBLE, 75
the only advantage women have over men . . . they can c.
RHYS, 2

the stones would immediately c. out	BIBLE, 337
We think caged birds sing, when indeed they c.	WEBSTER, J, 5
when we c. to Thee	WHITING, 1
crying An infant c. in the night	TENNYSON, 30
It is no use c.	PROVERBS, 229
cubic One c. foot less	BENCHLEY, 1
cuckoo the c. clock was invented . . . to give tourists something solid	COREN, 5
The c. comes in April	PROVERBS, 382
This is the weather the c. likes	HARDY, 12
cucumber A c. should be well sliced	JOHNSON, S, 161
cucumbers they are but c. after all	JOHNSON, S, 132
cui C. bono	CICERO, 5
cul-de-sac A committee is a c.	COCKS, 1
cult local c. called Christianity	HARDY, 5
What's a c.	ALTMAN, 1
cultivate c. our garden	VOLTAIRE, 9
cultivated I do not want to die . . . until I have . . . c. the seed	KOLLWITZ, 1
culture C. being a pursuit of our total perfection	ARNOLD, M, 3
C. is an instrument wielded by professors	WEIL, 1
C. is the passion for sweetness and light	ARNOLD, M, 23
C., the acquainting ourselves with the best	ARNOLD, M, 4
ladies who pursue C. in bands	WHARTON, 4
two half-cultures do not make a c.	KOESTLER, 4
Whenever I hear the word 'c.'	JOHST, 1
When I hear anyone talk of C.	GOERING, 1
You can lead a whore to c.	PARKER, D, 25
cup Ah, fill the C.	FITZGERALD, E, 12
Come, fill the C., and in the Fire of Spring	FITZGERALD, E, 3
my c. runneth over	PSALMS, 13
my c. shall be full	PSALMS, 11
tak a c. o' kindness yet	BURNS, R, 5
the c. of the vales	THOMAS, D, 28
cupboard But when she got there The c. was bare	NURSERY RHYMES, 39
Cupid wing'd C. painted blind	SHAKESPEARE, 258
cups c., That cheer but not inebriate	COWPER, 25
curates abundant shower of c.	BRONTË, C, 4
curators more philosophical than . . . c. of the museums	FRANCE, 4
cur'd C. . . . of my disease	PRIOR, 1
curds Eating her c. and whey	NURSERY RHYMES, 3
cure C. the disease	BACON, FRANCIS, 25
no c. for birth and death	SANTAYANA, 1
Show me a sane man and I will c. him for you	JUNG, 9
the c. for admiring the House of Lords	BAGEHOT, 2
There are maladies we must not seek to c.	PROUST, 10
Work is the grand c.	CARLYLE, T, 31
cured Poverty of goods is easily c.	MONTAIGNE, 10
the only disease you don't look forward to being c. of	MANKEIWICZ, 1
What can't be c.	PROVERBS, 454
curfew C. shall not ring tonight!	THORPE, R, 1
The C. tolls the knell of parting day	GRAY, 1
curiosities How these c. would be quite forgot	AUBREY, 2
curiosity C. killed the cat	PROVERBS, 104
C. will conquer fear	STEPHENS, 2
Disinterested intellectual c. . . . life blood of . . . civilisation	TREVELYAN, 1
I would rather be a brilliant memory than a c.	EAMES, 1
My c. was aroused to fever-pitch	VERNE, 1
curious Be not c. in unnecessary matters	BIBLE, 81
I am c. to see what happens . . . to one who dies unshriven	PERUGINO, 1
'That was the c. incident,' remarked . . . Holmes	DOYLE, 15
curiouser C. and c.	CARROLL, 5
curl There was a little girl Who had a little c.	MILLER, M, 1
curly C. locks, C. locks, Wilt thou be mine	NURSERY RHYMES, 8
currency I will not be a party to debasing the c.	KEYNES, 8
curse A c. is on her if she stay	TENNYSON, 44
Christianity the one great c.	NIETZSCHE, 4
c. God, and die	BIBLE, 224
She would rather light candles than c. the darkness	STEVENSON, A, 8
The c. is come upon me	TENNYSON, 46
the c. of all the human race	NAPOLEON I, 1
the c. of the present British Prime Minister	CHAMBERLAIN, N, 1
Work is the c. of the drinking classes	WILDE, 75
cursed thou art c. above all cattle	BIBLE, 151
curses C. . . . always come home to roost	SOUTHEY, 2
curst C. be the verse	POPE, 15

curtain An iron c.	CHURCHILL, W, 65
I saw it at a disadvantage – the c. was up	WINCHELL, 1
Ring down the c.	RABELAIS, 9
The Iron C.	GOEBBELS, 1
There is an iron c. across Europe	TROUBRIDGE, 1
cushion Like a c., he always bore	LLOYD GEORGE, 16
custodiet *Quis c. ipsos custodes*	JUVENAL, 5
custom A c. loathsome to the eye, hateful to the nose	JAMES I, 1
Age . . . nor c. stale her infinite virginity	WEBSTER, D, 3
C. calls me to't	SHAKESPEARE, 58
c. More honour'd in the breach than the observance	SHAKESPEARE, 75
c. stale Her infinite variety	SHAKESPEARE, 30
C., then, is the great guide of human life	HUME, D, 1
customer The c. is always right	SELFRIDGE, 1
customers When you are skinning your c.	KHRUSHCHEV, 2
cut c. to the heart	BIBLE, 5
C. your coat	PROVERBS, 105
Don't c. off your nose	PROVERBS, 117
in the evening . . . c. down	PSALMS, 49
the human pack is shuffled and c.	LODGE, 3
cuts he that c. off twenty years of life	SHAKESPEARE, 148
cutting busy driving cabs and c. hair	BURNS, G, 1
cymbal a tinkling c.	BIBLE, 38
cymbals Praise him in the c. and dances	PSALMS, 77
Cynara faithful to thee, C.	DOWSON, 1
cynicism C. is an unpleasant way of saying the truth	HELLMAN, 1
C. is humour in ill-health	WELLS, 17
no literature can outdo the c. of real life	CHEKHOV, 13

D

dad if the d. is present at the conception	ORTON, 2
They fuck you up, your mum and d.	LARKIN, 4
Daddy D. wouldn't buy me a bow-wow	TABRAR, 1
daffodils Fair d., we weep to see	HERRICK, 4
host, of golden d.	WORDSWORTH, W, 7
I never saw d. so beautiful	WORDSWORTH, D, 1
dagger d. which I see before me	SHAKESPEARE, 211
never be left holding the d.	WILSON, HAROLD, 1
dainties d. that are bred in a book	SHAKESPEARE, 196
dainty Nothing's so d. sweet	BEAUMONT, 7
Daisy D., give me your answer, do	DACRE, 1
Dalhousie Alas! Lord and Lady D. are dead	MCGONAGALL, 1
dalliance primrose path of d.	SHAKESPEARE, 72
damage nothing which might d. his career	BARRIE, 10
dame one for the d.	NURSERY RHYMES, 4
dammed Holland . . . lies so low they're only saved by being d.	HOOD, 13
damn D. braces	BLAKE, W, 28
D. the age. I'll write for antiquity	LAMB, CHARLES, 21
D. with faint praise	POPE, 14
I don't care a twopenny d.	WELLINGTON, 24
not worth a d.	WELLINGTON, 6
The public doesn't give a d.	BEECHAM, 1
damnation there would be no d.	TOURNEUR, 1
the terminal point of addiction is . . . d.	AUDEN, 7
damnations Twenty-nine distinct d.	BROWNING, R, 54
damn'd thou must be d. perpetually	MARLOWE, 1
damned a d. serious business	WELLINGTON, 7
d. good-natured friend	SHERIDAN, R, 3
d. if you do – And . . . d. if you don't	DOW, 1
if I am ever d.	HAZLITT, 1
Life is just one d. thing after another	HUBBARD, 3
Publish and be d.	WELLINGTON, 23
The public be d.. I am working for my stockholders	VANDERBILT, 1
damp Avoid d. beds and think of me	ANONYMOUS, 5
Danaos *timeo D. et dona ferentis*	VIRGIL, 9
dance d. an antic hay	MARLOWE, 7
D., d., d. little lady	COWARD, 6
I have discovered the d.	DUNCAN, 1
On with the d.	BYRON, 14
will you join the d.	CARROLL, 17
danced I've d. with a man	FARJEON, 1
dancers a perfectly ghastly season . . . for you Spanish d.	BANKHEAD, 9
dances Praise him in the cymbals and d.	PSALMS, 77
dancing And d. dogs and bears	HODGSON, 1
d. on a volcano	SALVANDY, 1
the morals of a whore, and the manners of a d. master	JOHNSON, S, 51

dandy Arnold is a d. Isaiah ARNOLD, M, 2
danger A nation is not in d. of financial disaster MELLON, 1
d. . . . lies in acting well CHURCHILL, C, 1
Euthanasia is a long, smooth-sounding word, and . . . conceals its d. BUCK, 1
I realized there was a measure of d. EARHART, 2
Oft in d., oft in woe WHITE, H, 1
Out of this nettle, d. SHAKESPEARE, 111
the only real d. that exists is man himself JUNG, 11
when we conquer without d. CORNEILLE, 2
dangerous A little learning is a d. thing POPE, 23
He thinks too much. Such men are d. SHAKESPEARE, 144
If a little knowledge is d., where is the man . . . out of danger HUXLEY, T, 8
if a little knowledge was a d. thing SHARPE, 3
Mad, bad, and d. to know LAMB, CAROLINE, 1
man is a d. creature ADAMS, A, 1
misery that may be caused by a single d. intimacy LACLOS, 1
more d. the abuse BURKE, E, 25
Napoleon is a d. man in a free country NAPOLEON I, 2
dangerously live d. NIETZSCHE, 4
dangers D. by being despised BURKE, E, 29
Daniel A D. come to judgment SHAKESPEARE, 247
brought D., and cast him into the den BIBLE, 53
Daniels I should be like a lion in a cave of savage D. WILDE, 77
Danny Deever they're hangin' D. in the mornin'. KIPLING, 12
Dante D. makes me sick VEGA CARPIO, 1
dappled Glory be to God for d. things HOPKINS, 4
dare d. to eat a peach ELIOT, T, 15
Darien Silent, upon a peak in D. KEATS, 42
daring d. to excel CHURCHILL, C, 1
Darjeeling There was an old man from D. ANONYMOUS, 91
dark A blind man in a d. room BOWEN, C, 2
children fear . . . the d. BACON, FRANCIS, 18
colours will agree in the d. BACON, FRANCIS, 57
Genuineness only thrives in the d. HUXLEY, A, 34
great leap in the d. HOBBES, 4
never to refuse a drink after d. MENCKEN, 18
O d., d., d., amid the blaze of noon MILTON, 58
slow, sure doom falls pitiless and d. RUSSELL, B, 16
The d. night of the soul JOHN OF THE CROSS, 2
they grope in the d. BIBLE, 229
Turn up the lights, I don't want to go home in the d. HENRY, O, 3
we are for the d. SHAKESPEARE, 37
What in me is d. Illumine MILTON, 31
darken never d. my towels again MARX, G, 8
darkest The d. hour PROVERBS, 383
darkling as on a d. plain ARNOLD, M, 11
D. I listen KEATS, 40
darkly through a glass, d. BIBLE, 38
darkness Before us pass'd the door of D. FITZGERALD, E, 17
cast away the works of d. BOOK OF COMMON PRAYER, 4
d. was upon the face of the deep BIBLE, 137
fool walketh in d. BIBLE, 66
God shall make my d. to be light PSALMS, 7
Lighten our d. BOOK OF COMMON PRAYER, 9
men loved d. . . . because their deeds were evil BIBLE, 246
outer d. BIBLE, 381
She would rather light candles than curse the d. STEVENSON, A, 8
The d. falls at Thy behest ELLERTON, 1
the d. inside houses DELANEY, 1
the people that walked in d. BIBLE, 200
the pestilence that walketh in d. PSALMS, 51
we wrestle . . . against the rulers of the d. BIBLE, 96
darlin' he's a d. man O'CASEY, 2
darling Charlie is my d. NAIRNE, 2
d. of the Gods was born MARVELL, 7
Thrice welcome, d. of the spring WORDSWORTH, W, 74
darn A hole is the accident . . . a d. is . . . poverty SHUTER, 1
Darwin D. was to the nineteenth DARWIN, C R, 2
dates Its history d. from today WHISTLER, 2
daughter as is the mother, so is her d. BIBLE, 125
d. of Earth and Water SHELLEY, 6
Don't put your d. on the stage COWARD, 8
Dwelt a miner, Forty-niner, And his d., Clementine MONTROSE, 1
I always remember that I am Caesar's d. JULIA, 2
My d.! O my ducats SHAKESPEARE, 243
skipper had taken his little d. LONGFELLOW, 18
daughters old cemetery in which nine of his d. were lying THURBER, 7
Words are men's d. MADDEN, 1
dauntless faithful in love, . . . d. in war SCOTT, WALTER, 15

David D. Copperfield kind of crap SALINGER, 1
D. his ten thousands BIBLE, 481
Once in royal D.'s city ALEXANDER, 2
Davy Sir Humphry D. Abominated gravy BENTLEY, E, 4
dawn a grey d. breaking MASEFIELD, 5
Bliss was it in that d. to be alive WORDSWORTH, W, 40
the dappled d. doth rise MILTON, 17
They sighed for the d. and thee TENNYSON, 57
dawned each day that has d. is your last HORACE, 18
day As I was saying the other d. LÉON, 1
compare thee to a summer's d. SHAKESPEARE, 358
count as profit every d. that Fate allows you HORACE, 29
death will have his d. SHAKESPEARE, 297
drinking it for sixty-five years and I am not d. yet VOLTAIRE, 35
each d. is like a year WILDE, 9
each d. that has dawned is your last HORACE, 18
every dog has his d. BORROW, 3
from this d. forward BOOK OF COMMON PRAYER, 27
God called the light D. BIBLE, 137
Good morning to the d.: and, next, my gold JONSON, 14
If every d. in the life of a school LEACOCK, 1
I look upon every d. to be lost JOHNSON, S, 154
in the d. of judgement BOOK OF COMMON PRAYER, 18
It takes place every d. CAMUS, 9
It was such a lovely d. MAUGHAM, 16
let the d. perish wherein I was born BIBLE, 225
live murmur of a summer's d. ARNOLD, M, 35
Live this d., as . . . thy last KEN, 2
long d.'s task is done SHAKESPEARE, 34
Night and d. PORTER, C, 4
Now the d. is over BARING-GOULD, 1
one d. in thy courts is better than a thousand PSALMS, 45
Our little systems have their d. TENNYSON, 26
Seize the d. HORACE, 32
So foul and fair a d. SHAKESPEARE, 201
spend a single d. really well KEMPIS, 5
Stay, stay, Until the hasting d. Has run HERRICK, 4
Sweet d., so cool, so calm HERBERT, G, 9
That fellow would vulgarize the d. of judgment JERROLD, 3
the arrow that flieth by d. PSALMS, 51
The better the d. PROVERBS, 381
The bright d. is done SHAKESPEARE, 37
The d. begins to droop BRIDGES, 3
the d. I was meant not to see THATCHER, M, 22
the d. returns too soon BYRON, 42
the twenty-four hour d. BEERBOHM, 6
thou knowest not what a d. may bring forth BIBLE, 457
when the d. of Pentecost was fully come BIBLE, 2
Without all hope of d. MILTON, 58
daylight a rule never to drink by d. MENCKEN, 18
Dayrolles Give D. a chair CHESTERFIELD, 23
days D. and moments quickly flying CASWALL, 1
D. off TRACY, 2
d. of man are but as grass PSALMS, 58
d. of wine and roses DOWSON, 4
Do not let us speak of darker d. CHURCHILL, W, 58
Shuts up the story of our d. RALEIGH, W, 3
Sweet childish d. WORDSWORTH, W, 71
the d. of our age are threescore years and ten PSALMS, 50
Thirty d. hath November GRAFTON, 1
dead Add: 'provided he is really d.' LA BRUYÈRE, 12
A master is d. BRAHMS, 2
And what was d. was Hope WILDE, 7
A statesman is a politician who's been d. TRUMAN, 5
But he's just as d. as if he'd been wrong ANONYMOUS, 102
Come not, when I am d. TENNYSON, 11
D.! and . . . never called me mother WOOD, 1
d., but in the Elysian fields DISRAELI, 41
D. men tell no tales PROVERBS, 106
Either he's d. or my watch has stopped MARX, G, 5
England mourns for her d. across the sea BINYON, 2
Fifteen men on the d. man's chest STEVENSON, R, 8
forgotten, as a d. man out of mind PSALMS, 20
for those who like it better d. MACAULAY, R, 6
God is d. NIETZSCHE, 5
great deal to be said for being d. BENTLEY, E, 3
Here lies Fred, Who was alive and is d. ANONYMOUS, 30
He was a great patriot . . . provided . . . that he really is d. VOLTAIRE, 36
if I am d. he would like to see me HOLLAND, 1
If the d. talk to you, you are a spiritualist SZASZ, 8
It does not then concern either the living or the d. EPICURUS, 2

I've just read that I am d.   KIPLING, 32
I wouldn't believe Hitler was d.   HITLER, 6
let the d. bury their d.   BIBLE, 382
more to say when I am d.   ROBINSON, E., 1
most of 'em d.   SASSOON, S., 4
Mother is the d. heart of the family   GREER, 2
move in a world of the d.   FORSTER, 1
My husband is d.   MARX, G., 7
Nobody heard him, the d. man   SMITH, STEVIE, 2
Now he is d.   ARNOLD, M., 30
Now I'm d. in the grave with my lips moving   MANDELSTAM, 2
O pity the d. that are d.   LAWRENCE, D., 10
Over my d. body   KAUFMAN, 1
Queen Anne's d.   COLMAN, THE YOUNGER, 2
she was d.; but my father he kept ladling gin   SHAW, 37
The d. don't die   LAWRENCE, D., 44
The d. . . . look on and help   LAWRENCE, D., 44
The d. Only are pleased to be alone   FULLER, ROY, 1
the d. shall be raised incorruptible   BIBLE, 42
the d. shall hear the voice of the Son of God   BIBLE, 248
The noble living and the noble d.   WORDSWORTH, W., 43
The novel being d.   VIDAL, 1
The only completely consistent people are the d.   HUXLEY, A., 14
The only good Indians I ever saw were d.   SHERIDAN, P., 1
The past is the only d. thing   THOMAS, E., 2
the people we should have been seen d. with   WEST, R., 7
To one d. deathless hour   ROSSETTI, D., 1
to resuscitate the d. art Of poetry   POUND, 12
to the d. we owe only truth   VOLTAIRE, 24
we are all d.   KEYNES, 1
we survive amongst the d. and the dying as on a battlefield   SPARK, 5
When I am d., and laid in grave   ANONYMOUS, 106
When I am d., my dearest   ROSSETTI, C., 8
who quoted d. languages   TREE, 5
deadener Habit is a great d.   BECKETT, 6
deadly Soap and education . . . are more d.   TWAIN, 5
the female of the species is more d. than the male   KIPLING, 9
deaf Historians are like d.   TOLSTOY, L., 15
union of a d. man to a blind woman   COLERIDGE, S., 22
deal a new d. for the American people   ROOSEVELT, F., 9
Dean no dogma, no D.   DISRAELI, 35
the queer old D.   SPOONER, 4
dear D. 338171   COWARD, 23
that bread should be so d.   HOOD, 12
dearer d. still is truth   ARISTOTLE, 10
met with anything that was d. to anyone than his own self   BUDDHA, 2
death a covenant with d.   GARRISON, 2
added a new terror to d.   WETHERELL, 1
added another terror to d.   LYNDHURST, 1
After the first d., there is no other   THOMAS, D., 16
After your d. you will be   SCHOPENHAUER, 7
Angel of D. has been abroad   BRIGHT, 1
Any man's d. diminishes me   DONNE, 8
a Reaper whose name is D.   LONGFELLOW, 11
a remedy for everything except d.   CERVANTES, 12
artist is in danger of d.   HEMINGWAY, 4
A single d. is a tragedy   STALIN, 6
a tie that only d. can sever   MAUGHAM, 6
A useless life is an early d.   GOETHE, 5
Because I could not stop for D.   DICKINSON, 1
Birth, and copulation, and d.   ELIOT, T., 21
Christianity has made of d. a terror   OUIDA, 1
d. after life does greatly please   SPENSER, 1
D. and taxes and childbirth   MITCHELL, M., 3
D. be not proud   DONNE, 14
D. cometh soon or late   MACAULAY, T., 11
D. defies the doctor   PROVERBS, 107
D. destroys a man   FORSTER, 8
D. hath so many doors   FLETCHER, 1
D. is my neighbour now   EVANS, E., 2
D. is still working like a mole   HERBERT, G., 5
D. is the great leveller   PROVERBS, 108
D. is the veil   SHELLEY, 22
d. itself must be . . . a mockery   SHELLEY, 23
d. looked lovely in her lovely face   PETRARCH, 2
d. of Little Nell without laughing   WILDE, 64
d. shall have no dominion   THOMAS, D., 3
d.'s own hand is warmer than my own   MAUGHAM, 27
d. . . . the least of all evils   BACON, FRANCIS, 6
d., the most terrifying of ills   EPICURUS, 2

D. took him by the heart   OWEN, W., 2
D. was absorbing   LEE, L., 2
D. was but A scientific fact   WILDE, 6
D. . . . we haven't succeeded in . . . vulgarizing   HUXLEY, A., 17
D. will disprove you   TURGENEV, 3
d. will have his day   SHAKESPEARE, 297
Do not suppose that I do not fear d.   JENNINGS, E., 1
dread of something after d.   SHAKESPEARE, 90
enormously improved by d.   SAKI, 4
give me liberty or give me d.   HENRY, P., 2
Go and try to disprove d.   TURGENEV, 3
Growth is a greater mystery than d.   MAILER, 3
half in love with easeful D.   KEATS, 40
He has seen too much d.   PLATH, 2
He who pretends to look on d. without fear lies   ROUSSEAU, 2
His d., which happen'd in his berth   HOOD, 5
I am able to follow my own d. step by step   JOHN XXIII, 1
I am become d., the destroyer of worlds   OPPENHEIMER, 3
I am disappointed by that stroke of d.   JOHNSON, S., 21
I am signing my d. warrant   COLLINS, MICHAEL, 1
Ideal mankind would abolish d.   LAWRENCE, D., 23
I do really think that d. will be marvellous   SMITH, STEVIE, 5
I here importune d. awhile   SHAKESPEARE, 35
in their d. they were not divided   BIBLE, 482
In the midst of life we are in d.   BOOK OF COMMON PRAYER, 3
Into the jaws of D.   TENNYSON, 10
Into the valley of D.   TENNYSON, 10
I prepare for a journey . . . as though for d.   MANSFIELD, K., 2
I shall but love thee better after d.   BROWNING, E., 4
it is not d., but dying, which is terrible   FIELDING, 1
it may be so the moment after d.   HAWTHORNE, 1
I've been accused of every d.   CAPONE, 1
I wanted to be bored to d.   DE VRIES, 4
man fears . . . only the stroke of d.   BACON, FRANCIS, 2
Many men would take the d.-sentence   LAWRENCE, T., 6
Men fear d.   BACON, FRANCIS, 18
no cure for birth and d.   SANTAYANA, 11
no drinking after d.   FLETCHER, 1
nothing is certain but d. and taxes   FRANKLIN, 17
O d., where is thy sting   BIBLE, 42; POPE, 46
O D., where is thy sting-a-ling-a-ling   ANONYMOUS, 65
one of those unfortunates to whom d. is   LEWIS, D., 1
one that had been studied in his d.   SHAKESPEARE, 204
Pale D. kicks his way equally   HORACE, 27
passed from d. unto life   BIBLE, 248
Railing at life, and yet afraid of d.   CHURCHILL, C., 4
Reports of my d. are greatly exaggerated   TWAIN, 18
sad stories of the d. of kings   SHAKESPEARE, 298
sentenced to d. in my absence   BEHAN, 2
Sickness, sin and d. . . . do not originate in God   EDDY, 4
Sin brought d.   EDDY, 5
Sleeping as quiet as d.   THOMAS, D., 20
Sleep is good, d. is better   HEINE, 2
Sleep . . . knows not D.   TENNYSON, 32
snares of d. compassed me round   PSALMS, 65
Soldiers are citizens of d.'s grey land   SASSOON, S., 3
Swarm over, D.   BETJEMAN, 10
that . . . turneth the shadow of d. into the morning   BIBLE, 18
the idea of d. as an individual   KOESTLER, 2
the land of the shadow of d.   BIBLE, 200
there's always d.   NAPOLEON I, 12
the struggle against d.   HESSE, 3
the valley of the shadow of d.   PSALMS, 21
this is d., and the sole d.   BROWNING, R., 20
this may be play to you, 'tis d. to us   L'ESTRANGE, 2
Thou wast not born for d.   KEATS, 39
till d. us do part   BOOK OF COMMON PRAYER, 27
Time flies, d. urges   YOUNG, 2
to abolish the d. penalty   KARR, 2
tragedies are finished by a d.   BYRON, 22
valiant never taste of d. but once   SHAKESPEARE, 146
way to dusty d.   SHAKESPEARE, 225
we all contain failure and d. within us   MAILER, 1
we owe God a d.   SHAKESPEARE, 123
what a man still plans . . . shows the . . . injustice in his d.   CANETTI, 2
When Byron's eyes were shut in d.   ARNOLD, M., 1
who fears dishonour more than d.   HORACE, 43
worse than d.   COWPER, 8
deaths Any amusing d.   BOWRA, 2
it is chiefly our own d. that we mourn for   BRENAN, 1
debasing I will not be a party to d. the currency   KEYNES, 8

debate   I love argument, I love d.   THATCHER, M, 7
debauch   a man may d. his friend's wife   BOSWELL, 2
debauchee   *D.*, n. One who has . . . pursued pleasure   BIERCE, 5
debt   A promise made is a d. unpaid   SERVICE, 1
d. which cancels all others   COLTON, 5
Out of d.   PROVERBS, 332
The nations which have put mankind and posterity most in their
d.   INGE, 12
debtor   Not everyone is a d.   RABELAIS, 6
debts   He that dies pays all d.   SHAKESPEARE, 324
decade   fun to be in the same d.   ROOSEVELT, F, 4
decadence   The difference between our d. and the Russians'
THURBER, 13
decades   D. have a delusive edge   MACAULAY, R, 2
decay   as short a Spring; As quick a growth to meet d.
HERRICK, 4
Macmillan seemed . . . to embody the national d.   MUGGERIDGE, 3
Time drops in d.   YEATS, 21
woods d. and fall   TENNYSON, 75
deceit   love we swore . . . seems d.   DAY LEWIS, 1
philosophy and vain d.   BIBLE, 19
temper discretion with d.   WAUGH, E, 6
Where rumour of oppression and d.   COWPER, 27
deceitfulness   a Cat of such d.   ELIOT, T, 16
deceive   if we say that we have no sin, we d.   BIBLE, 281
Oh, don't d. me; Oh, never leave me   ANONYMOUS, 16
To d. oneself   PROVERBS, 436
deceived   take heed . . . that your heart be not d.   BIBLE, 55
deceiving   Propaganda . . . consists in nearly d. your friends
CORNFORD, 2
without quite d. your enemies   CORNFORD, 2
decent   d. means poor   PEACOCK, 1
Every man's house will be fair and d.   MORRIS, W, 4
riff-raff apply to what is respectable . . . aristocracy to what is d.
HOPE, 6
the only d. thing . . . is to die at once   BUTLER, S, 28
decision   he is going to make 'a realistic d.' . . . resolved to do
something bad   MCCARTHY, M, 1
if usage so choose, with whom resides the d.   HORACE, 4
decisive   Marriage is a step so grave and d.   STEVENSON, R, 23
declaim   Nay, Madam, when you are declaiming, d.
JOHNSON, S, 112
declaration   D. of Independence . . . no relation to half of the
human race   MARTINEAU, 6
declare   they should d. the causes which impel them to . . .
separation   JEFFERSON, 4
declining   pass my d. years saluting strange women and
grandfather clocks   NASH, 9
decomposing   d. in the eternity of print   WOOLF, 3
decorated   proverb . . . much matter d.   FULLER, T, 2
decorum   *Dulce et d. est*   HORACE, 34
Let them cant about d.   BURNS, R, 13
decrepit   He is . . . d. and forgetful . . . a bore   BELLOC, 2
you are not yet d. enough   ELIOT, T, 28
decussated   Anything reticulated or d. at equal distances
JOHNSON, S, 11
dedicated   never d. to something you have complete confidence in
PIRSIG, 1
Dee   Across the sands of D.   KINGSLEY, 4
deed   a good d. to forget a poor joke   BRACKEN, 1
good d. in a naughty world   SHAKESPEARE, 252
right d. for the wrong reason   ELIOT, T, 18
The better day, the worse d.   HENRY, M, 1
deeds   better d. shall be in water writ   BEAUMONT, 8
Don't listen to their words, fix your attention on their d.
EINSTEIN, 5
Foul d. will rise   SHAKESPEARE, 71
means to do ill d.   SHAKESPEARE, 166
deep   beauty is only sin d.   SAKI, 21
D. and crisp and even   NEALE, 2
Rocked in the cradle of the d.   MILLARD, 1
what a very singularly d. young man   GILBERT, W, 35
deeper   d. than did ever plummet sound   SHAKESPEARE, 326
whelm'd in d. gulphs   COWPER, 6
deeth   D. is an ende of every worldly sore   CHAUCER, 10
defeat   a d. without a war   CHURCHILL, W, 47
d. is an orphan   KENNEDY, JOHN, 18
D. of Germany means   ROOSEVELT, F, 6
every victory turns into a d.   BEAUVOIR, 1
In d. unbeatable   CHURCHILL, W, 33
The greatest tragedy . . . except a d.   WELLINGTON, 13

defeated   Like an army d. The snow hath retreated
WORDSWORTH, W, 77
man can be destroyed . . . not d.   HEMINGWAY, 7
No general in the midst of battle has a great discussion . . . if d.
OWEN, D, 2
defect   Chief D. of Henry King   BELLOC, 5
defence   Never make a d. or apology   CHARLES I, 1
The best immediate d. of the United States   ROOSEVELT, F, 7
the d. of England   BALDWIN, S, 6
The only d. is in offence   BALDWIN, S, 4
defend   D., O Lord, this thy Child   BOOK OF COMMON PRAYER, 20
will d. to the death your right to say it   VOLTAIRE, 39
defiance   in defeat,   CHURCHILL, W, 27
poorest man may in his cottage bid d. to . . . the Crown
PITT THE ELDER, 1
The d. of established authority   ARENDT, 1
defied   Age will not be d.   BACON, FRANCIS, 42
defining   Language is . . . a d. framework   WHORF, 1
definite   a d. maybe   GOLDWYN, 14
definition   This d. . . . would not do for a policeman
NIGHTINGALE, 2
deflowered   At last you are d.   COWARD, 25
defying   by d. their parents and copying one another   CRISP, 2
degenerates   everything d. in the hands of man   ROUSSEAU, 3
degeneration   fatty d. of his moral being   STEVENSON, R, 24
degradation   a . . . sense of intellectual d. after an interview with
a doctor   JAMES, A, 3
degree   d. of delight   BURKE, E, 6
when d. is shak'd   SHAKESPEARE, 329
degrees   Crime, like virtue, has its d.   RACINE, 4
We boil at different d.   EMERSON, 24
dei   *Vox populi, vox d.*   ALCUIN, 1
deid   Gey few, and they're a' d.   ANONYMOUS, 36
deities   the d. so kindly   RABELAIS, 5
Deity   to distinguish between the D. and the Drains
STRACHEY, L, 1
deleted   D. by French censor   BENNETT, J, 1
deliberate   with a slow d. carelessness   LAWRENCE, T, 9
deliberates   woman that d. is lost   ADDISON, 6
deliberation   D. is the work of many men   DE GAULLE, 4
delicacy   the talent of flattering with d.   AUSTEN, 22
delight   a degree of d.   BURKE, E, 6
Commodity, Firmness, and *D.*   WOTTON, 1
Energy is Eternal D.   BLAKE, W, 32
go to't with d.   SHAKESPEARE, 33
his d. is in the law of the Lord   PSALMS, 1
Studies serve for d.   BACON, FRANCIS, 49
Teach us d. in simple things   KIPLING, 5
The leaping light for your d. discovers   AUDEN, 19
very temple of d.   KEATS, 34
wept with d. when you gave her a smile   ENGLISH, 1
delighted   Whosoever is d. in solitude   BACON, FRANCIS, 24
You have d. us long enough   AUSTEN, 23
delightful   make his conversation perfectly d.   SMITH, SYDNEY, 11
What a d. thing this perspective is   UCCELLO, 1
delights   Man d. not me   SHAKESPEARE, 84
deliver   d. me from myself   BROWNE, T, 9
delivered   thou hast d. my soul from death   PSALMS, 35
delivers   the Man Who D. the Goods   MASON, 1
deluge   After us the d.   POMPADOUR, 1
déluge   *Après nous le d.*   POMPADOUR, 1
delusion   nation is a society united by a d. about its ancestry
INGE, 10
delusions   Many people have d. of grandeur   IONESCO, 1
delusive   Decades have a d. edge   MACAULAY, R, 2
delved   When Adam d.   BALL, 1
demagogues   the vilest specimens . . . found among d.
MACAULAY, T, 10
demands   the populace cannot exact their d.   WELLINGTON, 14
democracy   arsenal of d.   ROOSEVELT, F, 13
D. . . . government by the uneducated   CHESTERTON, 43
D. is only an experiment in government   INGE, 7
D. means government by discussion   ATTLEE, 1
D. passes into despotism   PLATO, 5
D. resumed her reign   BELLOC, 9
extreme d. or absolute oligarchy, or despotism will come
ARISTOTLE, 8
In Switzerland . . . five hundred years of d. and peace   WELLES, 1
Man's capacity for evil makes d. necessary   NIEBUHR, 1
they which find themselves grieved under a d., call it *anarchy*
HOBBES, 6
world . . . made safe for d.   WILSON, W, 11

democratic a d. and free society in which all persons live together in harmony — MANDELA, 3
demon woman wailing for her d.-lover — COLERIDGE, S, 16
demons thanks to words, we have often sunk to the level of the d. — HUXLEY, A, 3
demure Being surrounded by d., black-stockinged creatures does not induce academic calm — CAREY, J, 2
den a d. of thieves — BIBLE, 408
denial the highest praise of God consists in the d. of Him — PROUST, 8
denies spirit that always d. — GOETHE, 4
Denmark rotten in the state of D. — SHAKESPEARE, 76
denounce We thus d. . . . the arms race — JOHN PAUL II, 2
dentist fuss about sleeping together . . . sooner go to my d. — WAUGH, E, 44
  like going to the d. — WILDER, B, 2
dentists I have let d. ride roughshod over my teeth — PERELMAN, 1
  Our gratitude to most benefactors is the same as . . . for d. — CHAMFORT, 3
  The thought of d. gave him just the same sick horror — WELLS, 8
deny before the cock crow, thou shalt d. me thrice — BIBLE, 425
  let him d. himself — BIBLE, 398
  Those who d. freedom — LINCOLN, 12
depart D. . . . and let us have done with you — AMERY, 2
  lettest thou thy servant d. in peace — BIBLE, 317
  when the great and good d. — WORDSWORTH, W, 15
departure the time of my d. is at hand — BIBLE, 514
depends It all d. upon that article there — WELLINGTON, 3
depraved No one . . . suddenly became d. — JUVENAL, 2
depression we went through . . . the Great D. without missing a meal — ASIMOV, 1
depth out of your d. — TEMPLE, W, 3
derangement a nice d. of epitaphs — SHERIDAN, R, 9
derision Ambition, Distraction, Uglification, and D. — CARROLL, 15
descend Never d. to the ways of those above you — MALLABY, 1
description beggar'd all d. — SHAKESPEARE, 29
descriptions d. of the fairest wights — SHAKESPEARE, 367
desert The sand of the d. is sodden red — NEWBOLT, 7
  Use every man after his d. — SHAKESPEARE, 87
deserts D. of vast eternity — MARVELL, 10
deserve I have arthritis, and I don't d. that either — BENNY, 1
deserved I wasn't lucky. I d. it — THATCHER, M, 25
deserves At 50, everyone has the face he d. — ORWELL, 36
  the government it d. — MAISTRE, 1
designing I am d. St Paul's — BENTLEY, E, 6
desire antidote to d. — CONGREVE, 17
  a universal innate d. — BUTLER, S, 11
  d. is got without content — SHAKESPEARE, 215
  D. is the very essence of man — SPINOZA, 4
  d. should so many years outlive performance — SHAKESPEARE, 120
  d. to be praised twice over — ROCHEFOUCAULD, 18
  I am my beloved's, and his d. is toward me — BIBLE, 499
  is yet also consumed with this d. — KEATS, 1
  It provokes the d. — SHAKESPEARE, 213
  my soul hath a d. — PSALMS, 44
  nothing like d. for preventing the thing one says — PROUST, 13
  not really d. the things they failed to obtain — MAUROIS, 1
  The D. of Man being Infinite — BLAKE, W, 50
  Those who restrain D. — BLAKE, W, 30
  to have few things to d. — BACON, FRANCIS, 21
  to lose your heart's d. — SHAW, 24
desired more to be d. . . . than gold — PSALMS, 9
  war which . . . left nothing to be d. — BRECHT, 7
desires He who d. but acts not — BLAKE, W, 26
  him who d. his own advantage not harm another — BUDDHA, 2
  made young with young d. — THOMPSON, F, 3
  Man's D. are limited by his Perceptions — BLAKE, W, 49
  Strong enough to answer back to d., to despise distinctions — HORACE, 47
  than nurse unacted d. — BLAKE, W, 21
desireth like as the hart d. the water-brooks — PSALMS, 34
desiring pessimists end up by d. the things they fear — MALLET, 1
desist to d. from the experiment in despair — LAMB, CHARLES, 6
desk what risks you take . . . to find money in a d. — BALZAC, 4
desks Stick . . . to your d. and never go to sea — GILBERT, W, 11
desolate d. and sick of an old passion — DOWSON, 3
despair carrion comfort, D., not feast on thee — HOPKINS, 1
  Don't d., not even over . . . d. — KAFKA, 1
  Look on my works, ye Mighty, and d. — SHELLEY, 17
  Patience, n. A minor form of d. — BIERCE, 9
  some divine d. — TENNYSON, 62
  to desist from the experiment in d. — LAMB, CHARLES, 6

despairs He who d. over an event is a coward — CAMUS, 16
desperate D. cuts — PROVERBS, 109
desperation lives of quiet d. — THOREAU, 9
despise I d. Shakespeare — SHAW, 11
  some other Englishman d. him — SHAW, 36
despised A poor man is d. the whole world over — JEROME, 3
  d. by a street boy — HUXLEY, T, 5
despises A woman d. a man for loving her — STODDARD, 1
despond name of the slough was D. — BUNYAN, 2
despot A country governed by a d. — JOHNSON, S, 122
despotism Democracy passes into d. — PLATO, 5
  extreme democracy or absolute oligarchy, or d. will come — ARISTOTLE, 8
  France was a long d. — CARLYLE, T, 14
destination I do not think this poem will reach its d. — VOLTAIRE, 37
destiny I were walking with d. — CHURCHILL, W, 13
  Riddle of d. — LAMB, CHARLES, 20
destroy Doth the wingèd life d. — BLAKE, W, 15
  He would like to d. his old diaries — TOLSTOY, S, 3
  sought to d. institutions — WHITMAN, 4
  they shall not hurt nor d. in all my holy mountain — BIBLE, 203
  whom God wishes to d. — EURIPIDES, 1
  Whom God would d. — DUPORT, 1
  Whom the gods wish to d. — CONNOLLY, 9
destroy'd a bold peasantry . . . When once d. — GOLDSMITH, 6
destroyed man can be d. . . . not defeated — HEMINGWAY, 7
destroyer I am become death, the d. of worlds — OPPENHEIMER, 2
  Man . . . hasn't been a creator, only a d. — CHEKHOV, 10
destroying simplifying something by d. nearly everything — CHESTERTON, 5
destroys he who d. a good book, kills reason — MILTON, 6
destruction broad is the way, that leadeth to d. — BIBLE, 377
  It is time for the d. of error — AUDEN, 16
  one purpose . . . d. of Hitler — CHURCHILL, W, 14
  the d. of Hitler — HITLER, 3
detail life is frittered away by d. — THOREAU, 16
details with the thoroughness of a mind that reveres d. — LEWIS, S, 3
detective The d. novel is — PRITCHETT, 1
deterrent the d. is a phallic symbol — WIGG, 1
detest they d. at leisure — BYRON, 33
detestable He was a d. man — THOMAS, D, 2
detested D. sport — COWPER, 31
Deutschland D., D. über alles — HOFFMANN VON FALLERSLEBEN, 1
device A banner with the strange d., Excelsior — LONGFELLOW, 7
devil Abashed the D. . . . felt how awful goodness is — MILTON, 47
  cleft the D.'s foot — DONNE, 13
  D. always builds a chapel there — DEFOE, 5
  d. can cite Scripture — SHAKESPEARE, 239
  d.'s walking parody — CHESTERTON, 12
  given up believing in the d. — KNOX, R, 1
  I do not see . . . why the d. should have all the good tunes — HILL, R, 1
  nickname is the heaviest stone that the d. can throw — HAZLITT, 12
  Renounce the d. — BOOK OF COMMON PRAYER, 22
  resist the d., and he will flee — BIBLE, 218
  sacrifice . . . of the d.'s leavings — POPE, 56
  Sarcasm . . . the language of the d. — CARLYLE, T, 26
  The d. finds work — PROVERBS, 384
  The D. is a gentleman — SHELLEY, 18
  The d. is not so black — PROVERBS, 385
  the D. knows Latin — KNOX, R, 2
  The d. looks after his own — PROVERBS, 386
  the d. played at chess with me — BROWNE, T, 4
  the world, the flesh, and the d. — MURRAY, 1
  world, the flesh, and the d. — BOOK OF COMMON PRAYER, 12
devils It is no good casting out d. — LAWRENCE, D, 36
  One more d.'-triumph and sorrow for angels — BROWNING, R, 32
devoted definition of . . . a nurse . . . than . . . "d. and obedient." — NIGHTINGALE, 2
devotion The almighty dollar, that great object of universal d. — IRVING, 4
devour he shall d. the prey — BIBLE, 182
  shed tears when they would d. — BACON, FRANCIS, 60
dew his body was wet with the d. of heaven — BIBLE, 50
  Just to save her from the foggy, foggy d. — ANONYMOUS, 63
dexterity Your d. seems a happy compound — DISRAELI, 33
diagram cat is a d. and pattern of subtle air — LESSING, D, 6
dialect a d. I understand very little — PEPYS, 10
  D. words – those terrible marks of the beast — HARDY, 9

diamond D.! D.! NEWTON, I, 6
more of rough than polished d. CHESTERFIELD, 13
diamonds D. Are ROBIN, 2
My goodness those d. are lovely WEST, M, 4
to give him d. back GABOR, 3
diaries He would like to destroy his old d. TOLSTOY, S, 3
Let d., therefore BACON, FRANCIS, 55
Only good girls keep d. BANKHEAD, 13
diary I never travel without my d. WILDE, 30
What is a d. as a rule TERRY, 3
Dickens D. . . . never quite took BENNETT, ALAN, 5
D.' world is not life-like CECIL, 1
does not matter that D.' world is not life-like DICKENS, 2
dictation I did not write it. God wrote it. I merely did his d.
STOWE, 4
dictator and finally a single d. substitutes himself TROTSKY, 11
I am painted as the greatest little d. THATCHER, M, 17
dictators D. ride to and fro upon tigers CHURCHILL, W, 32
dictatorship The d. of the proletariat MARX, K, 7
dictionaries To make d. is dull work JOHNSON, S, 8
dictionary this is the first time I ever made the d. WEST, M, 19
use a word that might send the reader to the d. HEMINGWAY, 2
words never seen . . . before outside of a d. LODGE, 5
diddle Hey d. d., The cat and the fiddle NURSERY RHYMES, 14
die A man can d. PROVERBS, 43
better to d. on your feet than to live on your knees IBARRURI, 2
but to do and d. TENNYSON, 9
curse God, and d. BIBLE, 224
D. the last thing I shall do PALMERSTON, 2
D. when I may . . . I have always plucked a thistle and planted a
flower LINCOLN, 7
either do, or d. BEAUMONT, 4
Everybody has got to d., ... Now what SAROYAN, 1
expedient that one man should d. for the people BIBLE, 264
for me to d., for you to go on living SOCRATES, 6
How often are we to d. POPE, 61
I d. a Christian CHARLES I, 2
I d. because I do not d. JOHN OF THE CROSS, 1
I d. happy FOX, C, 5
I do not want to d. . . . until I have . . . cultivated the seed
KOLLWITZ, 1
If a man hasn't discovered something that he would d. for
KING, M, 3
If I should d. BROOKE, 6
I have been learning how to d. LEONARDO DA VINCI, 6
in what peace a Christian can d. ADDISON, 19
I shall be like that tree; I shall d. from the top SWIFT, 20
it is an ideal for which I am prepared to d. MANDELA, 3
It is natural to d. BACON, FRANCIS, 19
it is youth that must fight and d. HOOVER, 4
I will d. in peace WOLFE, J, 2
I will d. in the last ditch WILLIAM III, 1
I would d. for my country KINNOCK, 12
let me d. drinking in an inn MAP, 1
Let us determine to d. here BEE, 1
Let us do or d. BURNS, R, 18
let us eat and drink; for tomorrow we d. BIBLE, 40
live for ever or d. in the attempt HELLER, 2
man can d. but once SHAKESPEARE, 123
Many people would sooner d. than think RUSSELL, B, 28
Never say d. PROVERBS, 305
No young man believes he shall ever d. HAZLITT, 19
one may d. without ever laughing LA BRUYÈRE, 8
pie in the sky when you d. ALI, 4
place . . . to d. in BROWNE, T, 10
Rather suffer than d. LA FONTAINE, 1
Ring out, wild bells, and let him d. TENNYSON, 35
save your world you asked this man to d. AUDEN, 13
The dead don't d. LAWRENCE, D, 44
The d. is cast CAESAR, 3
the only decent thing . . . is to d. at once BUTLER, S, 28
those who are about to d. salute you ANONYMOUS, 9
To achieve great things we must live as though . . . never going to
d. VAUVENARGUES, 2
to d., and go we know not where SHAKESPEARE, 232
To d. will be an awfully big adventure BARRIE, 5
trains all night groan on the rail To men that d. at morn
HOUSMAN, 8
we can d. but once to serve our country ADDISON, 8
We d. – does it matter when TENNYSON, 71
when good Americans d. they go to Paris WILDE, 57
died As estimated, you d. HILL, G, 2

dog it was that d. GOLDSMITH, 11
I d. . . . of my physician PRIOR, 1
Men have d. from time to time SHAKESPEARE, 55
there were people who d. of dropsies JOHNSON, S, 160
'Tis said that some have d. for love WORDSWORTH, W, 70
What can you say about a 25-year-old girl who d. SEGAL, 1
diem *Carpe d.* HORACE, 32
dies a young person, who . . . marries or d., is sure to be kindly
spoken of AUSTEN, 7
because a man d. for it WILDE, 65
Every moment d. a man BABBAGE, 1
he d. in pain LA BRUYÈRE, 6
He that d. pays all debts SHAKESPEARE, 324
It matters not how a man d. JOHNSON, S, 78
king never d. BLACKSTONE, 2
One d. only once MOLIÈRE, 4
Whatever is begotten, born, and d. YEATS, 27
When a friend d. out on us MACNEICE, 3
whom the gods favour d. young PLAUTUS, 1
diet Food is an important part of a balanced d. LEBOWITZ, 2
diots I feel about airplanes the way I feel about d. KERR, 4
difference Because there is no d. THALES, 1
d. between . . . prose and metrical composition
WORDSWORTH, W, 18
made the d. of forty thousand men WELLINGTON, 11
more d. within the sexes than between them COMPTON-
BURNETT, 2
the d. of sex, if there is any ANTHONY, 3
differences If we cannot now end our d. KENNEDY, JOHN, 14
The Jews and Arabs should . . . settle their d. AUSTIN, W, 2
different rich are d. FITZGERALD, F S, 5
differently I would have done it d. WHISTLER, 16
differeth one star d. from another . . . in glory BIBLE, 41
difficult D. do you call it, Sir JOHNSON, S, 40
It is d. to be humble DOBRÉE, 1
It is very d. to get up resentment NEWMAN, J, 1
never let them persuade you that things are too d. BADER, 2
When a piece gets d. SCHNABEL, 4
difficulties settle up these little local d. MACMILLAN, 6
difficulty A d. for every solution SAMUEL, 6
I feel . . . a certain d. in continuing to exist FONTENELLE, 1
digest mark, learn, and inwardly d. BOOK OF COMMON PRAYER, 7
Well, then, my stomach must just d. in its waistcoat
SHERIDAN, R, 12
digestion Things sweet to taste prove in d. sour
SHAKESPEARE, 293
digestions Few radicals have good d. BUTLER, S, 16
dignity All human beings are born free and equal in d. and rights
ANONYMOUS, 3
man is capable of a certain degree of d. CAMUS, 2
Official d. . . . in inverse ratio to . . . importance HUXLEY, A, 10
digression a prosaic d. BUCHAN, 3
dilemmas d. of conscience and egotism SNOW, 2
diligently Had I . . . served God as d. as I have served the king
WOLSEY, 1
dim my lamp burns low and d. ADAMS, F, 2
dime Brother, can you spare a d. HARBURG, 2
dimensions sickness enlarges the d. of a man's self
LAMB, CHARLES, 17
diminished ought to be d. DUNNING, 1
dimmed The eyes that shone, Now d. and gone MOORE, T, 7
dimple A d. in the chin, a devil within PROVERBS, 13
dine wretches hang that jury-men may d. POPE, 51
dined More d. against than dining BOWRA, 1
when Thomas Jefferson d. alone KENNEDY, JOHN, 12
you have d. in every house in London – *once* WILDE, 78
diners Observe d. arriving at any restaurant MORRIS, D, 2
diners-out d. from whom we guard our spoons MACAULAY, T, 19
ding D. dong, bell, Pussy's in the well NURSERY RHYMES, 9
dinkum a 'd. hard-swearing Aussie' HASKELL, 1
dinner A d. lubricates business SCOTT, WILLIAM, 1
A man is . . . better pleased when he has a good d. upon his table
JOHNSON, S, 37
Breakfast, D., Lunch and Tea BELLOC, 6
people . . . would ask him to d. CARLYLE, T, 28
This was a good d. enough JOHNSON, S, 70
dinner-table dominate a London d. WILDE, 68
diplomacy All d. is a continuation of war CHOU EN LAI, 1
diplomat A d. . . . always remembers a woman's birthday
FROST, R, 10
d. these days is nothing but a head-waiter USTINOV, 8
diplomats aged d. to be bored AUSTIN, W, 1

Dirce With D. in one boat conveyed — LANDOR, 1
direction God knows how you Protestants . . . have any sense of
  d. — WILSON, A, 3
  in which d. the car was travelling — LLOYD GEORGE, 3
directions rode madly off in all d. — LEACOCK, 10
director Every d. bites the hand — GOLDWYN, 13
  Theatre d.: a person — AGATE, 2
dirt After the first four years the d. doesn't get any worse
  — CRISP, 4
  Throw d. enough — PROVERBS, 431
dirty bathing in someone else's d. water — PROUST, 1
  Is sex d. — ALLEN, W, 1
  The permissive society has . . . become a d. phrase — JENKINS, 1
  You d. double-crossing rat — CAGNEY, 1
disadvantage d. of merely counting votes — INGE, 7
disagree Who shall decide when doctors d. — POPE, 46
disappointed I am d. by that stroke of death — JOHNSON, S, 21
disappointment Grief and d. give rise to anger — HUME, D, 7
disapprove I d. of what you say, but I will defend to the death
  your right to say it — VOLTAIRE, 39
disarmament precede the d. of the victors — CHURCHILL, W, 12
disaster audience was a d. — WILDE, 70
  meet with Triumph and D. — KIPLING, 16
disasters the middle station had the fewest d. — DEFOE, 3
  trace . . . the d. of English history to . . . Wales — WAUGH, E, 15
disbelief willing suspension of d. — COLERIDGE, S, 8
disciples d. . . . mark its ways and note . . . its mysteries
  — BRADLEY, F, 2
discomforts d. that will accompany my being blind — PEPYS, 17
discommendeth He who d. others — BROWNE, T, 1
discontent d. that goes with unemployed activies — ANDERSON, 2
  lent To youth and age . . . d. — ARNOLD, M, 46
  To be discontented with the divine d. — KINGSLEY, 2
  winter of our d. — SHAKESPEARE, 300
discontented you already have a d. work force — MORGAN, E, 2
discontents the family . . . source of all our d. — LEACH, 1
discourse their d. was about hunting — PEPYS, 10
discover not d. new lands — GIDE, 2
discovered in the morning we d. a bay — COOK, J, 1
  We have d. the secret of life — CRICK, 1
discoverers They are ill d. that think there is no land
  — BACON, FRANCIS, 3
discovery behind the d. of America — RICHLER, 2
  D. consists of seeing what everybody has seen — SZENT-GYÖRGYI, 1
  he who never made a mistake never made a d. — SMILES, 1
  Scientific d. is a private event — MEDAWAR, 1
discretion better part of valour is d. — SHAKESPEARE, 115
  temper d. with deceit — WAUGH, E, 6
  the years of d. — BOOK OF COMMON PRAYER, 19
discrimination sympathetic without d. — FIRBANK, 3
discussion D. in class, which means — NABOKOV, 4
disdains He d. all things above his reach — OVERBURY, 1
disease an incurable d. – colour blindness — DE BLANK, 2
  Consciousness is a d. — UNAMUNO Y JUGO, 2
  Cur'd . . . of my d. — PRIOR, 1
  Cure the d. — BACON, FRANCIS, 25
  desperate d. requires a dangerous remedy — FAWKES, 1
  D. is an image of thought externalized — EDDY, 5
  Evil comes . . . like the d.; good . . . like the doctor
  — CHESTERTON, 26
  if the physician had the same d. upon him that I have — SELDEN, 5
  Life is an incurable d. — COWLEY, 2
  Only those in the last stage of d. — AUDEN, 23
  remedies . . . suggested for a d. — CHEKHOV, 5
  remedy is worse than the d. — BACON, FRANCIS, 46
  strange d. of modern life — ARNOLD, M, 37
  the d. of writing books — MONTESQUIEU, 8
  the incurable d. of writing — JUVENAL, 7
  the only d. you don't look forward to being cured of
  — MANKEIWICZ, 1
  this long d., my life — POPE, 13
diseased women possess but one class of physical organs . . .
  always d. — LIVERMORE, 1
diseases Extreme remedies . . . for extreme d. — HIPPOCRATES, 2
  Hungry Joe collected lists of fatal d. — HELLER, 6
disfranchisement woman . . . feels as keenly as man the injustice
  of d. — STANTON, E, 2
disgrace a d. to our family name of Wagstaff — MARX, G, 11
disgracefully The world is d. managed — FIRBANK, 2
disguise his ability to d. charmingly the seriousness . . . of his
  work — CARROLL, 3
  virtues are . . . vices in d. — ROCHEFOUCAULD, 27

disgusting A crawling and d. parasite — VIRGIL, 1
  an ugly, affected, d. fellow — GIBBON, 1
dish And the d. ran away with the spoon — NURSERY RHYMES, 14
  a side d. he hadn't ordered — LARDNER, 1
  butter in a lordly d. — BIBLE, 293
  The national d. of America — ROBINSON, R, 1
dishes Thou shalt not wash d. — NURSERY RHYMES, 8
dishonour honour rooted in d. — TENNYSON, 17
  who fears d. more than death — HORACE, 43
disillusionments d. in the lives of the medieval saints — SAKI, 13
disinclination d. to inflict pain upon oneself — MEREDITH, G, 3
disinterested D. intellectual curiosity . . . life blood of . . .
  civilisation — TREVELYAN, 1
dislike I d. what I fancy I feel — ANONYMOUS, 90
  that *my* statue should be moved, which I should much d.
  — VICTORIA, 11
  The law of d. for the unlike — ZANGWILL, 3
disliked I have always d. myself — CONNOLLY, 12
dismal the D. Science — CARLYLE, T, 20
Disney D. the most significant figure . . . since Leonardo — LOW, 1
disobedience Of Man's first d. — MILTON, 30
disorder A sweet d. in the dress — HERRICK, 2
disposes God d. — KEMPIS, 4
dispute Many a long d. among divines — FRANKLIN, 10
disputing The itch of d. will prove the scab of churches
  — WOTTON, 2
Disraeli D. lacked two qualities — DISRAELI, 3
disreputable I've been offered titles . . . get one into d. company
  — SHAW, 44
disrespectfully Never speak d. of Society — WILDE, 33
dissipated still keep looking so d. — BENCHLEY, 2
dissipation At what time does the d. of energy begin — KELVIN, 1
  d. without pleasure — GIBBON, 4
  other things than d. . . . thicken the features — WEST, R, 1
dissolve Fade far away, d. — KEATS, 38
distance The d. doesn't matter — DEFFAND, 1
disthressful She's the most d. country that iver yet was seen
  — ANONYMOUS, 46
distinctions woman feels the invidious d. of sex — STANTON, E, 2
distinguish all there is to d. us from other animals
  — BEAUMARCHAIS, 2
distinguished a sparrow alight upon my shoulder . . . I was more
  d. by that — THOREAU, 18
  So it has come at last, the d. thing — JAMES, H, 15
  When a d. but elderly scientist states — CLARKE, A, 1
distraction Ambition, D., Uglification, and Derision — CARROLL, 15
distress All pray in their d. — BLAKE, W, 43
  the mean man is always full of d. — CONFUCIUS, 10
distrust shameful to d. one's friends — ROCHEFOUCAULD, 12
  stay together, but we d. one another — BRADBURY, 3
distrusts him who d. himself — ROCHEFOUCAULD, 11
disturb What isn't part of ourselves doesn't d. us — HESSE, 1
ditchwater Is d. dull — CHESTERTON, 37
diversion Most sorts of d. . . . are an imitation of fighting
  — SWIFT, 17
  'tis a country d. — CONGREVE, 15
diversity make the world safe for d. — KENNEDY, JOHN, 14
divide D. and rule — PROVERBS, 110
divided in their death they were not d. — BIBLE, 482
  Obstinate people can be d. into — ARISTOTLE, 3
  Thought must be d. against itself — HUXLEY, A, 15
divides Nothing d. them like Picasso — PICASSO, 1
divine a pleasant smile that it seems rather d. than human
  — LEONARDO DA VINCI, 4
  attain to the d. perfection — LONGFELLOW, 9
  The *d. right* of husbands — WOLLSTONECRAFT, 4
  The Hand that made us is d. — ADDISON, 15
  The right of d. of kings to govern wrong — POPE, 4
  To be discontented with the d. discontent — KINGSLEY, 2
  To err is human, to forgive, d. — POPE, 28
divines Many a long dispute among d. — FRANKLIN, 10
divinity a d. that shapes our ends — SHAKESPEARE, 106
  a piece of d. in us — BROWNE, T, 11
  d. in odd numbers — SHAKESPEARE, 256
  There's such d. doth hedge a king — SHAKESPEARE, 102
divisions How many d. has *he* got — STALIN, 1
divorce D.? Never. But murder often — THORNDIKE, 1
Dizzy The soul of D. was a chandelier — DISRAELI, 1
do Can I d. you now — KAVANAGH, 1
  D. as you would be done by — CHESTERFIELD, 9
  D. other men — DICKENS, 27
  d. what the mob d. — DICKENS, 44

doubting castle called D. Castle — BUNYAN, 7
doubts end in d. — BACON, FRANCIS, 2
His d. are better than . . . certainties — HARDWICKE, 1
douche the rattling of a thousand d. bags — LOWRY, 1
dove and the d. came in to him — BIBLE, 159
the Spirit of God descending like a d. — BIBLE, 355
the wings of a d. — COWPER, 33
wings like a d. — PSALMS, 33
Dove Cottage No visit to D., Grasmere, is complete — COREN, 1
Dover It is burning a farthing candle at D. — JOHNSON, S, 68
the chalk cliffs of D. — BALDWIN, S, 6
doves The moans of d. in immemorial elms — TENNYSON, 68
Dowel D., Dobet and Dobest — LANGLAND, 2
dower forfeited their ancient English d. — WORDSWORTH, W, 55
down for coming d. let me shift for myself — MORE, 3
He that is d. — BUNYAN, 10
I started at the top and worked my way d. — WELLES, 2
put it d. a we — DICKENS, 52
Yes, and they went d. very well too — WELLINGTON, 4
downcast causes many people to feel a little d. — MCGONAGALL, 1
downhearted Are we d.? No — ANONYMOUS, 7
Downing the first comic genius who ever installed himself in D. Street — DISRAELI, 2
downstairs he had known many kicked d. — BURNET, 1
dozen a d. are only a chorus — FITZGERALD, F S, 9
drain you will leave Oxford by the town d. — SPOONER, 5
drainpipe wrong end of a municipal d. — LLOYD GEORGE, 5
drains to distinguish between the Deity and the D. — STRACHEY, L, 1
Drake D. he's in his hammock — NEWBOLT, 3
drama A good d. critic is — TYNAN, 3
dramatic a playwright . . . void of d. interest — SARTRE, 2
dramatist Sherard Blaw, the d. who had discovered himself — SAKI, 23
Drang *Sturm und D.* — KLINGER, 1
draught O, for a d. of vintage — KEATS, 36
draw I d. what I feel in my body — HEPWORTH, 1
When I was their age, I could d. like Raphael . . . it took me a lifetime to learn to d. like them — PICASSO, 10
drawbacks everything has its d. — JEROME, 6
One of the d. of Fame — MELBA, 3
drawing room the Suez Canal was flowing through my d. — EDEN, C, 1
dread the d. of doing what has been done before — WHARTON, 3
dreadful d. is the check — BRONTË, E, 3
Other people are quite d. — WILDE, 16
Portions and parcels of the d. Past — TENNYSON, 54
some have called thee Mighty and d. — DONNE, 14
Dreadnoughts A . . . Duke costs as much . . . as two D. — LLOYD GEORGE, 10
dream Abou Ben Adhem . . . Awoke one night from a deep d. of peace — HUNT, L, 1
All men d.: but not equally — LAWRENCE, T, 7
A sight to d. of — COLERIDGE, S, 10
awakened from the d. of life — SHELLEY, 4
behold it was a d. — BUNYAN, 8
d. of perfect bliss — BAYLY, 2
For life is but a d. — THOMSON, JAMES, 1
God will cease to d. you — UNAMUNO Y JUGO, 1
Happiness is no vague d. — SAND, 1
hope is . . . the d. of those that wake — PRIOR, 2
I d. when I am awake — CALDERÓN DE LA BARCA, 2
I have a d. — KING, M, 4
Napoleon – mighty somnambulist of a vanished d. — NAPOLEON I, 3
The young men's vision, and the old men's d. — DRYDEN, 14
To sleep, perchance to d. — SHAKESPEARE, 89
warned of God in a d. — BIBLE, 352
Where is it now, the glory and the d. — WORDSWORTH, W, 25
you d. you are crossing the Channel — GILBERT, W, 21
dreamer that prophet, or . . . d. of dreams — BIBLE, 56
The poet and the d. are distinct — KEATS, 16
this d. cometh — BIBLE, 175
dreamers the d. of the day are dangerous men — LAWRENCE, T, 7
dreamin' d. . . . o' Plymouth Hoe — NEWBOLT, 3
dreaming after-dinner's sleep, d. on both — SHAKESPEARE, 231
a man d. I was a butterfly — CHUANG TSE, 1
City with her d. spires — ARNOLD, M, 45
dreams doubtful d. of d. — SWINBURNE, 2
do we not live in d. — TENNYSON, 16
dream our d. away — FLANAGAN, 1
D. and predictions — BACON, FRANCIS, 41
Fanatics have their d. — KEATS, 15

For one person who d. of making fifty thousand pounds — MILNE, 3
I, being poor, have only my d. — YEATS, 35
In d. begins responsibility — YEATS, 23
show life . . . as we see it in our d. — CHEKHOV, 3
Than this world d. of — TENNYSON, 24
the city of perspiring d. — RAPHAEL, 1
We are nothing; less than nothing, and d. — LAMB, CHARLES, 4
We are such stuff As d. are made on — SHAKESPEARE, 325
what d. may come — SHAKESPEARE, 89
dreamt d. of in your philosophy — SHAKESPEARE, 78
I d. that I was making a speech — DEVONSHIRE, SPENCER, DUKE OF, 1
dreary intercourse of daily life — WORDSWORTH, W, 14
Dying is a very dull, d. affair — MAUGHAM, 26
If your morals make you d. — STEVENSON, R, 3
Once upon a midnight d. — POE, 1
dress I have no d. except the one I wear — CURIE, 6
put on a d. of guilt — MCGOUGH, 1
sweet disorder in the d. — HERRICK, 2
The Englishman's d. is like a traitor's body — DEKKER, 2
Those who make their d. . . . themselves — HAZLITT, 15
dress'd D. in a little brief authority — SHAKESPEARE, 228
dressed All d. up, with nowhere to go — WHITE, W, 1
Some fruit for Him that d. me — HERBERT, G, 3
Today I d. to meet my father's eyes — JULIA, 1
dresses long d. . . . cover a multitude of shins — WEST, M, 1
drink A good d. — PROVERBS, 22
A little in d. — STEELE, 2
A population sodden with d. — BOOTH, 1
a rule never to d. by daylight — MENCKEN, 18
A taste for d., combined with gout — GILBERT, W, 3
D. and the devil — STEVENSON, R, 8
D. deep, or taste not the Pierian spring — POPE, 23
D.! for you know not whence you came — FITZGERALD, E, 18
d. may be said to be an equivocator with lechery — SHAKESPEARE, 213
D. to me only with thine eyes — JONSON, 7
First you take a d. . . . then the d. takes you — FITZGERALD, F S, 14
I commended mirth . . . to eat . . . to d., and to be merry — BIBLE, 72
let us eat and d.; for tomorrow we . . . die — BIBLE, 205
never to refuse a d. after dark — MENCKEN, 17
no one has yet found a way to d. for a living — KERR, 3
Nor any drop to d. — COLERIDGE, S, 30
that he has taken to d. — TARKINGTON, 1
There are five reasons we should d. — ALDRICH, 1
we d. too much tea — PRIESTLEY, 6
willing to taste any d. once — CABELL, 1
woe unto them that . . . follow strong d. — BIBLE, 195
you shall d. twice while I d. once — WALPOLE, 3
drinkers no verse can give pleasure . . . written by d. of water — HORACE, 23
drinking D. . . . and making love — BEAUMARCHAIS, 2
d. deep of that divinest anguish — BRONTË, E, 4
I have been d. it for sixty-five years and I am not dead yet — VOLTAIRE, 35
let me die d. in an inn — MAP, 1
no d. after death — FLETCHER, 1
resolve to give up smoking, d. and loving — FREUD, C, 1
smoking cigars and . . . d. of alcohol before, after, and if need be during all meals — CHURCHILL, W, 25
there's nothing like d. — DIBDIN, 2
'Tis not the d. . . . but the excess — SELDEN, 8
two reasons for d. — PEACOCK, 6
Work is the curse of the d. classes — WILDE, 25
drinks He who d. a little too much — PROVERBS, 198
dripping Constant d. hollows out a stone — LUCRETIUS, 2
electricity was d. invisibly — THURBER, 10
driver in the d.'s seat — BEAVERBROOK, 2
driving busy d. cabs and cutting hair — BURNS, G, 1
I would spend my life in d. briskly in a post-chaise — JOHNSON, S, 115
drizzle the blasted English d. — KIPLING, 24
droghte d. of Marche — CHAUCER, 3
dromedary whose muse on d. trots — COLERIDGE, S, 3
droop The day begins to d. — BRIDGES, 3
drop d. thy 'H's' — CALVERLEY, 3
Nor any d. to drink — COLERIDGE, S, 30
there are people whom one should like very well to d. — JOHNSON, S, 136
dropping peace comes d. slow — YEATS, 18
dropsies there were people who died of d. — JOHNSON, S, 160
dropt Mrs Montagu has d. me — JOHNSON, S, 136

E

earning   learning, e. and yearning   MORLEY, C, 1
ears   A hungry stomach has no e.   LA FONTAINE, 9
device to keep the e. from grating   DE VRIES, 1
e. to hear, let him hear   BIBLE, 388
guard over your eyes and e.   BRONTÉ, A, 3
Romans, countrymen, lend me your e.   SHAKESPEARE, 153
the seven thin e.   BIBLE, 178
earth   a covenant between me and the e.   BIBLE, 161
a new heaven and a new e.   BIBLE, 473
axis of the e. sticks out visibly through . . . every town or city   HOLMES, O, 4
But did thee feel the e. move   HEMINGWAY, 5
Cool'd . . . in the deep-delved e.   KEATS, 36
E. fills her lap with pleasures   WORDSWORTH, W, 26
E. has not anything to show more fair   WORDSWORTH, W, 52
e. of England is in my two hands   WILLIAM THE CONQUEROR, 1
from whose face the e. and the heaven fled   BIBLE, 472
God called the dry land E.   BIBLE, 139
God created . . . the e.   BIBLE, 137
heaven and e. shall pass away   BIBLE, 415
heav'n on e.   MILTON, 45
hell upon e. . . . in a melancholy man's heart   BURTON, ROBERT, 2
in his hand are all the corners of the e.   PSALMS, 54
I will move the e.   ARCHIMEDES, 1
lards the lean e. as he walks   SHAKESPEARE, 110
let all the e. keep silence before him   BIBLE, 183
mine were princes of the e.   BENJAMIN, 1
more things in heaven and e.   SHAKESPEARE, 78
No grave upon the e.   SHAKESPEARE, 39
passenger on the spaceship, E.   FULLER, RICHARD, 1
so much of e. . . . of heaven   WORDSWORTH, W, 47
the cool flowery lap of e.   ARNOLD, M, 27
The e. does not argue   WHITMAN, 14
the e. is full of the goodness of the Lord   PSALMS, 21
the e. is the Lord's, and the fulness   BIBLE, 35
the e. shall melt away   PSALMS, 27
the e. where cares abound   WORDSWORTH, W, 73
The meek do not inherit the e.   LASKI, 1
then shall the e. bring forth her increase   PSALMS, 38
This e. of majesty   SHAKESPEARE, 295
When e. was nigher heaven   BROWNING, R, 46
earthquake   a story that starts with an e. and . . . a climax   GOLDWYN, 5
ease   done with so much e.   DRYDEN, 4
Joys in another's loss of e.   BLAKE, W, 37
No warmth, no cheerfulness, no healthful e.   HOOD, 10
Prodigal of E.   DRYDEN, 6
True e. in writing comes from art   POPE, 26
easeful   half in love with e. Death   KEATS, 40
easier   E. said than done   PROVERBS, 125
it is much e. to say what it is not   JOHNSON, S, 111
east   E. is E., and West is West   KIPLING, 3
E., west   PROVERBS, 126
hold the gorgeous e. in fee   WORDSWORTH, W, 58
made flesh   APPLETON, T, 2
to have the E. come to the Atlantic   GOERING, 1
to prevent us from going into the E.   GOERING, 1
wise men from the e.   BIBLE, 351
East End   Now we can look the E. in the face   ELIZABETH THE QUEEN MOTHER, 1
easy   E. come   PROVERBS, 127
It is e. to bear   PROVERBS, 227
It is e. to be wise   PROVERBS, 228
It's either e. or impossible   DALI, 1
eat   Don't e. too many almonds   COLETTE, 5
E. as much as you like   SECOMBE, 1
E. to live   PROVERBS, 128
e. to live, not live to e.   MOLIÈRE, 2
gave me of the tree, and I did e.   BIBLE, 151
great ones e. up the little ones   SHAKESPEARE, 290
I commended mirth . . . to e. . . . to drink, and to be merry   BIBLE, 72
I could e. one of Bellamy's veal pies   PITT THE YOUNGER, 3
I do not e. for the sake of enjoyment   GANDHI, 5
I e. to live   GANDHI, 6
if any would not work, neither should he e.   BIBLE, 505
Let them e. the lie   CERVANTES, 10
let us e. and drink; for tomorrow we die   BIBLE, 40
let us e. and drink; for tomorrow we . . . die   BIBLE, 205
man did e. angels' food   PSALMS, 42
So I did sit and e.   HERBERT, G, 7
Some hae meat, and canna e.   BURNS, R, 19

eaten   daring . . . to explain . . . that cows can be e.   GANDHI, I, 2
e. me out of house and home   SHAKESPEARE, 119
e. of worms   BIBLE, 11
eater   out of the e. came forth meat   BIBLE, 294
eating   Appetite comes with e.   RABELAIS, 3
E. people is wrong   FLANDERS, 1
sign something is e. us   DE VRIES, 2
eats   e., sleeps and watches the television   GREER, 2
Man . . . friendly terms with the victims . . . he e.   BUTLER, S, 20
ecce   e. homo   BIBLE, 268
eccentrics   As a poet, Milton seems . . . the greatest of e.   MILTON, 4
ecclesiastic   E. tyranny's the worst   DEFOE, 6
ecclesiastical   lay interest in e. matters . . . often a prelude to insanity   WAUGH, E, 16
echo   The sound must seem an e. to the sense   POPE, 26
eclipse   A gentleman of thirty-two who could calculate an e.   JEFFERSON, 2
his departure was the e. of a genius   MOUNTBATTEN, 1
economic   bottom of the e. pyramid   ROOSEVELT, F, 8
lack of efficiency in using scientific achievements for e. needs   GORBACHOV, 2
economist   Give me a one-handed e.   TRUMAN, 9
Jesus was . . . a first-rate political e.   SHAW, 3
Practical men . . . are usually the slaves of some defunct e.   KEYNES, 7
economists   All races have . . . e., with the exception of the Irish   GALBRAITH, 5
If all e. were laid end to end   SHAW, 53
economy   E. is going without something you do want   HOPE, 3
Everybody is always in favour of general e.   EDEN, A, 2
eczema   style . . . often hides e.   CAMUS, 5
Eden   a garden eastward in E.   BIBLE, 144
futile to attempt a picnic in E.   BOWEN, ELIZABETH, 5
Sir Anthony E.   MUGGERIDGE, 6
the garden of E.   BIBLE, 145
This other E., demi-paradise   SHAKESPEARE, 295
Through E. took their solitary way   MILTON, 52
edge   his keener eye The axe's e. did try   MARVELL, 4
We stand today on the e. of a new frontier   KENNEDY, JOHN, 10
editor   An e. . . . separates the wheat from the chaff   STEVENSON, A, 1
editorial   the nineteenth century was the age of the e. chair   MCLUHAN, 3
Edmonton   If wife should dine at E.   COWPER, 13
Unto the Bell at E.   COWPER, 14
educate   e. a woman you e. a family   MANIKAN, 1
e. with the head instead of with the hand   KEY, E, 3
got to e. him first   SAKI, 15
'tis the schoolboys that e. my son   EMERSON, 19
education   E. . . . has produced a vast population able to read   TREVELYAN, 2
e. is a leading out of what is . . . in the pupil's soul   SPARK, 10
E. is . . . the soul of a society   CHESTERTON, 44
E. is what survives   SKINNER, B, 2
E. made us what we are   HELVÉTIUS, 1
fortunate in escaping regular e.   MACDIARMID, 3
if e. is . . . a mere transmission of knowledge   MONTESSORI, 1
make your children *capable of honesty* is the beginning of e.   RUSKIN, 12
one of the ultimate advantages of an e.   SKINNER, B, 1
part of English middle-class e. is devoted to the training of servants   WILLIAMS, R, 1
Soap and e. are not as sudden as a massacre, but they are more deadly   TWAIN, 5
'Tis e. forms the common mind   POPE, 40
Travel . . . is a part of e.   BACON, FRANCIS, 54
with e. and whisky the price it is   WAUGH, E, 3
woman of e.   VANBURGH, 2
Edwardian   plants left over from the E. Wilderness   OSBORNE, 2
Edwardians   The E. . . . were nomadic   WHITE, T, 1
eena   E., meena, mina, mo   NURSERY RHYMES, 11
effect   little e. after much labour   AUSTEN, 32
effervesced   She should have waited till it e.   ANONYMOUS, 32
efficient   be e. if you're going to be lazy   CONRAN, 2
effort   What is written without e.   JOHNSON, S, 41
efforts   One is happy as a result of one's own e.   SAND, 1
egalitarianism   The majestic e. of the law   FRANCE, 9
Egalité   *Liberté! E.! Fraternité*   ANONYMOUS, 50
egg   a broody hen sitting on a china e.   FOOT, 1
Better an e. today   PROVERBS, 86
hand that lays the golden e.   GOLDWYN, 13

like an e. without salt — CAWEIN, 1
the learned roast an e. — POPE, 53
The vulgar boil . . . an e. — POPE, 53
throw an e. into an electric fan — HERFORD, 1
eggs Don't put all your e. in one basket — PROVERBS, 119
I've met a lot of hardboiled e. — WILDER, B, 1
putting all my e. in one bastard — PARKER, D, 21
to cook himself a couple of e. — CHAMFORT, 1
ways to dress e. — MOORE, T, 1
eggyellow his nicotine e. weeping walrus Victorian moustache — THOMAS, D, 26
egoistic the emancipation of women is . . . the greatest e.
movement — KEY, E, 1
egotism dilemmas of conscience and e. — SNOW, 2
his e. was all but second childhood — CARROLL, 2
egotist *E.*, n. A person . . . more interested in himself — BIERCE, 6
Egypt I am dying, E., dying — SHAKESPEARE, 35
Remember you're in E. — TREE, 7
We are not at war with E. — EDEN, A, 3
Egyptians the E. worshipped an insect — DISRAELI, 34
eight E. for the e. bold rangers — ANONYMOUS, 45
E. maids a-milking — NURSERY RHYMES, 60
Pieces of e. — STEVENSON, R, 9
eighteen From birth to age e., a girl needs good parents — TUCKER, 3
I knew almost as much at e. as I do now — JOHNSON, S, 43
she speaks e. languages. And she can't say 'No' in any of them — PARKER, D, 26
eighty fate would not drag him round the world in e. days — VERNE, 2
Ein And no one can understand E. — ANONYMOUS, 89
Einstein E. – the greatest Jew since Jesus — EINSTEIN, 1
Let E. be — SQUIRE, 3
The genius of E. leads to Hiroshima — EINSTEIN, 2
Eisenhower E. proved we don't need a president — EISENHOWER, 1
elations the impalpable e. and apprehensions of growth — MAILER, 1
elderly When a distinguished but e. scientist states — CLARKE, A, 1
elders miss not the discourse of the e. — BIBLE, 82
elected audacity of e. persons — WHITMAN, 11
election I am certain that we will win the e. with a good majority — THATCHER, M, 23
electric the e. display of God the Father — O'NEILL, 3
electrical E. force . . . causes motion of e. charge — EDDINGTON, 1
electricity e. was dripping invisibly — THURBER, 10
electrification Communism is Soviet power plus the e. — LENIN, 3
elegant English women are e. — MITFORD, N, 2
the e. nonchalance of a duke — CHAPLIN, 3
element One God, one law, one e. — TENNYSON, 38
elementary 'E.,' said he — DOYLE, 9
elements I tax not you, you e., with unkindness — SHAKESPEARE, 177
something that was before the e. — BROWNE, 1, 11
elephant I shot an e. in my pajamas — MARX, G, 2
Nonsense, they couldn't hit an e. at this dist — SEDGWICK, J, 1
elevate E. them guns a little lower — JACKSON, A, 3
eleven E. for the e. who went to heaven — ANONYMOUS, 45
E. ladies dancing — NURSERY RHYMES, 60
Elijah E. went up by a whirlwind into heaven — BIBLE, 301
Eliot to write like Tennyson . . . rather than E. or Auden — BETJEMAN, 2
elms The moans of doves in immemorial e. — TENNYSON, 68
eloquence Talking and e. are not the same — JONSON, 5
eloquent the most e. expressions — KEATS, 4
else Lord High Everything E. — GILBERT, W, 22
Suppose it had been someone e. who found you like this — RICHELIEU, DUC DE, 1
elusive One's prime is e. — SPARK, 2
Elysian dead, but in the E. fields — DISRAELI, 41
emancipated e. from . . . time and space — COLERIDGE, S, 6
emancipation imagine that they are upholding women's e. — STOPES, 6
the e. of women is . . . the greatest egoistic movement — KEY, E, 1
embalmer A triumph of the e.'s art — REAGAN, 3
soft e. of the still midnight — KEATS, 47
embarras *l'e. des richesses* — ALLAINVAL, 1
embarrassment God could cause us considerable e. — GOETHE, 8
embittered He was an e. atheist — ORWELL, 12
embody I, my lords, e. the Law — GILBERT, W, 18
embrace I e. the purpose of God — TENNYSON, 58
none, I think, do there e. — MARVELL, 12
to e. tenderly in a darkened room — YEVTUSHENKO, 2

whether I e. your lordship's principles or your mistress — WILKES, 1
Emerson E. is one who lives . . . on ambrosia — EMERSON, 2
I could . . . see in E. a gaping flaw — EMERSON, 1
emotion Poetry is not a turning loose of e. — ELIOT, T, 24
Sorrow is tranquillity remembered in e. — PARKER, D, 9
the degree of my aesthetic e. — BELL, C, 2
emotional a well-bred sort of e. anarchy — LAWRENCE, D, 16
emotions a sort of metaphysical brothel for e. — KOESTLER, 2
big e. come from big words — HEMINGWAY, 9
noble grounds for the noble e. — RUSKIN, 5
She ran . . . e. from A to B — PARKER, D, 29
emperor An e. ought at least to die on his feet — VESPASIAN, 1
I am the e., and I want dumplings — FERDINAND I, 1
the E. has nothing on — ANDERSEN, 1
emperors e. can't do it all by themselves — BRECHT, 6
empire An e. founded by war — MONTESQUIEU, 1
Great Britain has lost an E. — ACHESON, 6
How is the E. — GEORGE V, 3
Our Eastern E. . . . *made* the English middle class — SCOTT, P, 1
the Holy Roman E. was neither holy, nor Roman, nor an e. — VOLTAIRE, 16
the man who liquidated the E. — MOUNTBATTEN, 3
to the French the e. of the land — RICHTER, 1
empires The day of E. has come — CHAMBERLAIN, J, 2
employed innocently e. than in getting money — JOHNSON, S, 91
The rise in the . . . e. is governed by Parkinson's Law — PARKINSON, 0
employees e. who have not yet reached . . . incompetence — PETER, 2
employment I will undoubtedly have to seek . . . gainful e. — ACHESON, 5
empty Bring on the e. horses — CURTIZ, 1
E. vessels — PROVERBS, 129
You can't think rationally on an e. stomach — REITH, 1
enchantment distance lends e. to the view — CAMPBELL, T, 3
Yeats stood for e. — YEATS, 1
enclose A vacuum can only exist . . . by the things which e. it — FITZGERALD, Z, 3
enclosed Check e. — PARKER, D, 28
encourage the right to be consulted . . . to e. . . . to warn — BAGEHOT, 7
to e. the others — VOLTAIRE, 7
encourager *pour e. les autres* — VOLTAIRE, 7
encyclopaedia a whole E. behind the rest of the world — LAMB, CHARLES, 8
end a beginning, a muddle, and an e. — LARKIN, 5
an e. to the beginnings of all wars — ROOSEVELT, F, 17
a whole is that which has a beginning, a middle, and an e. — ARISTOTLE, 4
beginning of the e. — TALLEYRAND, 3
God be at my e., And at my departing — ANONYMOUS, 20
I like a film to have a beginning, a middle and an e. — GODARD, 2
I move softly towards the e. — JOHN XXIII, 1
Keep right on to the e. of the road — LAUDER, 5
of making many books there is no e. — BIBLE, 78
our minutes hasten to their e. — SHAKESPEARE, 363
the e. is not yet — BIBLE, 413
The *e.* is to build well — WOTTON, 2
The e. justifies the means — PROVERBS, 388
the e. of the beginning — CHURCHILL, W, 60
Walt Whitman who laid e. to e. — LODGE, 5
we're forbidden to know – what e. the gods have in store — HORACE, 30
world without e. — BOOK OF COMMON PRAYER, 15
Yes, to the very e. — ROSSETTI, C, 6
endeavour To e. to forget anyone — LA BRUYÈRE, 14
ended My life with girls has e. — HORACE, 38
The day Thou gavest, Lord, is e. — ELLERTON, 1
ending beginning and the e. — BIBLE, 459
The quickest way of e. a war — ORWELL, 30
endless History is an e. repetition — DURRELL, L, 3
ends divinity that shapes our e. — SHAKESPEARE, 106
my family begins . . . yours e. with you — IPHICRATES, 1
endurance patient e. is godlike — LONGFELLOW, 6
endure For his mercies ay e. — MILTON, 55
It is flattering some men to e. them — HALIFAX, 3
Youth's a stuff will not e. — SHAKESPEARE, 338
endured Human life is everywhere a state in which much is to be e. — JOHNSON, S, 28
Job e. everything – until his friends came — KIERKEGAARD, 1

endures When a man is in love he e. more | NIETZSCHE, 2
endureth blessed is the man that e. temptation | BIBLE, 216
enemies Better a thousand e. | PROVERBS, 87
designing mausoleums for his e. | LINKLATER, 1
do not have to forgive my e. | NARVÁEZ, 1
Even a paranoid can have e. | KISSINGER, 5
He could not make e. | SHERIDAN, R, 2
his e. shall lick the dust | PSALMS, 41
love your e. | BIBLE, 365
mine e. shall be confounded | PSALMS, 2
Mountains interposed Make e. of nations | COWPER, 28
The e. of Freedom | INGE, 2
we have been mortal e. ever since | LESAGE, 2
enemy Every man is his own worst e. | PROVERBS, 139
hasn't an e. in the world | WILDE, 66
in politics to chastise his own side than the e. | ORWELL, 2
It takes your e. and your friend . . . to hurt you | TWAIN, 6
no more sombre e. of good art | CONNOLLY, 10
Poverty is a great e. to human happiness | JOHNSON, S, 140
We have met the e., and they are ours | PERRY, 1
we must be just to our e. | CAMPBELL, T, 7
energies quarrel . . . e. displayed in it are fine | KEATS, 68
energy At what time does the dissipation of e. begin | BLAKE, W, 32
E. is Eternal Delight | BLAKE, W, 32
enfants Allons, e., de la patrie | ROUGET DE LISLE, 1
Les e. terribles | GAVARNI, 1
engaged one of the nicest girls I was ever e. to | WODEHOUSE, 17
engine indefatigable and unsavoury e. of pollution | SPARROW, 1
England A grain, which in E. is generally given to horses | JOHNSON, S, 12
Be E. what she will | CHURCHILL, C, 2
but the King of E. cannot enter | PITT THE ELDER, 2
Christianity is part of the Common Law of E. | HALE, M, 1
Common Law of E. | HERBERT, A, 3
earth of E. is in my two hands | WILLIAM THE CONQUEROR, 1
E. elects a Labour Government | ROGERS, W, 2
E. expects every man will do his duty | NELSON, 4
E. is a nation of shopkeepers | NAPOLEON I, 13
E. is a paradise for women | BURTON, ROBERT, 4
E. is the mother of parliaments | BRIGHT, 1
E. is the paradise of women | FLORIO, 1
E. is the paradise of individuality | SANTAYANA, 9
E. mourns for her dead across the sea | BINYON, 2
E.'s green and pleasant land | BLAKE, W, 33
E.'s pleasant pastures | BLAKE, W, 33
E. . . . the workshop of the world | DISRAELI, 21
E.! . . . What love I bore to thee | WORDSWORTH, W, 6
E. will have her neck wrung like a chicken | WEYGAND, 1
E., with all thy faults | COWPER, 23
For E.'s the one land | BROOKE, 1
For God's sake, madam, don't say that in E. for . . . they will surely tax it | SWIFT, 19
go back to thy stately homes of E. | LAWRENCE, D, 18
God for Harry! E. and Saint George | SHAKESPEARE, 130
he bores for E. | MUGGERIDGE, 1
in E. people have good table manners | MIKES, 1
In E., pop art and fine art | MACINNES, 1
In E. there is only silence or scandal | MAUROIS, 1
It was twenty-one years ago that E. and I | MIKES, 4
Living in E. . . . must be like being married to a stupid . . . wife | HALSEY, 3
no man in E. will take away my life | CHARLES II, 4
occurred nowhere but in E. | CONRAD, 9
Oh, to be in E. | BROWNING, R, 25
Old E. is lost | JOHNSON, S, 113
rather hew wood than be . . . King of E. | CHARLES X, 1
should they know of E. who only E. know | KIPLING, 8
Speak for E. | AMERY, 1
that is forever E. | BROOKE, 6
The best thing I know between France and E. | JERROLD, 2
the defence of E. | BALDWIN, S, 6
the Kings of E., Diamonds, Hearts, Spades and Clubs | FAROUKI, 1
The Law of E. is a very strange one | DARLING, 5
the little ships of E. brought the Army home | GUEDALLA, 2
The national sport of E. | TREE, 6
the old savage E., whose last blood flows still | LAWRENCE, D, 22
There'll always be an E. | PARKER, CLARKE, 1
The roast beef of E. | FIELDING, 6
The stately homes of E. | HEMANS, 2
this generation . . . found E. a land of beauty | JOAD, 3
this realm, this E. | SHAKESPEARE, 295
we are the people of E. | CHESTERTON, 36

English Dr Johnson's morality was as E. . . . as a beefsteak | HAWTHORNE, 2
E. people . . . are surely the nicest people in the world | LAWRENCE, D, 4
E. soldiers fight like lions | HOFFMANN, M, 1
E. . . . the language of an imaginative race | BRENAN, 4
E. women are elegant | MITFORD, N, 2
especially if he went among the E. | BARRIE, 9
exterminate . . . the treacherous E. | WILHELM II, 4
forfeited their ancient E. dower | WORDSWORTH, W, 55
give him seven feet of E. ground | HAROLD II, 1
He is a writer of something occasionally like E. | WHITMAN, 2
I do love cricket – it's so very E. | BERNHARDT, 2
If the E. language had been properly organized | MILNE, 2
If you get the E. people into the way of making kings | MELBOURNE, 5
one of the few E. novels for grown up people | WOOLF, 2
Opera in E. | MENCKEN, 17
our E. nation, if they have a good thing, to make it too common | SHAKESPEARE, 117
part of E. middle-class education is devoted to the training of servants | WILLIAMS, R, 1
stones kissed by the E. dead | OWEN, W, 1
The attitude of the E. . . . toward E. history | HALSEY, 1
The baby doesn't understand E. | KNOX, R, 2
the E. are . . . the least a nation of pure philosophers | BAGEHOT, 6
the E. have hot-water bottles | MIKES, 3
The E. have no respect for their language | SHAW, 36
The E. instinctively admire | AGATE, 2
The E. (it must be owned) are rather a foul-mouthed nation | HAZLITT, 16
The E. may not like music | BEECHAM, 4
the E. seem . . . to have conquered and peopled half the world | SEELEY, 1
The E. take their pleasures | SULLY, 1
The E. want inferiors | TOCQUEVILLE, 1
This is the sort of E. | CHURCHILL, W, 38
To Americans E. manners are . . . frightening | JARRELL, 2
to the E. that of the sea | RICHTER, 1
two most beautiful words in the E. language | JAMES, H, 14
typically E. characteristic | ADCOCK, 1
writes like a Pakistani who has learned E. when he was twelve years old | SHAW, 2
Englishman Am I not punished enough in not being born an E. | VOLTAIRE, 34
An E. . . . forms an orderly queue of one | MIKES, 2
an E.'s heaven-born privilege of doing as he likes | ARNOLD, M, 9
An E.'s home | PROVERBS, 51
An E.'s way of speaking | LERNER, 2
An E.'s word | PROVERBS, 52
an . . . young E. of our upper class | ARNOLD, M, 6
E. . . . is afraid to feel | FORSTER, 2
E. never enjoys himself except for a noble purpose | HERBERT, A, 6
He was born an E. | BEHAN, 3
If I were an American, as I am an E. | PITT THE ELDER, 6
in spite of all temptations . . . He remains an E. | GILBERT, W, 13
it takes a great deal to produce ennui in an E. | HALSEY, 1
never find an E. among the underdogs | WAUGH, E, 28
Remember that you are an E. | RHODES, 2
some other E. despise him | SHAW, 36
tale . . . which would have stirred . . . E. | SCOTT, R, 2
To be an E. | NASH, 2
to behold the E. at his best | FIRBANK, 1
You may be the most liberal Liberal E. | LAWRENCE, D, 12
Englishmen Mad dogs and E. | COWARD, 11
to create Frenchmen in the image of E. | CHURCHILL, W, 62
to see the absurd nature of E. | PEPYS, 7
When two E. meet, their first talk is of the weather | JOHNSON, S, 15
Englishwoman This E. is so refined | SMITH, STEVIE, 4
enigma a riddle wrapped in a mystery inside an e. | CHURCHILL, W, 48
enjoy Certainly, there is nothing else here to e. | SHAW, 49
He knew everything about literature except how to e. it | HELLER, 4
Since God has given us the papacy . . . e. it | LEO X, 1
enjoyment a capacity for e. | HEMINGWAY, 6
I do not eat for the sake of e. | GANDHI, 6
enlightened in this e. age | WOLLSTONECRAFT, 1
enlightened in this e. age | WOLLSTONECRAFT, 1
ennui it takes a great deal to produce e. in an Englishman | HALSEY, 1
enough It comes soon e. | EINSTEIN, 13

patriotism is not e.   CAVELL, 1
entente *La cordiale e.*   LOUIS PHILIPPE, 1
enter but the King of England cannot e.   PITT THE ELDER, 1
enterprises e. that require new clothes   THOREAU, 13
entertained have e. angels unawares   BIBLE, 187
Television . . . permits you to be e. in your living room
         FROST, D, 1
three unhappy women . . . being e. within an inch of their lives
         SOMERVILLE, 3
entertainment what cats most appreciate . . . is . . . e. value
         HOUSEHOLD, 1
enthusiasm all the e. and perseverance that he withheld from
  books and ideas   EISENHOWER, 2
He never . . . felt any real e. for any subject   DRYDEN, 1
Nothing great was ever achieved without e.   EMERSON, 2
Nothing is so contagious as e.   BULWER-LYTTON, 2
We were as nearly bored as e. would permit   GOSSE, 1
enthusiastic Latins are tenderly e.   DIETRICH, 2
enthusiasts so few e. can be trusted   BALFOUR, 5
entities E. should not be multiplied   OKHAM, 1
entrance all men have one e, into life   BIBLE, 520
entrances the e. of this world made narrow   BIBLE, 98
entuned E. in hir nose   CHAUCER, 6
envied Better be e.   PROVERBS, 90
There are two things for which animals are . . . e.   VOLTAIRE, 28
environment President Robbins was so well adjusted to his e.
         JARRELL, 1
envy 2 percent moral, 48 percent indignation and 50 percent e.
         DE SICA, 1
e. is a kind of praise   GAY, 9
prisoners of addiction and . . . prisoners of e.   ILLICH, 4
The dullard's e. of brilliant men   BEERBOHM, 11
the upbringing a nun would e.   ORTON, 1
Epicurus one of E.' herd of pigs   HORACE, 18
epigram it purrs like an e.   MARQUIS, 2
epigrams long despotism tempered by e.   CARLYLE, T, 14
epilogue good play needs no e.   SHAKESPEARE, 57
Epipsychidion You understand *E.* best when you are in love
         MACCARTHY, 2
epitaph 'Can't' will be the e. of the British Empire   MOSLEY, 3
epitaphs a nice derangement of e.   SHERIDAN, R, 9
epithet *Bourgeois* . . . is an e.   HOPE, 6
epitome all Mankind's E.   DRYDEN, 9
epoch A great e. has begun   LE CORBUSIER, 2
From today . . . there begins a new e. in the history of the world
         GOETHE, 9
Epp E.'s statues are junk   ANONYMOUS, 89
Epsom Had we but stick to E. salts   ANONYMOUS, 25
Epstein If people . . . a thousand years hence . . . found E.'s
  statues   LESSING, D, 4
equal All animals are e.   ORWELL, 7
all men and women are created e.   STANTON, E, 6
all men are created e. and independent   JEFFERSON, 5
all men are created e.   KING, M, 4
All shall e. be   GILBERT, W, 4
Everybody should have an e. chance   WILSON, HAROLD, 3
Inferiors revolt . . . that they may be e.   ARISTOTLE, 9
some animals are more e. than others   ORWELL, 7
That all men are e. is a proposition   HUXLEY, A, 30
When you meet someone better . . . turn your thoughts to
  becoming his e.   CONFUCIUS, 1
equality E. . . . is the thing   PEAKE, 1
E. may perhaps be a right, but no . . . fact   BALZAC, 1
e. . . . with our superiors   BECQUE, 1
Freedom! E.! Brotherhood   ANONYMOUS, 50
there never will be . . . e. until women . . . make laws   ANTHONY, 2
equally I hate everyone e.   FIELDS, 4
It comes e. to us all   DONNE, 15
Pale Death kicks his way e.   HORACE, 27
That all who are happy, are e. happy   JOHNSON, S, 73
equanimity an e. bordering on indifference   GILBERT, W, 46
equipping e. us with a neck   KOESTLER, 3
erect he faced the firing squad; e. and motionless   THURBER, 11
ergo *Cogito, e. sum*   DESCARTES, 1
erogenous The mind can also be an e. zone   WELCH, 1
Eros Unarm, E.   SHAKESPEARE, 34
erotics e. is a perfectly respectable function of medicine
         AVICENNA, 1
err The Most may e. as grossly   DRYDEN, 14
those Who e. each other must respect   PATMORE, 1
To e. is human   POPE, 28; PROVERBS, 437
errand What thy e. here below   LAMB, CHARLES, 20

erred We have e., and strayed from thy ways
    BOOK OF COMMON PRAYER, 13
error A new maxim is often a brilliant e.   MALESHERBES, 1
It is time for the destruction of e.   AUDEN, 18
show a man that he is in an e.   LOCKE, 2
the e. of his way   BIBLE, 220
errors E., like Straws, upon the surface flow   DRYDEN, 17
few e. they have ever avoided   CHURCHILL, W, 64
the e. of those who think they are strong   BIDAULT, 1
Esau E. . . . a hairy man   BIBLE, 171
escape Gluttony is an emotional e.   DE VRIES, 2
Let no guilty man e.   GRANT, U, 7
escaped e. from a mad and savage master   SOPHOCLES, 3
escaping fortunate in e. regular education   MACDIARMID, 3
esprit de corps English characteristic . . . *e.*   ADCOCK, 1
essay an over-ambitious e. by a second-year student
         PRIESTLEY, 2
essence Desire is the very e. of man   SPINOZA, 4
The poet gives us his e.   WOOLF, 1
establishment to refer to your friend's country e. as a 'cottage'
         POTTER, S, 3
estate e. o' th' world were now undone   SHAKESPEARE, 226
estates Three E. in Parliament   CARLYLE, T, 13
état *L'E. c'est moi*   LOUIS XIV, 1
etchings I'll bring the e. down   THURBER, 16
eternal Hope springs e. in the human breast   POPE, 32
The e. *not ourselves* that makes for righteousness   ARNOLD, M, 24
to the transitory will then succeed the e.   PETRARCH, 1
We feel . . . we are e.   SPINOZA, 3
eternity All things from e. . . . come round in a circle
         MARCUS AURELIUS, 4
Deserts of vast e.   MARVELL, 10
E. by term   DICKINSON, 3
E. in an hour   BLAKE, W, 9
E.'s a terrible thought   STOPPARD, 8
from e. spinning the thread of your being   MARCUS AURELIUS, 12
Its narrow measure spans Tears of e., and sorrow   HOUSMAN, 5
I will burn, but . . . continue our discussion in e.   SERVETUS, 1
over the Bridge of Sighs into e.   KIERKEGAARD, 2
without injuring e.   THOREAU, 8
ethereal E. minstrel   WORDSWORTH, W, 73
Ethiopians The E. say that their gods are . . . black
         XENOPHANES, 1
Eton the Battle of Waterloo *was* won on the playing-fields of E.
         ORWELL, 13
the playing fields of E.   WELLINGTON, 19
eunuch a kind of moral e.   SHELLEY, 20
eureka *E.*   ARCHIMEDES, 2
Euripides E. portrays them as they are   SOPHOCLES, 2
Europe another war in E.   BISMARCK, 8
Communism continued to haunt E. as a spectre   TAYLOR, A, 3
E. is the unfinished negative   MCCARTHY, M, 4
glory of E. is extinguished   BURKE, E, 9
In Western E. there are now only small countries   LEFÈVRE, 1
lamps are going out over all E.   GREY, 2
last gentleman in E.   LEVERSON, 3
part of the community of E.   GLADSTONE, 3
'sick man of E.'   NICHOLAS I, 1
That E.'s nothin' on earth   WILLIAMS, T, 3
the community of E.   SALISBURY, 2
the race of men is almost extinct in E.   LAWRENCE, D, 27
There is an iron curtain across E.   TROUBRIDGE, 1
The spacious philanthropy which he exhaled upon E.   WILSON, W, 1
This going into E.   THOMPSON, E, 1
United States of E.   CHURCHILL, W, 66
European the feminization of the white E. and American is
  already far advanced   LEWIS, W, 3
to shoot down a E. is to kill two birds with one stone   SARTRE, 18
Europeanism Their E. is . . . imperialism with an inferiority
  complex   HEALEY, 2
Europeans only really materialistic people . . . E.   MCCARTHY, M, 3
euthanasia E. is a long, smooth-sounding word, and . . . conceals
  its danger   BUCK, 1
evacuations Wars are not won by e.   CHURCHILL, W, 29
evah Well, did you e.! What a swell party   PORTER, C, 6
Eva Peron If a woman like E. with no ideals   THATCHER, M, 8
Eve E. . . . the mother of all living   BIBLE, 152
from noon to dewy e.   MILTON, 38
When E. ate this particular apple   LAWRENCE, D, 9
even Deep and crisp and e.   NEALE, 2
evening e. is spread out against the sky   ELIOT, T, 11
in the e. . . . cut down, dried up   PSALMS, 49

Now came still E. on | MILTON, 46
Soup of the e. | CARROLL, 18
the quiet-coloured end of e. | BROWNING, R, 34
thou art fairer than the e. air | MARLOWE, 3
event greatest e. . . . that ever happened | FOX, C, 3
hurries to the main e. | HORACE, 7
one far-off divine e. | TENNYSON, 38
thinking too precisely on th' e. | SHAKESPEARE, 100
eventide Abide with me; fast falls the e. | LYTE, 1
events all great e. and personalities in . . . history reappear | MARX, K, 6
E. which . . . never happened | INGE, 1
many e. in the womb of time | SHAKESPEARE, 278
There are only three e. in a man's life | LA BRUYÈRE, 6
When in the course of human e., it becomes necessary for one people to dissolve . . . political bonds | JEFFERSON, 4
ever for e. hold his peace | BOOK OF COMMON PRAYER, 25
I go on for e. | TENNYSON, 6
Everest the summit of E. was hardly the place | HILLARY, 1
treating the *mons Veneris* as . . . Mount E. | HUXLEY, A, 16
everlasting God from e. | PSALMS, 48
every E. day in e. way | COUÉ, 1
God bless us, e. one | DICKENS, 10
everybody E. has got to die . . . . Now what | SAROYAN, 1
E. is always in favour of general economy | EDEN, A, 2
E. was up to something | COWARD, 9
Everyman E., I will go with thee, and be thy guide | ANONYMOUS, 17
everyone e. against e. | HOBBES, 1
I hate e. equally | FIELDS, 4
stop e. from doing it | HERBERT, A, 2
everything A place for e. | SMILES, 2
destroying nearly e. | CHESTERTON, 5
e. in its place | SMILES, 2
E. is funny | ROGERS, W, 4
E. is only for a day | MARCUS AURELIUS, 7
E.'s got a moral | CARROLL, 13
e. that lives is holy | BLAKE, W, 3
God made e. out of nothing | VALÉRY, 1
making e. the concern of all | SOLZHENITSYN, 15
men we like are good for e. | HALIFAX, 2
One fifth of the people are against e. | KENNEDY, R, 3
Was E. by starts | DRYDEN, 9
evidence If ever there was a case of clearer e. | ARABIN, 1
Most men . . . give e. against their own understanding | HALIFAX, 8
evil about the dreadful wood Of conscious e. | AUDEN, 14
a chief magistrate of whom so much e. has been predicted | JACKSON, A, 1
as gods, knowing good and e. | BIBLE, 149
a thing may look e. in theory . . . in practice excellent | BURKE, E, 28
belief in a supernatural source of e. | CONRAD, 7
better is he . . . who hath not seen the e. work under the sun | BIBLE, 68
deliver us from e. | BIBLE, 367
E., be thou my Good | MILTON, 44
E. be to him who e. thinks | ANONYMOUS, 39
E. comes . . . like the disease; good . . . like the doctor | CHESTERTON, 26
e. communications corrupt good manners | BIBLE, 40
e. is wrought by want of thought | HOOD, 8
e. men and seducers | BIBLE, 513
Government . . . is but a necessary e. | PAINE, 2
how can ye, being e., speak good | BIBLE, 389
know all the e. he does | ROCHEFOUCAULD, 21
love of money is the root of all e. | BIBLE, 511
Man's capacity for e. makes democracy necessary | NIEBUHR, 1
men loved darkness . . . because their deeds were e. | BIBLE, 246
Men's e. manners live in brass | SHAKESPEARE, 141
No man is justified in doing e. | ROOSEVELT, T, 3
Only lies and e. come from letting people off | MURDOCH, 5
Put off the e. hour | PROVERBS, 345
Socrates is a doer of e. | SOCRATES, 1
The e. that men do lives after them | SHAKESPEARE, 153
the fear of one e. | BOILEAU, 2
the love of money is the root of all e. | BUTLER, S, 6
There is no e. in the atom | STEVENSON, A, 5
the righteous is taken away from the e. to come | BIBLE, 215
Touch for the E. according to costome | EVELYN, 1
Vice itself lost half its e. | BURKE, E, 8
we are the origin of all coming e. | JUNG, 11
woe unto them that call e. good | BIBLE, 196

evils death, . . . the least of all e. | BACON, FRANCIS, 6
He . . . must expect new e. | BACON, FRANCIS, 30
There exist some e. so terrible | LABRUYÈRE, 10
To great e. we submit; we resent little provocations | HAZLITT, 22
We cannot remove the e. of capitalism | KINNOCK, 4
Whenever I'm caught between two e. | WEST, M, 18
Work banishes those three great e. | VOLTAIRE, 10
evolution Coolidge is a better example of e. | ROGERS, W, 6
e. of the human race | DARWIN, C G, 1
sex . . . must itself be subject . . . to e. | BLACKWELL, 1
exact Politics is not an e. science | BISMARCK, 2
exaggerated Reports of my death are greatly e. | TWAIN, 18
exalted Every valley shall be e. | BIBLE, 210
I will be e. among the heathen | PSALMS, 28
examine One should e. oneself . . . before . . . condemning others | MOLIÈRE, 7
example E. is the school of mankind | BURKE, E, 3
George the Third – ('Treason,' cried the Speaker) . . . *may profit by their e.* | HENRY, P, 1
exasperating that the afterlife will be any less e. than this one | COWARD, 3
excel daring to e. | CHURCHILL, C, 1
excellence acute limited e. at twenty-one | FITZGERALD, F S, 7
excellences e. carried to an excess | COLERIDGE, S, 20
excellent everything that's e. | GILBERT, W, 18
very e. things are spoken of thee, thou city of God | PSALMS, 47
Excelsior A banner with the strange device, E. | LONGFELLOW, 7
exception I never forget a face, but I'll make an e. | MARX, G, 20
The e. proves the rule | PROVERBS, 389
excess excellences carried to an e. | COLERIDGE, S, 20
e. is most exhilarating | ANOUILH, 6
Give me e. of it | SHAKESPEARE, 334
In charity there is no e. | BACON, FRANCIS, 27
Nothing succeeds like e. | WILDE, 61
The road of e. | BLAKE, W, 25
'Tis not the drinking . . . but the e. | SELDEN, 8
exchange conversation must be an e. of thought | POST, 1
I stopped . . . to e. ideas | HEINE, 3
Exchequer Chancellor of the E. | LOWE, 1
exciting He found it less e. | GILBERT, W, 1
Jam today, and men aren't at their most e. | SNOW, 1
exclude we cannot e. the intellect from . . . any of our functions | JAMES, W, 3
excluded when you have e. the impossible | DOYLE, 1
exclusive the most e. club there is | NASH, 3
excuse bet he's just using that as an e. | MARX, G, 7
E. my dust | PARKER, D, 30
execution some are daily led to e. | RALEIGH, W, 4
executioner I am mine own E. | DONNE, 6
executioners victims who respect their e. | SARTRE, 1
executive the e. expression of human immaturity | BRITTAIN, 3
exemplary His attachment to . . . his friends . . . was thoroughgoing and e. | JEFFERSON, 1
exercise E. is bunk | FORD, H, 3
Prostitution . . . provides fresh air and wholesome e. | HELLER, 7
exertion success depends . . . upon individual initiative and e. | PAVLOVA, 2
the e. is too much for me | PEACOCK, 9
exhausted Our agenda is now e. . . . . we find ourselves in such complete unanimity | SPAAK, 1
exhibitionist he was sincerely shy and naively e. | LAWRENCE, T, 4
exile cause of Ovid's sudden e. is not known | OVID, 2
his attitude of a king in e. | DE GAULLE, 2
New York . . . where every one is an e. | GILMAN, 2
exist Facts do not cease to e. | HUXLEY, A, 32
I e. by what I think | SARTRE, 3
I feel . . . a certain difficulty in continuing to e. | FONTENELLE, 2
If God did not e. | VOLTAIRE, 14
liberty cannot long e. | BURKE, E, 22
No more things should be presumed to e. | OKHAM, 1
existence A God who let us prove his e. | BONHOEFFER, 2
disregard for the necessities of e. | MAUGHAM, 14
individual e. goes out in a lonely spasm of helpless agony | JAMES, W, 1
Let us contemplate e. | DICKENS, 26
mere e. is swollen to a horror | LAWRENCE, D, 23
the sole purpose of human e. is to kindle a light | JUNG, 4
the struggle for e. | DARWIN, C R, 9
to deny the e. of an unseen kingdom is bad | BUTLER, S, 2
to do something is to create . . . | SARTRE, 10
woman's whole e. | BYRON, 20
exit E., pursued by a bear | SHAKESPEARE, 351

exits They have their e. and their entrances SHAKESPEARE, 47
expect all any reasonable child can e. ORTON, 2
I e. a judgment DICKENS, 6
people e. me to neigh, grind my teeth ANNE, 1
the audience want to be surprised . . . by things that they e. BERNARD, T, 1
you e. other people to be . . . to your liking KEMPIS, 3
expectation the distinction between hope and e. ILLICH, 3
expectations the difference between our talents and our e. BONO, 1
expects Blessed is the man who e. nothing POPE, 60
England e. every man will do his duty NELSON, 4
expediency the most useful thing about a principle . . . sacrificed to e. MAUGHAM, 4
expedient all things are not e. BIBLE, 34
e. that one man should die for the people BIBLE, 264
expenditure annual e. nineteen nineteen six DICKENS, 13
in favour of . . . particular e. EDEN, A, 2
expense flatterers live at the e. of those who listen LAFONTAINE, 2
who Would be at the e. of two CLOUGH, 5
experience All e. is an arch TENNYSON, 80
An e. of women DOYLE, 14
E. is a good teacher ANTRIM, 3
E. is never limited JAMES, H, 10
E. isn't interesting BOWEN, ELIZABETH, 1
E. is the best teacher PROVERBS, 145
E. is the mother PROVERBS, 146
I can't see that it's wrong to give him a little legal e. KENNEDY, JOHN, 1
Language is not simply a reporting device for e. WHORF, 1
moment's insight . . . worth a life's e. HOLMES, O, 7
my e. of life has been drawn from life itself BEERBOHM, 16
Notwithstanding the poverty of my . . . e. JAMES, A, 2
she has written . . . a few moments of human e. PARKER, D, 1
the light which e. gives COLERIDGE, S, 23
The triumph of hope over e. JOHNSON, S, 81
experiences the child should be allowed to meet the real e. of life KEY, E, 2
experiment A theory can be proved by e. EINSTEIN, 11
existence remains a . . . lamentable e. SANTAYANA, 5
E. alone crowns the efforts of medicine PAVLOV, 2
no path leads from e. to . . . theory EINSTEIN, 11
to desist from the e. in despair LAMB, CHARLES, 6
experimental Does it contain any e. reasoning? HUME, D, 2
expert An e. . . . has made all the mistakes . . . in a very narrow field BOHR, 2
An e. . . . knows some of the worst mistakes that can be made HEISENBERG, 1
Prince Philip. He's a world e. on leisure KINNOCK, 5
explanations less hideous than e. LEWIS, D, 1
export I integrate the current e. drive BETJEMAN, 5
exposes A man who e. himself when he is intoxicated JOHNSON, S, 129
ex-president No candidate . . . elected e. by such a large majority TAFT, 1
expression supreme e. of the mediocrity TROTSKY, 10
the executive e. of human immaturity BRITTAIN, 3
expressions the most eloquent is e. KEATS, 4
expulsion arbitrary arrest and e. SOLZHENITSYN, 1
exquisite e. showman minus the show POUND, 1
It is e., and it leaves one unsatisfied WILDE, 51
the e. touch . . . is denied to me SCOTT, WALTER, 5
ex-secretary attacking an e. of state ACHESON, 5
exterminate E. all brutes CONRAD, 1
e. . . . the treacherous English WILHELM II, 4
extinct convention which says you must not make species e. PHILIP, PRINCE, 4
the Tasmanians, who never committed adultery, are now e. MAUGHAM, 1
extinguished glory of Europe is e. BURKE, E, 9
extraordinary Little minds are interested in the e. HUBBARD, 2
the most e. collection of talent KENNEDY, JOHN, 12
this is an e. man BURKE, E, 148
extravagance e. . . . thrift and adventure seldom go hand in hand CHURCHILL, J, 2
Our love of what is beautiful does not lead to e. PERICLES, 1
extreme E. remedies . . . for e. diseases HIPPOCRATES, 2
extremism e. in the defence of liberty is no vice GOLDWATER, 2
exuberance E. is Beauty BLAKE, W, 29
e. of his own verbosity DISRAELI, 32

exultations Thy friends are e., agonies, And love WORDSWORTH, W, 62
ex-wife no fury like an e. searching for a new lover CONNOLLY, 17
eye A custom loathsome to the e., hateful to the nose JAMES I, 1
a limit to what one can listen to with the naked e. SPARK, 11
a sober colouring from an e. WORDSWORTH, W, 32
as the apple of his e. BIBLE, 59
At last God caught his e. SECOMBE, 2
clapped the glass to his sightless e. NEWBOLT, 1
Every tear from every e. BLAKE, W, 7
e. for e. BIBLE, 116
e. hath not seen BIBLE, 25
God . . . caught his e. KAUFMAN, 2
He had but one e. DICKENS, 31
he that made the e., shall he not see PSALMS, 53
his keener e. The axe's edge did try MARVELL, 4
I have only one e. NELSON, 3
indebted for a nose or an e. . . . to a great-aunt HAZLITT, 25
keep me as the apple of an e. PSALMS, 6
less in this than meets the e. BANKHEAD, 8
man who looks you . . . in the e. . . . hiding something FADIMAN, 2
nearest thing . . . to the e. of God SHAKESPEARE, 14
neither e. to see, nor tongue to speak LENTHALL, 1
such beauty as a woman's e. SHAKESPEARE, 197
The e. is bigger PROVERBS, 390
the e. . . . shall see me no more BIBLE, 226
There is a road from the e. to the heart CHESTERTON, 9
the sort of e. that can open an oyster at sixty paces WODEHOUSE, 6
the twinkling of an e. PSALMS, 17
with an e. made quiet . . . We see into the life of things WORDSWORTH, W, 11
with the jaundiced e. TENNYSON, 52
eyeless E. in Gaza MILTON, 57
eye-lids the opening e. of the morn MILTON, 22
eyelids tir'd e. upon tir'd eyes TENNYSON, 55
When she raises her e. COLETTE, 2
eyes And on his grave, with shining e. ARNOLD, M, 30
and throws . . . sand in their e. HOFFMANN, E, 1
Dead e. and a red beard LAWRENCE, D, 1
Drink to me only with thine e. JONSON, 7
e. have they, and see not PSALMS, 64
fortune and men's e. SHAKESPEARE, 360
God be in my e., And in my looking ANONYMOUS, 20
guard over your e. and ears BRONTË, A, 3
His e. . . . had a very disconcerting trick COLLINS, W, 1
I first set my e. on sweet Molly Malone ANONYMOUS, 47
I was e. to the blind BIBLE, 235
I will lift up mine e. unto the hills PSALMS, 67
Look at that man's e. LAW, 5
Look not in my e., for fear They mirror true the sight I see HOUSMAN, 9
Love looks not with the e. SHAKESPEARE, 258
Mine e. have seen the glory of the coming of the Lord HOWE, 1
pearls that were his e. SHAKESPEARE, 321
the creature hath a purpose and its e. are bright with it KEATS, 69
the e. are the windows of the soul BEERBOHM, 12
The e. are the window PROVERBS, 391
the e. of the blind shall be opened BIBLE, 209
The e. that shone, Now dimmed and gone MOORE, T, 7
the whites of their e. PRESCOTT, 1
Thy rapt soul sitting in thine e. MILTON, 12
Two lovely black e. COBORN, 1
When Byron's e. were shut in death BYRON, 1
you'll wear your e. out ZOLA, 1
Your e. shine like the pants MARX, G, 4
eyesight with blinded e. TENNYSON, 53

F

Fabian Britain . . . F. Society writ large HAMILTON, W, 2
Fabians A good man fallen among F. LENIN, 10
fabric chemical barrage has been hurled against the f. of life CARSON, 2
the baseless f. of this vision SHAKESPEARE, 325
face Accustomed to her f. LERNER, 7
a garden in her f. CAMPION, 2
A good f. is a letter of recommendation PROVERBS, 23
And hid his f. amid a crowd of stars YEATS, 34
At 50, everyone has the f. he deserves ORWELL, 36

everybody's f. but their own — SWIFT, 3
every man is responsible for his f. — CAMUS, 4
False f. must hide — SHAKESPEARE, 210
from whose f. the earth and the heaven fled — BIBLE, 472
he turned his f. to the wall — BIBLE, 304
I have looked upon the f. of Agamemnon — SCHLIEMANN, 1
I never forget a f., but I'll make an exception — MARX, G, 20
Look in my f.; my name is Might-have-been — ROSSETTI, D, 2
Looks the whole world in the f. — LONGFELLOW, 17
My f. is my fortune, sir, she said — NURSERY RHYMES, 71
painting a f. and not washing — FULLER, T, 1
Socialism with a human f. — DUBČEK, 1
the f. that launch'd a thousand ships — MARLOWE, 2
There is a garden in her f. — ALISON, 2
There is not any book Or f. — THOMAS, E, 3
to order a new stamp . . . with my f. on it — CHARLES FRANCIS JOSEPH, 1
faces All, all are gone, the old familiar f. — LAMB, CHARLES, 19
among so many million of f. — BROWNE, T, 6
make f. — SCHNABEL, 4
facetious You must not think me . . . foolish because I am f. — SMITH, SYDNEY, 16
fact the slaying of a beautiful hypothesis by an ugly f. — HUXLEY, T, 1
faction To die for f. — DRYDEN, 15
factory In the f. we make cosmetics — REVSON, 1
facts Comment is free but f. are sacred — SCOTT, C, 1
F. alone are wanted in life — DICKENS, 21
F. . . . are as water to a sponge — HOOVER, 1
F. do not cease to exist — HUXLEY, A, 32
F. speak louder than statistics — STREATFIELD, 1
Learn, compare, collect the f. — PAVLOV, 1
Once a newspaper touches a story, the f. are lost — MAILER, 2
fade the cheek that doth not f. — KEATS, 18
faded interviewing a f. female in a damp basement — HARDING, 1
fail If they succeed, they f. — CRISP, 9
Others must f. — VIDAL, 6
to f. conventionally — KEYNES, 5
failed Here lies Joseph, who f. in everything he undertook — JOSEPHII, 1
Light that F. — KIPLING, 19
faileth charity never f. — BIBLE, 38
fails If thy heart f. thee — ELIZABETH I, 10
failure no success like f. — DYLAN, 6
Rejection, derision, poverty, f. — VIZINCZEY, 2
we all contain f. and death within us — MAILER, 1
faint Damn with f. praise — POPE, 14
fair All is f. — PROVERBS, 34
all's f. in love and war — FORREST, 2
Every man's house will be f. and decent — MORRIS, W, 4
F. stood the wind for France — DRAYTON, 1
Grief has turned her f. — WILDE, 74
how f. . . . art thou, O love, for delights — BIBLE, 498
Monday's child is f. of face — NURSERY RHYMES, 35
Serious sport has nothing to do with f. play — ORWELL, 32
So foul and f. a day — SHAKESPEARE, 201
the Brave deserves the F. — DRYDEN, 16
the name of Vanity F. — BUNYAN, 3
There was a f. maid dwellin' . . . Her name was Barbara Allen — ANONYMOUS, 49
faire *Laissez f.* — QUESNAY, 1
fairer I can't say no f. than that — DICKENS, 18
thou art f. than the evening air — MARLOWE, 3
fairest the f. things have the worst fate — MALHERBE, 1
fairies I don't believe in f. — BARRIE, 4
the beginning of f. — BARRIE, 3
There are f. at the bottom of our garden — FYLEMAN, 1
fairy the f. tales of science — TENNYSON, 49
fairyland The Fleet's lit up. It is like f. — WOODROOFE, 1
fairy story A myth is, of course, not a f. — RYLE, 2
faith a life of doubt diversified by f. — BROWNING, R, 11
an absolute f. that all things are possible to God — EDDY, 1
And f. shines equal — BRONTË, E, 1
by f. the walls of Jericho fell down — BIBLE, 186
F. . . . an illogical belief in . . . the improbable — MENCKEN, 14
F. . . . believing when it is beyond the power of reason — VOLTAIRE, 25
f. is the substance of things hoped for — BIBLE, 189
f. unfaithful kept him falsely true — TENNYSON, 17
F. will move mountains — PROVERBS, 147
Lincoln had f. in time — LINCOLN, 3
no need for any other f. than . . . f. in human beings — BUCK, 6

now abideth f., hope, charity — BIBLE, 38
O thou of little f., wherefore didst thou doubt — BIBLE, 395
O ye of little f. — BIBLE, 383
Reason is itself a matter of f. — CHESTERTON, 31
the f. and morals hold Which Milton held — WORDSWORTH, W, 54
thy f. hath saved thee — BIBLE, 322
'Tis not the dying for a f. — THACKERAY, 3
we walk by f., not by sight — BIBLE, 44
When your ladyship's f. has removed them — CHESTERFIELD, 22
whoever is moved by f. . . . conscious of a continued miracle — HUME, D, 3
faithful f. in love, . . . dauntless in war — SCOTT, WALTER, 15
f. to thee, Cynara — DOWSON, 1
happiness of man that he be mentally f. — PAINE, 1
If this man is not f. to his God — THEODORIC, 1
if you had been f. — RACINE, 3
my heart shall be The f. compass — GAY, 12
O come all ye f. — OAKELEY, 1
thou good and f. servant — BIBLE, 418
Translations (like wives) are seldom f. — CAMPBELL, R, 2
faithfully those things which we ask f. — BOOK OF COMMON PRAYER, 6
faithfulness his f. and truth shall be thy shield and buckler — PSALMS, 51
fake a sonorous f. as a writer — LAWRENCE, T, 1
fakir It is nauseating to see Mr Gandhi . . . posing as a f. — GANDHI, 2
Falklands F. . . . a fight between two bald men over a comb — BORGES, 4
fall and an haughty spirit before a f. — BIBLE, 451
a thousand shall f. beside thee — PSALMS, 51
Fain would I climb, yet fear I to f. — RALEIGH, W, 2
harder they f. — FITZSIMMONS, 1
The airplane stays up because it doesn't have the time to f. — WRIGHT, O, 1
Whenever you f., pick up something — AVERY, 1
fallen A good man f. among Fabians — LENIN, 10
y-f. out of heigh degree. Into miserie — CHAUCER, 15
falleth woe to him that is alone when he f. — BIBLE, 69
falling Fish die belly-upward and rise . . . their way of f. — GIDE, 3
fallow lie f. for a while — TUPPER, 1
false beware of f. prophets — BIBLE, 378
F. face must hide what the f. heart — SHAKESPEARE, 210
f. to his friends . . . true to the public — BERKELEY, 1
natural f. teeth — ROBINSON, R, 2
The religions we call f. were once true — EMERSON, 6
the true and the f. and . . . extracting the plausible — LLOYD GEORGE, 2
Thou canst not then be f. — SHAKESPEARE, 74
thou shalt not bear f. witness — BIBLE, 115
True and F. are attributes of speech, not of things — HOBBES, 2
Vain wisdom all, and f. philosophy — MILTON, 41
falsehood Let her and F. grapple — MILTON, 8
falsely a verb meaning 'to believe f.' — WITTGENSTEIN, 7
Falstaff F. sweats to death — SHAKESPEARE, 110
fame blush to find it f. — POPE, 10
F. is a powerful aphrodisiac — GREENE, 10
F. is like a river — BACON, FRANCIS, 40
F. is sometimes like unto a . . . mushroom — FULLER, T, 3
F. is the spur — MILTON, 25
Here rests . . . A youth to fortune and to f. unknown — GRAY, 8
lifted Pasteur into indisputable f. — PASTEUR, 2
Love of f. is the last thing . . . to be parted from — TACITUS, 3
One of the drawbacks of F. — MELBA, 3
one whom f. has not corrupted — CURIE, 2
The book written against f. . . . has the author's name on the title-page — EMERSON, 20
familiar mine own f. friend — PSALMS, 25
old f. faces — LAMB, CHARLES, 19
familiarity F. breeds contempt — PROVERBS, 148
F. breeds contempt – and children — TWAIN, 12
families All happy f. resemble one another — TOLSTOY, L, 5
Good f. are generally worse than any others — HOPE, 8
Murder, like talent, seems . . . to run in f. — LEWES, 2
the best-regulated f. — DICKENS, 17
There are only two f. in the world — CERVANTES, 2
family A f. with the wrong members in control — ORWELL, 14
a tense and peculiar f., the Oedipuses — BEERBOHM, 21
average American loves his f. — TWAIN, 2
educate a woman you educate a f. — MANIKAN, 1
Mother is the dead heart of the f. — GREER, 2
my f. begins with me — IPHICRATES, 1

the f. . . . source of all our discontents | LEACH, 1
The f. that prays together | PROVERBS, 392
The sink is the great symbol . . . of f. life | MITCHELL, JULIAN, 1
famine f. was sore in the land | BIBLE, 179
They that die by f. die by inches | HENRY, M, 2
you look as if there were f. in the land | SHAW, 52
famous everyone will be f. for 15 minutes | WARHOL, 5
get rich, get f. and get laid | GELDOF, 2
I awoke . . . found myself f. | BYRON, 45
I'm never going to be f. | PARKER, D, 7
let us now praise f. men | BIBLE, 91
so f., that it would permit me . . . to break wind in society | BALZAC, 5
What are you f. _for?_' | MURDOCH, 3
fan 'F. vaulting' . . . belongs to the 'Last-supper-carved-on-a-peach-stone' | LANCASTER, 1
throw an egg into an electric f. | HERFORD, 1
fanatic f. . . . over-compensates a . . . doubt | HUXLEY, A, 39
fanaticism They charge me with f. | WILBERFORCE, W, 2
fanatics F. have their dreams | KEATS, 15
when f. are on top there is no limit to oppression | MENCKEN, 8
fancies All universal moral principles are idle f. | SADE, 1
fancy a young man's f. . . . turns to . . . love | TENNYSON, 50
Ever let the f. roam | KEATS, 17
F. is . . . a mode of memory | COLERIDGE, S, 6
f. wit will come | POPE, 9
hopeless f. feign'd | TENNYSON, 63
little of what you f. does you good | LLOYD, M, 2
sweetest Shakespeare, F.'s child | MILTON, 19
Fanny F. by Gaslight | SADLEIR, 1
fantastic the light f. toe | MILTON, 16
far a f., f., better thing | DICKENS, 57
how f. we may go too f. | COCTEAU, 1
The night is dark, and I am f. from home | NEWMAN, J, 3
Thursday's child has f. to go | NURSERY RHYMES, 35
Faraday remain plain Michael F. to the last | FARADAY, 1
farce F. is the essential theatre | CRAIG, 1
Parliament is the longest running f. | SMITH, SIR CYRIL, 2
the f. is over | RABELAIS, 9
the wine was a f. and the food a tragedy | POWELL, A, 2
farewell F., a long f., to all my greatness | SHAKESPEARE, 139
F., my poor hands | RACHMANINOV, 1
F.! thou art too dear for my possessing | SHAKESPEARE, 365
hail and f. | CATULLUS, 3
long journey . . . must bid the company f. | RALEIGH, W, 7
farmer This is the f. sowing his corn | NURSERY RHYMES, 62
farm-yard nothing to distinguish human society from the f. | SHAW, 12
the f. world of sex | GRANVILLE-BARKER, 2
far-reaching Life's short span forbids us to enter on f. hopes | HORACE, 28
far-sighted Green politics is . . . being f. | ICKE, 1
fart he can't f. and chew gum at the same time | JOHNSON, L, 4
farthing It is burning a f. candle at Dover | JOHNSON, S, 68
steal one poor f. without excuse | NEWMAN, J, 4
fascinates I like work; it f. me | JEROME, 7
fascination Philosophy, . . . is a fight against . . . f. | WITTGENSTEIN, 1
war . . . will always have its f. | WILDE, 10
Fascism F. . . . future refusing to be born | BEVAN, 12
F. is a religion | MUSSOLINI, 4
F. is not an article for export | MUSSOLINI, 5
F. means war | STRACHEY, J, 2
the twentieth century will be . . . the century of F. | MUSSOLINI, 3
fascist Every communist has a f. frown | SPARK, 3
fashion after the f. of their country | SULLY, 1
as . . . be . . . out of the f. | CIBBER, 1
Every man after his f. | PROVERBS, 137
faithful to thee, Cynara! in my f. | DOWSON, 1
F. is architecture | CHANEL, 4
Nothing else holds f. | SHAKESPEARE, 333
the unreasoning laws of markets and f. | ALBERT, 1
true to you, darlin', in my f. | PORTER, C, 8
fashionable an idea . . . to be f. is ominous | SANTAYANA, 13
fashions I cannot . . . cut my conscience to fit this year's f. | HELLMAN, 2
fast none so f. as stroke | COKE, D, 1
they stumble that run f. | SHAKESPEARE, 313
US has to move very f. | KENNEDY, JOHN, 7
faster the world would go round a deal f. | CARROLL, 7
Will you walk a little f. | CARROLL, 16

fastidious to set a chime of words tinkling in . . . a few f. people | SMITH, L, 9
fat butter will only make us f. | GOERING, 3
Enclosing every thin man, there's a f. man | WAUGH, E, 30
in every f. man a thin one | CONNOLLY, 18
Let me have men about me that are f. | SHAKESPEARE, 144
O f. white woman | CORNFORD, 1
Outside every f. man . . . an even fatter man | AMIS, 1
the f. of the land | BIBLE, 180
there's a thin man inside every f. man | ORWELL, 9
Who's your f. friend | BRUMMEL, 1
you will come and find me f. and sleek | HORACE, 18
fatal Anno domini . . . the most f. complaint | HILTON, 1
f. period when _old age_ must be endured | SÉVIGNÉ, 1
Nature has never put the f. question as to the meaning of their lives | JUNG, 1
when he does it is nearly always f. | MACDIARMID, 2
fate count as profit every day that F. allows you | HORACE, 29
Each man the architect of his own f. | APPIUS CAECUS, 1
F. sits on these dark battlements | RADCLIFFE, 1
hostages given to f. | LUCAN, 1
How wayward the decrees of F. | THACKERAY, 8
it is not only our f. but our business to lose innocence | BOWEN, ELIZABETH, 5
jeers at F. | ADAMS, F, 1
Leave the flesh to the f. it was fit for | BROWNING, R, 51
master of his f. | TENNYSON, 19
mortifying f. of most English universities | LODGE, 2
Prudence . . . when one is determining the f. of others | LACLOS, 2
the fairest things have the worst f. | MALHERBE, 1
Their f. must always be the same as yours | AUDEN, 25
the life-sentence which f. carries | LAWRENCE, T, 6
the master of my f. | HENLEY, 2
the severity of f. | FORD, JOHN, 1
We may become the makers of our f. | POPPER, 6
when F. summons | DRYDEN, 26
Wilde performed his life . . . even after f. had taken the plot | WILDE, 1
father a wise f. that knows his own child | SHAKESPEARE, 241
'Box about: 'twill come to my f. anon' | AUBREY, 1
brood of Folly without f. | MILTON, 11
Dreading to find its F. | AUDEN, 14
except to shoot rabbits and hit his f. on the jaw | MASEFIELD, 1
F. . . . come home with me now | WORK, 1
Full fathom five thy f. lies | SHAKESPEARE, 321
God is . . . an exalted f. | FREUD, S, 5
have we not all one f. | BIBLE, 342
he had rather Have a turnip than his f. | JOHNSON, S, 33
If poverty is the mother of crime, stupidity is its f. | LABRUYÈRE, 11
in my F.'s house are many mansions | BIBLE, 258
left me by my F. | CHARLES I, 2
Like f., like son | PROVERBS, 262
My f. didn't create you to arrest me | PEEL, 1
No man is responsible for his f. | TURNBULL, 1
our F. | BIBLE, 367
The Child is F. of the Man | WORDSWORTH, W, 23
the night the bed fell on my f. | THURBER, 9
Today I dressed to meet my f.'s eyes | JULIA, 1
You are old, F. William | SOUTHEY, 4
fatherhood Mirrors and f. are abominable | BORGES, 2
fathers atone for the sins of your f. | HORACE, 36
Come mothers and f. Throughout the land | DYLAN, 7
f., provoke not your children | BIBLE, 22
land of my f. | THOMAS, D, 29
the f. have eaten sour grapes | BIBLE, 126
Victory has a thousand f. | KENNEDY, JOHN, 18
fathom f. the inscrutable workings of Providence | BIRKENHEAD, 3
Full f. five thy father lies | SHAKESPEARE, 321
fatted the f. calf | BIBLE, 332
fattening the things I really like . . . are either immoral, illegal, or f. | WOOLLCOTT, 4
fatter But the valley sheep are f. | PEACOCK, 7
fatty f. degeneration of his moral being | STEVENSON, R, 24
fatuity the English seem . . . to act with . . . the f. of idiots | SMITH, SYDNEY, 2
fault only one f.. It was . . . lousy | THURBER, 20
Shakespeare never had six lines together without a f. | JOHNSON, S, 75
The f., dear Brutus, is not in our stars | SHAKESPEARE, 143
the f. were on only one side | ROCHEFOUCAULD, 26
The fundamental f. of the female character | SCHOPENHAUER, 4

faultless Whoever thinks a f. piece to see POPE, 24
faults best men are moulded out of f. SHAKESPEARE, 235
by pointing out to a man the f. of his mistress PROUST, 3
England, with all thy f. COWPER, 23
f., do not fear to abandon them CONFUCIUS, 8
If we had no f. of our own ROCHEFOUCAULD, 4
not quite clever enough to compensate for his f. MOUNTBATTEN, 2
only confess our little f. ROCHEFOUCAULD, 22
vile ill-favour'd f. Looks handsome in three hundred pounds SHAKESPEARE, 255
When you have f. CONFUCIUS, 8
favour accepts a smaller as a f. CARLYLE, J, 1
Many terms . . . out of f., will be revived HORACE, 4
she obtained grace and f. BIBLE, 101
truths being in and out of f. FROST, S, 6
whom the gods f. dies young PLAUTUS, 1
favoured they're a f. race CERVANTES, 18
thou that art highly f. BIBLE, 308
favours On whom their f. fall TENNYSON, 73
Whether a pretty woman grants or withholds her f. OVID, 3
fav'rite A f. has no friend GRAY, 12
fawning How like a f. publican he looks SHAKESPEARE, 238
fear ceased to be an object of f. as soon as one is pitied NIETZSCHE, 18
concessions of f. BURKE, E, 13
Curiosity will conquer f. STEPHENS, 2
do I f. thy nature SHAKESPEARE, 205
Do not suppose that I do not f. death JENNINGS, E, 1
f. clawed at my mind and body FRANK, 2
f. God, and keep his commandments BIBLE, 79
F. has many eyes CERVANTES, 7
f. in a handful of dust ELIOT, T, 27
F. is the parent of cruelty FROUDE, 3
F. lent wings to his feet VIRGIL, 15
f. made manifest on the body EDDY, 5
F. no more the heat o' th' sun SHAKESPEARE, 62
F. of death PROVERBS, 149
f. of the Lord is the beginning of wisdom PSALMS, 62
fools rush in where angels f. to tread POPE, 29
Fostered alike by beauty and by f. WORDSWORTH, W, 35
freedom from f. ROOSEVELT, F, 14
hate that which we often f. SHAKESPEARE, 26
have . . . many things to f. BACON, FRANCIS, 21
He who pretends to look on death without f. lies ROUSSEAU, 2
Men f. death BACON, FRANCIS, 18
None but a coward . . . has never known f. FOCH, 3
only thing we have to f. is f. itself ROOSEVELT, F, 10
perfect love casteth out f. BIBLE, 283
Perhaps your f. in passing judgement BRUNO, 1
pessimists end up by desiring the things they f. MALLET, 1
The concessions of the weak are the concessions of f. BURKE, E, 13
the f. of one evil BOILEAU, 2
the f. of the Lord . . . endureth for ever PSALMS, 9
feared neither f. nor flattered any flesh DOUGLAS, J, 1
fearful facing f. odds MACAULAY, T, 11
thy f. symmetry BLAKE, W, 39
fears A man who f. suffering MONTAIGNE, 11
enough for fifty hopes and f. BROWNING, R, 9
man f. . . . only the stroke of death BACON, FRANCIS, 7
The sum of their f. CHURCHILL, W, 34
feast Life is not a . . . f. SANTAYANA, 8
Paris is a moveable f. HEMINGWAY, 6
feather a f. to tickle the intellect LAMB, CHARLES, 16
feathers Fine f. PROVERBS, 152
not only fine f. AESOP, 5
thou shalt be safe under his f. PSALMS, 51
February dreadful pictures of January and F. TROLLOPE, 7
Excepting F. alone And that has twenty-eight days clear NURSERY RHYMES, 61
F., fill the dyke TUSSER, 1
fecund to mistake for the first-rate, the f. rate PARKER, D, 17
fed bite the hand that f. them BURKE, E, 19
fee hold the gorgeous east in f. WORDSWORTH, W, 58
feeble-minded woman . . . so vicious, or so f., that she cannot withstand temptation BRONTË, A, 1
feed f. my lambs BIBLE, 279
f. my sheep BIBLE, 280
he shall f. his flock BIBLE, 211
he shall f. me in a green pasture PSALMS, 10
Why rob one to f. the other JUANG-ZU, 1
You cannot f. the hungry on statistics LLOYD GEORGE, 7

feedeth he f. among the lilies BIBLE, 491
feeding Spoon f. . . . teaches us nothing but the shape of the spoon FORSTER, 12
feel Englishman . . . is afraid to f. FORSTER, 2
I can f. him ten feet away BIERCE, 2
I draw what I f. in my body HEPWORTH, 1
what I f. really bad about FRAYN, 3
feeling A man is as old as he's f. COLLINS, MORTIMER, 1
Compassion is not a sloppy, sentimental f. KINNOCK, 6
forgetting . . . womanly f. and propriety VICTORIA, 7
feelings First f. are always the most natural LOUIS XIV, 3
feels A really intelligent man f. what other men . . . know MONTESQUIEU, 2
feet Alan will always land on somebody's f. PARKER, D, 22
An emperor ought at least to die on his f. VESPASIAN, 1
better to die on your f. than to live on your knees IBARRURI, 2
both f. firmly planted in the air SCANLON, 1
Fear lent wings to his f. VIRGIL, 15
those f. in ancient time BLAKE, W, 33
feigning truest poetry is the most f. SHAKESPEARE, 54
felicity likely to mar the general f. BUTLER, S, 19
Fell Doctor F. BROWN, T, 1
fell by faith the walls of Jericho f. down BIBLE, 186
crumbs which f. from the rich man's table BIBLE, 333
f. among thieves BIBLE, 324
men f. out BUTLER, S, 1
felled The poplars are f. COWPER, 19
fellow f. of infinite jest SHAKESPEARE, 105
fellow-men Write me as one that loves his f. HUNT, L, 2
fellows Boys are capital f. in their own way LAMB, CHARLES, 9
fellowship such a f. of good knights shall never be together MALORY, 3
female male and f. created he them BIBLE, 142
the f. character . . . has no sense of justice SCHOPENHAUER, 4
the f. of the species is more deadly than the male KIPLING, 9
The fundamental fault of the f. character SCHOPENHAUER, 4
The seldom f. PITTER, 1
What f. heart can gold despise GRAY, 11
feminine reflection of a boy too long exposed to f. eyes CARROLL, 1
Taste is the f. of genius FITZGERALD, E, 1
feminist the best home for a f. WATSON, 1
feminization the f. of the white European . . . far advanced LEWIS, W, 3
fence The . . . gentleman has sat so long on the f. LLOYD GEORGE, 14
fences Good f. PROVERBS, 179
Good f. make good neighbours FROST, R, 6
ferries the snow blind twilight f. THOMAS, D, 28
fettered so f. fast we are BROWNING, R, 3
fever hand that signed the treaty bred a f. THOMAS, D, 11
Février Generals Janvier and F. NICHOLAS I, 2
few err as grosly as the F. DRYDEN, 12
How f. of his friends' houses JOHNSON, S, 142
I don't want art for a f. MORRIS, W, 3
so much owed by so many to so f. CHURCHILL, W, 54
fiat f. lux BIBLE, 138
fickle Woman is always f. and changing VIRGIL, 12
fiction ancient history . . . is no more than accepted f. VOLTAIRE, 17
an improbable f. SHAKESPEARE, 343
Children should acquire . . . heroes and villains from f. AUDEN, 4
one form of continuous f. BEVAN, 2
Poetry is a comforting piece of f. MENCKEN, 12
Stranger than f. BYRON, 35
fiddle consider your puny little f. when He speaks to me BEETHOVEN, 2
Hey diddle diddle, The cat and the f. NURSERY RHYMES, 14
keep it shut up . . . like a rare, rare f. MANSFIELD, K, 1
When I play on my f. in Dooney YEATS, 12
fiddlers he called for his f. three NURSERY RHYMES, 38
field A cow is a very good animal in the f. JOHNSON, S, 156
Behold her, single in the f. WORDSWORTH, W, 50
Man for the f. and woman for the hearth TENNYSON, 66
shepherds abiding in the f. BIBLE, 314
some corner of a foreign f. BROOKE, 1
What though the f. be lost MILTON, 32
fields 'a babbl'd of green f. SHAKESPEARE, 127
Now there are f. where Troy once was OVID, 5
We plough the f., and scatter CAMPBELL, JANE, 1
fiend a f. hid in a cloud BLAKE, W, 38
a frightful f. Doth close behind him tread COLERIDGE, S, 36

fierce f. and bald and short of breath   SASSOON, S, 1
fiercest scene of the f. fight   MANDELA, 1
fiery Nightingale . . . A creature of a 'f. heart'   WORDSWORTH, W, 34
fifteen F. men on the dead man's chest   STEVENSON, R, 8
fifth Beethoven's F. Symphony is the most sublime noise   FORSTER, 7
One f. of the people are against everything   KENNEDY, R, 3
fifty For one person who dreams of making f. thousand pounds   MILNE, 3
Sit on your arse for f. years   MACNEICE, 1
'You'll see, when you're f.'   SATIE, 2
fifty-fifty There can be no f. Americanism   ROOSEVELT, T, 10
fig they sewed f. leaves together   BIBLE, 149
fight a great cause to f. for   PANKHURST, C, 2
do not f. with the world   BUDDHA, 1
easier to f. for one's principles   ADLER, 1
f., f., f., and f. again   GAITSKELL, 3
F. fire   PROVERBS, 150
f. the good f.   BIBLE, 512
F. the good f. with all thy might   MONSELL, 1
Good at a f.   SHERIDAN, R, 4
I dare not f.   SHAKESPEARE, 125
I have not yet begun to f.   JONES, 1
I purpose to f. it out on this line   GRANT, U, 4
I will not cease from mental f.   BLAKE, W, 33
Nor law, nor duty bade me f.   YEATS, 16
soil of our country . . . scene of the fiercest f.   MANDELA, 1
There'll be a hard f. tomorrow   SAKHAROV, 1
To f. and not to heed the wounds   LOYOLA, 1
too proud to f.   WILSON, W, 10
Ulster will f.   CHURCHILL, R, 3
We don't want to f., but, by jingo if we do   HUNT, G, 1
We'll f. and we'll conquer   GARRICK, 2
we shall f. on the beaches   CHURCHILL, W, 51
when the f. begins within   BROWNING, R, 12
With our backs to the wall . . . each . . . must f. on to the end   HAIG, 1
You cannot f. against the future   GLADSTONE, 1
fighting F. is like champagne   MITCHELL, M, 2
Most sorts of diversion . . . are an imitation of f.   SWIFT, 17
not conquering but f. well   COUBERTIN, 1
'What are we f. for?'   SERVICE, 4
fights He that f. and runs away   ANONYMOUS, 38
I can't spare this man; he f.   LINCOLN, 20
figure an oblong angular f.   LEACOCK, 6
figures prove anything by f.   CARLYLE, T, 4
film A wide screen . . . makes a bad f. twice as bad   GOLDWYN, 9
I like a f. to have a beginning, a middle and an end   GODARD, 2
films Why . . . pay money to see bad f.   GOLDWYN, 2
finality F. is death. Perfection is f.   STEPHENS, 1
find terrible thing for a man to f. out   WILDE, 36
your sin will f. you out   BIBLE, 439
finders F. keepers   PROVERBS, 151
fine Give me books, fruit, French wine and f. weather   KEATS, 66
not only f. feathers   AESOP, 5
The big print giveth and the f. print taketh away   SHEEN, 2
fine art In England, pop art and f.   MACINNES, 1
finer every baby . . . is a f. one   DICKENS, 33
finest their f. hour   CHURCHILL, W, 52
finger Moving F. writes   FITZGERALD, E, 14
The least pain in our little f.   HAZLITT, 3
fingernails See what will happen . . . if you don't stop biting your f.   ROGERS, W, 11
fingers about time we pulled our f. out   PHILIP, PRINCE, 2
f. of a man's hand, and wrote   BIBLE, 51
F. were made before forks   PROVERBS, 154
ill cook that cannot lick his own f.   SHAKESPEARE, 317
our f. are circumcised   PERLMAN, 1
thy heavens, even the works of thy f.   PSALMS, 46
finger-tips An accomplished man to his f.   HORACE, 46
Fings F. Ain't Wot They Used T'Be   NORMAN, F, 1
finished it is f.   BIBLE, 271
finite Our knowledge can only be f.   POPPER, 1
fir The f. trees dark and high   HOOD, 7
fire a chariot . . . of f.   BIBLE, 301
All things, oh priests, are on f.   BUDDHA, 1
a pillar of f.   BIBLE, 111
Billy . . . Fell in the f.   GRAHAM, H, 2
bound Upon a wheel of f.   SHAKESPEARE, 191
cloven tongues like as of f.   BIBLE, 2
f. and brimstone, storm and tempest   PSALMS, 5
F. – without hatred   RIVERA, 1

French Guard, f. first   HAY, C, 1
heap coals of f. upon his head   BIBLE, 454
Ideas that enter the mind under f.   TROTSKY, 9
It is with our passions as it is with f. and water   L'ESTRANGE, 1
I warmed both hands before the f. of life   LANDOR, 7
London burnt by f. in three times twenty plus six   NOSTRADAMUS, 2
that deplorable f. near Fish Street in London   EVELYN, 3
the bush burned with f.   BIBLE, 105
The f. which in the heart resides   ARNOLD, M, 29
two irons in the f.   BEAUMONT, 3
what wind is to f.   BUSSY-RABUTIN, 1
firearms Though loaded f. were strictly forbidden at St Trinian's   SEARLE, 1
fire-folk the f. sitting in the air   HOPKINS, 5
fireirons Saint Preux never kicked the f.   CARLYLE, J, 2
fires Husbands are like f.   GABOR, 1
fireside A man may surely be allowed to take a glass of wine by his own f.   SHERIDAN, R, 16
firing he faced the f. squad; erect and motionless   THURBER, 11
firm not a family, we're a f.   GEORGE VI, 1
firmness *Commodity, F., and Delight*   WOTTON, 1
first Because of my title, I was the f.   ALENÇON, 1
F. come   PROVERBS, 155
F. impressions   PROVERBS, 156
f. in peace   WASHINGTON, 1
F. in war   WASHINGTON, 1
F. things f.   PROVERBS, 157
f. time I saw Dylan Thomas   THOMAS, D, 1
If at f. you don't succeed   HICKSON, 1
many that are f. shall be last   BIBLE, 406
The constitution . . . f. and second class citizens   WILLKIE, 1
The f. day a guest   PROVERBS, 393
there is no last or f.   BROWNING, R, 48
which came f., the Greeks or the Romans   DISRAELI, 39
Who ever loved, that loved not at f. sight   MARLOWE, 8
first-aid His ideas of f.   WODEHOUSE, 11
firstborn I . . . will smite all the f.   BIBLE, 110
firstfruits first of the f.   BIBLE, 118
first-rate the powers of a f. man and the creed of a second-rate man   BAGEHOT, 9
to mistake for the f., the fecund rate   PARKER, D, 17
fish a great f. to swallow up Jonah   BIBLE, 286
F. and guests   PROVERBS, 158
F. die belly-upward and rise . . . their way of falling   GIDE, 3
F. fuck in it   FIELDS, 2
I have my own f. to fry   CERVANTES, 10
No human being . . . was ever so free as a f.   RUSKIN, 15
Phone for the f. knives Norman   BETJEMAN, 1
queen did f. for men's souls   ELIZABETH I, 1
This man . . . is a poor f.   DENNIS, N, 1
What cat's averse to f.   GRAY, 11
fishbone The monument sticks like a f.   LOWELL, 2
fishermen a bite every time for f.   MORTON, 4
fishers f. of men   BIBLE, 359
fishes f. live in the sea   SHAKESPEARE, 290
five barley loaves, and two small f.   BIBLE, 249
So are the f.   CHURCHILL, W, 55
fishing Time is but the stream I go a-f. in   THOREAU, 17
fishmonger She was a f., but sure 'twas no wonder   ANONYMOUS, 47
fishy something f. about the French   COWARD, 5
fist You cannot shake hands with a clenched f.   GANDHI, I, 3
fit a pleasing f. of melancholy   MILTON, 10
It is not f. that you should sit here   CROMWELL, O, 7
let the punishment f. the crime   GILBERT, W, 29
news that's f. to print   OCHS, 1
only the F. survive   SERVICE, 3
fits periodical f. of morality   MACAULAY, T, 16
Strange f. of passion   WORDSWORTH, W, 66
fittest Survival of the f.   SPENCER, H, 3
Survival of the F.   DARWIN, C R, 10
Fitzgerald F. was an alcoholic   FITZGERALD, F S, 1
five child of f. would understand this   MARX, G, 6
F. for the symbol at your door   ANONYMOUS, 45
F. gold rings   NURSERY RHYMES, 60
If you don't find a God by f. o'clock this afternoon   JOWETT, 7
Mister John Keats f. feet high   KEATS, 61
practise f. things   CONFUCIUS, 9
The formula 'Two and two make f.'   DOSTOEVSKY, F, 1
five-pound note get a f. as . . . a light for a cigarette   JAMES, H, 5
flabbiness The moral f. born of . . . Success   JAMES, W, 4

flag But spare your country's f.   WHITTIER, 2
keep the red f. flying here   CONNELL, 1
Tonight the American f. floats from yonder hill or Molly Stark
sleeps a widow   STARK, 1
flagons stay me with f.   BIBLE, 487
flame like a moth, the simple maid Still plays about the f.   GAY, 2
flames Commit it then to the f.: for it can contain nothing but
sophistry and illusion   HUME, D, 2
Superstition sets the whole world in f.   VOLTAIRE, 13
Flanders In F. fields   MCCRAE, 1
You have sent me a F. mare   HENRY VIII, 1
flash the f. cut him, and he lies in the stubble   ANONYMOUS, 27
flashing His f. eyes, his floating hair   COLERIDGE, S, 17
flat f. road to heaven   SANTAYANA, 1
Very f., Norfolk   COWARD, 16
Vile snub-nose, f.-nosed ass   ROSTAND, E, 1
flatter not f. me   CROMWELL, O, 4
We f. those we scarcely know   WILCOX, 1
flattered neither feared nor f. any flesh   DOUGLAS, J, 1
flatterer the brave beast is no f.   JONSON, 8
flatterers f. live at the expense of those who listen
       LAFONTAINE, 2
Self-love . . . greatest of all f.   ROCHEFOUCAULD, 13
flattering It is f. some men to endure them   HALIFAX, 3
the talent of f. with delicacy   AUSTEN, 22
flattery consider whether . . . your f. is worth his having
       JOHNSON, S, 31
f.'s the food of fools   SWIFT, 4
Imitation is the sincerest form of f.   COLTON, 3
ne'er Was f. lost   SCOTT, WALTER, 6
woman . . . to be gained by . . . f.   CHESTERFIELD, 17
flaunt if you've got it, f. it   BROOKS, M, 2
flautists f. . . . know something we don't know   JENNINGS, P, 1
flavour Does the Spearmint Lose Its F.   ROSE, 1
flea English literature's performing f.   O'CASEY, 4
man's whole frame is obvious to a f.   POPE, 5
The guerrilla fights the war of the f.   TABER, 1
the point of precedency between a louse and a f.   JOHNSON, S, 144
fleas dog that praised his f.   YEATS, 31
F. . . . upon the body of a giant   LANDOR, 6
Great f. have little f. upon their backs   MORGAN, A, 1
the f. in my bed were as good   CERVANTES, 13
The f. that tease in the high Pyrenees   BELLOC, 15
these have smaller f. to bite 'em   SWIFT, 9
fled I f. Him, down the nights   THOMPSON, F, 1
flee then would I f. away, and be at rest   PSALMS, 33
fleece On Wenlock Edge the wood's in trouble; His forest f. the
Wrekin heaves   HOUSMAN, 1
Fleet The F.'s lit up. It is like fairyland   WOODROOFE, 1
flesh all f. is as grass   BIBLE, 440
a thorn in the f.   BIBLE, 47
f. and blood so cheap   HOOD, 12
f. to feel the chain   BRONTË, E, 3
I, born of f. and ghost   THOMAS, D, 4
I have more f. than another man   SHAKESPEARE, 112
Ishmaelites . . . will not publicly eat human f. uncooked in Lent
       WAUGH, E, 38
I wants to make your f. creep   DICKENS, 43
Leave the f. to the fate it was fit for   BROWNING, R, 51
Rehearsing a play is making the word f.   SHAFFER, 3
take off my f. and sit in my bones   SMITH, SYDNEY, 3
that which is born of the f. is f.   BIBLE, 244
the f. is weak   BIBLE, 426
the f. lusteth against the Spirit   BIBLE, 134
the way of all f.   CONGREVE, 12
the way of all f. . . . towards the kitchen   WEBSTER, J, 4
'Tis the way of all f.   SHADWELL, 2
world, the f., and the devil   BOOK OF COMMON PRAYER, 12;
       MURRAY, 4
fleshly The F. School of Poetry   BUCHANAN, 2
flies As f. to wanton boys   SHAKESPEARE, 185
certain, that Life f.   FITZGERALD, E, 10
Time f., death urges   YOUNG, E, 7
flight Above the vulgar f. of common souls   MURPHY, A, 1
fling I'll have a f.   BEAUMONT, 11
flirt f. with their own husbands   WILDE, 22
Young women have a duty to f.   BROOKNER, 1
float rather be an opportunist and f.   BALDWIN, S, 10
flock he shall feed his f.   BIBLE, 211
keeping watch over their f. by night   BIBLE, 314
flogging There is now less f. in our great schools
       JOHNSON, S, 100

flood the f. was forty days upon the earth   BIBLE, 158
Which, taken at the f.   SHAKESPEARE, 159
floor stood ninety years on the f.   WORK, 2
flowed water f. like champagne   EVARTS, 1
flower A lovelier f. . . . was never sown   WORDSWORTH, W, 69
Die when I may . . . I have always plucked a thistle and planted a
f.   LINCOLN, 7
just miss the prizes at the f. show   BRONOWSKI, 5
many a f. is born to blush unseen   GRAY, 5
The F. that once has blown   FITZGERALD, E, 10
the meanest f. . . . can give Thoughts   WORDSWORTH, W, 30
flowers a book that is a book f. once   LAWRENCE, D, 40
Do spring May f.   TUSSER, 2
Gather the f., but spare the buds   MARVELL, 8
Letting a hundred f. blossom   MAO TSE-TUNG, 6
No fruits, no f., no leaves, no birds   HOOD, 10
Say it with f.   O'KEEFE, 1
The f. that bloom in the spring   GILBERT, W, 33
Their f. the tenderness of patient minds   OWEN, W, 1
Too late for fruit, too soon for f.   DE LA MARE, 3
When people come together, f. always flourish   JACKSON, J, 1
Where have all the f. gone   SEEGER, P, 1
flowery A little thin, f. border   LAMB, CHARLES, 25
flows Everything f. and nothing stays   HERACLITUS, 1
flung he f. himself from the room   LEACOCK, 10
flutes Gibbon moved to f. and hautboys   GIBBON, 2
fluxions Sir Isaac Newton . . . deep in algebra and f.   NEWTON, I, 2
fly A f., Sir, may sting a stately horse   JOHNSON, S, 49
f. . . . said, what a dust do I raise   BACON, FRANCIS, 58
said a spider to a f.   HOWITT, 1
small gilded f. Does lecher   SHAKESPEARE, 187
Who saw him die? I, said the F.   NURSERY RHYMES, 73
flying Days and moments quickly f.   CASWALL, 1
He ought to have stuck to his f. machines   LEONARDO DA VINCI, 3
foam the f. Of perilous seas   KEATS, 39
the white f. flew   COLERIDGE, S, 29
foe Heat not a furnace for your f.   SHAKESPEARE, 107
he is the sworn f. of our nation   CAMPBELL, T, 7
He . . . who never made a f.   TENNYSON, 18
foeman When the f. bares his steel   GILBERT, W, 39
foes judge of a man by his f.   CONRAD, 4
fog a London particular . . . A f.   DICKENS, 5
Folies-Bergère A psychiatrist is a man who goes to the F.
       STOCKWOOD, 1
folk-dancing except incest and f.   BAX, 1
folks for de old f. at home   FOSTER, 3
follies f. as the special evidences of our wisdom   TROLLOPE, 10
lovers cannot see the pretty f.   SHAKESPEARE, 242
the f. of the town crept slowly among us   GOLDSMITH, 20
The f. which a man regrets   ROWLAND, H, 2
follow F. up! . . . Till the field ring again   BOWEN, E. E., 2
I have to f. them, I am their leader   LEDRU-ROLLIN, 1
I must f. them   LAW, 1
take up his cross, and f. me   BIBLE, 398
folly brood of F. without father   MILTON, 11
His foe was f. and his weapon wit   HOPE, 9
the slightest f. That ever love did make thee run into
       SHAKESPEARE, 44
When lovely woman stoops to f.   GOLDSMITH, 29
where ignorance is bliss, 'Tis f. to be wise   GRAY, 10
fond He is very f. of making things   HOPE, 2
fonder Absence makes the heart grow f.   BAYLY, 1
fondness inordinate f. for beetles   HALDANE, 3
food flattery's the f. of fools   SWIFT, 4
f. in music   LILLO, 1
F. is an important part of a balanced diet   LEBOWITZ, 2
f. to one man is bitter poison to others   LUCRETIUS, 4
man did eat angels' f.   PSALMS, 42
my Uncle George . . . discovered that alcohol was a f.
       WODEHOUSE, 8
Nothing to eat but f.   KING, B, 1
On the Continent people have good f.   MIKES, 1
Spleen can subsist on any kind of f.   HAZLITT, 31
The perpetual struggle for room and f.   MALTHUS, 1
the wine was a farce and the f. a tragedy   POWELL, A, 2
fool a f. among fools or a f. alone   WILDER, T, 4
A f. and his money   PROVERBS, 15
A f. at forty   PROVERBS, 16
A f. believes everything   PROVERBS, 17
A f. bolts pleasure, then complains of . . . indigestion   ANTRIM, 1
A f. sees not the same tree   BLAKE, W, 27
a greater f. to admire him   BOILEAU, 3

answer a f. according to his folly — BIBLE, 456
a worm at one end and a f. at the other — JOHNSON, S, 164
Better be a f. than a knave — PROVERBS, 88
born f. who voluntarily engages in controversy with Mr. Adams — ADAMS, J, 1
brains enough to make a f. of himself — STEVENSON, R, 21
Busy old f., unruly Sun — DONNE, 16
f. his whole life long — LUTHER, 5
f. walketh in darkness — BIBLE, 66
He who holds hopes . . . is a f. — CAMUS, 16
it needs a very clever woman to manage a f. — KIPLING, 21
Love is the wisdom of the f. — JOHNSON, S, 42
more of the f. than of the wise — BACON, FRANCIS, 13
No creature smarts . . . as a f. — POPE, 17
One f. . . . in every married couple — FIELDING, 4
Send a f. to the market — PROVERBS, 361
The dupe of friendship, and the f. of love — HAZLITT, 26
the greatest f. may ask more — COLTON, 5
the old man who will not laugh is a f. — SANTAYANA, 3
There's no f. like an old f. — PROVERBS, 416
The wisest f. in Christendom — HENRI IV, 3
Wise Man or a F. — BLAKE, W, 17
You can f. too many of the people — THURBER, 5
foolish A f. consistency — EMERSON, 15
a f. man, which built his house upon the sand — BIBLE, 380
anything very f. — MELBOURNE, 8
He never said a f. thing — ROCHESTER, 1
If you are f. enough to be contented, don't show it — JEROME, 4
more f. when he had not a pen in his hand — GOLDSMITH, 1
O f. Galatians — BIBLE, 131
You must not think me . . . f. because I am facetious — SMITH, SYDNEY, 16
foolishness by the f. of preaching — BIBLE, 24
Mix a little f. with your serious plans — HORACE, 44
fools Christianity . . . says that they are all f. — CHESTERTON, 22
flattery's the food of f. — SWIFT, 4
f. and passengers drink at sea — VILLIERS, 1
F. are in a terrible, overwhelming majority — IBSEN, 1
F. build houses — PROVERBS, 159
F. live poor — PROVERBS, 160
f. rush in where angels fear to tread — POPE, 29
Fortune always favours f. — GAY, 8
Fortune, that favours f. — JONSON, 3
I am two f. — DONNE, 17
Is Pride, the never-failing vice of f. — POPE, 22
Many have been the wise speeches of f. — FULLER, T, 4
not suffer f. gladly — ACHESON, 2
suffer f. gladly — BIBLE, 46
the greater part of the law is learning to tolerate f. — LESSING, D, 5
Thirty millions, mostly f. — CARLYLE, T, 36
this great stage of f. — SHAKESPEARE, 190
To suckle f. and chronicle — SHAKESPEARE, 280
what delight we married people have to see . . . f. decoyed into our condition — PEPYS, 13
what f. these mortals be — SHAKESPEARE, 262
world is made up . . . of f. and knaves — BUCKINGHAM, 2
foot noiseless f. of Time — SHAKESPEARE, 104
footprints F. on the sands of time — PROVERBS, 161
footsteps home his f. he hath turn'd — SCOTT, WALTER, 8
foppery excellent f. of the world — SHAKESPEARE, 169
for neither f. nor against institutions — WHITMAN, 4
forbearance f. ceases to be a virtue — BURKE, E, 5
forbid I f. my tears — SHAKESPEARE, 104
forbidden F. fruit — PROVERBS, 162
he wanted it only because it was f. — TWAIN, 15
we're f. to know – what end the gods have in store — HORACE, 30
Ye are f. to eat that which dieth of itself — KORAN, 5
force f. alone is but *temporary* — BURKE, E, 15
F., if unassisted by judgement, collapses — HORACE, 35
F. is not a remedy — BRIGHT, 3
F. that through the green fuse — THOMAS, D, 10
Hence no f. however great — WHEWELL, 1
May the F. be with you — LUCAS, 1
Other nations use 'f.'; we Britons . . . use 'Might' — WAUGH, E, 39
Who overcomes By f. — MILTON, 37
forced f. to commend her highly — PEPYS, 9
force-feeding This universal, obligatory f. with lies — SOLZHENITSYN, 11
forces one of the f. of nature — MICHELET, 1
Ford Jerry F. is so dumb — JOHNSON, L, 4
The time of our F. — HUXLEY, A, 11
forefathers Think of your f. — ADAMS, J, 3

forehead A burning f., and a parching tongue — KEATS, 31
foreign pronounce f. names as he chooses — CHURCHILL, W, 37
wandering on a f. strand — SCOTT, WALTER, 8
foreigner f. should . . . be wiser than ourselves — TROLLOPE, 10
foreigners f. speak English when our backs are turned — CRISP, 8
f. . . . spell better than they pronounce — TWAIN, 10
Sympathy . . . for being f. — BRADBURY, 1
forest His f. fleece the Wrekin heaves — HOUSMAN, 13
Wandering in a vast f. at night — DIDEROT, 1
forests the f. of the night — BLAKE, W, 39
foretaste Every parting gives a f. of death — SCHOPENHAUER, 3
forever That is f. England — BROOKE, 6
forewarned F. is forearmed — PROVERBS, 163
forget Better by far you should f. and smile — ROSSETTI, C, 5
Fade far away, dissolve, and . . . f. — KEATS, 38
I f. what I was taught — WHITE, P, 2
I'll not f. old Ireland — BLACKWOOD, 2
I never f. a face, but I'll make an exception — MARX, G, 20
Oh Lord! . . . if I f. thee, do not thou f. me — ASTLEY, 1
Old men f. — SHAKESPEARE, 134
To endeavour to f. anyone — LA BRUYÈRE, 14
Were it not better to f. — LANDON, 1
When I f. my sovereign — THURLOW, 1
forgetful He is . . . decrepit and f. . . . a bore — BELLOC, 2
forgivable Few books today are f. — LAING, 3
forgive do not have to f. my enemies — NARVÁEZ, 1
Father, f. them — BIBLE, 339
F. and forget — PROVERBS, 164
how oft shall . . . I f. him — BIBLE, 402
Men will f. a man — CHURCHILL, W, 39
To err is human, to f., divine — POPE, 28
forgiven man can be f. a lot if he can quote Shakespeare — SHAKESPEARE, 15
Once a woman has f. her man — DIETRICH, 1
forgot auld acquaintance be f. — BURNS, R, 4
How these curiosities would be quite f. — AUBREY, 2
I have f. my part — SHAKESPEARE, 59
forgotten East and west on fields f. — HOUSMAN, 14
five sparrows . . . not one of them is f. — BIBLE, 328
Has God then f. — LOUIS XIV, 2
I am clean f., as a dead man — PSALMS, 20
I have f. more law than you ever knew — MAYNARD, 1
Nobody is f. when it is convenient to remember him — DISRAELI, 36
The f. man — ROOSEVELT, F, 8
what has been learnt has been f. — SKINNER, B, 2
fork he had a f. — LEVERSON, 4
forks I had a knife and two f. left — RIDGE, 2
forlorn faery lands f. — KEATS, 39
The British postgraduate student is a lonely f. soul — LODGE, 3
form significant f. — BELL, C, 1
formed not f. by nature to bear — MARCUS AURELIUS, 9
former there is no remembrance of f. things — BIBLE, 63
formidable Examinations are f. — COLTON, 4
forms from outward f. to win — COLERIDGE, S, 11
formula Matter . . . a convenient f. — RUSSELL, B, 18
fornicated f. and read the papers — CAMUS, 6
fornication F.: but that was in another country — MARLOWE, 11
forsaken my God, why hast thou f. me — BIBLE, 431
fortress f. built by Nature — SHAKESPEARE, 295
fortuitous Accidental and f. concurrence of atoms — PALMERSTON, 1
fortune deficiences of f. — GOLDSMITH, 28
F. always favours fools — GAY, 8
f. and men's eyes — SHAKESPEARE, 360
F. favours fools — PROVERBS, 165
F. favours the brave — TERENCE, 3
F., that favours fools — JONSON, 3
greater virtues to sustain good f. — ROCHEFOUCAULD, 3
Here rests . . . A youth to f. and to fame unknown — GRAY, 4
hostages to f. — BACON, FRANCIS, 33
people of f. . . . a few delinquencies — ELIOT, G, 5
slings and arrows of outrageous f. — SHAKESPEARE, 89
to make your f. . . . let people see . . . it is in their interests to promote yours — LA BRUYÈRE, 16
What is your f., my pretty maid — NURSERY RHYMES, 71
fortunes f. sharp adversitee — CHAUCER, 20
share in the good f. of the mighty — BRECHT, 1
forty f. days and f. nights — BIBLE, 356
F. years on — BOWEN, E, E, 1
I am just turning f. — LLOYD, H, 1
I have been talking prose for over f. years — MOLIÈRE, 3
Life begins at f. — TUCKER, 4
look young till f. — DRYDEN, 27

made the difference of f. thousand men — WELLINGTON, 11
When you are f. — ANOUILH, 7
forty-five That should assure us of . . . f. minutes of undisturbed privacy — PARKER, D, 12
Forty-niner In a cavern . . . Dwelt a miner, F., And his daughter, Clementine — MONTROSE, 1
forty-three She may very well pass for f. — GILBERT, W, 45
forward looking f. to the past — OSBORNE, 5
foster-child f. of silence and slow time — KEATS, 27
fou I wasna f. — BURNS, R, 7
fought better to have f. and lost — CLOUGH, 7
f. with us upon Saint Crispin's day — SHAKESPEARE, 135
I have f. a good fight — BIBLE, 514
foul F. deeds will rise — SHAKESPEARE, 71
Murder most f. — SHAKESPEARE, 77
So f. and fair a day — SHAKESPEARE, 201
foul-mouthed English . . . are rather a f. nation — HAZLITT, 16
found he f. it brick — AUGUSTUS, 1
I have f. it — ARCHIMEDES, 2
I have f. my sheep which was lost — BIBLE, 330
Pleasure is . . . seldom f. where it is sought — JOHNSON, S, 16
Suppose it had been someone else who f. you like this — RICHELIEU, DUC DE, 1
they f. no more of her than . . . the palms of her hands — BIBLE, 303
When f., make a note of — DICKENS, 19
foundation The Church's one f. — STONE, S, 1
foundations her f. are upon the holy hills — PSALMS, 47
fountain a f. of gardens — BIBLE, 492
fountains their f. piped an answer — LAWRENCE, D, 6
four at the age of f. . . . we're all Generals — USTINOV, 7
F. colly birds — NURSERY RHYMES, 60
f. essential human freedoms — ROOSEVELT, F, 14
F. for the Gospel makers — ANONYMOUS, 45
F. legs good — ORWELL, 4
f. seasons in the mind of men — KEATS, 19
'Great God grant that twice two be not f.' — TURGENEV, 4
fourth a f. estate of the realm — MACAULAY, T, 4
Because there's no f. class — SANTAYANA, 7
on the f. day they will say 'To hell with you!' — KHRUSHCHEV, 8
there sat a *F. Estate* — CARLYLE, T, 13
four-year-old You've got the brain of a f. boy — MARX, G, 12
Fox Charles James F. — WORDSWORTH, W, 15
fox a f. from his lair — GRAVES, J, 1
Let me remind you what the wary f. said . . . to the sick lion — HORACE, 1
The f. came home and he went to ground — MASEFIELD, 4
The f. knows many things — ARCHILOCHUS, 1
You don't set a f. to watching the chickens — TRUMAN, 11
foxes the little f., that spoil the vines — BIBLE, 490
fox-hunting athletics as inferior forms of f. — WAUGH, E, 17
fraction Only a residual f. is thought — SANTAYANA, 2
fragrant a thousand f. posies — MARLOWE, 14
frailty F., thy name is woman — SHAKESPEARE, 68
more flesh . . . more f. — SHAKESPEARE, 112
frame all the Human F. requires — BELLOC, 1
change their clime, not their f. of mind, who rush across the sea — HORACE, 21
man's whole f. is obvious to a flea — POPE, 5
frames The finest collection of f. — DAVY, 1
framework Language is . . . a defining f. — WHORF, 1
France all roads lead to F. — THOMAS, E, 4
Fair stood the wind for F. — DRAYTON, 11
F. has more need of me — NAPOLEON I, 10
F. is a country where the money falls apart — WILDER, B, 3
F. was a long despotism — CARLYLE, T, 14
Like Brighton pier, . . . inadequate for getting to F. — KINNOCK, 7
The best thing I know between F. and England — JERROLD, 2
Francis My cousin F. and I are in perfect accord — CHARLES V, 1
frankincense gold, and f., and myrrh — BIBLE, 352
Franklin body of Benjamin F. — FRANKLIN, 18
fraternité *Liberté! Egalité! F.* — ANONYMOUS, 50
fraud Bonaparte's whole life . . . was a f. — NAPOLEON I, 4
frauds pious f. of friendship — FIELDING, 1
then . . . many of the great men of history are f. — LAW, 1
free a democratic and f. society in which all persons live together in harmony — MANDELA, 3
a f. society . . . where it is safe to be unpopular — STEVENSON, A, 6
All f. men . . . are citizens of Berlin — KENNEDY, JOHN, 15
All human beings are born f. and equal in dignity and rights — ANONYMOUS, 3
all men everywhere could be f. — LINCOLN, 8
f. as the road — HERBERT, G, 1

F. Will and Predestination — CHURCHILL, W, 20
Greece might still be f. — BYRON, 27
I'm with you on the f. press. It's the newspapers — STOPPARD, 7
In a f. society the state . . . administers justice among men — LIPPMAN, 1
I was f. born — BIBLE, 15
land of the f., and the home of the brave — KEY, F, 1
Man is condemned to be f. — SARTRE, 6
Man was born f. — ROUSSEAU, 1
Napoleon is a dangerous man in a f. country — NAPOLEON I, 2
No human being . . . was ever so f. as a fish — RUSKIN, 15
none the less f. than you were — MARCUS AURELIUS, 11
safer to be in chains than to be f. — KAFKA, 1
So f. we seem — BROWNING, R, 3
the truth shall make you f. — BIBLE, 246
Thou art f. — ARNOLD, M, 40
truth that makes men f. — AGAR, 1
We have to believe in f. will. We've got no choice — SINGER, 2
We must be f. or die — WORDSWORTH, W, 54
Who would be f. — BYRON, 12
freedom enemies of F. — INGE, 2
flame of f. in their souls — SYMONDS, 1
F.! Equality! Brotherhood — ANONYMOUS, 50
F. is an indivisible word — WILLKIE, 3
F. is Slavery — ORWELL, 18'
f. of speech — TWAIN, 7
F.'s just another word — KRISTOFFERSON, 1
f. to print . . . proprietor's prejudices — SWAFFER, 1
In solitude alone can he know true f. — MONTAIGNE, 2
Me this unchartered f. tires — WORDSWORTH, W, 33
Necessity is the plea for every infringement of human f. — PITT THE YOUNGER, 1
None can love f. heartily, but good men — MILTON, 64
only f. can make security secure — POPPER, 2
So long as the state exists there is no f. — LENIN, 4
The worst enemy of truth and f. — IBSEN, 3
Those who deny f. to others — LINCOLN, 12
Until you've lost your reputation, you never realize . . . what f. really is — MITCHELL, M, 1
we suffragettes aspire to be . . . ambassadors of f. to women — PANKHURST, C, 4
what is F. — COLERIDGE, H, 1
wind of nationalism and f. blowing — BALDWIN, S, 7
Your f. and mine cannot be separated — MANDELA, 2
You took my f. away a long time ago — SOLZHENITSYN, 7
freedoms four essential human f. — ROOSEVELT, F, 14
free-loader A f. is a confirmed guest — RUNYON, 8
freely nothing so f. as advice — ROCHEFOUCAULD, 16
freemasonry a kind of bitter f. — BEERBOHM, 13
French Bouillabaisse is only good because cooked by the F. — DOUGLAS, N, 2
everyone would always have spoken F. — VOLTAIRE, 32
F. governments are more selfish than most — ECCLES, 1
F. Guard, fire first — HAY, C, 1
Give me books, fruit, F. wine and fine weather — KEATS, 66
I do not dislike the F. from . . . vulgar antipathy — WALPOLE, H, 9
I hate the F. — GOLDSMITH, 12
Imagine the Lord talking F. — DAY, 1
I speak . . . Italian to women, F. to men — CHARLES V, 3
My suit is pale yellow. My nationality is F. — WILLIAMS, T, 1
something fishy about the F. — COWARD, 5
the F. — STERNE, 2
The F. are wiser than they seem — BACON, FRANCIS, 47
The F. want no-one to be their *superior*. The English want *inferiors* — TOCQUEVILLE, 3
The F. will only be united under the threat of danger — DEGAULLE, 8
the German text of F. operas — WHARTON, 1
There's something Vichy about the F. — NOVELLO, 2
to the F. the empire of the land — RICHTER, 1
Frenchman F. must be always talking — JOHNSON, S, 133
Louis Pasteur was the greatest F. — PASTEUR, 1
You must have a F. — NELSON, 2
Frenchmen F. drink wine just like — LARDNER, 3
to create F. in the image of Englishmen — CHURCHILL, W, 62
frenzy poet's eye, in a fine f. rolling — SHAKESPEARE, 264
fresh f. as is the month of May — CHAUCER, 4
Gentlemen know that f. air — MACAULAY, R, 1
the cod's wallop is always f. made — MORLEY, R, 2
freshen a mighty storm . . . to f. us up — CHEKHOV, 9
fret weariness, the fever, and the f. — KEATS, 38
fretting a moth f. a garment — PSALMS, 23

Fuzzy-Wuzzy to you, F., at your 'ome in the Soudan   KIPLING, 10

G

gabble giggle – g. – gobble – 'n' git   HOLMES, O, 8
gaiety G. . . . of the Soviet Union   STALIN, 5
the only concession to g.   THOMAS, G, 5
gain never broke the Sabbath, but for G.   DRYDEN, 10
richest g. I count but loss   WATTS, 8
gained learning hath g. most   FULLER, T, 6
gainful I will undoubtedly have to seek . . . g. employment   ACHESON, 5
gains no g. without pains   STEVENSON, A, 4
gaiters gas and g.   DICKENS, 34
Galatians a great text in G.   BROWNING, R, 54
O foolish G.   BIBLE, 131
Galileo If G. had said in verse that the world moved   HARDY, 14
What G. and Newton were to the seventeenth century   DARWIN, CR, 2
gall the wormwood and the g.   BIBLE, 305
gallant a loyal, a g. . . . people   STERNE, 2
Hereabouts died a very g. gentleman   ATKINSON, 1
He was a braw g.   ANONYMOUS, 109
gallantry What men call g.   BYRON, 19
galleon The moon was a ghostly g.   NOYES, 1
gallery The boy I love is up in the g.   WARE, 1
galloped I g., Dirck g.   BROWNING, R, 28
gallops g. night by night Through lovers' brains   SHAKESPEARE, 305
gallows You will die either on the g., or of the pox   WILKES, 1
gamble Life is a g.   STOPPARD, 10
gambling primary notion back of most g. is the excitement   KENNEDY, JOSEPH, 1
game how you played the g.   RICE, G, 1
I don't like this g.   MILLIGAN, 4
It's more than a g.. It's an institution   HUGHES, THOMAS, 2
'Play up! play up! and play the g.!'   NEWBOLT, 7
win this g. and thrash the Spaniards   DRAKE, 2
woman is his g.   TENNYSON, 65
games The British, being brought up on team g.   PARKINSON, 3
gamesmanship G. or The Art of Winning Games   POTTER, S, 1
gaming Man is a g. animal   LAMB, CHARLES, 2
gangsters The great nations have always acted like g.   KUBRICK, 1
garbage G. in   PROVERBS, 170
Garbo one sees in G. sober   TYNAN, 6
garden a g. in her face   ALISON, 2; CAMPION, 2
A g. is a lovesome thing   BROWN, T E, 2
Come into the g., Maud   TENNYSON, 56
cultivate our g.   VOLTAIRE, 9
Don't go into Mr McGregor's g.   POTTER, B, 2
God Almighty first planted a g.   BACON, FRANCIS, 26
God the first g. made   COWLEY, 1
I have a g. of my own   MARVELL, 6
My heart shall be thy g.   MEYNELL, 1
nearer God's Heart in a g.   GURNEY, 1
The chairs are being brought in from the g.   AUDEN, 18
the g. of Eden   BIBLE, 145
There are fairies at the bottom of our g.   FYLEMAN, 1
gardener Every time I talk to . . . my g., I'm convinced of the opposite   RUSSELL, B, 33
Nor does a . . . g. scent his roses   COCTEAU, 1
Oh, Adam was a g.   KIPLING, 12
supposing him to be the g.   BIBLE, 275
gardens a fountain of g.   BIBLE, 492
closing time in the g. of the West   CONNOLLY, 3
garland wither'd is the g. of the war   SHAKESPEARE, 36
garlands consumptive youth weaving g. of sad flowers   STEVENSON, R, 2
gather g. there   SCOTT, WALTER, 20
garment a moth fretting a g.   PSALMS, 23
garrulous That g. monk   HITLER, 5
Garter I like the G.   MELBOURNE, 4
gas g. and gaiters   DICKENS, 34
If silicon had been a g. I should have been a major-general   WHISTLER, 6
gaslight Fanny by G.   SADLEIR, 1
gas masks digging trenches and trying on g.   CHAMBERLAIN, N, 5
gate I am here at the g. alone   TENNYSON, 56
I said to the man who stood at the g. of the year   HASKINS, 1
matters not how strait the g.   HENLEY, 2

gatekeeper After I die, I shall return to earth as a g. of a bordello   TOSCANINI, 3
gates Battering the g. of heaven   TENNYSON, 74
lift up your heads, O ye g.   PSALMS, 14
the g. of the day   YEATS, 19
the iron g. of life   MARVELL, 11
thou leadest to the g. of hell   BIBLE, 522
gather G. the flowers . . .   MARVELL, 8
G. ye rosebuds while ye may   HERRICK, 5
gathered two or three are g. together   BOOK OF COMMON PRAYER, 16
where two or three are g. together   BIBLE, 401
gatling The g.'s jammed and the colonel dead   NEWBOLT, 7
gaudy round, neat, not g.   LAMB, CHARLES, 25
Gaul G. is divided into three   CAESAR, 1
Gaullist I . . . have become a G. . . . little by little   DE GAULLE, 5
gave God . . . g. his only begotten Son   BIBLE, 245
the Lord g., and the Lord hath taken away   BIBLE, 223
gay g. without frivolity   ARNOLD, M, 20
Gaza Eyeless in G.   MILTON, 57
gazelle never nurs'd a dear g.   MOORE, T, 6
general caviare to the g.   SHAKESPEARE, 86
In a civil war, a g. must know   REED, H, 4
generalizations All g. are dangerous   DUMAS, FILS, 2
generalize To g. is to be an idiot   BLAKE, W, 52
General Motors was good for G.   WILSON, C, 1
generals at the age of four with paper hats and wooden swords we're all G.   USTINOV, 7
Dead battles, like dead g.   TUCHMAN, 1
It is not the business of g. to shoot one another   WELLINGTON, 17
that's not against the law for g.   TRUMAN, 8
to be left to the g.   CLEMENCEAU, 2
wish he would *bite* . . . my g.   GEORGE II, 2
generation Each g. imagines itself . . . more intelligent than the one . . . before   ORWELL, 35
The beat g.   KEROUAC, 4
the neurotic ills of an entire g.   LAWRENCE, T, 3
You are a lost g.   STEIN, 6
generations all g. shall call me blessed   BIBLE, 309
g. . . . have struggled in poverty to build these altars   STANTON, E, 1
g. . . . pass in a short time   LUCRETIUS, 3
No hungry g. tread thee down   KEATS, 39
generosity The poor . . . their function . . . is to exercise our g.   SARTRE, 14
generous a loyal, a gallant, a g., an ingenious, and good-temper'd people   STERNE, 2
He was too g. to be frugal   JACKSON, A, 2
Genesis The man who started more creations since G.   ROOSEVELT, F, 2
genial about as g. as an *auto da fé* of teetotallers   CHESTERTON, 2
genius a country full of g., but with absolutely no talent   LEONARD, 1
a g. for backing into the limelight   LAWRENCE, T, 5
A g.! For thirty-seven years I've practiced . . . and now they call me a g.   SARASATE, 1
a g. that could cut a Colossus   MILTON, 5
a German and a g.   SWIFT, 22
a man of something occasionally like g.   WHITMAN, 2
G. . . . capacity of taking trouble   CARLYLE, T, 10
G. does what it must   MEREDITH, O, 1
G. is an infinite capacity   PROVERBS, 171
G. is one per cent inspiration   EDISON, 1
his departure was the eclipse of a g.   MOUNTBATTEN, 1
Milton, Madam, was a g.   JOHNSON, S, 150
Nothing, except my g.   WILDE, 76
Only an organizing g.   BEVAN, 1
Rules and models destroy g. and art   HAZLITT, 29
Since when was g. . . . respectable   BROWNING, E, 1
talent instantly recognizes g.   DOYLE, 17
Taste is the feminine of g.   FITZGERALD, E, 1
the difference between talent and g.   ALCOTT, 2
the first comic g. who ever installed himself in Downing Street   DISRAELI, 1
The g. of Einstein leads to Hiroshima   EINSTEIN, 2
the most remarkable and seductive g.   BEERBOHM, 2
true g. is a mind of large general powers   JOHNSON, S, 20
True g. walks along a line   GOLDSMITH, 3
Unless one is a g.   HOPE, 1
What a commonplace g. he has   HARDY, 3
When a true g. appears   SWIFT, 14
geniuses One of the greatest g.   SHAKESPEARE, 19

gent   what a man is to a g.   BALDWIN, S, 11
genteel   A man . . . is not g. when he gets drunk   BOSWELL, 2
gentil   verray parfit g. knight   CHAUCER, 2
Gentiles   a light to lighten the G.   BIBLE, 317
gentleman   A g. need not know Latin   MATTHEWS, 1
a g. . . . never inflicts pain   NEWMAN, J, 2
A g. of thirty-two who could calculate an eclipse   JEFFERSON, 2
A g. . . . wouldn't hit a woman with his hat on   ALLEN, F, 3
a nice old g.   CHAMBERLAIN, N, 2
g. of leisure   VEBLEN, 2
God is a g.   ORTON, 6
last g. in Europe   LEVERSON, 3
Not a g.; dresses too well   RUSSELL, B, 27
The Devil is a g.   SHELLEY, 18
the g. is an *attorney*   JOHNSON, S, 80
Who was then the g.   BALL, 1
gentlemanly   secondly, g. conduct   ARNOLD, T, 2
gentlemen   by g. for g.   THACKERAY, 6
extremely difficult to behave like g.   MACKENZIE, 1
g., let us do something today   COLLINGWOOD, C, 1
G. . . . remember blondes   LOOS, 1
God rest you merry, g.   ANONYMOUS, 21
Good-morning, g. both   ELIZABETH I, 6
one of Nature's G.   LINTON, 1
religion for g.   CHARLES II, 2
Scholars and g.   WORDSWORTH, W, 39
the British bourgeoisie have spoken of themselves as g.
                                                WAUGH, E, 12
There were g. and . . . seamen in the navy of Charles the Second
                                                MACAULAY, T, 9
genuineness   G. only thrives in the dark   HUXLEY, A, 34
geographical   India is a g. term   CHURCHILL, W, 46
geography   G. is about Maps   BENTLEY, E, 2
geometrical   Population, . . . increases in a g. ratio   MALTHUS, 1
geometricians   we are g. only by chance   JOHNSON, S, 22
geometry   G. is not true   PIRSIG, 2
Poetry is as exact a science as g.   FLAUBERT, 1
There is no 'royal road' to g.   EUCLID, 2
George   *Death of King G. V*   BETJEMAN, 4
G. the third . . . *may profit by their example*   HENRY, P, 1
King G. will be able to read that   HANCOCK, 1
Lloyd G.   BEAVERBROOK, 2
George Bernard Shaw   G. is sadly miscast   SHERWOOD, 2
Georgia   marching through G.   WORK, 4
Georgie   G. Porgie, pudding and pie   NURSERY RHYMES, 12
German   a G. and a genius   SWIFT, 22
I speak . . . G. to my horse   CHARLES V, 3
Life is too short to learn G.   PORSON, 1
the G. text of French operas   WHARTON, 1
Germans   Don't let's be beastly to the G.   COWARD, 7
How . . . thorough these G. always managed to be   HUXLEY, A, 36
Man, . . . had been created to jab the life out of G.   SASSOON, S, 5
The G., . . . are going to be squeezed, as a lemon   GEDDES, 1
to the G. that of the air   RICHTER, 1
Germany   Defeat of G. means   ROOSEVELT, F, 6
G. calling   HAW-HAW, 1
G., G. before all else   HOFFMANN VON FALLERSLEBEN, 1
G. was the cause of Hitler   HITLER, 8
G. will be . . . a world power   HITLER, 12
If we see that G. is winning   TRUMAN, 4
In G., the Nazis came for the Communists   NIEMÖLLER, 1
Nazi G. had become a menace to all mankind   NEVINS, 1
Gert   G.'s poems are bunk   ANONYMOUS, 89
gesture   g. by the individual to himself   GALBRAITH, 8
getting   a secret way . . . of g. at a boy   WORDSWORTH, W, 64
G. and spending   DICKENS, 20
getting married   Writing is like g.   MURDOCH, 2
get up   I thought it was a pity to g.   MAUGHAM, 16
ghastly   kind of g. object   SHELLEY, 2
ghost   I, born of flesh and g.   THOMAS, D, 4
oh that I had given up the g.   BIBLE, 227
the G. in the Machine   RYLE, 3
The Papacy is not other than the G. of the deceased Roman
Empire   HOBBES, 7
There is a g. That eats handkerchiefs   MORGENSTERN, 1
yielded up the g.   BIBLE, 432
ghoulies   From g. and ghosties and long-leggety beasties
                                                ANONYMOUS, 19
giant   Fleas . . . upon the body of a g.   LANDOR, 6
like a g. refreshed with wine   PSALMS, 43
owner whereof was G. Despair   BUNYAN, 7
the sun . . . rejoiceth as a g.   PSALMS, 8

we have only awakened a sleeping g.   YAMAMOTO, 1
giants   A battle of g.   WELLINGTON, 26
it is by standing on the shoulders of g.   NEWTON, I, 7
not g. but windmills   CERVANTES, 4
war of the g. is over   CHURCHILL, W, 31
Gideon   Why do they put the G. Bibles   MORLEY, C, 2
gift   Never look a g. horse   PROVERBS, 303
the timeliness of the g.   LA BRUYÈRE, 5
True love's the g. which God has given To man alone
                                                SCOTT, WALTER, 7
worth more than the g.   CORNEILLE, 3
gifts   deserves the name of happy who knows how to use the
gods' g. wisely   HORACE, 43
God's g. put man's best g.   BROWNING, E, 3
I fear the Greeks even when they bring g.   VIRGIL, 9
The Gods themselves cannot recall their g.   TENNYSON, 76
giggle   g. – gabble – gobble – 'n' git   HOLMES, O, 8
gild   To g. refined gold   SHAKESPEARE, 165
gilded   A best-seller is the g. tomb of a mediocre talent
                                                SMITH, L, 1
She's only a bird in a g. cage   LAMB, A, 1
Gilpin   John G. was a citizen   COWPER, 9
gin   G. was mother's milk   SHAW, 38
No man is genuinely happy, married, who has to drink worse g.
                                                MENCKEN, 13
Of all the g. joints in all the towns in all the world   BOGART, H, 3
she was dead; but my father he kept ladling g.   SHAW, 37
giraffe   a human g., sniffing . . . at mortals beneath his gaze
                                                DE GAULLE, 3
gird   g. up now thy loins like a man   BIBLE, 236
girded   Pavilioned in splendour, and g. with praise   GRANT, R, 1
girl   Every little g. knows about love   SAGAN, 1
From birth to age eighteen, a g. needs good parents   TUCKER, 3
g. with brains   LOOS, 2
Give me a g. at an impressionable age   SPARK, 6
If you were the only g. in the world   GROSSMITH THE YOUNGER, 1
one can . . . see in a little g. the threat of a woman
                                                DUMAS, FILS, 3
One g. can be pretty   FITZGERALD, F S, 9
park, a policeman and a pretty g.   CHAPLIN, 5
There was a little g. Who had a little curl   MILLER, M, 1
What can you say about a 25-year-old g. who died   SEGAL, 1
girlfriend   Not every problem someone has with his g.
                                                MARCUSE, 1
girls   Boys and g. come out to play   NURSERY RHYMES, 6
g. are so queer   ALCOTT, 3
g. from being g.   HOPE, 5
g. . . . say No when they mean Yes   ALCOTT, 3
g. who wear glasses   PARKER, D, 27
if ever I was to have a dozen g., I'd call 'em all Jane   WELLS, 13
little g. . . . slamming doors   BELLOC, 7
My life with g. has ended   HORACE, 38
one of the nicest g. I was ever engaged to   WODEHOUSE, 17
teaching one set of catchwords to the g.   STEVENSON, R, 14
Treaties are like roses and young g.   DE GAULLE, 12
When you see what some g. marry   ROWLAND, H, 1
Where . . . boys plan for what . . . young g. plan for whom
                                                GILMAN, 3
git   giggle – gabble – gobble – 'n' g.   HOLMES, O, 8
give   freely ye have received, freely g.   BIBLE, 385
g. me liberty or g. me death   HENRY, P, 2
G. me your tired, . . . Your huddled masses   LAZARUS, 1
like the grave, cries 'G., g..'   ADAMS, A, 1
such as I have g. I thee   BIBLE, 4
To g. and not to count the cost   LOYOLA, 1
When I g. I g. myself   WHITMAN, 8
given   I wish that God had not g. me what I prayed for   SPYRI, 1
I would have g. you another   JARRY, 1
unto every one that hath shall be g.   BIBLE, 419
gives   He g. twice who g. promptly   SYRUS, 4
giving   The manner of g.   CORNEILLE, 3
gizzard   My wife hath something in her g.   PEPYS, 16
glad   She had A heart . . . too soon made g.   BROWNING, R, 35
with a love like that you know you should be g.   LENNON, 10
you would have been very g. if I had written it   PIRON, 1
gladsome   Let us with a g. mind Praise the Lord   MILTON, 55
Gladstone   G.   BAGEHOT, 10
Mr G. read Homer for fun   CHURCHILL, W, 19
to G.'s always having the ace of trumps   LABOUCHÈRE, 1
Glasgow   never played the G. Empire   DODD, 1
glass   baying for broken g.   WAUGH, E, 4

Like many of the upper class He liked the sound of broken g.
BELLOC, 14

on the other side of the g. BENNETT, ALAN, 4
Satire is a sort of g. SWIFT, 3
through a g., darkly BIBLE, 38
you won't intoxicate with one g. CHEKHOV, 13
glasses girls who wear g. PARKER, D, 27
glimpse I . . . catch a g. of a stoat KEATS, 69
Same old g. of Paradise LAMPTON, 1
glisters Nor all that g. gold GRAY, 13
glittering long grey beard and g. eye COLERIDGE, S, 24
The world continues to offer g. prizes BIRKENHEAD, 4
glitters All that g. is not gold PROVERBS, 39
gloamin Roamin' in the g.' LAUDER, 3
global my wars Were g. REED, H, 1
the world in the image of a g. village MCLUHAN, 1
globe the great g. itself SHAKESPEARE, 325
globule I can trace my ancestry back to a . . . g. GILBERT, W, 24
gloire Le jour de g. est arrivé ROUGET DE LISLE, 1
gloria Sic transit g. mundi KEMPIS, 1
glorious G. things of thee are spoken NEWTON, J, 1
Happy and g. CAREY, H, 1
glory because he gave not God the g. BIBLE, 11
But trailing clouds of g. WORDSWORTH, W, 25
G. be to God for dappled things HOPKINS, 4
g., jest, and riddle of the world POPE, 33
g. to God in the highest BIBLE, 315
His face . . . hath its ancient g. COLERIDGE, S, 2
I go on to g. DUNCAN, 5
It is a great g. in a woman THUCYDIDES, 2
Land of Hope and G. BENSON, 1
Mine eyes have seen the g. of the coming of the Lord HOWE, 1
paths of g. lead but to the grave GRAY, 3
Popularity? . . . g.'s small change HUGO, 7
the g. of Europe is extinguished for ever BURKE, E, 9
the Son of man coming . . . with power and great g. BIBLE, 414
To the greater g. of God ANONYMOUS, 2
we left him alone with his g. WOLFE, C, 2
Wellington has exhausted nature and . . . g. WELLINGTON, 2
Where is it now, the g. and the dream WORDSWORTH, W, 25
who is the King of g. PSALMS, 14
Gloucester Doctor Foster went to G. NURSERY RHYMES, 10
glow make the corpuscles of the blood g. LAWRENCE, D, 14
Glum I've examined your son's head, Mr G. MUIR, 1
glum He is very yellow and g. ELIOT, T, 2
speed g. heroes . . . to death SASSOON, S, 1
gluttony G. is an emotional escape DE VRIES, 2
gnashing weeping and g. of teeth BIBLE, 381
gnomes the little g. of Zürich WILSON, HAROLD, 6
go a good cook, as cooks g. SAKI, 16
g., and do thou likewise BIBLE, 326
I don't want to g. home in the dark HENRY, O, 3
In the name of God, g.! AMERY, 2
I shall be the last to g. out ALENÇON, 1
Let's g. BECKETT, 4
Let us g. then, you and I ELIOT, T, 11
not to g. anywhere, but to g. STEVENSON, R, 7
stopped short – never to g. again WORK, 3
whither thou goest, I will g. BIBLE, 475
goal The g. stands up HOUSMAN, 12
goat-footed This g. bard KEYNES, 4
goats as a shepherd divideth his sheep from the g. BIBLE, 420
gobble giggle – gabble – g. – 'n' git HOLMES, O, 8
God A bit like G. THOMAS, G, 3
A G. who let us prove his existence BONHOEFFER, 2
A man with G. KNOX, J, 1
America is G.'s Crucible ZANGWILL, 2
an absolute faith that all things are possible to G. EDDY, 1
an atheist half believes a G. YOUNG, E, 4
An honest G. INGERSOLL, 1
Are G. and Nature then at strife TENNYSON, 31
At last G. caught his eye SECOMBE, 2
better to have no opinion of G. BACON, FRANCIS, 52
but for the grace of G. goes BRADFORD, 1
charged with the grandeur of G. HOPKINS, 3
concept of G. has any validity BALDWIN, J, 1
Dr Donne's verses are like the peace of G. JAMES I, 5
effect Whose cause is G. COWPER, 26
Either a beast or a g. ARISTOTLE, 2
either a wild beast or a g. BACON, FRANCIS, 24
Even G. cannot change the past AGATHON, 1
even G. was born too late LOWELL, 3

Every man thinks G. is on his side ANOUILH, 4
final proof of G.'s omnipotence DE VRIES, 6
G. alone deserves to be loved SAND, 2
G. as a working hypothesis BONHOEFFER, 1
G. bless . . . G. damn THURBER, 21
'G. bless us every one!' DICKENS, 10
G. can stand being told PRIESTLEY, 8
G. could cause us considerable embarrassment GOETHE, 8
G. defend me from my friends PROVERBS, 176
G. did send me JOAN OF ARC, 3
G. disposes KEMPIS, 4
G. does not play dice EINSTEIN, 5
G. erects a house of prayer DEFOE, 5
G., even our own G. PSALMS, 38
G. . . . first planted a garden BACON, FRANCIS, 26
G. from everlasting PSALMS, 48
G. has written all the books BUTLER, S, 13
G. helps them PROVERBS, 177
G. is a gentleman ORTON, 6
G. is always on the side of the big battalions TURENNE, 1
G. is beginning to resemble . . . the last fading smile of a cosmic Cheshire cat HUXLEY, J, 2
G. is dead NIETZSCHE, 6
G. Is distant, difficult HILL, G, 1
G. is nothing more than an exalted father FREUD, S, 5
G. is on the side . . . of the best shots VOLTAIRE, 7
G. is really only another artist PICASSO, 7
G. is subtle but he is not malicious EINSTEIN, 6
G. is the immemorial refuge of the incompetent MENCKEN, 9
G. is the only president WEBSTER, D, 2
G. . . . just had the power to kill her ADAMS, R, 2
G. made everything out of nothing VALÉRY, 1
G. made the country COWPER, 22
G. said, Let Newton be POPE, 130
G. save our gracious King CAREY, H, 1
G.'s gifts put man's best gifts BROWNING, E, 3
G. should go before such villains SHAKESPEARE, 274
G.'s in His heaven BROWNING, R, 45
G. the first garden made COWLEY, 1
G. will cease to dream you UNAMUNO Y JUGO, 1
G. will grant an end to these too VIRGIL, 6
G. will pardon me. It is His trade HEINE, 5
going back to G. BRUCE, 1
Good G., said G. SQUIRE, 4
gravest sins it was possible for a gentlewoman to VOLTAIRE, 14
'Great G. grant that twice two be not four.' TURGENEV, 4
Had I but serv'd my G. with half the zeal I serv'd my King SHAKESPEARE, 140
Had I . . . served G. as diligently as I have served the king WOLSEY, 1
Has G. then forgotten LOUIS XIV, 2
have one G. only CLOUGH, 1
her conception of G. was certainly not orthodox STRACHEY, L, 1
Holy, holy, holy, Lord G. Almighty HEBER, 3
How could G. do this to me LOUIS XIV, 1
'I am glad . . . he thanks G. for anything.' JOHNSON, S, 14
I believe I am becoming a g. VESPASIAN, 1
I did not write it. G. wrote it. I merely did his dictation STOWE, 4
If G. did not exist VOLTAIRE, 14
If G. made us in His image VOLTAIRE, 19
If G. were suddenly condemned to live the life DUMAS, FILS, 1
If this man is not faithful to his G. THEODORIC, 1
if triangles invented a g., they would make him three-sided MONTESQUIEU, 1
If you don't find a G. by five o'clock this afternoon JOWETT, 7
If you talk to G., you are praying SZASZ, 2
It takes a long while for a . . . trustful person to reconcile himself to . . . G. MENCKEN, 10
I wouldn't give up writing about G. WAUGH, E, 45
I wretch lay wrestling with . . . my G. HOPKINS, 2
justify the ways of G. to men MILTON, 31
Just what G. would have done if he had the money WOOLLCOTT, 3
Kill everyone, and you are a g. ROSTAND, J, 3
Know then thyself, presume not G. to scan POPE, 34
Live among men as if G. beheld you SENECA, 1
Many people believe that they are attracted by G. INGE, 5
May G. deny you peace UNAMUNO Y JUGO, 3
nature is the art of G. BROWNE, T, 3
Nearer, my G., to thee ADAMS, SARAH, 1
none deny there is a G. BACON, FRANCIS, 10
One G., one law, one element TENNYSON, 38

One on G.'s side is a majority — PHILLIPS, 2
only G. can make a tree — KILMER, 2
Our G., our help in ages past — WATTS, 6
poems . . . for the love of Man and in praise of G. — THOMAS, D, 5
Praise be to G., the Lord of all creatures — KORAN, 1
proof that G. is a bore — MENCKEN, 7
prose for G. — GRANVILLE-BARKER, 3
put your hand into the hand of G. — HASKINS, 1
'Resistance to tyranny is obedience to G..' — ANTHONY, 4
Sickness, sin and death . . . do not originate in G. — EDDY, 4
Since G. has given us the papacy . . . enjoy it — LEO X, 1
speak to G. as if men were listening — SENECA, 1
that G. is interested only . . . in religion — TEMPLE, W, 2
that great Leviathan, or rather . . . that *Mortal G.* — HOBBES, 5
The Act of G. designation — COREN, 2
the dear G. who loveth us — COLERIDGE, S, 39
the electric display of G. the Father — O'NEILL, 3
the highest praise of G. consists in the denial of Him — PROUST, 8
the nearer you are to G. — WOTTON, 4
the one G. whose worshippers . . . still trust in Him — BRADLEY, F, 2
There, but for the Grace of G., goes I. — MANKEIWICZ, 2
There once was a man who said 'G.' — KNOX, R, 4
The true G. . . . G. of ideas — VIGNY, 1
Those who marry G. . . . can become domesticated too — GREENE, 1
to obstruct the way of G. . . . is more grievous than to kill in the sacred months — KORAN, 8
we come From G., who is our home — WORDSWORTH, W, 25
we owe G. a death — SHAKESPEARE, 123
What G. does, He does well — LA FONTAINE, 10
When I composed that, I was . . . inspired by G. — BEETHOVEN, 2
when one has loved a man it is very different to love G. — SAND, 2
whom G. wishes to destroy — EURIPIDES, 1
Whom G. would destroy — DUPORT, 1
why G. withheld the sense of humour from women — CAMPBELL, MRS PATRICK, 3
yearning like a G. in pain — KEATS, 12
you hardly ever mention G. any more — MILLER, A, 4
you must believe in G. — JOWETT, 1
goddamm Lhude sing G. — POUND, 7
godlike patient endurance is g. — LONGFELLOW, 2
Godot waiting for G. — BECKETT, 4
gods Against stupidity the g. . . . struggle in vain — SCHILLER, 1
a great king above all g. — PSALMS, 54
by force of the g. — VIRGIL, 5
deserves the name of happy who knows how to use the g.' gifts wisely — HORACE, 43
for what high cause This darling of the G. — MARVELL, 7
g. help them — AESOP, 4
g. . . . Make instruments to plague us — SHAKESPEARE, 193
Kings are earth's g. — SHAKESPEARE, 289
leave the rest to the G. — CORNEILLE, 1
Live with the g. — MARCUS AURELIUS, 10
man's ignorance of the g. — BUTLER, S, 7
no other g. before me — BIBLE, 115
So many g., so many creeds — WILCOX, 4
The Ethiopians say that their g. are . . . black — XENOPHANES, 1
The G. themselves cannot recall their gifts — TENNYSON, 76
To understand G.'s thoughts — NIGHTINGALE, 3
gods we're forbidden to know – what end the g. have in store — HORACE, 30
whom the g. favour — PLAUTUS, 1
Whom the g. love — MENANDER, 1
Whom the g. wish to destroy — CONNOLLY, 9
goe to morowe longe I to g. to God — MORE, 2
Goethe G.'s sage mind and Byron's force — WORDSWORTH, W, 1
Gog G. and Magog — BIBLE, 471
going I am just g. outside — OATES, 1
Men must endure Their g. hence — SHAKESPEARE, 192
Stand not upon the order of your g. — SHAKESPEARE, 216
gold A g. rush is what happens when — WEST, M, 7
all the g. that the goose could give — AESOP, 3
An angel writing in a book of g. — HUNT, L, 1
cursed craving for g. — VIRGIL, 11
For g. in phisik is a cordial — CHAUCER, 11
gild refined g. — SHAKESPEARE, 165
Good morning to the day: and next my g. — JONSON, 14
I stuffed their mouths with g. — BEVAN, 13
more to be desired . . . than g. — PSALMS, 9
Nor all that glisters is g. — GRAY, 13
picking g. out of the dunghills of old Roman writers — VIRGIL, 3
silver and g. have I none — BIBLE, 4
Silver threads among the g. — REXFORD, 1

Their idols are silver and g. — PSALMS, 64
The ring so worn . . . is yet of g. — CRABBE, 2
To a shower of g. — CARLYLE, T, 15
travell'd in the realms of g. — KEATS, 41
Were't not for g. and women — TOURNEUR, 1
What female heart can g. despise — GRAY, 11
When every . . . thing you hold Is made of silver, or of g. — GILBERT, W, 5
golden G. slumbers kiss your eyes — DEKKER, 1
In good King Charles's g. days — ANONYMOUS, 48
In old time we had treen chalices and g. priests — JEWEL, 1
Jerusalem the g. — NEALE, 3
perhaps, the g. rule — STEVENSON, R, 22
silence is g. — PROVERBS, 368
The g. apples of the sun — YEATS, 30
the G. Road to Samarkand — FLECKER, 1
there are no g. rules — SHAW, 31
Goldsmith To Oliver G. — JOHNSON, S, 114
Goldwyn Mr G. . . . you are only interested in art — SHAW, 47
golf an earnest protest against g. — BEERBOHM, 19
G. . . . a form of moral effort — LEACOCK, 11
he bestowed upon the games of g. and bridge — EISENHOWER, 2
Gomorrah Sodom and . . . G. — BIBLE, 167
gone g. with the wind — DOWSON, 2; MITCHELL, M, 5
gongs women should be struck . . . like g. — COWARD, 18
good a g. friend, but bad acquaintance — BYRON, 23
A g. man fallen among Fabians — LENIN, 10
A g. novel tells us the truth — CHESTERTON, 23
A G. Time Was Had by All — SMITH, STEVIE, 1
All g. writing — FITZGERALD, F S, 16
Anybody can be g. in the country — WILDE, 52
as gods, knowing g. and evil — BIBLE, 149
Be g., sweet maid, and let who can be clever — KINGSLEY, 1
being really g. all the time — WILDE, 27
dedicate this nation to the policy of the g. neighbor — ROOSEVELT, F, 11
Do g. by stealth — POPE, 10
doing g. . . . professions which are full — THOREAU, 12
doing g. to base fellows — CERVANTES, 9
dull prospect of a distant g. — DRYDEN, 25
every creature of God is g. — BIBLE, 508
every man at the beginning doth set forth g. wine — BIBLE, 242
Every man loves what he is g. at — SHADWELL, 3
Evil, be thou my G. — MILTON, 44
Evil comes . . . like the disease; g. . . . like the doctor — CHESTERTON, 26
Far too g. to waste on children — SHAW, 50
Four legs g. — ORWELL, 4
General G. is the plea of the scoundrel — BLAKE, W, 16
God saw that it was g. — BIBLE, 139
G. at a fight — SHERIDAN, R, 1
G., but not religious-g. — HARDY, 10
G. isn't the word — GILBERT, W, 47
G. things, when short, are twice as g. — GRACIÁN, 1
g. tidings of great joy — BIBLE, 314
greatest g. — CICERO, 3
happiness makes them g. — LANDOR, 3
He who would do g. to another — BLAKE, W, 16
hold fast that which is g. — BIBLE, 504
how *can* they become g. people — VICTORIA, 6
how can ye, being evil, speak g. — BIBLE, 389
How g. is man's life, the mere living — BROWNING, R, 50
If . . . 'feeling g.' could decide, drunkenness would be . . . supremely valid — JAMES, W, 2
If to do were as easy as to know what were g. — SHAKESPEARE, 237
If you can't be g. — PROVERBS, 217
I have fought a g. fight — BIBLE, 514
it cannot come to g. — SHAKESPEARE, 69
It is g. to know what a man is — BRADLEY, F, 3
It is seldom . . . one parts on g. terms — PROUST, 17
letting the best be the enemy of the g. — JENKINS, 2
little of what you fancy does you g. — LLOYD, M, 2
Men have never been g. — BARTH, 1
never was a g. war — FRANKLIN, 16
no hint throughout the universe Of g. or ill — THOMSON, JAMES, 2
Nothing can harm a g. man — SOCRATES, 4
nothing either g. or bad — SHAKESPEARE, 83
nothing g. to be had in the country — HAZLITT, 13
on earth peace, g. will toward men — BIBLE, 315
One man is as g. as another — JOWETT, 2
Only g. girls keep diaries — BANKHEAD, 13
our people have never had it so g. — MACMILLAN, 5

Roman Conquest . . . a G. Thing — SELLAR, 4
strong antipathy of g. to bad — POPE, 11
Such persons are often g. — HUME, B, 1
suppose the people g. — ROBESPIERRE, 1
the g. are always the merry — YEATS, 13
The g. die early — DEFOE, 1
The g. die first — WORDSWORTH, W, 4
The g. die young — PROVERBS, 396
The g. is oft interred with their bones — SHAKESPEARE, 153
The g. is the beautiful — PLATO, 1
the g. must associate — BURKE, E, 20
The g. of the people — CICERO, 2
The 'g. old times' — BYRON, 4
The king has been very g. to me — BOLEYN, 1
the name of perseverance in a g. cause — STERNE, 6
The only g. Indians I ever saw were dead — SHERIDAN, P, 1
There is so much g. in the worst of us — ANONYMOUS, 88
the thing which is g. — BIBLE, 94
they are . . . surprised at hearing of a g. action — KEATS, 70
those who go about doing g. — CREIGHTON, 1
thou g. and faithful servant — ANONYMOUS, 70; BIBLE, 418
what g. came of it at last — SOUTHEY, 1
What's the g. of a home — GROSSMITH, G, 1
Whenever two g. people argue over principles — ESCHENBACH, 1
When I'm g. I'm very g. — WEST, M, 17
when the great and g. depart — WORDSWORTH, W, 15
Why care for grammar as long as we are g. — WARD, 4
You shouldn't say it is not g. — WHISTLER, 10
goodbye G. to All That — GRAVES, R, 1
Without a single kiss or a g. — PATMORE, 2
good-bye-ee G.! – g. — WESTON, 1
good knights sorrier for my g.' loss than for . . . my fair queen — MALORY, 3
good life three ingredients in the g. — MORLEY, C, 1
goodly make us love your g. gifts And snatch them — SHAKESPEARE, 291
good manners The Japanese have perfected g. — THEROUX, 2
to write good prose is an affair of g. — MAUGHAM, 17
goodness Abashed the devil . . . felt how awful is — MILTON, 47
G. does not . . . make men happy — LANDOR, 2
My g. those diamonds are lovely — WEST, M, 4
Not to be wronged is to forgo . . . g. — WELLS, 4
surely g. and mercy shall follow me — PSALMS, 13
the earth is full of the g. of the Lord — PSALMS, 21
goods isn't a bad bit of g., the Queen — CERVANTES, 3
Poverty of g. is easily cured — MONTAIGNE, 10
the Man Who Delivers the G. — MASON, 1
your wife . . . is a receiver of stolen g. — JOHNSON, S, 134
Good Samaritan No one would have remembered the G. — THATCHER, M, 11
good-temper'd a loyal, a gallant, a generous, an ingenious, a good people — STERNE, 2
good will a gigantic reservoir of g. — WILLKIE, 2
in peace, g. — CHURCHILL, W, 27
goose all the gold that the g. could give — AESOP, 3
goosey G., g. gander — NURSERY RHYMES, 13
gored you tossed and g. several persons — BOSWELL, 2
gorgeous hold the g. east in fee — WORDSWORTH, W, 58
gorilla these g. damnifications of humanity — DARWIN, C R, 1
gormed I'm G. — DICKENS, 18
Gospels We had no use for the policy of the G. — KHRUSHCHEV, 1
gossips No one go about . . . secret virtues — RUSSELL, B, 17
got Which in our case we have not g. — REED, H, 3
gout A taste for drink, combined with g. — GILBERT, W, 3
I refer to g. — ELLIS, 2
that old enemy the g. Had taken him in toe — HOOD, 9
govern Every class is unfit to g. — ACTON, 1
Grammar, which is g. even kings — MOLIÈRE, 1
He that would g. others — MASSINGER, 1
I will g. according to the common weal — JAMES I, 3
king reigns, but does not g. — ZAMOYSKI, 1
Kings g. by . . . assemblies only when — FOX, C, 4
Labour is not fit to g. — CHURCHILL, W, 44
No man is good enough to g. another man — LINCOLN, 10
Under socialism *all* will g. — LENIN, 5
govern'd Woe to the land that's g. by a child — SHAKESPEARE, 302
governed with how little wisdom the world is g. — OXENSTIERNA, 1
governing the right of g. was not property but a trust — FOX, C, 1
government A g. . . . big enough to give you all you want — GOLDWATER, 1
a g. organization could do it that quickly — CARTER, J, 1
All g. . . . is founded on compromise and barter — BURKE, E, 14

As to religion, I hold it to be the . . . duty of g. to protect all . . . professors thereof — PAINE, 4
Democracy is only an experiment in g. — INGE, 7
every g. . . . should have its old speeches burned — SNOWDEN, 1
g. by crony — ICKES, 1
G., . . . is but a necessary evil — PAINE, 3
g. of the people, by the people, and for the people — LINCOLN, 17
I would not give half a guinea to live under one form of g. — JOHNSON, S, 83
Monarchy is a strong g. — BAGEHOT, 3
no man believes, that want of g., is any new kind of g. — HOBBES, 6
people's g. — WEBSTER, D, 4
prepare for g. — STEEL, 1
The g. burns down whole cities — MAO TSE-TUNG, 10
the g. it deserves — MAISTRE, 1
the President is dead, but the G. lives — GARFIELD, 1
there was no form of g. common to the peoples — WAUGH, E, 37
the things which g. does . . . social progress — WARREN, 1
The worst g. is the most moral — MENCKEN, 8
We live under a g. of men and . . . newspapers — PHILLIPS, 1
governments all G. are selfish — ECCLES, 1
G. need to have both shepherds and butchers — VOLTAIRE, 22
G. will get out of the way and let them have peace — EISENHOWER, 9
The Beast stands for strong mutually antagonistic g. — WAUGH, E, 32
governors Our supreme g., the mob — WALPOLE, H, 3
Gower moral G. — CHAUCER, 21
grace but for the g. of God, goes — BRADFORD, 1
God in his mercy lend her g. — TENNYSON, 47
g. a summer queen — SCOTT, WALTER, 20
g. of our Lord Jesus Christ be with you — BIBLE, 43
He had at least the g. — BENTLEY, E, 1
Lord, I ascribe it to Thy g. — WATTS, 4
she obtained g. and favour — BIBLE, 101
Such g. had kings — BROWNING, R, 47
Tuesday's child is full of g. — NURSERY RHYMES, 35
Graces the G. do not seem . . . natives of Great Britain — CHESTERFIELD, 13
gracious A life that moves to g. ends — TENNYSON, 77
gradually Boys do not grow up g. — CONNOLLY, 13
gradualness The inevitability of g. — WEBB, S, 2
Grail What were they going to do with the G. — BEERBOHM, 22
grain A g., which in England is generally given to horses — JOHNSON, S, 12
He reaps the bearded g. at a breath — LONGFELLOW, 11
grammar down to posterity talking bad g. — DISRAELI, 17
G., which can govern even kings — MOLIÈRE, 9
I am . . . above g. — SIGISMUND, 2
Why care for g. as long as we are good — WARD, 4
grammatical I have laboured to refine our language to g. purity — JOHNSON, S, 24
gramophones waxworks inhabited by g. — DE LA MARE, 2
grand A 'G. Old Man' — LEACOCK, 2
that g. old man — NORTHCOTE, 1
The g. Perhaps — BROWNING, R, 10
the g. style arises in poetry — ARNOLD, M, 32
to be baith g. and comfortable — BARRIE, 2
grandeur g. is a dream — COWPER, 30
g. of God — HOPKINS, 2
Many people have delusions of g. — IONESCO, 1
grandfather a man has no reason to be ashamed of having an ape for his g. — HUXLEY, T, 11
g.'s clock — WORK, 2
I don't know who my g. was — LINCOLN, 22
pass my declining years saluting strange women and g. clocks — NASH, 9
grandmother I murdered my g. this morning — ROOSEVELT, F, 3
grandson I am much more concerned to know what his g. will be — LINCOLN, 22
your g. will . . . be a Communist — KHRUSHCHEV, 5
granted human beings have an . . . infinite capacity for taking things for g. — HUXLEY, A, 33
grape Beulah, peel me a g. — WEST, M, 6
grapes He is trampling out the vintage where the g. of wrath — HOWE, 1
I am sure the g. are sour — AESOP, 6
grapeshot A whiff of g. — CARLYLE, T, 16
grasp man's reach should exceed his g. — BROWNING, R, 4
grasping that power . . . , is ever g. — ADAMS, A, 1
grass all flesh is as g. — BIBLE, 440
days of man are but as g. — PSALMS, 58

There's a snake hidden in the g.   VIRGIL, 17
grassgreen down the g. gooseberried double bed   THOMAS, D, 22
gratification I have had no real g. . . . more than my neighbor . . .
    who is worth only half a million   VANDERBILT, 2
gratifying It is quite g. to feel guilty   ARENDT, 2
gratuite *L'acte g.*   GIDE, 1
grave a-mouldering in the g.   HALL, 1
And digs my g. at each remove   HERBERT, G, 5
And on his g., with shining eyes   ARNOLD, M, 30
Between the cradle and the g.   DYER, 2
Dig the g. and let me lie   STEVENSON, R, 12
Funeral marches to the g.   LONGFELLOW, 10
her heart in his g. is lying   MOORE, T, 4
If Roosevelt were alive he'd turn in his g.   GOLDWYN, 19
I may dread The g. as little   KEN, 1
I shall soon be laid in the quiet g.   KEATS, 72
like the g., cries 'Give, give.'   ADAMS, A, 1
Marriage is a step so g. and decisive   STEVENSON, R, 23
No g. upon the earth   SHAKESPEARE, 39
no work, nor device, nor knowledge . . . in the g.   BIBLE, 73
O g., where is thy victory   BIBLE, 43; POPE, 6
paths of glory lead but to the g.   GRAY, 3
The g.'s a fine and private place   MARVELL, 12
the g. yawns for him   TREE, 3
To that dark inn, the g.   SCOTT, WALTER, 12
grave-digger if I were a g., or . . . a hangman   JERROLD, 6
graven any g. image   BIBLE, 115
graves The bitterest tears shed over g.   STOWE, 1
The dust of great persons' g.   DONNE, 15
gravity He rose by g.; I sank by levity   SMITH, SYDNEY, 18
gravy Sir Humphry Davy Abominated g.   BENTLEY, E, 4
gray When you are old and g.   YEATS, 33
grazed He is the richest author that ever g.   JOHNSON, S, 60
great All my shows are g.   GRADE, 1
All things both g. and small   COLERIDGE, S, 39
deep consent of all g. men   RUSKIN, 14
Everything g. in the world is done by neurotics   PROUST, 20
everything that is g. . . . done by youth   DISRAELI, 9
fate of the g. wen   COBBETT, 3
G. men are but life-sized   BEERBOHM, 5
g. men have not commonly been g. scholars   HOLMES, O, 3
G. oaks   PROVERBS, 182
History is full of ignominious getaways by the g.   ORWELL, 3
How very small the very g.   THACKERAY, 8
If I am a g. man   LAW, 4
No g. man lives in vain   CARLYLE, T, 11
On earth there is nothing g. but man   HAMILTON, W, 2
Some are born g.   SHAKESPEARE, 341
the g. break through   SHENSTONE, 1
The g. man . . . walks across his century   LEACOCK, 9
the g. ones eat up the little ones   SHAKESPEARE, 290
then . . . many of the g. men of history are frauds   LAW, 4
the shade Of that which once was g.   WORDSWORTH, W, 61
To be g. is to be misunderstood   EMERSON, 26
when the g. and good depart   WORDSWORTH, W, 15
you, . . . who have made me too g. for my house   BACON, FRANCIS, 66
great-aunt A person may be indebted for a nose or an eye . . . to
    a g.   HAZLITT, 25
Great Britain G. could say that she supported both sides   MACDONALD, R, 1
G. has lost an Empire   ACHESON, 6
To make a union with G.   PÉTAIN, 2
greater g. love hath no man   BIBLE, 260
The g. the power   BURKE, E, 25
Thy need is yet g. than mine   SIDNEY, P, 4
greatest great city . . . has the g. men and women   WHITMAN, 12
I'm the g.   ALI, 1
Louis Pasteur was the g. Frenchman   PASTEUR, 1
One of the g. geniuses   SHAKESPEARE, 19
the g. deeds require a certain insensitiveness   LICHTENBERG, 3
The g. happiness of the g. number   BENTHAM, 1
the g. of these is charity   BIBLE, 38
great-grandfathers Classicism, . . . presents . . . the literature that
    gave . . . pleasure to their g.   STENDHAL, 2
Great-heart One G.   BUNYAN, 1
greatness long farewell to all my g.   SHAKESPEARE, 139
Men who have g. . . . don't go in for politics   CAMUS, 10
some have g. thrust upon 'em   SHAKESPEARE, 341
Great War A Soldier of the G.   KIPLING, 33
Greece Athens holds sway over all G.   THEMISTOCLES, 1
G. might still be free   BYRON, 27

The isles of G.   BYRON, 26
greedy be not g. to add money to money   BIBLE, 516
Greek it was G. to me   SHAKESPEARE, 145
neither Jew nor G.   BIBLE, 132
Nobody can say a word against G.   SHAW, 15
small Latin and less G.   JONSON, 10
the intrigue of a G. of the lower empire   DISRAELI, 33
The word is half G. and half Latin   SCOTT, C, 2
We were taught . . . Latin and G.   WELLS, 16
Greek literature I . . . impress upon you the study of G.
    GAISFORD, 1
Greeks G. Had a Word   AKINS, 1
G. seek after wisdom   BIBLE, 24
I fear the G. even when they bring gifts   VIRGIL, 9
The Romans and G. found everything human   LAWRENCE, D, 6
To the G. the Muse gave native wit   HORACE, 8
uncertainty: a state unknown to the G.   BORGES, 1
where the G. had modesty, we have cant   PEACOCK, 2
which came first, the G. or the Romans   DISRAELI, 39
green a g. thought in a g. shade   MARVELL, 2
for the wearin' o' the G.   ANONYMOUS, 46
G. grow the rashes O   BURNS, R, 11
G. politics is not about being far left or far right   ICKE, 1
in the morning it is g.   PSALMS, 49
I was g. in judgment   SHAKESPEARE, 28
religious system that produced G. Chartreuse   SAKI, 17
There is a g. hill far away   ALEXANDER, 3
tree of life is g.   GOETHE, 2
green-ey'd jealousy . . . g. monster   SHAKESPEARE, 283
Greenland From G.'s icy mountains   HEBER, 1
green-rob'd g. senators of mighty woods   KEATS, 21
Greensleeves G. was all my joy   ANONYMOUS, 22
greenwood Under the g. tree   SHAKESPEARE, 45
green woods When the g. laugh   BLAKE, W, 47
greeting the sort of g. a corpse would give to an undertaker
    BALDWIN, S, 5
greetings g. where no kindness is   WORDSWORTH, W, 14
perhaps the g. are intended for me   BEETHOVEN, 3
grenadier The healthy bones of a single Pomeranian g.
    BISMARCK, 5
Grenadiers With a tow, . . . row for the British G.
    ANONYMOUS, 73
grew Three years she g.   WORDSWORTH, W, 69
grey G. hairs are death's blossoms   PROVERBS, 183
theory is all g.   GOETHE, 2
There is only one cure for g. hair. . . . the guillotine
    WODEHOUSE, 16
These little g. cells   CHRISTIE, 3
well-belovèd hair has threads of g.   YEATS, 14
grief A g. too much to be told   VIRGIL, 8
calms one's g. by recounting it   CORNEILLE, 5
G. and disappointment give rise to anger   HUME, D, 7
G. has turned her fair   WILDE, 74
heart which g. hath cankered . . . remedy – the Tankard
    CALVERLEY, 1
in much wisdom is much g.   BIBLE, 65
My heart burned within me with indignation and g.   LINCOLN, 2
Should be past g.   SHAKESPEARE, 349
grievances redress of the g. of the vanquished   CHURCHILL, W, 12
grieve G. not that I die young   HASTINGS, 1
Men are we, and must be   WORDSWORTH, W, 61
grill be careful not to look like a mixed g.   COWARD, 10
grimace the only pianist . . . who did not g.   STRAVINSKY, 2
grin All Nature wears one universal g.   FIELDING, 14
ending with a g., which remained some time   CARROLL, 8
grind mills of God g. slowly   LOGAU, 1
grinders Writers, like teeth, are divided into incisors and g.
    BAGEHOT, 8
grist All's g. that comes to the mill   PROVERBS, 37
groan men sit and hear each other g.   KEATS, 38
groans How alike are the g. of love to those of the dying
    LOWRY, 2
Gromyko the G. of the Labour party   HEALEY, 3
grooves specialists . . . tend to think in g.   MORGAN, E, 1
grope they g. in the dark   BIBLE, 229
Groucho had Marx been G. instead of Karl   BERLIN, 3
No, G. is not my real name   MARX, G, 24
group A g. of closely related persons   MACAULAY, R, 3
grovelled Whenever he met a great man he g.   THACKERAY, 10
groves And seek for truth in the g. of Academe   HORACE, 24
grow Green g. the rashes O   BURNS, R, 11
They shall g. not old   BINYON, 3

Whoever could make two ears of corn . . . g.   SWIFT, 8
grow'd 'I 'spect I g.'   STOWE, 2
growing old G. is like being increasingly penalized   POWELL, A, 6
Say I'm g., but add, Jenny kissed me   HUNT, L, 4
growl I hate a fellow . . . who does nothing . . . but sit and *g.*   JOHNSON, S, 141
grown Boys . . . are unwholesome companions for g. people   LAMB, CHARLES, 9
grown up one of the few English novels for g. people   WOOLF, 2
grow out some of us never g.   USTINOV, 7
grows Nothing g. well in the shade   BRANCUSI, 1
growth as short a Spring; As quick a g. to meet decay   HERRICK, 4
G. is a greater mystery than death   MAILER, 1
the impalpable elations and apprehensions of g.   MAILER, 1
grub it is poor g., poor pay, and easy work   LONDON, 1
grumblers some g. are to be expected   LINCOLN, 1
grumbling the muttering grew to a g.   BROWNING, R, 43
gruntled he was far from being g.   WODEHOUSE, 5
guarantee No one can g. success in war   CHURCHILL, W, 28
guard That g. our native seas   CAMPBELL, T, 6
guardian As g. of His Majesty's conscience   THURLOW, 2
guards Up, G., and at 'em   WELLINGTON, 18
Who is to guard the g. themselves   JUVENAL, 5
gudeman Robin Gray, he was g. to me   BARNARD, A, 1
guerre *ce n'est pas la g.*   BOSQUET, 1
guerrilla The g. fights the war of the flea   TABER, 1
The g. wins if he does not lose   KISSINGER, 1
guest A free-loader is a confirmed g.   RUNYON, 1
Earth, receive an honoured g.   AUDEN, 17
The g. who outstays   PROVERBS, 397
guests the g. must be chosen as carefully as the wine   SAKI, 1
guide Custom, then, is the great g. of human life   HUME, D, 1
Everyman, I will go with thee, and be thy g.   ANONYMOUS, 17
God sent a voice to g. me   JOAN OF ARC, 2
I have only a faint light to g. me   DIDEROT, 1
guiding little onward lend thy g. hand   MILTON, 56
guillotine There is only one cure for grey hair. . . . the g.   WODEHOUSE, 16
guilt g. of having a nice body   DRABBLE, 2
I have no sense of g.   PANKHURST, E, 3
Let other pens dwell on g. and misery   AUSTEN, 13
Life without industry is g.   RUSKIN, 4
put on a dress of g.   MCGOUGH, 1
guiltless Whose g. heart is free   CAMPION, 3
guilty g. of Noel Cowardice   DE VRIES, 2
It is quite gratifying to feel g.   ARENDT, 2
Let no g. man escape   GRANT, U, 7
Luther was g. of two great crimes   LUTHER, 3
ten g. persons escape than one innocent suffer   BLACKSTONE, 5
tremble like a g. thing surprised   WORDSWORTH, W, 31
guinea a round disc of fire somewhat like a g.   BLAKE, W, 12
I would not give half a g. to live under one form of government   JOHNSON, S, 83
there go two-and-forty sixpences . . . to one g.   JOHNSON, S, 34
guineas I have only five g. in my pocket   PETERBOROUGH, 1
gulphs whelm'd in deeper g. than he   COWPER, 6
gun it is necessary to take up the g.   MAO TSE-TUNG, 4
The difference between a g. and a tree   POUND, 10
we have got The Maxim G., and they have not   BELLOC, 12
gunfire Thanks to the movies, g. has always sounded unreal   USTINOV, 3
Gunga Din You're a better man than I am, G.   KIPLING, 15
gunpowder G., Printing, and the Protestant Religion   CARLYLE, T, 9
guns But it's 'Saviour of 'is country' when the g.   KIPLING, 29
Elevate them g. a little lower   JACKSON, A, 3
G. will make us powerful   GOERING, 3
gutless W. H. Auden, a sort of g. Kipling   ORWELL, 28
gutter We are all in the g.   WILDE, 41
guy He looks like the g. in the science fiction movie   FORD, G, 1
gypsies My mother said that I never should Play with the g. in the wood   NURSERY RHYMES, 36

H

habit a h. the pleasure of which increases with practise   ADAMS, A, 2
H. is a great deadener   BECKETT, 6
honour peereth in the meanest h.   SHAKESPEARE, 320
I must . . . try hard to control the talking h.   FRANK, 3
some h. of which he is deeply ashamed   CRISP, 1

habitation to airy nothing A local h.   SHAKESPEARE, 264
habits Curious things, h.   CHRISTIE, 5
h. that carry them far apart   CONFUCIUS, 3
Old h. die hard   PROVERBS, 321
hack Do not h. me   MONMOUTH, 1
had you h. it in you   PARKER, D, 24
hae Scots, wha h.   BURNS, R, 17
ha-ha Funny peculiar, or funny h.   HAY, I, 1
hail All h., the power of Jesus' name   PERRONET, 1
h. and farewell   CATULLUS, 3
the flail of the lashing h.   SHELLEY, 5
hair busy driving cabs and cutting h.   BURNS, G, 1
if a woman have long h.   BIBLE, 37
part my h. behind   ELIOT, T, 15
scant as h. In leprosy   BROWNING, R, 15
Take a h. of the dog   PROVERBS, 373
there shall not one h. of his head fall   BIBLE, 479
To Crystal, h. was the most important thing on earth   O'BRIEN, E, 1
you have lovely h.   CHEKHOV, 12
hairy Esau . . . a h. man   BIBLE, 171
half And when they were only h. way up, They were neither up nor down   NURSERY RHYMES, 37
H. a loaf   PROVERBS, 184
h. a loaf is better than a whole   CHESTERTON, 39
I am only h. there when I am ill   LAWRENCE, D, 43
I have not told h. of what I saw   MARCO POLO, 1
longest h. of your life   SOUTHEY, 3
One h. . . . cannot understand . . . the other   AUSTEN, 4
There is an old saying 'well begun is h. done'   KEATS, 55
half-a-dozen six of one and h. of the other   MARRYAT, 2
half-developed the working-class which, raw and h.   ARNOLD, M, 9
half-wits a wit out of two h.   KINNOCK, 3
halitosis h. of the intellect   ICKES, 2
hall one of the sparrows . . . flew . . . through the h.   BEDE, 1
We met . . . Dr H. in such very deep mourning   AUSTEN, 31
Hallelujah Here lies my wife, . . . H.   ANONYMOUS, 31
hallowed The place of justice is a h. place   BACON, FRANCIS, 31
halt the whole process has ground to a h. with a 14th Earl   WILSON, HAROLD, 9
halters talk of h. in the hanged man's house   CERVANTES, 12
halves Never do things by h.   PROVERBS, 301
Hamelin H. Town's in Brunswick   BROWNING, R, 41
hammer Art is not a mirror . . . but a h.   MAYAKOVSKY, 1
Hampden Some village-H.   GRAY, 6
hand bite the h. that fed them   BURKE, E, 19
educate with the head instead of with the h.   KEY, E, 3
fingers of a man's h., and wrote   BIBLE, 11
h. that signed the treaty bred a fever   THOMAS, D, 11
I . . . will cover thee with my h.   BIBLE, 122
little onward lend thy guiding h.   MILTON, 56
No, this right h. shall work it all off   SCOTT, WALTER, 1
one of those parties which got out of h.   BRUCE, 2
put your h. into the h. of God   HASKINS, 1
Sit thou on my right h.   PSALMS, 61
sweeten this little h.   SHAKESPEARE, 222
The H. that made us is divine   ADDISON, 15
The h. that rocks the cradle   PROVERBS, 398
the sheep of his h.   PSALMS, 56
This h. hath offended   CRANMER, 1
touch his weaknesses with a delicate h.   GOLDSMITH, 15
handbook have used the Bible as if it was a constable's h.   KINGSLEY, 3
handful for a h. of silver he left us   BROWNING, R, 31
handicraft Art is not a h.   TOLSTOY, L, 13
handkerchief blow his nose . . . state of the h. industry   ORWELL, 1
handkerchiefs There is a ghost That eats h.   MORGENSTERN, 1
handle I polished up the h. of the big front door   GILBERT, W, 12
hands don't raise your h. because I am also nearsighted   AUDEN, 28
earth of England is in my two h.   WILLIAM THE CONQUEROR, 1
Farewell, my poor h.   RACHMANINOV, 1
He hath shook h. with time   FORD, JOHN, 3
his h. prepared the dry land   PSALMS, 54
into thy h. I commend my spirit   BIBLE, 19
Licence my roving h.   DONNE, 11
Many h. make light work   PROVERBS, 283
Pale h. I loved beside the Shalimar   HOPE, 1
Pilate . . . washed his h.   BIBLE, 430
temples made with h.   BIBLE, 12

little man wears a shocking bad h.   YORK, 1
looking for a black h.   BOWEN, C, 2
My h. and wig will soon be here   COWPER, 12
Where did you get that h.   ROLMAZ, 1
hatched   chickens before they are h.   AESOP, 8
count their chickens ere they're h.   BUTLER, S, 3
hatchet   I did it with my little h.   WASHINGTON, 5
hate   feel no h. for him   RACINE, 1
Few . . . can be happy unless they h.   RUSSELL, B, 30
h. that which we often fear   SHAKESPEARE, 26
If you h. a person, you h. . . . yourself   HESSE, 1
I h. a fellow . . . who does nothing . . . but sit and *growl*   JOHNSON, S, 141
I h. and love   CATULLUS, 2
I h. everyone equally   FIELDS, 4
I h. the whole race . . . your professional poets   WELLINGTON, 10
I love or I h.   PICASSO, 8
Let them h.   ACCIUS, 1
not to weep at them, nor to h. them, but to understand them   SPINOZA, 5
only love sprung from my only h.   SHAKESPEARE, 307
scarcely h. any one that we know   HAZLITT, 17
time to love, and a time to h.   BIBLE, 67
to h. the man you have hurt   TACITUS, 2
You must h. a Frenchman   NELSON, 2
hated   as if I were a Jew   YEVTUSHENKO, 1
h. of all men for my name's sake   BIBLE, 386
I never h. a man enough   GABOR, 3
I never saw a brute I h. so   BROWNING, R, 30
hates   Anybody who h. children and dogs   FIELDS, 3
Everybody h. house-agents   WELLS, 15
Everybody h. me   DE VRIES, 4
hateth   love God, and h. his brother   BIBLE, 284
hating   patriotism which consists in h. all other nations   GASKELL, 3
hatred   An intellectual h.   YEATS, 26
deep burning h. for the Tory Party   BEVAN, 8
Fire – without h.   RIVERA, 1
h. is . . . the longest pleasure   BYRON, 33
love . . . looks more like h. than like friendship   ROCHEFOUCAULD, 9
hats   H. divide generally into three classes   WHITEHORN, 3
Hatter   'Not the same thing a bit!' said the H.   CARROLL, 9
haunted   e'er beneath a waning moon was h.   COLERIDGE, S, 16
hautboys   Gibbon moved to flutes and h.   GIBBON, 2
have   To h. and to hold   BOOK OF COMMON PRAYER, 27
haves   H. and the *Have-nots*   CERVANTES, 20
hawk   know a h. from a handsaw   SHAKESPEARE, 85
hay   Make h. while the sun shines   PROVERBS, 278
hazard   an occupational h. of being a wife   ANNE, 2
he   For every h. has got him a she   ANONYMOUS, 13
head   anyone who slapped us . . . would get his h. kicked off   KHRUSHCHEV, 1
call that thing under your hat a h.   HOLBERG, 1
educate with the h. instead of with the hand   KEY, E, 3
God be in my h., And in my understanding   ANONYMOUS, 20
Here comes a chopper to chop off your h.   NURSERY RHYMES, 41
If you can keep your h.   KIPLING, 16
I'll hold my h. so high it'll strike the stars   HORACE, 26
in politics there is no heart, only h.   NAPOLEON I, 5
John Baptist's h. in a charger   BIBLE, 307
Lay your sleeping h.   AUDEN, 20
no matter which way the h. lies   RALEIGH, W, 6
Off with his h.   CARROLL, 12
ought to have his h. examined   GOLDWYN, 12
Scheherazade . . . a woman saving her h.   WYNNE-TYSON, E, 1
shorter by a h.   ELIZABETH I, 7
show my h. to the people   DANTON, 2
the greatest asset a h. of state can have   WILSON, HAROLD, 12
there shall not one hair of his h. fall   BIBLE, 479
Uneasy lies the h. that wears a crown   SHAKESPEARE, 121
waters flowed over mine h.   BIBLE, 307
you are like a pin, but without . . . h. or . . . point   JERROLD, 8
you incessantly stand on your h.   CARROLL, 6
head-in-air   Johnny h.   PUDNEY, 1
Little Johnny H.   HOFFMAN, 2
headmasters   H. have powers   CHURCHILL, W, 18
heads   H. I win   CROKER, 1
Two h. are better than one   PROVERBS, 446
head-waiter   A pompous woman . . . complaining that the h.   SITWELL, E, 4
diplomat . . . is nothing but a h.   USTINOV, 8
heal   I will h. me of my grievous wound   TENNYSON, 25

physician, h. thyself   BIBLE, 320
healeth   h. those that are broken in heart   PSALMS, 75
healing   the leaves . . . were for the h. of the nations   BIBLE, 474
health   All h. is better than wealth   SCOTT, WALTER, 23
H. is better than wealth   PROVERBS, 187
he drank my h. with a little speech   HUGO, 2
Here's a h. unto his Majesty   ANONYMOUS, 35
in sickness and in h.   BOOK OF COMMON PRAYER, 26
Only do always in h. what you have often promised to do when you are sick   SIGISMUND, 1
healthy   h. and wealthy and dead   THURBER, 6
Nobody is h. in London   AUSTEN, 5
the h. type that was essentially middle-class   FITZGERALD, F S, 10
hear   any of you at the back who do not h. me   AUDEN, 28
ear begins to h.   BRONTË, E, 3
ears to h., and h. not   BIBLE, 124
ears to h., let him h.   BIBLE, 388
he that planted the ear, shall he not h.   PSALMS, 55
make any man sick to h. her   PEPYS, 9
one is always sure to h. of it   SHERIDAN, R, 3
swift to h.   BIBLE, 217
to-day if ye will h. his voice   PSALMS, 56
truth which men prefer not to h.   AGAR, 1
heard   I have already h. it   RIMSKY-KORSAKOV, 1
nor ear h.   BIBLE, 25
hearsay   to replace X-ray by h.   THOMAS, G, 4
heart   A broken and contrite h. . . . shalt thou not despise   PSALMS, 32
Absence makes the h. grow fonder   BAYLY, 1
a man after his own h.   BIBLE, 478
Because my h. is pure   TENNYSON, 72
by want of thought, as well as want of h.   HOOD, 8
cold untroubled h. of stone   CAMPBELL, T, 4
cut to the h.   BIBLE, 5
Death took him by the h.   OWEN, W, 2
first come to pass in the h. of America   EISENHOWER, 5
God be in my h., And in my thinking   ANONYMOUS, 20
Good-night, Dear H.   ANONYMOUS, 104
Great thoughts come from the h.   VAUVENARGUES, 1
healeth those that are broken in h.   PSALMS, 75
h. and stomach of a King   ELIZABETH I, 11
holiness of the h.'s affections   KEATS, 51
I am sick at h.   SHAKESPEARE, 64
If thou didst ever hold me in thy h.   SHAKESPEARE, 107
I love thee for a h. that's kind   DAVIES, W, 4
in politics there is no h., only head   NAPOLEON I, 5
lonely h. is withered away   YEATS, 19
look in thy h. and write.   SIDNEY, P, 1
Mary . . . pondered them in her h.   BIBLE, 316
Mother is the dead h. of the family   GREER, 2
My h. aches   KEATS, 35
My h. is a lonely hunter   MACLEOD, F, 1
my h.'s abhorrence   BROWNING, R, 52
my h. shall be The faithful compass   GAY, 12
My h. shall be thy garden   MEYNELL, 1
My h.'s in the Highlands   BURNS, R, 21
Once a woman has given you her h.   VANBURGH, 6
our h. is not quiet until it rests in Thee   AUGUSTINE OF HIPPO, 1
She had A h. . . . too soon made glad   BROWNING, R, 35
So the h. be right   RALEIGH, W, 6
strings . . . in the human h.   DICKENS, 4
take heed . . . that your h. be not deceived   BIBLE, 55
Take thy beak from out my h.   POE, 2
that mighty h. is lying still   WORDSWORTH, W, 53
The fire which in the h. resides   ARNOLD, M, 29
The h. has its reasons   PASCAL, 7
The h. that loved her   WORDSWORTH, W, 13
The history of every country begins in the h.   CATHER, 1
The intellect is always fooled by the h.   ROCHEFOUCAULD, 15
Their h.'s in the right place   MAUGHAM, 21
them which are true of h.   PSALMS, 34
The nation had the lion's h.   CHURCHILL, W, 5
There is a road from the eye to the h.   CHESTERTON, 9
the waters of the h. Push in their tides   THOMAS, D, 14
The way to a man's h. is through his stomach   FERN, 1
to lose your h.'s desire   SHAW, 24
What comes from the h.   COLERIDGE, S, 43
With rue my h. is laden   HOUSMAN, 16
with the palsied h.   TENNYSON, 62
hearth   Man for the field and woman for the h.   TENNYSON, 66
the cricket on the h.   MILTON, 14
hearts   first in the h. of his countrymen   WASHINGTON, 1

if ye will hear his voice, harden not your h.   PSALMS, 56
Kind h. are more than coronets   TENNYSON, 40
One equal temper of heroic h.   TENNYSON, 81
The Queen of H.   CARROLL, 19; NURSERY RHYMES, 56
the song that is sung in our h.   OUIDA, 3
The Worldly Hope men set their H. upon   FITZGERALD, E, 7
those who have stout h. and sharp swords   BIRKENHEAD, 4
Two h. that beat as one   LOVELL, 1
well-developed bodies . . . and undeveloped h.   FORSTER, 3
hearty he is so h., so straightforward, outspoken   ROOSEVELT, T, 1
heat Britain . . . is going to be forged in the white h. of this
    revolution   WILSON, HAROLD, 8
can't stand the h., get out of the kitchen   TRUMAN, 3
H., madam! . . . to take off my flesh and sit in my bones
    SMITH, SYDNEY, 4
If you don't like the h.   PROVERBS, 218
heathen I was born of Christian race, And not a H., or a Jew
    WATTS, 4
I will be exalted among the h.   PSALMS, 28
the h. make much ado   PSALMS, 27
heaven a H. in Hell's despair   BLAKE, W, 36
all H. in a rage   BLAKE, W, 10
All place shall be hell that is not h.   MARLOWE, 1
All this and h. too   HENRY, M, 3
a new h. and a new earth   BIBLE, 473
ascend to h.   FIRMONT, 1
between H. and Charing Cross   THOMPSON, F, 2
flat road to h.   SANTAYANA, 1
from whose face the earth and the h. fled   BIBLE, 472
God created the h.   BIBLE, 137
h. and earth shall pass away   BIBLE, 415
H. has granted me no offspring   WHISTLER, 13
H. in a wild flower   BLAKE, W, 5
H. . . . is a place so inane, so dull   SHAW, 34
H. was in him, before he was in h.   WALTON, 7
Home is h.   NASH, 5
If it's h. for climate   BARRIE, 1
If Max gets to H.   WELLS, 21
If this belief from h. be sent   WORDSWORTH, W, 16
In h. an angel is nobody in particular   SHAW, 25
it were better for sun and moon to drop from h.   NEWMAN, J, 4
make a H. of Hell, a Hell of H.   MILTON, 33
man is as H. made him   CERVANTES, 15
Marriage is . . . excluded from h.   BUTLER, S, 19
more things in h. and earth   SHAKESPEARE, 78
Mr Chesterton . . . to h. might have gone   CHESTERTON, 3
no invention came more easily to man than H.   LICHTENBERG, 1
Now: h. knows   PORTER, C, 1
Order is h.'s first law   POPE, 37
Parting is all we know of h.   DICKINSON, 2
Pennies do not come from h.   THATCHER, M, 13
Pennies from H.   BURKE, J, 1
so much of earth . . . of h.   WORDSWORTH, W, 47
steep and thorny way to h.   SHAKESPEARE, 72
the Hell I suffer seems a H.   MILTON, 43
there was war in h.   BIBLE, 465
the starry h. above me   KANT, 1
to be young was very h.   WORDSWORTH, W, 40
'Twould ring the bells of H.   HODGSON, 1
We are all going to H.   GAINSBOROUGH, 1
We are as near to h. by sea as by land   GILBERT, H, 1
what's a h. for   BROWNING, R, 4
What they do in h.   SWIFT, 15
When earth was nigher h.   BROWNING, R, 46
heavenward A homely face . . . aided many women h.   ANTRIM, 1
heavier O you who have borne even h. things   VIRGIL, 6
heaviest nickname is the h. stone that the devil can throw
    HAZLITT, 12
heav'n h. on earth   MILTON, 45
To know I'm farther off from h. Than when . . . a boy   HOOD, 7
hedge A leap over the h.   CERVANTES, 8
hedgehogs If you start throwing h. under me   KHRUSHCHEV, 4
heed To fight and not to h. the wounds   LOYOLA, 1
heels Time wounds all h.   MARX, G, 22
heesh If John or Mary comes h. will want to play   MILNE, 2
heifer plowed with my h.   BIBLE, 295
heights If suffer we must, let's suffer on the h.   HUGO, 3
heiress American h. wants to buy a man   MCCARTHY, M, 3
hell a H. in Heaven's despite   BLAKE, W, 37
A lifetime of happiness . . . h. on earth   SHAW, 21
All place shall be h. that is not heaven   MARLOWE, 1
all we need of h.   DICKINSON, 2

Better to reign in H.   MILTON, 34
buttered slides to h.   SANTAYANA, 1
h. a fury like a woman scorned   CONGREVE, 9
H. is a city much like London   SHELLEY, 21
H. is oneself   ELIOT, T, 5
h. upon earth . . . in a melancholy man's heart   BURTON, ROBERT, 2
Italy . . . h. for women   BURTON, ROBERT, 4
make a Heaven of H., a H. of Heaven   MILTON, 33
Old age is woman's h.   LENCLOS, 1
on the fourth day they will say 'To h. with you!'   KHRUSHCHEV, 8
out of h. leads up to light   MILTON, 40
Raises from H. a human soul   BLAKE, W, 5
the H. I suffer seems a Heaven   MILTON, 43
the h. of horses   FLORIO, 1
the little holiday steamers made an excursion to h.   PRIESTLEY, 10
The road to h. is paved   PROVERBS, 423
though h. should bar the way   NOYES, 2
thou leadest to the gates of h.   BIBLE, 522
Ugly h., gape not   MARLOWE, 5
War is h.   SHERMAN, 2
way down to H. is easy   VIRGIL, 7
Which way I fly is H.; myself am H.   MILTON, 43
hell-broth Like a h. boil and bubble   SHAKESPEARE, 218
help God shall h. her, and that right early   PSALMS, 27
gods h. them that h. themselves   AESOP, 4
going in without the h. of Russia   LLOYD GEORGE, 13
I am trying to be, and you can't h. it   BIRKENHEAD, 2
not so much our friends' h. that helps us   EPICURUS, 1
People must h. one another   LA FONTAINE, 8
Since there's no h.   DRAYTON, 3
The dead . . . look on and h.   LAWRENCE, D, 44
the h. of too many physicians   ALEXANDER THE GREAT, 1
the will to h. others   SCHWEITZER, 1
what is past my h. is past my care   BEAUMONT, 2
with a little h. from my friends   LENNON, 12
you will find light and h. and human kindness   SCHWEITZER, 3
helpless Help of the h.   LYTE, 1
wealth had rendered her h.   BROOKNER, 3
helps He h. little   PROVERBS, 188
not so much our friends' help that h. us   EPICURUS, 1
hem only touch the h. of his garment   BIBLE, 396
hen a broody h. sitting on a china egg   FOOT, 1
Two Owls and a H.   LEAR, 1
Henry How H. would have loved it   TERRY, 4
The work of H. James has always seemed divisible   GUEDALLA, 1
Herald Price of the H. three cents daily   BENNETT, J, 2
herb sweetest fragrance from the h. . . . tread on it and bruise it
    TROLLOPE, 9
herbs nature runs either to h., or to weeds   BACON, FRANCIS, 37
Hercules Some talk of Alexander, and some of H.
    ANONYMOUS, 73
herd the H. of such, Who think too little   DRYDEN, 8
herd-morality Morality . . . is h.   NIETZSCHE, 12
here bet you a hundred bucks he ain't in h.   DILLINGHAM, 1
h. today and gone tomorrow   BEHN, 2
What you are looking for is h., is at Ulubrae   HORACE, 21
hereditary I must . . . try hard to control the talking habit, but . . .
    my case is h.   FRANK, 3
heresies new truths . . . begin as h.   HUXLEY, T, 3
heresy h. signifies no more than private opinion   HOBBES, 3
heritage I summon age To grant youth's h.   BROWNING, R, 49
hero Being a h.   ROGERS, W, 5
better to be the widow of a h. than the wife of a coward
    IBARRURI, 3
Every h. becomes a bore   EMERSON, 22
No man is a h. to his valet   CORNUEL, 1
The h. is strangely akin   RILKE, 3
to his very valet seem'd a h.   BYRON, 6
herod It out-h.s H.   SHAKESPEARE, 94
heroes Children should acquire . . . h. and villains from fiction
    AUDEN, 4
fit country for h. to live in   LLOYD GEORGE, 11
speed glum h. . . . to death   SASSOON, S, 1
the tragedy of life is that . . . h. lose their glamour   DOYLE, 2
Unhappy the land that has no h.   BRECHT, 2
heroic human beings are h.   ORWELL, 8
heroines fearless, high-spirited, resolute and intelligent h.
    SHAKESPEARE, 18
hesitate A leader who doesn't h. . . . is not fit to be a leader
    MEIR, 1
hesitates A science which h. to forget   WHITEHEAD, 5
He who h. is lost   PROVERBS, 199

Hesperus the schooner H.   LONGFELLOW, 18
heterodoxy h. is another man's doxy   WARBURTON, 1
    H. or Thy-doxy   CARLYLE, T, 17
hewers h. of wood   BIBLE, 289
hickory H., dickory, dock   NURSERY RHYMES, 15
hidden Nature is often h.   BACON, FRANCIS, 36
hide He can run, but he can't h.   LOUIS, 1
    h. me under the shadow of thy wings   PSALMS, 6
    I have a big house – and I h. a lot   URE, 1
    Robes and furr'd gowns h. all   SHAKESPEARE, 188
hideous less h. than explanations   LEWIS, D, 1
hiding man who looks you . . . in the eye . . . h. something   FADIMAN, 2

high civil fury first grew h.   BUTLER, S, 1
    I had braces on my teeth and got h. marks   MACDONALD, B, 1
    She's the Broad and I'm the H.   SPRING-RICE, 2
    to put off my hat to . . . h. or low   FOX, G, 1
    up in the h. numbers   KEYNES, 10
    ye'll tak' the h. road   ANONYMOUS, 67
highbrow What is a h.   WALLACE, E, 2
higher the rock that is h. than I   PSALMS, 37
highest h. type of human nature   SPENCER, H, 1
Highland Yon solitary H. lass   WORDSWORTH, W, 50
Highlandman taking the breeks aff a wild H.   SCOTT, WALTER, 4
Highlands My heart's in the H.   BURNS, R, 21
    Ye H. and ye Lawlands   ANONYMOUS, 109
Highness His Royal H. . . . prides himself upon . . . the excellent harvest   SHERIDAN, R, 13
high-water h. mark of my youth   THURBER, 9
highwayman the h. came riding   NOYES, 1
hill If the h. will not come to Mahomet, Mahomet will go to the h.   BACON, FRANCIS, 14
    There is a green h. far away   ALEXANDER, 3
    they call you . . . from the h.   ARNOLD, M, 34
    thou . . . hast made my h. so strong   PSALMS, 17
    Tonight the American flag floats from yonder h. or Molly Stark sleeps a widow   STARK, 1
hills a fine thing to be out on the h. alone   KILVERT, 1
    her foundations are upon the holy h.   PSALMS, 47
    I will lift up mine eyes unto the h.   PSALMS, 67
    Over the h. and far away   GAY, 3
    What are those blue remembered h.   HOUSMAN, 15
him he could not avoid making H. set the world in motion   PASCAL, 5
himself ever written out of reputation but by h.   BENTLEY, R, 2
    Every man for h., and the devil   PROVERBS, 138
    gesture by the individual to h.   GALBRAITH, 8
    He would kill H.   DUMAS, FILS, 1
Hind Here lies the body of Richard H.   ANONYMOUS, 33
hinder men that . . . h. the reception of every work   JOHNSON, S, 27
hinky H., dinky par-lee-voo   ROWLAND, E, 1
Hippocrene the blushful H.   KEATS, 37
Hiroshima The genius of Einstein leads to H.   EINSTEIN, 2
historian A good h. is timeless   FÉNELON, 2
    A h. is a prophet in reverse   SCHLEGEL, 1
    Great abilities are not requisite for an H.   JOHNSON, S, 61
    The h. must have . . . some conception of how men . . . behave   FORSTER, 1
    the profession of h. fits a man for psychological analysis   SARTRE, 11
historians H. are like deaf people   TOLSTOY, L, 15
    h. left blanks in their writings   POUND, 5
    h. repeat each other   GUEDALLA, 4
    H. tell the story of the past   GONCOURT, 1
history ancient h. . . . is no more than accepted fiction   VOLTAIRE, 17
    Austria is Switzerland . . . with h. added   MORPURGO, 1
    deal of h. to produce . . . literature   JAMES, H, 6
    From today . . . there begins a new epoch in the h. of the world   GOETHE, 9
    He was . . . a student of h.   TAYLOR, A, 7
    H. gets thicker   TAYLOR, A, 1
    h. is . . . a tableau of crimes and misfortunes   VOLTAIRE, 20
    H. is more or less bunk   FORD, H, 1
    H. is past politics   SEELEY, 2
    H. is philosophy teaching by examples   DIONYSIUS OF HALICARNASSUS, 1
    H. is the essence of . . . biographies   CARLYLE, T, 6
    H. is . . . the wrong way of living   DURRELL, L, 3
    H. is too serious   MACLEOD, I, 1
    h. must be false   WALPOLE, R, 1

'H. . . . nightmare from which I am trying to awake'   JOYCE, 8
    h. of the human spirit   ARNOLD, M, 22
    H. repeats itself   PROVERBS, 204
    H. teaches us that men and nations behave wisely   EBAN, 1
    h. . . . the biography of great men   CARLYLE, T, 11
    h. . . . the register of the . . . misfortunes of mankind   GIBBON, 8
    If men could learn from h.   COLERIDGE, S, 23
    It is impossible to write ancient h.   PÉGUY, 1
    Its h. dates from today   WHISTLER, 14
    more h. than they can consume locally   SAKI, 6
    no h.; only biography   EMERSON, 9
    one of these is the h. of political power   POPPER, 3
    people . . . never have learned anything from h.   HEGEL, 1
    poetry is . . . more philosophical . . . than h.   ARISTOTLE, 5
    Political h. is far too criminal . . . to be . . . fit . . . for the young   AUDEN, 4
    Science, h., politics, all were within his compass   WELLS, 2
    Stratford . . . suggests powdered h.   HALSEY, 5
    The attitude of the English . . . toward English h.   HALSEY, 4
    the greatest week in the h. of the world   NIXON, 8
    The h. of all . . . society is the h. of class struggles   MARX, K, 1
    The h. of every country begins in the heart   CATHER, 1
    The most persistent sound . . . through men's h.   KOESTLER, 5
    the Thames is liquid h.   BURNS, J, 1
    the whole subsequent h. of civilisation takes its rise   LUTHER, 1
    This was the Angel of H.   GOEBBELS, 2
    trace . . . the disasters of English h. to . . . Wales   WAUGH, E, 16
    War makes . . . good h.   HARDY, 6
history-making Man is a h. creature   AUDEN, 9
hit If you would h. the mark   LONGFELLOW, 5
hither Come h.   SHAKESPEARE, 45
Hitler every time H. occupies a country   MUSSOLINI, 2
    H. has carried out a revolution on our lines   MUSSOLINI, 1
    H. has missed the bus   CHAMBERLAIN, N, 7
    H. showed surprising loyalty to Mussolini   BULLOCK, 2
    H. was a nuisance. Mussolini was bloody   MADARIAGA Y ROGO, 2
    one purpose, the destruction of H.   CHURCHILL, W, 14
    The people H. never understood   BULLOCK, 1
    tipster who . . . reached H.'s level of accuracy   TAYLOR, A, 5
hoarse raven himself is h.   SHAKESPEARE, 206
hobbit In a hole in the ground there lived a h.   TOLKIEN, 4
hobby-horse So long as a man rides his h.   STERNE, 1
hobgoblin the h. of little minds   EMERSON, 15
hog Rule all England under a h.   COLLINGBOURNE, 1
hoi polloi the multitude, the h.   DRYDEN, 24
hoist H. your sail   PROVERBS, 205
hold h. fast that which is good   BIBLE, 504
    h. your tongue and let me love   DONNE, 5
    To have and to h.   BOOK OF COMMON PRAYER, 27
    When every . . . thing you h. Is made of silver, or of gold   GILBERT, W, 5
holder office sanctifies the h.   ACTON, 2
holders H. of one position, wrong for years   AUDEN, 25
hole A h. is the accident . . . a darn is . . . poverty   SHUTER, 1
    if you knows of a better h.   BAIRNSFATHER, 1
    In a h. in the ground there lived a hobbit   TOLKIEN, 4
    smallest h. . . . man can hide his head in   CHESTERTON, 30
    What happens to the h. when the cheese is gone   BRECHT, 8
holiday the little h. steamers made an excursion to hell   PRIESTLEY, 10
holiness put off H.   BLAKE, W, 17
    the h. of the heart's affections   KEATS, 51
    who, like you, your H., is a Roman Catholic   CHURCHILL, R, 5
Holland H. . . . lies so low they're only saved by being dammed   HOOD, 13
hollers whatever you try to do, somebody jumps up and h.   GUTHRIE, 2
hollow We are the h. men   ELIOT, T, 9
    within the h. crown   SHAKESPEARE, 298
holly The h. and the ivy   ANONYMOUS, 81
Hollywood In H., if you don't have happiness   REED, R, 1
    I should not have been invited to H.   CHANDLER, R, 5
    the attitude of a H. director toward love   HALSEY, 2
holy everything that lives is h.   BLAKE, W, 3
    h., h., h., is the Lord of hosts   BIBLE, 197
    H., h., h., Lord God Almighty   HEBER, 3
    If you become h.   HUME, B, 3
    the H. Roman Empire was neither h., nor Roman, nor an empire   VOLTAIRE, 16
    'Twas on a H. Thursday   BLAKE, W, 45
home against books the H. Secretary is   WAUGH, E, 41
    Charity begins at h.   BROWNE, T, 8

Comin' for to carry me h. — ANONYMOUS, 76
eaten me out of house and h. — SHAKESPEARE, 119
Father . . . come h. with me now — WORK, 1
for de old folks at h. — FOSTER, 3
For h. is best — TUSSER, 4
For the old Kentucky H. far away — FOSTER, 2
give me a h. where the buffalo roam — HIGLEY, 1
h. his footsteps he hath turn'd — SCOTT, WALTER, 8
H. is heaven — NASH, 5
H. is h. — CLARKE, J, 1; PROVERBS, 206
H. is the sailor, h. from sea — STEVENSON, R, 12
H. is where — PROVERBS, 207
H. of lost causes — ARNOLD, M, 13
H. . . . where . . . they have to take you in — FROST, R, 3
I can get all that at h. — COOK, P, 2
Many a man who thinks to found a h. — DOUGLAS, N, 3
no h. . . . save in Paris — NIETZSCHE, 7
permits you to be entertained . . . by people you wouldn't have in your h. — FROST, D, 1
Pleasure never is at h. — KEATS, 17
She's leaving h. — LENNON, 11
The Life and Soul, the man who will never go h. — WHITEHORN, 3
there's no place like h. — PAYNE, 1
till the cow comes h. — BEAUMONT, 12
Turn up the lights, I don't want to go h. in the dark — HENRY, O, 3
we come From God, who is our h. — WORDSWORTH, W, 25
What's the good of a h. — GROSSMITH, G, 1
home-keeping h. youth — SHAKESPEARE, 346
homely A h. face . . . aided many women heavenward — ANTRIM, 1
be never so h. — CLARKE, J, 1
h. wits — SHAKESPEARE, 346
Homer Cicero And . . . H. were *Mad as the mist and snow* — YEATS, 20
even excellent H. nods — HORACE, 9
Mr Gladstone read H. for fun — CHURCHILL, W, 19
Seven cities warr'd for H., being dead — HEYWOOD, 1
The author of that poem is either H. — HUXLEY, A, 35
home-sickness In h. you must keep moving — STACPOOLE, 1
homo ecce h. — BIBLE, 268
The 'h.' is the legitimate child — LEWIS, W, 4
homos one of the stately h. of England — CRISP, 7
homosexuals h. . . . set out to win the love of a 'real' man — CRISP, 9
honest An h. broker — BISMARCK, 6
An h. God — INGERSOLL, 1
an h. man sent to lie abroad for . . . his country — WOTTON, 3
An h. man's word — PROVERBS, 53
give me six lines . . . by the most h. man — RICHELIEU, CARDINAL DE, 3
He is nothing more than a sensible, h. man — MELBOURNE, 1
I am as h. as any man living — SHAKESPEARE, 271
It's better to be quotable than . . . h. — STOPPARD, 12
not an h. man — WHATELY, 2
She was poor but she was h. — ANONYMOUS, 1
then they get *h.* — ROLLESTON, 1
Though I am not naturally h. — SHAKESPEARE, 353
Though I be poor, I'm h. — MIDDLETON, 1
too h. to live above his means — JACKSON, A, 2
honestly If possible h., if not, somehow, make money — HORACE, 15
honesty *h.* is the beginning of education — RUSKIN, 12
H. is the best policy — PROVERBS, 208; WHATELY, 2
Philosophers never balance between profit and h. — HUME, D, 8
honey a land flowing with milk and h. — BIBLE, 106
a land of oil olive, and h. — BIBLE, 54
gather h. all the day — WATTS, 2
h. still for tea — BROOKE, 4
sweeter also than h. — PSALMS, 9
They took some h., and plenty of money — LEAR, 8
what is sweeter than h. — BIBLE, 295
honey'd the h. middle of the night — KEATS, 11
honey-dew on h. hath fed — COLERIDGE, S, 17
honi *H. soit qui mal y pense* — ANONYMOUS, 39
honky-tonk a rambling h. hitter — GUTHRIE, 1
honour All is lost save h. — FRANCIS I, 1
a prophet is not without h. — BIBLE, 392
As h., love, obedience — SHAKESPEARE, 223
brothers all In h. — WORDSWORTH, W, 39
His h. rooted in dishonour — TENNYSON, 17
h. all men — BIBLE, 441
h. is for the poor — TERESA, MOTHER, 4
H. pricks me on — SHAKESPEARE, 113

h. sinks where commerce long prevails — GOLDSMITH, 23
h. thy father and thy mother — BIBLE, 115
if I accepted the h. . . . I would not answer for the integrity of my intellect — FARADAY, 1
Let us h. if we can — AUDEN, 12
man being in h. hath no understanding — PSALMS, 29
only h. and life have been spared — FRANCIS I, 1
peace I hope with h. — DISRAELI, 31
So h. peereth in the meanest habit — SHAKESPEARE, 320
That chastity of h. — BURKE, E, 10
then they get *h.* — ROLLESTON, 1
There is h. among thieves — PROVERBS, 408
they get *on*, then they get *h.* — ROLLESTON, 1
To h. we call you — GARRICK, 2
Wealth has never been a sufficient source of h. — GALBRAITH, 2
we're fighting for this woman's h. — MARX, G, 9
honourable His designs were strictly h. — FIELDING, 12
hoof I see many h.-marks going in — AESOP, 6
hook canst thou draw out leviathan with an h. — BIBLE, 237
Hooligan Even the H. was probably invented in China — SAKI, 18
Hoorah Henry He is without strict doubt a H. — RUNYON, 9
Hoo-ray H. and up she rises — ANONYMOUS, 105
hope Abandon h., all ye who enter here — DANTE, 1
a faint h. that he will die — EMERSON, 3
And what was dead was H. — WILDE, 7
H. for the best — PROVERBS, 209
h. is . . . the dream of those that wake — PRIOR, 2
H. is the power of being cheerful — CHESTERTON, 21
H. may vanish, but can die not — SHELLEY, 8
H. springs eternal in the human breast — POPE, 32
I do not h. to turn — ELIOT, T, 3
Land of H. and Glory — BENSON, 1
no other medicine but only h. — SHAKESPEARE, 230
Not to h. for things to last for ever, is what the year teaches — HORACE, 41
now abideth faith, h., charity — BIBLE, 38
Our h. for years to come — WATTS, 6
the distinction between h. and expectation — ILLICH, 3
The triumph of h. over experience — JOHNSON, S, 81
The Worldly H. men set their Hearts upon — FITZGERALD, E, 7
to h. for Paradise is to live in Paradise — SACKVILLE-WEST, 4
unconquerable h. — ARNOLD, M, 38
What a strange thing is memory, and h. — GRANDMA MOSES, 1
While there is life, there's h. — GAY, 7
Without all h. of day — MILTON, 58
hopeless that controversy is either superfluous or h. — NEWMAN, J, 6
hopes enough for fifty h. and fears — BROWNING, R, 9
Life's short span forbids us to enter on far-reaching h. — HORACE, 28
My h. no more must change their name — WORDSWORTH, W, 33
The h. and prayers of liberty-loving people — EISENHOWER, 4
Horatius brave H. — MACAULAY, T, 11
horde Society is now one polish'd h. — BYRON, 34
horizontal we value none But the h. one — AUDEN, 12
Horner Little Jack H. Sat in the corner — NURSERY RHYMES, 30
Hornie Auld H., Satan, Nick — BURNS, R, 3
horns Memories are hunting h. — APOLLINAIRE, 1
When you take the bull by the h. — RIDGE, 1
horny-handed H. sons of toil — KEARNEY, 1
Horowitz Vladimir H. — SCHNABEL, 4
horrible A strange, h. business . . . good enough for Shakespeare's day — VICTORIA, 10
horrid are they all h. — AUSTEN, 14
horror I have a h. of sunsets — PROUST, 16
mere existence is swollen to a h. — LAWRENCE, D, 23
The h.! The h. — CONRAD, 2
The thought of dentists gave him just the same sick h. — WELLS, 8
horrors I have supp'd full with h. — SHAKESPEARE, 224
horse A fly, Sir, may sting a stately h. — JOHNSON, S, 49
a pale h. — BIBLE, 462
A Protestant with a h. — BEHAN, 1
Do not trust the h., Trojans — VIRGIL, 9
good deal of physical courage to ride a h. — LEACOCK, 8
Go together like a h. and carriage — CAHN, 1
h. was king — LEE, L, 4
I feel as a h. must feel — DEGAS, 1
I know two things about the h. — ANONYMOUS, 44
like to be a h. — ELIZABETH II, 1
my kingdom for a h. — SHAKESPEARE, 303
nobody has any business to go around looking like a h. — PARKER, D, 5

Ride a cock-h. to Banbury Cross   NURSERY RHYMES, 46
the h., as a means of locomotion is obsolete   SOMERVILLE, 2
To confess that you are totally Ignorant about the H.   SELLAR, 2
victory under the belly of a Cossack's h.   TROTSKY, 4
You can lead a h. to the water   PROVERBS, 470
You may have my husband, but not my h.   LAWRENCE, D, 25
Horse Guards You can be in the H.   RATTIGAN, 2
horseman *H., pass by*   YEATS, 32
horsemanship They say princes learn no art truly, but . . . h.   JONSON, 8
horse-pond celibacy is . . . a muddy h.   PEACOCK, 5
horses A grain, which in England is generally given to h.   JOHNSON, S, 12
Bring on the empty h.   CURTIZ, 1
Dogs, like h., are quadrupeds   MUIR, 4
England . . . hell for h.   BURTON, ROBERT, 4
England . . . hell of h.   FLORIO, 1
frighten the h.   CAMPBELL, MRS PATRICK, 1
Men are . . . more careful of the breed of their h. and dogs than
of their children   PENN, 2
SIXTY H. WEDGED IN A CHIMNEY   MORTON, 2
swap h. in mid-stream   LINCOLN, 16
hosanna h. in the highest   BIBLE, 407
hospital first requirement in a H. . . . do the sick no harm   NIGHTINGALE, 1
the world, I count it not an inn, but an h.   BROWNE, T, 10
host an innumerable company of the heavenly h.   BLAKE, W, 12
h. of men not one will still be alive in a hundred years' time   XERXES, 1
h. with someone indistinct   ELIOT, T, 22
hostages h. given to fate   LUCAN, 1
h. to fortune   BACON, FRANCIS, 33
hostile The universe is not h.   HOLMES, J, 1
hostility your h. towards him   BRADBURY, 4
hosts the Lord of h. is with us   PSALMS, 28
hot blow h. and cold with the same breath   AESOP, 7
H. cross buns!   NURSERY RHYMES, 6
hotel He's someone who flies around from h. to h.   STOPPARD, 5
hotel-keepers h. continue to give them   TROLLOPE, 11
hotels I prefer temperance h.   WARD, 1
hot-water bottles the English have h.   MIKES, 3
Houdin Robert H. who . . . invented the vanishing bird-cage trick   WELLES, 4
Houdini Harry H.   DILLINGHAM, 1
hounded I will not be h.   THATCHER, M, 4
hounds And the cry of his h.   GRAVES, J, 1
I said the h. of spring   THURBER, 17
When the h. of spring are on winter's traces   SWINBURNE, 1
hour A child's a plaything for an h.   LAMB, M, 1
An h. in the morning   PROVERBS, 54
at the rate of sixty minutes an h.   LEWIS, C, 5
I also had my h.   CHESTERTON, 13
In the h. of death   BOOK OF COMMON PRAYER, 18
Milton! thou shouldst be living at this h.   WORDSWORTH, W, 55
mine h. is not yet come   BIBLE, 241
nobody knew whether . . . he would be alive the next h.   FRANK, 1
nothing can bring back the the h.   WORDSWORTH, W, 29
one bare h. to live   MARLOWE, 4
One h.'s sleep   PROVERBS, 54
Some h. . . . will prove lovely   HORACE, 18
the clocks were striking the h.   LONGFELLOW, 4
their finest h.   CHURCHILL, W, 52
Time and the h. runs through   SHAKESPEARE, 203
To one dead deathless h.   ROSSETTI, D, 1
hours h. will take care of themselves   CHESTERFIELD, 11
Three h. a day   TROLLOPE, 3
housbondes H. at chirche-dore   CHAUCER, 12
house A h. is a machine for living in   LE CORBUSIER, 1
A man in the h. is worth two   WEST, M, 3
Cleaning your h. while your kids are still growing   DILLER, 1
Every man's h. will be fair and decent   MORRIS, W, 4
get thee out . . . from thy father's h.   BIBLE, 165
I had rather be a door-keeper in the h. of my God   PSALMS, 45
in my Father's h. are many mansions   BIBLE, 258
in the last days . . . the Lord's h. shall be established   BIBLE, 193
my h. shall be called the h. of prayer   BIBLE, 408
peace be to this h.   BIBLE, 323
set thine h. in order   BIBLE, 304
The h. of every one is to him as his castle   COKE, E, 1
The h. where I was born   HOOD, 6
the sparrow hath found her an h.   PSALMS, 44
they all lived together in a little crooked h.   NURSERY RHYMES, 57

you . . . who have made me too great for my h.   BACON, FRANCIS, 66
house-agents Everybody hates h.   WELLS, 15
household Spiro Agnew is not a h. name   AGNEW, 1
housekeeping H. ain't no joke   ALCOTT, 1
housemaid He was a meticulous h.   CHAMBERLAIN, N, 3
housemaids damp souls of the h.   ELIOT, T, 17
House of Commons leader of the H.   DISRAELI, 34
House of Lords Every man has a H. in his own head   LLOYD GEORGE, 12
The H., an illusion   STOPPARD, 4
The H. is a perfect eventide home   STOCKS, 2
House of Peers The H. . . . Did nothing in particular   GILBERT, W, 20
houses H. are built to live in   BACON, FRANCIS, 15
plague o' both your h.   SHAKESPEARE, 315
Rich men's h. are seldom beautiful   ASQUITH, M, 2
the darkness inside h.   DELANEY, 4
how Everything he saw made him ask h. and why   LEONARDO DA VINCI, 1
I do not know h. to tell you   NEHRU, 1
Hubbard Old Mother H. Went to the cupboard   NURSERY RHYMES, 39
hue native h. of resolution   SHAKESPEARE, 91
Hugo *H. – hélas*   GIDE, 4
human Adam was but h.   TWAIN, 15
All that is h. must retrograde   GIBBON, 10
a pleasant smile that it seems rather divine than h.   LEONARDO DA VINCI, 4
evolution of the h. race   DARWIN, C G, 1
h. beings are heroic   ORWELL, 8
h. beings have an . . . infinite capacity for taking things for granted   HUXLEY, A, 33
H. beings were invented by water   ROBBINS, 1
H. beings, yes, but not surgeons   VIRCHOW, 2
H. kind cannot bear   ELIOT, T, 7
H. life is everywhere a state in which much is to be endured   JOHNSON, S, 28
h. nature . . . more of the fool   BACON, FRANCIS, 13
H. on my faithless arm   AUDEN, 2
If h. beings could be propagated . . . aristocracy would be . . .
sound   HALDANE, 3
I got disappointed in h. nature   DONLEAVY, 1
I have got lots of h. weaknesses   THATCHER, M, 15
imagine a boot stamping on a h. face   ORWELL, 16
Ishmaelites . . . will not publicly eat h. flesh uncooked in Lent   WAUGH, E, 38
I wish I loved the H. Race   RALEIGH, W A, 2
Jews . . . contribution to the h. condition out of all proportion   USTINOV, 5
Mercy has a h. heart   BLAKE, W, 44
my opinion of the h. race   MAUGHAM, 21
No h. being . . . was ever so free as a fish   RUSKIN, 15
no need for any other faith than . . . faith in h. beings   BUCK, 6
nothing h. foreign to me   TERENCE, 2
nothing to distinguish h. society from the farm-yard   SHAW, 12
not linen you're wearing out, But h. creatures' lives   HOOD, 11
Socialism with a h. face must function again   DUBČEK, 2
the city is not a concrete jungle, it is a h. zoo   MORRIS, D, 1
the curse of all the h. race   NAPOLEON I, 1
the full tide of h. existence is at Charing-Cross   JOHNSON, S, 93
The h. face is . . . a whole cluster of faces   PROUST, 4
The h. race . . . many of my readers   CHESTERTON, 28
the importance of the h. factor   CHARLES, PRINCE, 2
The Romans and Greeks found everything h.   LAWRENCE, D, 6
the title h. being . . . out-ranks every other   LIVERMORE, 2
the vilest specimens of h. nature are . . . found among
demagogues   MACAULAY, T, 10
To err is h., to forgive, divine   POPE, 28
To kill a h. being   JAMES, H, 8
When in the course of h. events, it becomes necessary for one
people to dissolve . . . political bonds   JEFFERSON, 4
you feel as if a h. being sitting inside were making fun of you   CANETTI, 1
humanity Every year h. takes a step towards Communism   KHRUSHCHEV, 5
Oh wearisome condition of h.   GREVILLE, 5
That unremitting h.   BENNETT, ALAN, 5
the crooked timber of h.   KANT, 4
these gorilla damnifications of h.   DARWIN, C R, 1
The still, sad music of h.   WORDSWORTH, W, 12
unremitting h. soon had me cheesed off   DICKENS, 1

Women have always been the guardians of wisdom and h.
WOLFF, 1

humble for the last time in my life, Your H. Servant
WALPOLE, H. 1
h. and meek are thirsting for blood ORTON, 3
It is difficult to be h. DOBRÉE, 5
Sherlock Holmes *is* literature on a h. . . . level DOYLE, 1
humiliate His great pleasure was to h. people THOMAS, D. 2
humiliating Corporal punishment is . . . h. for him who gives it
KEY, E. 4
humiliation the last h. of an aged scholar COLLINGWOOD, R. 1
the moment of greatest h. is . . . when the spirit is proudest
PANKHURST, C. 2
humility H. is only doubt BLAKE, W. 13
humour Cynicism is h. in ill-health WELLS, 17
deficient in a sense of h. COLERIDGE, S. 42
Freudian . . . low . . . sort of h. GRAVES, R. 2
His taste lay in . . . good-natured h. COWPER, 1
own up to a lack of h. COLBY, 1
Total absence of h. COLETTE, 1
why God withheld the sense of h. from women
CAMPBELL, MRS PATRICK, 3
hump A woman . . . without a positive h., may marry whom she
likes THACKERAY, 9
Humpty H. Dumpty sat on a wall NURSERY RHYMES, 18
hunchback The h. in the park THOMAS, D. 12
hundred a h. schools of thought contend MAO TSE-TUNG, 6
bet you a h. bucks he ain't in here DILLINGHAM, 1
host of men not one will still be alive in a h. years' time
XERXES, 1
it would be all the same a h. years hence DICKENS, 26
Letting a h. flowers blossom MAO TSE-TUNG, 4
to trade a h. contemporary readers for KOESTLER, 6
Hungarian It's not enough to be H. KORDA, 1
hunger best sauce . . . is h. CERVANTES, 16
convicted of sickness, h., wretchedness, and want SMOLLETT, 3
H. is the best sauce PROVERBS, 210
The war against h. KENNEDY, JOHN, 13
to banish h. by rubbing the belly DIOGENES, 2
hungred h., and ye gave me meat BIBLE, 421
hungry A h. stomach has no ears LA FONTAINE, 9
h. as a hunter LAMB, CHARLES, 24
h. hare has no frontiers WALESA, 3
h. sheep look up, and are not fed MILTON, 26
she makes h. Where most she satisfies SHAKESPEARE, 30
You cannot feed the h. on statistics LLOYD GEORGE, 7
Hungry Joe H. collected lists of fatal diseases HELLER, 6
hunt how much more dogs are animated when they h. in a pack
HUME, D. 6
let their motto be: – H. BRONTË, C. 1
hunted tell the others by their h. expression LEWIS, C. 6
hunter hungry as a h. LAMB, CHARLES, 23
Man is the h. TENNYSON, 65
My heart is a lonely h. MACLEOD, F. 1
Nimrod the mighty h. BIBLE, 162
the snare of the h. PSALMS, 51
hunting Memories are h. horns APOLLINAIRE, 1
their discourse was about h. PEPYS, 10
when his half-civilized ancestors were h. the wild boar
BENJAMIN, 1
hurrah h.! we bring the Jubilee WORK, 4
hurricanoes You cataracts and h. SHAKESPEARE, 176
hurries h. to the main event HORACE, 7
hurry An old man in a h. CHURCHILL, R. 4
H.! I never h. I have no time to h. STRAVINSKY, 7
So who's in a h. BENCHLEY, 7
hurrying I see a man h. along – to what KEATS, 69
hurt it h. too much to laugh STEVENSON, A. 7
It takes your enemy and your friend . . . to h. you TWAIN, 6
They say hard work never h. anybody REAGAN, 10
Those have most power to h. BEAUMONT, 6
wish to h. BRONOWSKI, 4
hurting Art . . . can go on mattering once it has stopped h.
BOWEN, ELIZABETH, 2
husband An archaeologist is the best h. CHRISTIE, 2
at all times yr faithful h. STEELE, 2
Being a h. is a whole-time job BENNETT, ARNOLD, 7
easier to be a lover than a h. BALZAC, 6
happened unawares to look at her h. AUSTEN, 29
h. render unto the wife due benevolence BIBLE, 29
in love with . . . Her own h. CHURCHILL, J. 1
light wife doth make a heavy h. SHAKESPEARE, 253

My h. and I ELIZABETH II, 2
My h. is dead MARX, G. 7
Never trust a h. too far ROWLAND, H. 4
that monstrous animal a h. and wife FIELDING, 13
The h. frae the wife despises BURNS, R. 20
You may have my h., but not my horse LAWRENCE, D. 25
husbandry borrowing dulls the edge of h. SHAKESPEARE, 74
husbands flirt with their own h. WILDE, 22
h. and wives . . . belong to different sexes DIX, DOROTHY, 4
h. and wives make shipwreck of their lives DIX, DOROTHY, 3
H. are like fires GABOR, 1
h., love your wives BIBLE, 21
h. remind me of an orangutang BALZAC, 3
h. to stay at home ELIOT, G. 6
The *divine right* of h. WOLLSTONECRAFT, 1
hush a breathless h. in the Close tonight NEWBOLT, 6
husks the h. that the swine did eat BIBLE, 331
hut Love in a h. KEATS, 24
The Arab who builds . . . a h. out of . . . a temple FRANCE, 4
Hyacinth Children with H.'s temperament . . . merely know more
SAKI, 5
every H. the Garden wears FITZGERALD, E. 8
hydrostatics It gives me the h. SHERIDAN, R. 6
hymn Aisle. Altar. H. MUIR, 2
hymn-book Cassock, band, and h. too WILBERFORCE, S. 2
hymns My poems are h. of praise SITWELL, E. 1
hyper-thyroid Shelley had a h. face SQUIRE, 2
hyphenated h. Americanism ROOSEVELT, T. 9
hypocrisy an organized h. DISRAELI, 24
H. . . . is a whole-time job MAUGHAM, 2
H. is the homage paid by vice to virtue ROCHEFOUCAULD, 19
H. is the most . . . nerve-racking vice MAUGHAM, 2
neither man nor angel can discern H. MILTON, 42
That would be h. WILDE, 27
hypocrite h. in his pleasures CAMUS, 8
No man is a h. in his pleasures JOHNSON, S. 152
see . . . into a h. CHESTERTON, 19
hypocritical Man . . . learns by being h. KERR, 1
hypothesis I have no need of that h. LAPLACE, 1
the slaying of a beautiful h. by an ugly fact HUXLEY, T. 1
to discard a pet h. every day LORENZ, 1
hyssop purge me with h. PSALMS, 31

I

I I also had my hour CHESTERTON, 13
I am for people CHAPLIN, 7
in the infinite I AM COLERIDGE, S. 5
I would have done it differently WHISTLER, 16
ice skating over thin i. EMERSON, 15
The i. was here, the i. was there COLERIDGE, S. 26
ice-cream just enjoy your i. while it's on your plate WILDER, T. 5
iced three parts i. over ARNOLD, M. 47
icicles When i. hang by the wall SHAKESPEARE, 199
id put the i. back in yid ROTH, 1
idea An i. isn't responsible for the people MARQUIS, 1
constant repetition . . . in imprinting an i. HITLER, 10
Dying for an i. LEWIS, W. 2
I think it would be a good i. GANDHI, 5
no stand can be made against invasion by an i. HUGO, 4
That fellow seems to me to possess but one i. JOHNSON, S. 79
the i. of death as an individual KOESTLER, 2
they will end by ruining our i. MUSSOLINI, 1
ideal every boy should be in love with some i. woman
NORMAN, B. 1
it is an i. for which I am prepared to die MANDELA, 3
the i. American CHESTERTON, 24
idealism He had a kind of i. in pleasure PEPYS, 4
idealist An i. . . . on noticing that a rose smells better than a
cabbage MENCKEN, 16
people call me an i. WILSON, W. 12
ideals Away with all i. LAWRENCE, D. 33
with all the i. that I have THATCHER, M. 8
ideas all the enthusiasm . . . he withheld from books and i.
EISENHOWER, 2
down which i. are lured and . . . strangled COCKS, 1
i. are of more importance than values BRENAN, 2
i. simply pass through him BRADLEY, F. 6
I. that enter the mind under fire TROTSKY, 9
I stopped . . . to exchange i. HEINE, 3
Learn our i., or otherwise get out LESSING, D. 2
lots of i., but stupid ones MONTHERLANT, 2

Many i. grow better when HOLMES, O. JR., 2
Morality which is based on i. LAWRENCE, D, 8
she's only got two i. in her head LINKLATER, 2
the addiction of political groups to the i. GALBRAITH, 3
The true God . . . God of i. VIGNY, 1
Ides Beware the i. of March SHAKESPEARE, 142
idiot An inspired i. GOLDSMITH, 2
now I feel like a complete i. HEINE, 3
tale told by an i. SHAKESPEARE, 225
The i. who praises . . . every country but his own GILBERT, W, 26
To generalize is to be an i. BLAKE, W, 52
idiots the English seem . . . to act with . . . the fatuity of i.
SMITH, SYDNEY, 2
idle As i. as a painted ship COLERIDGE, S, 28
I am happiest when I am i. WARD, 3
Satan finds . . . mischief . . . For i. hands WATTS, 1
We would all be i. JOHNSON, S, 107
Young people ought not to be i. THATCHER, M, 20
idleness compulsory and irreproachable i. TOLSTOY, L, 9
i. and indifference CHEKHOV, 9
I. . . . the refuge of weak minds CHESTERFIELD, 15
Research! A mere excuse for i. JOWETT, 5
idling It is impossible to enjoy i. JEROME, 5
idol one-eyed yellow i. to the north of Khatmandu HAYES, 1
idolatry There is no i. in the Mass JOHNSON, S, 77
idols Their i. are silver and gold PSALMS, 64
if I. you can keep your head KIPLING, 16
much virtue in I. SHAKESPEARE, 56
ifs If i. and ans PROVERBS, 214
ignominious History is full of i. getaways ORWELL, 33
ignorance for i. is never better than knowledge FERMI, 1
From i. our comfort flows PRIOR, 3
I. is like a delicate exotic fruit WILDE, 25
I. is Strength ORWELL, 18
I., madam, pure i. JOHNSON, S, 53
I. of the law excuses SELDEN, 3
journalism. . . . keeps us in touch with the i. of the community
WILDE, 15
Lawyers are the only persons in whom i. . . . is not punished
BENTHAM, 2
man's i. of the gods BUTLER, S, 7
no sin but i. MARLOWE, 9
than keeping women in a state of i. KNOX, V, 1
where i. is bliss, 'Tis folly to be wise GRAY, 10
Your i. cramps my conversation HOPE, 7
ignorant a parlourmaid as i. as Queen Victoria VICTORIA, 4
Let no one i. of mathematics enter here PLATO, 6
The i. man always adores LOMBROSO, 1
the i. man he pretends to be MELBOURNE, 1
the opinionated, the i., and the boorish ARISTOTLE, 3
To confess that you are totally I. about the Horse SELLAR, 2
what preceded it, we are absolutely i. BEDE, 1
ill Cannot be i.; cannot be good SHAKESPEARE, 202
I am only half there when I am i. LAWRENCE, D, 43
If . . . someone is speaking i. of you EPICTETUS, 1
I. met by moonlight SHAKESPEARE, 260
means to do i. deeds SHAKESPEARE, 166
no hint throughout the universe Of good or i. THOMSON, JAMES, 2
woman colour'd i. SHAKESPEARE, 373
illegal collect legal taxes from i. money CAPONE, 4
things I really like . . . are either immoral, i. WOOLLCOTT, 4
illegitimate There are no i. children YANKWICH, 1
ill-health Cynicism is humour in i. WELLS, 17
illiteracy The ratio of literacy to i. MORAVIA, 1
illiterate I. him . . . from your memory SHERIDAN, R, 5
illness I. is the night-side of life SONTAG, 1
reborn from a mortal i. every day of his life LAWRENCE, D, 2
illogical Faith . . . an i. belief in . . . the improbable MENCKEN, 14
ills sharp remedy . . . for all i. RALEIGH, W, 5
ill-spent sign of an i. youth SPENCER, H, 2
illumine What in me is dark I. MILTON, 31
illusion it can contain nothing but sophistry and i. HUME, D, 2
Religion is an i. FREUD, S, 3
The House of Lords, an i. STOPPARD, 4
visible universe was an i. BORGES, 2
illusions It's life's i. I recall MITCHELL, JONI, 1
image any graven i. BIBLE, 115
A photograph is not only an i. SONTAG, 1
fall down and worship the golden i. BIBLE, 48
If God made us in His i. VOLTAIRE, 19
make man in our own i. BIBLE, 142

Why should I consent to the perpetuation of the i. of this i.
PLOTINUS, 1
imagery the loveliest i. KEATS, 4
imaginary Happiness is an i. condition SZASZ, 5
no other way to conceive an i. world VIZINCZEY, 1
imagination A lady's i. is very rapid AUSTEN, 20
Art is ruled . . . by the i. CROCE, 1
His novels are marvels of sustained i. TOLSTOY, L, 1
I.! . . . I put it first years ago TERRY, 2
I. without skill gives us modern art STOPPARD, 1
indebted to his . . . i. for his facts SHERIDAN, R, 20
not an ideal of reason but of i. KANT, 3
of i. all compact SHAKESPEARE, 263
stand up for freedom of the i. RUSHDIE, 2
The primary i. COLERIDGE, S, 5
truth of i. KEATS, 51
imaginative he possessed . . . abounding i. power OVID, 1
imagine never so happy . . . as we i. ROCHEFOUCAULD, 6
imagined What is now proved was . . . i. BLAKE, W, 24
imagining How reconcile this world . . . with . . . my i. KELLER, 3
imitate An original writer is . . . one whom nobody can i.
CHATEAUBRIAND, 1
I i. the Saviour HUXLEY, A, 5
never failed to i. BALDWIN, J, 4
obliged to i. himself, and to repeat REYNOLDS, J, 3
people . . . usually i. each other HOFFER, 1
imitates Photography can never grow up if it i. ABBOTT, 1
imitation I. is the sincerest of flattery COLTON, 3
Man . . . is an i. OUSPENSKY, 1
Immaculate Conception the I. was spontaneous combustion
PARKER, D, 19
Immanuel call his name I. BIBLE, 198
immature the i. man . . . wants to die nobly STEKEL, 1
immaturity common symptom of i. WHARTON, 3
the executive expression of human i. BRITTAIN, 3
immoral moral or an i. book WILDE, 44
the things I really like . . . are either i. WOOLLCOTT, 4
worse than i. ACHESON, 4
immorality the most rigid code of i. BRADBURY, 2
immortal Did you imagine that I was i. LOUIS XIV, 7
I have lost the i. part SHAKESPEARE, 281
make me i. with a kiss MARLOWE, 2
Our souls have sight of that i. sea WORDSWORTH, W, 28
immortality I . . . want to achieve i. ALLEN, W, 10
just ourselves And I. DICKINSON, 1
immutable Few things are as i. GALBRAITH, 3
impassioned the average sensual man i. HUGO, 1
impediment cause, or just i. BOOK OF COMMON PRAYER, 23
imperative This i. is Categorical KANT, 2
imperfection i. itself may have its . . . perfect state
DE QUINCEY, 3
imperial be yourself, i., plain and true BROWNING, R, 7
on the moon as in I. Russia CHEKHOV, 1
imperialism i. is the monopoly stage of capitalism LENIN, 1
Their Europeanism is . . . i. with HEALEY, 2
impersonal In the philosopher there is nothing whatever i.
NIETZSCHE, 14
impertinent ask an i. question BRONOWSKI, 2
impetuous such i. blood WORDSWORTH, W, 47
importance Official dignity . . . in inverse ratio to . . . i.
HUXLEY, A, 10
important One doesn't recognize . . . the really i. moments
CHRISTIE, 1
some reference to I. Person Play POTTER, S, 2
the little things are infinitely the most i. DOYLE, 6
imposed wish to be i. on, and then are COWPER, 1
impossibility a physical and metaphysical i. CARLYLE, T, 3
impossible complete sorrow is as i. TOLSTOY, L, 12
I believe because it is i. TERTULLIAN, 3
It's either easy or i. DALI, 1
something is i., he is . . . wrong CLARKE, A, 1
when you have excluded the i. DOYLE, 3
impotent an i. people, Sick with inbreeding THOMAS, R, 2
impregnator the writer . . . is the i. WHITE, E, 2
impression an i. of pleasure BACON, FRANCIS, 1
impressionable Give me a girl at an i. age SPARK, 6
impressions i. . . . lasting as . . . an oar upon the water CHOPIN, 3
improbable an i. fiction SHAKESPEARE, 343
an illogical belief in . . . the i. MENCKEN, 14
however i., must be the truth DOYLE, 5
impromptu Winston . . . preparing his i. speeches CHURCHILL, W, 2
improper I only hope it is not i. GASKELL, 2

impropriety   I. is the soul of wit · MAUGHAM, 9
improved   enormously i. by death · SAKI, 4
Victoria has greatly i. · VICTORIA, 1
improvement   most schemes of political i. · JOHNSON, S, 76
impulse   the i. of the moment · AUSTEN, 22
the need to talk is a primary i. · CERVANTES, 14
impulses   Mistrust first i. · TALLEYRAND, 7
impure   To the Puritan all things are i. · LAWRENCE, D, 5
in   you had it i. you · PARKER, D, 24
inactivity   wise and masterly i. · MACKINTOSH, 1
inadequate   i. for getting to France · KINNOCK, 7
inarticulate   speak for the i. and the submerged · BEAVERBROOK, 4
inartistic   He was unperfect, unfinished, i. · JAMES, H, 7
inbreeding   an impotent people, Sick with i. · THOMAS, R, 3
incest   except i. and folk-dancing · BAX, 1
inch   entertained within an i. of their lives · SOMERVILLE, 3
every i. a king · SHAKESPEARE, 186
Give him an i. · PROVERBS, 174
inches   They that die by famine die by i. · HENRY, M, 2
incident   What is i. but the illustration of character · JAMES, H, 11
incisors   Writers, like teeth, are divided into i. · BAGEHOT, 8
inclination   A man ought to read just as i. leads him · JOHNSON, S, 63
include   'I. me out' · GOLDWYN, 10
incoherent   I'm not i. · ROSS, H, 2
income   Annual i. twenty pounds · DICKENS, 13
live beyond its i. · BUTLER, S, 11
must not . . . look upon me as a source of i. · KEMBLE, C, 1
incomes   people live beyond their i · PAUL, 8
incomparable   The I. Max · BEERBOHM, 1
incompetence   employees who have not yet reached . . . i. · PETER, 2
incompetent   God is the immemorial refuge of the i. · MENCKEN, 9
i. swine · SASSOON, S, 4
incomplete   A man in love is i. until . . . married · GABOR, 2
incomprehensible   almost i. to the human mind · HOOVER, 2
an old, wild, and i. man · VICTORIA, 8
inconvenience   Change is not made without i. · HOOKER, 1
inconveniences   A good many i. attend play-going · TYNAN, 4
inconvenient   i. to be poor · COWPER, 7
incorruptible   seagreen i. · CARLYLE, T, 18
the dead shall be raised i. · BIBLE, 42
increase   from fairest creatures we desire i. · SHAKESPEARE, 357
then shall the earth bring forth her i. · PSALMS, 38
increased   influence of the Crown has i. · DUNNING, 1
incurable   the i. disease of writing · JUVENAL, 1
Ind   Outshone the wealth of Ormus and of I. · MILTON, 39
indecency   case of a man charged with i. · GRIFFITH-JONES, 2
prejudicial . . . as a public i. · CERVANTES, 21
The older one grows the more one likes i. · WOOLF, 8
indecent   It requires one to assume such i. postures · WILDE, 72
much more i. . . . than a good smack · LAWRENCE, D, 7
sent down for i. behaviour · WAUGH, E, 3
indefatigable   i. and unsavoury engine of pollution · SPARROW, 1
indefensible   the defence of the i. · ORWELL, 20
independent   all men are created equal and i. · JEFFERSON, 5
an I. Labour Party · WAUGH, E, 43
one . . . must be i. · CURIE, 3
To be poor and i. · COBBETT, 1
India   From I.'s coral strand · HEBER, 1
I. is a geographical term · CHURCHILL, W, 46
What have we to say to I. · RUSKIN, 18
Indian   base I., threw a pearl away · SHAKESPEARE, 288
in a world of Gary Coopers you are the I. · BALDWIN, J, 6
lay out ten to see a dead I. · SHAKESPEARE, 322
Indians   The only good I. I ever saw · SHERIDAN, P, 1
indictment   an i. against an whole people · BURKE, E, 16
indifference   and cold i. came · ROWE, 1
equanimity bordering on i. · GILBERT, W, 46
idleness and i. · CHEKHOV, 9
i. and a coach and six · COLMAN, THE ELDER, 1
Nothing is so fatal to religion as i. · BURKE, E, 23
indignation   48 percent i. and 50 percent envy · DESICA, 1
Moral i. is in most cases · DE SICA, 1
My heart burned within me with i. and grief · LINCOLN, 2
puritan pours righteous i. · CHESTERTON, 49
the mists of righteous i. · MUGGERIDGE, 1
those who are not wronged feel the same i. · SOLON, 1
indiscreet   people so i. in appearing to know · BOCCACCIO, 2
indiscretion   A lover without i. is no lover · HARDY, 7
indispensable   woman . . . knows that she is i. · WYNDHAM, 2
indispensables   She was one of those i. · HUXLEY, A, 25

indistinguishable   i. from any other . . . business man · LEWIS, S, 2
individual   gesture by the i. to himself · GALBRAITH, 8
It is of no moment to the happiness of an i. · JOHNSON, S, 83
the idea of death as an i. · KOESTLER, 7
The liberty of the i. must be thus far limited · MILL, 4
The psychic development of the i. · FREUD, S, 2
individualism   American system of rugged i. · HOOVER, 3
Art is the most intense mode of i. · WILDE, 55
individuality   England is the paradise of i. · SANTAYANA, 9
indoors   God having given us i. and out-of-doors · MACAULAY, R, 1
indulgence   An only son, sir, might expect more i. · GOLDSMITH, 16
industrial   I. relations are like sexual relations · FEATHER, 1
industry   Captains of i. · CARLYLE, T, 22
i. will supply their deficiency · REYNOLDS, 2
Life without i. is guilt · RUSKIN, 4
national i. of Prussia · MIRABEAU, 1
inebriated   i. with . . . his own verbosity · DISRAELI, 32
ineffectual   A weak . . . i. man · COLERIDGE, S, 1
Shelley was indeed 'a beautiful and i. angel' · SHELLEY, 1
inelegance   a continual state of i. · AUSTEN, 28
ineptitude   i. of M. Sartre's political performance · SARTRE, 3
inevitability   The i. of gradualness · WEBB, S, 2
inexactitude   terminological i. · CHURCHILL, W, 40
infallible   an i. sign of the second-rate · LEVERSON, 1
No man is i. · PROVERBS, 312
The only i. criterion of wisdom · BURKE, E, 4
We are none of us i. · THOMPSON, W, 1
infamous   I have got an i. army · WELLINGTON, 16
infancy   Heaven lies about us in our i. · WORDSWORTH, W, 25
Gray Age, Grene youth, White I. · ANONYMOUS, 53
infant   a mixed i. · BEHAN, 4
An i. crying in the night · TENNYSON, 30
I doubt that the i. monster · KIPLING, 1
Sooner murder an i. in its cradle · BLAKE, W, 21
infanticide   as indefensible as i. · WEST, R, 4
infection   the only man who escaped i. · SOCRATES, 2
inferior   No one can make you feel i. · ROOSEVELT, E, 1
Switzerland . . . an i. sort of Scotland · SMITH, SYDNEY, 14
you will end up with an i. product · MORGAN, E, 2
inferiority   imperialism with an i. complex · HEALEY, 2
minds so impatient of i. · JOHNSON, S, 23
Ulysses . . . gives me an i. complex · JOYCE, 3
Wherever an i. complex exists · JUNG, 10
inferiors   I. revolt in order that · ARISTOTLE, 9
The English want i. · TOCQUEVILLE, 1
they treat children as i. · DISNEY, 1
inferno   the i. of his passions · JUNG, 8
infidelity   I. . . . consists in professing to believe · PAINE, 1
infidels   War is enjoined you against the I. · KORAN, 3
infinite   Space is almost i. · QUAYLE, 1
The Desire of Man being I. · BLAKE, W, 50
The sight . . . gave me i. pleasure · PARK, 1
infinitive   When I split an i. · CHANDLER, R, 6
infinity   I. in the palm of your hand · BLAKE, W, 9
i. torments me · MUSSET, 1
infirmities   friend should bear his friend's i. · SHAKESPEARE, 158
infirmity   last i. of noble mind · MILTON, 25
inflation   I. in the Sixties was a nuisance · LEVIN, 1
influence   How to . . . I. People · CARNEGIE, 1
i. of the Crown has increased · DUNNING, 1
proper time to i. the character of a child · INGE, 9
influenza   call it i. if ye like · BENNETT, ARNOLD, 3
inform   all occasions do i. against me · SHAKESPEARE, 99
not to i. the reader · ACHESON, 7
infortune   The worst kinde of i. is this · CHAUCER, 20
infringement   Necessity is the plea for every i. · PITT THE YOUNGER, 1
infusion   The i. of a China plant · ADDISON, 12
ingenious   an i., and good-temper'd people · STERNE, 2
inglorious   mute i. Milton · GRAY, 6
the i. arts of peace · MARVELL, 3
ingratitude   Austria will astound the world with . . . her i. · SCHWARZENBERG, 1
I hate i. more in a man · SHAKESPEARE, 345
I., thou marble-hearted fiend · SHAKESPEARE, 170
man's i. · SHAKESPEARE, 49
ingress   Our i. . . . Was naked and bare · LONGFELLOW, 14
inherit   Russia will certainly i. the future · LAWRENCE, D, 34
inherited   as if he had i. it · GRANT, U, 1
inhumanity   Man's i. to man · BURNS, R, 14
initial   decided to take a middle i. · SELZNICK, 1

initiative success depends . . . upon individual i. PAVLOVA, 2
injured Never trust the man who . . . hath i. you FIELDING, 7
injury An i. is much sooner forgotten CHESTERFIELD, 7
Recompense i. with justice CONFUCIUS, 12
injustice A lawyer has no business with . . . i. JOHNSON, S, 157
fear of suffering i. ROCHEFOUCAULD, 10
shows the . . . i. in his death CANETTI, 2
threatened with a great i. CARLYLE, J, 1
injustices thought only to justify their i. VOLTAIRE, 11
ink fills up his crossword puzzle in i. SHORTER, 1
inn no room for them in the i. BIBLE, 313
To that dark i., the grave SCOTT, WALTER, 12
inner Conscience is the i. voice MENCKEN, 2
Innisfree I will arise and . . . go to I. YEATS, 17
innocence I. is no earthly weapon HILL, G, 1
it is . . . our business to lose i. BOWEN, ELIZABETH, 5
my i. begins to weigh me down RACINE, 2
Ralph wept for the end of i. GOLDING, 2
innocent Every one is i. PROVERBS, 141
ten guilty persons escape than one i. suffer BLACKSTONE, 5
innocently i. employed than in getting money JOHNSON, S, 91
innovator time is the greatest i. BACON, FRANCIS, 30
inordinate i. fondness for beetles HALDANE, 5
inquiry The world is but a school of i. MONTAIGNE, 9
inquisitive the i. mind can . . . receive no answer JOHNSON, S, 127
insane Charles Lamb . . . i. LAMB, CHARLES, 1
Man is quite i. MONTAIGNE, 6
insanity often a prelude to i. WAUGH, E, 16
inscriptions In lapidary i. a man is not upon oath JOHNSON, S, 99
inscrutable Dumb, i. and grand ARNOLD, M, 33
fathom the i. workings of Providence BIRKENHEAD, 2
insect the Egyptians worshipped an i. DISRAELI, 34
insemination Surely you don't mean by unartificial i. THURBER, 19
insensitiveness the greatest deeds require a certain i. LICHTENBERG, 3
inside attention to the i. CHESTERFIELD, 14
insight moment's i. . . . worth a life's experience HOLMES, O, 7
insignificance A man of . . . the utmost i. CURZON, 1
insignificant as i. men as any in England WALPOLE, R, 4
insolence a wretch who supports with i. JOHNSON, S, 13
i. is not invective DISRAELI, 26
the i. of wealth JOHNSON, S, 124
insolent their i. . . . airs of superiority WALPOLE, H, 9
insomnia Amor vincit i. FRY, C, 5
inspiration Genius is one per cent i. EDISON, 1
Ninety per cent of i. PROVERBS, 308
inspired An i. idiot GOLDSMITH, 2
instinct the i. for being unhappy SAKI, 4
institution Any i. which does not suppose ROBESPIERRE, 1
more than a game. It's an i. HUGHES, THOMAS, 2
institutions working of great i. SANTAYANA, 2
instrument an i. . . . of the ruling class STALIN, 2
that magnificent i. between your legs TOSCANINI, 5
instruments gods . . . Make i. to plague us SHAKESPEARE, 193
insufferable Oxford that has made me i. BEERBOHM, 9
insult adding i. to injuries MOORE, E, 1
A man should not i. his wife publicly THURBER, 12
sooner forgotten than an i. CHESTERFIELD, 7
insulted anyone here whom I have not i. BRAHMS, 1
insured you cannot be i. for the accidents COREN, 2
insurrection I. is an art TROTSKY, 6
intangible great i. machine of commercial tyrrany MORRIS, W, 1
integrate I i. the current export drive BETJEMAN, 5
integrity I. without knowledge is weak JOHNSON, S, 30
not answer for the i. of my intellect FARADAY, 1
intellect a feather to tickle the i. LAMB, CHARLES, 16
a road . . . that does not go through the i. CHESTERTON, 9
halitosis of the i. ICKES, 2
his i. is not replenished SHAKESPEARE, 196
i. is . . . fooled by the heart ROCHEFOUCAULD, 15
I. is invisible SCHOPENHAUER, 2
put on I. BLAKE, W, 17
take care not to make the i. our god EINSTEIN, 4
the i. of an advocate BAGEHOT, 10
The voice of the i. is a soft one FREUD, S, 1
we cannot exclude the i. from JAMES, W, 3
intellects an old man decayed in his i. JOHNSON, S, 143
highest i., like the tops of mountains MACAULAY, T, 6
intellectual an i. . . . mind watches itself CAMUS, 1
artist who's an i. FITZGERALD, F S, 11
Every i. attitude is latently political MANN, 2
I call upon the i. community RUSHDIE, 2

i., but I found it too difficult SCHWEITZER, 2
i. . . . doesn't know how to park a bike AGNEW, 4
I've been called many things, but never an i. BANKHEAD, 6
Man is an i. animal HAZLITT, 5
The word I. suggests AUDEN, 21
thirdly, i. ability ARNOLD, T, 2
intellectuals characterize themselves as i. AGNEW, 3
vanishing race . . . the i. SHERWOOD, 1
intelligence I. is quickness to apprehend WHITEHEAD, 2
The more i. . . . the more . . . one finds original PASCAL, 6
intelligent A really i. man feels MONTESQUIEU, 2
Each generation imagines itself . . . more i. ORWELL, 35
resolute and i. heroines SHAKESPEARE, 18
The i. are to the intelligentsia BALDWIN, S, 11
the most i. Prime Minister MACMILLAN, 4
intelligentsia intelligent are to the i. BALDWIN, S, 11
intelligible to aim at being i. HOPE, 1
intended i. to give you some advice HARRIS, 1
intensity excellence of every art is its i. KEATS, 54
intent prick the sides of my i. SHAKESPEARE, 209
intercourse dreary i. of daily life WORDSWORTH, W, 14
interest a playwright . . . void of dramatic i. SARTRE, 2
How can I take an i. in my work BACON, F, 2
It is not my i. to pay the principal SHERIDAN, R, 19
interested always been i. in people MAUGHAM, 28
seldom i. in what he is saying POUND, 2
The average man is . . . i. in a woman DIETRICH, 2
interests all these great i. entrusted VICTORIA, 8
intérieur Vive l'i. SELLAR, 6
intermission Pleasure is . . . i. of pain SELDEN, 4
international science is essentially i. CURIE, 4
interpreter The soul fortunately, has an i. BRONTË, C, 2
interrupted Mr Wordsworth is never i. WORDSWORTH, M, 1
interval an opera without an i. NEWMAN, E, 1
interviewing i. a faded female in a damp basement HARDING, 1
intimacy a single dangerous i. LACLOS, 4
intolerably I would grow i. conceited WHISTLER, 8
intolerant extremists . . . are i. KENNEDY, R, 1
intoxicate you won't i. with one glass CHEKHOV, 13
intoxicated A man who exposes himself when he is i. JOHNSON, S, 129
I was born i. RUSSELL, G, 1
intoxication best of life is . . . i. BYRON, 21
intrigue the i. of a Greek of the lower empire DISRAELI, 33
introduce let me i. you to that leg of mutton CARROLL, 37
introduction I could buy back my i. MARX, G, 15
intrudes society, where none i. BYRON, 16
invade when religion is allowed t, i. . . . private life MELBOURNE, 11
invalid permanent i. called Bunbury WILDE, 20
invasion no stand can be made against i. by an idea HUGO, 4
the long-promised i. CHURCHILL, W, 55
invective insolence is not i. DISRAELI, 26
invent it would be necessary to i. Him VOLTAIRE, 14
inventing reviewing of books involves constantly i. reactions ORWELL, 11
invention A long poem is a test of i. KEATS, 50
He was his own greatest i. COWARD, 1
Woman's virtue is man's greatest i. SKINNER, C, 1
inventions All one's i. are true FLAUBERT, 1
inverted commas absence of i. guarantees FADIMAN, 1
investment There is no finer i. CHURCHILL, W, 63
To bear many children is . . . an i. GANDHI, I, 1
inviolable the i. shade ARNOLD, M, 38
invisible the only evil that walks I. MILTON, 42
invisibly electricity was dripping i. THURBER, 10
invited People were not i. FITZGERALD, F S, 10
involuntary It was i. KENNEDY, JOHN, 3
inward They flash upon that i. eye WORDSWORTH, W, 8
truth in the i. parts PSALMS, 31
inwards he looked i., and found her DRYDEN, 23
IRA I. would think me a worthwhile target MOUNTBATTEN, 5
Ireland a picture of a relief map of I. ASTOR, N, 2
delivered I. from plunder and oppression SWIFT, 1
How's poor ould I. ANONYMOUS, 46
I'll not forget old I. BLACKWOOD, 2
I. is the old sow JOYCE, 6
I would have liked to go to I. WILHELM II, 2
Now I. has her madness AUDEN, 16
The moment . . . I. is mentioned SMITH, SYDNEY, 2
The problem with I. LEONARD, 1

Irish All races have . . . economists, with the exception of the I. GALBRAITH, 5
inability in Britain to comprehend I. feelings HAUGHEY, 1
I. . . . devotion to higher arts GALBRAITH, 5
I. Home Rule is conceded ROSEBERY, 2
nephew who sings an I. ballad KENNEDY, JOHN, 1
That is the I. Question DISRAELI, 22
The English . . . dislike only *some* I. BEHAN, 8
The I. and the Jews have a psychosis BEHAN, 7
The I. are a fair people JOHNSON, S, 90
The I. . . . are needed in this cold age CHILD, 2
Irishman Put an I. on the spit PROVERBS, 344
iron An i. curtain CHURCHILL, W, 65
an i. curtain across Europe TROUBRIDGE, 1
blood and i. BISMARCK, 1
I do, and I also wash and i. them THATCHER, D, 1
muscles . . . Are strong as i. bands LONGFELLOW, 14
The I. Curtain GOEBBELS, 1
the i. enter into his soul STERNE, 1
the i. has entered his soul LLOYD GEORGE, 14
will wink and hold out mine i. SHAKESPEARE, 125
ironics Life's Little I. HARDY, 8
irons Many i. in the fire PROVERBS, 284
two i. in the fire BEAUMONT, 3
irrelevant the most i. thing in nature LAMB, CHARLES, 15
irreproachable compulsory and i. idleness TOLSTOY, L, 9
irresponsible better to be i. and right CHURCHILL, W, 67
Iser of I., rolling rapidly CAMPBELL, T, 2
Ishmaelites I. . . . will not publicly eat human flesh WAUGH, E, 38
Islam author of the Satanic Verses book, which is against I. KHOMEINI, 2
I. unashamedly came with a sword RUNCIMAN, 1
island No man is an I. DONNE, 7
isle Kelly from the I. of Man MURPHY, C, 1
this sceptred i. SHAKESPEARE, 295
isles The i. of Greece BYRON, 26
isolating by i. him . . . as if he were a leper PARNELL, 1
Israel When I. was in Egypt land ANONYMOUS, 107
Italian as sensible as baseball in I. MENCKEN, 17
I speak . . . I. to women CHARLES V, 3
Italians The I. will laugh at me MUSSOLINI, 2
Italy A man who has not been in I. JOHNSON, S, 110
I. a paradise for horses BURTON, ROBERT, 4
itch The i. of disputing WOTTON, 2
the i. of literature LOVER, 1
iteration i. of nuptials CONGREVE, 16
itself Love seeketh not i. to please BLAKE, W, 36
ivy The holly and the i. ANONYMOUS, 81

J

jab Man . . . had been created to j. the life out of Germans SASSOON, S, 5
j'accuse J. ZOLA, 2
Jack J. and Jill went up the hill NURSERY RHYMES, 25
J. – I'm all right BONE, D, 1
J. of all trades PROVERBS, 239
J. Sprat could eat no fat NURSERY RHYMES, 26
Little J. Horner Sat in the corner NURSERY RHYMES, 30
the house that J. built NURSERY RHYMES, 62
jackals J. piss at their foot FLAUBERT, 2
Jackson J. standing like a stone wall BEE, 1
Jacob Talk to him of J.'s ladder JERROLD, 4
the traffic of J.'s ladder THOMPSON, F, 2
Jael J. the wife of Heber BIBLE, 293
jail being in a ship is being in a j. JOHNSON, S, 56
jam J. today, and men aren't at their most exciting SNOW, 3
The rule is, j. tomorrow and j. yesterday CARROLL, 30
will teach you how to make strawberry j. TOLSTOY, L, 3
James Henry J. has a mind so fine JAMES, H, 1
Henry J. was one of the nicest old ladies I ever met JAMES, H, 2
The work of Henry J. has always seemed divisible . . . into three
reigns JAMES, H, 3
Jane if ever I was to have a dozen girls, I'd call 'em all J. WELLS, 13
Time's up for Sir John, an' for little Lady J. LAWRENCE, D, 18
January dreadful pictures of J. and February TROLLOPE, 7
Janvier Generals J. and Février NICHOLAS I, 2
Japan There was a young man of J. ANONYMOUS, 94
Japanese The J. have perfected good manners THEROUX, 2
jaundiced with the j. eye TENNYSON, 52
jaw-jaw To j. is better than to war-war CHURCHILL, W, 68

jazz The basic difference between classical music and j. PREVIN, 1
the J. Age . . . became less and less an affair of youth FITZGERALD, F S, 4
jealous a j. God BIBLE, 115
Art is a j. mistress EMERSON, 4
through his whole life j. and obstinate BURKE, E, 1
jealousy J. . . . feeling alone among smiling enemies BOWEN, ELIZABETH, 4
of j.; It is the green-ey'd monster SHAKESPEARE, 283
the ear of j. heareth all things BIBLE, 518
Jeepers J. Creepers MERCER, 1
jeering laughing and j. at everything . . . strange PEPYS, 1
jeers j. at Fate ADAMS, F, 1
Jeeves J. coughed one soft, low, gentle cough WODEHOUSE, 7
like P. G. Wodehouse dropping J. WAUGH, E, 45
Jefferson when Thomas J. dined alone KENNEDY, JOHN, 12
jelly Out vile j. SHAKESPEARE, 182
Jemmy Young J. Grove on his death-bed lay ANONYMOUS, 49
Jenny J. kissed me when we met HUNT, L, 4
Jericho by faith the walls of J. fell down BIBLE, 186
Jerusalem J, BLAKE, W, 33
J. the golden NEALE, 3
J. . . . the mother of us all BIBLE, 133
the holy city, new J. BIBLE, 473
Till we have built J. BLAKE, W, 33
jest a fellow of infinite j. SHAKESPEARE, 105
A j.'s prosperity lies in the ear SHAKESPEARE, 198
glory, j., and riddle of the world POPE, 33
Life is a j. GAY, 10
jester the sharp, narrow silhouette of an aggressive j. RUSSELL, B, 1
jesting j. Pilate BACON, FRANCIS, 56
jests He j. at scars SHAKESPEARE, 308
Jesus All hail, the power of J.' name PERRONET, 1
Gentle J. WESLEY, C, 1
How sweet the name of J. sounds NEWTON, J, 2
If J. Christ were to come to-day CARLYLE, T, 28
J. loves me – this I know WARNER, 1
J. was . . . a first-rate political economist SHAW, 3
J. was a sailor when he walked upon the water COHEN, 3
when J. was born in Bethlehem of Judaea BIBLE, 351
jeunesse Si j. savait ESTIENNE, 1
Jew An American is either a J., or an anti-Semite SARTRE, 5
difficult for a J. to be converted HEINE, 4
Einstein – the greatest J. since Jesus HALDANE, 2
hated by every anti-semite as if I were a J. YEVTUSHENKO, 1
Hath not a J. eyes SHAKESPEARE, 245
I'm a coloured, one-eyed J. DAVIS, S, 2
I'm not really a J.; just Jewish MILLER, J, 1
I was born of Christian race, And not a Heathen, or a J. WATTS, 4
neither J. nor Greek BIBLE, 132
no intellectual society can flourish where a J. feels . . . uneasy JOHNSON, P, 1
No J. was ever fool enough to turn Christian ZANGWILL, 1
Pessimism is a luxury that a J. never can allow himself MEIR, 4
jewellery Don't ever wear artistic j. COLETTE, 4
j. . . . wrecks a woman's reputation COLETTE, 4
jewelry she did not remember . . . her j. LOOS, 4
jewels a capital bosom to hang j. upon DICKENS, 24
Jewish A J. man with parents alive ROTH, 2
a *total solution* of the J. question GOERING, 2
best that is in the J. blood LAWRENCE, D, 14
establishment in Palestine of a national home for the J. people BALFOUR, 4
I'm not really a Jew; just J. MILLER, J, 1
spit upon my J. gaberdine SHAKESPEARE, 240
Jewry Modern Physics is an instrument of J. TOMASCHEK, 1
Jews J. require a sign BIBLE, 24
King of the J. BIBLE, 351
not enough prisons . . . in Palestine to hold all the J. MEIR, 7
The Irish and the J. have a psychosis BEHAN, 7
The J. and Arabs should . . . settle their differences AUSTIN, W, 2
the J. bring the unlike into the heart of *every milieu* ZANGWILL, 3
the J. have made a contribution to the human condition out of all
proportion USTINOV, 5
The J. have produced . . . Christ, Spinoza, and myself STEIN, 5
the place was run by J. CHESTERTON, 3
To choose The J. EWER, 1
Jezebel J. . . . painted her face BIBLE, 302
Jill Jack and J. went up the hill NURSERY RHYMES, 25
Jim Lucky J. AMIS, 3

jingo We don't want to fight, but, by j. if we do   HUNT, G, 1
jo John Anderson my j.   BURNS, R, 12
Joan greasy J. doth keel the pot   SHAKESPEARE, 199
Job hast thou considered my servant J.   BIBLE, 222
    J. endured everything – until his friends came   KIERKEGAARD, 1
    the Lord answered J. out of the whirlwind   BIBLE, 236
job Being a husband is a whole-time j.   BENNETT, ARNOLD, 7
    If two men on the same j. agree   ZANUCK, 1
    We have finished the j.   HAILE SELASSIE, 1
    we will finish the j.   CHURCHILL, W, 56
jockey the . . . cup is given to the j.   DEGAS, 1
Joe Poor old J.   FOSTER, 5
John Beneath this slab J. Brown is stowed   NASH, 6
    D'ye ken J. Peel   GRAVES, J, 1
    I play J. Wayne in every picture   WAYNE, 1
    J. Anderson my jo   BURNS, R, 12
    J. Brown's body   HALL, 1
    Matthew, Mark, Luke and J.   ADY, 1
    Time's up for Sir J., an' for little Lady Jane   LAWRENCE, D, 18
Johnny J. head-in-air   PUDNEY, 1
    J.-the-bright-star   PUDNEY, 2
    Little J. Head-in-Air   HOFFMAN, 1
Johnson Dr J.'s sayings   PEMBROKE, 1
    J. made the most brutal speeches   JOHNSON, S, 3
    Kennedy promised, J. delivered   JOHNSON, L, 3
    That great Cham of literature, Samuel J.   SMOLLETT, 1
    There is no arguing with J.   GOLDSMITH, 1
join He's gone to j. the majority   PETRONIUS, 2
    will you j. the dance   CARROLL, 17
joined what . . . God hath j. together, let not man put asunder   BIBLE, 403
joint The time is out of j.   SHAKESPEARE, 79
joke A j.'s a very serious thing   CHURCHILL, C, 3
    a j. with a double meaning   BARKER, 1
    A rich man's j. is always funny   BROWN, T E, 1
    good deed to forget a poor j.   BRACKEN, 1
    Housekeeping ain't no j.   ALCOTT, 1
    The coarse j. proclaims   LEWIS, C, 2
jokes A different taste in j. is a . . . strain on the affections   ELIOT, G, 4
    Forgive . . . my little j. on Thee   FROST, R, 4
    He cannot bear old men's j.   FRISCH, 1
    I don't make j.   ROGERS, W, 7
joking My way of j. is to tell the truth   SHAW, 13
jolly There was a j. miller   BICKERSTAFFE, 1
Jonah a great fish to swallow up J.   BIBLE, 286
    and the lot fell upon J.   BIBLE, 285
Jonathan my brother J.   BIBLE, 483
Joneses drag the J. down to my level   CRISP, 3
Jonson O Rare Ben J.   JONSON, 2
Jordan the people were passed clean over J.   BIBLE, 287
Joseph Here lies J., who failed in everything he undertook   JOSEPH II, 1
jot one j. or one tittle   BIBLE, 362
journalism Christianity . . . but why j.   BALFOUR, 2
    j. . . . keeps us in touch with the ignorance of the community   WILDE, 15
    j. what will be grasped at once   CONNOLLY, 6
journalist the functions of the modern j.   CURZON, 3
    You cannot hope to bribe or twist . . . the British j.   WOLFE, H, 1
journalists J. say a thing that they know isn't true   BENNETT, ARNOLD, 8
journey I prepare for a j. . . . as though for death   MANSFIELD, K, 2
    long j. . . . must bid the company farewell   RALEIGH, W, 7
    One of the pleasantest things in the world is going on a j.   HAZLITT, 20
    Our j. had advanced   DICKINSON, 3
Jowett First come I; my name is J.   BEECHING, 1
joy a father's j.   SCOTT, WALTER, 19
    A thing of beauty is a j. for ever   KEATS, 7
    j. cometh in the morning   PSALMS, 17
    j. . . . in heaven over one sinner that repenteth   BIBLE, 330
    let j. be unconfined   BYRON, 14
    One j. scatters a hundred griefs   PROVERBS, 328
    Silence is the perfectest herald of j.   SHAKESPEARE, 268
    Strength through j.   LEY, 1
    the Lord . . . give thee j. for this thy sorrow   BIBLE, 517
    the noise of the shout of j.   BIBLE, 130
    They that sow in tears shall reap in j.   PSALMS, 9
    we could never learn to be brave . . . if there were only j.   KELLER, 2
    you'll give happiness and j. to many other people   BEETHOVEN, 1

joys For present j.   DRYDEN, 25
    Hence, vain deluding J.   MILTON, 11
    j. of parents are secret   BACON, FRANCIS, 38
jubilee hurrah! we bring the J.   WORK, 4
judge A j. is not supposed to know   PARKER, HUBERT, 1
    A j. knows nothing   PROVERBS, 27
    in righteousness he doth j. and make war   BIBLE, 470
    j. not, that ye be not judged   BIBLE, 372
    J. not the play   DAVIES, J, 1
    j. of a man by his foes   CONRAD, 4
    Never j. from appearances   PROVERBS, 302
    out of thine own mouth will I j. thee   BIBLE, 336
    shallow people . . . do not j. by appearances   WILDE, 48
    the j. standeth before the door   BIBLE, 219
judged they were j. every man according to their works   BIBLE, 472
    why is my liberty j. of another man's conscience   BIBLE, 36
judgement day of j.   BOOK OF COMMON PRAYER, 18
    Don't wait for the Last J.   CAMUS, 9
    Force, if unassisted by j., collapses   HORACE, 35
    let my will replace reasoned j.   JUVENAL, 6
    no one complains of his j.   ROCHEFOUCAULD, 13
    Perhaps your fear in passing j.   BRUNO, 1
    your j. will probably be right   MANSFIELD, W, 1
    Your representative owes you . . . his j.   BURKE, E, 2
judging if greater want of skill Appear in writing or in j. ill   POPE, 20
judgment A Daniel come to j.   SHAKESPEARE, 247
    I expect a j.   DICKENS, 1
    That fellow would vulgarize the day of j.   JERROLD, 3
    the j. of the great whore   BIBLE, 468
judgments the j. of the Lord are true   PSALMS, 9
    'Tis with our j. as our watches   POPE, 21
jug Little brown j., don't I love thee   ANONYMOUS, 23
Julia Whenas in silks my J. goes   HERRICK, 7
Juliet J. is the sun   SHAKESPEARE, 308
Jumblies far and few, Are the lands where the J. live   LEAR, 5
jump We'd j. the life to come   SHAKESPEARE, 208
Juno fierce J.'s never-forgetting anger   VIRGIL, 5
jury how should you like . . . to be tried before a j.   JOHNSON, S, 106
    Trial by j. itself . . . will be a delusion   DENMAN, 1
jury-men wretches hang that j. may dine   POPE, 51
just it raineth on the j.   BOWEN, C, 1
    j. and merciful as Nero   ELIZABETH I, 2
    rain on the j. and on the unjust   BIBLE, 365
justice A lawyer has no business with . . . j. or injustice   JOHNSON, S, 157
    In a free society the state . . . administers j. among men   LIPPMAN, 1
    J. is open to all   MATHEW, 1
    J. is such a fine thing   LESAGE, 1
    J. is the means by which established injustices are sanctioned   FRANCE, 2
    J. is the . . . perpetual wish   JUSTINIAN I, 1
    j. must be seen to be more or less done   STOPPARD, 2
    J. should . . . be seen to be done   HEWART, 1
    J. should not only be done   HEWART, 1
    Let j. be done   FERDINAND I, 1
    moderation in the pursuit of j. is no virtue   GOLDWATER, 2
    Recompense injury with j.   CONFUCIUS, 12
    Revenge is a kind of wild j.   BACON, FRANCIS, 43
    She's like the old line about j.   OSBORNE, 7
    the female character . . . has no sense of j.   SCHOPENHAUER, 4
    The j. of my quarrel   MARLOWE, 1
    The love of j. in most men   ROCHEFOUCAULD, 10
    The place of j. is a hallowed place   BACON, FRANCIS, 31
    You never expected j. from a company   SMITH, SYDNEY, 5
justification carry its j. in every line   CONRAD, 5
justified No man is j. in doing evil   ROOSEVELT, T, 3
justify thought only to j. their injustices   VOLTAIRE, 11
justifying men are more interested in . . . j. themselves than in . . . behaving   SZASZ, 1

K

Kaiser signed photograph of the K.   WAUGH, E, 42
kaleidoscope a girl with k. eyes   LENNON, 7
Karl had Marx been Groucho instead of K.   BERLIN, 3
Katy K-K-K., beautiful K.   O'HARA, 1
Keats K.'s vulgarity   LEAVIS, 1
    Mister John K. five feet high   KEATS, 61

Shelley and K. were	HALDANE, 2
keen out of a k. city in the sky	CUMMINGS, 1
Satire should, like a polished razor k.	MONTAGU, 1
keep if they k. on saying it	BENNETT, ARNOLD, 8
k. me as the apple of an eye	PSALMS, 6
K. up appearances	CHURCHILL, C, 5
they should k. who can	WORDSWORTH, W, 46
keeper am I my brother's k.	BIBLE, 154
a poacher a k. turned inside out	KINGSLEY, 8
k. stands up	HOUSMAN, 12
Kelly Has anybody here seen K.	MURPHY, C, 1
ken When a new planet swims into his k.	KEATS, 42
Kennedy K. promised, Johnson delivered	JOHNSON, L, 3
K. the politician exuded that musk odour	KENNEDY, JOHN, 2
kind of nation . . . President K. died for	JOHNSON, L, 6
Kennedys I don't feel the attraction of the K. at all	
	MCCARTHY, M, 6
Kent K., sir – everybody knows K.	DICKENS, 42
Knocked 'em in the Old K. Road	CHEVALIER, A, 2
Kentucky For the old K. Home far away	FOSTER, 2
kept Married women are k. women	SMITH, L, 4
kettle Polly put the k. on	NURSERY RHYMES, 44
system that produced the k.	LODGE, 6
Kew I am His Highness' dog at K.	POPE, 62
key taken away the k. of knowledge	BIBLE, 327
turn the k. deftly	KEATS, 48
keys the k. of the kingdom of heaven	BIBLE, 397
khaki One black, and one white, and two k.	ANONYMOUS, 95
Khatmandu idol to the north of K.	HAYES, 1
kick every ass thinks he may k. at him	PARR, 1
if I were under water I would scarcely k.	KEATS, 60
k. you out, but . . . never let you down	WAUGH, E, 8
to k. against the pricks	BIBLE, 6
kicked he had known many k. down stairs	HALIFAX, 9
Saint Preux never k. the fireirons	CARLYLE, J, 2
would get his head k. off	KHRUSHCHEV, 1
kid a k. in his mother's milk	BIBLE, 118
Here's looking at you, k.	BOGART, H, 1
Listen k., take my advice	BERLIN, 4
kiddies k. have crumpled the serviettes	BETJEMAN, 6
kidnapped finally realize that I'm k.	ALLEN, W, 9
kids Cleaning your house while your k. are still growing	
	DILLER, 1
kill a man can't step up and k. a woman	BENCHLEY, 1
churchmen fain would k. their church	TENNYSON, 59
God . . . had the power to k. her	ADAMS, R, 2
good to k. an admiral	VOLTAIRE, 7
He would k. Himself	DUMAS, FILS, 1
it's a sin to k. a mockingbird	LEE, H, 2
K. a man, and you are a murderer	ROSTAND, J, 3
k. a wife with kindness	SHAKESPEARE, 319
K. not the goose	PROVERBS, 243
k. the patient	BACON, FRANCIS, 25
k. us for their sport	SHAKESPEARE, 185
more grievous than to k. in the sacred months	KORAN, 3
Next week . . . I'll k. myself	RHYS, 1
only k. you once	CARLYLE, T, 30
'revolution' is a word for which you k.	WEIL, 2
The bullet that is to k. me	NAPOLEON I, 11
they k. you a new way	ROGERS, W, 1
thou shalt not k.	BIBLE, 115
To k. a human being	JAMES, H, 8
When you have to k. a man	CHURCHILL, W, 15
killed He must have k. a lot of men	MOLIÈRE, 5
I don't mind your being k.	KITCHENER, 1
killing k. for their country	RUSSELL, B, 31
K. Is the ultimate	MACDIARMID, 1
k. time Is only	SITWELL, O, 1
More ways of k. a cat	KINGSLEY, 10
no difference between . . . k. and making decisions that . . . kill	
	MEIR, 1
The man is k. time	LOWELL, 1
To save a man's life against his will is . . . k. him	HORACE, 1
kills Time . . . k. all its pupils	BERLIOZ, 1
time quietly k. them	BOUCICAULT, 1
Who k. a man k. a reasonable creature	MILTON, 6
Yet each man k. the thing he loves	WILDE, 5
kin more than k., and less than kind	SHAKESPEARE, 65
kind a k. parent	PLINY THE ELDER, 1
being k. Is all the sad world needs	WILCOX, 4
charity suffereth long, and is k.	BIBLE, 38
He was a vicious man, but very k.	JOHNSON, S, 45

I love thee for a heart that's k.	DAVIES, W, 4
less than k.	SHAKESPEARE, 65
try to be k.	JACKSON, F, 1
kindle purpose of human existence is to k. a light	JUNG, 4
kindly person, who . . . marries or dies . . . k. spoken of	
	AUSTEN, 7
the deities so k.	RABELAIS, 5
kindness a cup o' k. yet	BURNS, R, 5
full o' th' milk of human k.	SHAKESPEARE, 205
greetings where no k. is	WORDSWORTH, W, 14
kill a wife with k.	SHAKESPEARE, 319
nothing of the milk of human k.	BIERCE, 1
recompense k. with k.	CONFUCIUS, 12
set a high value on spontaneous k.	JOHNSON, S, 139
the k. of strangers	WILLIAMS, T, 6
unremembered acts Of k. and of love	WORDSWORTH, W, 9
Woman Killed with K.	HEYWOOD, 2
you will find light and help and human k.	SCHWEITZER, 3
kindred Like k. drops, been mingled	COWPER, 28
king A constitutional k. must learn to stoop	LEOPOLD II, 1
a dainty dish, To set before the k.	NURSERY RHYMES, 52
a great k. above all gods	PSALMS, 54
A k. is a thing	SELDEN, 1
a k. may make a nobleman	BURKE, E, 24
A k. of shreds and patches	SHAKESPEARE, 98
All the k.'s horses	NURSERY RHYMES, 18
an atheist if the k. were	LA BRUYÈRE, 1
a new k. over Egypt	BIBLE, 102
Authority forgets a dying k.	TENNYSON, 21
A worse k. never left a realm undone	BYRON, 43
better . . . than an old and foolish k.	BIBLE, 71
but the k. of England cannot enter	PITT THE ELDER, 1
every inch a k.	SHAKESPEARE, 186
Every subject's duty is the K.'s	SHAKESPEARE, 133
fight for its K. and country	ANONYMOUS, 77
God save our Gracious K.	CAREY, H, 1
half the zeal I serv'd my K.	SHAKESPEARE, 140
heart and stomach of a K.	ELIZABETH I, 11
He played the K. as though	FIELD, 1
Here lies our sovereign lord the K.	ROCHESTER, 1
his attitude of a k. in exile	DE GAULLE, 1
horse was k.	LEE, L, 4
if I were not k.	LOUIS XIV, 6
I'm the k. of the castle	NURSERY RHYMES, 23
I think the K. is but a man	SHAKESPEARE, 132
k. reigns, but does not govern	ZAMOYSKI, 1
Old K. Cole	NURSERY RHYMES, 38
rather hew wood than be . . . K. of England	CHARLES X, 1
such divinity doth hedge a k.	SHAKESPEARE, 102
That whatsoever K. shall reign	ANONYMOUS, 48
the k. can do no wrong	BLACKSTONE, 4
The k. has been very good to me	BOLEYN, 1
The k. never dies	BLACKSTONE, 2
The K. of Spain's daughter	NURSERY RHYMES, 20
The K. over the Water	ANONYMOUS, 82
The k. reigns	THIERS, 1
The k. sits in Dunfermline town	ANONYMOUS, 83
The k. was in his counting-house	NURSERY RHYMES, 52
The present life of men on earth, O k.	BEDE, 1
wash the balm from an anointed k.	SHAKESPEARE, 296
who is the K. of glory	PSALMS, 14
would rather hew wood than be a k.	CHARLES X, 1
kingdom mistake the echo of a . . . coffee-house for the . . . k.	
	SWIFT, 5
my k. for a horse	SHAKESPEARE, 303
No k. has . . . had as many . . . wars as the k. of Christ	
	MONTESQUIEU, 5
repent: for the k. of heaven is at hand	BIBLE, 358
the k. of God is not in word, but in power	BIBLE, 26
the k. of God is within you	BIBLE, 334
to deny the existence of an unseen k.	BUTLER, S, 3
kings Conquering k. their titles take	CHANDLER, J, 1
Grammar, which can govern even k.	MOLIÈRE, 9
If you get the English people into the way of making k.	
	MELBOURNE, 5
K. are earth's gods	SHAKESPEARE, 289
K. . . . are just as funny	ROOSEVELT, T, 4
K. are naturally lovers of low company	BURKE, E, 17
K. govern by . . . assemblies only when	FOX, C, 4
Or walk with K.	KIPLING, 17
Pale Death kicks his way equally into . . . the castles of k.	
	HORACE, 27

L

later It is l. than you think — SERVICE, 2
Latin A gentleman need not know L. — MATTHEWS, 1
A silly remark can be made in L. — CERVANTES, 3
Don't quote L. — WELLINGTON, 25
small L., and less Greek — JONSON, 10
the Devil knows L. — KNOX, R, 2
The word is half Greek and half L. — SCOTT, C, 2
We were taught . . . L. and Greek — WELLS, 16
Latins L. are tenderly enthusiastic — DIETRICH, 1
laudanum Whipping and abuse are like l. — STOWE, 3
laugh Auden was someone you could l.-at-with — SPENDER, 4
I make myself l. at everything — BEAUMARCHAIS, 1
L. and grow fat — PROVERBS, 247
L., and the world laughs with you — WILCOX, 3
L. before breakfast — PROVERBS, 248
l. before one is happy — LA BRUYÈRE, 8
Make 'em l. — READE, 1
not to l. at human actions — SPINOZA, 5
old man who will not l. — SANTAYANA, 3
The Italians will l. at me — MUSSOLINI, 2
laughable schemes of political improvement are very l. — JOHNSON, S, 76
laughed Few women care to be l. at — AYCKBOURN, 1
No man who has once . . . l. — CARLYLE, T, 23
on which one has not l. — CHAMFORT, 2
When the first baby l. — BARRIE, 3
laughing death of Little Nell without l. — WILDE, 64
Happiness is no l. matter — WHATELY, 1
l. and jeering at everything . . . strange — PEPYS, 7
One cannot be always l. at a man — AUSTEN, 25
one may die without ever l. — LA BRUYÈRE, 8
the most fun I ever had without l. — ALLEN, W, 2
laughter L. is pleasant — PEACOCK, 9
L. is the best medicine — PROVERBS, 249
l. is weakness — ECO, 2
present l. — SHAKESPEARE, 338
you can draw l. from an audience — KAVANAGH, 1
Launcelot Sir L. saw her visage — MALORY, 1
launched l. into this vale of tears — BLACKMORE, 1
laundries Land of L. — BETJEMAN, 8
laundry Give me a l.-list — ROSSINI, 2
in any first-class l. — LEACOCK, 13
laurel burned is Apollo's l.-bough — MARLOWE, 6
Caesar's l. crown — BLAKE, W, 4
laurels once more, O ye l. — MILTON, 21
The l. all are cut — HOUSMAN, 3
law Born under one l. — GREVILLE, 1
Every l. is a contract — SELDEN, 2
heaven's first l. — POPE, 37
his delight is in the l. of the Lord — PSALMS, 1
Human l. . . . flows from Eternal l. — AQUINAS, 3
Ignorance of the l. — SELDEN, 1
I have forgotten more l. than you ever knew — MAYNARD, 1
l. holds . . . property is of greater value than life — FRY, E, 1
lesser breeds without the L. — KIPLING, 22
lest the moral l. become . . . separated — ADDAMS, 2
No brilliance is needed in the l. — MORTIMER, 2
Nor l., nor duty bade me fight — YEATS, 16
nothing is l. that is not reason — POWELL, J, 1
our duty . . . to break the l. — PANKHURST, E, 4
Prisons are built with stones of L. — BLAKE, W, 20
rich men rule the l. — GOLDSMITH, 24
The army ages men sooner than the l. — WELLS, 7
the greater part of the l. is — LESSING, D, 5
The l. does not concern itself — PROVERBS, 400
the l. is a ass — DICKENS, 38
The L. is the true embodiment — GILBERT, W, 18
The l. of dislike for the unlike — ZANGWILL, 3
The L. of England is a very strange one — DARLING, 5
the L. of the Yukon — SERVICE, 3
the magnificent fair play of the British criminal l. — DOYLE, 10
The majestic egalitarianism of the l. — FRANCE, 9
There is no universal l. — LAWRENCE, D, 33
There's one l. for the rich — PROVERBS, 420
th' windy side of the l. — SHAKESPEARE, 344
Lawrence For L., existence was — LAWRENCE, D, 2
laws I know not whether L. be right — WILDE, 9
L. are generally found to be nets — SHENSTONE, 1
L. are like cobwebs — SWIFT, 18
L. are like spider's webs — SOLON, 2
L. grind the poor — GOLDSMITH, 24
l. were like cobwebs — BACON, FRANCIS, 5

L. were made to be broken — NORTH, 2
Nature's l. lay hid in night — POPE, 19
not governed by the same l. — DISRAELI, 12
nothing to do with the l. but to obey them. — HORSLEY, 1
the l. of poetic truth and poetic beauty — ARNOLD, M, 15
the repeal of bad or obnoxious l. — GRANT, U, 6
until women . . . make l. — ANTHONY, 2
what we call the l. of Nature — HUXLEY, T, 6
Where l. end, tyranny begins — PITT THE ELDER, 4
you do not make the l. — GRIMKÉ, 1
lawyer A client is fain to hire a l. — BUTLER, S, 22
A l. has no business with — JOHNSON, S, 157
A l. never goes — PROVERBS, 28
A l.'s opinion — PROVERBS, 29
as a l. interprets truth — GIRAUDOUX, 2
He that is his own l. — PROVERBS, 192
lawyers L. are the only persons — BENTHAM, 2
woe unto you, l. — BIBLE, 327
laxative sweet l. of Georgian strains — CAMPBELL, R, 1
lay I never would l. down my arms — PITT THE ELDER, 6
L. your sleeping head — AUDEN, 20
lays l. it on with a trowel — CONGREVE, 3
Lazarus L. . . . laid at his gate, full of sores — BIBLE, 333
lazy be efficient if you're going to be l. — CONRAN, 2
There are no ugly women, only l. ones — RUBINSTEIN, 2
lead L., kindly Light — NEWMAN, J, 3
leader A l. who doesn't hesitate — MEIR, 1
I have to follow them, I am their l. — LEDRU-ROLLIN, 1
political l. for the Labour Party — BEVAN, 4
leadership men do not approach to l. — BEVERIDGE, 2
leadeth he l. me beside the still waters — PSALMS, 12
leaf his l. also shall not wither — PSALMS, 1
Leah L. was tender eyed — BIBLE, 173
leap a great l. in the dark — HOBBES, 8
A l. over the hedge — CERVANTES, 8
And twenty-nine in each l. year — NURSERY RHYMES, 61
I shall l. over the wall — PSALMS, 7
one giant l. for mankind — ARMSTRONG, N, 1
leapt Into the dangerous world I l. — BLAKE, W, 38
learn L., compare, collect the facts — PAVLOV, 1
the craft so long to l. — HIPPOCRATES, 1
took me a lifetime to l. to draw — PICASSO, 10
we could never l. to be brave — KELLER, 2
What we have to l. to do — ARISTOTLE, 1
learned He was naturally l. — DRYDEN, 23
I am . . . of the opinion with the l. — CONGREVE, 5
l. man who is not cleansed — KHOMEINI, 1
people . . . never have l. anything from history — HEGEL, 1
the l. roast an egg — POPE, 53
learning A little l. is a dangerous thing — POPE, 23
A progeny of l. — SHERIDAN, R, 4
beauty and the lust for l. — BEERBOHM, 15
I thought that I was l. how to live — LEONARDO DA VINCI, 6
l., earning and yearning — MORLEY, C, 1
L. hath gained most — FULLER, T, 6
L. is a treasure — PROVERBS, 250
L. is but an adjunct — SHAKESPEARE, 197
L. is good in and of itself — BUSH, 2
l. was painfully beaten into him — PEACOCK, 8
L. without thought is labour lost — CONFUCIUS, 5
Their l. is like bread in a besieged town — JOHNSON, S, 96
learnt l. only remember what I've l. — WHITE, P, 2
More can be l. from Miss Austen — AUSTEN, 1
Soon l. — PROVERBS, 365
what has been l. has been forgotten — SKINNER, B, 2
least death . . . the l. of all evils — BACON, FRANCIS, 6
L. said soonest mended — PROVERBS, 251
the l. of these my brethren — BIBLE, 422
the noisy world Hears l. — WORDSWORTH, W, 3
leather Mr Lincoln's soul seems made of l. — LINCOLN, 4
leave Fare thee well, for I must l. thee — ANONYMOUS, 87
How I l. my country — PITT THE YOUNGER, 4
If you l. a thing alone — CHESTERTON, 33
L. well alone — PROVERBS, 252
to l. his country as good as he had found it — COBBETT, 2
leaves before the l. have fallen — WILHELM II, 1
If poetry comes not . . . as l. to a tree — KEATS, 57
No fruits, no flowers, no l., no birds — HOOD, 10
the l. . . . were for the healing of the nations — BIBLE, 474
Though l. are many, the root is one — YEATS, 7
With vine l. in his hair — IBSEN, 5
Words are like l. — POPE, 30

Now l. in the Abbey	BYRON, 39	like runners hand on the torch of l.	LUCRETIUS, 3
Only l. and evil come from letting people off	MURDOCH, 5	longest half of your l.	SOUTHEY, 3
Optimistic l.	SHAW, 33	lot of trouble in his l.	CHURCHILL, W, 30
polite by telling l.	BRADBURY, 6	love . . . has one arch-enemy – and that is l.	ANOUILH, 1
The cruellest l. are . . . told in silence	STEVENSON, R, 15	meaninglessness of l. forces man to	KUBRICK, 2
which way the head l.	RALEIGH, W, 6	meddling with any practical part of l.	ADDISON, 10
life against the fabric of l.	CARSON, 2	money has something to do with l.	LARKIN, 1
a keen observer of l.	AUDEN, 21	my experience of l. has been drawn	BEERBOHM, 16
A l. that moves to gracious ends	TENNYSON, 77	My way of l. Is fall'n into the sear	SHAKESPEARE, 223
Anythin' for a quiet l.	DICKENS, 54	My wife . . . is troubled with her lonely l.	PEPYS, 8
a pure river of water of l.	BIBLE, 474	Nietzsche . . . was a confirmed L. Force worshipper	NIETZSCHE, 1
As our l. is very short	TAYLOR, JEREMY, 1	no man loses any other l. than	MARCUS AURELIUS, 3
A well-written L.	CARLYLE, T, 7	Nothing in his l. Became him like the leaving	SHAKESPEARE, 204
Bankrupt of L.	DRYDEN, 6	only honour and l. have been spared	FRANCIS I, 1
believe in the l. to come	BECKETT, 1	our l. is what our thoughts make it	MARCUS AURELIUS, 5
Books are . . . bloodless substitute for l.	STEVENSON, R, 18	passion and the l. . . . within	COLERIDGE, S, 11
brief is l. but love is long	TENNYSON, 64	property is of greater value than l.	FRY, E, 1
death after l. does greatly please	SPENSER, 1	secret of reaping the greatest fruitfulness . . . from l.	
doctrine of the strenuous l.	ROOSEVELT, T, 6		NIETZSCHE, 6
dreary intercourse of daily l.	WORDSWORTH, W, 14	self-willed determination to l.	HESSE, 3
For l. is but a dream	THOMSON, JAMES, 1	she is mine for l.	SPARK, 6
greatest secret . . . except l.	RUTHERFORD, 1	show l. neither as it is nor	CHEKHOV, 8
hiring their servants for l.	CARLYLE, T, 34	so long as you have your l.	JAMES, H, 4
Human l. is everywhere a state in which	JOHNSON, S, 28	strange disease of modern l.	ARNOLD, M, 37
hymns of praise to the glory of l.	SITWELL, E, 1	Superstition is the poetry of l.	GOETHE, 6
I am the bread of l.	BIBLE, 250	take my l.	FARQUHAR, 2
I am the resurrection, and the l.	BIBLE, 256	Than to ever let a woman in my l.	LERNER, 3
I am the way, the truth, and the l.	BIBLE, 259	that a man lay down his l. for his friends	BIBLE, 260
I detest l.-insurance agents	LEACOCK, 3	The Book of L. begins	WILDE, 60
I have but one l. to lose for my country	HALE, N, 1	the child should be allowed to meet the real experiences of l.	
I have measured out my l.	ELIOT, T, 13		KEY, E, 2
Illness is the night-side of l.	SONTAG, 1	the crown of l.	BIBLE, 216
I might give my l. for my friend	SMITH, L, 5	The essential thing in l.	COUBERTIN, 1
in his pleasure is l.	PSALMS, 17	The first rule in opera is the first rule in l.	MELBA, 1
In real l . . . . it is the hare who wins	BROOKNER, 2	The Leaves of L. keep falling	FITZGERALD, E, 4
In the midst of l. we are in death	BOOK OF COMMON PRAYER, 3	The L. and Soul, the man who	WHITEHORN, 3
Is l. a boon	GILBERT, W, 42	the l. of man . . . brutish, and short	HOBBES, 4
Is not l . . . . too short . . . to bore ourselves	NIETZSCHE, 13	the l.-sentence which fate carries	LAWRENCE, T, 6
isn't l. a terrible thing	THOMAS, D, 24	The l. so short, the craft so long to learn	HIPPOCRATES, 1
Is there another l.	KEATS, 71	the l. to come shall be better for thee	KORAN, 9
It's as large as l.	CARROLL, 34	The love of l. is necessary to	JOHNSON, S, 29
Its private l. is a disgrace	ANONYMOUS, 84	the painted veil which those who live Call l.	SHELLEY, 12
I've had a happy l.	HAZLITT, 32	The present l. of men on earth, O king	BEDE, 1
I've looked at l. from both sides now	MITCHELL, JONI, 1	The prime goal . . . not to prolong l.	BARNARD, C, 1
I warmed both hands before the fire of l.	LANDOR, 7	The purpose of human l. is to serve	SCHWEITZER, 1
lay down his friends for his l.	THORPE, J, 1	There are only three events in a man's l.	LA BRUYÈRE, 6
L. . . . a bad dream between two awakenings	O'NEILL, 2	therefore choose l.	BIBLE, 57
L. begins at forty	TUCKER, 2	the stuff l. is made of	FRANKLIN, 9
l. . . . effort to prevent . . . thinking	HUXLEY, A, 24	the tree of l.	BIBLE, 144
L. exists in the universe	JEANS, 1	The vanity of human l. is like a river	POPE, 58
L. flies	FITZGERALD, E, 10	the veil which those who live call l.	SHELLEY, 22
L. . . . happens . . . while you're busy	LENNON, 1	The Wine of L. keeps oozing	FITZGERALD, E, 4
L. is a gamble	STOPPARD, 16	they get about ten percent out of l.	DUNCAN, 2
L. is a great surprise	NABOKOV, 2	this l. Is nobler	SHAKESPEARE, 60
L. is a jest	GAY, 10	this long disease, my l.	POPE, 13
L. is a maze in which we take the wrong turning	CONNOLLY, 15	Three passions . . . have governed my l.	RUSSELL, B, 4
L. is an incurable disease	COWLEY, 2	To save a man's l. against his will	HORACE, 12
L. . . . is a predicament	SANTAYANA, 8	total of such moments is my l.	CONNOLLY, 12
L. is as tedious as a twice-told tale	SHAKESPEARE, 164	We'd jump the l. to come	SHAKESPEARE, 208
L. is a tragedy . . . in close-up	CHAPLIN, 9	We have discovered the secret of l.	CRICK, 1
L. is just a bowl	PROVERBS, 258	We see into the l. of things	WORDSWORTH, W, 11
L. is just one damned thing after another	HUBBARD, 3	what a queer thing L. is	WODEHOUSE, 14
L. is made up of sobs	HENRY, O, 1	when religion is allowed to invade . . . private l.	MELBOURNE, 11
L. is mostly froth and bubble	GORDON, 1	'While there is l., there's hope,'	GAY, 7
L. is not all beer	PROVERBS, 259	who . . . would go into the temple to save his l.	BIBLE, 435
L. is not a spectacle or a feast	SANTAYANA, 8	Who saw l. steadily	ARNOLD, M, 42
L. isn't all beer and skittles	HUGHES, THOMAS, 1	Wilde performed his l. . . . even after fate	WILDE, 1
L. is one long process	BUTLER, S, 9	worth a l.'s experience	HOLMES, O, 7
L. is something to do when	LEBOWITZ, 3	**life-blood** A good book is the precious l.	MILTON, 7
L. is sweet	PROVERBS, 260	**lifeboat** This is a movie, not a l.	TRACY, 3
L. is the art of drawing sufficient conclusions	BUTLER, S, 10	**life-lie** Take the l. away from the average man	IBSEN, 9
l. is the thing	SMITH, L, 3	**life-like** Dickens' world is not l.	DICKENS, 2
L. is too short to do anything for oneself	MAUGHAM, 19	**life-sized** Great men are but l.	BEERBOHM, 7
L. is too short to learn German	PORSON, 1	**lifetime** I ask it for the knowledge of a l.	WHISTLER, 7
l., liberty, and the pursuit of happiness	JEFFERSON, 6	it took me a l. to learn to draw like them	PICASSO, 10
L.'s but a walking shadow	SHAKESPEARE, 225	**lift** I will l. up mine eyes unto the hills	PSALMS, 67
l. . . . seems to me preparation for something	YEATS, 5	l. up your heads, O ye gates	PSALMS, 14
L.'s Little Ironies	HARDY, 8	**light** a l. to lighten the Gentiles	BIBLE, 317
L.'s short span forbids us	HORACE, 28	armour of l.	BOOK OF COMMON PRAYER, 4
L.'s too short for chess	BYRON, H, 1	as one got a l. for a cigarette	JAMES, H, 5
L. without industry is guilt	RUSKIN, 4	By the l. of the moon	BYRON, 42
L. would be tolerable	LEWIS, G, 1	Culture is the passion for sweetness and l.	ARNOLD, M, 23

Come l. with me — DONNE, 4
Come l. with me, and be my love — MARLOWE, 13
Do you want to l. for ever — DALY, 1
eat to l., not l. to eat — MOLIÈRE, 2
he forgets to l. — LA BRUYÈRE, 6
Houses are built to l. in — BACON, FRANCIS, 15
I eat to l. — GANDHI, 6
If God were suddenly condemned to l. the life — DUMAS, FILS, 1
If you l. long enough — STONE, I, 1
I have learned to l. each day as it comes — DIX, DOROTHY, 2
in him we l., and move — BIBLE, 13
in Rome, l. as the Romans — AMBROSE, 1
I thought that I was learning how to l. — LEONARDO DA VINCI, 6
I want to love first, and l. incidentally — FITZGERALD, Z, 1
Like a rose, she has lived as long as roses l. — MALHERBE, 1
L. all you can; it's a mistake not to — JAMES, H, 4
L. among men as if God beheld you — SENECA, 1
L. and learn — PROVERBS, 264
l. beyond its income — BUTLER, S, 11
l. dangerously — NIETZSCHE, 6
l. for ever or die in the attempt — HELLER, 2
L. that thou mayest desire to l. again — NIETZSCHE, 9
L. this day, as . . . thy last — KEN, 2
l. to fight another day — ANONYMOUS, 38
L. with the gods — MARCUS AURELIUS, 10
Man . . . hath but a short time to l. — BOOK OF COMMON PRAYER, 10
One can't l. on love alone — TOLSTOY, S, 1
People do not l. nowadays — DUNCAN, 2
people l. beyond their incomes — SAKI, 9
Rascals, would you l. for ever — FREDERICK THE GREAT, 1
Teach me to l. — KEN, 1
than to l. up to them — ADLER, 16
there shall no man see me, and l. — BIBLE, 121
They l. ill — SYRUS, 1
those who l. . . . believe . . . to be the truth — HAMPTON, 2
Those who l. by . . . a lie, and — HAMPTON, 2
To achieve great things we must l. as though — VAUVENARGUES, 2
To l. with thee, and be thy love — RALEIGH, W, 1
we l. but to make sport — AUSTEN, 26
We l. in stirring times — ISHERWOOD, 2
You might as well l. — PARKER, D, 3
lived Never to have l. is best — YEATS, 22
no man . . . hath l. better than I — MALORY, 1
She . . . has never l. — GAY, 5
slimy things L. on — COLERIDGE, S, 32
livelihood slave for l. — ADAMS, F, 2
lives He that l. long — PROVERBS, 195
He who l. by the sword — PROVERBS, 200
he who l. more l. than one — WILDE, 8
l. of quiet desperation — THOREAU, 6
men devote the greater part of their l. — LA BRUYÈRE, 2
no man loses any other life than . . . he now l. — MARCUS AURELIUS, 3
liveth their name l. for evermore — BIBLE, 93
living A house is a machine for l. in — LE CORBUSIER, 1
A l. is made . . . by selling something that — WILDER, T, 1
Civilization is a method of l. — ADDAMS, 2
History is . . . the wrong way of l. — DURRELL, L, 3
How good is man's life, the mere l. — BROWNING, R, 50
I make war on the l. — CHARLES V, 2
It does not then concern either the l. or the dead — EPICURUS, 2
let the earth bring forth the l. creature — BIBLE, 141
let them be wiped out of the book of the l. — PSALMS, 39
life had prepared Podduyev for l. — SOLZHENITSYN, 6
l. need charity — ARNOLD, G, 1
no one has yet found a way to drink for a l. — KERR, 3
search the land of l. men — SCOTT, WALTER, 13
Television . . . permits you to be entertained in your l. room — FROST, D, 1
The noble l. and the noble dead — WORDSWORTH, W, 43
Vietnam was lost in the l. rooms of America — MCLUHAN, 4
We owe respect to the l. — VOLTAIRE, 24
Livingstone Dr L., I presume — STANLEY, 1
loaf half a l. is better than a whole l. — CHESTERTON, 39
loafed It is better to have l. and lost — THURBER, 4
loan Time, like a l. from the bank — BRAINE, 2
loathe I l. the country — CONGREVE, 15
loaves five barley l., and two small fishes — BIBLE, 249
lobby not a man would go into the L. against us — BALDWIN, S, 8
local settle up these little l. difficulties — MACMILLAN, 6
Lochinvar young L. — SCOTT, WALTER, 14
locked l. up a man who wanted to rule — COHEN, 2

locusts l. and wild honey — BIBLE, 353
lodge a l. in some vast wilderness — COWPER, 27
log-cabin L. to White House — THAYER, 1
logic L. must take care of itself — WITTGENSTEIN, 5
That's l. — CARROLL, 26
the l. of our times — DAY LEWIS, 2
The principles of l. and metaphysics are true — AYER, 2
You can only find truth with l. — CHESTERTON, 27
logical L. consequences are the scarecrows of fools — HUXLEY, T, 9
logik un-to l. hadde longe y-go — CHAUCER, 7
loitered I l. my life away — HAZLITT, 9
loitering Alone and palely l. — KEATS, 22
Lolita L., light of my life — NABOKOV, 1
Lomon' On the bonnie . . . banks o' Loch L. — ANONYMOUS, 67
London agricultural labourers . . . commute from L. — POWELL, A, 4
dominate a L. dinner-table — WILDE, 68
Dublin . . . much worse than L. — JOHNSON, S, 153
hear more good things on . . . a stagecoach from L. to Oxford — HAZLITT, 10
Hell is a city much like L. — SHELLEY, 21
I've been to L. to look at the queen — NURSERY RHYMES, 45
L. . . . Clearing-house of the World — CHAMBERLAIN, J, 1
L., that great cesspool — DOYLE, 16
L., that great sea — SHELLEY, 10
Nobody is healthy in L. — AUSTEN, 5
the best club in L. — DICKENS, 40
the lowest and vilest alleys of L. — DOYLE, 4
When a man is tired of L. — JOHNSON, S, 117
you have dined in every house in L. – *once* — WILDE, 78
Londoner spirit of the L. stands resolute — GEORGE VI, 2
loneliness L. . . . is the most terrible poverty — TERESA, MOTHER, 2
l. may spur you into finding something — HAMMARSKJÖLD, 1
lonely All the l. people — LENNON, 3
l. of heart is withered away — YEATS, 19
My Dear One is mine as mirrors are l. — AUDEN, 24
She left l. for ever — ARNOLD, M, 17
the l. sea and the sky — MASEFIELD, 5
lonesome A l. man . . . who does not know — FRANKLIN, 13
one, that on a l. road — COLERIDGE, S, 36
long a l., l. way to Tipperary — WILLIAMS, H, 1
It is a l. lane — PROVERBS, 225
Like German opera, too l. and too loud — WAUGH, E, 52
L. is the way And hard — MILTON, 40
make no l. tarrying, O my God — PSALMS, 24
Not that the story need be l. — THOREAU, 20
longer I have made this letter l. — PASCAL, 1
Was there ever yet anything written . . . wished l. by its readers — JOHNSON, S, 36
longest chapter of accidents is the l. — WILKES, 2
l. half of your life — SOUTHEY, 1
The weariest nights, the l. days — ORCZY, 2
longeth so l. my soul after thee, O God — PSALMS, 26
longing l. to enter into the courts of the Lord — PSALMS, 14
the l. for love — RUSSELL, B, 4
longitude A l. with no platitude — FRY, C, 4
longueurs Very good, but it has its *l.* — RIVAROL, 1
look a proud l. and a high stomach — PSALMS, 57
Cassius has a lean and hungry l. — SHAKESPEARE, 144
l. at him! He might be Stalin — DE GAULLE, 2
l. at those to whom He gives it — BARING, 1
L. before you leap — PROVERBS, 267
L., stranger, at this island now — AUDEN, 19
sit and l. at it for hours — JEROME, 1
To l. down to Camelot — TENNYSON, 14
looked better to be l. over than overlooked — WEST, M, 12
looker-on sit thou a patient l. — QUARLES, 2
looking Don't go on l. at me — ZOLA, 1
Here's l. at you, kid — BOGART, H, 1
somebody may be l. — MENCKEN, 2
looking glass The cracked l. of a servant — JOYCE, 11
looking-glasses Women have served . . . as l. — WOOLF, 9
looks A woman as old as she l. — COLLINS, MORTIMER, 1
l. commercing with the skies — MILTON, 12
man who l. you . . . in the eye — FADIMAN, 4
Well, he l. like a man — LINCOLN, 21
loose let l. upon the world with £300 — BARRIE, 1
Lord a L. among wits — JOHNSON, S, 50
And I replied, 'My L..' — HERBERT, G, 2
Let us with a gladsome mind Praise the L. — MILTON, 55
L. High Everything Else — GILBERT, W, 22
l. of all things, yet a prey to all — POPE, 33
L. shall preserve thy going out — PSALMS, 68

Mine eyes have seen the glory of the coming of the L.   HOWE, 1
Praise be to God, the L. of all creatures   KORAN, 1
Praise the L. and pass the ammunition   FORGY, 1
the L. is a man of war   BIBLE, 113
the L. is my shepherd   PSALMS, 11
the voice of the L. breaketh the cedar-trees   PSALMS, 16
Works of the L.   BOOK OF COMMON PRAYER, 1
Lords   addressing a naked House of L.   CARLYLE, T, 25
Great l. have their pleasures   MONTESQUIEU, 6
the cure for admiring the House of L.   BAGEHOT, 2
lordships   good enough for their l. on a hot summer afternoon
   ANONYMOUS, 101
lorn   a lone l. creetur   DICKENS, 11
lose   A man who does not l. his reason   LESSING, G, 1
In every friend we l. a part of ourselves   POPE, 61
I shall l. no time in reading it   DISRAELI, 19
l. the substance   AESOP, 1
nothing to l. but their chains   MARX, K, 2
tails you l.   CROKER, 1
We Don't Want To L. You   RUBENS, 1
What you l. on the swings   PROVERBS, 458
losers   In war . . . all are l.   CHAMBERLAIN, N, 4
loses   no man l. any other life than   MARCUS AURELIUS, 3
The conventional army l. if it does not win   KISSINGER, 1
loss   richest gain I count but l.   WATTS, 8
To suffer the l. they were afraid of   AUDEN, 25
lost   All is l. save honour   FRANCIS I, 1
All is not l.   MILTON, 32
better to have fought and l.   CLOUGH, 7
better to have loved and l.   TENNYSON, 28
girl is l.   ECO, 1
he was l., and is found   BIBLE, 332
Home of l. causes   ARNOLD, M, 13
I can't say I was ever l.   BOONE, 1
I have discovered the art . . . l. for two thousand years
   DUNCAN, 1
I look upon every day to be l.   JOHNSON, S, 154
It is better to have loafed and l.   THURBER, 4
I've l. one of my children this week   TURNER, 2
l. and gone for ever   MONTROSE, 1
never to have l. at all   BUTLER, S, 27
What though the field be l.   MILTON, 32
woman that deliberates is l.   ADDISON, 6
You are a l. generation   STEIN, 6
lot   and the l. fell upon Jonah   BIBLE, 285
policeman's l. is not a happy one   GILBERT, W, 40
remember L.'s wife   BIBLE, 335
lots   they parted his raiment, and cast l.   BIBLE, 339
loud   A l. noise at one end   KNOX, R, 3
Like German opera, too long and too l.   WAUGH, E, 52
Louis   Son of Saint L.   FIRMONT, 1
louse   precedency between a l. and a flea   JOHNSON, S, 144
lousy   only one fault. It was kind of l.   THURBER, 20
lov'd   I never writ, nor no man ever l.   SHAKESPEARE, 369
Of one that l. not wisely, but too well   SHAKESPEARE, 288
love   Absence is to l.   BUSSY-RABUTIN, 1
a comfort in the strength of l.   WORDSWORTH, W, 21
a girl likes to be crossed in l. a little   AUSTEN, 24
Alcohol is like l.   CHANDLER, R, 3
alike are the groans of l. to . . . dying   LOWRY, 2
All mankind l. a lover   EMERSON, 10
all's fair in l. and war   FORREST, 2
all the world and l. were young   RALEIGH, W, 1
And l. to all men   KIPLING, 5
An ounce of l.   WESLEY, J, 2
ashamed of having been in l.   ROCHEFOUCAULD, 8
As honour, l., obedience   SHAKESPEARE, 223
Because women can do nothing except l.   MAUGHAM, 10
brief is life but l. is long   TENNYSON, 64
But L. has pitched his mansion   YEATS, 8
Christianity has done a great deal for l.   FRANCE, 6
Come live with me, and be my l.   MARLOWE, 13
corner in the thing I l.   SHAKESPEARE, 284
courage to l. . . . courage to suffer   TROLLOPE, 5
Dear Roger Fry whom I l. as a man   MARSH, 1
Deep as first l.   TENNYSON, 63
Do not l. your neighbour as yourself   SHAW, 27
don't believe in . . . true l. until   ESCHENBACH, 2
Drinking . . . and making l.   BEAUMARCHAIS, 2
England! . . . What l. I bore to thee   WORDSWORTH, W, 6
Every little girl knows about l.   SAGAN, 1
folly . . . l. did make thee run into   SHAKESPEARE, 44

For where there is l. of man, there is also l. of the art
   HIPPOCRATES, 3
God is l.   BIBLE, 282
greater l. hath no man   BIBLE, 260
He fell in l. with himself   POWELL, A, 1
help . . . of the woman I l.   EDWARD VIII, 1
he told men to l. their neighbour   BRECHT, 4
how did you l. my picture   GOLDWYN, 23
how fair . . . art thou, O l., for delights   BIBLE, 498
husbands, l. your wives   BIBLE, 21
I do not l. thee   NORTON, 1
I do not l. thee, Doctor Fell   BROWN, T, 1
if men and women marry those whom they do not l.
   MARTINEAU, 5
If music be the food of l.   SHAKESPEARE, 334
I hate and l.   CATULLUS, 2
I l. or I hate   PICASSO, 2
I'm tired of L.   BELLOC, 11
In l. . . . the amateur status   GRAVES, R, 3
In Switzerland they had brotherly l.   WELLES, 1
I rather suspect her of being in l.   CHURCHILL, J, 1
I shall but l. thee better after death   BROWNING, E, 4
Is thy l. a plant Of such weak fibre   WORDSWORTH, W, 22
I think my l. as rare   SHAKESPEARE, 372
it jumps from admiration to l.   AUSTEN, 20
I understand only because I l.   TOLSTOY, L, 10
I want to l. first, and live incidentally   FITZGERALD, Z, 1
labour of l.   BIBLE, 502
law of nature which l. alone can alter   LACLOS, 1
let brotherly l. continue   BIBLE, 187
Let's Fall in L.   PORTER, C, 9
let us prove . . . the sports of l.   JONSON, 16
let us too give in to L.   VIRGIL, 18
lightly turns to thoughts of l.   TENNYSON, 50
live with me, and be my l.   DONNE, 4
longing for l.   RUSSELL, B, 4
l. – all the wretched cant of it   GREER, 3
L. and all his pleasures   CAMPION, 5
l. and marriage   CAHN, 1
l. and murder will out   CONGREVE, 4
l. . . . intercourse between tyrants and slaves   GOLDSMITH, 14
l. a place the less for having suffered   AUSTEN, 17
L. bade me welcome   HERBERT, G, 6
L. built on beauty   DONNE, 9
L. ceases to be a pleasure   BEHN, 1
L. conquers all   PROVERBS, 269
L. conquers all things   VIRGIL, 18
l. dwells in gorgeous palaces   BOCCACCIO, 3
L. fled   YEATS, 34
l. flies out of the window   PROVERBS, 460
l. God, and hateth his brother   BIBLE, 284
l. . . . has one arch-enemy   ANOUILH, 1
L.? I make it constantly but   PROUST, 7
L. in a golden bowl   BLAKE, W, 11
L. in a hut   KEATS, 24
L. is a boy   BUTLER, S, 4
L. is a sickness   DANIEL, 1
L. is blind   ANONYMOUS, 54
l. is blind and lovers cannot see   SHAKESPEARE, 242
L. is like the measles   JEROME, 1
L. is moral even without . . . marriage   KEY, E, 5
L. is my religion   KEATS, 67
L. is not l. Which alters   SHAKESPEARE, 368
L. is the wisdom of the fool   JOHNSON, S, 42
L. laughs at locksmiths   PROVERBS, 271
l. . . . looks more like hatred   ROCHEFOUCAULD, 9
L. looks not with the eyes   SHAKESPEARE, 258
L. makes the world   PROVERBS, 272
L. means never having to say   SEGAL, 2
L. means the pre-cognitive flow   LAWRENCE, D, 45
L. me, l. my dog   PROVERBS, 273
L. of honour   SIDNEY, P, 3
L. of justice in most men   ROCHEFOUCAULD, 10
l. of liberty is the l. of others   HAZLITT, 30
l. of money is the root of all evil   BIBLE, 511
l. robs those who have it of their wit   DIDEROT, 2
L. seeketh not itself to please   BLAKE, W, 36
L. seeketh only Self to please   BLAKE, W, 37
L.'s like the measles   JERROLD, 5
L. sought is good   SHAKESPEARE, 342
L.'s pleasure lasts but a moment   FLORIAN, 1
l. that loves a scarlet coat   HOOD, 4

L. . . . the gift of oneself — ANOUILH, 2
L., the human form divine — BLAKE, W, 44
l. the Lord thy God with all thy heart — BIBLE, 411
l. thy neighbour as thyself — BIBLE, 411
l. . . . was not as l. is nowadays — MALORY, 2
l. we swore . . . seems deceit — DAY LEWIS, 1
L. will find a way — PROVERBS, 274
l. your enemies — BIBLE, 365
L. your neighbour — PROVERBS, 275
make us l. your goodly gifts — SHAKESPEARE, 291
Making l. is the sovereign remedy for anguish — LEBOYER, 2
Many a man has fallen in l. with a girl — CHEVALIER, M, 1
Men l. in haste — BYRON, 33
My l. and I would lie — HOUSMAN, 10
My L. in her attire doth show her wit — ANONYMOUS, 58
My l. is like a red red rose — BURNS, R, 16
My l. she's but a lassie yet — HOGG, 2
My true l. sent to me — NURSERY RHYMES, 54
No l. like the first l. — PROVERBS, 310
no man dies for l., but on the stage — DRYDEN, 29
Nuptial l. maketh mankind — BACON, FRANCIS, 32
office and affairs of l. — SHAKESPEARE, 267
O Lord, to what a state . . . those who l. Thee — TERESA OF ÁVILA, 1
One can l. . . . vulgarity — HUXLEY, A, 38
One can't live on l. alone — TOLSTOY, L, 2
One must keep l. affairs quiet — WINDSOR, 1
only l. sprung from my only hate — SHAKESPEARE, 307
O tell me the truth about l. — AUDEN, 26
Our l. of what is beautiful does not — PERICLES, 1
perfect l. casteth out fear — BIBLE, 283
poet without l. — CARLYLE, T, 3
real truth about his or her l. affairs — WEST, R, 8
Religion is l. — WEBB, B, 1
Saying 'Farewell, blighted l.' — ANONYMOUS, 71
She makes l. just like a woman — DYLAN, 3
She never told her l. — SHAKESPEARE, 340
Society, friendship, and l. — COWPER, 33
Such ever was l.'s way — BROWNING, R, 19
temperate in l. and wine — MILTON, 2
The boy I l. is up in the gallery — WARE, 1
the fool of l. — HAZLITT, 26
The King of l. my Shepherd is — BAKER, 1
The l. of life is necessary to — JOHNSON, S, 25
the L. that dare not speak its name — DOUGLAS, ALFRED, 1
There can be no peace of mind in l. — PROUST, 5
these Christians l. one another — TERTULLIAN, 2
Those have most power to hurt us that we l. — BEAUMONT, 6
Though loves be lost l. shall not — THOMAS, D, 3
Thy friends are exultations, agonies, And l. — WORDSWORTH, W, 62
time to l., and a time to hate — BIBLE, 67
'Tis said that some have died for l. — WORDSWORTH, W, 70
To be wise and l. — SHAKESPEARE, 330
To business that we l. we rise betime — SHAKESPEARE, 2
To live with thee, and be thy l. — RALEIGH, W, 1
to l. and to cherish — BOOK OF COMMON PRAYER, 27
To l. oneself is the beginning of a lifelong romance — WILDE, 4
True L.'s the gift which God has given — SCOTT, WALTER, 7
Try thinking of l. — FRY, C, 5
vanity and l. . . . universal characteristics — CHESTERFIELD, 16
violence masquerading as l. — LAING, 4
War is like l. — BRECHT, 9
what a mischievous devil L. is — BUTLER, S, 14
What are your views on l. — PROUST, 7
What is commonly called l. — FIELDING, 11
What is l.? 'Tis not hereafter — SHAKESPEARE, 338
When a man is in l. he endures more — NIETZSCHE, 2
when l. is grown To ripeness — TENNYSON, 78
when one . . . it is very different to l. God — SAND, 2
where the course of true l. may be expected to run smooth — MARTINEAU, 1
whom to look at was to l. — TENNYSON, 51
Wilt thou l. her, comfort her — BOOK OF COMMON PRAYER, 26
with a l. like that you know you should be glad — LENNON, 10
with l. from me to you — LENNON, 4
Without l. you will be merely skilful — LEBOYER, 3
worms have eaten them, but not for l. — SHAKESPEARE, 55
written for the l. of Man — THOMAS, D, 5
yet I l. her till I die — ANONYMOUS, 86
your l. but not your thoughts — GIBRAN, 1
loved And the l. one all together — BROWNING, R, 36
better to be left than never to have been l. — CONGREVE, 13

better to have l. and lost — BUTLER, S, 27
God alone deserves to be l. — SAND, 2
I have l. him too much — RACINE, 1
It seems to me that he has never l. — DOSTOEVSKY, A, 2
l., to have thought, to have done — ARNOLD, M, 12
never to have l. at all — TENNYSON, 28
She who has never l. has never lived — GAY, 5
'Tis better to have l. and lost — TENNYSON, 28
Who ever l., that l. not at first sight — MARLOWE, 8
lovelier A l. flower . . . was never sown — WORDSWORTH, W, 69
lovelies Fifty l. in the rude — THOMAS, D, 15
loveliest L. of trees, the cherry — HOUSMAN, 7
loveliness A woman of so shining l. — YEATS, 29
lovely It was such a l. day — MAUGHAM, 16
l. and pleasant in their lives — BIBLE, 482
Some hour . . . will prove l. — HORACE, 18
lover All mankind love a l. — EMERSON, 10
a l. with any other career in view — WELLS, 5
A l. without indiscretion is no l. — HARDY, 7
an ex-wife searching for a new l. — CONNOLLY, 17
easier to be a l. than a husband — BALZAC, 6
lunatic, the l., and the poet — SHAKESPEARE, 263
satisfied with her l.'s mind — TROLLOPE, 14
loverly Oh, wouldn't it be l. — LERNER, 2
lovers gallops . . . Through l.' brains — SHAKESPEARE, 305
Hello, Young L., Wherever You Are — HAMMERSTEIN, 1
l. cannot see The pretty follies — SHAKESPEARE, 242
l. fled away into the storm — KEATS, 14
make two l. happy — POPE, 3
one makes l. as fast as one pleases — CONGREVE, 14
pair of star-cross'd l. — SHAKESPEARE, 304
those of us meant to be l. — COHEN, 1
two young l. lately wed — TENNYSON, 43
loves Anyone who l. his country — GARIBALDI, 1
Every man l. what he is good at — SHADWELL, 3
He that l. not his wife and children — TAYLOR, JEREMY, 2
I have reigned with your l. — ELIZABETH I, 3
Though l. be lost love shall not — THOMAS, D, 3
Two l. I have, of comfort and despair — SHAKESPEARE, 373
Write love as one that l. his fellow-men — HUNT, L, 2
lovesome garden is a l. thing — BROWN, T E, 2
loveth God l. a cheerful giver — BIBLE, 45
He prayeth best who l. best — COLERIDGE, S, 39
loving A woman despises a man for l. her — STODDARD, 1
But if we stop l. animals — SOLZHENITSYN, 2
Friday's child is l. and giving — NURSERY RHYMES, 35
l. himself better than all — COLERIDGE, S, 3
most l. mere folly — SHAKESPEARE, 50
night was made for l. — BYRON, 42
loving-kindness thy l. and mercy shall follow me — PSALMS, 11
low Caesar! dost thou lie so l. — SHAKESPEARE, 149
He that is l. — BUNYAN, 10
Holland . . . lies so l. — HOOD, 13
I'll tak' the l. road — ANONYMOUS, 67
Kings are naturally lovers of l. company — BURKE, E, 17
my lamp burns l. and dim — ADAMS, F, 2
to put off my hat to . . . high or l. — FOX, G, 1
when your powder's runnin' l. — NEWBOLT, 2
Lowder Here lies the body of Mary Ann L. — ANONYMOUS, 32
lower if the l. orders don't set us a good example — WILDE, 19
No one ever describes himself as belonging to the l.-middle class — MIKES, 5
The l. one's vitality — BEERBOHM, 10
thou madest him l. than the angels — PSALMS, 3
lowly In l. pomp ride on to die — MILMAN, 1
Lowry Malcolm L. Late of the Bowery — LOWRY, 3
loyal as a l., a gallant . . . people — STERNE, 2
loyalty Hitler showed surprising l. to Mussolini — BULLOCK, 2
Party l. lowers the greatest of men — LA BRUYÈRE, 9
When l. no harm meant — ANONYMOUS, 48
Lucifer come not, L.! I'll burn my books — MARLOWE, 5
that same star, That fitful, fiery L. — YOUNG, A, 1
luck A self-made man . . . believes in l. — STEAD, 1
it brings you l. whether you believe . . . or not — BOHR, 1
luckiest People who need people are the l. — MERRILL, 1
lucky It is better to be born l. — PROVERBS, 226
I wasn't l. — THATCHER, M, 25
L. at cards — PROVERBS, 276
L. Jim — AMIS, 3
lumber put away in the l. room of his library — DOYLE, 12
luminous Dong with a l. Nose — LEAR, 3
lump a crowd . . . brings a l. to my wallet — WALLACH, 1

lunatic l., the lover, and the poet — SHAKESPEARE, 263
Those comfortably padded l. asylums — WOOLF, 4
luncheon to read a novel before l. was — WAUGH, E, 45
lungs don't keep using your l. — LEACOCK, 4
lured down which ideas are l. — COCKS, 1
lust l. in action — SHAKESPEARE, 370
Nonconformity and l. stalking — WAUGH, E, 11
lusteth the flesh l. against the Spirit — BIBLE, 134
Lutheran I have a . . . L. stomach — ERASMUS, 1
lux fiat l. — BIBLE, 138
luxuries Give me the l. of life — WRIGHT, F, 2
Give us the l. of life — MOTLEY, 1
luxury Blesses his stars, and thinks it l. — ADDISON, 5
Every l. . . . atheism, breast-feeding — ORTON, 4
The saddest thing . . . to get used to l. — CHAPLIN, 6
lyf That l. so short — CHAUCER, 19
lying One of you is l. — PARKER, D, 11
the air of someone who is l. . . . to a policeman — PHILIPPE, 1
lynching he could have attended a l. every day — SMITH, T, 1
Lyndon L. acts like there was never — JOHNSON, L, 2
lyre on this wall will hang my weapons and my l — HORACE, 38
lyric if you include me among the l. poets — HORACE, 26

M

Mab Queen M. hath been with you — SHAKESPEARE, 305
Macaroni And called it M. — BANGS, 1
Macaulay great apostle of the Philistines, Lord M. — ARNOLD, M, 21
Lord M. — SMITH, SYDNEY, 11
Macavity there's no one like M. — ELIOT, T, 16
Macbeth combination of Little Nell and Lady M. — PARKER, D, 2
M. doth murder sleep — SHAKESPEARE, 212
McCarthyism M. is Americanism — MCCARTHY, J R, 1
MacDonald Ramsay M. — MAXTON, 1
McGregor Don't go into Mr M.'s garden — POTTER, B, 2
machine a taxing m. — LOWE, 1
great intangible m. of commercial tyrrany — MORRIS, W, 1
One m. can do the work of fifty ordinary men — HUBBARD, 1
Our body is a m. for living — TOLSTOY, L, 11
tall modern office building is the m. — WRIGHT, F, 3
the Ghost in the M. — RYLE, 3
The m. is running away with *him* — WILHELM II, 5
The m. threatens — RILKE, 2
machine-gun a m. riddling her hostess — HUXLEY, A, 23
machines He ought to have stuck to his flying m.
— LEONARDO DA VINCI, 4
I see no reason to suppose that these m. will ever force
themselves into general use — WELLINGTON, 9
mackerel M. sky and mares' tails — PROVERBS, 277
Macmillan M. seemed . . . to embody the national decay
— MUGGERIDGE, 3
mad escaped from a m. and savage master — SOPHOCLES, 3
half of the nation is m. — SMOLLETT, 1
he ceased to be m. he became merely stupid — PROUST, 11
he first makes m. — EURIPIDES, 2
He first sends m. — DUPORT, 1
M. about the boy — COWARD, 11
M. as the mist and snow — YEATS, 20
M., bad, and dangerous to know — LAMB, CAROLINE, 1
m. north-north-west — SHAKESPEARE, 85
Men will always be m. — VOLTAIRE, 29
Never go to bed m. — DILLER, 2
O, let me not be m. — SHAKESPEARE, 171
The dog . . . Went m. and bit the man — GOLDSMITH, 10
We all are born m. — BECKETT, 5
who turns m. for a reason — CERVANTES, 11
madam M. I may not call you — ELIZABETH I, 4
madame All I could think of . . . was: *M. Bovary* — MCCARTHY, M, 5
Call me m. — PERKINS, 1
maddest those who think they can cure them are the m.
— VOLTAIRE, 29
made Annihilating all that's m. — MARVELL, 2
Don't you think I was m. for you — FITZGERALD, Z, 2
'Do you know who m. you?' — STOWE, 2
Little Lamb, who m. thee — BLAKE, W, 46
Nothing should be m. . . . which is not worth making — MORRIS, W, 2
we're all m. the same — COWARD, 1
Madeira We're from M. — SHAW, 42
madeleine taste was that of the little crumb of m. — PROUST, 2
mademoiselle A m. from Armenteers — ROWLAND, E, 1

Madison How were the receipts today in M. Square Garden
— BARNUM, 2
madman If a m. were to come into this room — JOHNSON, S, 105
The m. . . . has lost everything except his reason — CHESTERTON, 29
The m. thinks the rest of the world crazy — SYRUS, 2
Thou call'st me m. — BLAKE, W, 51
madness destroyed by m. — GINSBERG, 1
devil's m. – War — SERVICE, 4
Great Wits . . . to M. near alli'd — DRYDEN, 5
M. in great ones — SHAKESPEARE, 93
M. need not be all breakdown — LAING, 5
Now Ireland has her m. — AUDEN, 16
that way m. lies — SHAKESPEARE, 179
Maestro Music, M., Please — MAGIDSON, 1
maggot how to create a m. — MONTAIGNE, 6
magic men mistook m. for medicine — SZASZ, 3
That old black m. — MERCER, 2
magicians Do you . . . believe that the sciences would . . . have
. . . grown if the way had not been prepared by m.
— NIETZSCHE, 10
magistrate a chief m. of whom so much evil has been predicted
— JACKSON, A, 1
Obscenity . . . happens to shock some elderly . . . m.
— RUSSELL, B, 25
suppose . . . the m. corruptible — ROBESPIERRE, 1
Magna Charta M. is such a fellow — COKE, E, 2
magnanimity in victory, m. — CHURCHILL, W, 27
magnificent more than m. – . . . mediocre — GOLDWYN, 20
como m. myth — PLATO, 3
there you sit with that m. instrument between your legs
— TOSCANINI, 5
magnifique *c'est m., mais* — BOSQUET, 1
magnify my soul doth m. the Lord — BIBLE, 309
Magog Gog and M. — BIBLE, 471
Mahomet good a Christian as M. — ELIZABETH I, 2
If the hill will not come to M., M. will go to the hill
— BACON, FRANCIS, 14
maid await news of the M. — JOAN OF ARC, 1
Being an old m. is like death by drowning — FERBER, 1
The m. was in the garden — NURSERY RHYMES, 52
the simple m. Still plays about the flame — GAY, 3
Where are you going to, my pretty m. — NURSERY RHYMES, 72
maiden A simple m. in her flower — TENNYSON, 39
How could you use a poor m. so — ANONYMOUS, 16
I've a neater, sweeter m. — KIPLING, 24
many a rose-lipt m. — HOUSMAN, 16
That kissed the m. all forlorn — NURSERY RHYMES, 62
maids And pretty m. all in a row — NURSERY RHYMES, 34
Three little m. from school — GILBERT, W, 27
majesty A sight so touching in its m. — WORDSWORTH, W, 52
Her M. is not a subject — DISRAELI, 37
her M. . . . must not . . . look upon me as a source of income
— KEMBLE, C, 1
Her M.'s Opposition — BAGEHOT, 4
How can I . . . dislike a sex to which Your M. belongs — RHODES, 3
Ride on! ride on in m. — MILMAN, 1
This earth of m. — SHAKESPEARE, 295
Major-General very model of a modern M. — GILBERT, W, 37
majority A m. is always the best repartee — DISRAELI, 14
Fools are in a terrible . . . m. — IBSEN, 3
He's gone to join the m. — PETRONIUS, 2
No candidate . . . elected ex-president by such a large m. — TAFT, 1
One on God's side is a m. — PHILLIPS, 2
the damned, compact, liberal m. — IBSEN, 2
the great silent m. — NIXON, 2
The m. has the might — IBSEN, 2
we will win the election with a good m. — THATCHER, M, 23
majors scarlet M. — SASSOON, S, 1
make a Scotsman on the m. — BARRIE, 11
If possible honestly, if not, somehow, m. money — HORACE, 15
Love? I m. it constantly but I never talk about it — PROUST, 7
The white man knows how to m. everything — SITTING BULL, 1
maker he adores his m. — BRIGHT, 18
making He is very fond of m. things — HOPE, 2
If you get the English people into the way of m. kings
— MELBOURNE, 5
Nothing should be made . . . which is not worth m. — MORRIS, W, 2
maladies all the m. and miseries — CARLYLE, T, 31
Medical men . . . call all sorts of m. . . . by one name
— CARLYLE, J, 4
There are m. we must not seek to cure — PROUST, 11

malady It is the m. of our age   HOFFER, 3
malaise Wembley, adj. Suffering from a vague m.   JENNINGS, P, 2
male especially the m. of the species   LAWRENCE, D, 11
In the sex-war thoughtlessness is the weapon of the m.
                                                     CONNOLLY, 16
m. and female created he them   BIBLE, 142
preserve one last m. thing   LAWRENCE, D, 25
the female of the species is more deadly than the m.   KIPLING, 9
the peculiar situation of the human m.   BEAUVOIR, 2
malevolent the most perverse and m. creature   HAZLITT, 2
malice M. is like a game of poker   SPIEL, 1
malicious God is subtle but he is not m.   EINSTEIN, 6
malign rather m. oneself   ROCHEFOUCAULD, 17
malignant the only part of Randolph that was not m.
                                                     WAUGH, E, 51
malignity that peculiar m. . . . characteristic of apostates
                                                   MACAULAY, T, 7
malingering Neurosis has an absolute genius for m.   PROUST, 10
malt M. does more than Milton   HOUSMAN, 17
mamas The Last of the Red-Hot M.   TUCKER, 1
mammon M. wins his way where Seraphs might despair
                                                      BYRON, 8
ye cannot serve God and m.   BIBLE, 369
man A 'Grand Old M.'   LEACOCK, 12
all animals were created . . . for the use of m.   PEACOCK, 4
a m. after his own heart   BIBLE, 478
a m. can die but once   SHAKESPEARE, 123
a m. has no reason to be ashamed of having an ape for his
grandfather   HUXLEY, T, 11
A m. in the house is worth two   WEST, M, 3
a m. is always seeking for happiness   DIX, DOROTHY, 3
A m. is as old as he feels   PROVERBS, 44
A m. is only as old as the woman   MARX, G, 26
A m. . . . is so in the way   GASKELL, 1
A m. must serve his time to every trade   BYRON, 38
a m. of something occasionally like genius   WHITMAN, 2
A m. of straw   PROVERBS, 45
A m.'s a m. for a' that   BURNS, R, 10
A m. should never put on his best trousers   IBSEN, 4
A m. should . . . own he has been in the wrong   POPE, 54
A m. with God   KNOX, J, 1
an old M. in a dry month   ELIOT, T, 8
apparel oft proclaims the m.   SHAKESPEARE, 73
arms and the m.   VIRGIL, 5
'A was a m., take him for all in all   SHAKESPEARE, 70
behold the m.   BIBLE, 267
big m. has no time   FITZGERALD, F S, 13
Brutus is an honourable m.   SHAKESPEARE, 154
century of the common m.   WALLACE, H, 1
coming together of m. and wife . . . should be a fresh adventure
                                                    STOPES, 5
condition of m. is a condition of war   HOBBES, 1
disguised as a complete M.   HUXLEY, A, 6
England expects every m. will do his duty   NELSON, 4
every m. did that which was right in his own eyes   BIBLE, 296
Every m. is as Heaven made him   CERVANTES, 15
Every m. is wanted   EMERSON, 12
Every m. meets his Waterloo   PHILLIPS, 3
for m. or beast   FIELDS, 1
Glory to M. in the highest   SWINBURNE, 3
God made the woman for the m.   TENNYSON, 13
Go West, young m.   GREELEY, 1
grand old m.   NORTHCOTE, 1
hate ingratitude more in a m.   SHAKESPEARE, 345
he asks most insistently is about m.   LEONARDO DA VINCI, 2
He is a m. of brick   UPDIKE, 4
he owes not any m.   LONGFELLOW, 17
I care not whether a m. is Good   BLAKE, W, 17
If a m. be gracious and courteous   BACON, FRANCIS, 28
If a m. stays away from his wife   DARLING, 1
I just want every m., woman, and child in America to see it
                                                   GOLDWYN, 8
I love not M. the less   BYRON, 16
I myself also am a m.   BIBLE, 9
In wit a m.   POPE, 18
I said to the m. who stood at the gate of the year HASKINS, 1
I see a m. hurrying along – to what   KEATS, 69
It is good to know what a m. is   BRADLEY, F, 3
It's that m. again   KAVANAGH, 3
It takes . . . twenty years to make a m.   ROWLAND, H, 3
King is but a m.   SHAKESPEARE, 132

let no m. put asunder   BOOK OF COMMON PRAYER, 29
little m. wears a shocking bad hat   YORK, 1
make m. in our own image   BIBLE, 142
m. alone leaves traces of what he created   BRONOWSKI, 1
m. being in honour hath no understanding   PSALMS, 29
M., being reasonable, must get drunk   BYRON, 21
M. belongs wherever he wants to go   BRAUN, 1
m. . . . is . . . a disease animal   UNAMUNO Y JUGO, 2
M. . . . can neither repeat his past nor leave it behind   AUDEN, 9
M. . . . can only find relaxation from one . . . labour   FRANCE, 3
M. . . . consumes without producing   ORWELL, 3
M. delights not me   SHAKESPEARE, 84
m. did eat angels' food   PSALMS, 42
m. fell into his anecdotage   DISRAELI, 9
M. for the field and woman for the hearth   TENNYSON, 66
M., . . . grows beyond his work   STEINBECK, 2
M. has his will   HOLMES, O, 1
m. has stopped moving   TEILHARD DE CHARDIN, 1
m. hath penance done   COLERIDGE, S, 35
m. is a dangerous creature   ADAMS, A, 1
M. is a history-making creature   AUDEN, 9
M. is . . . an everlasting contradiction to himself   HAZLITT, 5
M. is an intellectual animal   HAZLITT, 5
M. is a noble animal   BROWNE, T, 12
M. is . . . a political animal   ARISTOTLE, 6
m. is . . . a religious animal   BURKE, E, 11
M. is a social animal   SPINOZA, 2
m. is as old as he's feeling   COLLINS, MORTIMER, 1
M. is a tool-making animal   FRANKLIN, 12
m. is . . . a wild animal   DARWIN, C G, 1
m. is capable of a certain degree of dignity   CAMUS, 2
M. is like a thing of nought   PSALMS, 72
M. is not a solitary animal   RUSSELL, B, 10
M. is something that is to be surpassed   NIETZSCHE, 17
M. is the hunter   TENNYSON, 65
M. is the master of things   SWINBURNE, 3
M. . . . Laid the crops low   THOMAS, D, 17
m. made the town   COWPER, 22
M. . . . on friendly terms with the victims . . . he eats
                                                BUTLER, S, 20
M. proposes   KEMPIS, 4
m. right fair   SHAKESPEARE, 373
m.'s greatest crime   CALDERÓN DE LA BARCA, 1
M.'s inhumanity to m.   BURNS, R, 14
M.'s life is cheap as beast's   SHAKESPEARE, 175
M.'s love is of m.'s life a thing apart   BYRON, 20
m. so various   DRYDEN, 9
m.'s worth something   BROWNING, R, 12
m. that hath no music in himself   SHAKESPEARE, 251
m. that hath not walked in the counsel of the ungodly PSALMS, 1
m. that is born of a woman   BIBLE, 230
m. that is young in years   BACON, FRANCIS, 61
M. to command and woman to obey   TENNYSON, 66
M. wants but little   GOLDSMITH, 8
M. was born free   ROUSSEAU, 1
M. Who Delivers the Goods   MASON, 1
m. who . . . had the largest . . . soul   DRYDEN, 22
m. who makes no mistakes   PHELPS, 1
m. whose second thoughts are good   BARRIE, 12
m. who's untrue to his wife   AUDEN, 21
m. with all his noble qualities   DARWIN, C R, 7
M. with the head and woman with the heart   TENNYSON, 66
mean m. is always full of distress   CONFUCIUS, 10
no m. . . . hath lived better than I   MALORY, 1
No m. is a hypocrite in his pleasures   CAMUS, 8
No m. is an Island   DONNE, 7
No m. is good enough to govern another   LINCOLN, 10
Nor in the critic let the m. be lost   POPE, 31
Nothing happens to any m.   MARCUS AURELIUS, 9
Nothing links m. to m. like . . . cash   SICKERT, 1
No young m. believes he shall ever die   HAZLITT, 19
Of M.'s first disobedience   MILTON, 30
On earth there is nothing great but m.   HAMILTON, W, 2
One cannot be always laughing at a m.   AUSTEN, 25
one m. pick'd out of ten thousand   SHAKESPEARE, 81
One m. shall have one vote   CARTWRIGHT, 1
one small step for m.   ARMSTRONG, N, 1
only m. is vile   HEBER, 2
only place where a m. can feel . . . secure   GREER, 1
proper study of Mankind is M.   POPE, 34

rarely . . . one can see in a little boy the promise of a m.
DUMAS, FILS, 3
reason to lament What m. has made of m. WORDSWORTH, W, 16
She's more of a m. than I expected VICTORIA, 3
single sentence . . . for modern m. CAMUS, 6
some meannesses . . . too mean even for m. THACKERAY, 7
Style is the m. himself BUFFON, 1
superior m. is distressed by his want of ability CONFUCIUS, 13
superior m. is satisfied CONFUCIUS, 10
Tears of eternity, and sorrow, Not mine, but m.'s HOUSMAN, 2
That married the m. all tattered and torn NURSERY RHYMES, 62
The atrocious crime of being a young m. PITT THE ELDER, 2
The Child is Father of the M. WORDSWORTH, W, 23
the field of the stars is so vast, but . . . m. has measured it
FRANCE, 5
the honest m. who married GOLDSMITH, 27
the only real danger that exists is m. himself JUNG, 11
The really original woman . . . imitates a m. SVEVO, 1
There must be a m. behind the book EMERSON, 18
There once was a m. who said 'God' KNOX, R, 4
The silliest woman can manage a clever m KIPLING, 31
the state . . . M. is in NIETZSCHE, 5
This is the state of m. SHAKESPEARE, 139
this is the whole duty of m. BIBLE, 79
'This was a m.!' SHAKESPEARE, 161
'Tis strange what a m. may do THACKERAY, 4
To the m.-in-the-street, who AUDEN, 2
True love's the gift which God has given To m. alone
SCOTT, WALTER, 1
uneducated m. to read books of quotations CHURCHILL, W, 21
We have on our hands a sick m. NICHOLAS I, 1
We know nothing of m., far too little JUNG, 11
Well, he looks like a m. LINCOLN, 21
what a m. is to a gent BALDWIN, S, 11
What a piece of work is a m. SHAKESPEARE, 84
what a very singularly deep young m. GILBERT, W, 35
What is a m. SHAKESPEARE, 99
what is m., that thou art mindful of him PSALMS, 3
What's a m.'s first duty IBSEN, 8
when a m. bites a dog DANA, 1
When a m. is in love he endures more NIETZSCHE, 2
When a woman behaves like a m. EVANS, E, 1
whether he is a Wise M. or a Fool BLAKE, W, 17
Whoso would be a m. EMERSON, 14
Why can't a woman be more like a m. LERNER, 6
Women who love the same m. BEERBOHM, 13
you asked this m. to die AUDEN, 14
You cannot make a m. by standing a sheep BEERBOHM, 17
you'll be a M. my son KIPLING, 17
young m. not yet BACON, FRANCIS, 35
Mandalay On the road to M. KIPLING, 23
Manderley I dreamt I went to M. again DU MAURIER, 2
mandrake Get with child a m. root DONNE, 13
manger In a m. for His bed ALEXANDER, 2
laid him in a m. BIBLE, 313
Manhattan I like to walk around M. STOUT, 2
manhood m. a struggle DISRAELI, 4
No sounder piece of British m. SCOTT, WALTER, 1
mankind about the dreadful wood . . . runs a lost m. AUDEN, 14
a decent respect to the opinions of m. JEFFERSON, 4
all M.'s epitome DRYDEN, 9
As I know more of m. JOHNSON, S, 147
giant leap for m. ARMSTRONG, N, 1
Human reason won. M. won KHRUSHCHEV, 4
I am willing to love all m. JOHNSON, S, 123
Ideal m. would abolish death LAWRENCE, D, 23
I love m. SCHULZ, 1
M. are always happy for having been happy SMITH, SYDNEY, 1
M. is a closed society SCHUMACHER, 2
M. is a club CHESTERTON, 40
M. is not a tribe of animals CHESTERTON, 40
nations which have put m. . . . in their debt INGE, 12
Nazi Germany had become a menace to all m. NEVINS, 4
proper study of m. is books HUXLEY, A, 12
proper study of M. is Man POPE, 34
Spectator of m. ADDISON, 10
truly m.'s war of liberation KENNEDY, JOHN, 13
Upon the whole I dislike m. KEATS, 70
We should expect the best and the worse from m.
VAUVENARGUES, 3
Whatever Nature has in store for m. FERMI, 1

manna gave you m. . . . angels' bread BIBLE, 97
manners in England people have good table m. MIKES, 1
leave off first for m.' sake BIBLE, 88
M. are . . . the need of the plain WAUGH, E, 48
M. maketh man WILLIAM OF WYKEHAM, 1
m. of a dancing master JOHNSON, S, 51
m. of a Marquis GILBERT, W, 41
To Americans English m. are . . . frightening JARRELL, 2
Tom Jones . . . picture of human m. GIBBON, 5
mansion Can storied urn . . . Back to its m. GRAY, 4
mansions in my Father's house are many m. BIBLE, 258
manure The tree of liberty must be refreshed . . . It is its
natural m. JEFFERSON, 8
many m. men, m. women, and m. children JOHNSON, S, 58
so much owed by so m. CHURCHILL, W, 54
what are they among so m. BIBLE, 249
what can two do against so m. SHAW, 48
Mao the degree of acceptance . . . M. has acquired MAO TSE-
TUNG, 1
map a picture of a relief m. of Ireland ASTOR, N, 2
Roll up that m. PITT THE YOUNGER, 2
The books one reads in childhood . . . false m. ORWELL, 21
maps Geography is about M. BENTLEY, E, 2
mar likely to m. the general felicity BUTLER, S, 19
Marathon mountains look on M. BYRON, 27
marble he . . . left it m. AUGUSTUS, 1
Not m., nor the gilded monuments SHAKESPEARE, 362
March Beware the ides of M. SHAKESPEARE, 142
M. comes in like a lion PROVERBS, 285
M., whan God first maked man CHAUCER, 16
M. winds and April showers PROVERBS, 286
months . . . look gloomy in England are M. and April TROLLOPE, 7
'Then you should say what you mean,' the M. Hare went on
CARROLL, 9
Napoleon's armies used to m. on their stomachs SELLAR, 6
Truth is on the m. ZOLA, 3
Marche The droghte of M. CHAUCER, 3
marched He m. them up to the top of the hill, And he m. them
down again NURSERY RHYMES, 37
marching m. through Georgia WORK, 4
mare Though patience be a tired m. SHAKESPEARE, 126
You have sent me a Flanders m. HENRY VIII, 1
Margery See-saw, M. Daw NURSERY RHYMES, 50
Marie I have sometimes regretted living so close to M.
PROUST, 15
mariner It is an ancient M. COLERIDGE, S, 24
mariners Ye M. of England CAMPBELL, T, 6
mark an ever-fixed m. SHAKESPEARE, 368
If you would hit the m. LONGFELLOW, 6
the Lord set a m. upon Cain BIBLE, 155
the m. . . . of the beast BIBLE, 466
markets the unreasoning laws of m. and fashion ALBERT, 1
marmalade tangerine trees and m. skies LENNON, 7
Marquis the manners of a M. GILBERT, W, 41
marred young man married . . . m. SHAKESPEARE, 21
marriage comedies are ended by a m. BYRON, 22
hanging prevents a bad m. SHAKESPEARE, 336
Happiness in m. AUSTEN, 21
In no country . . . are the m. laws so iniquitous as in England
MARTINEAU, 4
It should be a very happy m. THOMAS, I, 2
It takes two to make a m. SAMUEL, 1
love and m. CAHN, 1
Love is moral even without . . . m. KEY, E, 5
M. has many pains JOHNSON, S, 29
m. in a registry office ADAMS, R, 1
M. is a step so grave and decisive STEVENSON, R, 23
M. is . . . but a civil contract SELDEN, 9
M. is . . . excluded from heaven BUTLER, S, 19
M. is like a cage MONTAIGNE, 7
M. is like life in this STEVENSON, R, 25
M. is the only adventure open to the cowardly VOLTAIRE, 26
M. may often be a stormy lake PEACOCK, 3
M., n. . . . a community . . . making in all two BIERCE, 8
m. of true minds SHAKESPEARE, 368
m. . . . resembles a pair of shears SMITH, SYDNEY, 10
rob a lady of her fortune by way of m. FIELDING, 12
they neither marry, nor are given in m. SWIFT, 15
twenty years of m. make her . . . like a public building WILDE, 56
Women . . . care fifty times more for a m. than a ministry
BAGEHOT, 5

marriages M. are made in heaven — PROVERBS, 287
M. are not normally made — VIRCHOW, 1
Nearly all m. . . . are mistakes — TOLKIEN, 7
the early m. of silly children — MARTINEAU, 3
When widows exclaim loudly against second m. — FIELDING, 3
married A man in love is incomplete until . . . m. — GABOR, 2
A m. couple are well suited — ROSTAND, J. 1
a woman's business to get m. — SHAW, 23
complacency and satisfaction . . . in . . . a new-m. couple — LAMB, CHARLES, 3
Every night of her m. life she has been late for school — THOMAS, D. 23
he that is m. careth . . . how he may please his wife — BIBLE, 31
I am . . . thankful for not having m. — MARTINEAU, 1
if ever we had been m. — GAY, 4
I have m. a wife — BIBLE, 329
I m. beneath me — ASTOR, N. 1
I'm getting m. in the morning — LERNER, 5
In m. life three is company and two is none — WILDE, 24
Living in England . . . like being m. to a stupid . . . wife — HALSEY, 3
m. past redemption — DRYDEN, 28
m. to the only man . . . untidier than I am — WHITEHORN, 2
M. women are kept women — SMITH, L. 4
No man is genuinely happy, m., who has to drink worse gin — MENCKEN, 13
no taste when you m. me — SHERIDAN, R. 10
Reader, I m. him — BRONTË, C. 3
that Albert m. beneath him — COWARD, 24
The best part of m. life is the fights — WILDER, T. 2
the honest man who m. — GOLDSMITH, 27
what delight we m. people have — PEPYS, 13
When m. people don't get on — MAUGHAM, 6
You are playing it like m. men — TOSCANINI, 4
young man m. . . . marred — SHAKESPEARE, 21
marries a young person, who . . . m. or dies — AUSTEN, 7
doesn't much signify whom one m. — ROGERS, S. 1
When a man m., dies — SHELLEY, 11
marry as easy to m. a rich woman as a poor woman — THACKERAY, 5
A woman . . . may m. whom she likes — THACKERAY, 9
better to m. than to burn — BIBLE, 30
Every woman should m. — DISRAELI, 10
if men and women m. those whom they do not love — MARTINEAU, 5
if men knew . . . they'd never m. — HENRY, O. 2
if only you could persuade him to m. — LEWIS, C. 4
M. in haste — PROVERBS, 288
M. in Lent — PROVERBS, 289
M. in May — PROVERBS, 290
M. those who are single — KORAN, 6
no woman should m. a teetotaller — STEVENSON, R. 22
Then I can't m. you, my pretty maid — NURSERY RHYMES, 71
Those who m. God . . . can become domesticated too — GREENE, 1
To m. a man out of pity is folly — ASQUITH, M. 1
We invite people like that to tea, but we don't m. them — BETJEMAN, 3
when a man should m. — BACON, FRANCIS, 35
When you see what some girls m. — ROWLAND, H. 1
while ye may, go m. — HERRICK, 6
marry'd M. in haste — CONGREVE, 10
Mars seat of M. — SHAKESPEARE, 295
marshal We may pick up a m. or two — WELLINGTON, 2
Martini out of these wet clothes and into a dry M. — WOOLLCOTT, 2
martyr a m. to music — THOMAS, D. 25
Now he will raise me to be a m. — BOLEYN, 1
the soul of a m. with the intellect of an advocate — BAGEHOT, 1
martyrdom M. is the test — JOHNSON, S. 131
martyrs The blood of the m. is the seed of the Church — TERTULLIAN, 1
marvel To m. at nothing is just about the one and only thing — HORACE, 19
Marx had M. been Groucho instead of Karl — BERLIN, 3
M. is a case in point — GALBRAITH, 6
not even M. is more precious . . . than the truth — WEIL, 3
Marxian M. Socialism must always remain a portent — KEYNES, 3
Marxist The M. analysis . . . like blaming Jesus Christ for the Inquisition — BENN, 2
to banish . . . M. socialism — THATCHER, M. 19
Mary Hail M., full of grace — ANONYMOUS, 24
I'm sitting on the stile, M. — BLACKWOOD, 1
M. had a little lamb — HALE, S. 1

M., M., quite contrary — NURSERY RHYMES, 34
O M., go and call the cattle home — KINGSLEY, 4
Maryland the hills of M. — WHITTIER, 1
It makes me feel m. to tell you — HELLMAN, 3
masculine It makes me feel m. to tell you — HELLMAN, 3
Mass I am a Catholic. . . . I go to M. every day — BELLOC, 17
Paris is worth a m. — HENRI IV, 2
There is no idolatry in the M. — JOHNSON, S. 77
masses Give me . . . Your huddled m. — LAZARUS, 1
I will back the m. against the classes — GLADSTONE, 2
The uprising of the m. — ORTEGA Y GASSET, 1
master A m. is dead — BRAHMS, 2
commerce between m. and slave — JEFFERSON, 3
Man is the m. of things — SWINBURNE, 3
m., is it I — BIBLE, 423
m. of himself — MASSINGER, 1
Not bound to swear allegiance to any m. — HORACE, 13
One for the m. — NURSERY RHYMES, 4
the manners of a dancing m. — JOHNSON, S. 51
the M. Mistress of my passion — SHAKESPEARE, 359
the m. of my fate — HENLEY, 2
Thou are my m. and my author — VIRGIL, 2
masterpiece the m. of Nature — EMERSON, 8
Who am I to tamper with a m. — WILDE, 71
masters an ambitious man has as many m. as . . . may be useful — LA BRUYÈRE, 15
Assistant m. . . . liked little boys — WAUGH, E. 27
Buy old m. — BEAVERBROOK, 5
By studying the m. — ABEL, 1
good servants, but bad m. — L'ESTRANGE, 1
no man can serve two m. — BIBLE, 369
people are the m. — BURKE, E. 18
that the m. willingly concede to slaves — CAMUS, 12
We are the m. at the moment — SHAWCROSS, 1
masturbation m. of war — RAE, 1
M.: the primary sexual activity — SZASZ, 3
Such writing is a sort of mental m. — KEATS, 2
material he would put that which was most m. in the postscript — BACON, FRANCIS, 17
materialistic Christianity is the most m. of all great religions — TEMPLE, W. 1
only really m. people . . . Europeans — MCCARTHY, M. 3
materialists books with which m. have pestered the world — STERNE, 3
mates moves, and m., and slays — FITZGERALD, E. 13
mathematical Russell's beautiful m. mind — RUSSELL, B. 2
mathematician the most revolutionary m. — NEWTON, I. 3
mathematics Angling may be said to be . . . like the m. — WALTON, 1
As far as the laws of m. refer to reality — EINSTEIN, 12
How are you at M. — MILLIGAN, 6
Let no one ignorant of m. enter here — PLATO, 6
M. may be defined as the subject — RUSSELL, B. 13
M. possesses not only truth, but supreme beauty — RUSSELL, B. 21
quite lawful for a Catholic woman to avoid pregnancy by . . . m. — MENCKEN, 4
the theoreticians, whose language was m. — BUCK, 2
Matilda You'll come a-waltzing, M. — PATERSON, 1
matinée Robert Houdin who . . . invented . . . the theater m. — WELLES, 4
mating Only in the m. season — MILLIGAN, 3
matrimony critical period in m. is breakfast-time — HERBERT, A. 4
Even if we take m. at its lowest — STEVENSON, R. 13
it jumps from . . . love to m. — AUSTEN, 20
m. . . . a highly overrated performance — DUNCAN, 4
matter It is not much m. which we say — MELBOURNE, 3
M. . . . a convenient formula — RUSSELL, B. 18
proverb is much m. decorated — FULLER, T. 2
We die – does it m. when — TENNYSON, 71
Women represent . . . m. over mind — WILDE, 50
mattering Art . . . can go on m. — BOWEN, ELIZABETH, 2
matters Nothing m. very much — BALFOUR, 6
Matthew M., Mark, Luke and John — ADY, 1
maturing Do you think my mind is m. late — NASH, 7
maturity m. is only a short break in adolescence — FEIFFER, 1
Maud Come into the garden, M. — TENNYSON, 56
maunder m. and mumble — CARLYLE, T. 19
mausoleums designing m. for his enemies — LINKLATER, 1
Max If M. gets to Heaven — WELLS, 21
The Incomparable M. — BEERBOHM, 1
maxim A new m. is often a brilliant error — MALESHERBES, 1
we have got The M. Gun, and they have not — BELLOC, 12

May And after April, when M. follows BROWNING, R, 26
as fresh as is the month of M. CHAUCER, 5
darling buds of M. SHAKESPEARE, 358
Do spring M. flowers TUSSER, 2
got through the perils of winter till at least the seventh of M.
  TROLLOPE, 7
Here we come gathering nuts in M. ANONYMOUS, 37
I'm to be Queen o' the M. TENNYSON, 60
the merry month of M. ANONYMOUS, 85
wish a snow in M. SHAKESPEARE, 195
maybe I'll give you a definite m. GOLDWYN, 14
mayest if 'Thou m.' – it is also true that 'Thou m. not'
  STEINBECK, 1
maze Life is a m. in which we take the wrong turning
  CONNOLLY, 15
mazes The melting voice through m. running MILTON, 20
MCC where M. ends and the Church of England begins
  PRIESTLEY, 7
me Besides Shakespeare and m. STEIN, 4
between m. and the sun DIOGENES, 1
My thought is m. SARTRE, 9
on m. PARKER, D, 20
we never talk about anything except m. WHISTLER, 5
meal A m. without flesh PROVERBS, 46
meals Any two m. at a boarding-house LEACOCK, 7
mean Down these m. streets CHANDLER, 4
He nothing common did or m. MARVELL, 4
He who meanly admires m. things is a Snob THACKERAY, 1
it means just what I choose it to m. CARROLL, 32
She was a woman of m. understanding AUSTEN, 19
'Then you should say what you m.' CARROLL, 9
meaner A patronizing disposition . . . has its m. side ELIOT, G, 1
motives m. than your own BARRIE, 13
meanest the m. . . . deeds require spirit and talent
  LICHTENBERG, 3
the m. of his creatures Boasts two soul-sides BROWNING, R, 40
meaning birth had no m. LEE, L, 2
Even when poetry has a m. HOUSMAN, 6
Literature is simply language charged with m. POUND, 11
Nature has never put the fatal question as to the m. of their lives
  JUNG, 4
The least of things with a m. is worth more . . . than the greatest
  JUNG, 7
meannesses some m. . . . too mean even for man THACKERAY, 4
means Errors look so very ugly in persons of small m.
  ELIOT, G, 5
I shall have to die beyond my m. WILDE, 63
Let us all be happy, and live within our m. WARD, 5
m. just what I choose it to mean CARROLL, 32
Private M. is dead SMITH, STEVIE, 3
We are living beyond our m. MEAD, 1
measles Love is like the m. JEROME, 1
Love's like the m. JERROLD, 5
measure M. still for M. SHAKESPEARE, 234
Shrunk to this little m. SHAKESPEARE, 149
measured purpose of its own And m. motion WORDSWORTH, W, 37
the field of the stars is so vast, but . . . man has m. it FRANCE, 5
measureless caverns to man COLERIDGE, S, 14
meat man loves the m. in his youth SHAKESPEARE, 269
one man is appointed to buy the m. SELDEN, 1
One man's m. PROVERBS, 329
out of the eater came forth m. BIBLE, 294
Some hae m., and canna eat BURNS, R, 19
The public buys its opinions as it buys its m. BUTLER, S, 15
meats m. for the belly BIBLE, 27
meddling He was m. too much in my private life WILLIAMS, T, 8
media The m. . . . a convention of spiritualists STOPPARD, 6
medicine erotics is a perfectly respectable function of m.
  AVICENNA, 1
Experiment alone crowns the efforts of m. PAVLOV, 1
men mistook magic for m. SZASZ, 3
miserable have no other m. SHAKESPEARE, 230
Sleep's the only m. that gives ease SOPHOCLES, 1
Tolstoy . . . wasn't taken in by . . . science and m. TOLSTOY, L, 4
medieval disillusionments in the lives of the m. saints SAKI, 3
mediocre A best-seller is the gilded tomb of a m. talent
  SMITH, L, 1
m. . . . always at their best GIRAUDOUX, 3
more than magnificent – . . . m. GOLDWYN, 20
Some men are born m. HELLER, 5
Titles distinguish the m. SHAW, 28

Women want m. men MEAD, 2
mediocrities sanity of any number of artistic m. BLAKE, W, 1
mediocrity M. knows nothing higher DOYLE, 17
supreme expression of the m. TROTSKY, 10
Mediterranean All my wife has ever taken from the M.
  SHAFFER, 1
medium The m. is the message MCLUHAN, 4
meek humble and m. are thirsting for blood ORTON, 3
m. and mild WESLEY, C, 1
The m. do not inherit the earth LASKI, 1
The m. . . . not the mineral rights GETTY, 2
the m. shall inherit the Earth BIRKENHEAD, 4
Wisdom has taught us to be calm and m. HOLMES, O, 5
meet M. on the stairs PROVERBS, 291
never the twain shall m. KIPLING, 3
The only way for writers to m. CONNOLLY, 14
Two may talk . . . yet never really m. CATHERWOOD, 1
We only part to m. again GAY, 12
When shall we three m. again SHAKESPEARE, 200
meeting as If I was a public m. VICTORIA, 9
My life's been a m., Dad THOMAS, G, 2
this m. is drunk DICKENS, 49
megalomaniac m. differs from the narcissist RUSSELL, B, 8
m. . . . seeks to be feared RUSSELL, B, 8
melancholia little about m. that he didn't know TENNYSON, 1
melancholy a pleasing fit of m. MILTON, 10
hell upon earth . . . in a m. man's heart BURTON, ROBERT, 2
M. has her sovran shrine KEATS, 34
Most musical, most m. MILTON, 13
so sweet as M. BURTON, ROBERT, 1
Melba Dame Nellie M. HASKELL, 1
mellows A tart temper never m. with age IRVING, 2
melodies Heard m. are sweet KEATS, 28
melody m. imposes continuity upon the disjointed MENUHIN, 1
melt crown o' the earth doth m. SHAKESPEARE, 36
melting the races of Europe are m. ZANGWILL, 2
melting-pot America is . . . the great M. ZANGWILL, 2
même plus c'est la m. chose KARR, 1
memorandum A m. is written ACHESON, 7
memorial executed a m. longer lasting than bronze HORACE, 39
some there be, which have no m. BIBLE, 92
memories M. are hunting horns APOLLINAIRE, 1
memory Everyone complains of his m. ROCHEFOUCAULD, 1
Fond M. brings the light Of other days MOORE, T, 7
For my name and m., I leave it to . . . the next ages
  BACON, FRANCIS, 68
good m. is needed after one has lied CORNEILLE, 4
'His m. is going.' JOHNSON, S, 143
How sweet their m. still COWPER, 14
Illiterate him . . . from your m. SHERIDAN, R, 5
I would rather be a brilliant m. than a curiosity EAMES, 1
m. is a painter GRANDMA MOSES, 1
Music . . . Vibrates in the m. SHELLEY, 25
O m., hope, love of finished years ROSSETTI, C, 1
Time whereof the m. of man BLACKSTONE, 3
Unless a man feels he has a good enough m. MONTAIGNE, 3
What a strange thing is m., and hope GRANDMA MOSES, 1
men All m. are liars PSALMS, 66
all m. have one entrance into life BIBLE, 520
all m. would be tyrants DEFOE, 2
depict m. as they ought to be SOPHOCLES, 2
England . . . purgatory of m. FLORIO, 1
fishers of m. BIBLE, 359
For m. may come TENNYSON, 6
give place to better m. CROMWELL, O, 7
great city . . . has the greatest m. and women WHITMAN, 12
Great m. are almost always bad m. . . . ACTON, 2
great m. have not commonly been great scholars HOLMES, O, 3
happy breed of m. SHAKESPEARE, 295
honour all m. BIBLE, 441
If m. knew how women pass the time HENRY, O, 2
I, in common with all other m. SOMERVILLE, 1
It brings m. together in crowds and mobs in bar-rooms
  THOREAU, 7
Many m. would take the death-sentence LAWRENCE, T, 6
m. about me that are fat SHAKESPEARE, 144
m. and sea interpenetrate CONRAD, 9
M. are but children of a larger growth DRYDEN, 18
M. are . . . more careful of the breed of their horses PENN, 2
M. are not hanged for stealing horses HALIFAX, 1
M. are we, and must grieve WORDSWORTH, W, 61

m. . . . capable of every wickedness   CONRAD, 7
M. come of age at sixty   STEPHENS, 3
m. devote the greater part of their lives   LA BRUYÈRE, 2
m. everywhere could be free   LINCOLN, 8
M. fear death   BACON, FRANCIS, 18
M. have never been good   BARTH, 1
M. of few words are the best m.   SHAKESPEARE, 131
m. represent . . . mind over morals   WILDE, 50
m.'s attitude to women   BRITTAIN, 1
M.'s natures are alike   CONFUCIUS, 3
m. think all m. mortal   YOUNG, E, 3
M. will always be mad   VOLTAIRE, 29
M. will confess   COLBY, 1
Most m. admire Virtue   MILTON, 53
O! m. with sisters dear   HOOD, 11
power over m.   WOLLSTONECRAFT, 2
proclaiming that women are brighter than m.   LOOS, 5
rich m. rule the law   GOLDSMITH, 24
schemes o' mice an' m.   BURNS, R, 22
So many m., so many opinions   TERENCE, 4
Such m. are dangerous   SHAKESPEARE, 144
That all m. are equal   HUXLEY, A, 30
the hearts of M. should seek beyond the world   TOLKIEN, 6
The many m., so beautiful   COLERIDGE, S, 32
The mass of m. lead lives   THOREAU, 9
the m. who borrow, and the m. who lend   LAMB, CHARLES, 10
The more I see of m., the more I admire dogs   SÉVIGNÉ, 2
the only advantage women have over m.   RHYS, 2
the race of m. is almost extinct in Europe   LAWRENCE, D, 27
the tongues of m. and of angels   BIBLE, 38
The War between M. and Women   THURBER, 14
those m. have their price   WALPOLE, R, 3
tide in the affairs of m.   SHAKESPEARE, 159
To famous m. all the earth is a sepulchre   THUCYDIDES, 1
to form Christian m.   ARNOLD, T, 1
We are the hollow m.   ELIOT, T, 9
We live under a government of m. and . . . newspapers   PHILLIPS, 1
when m. and mountains meet   BLAKE, W, 14
Why are women . . . so much more interesting to m.   WOOLF, 10
Women . . . are either better or worse than m.   LA BRUYÈRE, 7
Women had always fought for m.   PANKHURST, E, 2
menace Nazi Germany had become a m. to all mankind   NEVINS, 1
mend God won't, and we can't m. it   CLOUGH, 4
mendacity clergyman whose mendicity is only equalled by their m.   TEMPLE, F, 2
mental Christian Science explains all cause and effect as m.   EDDY, 2
philosophy ought to . . . unravel people's m. blocks   RAPHAEL, 2
Such writing is a sort of m. masturbation   KEATS, 2
mentally happiness of man that he be m. faithful   PAINE, 1
merci La belle Dame sans M.   KEATS, 23
mercies For his m. ay endure   MILTON, 55
merciful just and m. as Nero   ELIZABETH I, 2
merciless a kind parent . . . or a m. step-mother   PLINY THE ELDER, 3
mercury ''Twas a chilly day for Willie When the m. went down'   ANONYMOUS, 51
mercy And that is M.'s door   COWPER, 16
For M. has a human heart   BLAKE, W, 44
God ha' m. on such as we, Baa! Yah! Bah   KIPLING, 11
his m. endureth for ever   PSALMS, 59
'La belle dame sans m.'   KEATS, 13
m. and truth are met together   PSALMS, 46
m. I asked, m. I found   CAMDEN, 1
m. unto you . . . be multiplied   BIBLE, 290
quality of m. is not strain'd   SHAKESPEARE, 246
surely goodness and m. shall follow me   PSALMS, 13
thy loving-kindness and m. shall follow me   PSALMS, 11
To M., Pity, Peace, and Love   BLAKE, W, 43
merit no damned m. in it   MELBOURNE, 6
Satan exalted sat, by m. raised   MILTON, 39
meritocracy The Rise of the M.   YOUNG, M, 1
mermaids I have heard the m. singing   ELIOT, T, 15
Mermaid Tavern Choicer than the M.   KEATS, 26
merry For tonight we'll m., m. be   ANONYMOUS, 12
I am never m. when I hear sweet music   SHAKESPEARE, 250
I commended mirth . . . to eat . . . to drink, and to be m.   BIBLE, 72
Old King Cole Was a m. old soul   NURSERY RHYMES, 38

the good are always the m.   YEATS, 13
merryman It's a song of a m.   GILBERT, W, 44
message ask me to take a m. to Albert   DISRAELI, 42
the electric m. came   AUSTIN, A, 1
The medium is the m.   MCLUHAN, 4
Messiah He was the M. of the new age   SLOCOMBE, 1
messing m. about in boats   GRAHAME, 1
met I m. a man who wasn't there   MEARNS, 1
We have m. too late   JOYCE, 14
metaphor all m. is poetry   CHESTERTON, 11
metaphysical a physical and m. impossibility   CARLYLE, T, 3
a sort of m. brothel for emotions   KOESTLER, 2
metaphysics M. is the finding of bad reasons   BRADLEY, F, 5
method madness, yet there is m. in't   SHAKESPEARE, 82
Traditional scientific m. has always been   PIRSIG, 3
You know my m.   DOYLE, 4
Methuselah all the days of M.   BIBLE, 156
meticulous He was a m. housemaid   CHAMBERLAIN, N, 3
metre Poetry is opposed to science . . . prose to m.   COLERIDGE, S, 18
without . . . understanding what m.   COLERIDGE, S, 44
metrical difference between . . . prose and m. composition   WORDSWORTH, W, 18
metropolitan My habits are formed on m. activity   SHAFTESBURY, 2
Mexico Poor M.   DÍAZ, 1
mice schemes o' m. an' men   BURNS, R, 22
Three blind m., see how they run   NURSERY RHYMES, 64
Michelangelo last words . . . name of – M.   REYNOLDS, J, 4
Talking of M.   ELIOT, T, 12
Mickey Mouse I love M. more than any woman   DISNEY, 2
mickle Many a m. makes a muckle   PROVERBS, 281
microbe The M. is so very small   BELLOC, 13
mid-day go out in the m. sun   COWARD, 12
middle a whole is that which has a beginning, a m., and an end   ARISTOTLE, 4
I like a film to have a beginning, a m. and an end   GODARD, 2
no m. course between the throne and the scaffold   CHARLES X, 2
people who stay in the m. of the road   BEVAN, 10
middle age One of the pleasures of m. is to *find out* that one WAS right   POUND, 4
middle class Our Eastern Empire . . . *made* the English m.   SCOTT, P, 1
part of English m. education is devoted to the training of servants   WILLIAMS, R, 1
respectable, m. . . . lady   RATTIGAN, 1
the healthy type that was essentially m.   FITZGERALD, F S, 10
middle classes Bow, bow, ye lower m.   GILBERT, W, 15
Midland M., bound for Cricklewood   BETJEMAN, 8
midnight chimes at m.   SHAKESPEARE, 122
I stood on the bridge at m.   LONGFELLOW, 4
It came upon the m. clear   SEARS, 1
M. brought on the dusky hour   MILTON, 48
m. never come   MARLOWE, 4
Not to be abed after m.   SHAKESPEARE, 337
Once upon a m. dreary   POE, 1
See her stood on the bridge at m.   ANONYMOUS, 71
soft embalmer of the still m.   KEATS, 47
To cease upon the m. with no pain   KEATS, 40
midst God is in the m. of her   PSALMS, 27
In the m. of life we are in death   BOOK OF COMMON PRAYER, 3
mid-stream best to swap horses in m.   LINCOLN, 16
mid-winter In the bleak m.   ROSSETTI, C, 3
might Fight the good fight with all thy m.   MONSELL, 1
Other nations use 'force'; we Britons . . . use 'M.'   WAUGH, E, 39
The majority has the m.   IBSEN, 2
We m. have been   LANDON, 3
might-have-been Look in my face; my name is M.   ROSSETTI, D, 2
mightier pen is m. than the sword   BULWER-LYTTON, 1
mighty Another m. empire overthrown   WORDSWORTH, W, 51
How are the m. fallen   BIBLE, 483
Napoleon – m. somnambulist of a vanished dream   NAPOLEON I, 3
put down the m.   BIBLE, 310
share in the good fortunes of the m.   BRECHT, 1
mike I'm being amplified by the m.   CHESTERTON, 45
Milan he wants M., and so do I   CHARLES V, 1
miles m. to go before I sleep   FROST, R, 8
militant I am an optimist, unrepentant and m.   USTINOV, 3
militarism m. . . . is one of the chief bulwarks of capitalism   KELLER, 1

military The chief attraction of m. service — TOLSTOY, L, 9
milk a kid in his mother's m. — BIBLE, 118
a land flowing with m. and honey — BIBLE, 106
as when you find a trout in the m. — THOREAU, 6
drunk the m. of Paradise — COLERIDGE, S, 17
Gin was mother's m. — SHAW, 38
putting m. into babies — CHURCHILL, W, 63
too full o' th' m. of human kindness — SHAKESPEARE, 205
milksop He is the bully . . . ready to twist the m.'s arm — HEMINGWAY, 1
Mill John Stuart M. By a mighty effort of will — BENTLEY, E, 5
miller There was a jolly m. — BICKERSTAFFE, 1
million man who has a m. dollars — ASTOR, J, 1
m. m. spermatozoa, All of them alive — HUXLEY, A, 18
my neighbor . . . who is worth only half a m. — VANDERBILT, 2
Son, here's a m. dollars — NIVEN, L, 1
millionaire 'He must be a m.' — GILBERT, F, 1
Who Wants to Be a M. — PORTER, C, 10
millions take m. off the caring services — KINNOCK, 8
unrewarded m. — SMITH, L, 6
mills m. of God grind slowly — LOGAU, 1
millstone a m. . . . hanged about his neck — BIBLE, 400
Milton after Shakespeare and M. are forgotten — PORSON, 2
Malt does more than M. can — HOUSMAN, 17
M., Madam, was a genius — JOHNSON, S, 150
M.! thou shouldst be living at this hour — WORDSWORTH, W, 5
mute inglorious M. — GRAY, 6
the faith and morals hold Which M. held — WORDSWORTH, W, 54
the making up of a Shakespeare or a M. — COLERIDGE, S, 47
mimsy All m. were the borogoves — CARROLL, 23
min' never brought to m. — BURNS, R, 4
mince dined on m. and slices of quince — LEAR, 9
mind A good critic . . . narrates the adventures of his m. — FRANCE, 7
an exaggerated stress on not changing one's m. — MAUGHAM, 11
an unseemly exposure of the m. — HAZLITT, 18
A short neck denotes a good m. — SPARK, 1
a sound m. in a sound body — JUVENAL, 10
Beauty in things exists in the m. — HUME, D, 4
best means of clearing . . . one's own m. — HUXLEY, T, 7
clear your m. of cant . . . — JOHNSON, S, 146
Do you think my m. is maturing late — NASH, 7
fear clawed at my m. and body — FRANK, 2
forgotten, as a dead man out of m. — PSALMS, 20
his m. is in perfect tranquillity — VOLTAIRE, 1
I don't m. if I do — KAVANAGH, 2
If it is for m. that we are seaching the brain — SHERRINGTON, 1
it's all in the m. — WOLFE, T, 1
man's unconquerable m. — WORDSWORTH, W, 62
Many ideas grow better when transplanted into another m. — HOLMES, O, JR., 2
men represent . . . m. over morals — WILDE, 50
m. that makes the body rich — SHAKESPEARE, 320
M. your own business — PROVERBS, 292
never to ransack any m. but his own — REYNOLDS, J, 3
No m. is thoroughly well organized — COLERIDGE, S, 42
our love . . . of the m. does not make us soft — PERICLES, 1
Pain of m. is worse than pain of body — SYRUS, 3
prodigious quantity of m. — TWAIN, 9
questions to which the inquisitive m. can . . . receive no answer — JOHNSON, S, 127
Reading is to the m. — STEELE, 1
Russell's beautiful mathematical m. — RUSSELL, B, 2
someone whose m. watches itself — CAMUS, 11
That's the classical m. at work — PIRSIG, 5
The m. can also be an erogenous zone — WELCH, 1
The m. is its own place — MILTON, 33
The pendulum of the m. — JUNG, 2
There is in the British Museum an enormous m. — WOOLF, 6
'Tis education forms the common m. — POPE, 40
to change your m. — MARCUS AURELIUS, 11
To know the m. of a woman — LAWRENCE, D, 45
true genius is a m. of large general powers — JOHNSON, S, 20
we consider as nothing the rape of the human m. — HOFFER, 2
Women represent . . . matter over m. — WILDE, 54
mindful what is man, that thou art m. of him — PSALMS, 3
minds All things can corrupt perverted m. — OVID, 7
Great m. think alike — PROVERBS, 181
Little m. are interested in the extraordinary — HUBBARD, 2
marriage of true m. — SHAKESPEARE, 368
M. are not ever craving — CRABBE, 1

M. like beds always made up — WILLIAMS, W, 1
m. so impatient of inferiority — JOHNSON, S, 23
Strongest m. . . . the noisy world Hears least — WORDSWORTH, W, 3
Superstition is the religion of feeble m. — BURKE, E, 12
the hobgoblin of little m. — EMERSON, 15
To be alone is the fate of all great m. — SCHOPENHAUER, 1
well-developed bodies, fairly developed m. — FORSTER, 3
When people will not weed their own m. — WALPOLE, H, 8
miner Dwelt a m., Forty-niner — MONTROSE, 1
mineral animal or vegetable or m. — CARROLL, 35
miners it is only because m. sweat their guts out — ORWELL, 22
the Vatican, the Treasury and the m. — BALDWIN, S, 12
mingled Like kindred drops, been m. — COWPER, 28
ministers I don't mind how much my m. talk — THATCHER, M, 24
my actions are my m.' — CHARLES II, 3
ministries The Times has made many m. — BAGEHOT, 1
ministry Women . . . care fifty times more for a marriage than a m. — BAGEHOT, 5
minorities M. . . . are almost always in the right — SMITH, SYDNEY, 12
minority not enough people to make a m. — ALTMAN, 1
The m. is always right — IBSEN, 2
minstrel A wandering m. I — GILBERT, W, 20
Ethereal m. — WORDSWORTH, W, 73
The M. Boy — MOORE, T, 3
minute M. Particulars — BLAKE, W, 16
not a m. on the day — COOK, A, 1
sucker born every m. — BARNUM, 1
To a philosopher no circumstance . . . is too m. — GOLDSMITH, 5
minutes at the rate of sixty m. an hour — LEWIS, C, 5
some of them are about ten m. long — DYLAN, 8
take care of the m. — CHESTERFIELD, 11
Yes, about ten m. — WELLINGTON, 20
miracle a m. of rare device — COLERIDGE, S, 15
man prays . . . for a m. — TURGENEV, 4
miracles before we know he is a saint, there will have to be m. — GREENE, 8
The Christian religion not only was at first attended with m. — HUME, D, 3
mirror A novel is a m. — STENDHAL, 1
Art is not a m. . . . but a hammer — MAYAKOVSKY, 1
Look not in my eyes, for fear They m. true the sight I see — HOUSMAN, 9
When a man confronts catastrophe . . . a woman looks in her m. — TURNBULL, 2
mirrors M. and fatherhood are abominable — BORGES, 1
My Dear One is mine as m. are lonely — AUDEN, 24
mirth I commended m. . . . to eat . . . to drink, and to be merry — BIBLE, 72
I love such m. as does not make friends ashamed — WALTON, 5
misbeliever You call me m., cut-throat dog — SHAKESPEARE, 240
miscarriage success and m. are empty sounds — JOHNSON, S, 7
miscast George Bernard Shaw is sadly m. — SHERWOOD, 2
mischief If you want to make m. . . . papers — BEAVERBROOK, 3
Satan finds . . . m. . . . For idle hands — WATTS, 1
thou little knowest the m. done — NEWTON, I, 6
To mourn a m. that is past — SHAKESPEARE, 276
mischievous what a m. devil Love is — BUTLER, S, 14
misdeeds put out all my m. — PSALMS, 31
miserable m. have no other medicine — SHAKESPEARE, 230
poring over m. books — TENNYSON, 53
The secret of being m. is to have leisure — SHAW, 35
two people m. instead of four — CARLYLE, T, 1
miserie y-fallen out of heigh degree. Into m. — CHAUCER, 15
miseries all the maladies and m. — CARLYLE, T, 31
misery certain amount of m. . . . to distribute — LOWE, 1
greatest m. is a battle gained — WELLINGTON, 8
he Who finds himself, loses his m. — ARNOLD, M, 39
Let other pens dwell on guilt and m. — AUSTEN, 11
M. acquaints a man with strange bedfellows — SHAKESPEARE, 323
Thou art so full of m. — TENNYSON, 79
misfortune In the m. of our best friends — ROCHEFOUCAULD, 14
next greatest m. to losing a battle — WELLINGTON, 12
the most unhappy kind of m. — BOETHIUS, 1
misfortunes any man . . . who could not bear another's m. — POPE, 57
history is . . . a tableau of crimes and m. — VOLTAIRE, 20
history . . . the register of the . . . m. of mankind — GIBBON, 8
if a man talks of his m. — JOHNSON, S, 135
strong enough to bear the m. of others — ROCHEFOUCAULD, 2
The m. of poverty — JUVENAL, 3

the real m. and pains of others — BURKE, E, 6
mislead One to m. the public, another to m. the Cabinet
— ASQUITH, H, 1

misleading Though analogy is often m. — BUTLER, S, 17
Miss M. J. Hunter Dunn — BETJEMAN, 11
Write to M. Lonelyhearts — WEST, N, 1
whatever M. T eats — DE LA MARE, 1
miss A m. is as good — PROVERBS, 47
to m. the one before it — CHESTERTON, 47
missed who never would be m. — GILBERT, W, 25
missionary I would eat a m. — WILBERFORCE, S, 2
mist Mad as the m. and snow — YEATS, 20
The rolling m. came down — KINGSLEY, 5
Mistah M. Kurtz – he dead — CONRAD, 3
mistake he who never made a m. never made a discovery
— SMILES, 1
Live all you can; it's a m. not to — JAMES, H, 4
Woman was God's second m. — NIETZSCHE, 3
mistaken think it possible you may be m. — CROMWELL, O, 5
mistakes An expert . . . knows some of the worst m. that can be
made — HEISENBERG, 1
Nearly all marriages . . . are m. — TOLKIEN, 7
The man who makes no m. — PHELPS, 1
Young men make great m. in life — JOWETT, 4
you've made plenty of m. if you've lived your life properly
— REAGAN, 7
mistress a m., and only then a friend — CHEKHOV, 11
A m. should be like a . . . retreat — WYCHERLEY, 1
Art is a jealous m. — EMERSON, 4
by pointing out to a man the faults of his m. — PROUST, 3
Master M. of my passion — SHAKESPEARE, 359
m. I am ashamed to call you — ELIZABETH I, 4
whether I embrace your lordship's principles or your m.
— WILKES, 1
why and how I became . . . m. of the Earl of Craven
— WILSON, HARRIETTE, 1
mistresses a better price than old m. — BEAVERBROOK, 5
No, I shall have m. — GEORGE II, 1
one wife and hardly any m. — SAKI, 14
Wives are young men's m. — BACON, FRANCIS, 34
mistrust M. first impulses — TALLEYRAND, 7
mistrusted If the white man says he does, he is instantly . . . m.
— MACINNES, 3
mists Season of m. — KEATS, 45
misunderstood To be great is to be m. — EMERSON, 16
Mitty Walter M., the undefeated — THURBER, 11
mix I m. them with my brains — OPIE, 1
mixed a m. infant — BEHAN, 4
not to look like a m. grill — COWARD, 10
mob do what the m. do — DICKENS, 44
Our supreme governors, the m. — WALPOLE, H, 3
mobs It brings men together in crowds and m. in bar-rooms
— THOREAU, 7
mock Let not Ambition m. — GRAY, 2
M. on, m. on, Voltaire, Rousseau — BLAKE, W, 34
mockery death itself must be . . . a m. — SHELLEY, 23
mockingbird it's a sin to kill a m. — LEE, H, 2
mode Fancy is . . . a m. of memory — COLERIDGE, S, 6
model The idea that there is a m. Labour voter — KINNOCK, 11
very m. of a modern Major-General — GILBERT, W, 37
models Rules and m. destroy genius and art — HAZLITT, 29
moderation astonished at my own m. — CLIVE, 1
M. in all things — PROVERBS, 293
m. in the pursuit of justice is no virtue — GOLDWATER, 2
M. is a virtue only in those — KISSINGER, 3
modern a m. poet's fate — HOOD, 14
Imagination without skill gives us m. art — STOPPARD, 3
invading her own privacy . . . first of the m. personalities
— BANKHEAD, 3
It is so stupid of m. civilization — KNOX, R, 1
The m. pantheist not only — LAWRENCE, D, 21
modest and is m. about it — AGATE, 2
Be m.! It is the kind of pride least likely to offend — RENARD, 1
modester People ought to be m. — CARLYLE, T, 33
modesty a woman . . . ought to lay aside . . . m. with her skirt
— MONTAIGNE, 4
Enough for m. — BUCHANAN, 1
I have often wished I had time to cultivate m. — SITWELL, E, 5
lay aside . . . m. . . . and put it on again with her petticoat
— MONTAIGNE, 4
There is false m., but there is no false pride — RENARD, 3

where the Greeks had m., we have cant — PEACOCK, 2
Mohammed If the mountain will not come to M.
— BACON, FRANCIS, 14
Mohicans The Last of the M. — COOPER, 1
moi L'Etat c'est m. — LOUIS XIV, 4
mole Death is still working like a m. — HERBERT, G, 5
Molly Stark M. sleeps a widow — STARK, 1
moment a m. of time — ELIZABETH I, 12
A m. of time may make us unhappy for ever — GAY, 1
Every m. one is born — TENNYSON, 82
in a m. of time — BIBLE, 319
Mona Lisa A lotta cats copy the M. — ARMSTRONG, L, 2
the portrait of his wife M. — LEONARDO DA VINCI, 4
Mona Lisas I have . . . . . . several original M. — MILLIGAN, 2
monarch m. of all I survey — COWPER, 34
Retirement, for a m., is not a good idea — VICTORIA, 2
monarchy M. is a strong government — BAGEHOT, 3
The m. is a labour-intensive industry — WILSON, HAROLD, 5
The Sovereign has, under a constitutional m. . . . three rights
— BAGEHOT, 6
They that are discontented under m., call it tyranny — HOBBES, 6
tourists . . . take in the M. . . . with . . . the pigeons
— HAMILTON, W, 1
Monday is going to do on M. — YBARRA, 1
M.'s child — NURSERY RHYMES, 35; PROVERBS, 294
Solomon Grundy, Born on a M. — NURSERY RHYMES, 53
money a bank that would lend m. to such a poor risk
— BENCHLEY, 5
a licence to print your own m. — THOMSON OF FLEET, 1
always try to rub up against m. — RUNYON, 2
art . . . of draining m. — SMITH, A, 3
be not greedy to add m. to m. — BIBLE, 506
Brigands demand your m. or your life — BUTLER, S, 29
Business . . . may bring m. — AUSTEN, 9
. . . collect legal taxes from illegal m. — CAPONE, 2
descriptions of m. changing hands — DENNIS, N, 2
except for large sums of m. — AYCKBOURN, 1
France is a country where the m. falls apart — WILDER, B, 3
Give him the m. — PICKLES, 1
Good Samaritan . . . had m. as well — THATCHER, M, 11
He that wants m., means, and content — SHAKESPEARE, 51
If you can . . . count your m. you are not . . . rich man — GETTY, 1
innocently employed in getting m. — JOHNSON, S, 91
Just what God would have done if he had the m. — WOOLLCOTT, 1
killed a lot of men to have made so much m. — MOLIÈRE, 5
love of m. is the root of all evil — BIBLE, 511
make m. — HORACE, 15
m. answereth all things — BIBLE, 76
M. can't buy friends — MILLIGAN, 10
m. can't buy me love — LENNON, 2
M. gives me pleasure — BELLOC, 11
m. has something to do with life — LARKIN, 1
M. is good for bribing yourself — REINHARDT, 1
M. is like a sixth sense — MAUGHAM, 13
M. is like muck — BACON, FRANCIS, 45
M., it turned out, was exactly like sex — BALDWIN, J, 2
M. . . . source of anxiety — GALBRAITH, 7
pleasant it is to have m. — CLOUGH, 3
Put m. in thy purse — SHAKESPEARE, 277
the love of m. is the root of all evil — BUTLER, S, 6
The man who leaves m. to charity in his will — VOLTAIRE, 33
the poor person . . . thinks m. would help — KERR, 2
The profession of letters . . . in which one can make no m.
— RENARD, 2
They had been corrupted by m. — GREENE, 6
they have more m. — FITZGERALD, F S, 5
time is m. — FRANKLIN, 4
To be clever enough to get . . . m., one must be stupid
— CHESTERTON, 25
to waste my time making m. — AGASSIZ, 1
We all know how the size of sums of m. appears to vary
— HUXLEY, J, 1
We haven't the m., so we've got to think — RUTHERFORD, 2
We've got the ships, we've got the men, we've got the m. too
— HUNT, G, 1
what risks you take . . . to find m. in a desk — BALZAC, 1
what the Lord God thinks of m. — BARING, 1
Where large sums of m. are concerned, . . . trust nobody
— CHRISTIE, 2
with m. . . . they have not got — HURST, 1
You can be young without m. — WILLIAMS, T, 2

monkey no reason to attack the m. when the organ-grinder is
    present   BEVAN, 9
  the biggest asset the m. possesses   ROGERS, W, 6
monopoly imperialism is the m. stage of capitalism LENIN, 1
Monroe Marilyn M.'s funeral   MILLER, A, 6
monster I doubt that the infant m.   KIPLING, 1
  jealousy . . . green-ey'd m.   SHAKESPEARE, 283
  m. gibbering   SWIFT, 2
mons Veneris treating the m. as . . . Mount Everest
                                                     HUXLEY, A, 16
Montagu Mrs M. has dropt me   JOHNSON, S, 136
Monte Carlo M.   BRADLEY, F, 2
  the man who broke the Bank at M.   GILBERT, F, 1
month April is the cruellest m.   ELIOT, T, 25
months The mother of m.   SWINBURNE, 4
  two m. of every year   BYRON, 7
monument If you seek my m., look around you   WREN, 2
  like Patience on a m.   SHAKESPEARE, 340
  sonnet is a moment's m.   ROSSETTI, D, 1
  The m. sticks like a fishbone   LOWELL, 2
monuments Not marble, nor the gilded m.   SHAKESPEARE, 362
monumentum Si m. requiris, circumspice   WREN, 2
moo You silly m.   SPEIGHT, 1
moon By the light of the m.   BYRON, 42
  If they had said the sun and the m. was gone   CARLYLE, J, 3
  I got the sun in the mornin' and the m. at night   BERLIN, 1
  I saw the new m. late yestreen Wi' the auld m. in her arm
                                                     ANONYMOUS, 83
  I see the m., And the m. sees me   NURSERY RHYMES, 24
  moving M. went up the sky   COLERIDGE, S, 33
  nothing left remarkable beneath the . . . m.   SHAKESPEARE, 36
  only a paper m.   HARBURG, 1
  on the m. as in Imperial Russia   CHEKHOV, 1
  shine on, shine on, harvest m.   NORWORTH, 1
  The m. doth shine as bright as day   NURSERY RHYMES, 6
  the m.'s a balloon   CUMMINGS, 1
  The M.'s a Balloon   NIVEN, D, 1
  The m. was a ghostly galleon   NOYES, 1
  They danced by the light of the m.   LEAR, 9
  th' inconstant m.   SHAKESPEARE, 311
  We're very wide awake, The m. and I   GILBERT, W, 28
moonlecht a braw brecht m. necht   LAUDER, 1
moonlight How sweet the m.   SHAKESPEARE, 249
  Ill met by m.   SHAKESPEARE, 260
  Look for me by m.   NOYES, 2
moons So sicken waning m. too near the sun   DRYDEN, 19
moral 2 percent m., 48 percent indignation   DESICA, 1
  All universal m. principles are idle fancies   SADE, 1
  each man must struggle, lest the m. law become . . . separated
                                                     ADDAMS, 2
  Everything's got a m.   CARROLL, 13
  it should preach a high m. lesson   STRACHEY, L, 2
  Let us be m.   DICKENS, 26
  Love is m. even without . . . marriage   KEY, E, 5
  m. attribute of a Scotsman   BARRIE, 10
  M. indignation is in most cases   DE SICA, 1
  m. law   KANT, 1
  m. or an immoral book   WILDE, 44
  more than a m. duty to speak one's mind   WILDE, 28
  one is unhappy one becomes m.   PROUST, 6
  putting him into a m. Coventry   PARNELL, 1
  The highest possible stage in m. culture   DARWIN, C R, 6
  The worst government is the most m.   MENCKEN, 8
moralist A Scotchman must be a very sturdy m.   JOHNSON, S, 18
  m. . . . must be truly wretched   BLACKMORE, 3
  no sterner m. than Pleasure   BYRON, 24
morality Dr Johnson's m. was as English . . . as a beefsteak
                                                     HAWTHORNE, 2
  M. . . . is herd-m.   NIETZSCHE, 12
  M.'s not practical   BOLT, 1
  M. which is based on ideas   LAWRENCE, D, 8
  No m. can be founded on authority   AYER, 1
  periodical fits of m.   MACAULAY, T, 16
  This imperative may be called that of M.   KANT, 2
  two kinds of m.   RUSSELL, B, 20
morals basing m. on myth   SAMUEL, 5
  If your m. make you dreary   STEVENSON, R, 3
  men represent . . . mind over m.   WILDE, 50
  the faith and m. hold Which Milton held   WORDSWORTH, W, 54
  the m. of a whore   JOHNSON, S, 51
mordre M. wol out   CHAUCER, 17

More Sir Thomas M.   WHITTINGTON, 1
more As I know m. of mankind   JOHNSON, S, 147
  M. than Somewhat   RUNYON, 3
  Oliver Twist has asked for m.   DICKENS, 36
  Specialist – A man who knows m. and m. about less and less
                                                     MAYO, 1
  take m. than nothing   CARROLL, 11
  The m. the merrier   PROVERBS, 401
mores O tempora! O m.   CICERO, 4
morn From m. to night, my friend   ROSSETTI, C, 6
  From m. To noon he fell   MILTON, 38
  He rose the morrow m.   COLERIDGE, S, 30
  the opening eye-lids of the m.   MILTON, 22
mornin' nice to get up in the m.   LAUDER, 2
morning Early one m., just as the sun was rising   ANONYMOUS, 16
  I awoke one m.   BYRON, 45
  I'm getting married in the m.   LERNER, 5
  in the m. it is green   PSALMS, 49
  joy cometh in the m.   PSALMS, 17
  M. in the Bowl of Night   FITZGERALD, E, 2
  Oh, what a beautiful m.   HAMMERSTEIN, 3
  she has lived . . . the space of one m.   MALHERBE, 1
  that . . . turneth the shadow of death into the m. BIBLE, 18
  the m. cometh, and also the night   BIBLE, 204
  'Tis always m. somewhere   HORNE, 1
morrow take . . . no thought for the m.   BIBLE, 371
mortal All men are m.   PROVERBS, 35
  I was not unaware that I had begotten a m.   GOETHE, 10
  men think all men m.   YOUNG, E, 3
  that great Leviathan, or rather . . . that M. God HOBBES, 5
  The doctor found . . . Her last disorder m.   GOLDSMITH, 9
  we have been m. enemies ever since   LESAGE, 2
mortality kept watch o'er man's m.   WORDSWORTH, W, 32
  M., behold and fear   BEAUMONT, 9
mortals a human giraffe, sniffing . . . at m.   DEGAULLE, 3
  A novelist is, like all m.   NABOKOV, 7
  We m. cross the ocean   BROWNING, R, 8
  what fools these m. be   SHAKESPEARE, 262
Moscow don't march on M.   MONTGOMERY OF ALAMEIN, 1
Moses he saw his role as being that of M.   JAY, 1
  there arose not a prophet . . . like unto M.   BIBLE, 60
Moslems I ask all M. to execute them   KHOMEINI, 2
most The M. may err as grossly   DRYDEN, 12
mostest I got there fustest with the m.   FORREST, 1
mote the m. that is in thy brother's eye   BIBLE, 373
moth a m. fretting a garment   PSALMS, 23
  like a m., the simple maid   GAY, 2
  The desire of the m. for the star   JOYCE, 12
mother And Her M. Came Too   NOVELLO, 1
  as is the m., so is her daughter   BIBLE, 125
  behold thy m.   BIBLE, 270
  Dead! and . . . never called me m.   WOOD, 1
  Eve . . . the m. of all living   BIBLE, 152
  I am old enough to be – in fact am – your m.   MILNE, 1
  If poverty is the m. of crime, stupidity is its father
                                                     LA BRUYÈRE, 11
  I was born . . . because my m. needed a fourth at meals
                                                     LILLIE, 1
  I wished to be near my m.   WHISTLER, 18
  Jerusalem . . . the m. of us all   BIBLE, 133
  May you be the m. of a bishop   BEHAN, 11
  M. is the dead heart of the family   GREER, 2
  M. of the Free   BENSON, 1
  My m., drunk or sober.   CHESTERTON, 8
  The m. of months   SWINBURNE, 1
  the m. of parliaments   BRIGHT, 2
  the titles of wife and m. . . . are transitory   LIVERMORE, 2
  this war . . . which did not justify the sacrifice of a single m.'s son
                                                     PANKHURST, S, 1
motherhood wifehood and m. are but incidental relations
                                                     STANTON, E, 5
mother-in-law as the man said when his m. died   JEROME, 1
  What a marvellous place to drop one's m.   FOCH, 2
mothers Come m. and fathers Throughout the land   DYLAN, 7
  O! men with m. and wives   HOOD, 11
  women become like their m.   WILDE, 21
mothers-in-law Two m.   RUSSELL, J, 1
motives m. meaner than your own   BARRIE, 13
motto let their m. be: – Hunt   BRONTÉ, C, 1
mould Breaking the m.   JENKINS, 3
  If you cannot m. yourself   KEMPIS, 3

Nature made him, and then broke the m.   ARIOSTO, 1
mountain   A m. in labour shouted so loud   LA FONTAINE, 6
hardly be a beast or a fool alone on a great m.   KILVERT, 2
If the m. will not come to Mohammed   BACON, FRANCIS, 14
If the m. will not come to Mahomet   PROVERBS, 215
Land of the m. and the flood   SCOTT, WALTER, 9
never see another m.   LAMB, CHARLES, 24
mountains   all faith, so that I could remove m.   BIBLE, 38
England's m. green   BLAKE, W, 33
highest intellects, like the tops of m.   MACAULAY, T, 6
if the Swiss had designed these m.   THEROUX, 3
M. interposed Make enemies of nations   COWPER, 28
m. look on Marathon   BYRON, 27
m. skipped like rams   PSALMS, 63
M. . . . the beginning and the end of all natural scenery   RUSKIN, 6
M. will heave in childbirth   HORACE, 6
Two voices . . . one is of the sea, One of the m.   WORDSWORTH, W, 63
when men and m. meet   BLAKE, W, 14
mourn   countless thousands m.   BURNS, R, 14
it is chiefly our own deaths that we m. for   BRENAN, 1
To m. a mischief that is past   SHAKESPEARE, 276
mourning   I'm in m. for my life   CHEKHOV, 7
in m. . . . for the world   SITWELL, E, 3
tedium is the very basis of m.   HUGO, 5
We met . . . Dr Hall in such very deep m.   AUSTEN, 31
What we call m. for our dead   MANN, 1
with my m. . . . and new periwig   PEPYS, 15
mouse   a silly little m. will be born   HORACE, 6
He bought a crooked cat, which caught a crooked m.   NURSERY RHYMES, 57
leave room for the m.   SAKI, 22
she brought forth a m.   LA FONTAINE, 6
The m. ran up the clock   NURSERY RHYMES, 15
mouse-trap   If a man make a better m.   EMERSON, 26
moustache   a kiss without a m.   CAWEIN, 1; SARTRE, 15
a man outside with a big black m.   MARX, G, 10
Being kissed by a man who didn't wax his m.   KIPLING, 26
his nicotine eggyellow weeping walrus Victorian m.   THOMAS, D, 26
mouth   A politician is a statesman . . . with an open m.   STEVENSON, A, 2
butter wouldn't melt in her m.   LANCHESTER, 1
God be in my m., And in my speaking   ANONYMOUS, 20
Keep your m. shut and your eyes open   PROVERBS, 241
out of the m. of . . . babes and sucklings   PSALMS, 3
out of thine own m. will I judge thee   BIBLE, 336
mouth-brothels   Great restaurants are . . . nothing but m.   RAPHAEL, 4
move   But did thee feel the earth m.   HEMINGWAY, 5
in him we live, and m., and have our being   BIBLE, 13
I will m. the earth   ARCHIMEDES, 1
The great affair is to m.   STEVENSON, R, 7
movement   I want to be a m.   MITCHELL, A, 1
We are the true peace m.   THATCHER, M, 18
moves   m., and mates, and slays   FITZGERALD, E, 13
Yet it m.   GALILEI, 2
movie   He looks like the guy in the science fiction m.   FORD, G, 1
This is a m., not a lifeboat   TRACY, 3
movies   Thanks to the m., gunfire has always sounded unreal   USTINOV, 1
moving   In home-sickness you must keep m.   STACPOOLE, 1
man has stopped m.   TEILHARD DE CHARDIN, 1
m. Moon went up the sky   COLERIDGE, S, 33
people under suspicion are better m.   KAFKA, 4
The M. Finger writes   FITZGERALD, E, 14
Mozart   The sonatas of M. are unique   SCHNABEL, 3
when M. was my age   LEHRER, 4
MPs   The prospect of a lot Of dull M.   GILBERT, W, 17
much   m. . . . said on both sides   ADDISON, 13
So little done, so m. to do   RHODES, 4
so m. owed by so many to so few   CHURCHILL, W, 54
muchness   Much of a m.   VANBURGH, 3
muck   Money is like m.   BACON, FRANCIS, 45
sing 'em m.   MELBA, 4
mud   One sees the m., and one the stars   LANGBRIDGE, 1
muddle   a beginning, a m., and an end   LARKIN, 5
muddle-headed   He's a m. fool   CERVANTES, 19
muddy   The hunter for aphorisms . . . has to fish in m. water   BRADLEY, F, 1
Muffet   Little Miss M. Sat on a tuffet   NURSERY RHYMES, 31
multiplied   Entities should not be m.   OKHAM, 1

mercy unto you . . . be m.   BIBLE, 290
multiply   be fruitful and m.   BIBLE, 142
multitude   a m. of sins   BIBLE, 220
long dresses, . . . cover a m. of shins   WEST, M, 10
The m. is always in the wrong   ROSCOMMON, 2
this massed m. of silent witnesses to . . . war   GEORGE V, 1
multitudes   I contain m.   WHITMAN, 10
mum   M.'s the word   COLMAN, THE YOUNGER, 1
They fuck you up, your m. and dad   LARKIN, 4
mumble   maunder and m.   CARLYLE, T, 19
mundi   Sic transit gloria m.   KEMPIS, 1
murder   Divorce? Never. But m. often   THORNDIKE, 1
love and m. will out   CONGREVE, 4
Macbeth doth m. sleep   SHAKESPEARE, 212
m. back into its rightful setting   HITCHCOCK, 1
M. considered as one of the Fine Arts   DE QUINCEY, 2
M. . . . had a mask like Castlereagh   SHELLEY, 13
M., like talent, seems . . . to run in families   LEWES, 1
M. most foul   SHAKESPEARE, 77
m. shrieks out   WEBSTER, J, 1
Never m. a man who is committing suicide   WILSON, W, 3
So it was m.   MARX, G, 7
Sooner m. an infant in its cradle   BLAKE, W, 21
murdered   I m. my grandmother this morning   ROOSEVELT, F, 1
murderer   Kill a man, and you are a m.   ROSTAND, J, 3
murderous   at Yuletide men are the more m.   HILL, G, 4
murmur   live m. of a summer's day   ARNOLD, M, 35
Murray   And the bonny Earl of M.   ANONYMOUS, 109
muscular   His Christianity was m.   DISRAELI, 20
muse   To the Greeks the M. gave native wit   HORACE, 8
With Donne, whose m. on dromedary trots   DONNE, 1
mused   Lancelot m. a little space   TENNYSON, 47
museum   the m. of this world   LAWRENCE, D, 25
museums   The Arab . . . more philosophical than . . . curators of the m.   FRANCE, 4
mushroom   a supramundane m.   LAURENCE, 1
Fame is sometimes like unto a . . . m.   FULLER, T, 3
to stuff a m.   CONRAN, 1
music   a martyr to m.   THOMAS, D, 25
Architecture . . . is frozen m.   SCHELLING, 1
art constantly aspires towards . . . m.   PATER, 2
capable of being well set to m.   ADDISON, 11
century of aeroplanes deserves its own m.   DEBUSSY, 3
chord of m.   PROCTER, 1
food in m.   LILLO, 1
how potent cheap m. is   COWARD, 1
How sour sweet m. is   SHAKESPEARE, 299
I don't write modern m.   STRAVINSKY, 6
If all the arts aspire to the condition of m.   SANTAYANA, 14
If m. be the food of love   SHAKESPEARE, 334
I'll set it to m.   ROSSINI, 2
I love m. passionately   DEBUSSY, 2
In m., the punctuation is absolutely strict   RICHARDSON, 2
I shan't be doing m.   VAUGHAN WILLIAMS, 1
I think popular m. in this country   CROSBY, 2
making m. throatily and palpitatingly sexual   HUXLEY, A, 4
man that hath no m. in himself   SHAKESPEARE, 251
M. and women I cannot but give way to   PEPYS, 14
M. begins to atrophy   POUND, 3
M. creates order out of chaos   MENUHIN, 1
m. critics . . . small and rodent-like   STRAVINSKY, 3
M. has charms to soothe   CONGREVE, 8
M. helps not   PROVERBS, 296
M. is not written in red, white and blue   MELBA, 2
M. is the arithmetic of sounds   DEBUSSY, 4
M. is the food of love   PROVERBS, 297
M. is your own experience   PARKER, CHARLIE, 1
M., Maestro, Please   MAGIDSON, 1
M. that gentlier on the spirit lies   TENNYSON, 55
M. . . . Vibrates in the memory   SHELLEY, 25
never merry when I hear sweet m.   SHAKESPEARE, 250
no more m. in them   ARMSTRONG, L, 2
No one really understood m. unless he was a scientist   BUCK, 4
Poetry . . . set to more or less lascivious m.   MENCKEN, 12
silence sank like m.   COLERIDGE, S, 37
The English may not like m.   BEECHAM, 1
The hills are alive with the sound of m.   HAMMERSTEIN, 5
The m. teacher came twice each week   ADE, 2
thy chosen m., Liberty   WORDSWORTH, W, 63
Van Gogh's ear for m.   WILDER, B, 4
musical   cashiers of the M. Banks   BUTLER, S, 2

Most m., most melancholy · MILTON, 13
music-hall   M. songs provide the dull with wit · MAUGHAM, 23
musicologist   A m. . . . can read music but can't hear it · BEECHAM, 1
Mussolini   Hitler showed surprising loyalty to M. · HITLER, 2
Hitler was a nuisance. M. was bloody · MADARIAGA Y ROGO, 2
must   Genius does what it m. · MEREDITH, O, 1
Is *m.* a word to be addressed to princes · ELIZABETH I, 9
muttering   the m. grew to a grumbling · BROWNING, R, 43
mutton   Alice – M.; M. – Alice · CARROLL, 37
I could no longer stand their eternal cold m. · RHODES, 1
myriad-minded   m. Shakespeare · COLERIDGE, S, 3
myrrh   gathered my m. with my spice · BIBLE, 493
myself   deliver me from m. · BROWNE, T, 9
I am always with m. · TOLSTOY, L, 7
I have always disliked m. · CONNOLLY, 12
I know m. · FITZGERALD, F S, 12
I like to go by m. · HAZLITT, 20
I've over-educated m. · COWARD, 21
not only witty in m. · SHAKESPEARE, 116
The Jews have produced . . . Christ, Spinoza, and m. · STEIN, 5
mysteries   disciples . . . mark its ways and note . . . its m. · BRADLEY, F, 2
mysterious   God moves in a m. way · COWPER, 17
the ancient cathedrals – grand, wonderful, m. · STANTON, E, 1
mystery   a riddle wrapped in a m. inside an enigma · CHURCHILL, W, 48
Growth is a greater m. than death · MAILER, 1
Happiness is a m. like religion · CHESTERTON, 89
In m. our soul abides · ARNOLD, M, 29
mystic   The m. sees the ineffable · MAUGHAM, 8
mystics   M. always hope that science · TARKINGTON, 5
myth   A m. is, of course, not a fairy story · RYLE, 2
basing morals on m. · SAMUEL, 5
some magnificent m. · PLATO, 3
mythopoeic   some of the characters will seem almost m. · TOLKIEN, 3
myths   Science must begin with m. · POPPER, 5

N

naff   Why don't you n. off · ANNE, 3
nails   I used to bite my n. · PARKER, D, 7
naive   the n. forgive · SZASZ, 6
naked   a n. Duke of Windlestraw addressing a n. House of Lords · CARLYLE, T, 25
a pretty girl who n. is · CUMMINGS, 2
I can't stand a n. light bulb · WILLIAMS, T, 5
n., and ye clothed me · DIDLE, 421
n. into the conference chamber · BEVAN, 11
No woman so n. as . . . underneath her clothes · FRAYN, 1
Our ingress   Was n. and bare · LONGFELLOW, 14
Poor n. wretches · SHAKESPEARE, 180
The exception is a n. ape · MORRIS, D, 3
they were both n. · BIBLE, 147
who told thee that thou wast n. · BIBLE, 150
nakedness   N. is uncomely · BACON, FRANCIS, 48
name   And lo! Ben Adhem's n. led all the rest · HUNT, L, 3
Good n. in man and woman · SHAKESPEARE, 282
his n. shall be called, Wonderful, Counsellor · BIBLE, 201
How I loathe that other with my n. · MANDELSTAM, 1
How sweet the n. of Jesus sounds · NEWTON, J, 2
I have no middle n. · SELZNICK, 1
I remember your n. perfectly · SPOONER, 2
local habitation and a n. · SHAKESPEARE, 264
No, Groucho is not my real n. · MARX, G, 24
no n. on the door · SELFRIDGE, 2
Oh liberty! . . . What crimes are committed in thy n. · ROLAND, 1
People you know, yet can't quite n. · LARKIN, 2
rose by any other n. · SHAKESPEARE, 310
signing his n. and forgetting to write the letter · BEECHER, 1
that was the n. thereof · BIBLE, 146
their n. liveth for evermore · BIBLE, 93
the n. of which was Beautiful · BUNYAN, 4
thou shalt not take the n. of . . . God in vain · BIBLE, 115
two or three . . . gathered together in my n. · BIBLE, 401
What's in a n. · SHAKESPEARE, 310
When I pass my n. in such large letters · TREE, 8
nameless   a n. deed · RADCLIFFE, 1
names   No n., no pack-drill · PROVERBS, 313
naming   Today we have n. of parts · REED, H, 2

Naples   See N. and die · PROVERBS, 359
Napoleon   ashes of N. · WELLINGTON, 24
N. · WELLINGTON, 11
the N. of crime · DOYLE, 11
narcissist   megalomaniac differs from the n. · RUSSELL, B, 8
nastier   she could have found anything n. to say · SAYERS, 1
nasty   how n. the nice people can be · POWELL, A, 5
Short, big-nosed men with n. conical caps · FULLER, ROY, 2
Something n. in the woodshed · GIBBONS, 1
nation   America became top n. · SELLAR, 7
An army is a n. within a n. · VIGNY, 3
A n. is not in danger of financial disaster · MELLON, 1
a n. of amateurs · ROSEBERY, 3
dedicate this n. to the policy of the good neighbor · ROOSEVELT, F, 11
England is a n. of shopkeepers · NAPOLEON I, 13
he is the sworn foe of our n. · CAMPBELL, T, 7
I will make of thee a great n. · BIBLE, 165
n. . . . fall victim to a big lie · HITLER, 11
n. is a society united by a delusion about its ancestry · INGE, 10
n. shall not lift up sword against n. · BIBLE, 194
n. shall rise against n. · BIBLE, 413
N. shall speak peace · ANONYMOUS, 1
No n. is fit to sit in judgement · WILSON, W, 9
No n. was ever ruined by trade · FRANKLIN, 4
one n. was not enough for him · BELLOC, 1
right to fix the boundary of . . . a n. · PARNELL, 2
Teddy Bear to the N. · BETJEMAN, 1
the English are . . . the least a n. of pure philosophers · BAGEHOT, 6
. . . the kind of n. . . . President Kennedy died for · JOHNSON, L, 6
the kind of n. that President Roosevelt hoped for · JOHNSON, L, 6
The n. had the lion's heart · CHURCHILL, W, 5
nationalism   wind of n. and freedom blowing · BALDWIN, S, 7
nationality   My suit is pale yellow. My n. is French · WILLIAMS, T, 1
Other people have a n. · BEHAN, 7
nations   Commonwealth of N. · ROSEBERY, 1
extends over many n. and three continents · DOYLE, 14
If people behaved in the way n. do · WILLIAMS, T, 7
languages are the pedigree of n. · JOHNSON, S, 159
The day of small n. has long passed away · CHAMBERLAIN, J, 2
The great n. have always acted like gangsters · KUBRICK, 1
the healing of the n. · BIBLE, 474
The n. which have put mankind and posterity most in their debt · INGE, 12
Two n.; between whom there is no intercourse · DISRAELI, 12
native   My n. Land – Good Night · BYRON, 10
my own, my n. land · SCOTT, WALTER, 8
to appear considerable in his n. place · JOHNSON, S, 82
To the Greeks the Muse gave n. wit · HORACE, 8
white man . . . looks into the eyes of a n. · LESSING, D, 3
natives   Britons were only n. · SELLAR, 4
natural   First feelings are always the most n. · LOUIS XIV, 3
It is n. to die · BACON, FRANCIS, 19
making so much of n. selection · DARWIN, C R, 4
n. false teeth · ROBINSON, R, 2
N. Selection · DARWIN, C R, 8
Nothing prevents us from being n. · ROCHEFOUCAULD, 25
'twas N. to please · DRYDEN, 4
naturally   Though I am not n. honest · SHAKESPEARE, 353
nature   Accuse not N., she hath done her part · MILTON, 50
All N. wears one universal grin · FIELDING, 1
Allow not n. more than n. needs · SHAKESPEARE, 175
a noble n., . . . treats . . . a serious subject · ARNOLD, M, 32
a poet to whom n. has denied the faculty of verse · CARLYLE, T, 7
but N. more · BYRON, 16
can't call yourself a great work of n. · WHISTLER, 12
Consistency is contrary to n. · HUXLEY, A, 14
drive out n. with a pitchfork · HORACE, 20
fortress built by N. · SHAKESPEARE, 295
Friend . . . masterpiece of N. · EMERSON, 8
God and N. then at strife · TENNYSON, 31
Human n. is so well disposed · AUSTEN, 7
I got disappointed in human n. · DONLEAVY, 1
I have learned To look on n. · WORDSWORTH, W, 12
In n. there are neither rewards nor punishments · INGERSOLL, 2
In n. there are no rewards · VACHELL, 1
law of n. which love alone can alter · LACLOS, 3
Let N. be your Teacher · WORDSWORTH, W, 67
Little we see in N. that is ours · WORDSWORTH, W, 64

my . . . interest in n. became focused — DURRELL, G, 1
N. abhors a vacuum — RABELAIS, 1
N. admits no lie — CARLYLE, T, 21
N. has left this tincture — DEFOE, 2
N. has never put the fatal question — JUNG, 1
N. is but a name for an effect — COWPER, 26
N. is creeping up — WHISTLER, 11
N. is often hidden — BACON, FRANCIS, 36
n. is the art of God — BROWNE, T, 3
N. is usually wrong — WHISTLER, 4
N. is very consonant and conformable — NEWTON, I, 4
N. made him, and then broke the mould — ARIOSTO, 1
N. . . . must be obeyed — BACON, FRANCIS, 62
N. never did betray — WORDSWORTH, W, 13
N. remains — WHITMAN, 13
N.'s ancient power was lost — TENNYSON, 33
N.'s handmaid, art — DRYDEN, 20
n.'s law — LA FONTAINE, 8
N.'s laws lay hid in night — POPE, 19
new sights of N. made me rejoice — CURIE, 5
not formed by n. to bear — MARCUS AURELIUS, 9
o'erstep not the modesty of n. — SHAKESPEARE, 95
one of N.'s Gentlemen — LINTON, 1
one of the forces of n. — MICHELET, 1
science . . . the interplay between n. and ourselves — HEISENBERG, 2
secret of the arts is to correct n. — VOLTAIRE, 1
the most irrelevant thing in n. — LAMB, CHARLES, 15
the spectacles of books to read n. — DRYDEN, 23
to see the absurd n. of Englishmen — PEPYS, 7
True wit is n. to advantage dress'd — POPE, 25
unassuming common-place Of N. — WORDSWORTH, W, 75
vacuum . . . better . . . stuff that n. replaces — WILLIAMS, T, 4
Wellington has exhausted n. and . . . glory — WELLINGTON, 2
We need more understanding of human n. — JUNG, 11
Whatever N. has in store for mankind — FERMI, 1
wonderful case of n. imitating art — WILDE, 62
natures Men's n. are alike — CONFUCIUS, 3
naught N. so sweet as Melancholy — BURTON, ROBERT, 1
nauseate I n. walking — CONGREVE, 15
nauseating n. to see Mr Gandhi . . . posing as a fakir — GANDHI, 2
navee Ruler of the Queen's N. — GILBERT, W, 12
navy There were gentlemen and . . . seamen in the n. of Charles the Second — MACAULAY, T, 9
Nazi N. Germany had become a menace to all mankind — NEVINS, 1
Nazis In Germany, the N. came for the Communists — NIEMÖLLER, 1

near I wished to be n. my mother — WHISTLER, 18
nearer N., my God, to thee — ADAMS, SARAH, 1
the n. you are to God — WOTTON, 4
nearest the n. run thing you ever saw — WELLINGTON, 7
nearsighted don't raise your hands because I am also n. — AUDEN, 28
neat round, n., not gaudy — LAMB, CHARLES, 25
Nebuchadnezzar N. . . . did eat grass as oxen — BIBLE, 50
necessary Government . . . is but a n. evil — PAINE, 1
necessities disregard for the n. of existence — MAUGHAM, 14
we will dispense with its n. — MOTLEY, 1
necessity I find alone N. Supreme — THOMSON, JAMES, 2
N. is the mother — PROVERBS, 298
N. is the plea — PITT THE YOUNGER, 1
N. knows no law — SYRUS, 5
no virtue like n. — SHAKESPEARE, 294
necht a braw brecht moonlecht n. — LAUDER, 1
neck A short n. denotes a good mind — SPARK, 1
England will have her n. wrung like a chicken — WEYGAND, 1
equipping us with a n. — KOESTLER, 3
go to the bottom with my principles round my n. — BALDWIN, S, 10
my n. is very short — MORE, 4
Some n. — CHURCHILL, W, 59
the Roman people had but one n. — CALIGULA, 1
necking Whoever named it n. — MARX, G, 25
neckline did so without even lowering her n. — WEST, M, 1
neckties men wore their beards, like they wear their n. — LAWRENCE, D, 20
Ned no more work for poor old N. — FOSTER, 6
need An artist . . . produces things that people don't n. — WARHOL, 1
reason not the n. — SHAKESPEARE, 175
Thy n. is yet greater than mine — SIDNEY, P, 4
needle easier for a camel to go through the eye of a n. — BIBLE, 405

needs N. must — PROVERBS, 299
to each according to his n. — MARX, K, 3
needy as for me, I am poor and n. — PSALMS, 24
negation Capitalist production begets . . . its own n. — MARX, K, 5
negative Europe is the unfinished n. — MCCARTHY, M, 4
N. Capability — KEATS, 53
neglect A little n. may breed mischief — FRANKLIN, 5
he devotes to the n. of his duties — THOMPSON, W, 2
negligent Celerity . . . admired . . . by the n. — SHAKESPEARE, 32
Negro One of the things that makes a N. unpleasant to white folk — MENCKEN, 6
neiges les n. d'antan — VILLON, 1
neighbor dedicate this nation to the policy of the good n. — ROOSEVELT, F, 11
my n. . . . who is worth only half a million — VANDERBILT, 2
neighbour better mouse-trap than his n. — EMERSON, 26
death . . . had been his next-door n. — SCOTT, WALTER, 10
Death is my n. now — EVANS, E, 2
Do not love your n. as yourself — SHAW, 27
It's a recession when your n. — TRUMAN, 7
love thy n. as thyself — BIBLE, 411
they helped every one his n. — BIBLE, 212
told men to love their n. — BRECHT, 4
neighbours improper thoughts about . . . n. — BRADLEY, F, 4
make sport for our n. — AUSTEN, 26
neither better if n. of us had been born — NAPOLEON I, 6
Nell Pretty witty N. — PEPYS, 11
Nelly let not poor N. starve — CHARLES II, 1
Nelson keep the N. touch — NEWBOLT, 5
N., born in a fortunate hour — TREVELYAN, 3
The N. touch — NELSON, 1
nephew The enviably attractive n. — KENNEDY, JOHN, 1
Nero just and merciful as N. — ELIZABETH I, 2
nerves It destroys one's n. to be amiable every day — DISRAELI, 15
nervous breakdown One of the symptoms of approaching n. — RUSSELL, B, 6
nest broods a n. of sorrows — TAYLOR, JEREMY, 2
nets Laws are generally found to be n. — SHENSTONE, 1
nettle Out of this n., danger — SHAKESPEARE, 111
stroke a n., And it stings you for your pains — HILL, A, 1
nettles apt to be overrun with n. — WALPOLE, H, 8
neurosis N. has an absolute genius for malingering — PROUST, 10
N. is the way of avoiding non-being — TILLICH, 1
neurotic a highly n. young don — NEWTON, I, 3
Psychiatrists classify a person as n. — SZASZ, 7
the n. ills of an entire generation — LAWRENCE, T, 3
neurotics Everything great in the world is done by n. — PROUST, 20
never Better n. than late — SHAW, 51
I n. would lay down my arms — PITT THE ELDER, 6
Love? I make it constantly but I n. talk about it — PROUST, 7
N., n., n., n. — SHAKESPEARE, 194
our people have n. had it so good — MACMILLAN, 5
Than n. to have loved at all — TENNYSON, 28
nevermore Quoth the Raven, 'N.' — POE, 2
Nevershit like you was Lady N. — WESKER, 3
new a n. heaven and a n. earth — BIBLE, 473
He that will not apply n. remedies — BACON, FRANCIS, 39
He was dull in a n. way — JOHNSON, S, 92
He was the Messiah of the n. age — SLOCOMBE, 1
n. book is published, read an old one — ROGERS, S, 2
n. deal for the American people — ROOSEVELT, F, 9
N. roads: n. ruts — CHESTERTON, 50
n. wine into old bottles — BIBLE, 384
Revolution . . . the setting-up of a n. order — ORTEGA Y GASSET, 2
something n. out of Africa — PLINY THE ELDER, 4
There are no n. truths — MCCARTHY, M, 2
there is no n. thing under the sun — BIBLE, 62
we shall find something n. — VOLTAIRE, 6
We stand today on the edge of a n. frontier — KENNEDY, JOHN, 10
You suddenly understand something . . . in a n. way — LESSING, D, 1
Youth is something very n. — CHANEL, 2
new-found-land my n. — DONNE, 12
newness Americans . . . respect n. — UPDIKE, 3
news Bad n. travels fast — PROVERBS, 77
good n. from a far country — BIBLE, 455
Literature is n. — POUND, 5
n. that's fit to print — OCHS, 1
No n. is good n. — PROVERBS, 314
only n. until he's read it — WAUGH, E, 36
when a man bites a dog that is n. — BOGART, J, 1
newspaper good n. . . . is a nation talking to itself — MILLER, A, 5

I read the n. avidly · BEVAN, 6
Once a n. touches a story, the facts are lost · MAILER, 2
Reading someone else's n. · BRADBURY, 5
With the n. strike on · DAVIS, B, 1
newspapers I'm with you on the free press. It's the n. · STOPPARD, 7
N. always excite curiosity · LAMB, CHARLES, 14
We live under a government of men and . . . n. · PHILLIPS, 1
newt Eye of n., and toe of frog · SHAKESPEARE, 218
Newton God said, *Let N. be* · POPE, 19
What Galileo and N. were to the seventeenth century · DARWIN, C R, 2
Newtons the souls of five hundred . . . N. · COLERIDGE, S, 47
New York From California to N. Island · GUTHRIE, 3
N. is a small place · WODEHOUSE, 18
N. . . . that unnatural city · GILMAN, 2
One belongs to N. instantly · WOLFE, T, 2
Niagara one wouldn't *live* under N. · CARLYLE, 3
nice Be n. to people on your way up · MIZNER, 1
how nasty the n. people can be · POWELL, A, 5
I am a n. man · BENNETT, ARNOLD, 2
N. guys finish last · DUROCHER, 1
Sugar and spice And all that's n. · NURSERY RHYMES, 70
Nicely-Nicely what N. dies of will be over-feeding · RUNYON, 10
nicest English people . . . the *n.* people in the world · LAWRENCE, D, 4
Nicholas St N. soon would be there · MOORE, C, 1
Nick Satan, N., or Clootie · BURNS, R, 3
nickname n. is the heaviest stone · HAZLITT, 12
nicotine his n. . . . moustache · THOMAS, D, 26
Nietzsche N. . . . a confirmed Life Force worshipper · NIETZSCHE, 1
nigger Catch a n. by his toe · NURSERY RHYMES, 11
niggers He's gone whar de good n. go · FOSTER, 6
nigh draw n. to God · BIBLE, 218
night afraid for any terror by n. · PSALMS, 51
An infant crying in the n. · TENNYSON, 30
as a thief in the n. · BIBLE, 503
calm passage . . . across many a bad n. · NIETZSCHE, 11
Come to me in the silence of the n. · ROSSETTI, C, 1
Do not go gentle into that good n. · THOMAS, D, 7
From morn to n., my friend · ROSSETTI, C, 6
Gwine to run all n. · FOSTER, 1
ignorant armies clash by n. · ARNOLD, M, 11
in such a n. Troilus methinks mounted · SHAKESPEARE, 248
It ain't a fit n. out · FIELDS, 1
money in a desk by n. · BALZAC, 4
Morning in the Bowl of N. · FITZGERALD, E, 2
Nature's laws lay hid in n. · POPE, 19
N. and day · PORTER, C, 4
n. was made for loving · BYRON, 42
Oft in the stilly n. · MOORE, T, 7
only one man . . . can count on steady work – the n. watchman · BANKHEAD, 5
real dark n. of the soul · FITZGERALD, F S, 3
returned home the previous n. · BULLER, 1
Ships that pass in the n. · LONGFELLOW, 15
So late into the n. · BYRON, 11
sound of revelry by n. · BYRON, 13
that is past as a watch in the n. · PSALMS, 49
the black bat, n., has flown · TENNYSON, 56
the darkness he called N. · BIBLE, 137
The dark n. of the soul · JOHN OF THE CROSS, 2
the honey'd middle of the n. · KEATS, 11
the morning cometh, and also the n. · BIBLE, 204
The n. is dark, and I am far from home · NEWMAN, J, 3
wish the n. Had borne my breath away · HOOD, 6
nightingale A N. Sang in Berkeley Square · MASCHWITZ, 1
N. . . . A creature of a 'fiery heart' · WORDSWORTH, W, 34
The n. does sit so late · MARVELL, 5
nightingales From Wales Whose n. · THOMAS, E, 5
The n. are singing · ELIOT, T, 22
nightmare History . . . n. from which I am trying to awake · JOYCE, 8
nights a Chequer-board of N. and Days · FITZGERALD, E, 13
The weariest n. . . . must . . . end · ORCZY, 2
They shorten tedious n. · CAMPION, 5
nihilist a part-time n. · CAMUS, 1
Nile dam . . . the N. with bulrushes · CHILD, 3
my serpent of old N. · SHAKESPEARE, 27
Nimrod N. the mighty hunter · BIBLE, 162

nine N. drummers drumming · NURSERY RHYMES, 60
N. for the n. bright shiners · ANONYMOUS, 45
ninepence I have but n. in ready money · ADDISON, 18
ninety stood n. years on the floor · WORK, 2
Nineveh Quinquireme of N. · MASEFIELD, 2
nip I'll n. him in the bud · ROCHE, 2
Nixon N. is the kind of politician · NIXON, 2
N.'s motto · NIXON, 1
standing between N. and the White House · KENNEDY, JOHN, 9
You won't have N. to kick around · NIXON, 5
no . . . girls . . . say N. when they mean Yes · ALCOTT, 3
rebel . . . man who says n. · CAMUS, 1
she can't say 'N.' · PARKER, D, 26
Noah Out of their cataclysm but one poor N. · HUXLEY, A, 18
nobility N. has its own obligations · LÉVIS, 1
The n. . . . snored through the Sermon · BOLT, 2
noble a n. nature . . . treats . . . a serious subject · ARNOLD, M, 32
Englishman never enjoys himself except for a n. purpose · HERBERT, A, 6
n. grounds for the n. emotions · RUSKIN, 5
Ridicule . . . smothers that which is n. · SCOTT, WALTER, 17
The n. living and the n. dead · WORDSWORTH, W, 43
nobleman a king may make a n. · BURKE, E, 24
nobleness perfect n. · ARNOLD, M, 31
noblest n. man That ever lived · SHAKESPEARE, 150
n. Roman of them all · SHAKESPEARE, 160
nobly the immature man . . . wants to die n. for a cause · STEKEL, 1
nobody a man is n. unless his biography · TROLLOPE, 6
I care for n. . . . If no one cares for me · BICKERSTAFFE, 2
N. asked you, sir, she said · NURSERY RHYMES, 71
whom n. loves · CORNFORD, 1
nod A n. is as good as a wink · PROVERBS, 55
the land of N. · BIBLE, 155
nods even excellent Homer n. · HORACE, 9
no go It's n. the picture palace · MACNEICE, 1
noise A loud n. at one end · KNOX, R, 3
dreadful n. of waters in my ears · SHAKESPEARE, 301
the less they have . . . the more n. they make · POPE, 55
the n. of the shout of joy · BIBLE, 130
they . . . love the n. it makes · BEECHAM, 4
Those people . . . are making such a n. · PARKER, HENRY, 1
noises Like n. in a swound · COLERIDGE, S, 26
noisome the n. pestilence · PSALMS, 51
noisy Strongest minds . . . the n. world Hears least · WORDSWORTH, W, 3
The people would be just as n. · CROMWELL, O, 9
noli n. me tangere · BIBLE, 276
nomadic the charm . . . of a n. existence · SACKVILLE-WEST, 5
No Man's Land Absurdist plays take place in N. · ADAMOV, 1
nominated I will not accept if n. · SHERMAN, 1
No-more I am also called N. · ROSSETTI, D, 2
non-being Neurosis is the way of avoiding n. · TILLICH, 1
nonchalance the elegant n. of a duke · CHAPLIN, 3
non-combatant War hath no fury like a n. · MONTAGUE, 1
nonconformist a N. conscience · WILDE, 42
man must be a n. · EMERSON, 14
Why do you have to be a n. · THURBER, 18
nonconformity N. and lust stalking hand in hand · WAUGH, E, 11
none N. but the Brave · DRYDEN, 16
nonsense you intend to talk n. · KEYNES, 1
Non-U U and N. · ROSS, A, 1
non-violence to disagree . . . about . . . n. · HAMPTON, 4
noon From morn To n. he fell · MILTON, 38
from n. to dewy eve · MILTON, 38
O dark, dark, dark, amid the blaze of n. · MILTON, 58
noon-day the sickness that destroyeth in the n. · PSALMS, 51
no one become accustomed to n. governing · LENIN, 5
Norfolk bear him up the N. sky · BETJEMAN, 4
Very flat, N. · COWARD, 16
Norgay Tenzing N. · HILLARY, 1
Norma Jean Goodbye N. · TAUPIN, 1
normal 'n.' people . . . cause no trouble · TAYLOR, A, 6
the n. is so . . . interesting · STEIN, 1
Normans The Saxon is not like us N. · KIPLING, 20
north mad n.-n.-west · SHAKESPEARE, 85
The n. wind does blow · PROVERBS, 403
nose A custom loathsome to the eye, hateful to the n. · JAMES I, 1
A person may be indebted for a n. . . . to a great-aunt · HAZLITT, 25
Dong with a luminous N. · LEAR, 3

Entuned in hir n. ful semely | CHAUCER, 6
Had Cleopatra's n. been shorter | PASCAL, 6
Just as I'm picking my n. | AUDEN, 26
led by the n. with gold | SHAKESPEARE, 354
My n. is huge | ROSTAND, E, 1
Only the n. knows | ALI, 3
This fellow did not see further than his . . . n. | LA FONTAINE, 5
nostrils   God . . . breathed into his n. | BIBLE, 144
not   Believe it or n. | RIPLEY, 1
HOW N. TO DO IT | DICKENS, 22
note   make a n. of | DICKENS, 19
The world will little n., nor long remember | LINCOLN, 17
notes   the pauses between the n. | SCHNABEL, 2
nothin'   You ain't heard n. yet | JOLSON, 1
nothing   Blessed is the man who expects n. | POPE, 60
Certainly, there is n. else here to enjoy | SHAW, 49
certain we can carry n. out | BIBLE, 510
Children aren't happy with n. to ignore | NASH, 8
doing n. for each other | CROSBY, 1
from n. to a state of extreme poverty | MARX, G, 13
God made everything out of n. | VALÉRY, 1
have n. whatever to do with it | MAUGHAM, 26
I had n. to offer anybody | KEROUAC, 3
N. | LOUIS XVI, 1
N. can be created out of n. | LUCRETIUS, 1
n. can bring back the hour | WORDSWORTH, W, 29
n. either good or bad | SHAKESPEARE, 83
N., except my genius | WILDE, 76
N. happens | BECKETT, 2
n. if not critical | SHAKESPEARE, 279
n. is certain but death and taxes | FRANKLIN, 17
n. . . . is greater . . . than one's self | WHITMAN, 9
n. is had for n. | CLOUGH, 2
n. is law that is not reason | POWELL, J, 1
N. long | DRYDEN, 9
N. matters very much | BALFOUR, 6
N. to do but work | KING, B, 1
n. to do with the case | GILBERT, W, 33
N. will come of n. | SHAKESPEARE, 168
opened it only to find – n. | AESOP, 3
Signifying n. | SHAKESPEARE, 225
sooner read a time-table . . . than n. | MAUGHAM, 18
sort of woman . . . one would . . . bury for n. | DICKENS, 30
take *more* than n. | CARROLL, 11
The House of Peers . . . Did n. in particular | GILBERT, W, 20
The temerity to believe in n. | TURGENEV, 2
those who were up to n. | COWARD, 9
To marvel at n. is just about the one and only thing | HORACE, 19
We are n.; less than n., and dreams | LAMB, CHARLES, 4
When you have n. to say, say n. | COLTON, 1
Where some people are very wealthy and others have n. | ARISTOTLE, 8
nothingness   the n. shows through | VALÉRY, 1
notice   The State . . . takes no n. of their opinions | CROMWELL, O, 8
notices   One never n. what has been done | CURIE, 7
nought   Man is like a thing of n. | PSALMS, 72
N.'s had, all's spent | SHAKESPEARE, 215
nourisher   a n. of thine old age | BIBLE, 476
Chief n. in life's feast | SHAKESPEARE, 212
novel   A n. is a mirror | STENDHAL, 1
A n. is a static thing | TYNAN, 1
because a n.'s invented, it isn't true | POWELL, A, 7
good n. tells us the truth | CHESTERTON, 23
I'm going to write the Great Australian N. | WHITE, P, 4
not a n. to be tossed aside lightly | PARKER, D, 16
scrofulous French n. | BROWNING, R, 55
the choice of the moment . . . to begin his n. | SACKVILLE-WEST, 1
the last fashionable n. on the tables of young ladies | MACAULAY, T, 20
The n. being dead | VIDAL, 1
the n. tells a story | FORSTER, 5
The only obligation to which . . . we may hold a n. | JAMES, H, 9
to read a n. before luncheon | WAUGH, E, 45
When I want to read a n. | DISRAELI, 40
novelist   A n. is, like all mortals | NABOKOV, 7
n. who writes nothing for 10 years | PRIESTLEY, 9
novelists   n. the story of the present | GONCOURT, 1
There are many reasons why n. write | FOWLES, 4
novels   characters in one of my n. | FITZGERALD, F S, 15
His n. are marvels of sustained imagination | TOLSTOY, L, 1

one of the few English n. for grown up people | WOOLF, 2
who have to perpetrate thirty bad n. | HUXLEY, A, 1
worse English than Mr Hardy in . . . his n. | HARDY, 4
novelty   N., n., n. | HOOD, 15
November   N. | HOOD, 10
Please to remember the Fifth of N. | ANONYMOUS, 69
Thirty days hath N. | GRAFTON, 1
now   We are all Socialists n. | HARCOURT, 1
nowhere   All dressed up, with n. to go | WHITE, W, 1
He's a real N. Man | LENNON, 8
noxious   the most n. is a tourist | KILVERT, 1
nuclear   the n. defence of Britain | OWEN, D, 1
Wars cannot be fought with n. weapons | MOUNTBATTEN, 6
nude   To keep one from going n. | KING, B, 1
nuisance   exchange of one n. for another n. | ELLIS, 3
Inflation in the Sixties was a n. | LEVIN, 1
Never compose . . . unless . . . not composing . . . becomes a positive n. | HOLST, 1
nuisances   a change of n. is as good as a vacation | LLOYD GEORGE, 17
number   a very interesting n. | RAMANUJAN, 1
Look after n. one | PROVERBS, 266
n. 1 n. 2 man | ACHESON, 1
The greatest happiness of the greatest n. | BENTHAM, 1
numbers   divinity in odd n. | SHAKESPEARE, 256
N. sanctify | CHAPLIN, 4
Round n. | JOHNSON, S, 119
the greatest happiness for the greatest n. | HUTCHESON, 1
up in the high n. | KEYNES, 10
numble   We live in a n. abode | DICKENS, 14
numbness   drowsy n. pains My sense | KEATS, 35
nun   the upbringing a n. would envy | ORTON, 1
nunnery   Get thee to a n. | SHAKESPEARE, 92
nuns   he n. who never take a bath | RUSSELL, B, 7
nuptials   prone to any iteration of n. | CONGREVE, 16
nurse   definition of . . . a n. | NIGHTINGALE, 2
N. unupblown | WAUGH, E, 50
nurses   old men's n. | BACON, FRANCIS, 34
nut   I had a little n. tree | NURSERY RHYMES, 20
nut-brown   the spicy n. ale | MILTON, 18
nutmeg   But a silver n. | NURSERY RHYMES, 20

O

oak   Absalom hanged in an o. | BIBLE, 484
Heart of o. are our ships | GARRICK, 2
To win the palm, the o., or bays | MARVELL, 1
oar   impressions . . . lasting as . . . an o. upon the water | CHOPIN, 3
oat   This bread I break was once the o. | THOMAS, D, 19
oat-cakes   land of Calvin, o., and sulphur | SMITH, SYDNEY, 7
oath   In lapidary inscriptions a man is not upon o. | JOHNSON, S, 99
oaths   O. are but words | BUTLER, S, 6
obedience   As honour, love, o. | SHAKESPEARE, 223
Resistance to tyranny is o. to God. | ANTHONY, 4
The reluctant o. of distant provinces | MACAULAY, T, 5
obedient   a nurse . . . "devoted and o." | NIGHTINGALE, 2
obey   born to o. | COMPTON-BURNETT, 3
children . . . o. your parents | BIBLE, 95
one of those born neither to o. nor to command | MASEFIELD, 1
safer to o. than to rule | KEMPIS, 2
obeyed   Nature . . . must be o. | BACON, FRANCIS, 62
She-who-must-be-o. | HAGGARD, 1
object   o. will be, if possible to form Christian men | ARNOLD, T, 1
objectionable   its own animality either o. or funny | LEWIS, C, 2
obligation   The only o. to which . . . we may hold a novel | JAMES, H, 9
To the University of Oxford I acknowledge no o. | GIBBON, 3
oblige   One should o. everyone to . . . one's ability | LA FONTAINE, 3
oblivion   alms for o. | SHAKESPEARE, 331
that ineluctable o. | HALDANE, 1
oblong   an o. angular figure | LEACOCK, 6
obscene   would not say that our Press is o. | LONGFORD, 2
obscenity   O. . . . happens to shock some elderly . . . magistrate | RUSSELL, B, 25
obscure   I strive to be brief, and I become o. | HORACE, 2
observance   More honour'd in the breach than the o. | SHAKESPEARE, 75
the o. of trifles | DOYLE, 4
observations   To o. which ourselves we make | POPE, 39
observe   Whenever you o. an animal closely | CANETTI, 1
obsessed   O. with self | LAWRENCE, D, 1

obstinacy the name of . . . o. in a bad one   STERNE, 6
obstinate O. people can be divided into   ARISTOTLE, 3
   through his whole life jealous and o.   BURKE, E, 1
obtain so run, that ye may o.   BIBLE, 33
occasions all o. do inform against me   SHAKESPEARE, 99
occupation for ever apologizing for his o.   MENCKEN, 15
occupies every time Hitler o. a country   HITLER, 4
occur Accidents will o.   DICKENS, 17
ocean A life on the o. wave   SARGENT, E, 1
   My Bonnie lies over the o.   ANONYMOUS, 57
   on the o. of life we pass   LONGFELLOW, 15
   We mortals cross the o.   BROWNING, R, 8
   whilst the great o. of truth lay all undiscovered   NEWTON, I, 5
o'clock Three o. is always too late or too early   SARTRE, 7
odd How o. Of God   EWER, 1
   This world is very o. we see   CLOUGH, 4
odds The o. is gone   SHAKESPEARE, 36
odi O. et amo   CATULLUS, 2
odious comparisons are o.   DONNE, 10
   little o. vermin   SWIFT, 7
   One . . . sees the world in an o. light   CHATEAUBRIAND, 2
odium He lived in the o.   BENTLEY, E, 4
odorous Comparisons are o.   SHAKESPEARE, 272
odours O. . . . Live within the sense they quicken   SHELLEY, 25
Odysseus Like O., he looked wiser when seated   WILSON, W, 2
Oedipuses a tense and peculiar family, the O.   BEERBOHM, 21
o'er Returning were as tedious as go o.   SHAKESPEARE, 217
o'er-leaps Vaulting ambition, which o. itself   SHAKESPEARE, 209
off Days o.   TRACY, 2
   O. with his head   CARROLL, 12
offence dire o. from am'rous causes springs   POPE, 48
   greatest o. against virtue   HAZLITT, 14
   It is a public scandal that gives o.   MOLIÈRE, 10
   rock of o.   BIBLE, 199
   The only defence is in o.   BALDWIN, S, 4
offend the kind of pride least likely to o.   RENARD, 1
   Those who o. us are generally punished   TROLLOPE, 16
offended This hand hath o.   CRANMER, 1
   This hath not o. the king   MORE, 5
   When people do not respect us we are sharply o.   TWAIN, 13
offender a most notorious o.   SMOLLETT, 3
offensive extremely o., young man   BIRKENHEAD, 2
office not describe holding public o.   ACHESON, 3
   o. sanctifies the holder   ACTON, 2
   Written by o. boys for o. boys   SALISBURY, 1
officer unbecoming the character of an o.   ANONYMOUS, 6
official O. dignity . . . in inverse ratio to . . . importance   HUXLEY, A, 10
offspring Heaven has granted me no o.   WHISTLER, 13
often Do you come here o.   MILLIGAN, 3
oiled Oozing charm . . . He o. his way   LERNER, 4
oil olive a land of o., and honey   BIBLE, 54
Okie O. use' to mean you was from Oklahoma   STEINBECK, 3
old All evil comes from the o.   ANOUILH, 3
   an o., wild, and incomprehensible man   VICTORIA, 8
   a nourisher of thine o. age   BIBLE, 476
   a sight to make an o. man young   TENNYSON, 14
   at twenty-eight I am a thoroughly o. man   BRONTË, B, 1
   Before we grow o. and die   YEATS, 9
   being o. is having lighted rooms   LARKIN, 2
   Better be an o. man's darling   PROVERBS, 89
   for de o. folks at home   FOSTER, 3
   gift of perpetual o. age   WILDE, 69
   He cannot bear o. men's jokes   FRISCH, 1
   I am o. enough to be – in fact am – your mother   MILNE, 1
   I grow o. . . . I grow o.   ELIOT, T, 14
   I love everything that's o.   GOLDSMITH, 19
   inclination . . . to suppose an o. man decayed in his intellects   JOHNSON, S, 143
   It is so comic to hear oneself called o.   JAMES, A, 1
   I was born o.   TREE, 1
   I will never be an o. man   BARUCH, 1
   man . . . as o. as the woman he feels   MARX, G, 26
   new book is published, read an o. one   ROGERS, S, 2
   no more work for poor o. Ned   FOSTER, 6
   O. men forget   SHAKESPEARE, 134
   O. people are always absorbed   WEBB, S, 1
   O. sins   PROVERBS, 322
   one has to be very o. before one learns how to be amused   BUCK, 3
   'Poor o. Joe'   FOSTER, 5

redress the balance of the O.   CANNING, 3
Tell me the o., o. story   HANKEY, 1
that grand o. man   NORTHCOTE, 1
That is no country for o. men   YEATS, 27
that o. serpent   BIBLE, 465
the misery of an o. man is interesting to nobody   HUGO, 6
the o. have reminiscences   SAKI, 12
the o. have rubbed it into the young that they are wiser   MAUGHAM, 3
the o. is better   BIBLE, 321
The o. man has his death   PROVERBS, 404
There are no o. men any more   USTINOV, 4
There is too much Asia and she is too o.   KIPLING, 18
They shall grow not o.   BINYON, 3
they think he is growing o.   IRVING, 1
thought the o. man . . . had so much blood in him   SHAKESPEARE, 221
too o. to go again to my travels   CHARLES II, 1
When you are o. and gray   YEATS, 33
Where are the boys of the O. Brigade   WEATHERLY, 1
'You are o., Father William'   CARROLL, 6
old age fatal period when o. must be endured   SÉVIGNÉ, 1
   first sign of o.: . . . how young the policemen look   HICKS, 1
   I prefer o. to the alternative   CHEVALIER, M, 2
   o. a regret   DISRAELI, 4
   O., a second child   CHURCHILL, C, 4
   O. brings . . . the comfort   EMERSON, 21
   o. is . . . older than I am   BARUCH, 1
   Why does he die ot o.   LEONARDO DA VINCI, 2
older make way for an o. man   MAUDLING, 1
   O. men declare war   HOOVER, 4
   o. than the rocks among which she sits   PATER, 5
   The o. one grows the more one likes indecency   WOOLF, 8
   to go on getting o.   ADENAUER, 1
old-fashioned o. respect for the young   WILDE, 23
   O. ways which no longer apply to changed conditions   ADDAMS, 1
olfactory an o. bar   WELLS, 6
oligarchy absolute o., or despotism will come   ARISTOTLE, 8
   they that are displeased with aristocracy, call it o.   HOBBES, 6
olive a land of oil o., and honey   BIBLE, 54
   an o. leaf plucked off   BIBLE, 159
Oliver Twist O. has asked for more   DICKENS, 36
Olympic Games The most important thing in the O.   COUBERTIN, 1
Omega Alpha and O.   BIBLE, 459
omelette You can't make an o.   PROVERBS, 474
ominous an idea . . . to be fashionable is o.   SANTAYANA, 13
omnibuses if he had only ridden more in o.   HELPS, 3
omnipotence final proof of God's o.   DE VRIES, 6
on O. with the dance   BYRON, 14
   they get o., then they get honour   ROLLESTON, 1
Onan O. knew that the seed should not be his   BIBLE, 177
Onaway O.! Awake, beloved   LONGFELLOW, 13
once For Christmas comes but o. a year   TUSSER, 3
   O. more unto the breach, dear friends   SHAKESPEARE, 128
   One dies only o.   MOLIÈRE, 4
   you have dined in every house in London – o.   WILDE, 78
   you shall drink twice while I drink o.   WALPOLE, H, 10
one All for o., and o. for all   DUMAS, PÈRE, 1
   have we not all o. father   BIBLE, 342
   if we knew o., we knew two   EDDINGTON, 2
   I have only o. eye   NELSON, 3
   O. could . . . have done so much better for them   WYNDHAM, 1
   O. is o. and all alone   ANONYMOUS, 45
   The number o. book . . . was written by a committee   MAYER, 1
one-eyed o. yellow idol to the north of Khatmandu   HAYES, 1
   the O. Man is King   WELLS, 9
One Great Scorer when the O. comes   RICE, G, 1
one-handed Give me a o. economist   TRUMAN, 9
oneself examine o. . . . before . . . condemning others   MOLIÈRE, 7
   only possible society is o.   WILDE, 18
   stupidity . . . to busy o. with the correction of the world   MOLIÈRE, 6
one up How to be o.   POTTER, S, 2
onions carry their own o. when cycling abroad   COREN, 3
onward little o. lend thy guiding hand   MILTON, 56
   O., Christian soldiers   BARING-GOULD, 2
   O., Christians, o. go   WHITE, H, 1
open I declare this thing o.   PHILIP, PRINCE, 6
   O. Sesame   THE ARABIAN NIGHTS, 2
opened the eyes of the blind shall be o.   BIBLE, 209

opening time   It is always o. in the Sailors Arms   THOMAS, D, 21
open society   the transition . . . to the 'o.'   POPPER, 2
opera   an o. without an interval, or an interval without an o.
NEWMAN, E, 1
Bed . . . is the poor man's o.   HUXLEY, A, 21
Like German o., too long and too loud   WAUGH, E, 52
O. in English   MENCKEN, 17
The first rule in o. is the first rule in life   MELBA, 1
what language an o. is sung in   APPLETON, E, 1
operas   the German text of French o.   WHARTON, 1
opinion   A man . . . must have a very good o. of himself
AUSTEN, 6
better to have no o. of God   BACON, FRANCIS, 52
give him my o.   DICKENS, 7
he is . . . Now but a climate of o.   AUDEN, 15
heresy signifies no more than private o.   HOBBES, 3
I agree with no man's o.   TURGENEV, 1
I am . . . of the o. with the learned   CONGREVE, 5
Nobody holds a good o. of a man who has a low o. of himself
TROLLOPE, 12
nothing to admire except his o.   FRY, C, 2
of his own o. still   BUTLER, S, 8
so vain . . . care for the o. of those we don't care for
ESCHENBACH, 3
the English think of an o. as something . . . to hide   HALSEY, 4
The superiority of one man's o. over another's   JAMES, H, 12
They that approve . . . call it o.   HOBBES, 3
opinionated   the o., the ignorant, and the boorish   ARISTOTLE, 3
opinions   a decent respect to the o. of mankind   JEFFERSON, 2
New o. are always suspected   LOCKE, 1
not a writer's business to hold o.   YEATS, 36
So many men, so many o.   TERENCE, 4
the proper o. for the time of year   AUDEN, 27
The public buys its o. as it buys its meat   BUTLER, S, 15
The State . . . takes no notice of their o.   CROMWELL, O, 4
The wish to spread those o. that we hold   BUTLER, S, 4
opium   an o.-dose for keeping beasts of burden   KINGSLEY, 3
Religion . . . is the o. of the people   MARX, K, 4
opponent   Never ascribe to an o. motives meaner   BARRIE, 13
opportunist   rather be an o. and float   BALDWIN, S, 10
opportunities   A wise man will make more o.   BACON, FRANCIS, 16
opportunity   follies . . . he didn't commit when he had the o.
ROWLAND, H, 2
Never miss an o. to relieve yourself   EDWARD VIII, 2
O. seldom knocks twice   PROVERBS, 331
There is no security . . . only o.   MACARTHUR, 2
oppose   duty . . . to o.   CHURCHILL, R, 1
opposition   Her Majesty's O.   BAGEHOT, 4
I have spent many years . . . in o.   ROOSEVELT, E, 4
The duty of an o.   CHURCHILL, R, 1
When I invented the phrase 'His Majesty's O.'   HOBHOUSE, 1
oppression   when fanatics are on top there is no limit to o.
MENCKEN, 8
Where rumour of o. and deceit   COWPER, 27
optimism   Pessimism . . . is just as agreeable as o.
BENNETT, ARNOLD, 5
optimist   an o. . . . fills up his crossword puzzle in ink   SHORTER, 1
I am an o., unrepentant and militant   USTINOV, 3
The o. proclaims   CABELL, 2
optimistic   O. lies   SHAW, 33
Oracle   'I am Sir O.'   SHAKESPEARE, 236
oracular   the use of my o. tongue   SHERIDAN, R, 9
oral   a terrific story about o. contraception   ALLEN, W, 11
orange   Oh that I were an o.-tree   HERBERT, G, 3
oranges   O. and lemons, Say the bell of St Clement's
NURSERY RHYMES, 41
orangutang   an o. trying to play the violin   BALZAC, 3
orator   Webster is his o.   WEBSTER, D, 2
oratorium   *Laboratorium est o.*   NEEDHAM, 1
orchard   Before the cherry o. was sold   CHEKHOV, 6
orchestra   two golden rules for an o.   BEECHAM, 2
orchestration   Literature is the o. of platitudes   WILDER, T, 7
ordained   o. for the procreation of children
BOOK OF COMMON PRAYER, 24
order   done decently and in o.   BIBLE, 39
O. is heaven's first law   POPE, 37
Revolution is . . . the setting-up of a new o.   ORTEGA Y GASSET, 2
The old o. changeth   TENNYSON, 23
upon the o. of your going   SHAKESPEARE, 216
wisdom . . . sweetly doth . . . o. all things   BIBLE, 521
words in the best o.   COLERIDGE, S, 41

ordered   a side dish he hadn't o.   LARDNER, 1
ordering   the better o. of the universe   ALFONSO THE WISE, 1
orderly   Being o. . . . can be excessively tiresome   BOGARDE, 1
so o. in his way of life   SOCRATES, 2
ordinary   One machine can do the work of fifty o. men
HUBBARD, 1
talent for describing the . . . characters of o. life   AUSTEN, 2
organ   my second favourite o.   ALLEN, W, 6
Seated . . . at the o.   PROCTER, 1
organ-grinder   no reason to attack the monkey when the o. is
present   BEVAN, 9
organic   O. life . . . has developed   RUSSELL, B, 15
organization   a government o. could do it that quickly
CARTER, J, 1
organized   War is an o. bore   HOLMES, O, JR., 1
organs   he'd have given us all more o.   BRADBURY, 7
orgasm   The o. has replaced the Cross   MUGGERIDGE, 2
orgies   o. are vile   NASH, 5
orgy   An o. looks particularly alluring   MUGGERIDGE, 1
you need an o., once in a while   NASH, 5
Orientals   If . . . O. . . . drank a liquor   LA BRUYÈRE, 13
origin   the indelible stamp of his lowly o.   DARWIN, C R, 7
original   An o. writer   CHATEAUBRIAND, 1
Mona did researches in o. sin   PLOMER, 3
o. is unfaithful to the translation   BORGES, 3
The more intelligence . . . the more . . . one finds o.   PASCAL, 2
the only absolutely o. creation   MAUGHAM, 2
thought is often o.   HOLMES, O, 2
originality   absence of inverted commas guarantees . . . o.
FADIMAN, 1
All good things . . . are the fruits of o.   MILL, 3
without o. or moral courage   SHAW, 8
originator   quotes . . . a nodding acquaintance with the o.
WILLIAMS, K, 1
Ormus   Outshone the wealth of O. and of Ind   MILTON, 39
ornamental   not merely . . . useful and o.   STRACHEY, L, 2
orphan   defeat is an o.   KENNEDY, JOHN, 18
orthodoxy   O. is my doxy   WARBURTON, 1
'o.' . . . no longer means being right   CHESTERTON, 16
O. or My-doxy   CARLYLE, T, 17
Oscar   If . . . O. Wilde had lived into his nineties   MUGGERIDGE, 4
We all assume that O. said it   WILDE, 1
You will, O., you will.   WHISTLER, 17
ostrich   the wings of an o.   MACAULAY, T, 2
other   O. people are quite dreadful   WILDE, 18
you expect o. people to be . . . to your liking   KEMPIS, 3
others   By persuading o. we convince ourselves   JUNIUS, 2
delight in . . . misfortunes . . . of o.   BURKE, E, 6
some more than o.   COWARD, 4
tell the o. by their hunted expression   LEWIS, C, 6
to encourage the o.   VOLTAIRE, 7
otherwise   Some folk . . . are o.   SMOLLETT, 4
Otis   Miss O. regrets   PORTER, C, 5
ounce   An o. of a man's own wit   STERNE, 10
ours   We have met the enemy, and they are o.   PERRY, 1
ourselves   all our knowledge is, o. to know   POPE, 36
By persuading others we convince o.   JUNIUS, 2
In every friend we lose a part of o.   POPE, 61
remedies oft in o. do lie   SHAKESPEARE, 20
we but praise o. in other men   POPE, 27
What isn't part of o. doesn't disturb us   HESSE, 1
out   Mordre wol o.   CHAUCER, 11
once o., what you've said can't be stopped   HORACE, 11
O., damned spot   SHAKESPEARE, 220
outlive   o. this powerful rhyme   SHAKESPEARE, 362
outlook   religious o. on life   JUNG, 2
out-of-doors   God having given us indoors and o.   MACAULAY, R, 1
outrun   We may o. . . . And lose by over-running
SHAKESPEARE, 137
outside   I am just going o.   OATES, 1
I support it from the o.   MELBOURNE, 10
outspoken   he is so hearty, so straightforward, o.
ROOSEVELT, T, 1
outward   I may not hope from o. forms   COLERIDGE, S, 11
over   Now the day is o.   BARING-GOULD, 1
overcomes   Who o. By force   MILTON, 27
over-confident   Not that I am ever o.   THATCHER, M, 23
overdressed   overshadowed by his o. . . . wife   STOPES, 6
over-educated   I've o. myself in all the things   COWARD, 21
overexposure   she should catch a cold on o.   BUTLER, S, 18

overfed They're overpaid, o., oversexed and over here
TRINDER, 1
over-feeding what Nicely-Nicely dies of will be o. RUNYON, 10
overlooked better to be looked over than o. WEST, M, 12
overlord o. of the M5 HILL, G, 3
overpaid They're o., overfed, oversexed and over here
TRINDER, 1
overpaying o. him but he's worth it GOLDWYN, 4
overrated matrimony . . . a highly o. performance DUNCAN, 4
overrun apt to be o. with nettles WALPOLE, H, 8
over-running and lose by o. SHAKESPEARE, 137
oversexed They're overpaid, overfed, o. and over here
TRINDER, 1
overtakers It is the o. who PITTS, 1
overthrown Another mighty empire o. WORDSWORTH, W, 51
overtures I tried to resist his o. PERELMAN, 3
owe I don't o. a penny to a single soul WODEHOUSE, 12
owed so much o. by so many to so few CHURCHILL, W, 54
owes he o. not any man LONGFELLOW, 17
owl The O. and the Pussy-Cat went to sea LEAR, 8
owls Two O. and a Hen LEAR, 1
own mine o. Executioner DONNE, 6
owner o. of the business arrived in a Bentley JAMES, C, 2
ownership its source of power: o. KINNOCK, 4
transform this society without . . . extension of public o.
KINNOCK, 1
own-goal Aids pandemic is a classic o. ANNE, 4
ox When he stands like an o. in the furrow KIPLING, 20
Oxenford Clerk . . . of O. CHAUCER, 11
Oxford a secret in the O. sense FRANKS, 1
It is O. that has made me insufferable BEERBOHM, 9
nice sort of place, O. SHAW, 22
O. is on the whole more attractive than Cambridge BAEDEKER, 1
The clever men at O. Know all that there is to be knowed
GRAHAME, 2
To O. sent a troop of horse TRAPP, 1
To the University of O. I acknowledge no obligation GIBBON, 3
You will hear more good things on . . . a stagecoach from London
to O. HAZLITT, 10
you will leave O. by the town drain SPOONER, 5
oyster bold man . . . swallowed an o. JAMES I, 6
bold man that first eat an o. SWIFT, 12
sympathetic unselfishness of an o. SAKI, 6
the sort of eye that can open an o. at sixty paces WODEHOUSE, 6
world's mine o. SHAKESPEARE, 254
oysters Poverty and o. DICKENS, 46
Ozymandias 'My name is O.' SHELLEY, 17

P

pace this petty p. from day to day SHAKESPEARE, 225
Pacific The Admiral of the Atlantic salutes the Admiral of the P.
WILHELM II, 3
pack dogs are animated when they hunt in a p. HUME, D, 6
the human p. is shuffled and cut LODGE, 3
paddle every man p. his own canoe MARRYAT, 3
padlocked music critics. . . . with p. ears STRAVINSKY, 3
pagan A P. suckled in a creed outworn WORDSWORTH, W, 65
pageant insubstantial p. faded SHAKESPEARE, 325
paid I do not answer questions like this without being p.
HELLMAN, 3
pain a gentleman . . . never inflicts p. NEWMAN, J, 2
Although p. isn't real ANONYMOUS, 90
critics . . . desire our blood, not our p. NIETZSCHE, 15
disinclination to inflict p. upon oneself MEREDITH, G, 3
I feel no p., dear mother, now ANONYMOUS, 43
I have no p., dear mother, now FARMER, 1
momentary intoxication with p. BRONOWSKI, 4
Neither shame nor physical p. have any . . . effect KEY, E, 4
owes its pleasures to another's p. COWPER, 31
P. – has an Element of Blank DICKINSON, 4
P. of mind is worse than p. of body SYRUS, 3
Pleasure is . . . intermission of p. SELDEN, 4
The least p. in our little finger HAZLITT, 3
The p. passes, but the beauty remains RENOIR, 1
they blest him in their p. TENNYSON, 70
what p. it was to drown SHAKESPEARE, 301
yearning like a God in p. KEATS, 12
pained greatly p. at how little he was p. WAUGH, E, 23
pains no gains without p. STEVENSON, A, 4

paint A professional is someone whose wife works to enable him
to p. SHAHN, 1
flinging a pot of p. in the public's face RUSKIN, 17
My business is to p. . . . what I see TURNER, 1
to p. the lily SHAKESPEARE, 165
two hundred guineas for flinging a pot of p. WHISTLER, 1
painted As idle as a p. ship COLERIDGE, S, 28
I am p. as the greatest little dictator THATCHER, M, 17
Most women are not so young as they are p. BEERBOHM, 7
p. . . . by the great artist Kodak MILLIGAN, 2
painter I am married to Beatrice Salkeld, a p. BEHAN, 10
I could have become a real p. HOKUSAI, 1
memory is a p. GRANDMA MOSES, 1
who is not a great . . . p. can be an architect RUSKIN, 3
painters Good p. imitate nature CERVANTES, 23
P. and poets . . . licence to dare anything HORACE, 1
Poets and p. are outside the class system BRENAN, 6
painting a great difference between p. a face FULLER, T, 1
If I didn't start p., I would have raised chickens
GRANDMA MOSES, 2
If people only knew . . . about p. LANDSEER, 1
I just keep p. till I feel like pinching RENOIR, 2
P. is a blind man's profession PICASSO, 6
paintings the women in his p. PICASSO, 4
pajamas I shot an elephant in my p. MARX, G, 2
Pakistani writes like a P. SHAW, 2
palace Love in a p. KEATS, 24
palaces Mid pleasures and p. though we may roam PAYNE, 1
pale a p. horse BIBLE, 407
Palestine establishment in P. of a national home for the Jewish
people BALFOUR, 4
not enough prisons . . . in P. to hold all the Jews MEIR, 7
pall The pallor of girls' brows shall be their p. OWEN, W, 1
Palladium Liberty of the press is the P. of . . . rights JUNIUS, 1
pallor The p. of girls' brows shall be their pall OWEN, W, 1
palm getting the victor's p. without the dust of racing
HORACE, 14
To win the p., the oak, or bays MARVELL, 1
palms p. before my feet CHESTERTON, 13
they found no more of her than . . . the p. of her hands
BIBLE, 303
palm-tree the righteous shall flourish like a p. PSALMS, 52
palsied with the p. heart TENNYSON, 52
pan Put on the p.; Says Greedy Nan NURSERY RHYMES, 7
Pandora open that P.'s Box . . . Trojan 'orses will jump out
BEVIN, 2
Panjandrum the grand P. FOOTE, 1
pantheist The modern p. not only LAWRENCE, D, 21
pants There were times my p. were so thin TRACY, 1
Your eyes shine like the p. MARX, G, 4
papacy Since God has given us the p. . . . enjoy it LEO X, 1
The P. is not other than the Ghost of the deceased Roman
Empire HOBBES, 7
paper only a p. moon HARBURG, 1
reactionaries are p. tigers MAO TSE-TUNG, 5
The atom bomb is a p. tiger MAO TSE-TUNG, 9
This p. will no doubt be found interesting DALTON, 1
Where were you fellows when the p. was blank ALLEN, F, 2
papers fornicated and read the p. CAMUS, 6
only two posh p. on a Sunday OSBORNE, 2
papyromania P. – compulsive accumulation PETER, 1
papyrophobia P. – abnormal desire PETER, 1
parables great p. . . . but false art LAWRENCE, D, 42
parade the chief employment of riches consists in the p. of riches
SMITH, A, 2
paradise A p. for a sect KEATS, 15
drunk the milk of P. COLERIDGE, S, 17
England is a p. for women BURTON, ROBERT, 4
England is the p. of women FLORIO, 1
England is the p. of individuality SANTAYANA, 9
Grant me p. in this world TINTORETTO, 1
If a man could pass through P. COLERIDGE, S, 4
Same old glimpse of P. LAMPTON, 1
to hope for p. on a Sunday SACKVILLE-WEST, 4
Wilderness is P. enow FITZGERALD, E, 5
paragon the p. of animals SHAKESPEARE, 84
parallel We never remark any passion . . . of which . . . we may
not find a p. HUME, D, 5
parallelogram The landlady . . . is a p. LEACOCK, 6
paralyse p. it by encumbering it with remedies TOLSTOY, L, 11
paranoid Even a p. can have enemies KISSINGER, 5

parasite A crawling and disgusting p. VIRGIL, 1
parcels Portions and p. of the dreadful Past TENNYSON, 54
pardon God may p. you, but I never can ELIZABETH I, 5
God will p. me. It is His trade HEINE, 5
the government that should ask me for a p. DEBS, 1
pardoned The women p. all BYRON, 30
parent a kind p. . . . or a merciless step-mother PLINY THE ELDER, 3
To lose one p. . . . a misfortune WILDE, 26
parents A Jewish man with p. alive ROTH, 2
by defying their p. and copying one another CRISP, 2
children, obey your p. BIBLE, 95
From birth to age eighteen, a girl needs good p. TUCKER, 3
joys of p. are secret BACON, FRANCIS, 38
P. learn a lot from their children SPARK, 2
Possessive p. rarely live long enough to see GARNER, 1
what p. were created for NASH, 8
Paris delivered of a city bigger than P. LA FONTAINE, 6
Good Americans, when they die, go to P. APPLETON, T, 1
I love P. PORTER, C, 3
Is P. burning HITLER, 17
no home . . . save in P. NIETZSCHE, 7
P. is worth a mass HENRI IV, 2
when good Americans die they go to P. WILDE, 57
parish all the world as my p. WESLEY, J, 1
He was born, bred, and hanged, all in the same p. ANONYMOUS, 34
park The hunchback in the p. THOMAS, D, 12
Parkinson's Law The rise in the . . . employed is governed by P. PARKINSON, 2
par-lee-voo Hinky, dinky, p. ROWLAND, E, 1
Parliament build your House of P. upon the river WELLINGTON, 14
He stood twice for P. WAUGH, E, 21
If Her Majesty stood for P. SPEIGHT, 2
P. is the longest running farce SMITH, SIR CYRIL, 2
Three Estates in P. CARLYLE, T, 13
parliaments England . . . mother of p. BRIGHT, 1
parlour 'Will you walk into my p.?' HOWITT, 1
parlourmaid a p. as ignorant as Queen Victoria VICTORIA, 4
parochial worse than provincial – he was p. JAMES, H, 7
parody devil's walking p. CHESTERTON, 12
parole Classical quotation is the *p.* of literary men JOHNSON, S, 137
parrot to sell the family p. ROGERS, W, 12
parsnips fine words butter no p. SCOTT, WALTER, 11
parson If P. lost his senses HODGSON, 1
In arguing too, the p. own'd his skill GOLDSMITH, 7
Once a p. PROVERBS, 324
p. in a tye-wig ADDISON, 2
part I have forgot my p. SHAKESPEARE, 59
In every friend we lose a p. of ourselves POPE, 61
it is a little flesh and breath, and the ruling p. MARCUS AURELIUS, 1
let us kiss and p. DRAYTON, 2
read p. of it all the way GOLDWYN, 18
till death us do p. BOOK OF COMMON PRAYER, 27
We only p. to meet again GAY, 12
particular a London p. . . . A fog DICKENS, 5
did nothing in p. GILBERT, W, 20
particulars Minute P. BLAKE, W, 16
parties it is always like that at p. PROUST, 14
one of those p. which got out of hand BRUCE, 2
parting Every p. gives a foretaste of death SCHOPENHAUER, 3
P. is all we know of heaven DICKINSON, 2
P. is such sweet sorrow SHAKESPEARE, 312
partisanship P. is our great curse ROBINSON, J, 2
partly Man p. is BROWNING, R, 21
partridge A p. in a pear tree NURSERY RHYMES, 54
well-shot woodcock, p., snipe BETJEMAN, 4
parts It is seldom . . . one p. on good terms PROUST, 17
one man in his time plays many p. SHAKESPEARE, 47
Today we have naming of p. REED, H, 2
truth in the inward p. PSALMS, 31
part-time p. nihilist CAMUS, 4
party A great p. is not to be brought down HAILSHAM, 3
best number for a dinner p. is two GULBENKIAN, 1
Heard there was a p. LILLIE, 2
I always voted at my p.'s call GILBERT, W, 10
The p. is the rallying-point for the . . . working class STALIN, 4
The sooner every p. breaks up the better AUSTEN, 8
Well, did you evah! What a swell p. PORTER, C, 6

pass but let it p., let it p. THURBER, 17
Horseman, p. by YEATS, 32
ideas simply p. through him BRADLEY, F, 6
I shall not p. this way again GRELLET, 1
p. for forty-three GILBERT, W, 45
p. through things temporal BOOK OF COMMON PRAYER, 5
Praise the Lord and p. the ammunition FORGY, 1
They shall not p. IBARRURI, 1
To p. away ere life hath lost its brightness HASTINGS, 1
passage calm p. . . . across many a bad night NIETZSCHE, 11
Patience and p. of time LA FONTAINE, 4
who could see the p. of a goddess HOMER, 1
passageways smell of steaks in p. ELIOT, T, 19
passed p. by on the other side BIBLE, 324
p. from death unto life BIBLE, 248
That p. the time BECKETT, 3
the people were p. clean over Jordan BIBLE, 287
We have all p. a lot of water GOLDWYN, 17
passengers fools and p. drink at sea VILLIERS, 1
passeront *Ils ne p. pas* PÉTAIN, 2
passes Men seldom make p. PARKER, D, 27
passeth the peace of God, which p. all understanding BIBLE, 445
passion All breathing human p. far above KEATS, 31
cheated into p., but . . . reasoned into truth DRYDEN, 30
Culture is the p. for sweetness and light ARNOLD, M, 23
desolate and sick of an old p. DOWSON, 3
Master Mistress of my p. SHAKESPEARE, 359
one master-p. . . . swallows up the rest POPE, 35
p. and party blind our eyes COLERIDGE, S, 23
P. . . . can be destroyed by a doctor SHAFFER, 2
p. in the human soul LILLO, 1
So I triumphed ere my p. TENNYSON, 52
Strange fits of p. WORDSWORTH, W, 66
The p. and the life, whose fountains are within COLERIDGE, S, 11
The ruling p. conquers reason still POPE, 45
We never remark any p. . . . in others HUME, D, 5
passions A man who has not passed through the inferno of his p. JUNG, 3
It is with our p. as it is with fire and water L'ESTRANGE, 1
Literature and butterflies are the two sweetest p. NABOKOV, 8
not his reason, but his p. STERNE, 8
The man who is master of his p. CONNOLLY, 20
Three p. . . . have governed my life RUSSELL, B, 4
passover it is the Lord's p. BIBLE, 110
past Even God cannot change the p. AGATHON, 1
half of you belongs to the p. ANOUILH, 2
Historians tell the story of the p. GONCOURT, 1
I do not . . . prejudge the p. WHITELAW, 2
Keep off your thoughts from things that are p. WALEY, 1
looking forward to the p. OSBORNE, 5
people who live in the p. BENNETT, ARNOLD, 4
Portions and parcels of the dreadful P. TENNYSON, 54
remembrance of things p. SHAKESPEARE, 361
something . . . absurd about the p. BEERBOHM, 3
Study the p. CONFUCIUS, 4
that is p. as a watch in the night PSALMS, 49
The p., at least, is secure WEBSTER, D, 5
The p. is a foreign country HARTLEY, 2
The p. is the only dead thing THOMAS, E, 2
The p. was a sleep BROWNING, R, 56
The p. was nothing CHOPIN, 2
Those who cannot remember the p. SANTAYANA, 6
Time present and time p. ELIOT, T, 6
to know nothing but . . . the p. KEYNES, 2
what is p. my help is p. my care BEAUMONT, 2
what's p. help Should be p. grief SHAKESPEARE, 349
What we know of the p. is INGE, 1
Who can afford to live in the p. PINTER, 3
Who controls the p. controls the future ORWELL, 15
Pastoral Cold P. KEATS, 29
pasture the people of his p. PSALMS, 56
pastures fresh woods, and p. new MILTON, 27
he maketh me to lie down in green p. PSALMS, 12
pat P.-a-cake, p.-a-cake, baker's man NURSERY RHYMES, 42
P. it and prick it, and mark it with B NURSERY RHYMES, 42
patches king of shreds and p. SHAKESPEARE, 98
thing of shreds and p. GILBERT, W, 23
pate You beat your p. POPE, 9
patent The people – could you p. the sun SALK, 1
path the primrose p. of dalliance SHAKESPEARE, 72
world will make a . . . p. to his door EMERSON, 26

P. are not fallen angels	LAWRENCE, D, 42
p. are the masters	BURKE, E, 18
p. may be made to follow a course of action	CONFUCIUS, 11
P. must help one another	LA FONTAINE, 8
p.'s government	WEBSTER, D, 4
p. standing in the corners of our rooms	COREN, 6
p. under suspicion are better moving	KAFKA, 4
p. . . . usually imitate each other	HOFFER, 1
P. who like this sort of thing	LINCOLN, 19
P. who need p. are the luckiest	MERRILL, 1
p. whose company is coveted	MACCARTHY, 1
p. who stay in the middle of the road	LINCOLN, 6
P. will cross the road . . . to say 'We saw you on the telly'	
	CRISP, 1
Religion . . . is the opium of the p.	MARX, K, 4
show my head to the p.	DANTON, 2
the bludgeoning of the p.	WILDE, 54
The Lord prefers common-looking p.	LINCOLN, 6
the p. are forbidden to light lamps	MAO TSE-TUNG, 10
The p. – could you patent the sun	SALK, 1
the p. of his pasture	PSALMS, 56
The p.'s flag is deepest red	CONNELL, 1
the p. we should have been seen dead with	WEST, R, 7
The p. would be just as noisy	CROMWELL, O, 9
The right p. are rude	MAUGHAM, 15
The Swiss . . . are not a p. so much as a . . . business	
	FAULKNER, 1
They didn't act like p.	SALINGER, 3
This country . . . belongs to the p.	LINCOLN, 3
thy p. shall be my p.	BIBLE, 475
two p. with one pulse	MACNEICE, 2
we are not a small p.	HEATH, 1
When . . . necessary for one p. to dissolve . . . political bonds	
	JEFFERSON, 4
When p. come together, flowers always flourish	JACKSON, J, 1
When the P. contend for their Liberty	HALIFAX, 6
You can fool too many of the p.	THURBER, 9
Pepper Sergeant P.'s Lonely Hearts Club Band	LENNON, 9
pepper Peter Piper picked a peck of pickled p.	
	NURSERY RHYMES, 43
perception any truth but from a clear p.	KEATS, 63
doors of p. were cleansed	BLAKE, W, 19
prime agent of all human p.	COLERIDGE, S, 5
perceptions Man's Desires are limited by his P.	BLAKE, W, 49
perestroika 'p.' has easily entered the international lexicon	
	GORBACHOV, 1
perfect A cigarette is . . . a p. pleasure	WILDE, 51
be ye therefore p.	BIBLE, 366
p. in a short time	BIBLE, 519
p. love casteth out fear	BIBLE, 283
perfection attain to the divine p.	LONGFELLOW, 9
Culture being a pursuit of our total p.	ARNOLD, M, 3
Finality is death. P. is finality	STEPHENS, 1
The pursuit of p.	ARNOLD, M, 5
performance desire should . . . outlive p.	SHAKESPEARE, 120
it takes away the p.	SHAKESPEARE, 213
verses . . . as a literary p.	WHITMAN, 2
performed p. worst when I . . . wished to do better	SIDDONS, 1
performing English literature's p. flea	O'CASEY, 4
perfume As a p. doth remain	SYMONS, 1
perfumes All the p. of Arabia	SHAKESPEARE, 222
perhaps I am going in search of a great p.	RABELAIS, 10
The grand P.	BROWNING, R, 10
peril For those in p. on the sea	WHITING, 1
perils smile at p. past	SCOTT, WALTER, 3
periods Decades . . . are not . . . p. at all	MACAULAY, R, 2
perish man . . . compared unto the beasts that p.	PSALMS, 29
P. the Universe	CYRANO DE BERGERAC, 1
they . . . shall p. with the sword	BIBLE, 428
though the world p.	FERDINAND I, 1
weak shall p.	SERVICE, 3
whoever believeth not . . . shall p.	KORAN, 1
periwig with my mourning . . . and new p.	PEPYS, 15
perjury P. . . . is truth that is shamefaced	DARLING, 4
permanence love p. more than . . . beauty	CASSON, 1
permissive The p. society	JENKINS, 1
pernicious the most p. race	SWIFT, 7
Perón If I had not been born P.	PERÓN, J, 1
perpetrate who have to p. thirty bad novels	HUXLEY, A, 1
perpetual gift of p. old age	WILDE, 69
Literary men are . . . a p. priesthood	CARLYLE, T, 8

perpetuation Why should I consent to the p. of the image of this	
image	PLOTINUS, 1
persecutest Saul, why p. thou me	BIBLE, 6
perseverance p. that he withheld from books and ideas	
	EISENHOWER, 2
the name of p. in a good cause	STERNE, 6
persistent The most p. sound . . . through men's history	
	KOESTLER, 5
person A p. may be indebted for a nose or an eye	HAZLITT, 25
My idea of an agreeable p.	DISRAELI, 11
the only p. . . . I should like to know	WILDE, 40
the only thing that can exist is an uninterested p.	CHESTERTON, 17
The world regards such a p. as . . . an unmuzzled dog	
	HUXLEY, T, 4
to the cheek of a young p.	DICKENS, 39
personal They do those little p. things	MILLER, J, 2
personalities all . . . p. in . . . history reappear	MARX, K, 6
first of the modern p.	BANKHEAD, 3
personality Simply a radio p.	WAUGH, E, 47
persons God is no respecter of p.	BIBLE, 10
I am made up of several p.	MAUGHAM, 24
Such p. are often good	HUME, B, 1
perspective What a delightful thing this p. is	UCCELLO, 1
perspire he never seemed to p.	FITZGERALD, F S, 10
persuade Beauty . . . doth . . . p. the eyes of men	
	SHAKESPEARE, 356
perverse the most p. and malevolent creature	HAZLITT, 2
perversion that melancholy sexual p.	HUXLEY, A, 8
War is . . . universal p.	RAE, 1
pervert Once: a philosopher; twice: a p.	VOLTAIRE, 38
p. climbs into the minds	BRONOWSKI, 4
pessimism P. is a luxury	MEIR, 4
P. . . . is just as agreeable as optimism	BENNETT, ARNOLD, 5
pessimist A p. is a man who	PETER, 3
Scratch a p.	BEVERIDGE, 2
the p. fears this is true	CABELL, 2
pessimists p. end up by desiring the things they fear	MALLET, 1
pestiferous Such teaching is p.	LIVERMORE, 1
pestilence the noisome p.	PSALMS, 51
the p. that walketh in darkness	PSALMS, 51
Peter has been wholly in P. Pan ever since	COWARD, 1
One named P.	NURSERY RHYMES, 68
P. Piper picked a peck of pickled pepper	NURSERY RHYMES, 43
Shock-headed P.	HOFFMAN, 1
thou art P.	BIBLE, 397
petrified a man suffering from p. adolescence	BEVAN, 3
petticoat modesty . . . put it on again with her p.	MONTAIGNE, 4
pettiness I have something to expiate; A p.	LAWRENCE, D, 29
petty the p. fools of rhyme	TENNYSON, 48
petulance A certain girlish p. of style	RUSKIN, 1
p. is not sarcasm	DISRAELI, 26
pews Talk about the p. and steeples	CHESTERTON, 1
phallic the deterrent is a p. symbol	WIGG, 1
Pharisees Now is the time of P.	PASTERNAK, 1
phenomena chess . . . pieces . . . the p. of the universe	
	HUXLEY, T, 6
philanthropy The spacious p. which he exhaled	WILSON, W, 1
Philistines great apostle of the P., Lord Macaulay	ARNOLD, M, 21
society distributes itself into . . . P.	ARNOLD, M, 4
the designation of P.	ARNOLD, M, 7
to distinguish . . . the aristocratic class from the P.	ARNOLD, M, 8
philosopher I doubt if the p. lives	HUXLEY, T, 5
In the p. there is nothing whatever impersonal	NIETZSCHE, 14
never yet p. That could endure	SHAKESPEARE, 275
Once: a p.; twice: a pervert	VOLTAIRE, 38
Organic life . . . has developed . . . from the protozoon to the p.	
	RUSSELL, B, 15
some p. has said it	CICERO, 1
To a p. no circumstance . . . is too minute	GOLDSMITH, 5
philosophers now-a-days professors of philosophy but not p.	
	THOREAU, 11
P. never balance between profit and honesty	HUME, D, 8
the English are . . . the least a nation of pure p.	BAGEHOT, 6
till p. become kings	PLATO, 4
philosophical The Arab . . . more p. than	FRANCE, 4
philosophy a great advantage for . . . p. to be . . . true	
	SANTAYANA, 12
Art and religion first; then p.	SPARK, 9
Axioms in p. are not axioms	KEATS, 59
collection of prejudices which is called political p.	RUSSELL, B, 26
dreamt of in your p.	SHAKESPEARE, 78

History is p. . . . by examples	DIONYSIUS OF HALICARNASSUS, 1	P. . . . washed his hands	BIBLE, 430
mere touch of cold p.	KEATS, 25	rather have blood on my hands . . . P.	GREENE, 3
necessary for a superstition to enslave a p.	INGE, 5	**pilgrim** p. of the sky	WORDSWORTH, W, 73
new P. calls all in doubt	DONNE, 3	**Pill** Protestant women may take the P.	THOMAS, I, 1
Not to care for p.	PASCAL, 2	**pillar** a p. of a cloud	BIBLE, 111
now-a-days professors of p. but not philosophers	THOREAU, 11	a p. of salt	BIBLE, 168
p. and vain deceit	BIBLE, 19	the lie has become . . . a p. of the State	SOLZHENITSYN, 14
P. . . . is a fight against . . . fascination	WITTGENSTEIN, 1	triple p. of the world	SHAKESPEARE, 24
P. is not a theory	WITTGENSTEIN, 4	**pillars** wisdom . . . hath hewn out her seven p.	BIBLE, 448
P. is the product of wonder	WHITEHEAD, 4	**pilot** Dropping the p.	TENNIEL, 1
P. is the replacement	RYLE, 1	**Pimpernel** That damned elusive P.	ORCZY, 1
p. ought to . . . unravel people's mental blocks	RAPHAEL, 2	**pin** If I sit on a p.	ANONYMOUS, 90
Socrates was the first to call p. down	SOCRATES, 1	See a p. and pick it up	PROVERBS, 357
Vain wisdom all, and false p.	MILTON, 41	you are like a p.	JERROLD, 3
Western p. . . . footnotes to Plato's p.	WHITEHEAD, 4	**Pinafore** Captain of the P.	GILBERT, W, 7
phobias I have three p.	BANKHEAD, 4	**pinch** time for me to enjoy another p. of snuff	BAILLY, 1
phone Death invented the p.	HUGHES, TED, 1	**pinching** I just keep painting till I feel like p.	RENOIR, 2
why did you answer the p.	THURBER, 15	**pine-apple** p. of politeness	SHERIDAN, R, 8
phoney to dismiss him as a p.	SARTRE, 1	**pinko-gray** white races are . . . p.	FORSTER, 10
phoneyness p. . . . a lot of it at Wimbledon	MCENROE, 1	**pint** one cannot put a quart in a p. cup	GILMAN, 1
phonus bolonus is nothing but a p.	RUNYON, 4	You spend half a p. and flush two gallons	PHILIP, PRINCE, 3
photograph A p. is not only an image	SONTAG, 2	**pious** A p. man . . . would be an atheist	LABRUYÈRE, 1
she took down the signed p. of the Kaiser	WAUGH, E, 42	p. bird with the scarlet breast	WORDSWORTH, W, 44
photography P. can never grow up if it imitates	ABBOTT, 1	p. frauds of friendship	FIELDING, 2
P. is truth	GODARD, 1	**pipe** Blow your p. there	BROWNING, R, 44
physic Take p., pomp	SHAKESPEARE, 181	He called for his p.	NURSERY RHYMES, 38
physical a p. and metaphysical impossibility	CARLYLE, T, 3	**piped** their fountains p. an answer	LAWRENCE, D, 6
physician I died . . . of my p.	PRIOR, 1	**Piper** Peter P. picked a peck of pickled pepper	NURSERY
if the p. had the same disease upon him that I have	SELDEN, 5		RHYMES, 41
p., heal thyself	BIBLE, 320	**pipers** Wi' a hundred p. an' a', an' a'	NAIRNE, 3
The p. can bury his mistakes	WRIGHT, F, 1	**piping** Helpless, naked, p. loud	BLAKE, W, 38
the p. cutteth off a long disease	BIBLE, 84	P. down the valleys wild	BLAKE, W, 41
young p. fattens the churchyard	PROVERBS, 76	**pips** squeezed – until the p. squeak	GEDDES, 1
physicians P. are like kings	WEBSTER, J, 2	**piss** I can p. the old boy	LIEBERMANN, 1
the help of too many p.	ALEXANDER THE GREAT, 1	**piss-a-bed** Here is Johnny Keats' p. poetry	KEATS, 5
physicists The p. have known sin	OPPENHEIMER, 2	**pissed** the last four strikes we've had, it's p. down	SPEIGHT, 4
to find out anything from the theoretical p.	EINSTEIN, 5	**pissing** inside my tent p. out	JOHNSON, L, 7
physics Modern P. is an instrument of Jewry	TOMASCHEK, 1	**pistol** a p. let off at the ear	LAMB, CHARLES, 16
physiology an important part of reproductive p.	AVICENNA, 1	**pitchfork** drive out nature with a p.	HORACE, 20
pianist do not shoot the p.	WILDE, 37	**pith** all the p. is in the postscript	HAZLITT, 6
the only p. . . . who did not grimace	STRAVINSKY, 2	**pitied** one has . . . ceased to be an object of *fear* as soon as one	
Piatigorsky Gregor P.	HEIFETZ, 1	is p.	NIETZSCHE, 18
Picardy Roses are flowering in P.	WEATHERLY, 2	**pitiless** slow, sure doom falls p. and dark	RUSSELL, B, 16
Picasso Nothing divides them like P.	MILLS, 1	**pits** You are the p.	MCENROE, 2
There's no such thing as a bad P.	PICASSO, 5	**Pitt** P. is to Addington	CANNING, 2
Piccadilly Crossing P. Circus	THOMSON, JAMES, 1	**pity** A p. beyond all telling	YEATS, 25
Good-bye P., Farewell Leicester Square	WILLIAMS, H, 1	knock him down first, and p. him afterwards	JOHNSON, S, 105
pick Whenever you fall, p. up something	AVERY, 1	My subject is War, and the p. of War	OWEN, W, 6
pickle weaned on a p.	LONGWORTH, 1	P. a human face	BLAKE, W, 4
picnic futile to attempt a p. in Eden	BOWEN, ELIZABETH, 5	p. for the suffering of mankind	RUSSELL, B, 4
picture Every p. tells a story	PROVERBS, 143	The Poetry is in the p.	OWEN, W, 5
Every time I make a p.	DE MILLE, 1	'Tis P, She's a Whore	FORD, JOHN, 2
how did you love my p.	GOLDWYN, 23	To marry a man out of p. is folly	ASQUITH, M, 1
If you want a p. of the future	ORWELL, 16	To show p. is felt as a sign of contempt	NIETZSCHE, 18
pictures book . . . without p.	CARROLL, 4	**place** A p. for everything	SMILES, 2
would never buy my p.	LANDSEER, 1	everything in its p.	SMILES, 2
pidgin-English I include 'p.'	PHILIP, PRINCE, 1	firm p. to stand	ARCHIMEDES, 1
Pie Amblongus P.	LEAR, 6	give p. to better men	CROMWELL, O, 7
pie p. in the sky when you die	ALI, 4	Home is the p. where	FROST, R, 3
piece p. of cod passes all understanding	LUTYENS, 2	I go to prepare a p. for you	BIBLE, 258
p. of divinity in us	BROWNE, T, 11	Never the time and the p.	BROWNING, R, 36
Prologues precede the p.	GARRICK, 1	running . . . to keep in the same p.	CARROLL, 24
What a p. of work is a man	SHAKESPEARE, 84	there's no p. like home	PAYNE, 1
When a p. gets difficult	SCHNABEL, 1	the summit of Everest was hardly the p.	HILLARY, 1
pieces P. of eight	STEVENSON, R, 9	the wrong p. at the wrong time	JOHNSON, L, 1
pie-crust Promises and p. are made to be broken	SWIFT, 10	this is an awful p.	SCOTT, R, 1
pieman Simple Simon met a p.	NURSERY RHYMES, 51	Upon the p. beneath	SHAKESPEARE, 246
pier Like Brighton p.	KINNOCK, 7	**plague** A p. o' both your houses	SHAKESPEARE, 315
Pierian Drink deep, or taste not the P. spring	POPE, 23	gods . . . Make instruments to p. us	SHAKESPEARE, 193
pies I could eat one of Bellamy's veal p.	PITT THE YOUNGER, 3	P. still increasing	EVELYN, 2
pig a sort of p. in clover	BENNETT, ARNOLD, 1	**plagues** of all p. with which mankind are curst	DEFOE, 6
pigeons tourists . . . take in the Monarchy . . . with . . . the		**plain** be yourself, imperial, p. and true	BROWNING, R, 7
	HAMILTON, W, 1	making things p. to uninstructed people	HUXLEY, T, 7
piggy This little p. went to market	NURSERY RHYMES, 63	Manners are . . . the need of the p.	WAUGH, E, 48
pigmy That shriek and sweat in p. wars	TENNYSON, 84	**plainness** perfect is of speech	ARNOLD, M, 31
pigs And whether p. have wings	CARROLL, 28	**plaisir** P. d'amour	FLORIAN, 1
one of Epicurus' herd of p.	HORACE, 18	**plan** save the p.	NIXON, 9
P. might fly	PROVERBS, 336	**plane** only two emotions in a p.	WELLES, 2
social virtues . . . the virtue of p. in a litter	THOREAU, 7	**planet** I have lived some thirty years on this p.	THOREAU, 10
pig-sty kissed her once by the p.	THOMAS, D, 19	it fell on the wrong p.	BRAUN, 2
Pilate jesting P.	BACON, FRANCIS, 56	When a new p. swims into his ken	KEATS, 42

plans Life ... happens ... while you're busy making other p.
                                                            LENNON, 1
  The finest p. have always been spoiled   BRECHT, 6
  what a man still p.   CANETTI, 2
plant Is thy love a p. Of such weak fibre WORDSWORTH, W, 22
  The infusion of a China p.   ADDISON, 12
planted like a tree p. by the water-side   PSALMS, 1
plants bottinney means a knowledge of p.   DICKENS, 32
  p. left over from the Edwardian Wilderness   OSBORNE, 6
plashy p. fen passes the questing vole   WAUGH, E, 31
plate clean your p.   ROSEBERY, 4
  the silver p. on a coffin   O'CONNELL, 1
platitude A longitude with no p.   FRY, C, 4
  A p. is simply a truth repeated   BALDWIN, S, 13
  To stroke a p. until it purrs   MARQUIS, 2
platitudes Literature is the orchestration of p. WILDER, T, 7
Plato P. is dear to me   ARISTOTLE, 10
  Western philosophy ... footnotes to P.'s philosophy WHITEHEAD, 6
plausible extracting the p.   LLOYD GEORGE, 2
play a good p. needs no epilogue   SHAKESPEARE, 225
  a p. is a dynamic thing   TYNAN, 1
  behold the Englishman ... p. tip-and-run   FIRBANK, 1
  Better than a p.   CHARLES II, 5
  If you p. with fire   PROVERBS, 219
  Judge not the half   DAVIES, J, 2
  p., I remember, pleas'd not the million   SHAKESPEARE, 86
  p.'s the thing   SHAKESPEARE, 88
  'P. up! p. up! and p. the game!'   NEWBOLT, 2
  Rehearsing a p. is making the word flesh   SHAFFER, 3
  The little victims p.   GRAY, 9
  this may be p. to you   L'ESTRANGE, 2
  unless the p. is stopped, the child cannot ... go on KEMBLE, J, 1
playboy p. of the western world   SYNGE, 1
player poor p., That struts and frets his hour SHAKESPEARE, 229
players men and women merely p.   SHAKESPEARE, 47
  to conceal the fact that the p. cannot act   AGATE, 3
play-going A good many inconveniences attend p. TYNAN, 4
plays p. about rape, sodomy and drug addiction COOK, P, 2
  Robert Browning, you writer of p.   BROWNING, R, 30
  Some of my p. peter out   BARRIE, 14
plaything A book that furnishes no quotations is ... a p.
                                                            PEACOCK, 3
  A child's a p. for an hour   LAMB, M, 1
playwright a p. ... void of dramatic interest SARTRE, 2
  the only sophisticated p. England has produced CONGREVE, 1
pleasant If we do not find anything p.   VOLTAIRE, 6
  lovely and p. in their lives   BIBLE, 482
  p. it is to have money   CLOUGH, 1
please go anywhere I damn well p.   BEVIN, 1
  he that is married careth ... how he may p. his wife BIBLE, 31
  I ... do what I p.   FREDERICK THE GREAT, 2
  Music, Maestro, P.   MAGIDSON, 1
  Natural to p.   DRYDEN, 4
  Nothing can permanently p.   COLERIDGE, S, 7
  They ... say what they p.   FREDERICK THE GREAT, 2
  You can't p. everyone   PROVERBS, 476
pleases every prospect p.   HEBER, 2
  one makes lovers as fast as one p.   CONGREVE, 14
pleasing The art of p. consists in   HAZLITT, 24
  the art of p. was the first duty in life   CHESTERFIELD, 8
  the surest method ... of p.   CHESTERFIELD, 9
pleasure A fool bolts p.   ANTRIM, 2
  a p. in the pathless woods   BYRON, 16
  as much p. as any of our poets   CHAUCER, 2
  as much p. in the reading   QUARLES, 1
  Debauchee, n. One who has ... pursued p.   BIERCE, 5
  did p. me in his top-boots   MARLBOROUGH, 1
  dissipation without p.   GIBBON, 4
  Everyone is dragged on by their favourite p.   VIRGIL, 16
  gave p. to the spectators   MACAULAY, T, 8
  greatest p. ... to do a good action   LAMB, CHARLES, 18
  hatred is by far the longest p.   BYRON, 33
  He had a kind of idealism in p.   PEPYS, 4
  He that takes p. to hear sermons   SELDEN, 7
  His great p. was to humiliate people   THOMAS, D, 4
  I make poetry and give p. ... because of you HORACE, 40
  in his p. is life   PSALMS, 17
  knowledge and wonder ... an impression of p. BACON, FRANCIS, 1
  Love ceases to be a p.   BEHN, 1
  Money gives me a p.   BELLOC, 11
  No p. without pain   PROVERBS, 315

no sterner moralist than P.   BYRON, 24
P. after all is a safer guide   BUTLER, S, 25
P. is ... intermission of pain   SELDEN, 4
P. is ... seldom found where it is sought   JOHNSON, S, 16
P. never is at home   KEATS, 17
p. of your company   LAMB, CHARLES, 24
p. ... sole motive force behind the union of the sexes LACLOS, 3
Romanticism ... literary works ... affording ... the greatest ...
                                                            STENDHAL, 2
The only sensual p. without vice   JOHNSON, S, 39
The p. of criticizing   LA BRUYÈRE, 4
the p. of offering my seat to three ladies   CHESTERTON, 41
The sight ... gave me infinite p.   PARK, 1
The ugliest of trades have their moments of p.   JERROLD, 6
understanding will ... extinguish p.   HOUSMAN, 6
what p. ... in taking their roguish tobacco   JONSON, 6
Writers like Connolly gave p. a bad name   CONNOLLY, 1
Youth is full of p.   SHAKESPEARE, 355
pleasure-dome A stately p. decree   COLERIDGE, S, 14
  sunny p. with caves of ice   COLERIDGE, S, 15
pleasures Earth fills her lap with p.   WORDSWORTH, W, 26
  Love and all his p.   CAMPION, 5
  Mid p. and palaces though we may roam   PAYNE, 1
  No man is a hypocrite in his p.   CAMUS, 152
  One half ... cannot understand the p.   AUSTEN, 4
  One of the p. of middle age   POUND, 4
  P. are all alike   SELDEN, 7
  p. are their only care   COWPER, 20
  P. newly found are sweet   WORDSWORTH, W, 76
  purest of human p.   BACON, FRANCIS, 26
  The English take their p.   SULLY, 1
  the paucity of human p.   JOHNSON, S, 35
plenty but just had p.   BURNS, R, 7
  that p. should attain the poor   BYRON, 5
plods plowman homeward p. his weary way   GRAY, 1
plot p. hath many changes   QUARLES, 2
  the p. thickens   BUCKINGHAM, 1
plough To get it ready for the p.   BETJEMAN, 10
  We p. the fields, and scatter   CAMPBELL, JANE, 1
ploughing Is my team p.   HOUSMAN, 11
plowed p. with my heifer   BIBLE, 295
plowman The p. homeward plods his weary way GRAY, 1
plowshares beat their swords into p.   BIBLE, 194
pluck if thy right eye offend thee, p. it out BIBLE, 363
  p. till time and times are done   YEATS, 30
plunder delivered Ireland from p. and oppression SWIFT, 1
plural in the p. and they bounce   LUTYENS, 1
plus P. *ça change*   KARR, 1
Plymouth dreamin' ... o' P. Hoe   NEWBOLT, 1
poacher a p. a keeper turned inside out   KINGSLEY, 8
pocket carried a ... brick in his p.   SWIFT, 6
  smile I could feel in my hip p.   CHANDLER, R, 2
  To be played with both hands in the p.   SATIE, 3
pockets the p. of the people   SMITH, A, 5
Podduyev life had prepared P. for living   SOLZHENITSYN, 4
poem A long p. is a test of invention   KEATS, 50
  A p. lovely as a tree   KILMER, 1
  I do not think this p. will reach its destination VOLTAIRE, 37
  P. me no poems   MACAULAY, R, 4
  toil That goes ... to the p.'s making   THOMAS, R, 1
poems A man does not write p.   SKELTON, ROBIN, 1
  My p. are hymns of praise   SITWELL, E, 1
  p. ... for the love of Man and in praise of God THOMAS, D, 5
  that Anon, who wrote so many p.   WOOLF, 11
  The few bad p. ... created during abstinence REICH, 1
  These p., with all their crudities   THOMAS, D, 5
  We all write p.   FOWLES, 1
poet a modern p.'s fate   HOOD, 14
  As a p., Milton seems   MILTON, 4
  A true p. does not bother to be poetical   COCTEAU, 1
  combination of scientist and would-be p.   STOPES, 1
  godly p. must be chaste himself   CATULLUS, 1
  He might have passed ... for anything but a p. BROWNING, R, 8
  lunatic, the lover, and the p.   SHAKESPEARE, 263
  Many brave men ... lack their sacred p.   HORACE, 42
  no person can be a p. ... without   MACAULAY, T, 14
  No p. ... has his complete meaning alone   ELIOT, T, 23
  p.'s eye, in a fine frenzy   SHAKESPEARE, 264
  p. to whom nature has denied   CARLYLE, T, 2
  p. without love   CARLYLE, T, 3
  That maniacal Calvinist and coddled p.   COWPER, 2

The p. and the dreamer are distinct — KEATS, 16
The p. gives us his essence — WOOLF, 1
To be a p. is a condition — GRAVES, R, 4
We have one p. of genius in Auden — AUDEN, 1
Yet obviously a nice man and a great p. — ELIOT, T, 2
poetic the laws of p. truth and p. beauty — ARNOLD, M, 15
poetical A true poet does not bother to be p. — COCTEAU, 1
that werges on the p. — DICKENS, 50
poetry Angling is somewhat like p. — WALTON, 2
As civilization advances, p. . . . declines — MACAULAY, T, 13
Even when p. has a meaning — HOUSMAN, 6
Here is Johnny Keats' piss-a-bed p. — KEATS, 3
If p. comes not . . . as leaves to a tree — KEATS, 57
I make p. and give pleasure . . . because of you — HORACE, 40
Mr Shaw . . . has never written any p. — CHESTERTON, 32
no man ever talked p. — DICKENS, 48
P. is a comforting piece of fiction — MENCKEN, 12
P. is as exact a science as geometry — FLAUBERT, 1
P. is baroque — MAUGHAM, 17
p. is . . . more philosophical . . . than history — ARISTOTLE, 5
P. is not a turning loose of emotion — ELIOT, T, 24
P. is opposed to science — COLERIDGE, S, 18
P. is the record of the best and happiest moments — SHELLEY, 7
P. is the spontaneous overflow — WORDSWORTH, W, 19
P. is to prose — WAIN, 1
P. is what gets lost in translation — FROST, R, 11
p. makes nothing happen — AUDEN, 16
p. reminds him of the richness — KENNEDY, JOHN, 16
P. . . . set to more or less lascivious music — MENCKEN, 11
P. should be great and unobtrusive — KEATS, 56
p. sinks and swoons under . . . prose — LANDOR, 2
P.'s unnatural — DICKENS, 48
p. = the best words in the best order — COLERIDGE, S, 41
p., 'The Cinderella of the Arts.' — MONROE, H, 1
read a little p. sometimes — HOPE, 7
Superstition is the p. of life — GOETHE, 6
that is p. — CAGE, 1
The difference between genuine p. — ARNOLD, M, 44
the grand style arises in p. — ARNOLD, M, 32
The one . . . p. . . . continually flowing is slang — CHESTERTON, 10
The P. is in the pity — OWEN, W, 5
there is p. in peaches — GRANVILLE-BARKER, 1
to resuscitate the dead art Of p. — POUND, 12
truest p. is the most feigning — SHAKESPEARE, 54
What is p. — RUSKIN, 5
poets among the English P. after my death — KEATS, 62
as much pleasure as any of our p. — CHAUCER, 2
excellent p. that have never versified — SIDNEY, P, 2
I hate . . . your professional p. — WELLINGTON, 10
Milton the prince of p. — MILTON, 1
Painters and p. . . . licence to dare anything — HORACE, 1
P. and painters are outside the class system — BRENAN, 6
p. are the ones who write in words — FOWLES, 3
p. being second-rate — HORACE, 10
Souls of p. dead and gone — KEATS, 26
what would be theft in other p. — JONSON, 1
point Up to a p., Lord Copper — WAUGH, E, 40
you are like a pin, but without . . . head or . . . p. — JERROLD, 8
poison food to one man is bitter p. to others — LUCRETIUS, 4
strongest p. ever known — BLAKE, W, 4
poker Malice is like a game of p. — SPIEL, 1
pokers Wreathe iron p. into true-love knots — COLERIDGE, S, 21
pole And see all sights from p. to p. — ARNOLD, M, 4
Beloved from p. to p. — COLERIDGE, S, 34
One step beyond the p. — PEARY, 2
Poles few virtues . . . the P. do not possess — CHURCHILL, W, 64
police a sort of friendship recognized by the p. — STEVENSON, R, 13
Reading isn't an occupation we encourage among p. officers — ORTON, 1
policeman A p.'s lot is not a happy one — GILBERT, W, 40
park, a p. and a pretty girl — CHAPLIN, 5
the air of someone who is lying . . . to a p. — PHILIPPE, 1
The terrorist and the p. — CONRAD, 6
This definition . . . would not do for a p. — NIGHTINGALE, 2
policemen P. are numbered — MILLIGAN, 9
repressed sadists . . . become p. or butchers — CONNOLLY, 8
sign of old age: . . . how young the p. look — HICKS, 1
polished Satire should, like a p. razor keen — MONTAGU, 1
whole man in himself, p. and well-rounded — HORACE, 47
polite it costs nothing to be p. — CHURCHILL, W, 15
p. by telling lies — BRADBURY, 6

time to be p. — MONTESQUIEU, 7
politeness pine-apple of p. — SHERIDAN, R, 8
Punctuality is the p. of kings — LOUIS XVIII, 1
political addiction of p. groups to ideas — GALBRAITH, 3
After all, we are not p. whores — MUSSOLINI, 3
a man who . . . discovered a p. theory — CASTRO, 2
Every intellectual attitude is latently p. — MANN, 2
ineptitude of M. Sartre's p. performance — SARTRE, 3
Jesus was . . . a first-rate p. economist — SHAW, 3
most schemes of p. improvement — JOHNSON, S, 76
necessary for one people to dissolve . . . p. bonds — JEFFERSON, 4
one of these is the history of p. power — POPPER, 3
p. speech and writing — ORWELL, 20
That points clearly to a p. career — SHAW, 18
the formation of the p. will of the nation — HITLER, 14
politician a p. is an arse — CUMMINGS, 3
A p. is a statesman . . . with an open mouth — STEVENSON, A, 2
A statesman is a p. who — POMPIDOU, 1
A statesman is a p. who's been dead — TRUMAN, 5
at home you're just a p. — MACMILLAN, 7
Coffee which makes the p. wise — POPE, 52
Kennedy the p. exuded that musk odour — KENNEDY, JOHN, 2
like a scurvy p. — SHAKESPEARE, 189
Nixon is the kind of p. — NIXON, 2
p. never believes what he says — DE GAULLE, 11
the p. poses as the servant — DE GAULLE, 13
politicians a pity . . . that more p. are not bastards — WHITEHORN, 4
P. are the same all over — KHRUSHCHEV, 7
P. can never forgive being ignored — WHITEHORN, 7
P. neither love nor hate — DRYDEN, 7
politics are too serious . . . to be left to the p. — DE GAULLE, 14
politics A week is a long time in p. — WILSON, HAROLD, 11
Britain is no longer in the p. of the pendulum — THATCHER, M, 6
History is past p. — FREEMAN, 1
in p. there is no heart, only head — NAPOLEON I, 5
in p. to chastise his own side than the enemy — ORWELL, 2
making p. Christian — VAN DER POST, 1
Men who have greatness . . . don't go in for p. — CAMUS, 10
P. are now nothing more than — JOHNSON, S, 98
p. are too serious . . . to be left to the politicians — DE GAULLE, 14
P. is not an exact science — BISMARCK, 2
P. is not a science . . . but an art — BISMARCK, 7
P. is the art of preventing people from taking part — VALÉRY, 4
P. is the art of the possible — BISMARCK, 3
P. is . . . the only profession — STEVENSON, R, 4
p. was the second lowest profession — REAGAN, 8
Science, history, p., all were within his compass — WELLS, 2
that men enter local p. — PARKINSON, 4
The more you read about p. — ROGERS, W, 9
they can at least pretend that p. is a game — PARKINSON, 2
War is the continuation of p. — MAO TSE-TUNG, 3
pollution despite p. . . . I'm glad of the boom — BRAGG, 3
indefatigable and unsavoury engine of p. — SPARROW, 1
Polly P. put the kettle on — NURSERY RHYMES, 44
polygamy P. was made a Sin — DRYDEN, 3
Pomeranian The healthy bones of a single P. grenadier — BISMARCK, 5
pomp In lowly p. ride on to die — MILMAN, 1
Pride, p., and circumstance — SHAKESPEARE, 286
Take physic, p. — SHAKESPEARE, 181
pompous A p. woman — SITWELL, E, 4
p. in the grave — BROWNE, T, 12
Poms All the faces . . . seem to be bloody P. — CHARLES, PRINCE, 1
pondered Mary . . . p. them in her heart — BIBLE, 316
ponies And wretched, blind, pit p. — HODGSON, 1
pony I had a little p. — NURSERY RHYMES, 21
poodle Mr Balfour's P. — LLOYD GEORGE, 8
Pooh-Bah P. (Lord High Everything Else) — GILBERT, W, 22
poor A p. man is despised the whole world over — JEROME, 3
a p. society cannot be too p. — TAWNEY, 1
as for me, I am p. and needy — PSALMS, 24
Charity separates the rich from the p. — PERÓN, E, 2
cynical gestures of the p. — SPENDER, 2
decent means p. — PEACOCK, 1
Few, save the p., feel for the p. — LANDON, 2
give to the p. — BIBLE, 404
great men have their p. relations — DICKENS, 8
Hard to train to accept being p. — HORACE, 25
I, being p., have only my dreams — YEATS, 35
I can dare to be p. — GAY, 11
I have nothing; the rest I leave to the p. — RABELAIS, 8

inconvenient to be p. — COWPER, 7
it is p. grub, p. pay, and easy work — LONDON, 1
It's the p. wot gets the blame — ANONYMOUS, 71
Laws grind the p. — GOLDSMITH, 24
only the p. . . . are forbidden to beg — FRANCE, 1
only the p. who pay cash — FRANCE, 10
Pale Death kicks . . . into the cottages of the p. — HORACE, 27
p. have no right to the property of the rich — RUSKIN, 16
P. Little Rich Girl — COWARD, 15
P. old Joe — FOSTER, 5
p. relation — LAMB, CHARLES, 15
Resolve not to be p. — JOHNSON, S, 140
She was p. but she was honest — ANONYMOUS, 71
short and simple annals of the p. — GRAY, 2
that plenty should attain the p. — BYRON, 5
the p. are our brothers and sisters — TERESA, MOTHER, 1
the p. . . . need love — TERESA, MOTHER, 1
the p. person . . . thinks money would help — KERR, 2
The p. . . . their function — SARTRE, 14
THE RICH AND THE P. — DISRAELI, 12
Though I be p., I'm honest — MIDDLETON, 1
To be p. and independent — COBBETT, 1
What fun it would be to be p. — ANOUILH, 6
poorer for richer for p. — BOOK OF COMMON PRAYER, 27
poorest p. man may in his cottage — PITT THE ELDER, 1
pop art In England, p. and fine art — MACINNES, 1
Pope In P. I cannot read a line — POPE, 2
poplars The p. are felled — COWPER, 19
poppies the p. blow — MCCRAE, 1
populace society distributes itself into . . . P. — ARNOLD, M, 4
the p. cannot exact their demands — WELLINGTON, 14
this vast residuum we may . . . give the name of P. — ARNOLD, M, 9
popular I think p. music in this country — CROSBY, 2
librarian thought my books were far too p. — BLYTON, 2
Nothing can render them p. — SWIFT, 13
The worse I do, the more p. I get — KENNEDY, JOHN, 8
We're more p. than Jesus Christ — LENNON, 13
popularity P.? . . . glory's small change — HUGO, 7
P. is a crime — HALIFAX, 5
population a starving p. — DISRAELI, 28
P. . . . increases in a geometrical ratio — MALTHUS, 1
populi vox p., vox dei — ALCUIN, 1
porcupines I shall throw two p. under you — KHRUSHCHEV, 4
Porlock by a person on business from P. — COLERIDGE, S, 13
pornography P. is the attempt to insult sex — LAWRENCE, D, 35
p. of war — RAE, 1
You don't get any p. . . . on the telly — SPEIGHT, 3
port Any p. in a storm — PROVERBS, 56
it would be p. if it could — BENTLEY, R, 1
porter Oh, mister p., what shall I do — LLOYD, M, 1
portion best p. of a good man's life — WORDSWORTH, W, 9
portions P. and parcels of the dreadful Past — TENNYSON, 54
portrait Every man's work . . . is always a p. — BUTLER, S, 23
Every time I paint a p. I lose a friend — SARGENT, J, 1
portraits P. of famous bards and preachers — THOMAS, D, 27
posh only two p. papers on a Sunday — OSBORNE, 2
posies a thousand fragrant p. — MARLOWE, 14
beds of roses . . . fragrant p. — MARLOWE, 14
position only one p. for an artist — THOMAS, D, 31
Twain and I are in the same p. — TWAIN, 2
possessing too dear for my p. — SHAKESPEARE, 365
possession P. is nine points — PROVERBS, 337
The p. of a book — BURGESS, 5
the p. of it is intolerable — VANBURGH, 1
possessions Not the owner of many p. will you be right to call
happy — HORACE, 43
p. for a moment of time — ELIZABETH I, 12
possibility too much of a sceptic to deny the p. of anything
— HUXLEY, T, 10
possible Politics is the art of the p. — BISMARCK, 3
something is p., he is . . . right — CLARKE, A, 1
the art of the p. — BUTLER, R, 1
post p. of honour is a private station — ADDISON, 7
post-chaise I would spend my life in driving briskly in a p.
— JOHNSON, S, 115
posterity doing something for p. — ADDISON, 17
looked upon by p. as a brave, bad man — CROMWELL, O, 2
The nations which have put mankind and p. most in their debt
— INGE, 12
Think of your p. — ADAMS, J, 3
Thy p. shall sway — COWPER, 3

What has p. done for us — ROCHE, 1
postgraduate The British p. student — LODGE, 3
postscript all the pith is in the p. — HAZLITT, 6
that which was most material in the p. — BACON, FRANCIS, 17
postures It requires one to assume such indecent p. — WILDE, 72
pot greasy Joan doth keel the p. — SHAKESPEARE, 199
potent how p. cheap music is — COWARD, 17
potter Who *is* the P. — FITZGERALD, E, 16
poultry A p. matter — MARX, G, 3
pound the p. . . . in your pocket — WILSON, HAROLD, 10
pounds I only ask you for twenty-five p. — SHERIDAN, R, 14
Looks handsome in three hundred p. — SHAKESPEARE, 255
the p. will take care of themselves — CHESTERFIELD, 1
two hundred p. a year — BUTLER, S, 7
pouvait si vieillesse p. — ESTIENNE, 1
poverty a darn is . . . p. — SHUTER, 1
Almsgiving tends to perpetuate p. — PERÓN, 2
crime so shameful as p. — FARQUHAR, 1
Do you call p. a crime — SHAW, 19
from nothing to a state of extreme p. — MARX, G, 13
generations . . . have struggled in p. — STANTON, E, 1
If p. is the mother of crime, stupidity is its father — LA BRUYÈRE, 11
It is easy enough to say that p. is no crime — JEROME, 3
Loneliness . . . is the most terrible p. — TERESA, MOTHER, 1
Notwithstanding the p. of my . . . experience — JAMES, A, 2
P. and oysters — DICKENS, 46
p. . . . is a blunder — JEROME, 3
P. is a great enemy to human happiness — JOHNSON, S, 140
P. is an anomaly to rich people — BAGEHOT, 11
P. is not a crime — PROVERBS, 338
P. of goods is easily cured — MONTAIGNE, 10
p. of soul, impossible — MONTAIGNE, 10
P., therefore, was comparative — DRABBLE, 1
Rejection, derision, p., failure — VIZINCZEY, 2
The misfortunes of p. — JUVENAL, 2
three great evils, boredom, vice, and p. — VOLTAIRE, 10
When p. comes in — PROVERBS, 460
world p. is primarily a problem of — SCHUMACHER, 2
powder keep your p. dry — BLACKER, 1
She burst while drinking a seidlitz p. — ANONYMOUS, 32
when your p.'s runnin' low — NEWBOLT, 2
powdered Stratford . . . suggests p. history — HALSEY, 5
power As we make sex less secretive, we may rob it of its p.
— SZASZ, 2
corridors of p. — SNOW, 2
Germany will be . . . a world p. — HITLER, 12
greater the p. — BURKE, E, 25
He aspired to p. — TAYLOR, A, 4
If, drunk with sight of p., we loose — KIPLING, 22
its source of p.: ownership — KINNOCK, 4
Knowledge itself is p. — BACON, FRANCIS, 64
literature seeks to communicate p. — DE QUINCEY, 1
love of p. is the love of ourselves — HAZLITT, 30
one of these is the history of political p. — POPPER, 3
P. . . . and Liberty . . . are seldom upon good Terms — HALIFAX, 7
P. corrupts — STEVENSON, A, 3
p. is apt to corrupt — PITT THE ELDER, 3
P. is the ultimate aphrodisiac — KISSINGER, 4
P.? . . . like a dead sea fruit — MACMILLAN, 11
p. of life and death — BIBLE, 522
p. over men — WOLLSTONECRAFT, 2
P. tends to corrupt — ACTON, 2
p. without responsibility — BALDWIN, S, 3
self-sufficing p. of Solitude — WORDSWORTH, W, 38
that p. . . . is ever grasping — ADAMS, A, 1
The accursed p. which stands on Privilege — BELLOC, 1
The balance of p. — WALPOLE, R, 5
the kingdom of God is not in word, but in p. — BIBLE, 26
The wrong sort of people are always in p. — WYNNE-TYSON, J, 1
they . . . take, who have the p. — WORDSWORTH, W, 46
War knows no p. — BROOKE, 5
When p. narrows the areas of man's concern — KENNEDY, JOHN, 16
You only have p. over people — SOLZHENITSYN, 3
powerful Guns will make us p. — GOERING, 1
The rich and p. know — ANOUILH, 4
powerless Brief and p. — RUSSELL, B, 16
p. to be born — ARNOLD, M, 19
powers a taste for *hidden* and *forbidden* p. — NIETZSCHE, 10
Headmasters have p. — CHURCHILL, W, 18
the p. of a first-rate man — BAGEHOT, 9
pox P. take him and his wit — POPE, 2

You will die either on the gallows, or of the p.   WILKES, 1
practical Compassion is . . . an absolutely p. belief . . .
KINNOCK, 6
meddling with any p. part of life   ADDISON, 10
P. men . . . the slaves of some defunct economist   KEYNES, 7
practice a thing may look . . . in p. excellent   BURKE, E, 28
P. makes perfect   PROVERBS, 339
P. should always be based   LEONARDO DA VINCI, 7
practiced For thirty-seven years I've p.   SARASATE, 1
practise P. what you preach   PROVERBS, 340
morality . . . which we preach but do not p.   RUSSELL, B, 20
praise bury Caesar, not to p. him   SHAKESPEARE, 153
Damn with faint p.   POPE, 14
envy is a kind of p.   GAY, 9
his p. shall ever be in my mouth   PSALMS, 22
if we p. ourselves fearlessly   BACON, FRANCIS, 4
I will p. any man that will p. me   SHAKESPEARE, 31
Let us with a gladsome mind P. the Lord   MILTON, 55
My poems are hymns of p.   SITWELL, E, 1
Pavilioned in splendour, and girded with p.   GRANT, R, 1
People . . . only want p.   MAUGHAM, 12
P. him in the cymbals and dances   PSALMS, 77
P. the Lord and pass the ammunition   FORGY, 1
this blest man, let his just p. be given   WALTON, 7
To refuse p.   ROCHEFOUCAULD, 18
we but p. ourselves in other men   POPE, 27
written . . . in p. of God   THOMAS, D, 5
praises He who p. everybody   JOHNSON, S, 118
The idiot who p. . . . every country but his own   GILBERT, W, 26
yet he p. those who follow different paths   HORACE, 45
praising advantage of . . . p. . . . oneself   BUTLER, S, 26
pram sombre enemy of good art than the p.   CONNOLLY, 10
pray p. for you at St Paul's   SMITH, SYDNEY, 14
P. to God and say the lines   DAVIS, B, 3
watch and p.   BIBLE, 426
when ye p., use not vain repetitions   BIBLE, 367
praye Fare well . . . and p. for me   MORE, 2
prayed I wish that God had not given me what I p. for   SPYRI, 1
prayer As the drought continued, p. was abandoned   LEE, L, 1
More things are wrought by p.   TENNYSON, 24
most odious of . . . narcissisms – p.   FOWLES, 1
P. makes the Christian's armour bright   COWPER, 15
storms of p.   TENNYSON, 74
The people's p.   DRYDEN, 14
The p. that . . . heals the sick   EDDY, 1
prayers better than good men's p.   CERVANTES, 8
The hopes and p. of liberty-loving people   EISENHOWER, 4
prayeth He p. well   COLERIDGE, S, 38
prays man p. . . . for a miracle   TURGENEV, 4
preach morality . . . which we p.   RUSSELL, B, 20
p. Christ crucified   BIBLE, 24
preachers Portraits of famous bards and p.   THOMAS, D, 27
P. say, Do as I say, not as I do   SELDEN, 5
preaching A woman's p. is like   JOHNSON, S, 69
by the foolishness of p.   BIBLE, 24
precedency the point of p. between a louse and a flea
JOHNSON, S, 144
precedent A p. embalms a principle   DISRAELI, 2
precept for p. must be upon p.   BIBLE, 208
precious Right is more p.   WILSON, W, 7
so p. that it must be rationed   LENIN, 11
precisely thinking too p. on th' event   SHAKESPEARE, 100
pre-cognitive Love means the p. flow   LAWRENCE, D, 45
predestination Free Will and P.   CHURCHILL, W, 20
predicament Life . . . is a p.   SANTAYANA, 8
predictions Dreams and p.   BACON, FRANCIS, 41
prefabricated a better word than 'p.'   CHURCHILL, W, 11
preferment P.'s door   ARNOLD, M, 36
preferred he . . . coming after me is p. before me   BIBLE, 239
pregnancy avoid p. by . . . mathematics   MENCKEN, 4
prejudge I do not . . . p. the past   WHITELAW, 2
prejudice I am free of all p.   FIELDS, 4
skilled appeals to religious p.   HUXLEY, T, 11
prejudices collection of p. which is called political philosophy
RUSSELL, B, 26
Common sense is the collection of p.   EINSTEIN, 10
freedom to print . . . proprietor's p.   SWAFFER, 1
premise fundamental p. of a revolution   TROTSKY, 7
pre-natal the greatness of Russia is only her p. struggling
LAWRENCE, D, 34

preparation his life was a p. for elder statesmanship
MACMILLAN, 2
life . . . seems to me p. for something   YEATS, 5
no p. is thought necessary   STEVENSON, R, 4
prepare I go to p. a place for you   BIBLE, 258
I p. for a journey   MANSFIELD, K, 2
prepared Be P.   BADEN-POWELL, 2
Presbyter P. is but old Priest writ large   MILTON, 62
presence A certain person may have . . . a wonderful p.   SHAH, 1
come before his p. with thanksgiving   PSALMS, 54
present All p. and correct   ANONYMOUS, 4
an un-birthday p.   CARROLL, 31
novelists the story of the p.   GONCOURT, 1
P. mirth hath p. laughter   SHAKESPEARE, 338
Time p. and time past   ELIOT, T, 6
to know nothing but the p.   KEYNES, 2
preservation among which are the p. of life   JEFFERSON, 5
preserve Lord shall p. thy going out   PSALMS, 68
p. one last male thing   LAWRENCE, D, 25
president An extraordinarily gifted p.   JOHNSON, L, 1
Eisenhower proved we don't need a p.   EISENHOWER, 1
God is the only p.   WEBSTER, D, 2
I had rather be right than P.   CLAY, 1
in America anyone can be P.   FORD, G, 3
nobody is strongminded around a P.   REEDY, 1
one thing about being P.   EISENHOWER, 6
perfect for television is all a P. has to be   REAGAN, 2
P. spends . . . time kissing people   TRUMAN, 6
the P. is dead   GARFIELD, 1
We are all the P.'s men   KISSINGER, 4
While I'd rather be right than p.   THOMAS, N, 1
Press a gentleman of the P.   DISRAELI, 27
Never lose your temper with the P.   PANKHURST, C, 1
would not say that our P. is obscene   LONGFORD, 2
presume Dr Livingstone, I p.   STANLEY, 1
p. not God to scan   POPE, 34
pretending p. to be wicked   WILDE, 27
pretty a p. girl who naked is   CUMMINGS, 2
One girl can be p.   FITZGERALD, F S, 9
P. witty Nell   PEPYS, 11
There's only one p. child   PROVERBS, 421
preventing a means of p. it   PASTEUR, 5
Politics is the art of p. people   VALÉRY, 4
prevention P. is better than cure   PROVERBS, 341
prevents Nothing p. us from being natural   ROCHEFOUCAULD, 25
prey he shall devour the p.   BIBLE, 182
lord of all things, yet a p. to all   POPE, 33
price a better p. than old mistresses   BEAVERBROOK, 5
Courage is the p. . . . for granting peace   EARHART, 1
her p. is far above rubies   BIBLE, 458
P. of Herald three cents daily   BENNETT, J, 2
The p. . . . for pursuing any profession   BALDWIN, J, 3
the p. of everything and the value of nothing   WILDE, 43
those men have their p.   WALPOLE, R, 3
Who never knew the p. of happiness   YEVTUSHENKO, 3
prick If you p. us, do we not bleed   SHAKESPEARE, 245
p. the sides of my intent   SHAKESPEARE, 209
pricks to kick against the p.   BIBLE, 6
pride A mother's p.   SCOTT, WALTER, 19
Be modest! It is the kind of p.   RENARD, 1
contempt on all my p.   WATTS, 8
Is P., the never-failing vice of fools   POPE, 22
it is p., but understood in a different way   TOCQUEVILLE, 1
P. and Truth . . . shake their . . . sides at youth   YEATS, 24
p. goeth before destruction   BIBLE, 451
p. that licks the dust   POPE, 16
So sleeps the p. of former days   MOORE, T, 2
there is no false p.   RENARD, 3
prides His Royal Highness . . . p. himself   SHERIDAN, R, 13
priest A p. sees people at their best   PROVERBS, 61
For a p. to turn a man when he lies a-dying   SELDEN, 6
Presbyter is but old P. writ large   MILTON, 62
rid me of this turbulent p.   HENRY II, 1
That waked the p. all shaven and shorn   NURSERY RHYMES, 62
That whisky-p.   GREENE, 7
priest-craft e'r P. did begin   DRYDEN, 3
priesthood Literary men are . . . a perpetual p.   CARLYLE, T, 8
priests All things, oh p., are on fire   BUDDHA, 1
I always like to associate with a lot of p.   BELLOC, 16
In old time we had treen chalices and golden p.   JEWEL, 1
prig a bore and a bounder and a p.   LAWRENCE, T, 2

prim   A p. . . . rather querulous person   HOUSMAN, 1
prima donnas   They are for p. or corpses   TOSCANINI, 1
prime   having lost . . . your p.   HERRICK, 6
One's p. is elusive   SPARK, 7
Prime Minister   a P. has to be . . . a showman   MACMILLAN, 3
Macmillan would have been Labour P.   MACMILLAN, 1
Mr Macmillan is the best p. we have   BUTLER, R, 2
pays a harlot 25 times as much as it pays its P.   WILSON, HAROLD, 7
that of P. is filled by fluke   POWELL, E, 2
the curse of the present British P.   CHAMBERLAIN, N, 1
the most intelligent P. of the century   MACMILLAN, 2
when a British P. sneezed   LEVIN, 2
primitive   The classics are only p. literature   LEACOCK, 2
primroses   smiles, Wan as p.   KEATS, 8
prince   Milton the p. of poets   MILTON, 2
P. Philip. He's a world expert on leisure   KINNOCK, 5
who's danced with the P. of Wales   FARJEON, 1
princes   mine were p. of the earth   BENJAMIN, 1
O put not your trust in p.   PSALMS, 73
They say p. learn no art truly   JONSON, 8
principal   It is not my interest to pay the p.   SHERIDAN, R, 19
principle   A precedent embalms a p.   DISRAELI, 2
except from some strong p.   MELBOURNE, 8
the most useful thing about a p.   MAUGHAM, 4
the p. seems the same   CHURCHILL, W, 9
you never can tell. That's a p.   SHAW, 43
principles   All universal moral p. are idle fancies   SADE, 1
And wrote 'P. of Political Economy'   BENTLEY, E, 5
easier to fight for one's p.   ADLER, 1
If one sticks too rigidly to one's p.   CHRISTIE, 4
It is not . . . my principle to pay the interest   SHERIDAN, R, 19
The p. of a free constitution   GIBBON, 7
The p. of logic and metaphysics are true   AYER, 2
Whenever two good people argue over p.   ESCHENBACH, 1
whether I embrace your lordship's p. or your mistress   WILKES, 1
print   decomposing in the eternity of p.   WOOLF, 3
news that's fit to p.   OCHS, 1
pleasant, sure, to see one's name in p.   BYRON, 37
The big p. giveth and the fine p. taketh away   SHEEN, 2
printers   those books by which the p. have lost   FULLER, T, 6
printing   Gunpowder, P., and the Protestant Religion   CARLYLE, T, 9
priorities   The language of p. is   BEVAN, 2
prison   Anyone who has been to . . . public school . . . at home in p.   WAUGH, E, 22
ready to receive prizes as I am to be thrown into p.   WALESA, 1
Stone walls do not a p. make   LOVELACE, 1
the true place for a just man is also a p.   THOREAU, 3
The world . . . is but a large p.   RALEIGH, W, 4
prisoner   I object to your being taken p.   KITCHENER, 1
P., God has given you good abilities   ARABIN, 3
prisoners   If this is the way Queen Victoria treats her p.   WILDE, 73
p. of addiction and . . . p. of envy   ILLICH, 4
prisons   not enough p. . . . in Palestine   MEIR, 7
P. are built with stones of Law   BLAKE, W, 20
privacy   a right to share your p. in a public place   USTINOV, 5
forty-five minutes of undisturbed p.   PARKER, D, 12
invading her own p.   BANKHEAD, 2
the family, with its narrow p.   LEACH, 1
private   He was meddling too much in my p. life   WILLIAMS, T, 8
P. Means is dead   SMITH, STEVIE, 5
Scientific discovery is a p. event   MEDAWAR, 1
sex has been a very p., secretive activity   SZASZ, 2
The grave's a fine and p. place   MARVELL, 12
Travel is the most p. of pleasures   SACKVILLE-WEST, 3
Whatsoever . . . the p. calamity   SHERIDAN, R, 15
when religion is allowed to invade . . . p. life   MELBOURNE, 11
privatization   We must reject a p. of religion   RUNCIE, 1
privilege   a defender of p.   BEVERIDGE, 3
an Englishman's heaven-born p.   ARNOLD, M, 9
The accursed power which stands on P.   BELLOC, 9
privileged   only p. persons in our country   PERÓN, E, 1
prize   in a race run all, but one receiveth the p.   BIBLE, 33
Men p. the thing ungain'd   SHAKESPEARE, 328
Not all that tempts your . . . heedless hearts, is lawful p.   GRAY, 13
prizes   just miss the p. at the flower show   BRONOWSKI, 5
ready to receive p. as I am to be thrown into prison   WALESA, 1
The world continues to offer glittering p.   BIRKENHEAD, 4
P.R.O   partly a liaison man and partly P.   BETJEMAN, 5

problem   ineffectual liberal's p.   FRAYN, 3
Not every p. someone has with his girlfriend   MARCUSE, 1
Well, frankly, the p. as I see it . . . is   CHARLES, PRINCE, 5
problems   Among the many p. . . . the choice of the moment . . .   SACKVILLE-WEST, 1
to begin his novel   SACKVILLE-WEST, 1
There are two p. in my life   DOUGLAS-HOME, A, 2
procession   A torchlight p.   O'SULLIVAN, 1
procrastination   P. is the thief of time   YOUNG, E, 5
procreation   ordained for the p. of children   BOOK OF COMMON PRAYER, 24
prodigal   P. of Ease   DRYDEN, 6
producing   Man . . . consumes without p.   ORWELL, 3
production   Capitalist p. begets . . . its own negation   MARX, K, 5
profession   Politics is . . . the only p.   STEVENSON, R, 4
The price . . . for pursuing any p.   BALDWIN, J, 3
professional   A p. is someone whose wife works   SHAHN, 1
professor   A p. is one who talks in someone else's sleep   AUDEN, 29
professors   American p. like their literature   LEWIS, S, 4
As to religion . . . protect all . . . p. thereof   PAINE, 4
Culture is an instrument wielded by p.   WEIL, 1
now-a-days p. of philosophy   THOREAU, 11
profit   count as p. every day that Fate allows you   HORACE, 29
No p. grows where is no pleasure   SHAKESPEARE, 318
Philosophers never balance between p. and honesty   HUME, D, 8
profound   turbid look the most p.   LANDOR, 5
progeny   A p. of learning   SHERIDAN, R, 1
Programme   to help Britain to become a Third P.   WILKINSON, 1
progress   All p. is based   BUTLER, S, 11
Man's 'p.' is but a gradual discovery   SAINT-EXUPÉRY, 4
Our p. . . . Is trouble and care   LONGFELLOW, 14
P. . . . depends on retentiveness   SANTAYANA, 1
'p.' is simply a comparative   CHESTERTON, 18
the things which government does . . . social p.   WARREN, 1
What p. . . . In the Middle Ages   FREUD, S, 7
What we call p. is   ELLIS, 3
progression   Without Contraries is no p.   BLAKE, W, 18
prohibition   Communism is like p.   ROGERS, W, 3
proletarian   every time you are polite to a p.   WAUGH, E, 34
proletariat   The dictatorship of the p.   MARX, K, 7
the p. will . . . wage a class struggle for Socialism   LENIN, 3
prologues   P. precede the piece   GARRICK, 1
prolonged   the War is being deliberately p.   SASSOON, S, 6
Prometheus   as old as P.   NIETZSCHE, 1
promise   A p. made is a debt unpaid   SERVICE, 1
a young man of p.   CHURCHILL, W, 3
rarely . . . one can see . . . the p. of a man   DUMAS, FILS, 3
promised   Only do always in health what you have often p. to do when you are sick   SIGISMUND, 1
promises   a young man of p.   CHURCHILL, W, 3
P. and pie-crust are made to be broken   SWIFT, 10
P. are like pie-crust   PROVERBS, 342
young man of p.   BALFOUR, 3
promisin'   Once you were so p.   FRY, C, 1
promptly   He gives twice who gives p.   SYRUS, 4
pronounce   foreigners . . . spell better than they p.   TWAIN, 10
p. foreign names as he chooses   CHURCHILL, W, 37
spell it Vinci and p. it Vinchy   TWAIN, 10
pronouncements   Science should leave off making p.   JEANS, 2
proof   feeling p. against it   ADAMS, R, 3
propaganda   P. . . . nearly deceiving your friends   CORNFORD, 2
propagated   If human beings could be p.   HALDANE, 3
propensities   excite my amorous p.   JOHNSON, S, 46
proper   He never does a p. thing without   SHAW, 17
The p. study of Mankind is Man   POPE, 34
property   Few rich men own their p.   INGERSOLL, 4
law holds . . . p. is of greater value than life   FRY, E, 1
poor have no right to the p. of the rich   RUSKIN, 16
P. has its duties   DRUMMOND, 1
P. is theft   PROUDHON, 1
The future is the only kind of p.   CAMUS, 12
the right of governing was not p. but a trust   FOX, C, 1
prophecies   the verification of his own p.   TROLLOPE, 1
prophet   A historian is a p. in reverse   SCHLEGEL, 1
author of the Satanic Verses book, which is against . . . the P.   KHOMEINI, 2
p. is not without honour   BIBLE, 392
there arose not a p. . . . like unto Moses   BIBLE, 60
The sons of the p. were brave men and bold   ANONYMOUS, 98
proportion   strangeness in the p.   BACON, FRANCIS, 12

Proportional Representation P. . . . fundamentally counter-democratic KINNOCK, 2
proposes Man p. KEMPIS, 280
proposition undesirable to believe a p. RUSSELL, B, 19
propriety forgetting . . . womanly feeling and p. VICTORIA, 5
The p. of . . . having improper thoughts BRADLEY, F, 4
prosaic a p. digression BUCHAN, 3
prose anything except bad p. CHURCHILL, W, 39
difference between . . . p. and metrical composition WORDSWORTH, W, 18
I can only write p. today YEATS, 38
I have been talking p. for over forty years MOLIÈRE, 3
no one hears his own remarks as p. AUDEN, 3
Poetry is opposed to science . . . p. to metre COLERIDGE, S, 18
Poetry is to p. WAIN, 1
poetry sinks and swoons under . . . p. LANDOR, 2
P. . . . can bear a great deal of poetry LANDOR, 2
p. = words in their best order COLERIDGE, S, 41
the p. for God GRANVILLE-BARKER, 3
to write good p. is an affair of good manners MAUGHAM, 17
prosper Treason doth never p. HARINGTON, 1
whatsoever he doeth, it shall p. PSALMS, 1
prosperitee A man to have ben in p. CHAUCER, 20
him that stood in greet p. CHAUCER, 15
prosperity P. doth best discover vice BACON, FRANCIS, 8
prostitutes the small nations like p. KUBRICK, 1
prostitution P. . . . keeps her out of trouble HELLER, 7
P. . . . provides fresh air and wholesome exercise HELLER, 7
protect p. the writer ACHESON, 7
protest lady doth p. too much SHAKESPEARE, 96
Protestant A P. with a horse BEHAN, 1
Gunpowder, Printing, and the P. Religion CARLYLE, T, 9
P. women may take the Pill THOMAS, I, 1
what is worse, P. counterpoint BEECHAM, 6
Protestantism The chief contribution of P. to human thought MENCKEN, 7
Protestants God knows how you P. . . . have WILSON, A, 3
P. protesting against Protestantism LAWRENCE, D, 39
Proteus P. rising from the sea WORDSWORTH, W, 65
protozoon Organic life . . . has developed . . . from the p. to the philosopher RUSSELL, B, 15
proud a p. look and a high stomach PSALMS, 57
Death be not p. DONNE, 14
He who does not need to lie is p. NIETZSCHE, 16
no guarantee . . . you will not be p. of the feat DOBRÉE, 1
p. me no prouds SHAKESPEARE, 316
scattered the p. BIBLE, 310
too p. to fight WILSON, W, 10
Yes; I am p. POPE, 12
proudest greatest humiliation . . . when the spirit is p. PANKHURST, C, 2
prove p. anything by figures CARLYLE, T, 4
proved p. upon our pulses KEATS, 59
What is now P. was . . . imagined BLAKE, W, 24
Which was to be p. EUCLID, 1
proverb A p. is much matter FULLER, T, 2
no p. to you till your life has illustrated it KEATS, 64
p. is one man's wit and all men's wisdom RUSSELL, J, 2
proverbs p. provide them with wisdom MAUGHAM, 23
provided Add: 'p. he is really dead' LA BRUYÈRE, 12
Providence a kind of P. will . . . end . . . the acts of God DE VRIES, 7
fathom the inscrutable workings of P. BIRKENHEAD, 3
that P. dictates with the assurance of a sleepwalker HITLER, 15
This is the temple of P. BRADLEY, F, 2
Providential a case of P. interference TEMPLE, F, 1
province all knowledge to be my p. BACON, FRANCIS, 67
provinces The reluctant obedience of distant p. MACAULAY, T, 5
provincial worse than p. – he was parochial JAMES, H, 7
provincialism rather be taken in adultery than . . . p. HUXLEY, A, 7
provocations we resent little p. HAZLITT, 22
provoke p. not your children BIBLE, 22
P. The years WORDSWORTH, W, 27
provoked an opportunity of being p. PEPYS, 16
provokes No one p. me with impunity ANONYMOUS, 62
prude twenty is no age to be a p. MOLIÈRE, 8
prudence p. never to practise . . . them TWAIN, 7
P. . . . when one is determining the fate of others LACLOS, 2
Psyche Your mournful P. KEATS, 33
psychiatrist Anybody who goes to see a p. GOLDWYN, 12

A p. is a man who goes to the Folies-Bergère STOCKWOOD, 1
the century of the p.'s couch MCLUHAN, 6
psychiatrists P. classify a person as neurotic SZASZ, 7
psychic p. development of the individual FREUD, S, 2
psychological the profession of historian fits a man for p. analysis SARTRE, 11
There is no such thing as p. SARTRE, 17
psychology Children . . . have no use for p. SINGER, 1
psychopathologist the p. the unspeakable MAUGHAM, 8
psychotic Psychiatrists classify a person as . . . p. SZASZ, 7
puberty We are all American at p. WAUGH, E, 25
public a right to share your privacy in a p. place USTINOV, 6
false to his friends . . . true to the p. BERKELEY, 1
flinging a pot of paint in the p.'s face RUSKIN, 17
give the p. what they want to see SKELTON, RED, 1
If the British p. falls for this HAILSHAM, 4
I hope it will not interfere with the p. business of the country SHERIDAN, R, 15
more . . . ungrateful animal than the p. HAZLITT, 23
Never lose your temper with . . . the p. PANKHURST, C, 1
not describe holding p. office ACHESON, 5
Not even a p. figure CURZON, 1
strike against p. safety COOLIDGE, 4
The p. be damned VANDERBILT, 1
The p. buys its opinions as it buys its meat BUTLER, S, 15
The p. doesn't give a damn BEECHAM, 2
The P. is an old woman CARLYLE, T, 19
three things . . . the p. will always clamour for HOOD, 15
transform this society without a major extension of p. ownership KINNOCK, 1
twenty years of marriage make her . . . like a p. building WILDE, 56
two hundred guineas for flinging a pot of paint in the p.'s face WHISTLER, 1
publican How like a fawning p. he looks SHAKESPEARE, 238
publicity Any p. PROVERBS, 57
public school Anyone who has been to . . . p. WAUGH, E, 22
enjoy a p. CONNOLLY, 5
Keats's vulgarity with a P. accent LEAVIS, 1
p., where . . . learning was painfully beaten into him PEACOCK, 8
the p. system all over WAUGH, E, 8
public schools P. are the nurseries of all vice FIELDING, 10
publish I'll p., right or wrong BYRON, 36
P. and be damned WELLINGTON, 2
p. and be sued INGRAMS, 2
published you may destroy whatever you haven't p. HORACE, 11
publisher Barabbas was a p. CAMPBELL, T, 8
publishers those with irrational fear of life become p. CONNOLLY, 8
Puccini Wagner is the P. of music MORTON, 5
puffeth knowledge p. up BIBLE, 32
Puke Roger . . . would lead the procession, followed by Widdle and P. DURRELL, G, 2
pulled about time we p. our fingers out PHILIP, PRINCE, 2
pulse two people with one p. MACNEICE, 2
pulses proved upon our p. KEATS, 59
pun A man who could make so vile a p. DENNIS, J, 1
punctuality P. is the politeness of kings LOUIS XVIII, 1
P. is the politeness of princes PROVERBS, 343
P. is the virtue of the bored WAUGH, E, 26
punished Am I not p. enough in not VOLTAIRE, 34
Men are rewarded and p. not for what they do SZASZ, 1
Those who offend us are generally p. TROLLOPE, 16
punishing p. anyone who comes between them SMITH, SYDNEY, 10
punishment capital p. tend to the security of the people FRY, E, 1
Corporal p. is . . . humiliating for him who gives it KEY, E, 4
let the p. fit the crime GILBERT, W, 29
P. is not for revenge FRY, E, 2
punishments In nature there are neither rewards nor p. INGERSOLL, 2
pupils Time is a great teacher, but . . . kills all its p. BERLIOZ, 1
puppy Frogs and snails And p.-dogs' tails NURSERY RHYMES, 70
purchasers a pattern to encourage p. SWIFT, 6
pure All those who are not racially p. HITLER, 9
a p. river of water of life BIBLE, 474
Because my heart is p. TENNYSON, 72
p. as the driven slush BANKHEAD, 10
P. mathematics consists entirely of assertions RUSSELL, B, 14
purgatory the p. of men FLORIO, 1
purge p. me with hyssop PSALMS, 31

puritan A p.'s a person who pours righteous indignation

CHESTERTON, 49

The P. hated bear-baiting | MACAULAY, T. 8
To the P. all things are impure | LAWRENCE, D. 5
puritanism P. – The haunting fear | MENCKEN, 1
purity I have laboured to refine our language to grammatical p.

JOHNSON, S, 24

purple-stained And p. mouth | KEATS, 37
purpose p. of God and the doom assigned | TENNYSON, 58
p. of its own And measured motion | WORDSWORTH, W, 37
the creature hath a p. | KEATS, 59
You seem to have no real p. in life | CHURCHILL, J, 3
purrs it p. like an epigram | MARQUIS, 2
To stroke a platitude until it p. | MARQUIS, 2
purse consumption of the p. | SHAKESPEARE, 118
Put money in thy p. | SHAKESPEARE, 277
pursuit among which are . . . the p. of happiness | JEFFERSON, 5
pussy Ding dong, bell, P.'s in the well | NURSERY RHYMES, 9
P. cat, p. cat, where have you been | NURSERY RHYMES, 45
put I p. away childish things | BIBLE, 38
p. down the mighty | BIBLE, 310
p. up with bad things | TROLLOPE, 11
pygmies wars of the p. will begin | CHURCHILL, W, 31
pyjamas I in p. for the heat | LAWRENCE, D, 28
pylons P., those pillars Bare | SPENDER, 1
pyramid bottom of the economic p. | ROOSEVELT, F, 8
pyramids Books are made . . . like p. | FLAUBERT, 2
Pyrenees The fleas that tease in the high P. | BELLOC, 15
The P. have ceased to exist | LOUIS XIV, 5

Q

quack uses his words as a q. uses his remedies | FÉNELON, 1
Quad I am always about in the Q. | ANONYMOUS, 15
no one about in the Q. | KNOX, R, 1
quadrupeds Dogs, like horses, are q. | MUIR, 4
Quaker A philosophical Q. | FRANKLIN, 2
Quakers I was beaten up by Q. | ALLEN, W, 5
qualities Almost every man . . . attempts to display q.

JOHNSON, S, 26

He had . . . most of the q. that make a great scientist

FLEMING, A, 2

q. . . . necessary for success upon the stage | TERRY, 2
quantity a prodigious q. of mind | TWAIN, 9
quarks Three q. for Muster Mark | JOYCE, 5
quarrel a q. in a far-away country | CHAMBERLAIN, N, 5
a q. in the streets is . . . to be hated | KEATS, 68
It takes . . . one to make a q. | INGE, 6
Out of the q. . . . we make rhetoric | YEATS, 11
q. at the same time | ROSTAND, J, 1
q. . . . energies displayed in it are fine | KEATS, 68
The justice of my q. | MARLOWE, 12
quarrelled I did not know that we had ever q. | THOREAU, 22
I have q. with my wife | PEACOCK, 10
quarrels q. which vivify its barrenness | GREER, 3
Q. would not last | ROCHEFOUCAULD, 26
quart one cannot put a q. in a pint cup | GILMAN, 1
You can't get a q. | PROVERBS, 472
Quebec I would rather . . . than take Q. | WOLFE,J, 1
queen 'Fella belong Mrs Q.' | PHILIP, PRINCE, 1
he . . . happened to marry the Q. | STRACHEY, L, 3
how very different from the home life of our own dear Q.!'

ANONYMOUS, 40

I am your anointed Q. | ELIZABETH I, 8
If this is the way Q. Victoria treats her prisoners | WILDE, 73
isn't a bad bit of goods, the Q. | CERVANTES, 13
I've been to London to look at the q. | NURSERY RHYMES, 45
I would not be a q. For all the world | SHAKESPEARE, 138
Move Q. Anne? Most certainly not | VICTORIA, 1
Q. Anne's dead | COLMAN, THE YOUNGER, 2
q. did fish for men's souls | ELIZABETH I, 1
sorrier . . . than for . . . my fair q. | MALORY, 3
the British warrior q. | COWPER, 4
The Q. of Hearts | CARROLL, 19
The Q. of Hearts She made some tarts | NURSERY RHYMES, 56
the q. of Sheba | BIBLE, 299
The q. was in the parlour | NURSERY RHYMES, 52
queenly She keeps on being Q. | WHARTON, 2
queens for q. I might have enough | MALORY, 3
queer All the world is q. | OWEN, R, 1
girls are so q. | ALCOTT, 3

the q. old Dean | SPOONER, 4
There's nowt so q. | PROVERBS, 419
thou art a little q. | OWEN, R, 1
queerer the universe is . . . q. | HALDANE,4
querulous A prim . . . rather q. person | HOUSMAN, 1
questing plashy fen passes the q. vole | WAUGH, E, 31
question a good q. for you to ask | EDEN, A, 1
A timid q. will . . . receive a confident answer | DARLING,4
man who sees both sides of a q. | WILDE, 11
Nature has never put the fatal q. | JUNG, 1
No q. is ever settled Until | WILCOX, 2
not a wise q. for me to answer | EDEN, A, 1
q. . . . which I have not been able to answer | FREUD, S, 6
that is the q. | SHAKESPEARE, 89
the q. that we do not know | MACLEISH, 1
Whatever q. there may be of his talent | THOREAU, 1
questioning Q. is not the mode of conversation | JOHNSON, S, 103
questionings Those obstinate q. | WORDSWORTH, W, 31
questions all q. are open | BELL, C, 3
I do not answer q. like this without being paid | HELLMAN, 3
queue An Englishman . . . forms an orderly q. of one | MIKES, 1
quiet All Q. on the Western Front | REMARQUE, 1
Anythin' for a q. life | DICKENS, 54
Here, where the world is q. | SWINBURNE, 2
quietness unravish'd bride of q. | KEATS, 27
quince dined on mince, and slices of q. | LEAR, 9
quintessence this q. of dust | SHAKESPEARE, 84
quo q. vadis | BIBLE, 262
quod Q. erat demonstrandum | EUCLID, 1
quotable It's better to be q. than . . . honest | STOPPARD, 12
quotation Classical q. is the *parole* of literary men

JOHNSON, S, 137

Every q. contributes something | JOHNSON, S, 4
q. is a national vice | WAUGH, E, 29
the great spring of happy q. | MONTAGUE, 2
To say that anything was a q. | SAKI, 7
quotations A book that furnishes no q. | PEACOCK, 3
good thing . . . to read books of q. | CHURCHILL, W, 21
It needs no dictionary of q. | BEERBOHM, 12
q. from the Bible and the rest | JOYCE, 1
quote man can be forgiven a lot if he can q. Shakespeare

SHAKESPEARE, 15

q. Shakespeare in an economic crisis | PHILIP, PRINCE, 7
quoted Famous remarks are seldom q. correctly | STRUNSKY, 1
quotes q. . . . give us a nodding acquaintance with the originator

WILLIAMS, K, 1

R

rabbit The r. has a charming face | ANONYMOUS, 84
rabbits a tale of four little r. | POTTER, B, 1
except to shoot r. | MASEFIELD, 1
Rabelais R. is the wondrous mask of ancient comedy

RABELAIS, 1

rabies The victory over r. | PASTEUR, 2
race A loftier r. | SYMONDS, 1
in a r. run all, but one receiveth the prize | BIBLE, 33
my opinion of the human r. | MAUGHAM, 21
r. is not to the swift | BIBLE, 74
Slow and steady wins the r. | LLOYD, 1
races human species . . . two distinct r. | LAMB, CHARLES, 10
the r. of Europe are melting | ZANGWILL, 2
Rachmaninov R.'s immortalizing totality | STRAVINSKY, 1
racially those who are not r. pure | HITLER, 9
racing getting the victor's palm without the dust of r. | HORACE, 14
rack Leave not a r. behind | SHAKESPEARE, 325
radical A r. is a man | ROOSEVELT, F, 12
The r. invents the views | TWAIN, 11
radicals Few r. have good digestions | BUTLER, S, 16
radio I had the r. on | MONROE, M, 1
Simply a r. personality | WAUGH, E, 47
rage all Heaven in a r. | BLAKE, W, 10
R., r., against the dying of the light | THOMAS, D, 1
rages the weight of r. | SPOONER, 2
rags only men in r. . . . Mistake themselves | RALEIGH, W A, 1
no scandal like r. | FARQUHAR, 1
railing R. at life, and yet afraid of death | CHURCHILL, C, 4
railway when they think they are alone in r. carriages

MILLER, J, 2

raiment they parted his r., and cast lots | BIBLE, 339
rain A Hard R.'s A-Gonna Fall | DYLAN, 9

a hat that lets the r. in | FREDERICK THE GREAT, 3
drop of r. maketh a hole in the stone | LATIMER, 1
droppeth as the gentle r. | SHAKESPEARE, 246
falls not hail, or r., or any snow | TENNYSON, 25
He comes in the terrible R. | SITWELL, E, 2
R. before seven | PROVERBS, 346
R., r., go away | PROVERBS, 347
singing in the r. | FREED, 1
rainbow A r. in the morning | PROVERBS, 62
Somewhere over the r. | HARBURG, 4
the R. gave thee birth | DAVIES, W, 1
raineth it r. on the just | BOWEN, C, 1
rains It never r. but it pours | PROVERBS, 230
rainy Keep something for a r. day | PROVERBS, 240
when it is not r. | BYRON, 7
raise My God shall r. me up | RALEIGH, W, 3
Now he will r. me to be a martyr | BOLEYN, 1
rake every woman is at heart a r. | POPE, 42
lene . . . as is a r. | CHAUCER, 8
rallying-point The party is the r. | STALIN, 4
Ralph R. wept for the end of innocence | GOLDING, 2
ram a r. caught in a thicket | BIBLE, 170
Ramadan month of R. shall ye fast | KORAN, 4
rams mountains skipped like r. | PSALMS, 63
Randolph the only part of R. that was not malignant | WAUGH, E, 51
rapidly but not so r. | BECKETT, 3
rapping r. at my chamber door | POE, 1
rapture a r. on the lonely shore | BYRON, 16
The first fine careless r. | BROWNING, R, 27
rare as r. things will, it vanished | BROWNING, R, 39
keep it shut up . . . like a r., r. fiddle | MANSFIELD, K, 1
rascal Get down you dirty r. | NURSERY RHYMES, 23
rascals R., would you live for ever | FREDERICK THE GREAT, 1
rashes Green grow the r. O | BURNS, R, 11
rat face of a harassed r. | THURBER, 4
Mr Speaker, I smell a r. | ROCHE, 2
That killed the r. | NURSERY RHYMES, 62
You dirty double-crossing r. | CAGNEY, 1
ratchet politics . . . of the r. | THATCHER, M, 6
rationalized Happiness . . . should never be r. | CHESTERTON, 20
rats R.! They fought the dogs | BROWNING, R, 42
ravages What do the r. of time not injure | HORACE, 37
raven Quoth the R., 'Nevermore.' | POE, 2
r. himself is hoarse | SHAKESPEARE, 206
ravens There were three r. sat on a tree | ANONYMOUS, 96
ravished He . . . r. this fair creature | FIELDING, 8
raw the working-class which, r. and half-developed | ARNOLD, M, 9
razor Satire should, like a polished r. keen | MONTAGU, 1
razors R. pain you | PARKER, D, 3
reach a man's r. should exceed his grasp | BROWNING, R, 4
reactionaries r. are paper tigers | MAO TSE TUNG, 6
read A lonesome man . . . who does not know how to r. | FRANKLIN, 13
A man ought to r. | JOHNSON, S, 63
beautiful . . . for someone who could not r. | CHESTERTON, 48
books. . . . r. by people who don't understand them | LICHTENBERG, 2
do *you* r. books *through* | JOHNSON, S, 87
Education . . . has produced a vast population able to r. | TREVELYAN, 2
everybody wants to have r. | TWAIN, 17
give up writing today – r. Pepys instead | PEPYS, 3
Hares have no time to r. | BROOKNER, 2
He writes as fast as they can r. | HAZLITT, 7
His books were r. | BELLOC, 10
In my early years I r. very hard | JOHNSON, S, 43
I've just r. that I am dead . . . | KIPLING, 32
King George will be able to r. that | HANCOCK, 1
R., mark, learn and inwardly digest | BOOK OF COMMON PRAYER, 1
sooner r. a time-table . . . than nothing | MAUGHAM, 18
When I want to r. a novel | DISRAELI, 40
will bear to be r. twice | THOREAU, 5
reader A r. seldom peruses a book with pleasure | ADDISON, 9
not to inform the r. | ACHESON, 2
R., I married him | BRONTË, C, 3
the r. . . . is the respondent | WHITE, E, 2
use a word that might send the r. to the dictionary | HEMINGWAY, 2
readers his r. are proud to live in it | CONNOLLY, 4
The human race . . . many of my r. | CHESTERTON, 28
to trade a hundred contemporary r. for | KOESTLER, 6

Was there ever yet anything written . . . that was wished longer by its r. | JOHNSON, S, 36
reading as much pleasure in the r. | QUARLES, 1
a substitute for r. it | BURGESS, 5
a tragedy and therefore not worth r. | AUSTEN, 11
but I prefer r. | SMITH, L, 3
If a book is worth r. | RUSKIN, 7
I have . . . lost my taste for r. | WALPOLE, H, 2
I loitered my life away, r. books | HAZLITT, 9
I shall lose no time in r. it | DISRAELI, 19
Peace is poor r. | HARDY, 6
R. . . . . ingenious device for avoiding thought | HELPS, 1
R. isn't an occupation we encourage among police officers | ORTON, 5
R. is to the mind | STEELE, 1
R. maketh a full man | BACON, FRANCIS, 51
The r. of all good books | DESCARTES, 2
There are two motives for r. a book | RUSSELL, B, 9
When I am not walking, I am r. | LAMB, CHARLES, 13
ready I have but ninepence in r. money | ADDISON, 18
ready made critics are r. | BYRON, 38
Why not 'r.' | CHURCHILL, W, 11
Reagans the R. will be the rule | REAGAN, 2
real I could have become a r. painter | HOKUSAI, 1
Nothing ever becomes r. till it is experienced | KEATS, 64
whether Zelda and I are r. | FITZGERALD, F S, 15
realistic he is going to make 'a r. decision' | MCCARTHY, M, 1
reality art . . . r. which is . . . in our minds | MACCARTHY, 3
As far as the laws of mathematics refer to r. | EINSTEIN, 12
by r. I mean shops like Selfridges | LAWRENCE, T, 8
Cannot bear very much r. | ELIOT, T, 7
r. as a springboard into space | BLAKE, W, 2
statesmen . . . more estranged from 'r.' | LAING, 1
The whole of art is an appeal to a r. | MACCARTHY, 3
realize I saw it, but I did not r. it | PEABODY, 1
realm A worse king never left a r. undone | BYRON, 43
realms travell'd in the r. of gold | KEATS, 41
reap r. the whirlwind | BIBLE, 190
sow not, neither do they r. | BIBLE, 370
They that sow in tears shall r. in joy | PSALMS, 69
whatsoever a man soweth, that shall he also r. | BIBLE, 136
Reaper a R. whose name is Death | LONGFELLOW, 11
reaping No, r. | BOTTOMLEY, 1
reappear all great events . . . in . . . history r. | MARX, K, 6
reason A man who does not lose his r. | LESSING, G, 1
Faith consists in believing when it is beyond the power of r. to believe | VOLTAIRE, 25
happiness is not an ideal of r. | KANT, 3
He never does a proper thing without . . . an improper r. | SHAW, 17
he who destroys a good book, kills r. | MILTON, 6
Human r. won. | KHRUSHCHEV, 3
it was neither rhyme nor r. | MORE, 1
man . . . is R.'s slave | CONNOLLY, 20
nothing is law that is not r. | POWELL, J, 1
not to r. why | TENNYSON, 9
Once the people begin to r. | VOLTAIRE, 31
Only r. can convince us | BELL, C, 3
R. is itself a matter of faith | CHESTERTON, 31
r. not the need | SHAKESPEARE, 175
right deed for the wrong r. | ELIOT, T, 18
The madman . . . has lost everything except his r. | CHESTERTON, 29
the r. of the case | POWELL, J, 1
The ruling passion conquers r. still | POPE, 45
who turns mad for a r. | CERVANTES, 11
woman's r. | SHAKESPEARE, 347
reasonable Act of God . . . *something which no r. man could have expected* | HERBERT, A, 8
figure of 'The R. Man' | HERBERT, A, 3
Victoria has . . . become very r. | VICTORIA, 1
We are r. | PAISLEY, 1
Who kills a man kills a r. creature | MILTON, 6
reasoners most plausible r. | HAZLITT, 28
reasons Metaphysics is the finding of bad r. | BRADLEY, F, 5
never give your r. | MANSFIELD, W, 1
r. for not printing any list of subscribers | JOHNSON, S, 138
The heart has its r. | PASCAL, 7
two r. for drinking | PEACOCK, 6
rebel go on being a r. too long | DURRELL, L, 1
how to r. and conform at the same time | CRISP, 2

What is a r. CAMUS, 14
rebellion A little r. now and then JEFFERSON, 7
recall The Gods themselves cannot r. their gifts TENNYSON, 76
receipts How were the r. today BARNUM, 2
receive whoso shall r. one such little child BIBLE, 400
received a cloud r. him out of their sight BIBLE, 1
freely ye have r., freely give BIBLE, 385
receiver your wife . . . is a r. of stolen goods JOHNSON, S, 134
reception men that . . . hinder the r. of every work
JOHNSON, S, 27
recession It's a r. when your neighbour TRUMAN, 9
reckon'd beggary in the love that can be r. SHAKESPEARE, 25
reckoning take you . . . at your own r. TROLLOPE, 15
recognize did not r. me by my face TROLLOPE, 2
recoils Revenge . . . back on itself r. MILTON, 51
recompense R. injury with justice CONFUCIUS, 12
reconcile How r. this world . . . with . . . my imagining KELLER, 5
It takes a long while for a . . . trustful person to r. himself to . . . God MENCKEN, 10
recounting calms one's grief by r. it CORNEILLE, 5
recreation cooking . . . man . . . made of it a r. POST, 2
red Coral is far more r. SHAKESPEARE, 371
it's not even r. brick, but white tile OSBORNE, 4
leeches have r. blood CUVIER, 1
R. Badge of Courage CRANE, 1
R. lips are not so r. OWEN, W, 4
R. sky at night PROVERBS, 348
The people's flag is deepest r. CONNELL, 1
The sand of the desert is sodden r. NEWBOLT, 7
thin r. line tipped with steel RUSSELL, W, 1
redeemer I know that my r. liveth BIBLE, 233
O Lord, my strength, and my r. PSALMS, 10
redemption married past r. DRYDEN, 28
red-hot The Last of the R. Mamas TUCKER, 1
redundancy handing out r. notices to its own workers
KINNOCK, 9
reeling R. and Writhing CARROLL, 15
references Always verify your r. ROUTH, 1
reflection a r. of the British Museum Reading Room SPARK, 12
r. of a boy too long exposed to feminine eyes CARROLL, 1
reform All r. . . . will prove unavailing CARLYLE, T, 5
Any attempt to r. the university ILLICH, 1
reformation Every r. must have its victims SAKI, 19
refreshed like a giant r. with wine PSALMS, 43
The tree of liberty must be r. JEFFERSON, 8
refuge God is the immemorial r. MENCKEN, 9
Idleness . . . the r. of weak minds CHESTERFIELD, 15
Lord . . . our r. from one generation to another PSALMS, 48
Patriotism is the last r. JOHNSON, S, 95
the God of Jacob is our r. PSALMS, 28
refuse To r. praise ROCHEFOUCAULD, 18
refused She r. to begin the 'Beguine' COWARD, 19
refute I r. it *thus* JOHNSON, S, 71
regardless r. of their doom GRAY, 9
regime No r. has ever loved great writers SOLZHENITSYN, 10
regiment led his r. from behind GILBERT, W, 1
register I want to r. a complaint MARX, G, 14
the r. of the . . . misfortunes of mankind GIBBON, 1
registry marriage in a r. office ADAMS, R, 1
regret My r. Becomes an April violet TENNYSON, 37
remember and r. LANDON, 2
wild with all r. TENNYSON, 63
regrets I have no r. BERGMAN, 1
the Cup that clears TO-DAY OF PAST R. FITZGERALD, E, 9
The follies which a man r. ROWLAND, H, 2
rehearsing R. a play is making the word flesh SHAFFER, 3
reign Better to r. in Hell MILTON, 34
reigned I have r. with your loves ELIZABETH I, 3
reigns king r., but does not govern ZAMOYSKI, 1
The work of Henry James . . . into three r. JAMES, H, 3
reject If you r. me on account of my religion BELLOC, 17
rejection R., derision, poverty, failure VIZINCZEY, 1
rejoice let us heartily r. in the strength of our salvation
PSALMS, 54
new sights of Nature made me r. CURIE, 1
r. in the Lord alway BIBLE, 444
the bones which thou hast broken may r. PSALMS, 31
rejoiced my spirit hath r. in God my Saviour BIBLE, 309
related A group of closely r. persons MACAULAY, R, 3
relation If a man's character is to be abused . . . there's nobody like a r. THACKERAY, 11

relations Fate chooses your r. DELILLE, 1
great men have their poor r. DICKENS, 8
relaxation r. from one . . . labour FRANCE, 3
relaxes Bless r. BLAKE, W, 28
relief For this r. much thanks SHAKESPEARE, 64
There is a certain r. in change IRVING, 3
thou wilt give thyself r. MARCUS AURELIUS, 2
religion a feeling of inward tranquillity which r. is powerless to bestow FORBES, 1
Art and r. first; then philosophy SPARK, 9
As to r., I hold it to be the . . . duty PAINE, 4
brothels with bricks of R. BLAKE, W, 20
Cromwell . . . in whom ambition . . . suspended . . . r.
CROMWELL, O, 1
Fascism is a r. MUSSOLINI, 4
If you reject me on account of my r. BELLOC, 17
Love is my r. KEATS, 67
Many people think they have r. INGERSOLL, 3
Men will wrangle for r. COLTON, 1
no reason to bring r. into it O'CASEY, 3
Not a r. for gentlemen CHARLES II, 2
Nothing is so fatal to r. as indifference BURKE, E, 23
One's r. . . . yours is Success BARRIE, 7
R. Has made an honest woman of the supernatural FRY, C, 3
R. is an illusion FREUD, S, 3
R. is by no means a proper subject CHESTERFIELD, 19
R. is love WEBB, B, 1
R. . . . is the opium of the people MARX, K, 4
r. of feeble minds BURKE, E, 12
r. of Socialism BEVAN, 2
R.'s in the heart JERROLD, 1
Science without r. is lame EINSTEIN, 3
Sensible men are all of the same r. DISRAELI, 7
talks loudly against r. STERNE, 8
that God is interested only . . . in r. TEMPLE, W, 2
The Christian r. not only HUME, D, 3
To become a popular r. INGE, 5
We must reject a privatization of r. RUNCIE, 1
when r. is allowed to invade . . . private life MELBOURNE, 11
when r. was strong and science weak SZASZ, 2
religions a country with thirty-two r. TALLEYRAND, 1
sixty different r., and only one sauce CARACCIOLO, 1
The r. we call false were once true EMERSON, 6
religious a r. animal BURKE, E, 11
first, r. and moral principles ARNOLD, T, 2
not r.-good HARDY, 10
r. outlook on life JUNG, 6
skilled appeals to r. prejudice HUXLEY, T, 11
To be at ail is to be r. BUTLER, S, 21
relished the taste by which he is . . . r. WORDSWORTH, W, 20
reluctant The r. obedience of distant provinces
MACAULAY, T, 5
re-made emerged r., as from a chrysalis STAPLEDON, 2
remarkable nothing left r. SHAKESPEARE, 36
r. thing about Shakespeare SHAKESPEARE, 8
remedies Extreme r. . . . for extreme diseases HIPPOCRATES, 2
He that will not apply new r. BACON, FRANCIS, 30
Our r. oft in ourselves do lie SHAKESPEARE, 20
paralyse it by encumbering it with r. TOLSTOY, L, 11
r. . . . suggested for a disease CHEKHOV, 1
remedy a r. for everything except death CERVANTES, 17
Force is not a r. BRIGHT, 3
I never think of finding a r. PASTEUR, 5
r. is worse than the disease BACON, FRANCIS, 46
'Tis a sharp r., but a sure one RALEIGH, W, 5
remember I only r. what I've learnt WHITE, P, 2
I r., I r. HOOD, 5
Oh! don't you r. sweet Alice ENGLISH, 1
r. and regret LANDON, 1
r. Lot's wife BIBLE, 335
R. me when I am gone away ROSSETTI, C, 4
she did not r. . . . her jewelry LOOS, 1
The world will little note, nor long r. LINCOLN, 17
we shall be glad to r. even these hardships VIRGIL, 7
We will r. them BINYON, 1
When I meet a man whose name I can't r. DISRAELI, 38
remembered By this may I r. be ANONYMOUS, 106
I r. my God SOUTHEY, 5
we r. thee, O Sion PSALMS, 70
remembrance r. of things past SHAKESPEARE, 361
there is no r. of former things BIBLE, 63

There's rosemary, that's for r.	SHAKESPEARE, 103
reminiscences the old have r.	SAKI, 12
remorse r. for what you have thought about your wife	
	ROSTAND, J, 2
remove faith, so that I could r. mountains	BIBLE, 38
Renaissance the R. was . . . the green end	FOWLES, 2
render husband r. unto the wife due benevolence	BIBLE, 29
r. . . . unto Caesar	BIBLE, 410
rendezvous a r. with Death	SEEGER, A, 1
renegades Political r. always start their career	KINNOCK, 10
renew r. a right spirit within me	PSALMS, 31
renewal urban r. in New York City	ILLICH, 1
rent they r. out my room	ALLEN, W, 9
repair the landlord does not intend to r.	ADAMS, J, 4
repartee A majority is always the best r.	DISRAELI, 14
repast A new r., or an untasted spring	ADDISON, 5
repay whatsoever thou spendest . . . I will r.	BIBLE, 325
repeal the r. of bad or obnoxious laws	GRANT, U, 6
repeat obliged to imitate himself, and to r.	REYNOLDS, J, 3
repeated A platitude is simply a truth r.	BALDWIN, S, 13
repellent His sickness has created atrocities that are r.	
	PICASSO, 2
repent Do you . . . Never, my Love, r.	PATMORE, 2
r. at leisure	CONGREVE, 10
r.: for the kingdom of heaven is at hand	BIBLE, 358
r. you of your sins	BOOK OF COMMON PRAYER, 10
you may r. before you die	PROVERBS, 220
repentance A Christian . . . feels R. on a Sunday	YBARRA, 1
There's no r. in the grave	WATTS, 5
with the morning cool r.	SCOTT, WALTER, 18
repented it r. the Lord that he had made man	BIBLE, 157
repenteth joy . . . over one sinner that r.	BIBLE, 330
repetition constant r. will finally succeed	HITLER, 10
History is an endless r.	DURRELL, L, 3
replace no one can r. him	FRANKLIN, 1
replenished His intellect is not r.	SHAKESPEARE, 196
replied And I r., 'My Lord.'	HERBERT, G, 2
reporter A r. is a man who has renounced everything	MURRAY, 1
I am a r.	GREENE, 9
reporting Language is not simply a r. device	WHORF, 1
reprehend If I r. any thing	SHERIDAN, R, 9
representation Proportional R. . . . counter-democratic	
	KINNOCK, 2
Taxation without r.	OTIS, 1
reproduce butlers and lady's maids do not r.	WELLS, 3
reproductions accurate r. of Anne Hathaway's cottage	
	LANCASTER, 2
I've seen colour r.	ROSS, H, 1
republic An aristocracy in a r. is like	MITFORD, N, 1
the r. of letters	ADDISON, 3
Republican The R. form of Government	SPENCER, H, 1
Republicans Please assure me that you are all R.	REAGAN, 5
republics Revolts, r., revolutions	TENNYSON, 69
repulsive Roundheads (Right but R.)	SELLAR, 5
reputability Conspicuous consumption . . . is a means of r.	
	VEBLEN, 3
reputation ever written out of r. but by himself	BENTLEY, R, 2
it is better for the r.	KEYNES, 5
it wrecks a woman's r.	COLETTE, 4
O, I have lost my r.	SHAKESPEARE, 281
spotless r.	SHAKESPEARE, 292
Until you've lost your r., you never realize	MITCHELL, M, 1
requests thou wilt grant their r.	BOOK OF COMMON PRAYER, 16
requires all the Human Frame r.	BELLOC, 6
research R.! A mere excuse for idleness	JOWETT, 5
The outcome of any serious r.	VEBLEN, 2
resent we r. little provocations	HAZLITT, 2
resentment It is very difficult to get up r.	NEWMAN, J, 1
reservoir a gigantic r. of good will	WILLKIE, 2
residuum this vast r. . . . Populace	ARNOLD, M, 9
resign'd R. unto the Heavenly will	ANONYMOUS, 11
resist r. everything except temptation	WILDE, 38
r. the devil, and he will flee	BIBLE, 218
there is almost nothing to r. at all	LAWRENCE, D, 1
resistance 'R. to tyranny is obedience to God.'	ANTHONY, 1
resisting fond of r. temptation	BECKFORD, 1
resolute Be bloody bold, and r.	SHAKESPEARE, 219
resolution In war, r.	CHURCHILL, W, 27
native hue of r.	SHAKESPEARE, 91
resources statistics, born to consume r.	HORACE, 17
respect A child deserves the maximum r.	JUVENAL, 12

Civilization is . . . equal r. for all men	ADDAMS, 3
old-fashioned r. for the young	WILDE, 23
The English have no r. for their language	SHAW, 36
those Who err each other must r.	PATMORE, 1
We must r. the other fellow's religion	MENCKEN, 3
We owe r. to the living	VOLTAIRE, 24
When people do not r. us	TWAIN, 13
respectable made contraceptive devices r.	STOPES, 3
R. means rich	PEACOCK, 1
r., middle-class . . . lady	RATTIGAN, 1
riff-raff apply to what is r.	HOPE, 6
respecter God is no r. of persons	BIBLE, 10
respects no man much r. himself	TWAIN, 13
respondent the reader . . . is the r.	WHITE, E, 2
responsibility He had . . . a total lack of r.	HOPPER, 1
In dreams begins r.	YEATS, 23
no sense of r. at the other	KNOX, R, 3
No sex without r.	LONGFORD, 1
power without r.	BALDWIN, S, 3
responsible An idea isn't r. for the people	MARQUIS, 3
every man is r. for his face	CAMUS, 4
No man is r. for his father	TURNBULL, 1
r. and the irresponsible classes	LAWRENCE, D, 12
You are r. for your rose	SAINT-EXUPÉRY, 2
rest All the r. have thirty-one	NURSERY RHYMES, 61
get rid of the r. of her	VANBURGH, 5
leave the r. to the Gods	CORNEILLE, 1
Mary Ann has gone to r.	ANONYMOUS, 55
Seek home for r.	TUSSER, 4
then would I flee away, and be at r.	PSALMS, 33
the r. I leave to the poor	RABELAIS, 8
The r. is silence	SHAKESPEARE, 108
To toil and not to seek for r.	LOYOLA, 1
restaurants Great r. are . . . mouth-brothels	RAPHAEL, 4
rested God . . . r. on the seventh day	BIBLE, 143
restless r. who will volunteer for anything	NIVEN, D, 2
restore Time may r. us	ARNOLD, M, 28
rests our heart is not quiet until it r. in Thee	
	AUGUSTINE OF HIPPO, 1
result the long r. of Time	TENNYSON, 49
resurrection I am the r., and the life	BIBLE, 256
retain To expect a man to r. everything	SCHOPENHAUER, 6
reticulated Anything r. . . . at equal distances	JOHNSON, S, 11
retire can't put off being young until you r.	LARKIN, 1
retirement R., for a monarch	VICTORIA, 2
retreat A mistress should be like a . . . r.	WYCHERLEY, 1
retrograde All that is human must r.	GIBBON, 10
return I shall r.	MACARTHUR, 1
r., r., O Shulamite	BIBLE, 497
returning R. were as tedious as go o'er	SHAKESPEARE, 217
reveal words . . . half r. and half conceal	TENNYSON, 27
Revelations It ends with R.	WILDE, 80
revelry a sound of r. by night	BYRON, 13
revels Our r. now are ended	SHAKESPEARE, 325
revenge A man that studieth r.	BACON, FRANCIS, 44
he took his r. by speaking ill	VOLTAIRE, 27
if you wrong us, shall we not r.	SHAKESPEARE, 245
Punishment is not for r.	FRY, E, 2
R., at first though sweet	MILTON, 51
R. . . . back on itself recoils	MILTON, 51
R. is a dish	PROVERBS, 349
R. is a . . . wild justice	BACON, FRANCIS, 43
R. is sweet	PROVERBS, 350
revenue name a virtue that brings in as much r.	NAPOLEON III, 1
reverence Just a little more r.	SARGENT, M, 1
reviewers R. . . . would have been poets	COLERIDGE, S, 19
reviewing Prolonged . . . r. of books involves	ORWELL, 11
revolts R., republics, revolutions	TENNYSON, 69
revolution Britain is not . . . easily rocked by r.	HAMILTON, W, 2
forged in the white heat of this r.	WILSON, HAROLD, 8
fundamental premise of a r.	TROTSKY, 7
he'd go to church, start a r.	MILLER, A, 3
Hitler has carried out a r. on our lines	MUSSOLINI, 1
R. by its very nature	TROTSKY, 1
r. is a struggle to the death	CASTRO, 1
Russia is a collapse, not a r.	LAWRENCE, D, 37
socialism in terms of the scientific r.	WILSON, HAROLD, 8
The r. eats	RICHLER, 1
The word 'r.' is a word for which you kill	WEIL, 2
We invented the R.	WEISS, 1
revolutionary fierce and r. in a bathroom	LINKLATER, 3

nobody who does not r. early JOHNSON, S, 158
r. up and walk BIBLE, 4
we have been able to r. above the brutes HUXLEY, A, 3
risk a bank that would lend money to such a poor r. BENCHLEY, 5
risks what r. you take BALZAC, 4
Ritz like the R. hotel MATHEW, 1
river a pure r. of water of life BIBLE, 474
build your House of Parliament upon the r. WELLINGTON, 4
can't step into the same r. twice HERACLITUS, 2
Fame is like a r. BACON, FRANCIS, 40
Ol' man r. HAMMERSTEIN, 4
On either side the r. lie TENNYSON, 41
On the breast of the r. of Time ARNOLD, M, 18
the r. of knowledge has too often turned back on itself JEANS, 2
'the R. Tiber foaming with much blood' POWELL, E, 1
The vanity of human life is like a r. POPE, 58
They promise to build a bridge even where there's no r.
KHRUSHCHEV, 7
road All I seek . . . the r. below me STEVENSON, R, 6
a r. . . . that does not go through the intellect CHESTERTON, 9
Does the r. wind up-hill ROSSETTI, C, 6
free as the r. HERBERT, G, 1
He watched the ads And not the r. NASH, 6
Keep right on to the end of the r. LAUDER, 5
On the r. to Mandalay KIPLING, 23
people who stay in the middle of the r. BEVAN, 10
tell us of the R. FITZGERALD, E, 17
the Golden R. to Samarkand FLECKER, 1
There is a r. from the eye to the heart CHESTERTON, 9
The r. was a ribbon of moonlight NOYES, 1
the rolling English r. CHESTERTON, 35
They shut the r. through the woods KIPLING, 30
roads all r. lead to France THOMAS, E, 4
All r. lead to Rome PROVERBS, 36
How many r. must a man walk down DYLAN, 1
New r.: new ruts CHESTERTON, 50
Two r. diverged FROST, R, 7
roam Mid pleasures and palaces though we may r. PAYNE, 1
roamin' R. in the gloamin' LAUDER, 3
roast the learned r. an egg POPE, 53
rob Why r. one to feed the other JUANG-ZU, 1
robb'd He that is r., not wanting what is stol'n SHAKESPEARE, 285
robbed We was r. JACOBS, 1
when you've r. a man of everything SOLZHENITSYN, 8
robber now Barabbas was a r. BIBLE, 266
Robbins President R. was so well adjusted JARRELL, 1
robes R. and furr'd gowns hide all SHAKESPEARE, 188
robin A r. redbreast in a cage BLAKE, 9
Our little English r. WORDSWORTH, W, 44
Who killed Cock R. NURSERY RHYMES, 73
Robin Gray R., he was gudeman to me BARNARD, A, 1
Robinson Here's to you, Mrs R. SIMON, 1
robot the modern conception of a r. CHURCHILL, W, 24
rock built his house upon a r. BIBLE, 380
he smote the r. twice BIBLE, 437
R. of ages, cleft for me TOPLADY, 1
r. of offence BIBLE, 199
the r. that is higher than I PSALMS, 37
upon this r. I will build my church BIBLE, 397
With my little stick of Blackpool r. FORMBY, 1
rock and roll R. or Christianity LENNON, 13
rocked R. in the cradle of the deep MILLARD, 1
rocks older than the r. among which she sits PATER, 1
The hand that r. the cradle WALLACE, W, 1
rod Aaron's r. BIBLE, 108
he that spareth his r. hateth his son BIBLE, 450
spare the r. BUTLER, S, 4
thy r. and thy staff comfort me PSALMS, 11
rode r. madly off in all directions LEACOCK, 10
rodent-like music critics. . . . small and r. STRAVINSKY, 3
Roland *Childe R. to the Dark Tower came* BROWNING, R, 17
role he saw his r. as being that of Moses JAY, 1
roll our soul Had *felt* him like the thunder's r. ARNOLD, M, 26
R. up that map PITT THE YOUNGER, 2
rolled bottoms of my trousers r. ELIOT, T, 14
rolling Like a r. stone DYLAN, 4
The r. English drunkard CHESTERTON, 35
Rolls a small car . . . instead of my R. Royce MOUNTBATTEN, 1
She has a R. body and a Balham mind MORTON, 1
Roma *R. locuta est* AUGUSTINE OF HIPPO, 4
Roman noblest R. of them all SHAKESPEARE, 160

the Holy R. Empire was neither holy VOLTAIRE, 16
the Ghost of the deceased R. Empire HOBBES, 7
the R. people had but one neck CALIGULA, 1
romance The r. of *Tom Jones* GIBBON, 5
Twenty years of r. makes a woman look like a ruin WILDE, 56
Romans Friends, R., countrymen SHAKESPEARE, 153
The R. and Greeks found everything human LAWRENCE, D, 6
which came first, the Greeks or the R. DISRAELI, 39
Romanticism R. is STENDHAL, 2
Rome I lov'd R. more SHAKESPEARE, 152
R. has spoken AUGUSTINE OF HIPPO, 4
R.'s gross yoke Drops off BROWNING, R, 18
R. shall perish COWPER, 5
R.'s just a city like anywhere else BURGESS, 4
R. was not built PROVERBS, 351
The farther you go from the church of R. WOTTON, 4
When in R. AMBROSE, 1
when R. falls BYRON, 15
Romeo R.! wherefore art thou R. SHAKESPEARE, 309
room All I want is a r. somewhere LERNER, 2
before my little r. BROOKE, 2
Infinite riches in a little r. MARLOWE, 10
no r. for them in the inn BIBLE, 313
R. at the Top BRAINE, 1
The perpetual struggle for r. and food MALTHUS, 2
There is always r. at the top WEBSTER, D, 7
who sneaked into my r. MARX, G, 14
rooms being old is having lighted r. LARKIN, 2
Roosevelt If R. were alive he'd turn in his grave GOLDWYN, 10
the kind of nation that President R. hoped for JOHNSON, L, 6
roost Curses . . . always come home to r. SOUTHEY, 2
root love of money is the r. of all evil BIBLE, 511
the r. of all sins JAMES I, 2
Though leaves are many, the r. is one YEATS, 7
rootless We are not r. vagabonds ASHDOWN, 2
roots His r. were buried deep TOLKIEN, 1
rope Give a thief enough r. PROVERBS, 173
rose An unofficial English r. BROOKE, 3
a r. By any other name SHAKESPEARE, 310
A r. without a thorn MACNALLY, 1
At Christmas I no more desire a r. SHAKESPEARE, 195
killing as the canker to the r. MILTON, 23
Like a r., she has lived as long as roses live MALHERBE, 1
mighty lak' a r. STANTON, F, 1
One perfect r. PARKER, D, 8
R. is a r. STEIN, 3
R. . . . where some buried Caesar bled FITZGERALD, E, 8
The budding r. above the r. full blown WORDSWORTH, W, 41
the last r. of summer MOORE, T, 5
the r. of Sharon BIBLE, 486
You are responsible for your r. SAINT-EXUPÉRY, 2
rosebuds Gather ye r. while ye may HERRICK, 6
rosemary There's r., that's for remembrance SHAKESPEARE, 103
roses a wreath of r. BAYLY, 3
days of wine and r. DOWSON, 4
Everything's Coming Up R. SONDHEIM, 1
Flung r., riotously DOWSON, 2
I will make thee beds of r. MARLOWE, 14
I would like my r. to see you SHERIDAN, R, 18
Nor does a . . . gardener scent his r. COCTEAU, 1
not a bed of r. STEVENSON, R, 25
Plant thou no r. ROSSETTI, C, 8
Ring-a-ring o'r. NURSERY RHYMES, 47
R. are flowering in Picardy WEATHERLY, 2
Send two dozen r. to Room 424 MARX, G, 19
so with r. overgrown MARVELL, 6
The lilies and r. were all awake TENNYSON, 57
Treaties are like r. and young girls DE GAULLE, 12
rot lie in cold obstruction, and to r. SHAKESPEARE, 232
we r. and r. SHAKESPEARE, 46
Rotarians The astronauts! . . . R. in outer space VIDAL, 3
rotten r. in the state of Denmark SHAKESPEARE, 76
rough-hew R. them how we will SHAKESPEARE, 106
round R. and r. the garden Like a teddy bear
NURSERY RHYMES, 48
r., neat, not gaudy LAMB, CHARLES, 25
roundabouts What's lost upon the r. CHALMERS, 1
Roundheads R. (Right but Repulsive) SELLAR, 5
roving we'll go no more a r. BYRON, 41
row R. upon r. with strict impunity TATE, A, 1
rowed All r. fast COKE, D, 1

Rowley Heigh ho! says R.	NURSERY RHYMES, 1
royal A R. Commission is a broody hen	FOOT, 1
Once in r. David's city	ALEXANDER, 2
trying not to be different in the sense of being r.	
	MOUNTBATTEN, 4
rub R.-a-dub-dub, Three men in a tub	NURSERY RHYMES, 49
there's the r.	SHAKESPEARE, 89
try to r. up against money	RUNYON, 2
rubies her price is far above r.	BIBLE, 458
the price of wisdom is above r.	BIBLE, 234
Rubinstein Arthur R.	HEIFETZ, 1
rubs sentimentality . . . r. you up the wrong way	MAUGHAM, 25
rude Fifty lovelies in the r.	THOMAS, D, 15
The right people are r.	MAUGHAM, 15
rudeness oaf who has confused r. with blunt speech	JAMES, C, 1
rue With r. my heart is laden	HOUSMAN, 16
rug Stop . . . those dogs . . . peeing on my cheapest r.	HEARST, 1
Rugby Union R. which is a distillation	THOMAS, G, 1
ruin for the r. of our sex	SMOLLETT, 5
I am inclined to notice the r. in things	MILLER, A, 4
makes a woman look like a r.	WILDE, 56
ruined Such another victory and we are r.	PYRRHUS, 1
ruining they will end by r. our idea	MUSSOLINI, 1
ruins r. that Cromwell knocked about a bit	LLOYD, M, 3
rule a good r. in life never to apologize	WODEHOUSE, 9
A little r., a little sway	DYER, 2
a man who wanted to r. the world	COHEN, 2
I don't believe in black majority r.	SMITH, I, 1
One Ring to r. them all	TOLKIEN, 5
R. all England under a hog	COLLINGBOURNE, 1
safer to obey than to r.	KEMPIS, 2
The first r. in opera is the first r. in life	MELBA, 1
the Reagans will be the r.	REAGAN, 2
ruler I am the R. of the Queen's Navee	GILBERT, W, 5
rulers R. of the Queen's Navee	GILBERT, W, 11
rules R. and models destroy genius and art	HAZLITT, 29
r. of the game are what we call the laws of Nature	HUXLEY, T, 6
the hand that r. the world	WALLACE, W, 1
there are no golden r.	SHAW, 31
two golden r. for an orchestra	BEECHAM, 2
ruleth the cry of him that r. among fools	BIBLE, 75
ruling class The state is an instrument . . . of the r.	STALIN, 2
rum r., sodomy, and the lash	CHURCHILL, W, 35
Yo-ho-ho, and a bottle of r.	STEVENSON, R, 8
rumble R. thy bellyful	SHAKESPEARE, 177
rumour Where r. of oppression and deceit	COWPER, 27
run Gwine to r. all night	FOSTER, 1
He can r., but he can't hide	LOUIS, 1
in a race r. all, but one receiveth the prize	BIBLE, 33
so r., that ye may obtain	BIBLE, 33
You cannot r. with the hare	PROVERBS, 471
runcible ate with a r. spoon	LEAR, 3
He weareth a r. hat	LEAR, 7
runners like r. hand on the torch of life	LUCRETIUS, 3
runneth my cup r. over	PSALMS, 13
running it takes all the r. *you* can do	CARROLL, 24
nature . . . she'll be constantly r. back	HORACE, 20
The machine is r. away with *him*	WILHELM II, 5
runs He that fights and r. away	PROVERBS, 189
rushes Green grow the r. O	ANONYMOUS, 45
rushing a r. mighty wind	BIBLE, 2
Ruskin A certain girlish petulance of style that distinguishes R.	
	RUSKIN, 1
I doubt that art needed R.	RUSKIN, 13
Russell R.'s beautiful mathematical mind	RUSSELL, B, 2
Russia For us in R. communism is a dead dog	SOLZHENITSYN, 13
going in without the help of R.	LLOYD GEORGE, 13
on the moon as in Imperial R.	CHEKHOV, 3
R. is a collapse, not a revolution	LAWRENCE, D, 37
the greatness of R. is	LAWRENCE, D, 34
Why will America not reach out . . . to R.	DUNCAN, 2
Russian Scratch the R. and . . . find the Tartar	MAISTRE, 2
the R. people have become	TROTSKY, 8
Russians our decadence and the R.'	THURBER, 13
test the R., not the bombs	GAITSKELL, 1
rustling r. in unpaid-for silk	SHAKESPEARE, 60
ruts New roads: new r.	CHESTERTON, 50
rye Coming through the r.	BURNS, R, 6

S

Sabbath never broke the S., but for Gain	DRYDEN, 10
the child that is born on the S. day Is bonny and blithe, and good and gay	NURSERY RHYMES, 35
sabotage All business sagacity reduces itself . . . to . . . s.	
	VEBLEN, 1
sack Either back us or s. us	CALLAGHAN, 2
sacred the human body is s.	WHITMAN, 5
to obstruct the way of God . . . is more grievous than to kill in the s. months	KORAN, 3
We hold these truths to be s. and undeniable	JEFFERSON, 5
Sacred Heart Convent of the S.	ELIOT, T, 22
sacrifice A woman will always s. herself	MAUGHAM, 5
s. . . . of the devil's leavings	POPE, 56
this war . . . which did not justify the s. of a single mother's son	
	PANKHURST, S, 1
thou desirest no s., else would I give it thee	PSALMS, 32
sacrificed a principle . . . s. to expediency	MAUGHAM, 4
sad Becoming an Anglo-Catholic must . . . be a s. business	
	STRACHEY, J, 1
being kind Is all the s. world needs	WILCOX, 4
when thou art absent I am s.	NORTON, 1
sadder A s. and a wiser man	COLERIDGE, S, 40
sadists repressed s. . . . become policemen or butchers	
	CONNOLLY, 8
sadness Good day s.	ÉLUARD, 1
safe Better be s. than sorry	PROVERBS, 91
He . . . makes us feel s. and comfortable	MELBOURNE, 2
make the world s. for diversity	KENNEDY, JOHN, 14
thou shalt be s. under his feathers	PSALMS, 51
safeguard the s. of the west	WORDSWORTH, W, 58
safer s. to obey than to rule	KEMPIS, 2
safest Just when we are s.	BROWNING, R, 9
safety Safe though all s.'s lost	BROOKE, 5
s. is in our speed	EMERSON, 13
There is s. in numbers	PROVERBS, 411
sage without hardness will be s.	ARNOLD, M, 20
said a great deal to be s. For being dead	BENTLEY, E, 3
Nothing has yet been s. that's not been s. before	TERENCE, 1
the best which has been thought and s. in the world	
	ARNOLD, M, 3
they do not know what they have s.	CHURCHILL, W, 42
'Tis s. that some have died for love	WORDSWORTH, W, 70
sailor No man will be a s.	JOHNSON, S, 56
Tinker, Tailor, Soldier, S.	NURSERY RHYMES, 65
sailors It is always opening time in the S. Arms	THOMAS, D, 21
S. have a port	PROVERBS, 352
saint before we *know* he is a s., there will have to be miracles	
	GREENE, 8
being a novelist, I consider myself superior to the s., the scientist	
	LAWRENCE, D, 38
never a s. took pity on My soul	COLERIDGE, S, 31
possible for a woman to qualify as a s.	STOCKS, 1
St Agnes S.' Eve – Ah, bitter chill it was	KEATS, 9
Saint Crispin fought with us upon S.'s day	SHAKESPEARE, 135
St Ives As I was going to S.	NURSERY RHYMES, 3
St Paul I am designing S.'s	BENTLEY, E, 6
Saint Preux S. never kicked the fireirons	CARLYLE, J, 2
saints All are not s.	PROVERBS, 31
many bodies of the s. which slept arose	BIBLE, 432
St Trinian Though loaded firearms were strictly forbidden at S.'s	
	SEARLE, 1
sake Art for art's s.	COUSIN, 1
sakes king . . . men have made for their own s.	SELDEN, 1
salad My s. days	SHAKESPEARE, 28
salary The s. of the chief executive	GALBRAITH, 8
this is the week I earn my s.	KENNEDY, JOHN, 5
Salkeld I am married to Beatrice S., a painter	BEHAN, 10
Sally There's none like pretty S.	CAREY, H, 3
sally a sudden s.	TENNYSON, 7
salmon cider and tinned s.	WAUGH, E, 33
serve both cod and s.	LEVERSON, 2
the choice between smoked s. and tinned s.	WILSON, HAROLD, 2
salt a pillar of s.	BIBLE, 168
like an egg without s.	CAWEIN, 1
nobody likes having s. rubbed into their wounds	WEST, R, 3
S. water and absence	PROVERBS, 353
speech . . . seasoned with s.	BIBLE, 23
the s. of the earth	BIBLE, 361

salvation let us heartily rejoice in the strength of our s.
PSALMS, 54
the Lord is my light, and my s.
PSALMS, 15
There is no s. outside the church AUGUSTINE OF HIPPO, 3
The s. of mankind SOLZHENITSYN, 15
Sam Play it, S. BOGART, H, 2
Samaritan But a certain S. . . . had compassion on him BIBLE, 325
ready enough to do the S. SMITH, SYDNEY, 9
Samarkand the Golden Road to S. FLECKER, 1
same he is much the s. AUSTIN, A, 1
It will be all the s. PROVERBS, 238
it would be all the s. a hundred years hence DICKENS, 25
principle seems the the s. CHURCHILL, W, 9
the s. is my brother BIBLE, 390
we must all say *the s.* MELBOURNE, 3
we're all made the s. COWARD, 4
samite Clothed in white s. TENNYSON, 20
Samuel When they circumcised Herbert S. LLOYD GEORGE, 15
sanctify Numbers s. CHAPLIN, 4
sanction Happiness is the only s. of life SANTAYANA, 5
sand a foolish man, which built his house upon the s, BIBLE, 380
and throws . . . s. in their eyes HOFFMANN, E, 1
The s. of the desert is sodden red NEWBOLT, 7
They wept like anything to see Such quantities of s. CARROLL, 27
throw the s. against the wind BLAKE, W, 34
World in a grain of s. BLAKE, W, 9
sane Show me a s. man and I will cure him for you JUNG, 9
sanity s. of any number of artistic mediocrities BLAKE, W, 1
sans S. teeth, s. eyes, s. taste, s. every thing SHAKESPEARE, 48
Sappho Where burning S. loved BYRON, 26
sarcasm petulance is not s. DISRAELI, 26
S. . . . the language of the devil CARLYLE, T, 26
sardines Life is . . . like a tin of s. BENNETT, ALAN, 1
sat The . . . gentleman has s. so long on the fence LLOYD GEORGE, 14
Satan And S. trembles COWPER, 15
S. exalted sat, by merit raised MILTON, 39
S. finds . . . mischief . . . For idle hands WATTS, 1
S., Nick, or Clootie BURNS, R, 3
Satanic Verses The author of the S. book, which is against Islam KHOMEINI, 2
satire hard not to write s. JUVENAL, 1
not quite enough of the superb courage of his s. GALSWORTHY, 1
S. is a sort of glass SWIFT, 3
S. should, like a polished razor keen MONTAGU, 1
satirists S. should be heard and not seen SHERWOOD, 2
satisfaction complacency and s. . . . in . . . a new-married couple LAMB, CHARLES, 3
the s. of knowing that we are avenged TROLLOPE, 16
satisfied his soul is s. with what is assigned to him MARCUS AURELIUS, 10
The superior man is s, CONFUCIUS, 10
Saturday betwixt A S. and Monday CAREY, H, 2
Died on S. NURSERY RHYMES, 53
S.'s child works hard for his living NURSERY RHYMES, 35
what he did on S. YBARRA, 1
satyr man is . . . either a stoic or a s. PINERO, 1
sauce a country with thirty-two religions and only one s. TALLEYRAND, 1
Art is not a special s. LETHABY, 1
sixty different religions, and only one s. CARACCIOLO, 1
The best s. in the world CERVANTES, 16
Saul S. hath slain his thousands BIBLE, 481
savage a time when Britain had a s. culture BANDA, 1
s. place! as holy and enchanted COLERIDGE, S, 16
soothe a s. breast CONGREVE, 6
The young man who has not wept is a s. SANTAYANA, 3
savaged s. by a dead sheep HEALEY, 1
savait *Si jeunesse s.* ESTIENNE, 1
save Christ Jesus came into the world to s. sinners BIBLE, 506
s. the plan NIXON, 9
S. your breath PROVERBS, 354
To s. a man's life against his will is . . . killing him HORACE, 12
saved he that endureth to the end shall be s. BIBLE, 386
they only s. the world BELLOC, 8
thy faith hath s. thee BIBLE, 322
Saviour But it's 'S. of 'is country' KIPLING, 29
I imitate the S. HUXLEY, A, 5
saw I came; I s.; God conquered JOHN III SOBIESKI, 1
I came, I s., I conquered CAESAR, 4
I s. it, but I did not realize it PEABODY, 1

Saxon The S. is not like us Normans KIPLING, 20
say cannot s. what you have to s. in twenty minutes BRABAZON OF TARA, 1
Do as I s. PROVERBS, 111
if we s. that we have no sin, we deceive BIBLE, 281
I have nothing to s., I am saying it CAGE, 1
Preachers s., Do as I s., not as I do SELDEN, 5
S. it with flowers O'KEEFE, 1
s. what you have to s., and then sit down WELLINGTON, 25
The great consolation . . . is to s. what one thinks VOLTAIRE, 30
They are to s. what they please FREDERICK THE GREAT, 2
they do not know what they are going to s. CHURCHILL, W, 42
What have we to s. to India RUSKIN, 18
When you have nothing to s. COLTON, 2
saying S. is one thing PROVERBS, 355
seldom interested in what he is s. POUND, 2
when . . . speaking, they do not know what they are s. CHURCHILL, W, 42
sayings Dr Johnson's s. PEMBROKE, 1
His s. are generally like women's letters HAZLITT, 6
scab The itch of disputing will prove the s. of churches WOTTON, 2
scaffold no middle course between the throne and the s. CHARLES X, 2
scandal In England there is only silence or s. MAUROIS, 2
It is a public s. that gives offence MOLIÈRE, 10
s. by a woman . . . proved liar HAILSHAM, 3
There's no s. like rags FARQUHAR, 1
scape who shall s. whipping SHAKESPEARE, 87
scarce S., sir. Mighty s. TWAIN, 20
scare A good s. is worth more PROVERBS, 25
scarecrows Logical consequences are the s. of fools and the beacons of wise men HUXLEY, T, 9
scarlet His sins were s. BELLOC, 10
pious bird with the s. breast WORDSWORTH, W, 44
though your sins be as s. BIBLE, 191
scars He jests at s. SHAKESPEARE, 308
scatter We plough the fields, and s. CAMPBELL, JANE, 1
scattered s. the proud BIBLE, 310
scenery Mountains . . . the beginning and the end of all natural s. RUSKIN, 6
S. is fine KEATS, 58
scenes I'll come no more behind your s., David JOHNSON, S, 46
sceptic too much of a s. to deny the possibility of anything HUXLEY, T, 10
scepticism He combined s. . . . with credulity POWYS, 1
only her s. kept her from being an atheist SARTRE, 16
sceptred this s. isle SHAKESPEARE, 295
Scheherazade S. . . . a woman saving her head WYNNE-TYSON, E, 1
schemes best laid s. o' mice an' men BURNS, R, 22
schizophrenia if God talks to you, you have s. SZASZ, 8
S. cannot be understood LAING, 4
schizophrenic if God talks to you, you are a s. SZASZ, 8
scholar the last humiliation of an aged s. COLLINGWOOD, R, 1
scholars great men have not commonly been great s. HOLMES, O, 3
S. and gentlemen WORDSWORTH, W, 39
S. dispute HORACE, 1
school Every night of her married life she has been late for s. THOMAS, D, 23
Example is the s. of mankind BURKE, E, 3
fleshly s. of Poetry BUCHANAN, 1
If every day in the life of a s. LEACOCK, 1
The Stealthy S. of Criticism ROSSETTI, D, 4
The world is but a s. of inquiry MONTAIGNE, 9
Three little maids from s. GILBERT, W, 27
till he's been to a good s. SAKI, 15
schoolboy a s.'s barring out TENNYSON, 69
every s. repeating my words MANDELSTAM, 2
I see a s. when I think of him KEATS, 5
schoolboys 'tis the s. that educate my son EMERSON, 19
schoolmasters Let s. puzzle their brain GOLDSMITH, 21
schoolroom in the s. . . . does the difference of sex . . . need to be forgotten ANTHONY, 3
schools a hundred s. of thought contend MAO TSE-TUNG, 6
There is now less flogging in our great s. JOHNSON, S, 100
We class s. . . . into four grades WAUGH, E, 5
science A s. which hesitates to forget WHITEHEAD, 5
great tragedy of S. HUXLEY, T, 1
In everything that relates to s. LAMB, CHARLES, 8

Language is only the instrument of s.   JOHNSON, S, 6
lastly s.   SPARK, 9
Learn to inure yourself to drudgery in s.   PAVLOV, 1
only applications of s.   PASTEUR, 4
Poetry is opposed to s.,. . . prose to metre   COLERIDGE, S, 18
Politics is not an exact s.   BISMARCK, 2
Politics is not a s. . . . but an art   BISMARCK, 7
S., history, politics, all were within his compass   WELLS, 2
s. is essentially international   CURIE, 4
S. is nothing but trained and organized common sense   HUXLEY, T, 2
S. is the great antidote   SMITH, A, 4
s. . . . is . . . the interplay between nature and ourselves   HEISENBERG, 2
S. must begin with myths   POPPER, 5
S. should leave off making pronouncements   JEANS, 2
s. was the only career worth following   JOLIOT-CURIE, 1
S. without religion is lame   EINSTEIN, 3
Should we force s. down the throats   PORTER, G, 2
the essence of s.   BRONOWSKI, 2
the fairy tales of s.   TENNYSON, 49
the greatest collective work of s.   BRONOWSKI, 3
The highest wisdom has but one s.   TOLSTOY, L, 8
the incorporated ideal of a man of s.
The term S. should not be given to anything   VALÉRY, 2
Tolstoy . . . wasn't taken in by . . . s. and medicine   TOLSTOY, L, 4
when religion was strong and s. weak, men mistook magic for medicine   SZASZ, 3
science fiction   S. is no more written for scientists   ALDISS, 1
sciences   Books must follow s.   BACON, FRANCIS, 63
s. . . . way had not been prepared by magicians   NIETZSCHE, 10
scientific   it's not very s., but it helps   FLEMING, A, 4
lack of efficiency in using s. achievements for economic needs   GORBACHOV, 2
restating our socialism in terms of the s. revolution   WILSON, HAROLD, 8
S. discovery is a private event   MEDAWAR, 1
s. knowledge of the structure of our bodies   STOPES, 4
Traditional s. method has always been   PIRSIG, 3
scientist   A fascinating combination of s. and would-be poet   STOPES, 1
being a novelist, I consider myself superior to the saint, the s.   LAWRENCE, D, 38
He had . . . most of the qualities that make a great s.   FLEMING, A, 2
No one really understood music unless he was a s.   BUCK, 4
When a distinguished but elderly s. states   CLARKE, A, 1
scientists   in the company of s., I feel like a shabby curate   AUDEN, 7
The true men of action . . . are . . . the s.   AUDEN, 8
scissor-man   The great, long, red-legged s.   HOFFMAN, 3
scope   this man's art, and that man's s.   SHAKESPEARE, 360
scorn   Silence is the . . . perfect expression of s.   SHAW, 6
scorned   fury like a woman s.   CONGREVE, 9
scornful   the seat of the s.   PSALMS, 1
scorpions   dwell among s.   BIBLE, 123
Scotchman   A S. must be a very sturdy moralist   JOHNSON, S, 18
Much may be made of a S.   JOHNSON, S, 86
never met with any one S. but what was a man of sense   LOCKIER, 1
the noblest prospect which a S. ever sees   JOHNSON, S, 62
what it is that makes a S. happy   JOHNSON, S, 162
Scotchmen   trying . . . to like S.   LAMB, CHARLES, 6
Scotland   blow the Scots back again into S.   FAWKES, 2
I do indeed come from S.   JOHNSON, S, 57
I'll be in S. afore ye   ANONYMOUS, 67
Seeing S., Madam   JOHNSON, S, 121
Switzerland . . . an inferior sort of S.   SMITH, SYDNEY, 14
Scots   blow the S. back again into Scotland   FAWKES, 2
S., wha hae wi' Wallace bled   BURNS, R, 17
Scotsman   A young S. of your ability   BARRIE, 9
S. on the make   BARRIE, 11
the grandest moral attribute of a S.   BARRIE, 10
to distinguish between a S. with a grievance   WODEHOUSE, 23
Scott   C. P. S.   BONE, J, 1
Sir Walter S. . . . is an inspired butler   SCOTT, WALTER, 2
Scottish   a hard-handed S. peasant   BURNS, R, 2
scoundrel   given them to such a s.   SWIFT, 21
Patriotism . . . the last refuge of the s.   BRAGG, 1
scourge   whore, and the whoremonger, shall ye s.   KORAN, 7
Scout   A S. smiles and whistles   BADEN-POWELL, 1

scowl   Rachmaninov's immortalizing totality was his s.   STRAVINSKY, 1
scratch   S. my back   PROVERBS, 356
S. the Russian and . . . find the Tartar   MAISTRE, 2
screen   A wide s. . . . makes a bad film twice as bad   GOLDWYN, 9
scribble   Always s., s., s.   GLOUCESTER, 1
scribbling   My s. pays me zero francs per line   ROCHEFORT, 1
Scripture   devil can cite S.   SHAKESPEARE, 239
scrofulous   s. French novel   BROWNING, R, 55
sculptor   who is not a great s. or painter can be an architect   RUSKIN, 3
scum   Chesterton is like a vile s. on a pond   CHESTERTON, 1
of the s. of the earth   WELLINGTON, 22
The rich are the s. of the earth   CHESTERTON, 14
scutcheon   I bear no other s.   DISRAELI, 27
sea   all the s. were ink   ANONYMOUS, 42
Alone on a wide wide s.   COLERIDGE, S, 31
change their clime, not their frame of mind, who rush across the s.   HORACE, 21
Down to a sunless s.   COLERIDGE, S, 14
espouse the everlasting s.   WORDSWORTH, W, 60
fishes live in the s.   SHAKESPEARE, 290
For all at last return to the s.   CARSON, 1
For those in peril on the s.   WHITING, 1
go down to the s. in ships   PSALMS, 60
Jesus . . . walking on the s.   BIBLE, 394
kings of the s.   ARNOLD, M, 17
Learn the secret of the s.   LONGFELLOW, 12
like throwing water into the s.   CERVANTES, 9
men and s. interpenetrate   CONRAD, 9
Out of the s. came he   COLERIDGE, S, 25
Over the s. to Skye   BOULTON, 1
Owl and the Pussy-Cat went to s.   LEAR, 8
precious stone set in the silver s.   SHAKESPEARE, 295
Stick . . . to your desks and never go to s.   GILBERT, W, 11
the midst of the s. upon dry ground   BIBLE, 112
The s. is calm to-night   ARNOLD, M, 10
the s. is his   PSALMS, 54
The s.! the s.   XENOPHON, 1
The voice of the s. speaks to the soul   CHOPIN, 1
They went to s. in a sieve   LEAR, 1
to the English that of the s.   RICHTER, 1
Two voices . . . one is of the s., One of the mountains   WORDSWORTH, W, 63
We are as near to heaven by s. as by land   GILBERT, H, 1
when they can see nothing but s.   BACON, FRANCIS, 3
why the s. is boiling hot   CARROLL, 28
sea-change   doth suffer a s.   SHAKESPEARE, 321
seagreen   The s. Incorruptible   CARLYLE, T, 18
sealed   My lips are s.   BALDWIN, S, 8
sea-life   When men come to like a s.   JOHNSON, S, 101
seals   sealed with seven s.   BIBLE, 460
seam   And sew a fine s.   NURSERY RHYMES, 8
seamen   There were gentlemen and . . . s. in the navy of Charles the Second   MACAULAY, T, 9
sear   My way of life Is fall'n into the s.   SHAKESPEARE, 223
search   in s. of a great perhaps   RABELAIS, 1
s. for knowledge   RUSSELL, B, 4
s. the land of living men   SCOTT, WALTER, 13
seas   I must down to the s. again   MASEFIELD, 5
That guard our native s.   CAMPBELL, T, 6
the waters called he S.   BIBLE, 139
seaside   Beside the S.   GLOVER-KIND, 1
the drawback of all s. places   DOUGLAS, N, 1
season   a perfectly ghastly s. . . . for you Spanish dancers   BANKHEAD, 2
Only in the mating s.   MILLIGAN, 3
to every thing there is a s.   BIBLE, 67
seasoned   speech . . . s. with salt   BIBLE, 23
seasons   a man for all s.   WHITTINGTON, 1
seat   the pleasure of offering my s. to three ladies   CHESTERTON, 41
seated   S. . . . at the organ   PROCTER, 1
sea-water   Wealth is like s.   SCHOPENHAUER, 8
second   The constitution . . . first and s. class citizens   WILLKIE, 1
second-hand car   Would you buy a s.   SAHL, 1
second-rate   an infallible sign of the s.   LEVERSON, 1
nor even booksellers have put up with poets being s.   HORACE, 10
the powers of a first-rate man and the creed of a s. man   BAGEHOT, 9
secrecy   S. is the first essential   RICHELIEU, CARDINAL DE, 1

one must do some work s. and must be independent CURIE, 3
seriousness his ability to disguise charmingly the s. . . . of his
work CARROLL, 3
sermons Ever since his s. were discontinued TYRRELL, 1
He that takes pleasure to hear s. SELDEN, 7
S. in stones SHAKESPEARE, 42
serpent my s. of old Nile SHAKESPEARE, 27
s. beguiled me BIBLE, 151
sharper than a s.'s tooth DICKENS, 41; SHAKESPEARE, 171
that old s. BIBLE, 465
the s. was more subtil BIBLE, 148
servant for the last time in my life, Your Humble S.
WALPOLE, H, 1
good s. does not all commands SHAKESPEARE, 63
speak, Lord; for thy s. heareth BIBLE, 477
The cracked looking glass of a s. JOYCE, 11
the politician poses as the s. DE GAULLE, 13
thou good and faithful s. BIBLE, 418
servants Few men have been admired by their s. MONTAIGNE, 8
good s., but bad masters L'ESTRANGE, 4
half of them prefer hiring their s. for life CARLYLE, T, 34
part of English middle-class education is devoted to the training of
s. WILLIAMS, R, 1
Socialists treat their s. with respect STOPPARD, 3
We teachers can only help . . . as s. MONTESSORI, 2
serve capacity to permit his ministers to s. him
RICHELIEU, CARDINAL DE, 2
if thou . . . s. the Lord, prepare . . . for temptation BIBLE, 80
Mr. Lincoln . . . cannot s. them all at once LINCOLN, 1
They also s. who only stand and wait MILTON, 61
served I must have things daintily s. BETJEMAN, 6
Youth will be s. BORROW, 3
service 'I will see you in the vestry after s.' SMITH, SYDNEY, 8
life goes in the s. of the nation GANDHI, I, 5
Small s. is true s. WORDSWORTH, W, 72
services Sometimes give your s. for nothing HIPPOCRATES, 3
serviettes kiddies have crumpled the s. BETJEMAN, 6
Sesame Open S. THE ARABIAN NIGHTS, 2
sessions s. of sweet silent thought SHAKESPEARE, 361
set all, except their sun, is s. BYRON, 26
best plain s. BACON, FRANCIS, 11
s. thine house in order BIBLE, 304
sets on which the sun never s. NORTH, 1
setting clouds that gather round the s. sun WORDSWORTH, W, 32
settled No question is ever s. Until WILCOX, 2
Thank God, that's s. SHERIDAN, R, 17
seven his acts being s. ages SHAKESPEARE, 47
sealed with s. seals BIBLE, 460
S. for the s. stars in the sky ANONYMOUS, 45
S. swans a-swimming NURSERY RHYMES, 60
wisdom . . . hath hewn out her s. pillars BIBLE, 448
seventh God . . . rested on the s. day BIBLE, 143
seventy Being over s. is like being engaged in a war SPARK, 5
Being is not a sin MEIR, 5
Oh, to be s. again HOLMES, O, JR., 3
sever a tie that only death can s. MAUGHAM, 6
severity Summer has set in with its usual s. COLERIDGE, S, 46
sex As we make s. less secretive, we may rob it of its power
SZASZ, 2
Continental people have s. life MIKES, 3
farmyard world of s. GRANVILLE-BARKER, 2
Gandhi was very keen on s. GANDHI, 3
How can I . . . dislike a s. to which Your Majesty belongs
RHODES, 3
if there was a third s. VAIL, 1
in the schoolroom . . . does the difference of s. . . . need to be
forgotten ANTHONY, 3
In the s.-war thoughtlessness is the weapon of the male
CONNOLLY, 16
Is s. dirty ALLEN, W, 1
it's s. with someone you love ALLEN, W, 1
Literature is mostly about having s. LODGE, 1
meant us to have group s. BRADBURY, 7
Money, it turned out, was exactly like s. BALDWIN, J, 2
much more fundamental than s. DENNIS, N, 2
No more about s. DURRELL, L, 2
no more weakness than is natural to her s. THUCYDIDES, 2
No s. without responsibility LONGFORD, 1
Pornography is the attempt to insult s. LAWRENCE, D, 35
professed tyrant to their s. SHAKESPEARE, 266
s. has been a very private, secretive activity SZASZ, 2

S. is one of the nine reasons for reincarnation MILLER, H, 1
S. is something I really don't understand SALINGER, 2
S. is the biggest nothing WARHOL, 2
s. . . . must itself be subject . . . to evolution BLACKWELL, 1
the condition of our s. is so deplorable PANKHURST, E, 4
the difference of s., if there is any ANTHONY, 3
the s. novel is now normal SHAW, 40
woman feels the invidious distinctions of s. STANTON, E, 2
sexes husbands and wives . . . belong to different s.
DIX, DOROTHY, 4
more difference within the s. than between them
COMPTON-BURNETT, 2
several other old ladies of both s. DICKENS, 23
that pleasure . . . sole motive force behind the union of the s.
LACLOS, 3
the . . . rift between the s. is . . . widened by . . . teaching . . . to
the girls STEVENSON, R, 14
sexton went and told the s. HOOD, 1
sexual avowed purpose is to excite s. desire MUGGERIDGE, 5
Industrial relations are like s. relations FEATHER, 1
Masturbation: the primary s. activity SZASZ, 9
music throatily . . . s. HUXLEY, A, 4
surest guarantee of s. success is s. success AMIS, 1
shabby For tamed and s. tigers HODGSON, 1
shade a green thought in a green s. MARVELL, 2
inviolable s. ARNOLD, M, 38
No s., no shine, no butterflies, no bees HOOD, 10
Nothing grows well in the s. BRANCUSI, 1
the s. Of that which once was great WORDSWORTH, W, 61
shadow be caves . . . in which his s. will be shown NIETZSCHE, 5
hide me under the s. of thy wings PSALMS, 6
I am no s. . . . I am a wife PLATH, 3
lose the substance by grasping at the s. AESOP, 1
My S. ROSE, 2
the valley of the s. of death PSALMS, 11
unhappy s. CAMPION, 1
Who live under the s. of a war SPENDER, 3
Your s. at morning ELIOT, T, 27
shadows brooding tragedy and its dark s. can be lightened
GANDHI, I, 4
half sick of s. TENNYSON, 43
If we s. have offended SHAKESPEARE, 265
its degree is s. SHAKESPEARE, 329
Shakespeare after S. and Milton are forgotten PORSON, 2
A strange, horrible business . . . good enough for S.'s day
VICTORIA, 10
Besides S. and me, who do you think there is STEIN, 4
he had read S. and found him weak in chemistry WELLS, 18
I despise S. SHAW, 11
myriad-minded S. COLERIDGE, S, 9
reading S. by flashes of lightning COLERIDGE, S, 45
S. ARNOLD, M, 40
S., I come DREISER, 1
S. is . . . really very good GRAVES, R, 5
S. never had six lines together without a fault JOHNSON, S, 75
S. – the nearest thing OLIVIER, 1
S., undoubtedly wanted taste WALPOLE, H, 4
sweetest S., Fancy's child MILTON, 19
the making up of a S. or a Milton COLERIDGE, S, 47
the right to criticize S. SHAW, 41
tried lately to read S. DARWIN, C R, 5
We can say of S. ELIOT, T, 4
When I read S. I am struck LAWRENCE, D, 30
Wodehouse, whose works I place a little below S.'s
WODEHOUSE, 1
Wonderful women! . . . how much we . . . owe to S. TERRY, 1
shaking After s. hands with a Greek PROVERBS, 20
all these great interests entrusted to the s. hand VICTORIA, 8
Shakspeare who speak the tongue That S. spake
WORDSWORTH, W, 54
Shalimar Pale hands I loved beside the S. HOPE, 2
shambles Our civilization is founded on the s. JAMES, W, 1
shame expense of spirit in a waste of s. SHAKESPEARE, 370
Neither s. nor physical pain have any . . . effect KEY, E, 4
put to s. suddenly PSALMS, 1
shamefaced Perjury . . . is truth that is s. DARLING, 4
shapely it's . . . more important for a theory to be s., than . . .
true HAMPTON, 1
shapen I was s. in wickedness PSALMS, 31
shapes A Catalan wizard who fools with s. PICASSO, 1
share s. in the good fortunes of the mighty BRECHT, 1

Sharon   the rose of S.   BIBLE, 486
sharp   those who have stout hearts and s. swords   BIRKENHEAD, 4
sharper   the word of God is . . . s. than any two-edged sword
   BIBLE, 185
shaves   man who s. and takes a train   WHITE, E, 1
Shaw   Bernard S.   LENIN, 10
   G. B. S.   WILDE, 66
   Mr S. . . . has never written any poetry   CHESTERTON, 32
   S.   SHERWOOD, 1
she   s. is my country still   CHURCHILL, C, 2
   S.-who-must-be-obeyed   HAGGARD, 1
shears   marriage . . . resembles a pair of s.   SMITH, SYDNEY, 10
Sheba   the queen of S.   BIBLE, 299
shed   s. . . . for the remission of sins   BIBLE, 424
shedding   without s. of blood is no remission   BIBLE, 188
sheep   as a shepherd divideth his s. from the goats   BIBLE, 420
   A s. in s.'s clothing   GOSSE, 2
   Baa, baa, black s.   NURSERY RHYMES, 4
   feed my s.   BIBLE, 280
   hungry s. look up, and are not fed   MILTON, 26
   I have found my s. which was lost   BIBLE, 330
   like lost s.   BOOK OF COMMON PRAYER, 13
   make a man by standing a s.   BEERBOHM, 17
   not armies . . . but flocks of s.   CERVANTES, 5
   savaged by a dead s.   HEALEY, 1
   s.'s clothing   BIBLE, 378
   The mountain s. are sweeter, But the valley s. are fatter
   PEACOCK, 7
   the s. of his hand   PSALMS, 66
   The s.'s in the meadow   NURSERY RHYMES, 29
   the wolf in the s.'s clothing   AESOP, 10
   useless for the s. to pass resolutions in favour of vegetarianism
   INGE, 6
shelf   The dust and silence of the upper s.   MACAULAY, T, 12
Shelley   S. and Keats were . . . up to date in . . . chemical
   knowledge   HALDANE, 2
   S. had a hyper-thyroid face   SQUIRE, 2
   S. was indeed 'a beautiful and ineffectual angel'   SHELLEY, 1
   the right sphere for S.'s genius   ARNOLD, M, 25
shells   With silver bells and cockle s.   NURSERY RHYMES, 34
shelter   Our s. from the stormy blast   WATTS, 6
Shenandoah   O, S., I long to hear you   ANONYMOUS, 66
shepherd   Go, for they call you, S., from the hill   ARNOLD, M, 34
   The King of love my S. is   BAKER, 1
   the Lord is my s.   PSALMS, 11
   This is the weather the s. shuns   HARDY, 13
shepherds   Governments need to have both s. and butchers
   VOLTAIRE, 22
   s. abiding in the field   BIBLE, 314
   s. watch'd their flocks   TATE, N, 3
Sherard Blaw   S., the dramatist who had discovered himself
   SAKI, 23
sherry   With first-rate s. flowing into second-rate whores
   PLOMER, 2
shield   his faithfulness and truth shall be thy s. and buckler
   PSALMS, 51
shift   for coming down let me s. for myself   MORE, 3
shilling   I'm sorry to hear that, sir, you don't happen to have the
   s. about you now, do you   SHERIDAN, T, 1
shimmy   Put thy s. on, Lady Chatterley   LAWRENCE, D, 18
shine   s. on, s. on, harvest moon   NORWORTH, 1
shining   A woman of so s. loveliness   YEATS, 29
shins   long dresses, . . . cover a multitude of s.   WEST, M, 10
ship   all I ask is a tall s.   MASEFIELD, 5
   A whale s. was my Yale College   MELVILLE, 3
   being in a s. is being in a jail   JOHNSON, S, 56
   Don't give up the s.   LAWRENCE, J, 1
   places his s. alongside that of an enemy   NELSON, 5
   S. me somewheres east of Suez   KIPLING, 25
   The s. follows Soviet custom   THEROUX, 4
ships   go down to the sea in s.   PSALMS, 60
   Heart of oak are our s.   GARRICK, 2
   I spied three s. come sailing by   ANONYMOUS, 8
   S. that pass in the night   LONGFELLOW, 15
   something wrong with our bloody s.   BEATTY, 1
   stately s. go on   TENNYSON, 6
   the face that launch'd a thousand s.   MARLOWE, 2
   the little s. of England brought the Army home   GUEDALLA, 2
   We've got the s., we've got the men, we've got the money too
   HUNT, G, 1

shipwreck   husbands and wives make s. of their lives
   DIX, DOROTHY, 3
shirt   no s. or collar ever comes back twice   LEACOCK, 13
shit   I don't give a s. what happens   NIXON, 9
   the sun shining ten days a year and s. in the streets   KENEALLY, 1
   when you s.? Singing, it's the same thing   CARUSO, 1
shock   Anybody can s. a baby   STERN, 1
   deliberately set out to s.   OSBORNE, 8
shocked   how to be amused rather than s.   BUCK, 3
shock-headed   S. Peter   HOFFMAN, 4
shocking   little man wears a s. bad hat   YORK, 1
shocks   s. That flesh is heir to   SHAKESPEARE, 89
shoemaker   I take my shoes from the s.   GOLDSMITH, 32
   The s.'s son   PROVERBS, 424
shoes   before you let the sun in, mind it wipes its s.
   THOMAS, D, 18
   I take my s. from the shoemaker   GOLDSMITH, 32
   s. and ships and sealing wax   CARROLL, 28
shoot   do not s. the pianist   WILDE, 37
   except to s. rabbits and hit his father on the jaw   MASEFIELD, 1
   It is not the business of generals to s. one another
   WELLINGTON, 17
   S., if you must, this old gray head   WHITTIER, 2
   the ungodly . . . privily s. at them which are true of heart
   PSALMS, 4
   they could s. me in my absence   BEHAN, 2
shooting   war minus the s.   ORWELL, 32
shop   A man must keep a little back s.   MONTAIGNE, 2
shop-keepers   A nation of s.   ADAMS, SAMUEL, 1
shopkeepers   England is a nation of s.   NAPOLEON I, 13
shopping   Today you're unhappy? . . . Go s.   MILLER, A, 3
shore   adieu! my native s.   BYRON, 9
   waves make towards the pebbled s.   SHAKESPEARE, 363
Shoreditch   When I grow rich, Say the bells of S.
   NURSERY RHYMES, 41
shores   eternal whisperings around Desolate s.   KEATS, 43
short   Good things, when s., are twice as good   GRACIÁN, 1
   Is not life . . . too s. . . . to bore ourselves   NIETZSCHE, 13
   it will take a long while to make it s.   THOREAU, 20
   Life is too s. to do anything for oneself   MAUGHAM, 19
   make the beat keep time with s. steps   ANDERSEN, 3
   Man that is born of a woman . . . s. time to live
   BOOK OF COMMON PRAYER, 2
   s. and simple annals of the poor   GRAY, 2
   S., big-nosed men with nasty conical caps   FULLER, ROY, 2
   the life of man, solitary, poor, nasty, brutish, and s.   HOBBES, 4
   We have s. time to stay, as you   HERRICK, 4
shortage   a s. of coal and fish . . . at the same time   BEVAN, 2
shorter   not had the time to make it s.   PASCAL, 1
   s. by a head   ELIZABETH I, 7
shortest   I never realized that I'd end up being the s. knight of
   the year   RICHARDS, G, 1
   the s. works are always the best   LA FONTAINE, 11
shot   had them all s.   NARVÁEZ, 1
   he once s. a bookseller   CAMPBELL, T, 7
shots   God is on the side not of the heavy battalions, but of the
   best s.   VOLTAIRE, 23
   They really are bad s.   DE GAULLE, 7
should   nae better than he s. be   BURNS, R, 8
   no better than you s. be   BEAUMONT, 1
shoulder-blade   I have a left s.   GILBERT, W, 31
shoulders   it is by standing on the s. of giants   NEWTON, I, 7
shout   S. with the largest   DICKENS, 44
show   I have that within which passes s.   SHAKESPEARE, 66
   There's No Business Like S. Business   BERLIN, 2
showers   Sweet April s.   TUSSER, 2
showman   a Prime Minister has to be . . . a s.   MACMILLAN, 3
   exquisite s. minus the show   POUND, 1
show off   I often wish they would s. a little more   MACCARTHY, 1
shows   All my s. are great   GRADE, 1
shreds   A thing of s. and patches   GILBERT, W, 23
Shrewsbury   They hang us now in S. jail: The whistles blow
   forlorn   HOUSMAN, 8
shriek   That s. and sweat in pigmy wars   TENNYSON, 48
shrine   Melancholy has her . . . s.   KEATS, 34
shrink   all the boards did s.   COLERIDGE, S, 30
shuffled   s. off this mortal coil   SHAKESPEARE, 89
   the human pack is s. and cut   LODGE, 3
Shulamite   return, return, O S.   BIBLE, 497
shut   when I was there it seemed to be s.   FREUD, C, 2
shy   he was sincerely s. and naively exhibitionist   LAWRENCE, T, 4

Why so s., my pretty Thomasina — FRY, C. 1
sick A person seldom falls s. — EMERSON, 3
Dante makes me s. — VEGA CARPIO, 1
Hospital . . . do the s. no harm — NIGHTINGALE, 1
I am s. at heart — SHAKESPEARE, 64
Let me remind you what the wary fox said . . . to the s. lion — HORACE, 16
make any man s. to hear her — PEPYS, 9
so many poor s. people in the streets full of sores — PEPYS, 12
The prayer that . . . heals the s. — EDDY, 1
We have on our hands a s. man — NICHOLAS I, 1
sickness convicted of s., hunger, wretchedness, and want — SMOLLETT, 3
His s. has created atrocities that are repellent — PICASSO, 2
in s. and in health — BOOK OF COMMON PRAYER, 26
Love is a s. — DANIEL, 1
s. enlarges the dimensions of a man's self — LAMB, CHARLES, 17
S., sin and death . . . do not originate in God — EDDY, 4
the s. that destroyeth in the noon-day — PSALMS, 51
Sidcup If only I could get down to S. — PINTER, 1
side A door is what a dog is . . . on the wrong s. of — NASH, 2
a s. dish he hadn't ordered — LARDNER, 1
He who knows only his own s. . . . knows little — MILL, 2
passed by on the other s. — BIBLE, 324
Time is on our s. — GLADSTONE, 1
sides Do not . . . write on both s. of the paper — SELLAR, 8
said on both s. — ADDISON, 13
We . . . assume that everything has two s. — ROBINSON, J. 1
sieve They went to sea in a s. — LEAR, 4
sighed They s. for the dawn and thee — TENNYSON, 57
Sighs over the Bridge of S. into eternity — KIERKEGAARD, 2
sighs S. are the natural language of the heart — SHADWELL, 1
sight a s. to make an old man young — TENNYSON, 14
Lord giveth s. to the blind — PSALMS, 74
Out of s. — PROVERBS, 333
we walk by faith, not by s. — BIBLE, 44
sightless clapped the glass to his s. eye — NEWBOLT, 1
sights And see all s. from pole to pole — ARNOLD, M, 43
few more impressive s. in the world — BARRIE, 11
sign Jews require a s. — BIBLE, 24
Never s. a valentine — DICKENS, 51
s. documents which they do not read — HURST, 1
s. of an ill-spent youth — SPENCER, H, 2
writing a letter and forgetting to s. his name — BEECHER, 1
signal I really do not see the s. — NELSON, 3
significant s. form — BELL, C, 1
signifying S. nothing — SHAKESPEARE, 225
signing I am s. my death warrant — COLLINS, MICHAEL, 1
silence Come to me in the s. of the night — ROSSETTI, C, 1
foster-child of s. and slow time — KEATS, 27
In England there is only s. or scandal — MAUROIS, 1
let all the earth keep s. before him — BIBLE, 183
Make him a bishop, and you will s. him — CHESTERFIELD, 21
occasional flashes of s. — SMITH, SYDNEY, 11
S. is as full of potential wisdom — HUXLEY, A, 28
S. is become his mother tongue — GOLDSMITH, 18
s. is golden — PROVERBS, 368
S. is the best tactic — ROCHEFOUCAULD, 11
S. is the perfectest herald of joy — SHAKESPEARE, 268
S. is the . . . perfect expression of scorn — SHAW, 6
s. sank Like music — COLERIDGE, S, 37
Sorrow and s. are strong — LONGFELLOW, 6
That man's s. is wonderful to listen to — HARDY, 11
The cruellest lies are . . . told in s. — STEVENSON, R, 15
The dust and s. of the upper shelf — MACAULAY, T, 12
the impression that their normal condition is s. — SARTRE, 13
the more absolute s. of America — LAWRENCE, D, 24
the rest is s. — SHAKESPEARE, 108
With s. and tears — BYRON, 44
silent burst Into that s. sea — COLERIDGE, S, 29
the great s. majority — NIXON, 7
the man who can be s. in several languages — HARBORD, 1
thereon one must remain s. — WITTGENSTEIN, 6
silicon If s. had been a gas I should have been a major-general — WHISTLER, 6
silk rustling in unpaid-for s. — SHAKESPEARE, 60
s., too often hides eczema — CAMUS, 5
the s. stockings and white bosoms of your actresses excite my amorous propensities — JOHNSON, S, 46
silks Whenas in s. my Julia goes — HERRICK, 7
silly A s. remark can be made in Latin — CERVANTES, 3

it's lovely to be s. at the right moment — HORACE, 44
some damned s. thing in the Balkans — BISMARCK, 8
You s. twisted boy — MILLIGAN, 7
silver for a handful of s. — BROWNING, R, 31
Selling the family s. — MACMILLAN, 9
s. and gold have I none — BIBLE, 1
S. buckles on his knee — NURSERY RHYMES, 5
S. threads among the gold — REXFORD, 1
Their idols are s. and gold — PSALMS, 64
The s. apples of the moon — YEATS, 30
thirty pieces of s. — BIBLE, 429
When every . . . thing you hold Is made of s., or of gold — GILBERT, W, 5
silvery the s. adamant walls of life's exclusive city — LAWRENCE, D, 10
Silvia Who is S.? What is she — SHAKESPEARE, 348
Simon Simple S. met a pieman — NURSERY RHYMES, 5
simple A s. race — SCOTT, WALTER, 6
short and s. annals of the poor — GRAY, 2
Teach us delight in s. things — KIPLING, 3
simpleton The revolutionary s. — LEWIS, W, 6
simplicity O holy s. — HUSS, 1
s. a child — POPE, 18
simplify S., s. — THOREAU, 16
simplifying s. something by destroying nearly everything — CHESTERTON, 5
sin A branch of the s. of drunkenness — JAMES I, 2
All s. tends to be addictive — AUDEN, 5
a more dreadful record of s. than . . . countryside — DOYLE, 8
A private s. is not so prejudicial — CERVANTES, 21
beauty is only s. deep — SAKI, 21
Being seventy is not a s. — MEIR, 5
fall into no s. — BOOK OF COMMON PRAYER, 17
go, and s. no more — BIBLE, 252
he that is without s. . . . let him first cast a stone — BIBLE, 251
if we say that we have no s., we deceive — BIBLE, 281
it is no s. to s. in secret — MOLIÈRE, 10
it's a s. to kill a mockingbird — LEE, H, 2
my s. is ever before me — PSALMS, 30
nicest boy who ever committed the s. of whisky — SPARK, 4
no s. but to be rich — SHAKESPEARE, 162
no s. except stupidity — WILDE, 14
orders men to triumph over s. . . . But . . . 'Thou mayest' – that gives a choice — STEINBECK, 1
Sickness, s. and death . . . do not originate in God — EDDY, 4
S. brought death — EDDY, 3
s. no more, lest a worse thing come unto thee — BIBLE, 247
than that one soul . . . should commit one single venial s. — NEWMAN, J, 4
The physicists have known s. — OPPENHEIMER, 2
They are written as if s. were to be taken out . . . by . . . sleep — SMITH, SYDNEY, 3
which taketh away the s. of the world — BIBLE, 240
your s. will find you out — BIBLE, 439
Sinai S. was . . . on a smoke — BIBLE, 114
sincere for the moment, so absolutely s. — ROOSEVELT, T, 1
Some of the worst men in the world are s. — HAILSHAM, 1
sincerest Imitation . . . s. of flattery — COLTON, 3
sincerity A little s. is a dangerous thing — WILDE, 12
style, not s., is the vital thing — WILDE, 31
sinecure a widow . . . is a kind of s. — WYCHERLEY, 2
sinews Anger is one of the s. of the soul — FULLER, T, 5
Stiffen the s. — SHAKESPEARE, 129
sing Did certain persons die before they s. — COLERIDGE, S, 1
I will s. of the sun — POUND, 9
O come, let us s. unto the Lord — PSALMS, 54
s. the Lord's song in a strange land — PSALMS, 70
The Welsh . . . just s. — WAUGH, E, 14
we s. no more — BRAHMS, 2
singed s. the Spanish king's beard — DRAKE, 1
singing nightingales are s. near — ELIOT, T, 22
s. in the rain — FREED, 1
To hear the lark . . . s. . . . . From his watch-tower in the skies — MILTON, 5
when you shit? S., it's the same thing — CARUSO, 1
single a s. man in possession of a good fortune must be in want of a wife — AUSTEN, 18
Behold her, s. in the field — WORDSWORTH, W, 50
sink The s. is the great symbol . . . of family life — MITCHELL, JULIAN, 1
sinn'd More s. against than sinning — SHAKESPEARE, 178

sinned   father, I have s. against heaven   BIBLE, 331
sinner   one s. that repenteth   BIBLE, 330
sinners   At such an hour the s. are still in bed   RUNYON, 6
breeder of s.   SHAKESPEARE, 92
Christ Jesus came into the world to save s.   BIBLE, 506
It's your combination s. . . . who dishonour the vices
the way of s.   WILDER, T, 3
sinning   nothing so artificial as s. nowadays   PSALMS, 1
sins   atone for the s. of your fathers   LAWRENCE, D, 26
from Expensive S. refrain   HORACE, 36
gravest s. it was possible for a gentlewoman to commit   DRYDEN, 10
  WAUGH, E, 45
hide a multitude of s.   BIBLE, 220
His s. were scarlet   BELLOC, 10
One of the unpardonable s. . . . is . . . to go about unlabelled   HUXLEY, T, 4
shed . . . for the remission of s.   BIBLE, 424
she must not reheat his s. for breakfast   DIETRICH, 1
though your s. be as scarlet   BIBLE, 191
to read a novel before luncheon was one of the gravest s.   WAUGH, E, 45
truly and earnestly repent you of your s.   BOOK OF COMMON PRAYER, 10
Sion   the Lord loveth the gates of S.   PSALMS, 47
we remembered thee, O S.   PSALMS, 70
Sir   I am S. Oracle   SHAKESPEARE, 236
Sirens   Blest pair of S.   MILTON, 9
Sisera   the stars . . . fought against S.   BIBLE, 292
sister   I kissed her little s.   MONTROSE, 2
no friend like a s.   ROSSETTI, C, 2
sisters   all the S. virtuous   NEWCASTLE, 1
And so do his s.   GILBERT, W, 9
little s. to all the world   DIX, DOROTHY, 1
O! men with s. dear   HOOD, 11
sit   I will s. down now   DISRAELI, 20
men s. and hear each other groan   KEATS, 38
nobody can tell you when to s. down   EISENHOWER, 6
say what you have to say, and then s. down   WELLINGTON, 25
So I did s. and eat   HERBERT, G, 7
sitting   Are you s. comfortably? Then I'll begin   LANG, J, 1
by s. down round you   WELLINGTON, 14
I do most of my work s. down   BENCHLEY, 6
situation   s. excellent. I shall attack   FOCH, 1
six   Candidates should not attempt more than s.   BELLOC, 18
S. for the s. proud walkers   ANONYMOUS, 45
S. geese a-laying   NURSERY RHYMES, 60
s. of one and half-a-dozen of the other   MARRYAT, 2
two and two do not make s.   TOLSTOY, L, 16
sixpence   He found a crooked s. against a crooked stile   NURSERY RHYMES, 57
I love s., jolly little s.   NURSERY RHYMES, 22
Sing a song of s.   NURSERY RHYMES, 52
sixpences   there go two-and-forty s. . . . to one guinea   JOHNSON, S, 34
sixth   Money is like a s. sense   MAUGHAM, 13
sixty   at the rate of s. minutes an hour   LEWIS, C, 5
close-up of a woman past s.   ASTOR, N, 2
Men come of age at s.   STEPHENS, 3
S. HORSES WEDGED IN A CHIMNEY   MORTON, 2
sixty-five   I have been drinking it for s. years and I am not dead
yet   VOLTAIRE, 35
size   I am not this s., really   CHESTERTON, 45
skating   s. over thin ice   EMERSON, 13
skeleton   Every family has a s. in the cupboard   PROVERBS, 135
ski   unbecoming for a cardinal to s. badly   JOHN PAUL II, 1
skies   looks commercing with the s.   MILTON, 12
look up at the s.   HOPKINS, 5
skill   if greater want of s. Appear in writing or in judging ill   POPE, 20
In arguing too, the parson own'd his s.   GOLDSMITH, 7
S. without imagination is craftsmanship   STOPPARD, 1
skin   I've Got You Under My S.   PORTER, C, 2
never . . . sell the bear's s.   LA FONTAINE, 7
There is more than one way to s. a cat   PROVERBS, 409
skinning   When you are s. your customers   KHRUSHCHEV, 2
skins   beauty of their s.   TENNYSON, 65
skipper   s. had taken his little daughter   LONGFELLOW, 18
skirt   a woman . . . ought to lay aside . . . modesty with her s.   MONTAIGNE, 4
skittles   Life isn't all beer and s.   HUGHES, THOMAS, 1

sky   a Friend for little children Above the bright blue s.   MIDLANE, 1
inverted Bowl we call The S.   FITZGERALD, E, 15
pie in the s. when you die   ALI, 4
Which prisoners call the s.   WILDE, 4
Skye   Over the sea to S.   BOULTON, 1
slack   a man becomes s. and selfish   STEVENSON, R, 24
slain   Saul hath s. his thousands   BIBLE, 481
slamming   little girls . . . s. doors   BELLOC, 7
slander   it is always said of s. that something always sticks   BACON, FRANCIS, 4
slang   All s. is metaphor   CHESTERTON, 11
The one . . . poetry . . . continually flowing is s.   CHESTERTON, 10
slapped   We had shown that anyone who s. us . . . would get his
head kicked off   KHRUSHCHEV, 1
slaughter   as a lamb to the s.   BIBLE, 214
slave   Be not the s. of Words   CARLYLE, T, 24
commerce between master and s. is . . . exercise of . . . boisterous
passions   JEFFERSON, 3
man . . . is Reason's s.   CONNOLLY, 20
s. for livelihood   ADAMS, F, 2
slavery   Freedom is S.   ORWELL, 18
The prolonged s. of women   STANTON, E, 4
slaves   In a consumer society there are . . . two kinds of s.   ILLICH, 4
love, an . . . intercourse between tyrants and s.   GOLDSMITH, 14
Practical men . . . are usually the s. of some defunct economist   KEYNES, 7
S. cannot breathe in England   COWPER, 29
that the masters willingly concede to s.   CAMUS, 12
Slave Trade   suppression of the S.   WILBERFORCE, W, 1
slaying   the s. of a beautiful hypothesis by an ugly fact   HUXLEY, T, 1
slays   moves, and mates, and s.   FITZGERALD, E, 13
sleave   ravell'd s. of care   SHAKESPEARE, 212
sleek   you will come and find me fat and s.   HORACE, 18
sleep   A professor is one who talks in someone else's s.   AUDEN, 29
Better s. with a sober cannibal than a drunken Christian   MELVILLE, 1
haven't been to s. for over a year   WAUGH, E, 18
How do people go to s.   PARKER, D, 6
Let me s. the s. of the earth   VIGNY, 2
Now I lay me down to s.   ANONYMOUS, 64
Our birth is but a s.   WORDSWORTH, W, 25
our little life Is rounded with a s.   SHAKESPEARE, 325
s. begins for weary mortals . . . creeps over them most welcomely   VIRGIL, 10
S. is good, death is better   HEINE, 2
s.! it is a gentle thing   COLERIDGE, S, 34
S. . . . knows not Death   TENNYSON, 32
S.'s the only medicine that gives ease   SOPHOCLES, 3
S. that knits up the ravell'd sleave   SHAKESPEARE, 212
The past was a s.   BROWNING, R, 56
they are even as a s.   PSALMS, 49
They are written as if sin were to be taken out . . . by . . . s.   SMITH, SYDNEY, 3
To s., perchance to dream   SHAKESPEARE, 89
we must s.   SHAKESPEARE, 34
youth would s. out the rest   SHAKESPEARE, 350
sleepin'   Capten, art tha s.' there below   NEWBOLT, 3
sleeping   fuss about s. together . . . sooner go to my dentist   WAUGH, E, 44
Let s. dogs lie   PROVERBS, 255
like s. with someone else's wife   BRADBURY, 5
S. as quiet as death   THOMAS, D, 20
There will be s. enough   PROVERBS, 422
we have only awakened a s. giant   YAMAMOTO, 1
sleeps   eats, s. and watches the television   GREER, 2
sleepwalker   that Providence dictates with the assurance of a s.   HITLER, 15
sleepy   Come, let's to bed Says S.-head   NURSERY RHYMES, 7
sleeve   let the last man . . . brush the Channel with his s.   SCHLIEFFEN, 1
slept   David s. with his fathers   BIBLE, 297
Splendid couple – s. with both   BOWRA, 3
slick   I have three phobias which . . . would make my life as s. as
a sonnet   BANKHEAD, 1
slides   buttered s. to hell   SANTAYANA, 1
slimy   thousand thousand s. things   COLERIDGE, S, 32
sling   his s. was in his hand   BIBLE, 480

slings s. and arrows of outrageous fortune SHAKESPEARE, 89
slip he gave us all the s. BROWNING, R, 58
There's many a s. PROVERBS, 415
slippers Same old s. LAMPTON, 1
slipping Time is s. underneath FITZGERALD, E, 12
slogans If you feed people just with revolutionary s. KHRUSHCHEV, 8
Slough Come, friendly bombs, and fall on S. BETJEMAN, 10
slough the s. was Despond BUNYAN, 2
slow I am s. of study SHAKESPEARE, 259
On a s. boat to China LOESSER, 1
S. and steady wins the race LLOYD, R, 1
S. but sure PROVERBS, 363
s. to wrath BIBLE, 217
Tarry a while, says S. NURSERY RHYMES, 7
too swift arrives as tardy as too s. SHAKESPEARE, 314
with a s. deliberate carelessness LAWRENCE, T, 9
slug-horn the s. to my lips I set BROWNING, R, 17
slum if you've seen one city s. AGNEW, 2
slumber A s. did my spirit seal WORDSWORTH, W, 49
Oft in the stilly night, Ere S.'s chain MOORE, T, 7
slumber'd s. here While these visions did appear SHAKESPEARE, 265
slumbers Golden s. kiss your eyes DEKKER, 1
slush pure as the driven s. BANKHEAD, 10
smack much more indecent . . . than a good s. LAWRENCE, D, 7
small Errors look so very ugly in persons of s. means ELIOT, G, 5
From s. beginnings PROVERBS, 168
In Western Europe there are now only s. countries LEFÈVRE, 1
It's a s. world PROVERBS, 232
Microbe is so very s. BELLOC, 13
Popularity? . . . glory's s. change HUGO, 7
S. is beautiful PROVERBS, 364
The best things come in s. parcels PROVERBS, 379
virtue's still far too s. COLETTE, 3
smaller accepts a s. as a favour CARLYLE, J, 1
someone s. than oneself LA FONTAINE, 3
these have s. fleas to bite 'em SWIFT, 9
small-talking Where in this s. world FRY, C, 4
smartness the s. of an attorney's clerk DISRAELI, 33
smarts No creature s. . . . as a fool POPE, 17
smattering A s. of everything DICKENS, 2
smell rose . . . would s. as sweet SHAKESPEARE, 310
Sweet S. of Success LEHMAN, 1
smells the only dead thing that s. sweet THOMAS, E, 2
smile A dear old man with his . . . somewhat toothless s. GANDHI, 1
a pleasant s. that it seems rather divine than human LEONARDO DA VINCI, 4
a s. I could feel in my hip pocket CHANDLER, R, 2
nice s., but . . . iron teeth GROMYKO, 1
Oh, good gigantic s. BROWNING, R, 29
s. at perils past SCOTT, WALTER, 3
S. at us, pay us, pass us CHESTERTON, 36
s., s., s. ASAF, 1
the vain tribute of a s. SCOTT, WALTER, 6
smiled the soldiers he s. at SASSOON, S, 4
smiles A Scout s. and whistles BADEN-POWELL, 1
She is Venus when she s. JONSON, 13
s., Wan as primroses KEATS, 8
The s., the tears, Of boyhood's years MOORE, T, 7
smite whosoever shall s. thee on thy right cheek BIBLE, 364
Smith Chuck it, S. CHESTERTON, 6
smith The s., a mighty man is he LONGFELLOW, 16
smoke no woman should marry . . . a man who does not s. STEVENSON, R, 22
resembling the horrible Stygian s. of the pit JAMES I, 1
Sinai was . . . on a s. BIBLE, 114
S., my friend SATIE, 1
There's no s. without fire PROVERBS, 418
smoking resolve to give up s., drinking and loving FREUD, C, 1
s. at such a rate LAMB, CHARLES, 22
s. cigars and . . . drinking of alcohol before, after, and if need be during all meals CHURCHILL, W, 25
To cease s. is the easiest thing I ever did TWAIN, 21
What a blessing this s. is HELPS, 1
smooth course of true love never did run s. SHAKESPEARE, 257
many cities had rubbed him s. GREENE, 4
smote they s. the city with the edge of the sword BIBLE, 291
smyler The s. with the knyf CHAUCER, 13

snail said a whiting to a s. CARROLL, 16
s.'s on the thorn BROWNING, R, 45
snails Frogs and s. And puppy-dogs' tails NURSERY RHYMES, 70
snake A s. came to my water-trough LAWRENCE, D, 28
There's a s. hidden in the grass VIRGIL, 17
snapper-up s. of unconsidered trifles SHAKESPEARE, 352
snare a s. in which the feet of women have always become readily entangled ADDAMS, 1
the s. of the hunter PSALMS, 51
snares s. of death compassed me round PSALMS, 65
Snark For the S. *was* a Boojum CARROLL, 22
snatch make us love your goodly gifts And s. them SHAKESPEARE, 291
sneeze s. in English is the harbinger of misery DURRELL, G, 3
sneezed Not to be s. at COLMAN, THE YOUNGER, 3
when a British Prime Minister s. LEVIN, 2
snipe well-shot woodcock, partridge, s. BETJEMAN, 4
snob He who meanly admires . . . is a S. THACKERAY, 1
impossible, in our condition of society, not to be sometimes a S. THACKERAY, 2
Indian s. reasons, like calling an English person by his Christian name SCOTT, P, 3
Mr. Waugh . . . is . . . a s. in search of a class WAUGH, E, 1
snobbish Don't be s., we seek to abolish LOGUE, 1
He was . . . , s., sentimental and vain WILDE, 3
snobs His hatred of s. PROUST, 12
impudent s. who characterize themselves as intellectuals AGNEW, 3
snore s. and you sleep alone BURGESS, 2
snorer can't hear himself s. TWAIN, 16
snotgreen The s. sea JOYCE, 10
snow both its national products, s. and chocolate, melt COREN, 5
Like an army defeated The s. hath retreated WORDSWORTH, W, 77
S. had fallen, s. on s. ROSSETTI, C, 3
the s. blind twilight ferries THOMAS, D, 28
wish a s. in May SHAKESPEARE, 195
snows the s. of yesteryear VILLON, 1
Snow White I used to be S. WEST, M, 13
snub Vile s.-nose, flat-nosed ass ROSTAND, E, 1
snuff time for me to enjoy another pinch of s. BAILLY, 1
snug s. As a bug In a rug FRANKLIN, 14
so It is s.. It is not s. FRANKLIN, 10
soap S. and education . . . are more deadly MACAULAY, T, 2
soar to run, though not to s. WORDSWORTH, W, 32
sober a s. colouring from an eye FIELDING, 5
as s. as a Judge MELVILLE, 1
Better sleep with a s. cannibal than a drunken Christian MAGEE, 1
England should be compulsorily s. FLETCHER, 2
he that will go to bed s. LARDNER, 2
How do you look when I'm s. CHESTERTON, 8
'My mother, drunk or s.' TYNAN, 6
one sees in Garbo s. BURTON, RICHARD, 1
played drunks I had to remain s. HOOD, 1
sedate, s., silent, serious, sad-coloured sect ANONYMOUS, 12
Tomorrow we'll be s. BEHAN, 5
sociable I am a s. worker SHAKESPEARE, 61
Society is no comfort to one not s. SPINOZA, 2
social Man is a s. animal WILDE, 29
our s. spheres have been widely different WARREN, 1
the things which government does . . . s. progress KELLER, 3
the . . . world was stumbling . . . in s. blindness POPE, 36
true self-love and s. are the same KEYNES, 1
socialism Marxian S. must always remain a portent BEVAN, 1
religion of S. WILSON, HAROLD, 8
restating our s. in terms of the scientific revolution . . . THATCHER, M, 16
s. . . . alien to the British character VIERA GALLO, 1
S. can only arrive by bicycle DUBČEK, 1
S. with a human face LENIN, 6
the proletariat will . . . wage a class struggle for S. ORWELL, 2
the worst advertisement for S. is its adherents THATCHER, M, 19
To banish . . . the dark divisive clouds of Marxist s. ORWELL, 27
To the ordinary working man, . . . S. LENIN, 5
Under s. *all* will govern STOPPARD, 3
socialists S. treat their servants with respect HARCOURT, 1
We are all S. now LÉVI-STRAUSS, 1
societies range of human s. in time, the other in space TAWNEY, 1
society a poor s. cannot be too poor

A s. . . . of individuals . . . capable of original thought would
probably be unendurable MENCKEN, 11
Comedy, we may say, is s. PRIESTLEY, 1
if it be our clothes alone which fit us for s. ESCHENBACH, 4
impossible, in our condition of s., not to be sometimes a Snob
THACKERAY, 2
In a consumer s. there are . . . two kinds of slaves ILLICH, 4
it proved that I was in a civilized s. PARK, 1
Man was formed for s. BLACKSTONE, 1
nation is a s. united by a delusion about its ancestry INGE, 10
Never speak disrespectfully of S. WILDE, 33
no intellectual s. can flourish where a Jew feels . . . uneasy
JOHNSON, P, 1
no new baby in the womb of our s. LAWRENCE, D, 37
nothing to distinguish human s. from the farm-yard SHAW, 12
only possible s. is oneself WILDE, 18
S., friendship, and love COWPER, 33
S. goes on and on and on MACDONALD, R, 2
S. is no comfort To one not sociable SHAKESPEARE, 61
S. is now one polish'd horde BYRON, 34
s. . . . pays a harlot 25 times as much as it pays its Prime
Minister WILSON, HAROLD, 7
s., where none intrudes BYRON, 16
so famous, that it would permit me . . . to break wind in s.
BALZAC, 5
The history of all . . . s. is the history of class struggles
MARX, K, 1
transform this s. without a major extension of public ownership
KINNOCK, 1

sociology Children . . . have no use for psychology. They detest
s. SINGER, 1
sockets The candles burn their s. HOUSMAN, 4
socks His s. compelled one's attention SAKI, 11
sodium Of having discovered S. BENTLEY, E, 4
Sodom S. and . . . Gomorrah BIBLE, 167
the men of S. were wicked BIBLE, 166
sodomy Comedy, like s., is an unnatural act FELDMAN, 1
rum, s., and the lash CHURCHILL, W, 35
sofa rather lie on a s. than sweep beneath it CONRAN, 2
soft I'm not hard – I'm frightfully s. THATCHER, M, 4
our love . . . of the mind does not make us s. PERICLES, 1
solar the whole s. and stellar systems CARLYLE, T, 30
soldier a chocolate cream s. SHAW, 1
A S. of the Great War KIPLING, 33
Ben Battle was a s. bold HOOD, 2
I never expect a s. to think SHAW, 10
in the s. is flat blasphemy SHAKESPEARE, 229
The summer s. and the sunshine patriot PAINE, 5
Tinker, Tailor, S., Sailor NURSERY RHYMES, 65
soldiers English s. fight like lions HOFFMANN, M, 1
Old s. never die PROVERBS, 323
saucy, soft, short shirts for s., sister Susie sews WESTON, 2
S. are citizens of death's grey land SASSOON, S, 3
soliciting supernatural s. SHAKESPEARE, 202
Solidarity S. was born . . . when the shipyard strike evolved
WALESA, 2
solitary heard among the s. hills Low breathings
WORDSWORTH, W, 36
He lived the life of a s. NEWTON, I, 1
Life is for each man a s. cell O'NEILL, 1
Man is not a s. animal RUSSELL, B, 10
solitude In s. alone can he know true freedom MONTAIGNE, 2
In s. What happiness MILTON, 49
self-sufficing power of S. WORDSWORTH, W, 38
so companionable as s. THOREAU, 14
s.! where are the charms COWPER, 34
the bliss of s. WORDSWORTH, W, 8
Whosoever is delighted in s. BACON, FRANCIS, 24
Solomon S. Grundy, Born on a Monday NURSERY RHYMES, 53
solution A difficulty for every s. SAMUEL, 6
total s. of the Jewish question GOERING, 2
some I . . . may be s. time OATES, 1
s. more than others COWARD, 4
You can fool s. of the people all the time LINCOLN, 18
somebody s. may be looking MENCKEN, 1
someone I wouldn't be . . . talking to s. like you CARTLAND, 1
somer In a s. season LANGLAND, 1
Somerset corroboration . . . in the records of S. House
BIRKENHEAD, 1
something Everybody was up to s. COWARD, 9
S. must be done EDWARD VIII, 4

S. nasty in the woodshed GIBBONS, 1
Time for a little s. MILNE, 7
sometime Why don't you come up s. and see me WEST, M, 8
somewhat More than s. RUNYON, 3
somewhere 'Tis always morning s. HORNE, 1
son An only s., sir, might expect more indulgence GOLDSMITH, 16
I've examined your s.'s head, Mr Glum MUIR, 1
O Absalom, my s. BIBLE, 485
the S. of man coming . . . with power BIBLE, 414
woman, behold thy s. BIBLE, 270
sonatas The s. of Mozart are unique SCHNABEL, 3
song I have a s. to sing O GILBERT, W, 43
listening when the s. is over SAINT-LAMBERT, 1
the s. that is sung in our hearts OUIDA, 3
they shall not drink wine with a s. BIBLE, 206
Who loves not wine, woman and s. LUTHER, 5
songs Sing no sad s. ROSSETTI, C, 8
Where are the s. of Spring KEATS, 46
sonne when soft was the s. LANGLAND, 1
sonnet I have three phobias which . . . would make my life as
slick as a s. BANKHEAD, 4
s. is a moment's monument ROSSETTI, D, 1
son-of-a-bitch The poor s. PARKER, D, 13
sons I have a wife, I have s. LUCAN, 1
Now we are all s. of bitches BAINBRIDGE, 1
S. of Belial had a Glorious Time DRYDEN, 11
soon day returns too s. BYRON, 42
sophisticated the only s. playwright England has produced
CONGREVE, 1
sophistry Commit it then to the flames: for it can contain nothing
but s. and illusion HUME, D, 2
Universities incline wits to s. and affectation BACON, FRANCIS, 65
Sophonisba Oh! S. THOMSON, JAMES, 2
sores Lazarus . . . laid at his gate, full of s. BIBLE, 333
sorrow Down, thou climbing s. SHAKESPEARE, 174
Its narrow measure spans Tears of eternity, and s., Not
mine, but man's HOUSMAN, 5
Much in s., oft in woe WHITE, H, 1
One for s. PROVERBS, 325
Parting is such sweet s. SHAKESPEARE, 312
Pure and complete s. is as impossible TOLSTOY, L, 12
S. and silence are strong LONGFELLOW, 6
S. is tranquillity remembered in emotion PARKER, D, 9
s. makes us wise TENNYSON, 36
the Lord . . . give thee joy for this thy s. BIBLE, 517
There is no greater s. DANTE, 2
Through the night of doubt and s. BARING-GOULD, 3
sorrows When s. come, they come not single spies
SHAKESPEARE, 101
sort that like that s. of place SHAW, 22
Soudan to you, Fuzzy-Wuzzy, at your 'ome in the S. KIPLING, 10
sought Love s. is good SHAKESPEARE, 342
Pleasure is . . . seldom found where it is s. JOHNSON, S, 16
soul And never once possess our s. ARNOLD, M, 43
Anger is one of the sinews of the s. FULLER, T, 5
animated with the s. of a Briton VOLTAIRE, 2
Artists are not engineers of the s. KENNEDY, JOHN, 17
a . . . s. like season'd timber HERBERT, G, 10
become a living s. WORDSWORTH, W, 11
company, . . . have neither a s. to lose nor a body to kick
SMITH, SYDNEY, 5
education is a leading out of what is . . . in the pupil's s.
SPARK, 10
Education is . . . the s. of a society CHESTERTON, 44
Fair seed-time had my s. WORDSWORTH, W, 35
he shall convert my s. PSALMS, 11
His s. is marching on HALL, 1
his s. is satisfied with what is assigned to him
MARCUS AURELIUS, 10
I am positive I have a s. STERNE, 3
I am the captain of my s. HENLEY, 2
Impropriety is the s. of wit MAUGHAM, 9
In mystery our s. abides ARNOLD, M, 29
I pray the Lord my s. to keep ANONYMOUS, 64
Man has no Body distinct from his S. BLAKE, W, 31
Mr Lincoln's s. seems made of leather LINCOLN, 4
my s. doth magnify the Lord BIBLE, 309
my s. hath a desire PSALMS, 44
My s. in agony COLERIDGE, S, 31
my s. is among lions PSALMS, 36
my s. is athirst for God PSALMS, 26

558 • SOULS

my s. is white BLAKE, W, 48
my s. . . . should flee as a bird PSALMS, 4
Never mind about my s. . . . get my tie right JOYCE, 13
No coward s. is mine BRONTË, E, 1
Our Language . . . was unequal to that greatness of s. MILTON, 1
passion in the human s. LILLO, 1
possessive outrage done to a free solitary human s. POWYS, 2
poverty of s., impossible MONTAIGNE, 10
Raises from Hell a human s. BLAKE, W, 5
real dark night of the s. FITZGERALD, F S, 3
seal the hushed casket of my s. KEATS, 48
than that one s. . . . should commit one single venial sin NEWMAN, J, 4
The British postgraduate student is a lonely forlorn s. LODGE, 3
The dark night of the s. JOHN OF THE CROSS, 2
the . . . essence of a human s. CARLYLE, T, 27
the eyes are the windows of the s. BEERBOHM, 12
the iron enter into his s. STERNE, 1
the iron has entered his s. LLOYD GEORGE, 14
the largest and most comprehensive s. DRYDEN, 22
The Life and S., the man who will never go home WHITEHORN, 3
The s. fortunately, has an interpreter BRONTË, C, 2
The s. hath not her generous aspirings implanted in her in vain LAMB, CHARLES, 26
the s. is not more than the body WHITMAN, 9
the s. of a martyr with the intellect of an advocate BAGEHOT, 10
The s. started at the knee-cap LEWIS, W, 1
The S. that rises with us, our life's Star WORDSWORTH, W, 25
The voice of the sea speaks to the s. CHOPIN, 1
Thy rapt s. sitting in thine eyes MILTON, 12
Thy s. was like a star, and dwelt apart WORDSWORTH, W, 56
souls Above the vulgar flight of common s. MURPHY, A, 1
damp s. of the housemaids ELIOT, T, 17
Our s. have sight of that immortal sea WORDSWORTH, W, 28
queen did fish for men's s. ELIZABETH I, 1
S. of poets dead and gone KEATS, 26
Stars . . . robbed men of their s. ASIMOV, 2
their s. dwell in the house of tomorrow GIBRAN, 1
the s. of five hundred . . . Newtons COLERIDGE, S, 47
The s. of women are so small BUTLER, S, 9
Two s. dwell, alas! in my breast GOETHE, 3
Two s. with but a single thought LOVELL, 1
You may house their bodies but not their s. GIBRAN, 1
soul-sides the meanest of his creatures Boasts two s. BROWNING, R, 40
sound full of s. and fury SHAKESPEARE, 225
s. of a great Amen PROCTER, 1
The hills are alive with the s. of music HAMMERSTEIN, 5
The most persistent s. . . . through men's history KOESTLER, 5
The s. must seem an echo to the sense POPE, 26
The s. of the English county families WAUGH, E, 4
the trumpet shall s. BIBLE, 42
whispering s. of the cool colonnade COWPER, 19
sounding s. brass BIBLE, 38
sounds Music is the arithmetic of s. DEBUSSY, 1
the s. will take care of themselves CARROLL, 14
soup concludes that it will . . . make better s. MENCKEN, 16
S. of the evening, beautiful S. CARROLL, 18
Take the s. away HOFFMAN, 1
sour How s. sweet music is SHAKESPEARE, 299
I am sure the grapes are s. AESOP, 2
source her Majesty . . . must not . . . look upon me as a s. of income KEMBLE, C, 1
sourest sweetest things turn s. SHAKESPEARE, 366
south beaker full of the warm S. KEATS, 37
go s. in the winter ELIOT, T, 26
hardly be a town in the S. of England ORWELL, 25
South African The S. Police would leave no stone unturned SHARPE, 1
southern mother bore me in the s. wild BLAKE, W, 48
sovereign he will have no s. COKE, E, 2
The S. has, under a constitutional monarchy . . . three rights BAGEHOT, 7
When I forget my s. THURLOW, 1
Soviet Communism is S. power plus the electrification LENIN, 9
S. people want full-blooded . . . democracy GORBACHOV, 3
The ship follows S. custom THEROUX, 4
sow Ireland is the old s. JOYCE, 6
like a s. that hath overwhelm'd all her litter SHAKESPEARE, 116
s. not, neither do they reap BIBLE, 370
They that s. in tears shall reap in joy PSALMS, 69
soweth whatsoever a man s., that shall he also reap BIBLE, 136
sown A lovelier flower . . . was never s. WORDSWORTH, W, 69
space annihilate but s. and time POPE, 3
In the United States there is more s. STEIN, 2
range of human societies in time, the other in s. LÉVI-STRAUSS, 1
S. is almost infinite QUAYLE, 1
spaceship passenger on the s., Earth FULLER, RICHARD, 1
spade When I see a s. I call it a s. WILDE, 29
Spain Farewell and adieu to you, Ladies of S. ANONYMOUS, 18
not left to S. TENNYSON, 70
span Life's short s. forbids us . . . far-reaching hopes HORACE, 28
Spaniards the S. seem wiser than they are BACON, FRANCIS, 47
time to win this game, and to thrash the S. DRAKE, 2
Spanish I speak S. to God CHARLES V, 3
singed the S. king's beard DRAKE, 1
spare bread enough and to s. BIBLE, 331
Brother, can you s. a dime HARBURG, 2
I can't s. this man; he fights LINCOLN, 20
S. all I have FARQUHAR, 3
s. the rod BUTLER, S, 4; PROVERBS, 366
Woodman, s. that tree MORRIS, G, 1
spareth he that s. his rod hateth his son BIBLE, 450
sparkle That youthful s. in his eyes is caused by his contact lenses REAGAN, 1
sparrow a s. alight upon my shoulder . . . I was more distinguished by that THOREAU, 18
I, said the S., With my bow and arrow NURSERY RHYMES, 73
It is a city where you can see a s. fall O'BRIEN, C, 1
the s. hath found her an house PSALMS, 44
sparrowhawks S., Ma'am WELLINGTON, 27
sparrows five s. . . . not one of them is forgotten BIBLE, 328
one of the s. . . . flew . . . through the hall BEDE, 1
spasm individual existence goes out in a lonely s. of helpless agony JAMES, W, 1
spat So he stood up and s. on the ceiling ANONYMOUS, 91
Today I s. in the Seine PATTON, 1
speak I didn't s. up NIEMÖLLER, 1
I only s. right on SHAKESPEARE, 157
Let him now s. BOOK OF COMMON PRAYER, 25
more than a moral duty to s. one's mind WILDE, 28
Never s. ill of the dead PROVERBS, 306
province of knowledge to s. HOLMES, O, 6
some . . . s. . . . before they think LA BRUYÈRE, 3
s., Lord; for thy servant heareth BIBLE, 477
S. softly and carry a big stick ROOSEVELT, T, 7
s. to God as if men were listening SENECA, 1
S. when you are spoken to PROVERBS, 367
S. when you're spoken to CARROLL, 36
time to think before I s. DARWIN, E, 1
When I think, I must s. SHAKESPEARE, 52
Whereof one cannot s. WITTGENSTEIN, 6
speaking An Englishman's way of s. LERNER, 1
People talking without s. SIMON, 3
when . . . s., they do not know what they are saying CHURCHILL, W, 42
spearmint Does the S. Lose Its Flavour ROSE, 1
specialist S. – A man who knows more and more about less and less MAYO, 1
specialists s. . . . tend to think in grooves MORGAN, E, 1
species the idea of its death as a s. KOESTLER, 7
the one s. I wouldn't mind seeing vanish BENNETT, ALAN, 3
spectacle Life is not a s. SANTAYANA, 8
spectator a S. of mankind ADDISON, 10
spectre Communism continued to haunt Europe as a s. TAYLOR, A, 3
speculation If the world were good for . . . s. HAZLITT, 4
speech freedom of s. TWAIN, 7
freedom of s. and expression ROOSEVELT, F, 14
he drank my health with a little s. HUGO, 2
I dreamt that I was making a s. DEVONSHIRE, SPENCER, DUKE OF, 1
let thy s. be short BIBLE, 89
perfect plainness of s. . . . perfect nobleness ARNOLD, M, 31
S. is silver PROVERBS, 368
s. only to conceal their thoughts VOLTAIRE, 11
s. . . . seasoned with salt BIBLE, 23
S. was given to man to disguise his thoughts TALLEYRAND, 4
The most precious things in s. RICHARDSON, 3
The true use of s. GOLDSMITH, 13
the whole earth was . . . of one s. BIBLE, 163
True and False are attributes of s., not of things HOBBES, 2

speeches every government . . . should have its old s. burned
SNOWDEN, 1
Many have been the wise s. of fools
FULLER, T, 4
solved by s. and majority votes
BISMARCK, 1
Statesmen are far too busy making s.
RUSSELL, B, 23
Winston . . . preparing his impromptu s.
CHURCHILL, W, 7
speechless *The Times* is s.
CHURCHILL, W, 41
speed safety is in our s.
EMERSON, 13
s. was faster than light
BULLER, 1
spell s. it Vinci and pronounce it Vinchy
TWAIN, 10
spend s. a single day really well
KEMPIS, 5
spendest whatsoever thou s. more . . . I will repay
BIBLE, 325
spending Getting and s.
WORDSWORTH, W, 64
Riches are for s.
BACON, FRANCIS, 23
Spens Before they see Sir Patrick S. Come sailing to the strand
ANONYMOUS, 83
spent Nought's had, all's s.
SHAKESPEARE, 215
When I consider how my light is s.
MILTON, 60
spermatozoa million million s., All of them alive
HUXLEY, A, 18
spheres our social s. have been widely different
WILDE, 29
spice gathered my myrrh with my s
BIBLE, 100
Sugar and s. And all that's nice
NURSERY RHYMES, 70
Variety's the very s. of life
COWPER, 24
spices a young hart upon the mountains of s.
BIBLE, 501
spider said a s. to a fly
HOWITT, 1
spies sorrows . . . come not single s.
SHAKESPEARE, 101
spillikins Stevenson . . . like a man playing s.
STEVENSON, R, 1
spilt the blood that she has s.
COWPER, 5
spin These are rare attainments . . . but . . . can she s.
JAMES I, 4
spinning from eternity s. the thread of your being
MARCUS AURELIUS, 12
Spinoza The Jews have produced . . . Christ, S., and myself
STEIN, 5
spires City with her dreaming s.
ARNOLD, M, 45
spirit and an haughty s. before a fall
BIBLE, 451
bound in the s.
BIBLE, 14
Give me the s.
SHAKESPEARE, 124
Hail to thee, blithe S.
SHELLEY, 24
history of the human s.
ARNOLD, M, 22
into thy hands I commend my s.
BIBLE, 19
Music that gentlier on the s. lies
TENNYSON, 55
my s. found outlet in the air
JOHNSON, A, 1
my s. hath rejoiced in God my Saviour
BIBLE, 309
renew a right s. within me
PSALMS, 31
s. of the Londoner stands resolute
GEORGE VI, 2
that which is born of the S. is s.
BIBLE, 244
the flesh lusteth against the S.
BIBLE, 134
the fruit of the S. is love, joy, peace
BIBLE, 135
the meanest . . . deeds require s. and talent
LICHTENBERG, 3
There exists a new s.
LE CORBUSIER, 2
the sacrifice of God is a troubled s.
PSALMS, 32
The s. burning but unbent
BYRON, 17
the s. . . . is willing
BIBLE, 426
the S. of God descending like a dove
BIBLE, 355
the S. of God moved upon . . . the waters
BIBLE, 137
the s. that always denies
GOETHE, 4
Th' expense of s. in a waste of shame
SHAKESPEARE, 370
waxed strong in s.
BIBLE, 311
spiritualist If the dead talk to you, you are a s.
SZASZ, 8
spiritualists The media . . . a convention of s.
STOPPARD, 6
spit s. upon my Jewish gaberdine
SHAKESPEARE, 240
spiteful I like to write when I feel s.
LAWRENCE, D, 41
spits Who s. against the wind
PROVERBS, 466
spleen S. can subsist on any kind of food
HAZLITT, 31
splendour Pavilioned in s., and girded with praise
GRANT, R, 1
small line of inconceivable s.
RADCLIFFE, 2
s. falls on castle walls
TENNYSON, 61
splinters teeth like s.
CAUSLEY, 1
split They s. the atom by firing particles at it
HAY, W, 1
When I s. an infinitive
CHANDLER, R, 6
spoil Don't s. the ship
PROVERBS, 120
s. the child
BUTLER, S, 4
spoiled s. by the world which he s.
VOLTAIRE, 5
spoke s. among your wheels
BEAUMONT, 1
spoken Speak when you're s. to
CARROLL, 36
very excellent things are s. of thee
PSALMS, 47
sponge Facts . . . are as water to a s.
HOOVER, 1
spontaneous set a high value on s. kindness
JOHNSON, S, 139
the Immaculate Conception was s. combustion
PARKER, D, 19
Worrying is the most natural and s. of . . . functions
THOMAS, L, 1

spoof even the weather forecast seemed to be some kind of s.
LODGE, 4
spoon And the dish ran away with the s.
NURSERY RHYMES, 14
S. feeding . . . teaches us nothing but the shape of the s.
FORSTER, 12
spoons diners-out from whom we guard our s.
MACAULAY, T, 19
let us count our s.
JOHNSON, S, 64
the faster we counted our s.
EMERSON, 5
sport In love as in s., the amateur status
GRAVES, R, 3
kill us for their s.
SHAKESPEARE, 185
Serious s. has nothing to do with fair play
ORWELL, 32
s. would be as tedious as to work
SHAKESPEARE, 109
The national s. of England
TREE, 6
The only athletic s. I ever mastered
JERROLD, 7
to make s. for our neighbours
AUSTEN, 26
sportsman But He was never . . . A S.
SITWELL, O, 2
spot Out, damned s.
SHAKESPEARE, 220
spotless s. reputation
SHAKESPEARE, 292
spots or the leopard his s.
BIBLE, 221
sprang I s. to the stirrup
BROWNING, R, 28
sprat Throw out a s.
PROVERBS, 402
spreading Under the s. chestnut tree
LONGFELLOW, 16
spring A new repast, or an untasted s.
ADDISON, 5
as short a S.; As quick a growth to meet decay
HERRICK, 4
By chilly finger'd s.
KEATS, 8
can S. be far behind
SHELLEY, 15
Drink deep, or taste not the Pierian s.
POPE, 23
flowers that bloom in the s.
GILBERT, W, 33
In the fi . . . a young man's fancy
TENNYSON, 30
In the s. . . . your lovely Chloë
SEARLE, 2
I said the hounds of s.
THURBER, 17
lived light in the s.
ARNOLD, M, 12
S. and summer did happen in Cambridge
NABOKOV, 6
S. Flow down the woods
SACKVILLE-WEST, 2
S. has returned
RILKE, 1
S. is come home
THOMPSON, F, 3
s. now comes unheralded by the return of the birds
CARSON, 3
there would be S. no more
TENNYSON, 33
They call it easing the S.
REED, H, 3
The year's at the s.
BROWNING, R, 45
Thrice welcome, darling of the s.
WORDSWORTH, W, 74
When the hounds of s. are on winter's traces
SWINBURNE, 1
Where are the songs of S.
KEATS, 46
springboard reality as a s. into space
BLAKE, W, 2
spur A s. in the head
PROVERBS, 65
Fame is the s.
MILTON, 25
spurs Let the boy win his s.
EDWARD III, 1
spurts They move forward in s.
CONNOLLY, 13
square deal Shed his blood . . . given a s.
ROOSEVELT, T, 8
squares walk on the lines or the s.
MILNE, 5
squeezed The Germans . . . are going to be s., as a lemon
GEDDES, 1
squire Bless the s. and his relations
DICKENS, 9
stable It's too late to shut the s. door
PROVERBS, 233
staff I'll break my s.
SHAKESPEARE, 326
stage All the world's a s.
SHAKESPEARE, 47
Don't put your daughter on the s.
COWARD, 8
If this were play'd upon a s.
SHAKESPEARE, 343
no man dies for love, but on the s.
DRYDEN, 29
qualities . . . necessary for success upon the s.
TERRY, 2
the Attic s.
ARNOLD, M, 42
this great s. of fools
SHAKESPEARE, 190
we go quite off this s.
POPE, 61
stagecoach You will hear more good things on . . . a s. from
London to Oxford
HAZLITT, 10
stair As I was going up the s.
MEARNS, 1
stairs he had known many kicked down s.
HALIFAX, 9
walks up the s. of his concepts
STEINBECK, 2
stake To the thumbscrew and the s.
TENNYSON, 70
Stalin If Mr S. dies
EDEN, A, 1
look at him! He might be S.
DE GAULLE, 2
S. hates the guts of
ROOSEVELT, F, 5
stammer You persisted . . . like a s.
LEWIS, W, 5
stamp If we can't s. out literature
WAUGH, E, 41
the indelible s. of his lowly origin
DARWIN, C R, 7
to order a new s. . . . with my face on it
CHARLES FRANCIS JOSEPH, 1
stand a firm place to s.
ARCHIMEDES, 1
I call upon the intellectual community . . . to s. up for freedom of
the imagination
RUSHDIE, 2
no time to s. and stare
DAVIES, W, 2

s. not upon the order of . . . going   SHAKESPEARE, 216
S. your ground . . . if they mean to have a war, let it begin here
    PARKER, J, 1
They also serve who only s. and wait   MILTON, 61
We s. today on the edge of a new frontier   KENNEDY, JOHN, 10
stands S. the Church clock   BROOKE, 4
star a s. or two beside   COLERIDGE, S, 33
Being a s. has made it possible   DAVIS, S, 1
Bright s., would I were steadfast   KEATS, 6
Go, and catch a falling s.   DONNE, 13
Hitch your wagon to a s.   EMERSON, 23
one s. differeth from another . . . in glory   BIBLE, 41
She was always a s. . . . intermittently a good actress
    BANKHEAD, 2
Someday I'll wish upon a s.   HARBURG, 3
Sunset and evening s.   TENNYSON, 12
that same s., That fitful, fiery Lucifer   YOUNG, A, 1
The desire of the moth for the s.   JOYCE, 12
The Soul that rises with us, our life's S.   WORDSWORTH, W, 25
Thy soul was like a s., and dwelt apart   WORDSWORTH, W, 56
Twinkle, twinkle, little s.   TAYLOR, JANE, 1
we have seen his s. in the east   BIBLE, 351
star-cross'd pair of s. lovers   SHAKESPEARE, 304
stare no time to stand and s.   DAVIES, W, 2
Starkie There was a young woman called S.   ANONYMOUS, 95
starry the s. heaven above me   KANT, 1
Under the wide and s. sky   STEVENSON, R, 12
stars Clad in the beauty of a thousand s.   MARLOWE, 3
he made the s. also   BIBLE, 140
I'll hold my head so high it'll strike the s.   HORACE, 26
Look at the s.   HOPKINS, 5
One sees the mud, and one the s.   LANGBRIDGE, 1
some of us are looking at the s.   WILDE, 41
Some s. . . . Fell like a falling tear   YOUNG, A, 2
S. . . . robbed men of their souls   ASIMOV, 2
strives to touch the s.   SPENSER, 3
Tempt not the s.   FORD, JOHN, 1
The fault, dear Brutus, is not in our s.   SHAKESPEARE, 143
the field of the s. is so vast, but . . . man has measured it
    FRANCE, 5
The s. grew bright in the winter sky   MASEFIELD, 4
the s. in their courses   BIBLE, 292
the Stone that puts the S. to Flight   FITZGERALD, E, 2
The Syrian s. look down   ARNOLD, M, 30
Through endeavour to the s.   ANONYMOUS, 68
We are merely the s.' tennis-balls   WEBSTER, J, 3
what is the s.   O'CASEY, 1
star-spangled 'Tis the s. banner   KEY, F, 1
start Wrong from the s.   POUND, 12
starts make certain it never s.   BRADLEY, O, 1
starve Let not poor Nelly s.   CHARLES II, 6
starving all around you people are s.   PANKHURST, 1
state a s. in the proper sense of the word   LENIN, 3
attacking an ex-secretary of s.   ACHESON, 5
I am the S.   LOUIS XIV, 4
In a free society the s. . . . administers justice among men
    LIPPMAN, 1
O Lord, to what a s. . . . those who love Thee
    TERESA OF ÁVILA, 1
Our object in the construction of the s.   PLATO, 2
reinforcement of the power of the S.   CAMUS, 15
So long as the s. exists there is no freedom   LENIN, 4
S. socialism is totally alien   THATCHER, M, 16
the lie has become . . . a pillar of the S.   SOLZHENITSYN, 14
The S., in choosing men . . . takes no notice of their opinions
    CROMWELL, O, 8
The s. is an instrument . . . of the ruling class   STALIN, 2
The s. is not 'abolished', it withers away   ENGELS, 1
the s. . . . Man is in   NIETZSCHE, 5
The worth of a S.   MILL, 5
stately homes go back to thy s. of England   LAWRENCE, D, 18
S. of England ope their doors   CAMPBELL, R, 1
the S. of England   COWARD, 13; HEMANS, 2
Those comfortably padded lunatic asylums . . . the s.   WOOLF, 4
statement Any general s. is like a cheque   POUND, 6
states S., like men, have their growth . . . their decay   LANDOR, 4
statesman abroad you're a s.   MACMILLAN, 7
A politician is a s. . . . with an open mouth   STEVENSON, A, 2
A s. is a politician who   POMPIDOU, 1
A s. is a politician who's been dead   TRUMAN, 5
a s. of literature   GALSWORTHY, 2

definition of a constitutional s.   BAGEHOT, 9
if you agree with him he is a s.   LLOYD GEORGE, 20
statesmanship the suspicion . . . his life was a preparation for
elder s.   MACMILLAN, 2
statesmen S. are far too busy making speeches   RUSSELL, B, 23
s. . . . estranged from reality   LAING, 1
static class people as s. and dynamic   WAUGH, E, 24
novel is a s. thing   TYNAN, 1
station honour is a private s.   ADDISON, 7
stationmaster The s.'s whiskers are of a Victorian bushiness
    WODEHOUSE, 19
stations always know our proper s.   DICKENS, 9
statistics Facts speak louder than s.   STREATFIELD, 1
He uses s. as a drunken man uses lamp-posts   LANG, A, 1
lies, damned lies and s.   DISRAELI, 16;
    TWAIN, 4
s., born to consume resources   HORACE, 17
There are two kinds of s.   STOUT, 1
unrewarded millions without whom S. would be a bankrupt science
    SMITH, L, 6
we must study s.   NIGHTINGALE, 3
You cannot feed the hungry on s.   LLOYD GEORGE, 7
statue that *my* s. should be moved, which I should much dislike
    VICTORIA, 11
there's a s. inside every block of stone   ORWELL, 9
statues worth a million s.   CUMMINGS, 2
status restored the s. quo   SQUIRE, 3
stay s. me with flagons   BIBLE, 487
S., s., Until the hasting day Has run   HERRICK, 4
Stay-at-Home Sweet S.   DAVIES, W, 3
steaks smell of s. in passageways   ELIOT, T, 19
steal A man who will s. *for* me will s. *from* me   ROOSEVELT, T, 5
thou shalt not s.   BIBLE, 115
stealing hanged for s. horses   HALIFAX, 1
steals A good composer . . . s.   STRAVINSKY, 1
what can plead that man's excuse Who s. a common from a goose
    ANONYMOUS, 80
Who s. my purse s. trash   SHAKESPEARE, 282
stealth Do good by s.   POPE, 10
greatest pleasure I know, is to do a good action by s.
    LAMB, CHARLES, 18
stealthy The S. School of Criticism   ROSSETTI, D, 4
steamer tossing about in a s. from Harwich   GILBERT, W, 21
steel arm'd with more than complete s.   MARLOWE, 12
the cold s.   ARMINSTEAD, 1
When the foeman bares his s.   GILBERT, W, 39
steep When things are s., remember to stay level-headed
    HORACE, 33
steeple clock in the s. strikes one   WORK, 1
steeples Talk about the pews and s.   CHESTERTON, 6
Till you have drench'd our s.   SHAKESPEARE, 176
steer You just press the accelerator to the floor and s. left
    VUKOVICH, 1
Stein There's a wonderful family called S.   ANONYMOUS, 89
stellar the whole solar and s. systems   CARLYLE, T, 30
stem a rod out of the s. of Jesse   BIBLE, 202
step a s. from the sublime to the ridiculous   NAPOLEON I, 9
one small s. for man   ARMSTRONG, N, 1
One s. forward, two steps back   LENIN, 2
only the first s. . . . is difficult   DEFFAND, 1
The first s.   PROVERBS, 394
step-mother a kind parent . . . or a merciless s.
    PLINY THE ELDER, 3
Stepney When will that be? Say the bells of S.
    NURSERY RHYMES, 41
stepp'd in blood s. in so far   SHAKESPEARE, 217
Stevenson S. . . . like a man playing spillikins   STEVENSON, R, 1
stick if we praise ourselves fearlessly, something will always s.
    BACON, FRANCIS, 4
kind of burr; I shall s.   SHAKESPEARE, 233
meant us to s. it out   KOESTLER, 3
Speak softly and carry a big s.   ROOSEVELT, T, 7
white s. and a dog   LEVIN, 2
sticks it is always said of slander that something always s.
    BACON, FRANCIS, 4
S. and stones   PROVERBS, 369
stiff a s. upper lip   CARY, P, 1
stiffen S. the sinews   SHAKESPEARE, 129
stigma Any s. . . . to beat a dogma   GUEDALLA, 3
stile He found a crooked sixpence against a crooked s.
    NURSERY RHYMES, 57

strive I s. to be brief, and I become obscure HORACE, 2
needst not s. . . . to keep alive CLOUGH, 6
To s., to seek, to find, and not to yield TENNYSON, 81
strives s. to touch the stars SPENSER, 3
stroke man fears . . . only the s. of death BACON, FRANCIS, 7
none so fast as s. COKE, D, 1
To s. a platitude until it purrs MARQUIS, 2
strong a s. ass BIBLE, 181
battle to the s. BIBLE, 74
be s. and of a good courage BIBLE, 58
be s. in the Lord BIBLE, 96
disarm the s. and arm the weak FRANCE, 2
how sublime . . . To suffer and be s. LONGFELLOW, 8
Sorrow and silence are s. LONGFELLOW, 6
S. enough to answer back to desires, to despise distinctions HORACE, 47
s. enough to bear the misfortunes of others ROCHEFOUCAULD, 2
the errors of those who think they are s. BIDAULT, 1
the s. shall thrive SERVICE, 3
the wall is s. WILDE, 9
thou . . . hast made my hill so s. PSALMS, 17
waxed s. in spirit BIBLE, 311
woe unto them that . . . follow s. drink BIBLE, 195
strongest S. minds . . . the noisy world Hears least WORDSWORTH, W, 3
strongminded nobody is s. around a President REEDY, 1
strove I s. with none LANDOR, 7
struck Certain women should be s. regularly COWARD, 18
structure s. of the . . . British sentence CHURCHILL, W, 17
struggle each man must s., lest the moral law become . . . separated ADDAMS, 2
I believe in the armed s. as the only solution GUEVARA, 1
manhood a s. DISRAELI, 4
The perpetual s. for room and food MALTHUS, 2
the s. for existence DARWIN, C R, 9
struggles The history of all . . . society is the history of class s. MARX, K, 1
struggling the greatness of Russia is only her pre-natal s. LAWRENCE, D, 34
strumpet a s.'s fool SHAKESPEARE, 24
struts player that s. and frets SHAKESPEARE, 225
stubborn s. spear-men SCOTT, WALTER, 16
student an over-ambitious essay by a second-year s. PRIESTLEY, 2
a s. to the end of my days CHEKHOV, 4
He was . . . a s. of history TAYLOR, A, 7
studies S. serve for delight BACON, FRANCIS, 49
study I am slow of s. SHAKESPEARE, 259
much s. is a weariness of the flesh BIBLE, 78
s. what you most affect SHAKESPEARE, 318
The proper s. of Mankind is Man POPE, 34
the result of previous s. AUSTEN, 22
studying By s. the masters ABEL, 1
stuff Ambition should be made of sterner s. SHAKESPEARE, 155
such s. as dreams are made on SHAKESPEARE, 325
The future is made of the same s. WEIL, 4
to s. a mushroom CONRAN, 1
stuffed We are the s. men ELIOT, T, 9
stumble they s. that run fast SHAKESPEARE, 313
stumbled s. when I saw SHAKESPEARE, 183
stumbling the . . . world was s. . . . in social blindness KELLER, 3
stupid anger makes us all s. SPYRI, 2
clever man . . . came of . . . s. people CARLYLE, T, 32
he ceased to be mad he became merely s. PROUST, 11
Living in England . . . must be like being married to a s. . . . wife HALSEY, 3
The s. neither forgive SZASZ, 6
To be clever enough to get . . . money, one must be s. CHESTERTON, 25
stupidity Against s. the gods . . . struggle in vain SCHILLER, 1
Human S. consists in having lots of ideas, but stupid ones MONTHERLANT, 2
If poverty is the mother of crime, s. is its father LA BRUYÈRE, 11
It is a s. . . . to busy oneself with the correction of the world MOLIÈRE, 6
no sin except s. WILDE, 14
Sturm S. und Drang KLINGER, 1
Stygian resembling the horrible S. smoke of the pit JAMES I, 1
ye S. set LANDOR, 1
style killed a calf he would do it in a high s. SHAKESPEARE, 2
s. is the man himself BUFFON, 1

s., not sincerity, is the vital thing WILDE, 31
s. . . . often hides eczema CAMUS, 5
the grand s. arises in poetry ARNOLD, M, 32
The s. is the man PROVERBS, 426
styles All s. are good except the tiresome sort VOLTAIRE, 18
stylist the greatest literary s. of his time JOYCE, 4
subject a noble nature . . . treats . . . a serious s. ARNOLD, M, 32
Every s.'s duty is the King's SHAKESPEARE, 133
Her Majesty is not a s. DISRAELI, 37
the individual s. . . . 'has nothing to do with the laws but to obey them.' HORSLEY, 1
subjects Although there exist many thousand s. PROVERBS, 42
subjunctive S. to the last, he preferred WOOLLCOTT, 1
sublime a step from the s. to the ridiculous NAPOLEON I, 9
Beethoven's Fifth Symphony is the most s. noise FORSTER, 7
From the s. to the ridiculous PROVERBS, 169
how s. . . . To suffer and be strong LONGFELLOW, 8
The s. and the ridiculous PAINE, 2
submerged speak for the inarticulate and the s. BEAVERBROOK, 4
This S. Tenth BOOTH, 2
submit To great evils we s.; we resent little provocations HAZLITT, 22
subscribers reasons for not printing any list of s. JOHNSON, S, 138
subsequence It is incident to physicians . . . to mistake s. for consequence JOHNSON, S, 44
substance faith is the s. of things hoped for BIBLE, 189
lose the s. by grasping at the shadow AESOP, 1
substantial he that chiefly owes himself . . . is the s. Man BROWNE, T, 2
substantives be able to tell the s. from the adjectives MADARIAGA Y ROGO, 2
substitute a s. for reading it BURGESS, 5
no s. for talent HUXLEY, A, 27
substitutes and finally a single dictator s. himself TROTSKY, 11
subterfuge We live in our own world . . . The adult s. THOMAS, R, 2
subtil the serpent was more s. BIBLE, 148
subtle Time, the s. thief of youth MILTON, 59
subtlety one-dimensional s. of a comic-strip THATCHER, M, 3
suburbia I come from s. RAPHAEL, 3
succeed If at first you don't s. HICKSON, 213
If they s., they fail CRISP, 9
I'm . . . ugly enough to s. on my own ALLEN, W, 4
It is not enough to s. VIDAL, 5
Never having been able to s. in the world VOLTAIRE, 27
those who ne'er s. DICKINSON, 5
to s. unconventionally KEYNES, 1
succeeds Nothing s. PROVERBS, 318
Whenever a friend s. VIDAL, 6
success a self-made man who owed his lack of s. to nobody HELLER, 1
I thought that s. spelled happiness PAVLOVA, 3
I was never affected by the question of the s. MEIR, 2
no s. like failure DYLAN, 5
not in mortals to command s. ADDISON, 4
no very lively hope of s. SMITH, SYDNEY, 13
only place where s. comes before work SASSOON, V, 1
religion . . . yours is S. BARRIE, 7
s. and miscarriage are empty sounds JOHNSON, S, 7
s. . . . by dint of hard work PAVLOVA, 2
s. depends . . . upon individual initiative and exertion PAVLOVA, 2
S. is counted sweetest DICKINSON, 5
surest guarantee of sexual s. is sexual s. AMIS, 1
Sweet Smell of S. LEHMAN, 1
The moral flabbiness born of . . . S. JAMES, W, 4
The penalty of s. ASTOR, N, 3
two to make a marriage a s. SAMUEL, 1
successful It was very s. BRAUN, 2
we do everything we can to appear s. ROCHEFOUCAULD, 7
sucker a s. born every minute BARNUM, 1
suckle To s. fools SHAKESPEARE, 280
sucklings out of the mouth of . . . babes and s. PSALMS, 3
sucks s. the nurse asleep SHAKESPEARE, 38
suddenly No one . . . s. became depraved JUVENAL, 2
sued publish and be s. INGRAMS, 2
Suez Ship me somewhere east of S. KIPLING, 25
the S. Canal was flowing through my drawing room EDEN, C, 1
suffer courage to love . . . courage to s. TROLLOPE, 2
how sublime . . . To s. and be strong LONGFELLOW, 8
If s. we must, let's s. on the heights HUGO, 1
Rather s. than die LA FONTAINE, 1

s. fools gladly   BIBLE, 46
suffered   love a place the less for having s.   AUSTEN, 17
suffering   A man who fears s.   MONTAIGNE, 11
pity for the s. of mankind   RUSSELL, B, 4
sympathize with everything, except s.   WILDE, 49
The prime goal is to alleviate s., and not to prolong life
   BARNARD, C, 1
we cannot be created for this sort of s.   KEATS, 71
sufficient   s. unto the day is the evil thereof   BIBLE, 371
suffragettes   we s. aspire to be . . . ambassadors of freedom to
women   PANKHURST, C, 4
sugar   like sulphuric acid and s.   TAINE, 1
S. and spice And all that's nice   NURSERY RHYMES, 70
suicide   If you must commit s.   BORROW, 2
Never murder a man who is committing s.   WILSON, W, 3
No one ever lacks a good reason for s.   PAVESE, 1
s. is God's best gift to man   PLINY THE ELDER, 2
the only man . . . who cannot commit s.   VARAH, 1
thought of s. is a great . . . comfort   NIETZSCHE, 11
suit   in a light so dim he would not have chosen a s. by it
   CHEVALIER, M, 1
My s. is pale yellow. My nationality is French   WILLIAMS, T, 1
suitable   no s. material to work on   COMPTON-BURNETT, 3
Sukey   S. take it off again   NURSERY RHYMES, 44
sulphur   land of Calvin, oat-cakes, and s.   SMITH, SYDNEY, 7
Puffed its s. to the sunset   BETJEMAN, 8
sulphuric   like s. acid and sugar   TAINE, 1
sultry   common where the climate's s.   BYRON, 19
sum   *Cogito, ergo s.*   DESCARTES, 1
sumer   S. is icumen in   ANONYMOUS, 75
summer   after many a s. dies the swan   TENNYSON, 75
All on a s. day   CARROLL, 19
Beauty sat with me all the s. day   BRIDGES, 2
Before the war . . . it was s. all the year round   ORWELL, 10
Made glorious s.   SHAKESPEARE, 300
Now the peak of s.'s past   DAY LEWIS, 1
Spring and s. did happen in Cambridge   NABOKOV, 6
S. afternoon – s. afternoon   JAMES, H, 14
S. has set in with its usual severity   COLERIDGE, S, 46
the last rose of s.   MOORE, T, 5
Warm s. sun shine kindly here   ANONYMOUS, 104
summit   the s. of Everest was hardly the place   HILLARY, 1
summits   snowy s. old in story   TENNYSON, 61
summons   when Fate s.   DRYDEN, 26
summum   *S. bonum*   CICERO, 3
sun   all, except their s. is set   BYRON, 26
aweary of the s.   SHAKESPEARE, 226
before you let the s. in, mind it wipes its shoes   THOMAS, D, 18
better is he . . . who hath not seen the evil work under the s.
   BIBLE, 68
between me and the s.   DIOGENES, 1
Busy old fool, unruly S.   DONNE, 6
Fear no more the heat o' th' s.   SHAKESPEARE, 62
Follow thy fair s.   CAMPION, 1
Furnish'd and burnish'd by Aldershot s.   BETJEMAN, 11
go out in the mid-day s.   COWARD, 12
If they had said the s. and the moon was gone   CARLYLE, J, 3
I got the s. in the mornin' and the moon at night   BERLIN, 1
it were better for s. and moon to drop from heaven   NEWMAN, J, 4
I will sing of the s.   POUND, 9
Juliet is the s.   SHAKESPEARE, 308
let not the s. go down upon your wrath   BIBLE, 94
Light breaks where no s. shines   THOMAS, D, 14
My s. sets   BROWNING, R, 6
nothing like the s.   SHAKESPEARE, 371
on which the s. never sets   NORTH, 1
side next the s. that's tempting   OUIDA, 2
So sicken waning moons too near the s.   DRYDEN, 19
s. came dazzling thro' the leaves   TENNYSON, 45
s. had risen to hear him crow   ELIOT, G, 3
S. remains fixed in the centre   GALILEI, 1
s. shall not burn thee by day   PSALMS, 68
Thank heavens the s. has gone in   SMITH, L, 8
The kiss of s. for pardon   GURNEY, 1
The people – could you patent the s.   SALK, 1
there is no new thing under the s.   BIBLE, 62
There rises the s. of Austerlitz   NAPOLEON I, 7
The S. came up upon the left   COLERIDGE, S, 25
the s. . . . cometh forth as a bridegroom   PSALMS, 8
The s. does not set in my dominions   SCHILLER, 2
the s. . . . rejoiceth as a giant   PSALMS, 8

the s. shining ten days a year and shit in the streets   KENEALLY, 1
this s. of York   SHAKESPEARE, 300
To have enjoy'd the s.   ARNOLD, M, 12
we cannot make our s. Stand still   MARVELL, 11
sunburn   S. is very becoming   COWARD, 10
Sunday   A Christian . . . feels Repentance on a S.   YBARRA, 1
Buried on S.   NURSERY RHYMES, 53
only two posh papers on a S.   OSBORNE, 2
The feeling of S. is the same everywhere   RHYS, 3
sung   I have s. women in three cities   POUND, 9
sunk   thanks to words, we have often s. to the level of the
demons   HUXLEY, A, 3
sunless   Down to a s. sea   COLERIDGE, S, 14
sunset   a s.-touch   BROWNING, R, 9
Puffed its sulphur to the s.   BETJEMAN, 8
S. and evening star   TENNYSON, 12
s. breezes shiver   NEWBOLT, 4
sunsets   I have a horror of s.   PROUST, 16
superfluous   that controversy is either s. or hopeless
   NEWMAN, J, 6
superior   being a novelist, I consider myself s. to the saint, the
scientist   LAWRENCE, D, 38
One is not s. . . . because one sees the world in an odious light
   CHATEAUBRIAND, 2
The French want no-one to be their s.. The English want *inferiors*
   TOCQUEVILLE, 1
superiority   Cultivate a s. to reason   COLLINS, W, 2
their insolent and unfounded airs of s.   WALPOLE, H, 9
The s. of one man's opinion over another's   JAMES, H, 12
superiors   equality . . . with our s.   BECQUE, 1
In America everybody is of the opinion that he has no social s.
   RUSSELL, B, 22
superlative   we have not settled the s.   CHESTERTON, 18
Super-Mac   Introducing S.   VICKY, 1
Superman   he . . . raked up the S.   NIETZSCHE, 1
I teach you the S.   NIETZSCHE, 17
supernatural   Religion Has made an honest woman of the s.
   FRY, C, 3
This s. soliciting   SHAKESPEARE, 202
superstition   necessary for a s. to enslave a philosophy   INGE, 5
S. is the poetry of life   GOETHE, 16
S. is the religion of feeble minds   BURKE, E, 12
S. sets the whole world in flames   VOLTAIRE, 13
superstitions   new truths . . . end as s.   HUXLEY, T, 3
s. of the human mind   VOLTAIRE, 21
superstructure   Sentimentality is a s. covering brutality   JUNG, 8
supp'd   I have s. full with horrors   SHAKESPEARE, 224
support   atheist . . . no invisible means of s.   FOSDICK, 1
s. me when I am . . . wrong   MELBOURNE, 4
supposing   s. him to be the gardener   BIBLE, 275
supreme   Our s. governors, the mob   WALPOLE, H, 3
sups   He who s. with the devil   PROVERBS, 203
surgeons   Human beings, yes, but not s.   VIRCHOW, 1
start with the s. . . . and work *up* to the gutter   THOMAS, D, 6
surgically   I had it s. removed   SELLERS, 2
surmise   with a wild s.   KEATS, 42
surpassed   Man is something that is to be s.   NIETZSCHE, 17
surprise   Life is a great s.   NABOKOV, 2
surprised   it is *I* who am s.; you are merely astonished
   WEBSTER, N, 1
the audience want to be s. . . . by things that they expect
   BERNARD, T, 1
they are . . . s. at hearing of a good action and never of a bad one
   KEATS, 70
surrender   No terms except . . . s.   GRANT, U, 3
we shall never s.   CHURCHILL, W, 51
survey   When I s. the wondrous Cross   WATTS, 8
survival   the S. of the Fittest   DARWIN, C R, 10; SPENCER, H, 3
without victory there is no s.   CHURCHILL, W, 50
survive   as fitted to s. . . . as a tapeworm   GOLDING, 1
only the Fit s.   SERVICE, 3
Out of their cataclysm but one poor Noah Dare hope to s.
   HUXLEY, A, 18
that far down you have to struggle to s.   KENNEDY, R, 2
survived   I s.   SIEYÈS, 1
survives   Education is what s.   SKINNER, B, 2
Susanna   O, S.   FOSTER, 4
Susie   saucy, soft, short shirts for soldiers, sister S. sews
   WESTON, 2
suspect   I rather s. her of being in love   CHURCHILL, J, 1
suspected   New opinions are always s.   LOCKE, 1

T

Whatever question there may be of his t.   THOREAU, 1
talents A vain . . . coxcomb without . . . solid t.   PEPYS, 1
If you have great t., industry will improve them   REYNOLDS, J, 1
the difference between our t. and our expectations   BONO, 1
very rich people who are rich because they have t. or vital
  statistics   SCOTT, P, 2
talk If you can t. with crowds and keep your virtue   KIPLING, 17
my ministers t. – as long as they do what I say   THATCHER, M, 24
T. of the devil   PROVERBS, 376
Teas, Where small t. dies   SHELLEY, 19
the need to t. is a primary impulse   CERVANTES, 14
think too little . . . t. too much   DRYDEN, 8
Two may t. . . . yet never really meet   CATHERWOOD, 1
we never t. about anything except me   WHISTLER, 5
when I hear anyone t. of Culture   GOERING, 4
When two Englishmen meet, their first t. is of the weather
  JOHNSON, S, 15
women should t. an hour   BEAUMONT, 10
talked He t. on for ever   HAZLITT, 11
The more you are t. about, the more you . . . wish to be t. about
  RUSSELL, B, 1
There is only one thing . . . worse than being t. about   WILDE, 46
talker A good listener is a good t. with a sore throat
  WHITEHORN, 7
a non-stop t. to whom someone has given a typewriter
  BRENAN, 5
Nothing is more despicable than a professional t.   FÉNELON, 1
talkers fluent t.   HAZLITT, 28
talking for thirty-five years he had not stopped t.   WAUGH, E
Frenchman must be always t.   JOHNSON, S, 133
good newspaper, . . . is a nation t. to itself   MILLER, A, 5
if you ain't t. about him, ain't listening   BRANDO, 3
I must . . . try hard to control the t. habit, but . . . my case is
  hereditary   FRANK, 3
I wouldn't be . . . t. to someone like you   CARTLAND, 1
People t. without speaking   SIMON, 3
T. and eloquence are not the same   JONSON, 9
T. of Michelangelo   ELIOT, T, 12
While we're t., time will have meanly run on   HORACE, 31
tall all I ask is a t. ship   MASEFIELD, 5
Let our children grow t.   THATCHER, M, 5
taller glad that the sons are six inches t. than their fathers
  BRAGG, 2
tambourine Hey! Mr T. Man   DYLAN, 6
tambourines a clashing of t. and wriggling   BUCHAN, 1
tamper Who am I to t. with a masterpiece   WILDE, 10
tangere noli me t.   BIBLE, 276
tangerine t. trees and marmalade skies   LENNON, 7
tankard heart which grief hath cankered . . . remedy – the T.
  CALVERLEY, 1
tanned getting more t. and more tired   PEGLER, 1
tapeworm as fitted to survive . . . as a t.   GOLDING, 1
Tara through T.'s halls   MOORE, T, 2
target IRA would think me a worthwhile t.   MOUNTBATTEN, 5
tarnished neither t. nor afraid   CHANDLER, R, 4
tarry having lost . . . your prime, You may for ever t.   HERRICK, 6
tarrying make no long t., O my God   PSALMS, 24
Tartar Scratch the Russian and . . . find the T.   MAISTRE, 2
tarts He's lost us the t.' vote   DEVONSHIRE, 1
she made some t.   CARROLL, 19
The Queen of Hearts She made some t.   NURSERY RHYMES, 56
Tarzan Me T.   BURROUGHS, 1
Me? T.   WEISSMULLER, 1
task No t. is a long one but the t. on which one dare not start
  BAUDELAIRE, 1
Tasmanians the T., who never committed adultery, are now
  extinct   MAUGHAM, 1
taste A different t. in jokes is a . . . strain on the affections
  ELIOT, G, 4
bad t. is better than no t.   BENNETT, ARNOLD, 9
Drink deep, or t. not the Pierian spring   POPE, 23
Every one to his t.   PROVERBS, 142
great common sense and good t.   SHAW, 8
If you want to see bad t.   LE CORBUSIER, 3
I suspect his t. in higher matters   LAMB, CHARLES, 5
no t. when you married me   SHERIDAN, R, 10
nowhere worse t., than in a churchyard   JOWETT, 3
Shakespeare, undoubtedly wanted t.   WALPOLE, 4
T. is the feminine of genius   FITZGERALD, E, 1
the bouquet is better than the t.   POTTER, S, 7
the t. by which he is . . . relished   WORDSWORTH, W, 20

The t. was that of the little crumb of madeleine   PROUST, 2
Things sweet to t. prove . . . sour   SHAKESPEARE, 293
willing to t. any drink once   CABELL, 1
tasted Sir, you have t. two whole worms   SPOONER, 5
Some books are to be t.   BACON, FRANCIS, 50
tastes It is like a cigar. . . . it never t. quite the same   WAVELL, 1
Our t. greatly alter   JOHNSON, S, 74
There is no accounting for t.   PROVERBS, 410
taught a woman who knows all . . . that can be t.   CHANEL, 1
I forget what I was t.   WHITE, P, 2
tavern A t. chair is the throne   JOHNSON, S, 38
he has . . . opened a t. for his friends   DOUGLAS, N, 3
There is a t. in the town   ANONYMOUS, 87
There is nothing . . . by which so much happiness is produced as
  by a good t.   JOHNSON, S, 102
tawney that t. weed tobacco   JONSON, 4
tax A hateful t.   JOHNSON, S, 9
For God's sake, madam, don't say that in England for . . . they
  will surely t. it   SWIFT, 19
taxation T. without representation   OTIS, 1
taxed all the world should be t.   BIBLE, 312
taxes . . . collect legal t. from illegal money   CAPONE, 3
Death and t. and childbirth   MITCHELL, M, 3
read my lips, no new t.   BUSH, 3
The avoidance of t. . . . still carries . . . reward   KEYNES, 11
taxi done almost every human activity inside a t.   BRIEN, 1
taxis hiring t. . . . handing out redundancy notices to its own
  workers   KINNOCK, 9
Tay Beautiful Railway Bridge of the Silv'ry T.   MCGONAGALL, 2
tea Dinner, Lunch and T.   BELLOC, 6
honey still for t.   BROOKE, 4
sometimes counsel take – and sometimes T.   POPE, 49
Take some more t.   CARROLL, 11
T. for Two, and Two for T.   HARBACK, 1
we drink too much t.   PRIESTLEY, 6
We invite people like that to t., but we don't marry them
  BETJEMAN, 3
When I makes t. I makes t.   JOYCE, 7
teach Don't t. your grandmother   PROVERBS, 121
For every person wishing to t.   SELLAR, 1
He who shall t. the child to doubt   BLAKE, W, 8
It is no matter what you t. them first   JOHNSON, S, 67
You can't t. an old dog   PROVERBS, 478
teacher Experience is a good t.   ANTRIM, 3
Time is a great t., but . . . kills all its pupils   BERLIOZ, 1
teachers We t. can only help . . . as servants   MONTESSORI, 2
teaches He who cannot, t.   SHAW, 32
teaching Such t. is pestiferous   LIVERMORE, 1
teacup Storm in a T.   BERNARD, W, 1
team Is my t. ploughing   HOUSMAN, 11
The British, being brought up on t. games   PARKINSON, 3
tear Every t. from every eye   BLAKE, W, 7
Some stars . . . Fell like a falling t.   YOUNG, 2
tears blood, toil, t. and sweat   CHURCHILL, W, 49
foolish t. upon my grave   TENNYSON, 11
He spoke, and loos'd our heart in t.   ARNOLD, M, 27
I forbid my t.   SHAKESPEARE, 104
If you have t., prepare to shed them   SHAKESPEARE, 156
in a flood of t. and a Sedan chair   DICKENS, 53
mine own t. Do scald   SHAKESPEARE, 191
No t. in the writer   FROST, R, 2
our t. Thaw not the frost   SHELLEY, 3
shed t. when they would devour   BACON, FRANCIS, 60
T., idle t.   TENNYSON, 62
T. such as angels weep   MILTON, 36
T. were to me   CRISP, 5
The bitterest t. . . . are for words . . . unsaid   STOWE, 1
The bitterest t. shed over graves   STOWE, 1
the land of t.   SAINT-EXUPÉRY, 1
The smiles, the t., Of boyhood's years   MOORE, T, 7
the women whose eyes have been washed . . . with t.
  DIX, DOROTHY, 1
They that sow in t. shall reap in joy   PSALMS, 69
Violet Elizabeth dried her t.   CROMPTON, 1
With silence and t.   BYRON, 44
teas T., Where small talk dies   SHELLEY, 19
tease The fleas that t. in the high Pyrenees   BELLOC, 15
tea-stirring t. times   ISHERWOOD, 2
teatray Like a t. in the sky   CARROLL, 10
teche gladly wolde he lerne, and gladly t.   CHAUCER, 9
technological For t. man it is time   MCLUHAN, 2

Time, the subtle t. of youth — MILTON, 59
thieves a den of t. — BIBLE, 408
fell among t. — BIBLE, 324
thin Enclosing every t. man, there's a fat man — WAUGH, E, 30
in every fat man a t. one — CONNOLLY, 18
One can never be too t. — WINDSOR, 2
there's a t. man inside every fat man — ORWELL, 9
There were times my pants were so t. — TRACY, 1
t. red line tipped with steel — RUSSELL, W, 1
Through thick and t. — BUTLER, S, 5
thing call that t. under your hat a head — HOLBERG, 1
good t., to make it too common — SHAKESPEARE, 117
It is a far, far, better t. that I do — DICKENS, 57
something between a t. and a thought — PALMER, 1
The play's the t. — SHAKESPEARE, 88
the t. which is good — BIBLE, 94
thing-in-itself The t., the will-to-live, exists . . . in every being — SCHOPENHAUER, 5
things all t. were made by him — BIBLE, 238
Glorious t. of thee are spoken — NEWTON, J, 1
T. are entirely what they appear to be — SARTRE, 8
To talk of many t. — CARROLL, 28
think apparatus with which we t. — BIERCE, 4
I cannot sit and t. — LAMB, CHARLES, 13
I exist by what I t. — SARTRE, 9
I never t. of the future — EINSTEIN, 13
I t. him so, because I t. him so — SHAKESPEARE, 347
I t. therefore I am — DESCARTES, 1
Many people would sooner die than t. — RUSSELL, B, 28
not so t. as you drunk — SQUIRE, 1
some . . . speak . . . before they t. — LA BRUYÈRE, 3
There exist some evils so terrible . . . that we dare not t. of them — LABRUYÈRE, 10
T. of your posterity — ADAMS, J, 3
t. only this of me — BROOKE, 6
t. too little . . . talk too much — DRYDEN, 8
time to t. before I speak — DARWIN, E, 1
To know how to say what others only . . . t. — CHARLES, E, 1
We haven't the money, so we've got to t. — RUTHERFORD, 2
When I t. of all the books I have read — YEATS, 5
You can't t. rationally on an empty stomach — REITH, 1
thinkers not always the justest t. — HAZLITT, 28
thinking In order to draw a limit to t. — WITTGENSTEIN, 2
It ain't t. about it — TROLLOPE, 8
one prolonged effort to prevent oneself t. — HUXLEY, A, 24
Plain living and high t. are no more — WORDSWORTH, W, 57
T. is to me the greatest fatigue in the world — VANBURGH, 4
t. makes it so — SHAKESPEARE, 83
try t. of love — FRY, C, 5
We are t. beings — JAMES, W, 3
thinks He t. too much . . . dangerous — SHAKESPEARE, 144
never t. of me — ANONYMOUS, 87
The great consolation . . . is to say what one t. — VOLTAIRE, 30
third if there was a t. sex — VAIL, 1
T. time lucky — PROVERBS, 430
to help Britain to become a T. Programme — WILKINSON, 1
third-rate And t. conversation — PLOMER, 2
thirst the t. to come — RABELAIS, 2
thirsty t., and ye gave me drink — BIBLE, 421
thirty T. days hath November — GRAFTON, 1
T. days hath September — ANONYMOUS, 99; NURSERY RHYMES, 61
T. millions, mostly fools — CARLYLE, T, 36
t. pieces of silver — BIBLE, 429
thirty-five for t. years he had not stopped talking — WATSON, 2
this All t. and heaven too — HENRY, M, 3
thistle I have always plucked a t. and planted a flower — LINCOLN, 7
Thomasina Why so shy, my pretty T. — FRY, C, 1
thorn A rose without a t. — MACNALLY, 1
a t. in the flesh — BIBLE, 47
thorough How . . . t. these Germans always managed to be — HUXLEY, A, 36
thoroughness with the t. of a mind that reveres details — LEWIS, S, 3
thou Book of Verse – and T. — FITZGERALD, E, 5
thought a green t. in a green shade — MARVELL, 2
A library is t. in cold storage — SAMUEL, 3
A society . . . of individuals . . . capable of original t. would probably be unendurable — MENCKEN, 11
A t. is often original — HOLMES, O, 2
conversation must be an exchange of t. — POST, 1

Disease is an image of t. externalized — EDDY, 5
evil is wrought by want of t. — HOOD, 8
Learning without t. is labour lost — CONFUCIUS, 5
My t. is me — SARTRE, 9
Only a residual fraction is t. — SANTAYANA, 2
pale cast of t. — SHAKESPEARE, 91
Reading . . . ingenious device for avoiding t. — HELPS, 1
sessions of sweet silent t. — SHAKESPEARE, 361
silent form, dost tease us out of t. — KEATS, 29
something between a thing and a t. — PALMER, 1
the best which has been t. and said in the world — ARNOLD, M, 3
T. must be divided against itself — HUXLEY, A, 15
t. only to justify their injustices — VOLTAIRE, 11
t. without learning is perilous — CONFUCIUS, 5
Two souls with but a single t. — LOVELL, 1
will bear to be read twice, . . . was t. twice — THOREAU, 5
wrong to have t. that I was wrong — DULLES, 1
thoughtlessness In the sex-war t. is the weapon of the male — CONNOLLY, 16
thoughts Great t. come from the heart — VAUVENARGUES, 1
Keep off your t. from things that are past — WALEY, 1
man whose second t. are good — BARRIE, 12
our life is what our t. make it — MARCUS AURELIUS, 5
sensations rather than of t. — KEATS, 52
speech only to conceal their t. — VOLTAIRE, 11
Speech . . . to disguise . . . t. — TALLEYRAND, 4
Suspicions amongst t. — BACON, FRANCIS, 53
the meanest flower . . . can give T. — WORDSWORTH, W, 30
To understand God's t. — NIGHTINGALE, 4
we ought to control our t. — DARWIN, C R, 6
your love but not your t. — GIBRAN, 1
thousand a t. shall fall beside thee — PSALMS, 51
a t. years . . . are but as yesterday — PSALMS, 49
I can draw for a t. pounds — ADDISON, 18
I could be a good woman if I had five t. — THACKERAY, 12
if I were a t. years old — BAUDELAIRE, 2
one day in thy courts is better than a t. — PSALMS, 45
One t. years more . . . Homo sapiens has before him — WELLS, 22
the face that launch'd a t. ships — MARLOWE, 2
The thought of two t. people crunching celery at the same time horrified me — SHAW, 45
Victory has a t. fathers — KENNEDY, JOHN, 18
What's a t. dollars — MARX, G, 3
thousands 'Why only twelve? . . . get t.' — GOLDWYN, 21
thread from eternity spinning the t. of your being — MARCUS AURELIUS, 12
not a blanket woven from one t., one color, one cloth — JACKSON, J, 2
threads well-beloved's hair has t. of grey — YEATS, 14
threat one can . . . see in a little girl the t. of a woman — DUMAS, FILS, 3
three Chi Wen Tzu always thought t. times before taking action — CONFUCIUS, 1
There are only t. events in a man's life — LA BRUYÈRE, 6
there are only t. things to see — ROSS, H, 1
T. Estates in Parliament — CARLYLE, T, 13
T. for the rivals — ANONYMOUS, 45
T. French hens — NURSERY RHYMES, 60
t. fundamental truths — BELL, C, 3
T. little maids from school — GILBERT, W, 27
t. o'clock in the morning courage — THOREAU, 15
T. o'clock is always too late or too early — SARTRE, 7
t. things . . . the public will always clamour for — HOOD, 15
T. years she grew — WORDSWORTH, W, 69
we galloped all t. — BROWNING, R, 28
When shall we t. meet again — SHAKESPEARE, 200
who sneaked into my room at t. o'clock this morning — MARX, G, 14
threefold a t. cord is not quickly broken — BIBLE, 70
three-pipe a t. problem — DOYLE, 13
threescore years the days of our age are t. and ten — PSALMS, 50
three-sided if triangles invented a god, they would make him t. — MONTESQUIEU, 4
thrice before the cock crow, thou shalt deny me t. — BIBLE, 425
thrift extravagance . . . t. and adventure seldom go hand in hand — CHURCHILL, J, 2
thrive strong shall t. — SERVICE, 3
throat A good listener is a good talker with a sore t. — WHITEHORN, 7
throats cutting each other's t. — CARLYLE, T, 34
throne A man may build . . . a t. of bayonets — INGE, 11
A tavern chair is the t. — JOHNSON, S, 38

barge . . . like a burnished t.   SHAKESPEARE, 29
High on a t. of royal state   MILTON, 39
It helps . . . to remind your bride that you gave up a t. for her
    EDWARD VIII, 5
no middle course between the t. and the scaffold   CHARLES X, 2
royal t. of kings   SHAKESPEARE, 295
something behind the t.   PITT THE ELDER, 5
through part of it all the way t.   GOLDWYN, 18
throve that on which it t. Falls off   TENNYSON, 78
throw t. an egg into an electric fan   HERFORD, 1
t. away the dearest thing he ow'd   SHAKESPEARE, 204
thrush That's the wise t.   BROWNING, R, 27
Thucydides the historical works of T.   COBDEN, 1
thumbscrew To the t. and the stake   TENNYSON, 70
thunder laugh as I pass in t.   SHELLEY, 5
our soul Had *felt* him like the t.'s roll   ARNOLD, M, 26
trivial people . . . t. In such lovely language   SHAKESPEARE, 12
Thurlow No man . . . so wise as T. looked   FOX, C, 2
Thursday T.'s child has far to go   NURSERY RHYMES, 35
Took ill on T.   NURSERY RHYMES, 53
thusness What is the reason of this t.   WARD, 2
thyself Be so true to t.   BACON, FRANCIS, 59
Know then t., presume not God to scan   POPE, 34
Resolve to be t.   ARNOLD, M, 39
Tiber married to the only man north of the T. . . . untidier than I
am   WHITEHORN, 2
the T. foaming with much blood   VIRGIL, 14
Tiberius Had T. been a cat   ARNOLD, M, 33
tickle a feather to t. the intellect   LAMB, CHARLES, 16
ticky-tacky They're all made out of t.   REYNOLDS, M, 1
tide a t. in the affairs of women   BYRON, 31
a t. in the affairs of men   SHAKESPEARE, 159
ever lived in the t. of times   SHAKESPEARE, 150
the full t. of human existence is at Charing-Cross   JOHNSON, S, 93
The t. is full   ARNOLD, M, 10
The western t. crept up   KINGSLEY, 5
tides the waters of the heart Push in their t.   THOMAS, D, 14
tidings good t. of great joy   BIBLE, 314
tie Never mind about my soul . . . get my t. right   JOYCE, 13
tiger It is not the ape, nor the t.   TEMPLE, W, 5
The atom bomb is a paper t.   MAO TSE-TUNG, 9
T.! T.! burning bright   BLAKE, W, 39
tigers Dictators ride to and fro upon t.   CHURCHILL, W, 32
reactionaries are paper t.   MAO TSE-TUNG, 8
tightrope You may reasonably expect a man to walk a t. safely
    RUSSELL, B, 29
tile it's not even red brick, but white t.   OSBORNE, 4
tiller a t. of the ground   BIBLE, 153
timber a . . . soul like season'd t.   HERBERT, G, 10
Timbuctoo On the plains of T.   WILBERFORCE, S, 2
time a book to kill t.   MACAULAY, R, 6
Aging . . . the only . . . way to live a long t.   AUBER, 2
A Good T. Was Had by All   SMITH, STEVIE, 1
And t., that takes survey of all the world, Must have a stop
    SHAKESPEARE, 114
annihilate but space and t.   POPE, 3
Art is long, and T. is fleeting   LONGFELLOW, 10
As if you could kill t.   THOREAU, 8
Ask him the t.   REAGAN, 4
As t. goes by   HUPFELD, 1
'As T. Goes By'   BOGART, H, 2
a t. to be born, and a t. to die   BIBLE, 67
big man has no t.   FITZGERALD, F S, 13
But get me to the church on t.   LERNER, 5
But t. is too large   SARTRE, 12
chronicle of wasted t.   SHAKESPEARE, 367
do not squander t.   FRANKLIN, 9
Even such is T.   RALEIGH, W, 3
For technological man it is t.   MCLUHAN, 2
Had we but world enough, and t.   MARVELL, 9
He hath shook hands with t.   FORD, JOHN, 2
Hurry! I never hurry. I have no t. to hurry   STRAVINSKY, 7
I haven't got t. to be tired   WILHELM I, 1
I . . . may be some t.   OATES, 1
in a moment of t.   BIBLE, 319
inaudible and noiseless foot of T.   SHAKESPEARE, 23
irretrievable t. is flying   VIRGIL, 19
I shall lose no t. in reading it   DISRAELI, 19
it's for such a long t.   MOLIÈRE, 4
killing t. . . . By which T. kills us   SITWELL, O, 1
Lincoln had faith in t.   LINCOLN, 3

make the beat keep t. with short steps   ANDERSEN, 3
many events in the womb of t.   SHAKESPEARE, 278
Men talk of killing t.   BOUCICAULT, 1
moment of t.   ELIZABETH I, 12
My t. has not yet come   NIETZSCHE, 8
Never before have we had so little t.   ROOSEVELT, F, 15
Never the t. and the place   BROWNING, R, 36
not had the t. to make it shorter   PASCAL, 1
No t. like the present   PROVERBS, 320
no t. to stand and stare   DAVIES, W, 2
not of an age, but for all t.   JONSON, 11
O aching t.   KEATS, 20
On the breast of the river of T.   ARNOLD, M, 18
peace for our t.   CHAMBERLAIN, N, 6
pluck till t. and times are done   YEATS, 20
Procrastination is the thief of t.   YOUNG, E, 5
range of human societies in t., the other in space   LÉVI-STRAUSS, 1
Redeem thy mis-spent t.   KEN, 2
that old common arbitrator, T.   SHAKESPEARE, 332
That passed the t.   BECKETT, 3
The Bird of T. . . . little way To fly   FITZGERALD, E, 3
the long result of T.   TENNYSON, 49
the original good t. that was had by all   DAVIS, B, 2
There is a t. and place   PROVERBS, 407
'The t. has come,' the Walrus said   CARROLL, 28
The t. is out of joint   SHAKESPEARE, 79
the t. of my departure is at hand   BIBLE, 514
the t. will come when you will hear me   DISRAELI, 20
the wrong place at the wrong t.   JOHNSON, L, 1
this bank and shoal of t.   SHAKESPEARE, 208
those feet in ancient t.   BLAKE, W, 33
t. and chance happeneth to them all   BIBLE, 74
T. and the hour runs through   SHAKESPEARE, 203
T. and tide   PROVERBS, 433
t. as a tool not as a couch   KENNEDY, JOHN, 6
T. driveth onward fast   TENNYSON, 54
T. drops in decay   YEATS, 21
T. flies, death urges   YOUNG, E, 7
T. for a little something   MILNE, 7
T. hath, my lord, a wallet at his back   SHAKESPEARE, 331
T. held me green and dying   THOMAS, D, 9
T. is a great healer   PROVERBS, 434
T. is a great teacher, but . . . kills all its pupils   BERLIOZ, 1
T. is but the stream I go a-fishing in   THOREAU, 17
T. is like a river made up of the events which happen
    MARCUS AURELIUS, 8
t. is money   FRANKLIN, 3
T. is on our side   GLADSTONE, 1
T. is slipping underneath our Feet   FITZGERALD, E, 12
t. is the greatest innovator   BACON, FRANCIS, 30
T., like a loan from the bank   BRAINE, 2
T. may restore us   ARNOLD, M, 28
T. present and t. past   ELIOT, T, 6
t. quietly kills them   BOUCICAULT, 1
T.'s up for Sir John, an' for little Lady Jane   LAWRENCE, D, 18
T.'s winged chariot   MARVELL, 10
T., the subtle thief of youth   MILTON, 59
t. to love, and a t. to hate   BIBLE, 67
T. was away and somewhere else   MACNEICE, 2
T. whereof the memory of man   BLACKSTONE, 3
T. will tell   PROVERBS, 435
T. wounds all heels   MARX, G, 22
To choose t. is to save t.   BACON, FRANCIS, 20
to waste my t. making money   AGASSIZ, 1
We take no note of t.   YOUNG, E, 6
What do the ravages of t. not injure   HORACE, 37
While we're talking, t. will have meanly run on   HORACE, 31
Work expands so as to fill the t.   PARKINSON, 1
timeliness the t. of the gift   LA BRUYÈRE, 5
times It was the best of t.   DICKENS, 56
Like a piece of litmus paper . . . take the colour of his t.
    HUXLEY, A, 2
logic of our t.   DAY LEWIS, 1
one copy of *The T.*   COBDEN, 1
The 'good old t.'   BYRON, 4
The T. has made many ministries   BAGEHOT, 1
The T. is speechless   CHURCHILL, W, 41
the true old t. are dead   TENNYSON, 22
We live in stirring t.   ISHERWOOD, 2
time-table I would sooner read a t.   MAUGHAM, 18
sooner read a t. . . . than nothing   MAUGHAM, 18

tim'rous Wee . . . t. beastie	BURNS, R, 21
tinker T., Tailor, Soldier, Sailor	NURSERY RHYMES, 65
tinkling a t. cymbal	BIBLE, 38
to set a chime of words t. in . . . a few fastidious people	
	SMITH, L, 9
tinned food t. is a deadlier weapon	ORWELL, 24
tip-and-run watch him play t.	FIRBANK, 1
Tipperary a long, long way to T.	WILLIAMS, H, 1
tipping Do they allow t. on the boat	MARX, G, 17
tipster A racing t. . . . Hitler's level of accuracy	HITLER, 7
A racing t. who only reached Hitler's level of accuracy	
	TAYLOR, A, 5
tiptoe T. through the tulips	DUBIN, 1
tired getting more tanned and more t.	PEGLER, 1
Give me your t. . . . Your huddled masses	LAZARUS, 1
I haven't got time to be t.	WILHELM I, 1
I'm t. of Love	BELLOC, 11
Life . . . process of getting t.	BUTLER, S, 9
tiresome All styles are good except the t. sort	VOLTAIRE, 18
Being orderly . . . can be excessively t.	BOGARDE, 1
Titian Nobody cares much at heart about T.	RUSKIN, 1
title Because of my t., I was the first	ALENÇON, 1
That t. from a better man I stole	STEVENSON, R, 11
title-page The book written against fame . . . has the author's	
name on the t.	EMERSON, 20
titles t. . . . get one into disreputable company	SHAW, 44
Kinquering Congs their t. take	SPOONER, 3
T. distinguish the mediocre	SHAW, 28
tittle one jot or one t.	BIBLE, 362
toast t. . . . But fell . . . on the buttered side	PAYN, 1
toasted cheese – t., mostly	STEVENSON, R, 10
tobacco leave off t.	LAMB, CHARLES, 26
that tawney weed t.	JONSON, 4
what pleasure . . . they have in taking their roguish t.	JONSON, 6
who lives without t.	MOLIÈRE, 1
today here t., and gone tomorrow	BEHN, 2
He who can call t. his own	DRYDEN, 31
if T. BE SWEET	FITZGERALD, E, 12
Its history dates from t.	WHISTLER, 14
the Cup that clears T. OF PAST REGRETS	FITZGERALD, E, 9
they will listen t., they will listen tomorrow	KHRUSHCHEV, 8
wiser t. than . . . yesterday	POPE, 54
toddle I'd t. safely home	SASSOON, S, 2
toe that old enemy the gout Had taken him in t.	HOOD, 9
the light fantastic t.	MILTON, 16
together And the loved one all t.	BROWNING, R, 36
We must . . . all hang t.	FRANKLIN, 15
toil as some men t. after virtue	LAMB, CHARLES, 22
blood, t., tears and sweat	CHURCHILL, W, 49
Horny-handed sons of t.	KEARNEY, 1
they t. not	BIBLE, 370
t. That goes like blood to the poem's making	THOMAS, R, 1
To t. and not to seek for rest	LOYOLA, 1
toilet *Ulysses* . . . can be read only in the t.	JOYCE, 2
tolerance lead this people into war and they'll forget . . . t.	
	WILSON, W, 4
magnificent t. and broadmindedness of the English	SHAW, 1
tolerant Eddy was a tremendously t. person	MORTIMER, 1
tolerate the greater part of the law is learning to t. fools	
	LESSING, D, 5
toleration t. produced . . . religious concord	GIBBON, 6
toll'd The sexton t. the bell	HOOD, 5
tolls for whom the bell t.	DONNE, 8
Tolstoy Like T., he is a man of great talent	SOLZHENITSYN, 1
Their teacher had advised them not to read T. novels	
	SOLZHENITSYN, 9
When I write, I keep T. around	BROOKS, M, 1
Tom Old Uncle T. Cobbleigh and all	ANONYMOUS, 103
The romance of *T. Jones*	GIBBON, 2
T., he was a piper's son	NURSERY RHYMES, 66
T., T., the piper's son	NURSERY RHYMES, 67
tomb A best-seller is the gilded t. of a mediocre talent	
	SMITH, L, 1
drink a dozen of Claret on my T.	KEATS, 65
Tommy Little T. Tucker, Sings for his supper	
	NURSERY RHYMES, 32
Oh, it's T. this, an' T. that	KIPLING, 28
tomorrow assure him that he'd live t.	RABELAIS, 5
here today and gone t.	BEHN, 2
jam t.	CARROLL, 30
let us eat and drink; for t. we die	BIBLE, 40

Lyndon acts like there was never going to be a t.	JOHNSON, L, 2
Never put off till t.	PROVERBS, 304
T., and t., and t.	SHAKESPEARE, 225
t. is another day	MITCHELL, M, 4; PROVERBS, 438
T. never comes	PROVERBS, 439
tom-tit little t. sang Willow	GILBERT, W, 34
tone Take the t. of the company	CHESTERFIELD, 8
tongue A burning forehead, and a parching t.	KEATS, 31
a sharp t. is the only edged tool	IRVING, 2
him whose strenuous t. Can burst Joy's grape	KEATS, 34
hold your t. and let me love	DONNE, 5
neither eye to see, nor t. to speak	LENTHALL, 1
One t. is sufficient for a woman	MILTON, 65
saying right off what comes to my t.	CERVANTES, 14
Silence is become his mother t.	GOLDSMITH, 18
their t. a sharp sword	PSALMS, 36
the use of my oracular t.	SHERIDAN, R, 9
who speak the t. That Shakspeare spake	WORDSWORTH, W, 54
tongues cloven t. like as of fire	BIBLE, 2
Self-interest speaks all sorts of t.	ROCHEFOUCAULD, 5
too You can have t. much	PROVERBS, 409
tool a sharp tongue is the only edged t.	IRVING, 2
time as a t., not as a couch	KENNEDY, JOHN, 6
tools Give us the t.	CHURCHILL, W, 56
tooth sharper than a serpent's t.	DICKENS, 41
t. for t.	BIBLE, 116
toothache philosopher that could endure the t.	SHAKESPEARE, 275
top I shall be like that tree; I shall die from the t.	SWIFT, 20
I started at the t. and worked my way down	WELLES, 2
looking at the men at the t.	COLBY, 2
People at the t. of the tree	USTINOV, 10
Room at the T.	BRAINE, 1
There is always room at the t.	WEBSTER, D, 7
top-boots did pleasure me in his t.	MARLBOROUGH, 1
torch like runners hand on the t. of life	LUCRETIUS, 3
Truth, like a t.	HAMILTON, W, 1
torches she doth teach the t. to burn bright	SHAKESPEARE, 306
tormentor it is I who am my t.	TOLSTOY, L, 7
torments I cannot help it; . . . infinity t. me	MUSSET, 1
in spite of myself, infinity t. me	MUSSET, 1
torrent The wind was a t. of darkness	NOYES, 1
When the t. sweeps a man against a boulder	STEVENSON, R, 16
Tory deep burning hatred for the T. Party	BEVAN, 8
end up in the T. knackery	KINNOCK, 10
to what is called the T., and which might . . . be called the	
Conservative, party	CROKER, 2
tossed you t. and gored several persons	BOSWELL, 1
total *t.* solution of the Jewish question	GOERING, 2
totter t. towards the tomb	SAYERS, 2
touch keep the Nelson t.	NEWBOLT, 5
mere t. of cold philosophy	KEATS, 25
only t. the hem of his garment	BIBLE, 396
sunset t.	BROWNING, R, 9
t. me not	BIBLE, 275
t. of a vanish'd hand	TENNYSON, 5
Wound with a t.	MONTAGU, 1
tourist the most vulgar, . . . is the British t.	KILVERT, 1
tourists t. . . . take in the Monarchy . . . with . . . the pigeons	
	HAMILTON, W, 1
toves slithy t. did gyre	CARROLL, 23
towels never darken my t. again	MARX, G, 8
tower Childe Roland to the Dark T.	BROWNING, R, 17
towered Tolstoy t. above his age	TOLSTOY, L, 1
towering the height of his own t. style	CHESTERTON, 38
towers The cloud-capp'd t.	SHAKESPEARE, 325
town axis of the earth sticks out visibly through . . . every t. or	
city	HOLMES, O, 4
man made the t.	COWPER, 22
towns Of all the gin joints in all the t. in all the world	
	BOGART, H, 3
toy but a childish t.	MARLOWE, 9
trade Every man to his t.	PROVERBS, 140
God will pardon me. It is His t.	HEINE, 1
half a t. and half an art	INGE, 8
It is not your t. to make tables	JOHNSON, S, 59
man must serve his time to every t.	BYRON, 38
no nation was ever ruined by t.	FRANKLIN, 4
Two of a t. can ne'er agree	GAY, 6
trades The ugliest of t. have their moments of pleasure	
	JERROLD, 6
trading t. on the blood of my men	LEE, R, 2

tradition   deadly weight of the terrible t. of a dialogue
  MANDELA, 4
  It's t.. We don't want t.   FORD, H, 1
traffic   the t. of Jacob's ladder   THOMPSON, F, 2
tragedie   go litel myn t.   CHAUCER, 21
  T. is to seyn a certeyn storie   CHAUCER, 15
tragedies   There are two t. in life   SHAW, 24
  t. are finish'd by a death   BYRON, 22
tragedy   a t. and therefore not worth reading   AUSTEN, 11
  brooding t. and its dark shadows can be lightened   GANDHI, I, 4
  farce brutalized becomes t.   CRAIG, 1
  great t. of Science   HUXLEY, T, 1
  That is their t.   WILDE, 21
  The greatest t. . . . except a defeat   WELLINGTON, 13
  the t. of life is that . . . heroes lose their glamour   DOYLE, 2
  the wine was a farce and the food a t.   POWELL, A, 2
  T. is if I cut my finger   BROOKS, M, 3
  We participate in a t.   HUXLEY, A, 13
  what t. means   STOPPARD, 9
  world is a comedy to those who think, a t. to those who feel   WALPOLE, H, 6
  You *may* abuse a t.   JOHNSON, S, 59
  You're a bloody t.   MAXTON, 1
tragically   Everything must be taken seriously, nothing t.   THIERS, 2
train   I have seldom heard a t. go by and not wished   THEROUX, 1
  man who shaves and takes a t.   WHITE, E, 1
  The only way . . . of catching a t.   CHESTERTON, 47
trained   Science is nothing but t. and organized common sense   HUXLEY, T, 2
trains   t. all night groan on the rail To men that die at morn   HOUSMAN, 8
traitor   grieves me that I should be noted a t.   CROMWELL, T, 1
tramp   He began to think the t. a fine . . . fellow   WELLS, 6
  the Lady Is a T.   HART, 2
  the t. of the twenty-two men   BOWEN, E. E., 2
trampling   He is t. out the vintage where the grapes of wrath   HOWE, 1
tranquillity   his mind is in perfect t.   VOLTAIRE, 1
  Sorrow is t. remembered in emotion   PARKER, D, 9
  T. Base here – the Eagle has landed   ARMSTRONG, N, 2
transform   t. this society without . . . extension of public ownership   KINNOCK, 1
transformation   The universe is t.   MARCUS AURELIUS, 5
transit   Sic t. gloria mundi   KEMPIS, 1
transition   I expect no very violent t.   SEDGWICK, C, 1
transitory   the titles of wife and mother . . . are t. and accidental   LIVERMORE, 2
  to the t. will then succeed the eternal   PETRARCH, 1
translation   original is unfaithful to the t.   BORGES, 3
  Poetry is what gets lost in t.   FROST, R, 11
translations   T. (like wives) are seldom faithful   CAMPBELL, R, 2
transplanted   Many ideas grow better when t. into another mind   HOLMES, O, JR., 2
trapeze   daring young man on the flying t.   LEYBOURNE, 1
trappings   the t. and the suits of woe   SHAKESPEARE, 66
trash   *Paradise Lost*, is such barbarous t.   MILTON, 30
  Who steals my purse steals t.   SHAKESPEARE, 282
travel   To t. hopefully is . . . better . . . than to arrive   STEVENSON, R, 26
  T. broadens the mind   PROVERBS, 441
  t. for t.'s sake   STEVENSON, R, 7
  T., in the younger sort   BACON, FRANCIS, 54
  T. is the most private of pleasures   SACKVILLE-WEST, 2
  T. light   JUVENAL, 9
  wherever the wind takes me I t. as a visitor   HORACE, 13
travelled   I t. among unknown men   WORDSWORTH, W, 6
traveller   a t. from an antique land   SHELLEY, 16
  from whose bourn no t. returns   SHAKESPEARE, 90
travelling   in which direction the car was t.   LLOYD GEORGE, 3
  The grand object of t.   JOHNSON, S, 110
  T. is . . . like talking with men of other centuries   DESCARTES, 3
travels   A man t. the world over   MOORE, G, 1
  He t. fastest   PROVERBS, 196
  too old to go again to my t.   CHARLES II, 1
treachery   Political renegades always start their career of t.   KINNOCK, 10
tread   fools rush in where angels fear to t.   POPE, 29
  frightful fiend . . . behind him t.   COLERIDGE, S, 36
  Where'er you t.   POPE, 47
treason   If *this* be t., make the most of it   HENRY, P, 1

T. doth never prosper   HARINGTON, 1
T. was no Crime   DRYDEN, 11
treasure   Preserve it as your chiefest t.   BELLOC, 3
  purest t. mortal times afford   SHAKESPEARE, 292
treasures   lay not up . . . t. upon earth   BIBLE, 368
Treasury   the Vatican, the T. and the miners   BALDWIN, S, 12
treated   Actors should be t. like cattle   HITCHCOCK, 2
treaties   T. are like roses and young girls   DE GAULLE, 12
treaty   hand that signed the t. bred a fever   THOMAS, D, 11
tree   A billboard lovely as a t.   NASH, 10
  A poem lovely as a t.   KILMER, 1
  as the twig is bent, the t.'s inclined   POPE, 40
  gave me of the t., and I did eat   BIBLE, 151
  If poetry comes not . . . as leaves to a t.   KEATS, 57
  I shall be like that t.; I shall die from the top   SWIFT, 20
  like a t. planted by the water-side   PSALMS, 1
  only God can make a t.   KILMER, 2
  Rock-a-bye baby on the t. top   BLAKE, C, 1
  same t. that a wise man sees   BLAKE, W, 27
  soon think of taking the arm of an elm t.   THOREAU, 2
  spare the beechen t.   CAMPBELL, T, 1
  The difference between a gun and a t.   POUND, 10
  the fruit Of that forbidden t.   MILTON, 30
  The t. of liberty must be refreshed   JEFFERSON, 8
  the t. of life   BIBLE, 144
  the t. of the knowledge of good and evil   BIBLE, 144
  t. of life is green   GOETHE, 2
treen   In old time we had t. chalices and golden priests   JEWEL, 1
trees   Loveliest of t., the cherry   HOUSMAN, 7
Trelawny   shall T. die   HAWKER, 1
tremble   t. like a guilty thing surprised   WORDSWORTH, W, 31
trembled   And t. with fear at your frown   ENGLISH, 1
trembles   And Satan t.   COWPER, 15
trenches   digging t. and trying on gas-masks   CHAMBERLAIN, N, 5
trial   T. by jury . . . a delusion   DENMAN, 1
triangles   if t. invented a god, they would make him three-sided   MONTESQUIEU, 4
tribe   Abou Ben Adhem (may his t. increase!)   HUNT, L, 1
  Mankind is not a t.   CHESTERTON, 40
  Richer than all his t.   SHAKESPEARE, 288
tribute   the vain t. of a smile   SCOTT, WALTER, 6
trick   When in doubt, win the t.   HOYLE, 1
trifle   Is t. sufficient for sweet   BETJEMAN, 7
trifles   observance of t.   DOYLE, 4
  snapper-up of unconsidered t.   SHAKESPEARE, 352
trigger   Whose Finger do you want on the T.   ANONYMOUS, 108
Trinity   I the T. illustrate   BROWNING, R, 103
Triton   Old T. blow his wreathed horn   WORDSWORTH, W, 65
triumph   meet with T. and Disaster   KIPLING, 16
  One more devils'-t. and sorrow for angels   BROWNING, R, 32
  We t. without glory   CORNEILLE, 2
triumphed   So I t. ere my passion   TENNYSON, 52
trivial   mighty contests rise from t. things   POPE, 48
  The t. round, the common task   KEBLE, 1
  t. people . . . thunder In such lovely language   SHAKESPEARE, 12
triviality   you're deluded by t.   IONESCO, 1
Troilus   such a night T. methinks mounted the Troyan walls   SHAKESPEARE, 248
Trojan   open that Pandora's Box . . . T. 'orses will jump out   BEVIN, 2
Trojans   Do not trust the horse, T.   VIRGIL, 9
troops   t. of unrecording friends   TENNYSON, 77
trot   I don't t. it out and about   COLETTE, 5
trouble   a lot of t. in his life   CHURCHILL, W, 30
  A t. shared   PROVERBS, 70
  a woman is on a . . . hunt for t.   DIX, DOROTHY, 3
  it saves me the t. of liking them   AUSTEN, 30
  man . . . is . . . full of t.   BIBLE, 230
  'normal' people . . . cause no t. either to themselves   TAYLOR, A, 6
  One stops being a child when . . . telling one's t. does not make it better   PAVESE, 1
  Our progress . . . Is t. and care   LONGFELLOW, 14
  Prostitution . . . keeps her out of t.   HELLER, 7
troubles   Don't meet t. half-way   PROVERBS, 118
  I have had t. enough   BROWNING, R, 38
  pack up your t. in your old kit-bag   ASAF, 1
  take arms against a sea of t.   SHAKESPEARE, 89
troublesome   t. . . . bondage of Rhyming   MILTON, 29
trousers   bottoms of my t. rolled   ELIOT, T, 14
  I shall wear white flannel t.   ELIOT, T, 15
  man should never put on his best t.   IBSEN, 4

trout as when you find a t. in the milk	THOREAU, 6	it cannot compel anyone to tell the t.	DARLING, 5
trowel laid on with a t.	SHAKESPEARE, 40	It takes two to speak the t.	THOREAU, 19
lays it on with a t.	CONGREVE, 3	Let us begin by committing ourselves to the t.	NIXON, 6
Troy from the shores of T. came destined an exile	VIRGIL, 5	loving Christianity better than T.	COLERIDGE, S, 3
Now there are fields where T. once was	OVID, 5	mainly he told the t.	TWAIN, 3
true a great advantage for . . . philosophy to be . . . t.		mercy and t. are met together	PSALMS, 46
	SANTAYANA, 12	Much is spoken . . . more . . . concealed	DARLING, 3
All one's inventions are t.	FLAUBERT, 1	My way of joking is to tell the t.	SHAW, 13
A thing is not necessarily t.	WILDE, 65	Nobody speaks the t. when	BOWEN, ELIZABETH, 3
because a novel's invented, it isn't t.	POWELL, A, 7	No poet ever interpreted nature . . . as a lawyer interprets t.	
Be so t. to thyself	BACON, FRANCIS, 59		GIRAUDOUX, 2
be yourself, imperial, plain and t.	BROWNING, R, 7	not even Marx is more precious . . . than the t.	WEIL, 3
false to his friends . . . t. to the public	BERKELEY, 1	Now I may wither into the t.	YEATS, 7
Geometry is not t.	PIRSIG, 2	Perjury . . . is t. that is shamefaced	DARLING, 4
He said t. things	BROWNING, R, 13	Photography is t.	GODARD, 1
if they keep on saying it . . . it will be t.	BENNETT, ARNOLD, 8	polite by telling the t.	BRADBURY, 6
I said the honorable member was a liar it is t.	SHERIDAN, R, 21	Pride and T. . . . shake their . . . sides at youth	YEATS, 24
it's . . . more important for a theory to be shapely, than . . . t.		put him in possession of t.	LOCKE, 2
	HAMPTON, 1	Some men love t. so much	BUTLER, S, 18
Journalists say a thing that they know isn't t.	BENNETT, ARNOLD, 8	speaking nothing but the t.	WILDE, 36
Many a t. word	PROVERBS, 282	the laws of poetic t. and poetic beauty	ARNOLD, M, 15
No man worth having is t. to his wife	VANBRUGH, 6	the t. is not in us	BIBLE, 281
Small service is t. service	WORDSWORTH, W, 72	the t. of imagination	KEATS, 51
them which are t. of heart	PSALMS, 4	the t. shall make you free	BIBLE, 254
The religions we call false were once t.	EMERSON, 6	the unclouded face of t. suffer wrong	SCOTT, C, 1
the t. and the false and . . . extracting the plausible		The worst enemy of t. and freedom	IBSEN, 3
	LLOYD GEORGE, 2	those who live . . . believe . . . to be the t.	HAMPTON, 2
to thine own self be t.	SHAKESPEARE, 74	to the dead we owe only t.	VOLTAIRE, 24
T. and False are attributes of speech, not of things	HOBBES, 2	T. be veiled	SHELLEY, 8
T. love never grows old	PROVERBS, 442	T. comes out in wine	PLINY THE ELDER, 5
t. to you, darlin', in my fashion	PORTER, C, 8	T. fears no trial	PROVERBS, 443
truism is . . . none the less t.	SAMUEL, 2	t. in the inward parts	PSALMS, 31
whatsoever things are t.	BIBLE, 446	t. is always strange	BYRON, 35
truffles a swine to show you where the t. are	ALBEE, 3	T. is on the march	ZOLA, 3
truism A t. is on that account none the less true	SAMUEL, 2	T. is stranger	PROVERBS, 444
truly A t. great man	PROVERBS, 71	T., like a torch	HAMILTON, W, 1
trumpet the t. shall sound	BIBLE, 42	t. shall flourish out of the earth	PSALMS, 46
trumps to Gladstone's always having the ace of t.		T., Sir, is a cow	JOHNSON, S, 65
	LABOUCHÈRE, 1	T. sits upon the lips of dying men	ARNOLD, M, 41
trunkless Two vast and t. legs of stone	SHELLEY, 16	t. that makes men free	AGAR, 1
trust I don't t. him. We're friends	BRECHT, 5	T. will out	PROVERBS, 445
If you t. before you try, you may repent before you die		Two half-truths do not make a t.	KOESTLER, 4
	PROVERBS, 220	whatever remains, however improbable, must be the t.	DOYLE, 3
in thee, O Lord, have I put my t.	PSALMS, 18	What is t.	BACON, FRANCIS, 56; BIBLE, 265
my t. shall be under the covering of thy wings	PSALMS, 37	When t. is discovered by someone else	SOLZHENITSYN, 6
Never t. a husband too far	ROWLAND, H, 4	whilst the great ocean of t. lay all undiscovered before me
never t. a woman	WILDE, 59		NEWTON, I, 5
Never t. the man who . . . hath injured you	FIELDING, 7	who ever knew T. put to the worse	MILTON, 8
O put not your t. in princes	PSALMS, 73	You can only find t. with logic	CHESTERTON, 27
the one God whose worshippers . . . still t. in Him	BRADLEY, F, 1	**truths** All great t. begin as blasphemies	SHAW, 4
the right of governing was not property but a t.	FOX, C, 1	all t. are half-t.	WHITEHEAD, 1
t. ye not in a friend	BIBLE, 434	commonplaces are the great poetic t.	STEVENSON, R, 27
t. yourself when all men doubt you	KIPLING, 1	He was a man of two t.	MURDOCH, 2
Where large sums of money are concerned . . . t. nobody		new t. . . . begin as heresies	HUXLEY, T, 3
	CHRISTIE, 2	There are no new t.	MCCARTHY, M, 2
trusted familiar friend, whom I t.	PSALMS, 25	those three fundamental t.	BELL, C, 3
trustful It takes a long while for a . . . t. person to reconcile		t. being in and out of favour	FROST, R, 1
himself to . . . God	MENCKEN, 10	We hold these t. to be sacred and undeniable	JEFFERSON, 5
trusting it never extended to t. him	BULLOCK, 2	We hold these t. to be self-evident	JEFFERSON, 6
truth And seek for t. in the groves of Academe	HORACE, 24	**try** t. everything once	BAX, 1
any t. but from a clear perception	KEATS, 63	T., t. again	HICKSON, 1
A platitude is simply a t. repeated	BALDWIN, S, 13	**trying** I am t. to be, and you can't help it	BIRKENHEAD, 2
Appearances are not . . . a clue to the t.	COMPTON-BURNETT, 1	**tu** Et t., Brute	CAESAR, 147
a short armistice with t.	BYRON, 25	**tub** Rub-a-dub-dub, Three men in a t.	NURSERY RHYMES, 49
A t. that's told with bad intent	BLAKE, W, 6	**tubby** a t. little chap	WODEHOUSE, 18
a t. universally acknowledged	AUSTEN, 18	**Tuesday** Christened on T.	NURSERY RHYMES, 53
Beauty is t., t. beauty	KEATS, 30	T.'s child is full of grace	NURSERY RHYMES, 35
before the t. has got its boots on	CALLAGHAN, 1	**tulips** Tiptoe through the t.	DUBIN, 1
cheated into passion, but . . . reasoned into t.	DRYDEN, 30	**tumbler** He who drinks a t. of London water	SMITH, SYDNEY, 15
cinema is t.	GODARD, 1	**tune** There's many a good t.	PROVERBS, 414
Cynicism is an unpleasant way of saying the t.	HELLMAN, 1	Whistle a Happy T.	HAMMERSTEIN, 2
dearer still is t.	ARISTOTLE, 10	write a t. you all say it's commonplace	ELGAR, 2
economical with the t.	ARMSTRONG, R, 1	**tunes** I do not see . . . why the devil should have all the good t.
Every man has a right to utter what he thinks t.	JOHNSON, S, 131		HILL, R, 1
few enthusiasts . . . speak the t.	BALFOUR, 5	**turbot** would give the price of a large t. for it	RUSKIN, 9
He believes . . . that there is such a thing as t.	BAGEHOT, 10	**turbulent** rid me of this t. priest	HENRY II, 1
his faithfulness and t. shall be thy shield and buckler	PSALMS, 51	**turf** The blue ribbon of the t.	DISRAELI, 8
I am the way, the t., and the life	BIBLE, 259	**Turkey** T.	NICHOLAS I, 1
if the people . . . can be reached with the t.	ROOSEVELT, E, 2	**turn** I do not hope to t.	ELIOT, T, 3
If you do not tell the t. about yourself	WOOLF, 7	I wouldn't have left a t. unstoned	WIMPERIS, 1
in the end the t. will conquer	WYCLIFFE, 1	One good t. deserves another	PROVERBS, 326

turned   mine enemies . . . shall be t. back   PSALMS, 2
turning   Life is a maze in which we take the wrong t.
                                                    CONNOLLY, 15
   The lady's not for t.   THATCHER, M, 9
turnip   he had rather Have a t. than his father   JOHNSON, S, 33
turtle   the voice of the t. is heard   BIBLE, 489
tu-whit   T., Tu-who   SHAKESPEARE, 199
twain   never the t. shall meet   KIPLING, 3
twang   the triumphant t. of a bedspring   PERELMAN, 6
Tweedledum   T. and Tweedledee Agreed to have a battle
                                                    CARROLL, 25
twelve   I was born at the age of t.   GARLAND, 1
   T. for the t. apostles   ANONYMOUS, 45
   T. lords a-leaping   NURSERY RHYMES, 60
   'Why only t.? . . . get thousands.'   GOLDWYN, 21
twentieth   the t. century will be . . . the century of Fascism
                                                    MUSSOLINI, 4
   T.-Century Blues   COWARD, 20
twenty   the first t. years   SOUTHEY, 3
   The United States . . . are t. years in advance of this country
                                                    HOBSON, 1
twenty-five   My dear fellow . . . I only ask you for t. pounds
                                                    SHERIDAN, R, 14
twenty-four   There are only t. hours in the day   PROVERBS, 406
twenty-four-hour   the t. day   BEERBOHM, 6
   the t. strike   MUIR, 3
twenty-nine   t. distinct damnations   BROWNING, R, 54
twenty-two   the tramp of the t. men   BOWEN, E. E., 2
twice   can't step into the same river t.   HERACLITUS, 2
   desire to be praised t. over   ROCHEFOUCAULD, 18
   Literature . . . something that will be read t.   CONNOLLY, 6
   no shirt or collar ever comes back t.   LEACOCK, 13
   t. as natural   CARROLL, 34
   will bear to be read t., . . . was thought t.   THOREAU, 5
   you shall drink t. while I drink once   WALPOLE, H, 10
Twickenham   wicked asp of T.   POPE, 1
twig   as the t. is bent, the tree's inclined   POPE, 40
twilight   T. grey   MILTON, 46
twinkle   T., t., little bat   CARROLL, 10
   T., t., little star   TAYLOR, JANE, 1
twinkling   his wrath endureth but the t. of an eye   PSALMS, 17
   in the t. of an eye   BIBLE, 42
Twist   Oliver T. has asked for more   DICKENS, 36
twist   last t. of the knife   ELIOT, T, 20
   You cannot hope to bribe or t. . . . the British journalist
                                                    WOLFE, H, 1
twisted   You silly t. boy   MILLIGAN, 7
two   'Great God grant that twice t. be not four.'   TURGENEV, 4
   if we knew one, we knew t.   EDDINGTON, 2
   into the ark, t. and t.   BIBLE, 158
   I quite agree with you, sir, but what can t. do against so many
                                                    SHAW, 48
   It takes t.   PROVERBS, 235
   It takes t. to speak the truth   THOREAU, 19
   It takes t. to tango   PROVERBS, 236
   One step forward, t. steps back   LENIN, 2
   Tea for T., and T. for Tea   HARBACK, 1
   The formula 'T. and t. make five'   DOSTOEVSKY, F, 1
   t. and t. do not make six   TOLSTOY, L, 16
   t. legs bad   ORWELL, 2
   T. of a trade can ne'er agree   GAY, 6
   T. turtle doves   NURSERY RHYMES, 60
   T., t., the lily-white boys   ANONYMOUS, 44
two-faced   'I grant you that he's not t.'   SNOW, 1
twopenny   I don't care a t. damn   WELLINGTON, 24
tye-wig   parson in a t.   ADDISON, 2
typewriter   a non-stop talker to whom someone has given a t.
                                                    BRENAN, 5
tyrannize   man should t. over his bank balance   KEYNES, 6
tyranny   Ecclesiastic t.'s the worst   DEFOE, 6
   'Resistance to t. is obedience to God.'   ANTHONY, 4
   resumption of t. in our fair land   LINCOLN, 13
   They that are discontented under monarchy, call it t.   HOBBES, 6
   Where laws end, t. begins   PITT THE ELDER, 4
tyrant   professed t. to their sex   SHAKESPEARE, 266
   the makings of a t.   NAPOLEON I, 2
tyrants   all men would be t.   DEFOE, 2
   love, an . . . intercourse between t. and slaves   GOLDSMITH, 14
   the English seem . . . to act with the barbarity of t.
                                                    SMITH, SYDNEY, 2
   'Twixt kings and t. there's this difference   HERRICK, 3

U

U   U and Non-U   ROSS, A, 1
ugliest   The u. of trades have their moments of pleasure
                                                    JERROLD, 6
uglification   Ambition, Distraction, U., and Derision   CARROLL, 15
ugly   an intimate knowledge of its u. side   BALDWIN, J, 3
   an u., affected, disgusting fellow   GIBBON, 1
   an u. woman is a blot on the fair face of creation   BRONTE, C, 1
   better to be first with an u. woman than the hundredth with a
   beauty   BUCK, 5
   I'm . . . u. enough to succeed on my own   ALLEN, W, 4
   There are no u. women, only lazy ones   RUBINSTEIN, 2
   There is nothing u.   CONSTABLE, 1
   The U. Duckling   ANDERSEN, 2
Ulster   U. will fight; U. will be right   CHURCHILL, R, 3
Ulysses   U. . . . can be read only in the toilet   JOYCE, 1
   U. . . . gives me an inferiority complex   JOYCE, 3
umbrella   The unjust steals the just's u.   BOWEN, C, 1
unacceptable   u. face of capitalism   HEATH, 2
unacted   than nurse u. desires   BLAKE, W, 21
unanimity   Our agenda is now exhausted . . . we find ourselves in
   such complete u.   SPAAK, 1
unartificial   Surely you don't mean by u. insemination
                                                    THURBER, 19
unassuming   u. common-place Of Nature   WORDSWORTH, W, 75
unavailing   All reform . . . will prove u.   CARLYLE, T, 5
unawares   happened u. to look at her husband   AUSTEN, 29
unbaptized   Fraser . . . left his children u.   WOOLF, 5
unbearable   in victory u.   CHURCHILL, W, 33
unbecoming   nothing . . . so u. to a woman   WILDE, 42
   u. the character of an officer   ANONYMOUS, 6
un-birthday   an u. present   CARROLL, 31
unbowed   My head is bloody, but u.   HENLEY, 1
unbribed   seeing what the man will do u.   WOLFE, H, 1
uncertainty   I have known u.   BORGES, 1
unchartered   Me this u. freedom tires   WORDSWORTH, W, 33
unchivalrous   just a bit u.   BENCHLEY, 1
unclouded   the u. face of truth suffer wrong   SCOTT, C, 1
unclubable   A very u. man   JOHNSON, S, 72
uncomely   Nakedness is u.   BACON, FRANCIS, 48
uncommon   woman of common views but u. abilities
                                                    THATCHER, M, 1
unconcern   a Patron . . . one who looks with u.   JOHNSON, S, 48
unconfined   let joy be u.   BYRON, 14
unconquerable   man's u. mind   WORDSWORTH, W, 62
   the u. hope   ARNOLD, M, 38
unconscionable   most u. time dying   CHARLES II, 7
unconventionally   to succeed u.   KEYNES, 5
uncreative   that ineluctable oblivion which awaits the u. mind
                                                    HALDANE, 1
undecorated   No part of the walls is left u.   PEVSNER, 1
undefeated   Walter Mitty, the u.   THURBER, 11
undeniable   We hold these truths to be sacred and u.
                                                    JEFFERSON, 5
under   U. the greenwood tree   SHAKESPEARE, 45
underdogs   never find an Englishman among the u.   WAUGH, E, 28
underestimated   effect of boredom is . . . u.   INGE, 3
underground   Johnny u.   PUDNEY, 1
   Just the other day in the U.   CHESTERTON, 41
underprivileged   Compassion is not a sloppy, sentimental feeling
   for people who are u.   KINNOCK, 6
undersexed   he was somewhat u.   CHEKHOV, 2
understand   books. . . . criticized and read by people who don't u.
   them   LICHTENBERG, 2
   child of five would u. this   MARX, G, 6
   if he could make me u. . . . it would be clear to all
                                                    ROOSEVELT, E, 3
   I u. only because I love   TOLSTOY, L, 10
   not to weep at them, nor to hate them, but to u. them
                                                    SPINOZA, 5
   people . . . may not be made to u.   CONFUCIUS, 11
   When men u. what each other mean   NEWMAN, J, 6
   Wot do they u.   KIPLING, 24
   You suddenly u. something . . . in a new way   LESSING, D, 1
understanding   a candle of u.   BIBLE, 100
   God grant him peace . . . but never u.   BALDWIN, S, 9
   his clear knowledge of the limits of human u.   VOLTAIRE, 3
   man being in honour hath no u.   PSALMS, 29
   Most men . . . give evidence against their own u.   HALIFAX, 8

piece of cod passes all u.   LUTYENS, 2
the peace of God, which passeth all u.   BIBLE, 445
u. will . . . extinguish pleasure   HOUSMAN, 6
We need more u. of human nature   JUNG, 11
understood   Only one man ever u. me   HEGEL, 2
undertaker   the sort of greeting a corpse would give to an u.
    BALDWIN, S, 5
undertakers   I have nothing against u. personally   MITFORD, J, 1
undertaking   The love of life is necessary to . . . any u.
    JOHNSON, S, 25
under water   if I were u. I would scarcely kick   KEATS, 60
undiscovered   whilst the great ocean of truth lay all u. before me
    NEWTON, I, 5
undone   estate o' th' world were now u.   SHAKESPEARE, 226
left u. those things   BOOK OF COMMON PRAYER, 14
Things hitherto u. should be given . . . a wide berth   BEERBOHM, 8
uneasy   U. lies the head that wears a crown   SHAKESPEARE, 121
uneatable   the unspeakable in full pursuit of the u.   WILDE, 58
uneducated   Democracy . . . government by the u.
    CHESTERTON, 43
unemployed   discontent that goes with u. activities   ANDERSON, 2
unendurable   A society . . . of individuals . . . capable of original
thought would probably be u.   MENCKEN, 11
unequal   Men are made by nature u.   FROUDE, 2
Our Language . . . was u. to that greatness of soul   MILTON, 1
unexamined   U. life   SOCRATES, 1
unexpected   Old age is the most u. of all . . . things   TROTSKY, 2
unfaithful   My wife had been u. to me   BRAINE, 3
original is u. to the translation   BORGES, 3
unfortunates   one of those u. to whom death is   LEWIS, D, 1
ungain'd   Men prize the thing u. more   SHAKESPEARE, 328
ungodliness   the tents of u.   PSALMS, 45
ungodly   the u. . . . . privily shoot at them which are true of heart
    PSALMS, 4
unhappily   The bad end u.   STOPPARD, 9
unhappy   A moment of time may make us u. for ever   GAY, 1
don't believe one can ever be u. for long   WAUGH, E, 10
each u. family is u. in its own way   TOLSTOY, L, 5
It is better that some should be u.   JOHNSON, S, 109
making their remaining years u.   LA BRUYÈRE, 2
most u. kind of misfortune   BOETHIUS, 1
one is u. one becomes moral   PROUST, 6
only when I am unbearably u.   KAFKA, 2
the instinct for being u.   SAKI, 8
Today you're u.? . . . Go shopping   MILLER, A, 3
U. the land that has no heroes   DRECHT, 2
unheralded   spring now comes u. by the return of the birds
    CARSON, 3
unicorn   The lion and the u.   NURSERY RHYMES, 55
uniform   love that loves a scarlet coat Should be more u.   HOOD, 4
The u. 'e wore   KIPLING, 13
uniformity   let use be preferred before u.   BACON, FRANCIS, 15
U. isn't bad   HARTLEY, 1
uninstructed   making things plain to u. people was . . . best means
of clearing . . . one's own mind   HUXLEY, T, 7
uninteresting   no . . . u. subject   CHESTERTON, 17
union   that pleasure, which is undeniably the sole motive force
behind the u. of the sexes   LACLOS, 3
To make a u. with Great Britain   PÉTAIN, 1
U. is strength   PROVERBS, 448
unite   Workers of the world, u.   MARX, K, 2
united   U. we stand   PROVERBS, 449
U. States of Europe   CHURCHILL, W, 66
United States   In the U. there is more space   STEIN, 2
so near to the U.   DÍAZ, 1
The best immediate defence of the U.   ROOSEVELT, F, 7
The U. . . . are twenty years in advance of this country
    HOBSON, 1
The U. has to move very fast   KENNEDY, JOHN, 7
The U. is like a gigantic boiler   GREY, 1
The U. . . . . six hours behind   HOBSON, 1
U. is the best and fairest . . . nation   BUSH, 1
unites   Nothing u. the English like war   PICASSO, 3
universal   Aunt Edna is u.   RATTIGAN, 1
There is no u. law   LAWRENCE, D, 33
universe   chess-board is the world; the pieces . . . the phenomena
of the u.   HUXLEY, T, 6
He would take his attention away from the u.   CRISP, 10
I accept the u.   CARLYLE, T, 35
I don't pretend to understand the U.   CARLYLE, T, 33
I regarded the u. as an open book   KOESTLER, 1

Life exists in the u.   JEANS, 1
no hint throughout the u. Of good or ill   THOMSON, JAMES, 2
Perish the U.   CYRANO DE BERGERAC, 1
the better ordering of the u.   ALFONSO THE WISE, 1
the u. and all that surrounds it   COOK, P, 1
the u. is expanding and contracting   DE VRIES, 5
The u. is not hostile   HOLMES, J, 1
the u. is . . . queerer than we *can* suppose   HALDANE, 4
The u. is transformation   MARCUS AURELIUS, 5
The u. ought to be presumed too vast   PEIRCE, 1
The visible u. was an illusion   BORGES, 2
universities   mortifying fate of most English u.   LODGE, 2
The King, observing . . . the state of both his u.   TRAPP, 1
U. incline wits to sophistry and affectation   BACON, FRANCIS, 65
university   Any attempt to reform the u.   ILLICH, 1
it is necessary to go to a u. . . . . to become a successful writer
    BRITTAIN, 2
true U. . . . . collection of books   CARLYLE, T, 12
u., where it was carefully taken out   PEACOCK, 8
unjust   The u. steals the just's umbrella   BOWEN, C, 1
unkind   Thou art not so u.   SHAKESPEARE, 49
unkindness   I tax not you, you elements, with u.
    SHAKESPEARE, 177
unknown   apart from the known and the u.   PINTER, 2
'Give me a light that I may tread safely into the u.'   HASKINS, 1
I travelled among u. men   WORDSWORTH, W, 6
Many brave men . . . before Agamemnon's time . . . are
all, unmourned and u.   HORACE, 42
the U. Prime Minister   ASQUITH, H, 2
To go into the u.   THOMAS, E, 3
unlabelled   unpardonable sins . . . is . . . to go about u.
    HUXLEY, T, 4
unlike   the Jews bring the u. into the heart of *every milieu*
    ZANGWILL, 3
The law of dislike for the u.   ZANGWILL, 3
unluckily   the good u.   STOPPARD, 9
unmarried   to keep u.   SHAW, 23
unmotivated   The u. action   GIDE, 1
unmuzzled   The world regards such a person as . . . an u. dog
    HUXLEY, T, 4
unnatural   so u. as the commonplace   DOYLE, 2
unobtrusive   Poetry should be great and u.   KEATS, 56
unofficial   An u. English rose   BROOKE, 3
unpaid   A promise made is a debt u.   SERVICE, 1
unpardonable   One of the u. sins . . . is . . . to go about unlabelled
    HUXLEY, T, 4
unperfect   He was u., unfinished, inartistic   JAMES, H, 7
unpleasant   Cynicism is an u. way of saying the truth
    HELLMAN, 1
without mentioning a single book, or *in fact anything u.*
    REED, H, 6
unpopular   a free society . . . where it is safe to be u.
    STEVENSON, A, 6
unprofitable   How weary, stale, flat, and u.   SHAKESPEARE, 67
unrecording   troops of u. friends   TENNYSON, 77
unremembered   u. acts Of kindness and of love
    WORDSWORTH, W, 9
unremitting   That u. humanity   BENNETT, ALAN, 5
unrequited   Self-love seems so often u.   POWELL, A, 1
unsaid   The bitterest tears . . . are for words . . . u.   STOWE, 1
words left u. and deeds left undone   STOWE, 1
unsatisfied   It is exquisite, and it leaves one u.   WILDE, 51
unsavoury   indefatigable and u. engine of pollution   SPARROW, 1
unsealed   my lips are not yet u.   BALDWIN, S, 8
unseemly   an u. exposure of the mind   HAZLITT, 18
unseen   to deny the existence of an u. kingdom is bad
    BUTLER, S, 3
We keep passing u.   PIRSIG, 4
unshriven   I am curious to see what happens . . . to one who dies
u.   PERUGINO, 1
unsoundness   no person can be a poet . . . without . . . u. of mind
    MACAULAY, T, 14
unspeakable   the psychopathologist the u.   MAUGHAM, 8
the u. in full pursuit of the uneatable   WILDE, 58
unstoned   I wouldn't have left a turn u.   WIMPERIS, 1
untidier   married to the only man north of the Tiber . . . u. than I
am   WHITEHORN, 2
untravelled   Gleams that u. world   TENNYSON, 80
untruth   The camera . . . an accessory to u.   EVANS, H, 1
unupblown   Nurse u.   WAUGH, E, 50
unused   left over from last year u.   HARRIS, 1

The only sensual pleasure without v. — JOHNSON, S, 39
there is no distinction between virtue and v. — JOHNSON, S, 64
This v. brings in one hundred million francs . . . every year — NAPOLEON III, 1
three great evils, boredom, v., and poverty — VOLTAIRE, 10
V. and virtues are products — TAINE, 1
V. is its own reward — CRISP, 6
V. is often clothed — PROVERBS, 450
V. itself lost half its evil — BURKE, E, 8
When v. prevails — ADDISON, 7
vices   It's your combination sinners . . . who dishonour the v. — WILDER, T, 3
most v. may be committed very genteelly — BOSWELL, 2
one of the v. of our age — VIGNY, 3
small v. do appear — SHAKESPEARE, 188
virtues and v. couple with one another — HALIFAX, 4
virtues are . . . v. in disguise — ROCHEFOUCAULD, 27
We make ourselves a ladder out of our v. — AUGUSTINE OF HIPPO, 5
Vichy   There's something V. about the French — NOVELLO, 2
vicious   can't expect a boy to be v. — SAKI, 15
He was a v. man, but very kind — JOHNSON, S, 45
woman . . . so v., or so feeble-minded, that she cannot withstand temptation — BRONTË, A, 1
victim   more easily fall v. to a big lie — HITLER, 11
v. must be found I've got a little list — GILBERT, W, 25
victims   Every reformation must have its v. — SAKI, 19
Man is the only animal that can remain on friendly terms with the v. . . . he eats — BUTLER, S, 20
The little v. play — GRAY, 9
v. who respect their executioners — SARTRE, 12
victor   happy state of getting the v.'s palm without the dust of racing — HORACE, 14
Victoria   Mrs Thatcher . . . looking like Queen V. — TEBBITT, 2
take a ticket at V. Station — BEVIN, 3
Victorian   the most antagonistic to the V. age — WILSON, E, 1
V. values . . . were the values when our country — THATCHER, M, 14
Victorians   The V. had not been anxious to go away — WHITE, T, 1
victories   Peace hath her v. — MILTON, 63
victorious   Send him v. — CAREY, H, 1
victory   Before Alamein we never had a v. — CHURCHILL, W, 16
death is swallowed up in v. — BIBLE, 42
every v. turns into a defeat — BEAUVOIR, 4
in v. unbearable — CHURCHILL, W, 33
In . . . war it is not right that matters, but v. — HITLER, 13
O grave! where is thy v. — POPE, 6
Such another v. and we are ruined — PYRRHUS, 1
to gain such a v. as this — WELLINGTON, 12
'twas a famous v. — SOUTHEY, 1
V. at all costs — CHURCHILL, W, 50
V. has a thousand fathers — KENNEDY, JOHN, 18
v. under the belly of a Cossack's horse — TROTSKY, 4
without v. there is no survival — CHURCHILL, W, 50
vidders   be very careful o' v. — DICKENS, 45
vieillesse   si v. pouvait — ESTIENNE, 1
Vietnam   To win in V. — SPOCK, 1
V. was lost in the living rooms of America — MCLUHAN, 6
vigilance   eternal v. — CURRAN, 1
vile   Chesterton is like a v. scum on a pond — CHESTERTON, 1
every prospect pleases, And only man is v. — HEBER, 2
orgies are v. — NASH, 5
vilest   the v. specimens of human nature are . . . found among demagogues — MACAULAY, T, 10
village   the world in the image of a global v. — MCLUHAN, 1
villages   world poverty is primarily a problem of two million v. — SCHUMACHER, 1
villains   Children should acquire . . . heroes and v. from fiction — AUDEN, 4
God should go before such v. — SHAKESPEARE, 274
vine   With v. leaves in his hair — IBSEN, 5
vines   the little foxes, that spoil the v. — BIBLE, 490
vino   In v. veritas — PLINY THE ELDER, 5
vintage   He is trampling out the v. where the grapes of wrath — HOWE, 1
O, for a draught of v. — KEATS, 36
violate   men never v. the laws of God without suffering the consequences — CHILD, 1
violence   used words with the v. of a horse-breaker — BROWNING, R, 1
v. masquerading as love — LAING, 4
violent   better to be v. . . . than . . . cover impotence — GANDHI, 4
I expect no very v. transition — SEDGWICK, C, 1

virtue in ambition is v. — BACON, FRANCIS, 29
violet   My regret Becomes an April v. — TENNYSON, 37
violets   Good God, I forgot the v. — LANDOR, 8
violin   an orangutan trying to play the v. — BALZAC, 3
If the Almighty himself played the v. — HEIFETZ, 1
vipers   O generation of v. — BIBLE, 354
virgin   a v. shall conceive — BIBLE, 198
v. territory for whorehouses — CAPONE, 2
Virginia Woolf   Afraid of V. — ALBEE, 1
V. — SITWELL, E, 6
virginity   Age . . . nor custom stale her infinite v. — WEBSTER, D, 3
a little more v., if you don't mind — TREE, 1
that v. could be a virtue — VOLTAIRE, 21
virgins   those v. arose, and trimmed their lamps — BIBLE, 416
virtue   adversity doth best discover v. — BACON, FRANCIS, 8
a man of much wit . . . void of v. — CHESTERFIELD, 1
as some men toil after v. — LAMB, CHARLES, 22
Crime, like v., has its degrees — RACINE, 4
Fine words . . . seldom associated with v. — CONFUCIUS, 6
forbearance ceases to be a v. — BURKE, E, 5
greatest offence against v. — HAZLITT, 14
Let the blessing . . . be . . . upon all that are lovers of v. — WALTON, 6
moderation in the pursuit of justice is no v. — GOLDWATER, 2
Most men admire V. — MILTON, 53
much v. in If — SHAKESPEARE, 56
My v.'s still far too small — COLETTE, 3
name a v. that brings in as much revenue — NAPOLEON III, 1
no v. like necessity — SHAKESPEARE, 294
Self-denial is not a v. — SHAW, 29
That vice pays homage to v. — BUTLER, S, 24
there is no distinction between v. and vice — JOHNSON, S, 64
to practise five things . . . constitutes perfect v. — CONFUCIUS, 9
v. in ambition is violent — BACON, FRANCIS, 29
V. is like a rich stone — BACON, FRANCIS, 11
v. is only elicited by temptation — BRONTË, A, 1
What is it that constitutes v. — BRONTË, A, 2
Woman's v. is man's greatest invention — SKINNER, C, 1
virtues   ape-like v. without which — CONNOLLY, 5
few v. . . . the Poles do not possess — CHURCHILL, W, 64
greater v. to sustain good fortune — ROCHEFOUCAULD, 3
No one gossips about . . . secret v. — RUSSELL, B, 17
Vice and v. are products — TAINE, 1
v. and vices couple with one another — HALIFAX, 4
v. are . . . vices in disguise — ROCHEFOUCAULD, 27
v. We write in water — SHAKESPEARE, 141
What men call social v. . . . but the virtue of pigs in a litter — THOREAU, 7
world to hide v. in — SHAKESPEARE, 335
you meet Winston . . . you spend in discovering his v. — CHURCHILL, W, 6
virtuous   all the Sisters v. — NEWCASTLE, 1
the v. poor — WILDE, 53
When men grow v. in their old age — POPE, 56
who can find a v. woman — BIBLE, 458
visage   Sir Launcelot saw her v., but he wept not greatly — MALORY, 4
vision   I have a v. of the future — BETJEMAN, 9
The young men's v., and the old men's dream — DRYDEN, 14
turn to the wider v. of the Commonwealth — MACMILLAN, 6
visionary   Whither is fled the v. gleam — WORDSWORTH, W, 25
visions   slumber'd here While these v. did appear — SHAKESPEARE, 265
visits   Its v., Like those of angels — BLAIR, R, 2
vitai   v. lampada — LUCRETIUS, 3
vitality   a symptom of deficient v. — STEVENSON, R, 19
The lower one's v. — BEERBOHM, 10
vivify   quarrels which v. its barrenness — GREER, 3
vogue   It is charming to totter into v. — WALPOLE, H, 5
voice   a still small v. — BIBLE, 300
A still small v. — TENNYSON, 79
Conscience is the inner v. — MENCKEN, 2
God sent a v. to guide me — JOAN OF ARC, 1
the dead shall hear the v. of the Son of God — BIBLE, 248
The higher the v. — NEWMAN, E, 2
The melting v. through mazes running — MILTON, 20
the v. of my beloved — BIBLE, 488
The v. of the intellect is a soft one — FREUD, S, 1
the v. of the Lord breaketh the cedar-trees — PSALMS, 16
the v. of the turtle is heard — BIBLE, 489
to-day if ye will hear his v. — PSALMS, 56

v. of the people is the v. of God   ALCUIN, 1
voices Two v. . . . one is of the sea, One of the mountains
    WORDSWORTH, W, 63
volcano dancing on a v.   SALVANDY, 1
vole plashy fen passes the questing v.   WAUGH, E, 31
Voltaire I have seen V.   VOLTAIRE, 4
One does not arrest V.   DE GAULLE, 10
volunteer restless who will v. for anything   NIVEN, D, 2
volunteers V. usually fall into two groups   NIVEN, D, 2
vomit If . . . Orientals . . . drank a liquor which . . . made them v.
    LABRUYÈRE, 13
vote Give women the v.   SHAW, 20
He's lost us the tarts' v.   DEVONSHIRE, 1
One man shall have one v.   CARTWRIGHT, 1
The v., I thought, means nothing to women   O'BRIEN, E, 2
voted I always v. at my party's call   GILBERT, W, 10
voter The idea that there is a model Labour v. . . . is patronizing
    KINNOCK, 11
votes disadvantage of merely counting v.   INGE, 7
solved by speeches and majority v.   BISMARCK, 1
vow I v. to thee, my country   SPRING-RICE, 1
Vox *V. populi, v. dei*   ALCUIN, 1
vulgar Above the v. flight of common souls   MURPHY, A, 1
Funny without being v.   GILBERT, W, 48
I do not dislike the French from . . . v. antipathy   WALPOLE, H, 9
the most v. . . . is the British tourist   KILVERT, 1
The v. boil . . . an egg   POPE, 53
war . . . is looked upon as v.   WILDE, 10
vulgarity One can love a certain kind of v. for its own sake
    HUXLEY, A, 38
v. begins at home   WILDE, 67
vulgarise That fellow would v. the day of judgment   JERROLD, 3
vulgarizing Death . . . It's the only thing we haven't succeeded in
completely v.   HUXLEY, A, 17

W

wabe gyre and gimble in the w.   CARROLL, 23
wag A case of the tail dogging the w.   PERELMAN, 5
Every man has . . . an ambition to be a w.   JOHNSON, S, 32
wage One man's w. rise is another man's price increase
    WILSON, HAROLD, 4
Wagner W.   BRAHMS, 2
W. has lovely moments   ROSSINI, 1
W. is the Puccini of music   MORTON, 5
wagon Hitch your w. to a star   EMERSON, 23
Wagstaff a disgrace to our family name of W.   MARX, G, 11
waistcoat my stomach must just digest in its w.   SHERIDAN, R, 12
wait I thought I told you to w. in the car   BANKHEAD, 12
They also serve who only stand and w.   MILTON, 61
W. and see   ASQUITH, H, 3
waiting people w. for you stand out far less clearly   GIRAUDOUX, 1
There was I, w. at the church   LEIGH, 1
w. for the cock to crow   HUGHES, W, 1
We're w. for Godot   BECKETT, 4
wake hope is . . . the dream of those that w.   PRIOR, 2
waking w. from a troubled dream   HAWTHORNE, 1
walentine Never sign a w.   DICKENS, 51
Wales From W. Whose nightingales   THOMAS, E, 5
trace . . . the disasters of English history to . . . W.   WAUGH, E, 15
walk How does he w.   LEONARDO DA VINCI, 2
in the name of Jesus . . . rise up and w.   BIBLE, 4
I w. down the Strand   HARGREAVES, 2
Or w. with Kings   KIPLING, 17
w. before God in the light of the living   PSALMS, 35
w. on the lines or the squares   MILNE, 5
We must learn to w. before we can run   PROVERBS, 453
Where'er you w.   POPE, 47
walked man that hath not w. in the counsel of the ungodly
    PSALMS, 1
walking I'm w. backwards till Christmas   MILLIGAN, 5
I nauseate w.   CONGREVE, 15
I were w. with destiny   CHURCHILL, W, 13
Jesus . . . w. on the sea   BIBLE, 394
W. My Baby Back Home   TURK, 1
w. round him has always tired me   BEERBOHM, 20
When I am not w., I am reading   LAMB, CHARLES, 13
walks She w. in beauty   BYRON, 40
wall he turned his face to the w.   BIBLE, 304
Humpty Dumpty sat on a w.   NURSERY RHYMES, 18
I shall leap over the w.   PSALMS, 7

it is your business, when the w. next door catches fire
    HORACE, 22
Something . . . doesn't love a w.   FROST, R, 5
the w. fell down flat   BIBLE, 288
thou whited w.   BIBLE, 16
W. is the name – Max W.   WALL, 1
With our backs to the w. . . . each . . . must fight on to the end
    HAIG, 1
wallet a crowd like that . . . brings a lump to my w.   WALLACH, 1
Time hath . . . a w. at his back   SHAKESPEARE, 331
wallop the cod's w. is always fresh made   MORLEY, R, 2
wall paper Either that w. goes, or I do   WILDE, 79
walls by faith the w. of Jericho fell down   BIBLE, 186
No part of the w. is left undecorated   PEVSNER, 1
splendour falls on castle w.   TENNYSON, 61
Stone w. do not a prison make   LOVELACE, 1
W. have ears   PROVERBS, 451
walrus The W. and the Carpenter   CARROLL, 27
waltzing You'll come a-w., Matilda   PATERSON, 1
wandered I w. lonely as a cloud   WORDSWORTH, W, 7
wanderer A w. is man from his birth   ARNOLD, M, 18
wandering Poor w. one   GILBERT, W, 36
W. in a vast forest at night   DIDEROT, 1
w. minstrel I   GILBERT, W, 23
want convicted of sickness, hunger, wretchedness, and w.
    SMOLLETT, 3
Economy is going without something you do w.   HOPE, 3
evil is wrought by w. of thought   HOOD, 8
for w. of a nail   FRANKLIN, 5; PROVERBS, 166
freedom from w.   ROOSEVELT, F, 14
give the public what they w. to see and they'll come out for it
    SKELTON, RED, 1
If you w. a thing well done   PROVERBS, 221
the Lord is my shepherd; I shall not w.   PSALMS, 12
The w. of a thing is perplexing enough   VANBURGH, 1
What does a woman w.   FREUD, S, 6
wanted bought things because she w. 'em   VANBURGH, 2
Every man is w.   EMERSON, 12
I have w. only one thing to make me happy   HAZLITT, 9
wants Man w. but little   YOUNG, E, 1
war after the w. he should be publicly castrated   LLOYD GEORGE, 4
Against the beautiful . . . one can wage a pitiless w.   GREENE, 5
All diplomacy is a continuation of w.   CHOU EN LAI, 1
all's fair in love and w.   FORREST, 2
An empire founded by w.   MONTESQUIEU, 1
As long as w. is regarded as wicked   WILDE, 10
Before the w. . . . it was summer all the year round   ORWELL, 10
Being over seventy is like being engaged in a w.   SPARK, 5
blast of w.   SHAKESPEARE, 129
could lose the w. in an afternoon   CHURCHILL, W, 36
defeat without a w.   CHURCHILL, W, 47
done very well out of the w.   BALDWIN, S, 1
First in w.   WASHINGTON, 1
him who desires peace, prepare for w.   VEGETIUS, 1
I could have lost the w. in an afternoon   JELLICOE, 1
I don't care for w.   NAPOLEON III, 2
If we lose this w.   DAYAN, 2
I make w. on the living   CHARLES V, 2
in righteousness he doth judge and make w.   BIBLE, 470
In w. . . . there are no winners   CHAMBERLAIN, N, 4
It is well that w. is so terrible; . . .   LEE, R, 1
lead this people into w. and they'll forget . . . tolerance
    WILSON, W, 4
Lenin was the first to discover that capitalism 'inevitably' caused
w.   TAYLOR, A, 4
let slip the dogs of w.   SHAKESPEARE, 151
little woman who wrote the book that made this great w.
    LINCOLN, 5
makes a good w. makes a good peace   HERBERT, G, 8
My subject is W., and the pity of W.   OWEN, W, 5
never was a good w.   FRANKLIN, 16
No one can guarantee success in w.   CHURCHILL, W, 28
Now w. has a bad conscience   KEY, E, 6
Older men declare w.   HOOVER, 4
on this wall will hang my weapons and my lyre, discharged from
the w.   HORACE, 38
Stand your ground . . . if they mean to have a w., let it begin here
    PARKER, J, 1
Television brought the brutality of w.   MCLUHAN, 6
that devil's madness – W.   SERVICE, 4

the . . . barbarity of w. . . . forces men . . . to commit acts
KEY, E, 7
The first casualty when w. comes | JOHNSON, H, 1
the Lord is a man of w. | BIBLE, 113
The quickest way of ending a w. | ORWELL, 30
there was w. in heaven | BIBLE, 465
the second rule of w. | MONTGOMERY OF ALAMEIN, 1
The W. between Men and Women | THURBER, 14
the W. is being deliberately prolonged | SASSOON, S, 6
the w. of the giants is over | CHURCHILL, W, 31
The W. to End W. | WELLS, 20
The w. we have just been through . . . is not to be compared
WILSON, W, 6
The wrong w., at the wrong place | BRADLEY, O, 2
they'll give a w. and nobody will come | SANDBURG, 1
this liking for w. | BENNETT, ALAN, 2
this massed multitude of silent witnesses to . . . w. | GEORGE V, 1
This w. . . . is a w. to end w. | LLOYD GEORGE, 18
this w. . . . which did not justify the sacrifice of a single mother's son | PANKHURST, S, 1
Those who can win a w. well | CHURCHILL, W, 23
waging a w. it is not right that matters | HITLER, 13
w. can only be abolished through w. | MAO TSE-TUNG, 4
W. even to the knife | BYRON, 11
W. hath no fury like a non-combatant | MONTAGUE, 1
W. is, after all, the universal perversion | RAE, 1
W. is a great accelerator of events | NIVEN, D, 3
W is an organized bore | HOLMES, O, JR., 1
W. is enjoined you against the Infidels | KORAN, 3
W. is hell | SHERMAN, 2
W. is like love | BRECHT, 9
W. is much too serious a thing to be left to military men
TALLEYRAND, 6
W. is Peace | ORWELL, 18
W. is the continuation of politics | CLAUSEWITZ, 1
W. is too important | CLEMENCEAU, 2
W. is w. | ORWELL, 5
W. knows no power | BROOKE, 5
W. makes rattling good history | HARDY, 6
w. minus the shooting | ORWELL, 32
W. should belong to the tragic past | JOHN PAUL II, 3
w. which . . . left nothing to be desired | BRECHT, 7
W. will never cease until babies | MENCKEN, 5
we are . . . in the midst of a cold w. | BARUCH, 2
We are not at w. with Egypt | EDEN, A, 3
We have all lost the w. | LAWRENCE, D, 15
What they could do with round here is a good w. | BRECHT, 3
when there was w., he went | AUDEN, 27
when they learn how we began this w. | PRIESTLEY, 10
When you're at w. you think about a better life | WILDER, T, 6
Who live under the shadow of a w. | SPENDER, 3
ward as if I were locked up in a w. too | CHEKHOV, 3
wards key deftly in the oiled w. | KEATS, 48
Ware And I should dine at W. | COWPER, 13
warehouses One of the best w. I ever see was the Vatican
WESKER, 2
Waring What's become of W. | BROWNING, R, 58
warmongers w. who . . . have others pull the chestnuts out of the fire | STALIN, 3
warmth No w., no cheerfulness, no healthful ease | HOOD, 10
warn the right to be consulted . . . to encourage . . . to w.
BAGEHOT, 7
warned my Friends, be w. by me | BELLOC, 6
warning will it come without w. Just as I'm picking my nose
AUDEN, 26
War Office except the British W. | SHAW, 9
warrior a valiant w. Who never drew a sword | ANONYMOUS, 28
the British w. queen | COWPER, 4
wars end to the beginnings of all w. | ROOSEVELT, F, 17
he maketh w. to cease in all the world | PSALMS, 28
Just like an old liberal Between the w. | PLOMER, 1
my w. Were global | REED, H, 1
No kingdom has . . . had as many . . . w. as the kingdom of Christ
MONTESQUIEU, 5
Still w. and lechery | SHAKESPEARE, 333
the men who conduct their w. | GOEBBELS, 3
W. are not won by evacuations | CHURCHILL, W, 29
W. cannot be fought with nuclear weapons | MOUNTBATTEN, 6
W., conflict, it's all business | CHAPLIN, 4
w., horrible w. | VIRGIL, 14
Warsaw calm reigned in W. | SÉBASTIANI, 1

warts pimples, w., and everything as you see me
CROMWELL, O, 4
war-war To jaw-jaw is better than to w. | CHURCHILL, W, 68
wary Let me remind you what the w. fox said . . . to the sick lion
HORACE, 16
wash Don't w. your dirty linen | PROVERBS, 123
I do, and I also w. and iron them | THATCHER, D, 1
w. me throughly from my wickedness | PSALMS, 30
washed Pilate . . . w. his hands | BIBLE, 430
w. their robes . . . in the blood of the lamb | BIBLE, 463
washing painting a face and not w. | FULLER, T, 1
wasps w. and hornets break through | SWIFT, 18
waste Far too good to w. on children | SHAW, 50
The years to come seemed w. of breath | YEATS, 16
W. not, want not | PROVERBS, 452
wasted most w. of all days | CHAMFORT, 2
wasting she did not believe in w. her effects | CROMPTON, 1
watch Either he's dead or my w. has stopped | MARX, G, 5
keeping w. over their flock by night | BIBLE, 314
The W. on the Rhine | SCHNECKENBURGER, 1
w. and pray | BIBLE, 426
why not carry a w. | TREE, 2
watch-dog to hear the w.'s honest bark | BYRON, 18
watched A w. pot | PROVERBS, 73
watches 'Tis with our judgments as our w. | POPE, 21
watchmaker I should have become a w. | EINSTEIN, 9
watch-tower his w. in the skies | MILTON, 17
water a pure river of w. of life | BIBLE, 474
better deeds Shall be in w. writ | BEAUMONT, 8
biggest waste of w. in the country | PHILIP, PRINCE, 3
Dripping w. hollows out a stone | OVID, 4
half the landscape is . . . covered by useless w. | DOUGLAS, N, 1
Here lies one whose name was writ in w. | KEATS, 49
He who drinks a tumbler of London w. | SMITH, SYDNEY, 15
Human beings were invented by w. | ROBBINS, 1
I came like W. | FITZGERALD, E, 11
impressions . . . lasting as . . . an oar upon the w. | CHOPIN, 3
It is with our passions as it is with fire and w. | L'ESTRANGE, 1
Jesus was a sailor when he walked upon the w. | COHEN, 3
Like a bridge over troubled w. | SIMON, 1
like throwing w. into the sea | CERVANTES, 9
no verse can give pleasure for long . . . written by drinkers of w.
HORACE, 23
Streets full of w. | BENCHLEY, 8
The first possibility of rural cleanliness lies in *w. supply.*
NIGHTINGALE, 4
the w. that was made wine | BIBLE, 242
Too much of w. hast thou | SHAKESPEARE, 104
virtues we write in w. | SHAKESPEARE, 141
w. flowed like champagne | EVARTS, 1
W. is H$_2$O, hydrogen two parts, oxygen one | LAWRENCE, D, 19
w., is unsuitable in colour | HERBERT, A, 5
w. still keeps falling over | CHURCHILL, W, 9
W., w., every where | COLERIDGE, S, 30
We have all passed a lot of w. | GOLDWYN, 17
when I makes w. I makes w. | JOYCE, 7
watering a-w. the last year's crop | ELIOT, G, 2
Waterloo Battle of W. | WELLINGTON, 26
Every man meets his W. | PHILLIPS, 3
watermark high w. . . . of Socialist literature is W. H. Auden
AUDEN, 2
waters By the w. of Babylon | PSALMS, 70
dreadful noise of w. in my ears | SHAKESPEARE, 301
he leadeth me beside the still w. | PSALMS, 12
stolen w. are sweet | BIBLE, 449
the earth shall be full . . . as the w. cover the sea | BIBLE, 203
the Spirit of God moved upon . . . the w. | BIBLE, 137
the w. of comfort | PSALMS, 11
the w. of the heart Push in their tides | THOMAS, D, 14
w. flowed over mine head | BIBLE, 307
water-trough A snake came to my w. | LAWRENCE, D, 28
Watson Mr W., come here; I want you | BELL, A, 1
Waugh Evelyn W. . . . is a Roman Catholic | WAUGH, E, 1
Mr. W. . . . is . . . a snob in search of a class | WAUGH, E, 2
waves the w. make towards the pebbled shore | SHAKESPEARE, 363
waxworks w. inhabited by gramophones | DE LA MARE, 2
way A man . . . is *so* in the w. | GASKELL, 1
blow out your candle . . . to find your w. | DIDEROT, 1
catch the nearest w. | SHAKESPEARE, 205
I am the w., the truth, and the life | BIBLE, 259
I go my w. to him that sent me | BIBLE, 261

in every war they kill you a new w.   ROGERS, W, 1
plowman homeward plods his weary w.   GRAY, 1
That's the w. for Billy and me   HOGG, 1
the error of his w.   BIBLE, 220
The w. to a man's heart   PROVERBS, 427
The w. to dusty death   SHAKESPEARE, 225
though hell should bar the w.   NOYES, 2
Through Eden took their solitary w.   MILTON, 52
w. of all flesh   CONGREVE, 12; SHADWELL, 2
woman has her w.   HOLMES, O, 1
ways consider your w.   BIBLE, 184
She dwelt among the untrodden w.   WORDSWORTH, W, 48
we put it down a w.   DICKENS, 52
weak A w., diffusive, weltering, ineffectual man   COLERIDGE, S, 1
Beauty stands In the admiration . . . of w. minds   MILTON, 54
concessions of the w.   BURKE, E, 13
disarm the strong and arm the w.   FRANCE, 2
Idleness . . . the refuge of w. minds   CHESTERFIELD, 15
I inhabit a w., frail, decayed tenement   ADAMS, J, 4
Is thy love a plant Of such w. fibre   WORDSWORTH, W, 22
Like all w. men . . . an exaggerated stress   MAUGHAM, 11
surely the w. shall perish   SERVICE, 3
The concessions of the w. are the concessions of fear   BURKE, E, 13
The w. have one weapon   BIDAULT, 1
weaker the w. vessel   BIBLE, 442
weakest The w. goes to the wall   PROVERBS, 428
weakness no more w. than is natural to her sex   THUCYDIDES, 2
weaknesses I have got lots of human w.   THATCHER, M, 15
Never support two w.   WILDER, T, 3
touch his w. with a delicate hand   GOLDSMITH, 15
weal I will govern according to the common w.   JAMES I, 3
wealth All health is better than w.   SCOTT, WALTER, 23
His w. a well-spent age   CAMPION, 4
Outshone the w. of Ormus and of Ind   MILTON, 39
the insolence of w.   JOHNSON, S, 124
w. had rendered her helpless   BROOKNER, 3
W. has never been a sufficient source of honour   GALBRAITH, 3
W. I ask not   STEVENSON, R, 6
W. is like sea-water   SCHOPENHAUER, 8
W. is not without its advantages   GALBRAITH, 1
Where w. and freedom reign, contentment fails   GOLDSMITH, 23
wealthy Where some people are very w. and others have nothing   ARISTOTLE, 8
weaned w. on a pickle   LONGWORTH, 1
weapon art is not a w.   KENNEDY, JOHN, 17
Innocence is no earthly w.   HILL, G, 1
In the sex-war thoughtlessness is the w. of the male   CONNOLLY, 16
The weak have one w.   BIDAULT, 1
tinned food is a deadlier w.   ORWELL, 24
weapons books are w.   ROOSEVELT, F, 16
If sunbeams were w.   PORTER, G, 1
on this wall will hang my w. and my lyre, discharged from the war   HORACE, 38
wear I . . . chose my wife . . . for qualities as would w. well   GOLDSMITH, 26
I want you to w. me   FITZGERALD, Z, 2
you'll w. your eyes out   ZOLA, 1
weariest The w. nights . . . must . . . end   ORCZY, 2
The w. nights, the longest days   ORCZY, 2
weariness much study is a w. of the flesh   BIBLE, 78
The w., the fever, and the fret   KEATS, 38
weary Art thou w.   NEALE, 1
weasel w. under the cocktail cabinet   PINTER, 4
weather even the w. forecast seemed to be some kind of spoof   LODGE, 4
I like the w.   BYRON, 7
This is the w. the cuckoo likes   HARDY, 12
This is the w. the shepherd shuns   HARDY, 13
When two Englishmen meet, their first talk is of the w.   JOHNSON, S, 15
weather-eye Keep your w. open   PROVERBS, 242
weather-wise Some are w.   FRANKLIN, 6
web The w. of our life is of a mingled yarn   SHAKESPEARE, 24
webs Laws are like spider's w.   SOLON, 1
Webster W. is his orator   WEBSTER, D, 2
W. struck me much like a steam engine in trousers   WEBSTER, D, 1
wed With this Ring I thee w.   BOOK OF COMMON PRAYER, 28
wedding the bride at every w.   ROOSEVELT, T, 2

weddings w. is sadder than funerals   BEHAN, 6
wedlock W. . . . deep peace of the double bed   CAMPBELL, MRS PATRICK, 2
Wednesday Married on W.   NURSERY RHYMES, 53
W.'s child is full of woe   NURSERY RHYMES, 35
wee W. . . . tim'rous beastie   BURNS, R, 21
weed that tawney w. tobacco   JONSON, 4
What is a w.   EMERSON, 17
weed-killer Lovely day: sun . . . w.   ELGAR, 2
weeds Lilies that fester smell far worse than w.   SHAKESPEARE, 366
nature runs either to herbs, or to w.   BACON, FRANCIS, 37
Worthless as wither'd w.   BRONTÉ, E, 2
week A w. is a long time in politics   WILSON, HAROLD, 11
greatest w. . . . since the creation   NIXON, 8
Of all the days that's in the w.   CAREY, H, 2
the greatest w. in the history of the world   NIXON, 8
weekendmanship that basic w.   POTTER, S, 4
weep By the waters of Babylon we sit down and w.   WALPOLE, H, 7
Fair daffodils, we w. to see   HERRICK, 4
For men must work, and women must w.   KINGSLEY, 7
not to w. at them, nor to hate them, but to understand them   SPINOZA, 5
'She must w. or she will die.'   TENNYSON, 67
so that I do not w.   BEAUMARCHAIS, 1
Tears such as angels w.   MILTON, 36
w. for her sins at the other   CARY, J, 1
W. no more, my lady   FOSTER, 1
weeping Do you hear the children w.   BROWNING, E, 2
w. and gnashing of teeth   BIBLE, 381
Why are you w.? Did you imagine that I was immortal   LOUIS XIV, 7
weigh my innocence begins to w. me down   RACINE, 2
weighed thou art w. in the balances, and art found wanting   BIBLE, 52
weight deadly w. of the terrible tradition of a dialogue   MANDELA, 4
the w. of rages   SPOONER, 1
welcome Advice is seldom w.   CHESTERFIELD, 12
Love bade me w.   HERBERT, G, 6
Thrice w., darling of the spring   WORDSWORTH, W, 74
well At last I am going to be w.   SCARRON, 1
do not speak w. of yourself   PASCAL, 4
I am not w.; pray get me . . . brandy   GEORGE IV, 1
lov'd not wisely; but too w.   SHAKESPEARE, 288
nothing . . . and did it very w.   GILBERT, W, 20
reward of a thing w. done   EMERSON, 11
There are two things which I am confident I can do very w.   JOHNSON, S, 52
the world's work . . . is done by men who do not feel . . . w.   GALBRAITH, 6
W. building hath three Conditions   WOTTON, 1
We never do anything w.   HAZLITT, 27
worth doing w.   CHESTERFIELD, 6
well-bred a w. sort of emotional anarchy   LAWRENCE, D, 16
well-dressed The sense of being w.   FORBES, 1
Wellington W. has exhausted nature and . . . glory   WELLINGTON, 2
well-knownness The celebrity . . . known for his w.   BOORSTIN, 1
well off as w. as if he were rich   ASTOR, J, 1
Wells Whatever W. writes is not only alive   WELLS, 1
well-spent as rare as a w. one   CARLYLE, T, 7
well-written A w. Life   CARLYLE, T, 7
Welsh but he wouldn't put up with the W.   MORTIMER, 1
The W. . . . just sing   WAUGH, E, 14
Wembley W., adj. Suffering from a vague *malaise*   JENNINGS, P, 2
wen the fate of the great w.   COBBETT, 3
Wenceslas Good King W. looked out   NEALE, 2
wench beside the w. is dead   MARLOWE, 11
Wenlock Edge On W. the wood's in trouble   HOUSMAN, 13
went as cooks go she w.   SAKI, 16
wept Jesus w.   BIBLE, 257
They w. like anything to see   CARROLL, 27
young man who has not w.   SANTAYANA, 4
west closing time in the gardens of the W.   CONNOLLY, 3
East is East, and w. is W.   KIPLING, 3
Go W., young man   GREELEY, 1; SOULE, 1
the safeguard of the w.   WORDSWORTH, W, 58
western All Quiet on the W. Front   REMARQUE, 1

W. philosophy is . . . a series of footnotes to Plato's philosophy
WHITEHEAD, 6
wet joly whistle wel y-w. CHAUCER, 18
out of these w. clothes and into a dry Martini WOOLLCOTT, 2
whale A w. ship was my Yale College MELVILLE, 2
Very like a w. SHAKESPEARE, 97
what Aye, and w. then COLERIDGE, S, 4
W. is truth BACON, FRANCIS, 56
wheat An editor . . . separates the w. from the chaff
STEVENSON, A, 1
wheel bound upon a w. of fire SHAKESPEARE, 191
wheels A cruel story runs on w. OUIDA, 4
spoke among your w. BEAUMONT, 5
when have they fixed the where and w. HAWKER, 1
w. a man should marry BACON, FRANCIS, 35
where have they fixed the w. and when HAWKER, 1
to die, and go we know not w. SHAKESPEARE, 232
W. are you now HOPE, 2
W. were you fellows when the paper was blank ALLEN, F, 2
where'er W. you walk POPE, 47
wherefore There is occasions and causes why and w.
SHAKESPEARE, 136
w. art thou Romeo SHAKESPEARE, 309
whey Eating her curds and w. NURSERY RHYMES, 31
whiff w. of grapeshot CARLYLE, T, 16
Whig Sir, I perceive you are a vile W. JOHNSON, S, 84
Whigs caught the W. bathing DISRAELI, 23
whim The strangest w. CHESTERTON, 7
whimper not with a bang but a w. ELIOT, T, 10
whipping W. and abuse are like laudanum STOWE, 2
who shall scape w. SHAKESPEARE, 87
whirlwind Elijah went up by a w. into heaven BIBLE, 301
sown the wind . . . reap the w. BIBLE, 190
whisker can't speak above a w. MANKEIWICZ, 3
whisky A good gulp of hot w. at bedtime FLEMING, A, 6
nicest boy who ever committed the sin of w. SPARK, 4
That w. priest GREENE, 7
with education and w. the price it is WAUGH, E, 13
whispered it's w. every where CONGREVE, 7
whispering w. sound of the cool colonnade COWPER, 19
whisperings It keeps eternal w. around KEATS, 43
whistle I heard the bullets w. . . . charming in the sound
WASHINGTON, 4
So was hir joly w. wel y-wet CHAUCER, 18
W. a Happy Tune HAMMERSTEIN, 2
W. and she'll come to you BEAUMONT, 13
Whistler James W. WILDE, 67
W. himself entirely concurs WHISTLER, 2
whistles A Scout smiles and w. BADEN-POWELL, 1
They hang us now in Shrewsbury jail: The w. blow forlorn
HOUSMAN, 8
whistling W. aloud to bear his courage up BLAIR, R, 1
white Britain . . . is going to be forged in the w. heat of this
revolution WILSON, HAROLD, 8
'E was w., clear w., inside KIPLING, 14
If the w. man *says* he does, he is instantly . . . mistrusted
MACINNES, 3
it's not even red brick, but w. tile OSBORNE, 4
I want to be the w. man's brother KING, M, 2
my soul is w. BLAKE, W, 48
One black, and one w., and two khaki ANONYMOUS, 95
so-called w. races FORSTER, 10
Take up the W. Man's burden KIPLING, 31
the figure of a solitary Woman . . . in w. garments COLLINS, W, 3
the silk stockings and w. bosoms of your actresses JOHNSON, S, 46
The w. man knows how to make everything SITTING BULL, 1
When a w. in Africa LESSING, D, 3
When the w. man came we had the land GEORGE, 1
w. stick and a dog LEVIN, 3
whited thou w. wall BIBLE, 16
White House gathered together at the W. KENNEDY, JOHN, 12
Log-cabin to W. THAYER, 1
no whitewash at the W. NIXON, 3
standing between Nixon and the W. KENNEDY, JOHN, 9
whites the w. of their eyes PRESCOTT, 1
whitewash no w. at the White House NIXON, 3
whither w. thou goest, I will go BIBLE, 475
Whitman Walt W. who laid end to end LODGE, 5
W. who laid end to end words WHITMAN, 1
who I do not know w. or what I am SELLERS, 1
If you have to tell them w. you are, you aren't anybody PECK, 1

W. is Silvia SHAKESPEARE, 348
whole a w. is that which has a beginning, a middle, and an end
ARISTOTLE, 4
if she knew the w. of it TROLLOPE, 14
the greatest happiness of the w. PLATO, 2
w. man in himself, polished and well-rounded HORACE, 47
whom for w. the bell tolls DONNE, 8
'W. are you?' said he ADE, 1
whore I am the Protestant w. GWYN, 1
the judgment of the great w. BIBLE, 468
the morals of a w., and the manners of a dancing master
JOHNSON, S, 51
the old man does not care for the young man's w. JOHNSON, S, 74
The woman's a w. JOHNSON, S, 89
'Tis Pity She's a W. FORD, JOHN, 3
w., and the whoremonger, shall ye scourge KORAN, 7
You can lead a w. to culture PARKER, D, 25
whorehouses virgin territory for w. CAPONE, 14
whores After all, we are not political w. MUSSOLINI, 3
With first-rate sherry flowing into second-rate w. PLOMER, 2
whoreson w. zed SHAKESPEARE, 173
whoso W. would be a man EMERSON, 14
why Everything he saw made him ask how and w.
LEONARDO DA VINCI, 1
For every w. BUTLER, S, 2
occasions and causes w. and wherefore SHAKESPEARE, 136
they knew not w. BUTLER, S, 1
W. should I go MILLER, A, 6
wicked As long as war is regarded as w. WILDE, 10
no peace . . . unto the w. BIBLE, 213
the men of Sodom were w. BIBLE, 166
There is a w. inclination . . . to suppose an old man decayed in his
intellects JOHNSON, S, 143
to see men w. SWIFT, 16
wickedness I was shapen in w. PSALMS, 31
men alone are quite capable of every w. CONRAD, 7
The w. of the world BRECHT, 11
wash me throughly from my w. PSALMS, 30
Widdle Roger . . . would lead the procession, followed by W. and
Puke DURRELL, G, 2
wide Things hitherto undone should be given . . . a w. berth
BEERBOHM, 8
Widnes men become attached even to W. TAYLOR, A, 8
widow a w. . . . is a kind of sinecure WYCHERLEY, 2
better to be the w. of a hero than the wife of a coward
IBARRURI, 3
Molly Stark sleeps a w. STARK, 1
you, my dear, will be my w. GUITRY, 1
widows When w. exclaim loudly against second marriages
FIELDING, 3
wife A man should not insult his w. publicly THURBER, 12
A man who's untrue to his w. AUDEN, 21
an occupational hazard of being a w. ANNE, 1
A professional is someone whose w. works to enable him to paint
SHAHN, 1
better to be the widow of a hero than the w. of a coward
IBARRURI, 3
Caesar's w. must be above suspicion CAESAR, 2
chose my w. . . . for . . . qualities as would wear well
GOLDSMITH, 26
coming together of man and w. . . . should be a fresh adventure
STOPES, 5
Commuter . . . riding to and from his w. WHITE, E, 1
Here lies my w. DRYDEN, 21
Here lies my w., . . . Hallelujah ANONYMOUS, 31
He that has no w. PROVERBS, 191
he that is married careth . . . how he may please his w. BIBLE, 31
He that loves not his w. and children TAYLOR, JEREMY, 2
His w. could eat no lean NURSERY RHYMES, 26
his w. is beautiful and his children smart MENCKEN, 3
I am no shadow . . . I am a w. PLATH, 3
If a man stays away from his w. DARLING, 1
I have a w., I have sons LUCAN, 1
I have married a w. BIBLE, 329
I have quarrelled with my w. PEACOCK, 10
light w. doth make a heavy husband SHAKESPEARE, 253
like sleeping with someone else's w. BRADBURY, 5
man . . . shall cleave unto his w. BIBLE, 147
Mother to dozens, And nobody's w. HERBERT, A, 1
My w. had been unfaithful to me BRAINE, 3
My w. hath something in her gizzard PEPYS, 16

My w. . . . is troubled with her lonely life — PEPYS, 8
My w. won't let me — LEIGH, 1
No man worth having is true to his w. — VANBURGH, 6
one w. and hardly any mistresses — SAKI, 14
overshadowed by his overdressed, extravagant and idle w. — STOPES, 6
remorse for what you have thought about your w. — ROSTAND, J, 2
single man . . . must be in want of a w. — AUSTEN, 18
taking out his false teeth and hurling them at his w. — DOYLE, 5
that a man lay down his w. for a friend — JOYCE, 9
that monstrous animal a husband and w. — FIELDING, 13
The first w. is matrimony — PROVERBS, 395
The husband frae the w. despises — BURNS, R, 20
the titles of w. and mother . . . are transitory and accidental — LIVERMORE, 2
the w. . . . the weaker vessel — BIBLE, 442
times . . . it would be marvellous to have a w. — HUME, B, 2
Whose w. shall it be — TOOKE, 1
with a w. to tell him what to do — MANCROFT, 1
Would you allow your w. . . . to read this book — GRIFFITH-JONES, 1
your w. . . . is a receiver of stolen goods — JOHNSON, S, 134
wifehood w. and motherhood are but incidental relations — STANTON, E, 5
wig man with a w. to keep order — WAUGH, E, 7
My hat and w. will soon be here — COWPER, 12
wild an old, w., and incomprehensible man — VICTORIA, 8
mother bore me in the southern w. — BLAKE, W, 48
Wilde if . . . Oscar W. had lived into his nineties — MUGGERIDGE, 4
Oscar W. — LEVERSON, 3; WHISTLER, 17
W. performed his life . . . even after fate had taken the plot out of his hands — WILDE, 1
wilderness a little w. — MARVELL, 6
a lodge in some vast w. — COWPER, 27
plants left over from the Edwardian W. — OSBORNE, 6
the day of temptation in the w. — PSALMS, 56
the voice of him that crieth in the w. — BIBLE, 210
the voice of one crying in the w. — BIBLE, 353
the w. of this world — BUNYAN, 1
W. is Paradise enow — FITZGERALD, E, 5
wild-fowl more fearful w. than your lion — SHAKESPEARE, 261
will complies against his w. — BUTLER, S, 8
Do what you w. — RABELAIS, 4
formation of the political w. of the nation — HITLER, 14
His right was clear, his w. was strong — ANONYMOUS, 102
John Stuart Mill By a mighty effort of w. — BENTLEY, E, 5
let my w. replace reasoned judgement — JUVENAL, 6
Man has his w. — HOLMES, O, 1
The man who leaves money to charity in his w. — VOLTAIRE, 33
We have to believe in free w.. We've got no choice — SINGER, 2
Where there's a w. — PROVERBS, 463
W. ye no come back again — NAIRNE, 1
You w., Oscar, you w. — WHISTLER, 17
William That W. Blake Who beat upon the wall — YEATS, 3
You are old, Father W. — CARROLL, 4
Willie Here lie W. Michie's banes — BURNS, R, 9
Wee W. Winkie runs through the town — NURSERY RHYMES, 69
willin' Barkis is w. — DICKENS, 12
willow a little tom-tit Sang 'W., titwillow, titwillow — GILBERT, W, 34
willows W. whiten, aspens quiver — TENNYSON, 42
will-power There is no such thing as a great talent without great w. — BALZAC, 2
will-to-live The thing-in-itself, the w., exists . . . in every being — SCHOPENHAUER, 5
Wilson Harold W. — BULMER-THOMAS, 1
Mr W. . . . is the 14th Mr W. — DOUGLAS-HOME, A, 1
Wimbledon phoneyness . . . a lot of it at W. — MCENROE, 1
win Heads I w. — CROKER, 1
high sentiments always w. in the end — ORWELL, 8
I am certain that we will w. the election with a good majority — THATCHER, M, 23
The conventional army loses if it does not w. — KISSINGER, 1
Those who can w. a war well — CHURCHILL, W, 23
wind a rushing mighty w. — BIBLE, 2
Blow, blow, thou winter w. — SHAKESPEARE, 49
gone with the w. — DOWSON, 2
Gone With the W. — MITCHELL, M, 5
It's an ill w. — PROVERBS, 231
I will not permit thirty men . . . to agitate a bag of w. — WHITE, A, 1
like W. I go — FITZGERALD, E, 11
of w. and limb — BUTLER, S, 5
O Wild West W. — SHELLEY, 14

so famous, that it would permit me . . . to break w. in society — BALZAC, 5
The answer . . . is blowin' in the w. — DYLAN, 2
'The story is like the w.' — VAN DER POST, 1
The w. was a torrent of darkness — NOYES, 1
throw the sand against the w. — BLAKE, W, 34
what w. is to fire — BUSSY-RABUTIN, 1
wherever the w. takes me I travel as a visitor — HORACE, 13
Who has seen the w. — ROSSETTI, C, 9
w. of nationalism and freedom blowing — BALDWIN, S, 7
words but w. — BUTLER, S, 6
windmills not giants but w. — CERVANTES, 4
window Serve up . . . and throw . . . out of the w. — LEAR, 6
what light through yonder w. breaks — SHAKESPEARE, 308
wine A Flask of W. — FITZGERALD, E, 5
A man may surely be allowed to take a glass of w. by his own fireside — SHERIDAN, R, 16
And drink of my Algerian w. — BEHAN, 9
days of w. and roses — DOWSON, 6
drinks his w. 'mid laughter free — ANONYMOUS, 87
for its poisonous w. — KEATS, 32
Frenchmen drink w. just like — LARDNER, 3
full of new w. — BIBLE, 3
good w. needs no bush — SHAKESPEARE, 57
like a giant refreshed with w. — PSALMS, 43
new w. into old bottles — BIBLE, 384
no man . . . having drunk old w. straightway desireth new — BIBLE, 321
temperate in love and w. — MILTON, 2
the guests must be chosen as carefully as the w. — SAKI, 1
the water that was made w. — BIBLE, 242
the w. is in, the wit is out — BECON, 1
the w. was a farce and the food a tragedy — POWELL, A, 2
they shall not drink w. with a song — BIBLE, 206
This w. upon a foreign tree — THOMAS, D, 17
Truth comes out in w. — PLINY THE ELDER, 5
use a little w. for thy stomach's sake — BIBLE, 509
When the w. is in — PROVERBS, 462
Who loves not w., woman and song — LUTHER, 5
W. comes in at the mouth — YEATS, 9
w. is a mocker — BIBLE, 453
W. is the most healthful — PASTEUR, 3
winged Doth the w. life destroy — BLAKE, W, 15
Time's w. chariot — MARVELL, 10
wings Fear lent w. to his feet — VIRGIL, 15
hide me under the shadow of thy w. — PSALMS, 6
man with w. . . . might . . . overcome the resistance of the air — LEONARDO DA VINCI, 5
my trust shall be under the covering of thy w. — PSALMS, 37
O that I had w. like a dove — PSALMS, 33
shall . . . arise with healing in his w. — BIBLE, 343
the seraphims: each one had six w. — BIBLE, 197
the w. of a dove — COWPER, 33
whether pigs have w. — CARROLL, 28
wink I will w. and hold out mine iron — SHAKESPEARE, 125
never came a w. too soon — HOOD, 6
winners In war . . . there are no w. — CHAMBERLAIN, N, 4
winning not w. but taking part — COUBERTIN, 1
W. isn't everything, but wanting to win is — LOMBARDI, 1
Winston It hasn't taken W. long to get used to American ways — ACHESON, 3
The first time you meet W. — LYTTON, 1
W. . . . preparing his impromptu speeches — CHURCHILL, W, 7
W. with his hundred-horse-power mind — BALDWIN, S, 2
you meet W. . . . you spend in discovering his virtues — CHURCHILL, W, 6
winter got through the perils of w. till at least the seventh of May — TROLLOPE, 7
It is a w.'s tale — THOMAS, D, 7
Many . . . say that they enjoy the w. — ADAMS, R, 3
No one thinks of w. — KIPLING, 27
the furious w.'s rages — SHAKESPEARE, 62
The stars grew bright in the w. sky — MASEFIELD, 4
W. is icummen in — POUND, 7
w. of our discontent — SHAKESPEARE, 300
wintry sailed the w. sea — LONGFELLOW, 18
wiped let them be w. out of the book of the living — PSALMS, 39
wisdom fear of the Lord is the beginning of w. — PSALMS, 16
follies as the special evidences of our w. — TROLLOPE, 10
Greeks seek after w. — BIBLE, 24
in much w. is much grief — BIBLE, 65

Knowledge can be communicated but not w.   HESSE, 2
Love is the w. of the fool   JOHNSON, S, 42
privilege of w. to listen   HOLMES, O, 6
proverb is one man's wit and all men's w.   RUSSELL, J, 2
proverbs provide them with w.   MAUGHAM, 23
Silence is . . . full of potential w.   HUXLEY, A, 28
The highest w. has but one science   TOLSTOY, L, 8
The only infallible criterion of w.   BURKE, E, 4
the palace of W.   BLAKE, W, 25
the price of w. is above rubies   BIBLE, 234
Vain w. all, and false philosophy   MILTON, 41
want of human w.   LAW, 2
W. be put in a silver rod   BLAKE, W, 11
w. . . . cometh by opportunity of leisure   BIBLE, 90
W. has taught us to be calm and meek   HOLMES, O, 5
w. . . . hath hewn out her seven pillars   BIBLE, 448
W. in minds attentive   COWPER, 32
w. of the crocodiles   BACON, FRANCIS, 60
w. . . . sweetly doth . . . order all things   BIBLE, 521
with how little w. the world is governed   OXENSTIERNA, 1
with the ancient is w.   BIBLE, 228
Women . . . guardians of w. and humanity   WOLFF, 1
wise   a w. man, which built his house upon a rock   BIBLE, 380
A w. man will make more opportunities   BACON, FRANCIS, 16
Coffee which makes the politician w.   POPE, 52
How very weak the very w.   THACKERAY, 8
Many have been the w. speeches of fools   FULLER, T, 4
more of the fool than of the w.   BACON, FRANCIS, 13
No man . . . so w. as Thurlow looked   FOX, C, 2
Nor ever did a w. one   ROCHESTER, 1
sorrow makes us w.   TENNYSON, 36
The only wretched are the w.   PRIOR, 3
the w. forgive   SZASZ, 6
To be w. and love   SHAKESPEARE, 330
where ignorance is bliss, 'Tis folly to be w.   GRAY, 10
wisely   happy who knows how to use the gods' gifts w.   HORACE, 43
lov'd not w., but too well   SHAKESPEARE, 288
Wiseman   Mr Worldly W.   BUNYAN, 3
wiser   Be w. than other people   CHESTERFIELD, 5
foreigner should . . . be w. than ourselves   TROLLOPE, 10
Like Odysseus, he looked w. when seated   WILSON, W, 2
sadder and a w. man   COLERIDGE, S, 40
The French are w. than they seem   BACON, FRANCIS, 47
the old have rubbed it into the young that they are w.   MAUGHAM, 3
w. to-day than . . . yesterday   POPE, 54
wisest   The most attractive sentences are not perhaps the w.   THOREAU, 4
wish   Conscience is . . . rejection of a . . . w.   FREUD, 3
Justice is the . . . perpetual w.   JUSTINIAN I, 1
most . . . w. they were the only one alive   AUDEN, 11
quite a number fondly believe their w. . . . granted   AUDEN, 11
Someday I'll w. upon a star   HARBURG, 3
The w. to hurt   BRONOWSKI, 4
The w. to spread those opinions that we hold   BUTLER, S, 4
wished   consummation devoutly to be w.   SHAKESPEARE, 89
wishes   If w. were horses   PROVERBS, 216
wishful   There is w. thinking in Hell as well as on earth   LEWIS, C, 3
wit   a man of much w. . . . void of virtue   CHESTERFIELD, 4
An ounce of a man's own w.   STERNE, 10
Attic w.   PLINY THE ELDER, 1
a w. out of two half-wits   KINNOCK, 3
Brevity is the soul of w.   SHAKESPEARE, 80
cause that w. is in other men   SHAKESPEARE, 116
fancy w. will come   POPE, 9
His foe was folly and his weapon w.   HOPE, 9
I have neither w., nor words, nor worth   SHAKESPEARE, 157
Impropriety is the soul of w.   MAUGHAM, 9
In w. a man   POPE, 18
love robs those who have it of their w.   DIDEROT, 2
Music-hall songs provide the dull with w.   MAUGHAM, 23
Pox take him and his w.   POPE, 2
proverb is one man's w. and all men's wisdom   RUSSELL, J, 2
The universal monarchy of w.   CAREW, 1
True w. is nature to advantage dress'd   POPE, 25
wine in is, the w. is out   BECON, 1
W. that can creep   POPE, 16
witch   thou shalt not suffer a w. to live   BIBLE, 117
witches   I have ever believed . . . that there are w.   BROWNE, T, 5

wither   Age cannot w. her   SHAKESPEARE, 30
his leaf also shall not w.   PSALMS, 1
wither'd   w. is the garland of the war   SHAKESPEARE, 36
withered   lonely of heart is w. away   YEATS, 19
withers   The state is not 'abolished', it w. away   ENGELS, 1
within   that w. which passes show   SHAKESPEARE, 66
the kingdom of God is w. you   BIBLE, 334
when the fight begins w. himself   BROWNING, R, 12
without   I can do w.   SOCRATES, 7
You are not you w. me   FULLER, ROY, 1
witness   thou shalt not bear false w.   BIBLE, 115
witnesses   this massed multitude of silent w. to . . . war   GEORGE V, 1
wits   Great W. . . . to Madness near alli'd   DRYDEN, 5
homely w.   SHAKESPEARE, 346
their poetry is conceived and composed in their w.   ARNOLD, M, 44
This man I thought had been a Lord among w.   JOHNSON, S, 50
witty   a very w. prologue   CONGREVE, 11
I am not only w. in myself   SHAKESPEARE, 116
Pretty w. Nell   PEPYS, 11
stumbling on something w.   AUSTEN, 25
wives   Bricklayers kick their w. to death   WELLS, 19
husbands and w. . . . belong to different sexes   DIX, DOROTHY, 4
husbands and w. make shipwreck of their lives   DIX, DOROTHY, 3
husbands, love your w.   BIBLE, 21
I met a man with seven w.   NURSERY RHYMES, 3
O! men with mothers and w.   HOOD, 11
The others were only my w.   GUITRY, 1
Translations (like w.) are seldom faithful   CAMPBELL, R, 2
W. are young men's mistresses   BACON, FRANCIS, 34
you do not make the laws but . . . are the w. . . . of those who do   GRIMKÉ, 1
wiving   Hanging and w. goes by destiny   SHAKESPEARE, 244
wizard   A Catalan w. who fools with shapes   PICASSO, 1
Wodehouse   like P. G. W. dropping Jeeves   WAUGH, E, 45
W., whose works I place a little below Shakespeare's   WODEHOUSE, 1
woe   a sad variety of w.   POPE, 8
Much in sorrow, oft in w.   WHITE, H, 1
suits of w.   SHAKESPEARE, 66
Wednesday's child is full of w.   NURSERY RHYMES, 35
w. to him that is alone when he falleth   BIBLE, 69
W. to the land that's govern'd by a child   SHAKESPEARE, 302
W. to the vanquished   LIVY, 1
w. unto them that call evil good   BIBLE, 196
w. unto them that . . . follow strong drink   BIBLE, 195
wolf   The boy cried 'W., w.!'   AESOP, 9
the w. in the sheep's clothing   AESOP, 10
w. also shall dwell with the lamb   BIBLE, 203
wolf's-bane   neither twist W.   KEATS, 32
wolves   people being thrown to the w.   LAW, 3
send you forth as lambs among w.   BIBLE, 323
woman   A diplomat . . . always remembers a w.'s birthday   FROST, R, 10
A man is only as old as the w.   MARX, G, 26
And a w. is only a w.   KIPLING, 4
an ugly w. is a blot on the fair face of creation   BRONTË, C, 1
a w. is on a . . . hunt for trouble   DIX, DOROTHY, 3
A W. Killed with Kindness   HEYWOOD, 1
a w. . . . ought to lay aside . . . modesty with her skirt   MONTAIGNE, 4
A w.'s place is in the home   PROVERBS, 74
a w.'s reason   SHAKESPEARE, 347
A w.'s work   PROVERBS, 75
A w. will always sacrifice herself   MAUGHAM, 5
a w. yet think him an angel   THACKERAY, 4
body of a weak and feeble w.   ELIZABETH I, 11
Christ-like heroes and w.-worshipping Don Juans   LAWRENCE, D, 27
close-up of a w. past sixty   ASTOR, N, 2
educate a w. you educate a family   MANIKAN, 1
every w. is at heart a rake   POPE, 42
Every w. is infallibly to be gained   CHESTERFIELD, 17
Every w. should marry   DISRAELI, 10
Frailty, thy name is w.   SHAKESPEARE, 68
God made the w. for the man   TENNYSON, 13
good w. if I had five thousand   THACKERAY, 12
hell a fury like a w. scorned   CONGREVE, 9
I am a . . . w. — nothing more   TOLSTOY, S, 2
I am a w.? When I think, I must speak   SHAKESPEARE, 52
if a w. have long hair   BIBLE, 37
If a w. like Eva Peron with no ideals   THATCHER, M, 8

I had become a w. of . . . character — DOSTOEVSKY, A, 1
I love Mickey Mouse more than any w. — DISNEY, 2
It is a great glory in a w. — THUCYDIDES, 2
It's a sort of bloom on a w. — BARRIE, 8
I would . . . guess that Anon . . . was often a w. — WOOLF, 11
little w. who wrote the book that made this great war — LINCOLN, 5
Man for the field and w. for the hearth — TENNYSON, 66
Man to command and w. to obey — TENNYSON, 66
Man with the head and w. with the heart — TENNYSON, 66
none of w. born Shall harm Macbeth — SHAKESPEARE, 219
No one delights more in vengeance than a w. — JUVENAL, 11
nor w. neither — SHAKESPEARE, 84
No w. should ever be quite accurate about her age — WILDE, 34
No w. so naked as . . . underneath her clothes — FRAYN, 1
Old age is w.'s hell — LENCLOS, 1
Once a w. has given you her heart — VANBURGH, 5
one can . . . see in a little girl the threat of a w. — DUMAS, FILS, 3
One is not born a w. — BEAUVOIR, 3
one of w. born — SHAKESPEARE, 227
One tongue is sufficient for a w. — MILTON, 65
possible for a w. to qualify as a saint — STOCKS, 1
She makes love just like a w. — DYLAN, 3
She was a w. of mean understanding — AUSTEN, 19
such beauty as a w.'s eye — SHAKESPEARE, 197
Than to ever let a w. in my life — LERNER, 3
the figure of a solitary W. . . . in white garments — COLLINS, W, 3
the help and support of the w. I love — EDWARD VIII, 1
the most beautiful w. I've ever seen — MARX, G, 1
The really original w. . . . imitates a man — SVEVO, 1
There was an old w. Lived under a hill — NURSERY RHYMES, 58
There was an old w. who lived in a shoe — NURSERY RHYMES, 59
the rib . . . made he a w. — BIBLE, 147
The silliest w. can manage a clever man — KIPLING, 21
the sort of w. now . . . one would almost feel disposed to bury for nothing — DICKENS, 30
the sort of w. who lives for others — LEWIS, C, 6
The w.'s a whore — JOHNSON, S, 89
The w. that deliberates is lost — ADDISON, 5
the w. who is really kind to dogs — BEERBOHM, 14
this mad, wicked folly of 'W.'s Rights' — VICTORIA, 7
To know the mind of a w. — LAWRENCE, D, 45
Twenty years of romance makes a w. look like a ruin — WILDE, 56
want every man, w., and child in America to see it — GOLDWYN, 8
What does a w. want — FREUD, S, 6
When a w. behaves like a man — EVANS, E, 1
When lovely w. stoops to folly — GOLDSMITH, 29
who can find a virtuous w. — BIBLE, 458
Who loves not wine, w. and song — LUTHER, 5
Why can't a w. be more like a man — LERNER, 6
will not stand . . . being called a w. in my own house — WAUGH, E, 35
w. alone, can . . . commit them — THACKERAY, 7
w. as old as she looks — COLLINS, MORTIMER, 1
w., behold thy son — BIBLE, 270
w. governs America — MADARIAGA Y ROGO, 1
w. has her way — HOLMES, O, 1
W. is always fickle and changing — VIRGIL, 12
w. is his game — TENNYSON, 65
w. . . . knowing anything — AUSTEN, 16
w. . . . knows that she is indispensable — WYNDHAM, 2
w. of education — VANBURGH, 2
W.'s at best a contradiction — POPE, 43
w. seldom asks advice — ADDISON, 16
w. . . . so vicious, or so feeble-minded, that she cannot withstand temptation — BRONTË, A, 1
W.'s virtue is man's greatest invention — SKINNER, C, 1
w.'s whole existence — BYRON, 20
W. was God's second mistake — NIETZSCHE, 3
W. will be the last thing civilized by Man — MEREDITH, G, 1
wrecks a w.'s reputation — COLETTE, 1
You're a fine w., Lou — WEST, M, 9
womanhood W. is the great fact in her life — STANTON, E, 5
woman-kind whole race of w. is . . . made subject to man — BOCCACCIO, 4
womb How does a child live in the w. — LEONARDO DA VINCI, 2
many events in the w. of time — SHAKESPEARE, 278
mother's w. Untimely ripp'd — SHAKESPEARE, 227
no new baby in the w. of our society — LAWRENCE, D, 7
teeming w. of royal kings — SHAKESPEARE, 295
women A homely face . . . aided many w. heavenward — ANTRIM, 1
all men and w. are created equal — STANTON, E, 6

all w. do — ASTOR, N, 1
An experience of w. — DOYLE, 14
a snare in which the feet of w. have always become readily entangled — ADDAMS, 1
Because w. can do nothing except love — MAUGHAM, 10
Few w. care to be laughed at — AYCKBOURN, 1
Give w. the vote — SHAW, 20
great city . . . has the greatest men and w. — WHITMAN, 12
if civilisation is to advance . . . it must be through . . . w. — PANKHURST, E, 1
If men knew how w. pass the time — HENRY, O, 2
I have sung w. in three cities — POUND, 9
imagine that they are upholding w.'s emancipation — STOPES, 6
I'm furious about the W.'s Liberationists — LOOS, 5
Monstrous Regiment of W. — KNOX, J, 2
Most w. have no characters — POPE, 41
Most w. set out to try to change a man — DIETRICH, 4
Music and w. I cannot but give way to — PEPYS, 15
Older w. are best — FLEMING, I, 1
One would suppose . . . w. possess but one class of physical organs — LIVERMORE, 1
proclaiming that w. are brighter than men — LOOS, 5
proper function of w. — ELIOT, G, 6
several young w. . . . would render the Christian life intensely difficult — LEWIS, C, 4
souls of w. are so small — BUTLER, S, 9
stir up the zeal of w. — MILL, 6
Suffer the w. whom ye divorce — KORAN, 8
than keeping w. in a state of ignorance — KNOX, V, 1
The battle for w.'s rights — THATCHER, M, 12
the emancipation of w. is . . . the greatest egoistic movement — KEY, E, 1
The extension of w.'s rights — FOURIER, 1
the largest scope for change still lies in men's attitude to w. — BRITTAIN, 3
the only advantage w. have over men . . . they can cry — RHYS, 2
The prolonged slavery of w. — STANTON, E, 2
there never will be . . . equality until w. . . . make laws — ANTHONY, 2
The vote, I thought, means nothing to w. — O'BRIEN, E, 2
The War between Men and W. — THURBER, 14
the w. come and go — ELIOT, T, 12
the w. in his paintings — PICASSO, 4
the w. whose eyes have been washed . . . with tears — DIX, DOROTHY, 1
tide in the affairs of w. — BYRON, 31
We are here to claim our rights as w. — PANKHURST, C, 3
Were't not for gold and w. — TOURNEUR, 1
we suffragettes aspire to be . . . ambassadors of freedom to w. — PANKHURST, C, 1
When w. go wrong — WEST, M, 14
Why are w. . . . so much more interesting to men — WOOLF, 10
why God withheld the sense of humour from w. — CAMPBELL, MRS PATRICK, 3
Why need . . . w. know so much — BROWNING, R, 5
with peaches and w., it's . . . the side next the sun that's tempting — OUIDA, 2
W. . . . are either better or worse than men — LA BRUYÈRE, 7
W. are much more like each other — CHESTERFIELD, 16
w. become like their mothers — WILDE, 21
W. cannot be part of the Institute of France — CURIE, 1
W. . . . care fifty times more for a marriage than a ministry — BAGEHOT, 5
w. defend themselves so poorly — LACLOS, 1
w. dislike his books — ORWELL, 34
W. had always fought for men — PANKHURST, E, 2
W. have always been the guardians of wisdom and humanity — WOLFF, 1
W. have served . . . as looking-glasses — WOOLF, 9
w. . . . ill-using them and then confessing it — TROLLOPE, 9
W. never have young minds — DELANEY, 2
w. . . . not so young as . . . painted — BEERBOHM, 4
W. represent . . . matter over mind — WILDE, 50
w. require both — BUTLER, S, 29
w. should be struck . . . like gongs — COWARD, 18
w. their rights and nothing less — ANTHONY, 1
W. who love the same man — BEERBOHM, 13
W. would rather be right than reasonable — NASH, 4
Wonderful w.! . . . how much we . . . owe to Shakespeare — TERRY, 1
Young w. have a duty to flirt — BROOKNER, 1

womman   worthy w. al hir lyve   CHAUCER, 12
won   Human reason w.. Mankind w.   KHRUSHCHEV, 3
wonder   knowledge and w. . . . is an impression of pleasure   BACON, FRANCIS, 1
Many a man has been a w. to the world   MONTAIGNE, 8
Philosophy is the product of w.   WHITEHEAD, 4
the common w. of all men   BROWNE, T. 6
   Such knowledge is too w. and excellent for me   PSALMS, 71
the ancient cathedrals – grand, w., mysterious   STANTON, E, 1
w. case of nature imitating art   WILDE, 62
wonders   His w. to perform   COWPER, 17
wondrous   When I survey the w. Cross   WATTS, 8
wont   seen me as he was w. to see me   TROLLOPE, 2
woo   the . . . only thing that I ever did wrong Was to w. a fair
young maid   ANONYMOUS, 63
wood   about the dreadful w. Of conscious evil   AUDEN, 14
hewers of w.   BIBLE, 289
would rather hew w. than be a king   CHARLES X, 1
woodcock   well-shot w., partridge, snipe   BETJEMAN, 4
woodman   W., spare that tree   MORRIS, G, 1
w. spare the beechen tree   CAMPBELL, T, 1
woods   fresh w., and pastures new   MILTON, 27
Spring Flow down the w.   SACKVILLE-WEST, 2
The w. are lovely   FROST, R, 8
the w. decay and fall   TENNYSON, 75
They shut the road through the w.   KIPLING, 30
We'll to the w. no more   HOUSMAN, 3
woodshed   Something nasty in the w.   GIBBONS, 1
woodworm   the w. obligingly held hands   DU MAURIER, 4
word   better w. than prefabricated   CHURCHILL, W, 11
but a w. and a blow   BUNYAN, 6
Good isn't the w.   GILBERT, W, 47
Greeks had a W. for It   AKINS, 1
in the beginning was the w.   BIBLE, 238
in the captain's but a choleric w.   SHAKESPEARE, 229
Rehearsing a play is making the w. flesh   SHAFFER, 3
the kingdom of God is not in w., but in power   BIBLE, 26
the W. had breath   TENNYSON, 29
The w. is half Greek and half Latin   SCOTT, C, 2
the w. of God is . . . sharper than any two-edged sword   BIBLE, 185
use a w. that might send the reader to the dictionary   HEMINGWAY, 2
What is honour? A w.   SHAKESPEARE, 113
when I use a w.   CARROLL, 32
words   Be not the slave of W.   CARLYLE, T, 24
best w. in the best order   COLERIDGE, S, 41
big emotions come from big w.   HEMINGWAY, 9
by skilful arrangement of your w.   HORACE, 1
Don't listen to their w., fix your attention on their deeds   EINSTEIN, 5
Fine w. and an insinuating appearance   CONFUCIUS, 6
Fine w. butter no parsnips   PROVERBS, 153; SCOTT, WALTER, 11
For w., like Nature, half reveal   TENNYSON, 27
he was cautious of his own w.   CROMWELL, O, 3
I always try to get as many w.   ANONYMOUS, 94
In two w.: im - possible   GOLDWYN, 11
I put the w. down   WAUGH, E, 53
It wasn't the w. That frightened the birds   ANONYMOUS, 92
learn the use of living w.   DE LA MARE, 2
let the w. of my mouth . . . be alway acceptable in thy sight   PSALMS, 10
Men of few w. are the best   SHAKESPEARE, 131
my w. are my own   CHARLES II, 3
neither wit, nor w., nor worth   SHAKESPEARE, 157
shrank from w.   TAYLOR, E, 1
Thanks to w., we have been able to rise above the brutes   HUXLEY, A, 3
the barbarous, gothic times when w. had a meaning   FRANCE, 8
The bitterest tears . . . are for w. . . . unsaid   STOWE, 1
to set a chime of w. tinkling in . . . a few fastidious people   SMITH, L, 9
used w. with the violence of a horse-breaker   BROWNING, R, 1
uses his w. as a quack uses his remedies   FÉNELON, 1
use the most common . . . w.   WESLEY, J, 3
Whitman who laid end to end w.   WHITMAN, 1
W. are like leaves   POPE, 30
W. are men's daughters   MADDEN, 1
w. are the daughters of earth   JOHNSON, S, 6
W. are . . . the most powerful drug   KIPLING, 34

w. but wind   BUTLER, S, 6
w. left unsaid and deeds left undone   STOWE, 1
W. may be false and full of art   SHADWELL, 1
w. never seen . . . before outside of a dictionary   LODGE, 5
w. once spoke . . . never be recall'd   ROSCOMMON, 1
w. portray their users   CAREY, J, 3
Wordsworth   Mr W. is never interrupted   WORDSWORTH, M, 1
W. . . . never was a lake poet   WORDSWORTH, W, 2
W.'s healing power   ARNOLD, M, 1
wore   w. enough for modesty   BUCHANAN, 1
work   All w. and no play   PROVERBS, 41
can't call yourself a great w. of nature   WHISTLER, 12
Every man's w. . . . is always a portrait of himself   BUTLER, S, 23
For men must w., and women must weep   KINGSLEY, 7
His w. presents the feeling of the Absurd   CAMUS, 1
How can I take an interest in my w.   BACON, F, 1
if any would not w., neither should he eat   BIBLE, 505
I haven't had time to w. in weeks   KEROUAC, 2
I like w.; it fascinates me   JEROME, 7
it is poor grub, poor pay, and easy w.   LONDON, 1
My Nails are Drove, My W. is done   ANONYMOUS, 60
No, this right hand shall w. it all off   SCOTT, WALTER, 22
no w., nor device, nor knowledge . . . in the grave   BIBLE, 73
one must do some w. seriously . . . and not merely amuse oneself   JOLIOT-CURIE, 1
only place where success comes before w.   SASSOON, V, 1
prejudice against w.   CHEKHOV, 9
success . . . by dint of hard w.   PAVLOVA, 2
the w. comes out more beautiful   GAUTIER, 2
the world's w. . . . is done by men who do not feel . . . well   GALBRAITH, 6
they must hate to w. for a living   ROWLAND, H, 1
They say hard w. never hurt anybody   REAGAN, 10
To sport would be as tedious as to w.   SHAKESPEARE, 109
W. banishes those three great evils   VOLTAIRE, 10
W. . . . by those employees who have not yet reached . . . incompetence   PETER, 2
W. expands so as to fill the time   PARKINSON, 1
W. is much more fun than fun   COWARD, 22
W. is the curse of the drinking classes   WILDE, 75
W. is the grand cure   CARLYLE, T, 31
world of hard w.   LEE, L, 4
you already have a discontented w. force   MORGAN, E, 2
worker   a sociable w.   BEHAN, 5
workers   He is used to dealing with estate w.   DOUGLAS-HOME, C, 1
hiring taxis . . . handing out redundancy notices to its own w.   KINNOCK, 9
W. of the world, unite   MARX, K, 2
workhouse   'The W.' – always a word of shame   LEE, L, 3
working   God as a w. hypothesis   BONHOEFFER, 1
To the ordinary w. man . . . Socialism   ORWELL, 27
working class   The party is the rallying-point for the . . . w.   STALIN, 4
the w. which, raw and half-developed   ARNOLD, M, 9
working classes   No writer before the . . . 19th century wrote about the w.   WAUGH, E, 49
workman   A bad w.   PROVERBS, 2
works   all his w.   BOOK OF COMMON PRAYER, 22
cast away the w. of darkness   BOOK OF COMMON PRAYER, 4
He spoke of his w. as trifles   CONGREVE, 2
Look on my w., ye Mighty, and despair   SHELLEY, 17
more copies of my w. are left behind   BENCHLEY, 3
they were judged every man according to their w.   BIBLE, 472
thy heavens, even the w. of thy fingers   PSALMS, 3
W. done least rapidly   BROWNING, R, 37
W. of the Lord   BOOK OF COMMON PRAYER, 1
workshop   England . . . the w. of the world   DISRAELI, 21
worktime   the bustle of man's w.   BROWNING, R, 24
world   a citizen of the w.   SOCRATES, 8
A great writer creates a w. of his own   CONNOLLY, 4
All's right with the w.   BROWNING, R, 45
all the uses of this w.   SHAKESPEARE, 67
all the w. as my parish   WESLEY, J, 1
All the w. is queer   OWEN, R, 1
All the w. loves a lover   PROVERBS, 40
All the w.'s a stage   SHAKESPEARE, 47
all the w. should be taxed   BIBLE, 312
a man for whom the outside w. exists   GAUTIER, 1
A man travels the w. over   MOORE, G, 1
as good be out of the w.   CIBBER, 1
a W. in a grain of sand   BLAKE, W, 9

wring they will soon *w*. their hands	WALPOLE, R, 2
writ Here lies one whose name was w. in water	KEATS, 49
I never w., nor no man ever lov'd	SHAKESPEARE, 369
write A man may w. at any time	JOHNSON, S, 47
as much as a man ought to w.	TROLLOPE, 3
attempt to w. on both sides of the paper at once	SELLAR, 8
Better to w. for yourself	CONNOLLY, 19
he does not w. himself down	HAZLITT, 7
I began to w. them myself	BLYTON, 3
I like Leo Tolstoy . . . but . . . he won't w. much	TOLSTOY, L, 2
I like to w. when I feel spiteful	LAWRENCE, D, 41
'look in thy heart and w.'	SIDNEY, P, 1
signing his name and forgetting to w. the letter	BEECHER, 1
w. and read comes by nature	SHAKESPEARE, 270
w. for children . . . as you do for adults	GORKY, 1
writer A great w. creates a world of his own	CONNOLLY, 4
Asking a working w. . . . about critics	HAMPTON, 5
a sonorous fake as a w.	LAWRENCE, T, 1
A w.'s ambition should be	KOESTLER, 6
Every great and original w.	WORDSWORTH, W, 20
Galsworthy was a bad w.	GALSWORTHY, 3
He is a w. of something occasionally like English	WHITMAN, 2
it is necessary to go to a university . . . to become a successful w.	
	BRITTAIN, 2
not a w.'s business to hold opinions	YEATS, 36
No tears in the w.	FROST, R, 2
protect the w.	ACHESON, 5
Robert Browning, you w. of plays	BROWNING, R, 30
successful w. . . . is indistinguishable	LEWIS, S, 2
the w. . . . is the impregnator, . . . the reader . . . is the respondent	WHITE, E, 2
w.'s only responsibility is to his art	FAULKNER, 2
writers American w. want to be . . . great	VIDAL, 2
As w. become more numerous	GOLDSMITH, 4
Clear w., . . . do not seem so deep as they are	LANDOR, 5
Creative w. are . . . greater than the causes . . . they represent	
	FORSTER, 6
Irish w. – the ones that *think*.	BEHAN, 8
No regime has ever loved great w.	SOLZHENITSYN, 10
picking gold out of the dunghills of old Roman w.	VIRGIL, 3
The only way for w. to meet	CONNOLLY, 14
W. like Connolly gave pleasure a bad name	CONNOLLY, 1
W., like teeth, are divided into incisors and grinders	BAGEHOT, 8
writes He w. as fast as they can read	HAZLITT, 7
Moving Finger w.	FITZGERALD, E, 14
writhe Uriah, . . . made a ghastly w.	DICKENS, 16
writhing Reeling and W.	CARROLL, 15
writing All good w. is swimming under water	FITZGERALD, F S, 16
as I had in the w.	QUARLES, 1
give up w. today – read Pepys instead	PEPYS, 3
the disease of w. books	MONTESQUIEU, 4
the incurable disease of w.	JUVENAL, 7
True ease in w. comes from art	POPE, 26
When a man is in doubt about . . . his w.	BUTLER, S, 12
w. an exact man	BACON, FRANCIS, 51
W. . . . is but a different name for conversation	STERNE, 7
W. is like getting married	MURDOCH, 2
writings historians left blanks in their w.	POUND, 8
written Books are well w., or badly w.	WILDE, 44
No one has w. worse English than Mr Hardy in . . . his novels	
	HARDY, 4
she has w. . . . a few moments of human experience	PARKER, D, 1
what I have w. I have w.	BIBLE, 269
w. . . . for the sake of 'self-expression'	HARDY, 2
you would have been very glad if I had w. it	PIRON, 1
Wromantic Cavaliers (Wrong but W.)	SELLAR, 5
wrong A door is what a dog is . . . on the w. side of	NASH, 2
A man should . . . own he has been in the w.	POPE, 54
An extraordinarily gifted president who was the w. man	
	JOHNSON, L, 1
anxious to do the w. thing correctly	SAKI, 20
History is . . . the w. way of living	DURRELL, L, 3
Holders of one position, w. for years	AUDEN, 25
If anything can go w.	PROVERBS, 212
if I called the w. number, why did you answer the phone	
	THURBER, 15
I . . . may not always be right, but I am never w.	GOLDWYN, 6
Of course not . . . I may be w.	RUSSELL, B, 32
orthodoxy . . . practically means being w.	CHESTERTON, 16
our country, right or w.	DECATUR, 1
right deed for the w. reason	ELIOT, T, 18

sentimentality . . . rubs you up the w. way	MAUGHAM, 25
something is impossible, he is . . . w.	CLARKE, A, 1
something w. with our bloody ships	BEATTY, 1
support me when I am . . . w.	MELBOURNE, 4
their authors could not endure being w.	CAMUS, 7
The multitude is always in the w.	ROSCOMMON, 2
The right divine of kings to govern w.	POPE, 4
the unclouded face of truth suffer w.	SCOTT, C, 1
the w. place at the w. time under the w. circumstances	
	JOHNSON, L, 1
The w. sort of people are always in power	WYNNE-TYSON, J, 1
The w. war, at the w. place	BRADLEY, O, 2
When women go w.	WEST, M, 14
W. from the start	POUND, 12
w. to have *thought* that I was w.	DULLES, 1
wrongdoing W. can only be avoided if those who are not wronged feel the same indignation	SOLON, 1
wronged Not to be w. is to forgo . . . goodness	WELLS, 4
wrongs for one class to appreciate the w. of another	
	STANTON, E, 3
Nixon's motto was, if two w. don't make a right	NIXON, 1
Two w. do not make a right	PROVERBS, 447

XYZ

Xanadu In X. did Kubla Khan	COLERIDGE, S, 14
X-ray To replace X. by hearsay	THOMAS, G, 4
yacht I had to sink my y. to make my guests go home	
	FITZGERALD, F S, 6
Yale all the young ladies who attended the Y. promenade dance were laid end to end	PARKER, D, 14
A whale ship was my Y. College	MELVILLE, 2
Yankee Y. Doodle came to town	BANGS, 74
yard a y. . . . 3.37 inches longer than other people's	COREN, 3
yarn web of our life is of a mingled y.	SHAKESPEARE, 22
yawn When a book is boring, they y. openly	SINGER, 1
yawns grave y. for him	TREE, 3
year all the y. were playing holidays	SHAKESPEARE, 109
Another y.! – another deadly blow	WORDSWORTH, W, 51
each day is like a y.	WILDE, 9
I said to the man who stood at the gate of the y.	HASKINS, 1
Let it be kept till the ninth y.	HORACE, 11
Not to hope for things to last for ever, is what the y. teaches	
	HORACE, 41
That time of y. thou mayst in me behold	SHAKESPEARE, 364
two months of every y.	BYRON, 7
y.'s at the spring	BROWNING, R, 45
yearning learning, earning and y.	MORLEY, C, 1
years After long y.	BYRON, 44
a thousand y. . . . are but as yesterday	PSALMS, 49
he that cuts off twenty y. of life	SHAKESPEARE, 148
how many y. can some people exist	DYLAN, 2
I have been talking prose for over forty y.	MOLIÈRE, 3
It will keep for y.	LEACOCK, 4
One thousand y. more . . . *Homo sapiens* has before him	
	WELLS, 22
world must be made safe for . . . fifty y.	CHURCHILL, W, 10
Y. hence, perhaps, may dawn an age	ARNOLD, M, 20
y. of discretion	BOOK OF COMMON PRAYER, 19
Yeats In Drumcliff churchyard Y. is laid	YEATS, 32
Y. is not a man of this world	YEATS, 2
Y. stood for enchantment	YEATS, 1
yellow He is very y. and glum	ELIOT, T, 2
yeoman y. every inch of me	BLACKMORE, 2
yes . . . girls . . . say No when they mean Y.	ALCOTT, 3
yesterday a thousand years . . . are but as y.	PSALMS, 49
wiser to-day than . . . y.	POPE, 54
yesterdays And all our y.	SHAKESPEARE, 225
yesteryear snows of y.	VILLON, 1
yet A young man not y.	BACON, FRANCIS, 35
but not y.	AUGUSTINE OF HIPPO, 2
My time has not y. come	NIETZSCHE, 8
Yeti little in civilization to appeal to a Y.	HILLARY, 3
yid put the id back in y.	ROTH, 1
yield To strive, to seek . . . and not to y.	TENNYSON, 81
yo-ho-ho Y., and a bottle of rum	STEVENSON, R, 8
yoke good . . . that he bear the y. in his youth	BIBLE, 306
Rome's gross y. Drops off	BROWNING, R, 18
the inevitable y.	WORDSWORTH, W, 27
Yorick Alas, poor Y.	SHAKESPEARE, 105
York Oh! the grand old Duke of Y.	NURSERY RHYMES, 37

you For y. but not for me — ANONYMOUS, 65
Y. also — OVID, 6
Y. are not y. without me — FULLER, ROY, 1
young aged diplomats . . . bored than for y. men to die — AUSTIN, W, 1
ale from the Country of the Y. — YEATS, 15
a man of about a hundred and fifty who was rather y. — WODEHOUSE, 22
A man that is y. in years — BACON, FRANCIS, 61
a sight to make an old man y. — TENNYSON, 14
can't put off being y. until you retire — LARKIN, 1
country of y. men — EMERSON, 25
first sign of old age . . . how y. the policemen look — HICKS, 1
Grieve not that I die y. — HASTINGS, 1
I am sixty years y. — TREE, 1
look y. till forty — DRYDEN, 27
made y. with y. desires — THOMPSON, F, 3
man's friends begin to compliment him about looking y. — IRVING, 1
Most women are not so y. as they are painted — BEERBOHM, 7
old-fashioned respect for the y. — WILDE, 23
Political history is far too criminal . . . to be . . . fit . . . for the y. — AUDEN, 4
The atrocious crime of being a y. man — PITT THE ELDER, 2
The best careers advice to give to the y. — WHITEHORN, 6
the old have rubbed it into the y. that they are wiser — MAUGHAM, 3
The y. always have the same problem — CRISP, 2
the y. are so busy teaching us — HOFFER, 3
The y. Cambridge group — LAWRENCE, D, 16
The y. have aspirations — SAKI, 12
to be y. was very heaven — WORDSWORTH, W, 40
to make me y. again — ADENAUER, 1
When all the world is y., lad — KINGSLEY, 6
whom the gods favour dies y. — PLAUTUS, 1
You can be y. without money — WILLIAMS, T, 2
y. and easy under the apple boughs — THOMAS, D, 8
Y. men make great mistakes in life — JOWETT, 4
Y. people ought not to be idle — THATCHER, M, 20
younger I . . . get y. every day — TREE, 1
youngest not even the y. of us — THOMPSON, W, 1
yourself Better to write for y. — CONNOLLY, 19
If you do not tell the truth about y. — WOOLF, 7

If you hate a person, you hate . . . y. — HESSE, 1
no friends not equal to y. — CONFUCIUS, 7
What you do not want done to y. — CONFUCIUS, 14
youth age and y. cannot live together — SHAKESPEARE, 355
A y. to whom was given So much — WORDSWORTH, W, 47
everything that is great . . . done by y. — DISRAELI, 5
good . . . that he bear the yoke in his y. — BIBLE, 306
Here rests . . . A y. to fortune and to fame unknown — GRAY, 8
high-water mark of my y. — THURBER, 9
Home-keeping y. — SHAKESPEARE, 346
If only y. knew — ESTIENNE, 1
if thou has gathered nothing in thy y. — BIBLE, 87
I summon age To grant y.'s heritage — BROWNING, R, 49
it is y. that must fight and die — HOOVER, 4
Lye Gray Age, Grene y., White Infancy — ANONYMOUS, 53
man loves the meat in his y. — SHAKESPEARE, 269
Pride and Truth . . . shake their . . . sides at y. — YEATS, 24
sign of an ill-spent y. — SPENCER, H, 2
the Jazz Age . . . became less and less an affair of y. — FITZGERALD, F S, 4
the world hath lost his y. — BIBLE, 99
Thou hast nor y. nor age — SHAKESPEARE, 231
Time, the subtle thief of y. — MILTON, 59
Y. is a blunder — DISRAELI, 4
Y. is something very new — CHANEL, 2
Y.'s a stuff will not endure — SHAKESPEARE, 338
Y. will be served — BORROW, 3
Y. will come . . . beat on my door — IBSEN, 6
y. would sleep out the rest — SHAKESPEARE, 350
youthe Withouten other companye in y. — CHAUCER, 12
Yukon Law of the Y. — SERVICE, 3
Yuletide at Y. men are the more murderous — HILL, G, 4
zeal Not too much z. — TALLEYRAND, 5
stir up the z. of women — MILL, 6
zed whoreson z. — SHAKESPEARE, 173
zero My scribbling pays me z. francs per line — ROCHEFORT, 1
Zion Beneath this stone, in hope of Z. — ANONYMOUS, 11
zoo the city is not a concrete jungle, it is a human z. — MORRIS, D, 1
Zulus The Z. know Chaplin — CHAPLIN, 2
Zürich the little gnomes of Z. — WILSON, HAROLD, 6
Zyklon Just so much Z. and leather — HILL, G, 2